PATENT LAW

Aspen Treatise Series

PATENT LAW

Sixth Edition

JANICE M. MUELLER

Patent Attorney and Co-Founder
Chisum Patent Academy
Professor of Law at University
of Pittsburgh (2004-2011),
The John Marshall Law School (1999-2004),
and Suffolk University (1996-1999)

Wolters Kluwer

Published by Wolters Kluwer in New York.

Wolters Kluwer Legal & Regulatory U.S. serves customers worldwide with CCH, Aspen Publishers, and Kluwer Law International products. (www.WKLegaledu.com)

To contact Customer Service, e-mail customer.service@wolterskluwer.com, call 1-800-234-1660, fax 1-800-901-9075, or mail correspondence to:

Wolters Kluwer
Attn: Order Department
PO Box 990
Frederick, MD 21705

Printed in the United States of America.

1 2 3 4 5 6 7 8 9 0

ISBN 978-1-5438-0452-2

Library of Congress Cataloging-in-Publication Data

Names: Mueller, Janice M., 1963- author.
Title: Patent law / Janice M. Mueller, Patent Attorney and Co-Founder, Chisum Patent Academy, Professor of Law at University of Pittsburgh (2004-2011), The John Marshall Law School (1999-2004), and Suffolk University (1996-1999).
Description: Sixth edition. | New York : Wolters Kluwer, [2020] | Series: Aspen treatise series | Includes bibliographical references and index. | Summary: "A succinct, clearly-written, first-principles demystification of U.S. patent law for law school students enrolled in Patent Law courses"—Provided by publisher.
Identifiers: LCCN 2020007507 (print) | LCCN 2020007508 (ebook) | ISBN 9781543804522 (paperback) | ISBN 9781543821093 (ebook)
Subjects: LCSH: Patent laws and legislation—United States. | LCGFT: Textbooks.
Classification: LCC KF3114 .M84 2020 (print) | LCC KF3114 (ebook) | DDC 346.7304/86—dc23
LC record available at https://lccn.loc.gov/2020007507
LC ebook record available at https://lccn.loc.gov/2020007508

About Wolters Kluwer Legal & Regulatory U.S.

Wolters Kluwer Legal & Regulatory U.S. delivers expert content and solutions in the areas of law, corporate compliance, health compliance, reimbursement, and legal education. Its practical solutions help customers successfully navigate the demands of a changing environment to drive their daily activities, enhance decision quality and inspire confident outcomes.

Serving customers worldwide, its legal and regulatory portfolio includes products under the Aspen Publishers, CCH Incorporated, Kluwer Law International, ftwilliam.com and MediRegs names. They are regarded as exceptional and trusted resources for general legal and practice-specific knowledge, compliance and risk management, dynamic workflow solutions, and expert commentary.

This book is dedicated to Judge Giles Sutherland Rich, 1904-1999, the consummate teacher whose passion for patent law and a life fully lived continues to instruct and inspire us all.

Summary of Contents

Contents

Preface

Preface to the Sixth Edition

This is an exciting time to study patent law. One of its wonderful, if sometimes maddening, features is an almost constant and rapid rate of change. Patent law is never stagnant. Its evolution is driven by many factors: scientific and technological progress, global trade and borderless innovation, public policy debate over the proper role of patents in the U.S. free market economy, the marketplace for patents as a new class of capital asset, the rise of patent enforcement by non-practicing entities (sometimes pejoratively called "patent trolls"), the 2011 America Invents Act ("AIA") implementation of the most significant changes to the U.S. Patent Act since its 1952 codification, a steady stream of precedential decisions from the U.S. Court of Appeals for the Federal Circuit (having nationwide jurisdiction over patent-related appeals), and infrequent but often dramatic course corrections imposed by the U.S. Supreme Court. The extensive new content in the sixth edition of *Patent Law* reflects this dynamic milieu.

In the four years following publication of the fifth edition, the rapidity of change in patent law has, if anything, escalated. The considerable modifications worked by the 2011 AIA are now in full effect and have radically altered U.S. patent practice. The AIA shifted the U.S. patent system from its historic first-to-invent priority system to a hybrid first-inventor-to-file system. The new framework retains the traditional pre-filing "grace period" but limits its protections to inventor-generated or -obtained disclosures. The AIA also changed what qualifies as "prior art" to defeat patentability and expanded the universe thereof by removing geographic limitations, reflecting our global economy. But that universe has not transformed in its entirety. In its first encounter with the new statutory provisions, the Supreme Court in *Hellsin v. Teva* (2019) confirmed the continued applicability of the historic common law understanding that patent rights can be barred by excessive delays in seeking protection after a sale in which the details of an invention remained confidential to the public.

Critically, the AIA first-to-file changes were prospective only; over two million patents then in force were not impacted. The validity of patents issued from applications filed before March 16, 2013 continues to be assessed (in the USPTO, district courts, and the Federal Circuit) under pre-AIA rules for the remainder of the patents' lives and beyond. The upshot is that for the next twenty-plus years, the U.S. patent system will operate under a dual system of pre- and post-AIA rules. Students of patent law need to understand not one but two sets of rules. This text explains both.

Although the change to a "first-inventor-to-file" system upended 200 years of U.S. patent practice, the new AIA-implemented adjudicatory procedures for challenging the validity of issued patents in the U.S. Patent and Trademark Office (USPTO) carry even greater practical significance. Post-issuance review has catalyzed a booming new frontier in patent litigation. These USPTO adjudications now far outnumber patent lawsuits filed in the federal courts.

Although the AIA implemented myriad changes, its passage did not impact other fundamental aspects of patent law. For example, the AIA's enactment did not affect many traditionally contentious aspects of patent law practice including patent claim interpretation, standards for nonobviousness, venue for patent cases, infringement under the doctrine of equivalents, the standard for willful infringement, the defenses of laches and exhaustion of patent rights, remedies for infringement, and which types of inventions qualify as patent-eligible subject matter. This text explicates the major changes made by the Federal Circuit and Supreme Court in these areas of patent law since publication of the previous edition.

The Supreme Court's controversial 2012 decision in *Mayo v. Prometheus*, which announced wide-ranging exceptions to patent-eligibility, continues to generate the greatest fallout. *Mayo*'s unfortunate consequences are ongoing. In 2014 the Supreme Court issued *Alice Corp. v. CLS Bank*, furthering the exclusion of patents on "abstract ideas" that the Court emphasized in *Mayo* and *Bilski v. Kappos* (2010). Increasingly troubling are the mounting number of Federal Circuit decisions that have applied *Mayo* and its progeny to strike down as patent-ineligible "laws of nature" a wide variety of inventions in the life sciences. The consensus view is that medical diagnostics inventions are no longer patentable.

Frustratingly, the rules for discerning what subject matter is or is not patent-eligible are amorphous. The cases invoke vague, undefined concepts such as "abstract" and "inventive." The federal courts struggle with the lack of clear guidance, and the USPTO will soon face similar quandaries when post-grant review of AIA patents (which permits challenges to patent-eligibility) reaches full capacity. Distinguished Federal Circuit judges have publicly called for Congressional intervention, to no avail. Left without straightforward standards or metrics, the courts are forced to apply an "I know it when I see it" approach to decide patent-eligibility disputes by simply analogizing to the factually closest cases they can identify. Policy concerns typically receive short shrift.

While ignoring the patent-eligibility quandary left in the wake of its 2014 *Alice* and 2012 *Mayo* decisions, the Supreme Court has turned its attention to other aspects of patent law. In particular, the Court has granted review in a number of cases involving the new AIA-implemented post-issuance procedures. The Court has focused less on the substantive patent law questions raised in these proceedings and more on their procedural aspects. In some decisions, the Court had deferred to the USPTO and approved the agency's conduct of the new proceedings. For example, the Court affirmed the Article III Constitutionality of the AIA post-issuance proceedings and held that they did not deprive patentees of a jury trial right in *Oil States v. Greene's* (2018). And in *Cuozzo v. Lee* (2016), the Court agreed with the USPTO that barring certain limited exceptions, agency decisions to institute such proceedings are not judicially reviewable. In other decisions, however, the Court has forced the agency to shoulder a heavier workload than anticipated. In *SAS Institute v. Iancu* (2018), the Court interpreted new AIA statutory language to reject the USPTO's position that it could institute post-issuance review on a "pick and choose," claim-by-claim and ground-by-ground basis.

I am indebted to the many patent law students, academics, and practitioners whose feedback and suggestions for this text have proved invaluable during the revision process. Darren Kelly provided essential editorial assistance. Any errors are my own. Comments or questions are welcome and should be e-mailed to the author at Janice@chisum.com.

Janice M. Mueller
Lexington, Kentucky

April 2020

PATENT LAW

Chapter 1

Foundations of the U.S. Patent System

A. Introduction and Chapter Overview

Readers of this text do not need to be convinced of patent law's importance to the U.S. and international economies. The expanding recognition of patent rights and remedies as issues integral to domestic and global trade policy has brought this once relatively technical and arcane area of the law into the mainstream of legal practice.

This text is written for the many U.S. law students who are discovering, for these and many other reasons, that patent law is one of the most exciting, challenging, and relevant subjects in the law school curriculum. The information presented in this text also will be useful for practicing attorneys trained in general civil litigation and corporate practice who seek a more in-depth understanding of patent law. Engineers and scientists who seek patent protection for their inventions will also benefit. All of these individuals are finding it increasingly necessary to have a working comfort level with the finer points of patent, copyright, trademark, and trade secret (collectively, **intellectual property** or **IP**) law, reflecting the growing prominence of these legal specializations in our legal and economic infrastructure.[1]

After considering why patent law is an important subject for further exploration, the remainder of this chapter will introduce key foundational principles intended to enhance the reader's understanding of the rest of the text. This chapter places patents in context as a powerful form of IP protection that conveys the right to exclude all others from unauthorized imitation or use of a patented invention for a statutorily defined period of time. This chapter also provides the reader with a sample U.S. patent and an explanation of its component parts,

[1]U.S. Circuit Judge Richard A. Posner has written that "[l]egal disputes over intellectual property have exploded in recent years. No field of law is in greater ferment." Richard A. Posner, *The Law & Economics of Intellectual Property*, DAEDALUS, Spring 2002, at 5, *available at* https://www.amacad.org/publication/law-economics-intellectual-property.

emphasizing the importance of patent **claims**, which are meticulously drafted, single-sentence definitions of the patent owner's exclusionary right.[2] The chapter next surveys the fundamental economic theory and philosophical justifications upon which U.S. patent law is based. The various primary sources of U.S. patent law also are considered, including the Constitution, federal statutes and regulations, and common law (i.e., judicial decisions). Chapter 1 next introduces the "players" in the U.S. patent system, namely, the agencies and courts that grant and enforce patents in this country, and explains how these entities interact. Chapter 1 concludes with a summary of patent **prosecution**, the process of obtaining a patent by preparing and filing a patent application and interacting with the U.S. Patent and Trademark Office (USPTO).

B. Why Study Patent Law?

1. Rise of the Information-Based Economy

Not long ago, very few U.S. law schools offered many IP courses; most schools offered merely a basic course or two in patent law and copyright law, or perhaps an introductory "IP Survey" course covering patent, copyright, and trademark law. The twenty-first-century legal landscape has shifted dramatically. Many U.S. law schools now offer an impressive array of basic and advanced courses in all aspects of intellectual property,[3] and about 25 schools offer a post-J.D. degree known as the LL.M. (or "master of laws") in intellectual property law.[4]

[2]The drafting and interpretation of patent claims are considered in detail in Chapter 2, *infra*.

[3]*See* Kenneth L. Port, *Intellectual Property Curricula in the United States*, 46 IDEA 165, 165, 170 (2005) (reporting findings that 144 U.S. law schools offered an IP Survey course, 139 schools offered Patent Law, and that "[a]ll but seven law schools in America offer at least one course in IP"); Roberta R. Kwall, *The Intellectual Property Curriculum: Findings of Professor and Practitioner Surveys*, 49 J. LEGAL EDUC. 203, 205-216 (1999).

[4]The American Bar Association lists the following U.S. law schools offering an LL.M. degree in IP law: Akron, Albany, American, Boston, Case Western Reserve, Chicago-Kent, Connecticut, Dayton, DePaul, Drake, Fordham, George Mason, George Washington, Golden Gate, Houston, Indiana University-Indianapolis, John Marshall (Chicago), Michigan State, New Hampshire, San Francisco, Santa Clara, Seton Hall, Texas A&M, Univ. of Washington, Washington University, WMU Thomas Cooley, and Yeshiva. *See* American Bar Association Section of Legal Education & Admissions to the Bar, *Post J.D. Programs by Category (2016)*, http://www.americanbar.org/groups/legal_education/resources/llm-degrees_post_j_d_non_j_d/programs_by_category.html. Many other U.S. law schools offer an IP concentration or certificate program for J.D. students.

This increase in IP course offerings reflects dramatic changes in the U.S. and global economies, which have heightened the demand for lawyers trained to assist clients in the creation, protection, and enforcement of **IP rights** (**IPRs**) worldwide. In recent years the United States has seen a dramatic rise in the importance of the "IP industries" (e.g., high technology and entertainment) as a contributor to the nation's gross domestic product.[5] United States exports of the "knowledge goods" produced by these industries — information, entertainment, software, movies, books, and the like — are rapidly growing.[6] Corporations are recognizing and exploiting the potential

[5]*See, e.g.*, United States Patent and Trademark Office, *2018-2022 Strategic Plan* 2, *available at* uspto.gov/sites/default/files/documents/USPTO_2018-2022_Strategic_Plan,pdf (stating that "innovation is a national resource that forms a critical part of the country's economic base").

In 2014, "IP-intensive industries accounted for $6.6 trillion in value added . . . , up more than $1.5 trillion (30 percent) from $5.06 trillion in 2010. Accordingly, the share of total U.S. 6DP attributed to IP-intensive industries increased from 34.8 percent in 2010 to 38.2 percent in 2014." Econ. and Statistics Admin. and U.S. Patent and Trademark Off., *Intellectual Property and the U.S. Economy: 2016 Update ii (Sept. 2016)* ("ESA Report"), *available at* uspto.gov/sites/defaiult/files/documents/PandtheUSEconomySept2016.pdf. The ESA report identified 81 industries (among 313 studied) as "IP-intensive industries" that "directly accounted for 27.9 million American jobs in 2014." *Id.* at ii.

An earlier government report estimated that "[m]ore than half of the U.S. work force is in information-based jobs, and the telecommunications and information sector is growing faster than any other sector of the U.S. economy." Information Infrastructure Task Force, Intellectual Property and the National Information Infrastructure: The Report of the Working Group on Intellectual Property Rights (Sept. 1995), *available at* books.googleusercontent.com. The USPTO reports that

> [t]echnological innovation is linked to three-quarters of America's post–WW II growth rate. Two innovation-linked factors — capital investment and increased efficiency — represent 2.5 percentage points of the 3.4 percent average annual growth rate achieved since the 1940's. Invention, innovation, and diffusion benefit consumers not only through new products and processes that promote efficiency and improve health and lifestyle, but also by providing better, higher-paying jobs. Since 1990, the average compensation per employee in innovation-intensive sectors increased 50 percent — nearly two and one-half times the national average.

United States Patent and Trademark Office, *2010-2015 Strategic Plan* 2 (2010), https://www.uspto.gov/sites/default/about/stratplan/USPTO_2010-2015_Strategic_Plan.pdf (footnotes omitted).

[6]*See* Richard A. Posner, *The Law & Economics of Intellectual Property*, DAEDALUS, Spring 2002, at 5, *available at* https://www.amacad.org/publication/law-economics-intellectual-property (stating that "[t]he increase in intellectual property litigation was made inevitable by the rise of the information economy, an economy built on intellectual property — which is now, incidentally, America's largest export"). The World Bank reports that in 2013, about 18 percent of U.S. exports of manufactured goods were "[h]igh-technology exports," which it defines as "products with high R&D intensity, such as aerospace, computers, pharmaceuticals, scientific instruments, and electrical machinery." World Bank, *Data: High-Technology Exports (% of Manufactured Exports) (2016)*, http://data.worldbank.org/indicator/TX.VAL.TECH.MF.ZS/countries.

economic power conveyed by ownership of IP, as reflected by popular books such as *Rembrandts in the Attic.*[7] Many corporations now consider patents and other IP to be the key assets of the corporate balance sheet.

Law students also are drawn to patent law because the field is implicated in so many current issues of public interest and concern. Consider, for example, the controversies raised by patents sought on fragments of the human genome,[8] embryonic stem cells, drug targets,

[7]KEVIN G. RIVETTE & DAVID KLINE, REMBRANDTS IN THE ATTIC: UNLOCKING THE HIDDEN VALUE OF PATENTS (Harvard Bus. School Press 1999).

[8]Since the 1980s, the USPTO has granted more than 20,000 patents claiming isolated DNA molecules, almost 4,000 of which claim isolated human DNA encoding proteins. *See* Remarks of David Kappos, Under Secretary of Commerce for Intellectual Property and Director of the United States Patent and Trademark Office, BIO International Convention (May 3-6, 2010), *available at* http://www.ipwatchdog.com/2010/05/04/kappos-talks-patent-reform-and-gene-patents-at-bio-convention/id=10382 (May 4, 2010). Nevertheless, the topic of gene patenting continues to engender heated public debate.

For example, a New York federal district court in March 2010 granted summary judgment invalidating a number of biotechnology patents directed to the *BRCA1* and *BRCA2* human breast cancer genes. *See* Ass'n for Molecular Pathology (AMP) v. U.S. Patent and Trademark Office (USPTO) and Myriad Genetics, Inc., 702 F. Supp. 2d 181, 185-186 (S.D.N.Y. 2010) (as amended Apr. 5, 2010) ("[T]he challenged patent claims are directed to (1) isolated DNA containing all or portions of the *BRCA1* and *BRCA2* gene sequence and (2) methods for 'comparing' or 'analyzing' BRCA1 [sic, *BRCA1*] and *BRCA2* gene sequences to identify the presence of mutations correlating with a predisposition to breast or ovarian cancer."). One of the most highly publicized patent disputes in recent memory, the *Myriad* decision pitted patient care advocates against the patent-owning biotechnology industry.

In July 2011, the Federal Circuit issued its decision in *Myriad*, generating three separate opinions. *Association for Molecular Pathology v. U.S. Pat. and Trademark Off.*, 653 F.3d 1329 (Fed. Cir. 2011) ("*Myriad II*"). In the opinion "for the court" authored by Judge Lourie, the Federal Circuit majority reversed the district court's decision that the claimed isolated DNA molecules were patent-ineligible products of nature under 35 U.S.C. §101. Rather, the molecules qualified as §101 compositions of matter because "the molecules as claimed do not exist in nature." *Myriad II,* 653 F.3d at 1334; *see also id.* at 1350 (concluding that "the challenged claims to isolated DNAs, *whether limited to cDNAs or not*, are directed to patent-eligible subject matter under §101") (emphasis added). The Federal Circuit also reversed the district court with regard to Myriad's claim to a method of screening potential cancer therapeutics via changes in cell growth rates; in the appellate court's view, this claim recited a patent-eligible method within §101 rather than a patent-ineligible scientific principle. The Federal Circuit affirmed only one aspect of the district court's decision, agreeing with the lower court that "Myriad's method claims directed to 'comparing' or 'analyzing' DNA sequences are patent ineligible [because] such claims include no transformative steps and cover only patent-ineligible abstract, mental steps." *Myriad II,* 653 F.3d at 1334.

In March 2012, the Supreme Court vacated the Federal Circuit's *Myriad II* decision and directed the Circuit to reconsider it in view of the Supreme Court's decision in *Mayo v. Prometheus*, 132 S. Ct. 1289 (2012), discussed *infra* Chapter 7 ("Potentially Patentable Subject Matter (35 U.S.C. §101)"). Not satisfied with the Circuit's remand decision, the Supreme Court granted *certiorari* and issued its own decision in *Ass'n for Molecular Pathology v. Myriad Genetics, Inc.*, 133 S. Ct. 2107 (2013) ("*Myriad IV*"). The Court in

and monoclonal antibodies;[9] by the assertion of U.S. patents directed to business methods such as Amazon.com's "One-Click" ordering system;[10] consumer protests and government investigations over the high cost of prescription drugs (many of which are protected by patent);[11] and by the developing world's HIV/AIDS crisis and the corresponding need for low-cost access to patented drugs such as AZT and the "triple cocktail" that are used to treat those diseases.[12]

Students focused on international trade and business law also are finding an understanding of patent law important to their field. Once viewed as a rather specialized and obscure area of international commerce, the transnational aspects of recognizing and enforcing IP rights including patents have taken center stage as an issue of global trade. International intellectual property treaties such as the Trade-Related Aspects of Intellectual Property (TRIPS) Agreement of the World Trade Organization (WTO)[13] continue to spark philosophical and economic debate between the "north" and "south"— pitting the developed, industrialized countries that generally seek strong protection of IP

Myriad IV significantly limited the patenting of genetic material. It held that Myriad's patent claims to isolated DNA recited naturally-occurring subject matter that was not patent eligible under §101; rather, the claims were directed to a "natural phenomenon," a "law of nature," or a "product of nature." However, the Court also held that Myriad's claims to complementary DNA ("cDNA") *were* patent eligible subject matter under §101. In the Court's view, the cDNA claims were within §101 because they were drawn to synthetic DNA created in the laboratory. The *Myriad* cases are detailed *infra* Chapter 7, Section D.2.b ("Genetic Materials").

[9] *See, e.g.*, Eliot Marshall, *Patent on HIV Receptor Provokes an Outcry*, 287 SCIENCE 1375 (2000); Andrew Pollack, *The New High-Tech Battleground*, N.Y. TIMES, July 3, 1998, at 31 (describing patent battles involving Eli Lilly, Monoclonal Antibodies, Inc., and Abbott Laboratories over use of monoclonal antibodies in diagnostic testing with sandwich immuno-assays).

[10] *See* Patti Waldmeir & Louise Kehoe, *E-Commerce Companies Sue to Protect Patents: Intellectual Rights Given Legal Test*, FINANCIAL TIMES, Oct. 25, 1999, at 16.

[11] *See* Tatiana Boncompagni, *Patently Political*, AMERICAN LAWYER, Sept. 13, 2002, at 96 (describing Federal Trade Commission review of Hatch-Waxman Act litigation settlement practices between brand-name pharmaceutical firms and their generic rivals); Julie Appleby & Jayne O'Donnell, *Consumers Pay as Drug Firms Fight over Generics*, USA TODAY, June 6, 2002, at A1.

[12] *See* Tina Rosenberg, *Look at Brazil*, N.Y. TIMES, Jan. 28, 2001, §6 (Magazine) at 26 (reporting on HIV/AIDS catastrophe in Africa, differences in pharmaceutical patent protection around the world, challenges in treating patient populations in developing countries, and Brazil's use of compulsory licensing for the manufacture of HIV/AIDS drugs). *See also* A. Samuel Oddi, *Plagues, Pandemics, and Patents: Legality and Morality*, 51 IDEA 1 (2011) (addressing the tension between the need for life-saving medicines for least-developed nations and maintaining incentives for developing these medicines in developed nations).

[13] *See* Agreement on Trade-Related Aspects of Intellectual Property Rights, Marrakesh Agreement Establishing the World Trade Organization, Annex 1C, art. 31(1), Apr. 15, 1994, 1869 U.N.T.S. 299; 33 I.L.M. 1197 (1994) [hereinafter TRIPS].

rights against the less- and least-developed countries that have historically opposed strong IP protection because of economic and public health concerns.[14]

The 1995 entry into force of the TRIPS Agreement,[15] to which 164 countries are signatories as of December 2019,[16] was a watershed event for the protection of IP worldwide. Countries that are signatories to TRIPS must agree to maintain certain minimum standards of protection for innovation protectable under the law of patents, copyright, trademarks, and trade secrets. They also must commit to instituting minimum acceptable enforcement measures to protect IP rights. Through TRIPS' implementation of the WTO's Dispute Settlement Understanding (DSU), member countries now have a powerful mechanism — the imposition of trade sanctions — for challenging another member country's failure to live up to its obligations under the TRIPS Agreement.[17]

Yet another valuable reason to study patent law is to grasp the complexities of a legal system evolving through significant legislative reform. Discussed in greater detail elsewhere in this text,[18] the America Invents Act of 2011 (AIA) implemented landmark changes to U.S. patent law,[19] probably the most significant since 1952, when the current patent statute was codified at Title 35 of the *United States Code*. For example, the AIA changed the United States practice from its historic first-to-invent **priority system** to a unique first-inventor-to-file system, while retaining some (but not all) aspects of the traditional

[14]*See generally* KEITH E. MASKUS, INTELLECTUAL PROPERTY RIGHTS IN THE GLOBAL ECONOMY (Inst. for Int'l Econ. 2000). *See also* Laurence R. Helfer, *Pharmaceutical Patents and the Human Right to Health: The Contested Evolution of the Transnational Legal Order on Access to Medicines (2015),* in TRANSNATIONAL LEGAL ORDERS (Terence C. Halliday & Gregory Shaffer, eds. 2015) (exploring clash between entities concerned with IP protection (i.e., patent protection for new drugs) and those focused on the right to health (i.e., access to essential medicines)), *available at* SSRN: http://ssrn.com/abstract=2737170.

[15]The TRIPS Agreement was signed in Marrakesh, Morocco on April 15, 1994. The TRIPS Agreement entered into force on January 1, 1995.

[16]*See* World Trade Organization, *Members and Observers* https://www.wto.org/english/thewto_e/whatis_e/tif_e/org6_e.htm. All WTO member countries must comply with the WTO's TRIPS Agreement. *See* Scope of the WTO, Apr. 15, 1994, Marrakesh Agreement Establishing the World Trade Organization Art. II(2) — Results of the Uruguay Round, 33 I.L.M. 1125 (1994) (stating that "[t]he agreements and associated legal instruments included in Annexes 1, 2 and 3 . . . are integral parts of this Agreement, binding on all Members"). The referenced "Annex 1" includes the TRIPS Agreement as Annex 1C.

[17]These and other international topics are covered in Chapter 12 ("International Patenting Issues"), *infra*.

[18]*See infra* Chapter 4, Part III ("Novelty and Priority Post-America Invents Act of 2011"); Chapter 8, Section E ("AIA-Implemented Procedures for Challenging Issued Patents").

[19]Leahy-Smith America Invents Act, Pub. L. No. 112-29 (H.R. 1249), 125 Stat. 284 (2011).

U.S. pre-filing **grace period**.[20] The first-to-file system and associated changes are prospective, meaning that they apply only to patent applications filed on or after March 16, 2013, and patents issuing therefrom.[21] Patents and applications already existing on March 16, 2013, continue to be governed by the pre-AIA rules, also detailed in this text. Because a patent's validity may be subject to litigation challenge throughout the patent's lifetime, *practitioners of patent law will need to operate in a dual system, understanding and applying both pre- and post-AIA rules, for the next 25 years or more.*[22]

2. Educational Prerequisites

Many law students believe they must have an undergraduate degree in the sciences or engineering disciplines to study patent law. This is incorrect. The study of patent law will entail the application of legal rules to technology, of course, because patents are all about generating and protecting inventions. Although having scientific or technical training may be helpful to a student's understanding of the facts in some cases, it is certainly not a prerequisite for success. Consider that the first time she encounters it, even a nuclear engineer may be mystified by genetic engineering technology. Anyone with a genuine interest and curiosity about inventions and how the law treats them should be able to master patent law. This text endeavors to use straightforward examples of simple inventions to illustrate its points. Technical complexity should not obscure learning about the law.

Only one aspect of patent law practice requires a technical background. In order to sit for the patent bar examination administered by the USPTO, candidates must have an undergraduate degree or

[20] *See* Leahy-Smith America Invents Act, Pub. L. No. 112-29 (H.R. 1249), §3 ("First Inventor to File"), 125 Stat. 284, 285-293 (2011). The concepts of priority and grace period are further explored *infra* Chapter 4 ("Novelty, Loss of Right, and Priority Pre- and Post-America Invents Act of 2011 (35 U.S.C. §102)").

[21] *See* Leahy-Smith America Invents Act, Pub. L. No. 112-29 (H.R. 1249), §3(n) ("Effective Date"), 125 Stat. 284, 293 (2011).

[22] An unfortunate feature of the AIA is that Congress rewrote many critical sections of the Patent Act but retained the original statutory section numbers. Thus, for example, patent professionals will need to understand and apply the pre-AIA version of 35 U.S.C. §102 as well as the entirely new, post-AIA version of 35 U.S.C. §102. Both these sections define what potentially patentable subject matter is "novel" and what qualifies as "prior art" to preclude patenting, but the AIA changed the rules underlying those definitions. To distinguish between pre- and post-AIA versions of statutory sections, this text will generally use the citation format "35 U.S.C. §102(b) (2006)" or "35 U.S.C. §102(b) (pre-AIA)" when specifically referring to pre-AIA versions of statutory provisions. The statutory provisions amended or created by the AIA will generally be cited with their effective dates, for example, "35 U.S.C. §102(a)(1) (eff. Mar. 16, 2013)."

equivalent course work in one of the scientific and technical disciplines listed in the USPTO's *General Requirements Bulletin for Admission to the Examination for Registration to Practice in Patent Cases Before the United States Patent and Trademark Office.*[23] Passing the patent bar exam qualifies a person to be a registered patent agent or attorney, who may represent clients before the USPTO in matters such as filing and prosecuting applications for patent.

Many lawyers without a technical background practice in areas of patent law other than patent prosecution. Being a registered patent attorney (i.e., passing the USPTO bar exam) is *not* required to litigate issued patents, to license patents, or to practice other forms of IP law such as trademark, copyright, and trade secret law.

C. What Is a Patent?

1. Patents as a Form of Intellectual Property

Patents, along with copyrights, trademarks, and trade secrets, are a form of legal protection for intellectual property. Ownership of IP represents a proprietary right in intangible products of the human mind. These "knowledge goods" include inventions, ideas, information, artistic creations, music, brand names, celebrity persona, industrial secrets, and customer lists.

2. The Appropriability Problem of Intellectual Property

Our legal system recognizes separate forms of legal protection for knowledge goods, rather than analyzing them under the same law that applies to real property or tangible objects. Why? As explained below, the fundamentally different nature of knowledge goods dictates this separate structure.

Because they are intangibles, knowledge goods such as information suffer from an "appropriability problem." Knowledge is indivisible, inexhaustible, and nonexcludable. Unlike an item of tangible property, sharing my idea with another person neither splits up nor exhausts my possession of the idea. If I have only one football, giving that football to a friend divests me of its physical possession. But if I invent a

[23] *Available at* http://www.uspto.gov/sites/default/files/OED_GRB.pdf (Feb. 2020). Persons who have passed the Fundamentals of Engineering (FE) test, which is administered by individual state boards of engineering examiners, may also qualify to sit for the patent bar exam. *See id.* at 8 ("Category C: Practical Engineering or Scientific Experience").

way of manufacturing a football out of grooved foam so that it flies higher and farther than existing footballs, I retain possession of that idea even after disclosing it to my friend. As Thomas Jefferson wrote to his colleague Isaac McPherson in 1813, "he who lights his taper at mine, receives light without darkening me. . . . Inventions then cannot, in nature, be a subject of property."[24] After I have disclosed my idea to another, how am I to prevent subsequent uses of the idea? In this sense, knowledge is considered nonexcludable.

Because knowledge goods are inexhaustible and nonexcludable, how then are inventors to profit from the investments made to generate these goods? The key problem with generation of knowledge goods is that the cost of creating knowledge can be very high, but the cost of copying it is often trivial. To see why this is so, consider the discovery of a new drug that cures a life-threatening illness. Many years and millions of dollars of research, development, and testing have gone into the creation of this drug, but once its chemical structure is known, the drug can be copied for pennies. Because copying is so easy and inexpensive, how, then, do we motivate firms to invest in this technology? How do we encourage innovation in these technologies?

As detailed below, patents are one solution to these quandaries.[25] The ownership of a patent permits the patentee to recoup its investment in discovering and developing the new drug, by conveying a time-limited right to exclude all competitors from the marketplace for that drug. In other words, the patentee will be positioned as the sole source of the patented drug during the life of the patent. This possibility of recouping investment costs by the acquisition of monopoly profits acts as a powerful spur to technical innovation.

3. Public Goods

When adequate incentives for innovation do not exist, the result is underproduction of new inventions. Economists have referred to this

[24]Graham v. John Deere Co., 383 U.S. 1, 9 n.2 (1966) (quoting 6 Thomas Jefferson, The Writings of Thomas Jefferson 180-181) (H.A. Washington ed., Washington, D.C., Taylor & Maury 1854, 2d ed.).

[25]Alternative proposed solutions to the market failure problem have included government subsidization for research and development, and the grant of prizes or awards for technical achievement (such as the Nobel Prize). *See also* Robert P. Merges et al., Intellectual Property in the New Technological Age 13 (5th ed. 2010) (noting that to prevent underproduction of public goods such as national defense and lighthouses, government steps in and pays for them; in contrast, for many forms of information, government has "created intellectual property rights in an effort to give authors and inventors control over the use and distribution of their ideas, thereby encouraging them to invest in the production of new ideas and works of authorship").

"market failure" scenario as a "public goods problem."[26] Besides inventions, other classic examples of public goods include lighthouses and national defense. Consider also the example of a telethon to raise money for a public television station. Each of us watching the telethon on our television has an incentive not to make any donation, that is, to pay less than our pro rata share for these goods, because we know we will benefit (i.e., will be able to watch the station's programming) whether or not we contribute. Absent a mechanism to exclude "free riders"— people who enjoy the benefit of the good without paying for it — these public goods will be underproduced.

To overcome these market failures, society has created systems of intellectual property rights. When the right conveyed is a patent, this means the government conveys to an inventor a time-limited property right in her invention. More specifically, the patent property right is the right to prevent others from making, selling, offering to sell, importing, or even using the patented invention in the patent-granting country during the term of the patent.[27]

[26]*See* Robert P. Merges et al., Intellectual Property in the New Technological Age 11-14 (5th ed. 2010) (observing that economists refer to information as a "public good" that may be consumed by many without depletion, and that it is difficult to identify and stop those who use information without paying for it).

[27]35 U.S.C. §154(a)(1); 35 U.S.C. §271(a). Patents are owned by private parties but issued by the federal government and restrict the public from infringing activity. Hence the question whether a patent is best described as a private property right or a "public franchise" has never been cleanly resolved; it took on new significance with the Supreme Court's 2018 decision in *Oil States Energy Servs., LLC v. Greene's Energy Grp., LLC*, 138 S. Ct. 1365. In an opinion authored for the 7-2 majority by Justice Thomas, the Court stated that it

> has long recognized that the grant of a patent is a "'matte[r] involving public rights.'" United States v. Duell, 172 U.S. 576, 582-583, 19 S. Ct. 286, 43 L. Ed. 559 (1899) (quoting Murray's Lessee v. Hoboken Land & Improvement Co., 18 How. 272, 284, 15 L. Ed. 372 (1856)). It has the key features to fall within this Court's longstanding formulation of the public-rights doctrine.
>
> *Ab initio*, the grant of a patent involves a matter "arising between the government and others." Ex parte Bakelite Corp., *supra*, at 451, 49 S. Ct. 411. As this Court has long recognized, the grant of a patent is a matter between "'the public, who are the grantors, and . . . the patentee.'" *Duell, supra*, at 586, 19 S. Ct. 286 (quoting Butterworth v. United States ex rel. Hoe, 112 U.S. 50, 59, 5 S. Ct. 25, 28 L. Ed. 656 (1884)). By "issuing patents," the PTO "take[s] from the public rights of immense value, and bestow[s] them upon the patentee." United States v. American Bell Telephone Co., 128 U.S. 315, 370, 9 S. Ct. 90, 32 L. Ed. 450 (1888). Specifically, patents are "public franchises" that the Government grants "to the inventors of new and useful improvements." Seymour v. Osborne, 11 Wall. 516, 533, 20 L. Ed. 33 (1871); *accord*, Pfaff v. Wells Electronics, Inc., 525 U.S. 55, 63-64, 119 S. Ct. 304, 142 L. Ed. 2d 261 (1998). The franchise gives the patent owner "the right to exclude others from making, using, offering for sale, or selling the invention throughout the United States." 35 U.S.C. §154(a)(1). That right "did not exist at common law." Gayler v. Wilder, 10 How. 477, 494, 13 L. Ed. 504

The conveyance of a property right in inventions is by no means a new idea. A right to exclude others from the use of certain worthy inventions was provided in the first known general patent law, enacted by the Venetian Republic in the late fifteenth century.[28] In 1624, England enacted the Statute of Monopolies, which prohibited all monopolies but recognized an exception for "any manner of newe Manufacture within this Realm. . . ."[29] The U.S. patent system owes its origin to these predecessors.

4. Exception to the General Rule of Competition by Imitation

In a free market economy such as that of the United States, the general rule is that competition through imitation of a competitor's product or service is permitted, so long as that competition is not deemed legally "unfair."[30] Patent rights should be understood as carefully limited exceptions to the general rule of free and open competition through imitation.

Older cases referred to the notion of competition through imitation of others' products or services as the *privilege* to compete, but it is probably more precisely viewed as a *right* to compete, so long as that competition is fair. Although patents are not technically viewed as a subset of unfair competition law,[31] in a larger sense, the infringement of another's patent right is a manner of competition that society has decided is wrong and for which it will subject the copier to remedies such as an injunction and damages.[32]

(1851). Rather, it is a "creature of statute law." Crown Die & Tool Co. v. Nye Tool & Machine Works, 261 U.S. 24, 40, 43 S. Ct. 254, 67 L. Ed. 516 (1923).

Oil States, 138 S. Ct. at 1373-1374.

[28] *See* Bruce W. Bugbee, The Genesis of American Patent and Copyright Law 22-23 (Public Affairs Press, Washington, D.C., 1967) (reproducing Venetian enactment of March 19, 1474, which "appearing 150 years before England's Statute of Monopolies, established a legal foundation for the world's first patent system").

[29] *Id.* at 39 (quoting England's Statute of Monopolies (1624)).

[30] *See* 1 J. Thomas McCarthy, McCarthy on Trademarks and Unfair Competition §1.2 (4th ed. 2011) (characterizing public domain as "the rule," and intellectual property as "the exception").

[31] The traditional understanding of "unfair competition law" embraces commercial torts such as trademark infringement, false advertising, and trade secret misappropriation, but not violations of the patent or copyright laws, which are considered separate regimes. *See id.* §1.10 (listing examples of unfair competition).

[32] These remedies for violations of patent laws are explored in greater detail in Chapter 11 ("Remedies for Patent Infringement"), *infra*.

5. The Patent Document and Its Components

The meaning of *patent* can be viewed in at least two senses. One use of "patent" refers to an official document issued by the U.S. government. Figure 1.1 reproduces a typical U.S. patent, directed to an insulating sleeve for a hot beverage cup. Skim over this document and familiarize yourself with its various parts. The entirety of the document is referred to as the patent's **specification**, which is composed of (1) the **written description**, (2) drawings (where necessary, as here in the patent's figures, to fully enable others to make and use the invention), and (3) the claims.

The patent's **claims**, which are the numbered, single-sentence paragraphs found at the very end of the patent document, are its most important part. Although Chapter 2 ("Patent Claims"), *infra,* is devoted to the topic, a brief introduction is helpful here. The claims define the scope of the patent owner's right to exclude others from making, using, selling, offering to sell, or importing her invention, much as a deed to a plot of land defines the geographic boundaries of its owner's right to exclude others from coming onto the land (i.e., trespassing). Patent claims form a sort of lingual fence around an invention. For the patent system to function properly, patent claims must provide clear notice on which marketplace participants can rely.[33] The interpretation and scope of the claims will be the focal point of any litigation involving the patent. The language of the claims is scrutinized intensely in analyzing both the validity of the patent and whether it has been infringed. In determining whether to grant the patent in the first instance, the USPTO will compare the language of the claims with relevant prior technology. This process is described in Section H ("Patent Prosecution Overview"), *infra.*

[33]Professors Bessen and Meuer succinctly capture this idea in their book chapter titled "If You Can't Tell the Boundaries, Then It Ain't Property." JAMES BESSEN & MICHAEL J. MEURER, PATENT FAILURE: HOW JUDGES, BUREAUCRATS, AND LAWYERS PUT INNOVATORS AT RISK 46 (2008). They contend that

> increasingly, patents fail to provide *clear notice* of the scope of patent rights. Thus, innovators find it increasingly difficult to determine whether a technology will infringe upon anyone's patents, giving rise to inadvertent infringement. Similarly, they find it increasingly costly to find and negotiate the necessary patent licenses in advance of their technology development and adoption decisions. Thus, clearance procedures that work well for tangible property are undercut by a profusion of fuzzy patent rights.

Id.

US005425497A

United States Patent [19]

Sorensen

[11] **Patent Number:** **5,425,497**

[45] **Date of Patent:** **Jun. 20, 1995**

[54] **CUP HOLDER**

[76] Inventor: **Jay Sorensen,** 3616 NE. Alberta Ct., Portland, Oreg. 97211

[21] Appl. No.: **150,682**

[22] Filed: **Nov. 9, 1993**

[51] **Int. Cl.⁶** **B65D 3/22**

[52] **U.S. Cl.** **220/738;** 220/903; 294/31.2

[58] **Field of Search** .... 294/27.1, 31.2, 33, 294/149, 152; 220/710.5, 753, 758, 759, 412, 738, 739, 903; 229/1.5 B, 1.5 H, 89, 90

[56] **References Cited**

U.S. PATENT DOCUMENTS

1,632,347	6/1927	Pipkin .	
1,771,765	7/1930	Benson .	
1,866,805	7/1932	Haywood	294/31.2
2,028,566	1/1936	Seipel et al. .	
2,266,828	12/1941	Sykes .	
2,591,578	4/1952	McNealy et al. .	
2,617,549	11/1952	Egger .	
2,661,889	12/1953	Phinney .	
2,675,954	4/1954	Vogel .	
2,853,222	9/1958	Gallagher .	
2,979,301	4/1961	Reveal	229/1.5 H X
3,049,277	8/1962	Shappell .	
3,123,273	3/1964	Miller	229/1.5 B
3,157,335	11/1964	Maier	229/1.5 B
3,908,523	9/1975	Shikaya .	
4,685,583	8/1987	Noon	294/31.2 X
5,092,485	3/1992	Lee .	
5,145,107	9/1992	Silver et al. .	

Primary Examiner—Johnny D. Cherry
Attorney, Agent, or Firm—Kolisch, Hartwell, Dickinson, McCormack & Heuser

[57] **ABSTRACT**

A cup holder is disclosed in the form of a sheet with distal ends. A web is formed in one of the ends, and a corresponding slot is formed in the other end such that the ends interlock. Thus the cup holder is assembled by rolling the sheet and interlocking the ends. The sheet can be an elongate band of pressed material, preferably pressed paper pulp, and is preferably formed with multiple nubbins and depressions. In one embodiment, the sheet has a top and bottom that are arcuate and concentric, and matching webs and cuts are formed in each end of the sheet, with the cuts being perpendicular to the top of the sheet.

6 Claims, 1 Drawing Sheet

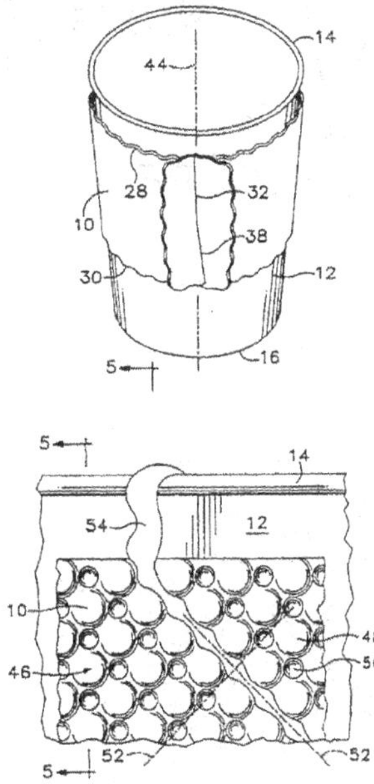

Figure 1.1

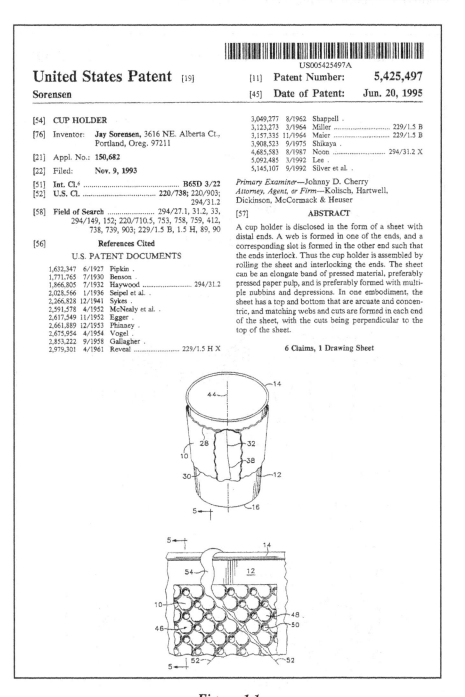

Java Jacket®
U.S. Patent No. 5,425,497 (issued 1995)

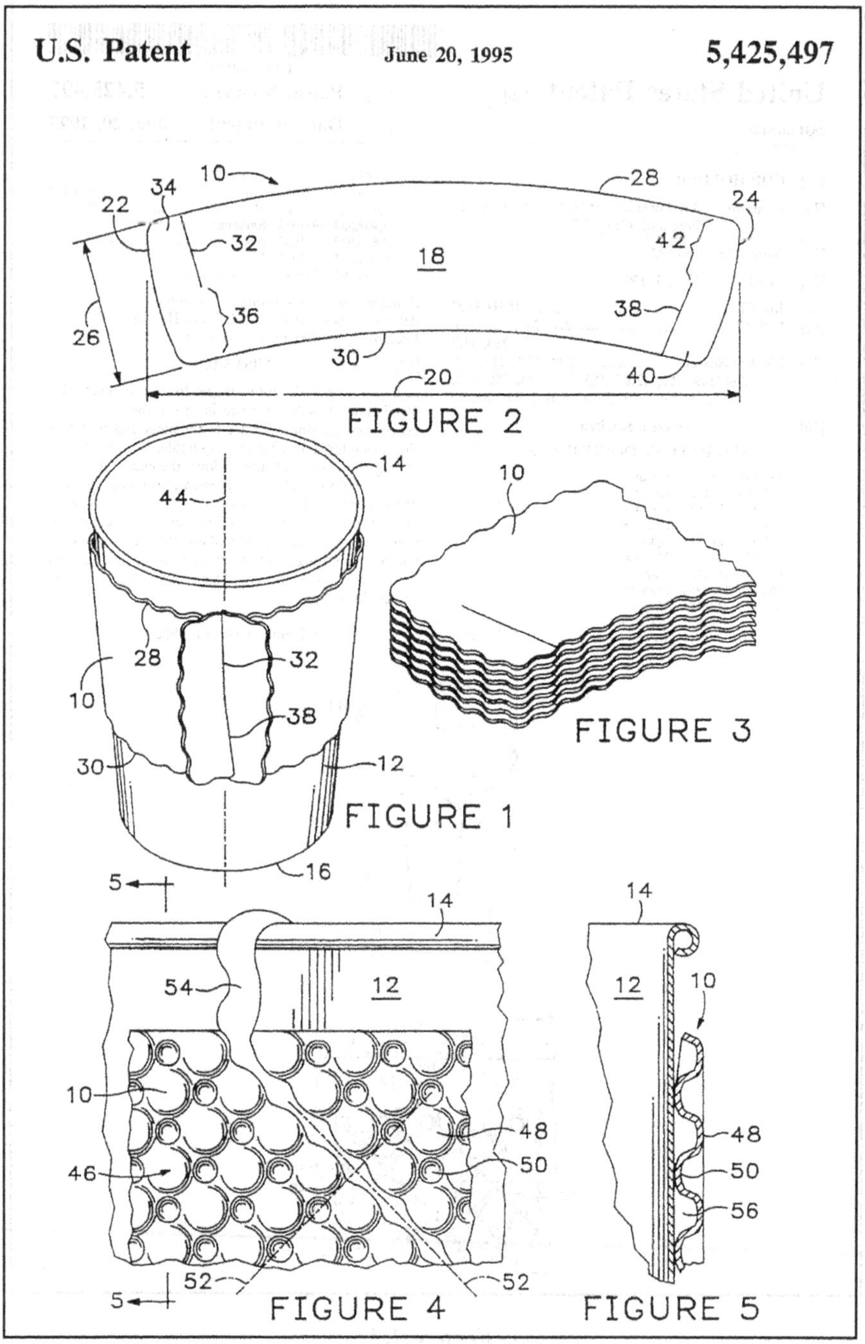
U.S. Patent
June 20, 1995
5,425,497
FIGURE 2
FIGURE 1
FIGURE 3
FIGURE 4
FIGURE 5

Figure 1.1

5,425,497

1

CUP HOLDER

FIELD OF THE INVENTION

The present invention relates generally to holders for cups. More particularly, the invention relates to a disposable cup holder that can be stored flat and then assembled by a user to fit around a cup. The resulting cup and holder combination increases the gripability and insulation value of the cup.

BACKGROUND ART

A cup holder is a removable device that encompasses a cup to provide added features to the cup. These features can include gripability, insulation value, and decoration. By gripability it is meant that the cup and holder combination is easier to hold in a human hand. Insulation value is important if the cup is holding hot or cold liquids, particularly if the cup is a thin disposable paper cup which has little inherent insulation value. Decoration can include features that make the cup more appealing, such as texture or color, or features that communicate to the user of the holder, such as advertising or instructions.

A conventional cup holder includes a three-dimensional body into which the cup is inserted. These bodies can be in the shape of an annular ring, such as that shown in U.S. Pat. No. 2,028,566, or in the shape of a cup that is oversized relative to the cup to be held, such as that shown in U.S. Pat. No. 2,617,549. In order to provide insulation value from a material that is thermally conductive, such as paper, the cup holders are usually provided with annular grooves or vertical flutes so that the holder is only in contact with the cup at the valleys in the grooves or flutes. These grooves or flutes provide a structural integrity to the cup holders such that they must be packaged in substantially the same form as they will be used. Thus a significant volume is required to store a quantity of the cup holders. Therefore it is cumbersome for a retailer selling drinks in cups to use the cup holders because a significant amount of shelf space is required just to have a sufficient quantity of cup holders accessible for immediate use.

It is an object of the invention to reduce the volume required to store cup holders.

Conventional cup holders may also require significant amounts of handling and operations to be assembled. It is a further object of this invention to reduce the number of steps involved in making a cup holder ready for ultimate use by the consumer.

An object of the invention is to produce a cup holder by bending a sheet and interlocking the ends.

It is a further object of the invention to improve the gripability of a cup.

Yet another object of the invention is to thermally insulate the hand of a user from the liquid held in a cup.

Another object of the invention is to form a cup holder from a substantially flat sheet of pressed paper pulp.

SUMMARY OF THE INVENTION

The invented cup holder is designed for use with an upright cup. The cup is in turn designed for holding hot or cold liquids, and has an open rim and closed base.

The invented cup holder is formed from a sheet of flat material, preferably pressed paper pulp. The sheet is formed to have a length defined by a first end and a second end. The sheet has a width defined by a top and

2

a bottom. Two cuts are made in the sheet, the first cut extending partially across the width of the sheet and adjacent one end. The second cut also extends partially across the width of the sheet, but is adjacent the end of the sheet opposite from the first cut. Preferably, one of the cuts severs the top of the sheet and the other of the cuts severs the bottom of the sheet. A holder conforming to a cup can then be made by rolling the sheet into a substantially cylindrical shape and interlocking the first end with the second end by interlocking the first cut with the second cut. Once the cylindrically shaped cup holder is made, a cup can be inserted into the cup holder.

The sheet includes a texture to increase the gripability and insulation value of the cup holder. In one embodiment, the texture includes multiple nubbins and depressions interspersed about the sheet, preferably in a uniform repeating geometrical pattern. The depressions can be aligned in rows forming troughs, so that any liquid that should spill on the cup holder will tend to trickle along the troughs.

If the cup holder is to hold a tapered cup, the holder fits the cup better if the top and bottom of the sheet are arcuate and essentially concentric. Preferably, the first cut is substantially non-parallel to the second cut such that the first cut and the second cut extend along lines that are substantially perpendicular to the arcuate top. When a sheet so formed is made into a cup holder, the resulting holder is tapered with a top and bottom that define planes essentially parallel to the planes defined by the rim and base of the cup to be held. The cuts will also be aligned with the taper of the cup when the holder is assembled, that is, the cuts will extend along a line that is substantially perpendicular to the above planes.

Alternatively, the present invention can be viewed as a combination of a cup and a cup holder. The cup holder is an elongate band having ends that detachably interlock. When the ends are so interlocked, the elongate band extends in a continuous loop. One method of interlocking the ends is by forming interlocking slots in the band. Preferably, the band includes a texture to increase the gripability and insulation value of the combination. The texture can include multiple nubbins and depressions interspersed about the band, preferably in a uniform repeating geometrical pattern. If the cup used as part of the combination is tapered, the tipper and lower surfaces of the band can be concentric arcuate shapes so that the continuous loop formed from the band is approximately conformed with the cup.

BRIEF DESCRIPTION OF THE DRAWINGS

FIG. 1 is a perspective view of an assembled cup holder formed in accordance with one embodiment of the present invention, in combination with a cup.

FIG. 2 is a top plan view of the cup holder of the present invention, shown unassembled.

FIG. 3 is a perspective partial view of a stack of the cup holders shown in FIG. 2.

FIG. 4 is a partial :front elevation of the combination shown in FIG. 1, shown with liquid spilled on the cup holder.

FIG. 5 is a partial front sectional view of the combination shown in FIG. 4, taken along the line 5—5 shown in FIG. 4.

Figure 1.1

(Continued)

5,425,497

3

DETAILED DESCRIPTION AND BEST MODE OF CARRYING OUT THE INVENTION

Referring to FIG. 1, the cup holder **10** is shown in combination with a cup **12**. Cup **12** is usually a tapered paper cup with an open rim **14** and a closed base **16**. Cup holder **10** is shown in its assembled state in FIG. **1**, and can be described as a continuous loop.

Cup holder **10** is shown unassembled in FIGS. **2** and **3**, and is in the form of a sheet **18**, also described as an elongate band having distal ends. Sheet **18** has a length **20** defined by a first end **22** and a second end **24**. Sheet **18** also has a width **26**, defined by a top **28** and a bottom **30**. Top **28** and bottom **30** are preferably arcuate in shape. Thus top **28** can be described as an elongate arcuate surface and bottom **30** can also be described as an elongate arcuate surface. Elongate arcuate surface **28** is essentially concentric with elongate arcuate surface **30**, such that the radius of surface **28** is longer than the radius of surface **30** by an amount approximately equal to width **26**.

A first cut **32** is made in sheet **18** adjacent first end **22**. First cut **32** extends partially across width **26**, and preferably severs top **28** such that a first tab **34** and first web **36** are formed. A second cut **38** is made in sheet **18** adjacent second end **24**. Second cut **38** extends partially across width **26**, and preferably severs bottom **30** to form a second tab **40** and second web **42**.

When sheet **18** is configured as described above, a cup holder can be assembled as follows. Sheet **18** is rolled into a substantially cylindrical shape, and cuts **32** and **38** are interlocked with webs **42** and **36**, respectively, thereby interlocking first end **22** with second end **24**. The resulting cup holder forms a continuous loop as shown in FIG. **1**, and can hold cup **12** by inserting cup **12** into cup holder **10**. Elongate arcuate surface **28** forms an open annular top that is substantially parallel with rim **14** of cup **12**. Elongate arcuate surface **30** forms an open annular bottom that is substantially parallel to base **16** of cup **12**. Cup **12** extends through the open top and open bottom and, as shown in FIG. **5**, encircles cup **12** so that cup holder **10** has an inner surface **58** and an outer surface **60**. First cut **32** and second cut **38** extend along a line shown generally at **44**. Line **44** is substantially perpendicular to rim **14** of cup **12**. Alternatively, line **44** can be described as extending along the taper of cup **12**.

As shown in FIGS. **4** and **5**, sheet **18** is provided with a texture indicated generally at **46**. Texture **46** includes multiple nubbins **48** and oppositely shaped discrete, approximately semi-spherically shaped depressions **50** distributed on substantially the entire inner surface **58** of sheet **18**. Nubbins **48** and depressions **50** are arranged in a repeating geometrical pattern. Preferably, depressions **50** are aligned in rows forming troughs indicated generally by line **52** in FIG. **4**.

Should liquid spill on cup holder **10**, as indicated generally at **54** in FIG. **5**, liquid **54** will tend to trickle along troughs **52**. When the combination of cup holder **10** and cup **12** is held by a human hand, the hand will tend to be held away from troughs **52** by nubbins **48**. Thus the hand will be kept out of contact with liquid **54**. Furthermore, as shown in FIG. **4**, when cup holder **10** is placed on an upright cup **12**, troughs **52** extend along lines that intersect both rim **14** and lines extending along the taper of cup **12** at acute angles. Thus the flow of liquid **54** down cupholder **10** is slowed relative to the flow of liquid down vertically oriented flutes.

4

In addition, texture **46** provides an increased gripability to the cup and cup holder combination. Specifically, nubbins **48** provide a surface texture which is more easily held by a human hand.

Texture **46** also adds an insulation value to the combination because depressions **50** define non-contacting regions **56** of sheet **18**, and thus reduce the surface contact between cup holder **10** and the hand of a user and cup **12**, respectively. Thus conductive heat transfer is reduced. The insulation value is also increased by air gaps **56** formed by texture **46**.

Furthermore, texture **46** is pleasing in appearance, and therefore provides decoration for cup holder **10**.

Cup holder **10** as described above and shown in the figures is made from a reversible, two-sided sheet **18**. That is, when sheet **18** is rolled to form a continuous loop, either of the textured sides can serve as the outside of cup holder **10**. The reversibility of cup holder **10** is particularly evident when, as shown in FIG. **5**, inner surface **58** and outer surface **60** are mirrored, that is, when each depression **62** on inner surface **58** defines a nubbine **48** on outer surface **60** and each depression **50** on outer surface **60** defines a nubbin **64** on inner surface **58**. Non-reversible cup holders are, however, envisioned within the scope of the present invention.

Alternatively, the present invention can be viewed as a method of making a cup and cup holder combination. The method includes the steps of providing a flat sheet with a texture, forming the flat sheet into an elongate band **18** having a top elongate arcuate surface **28** and a bottom elongate arcuate surface **30**. Elongate arcuate surface **28** is severed with a first cut **32** extending partially across elongate band **18**. Elongate arcuate surface **30** is severed with a second cut **38** extending partially across elongate band **18**. Elongate band **18** is then rolled to form a substantially cylindrical shape, and first cut **32** is interlocked with second cut **38** to form a continuous loop. A cup **12** is then inserted into cup holder **10**.

Many materials are envisioned for use in making sheet **10**, however pressed paper pulp is preferred. Pressed pulp, similar in properties to that used to make semi-rigid paper products such as egg cartons, is pleasing to the touch, partially absorbent, easily formed and relatively inexpensive.

INDUSTRIAL APPLICABILITY

The invented cup holder and cup and cup holder combination are applicable in any situation where the gripability, insulation value, or decoration of a cup needs to be augmented. It is particularly applicable for a cup holder for holding paper coffee cups.

While a preferred embodiment of the invented cup holder and cup and cup holder combination have been disclosed, changes and modifications can be made without departing from the spirit of the invention.

We claim:

1. A cup and holder combination comprising:

a cup for holding hot or cold liquids; and

a holder defined by a band mounted on and encircling the cup, the band having an open top and an open bottom through which the cup extends and an inner surface immediately adjacent the cup with a plurality of discrete, spaced-apart, approximately semi-spherically shaped depressions distributed on substantially the entire inner surface of the band so that each depression defines a non-contacting region of the band creating an air gap between the

Figure 1.1

5,425,497

5

band and the cup, thereby reducing the rate of heat transfer through the holder.

2. The cup and holder combination of claim 1, wherein the band also has an outer surface opposite the inner surface, with a plurality of discrete, spaced-apart, approximately semi-spherically shaped depressions distributed on substantially the entire outer surface of the band.

3. The cup and holder combination of claim 2, wherein the inner and outer surfaces of the band are mirrored, with each depression on the inner surface defining a nubbin on the outer surface and each depression on the outer surface defining a nubbin on the inner surface.

4. A holder for encircling a liquid-containing cup to reduce the rate of heat transfer between the liquid contained in the cup and a hand gripping the holder encircling the cup, comprising a band of material formed with an open top and an open bottom through which

6

the cup can extend and an inner surface immediately adjacent the cup, the band including a plurality of discrete, spaced-apart, approximately semi-spherically shaped depressions distributed on substantially the entire inner surface of the band so that each depression defines a non-contacting region of the band creating an air gap between the band and the cup, thereby reducing the rate of heat transfer through the holder.

5. The holder of claim 4, wherein the band also has an outer surface opposite the inner surface, with a plurality of discrete, spaced-apart, approximately semi-spherically shaped depressions distributed on substantially the entire outer surface of the band.

6. The holder of claim 5, wherein the inner and outer surfaces of the band are mirrored, with each depression on the inner surface defining a nubbin on the outer surface and each depression on the outer surface defining a nubbin on the inner surface.

* * * * *

Figure 1.1

(Continued)

6. The Negative Right to Exclude

A patent, in one sense, is an official government document like the one reproduced at Figure 1.1. More importantly, the patent represents a property right. The paper document is merely a tangible representation of the boundaries of a time-limited property right granted by the U.S. federal government. Importantly, this property right is a *negative* right; that is, a right to exclude others from making, using, selling, offering to sell, or importing the patented invention in the United States during the term of the patent.[34] Much as the owner of real property generally has a right to prevent others from entering onto her land,[35] the owner of a patent can ask a court to enjoin those who make, use, sell, offer to sell, or import her invention into this country without authorization. The patent owner also can grant **licenses** to third parties, authorizing them to make, use, sell, offer to sell, or import the patented invention without fear of being sued for infringement. Licenses are contracts, typically requiring financial payments to the patentee called *royalties*.[36]

Notably, a patent does not convey any *positive* or affirmative right to make, use, sell, offer to sell, or import an invention.[37] Any such positive right to exploit one's own creations arises from the common law, not federal patent law.[38] In fact, there are any number of reasons

[34] 35 U.S.C. §154(a)(1); 35 U.S.C. §271(a).

[35] *See* Restatement (First) of Property §1 cmt. a, illus. 1 (1936) (definition of *right*) (stating that A, the owner of Blackacre, "normally has a right that B [any other person] shall not walk across Blackacre," and that B "normally has a duty not to walk across Blackacre").

[36] *See generally* Michael A. Epstein & Frank L. Politano, Drafting License Agreements (4th ed. 2011); Robert W. Gomulkiewicz et al., Licensing Intellectual Property: Law and Application (2d ed. 2011).

[37] *See* Leatherman Tool Group Inc. v. Cooper Indus., Inc., 131 F.3d 1011, 1015 (Fed. Cir. 1997) (explaining that "the federal patent laws do not create any affirmative right to make, use, or sell anything. As the Supreme Court has stated, '[t]he franchise which the patent grants, consists altogether in the right to exclude every one from making, using, or vending the thing patented, without the permission of the patentee. This is all that he obtains by the patent.' ") (quoting Bloomer v. McQuewan, 55 U.S. 539, 548 (1852)).

[38] *See* Crown Die & Tool Co. v. Nye Tool & Machine Works, 261 U.S. 24, 36 (1923) (noting that "[i]t is the fact that the patentee has invented or discovered something useful[,] and thus has the common-law right to make, use, and vend it himself[,] which induces the government to clothe him with power to exclude every one else from making, using[,] or vending it."). The common law did not provide the inventor with any right to exclude *others*, however. *See* Deepsouth Packing Co. v. Laitram Corp., 406 U.S. 518, 525-526 (1972). The negative right to exclude is provided only through the Patent Act. *See* 406 U.S. at 526 n.8 ("But the right of property which a patentee has in his invention, and his right to its exclusive use, is derived altogether from these statutory provisions; and this court [has] always held that an inventor has no right of property in his invention, upon which he can maintain a suit, unless he obtains a patent for it, according to the acts of Congress; and that his rights are to be regulated and

why one might own a patent and yet not be able to practice (i.e., make or sell) her patented invention. For example, criminal laws may forbid the manufacture of certain patented weapons banned by the government. If the patent is directed to a new medicine or method of treatment, the Food and Drug Administration (FDA) may not yet have granted approval for the sale of the item to U.S. consumers. Under certain narrow circumstances, moreover, the practice of a patent in an anticompetitive manner may result in liability under the antitrust laws.[39]

Yet another situation that may prohibit the practice of a patent involves the issuance of a **blocking patent** to another entity. In this scenario, Inventor A's subservient patent is blocked by a dominant patent owned by Inventor B, even though both A and B independently qualified for patent protection on their respective inventions. Consider an example from the time of cave dwellers, before furniture, at least as we know it today, existed. Assume that the cave dwellers' society has implemented a primitive patent system, and that Inventor A has been issued the first patent claiming a "chair." In her patent, Inventor A discloses only a single embodiment (i.e., one specific example) of a chair, the design of which is a simple straight-backed, four-legged chair of the type seen (in modern times) in classrooms or offices. Because Inventor A is considered a "pioneer," her patent should be entitled to a relatively broad interpretation, so as to offer incentives for the creation of basic inventions such as the first "chair."[40]

Assume further that during the period of time while Inventor A's chair patent is still in force, unrelated Inventor B independently invents a rocking chair. Inventor B obtains what patent attorneys refer to as an "improvement patent" that claims the rocking chair. Inventor B's rocking chair is sufficiently new and nonobvious, as compared to the chair disclosed in A's patent, that B is independently entitled to his own patent. If Inventor B makes or sells his rocking chair in

---

measured by these laws, and cannot go beyond them.") (quoting Brown v. Duchesne, 60 U.S. (19 How.) 183, 195 (1857)).

[39] *See infra* Chapter 10 ("Defenses to Patent Infringement"), discussing potential antitrust liability for enforcement of patent rights.

[40] *See* In re Hogan, 559 F.2d 595, 606 (C.C.P.A. 1977) (Markey, C.J.) (contending that if applicants were in fact "pioneers," "they would deserve broad claims to the broad concept," and that to restrict them to claim scope no broader than single disclosed embodiment "is merely to state a policy against broad protection for pioneer inventions, a policy both shortsighted and unsound from the standpoint of promoting progress in the useful arts, the constitutional purpose of the patent laws").

the patent-granting country, however, he will literally infringe Inventor A's patent, which broadly covers all types of chairs.[41]

Note that although Inventor B obtained his own patent based on his novel and nonobvious improvement invention, nevertheless Inventor B did not receive any *affirmative* right to practice his invention. By the same token, because his patent did give Inventor B a negative right to exclude others from making and selling a rocking chair, Inventor A is now blocked from producing rocking chairs, even though her patent broadly covers any type of chair (including a rocking chair). In other words, if Inventor A wants to manufacture and sell a rocking chair, she must obtain a **license** from Inventor B in order to avoid infringement liability.[42]

In practice, the dilemma of blocking patents in the United States is sometimes resolved by contract; that is, the parties cross-license each other.[43] If the parties are unable to negotiate a solution, however, the public is harmed because no one gets the benefit of the improvement.[44] Alternatively, some foreign patent systems authorize compulsory licensing of a blocking basic patent where the subject matter of the blocked improvement patent qualifies as an "important

[41]Professor Mark Lemley has noted that "this infringement determination does not take into account the value of the improvement made by the accused infringer," citing as an example *Hughes Aircraft Co. v. United States*, 717 F.2d 1351 (Fed. Cir. 1983) (holding that government's accused satellite control system, implemented by onboard computers, infringed patent on ground-based analog control system). Mark A. Lemley, *The Economics of Improvement in Intellectual Property Law*, 75 TEX. L. REV. 989, 1006 (1997).

[42]A license is simply an agreement between the patent owner (licensor) and another party (licensee) that the licensor will not sue the licensee for making, using, selling, offering to sell, or importing the patented invention. The consideration for the licensor's promise not to sue is typically a payment called a royalty, which is computed based on the level of the licensee's use of the invention. *See generally* MICHAEL A. EPSTEIN & FRANK L. POLITANO, DRAFTING LICENSE AGREEMENTS (4th ed. 2011); ROBERT W. GOMULKIEWICZ ET AL., LICENSING INTELLECTUAL PROPERTY: LAW AND APPLICATION (2d ed. 2011); *see also infra* Chapter 10 ("Defenses to Patent Infringement"), discussing license defenses.

[43]*See generally* Robert P. Merges, *Intellectual Property Rights and Bargaining Breakdown: The Case of Blocking Patents*, 62 TENN. L. REV. 75 (1994).

[44]*See* Mark A. Lemley, *The Economics of Improvement in Intellectual Property Law*, 75 TEX. L. REV. 989, 1010 (1997). Lemley also notes that, although the defense of the "reverse doctrine of equivalents" is theoretically available to excuse B's infringement, the doctrine has rarely been applied to excuse literal infringement. *See id.* at 1011. For a more optimistic view of the reverse doctrine of equivalents as a solution to the blocking patents problem, *see* Robert P. Merges, *Intellectual Property Rights and Bargaining Breakdown: The Case of Blocking Patents*, 62 TENN. L. REV. 75 (1994). The concepts of literal infringement, infringement under the doctrine of equivalents, and the reverse doctrine of equivalents are addressed in further detail *infra* Chapter 9 ("Patent Infringement").

technical advance of considerable economic significance."[45] The United States has not implemented this type of compulsory licensing.

7. The Patent Term

How long does a patent last? The U.S. Constitution specifies that inventors are to be secured exclusive rights to their discoveries "for limited times," but does not specify any particular number of years. The first U.S. patents lasted 14 years from issuance (i.e., the date that the Patent Office issued the patent), based on the **patent term** in England at that time.[46] The U.S. patent term was extended to 17 years from issuance by the Patent Act of 1861.[47] The length of time during which the patent application was pending in the Patent Office before patent issuance was not relevant to the patent's term.[48]

United States law on the term of patents underwent a major change effective June 8, 1995. This change harmonized U.S. law on patent term with that of other countries. It also dramatically reduced incentives to obtain *submarine patents,* the colloquial term for patents that issue after secretly pending in the USPTO for many years.[49] For any patent application filed on or after June 8, 1995, that patent will expire 20 years after the earliest effective U.S. filing date.[50] For patents that were in force on June 8, 1995, or for patent applications already pending on that

[45]*See* Agreement on Trade-Related Aspects of Intellectual Property Rights [TRIPS], Marrakesh Agreement Establishing the World Trade Organization, Annex 1C, art. 31(l), Apr. 15, 1994, 1869 U.N.T.S. 299; 33 I.L.M. 1197 (1994) (setting forth special criteria for compulsory licensing in the case of blocking patents).

[46]Moreover, early U.S. Congresses extended the term of numerous individual patents; the courts saw no "limited times" impediments to these extensions. Eldred v. Ashcroft, 537 U.S. 186, 201-202 (2003).

[47]Act of March 2, 1861, ch. 88, §16, 12 Stat. 246, 249 (1861).

[48]In rare cases, an extended pendency can give rise to a defense against a patent's enforcement. The Federal Circuit has recognized the equitable defense of "prosecution laches," which may be raised as an affirmative defense to charges of infringement even though the patent applicant's delay in issuing its patent was in compliance with the Patent Act and all pertinent USPTO regulations. *See* Cancer Research Tech. Ltd. v. Barr Labs., Inc., 625 F.3d 724, 728 (Fed. Cir. 2010) (recognizing defense but concluding that district court committed legal error in holding patent unenforceable for prosecution laches in the absence of any evidence of intervening rights); Symbol Techs., Inc. v. Lemelson Med., 422 F.3d 1378 (Fed. Cir. 2005); Symbol Techs., Inc. v. Lemelson Med., 277 F.3d 1361 (Fed. Cir. 2002). For discussion of prosecution in further detail, *see infra* Chapter 10 ("Defenses to Patent Infringement").

[49]In *Ricoh Co. v. Nashua Corp.*, No. 97-1344, 1999 U.S. App. LEXIS 2672, at *8 (Fed. Cir. Feb. 18, 1999) (non-precedential), the Federal Circuit described the legislative change in U.S. patent term as "in effect address[ing] the perceived problem of so-called 'submarine patents,' i.e., the use of continuation applications to claim previously disclosed but unclaimed features of an invention many years after the filing of the original patent application").

[50]35 U.S.C. §154(a)(2). In some cases the 20-year term will be extended by *patent term adjustment*. *See infra* this section.

date, the patent will expire on the later of the two dates — either 20 years from filing, or 17 years from issuance, whichever is later.[51]

Although patent attorneys often speak in shorthand of the "20-year patent term," this terminology is not precisely correct. The term, or enforceable life, of a patent does not begin until the date the patent is *issued* (i.e., on the "issue date") by the USPTO. A patent is entirely a creature of statute. While a patent application is still pending, there is no basis for a lawsuit alleging patent infringement, because there is not yet any patent in existence.[52]

The patent term *expires* on the date that is 20 years after the earliest effective U.S. filing date.[53] The application pendency period is subtracted from 20 years to obtain the patent term. Typical U.S. patent application pendencies last about 2.5 years, at least for mechanical inventions.[54] Thus, the colloquial "20-year term" is, in reality, usually about 17.5 years, as illustrated in Figure 1.2.

The America Invents Act of 2011 added for the first time to the Patent Act a definition of "effective filing date." *See* Leahy-Smith America Invents Act, Pub. L. No. 112-29 (H.R. 1249), §3(a)(2), 125 Stat. 284, 285 (2011) (adding a new §100(i) to the definitional section 35 U.S.C. §100). The definition provides:

> (i)(1) The term "effective filing date" for a claimed invention in a patent or application for patent means —
>
> (A) if subparagraph (B) does not apply, the actual filing date of the patent or the application for the patent containing a claim to the invention; or
>
> (B) the filing date of the earliest application for which the patent or application is entitled, as to such invention, to a right of priority under section 119, 365(a), or 365(b) or to the benefit of an earlier filing date under section 120, 121, or 365(c).
>
> (2) The effective filing date for a claimed invention in an application for reissue or reissued patent shall be determined by deeming the claim to the invention to have been contained in the patent for which reissue was sought.

35 U.S.C. §100 (eff. Mar. 16, 2013).

Note that a U.S. patent's term ends 20 years after its earliest effective *U.S.* filing date, not 20 years from any earlier *foreign* priority date that the applicant may have asserted under 35 U.S.C. §119(a)-(b) or 35 U.S.C. §365(a)-(b) for reasons of patentability (e.g., establishing novelty and/or nonobviousness over prior art). *See* 35 U.S.C. §154(a)(3) ("Priority"). For further discussion of foreign priority, *see infra* Chapter 12 ("International Patenting Issues").

[51] 35 U.S.C. §154(c)(1).

[52] The possibility exists of recovering reasonable royalty damages for certain infringements between the date that a patent application was published by the USPTO at 18 months after filing and the date it issued as a patent, but such damages cannot be sought until the patent issues. *See* 35 U.S.C. §154(d) ("Provisional rights"); *see also infra* Chapter 11, Section I ("Provisional Compensation Remedy").

[53] 35 U.S.C. §154(a)(2).

[54] *See* United States Patent and Trademark Office, *Performance and Accountability Report Fiscal Year 2015*, at 186 tbl. 4 (2015), *available at* http:/www.uspto.gov/sites/default/files/documents/USPTOFY15PAR.pdf (listing total average pendency for applications classified in "Tech Center 3700 — Mechanical Engineering, Manufacturing & Products" as 30.8 months). More complicated technologies involve somewhat longer average pendencies. For example, total average pendency for applications classified in "Tech Center 2100 — Computer Architecture, Software & Information Security" is 31.1 months. *Id.*

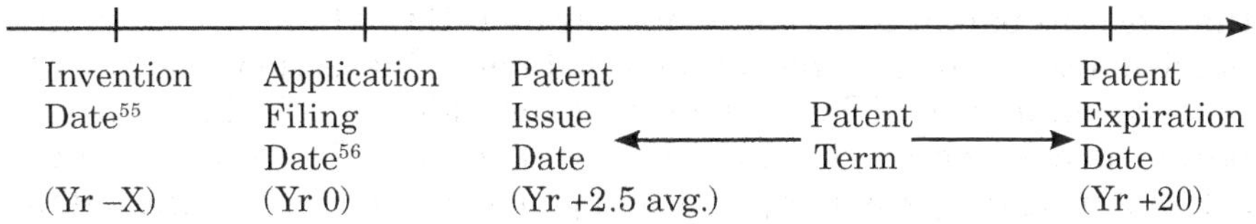

Figure 1.2

Typical U.S. Patent Timeline (not to scale)

Because under the current "20-year term" system the term of a patent will be reduced by the period of time in which the application was pending in the USPTO, it is necessary to ensure that patent owners are not penalized for pendency delays caused by the USPTO rather than by the applicants themselves. Accordingly, the 1999 American Inventors Protection Act (AIPA) added to U.S. patent law the concept

[55]The **invention date** of a claimed invention is a central concept under pre-AIA novelty and first-to-invent priority rules. (Post-AIA, however, the significance of invention dates is likely limited to derivation proceedings under 35 U.S.C. §135 (eff. Mar. 16, 2013).) For purposes of the example discussed in the text, invention date may be thought of as the date of actual reduction to practice of the invention, that is, the date on which the inventor had constructed a physical embodiment of the invention that worked for its intended purpose. The use of "Yr –X" in Figure 1.2 is intended to indicate that there is no set time period in which a patent application must be filed following the invention date, so long as the invention has not been injected into the public domain in some fashion. *See* 35 U.S.C. §102(b) (2006) (providing one-year grace period for application filing following the first patenting or description of invention in a printed publication anywhere in the world, or the first public use or placement on sale of the invention in the United States). In some cases, the invention date may date back to the date of conception, that is, the date on which the inventor had a complete mental picture of the operative invention, as it was thereafter reduced to practice, if the inventor displayed reasonable diligence in moving from the conception to a reduction to practice. *See* Mahurkar v. C.R. Bard, Inc., 79 F.3d 1572, 1577-1578 (Fed. Cir. 1996). The details of determining an invention date are further addressed *infra* Chapter 4 ("Novelty, Loss of Right, and Priority Pre- and Post-America Invents Act of 2011 (35 U.S.C. §102)").

The AIA transitioned the U.S. patent system away from its historic first-to-invent system, such that for patent applications filed on or after March 16, 2013, the invention date described above is no longer relevant to determining which of two rival claimants for a patent will prevail. Rather, the first inventor to file an application describing the invention generally will obtain the patent. *See infra* Chapter 4, Part III.

Nevertheless, concepts such as invention date, reduction to practice, conception, and diligence remain relevant to patents already in force or already applied for before March 16, 2013. These concepts will also be relevant in derivation proceedings, which replace interference proceedings under the AIA.

[56]The application filing date depicted in this figure refers to the filing date of a non-provisional application. Non-provisional and provisional applications are explained *infra* Section H of this chapter ("Patent Prosecution Overview").

of *patent term adjustment* for such delays.[57] The statutory provision that governs patent term adjustment is 35 U.S.C. §154(b),[58] a complex provision that will only be summarized here. Subsection 154(b)(1)(A) concerns prompt USPTO responses. It provides that if the issue of a patent is delayed by certain failures of the USPTO to take timely action during the patent application's pendency, the term of the patent will be extended by one day for each day of such delay. Importantly, subsection 154(b)(1)(B) provides a guarantee of no more than a three-year application pendency. If due to certain USPTO delays the patent is not issued within three years after its filing date, the term of the patent will be extended by one day for each day beyond the three-year window. The delay under this subsection does not include time consumed by requests for continued examination (RCEs),[59] by **interferences**,[60] by secrecy orders, by appeals to the Board or the Federal Circuit, or for processing delays requested by the applicant. Moreover, the period of adjustment under this section will be reduced by any delay on the part of the applicant in responding to USPTO actions more than three months after they were transmitted.[61] Section 154(b)(1)(C) provides adjustment for delays due to interferences, secrecy orders, and appeals in which the applicant succeeds in obtaining a reversal of an adverse determination of patentability.

Any period of patent term adjustment resulting from the USPTO delays described above is subject to being reduced by delays that are the fault of the applicant; namely, by any period of time during which the applicant failed to engage in "reasonable efforts to conclude prosecution" of his application.[62] The USPTO will make a determination of any patent term adjustment to which the applicant is entitled and will transmit notice of that determination along with the notice of

[57]*See* American Inventors Protection Act of 1999, Pub. L. No. 106-113, §4402 ("Patent Term Guarantee Authority"), 113 Stat. 1501 (1999).

[58]The corresponding USPTO rule for patent applications filed on or after May 29, 2000, is 37 C.F.R. §1.702 (2008) ("Grounds for adjustment of patent term due to examination delay under the Patent Term Guarantee Act of 1999 (original applications, other than designs, filed on or after May 29, 2000)"). *See also* 37 C.F.R. §1.703 ("Period of adjustment of patent term due to examination delay"); 37 C.F.R. §1.704 ("Reduction of period of adjustment of patent term"); and 37 C.F.R. §1.705 ("Patent term adjustment determination"). For applications that were filed between June 8, 1995 and May 28, 2000, *see* 37 C.F.R. §1.701 ("Extension of patent term due to examination delay under the Uruguay Round Agreements Act (original applications, other than designs, filed on or after June 8, 1995, and before May 29, 2000)").

[59]*See* 35 U.S.C. §132(b); *infra* Section H ("Patent Prosecution Overview").

[60]Interferences are *inter partes* proceedings conducted in the USPTO to determine priority of invention between rival claimants under the United States' pre-AIA historic first-to-invent priority system. *See infra* Chapter 4, Section N ("Prior Invention Under 35 U.S.C. §102(g) (Pre-AIA)").

[61]*See* 35 U.S.C. §154(b)(2)(C)(ii).

[62]*See* 35 U.S.C. §154(b)(2)(C)(i).

allowance.[63] A patent applicant who disagrees with the term adjustment determination can request reconsideration by the USPTO[64] or may seek judicial review by filing a civil action against the USPTO Director in the federal district court.[65]

Patent term adjustment under section 154(b) of the Patent Act should be distinguished from the separate concept of *patent term restoration* under section 156.[66] Section 156 was added to the Patent Act by Title II of the Drug Price Competition and Patent Term Restoration Act of 1984,[67] popularly known as the Hatch-Waxman Act. Pharmaceutical and health care firms often file for and obtain U.S. patents on new drugs and medical devices before they have obtained the requisite final approval of the U.S. FDA to sell these products to the public. To maintain incentives for costly drug and medical device research and development, the Hatch-Waxman legislation provided for limited restoration of patent term that would otherwise be lost due to this delay in pre-market federal regulatory approval. A patent owner seeking extension of the term of its patent under section 156 submits an application therefore to the USPTO Director.[68]

D. Economic Considerations

Patents have been described as "large-scale governmental intrusions into the free-market economy" that "involve manipulating social costs and benefits to increase the national wealth."[69] There is no dispute that patents have a very real impact on domestic and global economics. Patents are valuable government-created property rights with the potential to act as powerful incentives for innovation, affect the supply and prices of goods and services, and impact the flow of commerce across national borders. This section introduces some of the most basic economic theory relevant to patents.[70]

[63]*See* 35 U.S.C. §154(b)(3)(B)(i).

[64]*See* 35 U.S.C. §154(b)(3)(B)(ii).

[65]*See* 35 U.S.C. §154(b)(4)(A). The America Invents Act of 2011 changed the venue for such actions from the District of Columbia to the Eastern District of Virginia. *See* 35 U.S.C. §154(b)(4)(A) (eff. Sept. 16, 2011).

[66]*See* 35 U.S.C. §156 ("Extension of Patent Term").

[67]Pub. L. No. 98-417, 98 Stat. 1585 (1984).

[68]*See* 35 U.S.C. §156(d)(1).

[69]R. Carl Moy, *The History of the Patent Harmonization Treaty: Economic Self-Interest as an Influence,* 26 J. Marshall L. Rev. 457, 473 (1993).

[70]Those seeking more detailed treatment of the economic impact of the patent system should consult the materials presented during a 2002 series of public hearings on "Competition and Intellectual Property Law and Policy in the Knowledge-Based Economy," jointly sponsored by the U.S. Department of Justice and U.S. Federal Trade Commission. Testimony and presentations delivered on February 20, 25, and 26, 2002, concerning "Economic Perspectives on Intellectual Property, Competition, and

1. Is a Patent a Monopoly?

Courts and commentators sometimes refer to patents as "monopolies," usually in a pejorative manner to indicate the view that patent rights are being used for anticompetitive purposes.[71] A better way to think of patents is as time-limited government conveyances of *potential* monopoly power, which can be put to "good" or "bad" uses from a societal standpoint.[72]

In the days of Queen Elizabeth I of England, patents were handed out as personal favors to royal cronies.[73] For example, the Queen might award to one royal friend the sole right to sell salt, to another the sole right to sell vinegar, and to yet another the sole right to sell playing cards. These patents were truly "bad" or "odious" monopolies that took from the public what had previously been widely available from multiple suppliers. Because these "staple" articles of commerce were now available from only one source (the patent holder), their prices went up and quantities supplied went down. Such "patents" merely rewarded personal loyalty rather than innovation.

A patent as understood today is very different from the royal privileges conferred by the English monarchy. A modern patent conveys a right to exclude others from making, selling, offering to sell, using, or importing only "novel" and "nonobvious" inventions.[74] Thus a modern patent provides only the right to control new technical contributions, not the ability to extract existing technology from the public domain. Patents do not take from the public any innovations that it already possessed.

Today, the type of harmful patent monopoly with which the law is concerned is the use of patent rights for anticompetitive purposes in

---

Innovation" are available online. Federal Trade Commission, *Schedule of Hearings*, [hereinafter FTC/DOJ HEARINGS]. The final report generated from these hearings is Federal Trade Commission, *To Promote Innovation: The Proper Balance of Competition and Patent Law and Policy* (2003), *available at* https://www.ftc.gov/sites/default/files/documents/reports/promote-innovation-proper-balance-competition-and-patent-law-and-policy/innovationrpt.pdf [hereinafter FTC REPORT].

[71]*See, e.g.*, Jamesbury Corp. v. Litton Indus. Prod., Inc., 756 F.2d 1556, 1559 (Fed. Cir. 1985) (admonishing district court that jury instructions that "interject[] language to the effect that the public must be 'protected' against a 'monopoly,' a term found nowhere in the statute, are likely to be prejudicial and should be avoided"), *overruled on other grounds*, A.C. Aukerman Co. v. R.L. Chaides Const. Co., 960 F.2d 1020 (Fed. Cir. 1992); *See also* Schenck v. Nortron Corp., 713 F.2d 782, 786 n.3 (Fed. Cir. 1983) (stating that "[i]t is but an obfuscation to refer to a patent as "the patent monopoly" or to describe a patent as an "exception to the general rule against monopolies").

[72]*See* Giles S. Rich, *Are Letters Patent Grants of Monopoly?*, 15 W. NEW ENG. L. REV. 239, 251 (1993).

[73]*See id.* at 241-242.

[74]Chapters 4 and 5, *infra*, explore the statutory requirements for novelty and nonobviousness in further detail.

a manner that violates the U.S. antitrust laws, including the Sherman Act.[75] As addressed in further detail in Chapter 10 ("Defenses to Patent Infringement"), *infra,* an antitrust violation must be premised on anticompetitive conduct by a patent owner with "market power" as defined in the antitrust sense. Modern antitrust law recognizes that mere ownership of a patent does not necessarily confer monopoly power of the type necessary to establish a violation of the Sherman Act, however.[76] A number of alternatives to the patented invention may exist that consumers would consider acceptable substitutes. Thus the relevant market for antitrust purposes may be much broader than the market for the claimed invention. For example, if the problem is mouse infestation, the relevant market might be defined as all solutions, including not only a patented, proverbial "better mouse trap" but also all old, non-patented mousetraps as well as cats. Economic, not merely technological, substitutability is the key determiner of relevant market.[77]

2. Cost/Benefit Analysis for Patents

A government's decision to recognize and enforce patent rights brings with it certain societal costs as well as benefits. Understanding and recognizing both sides of the equation is an essential prerequisite to a thorough understanding of the patent system.[78]

[75]15 U.S.C. §§1 *et seq*. Antitrust allegations involving unilateral enforcement of patent rights are premised on Section 2 of the Sherman Act, which criminalizes monopolization and attempted monopolization of "any part of the trade or commerce among the several States, or with foreign nations." 15 U.S.C. §2; *see also infra* Chapter 10, Section F ("Antitrust Counterclaims").

[76]*See* U.S. Dep't of Justice, *Antitrust Guidelines for the Licensing of Intellectual Property* §2.2 (1995), *available at* http://www.usdoj.gov/atr/public/guidelines/0558.pdf. *See also* Richard A. Posner, *Transaction Costs and Antitrust Concerns in the Licensing of Intellectual Property,* 4 J. MARSHALL REV. INTELL. PROP. L. 325, 329 (2005), https://repository.jmls.edu/ripl/vol4/iss3/1/ (characterizing patent "monopoly" usage as "unfortunate" because it "confuses an exclusive right with an economic monopoly").

[77]*See* Unitherm Food Sys., Inc. v. Swift-Eckrich, Inc., 375 F.3d 1341, 1364 (Fed. Cir. 2004), *reversed on other grounds,* 546 U.S. 394 (2006); *see also* Illinois Tool Works Inc. v. Independent Ink, Inc., 547 U.S. 28, 44 (2006) (noting that "the vast majority of academic literature recognizes that a patent does not necessarily confer market power," and rejecting a *per se* presumption of market power for patents involved in tying arrangements).

[78]A classic study of the economic impact of patents is STAFF OF SUBCOMM. ON PAT. TRADEMARK & COPYRIGHT OF THE COMM. ON THE JUDICIARY, 85TH CONG., AN ECONOMIC REVIEW OF THE PATENT SYSTEM (Comm. Print 1958) (prepared by Fritz Machlup pursuant to S. Res. 236). Other leading works on the economics of patent law include WARD S. BOWMAN, JR., PATENT AND ANTITRUST LAW: A LEGAL AND ECONOMIC APPRAISAL 15-32 (1973), and F.M. SCHERER, INDUSTRIAL MARKET STRUCTURE and ECONOMIC PERFORMANCE 379-399 (1970). More recent scholarly work on the economics of the patent system was presented during a 2002 series of public hearings on "Competition and Intellectual

a. Costs

Patent systems place a number of short-term costs or burdens on the public. At a microeconomic level, one can see this by comparing a perfectly competitive market[79] for widgets that are not patented with a market in which one person holds a patent on widgets. The introduction of patent rights will result in a reduction in the quantity of widgets supplied, compared with what that quantity would have been in a perfectly competitive market. It will also raise the price of widgets above that which would have been set in a perfectly competitive market.[80]

Creating and maintaining a patent system also entails considerable administrative costs. The U.S. Patent and Trademark Office (USPTO), a bureau of the Department of Commerce, is the federal agency that grants U.S. patents. One of the very oldest federal agencies, the USPTO in fiscal year 2018 employed almost 12,600 federal personnel[81] and operated on a budget of nearly $3.75 billion.[82] To its credit, the USPTO has been fully "user fee-funded" for several years, although Congress has frequently diverted USPTO income to other government entities.[83]

Another cost of the patent system is duplicative, overlapping expenditures on research and development in the same technical field by different firms. It is not uncommon for multiple firms to focus their

---

Property Law and Policy in the Knowledge-Based Economy," jointly sponsored by the U.S. Department of Justice and U.S. Federal Trade Commission. *See* Federal Trade Commission, *Schedule of Hearings*. A helpful summary of recent empirical work on the patent system's impact on innovation is included in Bronwyn H. Hall, *Testimony for the FTC/DOJ (Antitrust) Hearings on Competition and Intellectual Property Law in the Knowledge-Based Economy* (Feb. 26, 2002), https://www.ftc.gov/sites/default/files/documents/reports/promote-innovation-proper-balance-competition-and-patent-law-and policy/innovationrpt.pdf.

[79] *Perfectly competitive market* refers to the economics concept of a hypothetical market operating at "perfect" competition, in which there are such a large number of firms that no individual firm can influence the market price, and where all parties have "perfect" information. For helpful definitions of these microeconomic terms, *see* THE ECONOMIST, *Economics A-Z terms (2016)*, http://www.economist.com/economics-a-to-z.

[80] For a useful introduction to the microeconomics of patent law, *see* Paul E. Schaafsma, *An Economic Overview of Patents*, 79 J. PAT. & TRADEMARK OFF. SOC'Y 241 (1997).

[81] *See* United States Patent and Trademark Office, *Performance and Accountability Report Fiscal Year 2018*, at 2 (chart titled "Financial and Related Highlights"), https://www.uspto.gov/sites/default/files/documents/USPTOFY18PAR.pdf.

[82] *See* United States Patent and Trademark Office, *Performance and Accountability Report Fiscal Year 2018*, at 2 (chart titled "Financial and Related Highlights"), https://www.uspto.gov/sites/default/files/documents/USPTOFY18PAR.pdf (including line item titled "Budgetary Resources Available for Spending").

[83] *See* Intellectual Prop. Owners Ass'n, *Background and Status on USPTO Funding, Adequate Funding for the USPTO and Ending Fee Diversion,* http://www.ipo.org/AM/Template.cfm?Section=Home&Template=/CM/ContentDisplay.cfm&ContentID=3360 (last visited June 16, 2011) (stating that "[s]ince 1990, a total of over $800 Million of USPTO User Fees have been withheld from the agency. . . .").

research and development efforts on the same or similar technical or scientific problem. If, in so doing, two (or more) entities independently invent the same invention, only one can receive a U.S. patent on the invention.[84] Under the historic U.S. **priority system**, the patent was awarded to the first in time to invent;[85] for patent applications filed on or after March 16, 2013, in accordance with the America Invents Act of 2011, the U.S. patent generally will be awarded to the first inventor to file a patent application describing the invention.[86] In either case, an independent inventor of the same invention, if later in time (later to invent or later to file, respectively, under pre- and post-AIA systems), will not be entitled to the patent and generally will need a license from the first inventor in order to avoid infringement liability.[87] Thus the research and development work on the invention by the unsuccessful later inventor or filer can be viewed as duplicative and wasteful from an economic standpoint.[88]

The patent system also places costs on society in terms of forgone research and development that is not conducted because of existing patents owned by others. These patents may or may not be valid. Like a "scarecrow," extant patents of questionable validity may dissuade others from doing follow-on work in the same area of the invention. When an invalid patent operates in this manner, society bears the cost of losing potentially important innovation that might otherwise have been generated.[89]

[84]*See* 35 U.S.C. §101 (providing that "[w]hoever invents or discovers any new and useful process, machine, manufacture, or composition of matter, or any new and useful improvement thereof, may obtain *a* patent therefor, subject to the conditions and requirements of this title") (emphasis added).

[85]35 U.S.C. §102(g)(1) (2006).

[86]*See* 35 U.S.C. §102(a)(2) (eff. Mar. 16, 2013) (providing that "a person shall be entitled to a patent unless . . . the claimed invention was described in a patent issued under section 151, or in an application for patent published or deemed published under section 122(b), in which the patent or application, as the case may be, names another inventor and was effectively filed before the effective filing date of the claimed invention"); *see also* Leahy-Smith America Invents Act, Pub. L. No. 112-29 (H.R. 1249), §3 ("First Inventor to File"), 125 Stat. 284, 285-293 (2011).

[87]The America Invents Act of 2011 broadened the availability of prior user rights to shield later filers in this scenario who have already made commercial use of their inventions. *See* 35 U.S.C. §273 (eff. Sept. 16, 2011) ("Defense to infringement based on prior commercial use").

[88]The problem of wasteful, duplicative research expenditures was exacerbated by the fact that U.S. patent applications were traditionally maintained in secrecy until they issued as patents. Thus, researchers were unable to discover, at least through the mechanism of patent disclosures, what their competitors were working on until the competitors' patents issued. The secrecy problem has been ameliorated to some degree by the passage of the American Inventors Protection Act of 1999, which enacted 18-month publication for most U.S. patent applications. *See* 35 U.S.C. §122(b); *infra* Section H ("Patent Prosecution Overview").

[89]A contrary view is the "prospect theory" of patents. *See* Edmund W. Kitch, *The Nature and Function of the Patent System*, 20 J.L. & ECON. 265 (1977). Kitch analogized

Litigation expense represents another cost of the patent system, particularly when infringement is inadvertent.[90] Only a small percentage of issued patents are ever litigated in court, but each such litigation is potentially lengthy and expensive. For example, total litigation costs for a patent infringement suit with $10-25 million at risk averaged an estimated $2 million in 2017.[91]

Policymakers are increasingly concerned about the high costs of patent litigation, which may be a deterrent to patent enforcement by small firms.[92] Although the parties pay attorney fees and litigation

---

the grant of patents to the award of mining claims in nineteenth-century America, which reserved for the first claimant to arrive on the scene the exclusive right to mine all territory within the claim. Kitch contended that giving patent rights of broad scope to the first inventor of a particular technological advance would enhance, rather than reduce, incentives for follow-on improvements, and serve the larger social welfare. He described the process of technological innovation as one in which a variety of resources are brought to bear on an array of "prospect[s]," or "particular opportunit[ies] to develop a known technological possibility." *Id.* at 266. Because each prospect can be pursued by multiple firms, the process is efficient only if some system ensures "efficient allocation of the resources among the prospects at an efficient rate and in an efficient amount." *Id.* Kitch contended that the patent system functions in this manner "by awarding exclusive and publicly recorded ownership of a prospect shortly after its discovery." *Id.*

[90]Professors Bessen and Meurer explain that infringement occurs inadvertently when patents fail to provide clear, up-front notice of permitted and non-permitted activity. *See* James Bessen & Michael J. Meurer, Patent Failure: How Judges, Bureaucrats, and Lawyers Put Innovators at Risk 147 (2008) (finding that "inadvertent infringement plays a crucial role in explaining the pattern of litigation over time and . . . across technology. Simply put, notice failure and the resulting inadvertent infringement are central to the failure of patents to provide positive innovation incentives.").

[91]*See* Am. Intellectual Prop. Law Ass'n, Report of the Economic Survey 41 (2017). The AIPLA survey lists median litigation costs for such suits from the commencement of suit to the "[e]nd of discovery" as $1 million, and "[i]nclusive, all costs" as $2 million. *Id.* For patent infringement lawsuits with less than $1 million at risk, the median litigation cost figures were $250,000 and $5000,000, respectively. *Id.* For patent infringement lawsuits with more than $25 million at risk, the median cost figures were $1.7 million and $3 million, respectively. *Id.*

Although a primary goal of the America Invents Act of 2011 was to create new procedures for challenging the validity of issued patents in the USPTO that would be less time-consuming and expensive than patent litigation in federal court, *see infra* Chapter 8, Section E ("AIA-Implemented Procedures for Challenging Issued Patents"), the new AIA-implemented procedures are by no means costless. The AIPLA's 2015 survey reports median litigation costs for taking an *inter partes* review through Patent Trial and Appeal Board (PTAB) hearing as $275,000. *Id.* at 38. If the PTAB's decision is appealed to the Federal Circuit, median costs through appeal increase to $350,000.

[92]*See* Federal Trade Commission, *Schedule of Hearings*, ch. 5, at 3 (stating that "[t]he record is replete with discussion of the cost of litigation and its potential to operate as a drag on the system"); *id.* at 25 (reporting concern of several panelists "that the high cost of litigation may work to the disadvantage of small firms, pressuring them to settle when accused and discouraging them from asserting their own patent rights"). *See also* Federal Trade Commission, *The Evolving IP Marketplace — Aligning Patent Notice and*

expenses, the public also shoulders the costs because taxes support the judicial system. Moreover, as the frequency of patent litigation increases,[93] judicial system resources allocated to protracted patent lawsuits are not available for other types of cases.

b. Benefits

Costs of our patent system must be weighed against the many important benefits that it provides to the public. As Abraham Lincoln famously described it, the patent system "added the fuel of interest to the fire of genius."[94] Patents are fundamentally incentive systems. The time-limited right to exclude others that a patent represents is a powerful incentive for the creation of new innovation from which society benefits.[95]

The specific benefits conferred by the existence and recognition of patents are observable at different stages in the timeline of patent life. When patent applications are published, in most cases 18 months after their effective filing date,[96] the public domain is enhanced by the disclosure of the information in the application. The Patent Act

---

Remedies with Competition 147 (Mar. 2011), https://www.ftc.gov/sites/default/files/documents/reports/evolving-ip-marketplace-aligning-patent-notice-and-remedies-competition-report-federal-trade/110307patentreport.pdf (recognizing that "[t]he problem of high litigation costs should be addressed directly. . . ."); Deborah Platt Majoras, Chairman, Federal Trade Commission, *A Government Perspective on IP and Antitrust Law* (June 21, 2006) (transcript available at https://www.ftc.gov/public-statements/2006/06/government-perspective-ip-and-antitrust-law) (stating that "[e]xpensive and time-consuming litigation to challenge a patent on an obvious technology wastes resources").

[93]In fiscal year 2015, over 5,500 patent cases were filed in the federal district courts. *See* Administrative Office of the U.S. Courts, *Judicial Business 2015*, Table C-7 — U.S. District Courts-Civil Judicial Business (Sept. 30, 2015), *available at* http://www.uscourts.gov/statistics/table/c-7/judicial-business/2015/09/30 (reporting that a total of 5,564 patent cases were filed in the U.S. District Courts during 12-month period ending Sept. 30, 2015). Litigants filed more than 3,300 patent infringement actions in 2010. In comparison, only about 800 such suits were brought in 1980. *See Making Sense of Patent Law,* N.Y. TIMES, Nov. 18, 2011, at B2.

[94]This quote from a speech given by Abraham Lincoln is inscribed over a door of the building that houses the U.S. Department of Commerce in Washington, D.C. The USPTO, a bureau of the Department of Commerce, was once housed in this building, but is currently located in northern Virginia.

[95]Some scholars question the traditional view that the right to exclude conveyed by patent ownership is the "alpha and omega of the private value of patent rights." Clarisa Long, *Patent Signals*, 69 U. CHI. L. REV. 625, 627 (2002). Professor Long views patents as "a means of credibly publicizing information," which can "reduc[e] informational asymmetries between patentees and observers." *Id.* She contends that the ability of patents to signal information about their owners may be of greater value in some cases than the substance of the exclusionary right. *See id.* at 627-628.

[96]*See* 35 U.S.C. §122(b). Eighteen-month publication was a major change to the U.S. patent system, implemented as part of the American Inventors Protection Act of 1999. Prior to that implementation, pending U.S. patent applications were maintained in secret until they issued as patents. *See infra* Section H ("Patent Prosecution Overview").

requires that this disclosure be **enabling**, such that it will permit others to make and use the invention (either with the patent owner's authorization during the term of the patent, or after it expires) without undue experimentation.[97] Patents perform an important role in the dissemination of new technologic information. As soon as the application is published, members of the public can read, study, and learn from the information contained therein. Some may even attempt to "invent around" the patent; that is, they develop alternative devices or methods that accomplish the same purpose as the patented invention but that are sufficiently different to avoid infringement. The U.S. domestic economy also is enhanced when the patent is "practiced" or "worked" in this country, meaning that the patent owner and/or her licensee(s) actually manufactures and sells the patented item in the United States during the term of the patent. This activity generates sales, creates jobs, and spurs investment. Once a patent expires, the invention enters the public domain and is free for all to make and use[98] (assuming that such use is not blocked by another patent, government regulation, or the like).

Utilitarian theory (described below) views the short-term costs of having a patent system as a necessary trade-off to obtain the long-term benefits mentioned above. But determining the precise balance between incentive and reward has eluded economists for centuries.[99] What is the "optimal" level of protection that must be offered, both in terms of patent scope and duration, to call forth the "right" level of

[97]35 U.S.C. §112, ¶1 (2006); 35 U.S.C. §112(a) (eff. Sept. 16, 2012); *see also* In re Wands, 858 F.2d 731, 737 (Fed. Cir. 1988).

[98]*See* Bonito Boats, Inc. v. Thunder Craft Boats, Inc., 489 U.S. 141, 152 (1989) (stating that "[w]e have long held that after the expiration of a federal patent, the subject matter of the patent passes to the free use of the public as a matter of federal law") (citing Coats v. Merrick Thread Co., 149 U.S. 562, 572 (1893) ("[P]laintiffs' right to the use of the embossed periphery expired with their patent, and the public had the same right to make use of it as if it had never been patented"); Kellogg Co. v. National Biscuit Co., 305 U.S. 111 (1938); Singer Mfg. Co. v. June Mfg. Co., 163 U.S. 169 (1896)).

[99]Johns Hopkins University economist Fritz Machlup authored one of the most important modern studies of the patent system. Staff of Subcomm. on Pat. Trademark & Copyright of the Comm. on the Judiciary, 85th Cong., *An Economic Review of the Patent System* 1-80 (Comm. Print 1958) (prepared by Fritz Machlup pursuant to S. Res. 236), *available at* http://mises.org/etexts/patentsystem.pdf. Machlup's study is famously noted for his lukewarm conclusion about the value of the U.S. patent system:

> If one does not know whether a system "as a whole" (in contrast to certain features of it) is good or bad, the safest "policy conclusion" is to "muddle through"—either with it, if one has long lived with it, or without it, if one has lived without it. If we did not have a patent system, it would be irresponsible, on the basis of our present knowledge of its economic consequences, to recommend instituting one. But since we have had a patent system for a long time, it would be irresponsible, on the basis of our present knowledge, to recommend abolishing it.

Id. at 80.

innovation? Scholars have long debated this question,[100] and it may never be fully resolved. Most likely the answers will differ depending on the type of technology involved.[101] For example, a longer term of protection is more critical for pharmaceutical innovation than for spurring the development of new computer software products, which typically have a much shorter marketplace life cycle.

E. Philosophical Rationales for Patent Protection

Scholars have identified four primary theories or rationales for the protection of intellectual property, including patents.[102] The "natural rights" and "reward for services rendered" theories are grounded on notions of fundamental fairness and doing justice to individuals who innovate. In contrast, the "monopoly profits incentive" and "exchange for secrets" rationales are considered "utilitarian," or economically

[100]*See, e.g.*, Ted M. Sichelman, *Markets for Patent Scope,* 1 IP THEORY 41 (2010), *available at* http://www.repository.law.indiana.edu/ipt/vol1/iss2/1 (considering the "recurring issue in intellectual property theory is how the scope of patent rights affects invention and commercialization"); Fed. Trade Comm'n, *Ideas Into Action: Implementing Reform of the Patent System: To Promote Innovation: The Proper Balance of Competition and Patent Law and Policy,* 19 BERKELEY TECH. L.J. 861 (2004); Frederic M. Scherer, *Nordhaus' Theory of Optimal Patent Life: A Geometric Reinterpretation*, 62 AM. ECON. REV. 422 (1972); WILLIAM D. NORDHAUS, INVENTION, GROWTH, AND WELFARE: A THEORETICAL TREATMENT OF TECHNOLOGICAL CHANGE (MIT Press 1969).

[101]A Carnegie Mellon survey of R&D laboratories in the U.S. manufacturing sector concluded that patents are far more important for stimulating innovation in the pharmaceutical industry than in any other. Wesley M. Cohen et al., *Protecting Their Intellectual Assets: Appropriability Conditions and Why U.S. Manufacturing Firms Patent (or Not)* (Nat'l Bureau of Econ. Research, Working Paper No. 7522, 2000), *available at* http://www.nber.org/papers/w7552.pdf. The Carnegie Mellon study is summarized at Wesley M. Cohen, *Patents: Their Effectiveness and Role* (Feb. 20, 2002), researchgate.net/publication/247121253_Patents_Their_Effectiveness_and_Role [hereinafter Cohen 2002] (prepared for the FTC/DOJ Hearings on Competition and Intellectual Property Law in the Knowledge-Based Economy). Professor Cohen finds that patents are used differently in "[c]omplex product industries," where products (such as computers or communications equipment) are typically protected by numerous (possibly hundreds) of patents, than in "[d]iscrete product industries," where products (such as drugs and chemicals) are protected by relatively few patents. *See id.* at 13. In the complex product industries it is unlikely that any one firm owns all the patent rights in a particular product (such as a computer). Thus, firms are mutually dependent and more likely to use their patents to ensure inclusion in cross-licensing negotiations to gain access to rivals' complementary technology. *Id.* at 14. In discrete product industries, by contrast, patents are used to block substitute products by building "patent fences" rather than to compel cross-licensing. *Id.*

[102]Some of the most important studies of the philosophical foundations of IP law include Edwin C. Hettinger, *Justifying Intellectual Property*, 18 PHIL. & PUB. AFF. 31 (1989); Justin Hughes, *The Philosophy of Intellectual Property*, 77 GEO. L.J. 287 (1988); ROBERT P. MERGES, JUSTIFYING INTELLECTUAL PROPERTY (Harvard Univ. Press 2011); and EDITH TILTON PENROSE, THE ECONOMICS OF THE INTERNATIONAL PATENT SYSTEM (Baltimore: Johns Hopkins Press, 1951).

focused, theories. The utilitarian view seeks to maximize the overall happiness of society at large, rather than focusing on rewarding the individual inventor. The utilitarian theories, rather than natural rights–based rationales, are generally considered to be the most aligned with the U.S. patent system.

1. Natural Rights

The natural rights (or "deontological") justification, which has most strongly influenced the intellectual property systems of continental Europe, is based on the work of John Locke, the seventeenth-century English philosopher who developed a "labor theory" of property.[103] Locke believed that God gave the earth to people "in common," and that all persons have a property interest in their own body and own their own labor. When a person mixes her labor with objects found in the common, she makes it her property. For example, if a person gathers a pile of acorns in a public park, she has mixed her labor with the acorns and by so doing has acquired a property interest in that pile of acorns; if another takes away the acorns without permission, it constitutes stealing. The gatherer in this example must not attempt to appropriate all the available acorns, however; Locke's "proviso" mandates that the right to private ownership is conditional on a person leaving in common "enough and as good" for others. Nor must she take more from the common than she can make use of (i.e., Locke's "nonwaste condition").

Some of the problems with Locke's theory as applied to intellectual property are that it would appear to award property rights that are perpetual, and never permit the intellectual property to pass into the public domain. Natural rights theory does not address the central question of balancing proprietary rights against enhancement of the public domain. The theory also fails to grapple with allocation of efforts by multiple innovators; modern scholars recognize that the process of invention is generally cumulative,[104] meaning that the work of one inventor typically builds on the work of earlier inventors.[105]

[103]John Locke, *Second Treatise of Government*, ch. V, §27 (1690).

[104]*See, e.g.*, Ofer Tur-Sinai, *Cumulative Innovation in Patent Law: Making Sense of Incentives*, 50 IDEA 723 (2010); Christopher A. Cotropia, *"After-Arising" Technologies and Narrowing Patent Scope*, 61 N.Y.U. ANN. SURV. AM. L. 151, 178 (2005) (stating that "most inventions build upon earlier inventions"); Arti K. Rai, *Fostering Cumulative Innovation in the Biopharmaceutical Industry: The Role of Patents and Antitrust*, 16 BERKELEY TECH. L.J. 813 (2001); Clarisa Long, *Patents and Cumulative Innovation*, 2 WASH. U. J.L. & POL'Y 229 (2000); Suzanne Scotchmer, *Standing on the Shoulders of Giants: Cumulative Research and the Patent Law,* 5 J. ECON. PERSP. 29 (1991).

[105]Isaac Newton said of his inventive genius that "[i]f I have seen further [than certain other men,] it is by standing on the shoulders of giants." THE COLUMBIA WORLD OF QUOTATIONS No. 41418 (Robert Andrews et al. eds. 1996).

2. Reward for Services Rendered

A second rationale for conveying proprietary rights in intellectual property characterizes these rights as a reward for services rendered. This theory posits that inventors render a useful service to society and that society must reward them for it. An inventor has a right to receive, and therefore society is morally obligated to give, a reward for the inventor's services in proportion to their usefulness to society.

One concern with the reward for services theory is that it does not guide us in rewarding the invention made by accident, rather than conscious effort and hard work. Another problem is that the reward theory assumes that the price a patentee can attain for her invention in the marketplace is the correct measure of its usefulness to society. In reality, however, that price reflects the fact that the patentee is the sole source of the patented invention and can thus set prices without having to meet competition. To see why the price obtained by the patentee for her invention may not always be an accurate reflection of its societal utility, consider inventions created "before their time." Such inventions ultimately become very important to society, but are not recognized as beneficial and in fact are criticized at the time of their introduction to the marketplace on "moral" or other grounds, for example, contraceptives. Conversely, other inventions may be overvalued by the marketplace, well beyond their intrinsic value to society; consider "fad" items such as mood-revealing jewelry or herb gardens grown in clay shaped like animals.[106]

3. Monopoly Profits Incentive

The monopoly profits incentive rationale assumes that innovation is good for society, and that the correct incentive to bring forth the societally optimal level of innovation is the (currently) 20-year period of exclusivity that a patent represents. Economists are divided over whether a 20-year term makes sense. The answer most likely differs according to the type of technology involved.[107] While patents of this

[106]*See* Joseph Enterprises, *Original Chia Products* (2015), chia.com/chia-pets/original-chia-products.

[107]*See* Wesley M. Cohen, *Patents: Their Effectiveness and Role* (Feb. 20, 2002), research.net/publication/247121253_Patents_Their_Efectiveness_and-Role [hereinafter Cohen 2002] (prepared for the FTC/DOJ Hearings on Competition and Intellectual Property Law in the Knowledge-Based Economy); *see also* Bronwyn H. Hall, *The Use and Value of Patent Rights,* at 7, tbl. 2 (2009), *available at* https://eml.berheley.edu//-bhhall/papers/BHH09_IPMinisterial_June.pdf (gathering survey results in report to the UK IP Ministerial Forum on the Economic Value of Intellectual Property that present "a rough ranking of the industries in which patents are considered the most important. In almost all cases where it is broken out separately, the pharmaceutical industry ranks at or near the top, followed by specialized machinery and instruments, other chemicals, and occasionally transport equipment including motor vehicles and parts.").

term are considered essential to the pharmaceutical industry, it is not so clear that 20-year patents are needed to bring forth the optimal level of innovation in computer software or business methods. In many cases, the "first-mover advantage" may be enough to spur innovation in these technological fields. Witness the case of Federal Express, which revolutionized the shipping industry with its new method of overnight package delivery but never sought patent protection.

4. Exchange for Secrets

The exchange for secrets model assumes that most innovation would remain secret, but for the incentive to disclose that the patent system provides. Seen in this light the patent system often has been described as a *quid pro quo,* or bargain-exchange, in that the inventor is conveyed a time-limited right to exclude others from exploiting her invention, in exchange for disclosing how to make and use the invention in an enabling fashion that will facilitate practice of the invention by all once the patent expires.

One criticism of the exchange for secrets theory is that it fails to account for the "ripeness of time" concept of innovation. This theory posits that multiple inventors are often working simultaneously on the same problem, and that if one of them does not find and disclose her solution, someone else probably will in a relatively short while. For example, the Supreme Court contended in *Kewanee Oil Co. v. Bicron Corp.,*[108] its decision holding that state trade secret laws are not preempted by the federal patent laws, that had Watson and Crick not discovered the doubled-stranded helix structure of DNA, it is very likely that Linus Pauling would have.[109] Thus it is not clear that the patent system is needed to guarantee the disclosure of inventions that would otherwise be kept secret.

One response to this criticism of the patent system is that, although the same invention is often being developed in parallel by two or more independent parties, there is nothing that prevents *both* parties from

[108] 416 U.S. 470 (1974).

[109] *See Kewanee Oil*, 416 U.S. at 491 n.19. More recent scholarship suggests that x-ray crystallographer Rosalind Franklin, a collaborator of James Watson, Francis Crick, and Maurice Wilkins, also played a leading role in the discovery of DNA's double-helix structure, but was never officially credited. *See generally* BRENDA MADDOX, ROSALIND FRANKLIN: THE DARK LADY of DNA (Harper Collins 2002); ANNE SAYRE, ROSALIND FRANKLIN AND DNA (2d ed., W.W. Norton 2000). Watson, Crick, and Wilkins received a Nobel Prize for the double-helix model of DNA in 1962, four years after Franklin's death at age 37 from ovarian cancer. *See* Merry Maisel & Laura Smart, San Diego Supercomputer Center, *Women in Science: A Selection of 16 Significant Contributors* 3 (1997), http://www.sdsc.edu/ScienceWomen/GWIS.pdf ("Rosalind Elsie Franklin (1920-1958) *Pioneer Molecular Biologist*").

keeping their inventions secret. Absent a patent system, it may make economic sense for *all* parties to maintain the invention in secrecy. Thus, parallel development does not necessarily guarantee disclosure of inventions if maintaining secrecy is a more economically viable option for all. The patent system represents what is, in many cases, a sufficient economic incentive to overcome the attractions of trade secrecy, thus facilitating the disclosure of new inventions in exchange for a time-limited right to exclude others.[110]

F. Primary Sources of U.S. Patent Law

The three primary sources of U.S. patent law are (1) the U.S. Constitution, (2) the federal patent law found in U.S. statutes and regulations, and (3) federal judicial decisions interpreting and applying these statutory and regulatory provisions.[111]

1. The Constitution

Congressional power to establish a patent system derives from the Intellectual Property (IP) Clause of the U.S. Constitution. The IP Clause appears in the Constitution's Article I, section 8 statement of Congress's enumerated powers, which also include the power to collect taxes, provide for the national defense, and the like. In more detailed terms than the other clauses of section 8, the IP Clause provides that Congress shall have the power

> to promote the Progress of Science and useful Arts by securing for limited Times to Authors and Inventors the exclusive Right to their respective Writings and Discoveries.[112]

The IP Clause (sometimes also referred to as the "Progress Clause") has an interesting parallel structure, for it is really two grants of congressional power rolled into one — the patent power as well as the copyright power. At the time the IP Clause was ratified in 1787, the word "Science" had a much broader connotation than it does today. "Science" then meant knowledge and learning in general.[113] As such, the

[110] The author thanks Professor Timothy Holbrook for this insight.

[111] In addition to these domestic sources, U.S. patent law is impacted by, and exerts a strong influence on, the patent laws of other countries and on the multinational treaties and agreements that govern patent procurement and enforcement in foreign countries. These international patenting issues are treated separately *infra* Chapter 12.

[112] U.S. CONST., art. I, §8, cl. 8.

[113] Edward Walterscheid, *The Nature of the Intellectual Property Clause: A Study in Historical Perspective (Part 1)*, 83 J. PAT. & TRADEMARK OFF. SOC'Y 763, 781 (2001); Giles S. Rich,

word "Science" in the IP Clause is viewed as referring to copyrightable subject matter. The phrase "useful Arts" is understood as referring to patentable subject matter, because "Arts" meant "technologies" or "industries." Thus, the portion of the IP Clause pertaining to copyright provides that to promote the progress of "Science," "Authors" shall have a time-limited exclusive right in their "Writings," while the patent portion of the Clause provides that to promote the progress of the "useful Arts," "Inventors" shall have a time-limited exclusive right in their "Discoveries."

Although the IP Clause is a *grant* of congressional power, the Supreme Court also has interpreted it as a *limitation* on Congress's authority to carry out the constitutional goal of "promot[ing] the progress of Science and Useful Arts." Congress may not establish a legal system in which patents can be attained for technology that is already in the public domain, or that is a merely obvious extension thereof. As expressed by the Court in the landmark decision, *Graham v. John Deere Co.*:[114]

> The Congress in the exercise of the patent power may not overreach the restraints imposed by the stated constitutional purpose. Nor may it enlarge the patent monopoly without regard to the innovation, advancement or social benefit gained thereby. Moreover, Congress may not authorize the issuance of patents whose effects are to remove existent knowledge from the public domain, or to restrict free access to materials already available. Innovation, advancement, and things which add to the sum of useful knowledge are inherent requisites in a patent system which by constitutional command must "promote the Progress of . . . useful Arts."[115]

2. Federal Statutes and Regulations

Pursuant to the constitutional grant, the U.S. Congress enacted the first federal patent statute in 1790.[116] During the first three years after this enactment, patent applications were substantively examined by comparison to earlier-developed technology (i.e., the **prior art**) to determine whether the invention sought to be patented was new and useful.

The "Exclusive Right" Since Aristotle, Address at the Foundation for a Creative American Bicentennial Celebration (May 9, 1990), *reprinted in* 14 Fed. Cir. B.J. 217 (2004-2005).

[114]383 U.S. 1 (1966). The watershed *Graham* case is explored in greater detail *infra* Chapter 5 ("The Nonobviousness Requirement (35 U.S.C. §103)").

[115]*Graham,* 383 U.S. at 5-6. *See also* Bonito Boats, Inc. v. Thunder Craft Boats, Inc., 489 U.S. 141, 146 (1989) (stating that "the Clause contains both a grant of power and certain limitations upon the exercise of that power. Congress may not create patent monopolies of unlimited duration, nor may it 'authorize the issuance of patents whose effects are to remove existent knowledge from the public domain, or to restrict free access to materials already available'") (quoting Graham v. John Deere Co. of Kansas City, 383 U.S. 1, 6 (1966)).

[116]Act of April 10, 1790, ch. 7, 1 Stat. 109.

The administrative burden of this on-the-merits examination quickly proved too great, however, and with the Patent Act of 1793, the U.S. patent system became a *pro forma* "registration" system without substantive examination against the prior art. In time, the registration system came under severe criticism for permitting the grant of many invalid patents, and by means of the Patent Act of 1836, Congress reverted to the substantive examination system that we still have today.

The two most important revisions of the U.S. patent statute thereafter were the Patent Act of 1870, which required that patents contain claims, single-sentence definitions of the scope of the patent owner's right to exclude others from her invention,[117] and the Patent Act of 1952, which in amended form is the statute that governs U.S. patent law today. Co-authored by then-attorney and later-judge Giles S. Rich and Pasquale J. Federico, a USPTO official,[118] the Patent Act of 1952 included for the first time the statutory requirement for **nonobviousness**, codified in 35 U.S.C. §103.[119] The 1952 Act also included the first statutory provisions on direct, inducing, and contributory **infringement**, set forth at 35 U.S.C. §271(a)-(c), respectively.[120]

In the twenty-first century, the America Invents Act of 2011 (AIA) implemented what are probably the most significant revisions of the Patent Act since its 1952 codification at Title 35 U.S.C.[121] The AIA transitioned the U.S. patent system from its historic first-to-invent priority system to a unique first-inventor-to-file regime.[122] The AIA

[117] *See infra* Chapter 2 ("Patent Claims").

[118] Although not officially "legislative history," Federico's *Commentary on the 1952 Patent Act*, 35 U.S.C.A. 1 (1954 ed.), *reprinted at* 75 J. PAT. & TRADEMARK OFF. SOC'Y 161 (1993), is considered by the Federal Circuit to be "an invaluable insight into the intentions of the drafters of the Act." Symbol Techs., Inc. v. Lemelson Med., 277 F.3d 1361, 1366 (Fed. Cir. 2002). The Federal Circuit has observed that "the Supreme Court has trusted Federico as an authority on the Patent Act at least thrice." SCA Hygiene Prods. Aktiebolag v. First Quality Baby Prods., LLC, 807 F.3d 1311, 1322-1323 (Fed. Cir. 2015) (*en banc*) (citing Warner-Jenkinson Co. v. Hilton Davis Chem. Co., 520 U.S. 17, 28 (1997) (citing 2 D. CHISUM, PATENTS §8.04 [2], pp. 63-64 (1996) (discussing Federico *Commentary*)); Diamond v. Diehr, 447 U.S. 303, 321 (1980) (citing Hearings on H.R. 3760 before Subcommittee No. 3 of the House Committee on the Judiciary, 82d Cong., 1st Sess., 37 (1951) (statement of P.J. Federico)); Aro Mfg. Co. v. Convertible Top Replacement Co., 365 U.S. 336, 342 n.8 (1961) (citing Federico *Commentary*)).

[119] The nonobviousness requirement of 35 U.S.C. §103 is the subject of Chapter 5, *infra*.

[120] These theories of patent infringement are discussed in further detail in Chapter 9, *infra*.

[121] Leahy-Smith America Invents Act, Pub. L. No. 112-29 (H.R. 1249), 125 Stat. 284 (2011). A useful resource providing both pre- and post-AIA text of the Patent Act (35 U.S.C.) is THE NEW UNITED STATES PATENT LAW, BLACK LINE EDITION (2011), *available at* www.LegalPub.com.

[122] *See* 35 U.S.C. §102(a)(2) (eff. Mar. 16, 2013) (providing that "a person shall be entitled to a patent unless . . . the claimed invention was described in a patent issued under section 151, or in an application for patent published or deemed published under section 122(b), in which the patent or application, as the case may be, names another

also established a post-grant opposition system, intended to provide a new early-stage means of challenging the validity of issued patents by proceeding in the USPTO rather than federal court.[123] Other notable AIA changes are discussed throughout this text.

---

inventor and was effectively filed before the effective filing date of the claimed invention"); *see also* Leahy-Smith America Invents Act, Pub. L. No. 112-29 (H.R. 1249), §3 ("First Inventor to File"), 125 Stat. 284, 285-293 (2011); H.R. Rep. No. 112-98 [House Judiciary Comm. Rep. on the America Invents Act], at 53 (2011), which explains that the AIA

> creates a new "first-inventor-to-file" system. This new system provides patent applicants in the United States the efficiency benefits of the first-to-file systems used in the rest of the world by moving the U.S. system much closer to a first-to-file system and making the filing date that which is most relevant in determining whether an application is patentable. The new system continues, however, to provide inventors the benefit of the 1-year grace period. As part of the transition to a simpler, more efficient first-inventor-to-file system, this provision eliminates costly, complex interference proceedings, because priority will be based on the first application. A new administrative proceeding — called a "derivation" proceeding — is created to ensure that the first person to file the application is actually a true inventor. This new proceeding will ensure that a person will not be able to obtain a patent for the invention that he did not actually invent. If a dispute arises as to which of two applicants is a true inventor (as opposed to who invented it first), it will be resolved through an administrative proceeding by the Patent Board. The Act also simplifies how prior art is determined, provides more certainty, and reduces the cost associated with filing and litigating patents.

See also infra Chapter 4 ("Novelty, Loss of Right, and Priority Pre- and Post-America Invents Act of 2011 (35 U.S.C. §102)").

[123]*See* Leahy-Smith America Invents Act, Pub. L. No. 112-29 (H.R. 1249), §6(d), 125 Stat. 284, 305 (2011) (adding to 35 U.S.C. a new Chapter 32 titled "Post-Grant Review"); 35 U.S.C. §§321-329 (eff. Sept. 16, 2012); *see also* H.R. Rep. No. 112-98 [House Judiciary Comm. Rep. on the America Invents Act], at 58 (2011), which explains that the AIA

> creates a new post-grant opposition procedure that can be utilized during the first 12 months after the grant of a patent or issue of a reissue patent. Unlike reexamination proceedings, which provide only a limited basis on which to consider whether a patent should have issued, the post-grant review proceeding permits a challenge on any ground related to invalidity under [35 U.S.C.] section 282. The intent of the post-grant review process is to enable early challenges to patents, while still protecting the rights of inventors and patent owners against new patent challenges unbounded in time and scope. The Committee believes that this new, early-stage process for challenging patent validity and its clear procedures for submission of art will make the patent system more efficient and improve the quality of patents and the patent system. This new, but time-limited, post-grant review procedure will provide a meaningful opportunity to improve patent quality and restore confidence in the presumption of validity that comes with issued patents in court.

In the AIA as signed into law, the window for filing a petition for post-grant review was changed from 12 months (as indicated in the House Report above) to 9 months post-issuance. *See* Leahy-Smith America Invents Act, Pub. L. No. 112-29 (H.R. 1249), §6(d), 125 Stat. 284, 305 (2011) (adding new §321(c) to 35 U.S.C.); 35 U.S.C. §321(c) (eff. Sept. 16, 2012).

The statutory provisions of Title 35, U.S.C., governing patentability, which most directly impact the operations of the USPTO, are implemented through the agency's governing regulations. These regulations (sometimes referred to as USPTO "rules"), are found in Title 37 of the Code of Federal Regulations (C.F.R.). The USPTO also publishes the *Manual of Patent Examining Procedure* (MPEP), a detailed internal operating manual for patent examiners.[124] The MPEP is a very useful resource for patent practitioners and courts, but does not have the force and effect of law.[125]

3. Case Law

Since 1982, the primary source of decisional authority interpreting the patent statute and regulations is the U.S. Court of Appeals for the Federal Circuit. The Federal Circuit (or CAFC) generally hears appeals in patent cases, sitting in panels of three Circuit judges. Prior decisions of Federal Circuit panels are considered binding precedent on later panels, and only the *en banc* court (i.e., all "active" status judges on the CAFC, a maximum of 12) can overrule binding precedent.[126] The Federal Circuit also has adopted as binding precedent the decisions of its two predecessor courts, the Court of Customs and Patent Appeals (CCPA), which no longer exists, and the appellate decisions of the Court of Claims, which exists today in the form of a specialized trial court called the Court of Federal Claims.[127]

The U.S. Supreme Court infrequently reviews the Federal Circuit's decisions in patent matters. When the Supreme Court does grant writs of *certiorari* from the Federal Circuit, the resulting Supreme Court decisions are very important and, of course, bind the Federal Circuit.[128]

[124]The MPEP is available electronically. UNITED STATES PATENT AND TRADEMARK OFFICE, MANUAL OF PATENT EXAMINING PROCEDURE (9th ed., last rev. Jan. 2018), *available at* https://www.uspto.gov/web/offices/pac/mpep/index.html.

[125]*See* Critikon, Inc. v. Becton Dickinson Vascular Access, Inc., 120 F.3d 1253, 1257 (Fed. Cir. 1997) (observing that "the Manual of Patent Examining Procedure (MPEP), . . . although it does not have the force of law, is well known to those registered to practice in the PTO and reflects the presumptions under which the PTO operates").

[126]*See* Fed. Cir. R. 35(a)(1) (Dec. 1, 2019), *available at* http://www.cafc.uscourts.gov/sites/default/files/rules-of-practice/FederalCircuitRulesofPractice-December2019.pdf.

[127]*See* South Corp. v. United States, 690 F.2d 1368, 1369 (Fed. Cir. 1982).

[128]Notable U.S. Supreme Court patent decisions since 1996 include *Return Mail, Inc. v. United States Postal Serv.*, 139 S. Ct. 1853 (June 10, 2019) (Sotomayor, J.) (holding that a federal agency is not a "person" entitled to challenge the validity of a patent post-issuance in the USPTO via an *inter partes* review (IPR), post-grant review (PGR), or covered business method (CBM) proceeding); *Helsinn Healthcare S.A. v. Teva Pharm. USA, Inc.,* 139 S. Ct. 628 (Jan. 22, 2019) (Thomas, J.) (holding that under 35 U.S.C. §102(b) (America Invents Act of 2011 (AIA) version), the on sale bar to patentability may be triggered by a sale in which the purchaser is required to keep the details of the invention confidential);

WesternGeco LLC v. ION Geophysical Corp., 138 S. Ct. 2129 (June 22, 2018) (Thomas, J.) (by 7-2 vote, holding that patentee who established infringement under 35 U.S.C. §271(f)(2) based on defendant's export of specially adapted components from United States was entitled to remedy of foreign lost profits for ten contracts patentee failed to obtain with foreign customers due to the infringement; the infringing act of export occurred in the United States and this domestic infringement was "the object[t] of the statute's [i.e., of 35 U.S.C. §284] solicitude"); *SAS Inst., Inc. v. Iancu*, 138 S. Ct. 1348 (Apr. 24, 2018) (Gorsuch, J.) (by 5-4 vote, interpreting 35 U.S.C. §318(a)'s mandate that the Board's final written decision "shall" resolve the patentability of "any patent claim challenged by the petitioner" to mean that the Board must address every claim the petitioner has challenged in an America Invents Act of 2011 (AIA)-implemented *inter partes* review (IPR) proceeding; rejecting agency's position that it can institute IPR on a claim-by-claim and ground-by-ground basis); *Oil States Energy Servs., LLC v. Greene's Energy Grp., LLC*, 138 S. Ct. 1365 (Apr. 24, 2018) (Thomas, J.) (affirming Article III constitutionality of AIA-implemented *inter partes* review; holding that a patentee has no Seventh Amendment right to jury trial on the validity of its patents; patents are public rights; patentability can be decided by actors other than federal courts, such as the legislative or executive branch (i.e., USPTO)); *Impression Prods., Inc. v. Lexmark Int'l, Inc.*, 137 S. Ct. 1523 (May 30, 2017) (Roberts, C.J.) (reversing Federal Circuit and holding that "a patentee's decision to sell a product exhausts all of its patent rights in that item, regardless of any restrictions the patentee purports to impose or the location of the sale"); *TC Heartland LLC v. Kraft Foods Grp. Brands LLC*, 137 S. Ct. 1514 (2017) (Thomas, J.) (reversing Federal Circuit and holding that under the patent venue statute 28 U.S.C. §1400(b), a domestic corporation "resides" only in its state of incorporation); *SCA Hygiene Prods. Aktiebolag v. First Quality Baby Prods., LLC*, 137 S. Ct. 954 (Mar. 21, 2017) (Alito, J.) (rejecting 25 years of Federal Circuit patent laches precedent and holding that laches is not a defense to a patent infringement suit seeking damages for infringements that occurred during the 35 U.S.C. §286 six-year period before filing suit); *Life Techs. Corp. v. Promega Corp.*, 137 S. Ct. 734 (2017) (Sotomayor, J.) (reversing Federal Circuit and holding that "substantial portion of the components of a patented invention" in 35 U.S.C. §271(f)(1) should be interpreted quantitatively rather than qualitatively; determining that accused infringer's export from U.S. of single component (*Taq* polymerase) for inclusion in a genetic testing toolkit to be assembled with four other components in United Kingdom did not trigger §271(f)(1) liability; holding that "the supply of a single component of a multicomponent invention" is *not* an infringing act under §271(f)(1)); *Samsung Elecs. Co. v. Apple Inc.*, 137 S. Ct. 429 (2016) (Sotomayor, J.) (reversing Federal Circuit and holding that "article of manufacture" to which patented design is applied for purposes of computing infringer's "total profit" under 35 U.S.C. §289 "encompasses both a product sold to a consumer *and a component of that product*"; rejecting Federal Circuit's holding that only permissible "article of manufacture" for calculating §289 profits was entire accused smartphone as available for purchase by consumers) (emphasis added); *Halo Elecs., Inc. v. Pulse Elecs., Inc.*, 136 S. Ct. 1923 (2016) (Roberts, C.J.) (abrogating-in-part Federal Circuit's 2007 *en banc Seagate* decision and rejecting its rigid two-part test for establishing willful infringement for damages enhancement under 35 U.S.C. §284); *Cuozzo v. Lee*, 136 S. Ct. 2131 (2016) (Breyer, J.) (broadly affirming USPTO's authority to issue regulations governing *inter partes* review, and in particular those requiring use of controversial "broadest reasonable construction" standard for claim interpretation; also affirming position of USPTO that barring certain limited exceptions, PTAB decisions to *institute inter partes* review are not reviewable on appeal under 35 U.S.C. §314(d); *Kimble v. Marvel Ent., LLC,* 135 S. Ct. 2401 (2015) (declining to overturn *Brulotte v. Thys Co.,* 379 U.S. 29 (1964), and reaffirming *Brulotte*'s bright-line rule that a patent owner cannot charge royalties for use of its patented invention after the patent has expired); *Commil USA, LLC v. Cisco Sys., Inc.*, 135 S. Ct. 1920 (2015) (holding that accused inducer's belief in patent's invalidity is not a defense to liability for inducing infringement under 35 U.S.C. §271(b)); *Teva Pharm. USA, Inc. v. Sandoz, Inc.*, 135 S. Ct. 831 (2015) (holding that when district court's patent claim interpretation involves "evidentiary underpinnings" (i.e., requires subsidiary fact findings), such factual findings cannot be reversed unless "clearly erroneous" under Fed. R. Civ. P. 52); *Alice Corp. Pty. v. CLS Bank Int'l*, 134 S. Ct. 2347 (2014) (applying framework of *Mayo Collaborative Serv. v. Prometheus Labs., Inc.*, 132 S. Ct. 1289 (2012), to determine that claims drawn to a method using computers to minimize settlement risk in financial transactions were attempts to patent an "abstract idea" and thus not patent-eligible subject matter under 35 U.S.C. §101); *Nautilus, Inc. v. Biosig Instruments, Inc.*, 134 S. Ct. 2120 (2014) (rejecting Federal Circuit's overly lenient and uncertain formulation of the patent claim definiteness standard of 35 U.S.C. §112 and replacing it with a new standard turning on "reasonable certainty" of claim scope to a skilled artisan); *Limelight Networks, Inc. v. Akamai Techs., Inc.*, 134 S. Ct. 2111 (2014) (renouncing *en banc* Federal Circuit's reasoning that a defendant can be liable for inducing infringement under §271(b) even if no one committed direct infringement within the terms of §271(a), and holding that a method patent is not directly infringed unless a single actor can be held responsible for the performance of all steps of the claimed method); *Octane Fitness, LLC v. Icon Health & Fitness, Inc.*, 134 S. Ct. 1749 (2014) (rejecting Federal Circuit's unduly rigid *Brooks Furniture* framework for determining whether attorney fee shifting is warranted under 35 U.S.C. §285 and holding that an "exceptional" case §285 is simply "one that stands out from others with respect to the substantive strength of a party's litigating position (considering both the governing law and the facts of the case) or the unreasonable manner in which the case was litigated"); *Highmark Inc. v. Allcare Health Mgmt. Sys., Inc.*, 134 S. Ct. 1744 (2014) (holding that Federal Circuit should apply an abuse-of-discretion standard in reviewing all aspects of a district court's "exceptional case" attorney fee shifting determination under 35 U.S.C. §285); *Medtronic, Inc. v. Mirowski Family Ventures, LLC*, 134 S. Ct. 843 (2014) (holding that when a patent licensee seeks a declaratory judgement of non-infringement, the burden of proving infringement remains on the patentee); *Federal Trade Comm'n v. Actavis, Inc.*, 133 S. Ct. 2223 (2013) (holding that "reverse payment" settlement in Hatch-Waxman pharmaceutical patent litigation must be assessed under antitrust law's rule of reason); *Ass'n for Molecular Pathology v. Myriad Genetics, Inc.*, 133 S. Ct. 2107, 2111 (2013) (holding that "a naturally occurring DNA segment is a product of nature and not patent eligible [under 35 U.S.C. §101] merely because it has been isolated, but that cDNA [complementary DNA] is patent eligible because it is not naturally occurring"); *Bowman v. Monsanto Co.*, 133 S. Ct. 1761 (holding that doctrine of patent exhaustion did not permit farmer who bought patented seeds to reproduce them through planting and harvesting without the patent holder's permission); *Gunn v. Minton*, 133 S. Ct. 1059 (2013) (holding that federal court did not have exclusive "arising under" jurisdiction under 28 U.S.C. §1338 over a state law claim alleging legal malpractice in the handling of a patent case); *Caraco Pharm. Labs., Ltd. v. Novo Nordisk A/S*, 132 S. Ct. 1670 (2012) (holding that a generic pharmaceutical manufacturer may employ 21 U.S.C. §355(j)(5)(C)(ii)(I) to force correction of a "use code," i.e., a brand-name pharmaceutical manufacturer's description of its patent's scope, which inaccurately describes the brand's patent as covering a particular method of using the drug in question); *Kappos v. Hyatt*, 132 S. Ct. 1690 (2012) (holding that in a civil action to obtain a patent under 35 U.S.C. §145, there are no limitations on a patent applicant's ability to introduce new evidence beyond those already present in the Federal Rules of Evidence and the Federal Rules of Civil Procedure, and that if new evidence is presented on a disputed question of fact the district court must make *de novo* factual findings that take account of both the new evidence and the administrative record before the USPTO); *Mayo Collaborative Serv. v. Prometheus Labs., Inc.*, 132 S. Ct. 1289 (2012) (holding that claimed methods of optimizing therapeutic efficacy for treatment of an immune-mediated gastrointestinal disorder were not patent-eligible subject matter under 35 U.S.C. §101 because claims merely recited "laws of nature" plus additional steps consisting of "well-understood, routine, conventional activity already engaged in by the scientific community"); *Global-Tech Appliances, Inc. v. SEB S.A.*, 131 S. Ct. 2060, 2068, 2070-2071 (2011) (holding that to be liable for actively inducing infringement of a patent under 35 U.S.C. §271(b), the inducer must have "knowledge that the induced acts constitute patent infringement," that "willful blindness" may satisfy the knowledge requirement, and that a willfully blind defendant is "one who takes deliberate actions to avoid confirming a high probability of wrongdoing and who can almost be said to have actually known the critical facts"); *Microsoft Corp. v. i4i Ltd. P'ship*, 131 S. Ct. 2238, 2251, 2252-2253 (2011) (affirming Federal Circuit's interpretation of 35 U.S.C. §282 that invalidity of a patent must be established by clear and convincing evidence, but also stating that "if the PTO did not have all material facts [e.g., prior art] before it, its considered judgment may lose significant force . . . [a]nd, concomitantly, the challenger's burden to persuade the jury of its invalidity defense by clear and convincing evidence may be easier to sustain."); *Bilski v. Kappos*, 130 S. Ct. 3218 (2010) (holding that Federal Circuit erred in denominating its "machine-or-transformation test" as the exclusive standard of eligibility for patenting a process under 35 U.S.C. §101, but concluding that Bilski's claims to methods for protecting buyers and sellers against the risk of demand fluctuations in energy markets did not qualify as §101 processes because they attempted to patent an abstract idea); *Quanta Comp., Inc. v. LG Elecs., Inc.*, 553 U.S. 617 (2008) (holding that doctrine of patent exhaustion applies to method patents; Intel's sale of licensed computer microprocessors and chipsets, in which LG's patented methods were "embodied," exhausted LG's right to sue Quanta and other computer manufacturers for infringement based on their combination of the licensed Intel products with non-Intel computer memory and buses); *KSR Int'l Co. v. Teleflex, Inc.*, 550 U.S. 398 (rejecting Federal Circuit's overly rigid application in that case of teaching/suggestion/motivation test for combining references in nonobviousness analysis); *Microsoft Corp. v. AT&T Corp.*, 550 U.S. 437 (2007) (holding that Microsoft's export of "master disk" containing Windows software for copying and installation on foreign-made computers did not trigger infringement liability under 35 U.S.C. §271(f), which prohibits export of a U.S.-patented invention's "component(s)" for "combination" outside U.S.); *MedImmune, Inc. v. Genentech, Inc.*, 549 U.S. 118 (2007) (holding that subject-matter jurisdiction existed over licensee's Declaratory Judgment Act lawsuit challenging validity, enforceability, and infringement of licensed patent; justiciable case, or controversy under U.S. Constitution Art. III existed despite licensee's payment of royalties under protest); *eBay Inc. v. MercExchange, L.L.C.*, 547 U.S. 388 (2006) (applying equity courts' traditional four-factor test for determining whether to award permanent injunctive relief in patent infringement dispute; Federal Circuit erred by "categorical[ly]" granting such relief when patents are adjudged valid and infringed); *Ill. Tool Works, Inc. v. Indep. Ink, Inc.*, 547 U.S. 28 (2006) (holding that when a seller conditions its sale of a "tying" product on the purchase of a second, "tied" product, the mere fact that the tying product is patented does not support a presumption that its seller has market power as a matter of antitrust law); *Merck KgaA v. Integra Lifesciences I, Ltd.*, 545 U.S. 193 (2005) (broadly interpreting scope of 35 U.S.C. §271(e)(1) safe harbor for regulatory drug testing); *Holmes Group, Inc. v. Vornado Air Circulation Sys., Inc.*, 535 U.S. 826 (2002) (holding that Federal Circuit's appellate jurisdiction does not extend to cases in which a counterclaim, rather than the well-pleaded complaint, asserts a claim arising under the patent laws); *Festo Corp. v. Shoketsu Kinzoku Kogyo Kabushiki Co.*, 535 U.S. 722 (2002) (rejecting Federal Circuit's "complete bar" rule for prosecution history estoppel; holding that, by amending a claim to narrow a limitation, a patentee presumptively surrenders all equivalents to the limitation, but that the patentee may rebut the presumption by showing that (1) an alleged equivalent was unforeseeable, (2) the rationale underlying the amendment bore no more than a tangential relation to the equivalent in question, or (3) there was some other reason why the patentee could not reasonably have been expected to have literally claimed the equivalent); *Dickinson v. Zurko*, 527

G. Adjudicatory Forums for Patent Matters

A number of different administrative and judicial entities render decisions in U.S. patent matters. To summarize, the USPTO examines patent applications and grants patents, which are then enforced (or challenged) in the U.S. federal court system. Figure 1.3 below depicts the adjudicatory framework that is further described in the text below.

1. U.S. District Courts

a. Subject Matter Jurisdiction and Venue

(i) Subject Matter Jurisdiction

The fundamental substance of subject matter jurisdiction concerns the types of cases that courts may hear. In accordance with 28 U.S.C. §1338,[129] the U.S. District Courts have original *subject matter jurisdiction*, exclusive of state courts, over cases that are considered "arising under" the patent laws, in whole or in part.[130] The America Invents

U.S. 150 (1999) (holding Administrative Procedure Act standards of judicial review applicable to Federal Circuit review of USPTO patentability fact-findings); *Pfaff v. Wells Elecs. Inc.*, 525 U.S. 55 (1998) (announcing "ready for patenting" test as triggering on sale bar under 35 U.S.C. §102(b)); *Warner-Jenkinson Co. v. Hilton Davis Chem. Co.*, 520 U.S. 17 (1997) (reaffirming viability of doctrine of equivalents); *Markman v. Westview Instruments, Inc.*, 517 U.S. 370 (1996) (assigning patent claim interpretational responsibility in jury trials to judges).

[129]28 U.S.C. §1338 (eff. Sept. 16, 2011) provides:

> **§1338.** Patents, plant variety protection, copyrights, mask works, designs, trademarks, and unfair competition
>
> (a) The district courts shall have original jurisdiction of any civil action arising under any Act of Congress relating to patents, plant variety protection, copyrights and trademarks. No State court shall have jurisdiction over any claim for relief arising under any Act of Congress relating to patents, plant variety protection, or copyrights. For purposes of this subsection, the term "State" includes any State of the United States, the District of Columbia, the Commonwealth of Puerto Rico, the United States Virgin Islands, American Samoa, Guam, and the Northern Mariana Islands.
>
> (b) The district courts shall have original jurisdiction of any civil action asserting a claim of unfair competition when joined with a substantial and related claim under the copyright, patent, plant variety protection or trademark laws.
>
> (c) Subsections (a) and (b) apply to exclusive rights in mask works under chapter 9 of title 17 [17 USCS §§901 et seq.], and to exclusive rights in designs under chapter 13 of title 17 [17 USCS §§1301 et seq.], to the same extent as such subsections apply to copyrights.

[130]*See* Gunn v. Minton, 133 S. Ct. 1059, 1064 (2013) (stating that "[f]or cases falling within the patent-specific arising under jurisdiction of §1338(a), however, Congress has

Act of 2011 (AIA) amended the wording of §1338(a) to "more fully preclud[e] state court jurisdiction over patent legal claims."[131]

---

not only provided for federal jurisdiction but also eliminated state jurisdiction, decreeing that '[n]o State court shall have jurisdiction over any claim for relief arising under any Act of Congress relating to patents.'") (quoting 28 U.S.C. §1338(a) (2006 ed., Supp. V)).

[131]The pre-AIA version of §1338(a) provided in its second sentence that "such jurisdiction shall be exclusive of the courts of the states in patent, plant variety protection, and copyright cases." 28 U.S.C. §1338(a) (2006). Section 1338(a), as interpreted by the Supreme Court in *Holmes Group, Inc. v. Vornado Air Circulation Sys., Inc.*, 535 U.S. 826 (2002), left some ambiguity concerning the power of state courts to assert jurisdiction over certain patent law–related claims for relief. The AIA deleted the second sentence of §1338(a) and replaced it with the following text (as also quoted *supra*):

> No State court shall have jurisdiction over any claim for relief arising under any Act of Congress relating to patents, plant variety protection, or copyrights. For purposes of this subsection, the term "State" includes any State of the United States, the District of Columbia, the Commonwealth of Puerto Rico, the United States Virgin Islands, American Samoa, Guam, and the Northern Mariana Islands.

Leahy-Smith America Invents Act, Pub. L. No. 112-29 (H.R. 1249), §19(a), 125 Stat. 284, 331 (2011) (titled "State Court Jurisdiction"). The intent of the AIA amendment appeared to be "more fully precluding state court jurisdiction over patent legal claims," although the legislative history does not define the phrase "patent legal claims." *See* H.R. Rep. No. 112-98 [House Judiciary Comm. Rep. on the America Invents Act], at 81 (2011) (explaining that "Subsection (a) through (d) [of Section 19 of the AIA] enact the so-called *Holmes Group* fix (H.R. 2955, 109th Congress), which the House Judiciary Committee reported favorably in 2006. The Committee Report accompanying H.R. 2955 (House Rep. 109-407), which we reaffirm, explains the bill's reasons for abrogating *Holmes Group, Inc. v. Vornado Air Circulation Systems, Inc.*, 535 U.S. 826 (2002), *and more fully precluding state court jurisdiction over patent legal claims*") (emphasis added).

The AIA amendment to 28 U.S.C. §1338 corrected a ten-year aberration in Federal Circuit jurisdiction over cases involving patent issues. In *Holmes Group, Inc. v. Vornado Air Circulation Sys., Inc.*, 535 U.S. 826 (2002) (Scalia, J.), the Supreme Court had very literally interpreted the "arising under" language of 28 U.S.C. §1338(a) (2000) to mean that the Federal Circuit's appellate jurisdiction over patent cases did *not* extend to those cases in which a *counterclaim*, rather than the *complaint*, asserted a patent-based cause of action (e.g., in a lawsuit initially brought on a non-patent basis such as trade dress misappropriation). Assuming such cases were tried in federal district court, *Holmes Group* meant that they would be appealed to the appropriate U.S. Court of Appeals for the regional circuit in which the federal district court was located rather than to the Federal Circuit. For example, an antitrust case litigated in the Northern District of Illinois in which the defendant invoked a patent law–based counterclaim would be appealed to the U.S. Court of Appeals for the Seventh Circuit rather than to the Federal Circuit.

In the view of this author, such an outcome was contrary to the policy goals underlying the 1982 formation of the Federal Circuit. *See infra* Section G.2. For critiques of the *Holmes Group* decision, *see* Molly Mosley-Goren, *Jurisdictional Gerrymandering? Responding to* Holmes Group v. Vornado Air Circulation Systems, 36 J. MARSHALL L. REV. 1 (2002); Janice M. Mueller, *"Interpretive Necromancy" or Prudent Patent Policy? The Supreme Court's "Arising Under" Blunder in* Holmes Group v. Vornado, 2 J. MARSHALL REV. INTELL. PROP. L. 57 (2002), https://repository.jmls.edu/cgi/viewcontent.cgi?article=1023&context=ripl, *available at* SSRN: http://ssrn.com/abstract=1367857. More generally, *see* Christopher A. Cotropia, *Counterclaims, The Well-Pleaded Complaint, and Federal Jurisdiction,* 33 HOFSTRA L. REV. 1, 1 (2004) (observing that the *Holmes Group* decision "represented a significant departure from over ten years of established Federal

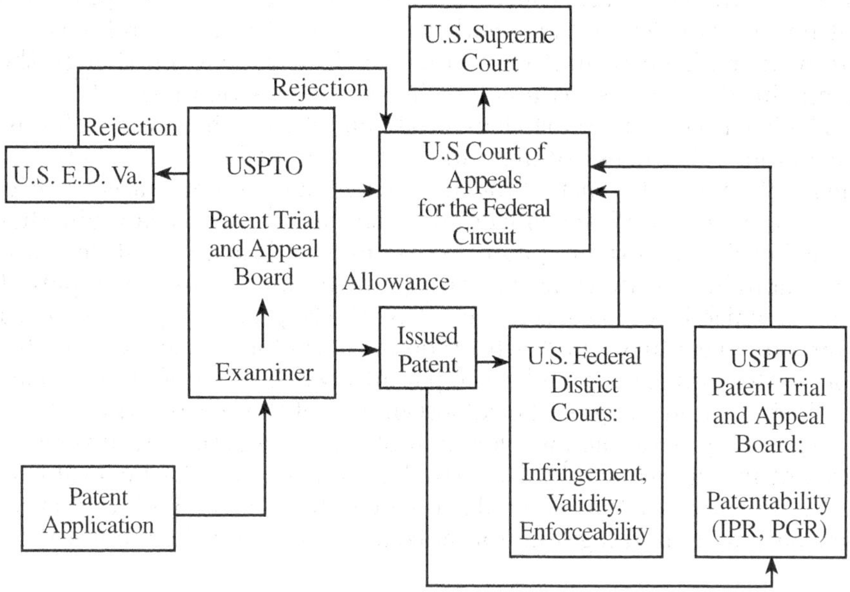

Figure 1.3

Interaction of USPTO, U.S. Federal District Courts, U.S. Court of Appeals for the Federal Circuit, and U.S. Supreme Court in Patent Matters

In *Christianson v. Colt Indus. Operating Corp.*,[132] the Supreme Court set forth the "well-pleaded complaint rule," which provides that §1338 "arising under" subject matter jurisdiction extends only to those cases in which a well-pleaded complaint establishes either that (1) federal patent law creates the cause of action, or (2) the plaintiff's right to relief necessarily depends on resolution of a substantial question of federal patent law, in that patent law is a necessary element of one of the well-pleaded claims.[133] Garden-variety patent infringement suits, as well as **declaratory judgment** actions seeking a declaration of non-infringement and/or patent invalidity,[134] fall within category (1) of the well-pleaded complaint rule. More problematic are litigations such as *Christianson,* an antitrust lawsuit that raised patent law

Circuit patent law jurisprudence confirming that even if the only patent claim present in a case was a counterclaim, the Federal Circuit still had appellate jurisdiction. Federal Circuit jurisdiction over such cases made sense, considering that the Federal Circuit was created by Congress to be the exclusive venue for patent appeals.") (footnotes omitted).

[132] 486 U.S. 800 (1988).

[133] *Christianson*, 486 U.S. at 808-809.

[134] Declaratory judgment actions by accused patent infringers are discussed in Chapter 10, Section G, *infra.*

issues.[135] In such cases, courts must decide whether the dispute falls within category (2), that is, whether the plaintiff's right to relief *necessarily* depends on resolution of a patent law issue, even though the complaint does not assert a patent law cause of action per se.[136]

The federal district courts lack §1338 jurisdiction, however—that is, a claim for relief does *not* arise under the patent laws—"if there is a theory of liability for each of the asserted claims for which it is not necessary to resolve an issue of federal patent law."[137] Thus, lawsuits that raise, but do not turn on, patent issues may be brought in state court. For example, a state court might adjudicate a dispute over a patent license, which is a type of contract.[138] As the Supreme Court recognized more than a century ago, "'[t]he Federal courts have exclusive jurisdiction of all cases arising under the patent laws, but not of all questions in which a patent may be the subject-matter of the controversy.'"[139]

Legal malpractice actions, for example, are tort actions traditionally brought in state courts.[140] Nevertheless, until 2013, the Federal Circuit held the view that the federal courts had exclusive jurisdiction over patent-related legal malpractice actions "when the adjudication

[135] *See Christianson*, 486 U.S. at 804-805 (describing antitrust action by former employee Christianson against patentee Colt, manufacturer of automatic rifles, alleging that Colt drove Christianson out of business by warning former clients against doing business with Christianson because he was allegedly misappropriating Colt's trade secrets).

[136] *See Christianson*, 486 U.S. at 808.

[137] Warrior Sports, Inc. v. Dickinson Wright, P.L.L.C., 631 F.3d 1367, 1370-1371 (quoting ClearPlay, Inc. v. Abecassis, 602 F.3d 1364, 1367 (Fed. Cir. 2010)); *see also* Air Measurement Techs., Inc. v. Akin Gump Strauss Hauer & Feld, L.L.P., 504 F.3d 1262, 1267-1268 (Fed. Cir. 2007).

[138] *See, e.g.*, Applera Corp. v. MP Biomedicals, LLC, 93 Cal. Rptr. 3d 178, 190 (Cal. App. 2009) (stating in resolving license dispute that post-*Christianson*, "it remains true that '[a] case does not arise under the patent laws merely because questions of patent law may arise in the course of interpreting a contract. . . .' The fact that an issue of patent law may be relevant in the interpretation of a contractual dispute 'cannot possibly convert a suit for breach of contract into one 'arising under' the patent laws as required to render the jurisdiction of the district court based on section 1338'") (quoting Linear Tech. Corp. v. Applied Materials, Inc., 61 Cal. Rptr. 3d 221, 228 (Cal. App. 2007)).

In a non-precedential decision, the Federal Circuit has stated that "the interpretation of contracts for rights under patents is generally governed by state law." Rhone-Poulenc Agro, S.A. v. DeKalb Genetics Corp., No. 00-1266, 2002 WL 501122, at *3 (Fed. Cir. 2002) (non-precedential) (citing Aronson v. Quick Point Pencil Co., 440 U.S. 257, 262 (1979); Lear, Inc. v. Adkins, 395 U.S. 653, 661-662 (1969); Sun Studs, Inc. v. Applied Theory Assocs., Inc., 772 F.2d 1557, 1561 (Fed. Cir. 1985); Studiengesellschaft Kohle, M.B.H. v. Hercules, Inc., 105 F.3d 629, 632 (Fed. Cir. 1997); Gjerlov v. Schuyler Labs., Inc., 131 F.3d 1016, 1020 (Fed. Cir. 1997)).

[139] Gunn v. Minton, 133 S. Ct. 1059, 1068 (2013) (quoting New Marshall Engine Co. v. Marshall Engine Co., 223 U.S. 473, 478 (1912)).

[140] *See, e.g.*, *Gunn*, 133 S. Ct. at 1065 (stating that "[u]nder Texas law, a plaintiff alleging legal malpractice must establish four elements: (1) that the defendant attorney owed the plaintiff a duty; (2) that the attorney breached that duty; (3) that the breach was the proximate cause of the plaintiff's injury; and (4) that damages occurred") (citing Alexander v. Turtur & Assocs., Inc., 146 S.W.3d 113, 117 (Tex. 2004)).

of the malpractice claim requires the court to address the merits of the plaintiff's underlying patent infringement lawsuit."[141] The Supreme Court rejected the Federal Circuit's view in an important 2013 decision, *Gunn v. Minton*.[142]

(ii) Venue

The issue of *venue* for patent disputes asks *which* U.S. District Court may properly hear the case. Venue doctrine deals largely with the convenience of the forum to the accused infringer.[143]

Section 1400(b) of Title 28, United States Code ("Judiciary and Judicial Procedure") is a patent-specific statute providing that "[a]ny civil action for patent infringement may be brought in the judicial district where the defendant resides, *or* where the defendant has committed acts of infringement and has a regular and established place of business."[144] For the many defendants that are corporations rather than natural persons, Title 28 provides elsewhere a general provision stating that "[f]or purposes of venue under this chapter, a defendant that is a corporation shall be deemed to reside in any judicial district in which it is subject to personal jurisdiction at the time the action is commenced."[145] In view

[141] Warrior Sports, Inc. v. Dickinson Wright, P.L.L.C., 631 F.3d 1367, 1371 (Fed. Cir. 2011) (citing Air Measurement Techs., Inc. v. Akin Gump Strauss Hauer & Feld, L.L.P., 504 F.3d 1262, 1269 (Fed. Cir. 2007)).

[142] 133 S. Ct. 1059, 1068 (2013) (holding unanimously that §1338(a) jurisdiction did not exist over Minton's patent-related malpractice action because it raised no "serious federal issue").

[143] *See* VE Holding Corp. v. Johnson Gas Appliance Co., 917 F.2d 1574, 1576 (Fed. Cir. 1990) (explaining that "[v]enue, which connotes locality, serves the purpose of protecting a defendant from the inconvenience of having to defend an action in a trial court that is either remote from the defendant's residence or from the place where the acts underlying the controversy occurred. . . . The venue statutes achieve this by limiting a plaintiff's choice of forum to only certain courts from among all those which might otherwise acquire personal jurisdiction over the defendant.") (citation and footnote omitted).

[144] 28 U.S.C. §1400(b) (2012) (emphasis added).

[145] 28 U.S.C. §1391(c) (2010). The Federal Circuit announced the applicability of §1391(c) to corporate patent defendants in its controversial decision, *VE Holding Corp. v. Johnson Gas Appliance Co.*, 917 F.2d 1574 (Fed. Cir. 1990). The Circuit in *VE Holding* considerably broadened patent venue by holding that for patent infringement actions in which the defendant was a corporation, the phrase "where the defendant resides" in the patent-specific venue statute, 28 U.S.C. §1400(b), had to be read in accordance with the broader definition of "residence" provided for corporate defendants in the general federal venue statute, 28 U.S.C. §1391(c).

Prior to the Circuit's 1990 decision in *VE Holding*, venue for patent suits against corporations was considerably narrower — the Supreme Court had confirmed in a 1957 decision that a corporation's "residence" for patent suits was limited to its state of incorporation. *See VE Holding*, 917 F.2d at 1578 (explaining that "[t]he Supreme Court in *Fourco* [Fourco Glass Co. v. Transmirra Prods. Corp., 353 U.S. 222 (1957)] confirmed that for defendants that are corporations, 'resides' meant the state of incorporation only. Section 1391(c), the general venue section which addressed the question of where corporations may be sued,

of unresolved Supreme Court "minimum contacts" precedent governing personal jurisdiction, many corporations accused of patent infringement were once deemed to "reside" in any judicial district in which their alleged infringing product could be purchased, e.g., in a local retail outlet.[146]

Given the seemingly very broad scope of venue choice for plaintiff patent owners, certain U.S. District Courts became extremely popular fora for patent litigation in the 1990s-2010s.[147] For example, patent litigation lore suggested that the U.S. District Court for the Eastern District of Texas provided a jury pool tending to award large verdicts to patent owners.[148] Whether or not empirical evidence actually

---

and which contained language about the residence of corporations, did not supplement the specific provisions of §1400(b).") (citing *Fourco*, 353 U.S. at 229)).

The Federal Courts Jurisdiction and Venue Clarification Act of 2011, Pub. L. No. 112-63, Title II, §202(1), 125 Stat. 763 (2011), amended the language of 28 U.S.C. §1391(c) but did not substantively impact the deemed residence of a corporate defendant. For lawsuits filed on or after January 7, 2012, *see id.* §105 ("Effective Date"), subsection (c) of 28 U.S.C. §1391 now provides that "[f]or all venue purposes — (2) an entity with the capacity to sue and be sued in its common name under applicable law, whether or not incorporated, shall be deemed to reside, if a defendant, in any judicial district in which such defendant is subject to the court's personal jurisdiction with respect to the civil action in question and, if a plaintiff, only in the judicial district in which it maintains its principal place of business. . . ." 35 U.S.C. §1391(c) (eff. Jan. 7, 2012).

The Federal Circuit's 1990 *VE Holding* decision and its broad venue ruling for corporate defendants remained controversial amid allegations of forum shopping by patent owners. The continued propriety of *VE Holding* was the focal point of a closely-watched mandamus petition pending before the Federal Circuit as of January 2016. *See* Petition for Writ of Mandamus, Case 16-105, In re: TC Heartland, LLC (filed Oct. 23, 2015), *available at* http://patentlyo.com/media/2016/01/Heartland.Petition.pdf. As described in the text, the Supreme Court in 2017 would review the venue issue in *TC Heartland* and return patent venue to its earlier, narrower scope in accordance with the Court's 1957 *Fourco* decision.

[146] *See, e.g.*, Beverly Hills Fan Co. v. Royal Sovereign Corp., 21 F.3d 1558 (Fed. Cir. 1994) (finding that personal jurisdiction over accused out-of-state infringers existed in Virginia, where 52 accused infringing items were available for sale in retail outlets). However, the presence of the accused products in the forum was not the only factor conferring personal jurisdiction in *Beverly Hills Fan.* The "minimum contacts" case law of the Supreme Court is less than crystal clear, so each case should be analyzed on its own facts.

[147] For the decade of 2005-2015, the four most popular federal district courts (in terms of new patent case filings) were (in descending order): the Eastern District of Texas; the District of Delaware; the Central District of California; and the Northern District of California. *See* Dennis Crouch, *The Concentrated Market of Patent Jurisdictions,* PATENTLY-O (Oct. 8, 2015), http://patentlyo.com/patent/2015/10/concentrated-patent-jurisdictions.html. Professor Crouch notes that "E.D. Tex. has been the leading district almost every year for the past decade, but that growth has increased since the AIA (2011) and even further increased in 2014 and 2015."

[148] *See, e.g.*, Danny Hakim, *Tech Giants Fear Spread of Patent Wars to Europe*, N.Y. TIMES, Sept. 26, 2013, at B3 (stating that the Eastern District of Texas "has become an American capital of patent litigation known for sympathetic juries and speedily moving cases").

supported this belief,[149] the Eastern District of Texas indisputably attracted a great deal of patent litigation, making it one of the busiest patent dockets in the nation.[150] Despite vocal criticism of forum shopping by patentees at the trial court level,[151] the American Invents Act of 2011 (AIA) did not change this aspect of the patent venue rules.

However, a 2017 U.S. Supreme Court decision did change the patent venue rules, and dramatically so, returning venue to a much narrower range of options for patent owners than in the previous 25-plus years. In *TC Heartland LLC v. Kraft Foods Grp. Brands LLC*,[152] the Supreme Court reversed the Federal Circuit, rejecting the Circuit's 1990 *VE Holding v. Johnson Gas Appliance Co.* reasoning to the contrary,[153] and interpreted the patent venue statute 28 U.S.C. §1400(b) to mean that a domestic corporation "resides" only in its state of incorporation.[154] The result of the Supreme Court's 2017 decision in *TC*

[149]*See* University of Houston Law Center, patstats.org (Sept. 18, 2013), http://patstats.org/Patstats3.html (stating that "[j]ury verdicts are now updated to May 31, 2013. Little has changed. Patentees who make it to a jury trial win a verdict in 75% of the cases. The figure for the Eastern District of Texas is about the same.").

[150]*See generally* XIV SMU SCI. & TECH. L. REV. 191, 191-320 (2011) (symposium issue titled "Emerging Intellectual Property Issues" focusing on Eastern District of Texas). In their symposium article, *Real Reasons the Eastern District of Texas Draws Patent Cases — Beyond Lore and Anecdote*, XIV SMU SCI. & TECH. L. REV. 299 (2011), attorneys Andrei Iancu and Jay Chung report that the Eastern District of Texas, along with the Central District of California, "is perennially among the busiest patent dockets in the nation, although that that has not always been the case." *Id.* at 299. Based on their statistical analysis, Iancu and Chung disagree with the popular perception that juries in the Eastern District of Texas are "unsophisticated and predisposed to find for plaintiffs." *Id.* at 300. The authors find "little evidence that the District's popularity arises primarily from its jury pool." *Id.* Rather, they contend, a confluence of factors combine "to render a much more satisfactory explanation." *Id.*

[151]*See* Paul M. Janicke, *Venue Transfers from the Eastern District of Texas: Case by Case or an Endemic Problem?*, 2 LANDSLIDE 14 (2010) (describing "[a]dverse commentary and congressional proposals to limit patent venue"); *see generally* Kimberly A. Moore, *Forum Shopping in Patent Cases: Does Geographic Choice Affect Innovation?*, 79 N.C. L. REV. 889 (2001).

[152]137 S. Ct. 1514 (2017) (Thomas, J.).

[153]917 F.2d 1574, 1576 (Fed. Cir. 1990) (establishing broad patent venue by holding that for patent infringement actions in which the defendant/accused infringer was a corporation, the phrase "where the defendant resides" in the patent-specific venue statute, 28 U.S.C. §1400(b), had to be interpreted in accordance with the broader definition of "residence" provided for corporate defendants in the general federal venue statute, 28 U.S.C. §1391(c)). The latter statute stated that "[f]or purposes of venue under this chapter, a defendant that is a corporation shall be deemed to reside in any judicial district in which it is subject to personal jurisdiction at the time the action is commenced." 28 U.S.C. §1391(c) (2010).

[154]In so holding, the Supreme Court in 2017 returned U.S. patent venue to its narrower confines as earlier set forth in *Fourco Glass Co. v. Transmirra Prods. Corp.*, 353 U.S. 222 (1957). Under *Fourco*, venue for patent suits against corporations was considerably narrower — the Supreme Court confirmed in that case that a corporation's "residence" for patent suits was limited to its state of incorporation. *See* VE Holding Corp. v. Johnson Gas Appliance Co., 917 F.2d 1574, 1578 (Fed. Cir. 1990) (explaining that "[t]he

Heartland is that, under current law, corporate accused infringers must be sued either in (1) the state of their "residence"; i.e., the state in which they are incorporated; or (2) the state in which the corporation "has committed acts of infringement *and* has a regular and established place of business." Pursuing prong (2) can create a type of "satellite litigation" because complex questions often arise concerning what counts as a corporation's "regular and established place of business."[155]

Note that the 28 U.S.C. §1400(b) patent-specific venue rules also apply to civil actions for patent infringement filed against individuals. The judicial debates about patent venue described above have focused almost exclusively on where domestic corporations reside, not where individuals reside.

Lastly, venue for suits against *foreign* corporations (i.e., those not incorporated in a state of the United States) accused of patent infringement is proper "in any judicial jurisdiction." Subsection 3 of 28 U.S.C. §1391(c) provides "a defendant not resident in the United States may be sued in *any* judicial district. . . ."[156]

Supreme Court in *Fourco* confirmed that for defendants that are corporations, 'resides' meant the state of incorporation only. Section 1391(c), the general venue section which addressed the question of where corporations may be sued, and which contained language about the residence of corporations, did not supplement the specific provisions of §1400(b).") (citing *Fourco*, 353 U.S. at 229)).

[155]*See, e.g.*, In re Cray, 871 F.3d 1355 (Fed. Cir. Sept. 21, 2017) (Lourie, J.) (announcing a narrow definition for "regular and established place of business" that hewed closely to nineteenth-century definitions of "place" as a physical, permanent location; setting forth three-factor test for establishing that defendant had "regular and established place of business" in the forum: (1) there must be a *physical place* in the district (which cannot be a "virtual space" or involve "electronic communications" between individuals); (2) it must be a *regular and established* place of business, which must have "sufficient permanence" such that it cannot be "transient" or "sporadic"; and (3) it must be the place *of the defendant*, not merely the place of its employee working from a home office, for example); In re Cordis Corp., 769 F.2d 733 (Fed. Cir. 1985) (Friedman, J.) (pre-*VE Holding* case holding that although accused infringer Cordis was incorporated in Florida and maintained its principal place of business there, venue was proper in Minnesota (in suit brought by patentee Medtronic); activities of the accused infringer Cordis's two Minnesota-based sales representatives amounted to a "permanent and continuous presence" by Cordis in Minnesota, although Cordis had no formal office or store in Minnesota). *See also* In re ZTE (USA) Inc., 890 F.3d 1008 (Fed. Cir. May 14, 2018) (Linn, J.) (deciding an issue of first impression: that when a defendant objects to venue in a patent case, the plaintiff is the party that bears the burden of persuasion (proof) to show that venue is proper).

[156]28 U.S.C. §1391(c)(3) (2012) (emphasis added). *See also Brunette Machine Works, Ltd. v. Kockum Indus., Inc.*, 406 U.S. 706 (1972), the leading case on venue for suing foreign corporations for patent infringement in the U.S. courts. In its 2017 *TC Heartland* decision, the Supreme Court had no need to reach or reconsider *Brunette,* so it remains controlling law.

b. *Civil Actions Against the USPTO Director in the Eastern District of Virginia*

Certain U.S. district courts occasionally preside over civil actions to obtain a patent under 35 U.S.C. §145 and civil actions in the case of a derivation proceeding under 35 U.S.C. §146 (a proceeding newly created by the AIA).[157] In these proceedings, parties who have had their claims rejected by a USPTO examiner in *ex parte* prosecution and failed to obtain a reversal thereof from the USPTO Patent Trial and Appeal Board (PTAB), or parties who have lost a derivation proceeding before the PTAB, will bring a lawsuit against the Director of the agency in federal district court. Should the plaintiff prevail in the civil action, the District Court will issue an order authorizing the USPTO to issue a patent. If the plaintiff does not prevail, he or she may appeal the District Court's decision to the Federal Circuit.

The America Invents Act of 2011 changed the venue for §145 and §146 actions (and also changed the nature of §146 actions).[158] Prior to the AIA, a civil action to obtain a patent under 35 U.S.C. §145 was brought in the U.S. District Court for the District of Columbia.[159] Effective September 16, 2011, §145 actions must be brought in the U.S. District Court for the Eastern District of Virginia. Also prior to

[157]*See* 28 U.S.C. §1295(a)(4)(C). However, Congress in enacting the America Invents Act of 2011 (AIA) did *not* provide for a §145-style civil action for unsuccessful parties in an AIA-implemented post-issuance review proceeding (i.e., *inter partes* review, post-grant review, or covered business method review). Such parties have only the option of a direct appeal to the Federal Circuit under 35 U.S.C. §§141-144, assuming they possess standing under Article III of the U.S. Constitution. *See, e.g.,* Samsung Elecs. Co. v. Infobridge Pte. Ltd., 929 F.3d 1363, 1367-1368 (Fed. Cir. 2019) (O'Malley, J.) (holding that IPR petitioner Samsung, owner and licensee of patents in a standard-essential patent pool that also included the challenged Infobridge patent, possessed Article III standing to appeal its loss in the IPR to the Federal Circuit; explaining that Samsung's "concrete and particularized" economic injury (i.e., having to pay royalties on Infobridge's allegedly invalid patent) "can be traced directly to the validity of Infobridge's patent and would be redressed by a favorable decision for Samsung").

[158]*See* Leahy-Smith America Invents Act, Pub. L. No. 112-29 (H.R. 1249), §9(a), 125 Stat. 284, 316 (2011) ("Technical Amendments Relating to Venue. — Sections 32, *145, 146*, 154(b)(4)(A), and 293 of title 35, United States Code, and section 21(b)(4) of the Trademark Act of 1946 (15 U.S.C. 1071(b)(4)), are each amended by striking 'United States District Court for the District of Columbia' each place that term appears and inserting 'United States District Court for the Eastern District of Virginia.' ") (emphasis added); 35 U.S.C. §145 (eff. Sept. 16, 2011); 35 U.S.C. §146 (eff. Sept. 16, 2011).

[159]Before the AIA, §145 actions were filed in the U.S. District Court for the District of Columbia. *See* 35 U.S.C. §145 (2006) (providing in part that "[a]n applicant dissatisfied with the decision of the Board of Patent Appeals and Interferences in an appeal under section 134(a) of this title may, unless appeal has been taken to the United States Court of Appeals for the Federal Circuit, have remedy by civil action against the Director in the United States District Court for the District of Columbia . . ."). Pre-AIA, analogous civil actions in the case of interferences could be brought in any U.S. district court in accordance with 35 U.S.C. §146 (2006).

the AIA, a civil action could be brought under 35 U.S.C. §146 to contest an adverse USPTO decision in an interference.[160] Such §146 actions could be brought in any U.S. District Court and were not limited to the District of Columbia (unlike a pre-AIA §145 action). The AIA eliminated interferences as well as the §146 civil action in case of interference. The AIA replaced the old §146 civil action in case of interference with a new §146 civil action in case of derivation proceeding. Section 146 derivation actions, like §145 (post-AIA) civil actions to obtain a patent, must be brought in the U.S. District Court for the Eastern District of Virginia.

Although this civil action route is generally more expensive and lengthy than a direct appeal from the USPTO to the Federal Circuit under 35 U.S.C. §141,[161] the advantage provided by the civil action is that the plaintiff can put before the federal district court new evidence that was not considered by the USPTO.[162] The civil action is essentially a *trial de novo* of patentability with the opportunity for pretrial discovery. In contrast, new evidence cannot be presented in a direct appeal from the USPTO to the Federal Circuit because this type of appeal must be "on the record" that was before the agency in accordance with 35 U.S.C. §144.

2. U.S. Court of Appeals for the Federal Circuit

The U.S. Court of Appeals for the Federal Circuit plays a unique and powerful role in the American patent system.[163] The court has

[160]Interferences are *inter partes* proceedings conducted in the USPTO to determine priority of invention between rival claimants under the United States' pre-AIA historic first-to-invent priority system. *See infra* Chapter 4, Section N ("Prior Invention Under 35 U.S.C. §102(g) (Pre-AIA)").

[161]Depending on the outcome of a case under review in 2019 by the U.S. Supreme Court, the not-insignificant expenses associated with prosecuting a Section 145 action may increase even beyond current levels. *See* Iancu v. NantKwest, Inc., 139 S. Ct. 1292 (Mar. 4, 2019) (order granting petition for writ of *certiorari* to Federal Circuit in *Nantkwest, Inc. v. Iancu*, 898 F.3d 1177 (Fed. Cir. 2018) (Stoll, J.) (*en banc* Circuit majority holding that 35 U.S.C. §145's provision that patent applicant/plaintiff shall pay "[a]ll the expenses of the proceedings" does *not* compel plaintiff to pay attorney fees incurred by USPTO in defending lawsuit; the quoted statutory text falls short of the "stringent standard" adopted by the American Rule on attorney fees, which prohibits courts from shifting attorney fees from one party to another absent a "specific and explicit" directive from Congress)).

[162]The Supreme Court has confirmed that in a §145 proceeding, introduction of new evidence not previously presented to the USPTO is limited only by the Federal Rules of Evidence and the Federal Rules of Civil Procedure. Kappos v. Hyatt, 132 S. Ct. 1690 (2012). "Moreover, if new evidence is presented on a disputed question of fact, the district court must make *de novo* factual findings that take account of both the new evidence and the administrative record before the PTO." *Id.* at 1701.

[163]*See* Rochelle C. Dreyfuss, *In Search of Institutional Identity: The Federal Circuit Comes of Age*, 23 Berkeley Tech. L.J. 787, 788-789 (2008) (observing that "[t]he Federal

nationwide jurisdiction over appeals in patent cases. Created in 1982, the Federal Circuit is located in Washington, D.C.[164]

Circuit is now a quarter-century old and has proved to be a success in many important ways. The court freed regional circuit judges from the complexity of patent appeals. For patent law, forum shopping — at least at the appellate level — is now barely possible. Procedural developments, such as the *Markman* hearing, have brought down litigation costs, at least for a time. Patent law is not only more uniform across the nation, it is also considerably more determinate in that it is easier to predict outcomes.") (footnotes omitted); Timothy R. Holbrook, *Substantive Versus Process-Based Formalism in Claim Construction*, 9 Lewis & Clark L. Rev. 123, 151 (2005) (stating that "[b]oth the Supreme Court and the Federal Circuit recognize the unique role the Federal Circuit plays in U.S. patent law . . ."); R. Polk Wegner & Lee Petherbridge, *Is the Federal Circuit Succeeding? An Empirical Assessment of Judicial Performance*, 152 U. Pa. L. Rev. 1105, 1105 (2005) (observing that "[a]s an appellate body jurisdictionally demarcated by subject matter rather than geography, the United States Court of Appeals for the Federal Circuit occupies a unique role in the federal judiciary. This controversial institutional design has profoundly affected the jurisprudential development of legal regimes within its purview — especially in patent law, which the Federal Circuit has come to thoroughly dominate in its two decades of existence."); Ryan G. Vacca, *The Federal Circuit as an Institution,* University of Akron Research Paper No. 15-07 (Dec. 21, 2015), *available at* http://papers.ssrn.com/sol3/papers.cfm?abstract_id=2706849 (examining Federal Circuit's institutional development and describing "the evolving qualities that have helped the Federal Circuit distinguish itself, for better or worse, as an institution"); *Cf.* Ryan G. Vacca, *Acting Like an Administrative Agency: The Federal Circuit* En Banc, 76 Mo. L. Rev. 733, 733-734 (2011) (observing that "[t]he number and breadth of questions the Federal Circuit agrees to hear *en banc* and the means by which it hears them go beyond the limited role of a court — to decide the case before it. Instead of exercising restraint and addressing only what it must, the Federal Circuit raises wide-ranging questions and makes broad pronouncements of law that set or change patent policy") (footnotes omitted).

[164]For biographical, statistical, and other information on the work of the Federal Circuit, visit the court's website at http:/www.cafc.uscourts.gov. Precedential opinions of the Federal Circuit are available for download at http:/www.cafc.uscourts.gov/opinions-orders.

For additional background on the history of the Federal Circuit's creation, *see* Federal Circuit Historical Society, *History of the United States Court of Appeals for the Federal Circuit*, http:/www.federalcircuithistoricalsociety.org/historyofcourt.html; Pauline Newman, *After Twenty-Five Years*, 17 Fed. Cir. B.J. 123-234 (2007) (essays and articles compiled in "Federal Circuit 25th Anniversary Edition"); Jim Davis, *Formation of the Federal Circuit*, 11 Fed. Cir. B.J. 547 (2001); Donald R. Dunner, *Reflections on the Founding of the Federal Circuit*, 11 Fed. Cir. B.J. 545 (2001); Clarence T. Kipps, Jr., *Remarks*, 11 Fed. Cir. B.J. 563 (2001); Daniel J. Meador, *Retrospective on the Federal Circuit: The First 20 Years — A Historical View*, 11 Fed. Cir. B.J. 557 (2001); Pauline Newman, *Origins of the Federal Circuit: The Role of Industry*, 11 Fed. Cir. B.J. 541 (2001); Ryan G. Vacca, *The Federal Circuit as an Institution,* University of Akron Research Paper No. 15-07 (Dec. 21, 2015), *available at* https://papers.ssrn.com/sol3/papers.cfm?abstract_id=2706849.

The Federal Circuit has spearheaded the publication of a series of substantial books detailing the court's history. *See* Advisory Council to the United States Court of Appeals for the Federal Circuit, United States Court of Appeals for the Federal Circuit — A History: 1990-2002 (Kristin L. Yohannan, ed.) (informally referred to as "the Blue Book"); Judicial Conf. of the United States, The United States Court of

Prior to 1982, appeals of judgments in garden-variety patent infringement cases clearly "arising under" the patent laws were taken to the appropriate federal regional circuit court of appeals for the federal district court in question. For example, if a patent infringement case was tried prior to 1982 in Chicago before the U.S. District Court for the Northern District of Illinois, any appeal would have been taken to the U.S. Court of Appeals for the Seventh Circuit.

Concerns over forum shopping at the appellate level and lack of national uniformity in patent law prompted Congress to create in 1982 a new appellate court, the U.S. Court of Appeals for the Federal Circuit.[165] The Federal Circuit (or CAFC) has exclusive nationwide jurisdiction over appeals in which the well-pleaded complaint (or a compulsory counterclaim) asserts a cause of action arising under the patent laws. Section 1295 of 28 U.S.C. provides that the Federal Circuit's appellate jurisdiction encompasses all appeals from final decisions of a U.S. district court "in any civil action arising under, or in any civil action in which a party has asserted a compulsory counterclaim arising under, any Act of Congress relating to patents...."[166]

APPEALS FOR THE FEDERAL CIRCUIT: A HISTORY 1982-1990 (Marion T. Bennett, ed., 1991) (informally referred to as "the Red Book").

For a history of the CCPA, one of the Federal Circuit's two predecessor courts, *see* GILES S. RICH, JUDICIAL CONF. OF THE UNITED STATES, A BRIEF HISTORY OF THE UNITED STATES COURT OF CUSTOMS AND PATENT APPEALS (1980).

[165]The legislation that created the Federal Circuit is the Federal Courts Improvement Act (FCIA) of 1982, Pub. L. No. 97-164, 96 Stat. 25 (1982). The legislative history for the FCIA is S. Rep. No. 97-275 (Nov. 18, 1981), *reprinted in* 1982 U.S.C.C.A.N. 11. The legislative history states in part:

> The establishment of the Court of Appeals for the Federal Circuit also provides a forum that will increase doctrinal stability in the field of patent law. Based on the evidence it had compiled, the Hruska Commission singled out patent law as an area in which the application of the law to the facts of a case often produces different outcomes in different courtrooms in substantially similar cases. Furthermore, in a Commission survey of practitioners, the patent bar indicated that uncertainty created by the lack of national law precedent was a significant problem, and the Commission singled out patent law as an area in which widespread forum-shopping is particularly acute.

S. Rep. No. 97-275 (1981), at 15 (footnotes omitted).

[166]28 U.S.C. §1295 (eff. Sept. 16, 2011) provides in part:

§1295. Jurisdiction of the United States Court of Appeals for the Federal Circuit

> (a) The United States Court of Appeals for the Federal Circuit shall have exclusive jurisdiction —
>
> (1) of an appeal from a final decision of a district court of the United States, the District Court of Guam, the District Court of the Virgin Islands, or the District Court of the Northern Mariana Islands, in any civil action arising under, or in any civil action in which a party has asserted a compulsory counterclaim arising under, any Act of Congress relating to patents or plant variety protection....

Thus, if a patent infringement case is tried today in San Jose before the U.S. District Court for the Northern District of California, any appeal will be taken to the Federal Circuit, not to the U.S. Court of Appeals for the Ninth Circuit.

Although the Federal Circuit has its share of critics,[167] the consensus view is that the CAFC "experiment" has been a success.[168] As a practical

[167]*See, e.g.*, Diane P. Wood, *Keynote Address: Is It Time to Abolish the Federal Circuit's Exclusive Jurisdiction in Patent Cases?*, 13 CHI.-KENT J. INTELL. PROP. 1 (2013), *available at* http://studentorgs.kentlaw.iit.edu/ckjip/?attachment_id=1072 (speech by Chief Judge of U.S. Court of Appeals for the Seventh Circuit advocating abolition of Federal Circuit's exclusive appellate jurisdiction over patent cases and proposing system in which parties could choose whether to appeal their patent cases to Federal Circuit or to regional circuit where their case was filed); Lucas S. Osborn, *Instrumentalism at the Federal Circuit*, 56 ST. LOUIS U. L.J. 419, 424 (2012) (concluding that "[r]egardless of the reasons for it, the Federal Circuit's forced formalism tends to lead to opinions lacking full legitimacy and the adoption of sub-optimal legal rules"); Timothy B. Lee, *Bring Appellate Competition Back to Patent Law,* CATO INST. (July 28, 2008), https://www.cato.org/publications/techknowledge/bring-appellate-competition-back-patent-law (stating that "[w]hile the problems of too little uniformity in patent law were obvious in 1982, the policymakers who created the Federal Circuit failed to appreciate that excessive uniformity could be even worse"); Craig A. Nard & John F. Duffy, *Rethinking Patent Law's Uniformity Principle*, 101 NW. U. L. REV. 1619 (2007) (reviewing history and criticisms of the Federal Circuit and proposing a decentralized institutional architecture for patent law that would assign appeals from district court patent decisions to at least one other extant U.S. Court of Appeals); ADAM B. JAFFE & JOSHUA LERNER, INNOVATION AND ITS DISCONTENTS: HOW OUR BROKEN PATENT SYSTEM IS ENDANGERING INNOVATION AND PROGRESS, AND WHAT TO DO ABOUT IT 96-126 (Princeton Univ. Press 2004); Matthew F. Weil & William C. Rooklidge, *Stare Un-Decisis: The Sometimes Rough Treatment of Precedent in Federal Circuit Decision-Making*, 80 J. PAT. & TRADEMARK OFF. SOC'Y 791 (1998); Allan N. Littman, *Restoring the Balance of Our Patent System*, 37 IDEA 545 (1997).

[168]*See, e.g.*, Symposium, *Evolving the Court of Appeals for the Federal Circuit and Its Patent Law Jurisprudence,* 76 MO. L. REV. 629 (Summer 2011) (stating in Foreword by Professor Dennis Crouch that although the Circuit's evolution in response to questions presented by litigants, external political influences, changing judicial composition, and role of intellectual property in society "alters the law and its practice, it is this evolution that guarantees an ongoing role for the court and satisfies the public demand for a law shaped to fit the needs of society"); Ryan Vacca, *Acting Like an Administrative Agency: The Federal Circuit* En Banc, 76 MO. L. REV. 733, 759 (2011) (concluding that "[a]lthough the Federal Circuit's *en banc* practices strongly resemble an agency's procedure for substantive rulemaking, . . . until structural changes are made or enough political will is garnered, the Federal Circuit hearing cases *en banc* is not a bad solution to the ever-present problem of changing circumstances in patent law"); Elizabeth I. Winston, *Differentiating the Federal Circuit*, 76 MO. L. REV. 813, 837 (2011) (concluding that "[o]ften referred to as an experiment, the Federal Circuit has flourished. Born again from the ashes of its predecessors, the Phoenix Court continues to grow in significance, stature, and strength."); Paul D. Carrington & Paulina Orchard, *The Federal Circuit: A Model for Reform?*, 78 GEO. WASH. L. REV. 575 (2010); Symposium, *The U.S. Court of Appeals for the Federal Circuit: Its Critical Role in the Revitalization of U.S. Patent Jurisprudence, Past, Present, and Future,* 43 LOY. L.A. L. REV. 775 (2010); Daniel J. Meador, *Remarks in the United States Court of Appeals for the Federal Circuit, April 2, 2007*, 17 FED. CIR. B.J. 125, 126 (2007) ("The beauty of this court's design is that because of the wide-ranging jurisdiction inherited from its predecessor courts, it can

matter, the creation of the Federal Circuit has resulted in a single, relatively coherent body of patent case law on which district courts and litigants can rely with greater certainty than the disparate decisions reached by the regional circuits in patent cases prior to 1982.[169]

---

secure national uniformity in patent law and other fields without encountering the specialization stigma."); Jonathan Ringel, *A New Order: 20 Years of the Federal Circuit*, IP WORLDWIDE (Dec. 2001), at 40; Victoria Slind-Flor, *Formerly Obscure Court Is in Spotlight*, NAT'L L.J. (Apr. 30, 2001), at B9; Steven Andersen, *Federal Circuit Gets Passing Marks to Date But There's a Lot of Room for Improvement*, CORP. LEGAL TIMES (Mar. 2000), at 86; John F. Merz & Nicholas M. Pace, *Trends in Patent Litigation: The Apparent Influence of Strengthened Patents Attributable to the Court of Appeals for the Federal Circuit*, 79 J. PAT. & TRADEMARK OFF. SOC'Y 579 (1994).

[169]A leading study of the Federal Circuit's creation and evolution as a court is Rochelle Cooper Dreyfuss, *The Federal Circuit: A Case Study in Specialized Courts*, 64 N.Y.U. L. REV. 1 (1989). Professor Dreyfuss updated her examination of the Federal Circuit in *In Search of Institutional Identity: The Federal Circuit Comes of Age*, 23 BERKELEY TECH. L.J. 787 (2008). *See also* Rochelle Cooper Dreyfuss, *What the Federal Circuit Can Learn from the Supreme Court—And Vice Versa*, 59 AM. U. L. REV. 787 (2010). Professor Wagner revises and expands upon Dreyfuss's seminal work in R. Polk Wagner, *The Two Federal Circuits*, 43 LOY. L.A. L. REV. 785 (2010) (concluding that "the most important moving part is not so much the specialization of the [Federal Circuit] along subject matter lines but instead the emergence of two distinct understandings of the court's role in patent law [i.e., what Wagner terms its "decisional" versus "managerial" approaches to deciding patent appeals], and how that role should be reflected in its decisions").

A number of patent scholars now use empirical techniques including data gathering and statistical analysis to study the Federal Circuit's performance in several areas of its patent jurisprudence. For example, data on Federal Circuit decision making in validity matters are reported at John R. Allison & Mark A. Lemley, *How Federal Circuit Judges Vote in Patent Validity Cases*, 10 FED. CIR. B.J. 435 (2001). The Federal Circuit's treatment of nonobviousness, the most critical issue within the patentability/validity rubric (*see infra* Chapter 5), is empirically examined in Lee Petherbridge & R. Polk Wagner, *The Federal Circuit and Patentability: An Empirical Assessment of the Law of Obviousness*, 85 TEX. L. REV. 2051 (2007) (presenting data suggesting "that the Federal Circuit has developed a doctrine in this area that is relatively stable and appears reasonably predictable," despite controversy concerning the court's "teaching, suggestion, or motivation" inquiry). The Federal Circuit's oversight of the district courts' patent claim interpretation is analyzed in David L. Schwartz, *Practice Makes Perfect? An Empirical Study of Claim Construction Reversal Rates in Patent Cases*, 107 MICH. L. REV. 223, 267 (2008) (concluding that "the [Federal Circuit's] reversal rate may be essentially constant, regardless of the prior claim construction experience of the district court judge," and identifying three possible reasons for the district courts' lack of improvement: "(1) an indeterminate nature of claim construction; (2) a failure of the Federal Circuit to teach properly how to construe claims; and (3) a failure of district court judges to learn claim construction").

For a compact compendium of Federal Circuit patent decisions, *see* ROBERT L. HARMON ET AL., PATENTS AND THE FEDERAL CIRCUIT (12th ed. 2015). Abstracts of all significant Federal Circuit patent decisions appear in the single-volume work DONALD S. CHISUM, PATENT LAW DIGEST (2015 ed.). Chisum reviews all district court, Federal Circuit, and Supreme Court patent cases in the 53-volume treatise DONALD S. CHISUM, CHISUM ON PATENTS (2015), first published in 1978. Another important scholarly treatise is R. CARL MOY, MOY'S WALKER ON PATENTS (4th ed. 2015).

An overview of patent jurisprudence and a look toward the future by a former Chief Judge of the Federal Circuit is available at The Honorable Paul R. Michel, *A Review of*

A 2016 law review symposium examined the often-controversial manner in which Supreme Court review of the Federal Circuit's patent jurisprudence has significantly impacted U.S. patent law.[170]

3. USPTO Patent Trial and Appeal Board (PTAB)

In addition to its jurisdiction to hear appeals from decisions of district courts in litigation involving issued patents, the Federal Circuit also hears appeals from decisions of the Patent Trial and Appeal Board (Board or PTAB).[171] The Board is an administrative body within the USPTO that hears appeals from patent examiners' decisions in a variety of USPTO proceedings discussed in later chapters of this text, including refusals to grant patents in *ex parte* patent examination,[172] as well as adverse decisions in **reexamination** (in both its *ex parte*[173] and *inter partes*[174] forms) proceedings[175] as well as **reissue** proceedings.[176]

Recent Decisions of the United States Court of Appeals for the Federal Circuit: Afterword: Past, Present, and Future in the Life of the U.S. Court of Appeals for the Federal Circuit, 59 AM. U. L. REV. 1199 (2010).

[170]*See 2017 Symposium: Supreme Court Insight on Patent Law,* CHI-KENT J. INTELL. PROP. LAW, Issue 16, Vols. 1-2 (2016-2017), compiling articles including The Honorable Timothy B. Dyk, *Thoughts on the Relationship Between the Supreme Court and the Federal Circuit,* 16 CHI.-KENT J. INTELL. PROP. 67 (2016); Greg Reilly, *How Can the Supreme Court Not "Understand" Patent Law?,* 16 CHI.-KENT J. INTELL. PROP. 292 (2017); Timothy R. Holbrook, *Is the Supreme Court Concerned with Patent Law, the Federal Circuit, or Both: A Response to Judge Timothy B. Dyk,* 16 CHI.-KENT J. INTELL. PROP. 313 (2017); Donald R. Dunner, *Response to Judge Timothy B. Dyk,* 16 CHI.-KENT J. INTELL. PROP. 326 (2017); Paul R. Gugliuzza, *How Much Has the Supreme Court Changed Patent Law?,* 16 CHI.-KENT J. INTELL. PROP. 330 (2017). The symposium articles can be viewed in the public domain at https://scholarship.kentlaw.iit.edu/ckjip/vol16/iss1/ and https://scholarship.kentlaw.iit.edu/ckjip/vol16/iss2 (last visited Aug. 14, 2019).

[171]*See* 28 U.S.C. §1295(a)(4)(A); 35 U.S.C. §141. Prior to the America Invents Act of 2011 (AIA), the Board was known as the Board of Patent Appeals and Interferences (BPAI). The AIA changed the Board's name to the Patent Trial and Appeal Board, and broadened the Board's jurisdiction. *See* Leahy-Smith America Invents Act, Pub. L. No. 112-29 (H.R. 1249), §7, 125 Stat. 284, 313 (2011); 35 U.S.C. §6 (eff. Sept. 16, 2012) ("Patent Trial and Appeal Board").

[172]*See* 35 U.S.C. §134(a). *See also infra* Section H ("Patent Prosecution Overview").

[173]*See* 35 U.S.C. §§301-307. Reexamination, a USPTO administrative procedure for reexamining an issued patent based on a substantial new question of patentability, is covered in Chapter 8 ("Correcting and Challenging Issued Patents at the USPTO"), *infra.*

[174]*See* 35 U.S.C. §315. The *inter partes* reexamination proceeding is covered in Chapter 8 ("Correcting and Challenging Issued Patents at the USPTO"), *infra.*

The America Invents Act of 2011 phased out *inter partes* reexamination in favor of a new "*inter partes* review" procedure. *See* Leahy-Smith America Invents Act, Pub. L. No. 112-29 (H.R. 1249), §6(a) (2011); 35 U.S.C. §§311-319 (eff. Sept. 16, 2012).

[175]*See* 35 U.S.C. §134(b).

[176]*See* 35 U.S.C. §251; *id.* §134(a). Reissue, a USPTO administrative procedure for reissuing patents that are defective in certain respects, is covered in Chapter 8 ("Correcting and Challenging Issued Patents at the USPTO"), *infra.*

Importantly, the PTAB also presides over a rapidly growing number of AIA-implemented post-issuance review proceedings, including "*inter partes* review" (IPR) and "post-grant review" (PGR).[177] IPRs were first made available to challenge issued patents in September 2012. As of July 2019, the PTAB had granted a total of 5,330 petitions to institute post-issuance reviews (IPR was sought in 93 percent of the 10,299 total petitions filed) and had issued 2,796 final written decisions in those reviews.[178]

Lastly, the PTAB renders decisions in AIA-implemented "derivation proceedings," which are USPTO *inter partes* proceedings for determining whether one applicant derived her invention from another.[179]

4. U.S. International Trade Commission

Lastly, the International Trade Commission (ITC) is a forum of rapidly growing importance to patent owners in a global economy.[180] The ITC has jurisdiction over patent-related matters involving imports under Section 337 of the Tariff Act of 1930, as amended.[181] Section 337 makes it unlawful to import into the U.S. articles that "infringe a valid and enforceable United States patent" or that "are made, produced, processed, or mined under, or by means of, a process covered by the claims of a valid and enforceable United States patent."[182] The ITC investigates alleged

[177]*See* 35 U.S.C. §§311-319 (eff. Sept. 16, 2012) (*inter partes* review); 35 U.S.C. §§321-329 (eff. Sept. 16, 2012 for applications filed on or after Mar. 16, 2013) (post-grant review). *Inter partes* review and post-grant review proceedings are covered in Chapter 8 ("Correcting and Challenging Issued Patents at the USPTO"), *infra.*

[178]United States Patent and Trademark Office, *Trial Statistics: IPR, PGR, CBM* (June 2019), at 10, https://www.uspto.gov/sites/default/files/documents/Trial_Statistics_2019-06-30.pdf ("Status of Petitions (All Time: Sept. 16, 2012 to Jun. 30, 2019)").

[179]*See* 35 U.S.C. §135 (eff. Mar. 16, 2013) ("Derivation proceedings"). Before enactment of the AIA, 35 U.S.C. §135 (2006) governed interference proceedings. The AIA discontinued interferences but implemented a new derivation proceeding.

[180]*See* Suprema, Inc. v. International Trade Comm'n, 796 F.3d 1338 (Fed. Cir. 2015) (*en banc*), examined *infra* this section; *see also* Christopher A. Cotropia, *Strength of the International Trade Commission as a Patent Venue* (Mar. 2, 2011), https://papers.ssrn.com/sol3/papers.cfm?abstract_id=1774881 (describing ITC as a new "favored jurisdiction for patent infringement disputes," and reporting empirical data "suggest[ing] that [despite *Kyocera Wireless Corp. v. Int'l Trade Comm'n*, 545 F.3d 1340 (Fed. Cir. 2008), in which court narrowed scope of ITC's limited exclusion orders to cover only imports by explicitly named respondents,] the ITC is here to stay and almost all patent enforcement actions will take place, at least in part, in the ITC. The landscape of patent enforcement has permanently changed, and the ITC is a solid part of it."). *See generally* Tom M. Schaumberg, Ed., *A Lawyer's Guide to Section 337 Investigations Before the U.S. International Trade Commission, Second Edition* (American Bar Assoc. 2012).

[181]*See* 19 U.S.C. §1337 ("Unfair practices in import trade").

[182]19 U.S.C. §1337(a)(1)(B). This provision applies "only if an industry in the United States, relating to the articles protected by the patent . . . concerned, exists or is in the process of being established." 19 U.S.C. §1337(a)(2).

violations of Section 337, typically at the urging of U.S patent owners.[183] ITC investigations include trial proceedings conducted before an ITC administrative law judge, whose Initial Decision on the merits is reviewed by the Commission.[184]

If it finds patent infringement, the ITC will typically enter an order excluding the infringing articles from entry into the United States;[185] however, the ITC does not award damages for infringement. Patent litigation conducted before the ITC is resolved much more rapidly than infringement cases in the federal district courts, historically within fewer than 15 months.[186] For this and other reasons, enforcement at the ITC has become an increasingly attractive option for patent owners.[187] The ITC's Section 337 decisions do not bind the federal district courts, however, and many parties bring actions in both fora.[188]

Federal Circuit decisions are facilitating an expanded role for the ITC in policing transborder patent infringement. In 2015, the Federal Circuit considered *en banc* whether the ITC could properly issue an exclusion order, based on a theory of inducing infringement liability,[189] to bar the importation of articles (i.e., fingerprint scanners) which, after their importation, were (in some but not all cases) combined with domestically developed software and used by purchasers to directly infringe a patent drawn to a fingerprint scanning method.[190] Suprema,

[183] *See* 19 U.S.C. §1337(b) ("Investigation of violations by Commission").

[184] *See* 19 C.F.R. §§210.43-.45 (2010); United States International Trade Commission, *USITC — Intellectual Property Infringement and Other Unfair Acts*, https://www.usitc.gov/intellectual_property.htm (last visited Mar. 2, 2016).

[185] *See* 19 U.S.C. §1337(d) ("Exclusion of articles from entry"). An exclusion order is the ITC's "primary remedy." United States International Trade Commission, *USITC — Intellectual Property Infringement and Other Unfair Acts*, https://www.usitc.gov/intellectual_property.htm (last visited Mar. 2, 2016).

[186] *See* United States International Trade Commission, *Section 337 Investigations: Answers to Frequently Asked Questions* 23 (Mar. 2009), https://www.usitc.gov/intellectual_property/documents/337_faqs.pdf.

[187] *See generally* Christopher A. Cotropia, *Strength of the International Trade Commission as a Patent Venue*, 20 Tex. Intell. Prop. L.J. 1 (2011); *id.* at 2 (stating that "because of their exclusive jurisdiction over [Section 337] actions, ITC administrative judges are seen by many as patent law savvy and, in turn, patentholder friendly. As a result, the ITC has become a favored jurisdiction for patent infringement disputes, being used more and more by patentees.").

[188] *See* Colleen V. Chien, *Patently Protectionist? An Empirical Analysis of Patent Cases at the International Trade Commission,* 50 Wm. & Mary L. Rev. 63, 64 (2008).

[189] Suprema, Inc. v. International Trade Comm'n, 796 F.3d 1338 (Fed. Cir. 2015) (*en banc*) (Reyna, J.). Inducing infringement liability under 35 U.S.C. §271(b), a type of "aiding and abetting" another's direct infringement, is examined *infra* Chapter 9, Section E.1.

[190] Claim 10 of U.S. Patent No. 7,203,344, owned by Cross Match Techs., Inc., the intervenor/complainant in *Suprema*, recited:

> 1. A method for capturing and quality classifying fingerprint images, the method comprising:
> (a) scanning a plurality of fingers substantially simultaneously;

a Korean company, manufactured the scanners and sold them to Mentalix, Inc., a U.S. company that imported the scanners into the United States, bundled the scanners with Mentalix's custom software, and resold the bundles to end users in the United States.[191] By a 6-4 majority, the *en banc* court answered the question affirmatively and approved the ITC's exclusion order in *Suprema, Inc. v. International Trade Comm'n.*[192] The *Suprema en banc* majority rejected the "plain language" interpretation of "articles that infringe" relied on by the Circuit panel that in 2013 had decided to the contrary.[193]

(b) capturing data representing a combined image of a corresponding plurality of fingerprints;

(c) using concentrations of black pixels arranged in oval-like shapes in the combined image to determine individual fingerprint areas and shapes;

(d) separating the combined image into individual fingerprint images;

(e) comparing each of the separated individual fingerprint images to a corresponding previously captured acceptable fingerprint image;

(f) quality classifying the separated individual fingerprint images as being either acceptable, possibly acceptable, or unacceptable according to the comparing step (e);

(g) indicating the quality classification of each of the individual fingerprint images based on the quality classifying step (f); and

(h) determining whether the processed combined image is of a good quality.

[191]*See Suprema,* 796 F.3d at 1341-1342.

[192]796 F.3d 1338 (Fed. Cir. 2015) (*en banc*) (Reyna, J.).

[193]The panel decision was reported at *Suprema, Inc. v. International Trade Comm'n*, 742 F.3d 1350 (Fed. Cir. 2013). The 2015 *en banc* majority explained:

> A majority panel of this court . . . reason[ed] that there are no "articles that infringe" at the time of importation when direct infringement does not occur until after importation. *Suprema, Inc. v. Int'l Trade Comm'n*, 742 F.3d 1350, 1352 (Fed. Cir. 2013). In doing so, the panel effectively eliminated trade relief under Section 337 for induced infringement and potentially for all types of infringement of method claims.

Suprema, 796 F.3d at 1340 (*en banc*). As a policy matter, the *en banc* majority emphasized the ITC's broad role in fighting acts of unfair trade including patent infringement. The majority asserted that

> [t]he technical interpretation adopted by the panel weakens the Commission's overall ability to prevent unfair trade acts involving infringement of a U.S. patent. The panel's interpretation of Section 337 would eliminate relief for a distinct unfair trade act and induced infringement. There is no basis for curtailing the Commission's gap-filling authority in that way. Indeed, the practical consequence would be an open invitation to foreign entities (which might for various reasons not be subject to a district court injunction) to circumvent Section 337 by importing articles in a state requiring post-importation combination or modification before direct infringement could be shown.

Suprema, 796 F.3d at 1352 (*en banc*).

H. Patent Prosecution Overview

1. Introduction

Contrary to its name, patent **prosecution** has nothing to do with criminal law. Rather it refers to the process of preparing and filing a patent application in the USPTO and thereafter interacting with the agency to obtain a U.S. patent. This interaction typically involves a multi-year negotiation between the patent applicant and the USPTO examiner over the allowable scope of the patent claims in view of the relevant prior art. Patent prosecution is sometimes referred to as patent solicitation.[194]

2. Filing the Application

The process begins with the filing of a patent application in the USPTO. A patent applicant can file *pro se* and need not be represented by a patent attorney or agent, but obtaining competent representation is highly recommended in order to minimize the risk of losing important legal rights.[195] Two types of patent applications may be filed: **provisional** applications and **nonprovisional** applications. Provisional applications are the newer option, available for the first time as of June 8, 1995. Prior to that date, only nonprovisional applications (then known simply as "applications") could be filed.[196]

Provisional applications are governed by 35 U.S.C. §111(b), which provides that a provisional application must have a specification (and drawings, if necessary to understand the invention). Unlike a

[194]This discussion of patent prosecution is by necessity a summary overview. Good sources of more detailed guidance on patent application preparation and prosecution include Irah H. Donner, Patent Prosecution: Law, Practice and Procedure (9th ed. BNA 2015); Joshua P. Graham and Thomas G. Marlow, U.S. Patent Prosecutor's Desk Reference (LexisNexis 2015); James E. Hawes, Patent Application Practice (2d ed. Thomson/West 2008); David Pressman, Patent It Yourself (17th ed. Nolo 2014); Joseph E. Root, Rules of Patent Drafting: Guidelines from Federal Circuit Case Law (LexisNexis 2014); Ronald D. Slusky, Invention Analysis and Claiming: A Patent Lawyer's Guide (ABA 2013); Jeffrey G. Sheldon, How to Write a Patent Application (2d ed. PLI 2009); Thomas A. Turano, Obtaining Patents (James Pub. 1997). *See also* United States Patent and Trademark Office, Manual of Patent Examining Procedure *available at* https://www.uspto.gov/web/offices/pac/mpep/index.html.

[195]Persons who have been admitted to practice before the USPTO can represent inventors before the agency. Attorneys admitted to practice before the USPTO are called "patent attorneys" while non-attorneys admitted to practice before the agency are referred to as "patent agents." For a searchable list of registered patent attorneys and agents, *see* United States Patent and Trademark Office, Office of Enrollment and Discipline, *Persons Recognized to Practice in Patent Matters (2016),* https://oedci.uspto.gov/OEDCI. As of 2016, the list comprised "11035 active agents and 33092 active attorneys." *Id.*

[196]*See* Uruguay Round Agreements Act, Pub. L. No. 103-465, tit. V, subtit. C, §532, 108 Stat. 4983-88 (Dec. 8, 1994) ("Patent Term and Internal Priority").

nonprovisional application, however, the provisional application need not include any claims or an oath by the applicant. The provisional patent application has proven very popular as a quick and inexpensive means of establishing an early domestic priority date.[197] Its filing also allows the patent applicant to apply the words "patent pending" to her products that embody the invention disclosed in the provisional application.[198] She may also be able to rely on the provisional application as evidence that she had conceived the invention disclosed therein no later than the provisional application's filing date.[199] Lastly, the provisional application filing date may also be relied on as a priority date for the subsequent filing of foreign patent applications on the same invention in accordance with the right of priority of the Paris Convention.[200]

The provisional application is not substantively examined by the USPTO, but rather acts as a sort of placeholder. If the applicant elects to do so, she can file a corresponding nonprovisional application within 12 months of the provisional application's filing date. The nonprovisional ("regular" or "full-service") application will be substantively examined. So long as the invention she claims in the nonprovisional patent application was adequately supported by the disclosure of the provisional application in accordance with 35 U.S.C. §112, ¶1 (renamed §112(a) by the America Invents Act of 2011), the applicant can claim for the later nonprovisional application the benefit of the earlier provisional application's filing date, effectively "backdating" her application by up to 12 months.[201] This benefit means that when

[197]During fiscal year 2017, approximately 167,000 provisional patent applications were filed with the USPTO, in comparison with the approximately 647,000 nonprovisional utility patent applications filed during the same period. *See* United States Patent and Trademark Office, *Performance and Accountability Report Fiscal Year 2017*, tbl. 1, https://www.uspto.gov/sites/default/files/documents/USPTOFY17PAR.pdf, at 148 ("Summary of Patent Examining Activities"). As of January 2018, the filing fee for provisional applications filed by large entities was $280 and by small entities was $140. *See* United States Patent and Trademark Office, *USPTO Fee Schedule (effective Jan. 16, 2018; last revised Oct. 10, 2019)*, https://www.uspto.gov/learning-and-resources/fees-and-payment/uspto-fee-schedule#Patent%20Fees.

[198]*See* United States Patent and Trademark Office, *Provisional Application for Patent* (Jan. 2015), *available at* https://www.uspto.gov/patents-getting-started/patent-basics/types-patent-applications/provisional-application-patent.

[199]*See* Charles E. Van Horn, *Practicalities and Potential Pitfalls When Using Provisional Patent Applications*, 22 AIPLA Q.J. 259, 299-300 (Summer/Fall 1994). Post-AIA, dates of conception may still be relevant in derivation proceedings under 35 U.S.C. §135 (eff. Mar. 16, 2013).

[200]*See* Charles E. Van Horn, *Practicalities and Potential Pitfalls When Using Provisional Patent Applications*, 22 AIPLA Q.J. 259, 270-273 (Summer/Fall 1994) ("Claiming Benefit Outside the United States"); Paris Convention for the Protection of Industrial Property art. 4(A), *available at* https://wipolex.wipo.int/en/text/288514. The right of foreign priority is further discussed in Chapter 12, *infra*.

[201]*See* 35 U.S.C. §119(e)(1). This ability to "backdate" a patent to its provisional application filing date is by no means automatic and often fails. There is no

the USPTO examiner compares the claims of the nonprovisional application with the prior art for purposes of assessing novelty and nonobviousness, he will consider only that prior art that has an effective date earlier in time than the filing date of the provisional application.

When it is necessary for an applicant to claim the benefit of her earlier provisional filing date, and the examiner determines that the claims in question are adequately supported by the disclosure of the provisional application,[202] he will treat the provisional application filing date as either (1) the applicant's presumptive *invention date* for purposes of analyzing novelty, loss of right, and nonobviousness under the pre-AIA version of 35 U.S.C. §102;[203] or (2) the **effective filing date** for analyzing novelty and nonobviousness of the claimed invention(s) in the application if the application has been filed on or after March 16, 2013 (post-AIA).[204] In either case, if someone else filed for a U.S. patent on the same or similar invention during the provisional application's pendency period, or published a description of the invention during that time period, such materials will not count as prior art against the nonprovisional application; the examiner will effectively ignore them.

"presumption of priority" for an issued patent to the filing date of its provisional application; priority must be established on the merits by showing §112, first paragraph support in the provisional application's disclosure for the claims of the patent in question. For an example of an unsuccessful attempt to claim during litigation the benefit of a provisional application's filing date in order to avoid a 35 U.S.C. §102(b) (pre-AIA) statutory bar, *see* New Railhead Mfg., L.L.C. v. Vermeer Mfg. Co., 298 F.3d 1290 (Fed. Cir. 2002). For an example of an unsuccessful attempt by an *inter partes* review petitioner to claim the benefit of a provisional application's filing date as the effective date of a patent proffered as §102(e)(2) anticipatory prior art, *see* Dynamic Drinkware, LLC v. National Graphics, Inc., No. 2015-1214, 800 F.3d 1375, 2015 WL 5166366 (Fed. Cir. Sept. 4, 2015). *Dynamic Drinkware,* which relied in part on an important CCPA precedent, *In re Wertheim*, 646 F.2d 527, 537 (C.C.P.A. 1981) (Rich, J.), is further discussed *infra* Chapter 4, Section L.2 ("Attempted Reliance on Provisional Application Filing Date as Effective Date for §102(e) Reference (Rule of *In re Wertheim*)").

[202]This means that the disclosure (i.e., written description and drawings) of the provisional application supports the claims of the nonprovisional application in a manner that satisfies the requirements of 35 U.S.C. §112, first paragraph (renamed 35 U.S.C. §112(a) by the AIA (eff. Sept. 16, 2012)).

[203]*See* 35 U.S.C. §102 (2006); United States Patent and Trademark Office, Manual of Patent Examining Procedure §201.11.I.A (8th ed., Aug. 2001, last rev. July 2010) (stating that "[i]f the filing date of the earlier provisional application is necessary, for example, in the case of an interference or to overcome a reference, care must be taken to ensure that the disclosure filed as the provisional application adequately provides (1) a written description of the subject matter of the claim(s) at issue in the later filed nonprovisional application, and (2) an enabling disclosure to permit one of ordinary skill in the art to make and use the claimed invention in the later filed nonprovisional application without undue experimentation"). *See also infra* Chapter 3 ("Disclosure Requirements); *infra* Chapter 4 ("Novelty, Loss of Right, and Priority Pre- and Post-America Invents Act of 2011 (35 U.S.C. §102)").

[204]*See* 35 U.S.C. §100(i)(1)(B) (eff. Mar. 16, 2013) (defining "effective filing date" as including "the filing date of the earliest application for which the . . . application is entitled, as to such invention, to a right of priority under section 119 . . ."); 35 U.S.C. §119(e)(1) (domestic priority).

Moreover, if a patent is ultimately issued from the nonprovisional application, its expiration date will be 20 years after the later nonprovisional application filing date rather than from the earlier provisional application filing date.[205] The up-to-12-month pendency period of the provisional application does not cost the applicant any patent term.[206]

There is certainly no requirement that a patent applicant begin the patent prosecution process by filing a provisional application, however, and many applicants proceed by filing the regular nonprovisional application as their first filing. Section 111(a) of 35 U.S.C. sets forth the requirements for nonprovisional applications. They must include a specification concluding with at least one claim,[207] drawings (if necessary to understand the invention),[208] and (subject to certain exceptions) an oath or declaration by each named inventor that she believes herself to be an "original inventor" of the invention she seeks to patent.[209] The nonprovisional application (like the provisional application) must be accompanied by the appropriate fees.[210]

3. Examination by the USPTO

The Patent Act provides that "the Director [of the USPTO] shall cause an examination to be made of the application and the alleged new invention; and if on such examination it appears that the applicant is entitled to a patent under the law, the Director shall issue a patent therefor."[211] A USPTO examiner will be assigned to the

[205] *See* 35 U.S.C. §154(a)(3) (stating that "[p]riority under section 119 . . . shall not be taken into account in determining the term of a patent").

[206] *See* 35 U.S.C. §154(a)(3) (providing that priority under §119 [whether domestic or foreign priority] is not taken into account in determining expiration of 20-year patent term).

[207] *See* 35 U.S.C. §112(b) (eff. Sept. 16, 2012) ("The specification shall conclude with one or more claims particularly pointing out and distinctly claiming the subject matter which the applicant regards as his invention.").

[208] *See* 35 U.S.C. §113.

[209] *See* 35 U.S.C. §115(a), (b)(2) (eff. Sept. 16, 2012). Prior to the AIA, a patent applicant had to make oath that she believed herself to be "the original and first inventor" of the invention she sought to patent. *See* 35 U.S.C. §115 (2006). The AIA amendments to the Patent Act permit an assignee (that is, a person to whom the inventor has assigned or is under an obligation to assign the invention) to file a patent application under certain circumstances. *See* 35 U.S.C. 118 (eff. Sept. 16, 2012). *See also* United States Patent and Trademark Office, *Final Rule: Changes to Implement the Inventor's Oath or Declaration Provisions of the Leahy-Smith America Invents Act*, 77 Fed. Reg. 48776 (Aug. 14, 2012).

[210] The current schedule of USPTO fees, revised annually, is *available at* https://www.uspto.gov/sites/default/files/documents/USPTO%20fee%20schedule_current.pdf (last rev. Jan. 1, 2020). In addition to the filing fee, applicants filing nonprovisional applications on or after December 8, 2004, also pay a "search fee" and an "examination fee." All three fees are due at the time of filing. If the applicant is granted a patent, an issue fee is also due. Non-insubstantial maintenance fees must also be paid during the post-issuance life of the patent (i.e., at 3.5, 7.5, and 11.5 years) in order to keep it in force. *See id.*

[211] 35 U.S.C. §131.

application depending upon the type of technology involved. The examiner's job is to determine whether the application and the invention claimed therein satisfy the various statutory requirements for the issuance of a patent; each of these requirements is covered in greater detail in subsequent chapters of this text. To summarize here, however, the examiner will first study the application to understand the claimed invention. He will review the form and content of the application to determine whether it complies with the disclosure and claiming requirements.[212] He will also consider whether the claimed invention falls within one of the permissible categories of potentially patentable subject matter[213] and whether it is useful (i.e., possesses "utility").[214]

The examiner's most important and difficult task is to determine whether the invention, as recited by the claims of the patent application, is new ("novel")[215] and "nonobvious."[216] To make this determination the examiner will conduct a search of the prior art, including U.S. and foreign patents and non-patent printed publications, and will compare what is taught by that prior art with what the applicant has claimed as her invention. The examiner will also consider prior art submitted by the applicant (typically accompanying an Information Disclosure Statement).[217] Under certain circumstances, third parties may also submit information they believe relevant to patentability.[218]

Depending upon the results of his search and examination, the examiner may initially "allow" (i.e., approve) certain of the applicant's

[212] 35 U.S.C. §112; *see also infra* Chapter 2 ("Patent Claims") and Chapter 3 ("Disclosure Requirements (35 U.S.C. §112(a))").

[213] 35 U.S.C. §101 (defining potentially patentable subject matter as encompassing processes, machines, manufactures, compositions of matter, and improvements thereof); *see also infra* Chapter 7 ("Potentially Patentable Subject Matter (35 U.S.C. §101)").

[214] 35 U.S.C. §101; *see also infra* Chapter 6 ("The Utility Requirement (35 U.S.C. §101)").

[215] 35 U.S.C. §102; *see also infra* Chapter 4 ("Novelty, Loss of Right, and Priority Pre- and Post-America Invents Act of 2011 (35 U.S.C. §102)").

[216] 35 U.S.C. §103; *see also infra* Chapter 5 ("The Nonobviousness Requirement (35 U.S.C. §103)").

[217] *See* 37 C.F.R. §1.97 ("Filing of Information Disclosure Statement"); *id.* §1.98 ("Content of Information Disclosure Statement").

[218] Before enactment of the AIA, third parties could submit to the USPTO patents or publications they believed relevant to pending patent applications that had been published, but there was no requirement that the examiner consider such submissions. The information would simply be made part of the application file. The submitter could not include any explanation of asserted relevancy. *See* 37 C.F.R. §1.99 (2010).

Effective September 16, 2012, third parties could submit patents or publications of potential relevance to examination "for consideration" (presumably by the USPTO examiner). A concise description of asserted relevance must accompany any such submission. *See* Leahy-Smith America Invents Act, Pub. L. No. 112-29 (H.R. 1249), §8, 125 Stat. 284, 315-316 (2011) (adding a subsection (e) to 35 U.S.C. §122); 35 U.S.C. §122(e) (titled "Preissuance Submissions by Third Parties"); 37 C.F.R. §1.290 (eff. Dec. 18, 2013) (titled "Submissions by third parties in applications"). *See also* United States Patent and Trademark Office, *Final Rule: Changes to Implement the Preissuance Submissions by Third Parties Provision of the Leahy-Smith America Invents Act*, 77 Fed. Reg. 42150 (July 17, 2012).

claims and reject others, or (relatively rarely) may allow all the claims, or (more typically) may reject all the claims. The examiner may also make "objections" to the form of the written description and/or drawings. The examiner will convey all of these determinations (and explanations for them) to the applicant in writing in an official document known as an "examiner's action" or "office action";[219] subsection H.3.a of this chapter provides a sample. Due to USPTO backlog and examiner workload, this process does not occur quickly; currently it takes about 20 months after the filing of her application for the applicant to receive a first office action.[220]

After receiving the first office action, the applicant has a statutorily set period of time (maximum of six months) in which to respond.[221] Failure to make a timely response means that the application will be considered abandoned.[222] Assuming that the applicant decides to go forward with the prosecution rather than abandon her application, she will typically submit a written response to the examiner's rejections.[223] In this response she may make arguments for patentability in an attempt to "traverse" (i.e., overcome) the rejections. She may also submit test data or other evidence in support of her arguments.[224]

Frequently, an applicant will opt to narrow the scope of her claims by amendment in order to avoid the prior art and remove the rejection. Changing the wording of the claims during prosecution of an application (by either narrowing or broadening the claims' scope), or adding new claims, is perfectly proper *if* the application as filed adequately supports the amended or new claims in accordance with 35 U.S.C. §112, ¶1.[225] She may also amend the written description and/or

[219]*See* 35 U.S.C. §132(a) (providing in part that "[w]henever, on examination, any claim for a patent is rejected, or any objection or requirement made, the Director shall notify the applicant thereof, stating the reasons for such rejection, or objection or requirement, together with such information and references as may be useful in judging of the propriety of continuing the prosecution of his application . . .").

[220]In FY 2015, the first office action pendency was about 20 months for mechanical applications, about 19 months for chemical applications, and about 21 months for software applications. *See* United States Patent and Trademark Office, *Performance and Accountability Report Fiscal Year 2015,* at 186 tbl. 4 (2015), *available at* http://www.uspto.gov/sites/default/files/documents/USPTOFY15PAR.pdf.

[221]*See* 35 U.S.C. §133; 37 C.F.R. §1.134.

[222]*See* 35 U.S.C. §133.

[223]Responses can also be made orally, either in a telephone interview or in person at the USPTO. However, oral responses must be followed up with a written response. *See* 37 C.F.R. §1.133(b).

[224]*See* 37 C.F.R. §1.132 ("Affidavits or declarations traversing rejections or objections").

[225]Renamed 35 U.S.C. §112(a) by the AIA (eff. Sept. 16, 2012). *See* Liebel-Flarsheim Co. v. Medrad, Inc., 358 F.3d 898, 909 n.2 (Fed. Cir. 2004) ("[I]t is not improper for an applicant to broaden his claims during prosecution in order to encompass a competitor's products, as long as the disclosure supports the broadened claims."); Gentry Gallery, Inc. v. Berkline Corp., 134 F.3d 1473, 1479 (Fed. Cir. 1998) ("[O]ne can add claims to a pending application directed to adequately described subject matter.").

drawings to respond to the examiner's objections thereto, but not in a way that would fundamentally change what she has disclosed as her invention; this would violate the "new matter" prohibition.[226]

After the applicant has responded to the first office action, whether or not she has amended the claims, the application will be reexamined by the USPTO examiner.[227] The examiner will thereafter issue a second office action. As in the first action, the examiner in the second action may allow some or all of the claims or may reject some or all of the claims. The examiner's second office action is usually made final.[228]

If in a final action the examiner has maintained rejections with which the applicant disagrees, or has twice rejected any claim, the applicant cannot automatically continue to argue the rejections with the examiner. At this point she must either appeal from the examiner's decision to the USPTO's Patent Trial and Appeal Board,[229] or effectively "buy" more prosecution time. A streamlined way of exercising the latter option, without having to file a new application, is to file a request for continued examination (RCE), an option available since 2000 for nonprovisional applications that were filed on or after June 8, 1995.[230] Alternatively, while her application is still pending an applicant can file a second or "continuing" application that will

---

Although they may result in allowance of a patent, narrowing claim amendments made during a patent's prosecution may later limit the patentee's ability to rely on the doctrine of equivalents to enforce her patent against competitors. *See infra* Chapter 9, Section D.2 ("Prosecution History Estoppel").

[226]*See* 35 U.S.C. §132(a) ("No amendment shall introduce new matter into the disclosure of the invention.").

[227]*See* 35 U.S.C. §132(a). Note that the word "reexamined" in this context simply means a second examination of the same application, not reexamination of an issued patent under 35 U.S.C. §§301 *et seq.* (a separate proceeding). Reexamination proceedings are detailed *infra* Chapter 8 ("Correcting and Challenging Issued Patents at the USPTO").

[228]*See* 37 C.F.R. §1.113(a).

[229]*See* 35 U.S.C. §134(a) (eff. Sept. 16, 2012) ("Appeal to the Patent Trial and Appeal Board"). Prior to the AIA, the Board was known as the "Board of Patent Appeals and Interferences." *See* 35 U.S.C. §134(a) (2006) ("An applicant for a patent, any of whose claims has been twice rejected, may appeal from the decision of the primary examiner to the Board of Patent Appeals and Interferences, having once paid the fee for such appeal."). For further details on appeals to the Board, *see* United States Patent and Trademark Office, Manual of Patent Examining Procedure ch. 1200 (8th ed., Aug. 2001, last rev. July 2010), *available at* http://www.uspto.gov/web/offices/pac/mpep/mpep.htm.

[230]*See* 35 U.S.C. §132(b) (providing that "[t]he Director shall prescribe regulations to provide for the continued examination of applications for patent at the request of the applicant"); 37 C.F.R. §1.114 ("Request for continued examination"). *See generally* Robert Bahr, *Request for Continued Examination (RCE) Practice*, 82 J. Pat. & Trademark Off. Soc'y 336 (2000).

Filing an RCE may not be an ideal strategy. In late 2012, the USPTO disclosed that it was facing a backlog of over 90,000 unexamined RCE's and solicited public feedback "in an effort to better understand the full spectrum of factors that impact the decision to file an RCE." *See* United States Patent and Trademark Office, *Request for Comments on Request for Continued Examination (RCE) Practice*, 77 Fed. Reg. 72830 (Dec. 6, 2012).

carry forward the information in the first application and may add additional information thereto. Continuing application practice has its own complexities and is discussed separately *infra*.[231]

The preceding discussion is not intended to suggest that an examiner will always reject all of the applicant's claims. Depending upon the scope of the claims and the state of the prior art, some (or all) claims may be allowed by the examiner immediately (this is called a "first action allowance"). Alternatively, claims that were initially rejected may be allowed in the second office action in light of the applicant's response to the first office action, or after having been amended. Whenever in the process the examiner determines that the applicant is entitled to a patent on some or all of the claims, he will send the applicant a Notice of Allowance so indicating.[232] The applicant must then (within three months) pay an issue fee in order to obtain a patent encompassing the allowed claims. The USPTO will issue the patent within about three months after the applicant has paid the issue fee.[233] The issue date represents the first date on or after which the patent owner can enforce the patent in U.S. federal court by suing alleged infringers.

a. Sample Office Action and Applicant's Response

This subsection provides excerpts from a patent's prosecution file history to illustrate some of the basic mechanics of the process.[234] Figure 1.4 reproduces the title page of U.S. Patent No. 7,241,196 ("the '196 patent"), directed to a "Heated Stuffed Animal." The '196 patent was prosecuted in 2005-2007, well before implementation of America Invents Act of 2011 rules.[235]

The invention of the '196 patent modifies a conventional stuffed animal by incorporating a heating source inside the animal's torso.

[231]*See infra* Section H.5 ("Continuing Application Practice"). Yet another option for an applicant faced with a final rejection is to file an "amendment after final" under 37 C.F.R. §1.116.

[232]*See* 35 U.S.C. §151 ("Issue of Patent").

[233]*See* Mark Montague et al., *Examination Before the USPTO,* in Advising High-Technology Companies §3:5.1[F] (Nathaniel T. Trelease ed., PLI 2004).

[234]Beginning in 2004, members of the public have been able to view prosecution file histories for issued patents and published applications at no charge via the USPTO's Public PAIR (Patent Application and Information Retrieval) system. United States Patent and Trademark Office, *Patent Application Information Retrieval*, https://portal.uspto.gov/pair/PublicPair (last visited Mar. 2020). More restricted access to pending application status and history is available to registered users of the Private PAIR system, https://www.uspto.gov/patents-application-process/checking-application-status/check-filing-status-your-patent-application (last rev. Mar. 2020) (follow "Private PAIR" hyperlink).

[235]The first-to-file regime implemented by the AIA takes effect for applications filed on or after March 16, 2013. For more on the distinctions between pre- and post-AIA rules, *see infra* Chapter 4 ("Novelty, Loss of Right, and Priority Pre- and Post-America Invents Act of 2011 (35 U.S.C. §102)").

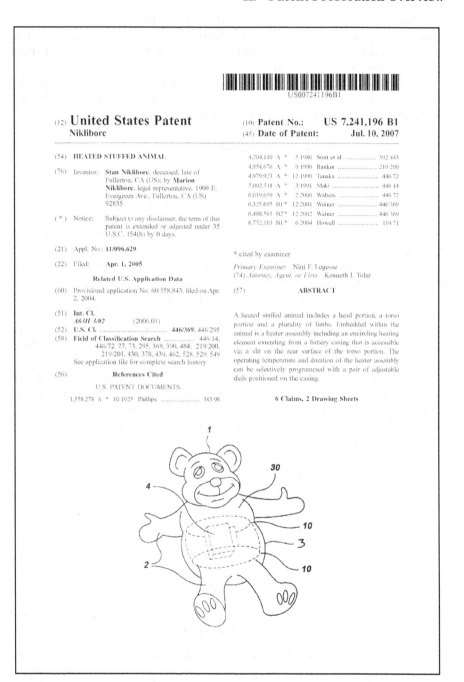

US007241196B1

(12) **United States Patent**
Nikliborc

(10) **Patent No.: US 7,241,196 B1**
(45) **Date of Patent: Jul. 10, 2007**

(54) **HEATED STUFFED ANIMAL**

(76) Inventor: **Stan Nikliborc**, deceased, late of Fullerton, CA (US); by **Marion Nikliborc**, legal representative, 1909 E. Evergreen Ave., Fullerton, CA (US) 92835

(*) Notice: Subject to any disclaimer, the term of this patent is extended or adjusted under 35 U.S.C. 154(b) by 0 days.

(21) Appl. No.: **11/096,629**

(22) Filed: **Apr. 1, 2005**

Related U.S. Application Data

(60) Provisional application No. 60/558,843, filed on Apr. 2, 2004.

(51) **Int. Cl.**
A63H 3/02 (2006.01)

(52) **U.S. Cl.** **446/369**; 446/295

(58) **Field of Classification Search** 446/14, 446/72, 77, 73, 295, 369, 390, 484; 219/200, 219/201, 430, 378, 439, 462, 528, 529, 549
See application file for complete search history.

(56) **References Cited**

U.S. PATENT DOCUMENTS

1,558,278 A *	10/1925	Phillips	....	383/96
4,204,110 A *	5/1980	Smit et al.	....	392/443
4,954,676 A *	9/1990	Rankin	....	219/200
4,979,923 A *	12/1990	Tanaka	....	446/72
5,002,511 A *	3/1991	Maki	....	446/14
6,019,659 A *	2/2000	Walters	....	446/72
6,325,695 B1 *	12/2001	Weiner	....	446/369
6,488,561 B2 *	12/2002	Weiner	....	446/369
6,752,103 B1 *	6/2004	Howell	....	119/71

* cited by examiner

Primary Examiner—Nini F. Legesse
(74) *Attorney, Agent, or Firm*—Kenneth L. Tolar

(57) **ABSTRACT**

A heated stuffed animal includes a head portion, a torso portion and a plurality of limbs. Embedded within the animal is a heater assembly including an encircling heating element extending from a battery casing that is accessible via a slit on the rear surface of the torso portion. The operating temperature and duration of the heater assembly can be selectively programmed with a pair of adjustable dials positioned on the casing.

6 Claims, 2 Drawing Sheets

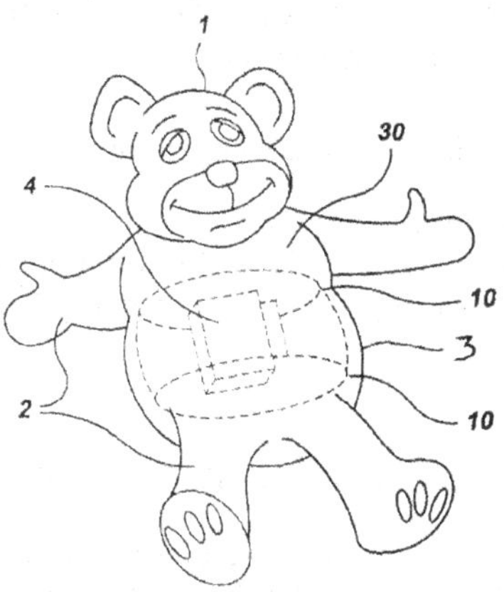

Figure 1.4

The heated animal provides a means for "warming, comforting and consoling a person embracing the animal."[236] The heating element is programmable such that its temperature and duration can be preselected by the user or a child's parent.

As is typical in patent prosecution practice, the application for the '196 patent was submitted to the USPTO with relatively broad claims. In Application No. 11/096,629, filed April 1, 2005, claim 1 recited:

> 1. A heated stuffed animal comprising:
>
> a head, limbs and a torso portion;
> a heater means embedded within the torso portion for warming, comforting and consoling a person embracing the animal.

Various dependent claims recited additional features, such as means for automatically disabling the heater means (claim 3) and means for automatically controlling an operating temperature range of the heater means (claim 4).[237]

In the first office action, the USPTO examiner rejected all the claims as anticipated under 35 U.S.C. §102(b) (2006).[238] The examiner took the position that each feature of the application claims was described in prior art patents that disclosed a heated stuffed animal.[239] Figure 1.5 is an excerpt of the USPTO office action.

In response to the rejection, the applicant effectively narrowed the scope of his claims by canceling the original claims and replacing them with a new set of claims, the broadest of which added features that previously had been recited in dependent claims. After amendment, the broadest application claim recited:

> 9. (New) A heated stuffed animal comprising:
>
> a head, limbs and a torso portion;
> a heater means embedded within the torso portion for warming, comforting and consoling a person embracing the animal;

[236] U.S. Patent No. 7,241,196, col. 2, ll. 57-58 (issued July 10, 2007) (reciting limitation of claim 1).

[237] Chapter 2 ("Patent Claims"), *infra,* explains the distinction between "independent" and "dependent" patent claims, and the special meaning of the phrase "means for [function]" as used in patent claim drafting.

[238] *See* U.S. Patent Application No. 11/096,629, Office Action Summary (mailed Aug. 3, 2006).

[239] The examiner cited each of U.S. Pat. No. 6,019,659 to Walters and U.S. Pat. No. 6,488,561 to Weiner as anticipatory under 35 U.S.C. §102(b) (pre-AIA). *See* Heated Stuffed Toy, U.S. Patent No. 6,019,659 (issued Feb. 1, 2000); Heated Stuffed Animal, U.S. Patent No. 6,488,561 (issued Dec. 3, 2002). Due to space limitations we do not reproduce the Walters and Weiner patents.

> means for automatically disabling said heater means after a selectively variable duration;
> means for automatically controlling an operating temperature range of said heater means.

The applicant's accompanying written remarks to the USPTO emphasized the criticality of the timed disabling means for the heating element as now recited in application claim 9. The child's parent or other user could feel comfortable falling asleep knowing that the heater would be disabled after a set time. The claimed invention was patentable over the prior art heated animals because the latter provided a thermostat but did not provide a timer for automatic shut-off of the heating element after a predetermined time.

These arguments apparently convinced the USPTO examiner that all the amended claims were allowable. After additional communications, including a telephone interview, the application issued as U.S. Patent No. 7,241,196 on July 10, 2007.[240]

4. Publication of Pending Patent Applications

Historically, all pending patent applications were maintained in secrecy throughout their pendency by the USPTO. The public did not see the content of the applications unless and until they issued as patents. This led to the problem of so-called "submarine" patents, applications for which would be kept pending in secrecy in the USPTO by their owners for many years through the filing of multiple continuation applications (discussed below). When patents finally issued on these applications, it was often to the great consternation of competitors who had no prior notice and were now suddenly liable as potential infringers.

[240]The title page of the patent lists the patent number as "7,241,196 B1." The "B1" notation (or "kind code") is a WIPO (World Intellectual Property Organization) standard code signifying that this document is a patent and is being published for the first time; i.e., there was no pre-issuance publication of this patent. *See* United States Patent and Trademark Office, *"Kind Codes" Included on the USPTO Patent Documents* (last rev. Sept. 18, 2013), https://www.uspto.gov/patents-application-process/patent-search/authority-files/uspto-kind-codes. Unlike the majority of patents, the applicant for the '196 patent chose to opt-out of automatic publication at 18 months after application filing. He did so by filing during prosecution a document titled "Non-Publication Request Under 35 U.S.C. 122(b)(2)(B)(i)," in which the applicant certified that his invention had not and would not be the subject of an application filed in another country or under a multilateral agreement (such as the Patent Cooperation Treaty) that would require publication at 18 months after filing.

Office Action Summary	Application No.	Applicant(s)
	11/096,629	NIKLIBORC ET AL.
	Examiner	**Art Unit**
	Nini F. Legesse	3711

-- The MAILING DATE of this communication appears on the cover sheet with the correspondence address --

Period for Reply

A SHORTENED STATUTORY PERIOD FOR REPLY IS SET TO EXPIRE 3 MONTH(S) OR THIRTY (30) DAYS, WHICHEVER IS LONGER, FROM THE MAILING DATE OF THIS COMMUNICATION.

- Extensions of time may be available under the provisions of 37 CFR 1.136(a). In no event, however, may a reply be timely filed after SIX (6) MONTHS from the mailing date of this communication.
- If NO period for reply is specified above, the maximum statutory period will apply and will expire SIX (6) MONTHS from the mailing date of this communication.
- Failure to reply within the set or extended period for reply will, by statute, cause the application to become ABANDONED (35 U.S.C. § 133). Any reply received by the Office later than three months after the mailing date of this communication, even if timely filed, may reduce any earned patent term adjustment. See 37 CFR 1.704(b).

Status

1)☒ Responsive to communication(s) filed on *01 April 2005*.

2a)☐ This action is **FINAL**. 2b)☒ This action is non-final.

3)☐ Since this application is in condition for allowance except for formal matters, prosecution as to the merits is closed in accordance with the practice under *Ex parte Quayle*, 1935 C.D. 11, 453 O.G. 213.

Disposition of Claims

4)☒ Claim(s) *1-8* is/are pending in the application.

4a) Of the above claim(s) _____ is/are withdrawn from consideration.

5)☐ Claim(s) _____ is/are allowed.

6)☒ Claim(s) *1-8* is/are rejected.

7)☐ Claim(s) _____ is/are objected to.

8)☐ Claim(s) _____ are subject to restriction and/or election requirement.

Application Papers

9)☐ The specification is objected to by the Examiner.

10)☐ The drawing(s) filed on _____ is/are: a)☐ accepted or b)☐ objected to by the Examiner.

Applicant may not request that any objection to the drawing(s) be held in abeyance. See 37 CFR 1.85(a).

Replacement drawing sheet(s) including the correction is required if the drawing(s) is objected to. See 37 CFR 1.121(d).

11)☐ The oath or declaration is objected to by the Examiner. Note the attached Office Action or form PTO-152.

Priority under 35 U.S.C. § 119

12)☐ Acknowledgment is made of a claim for foreign priority under 35 U.S.C. § 119(a)-(d) or (f).

a)☐ All b)☐ Some * c)☐ None of:

1.☐ Certified copies of the priority documents have been received.

2.☐ Certified copies of the priority documents have been received in Application No. _____.

3.☐ Copies of the certified copies of the priority documents have been received in this National Stage application from the International Bureau (PCT Rule 17.2(a)).

* See the attached detailed Office action for a list of the certified copies not received.

Attachment(s)

1)☒ Notice of References Cited (PTO-892)

2)☐ Notice of Draftsperson's Patent Drawing Review (PTO-948)

3)☐ Information Disclosure Statement(s) (PTO-1449 or PTO/SB/08) Paper No(s)/Mail Date _____.

4)☐ Interview Summary (PTO-413) Paper No(s)/Mail Date. _____.

5)☐ Notice of Informal Patent Application (PTO-152)

6)☐ Other: _____.

U.S. Patent and Trademark Office
PTOL-326 (Rev. 7-05) Office Action Summary Part of Paper No./Mail Date 20060802

Page 45 of 80

Figure 1.5

Excerpt of First Office Action

Application/Control Number: 11/096,629
Art Unit: 3711

DETAILED ACTION

Claim Rejections - 35 USC § 102

The following is a quotation of the appropriate paragraphs of 35 U.S.C. 102 that form the basis for the rejections under this section made in this Office action:

> A person shall be entitled to a patent unless –
>
> (b) the invention was patented or described in a printed publication in this or a foreign country or in public use or on sale in this country, more than one year prior to the date of application for patent in the United States.

Claims 1-8 are rejected under 35 U.S.C. 102(b) as being anticipated by Walters (US Patent No. 6,019,659).

Walter discloses a heated stuffed animal (see Fig. 1) as claimed comprising a heater means (22) with automatically temperature controlling means (40), and a power source (32) casing as claimed (see Fig. 2).

Claims 1-8 are rejected under 35 U.S.C. 102(b) as being anticipated by Weiner (US Patent No. 6,488,561).

Weiner discloses a heated stuffed animal (see Fig. 1) as claimed comprising a heater means (3) with automatically temperature controlling means (6), and a power source casing as claimed (see Fig. 1).

Conclusion

Any inquiry concerning this communication or earlier communications from the examiner should be directed to Nini F. Legesse whose telephone number is (571) 272-4412. The examiner can normally be reached on 9 AM - 5:30 PM.

Figure 1.5
(Continued)

This state of affairs improved significantly with the implementation of "18-month publication" procedure as part of the American Inventors Protection Act of 1999.[241] Under current law, the default rule is that a nonprovisional (i.e., regular, "full-service") U.S. utility patent application will be automatically published 18 months after its effective filing date.[242] Publication can be avoided by certifying to the USPTO that the applicant has not and will not file any other applications on the same invention in foreign countries or under multinational agreements that would require publication 18 months after filing.[243] In other words, an application must be purely domestic to avoid 18-month publication.[244] In fiscal year 2018, the USPTO published almost 372,000 applications.[245] A government study reported in 2004 that about 85 percent of U.S. patent applications filed by large entities were published at 18 months after filing.[246]

5. Continuing Application Practice

Suppose that an applicant receives from the examiner a final rejection of some of the claims in her application but an allowance of other claims. The applicant would like to obtain a patent (as soon as

[241]*See* American Inventors Protection Act of 1999, S. 1948, 106th Cong. tit. IV, §§4501-4502 (1999) ("Domestic Publication of Patent Applications Published Abroad") (as implemented by Pub. L. No. 106-113, 113 Stat. 1501 (1999)). Eighteen-month publication became the default rule for all applications filed on or after the Act's effective date of November 29, 2000. The first applications began to be published around March 2001.

[242]Publication of pending applications is online at the USPTO's website. *See* United States Patent and Trademark Office, *Patent Full-Text Databases* (last rev. May 1, 2015), http://patft.uspto.gov (follow links under "AppFT: Applications: Published since March 2001").

[243]*See* 35 U.S.C. §122(b)(2)(B)(i).

[244]Applications subject to a security order and design patent applications are also exempt from 18-month publication. *See* 35 U.S.C. §122(b)(2)(A)(ii), (iv).

[245]*See* United States Patent and Trademark Office, *Performance and Accountability Report Fiscal Year 2018*, tbl. 1, https://www.uspto.gov/sites/default/files/documents/USPTOFY18PAR.pdf, at 178 ("Summary of Patent Examining Activities FY 2014-FY 2018") (reporting that agency published 371,502 applications in FY 2018 pursuant to 18-month publication as provided for by the AIPA, Pub. L. No. 106-113). As a point of reference, the number of nonprovisional utility patent applications *filed* in FY 2016 (two fiscal years earlier) was 607,753. *Id.*

[246]United States General Accounting Office, *Report to Congressional Committees: Patents: Information About the Publication Provisions of the American Inventors Protection Act* 4 (2004), http://www.gao.gov/new.items/d04603.pdf (reporting that for applications received between November 29, 2000, and November 28, 2003, the USPTO "has published or plans to publish applications from about 85 percent of the applicants qualifying as large entities compared with only about 74 percent of those qualifying as small entities").

possible) on the allowed claims, perhaps because of a potential infringer in the marketplace, while at the same time continue prosecuting the rejected claims (rather than appealing their rejection to the Board of Patent Appeals and Interferences). The applicant in this situation has the option of filing what is known as a **continuation application**. Using continuation applications is a way of prolonging the application process; the continuation application extends the patenting transaction that began with the applicant's earlier-filed application.[247]

Currently there is no limit on the number of continuation applications that may be filed,[248] but abuse of the continuation process can give rise to the defense of "prosecution laches" if and when the patentee later attempts to enforce her patent.[249] Moreover, the longer that the prosecution of the original application is extended through the filing of continuations, the shorter the term of any resulting patent.[250]

The continuation application described in the preceding paragraphs is actually one of three kinds of **continuing applications**, a generic term for a later-filed patent application that contains some or all of the disclosure of that applicant's earlier-filed application (referred to hereafter as the "parent" application) and that names at least one inventor also named in the parent application.[251] The continuing application must be filed while the parent application is still pending

[247]*See* R. Carl Moy, Moy's Walker on Patents §3:43 (4th ed. 2007).

[248]A federal district court in 2007 preliminarily enjoined the USPTO from implementing new rules that would have limited the number of continuation applications and RCEs that an applicant could file from a given original application. *See* Tafas v. Dudas, 511 F. Supp. 2d 652 (E.D. Va. 2007) (finding that plaintiff/movant Glaxo SmithKline was likely to succeed on the merits of its claims that USPTO lacked authority under 35 U.S.C. §2(b)(2) (2006) to promulgate the new rules and that the rules were contrary to various other provisions of the Patent Act, including §120). After a Federal Circuit panel decision, *Tafas v. Doll*, 559 F.3d 1345 (2009), and a Federal Circuit order granting rehearing *en banc*, 328 F. App'x 658 (2009), the USPTO dropped the proposed new rules limiting the number of continuation applications and RCEs. *See* 74 Fed. Reg. 52688 (Oct. 14, 2009).

[249]The defense of prosecution laches is further detailed in Chapter 10 ("Defenses to Patent Infringement"), *infra*. *See generally* Mark A. Lemley & Kimberly A. Moore, *Ending Abuse of Patent Continuations*, 84 B.U. L. Rev. 63 (2004).

[250]*See* 35 U.S.C. §154(a)(2) (providing in part that "such grant shall be for a term beginning on the date on which the patent issues and ending 20 years from the date on which the application for the patent was filed in the United States or, if the application contains a specific reference to an earlier-filed application or applications under section 120, 121, or 365(c), from the date on which the earliest such application was filed").

[251]*See* United States Patent and Trademark Office, Manual of Patent Examining Procedure §201.11.II.B (8th ed., Aug. 2001, last rev. July 2010), *available at* http://www.uspto.gov/web/offices/pac/mpep/mpep.htm (stating that "[c]ontinuing applications include those applications which are called divisions, continuations, and continuations-in-part"); Transco Prods., Inc. v. Performance Contracting, Inc., 38 F.3d 551, 555 (Fed. Cir. 1994).

(i.e., has not been abandoned or issued as a patent).[252] Procedurally, the pertinent USPTO rule under which an applicant currently may file any type of continuing application is Rule 53(b).[253] The three types of continuing applications are

1. **Continuation application:** a second application for the same invention claimed in the parent application and filed during the lifetime of the parent application. The continuation application encompasses all the disclosure of the parent application and does not add any new matter to that disclosure. It claims the same invention claimed in the parent application, although there may be some variation in the scope of the subject matter claimed.
2. **Continuation-in-part application:** a second application filed during the lifetime of the parent application that encompasses some substantial portion or all of the disclosure of the parent application and also adds additional matter to that disclosure.[254]
3. **Divisional application:** a second application for an independent and distinct invention, carved out of the parent application during its lifetime and disclosing and claiming only subject matter disclosed in the parent application. A divisional application is appropriate when the parent application claimed more than one invention. A patent may claim only a single invention, so any other invention must be "divided out" and claimed in a separate application. The divisional application is often filed as a result of a **restriction requirement** made by the USPTO examiner.[255]

[252]*See* 35 U.S.C. §120 ("if filed before the patenting or abandonment of or termination of proceedings on the first application . . .").

[253]37 C.F.R. §1.53(b) (2008). Before December 1, 1997, continuing applications could be filed under 37 C.F.R. §1.60 (for continuations or divisionals) and 37 C.F.R. §1.62 ("file wrapper continuing" procedure for continuations, continuations-in-part, or divisionals). Rules 60 and 62 were superseded as of December 1, 1997, however, by the "continued prosecution application" (CPA) procedure of Rule 53(d) [37 C.F.R. §1.53(d)]. From 1997 to 2003, a continuation or divisional application (but not a continuation-in-part application) could be filed as a CPA. Effective July 14, 2003, CPA practice was made inapplicable to utility patent applications. *See* United States Patent and Trademark Office, Manual of Patent Examining Procedure §706.07(h), pt. XIII.B (8th ed., 2d rev. 2004) (showing comparison chart), *available at* https://www.uspto.gov/web/offices/pac/mpep/s706.html#d0e70778. Currently, CPAs under Rule 53(d) are available only for design patent applications. *See generally* Donald S. Chisum, 4A-13 Chisum on Patents §13.03[7] (2008).

[254]*See* PowerOasis, Inc. v. T-Mobile USA, Inc., 522 F.3d 1299, 1304 n.3 (Fed. Cir. 2008) (noting that "[w]hile the PTO has noted that the expressions 'continuation,' 'divisional,' and 'continuation-in-part' are merely terms used for administrative convenience, . . . the quintessential difference between a continuation and a continuation-in-part is the addition of new matter") (citation omitted).

[255]*See* 35 U.S.C. §121 (providing that "[i]f two or more independent and distinct inventions are claimed in one application, the Director may require the application to be restricted to one of the inventions").

The statutory bases for continuing application practice are Sections 120 and 121 of the Patent Act. Importantly, §120 provides that to the extent the claims of the continuing application are supported by the disclosure set forth in the parent application in accordance with the requirements of 35 U.S.C. §112, ¶1 (i.e., if the parent application's disclosure satisfies the enablement and written description requirements for the claims of interest in the continuing application),[256] those claims are entitled to the benefit of the filing date of the earlier-filed parent application.[257] The *effective filing date* of such claims is the parent application's filing date.[258] Practically speaking, this means that patents and publications of others, describing the same or similar invention but having an effective date in the interim period between the parent application's filing date and the continuing application's filing date, will be ignored. They are not considered prior art against the continuing application claims that are entitled to the parent application's filing date.

In contrast, those claims in a continuing application (namely, a continuation-in-part) that are *not* adequately supported by the disclosure of the parent application will not be entitled to the benefit of the

[256]The America Invents Act of 2011 (AIA) deleted the requirement that a parent application provide best mode disclosure support for the claims of a related continuing application. *See* 35 U.S.C. §120 (eff. Sept. 16, 2012) (referring to "[a]n application for patent for an invention disclosed in the manner provided by section 112(a) (other than the requirement to disclose the best mode) in an application previously filed in the United States . . ."). The AIA also renamed 35 U.S.C. §112's first paragraph as 35 U.S.C. §112(a) (eff. Sept. 16, 2012).

[257]*See* 35 U.S.C. §120 ("Benefit of Earlier Filing Date in the United States") (eff. Sept. 16, 2012). This rather wordy section provides in part (emphasis added and explanatory references in brackets):

> An [continuing] application for patent for an invention disclosed in the manner provided by section 112(a) (other than the requirement to disclose the best mode) in an [parent] application previously filed in the United States, or as provided by section 363 [35 U.S.C. §363] [i.e., an international application designating the U.S. and filed under the Patent Cooperation Treaty (PCT)], which names an inventor or joint inventor in the previously filed [parent] application *shall have the same effect, as to such invention, as though filed on the date of the prior [parent] application*, if filed before the patenting or abandonment of or termination of proceedings on the first [parent] application or on an application similarly entitled to the benefit of the filing date of the first [parent] application and if it [the continuing application] contains or is amended to contain a specific reference to the earlier-filed [parent] application.

The key language is "shall have the same effect," which in this context means "shall be entitled to the filing date of" the parent application.

[258]The America Invents Act of 2011 added to the Patent Act a definition of "effective filing date." *See* 35 U.S.C. §100(i)(1)(B) (eff. Mar. 16, 2013) (defining "effective filing date" as including "the filing date of the earliest application for which the . . . application is entitled, as to such invention, . . . to the benefit of an earlier filing date under section 120 . . ."); 35 U.S.C. §120 ("Benefit of earlier filing date in the United States").

parent application's filing date; rather, they will be considered filed on the continuing application's filing date. Such claims will not relate back to the filing date of the parent application for purposes of avoiding intervening prior art. Thus, patents and publications of others, describing the same invention but having an effective date in the interim period between the parent application's filing date and the continuing application's filing date, *will* be available as prior art against those claims.[259]

In sum, the claims of a continuing application are entitled to the benefit of the filing date of its parent application only as to commonly disclosed subject matter; claims directed to new matter will not get that benefit.[260]

For example, consider a parent application filed by inventor Jack on January 1, 2005 that disclosed only a widget made of wood and included no broadening language to indicate that the widget could be made of any other material besides wood. Claim 1 of the parent application recited:

1. A widget formed from wood.

Jack soon thereafter discovered that widgets of his invention could also be made of plastic, metal, or other solid materials. On January 1, 2006, while his parent application was still pending, Jack filed a second application, which he designated as a continuation-in-part (CIP) of the parent application, repeating all the disclosure of his parent application but adding new disclosure concerning the making of widgets from plastic, metal, or other solid materials. Jack's CIP application carried forward and rewrote his original claim 1 in dependent form as claim 2, and added a new, broader claim 1, as follows:

1. A widget formed from a solid material.
2. The widget of claim 1 wherein said solid material is wood.

After filing the CIP application, Jack abandoned the parent application.

During subsequent examination of the CIP application, the USPTO examiner's search located a publication authored by independent

[259]*See* PowerOasis, Inc. v. T-Mobile USA, Inc., 522 F.3d 1299, 1301 (Fed. Cir. 2008) (affirming district court's invalidation of two patents on ground that "none of the asserted claims . . . were entitled, under 35 U.S.C. §120, to the benefit of the filing date of PowerOasis's original application because the earlier application did not provide a written description of the invention claimed in the asserted patents, as required by 35 U.S.C. §112").

[260]*See Transco*, 38 F.3d at 556.

inventor Jill and published on June 1, 2005, that described identical widgets formed from wood and from metal. As we will see in Chapter 4 *infra,* the teaching of this printed publication would anticipate (i.e., destroy the novelty of) claim 1 of Jack's CIP application under 35 U.S.C. §102(a), because the species of metal widget (and likewise the species of wood widget) described in the publication destroys the novelty of Jack's claimed genus of "solid material" widgets. The printed publication by Jill would be prior art with respect to CIP claim 1 because CIP claim 1 is only entitled to the filing date of the CIP application (January 1, 2006), not to the filing date of the parent application (January 1, 2005).[261]

On the other hand, CIP claim 2 would not be anticipated by the teaching of wood widgets in the printed publication by Jill. This is because CIP claim 2 is entitled to the benefit of the January 1, 2005, filing date of the parent application (because the parent application provided a disclosure of wood widgets that satisfies the enablement, written description, and best mode criteria of 35 U.S.C. §112, ¶1 (2006)). January 1, 2005 is the effective filing date of CIP claim 2. Because Jill's article was published after that date, it is not section 102(a) prior art against CIP claim 2. Disregarding any other potential patentability issues, Jack will receive a patent on CIP claim 2 (but not on CIP claim 1).

In contrast with the claim-by-claim analysis described above for determining benefit of particular claims in a continuing application to a parent application's filing date, the analysis for determining when a patent issued from a continuing application will expire does not distinguish between claims.[262] If we change the facts in the example above and assume that no pertinent prior art was uncovered by the examiner and that Jack's CIP application issued with both claims 1 and 2, both of those claims (along with any other claims in the patent) would expire 20 years after January 1, 2005, Jack's parent application's filing date. It is *not* the case that claim 1 would expire on January 1, 2026, and claim 2 would expire on January 1, 2025.

[261]The same result would follow under the America Invents Act of 2011 if the applications were governed by the AIA.

[262]In accordance with 35 U.S.C. §154(a)(2), *all* the claims in a designated continuing application will be deemed to expire 20 years after the parent application's filing date, regardless of whether particular claims are supported in the §112 sense by the parent application's disclosure. *See also* United States Patent and Trademark Office, *Changes to Implement 20-Year Patent Term and Provisional Applications*, 60 FED. REG. 20195, 20205 (Apr. 25, 1995) (to be codified at 37 C.F.R. pts. 1, 3) (explaining in response to Comment 5 that "[t]he term of a patent is not based on a claim-by-claim approach"), *available at* https://www.govinfo.gov/content/pkg/FR-1995-04-25/pdf/95-9838.pdf (last visited May 26, 2012).

6. Double Patenting

a. Introduction

A patent applicant may obtain only one U.S. patent on a given invention. If a patent applicant is granted a patent on invention X and files another application that again claims invention X (or an obvious variant of invention X), the USPTO examiner will reject the claims of the later application as violating the prohibition on "double patenting."[263] In the litigation context, double patenting is often charged against pharmaceutical firms allegedly engaged in "evergreening," that is, obtaining a series of patents on closely related drug inventions in an attempt to improperly prolong the patent life of the firm's products.[264]

b. Two Forms

There are two forms of double patenting. In the example of the preceding paragraph, if the later-filed application claims the *identical* invention as the applicant's patent, the USPTO examiner's rejection will be for "same invention-type" double patenting, which is based on the language of 35 U.S.C. §101 that "[w]hoever invents or discovers any new and useful [invention] may obtain *a* patent therefor . . ." (emphasis added). Same invention-type double patenting is also referred to as "statutory" double patenting. On the other hand, if the later application does not claim the same invention, but rather claims a *merely obvious variant* of it, the rejection will be for "obviousness-type" double patenting. This form of double patenting, which is recognized in judicial decisions but which does not have an explicit basis in the patent statute, is also referred to as "nonstatutory" double patenting.

[263]The typical fact situation giving rise to double patenting concerns is one that involves an already issued patent and a pending patent application, both owned by the same entity. However, a double patenting issue may also arise between two or more pending applications or between one or more pending applications and a published application. *See* United States Patent and Trademark Office, Manual of Patent Examining Procedure §804 (8th ed., Aug. 2001, last rev. July 2010), *available at* https://www.uspto.gov/web/offices/pac/mpep/s804.html.

[264]*See* Rebecca S. Eisenberg, 13 Mich. Telecomm. & Tech. L. Rev. 345, 354 (2007) (commenting that "[i]n recent years drug innovators have sought to prolong their effective periods of patent protection through various 'evergreening' strategies that add new patents to their quivers as old ones expire. Examples include patents on "metabolites" (i.e., the products into which drugs are transformed in a patient's body); patents on intermediate products used in producing drugs; patents on new uses for drugs; and patents on new formulations or preparations.") (footnotes omitted).

c. *Policy Concerns*

The policy concern underlying the double patenting doctrine is *not* that an applicant is seeking to patent something that another has already invented.[265] Rather, the primary and traditional policy basis underlying the double patenting doctrine is to prevent the same patent owner, through obtaining a second patent on the same invention (or an obvious variant of the same invention) she has already patented, from improperly "extending her monopoly." In other words, the goal is to prevent the patentee from obtaining a second patent that will effectively extend the duration of the right to exclude others from practice of a given invention that was conveyed previously by her first patent.[266]

A second policy concern also drives double patenting jurisprudence — the potential for harassment of an accused infringer by multiple assignees (owners) has of patents claiming very similar subject matter.[267] This policy concern gained importance since the 1994 Uruguay Round Amendments Act implementation of the 20-year patent term. Recall that that statutory change required that multiple patents issuing from co-pending applications (e.g., a parent application and related continuation or continuation-in-part applications) expire on the same date. Thus, switching to the 20-year term went a long way towards eliminating the double patenting policy concern with timewise extension of monopoly.[268]

[265]Thus, a USPTO rejection of application claims (or a federal court's invalidation of claims in an issued patent) for double patenting is analytically distinct from a rejection (or invalidation) on the grounds of anticipation (*see infra* Chapter 4) or obviousness (*see infra* Chapter 5).

[266]*See* In re Zickendraht, 319 F.2d 225, 232 (C.C.P.A. 1963) (Rich, J., concurring) (observing that "[t]he public should . . . be able to act on the assumption that upon the expiration of the patent it will be free to use not only the invention claimed in the patent but also modifications or variants thereof which would have been obvious to those of ordinary skill in the art at the time the invention was made, taking into account the skill in the art and prior art other than the invention claimed in the issued patent").

[267]*See* In re Van Ornum, 686 F.2d 937, 947 (C.C.P.A. 1982) (Rich, J.) (stating that "extension of monopoly is not the only objection to double patenting" and that "[o]ther[] [objections] include possible harassment by multiple assignees"). If the ownership of two or more patents claiming inventions that are merely obvious variants of one another becomes divided between different owners, a competitor may find itself being sued by all of the patent owners for infringement based on the competitor's single allegedly infringing product or process.

[268]The 1994 enactment of the Uruguay Round Amendments Act (URAA) is described *supra* Section C.7 ("The Patent Term")). Many (though not all) obviousness-type double patenting situations stem from the issuance of multiple patents based on a chain of continuing applications (described *supra* Section H.5 ("Continuing Application Practice"). Although originally owned by the same entity, some of the resulting patents may be sold (i.e., assigned) by the original owner to different entities. Under the URAA-implemented 20-year term, all such patents would expire on the same date. The common expiration date eliminates the policy concern regarding improper extension of monopoly by the patentees, but leaves intact the possibility of harassment by multiple patentees. To respond to the harassment concern, certain provisions must be included

But it did *not* eliminate the possibility that a potential infringer might have to deal with multiple lawsuits if ownership of two (or more) patents on obvious variants of the same invention were split up and the two (or more) patentees each sued the same potential infringer.

The latter policy concern — potential harassment by multiple patent owners — drove the Federal Circuit's 2013 decision in *In re Hubbell.*[269] There a divided panel of the Federal Circuit affirmed a USPTO obviousness-type double patenting rejection of an application owned by the California Institute of Technology (CalTech) in view of an issued patent owned by a completely separate entity — the Eidgenossiche Technische Hochschule Zurich (ETHZ) and Universitat Zurich.

Importantly, the rejected CalTech application and ETHZ reference patent shared two common inventors, but lacked *identical* inventorship (each had two other, different inventors). The ETHZ reference patent was not prior art because its priority date was later than that of the CalTech application,[270] and the ETHZ patent claimed a species of a genus claimed in the CalTech application.[271] The parties did not

---

in terminal disclaimers, discussed *infra* Section H.6.f, that preclude the original patent owner from dividing ownership of the patents that result from the USPTO's allowance of the two or more patents claiming inventions that are obvious variants of one another.

[269]709 F.3d 1140 (Fed. Cir. 2013).

[270]*See Hubbell,* 709 F.3d at 1143 n.2 ("The application for the '685 patent was a continuation-in-part of Application No. 09/563,760, filed on May 1, 2000, now U.S. Patent No. 6,894,022, which is a continuation-in-part of Application No. 09/141,153, filed on August 27, 1998, now abandoned. Accordingly, though the '685 patent issued first, it is not available as prior art under 35 U.S.C. §§102 or 103 against the claims in the '509 application[, which had a priority date of April 3, 1997].").

[271]Representative claim 18 of CalTech's '509 application recited a genus of bidomain proteins or peptides:

> 18. A bidomain protein or peptide comprising a transglutaminase substrate domain and a polypeptide growth factor.

> Claim 1 of ETHZ's '685 patent recited a species within the genus recited in claim 18 of the '509 application:
>
> 1. A fusion protein, comprising:
>   (i) a first protein domain;
>   (ii) a second protein domain; and
>   (iii) an enzymatic or hydrolytic cleavage site between the first and second domains;
>
>   wherein the first domain is a growth factor selected from the group consisting of the platelet derived growth factor superfamily and the transforming growth factor beta (TGF[beta]) superfamily;
>
>   wherein the second domain is a crosslinking Factor XIIIa substrate domain;
>
>   wherein the enzymatic cleavage site is selected from the group consisting of proteolytic substrates and polysaccharide substrates; and
>
>   wherein the hydrolytic cleavage site comprises a substrate with a linkage which undergoes hydrolysis by an acid or a base catalyzed reaction.

Hubbell, 709 F.3d at 1142-1143.

dispute that if the double patenting rejection was permissible as a matter of law, the species claim recited in the ETHZ reference patent would "anticipate" the genus claim of the CalTech application.[272]

In holding that the double patenting rejection was properly entered as a matter of law, the *Hubbell* majority blessed the USPTO's position that obviousness-type double patenting does not require either common ownership or the identical inventive entity between a rejected application and a reference patent. In other words, *some* overlap in inventorship is enough to create double patenting problems. The *Hubbell* majority specifically cited in support of its ruling the USPTO's MANUAL OF PATENT EXAMINING PROCEDURE, which provided that "[d]ouble patenting may exist between an issued patent and an application filed by the same inventive entity, *or by a different inventive entity having a common inventor*, and/or by a common assignee/owner."[273] Notably, in a 2009 decision, *In re Fallaux,*[274] the Circuit had specifically *declined* to adopt the PTO's position that inventor overlap, without common ownership or identical inventive entity, was enough.[275] The 2013

[272]*See Hubbell,* 709 F.3d at 1145 ("On appeal, Hubbell does not dispute that Claim 1 of the '685 patent anticipates representative Claim 18 of the '509 application. Instead, Hubbell argues that obviousness-type double patenting should not apply where, as here, an application and a conflicting patent share common inventors but do not have *identical* inventive entities, were never commonly owned, and are not subject to a joint research agreement") (emphasis in original).

[273]UNITED STATES PATENT AND TRADEMARK OFFICE, MANUAL OF PATENT EXAMINING PROCEDURE (MPEP) §804(I)(A) (emphasis added by Federal Circuit). Although the Federal Circuit decided *Hubbell* in 2013, the language of §804(I)(A) as set forth in the current version of the MPEP (9th ed., Nov. 2015) at the time of this writing (Feb. 2016) is identical. The provision provides in full:

> Double patenting may exist between an issued patent and an application filed by the same inventive entity, or by a different inventive entity having a common inventor, and/or by a common assignee/owner. Double patenting may also exist where the inventions claimed in a patent and an application were made as a result of activities undertaken within the scope of a joint research agreement as defined in 35 U.S.C. 103(c)(2) and (3). Since the inventor/patent owner has already secured the issuance of a first patent, the examiner must determine whether the grant of a second patent would give rise to an unjustified extension of the rights granted in the first patent.

MPEP §804(I)(A) (9th ed., Nov. 2015).

[274]564 F.3d 1313 (Fed. Cir. 2009).

[275]*Fallaux,* 564 F.3d at 1315 n.1. The court stated:

> The reference patents for the double patenting rejection on appeal — the Vogels patents — are *related to the Fallaux application only by way of a single common inventor*— Abraham Bout. . . . [Footnote text:] Neither party raised or argued the question of whether a patent may be used as a reference for an obviousness-type double patenting rejection where the patent shares only a common inventor with the application, rather than an identical inventive entity or a common assignee. The *Manual of Patent Examination Procedure (MPEP)* allows such a rejection. See §804 ¶I.A (8th ed., rev.7, 2008) ("Double patenting may exist

Hubbell decision represents the court's endorsement (or at least endorsement by two Federal Circuit judges) of the USPTO view that the court had declined to adopt in 2009.[276]

d. Comparing Claims with Claims

The scope of the patentee's right to exclude is measured by the language of the patent claims. Therefore, the double patenting analysis necessarily involves comparing the *claims* of the patentee's later-filed application with the *claims* of the patent she has already obtained.[277] As we will see in later chapters, comparing the claims first requires that we understand what the words of the claims mean, and in so doing, we may consult the written description and drawings of the corresponding patent or application. However, it is analytically incorrect to view the double patenting analysis as involving the use of the content of the earlier-filed patent as prior art against the later-filed application.[278] Assuming that no statutory bars apply,[279] the earlier-filed patent to the same inventor does not qualify as prior art under 35 U.S.C. §102 (2006) because it does not disclose the invention of "another."[280]

e. Case Study

A classic case study for double patenting analysis is *In re Vogel,*[281] which involved methods of packaging meat products to prevent

---

> between an issued patent and an application filed by the same inventive entity, or by a different inventive entity having a common inventor, and/or by a common assignee/owner."). This opinion should not be read to decide or endorse the PTO's view on this issue.

Fallaux, 564 F.3d at 1315, 1315 n.1 (Fed. Cir. 2009) (emphasis added).

[276]On this point, dissenting Judge Newman charged that

> [t]he panel majority miscites *In re Fallaux*, 564 F.3d 1313 (Fed. Cir. 2009), for that ruling disclaimed the holding for which its authority is now asserted. The *Fallaux* court referred to a provision in the MPEP and stated that "This opinion should not be read to decide or endorse the PTO's view on this issue." Id. at 1316 n.1. My colleagues now cite this footnote as authority for the holding it declined to make.

Hubbell, 709 F.3d at 1153-1154 (Newman, J., dissenting).

[277]*See* General Foods Corp. v. Studiengesellschaft Kohle mbH, 972 F.2d 1272, 1277 (Fed. Cir. 1992) ("Double patenting is altogether a matter of what is claimed.").

[278]*See* In re Vogel, 422 F.2d 438, 441-442 (C.C.P.A. 1970) ("In considering the question [whether any claim in the application defines merely an obvious variation of an invention disclosed and claimed in the patent], the patent disclosure may not be used as prior art.").

[279]*See* 35 U.S.C. §102(b) (2006).

[280]*See* 35 U.S.C. §102(a), (e), (g)(2) (2006).

[281]422 F.2d 438 (C.C.P.A. 1970).

spoilage. Vogel initially obtained a patent on his method as applied to pork. Claim 1 of Vogel's patent recited:

> 1. A method of preparing pork products, comprising the steps of: boning a freshly slaughtered carcass while still hot into trimmings; grinding desired carcass trimming while still warm and fluent; mixing the ground trimmings while fluent and above approximately 80 degrees F., mixing to be completed not more than approximately 3 hours after the carcass has been bled and stuffing the warm and fluent mixed trimmings into air impermeable casings.

Vogel subsequently filed a second patent application that more broadly claimed the method as applied to "meat" generally, and also as applied specifically to beef. Application claim 10 recited:

> 10. A method for prolonging the storage life of packaged meat products comprising the steps of: removing meat from a freshly slaughtered carcass at substantially the body bleeding temperature thereof under ambient temperature conditions; comminuting the meat during an exposure period following slaughter while the meat is at a temperature between said bleeding and ambient temperatures; sealing the comminuted meat within a flexible packaging material having an oxygen permeability ranging from 0.01 × 10(-10) to 0.1 × 10(-10) cc.-mm/sec/cm(2)/cm Hg at 30 degrees C. during said exposure period and before the meat has declined in temperature to the ambient temperature; and rapidly reducing the temperature of the packaged meat to a storage temperature below the ambient temperature immediately following said packaging of the meat.

Application claim 11 depended from claim 10 but was limited to beef. The USPTO rejected Vogel's application claims 10 and 11 as unpatentable in view of claim 1 of Vogel's issued patent (in combination with a reference to one Ellies). The USPTO characterized the rejection as same invention-type double patenting under 35 U.S.C. §101.

In considering whether to affirm the rejection on appeal, the Court of Customs and Patent Appeals (CCPA) set forth the following roadmap for double patenting analysis. The first question to be asked, the court explained, is whether "the same invention [is] being claimed twice?"[282] By "same invention" the court meant "identical subject matter," which implies identical claim scope. Thus, "halogen" is not the same invention for double patenting purposes as "chlorine" (a species of the genus halogen), but a widget of length "36 inches" is the same invention as a widget of length "3 feet." The court further instructed that "[a] good test, and probably the only objective test, for 'same

[282]*Vogel*, 422 F.2d at 441.

invention,' is whether one of the claims could be literally infringed without literally infringing the other. If it could be, the claims do not define identically the same invention."[283] By applying this test, the court concluded that same invention-type double patenting did not apply to Vogel's application claims 10 and 11 and that the USPTO had erred in holding to the contrary. Application claims 10 (meat process) and 11 (beef process) did not define the same invention as patent claim 1 (pork process).[284] For example, performing the process of application claims 10 and 11 with beef would literally infringe those claims but would not literally infringe patent claim 1 (pork process).

The *Vogel* court then moved to the second question: "[d]oes any appealed claim define merely an obvious variation of an invention disclosed and claimed in the patent?"[285] With respect to application claim 11 (limited to beef methods), the answer was no. That claim did not define a merely obvious variation of the pork process of patent claim 1. "The specific time and temperature considerations with respect to pork might not be applicable to beef," the court observed. There was "nothing in the record to indicate that the spoliation characteristics of the two meats are similar."[286] Thus, neither same invention-type nor obviousness-type double patenting was implicated by application claim 11, and the USPTO's rejection of application claim 11 on the basis of double patenting was reversed.[287]

The *Vogel* court lastly applied the "mere obvious variation" test to compare patent claim 1 (pork process) and application claim 10 (meat process). This time, obviousness-type double patenting was present. The court explained that "'[m]eat' reads literally on pork. The only limitation appearing in [application] claim 10 which is not disclosed in the available portion of the patent disclosure is the permeability range of the packaging material; but this is merely an obvious variation as shown by Ellies." Allowance of application claim 10 for its full term would therefore improperly extend the duration of Vogel's monopoly on the pork process recited in patent claim 1.

[283]*Vogel*, 422 F.2d at 441.

[284]*Vogel*, 422 F.2d at 442 (reasoning that "[t]he patent claims are limited to pork. Appealed [application] claims 7 and 10 are limited to meat, which is not the same thing. [Application] Claims 7 and 10 could be infringed by many processes which would not infringe any of the patent claims. [Application] Claim 11 is limited to beef. Beef is not the same thing as pork.").

[285]*Vogel*, 422 F.2d at 442.

[286]*Vogel*, 422 F.2d at 442.

[287]Depending upon the order in which the pertinent patent applications were filed and certain other factors, the USPTO currently applies either a "one-way obviousness" or a "two-way obviousness" test for determining obviousness-type double patenting. For further details, *see* UNITED STATES PATENT AND TRADEMARK OFFICE, MANUAL OF PATENT EXAMINING PROCEDURE §804 (8th ed., Aug. 2001, last rev. July 2010), *available at* http://www.uspto.gov/web/offices/pac/mpep/mpep.htm.

f. Terminal Disclaimers

Unlike a same invention-type double patenting rejection,[288] an obviousness-type double patenting rejection is not fatal to the applicant's attempt at obtaining a second patent. An obvious-type double patenting rejection can be overcome by the filing of a **terminal disclaimer**, which is authorized by 35 U.S.C. §253.[289] A terminal disclaimer is a document in which the applicant formally agrees that if he is awarded a patent on the application claims that have been rejected for obviousness-type double patenting, that patent will be deemed to expire on the same date as the applicant's first patent (on which the double patenting rejection was based).[290] The terminal disclaimer thus alleviates the concern about extension of monopoly that would otherwise result from granting a patent on the later-filed application. As a result, a patentee may ultimately obtain two (or more) patents claiming inventions that are merely obvious variants of each other, but all of these patents will expire on the same date. In permitting this result, the patent system maintains incentives for the patentee to improve his original invention, but does not allow him to extend the period of time in which he can prevent others from practicing the patented invention and its obvious variations.

[288]The same invention-type double patenting rejection cannot be overcome by terminal disclaimer because the basis of the rejection is statutory. *See* In re Vogel, 422 F.2d 438, 441 (C.C.P.A. 1970) ("If it is determined that the same invention is being claimed twice, 35 USC 101 forbids the grant of the second patent, regardless of the presence or absence of a terminal disclaimer.").

[289]The second paragraph of 35 U.S.C. §253 (2006) provides that "[i]n like manner any patentee or applicant may disclaim or dedicate to the public the entire term, or any terminal part of the term, of the patent granted or to be granted."

[290]In the terminal disclaimer the applicant must also promise that the ownership of the two (or more) patents at issue will be commonly maintained throughout the term of the patents. *See* 37 C.F.R. §1.321(c)(3) (providing that terminal disclaimer filed to obviate obviousness-type double patenting rejection must "[i]nclude a provision that any patent granted on that application . . . shall be enforceable only for and during such period that said patent is commonly owned with the application or patent which formed the basis for the rejection"). This requirement addresses a second policy concern that would otherwise arise as to harassment of competitors through the filing of multiple lawsuits if ownership of two (or more) patents on obvious variants of the same invention were split up and the two (or more) patentees each sued the same potential infringer. The potential harassment concern was the subject of *In re Hubbell*, 709 F.3d 1140 (Fed. Cir. 2013), examined *supra* Section H.6.c.

Chapter 2

Patent Claims

A. Introduction

This chapter focuses on **claims**, arguably the most important part of a patent. A patent claim is a precision-drafted, single-sentence definition of the patent owner's right to exclude others.[1] Every U.S. utility patent must conclude with one or more claims that particularly point out and distinctly claim the subject matter which the applicant regards as his invention.[2]

This text addresses claims in Chapter 2 because of their importance to understanding all concepts covered in the remaining chapters. Claims play a central role in all aspects of the U.S. patent system. The USPTO examines the claims and compares them to the prior art in order to determine patentability. In federal court litigation involving issued patents, the claims are the central focus of judges and juries when determining validity and infringement.

The critical threshold step of interpreting the claims — that is, determining what the words in the claims mean — is quite often dispositive of the issues of infringement and validity. Consequently, the crafting of patent claims is one of the most challenging and important drafting tasks in all of legal practice. This chapter therefore covers not only the legal doctrines pertaining to claim interpretation but also a number of commonly used drafting techniques and claim formats. In patent law, "the name of the game is the claim."[3]

1. Historical Development of Patent Claiming

The development of claiming practice in the United States reflects a shift from a historical **central claiming** regime to the current system of **peripheral claiming**.

[1]*See* Chapter 1 ("Foundations of the U.S. Patent System"), *supra*, for further discussion of the nature of the exclusive right conveyed by a patent.

[2]35 U.S.C. §112(b) (eff. Sept. 16, 2012).

[3]Giles S. Rich, *Extent of Protection and Interpretation of Claims — American Perspectives*, 21 INT'L REV. INDUS. PROP. & COPYRIGHT L. 497, 499 (1990).

The earliest patent claims were written in central claiming style. Central claiming means that the claim recites the preferred embodiment of the invention but is understood to encompass all equivalents. Such claims will typically make an explicit reference to the preceding part of the patent specification. For example, a U.S. patent issued in 1858 included the following claim directed to a writing instrument:

> The combination of the lead and india-rubber or other erasing substance in the holder of a drawing-pencil, the whole being constructed and arranged substantially in the manner and for the purposes set forth.[4]

Claims were first mentioned in the U.S. Patent Act of 1836, but not mandated by statute until 1870. Prior to these enactments, patent applicants disclosed their invention to the world by means of a written description. This description provided a narrative explanation of how to make and use the invention, as well as a statement of how the invention differed from what had come before.[5] If a claim was included in the patent at all, it was something of an afterthought, having no more legal significance than the written description.

In the U.S. Patent Act of 1870, the inclusion of claims became mandatory. From this point on, claiming practice evolved to the peripheral claiming regime we have today in the United States. Peripheral claiming means that the claim recites a precise boundary or periphery of the patentee's property right, which is the patentee's time-limited right to exclude others. The following section elaborates on this idea.

2. Definition of a Patent Claim

A patent claim is a single-sentence definition of the scope of the patent owner's property right — that is, her right to exclude others from making, using, selling, offering to sell, or importing the invention, in this country, during the term of the patent.[6] A common analogy used to explain the concept of patent claiming is that a claim to an invention is like a deed to real property (land): the property description in the deed sets forth the metes and bounds of the plot, but it does not describe the interior of the land (i.e., whether the land is flat, hilly, wooded, boasts structures, or has water running through it).[7]

[4]U.S. Patent No. 19,783 (issued Mar. 30, 1858) ("Combination of Lead-Pencil and Eraser").
[5]Evans v. Eaton, 16 U.S. 454, 514-515 (1818).
[6]35 U.S.C. §§154(a)(1); 271(a).
[7]For example, consider the following property description from a deed to real estate:

> Beginning at a point (POB) on the North side of Wells Street 50 feet East from the corner formed by the intersection of the East boundary of Polk Road and the North boundary of Wells Street: thence East 90 degrees 200 feet; thence North 300 feet; thence West 200 feet; thence direct to the POB.

A patent claim, like a deed to real property, defines the boundaries of the patentee's right to exclude others. It acts as a verbal fence around the patentee's intangible property. But it is equally important to understand what a patent claim does *not* do: a patent claim does not *describe* the invention, in terms of how to make and use it, or its best mode. That is the role of the written description and drawings, parts of the patent document that are distinct from the claims.

In fact, the invention or inventive contribution of the patent applicant is often a far cry from what is ultimately recited in the patent claims. This variance results from the vagaries of patent prosecution: patent applications are typically filed with an array of claims of varying scope, ranging from very broad to very narrow. Over the course of the application's prosecution, as described in Chapter 1, *supra,* the USPTO often will identify prior art that the agency believes would anticipate or render obvious the subject matter of the broadest claims. Unless she believes the rejections are appealable, the patent applicant or her attorney will typically amend the claims so as to narrow them to subject matter that would be novel and nonobvious over the cited prior art.[8] In so doing, the claims, which set forth the literal boundaries of the patentee's right to exclude others, may evolve into something very different from the invention as originally envisioned by the inventor.[9] As expressed by a prominent patent jurist:

> What do we construe claims for, anyway? To find out what the inventor(s) invented? Hardly! Claims are frequently a far cry from what the inventor invented. In a suit, claims are construed to find out what the patentee can exclude the defendant from doing. CLAIMS ARE CONSTRUED TO DETERMINE THE SCOPE OF THE RIGHT TO EXCLUDE, regardless of what the inventor invented. I submit that that is the sole function of patent claims. I think this truism ought to be promoted in every seminar on the subject of claims. . . . Tell [readers] to stop talking about claims defining the invention. It's a bad habit. And it seems to be almost universal.[10]

Nor do patent claims define a tangible product or thing. Rather, claims may be best understood as *abstractions.* A noted patent law scholar explained:

[8]The applicant's ability to amend the claims in this fashion assumes that her application provides adequate support under 35 U.S.C. §112(a) (eff. Sept. 16, 2012) for the amended (narrower) claim(s). *See* Chapter 3 ("Disclosure Requirements (35 U.S.C. §112(a))"), *infra.*

[9]*See, e.g.*, Elekta Instrument S.A. v. O.U.R. Scientific Int'l, Inc., 214 F.3d 1302, 1308 (Fed. Cir. 2000) (concluding that amendments made during prosecution of patent in suit compelled an interpretation of the asserted claim that excluded the preferred and only embodiment of the invention disclosed in the specification).

[10]Janice M. Mueller, *A Rich Legacy*, 81 J. PAT. & TRADEMARK OFF. SOC'Y 755, 758-759 (1999) (quoting remarks of Judge Giles S. Rich).

> The difficulty which American courts [have had in comprehending patent claims] goes back to the primitive thought that an "invention" upon which the patent gives protection is something tangible. The physical embodiment or disclosure, which, in itself is something tangible, is confused with the definition or claim to the inventive novelty, and this definition or claim or monopoly, also sometimes called "invention" in one of that word's meanings, is not something tangible, but is an abstraction. Definitions are always abstractions. This primitive confusion of "invention" in the sense of physical embodiment with "invention" in the sense of definition of the patentable amount of novelty, survives to the present day, not only in the courts, but among some of the examiners in the Patent Office.[11]

Thus, patent claims delineate the patent owner's right to exclude others from practicing the claimed invention, which is intangible. The invention is probably best understood in the form of a physical, tangible embodiment, but that tangible embodiment is not, strictly speaking, what the patent protects.

3. A Key Reference Work

The leading reference work on U.S. patent claiming practice is Faber's *Mechanics of Patent Claim Drafting*.[12] Much of patent claiming technique has evolved in practice before the USPTO and is governed by convention rather than statute or regulation. Landis's work is an excellent compendium of these practices. All patent attorneys and agents should own, or at least make themselves familiar with, this work.

B. Claim Definiteness Requirement (35 U.S.C. §112(b))

1. Own Lexicographer Rule

The second paragraph of Section 112 of the Patent Act requires that each patent conclude with

> one or more claims particularly pointing out and distinctly claiming the subject matter which the inventor or a joint inventor regards as the invention.[13]

[11] EMERSON STRINGHAM, DOUBLE PATENTING 209 (1933).

[12] ROBERT C. FABER, FABER ON MECHANICS OF PATENT CLAIM DRAFTING (Practising Law Institute 7th ed. 2015). The Faber work (known for many years by the name of its former author, John L. Landis) is an excellent compendium of U.S. patent claim practice.

[13] 35 U.S.C. §112(b) (eff. Sept. 16, 2012). The America Invents Act of 2011 renamed the second paragraph of 35 U.S.C. §112 (generally referred to as "35 U.S.C. §112, ¶2") as 35 U.S.C. §112(b) and amended its wording. The pre-AIA statutory text required that "[t]he specification shall conclude with one or more claims particularly pointing out and

This statutory edict is known to patent lawyers as the claim **definiteness** requirement (although the statute does not use the word "definite").

One might reasonably ask how it is possible to satisfy the claim definiteness requirement, when the invention being claimed may represent novel and nonobvious technology that has never before been known or used or sold. In such a case, sufficient terminology may not even be present in the existing English lexicon to adequately describe the invention. In other cases, the mechanical operation of a more conventional device may be extremely difficult to convey in words. For example, consider the challenge of drafting a claim to the well-known children's SLINKY® toy.[14] Test your claim drafting skill by attempting to write a definite claim to a SLINKY® toy. How would your claim recite its structural features, such as its elongation, and coiled shape? Must the number of twists in the coil be specified? Can the SLINKY® toy be claimed as a spring? Must the material (metal or plastic?) from which the SLINKY® toy is made be specified in the claim?

Fortunately it is possible to write definite claims to novel technology, even if existing words are inadequate, because the patent law permits the applicant to create new words with which to claim her invention. In other words, a patent applicant can be her own lexicographer, meaning that she can make up and define terms to be used in her claims. In this manner the written description portion of a patent operates as a sort of dictionary or concordance that defines and explains terms found in the claims. Each newly created term may be expressly defined (e.g., the written description might state that "as used herein, 'gizmo' means a machine having two lever arms, three pulleys, and four gears, made entirely of aluminum"). In other cases, a claim term may be implicitly defined through consistent use of the term in the written description.[15]

If the applicant chooses *not* to supply definitions for the terms in her claims, either expressly or implicitly, how will they be defined? Case law provides that in the absence of such definitions, terms in patent claims will be given their ordinary and customary meaning to persons of ordinary skill in the art of the invention.[16] This treatment is

---

distinctly claiming the subject matter which the applicant regards as his invention." 35 U.S.C. §112, ¶2 (2006).

[14] *See* Alex Brands, *About Us* (2019) (describing SLINKY® toy, first invented in 1945, as a "quintessential childhood toy and an icon of classic fun"), http://www.alexbrands.com/about-us.

[15] *See* Bell Atlantic Network Servs., Inc. v. Covad Communications Group, Inc., 262 F.3d 1258, 1271 (Fed. Cir. 2001).

[16] *See* Vitronics Corp. v. Conceptronic, Inc., 90 F.3d 1576, 1582 (Fed. Cir. 1996). Following the *Vitronics* decision, the Federal Circuit became increasingly polarized over the use of dictionaries for this purpose rather than reliance on the patent's written

analogous to the contract law rule of interpreting undefined contractual terms in accordance with "usage in the trade."[17]

2. Definiteness Standards

a. Introduction

When the Patent Act requires that claims "particularly point[] out and distinctly claim[] the subject matter which the inventor . . . regards as his invention,"[18] from whose perspective must one determine if the claim language is sufficiently "particular" and "distinct" to satisfy the statute? The proper vantage point is that of the hypothetical **person having ordinary skill in the art (PHOSITA)**, whom we will encounter in many other patent law contexts. In other words, we do not interpret patent claims according to what a judge, jury, or scientific experts may understand the terms of the claim to mean. Rather, we must determine whether the claim terms are definite to a PHOSITA, a hypothetical construct that represents the skill and understanding of an "ordinary" person (e.g., whether a scientist, engineer, technician, or other worker) in the particular technology of the claimed invention.[19]

---

description. *See* Section B.4 ("The *Phillips* Debate: 'Contextualist' Versus 'Literalist' Approaches") in Chapter 9 ("Patent Infringement"), *infra*.

[17]*See* U.C.C. §2-202 (2008). Such undefined terms are to be read "on the assumption that . . . the usages of trade were taken for granted when the document was phrased." *Id.* at cmt. 2. Usage of trade is defined in U.C.C. §1-205(2) (2008) as "any practice or method of dealing having such regularity of observance in a place, vocation or trade as to justify an expectation that it will be observed with respect to the transaction in question." As Professor Corbin explains,

> Just as a court would interpret according to the French language a contract written in French by two French speakers, a court will interpret according to trade usage a contract written by two parties familiar with a term common in that trade . . . [t]he law requires the court to put itself as nearly as possible in the position of the parties, with their knowledge and their ignorance, with their language and their usage.

5 A. Corbin on Contracts §24.13, at 111 (Joseph M. Perillo ed., Lexis Publ. 1998) (1952).

[18]35 U.S.C. §112(b) (eff. Sept. 16, 2012).

[19]Professor John Golden argues for abandoning the commonly accepted notion that claims should be construed from a PHOSITA's perspective, on the ground that the views of ordinary engineers or scientists may be "too legally ill-informed and idiosyncratic to permit substantial predictability." Golden proposes that a better perspective would be that of "a patent attorney having access to the knowledge of a person of technological skill." Such a perspective would "more generally follow rules and techniques for claim construction that are publicly known and anchored in the practices of an active interpretive community." John M. Golden, *Construing Patent Claims According to Their "Interpretive Community": A Call for an Attorney-Plus-Artisan Perspective*, 21 Harv. J.L. & Tech. 321 (2008).

Solomon v. Kimberly-Clark Corp.[20] nicely illustrates this rule. Solomon's patent was directed to a disposable woman's protective undergarment for holding a sanitary napkin. The accused infringer, Kimberly-Clark, alleged that the patent was invalid under 35 U.S.C. §112, ¶2, because Solomon failed to claim the subject matter that she regarded as her invention. This argument was based on Solomon's deposition, in which she stated that the "depression" limitation of the claimed invention had a uniform thickness.[21] However, the district court (and on appeal, the Federal Circuit) interpreted the claim language to mean that the depression had a thickness that varied, contrary to Solomon's deposition testimony.

The Federal Circuit rejected Kimberly-Clark's challenge and upheld the validity of the patent claims under §112, ¶2. The definiteness of claims of an issued patent must be evaluated from the perspective of the PHOSITA, the court explained, and not based on evidence extrinsic to the patent such as the inventor's deposition testimony. The inventor's perspective may not be the same as that of the PHOSITA. If the claims of the patent, read in light of the written description, would reasonably give notice to the PHOSITA of the scope of the patentee's right to exclude others, this is all that the definiteness rule of §112, ¶2 requires. After a patent issues, statements by the inventor about what she subjectively intended or understood the claim language to mean are largely irrelevant, the court emphasized. After issuance, the claims must be viewed objectively, from the perspective of the hypothetical PHOSITA.[22]

Just how "definite" can the PHOSITA expect a patent claim to be? In *Orthokinetics, Inc. v. Safety Travel Chairs, Inc.*,[23] the patent in suit was directed to a portable folding wheelchair for children that could

[20]216 F.3d 1372 (Fed. Cir. 2000).

[21]Kimberly-Clark's invalidity argument also was based on the existence of a prototype of the invention, which depicted an area of uniform thickness in the region where the depression was located.

[22]In contrast, during examination of applications for patent by the USPTO, the examiner will assign the claims their broadest reasonable interpretation consistent with the specification. *See* In re Graves, 69 F.3d 1147, 1152 (Fed. Cir. 1995). Assigning claims a relatively broader interpretation for purposes of examination reduces the possibility that the "claims, finally allowed, will be given broader scope than is justified." In re Yamamoto, 740 F.2d 1569, 1571 (Fed. Cir. 1984). This USPTO practice is not considered unfair to applicants because "before a patent is granted the claims are readily amended as part of the examination process." Burlington Indus., Inc. v. Quigg, 822 F.2d 1581, 1583 (Fed. Cir. 1987).

[23]806 F.2d 1565 (Fed. Cir. 1986).

easily be installed on and removed from the seat of an automobile.[24] A depiction of the portable wheelchair is shown in Figure 2.1. The nature of this invention was such that the dimensions of the chair would need to be altered for a particular make of car. The claim recited "wherein said front leg portion is *so dimensioned* as to be insertable through the space between the doorframe of an automobile and one of the seats thereof."[25] The accused infringer alleged that this variability in dimensions rendered the claim indefinite under 35 U.S.C. §112, ¶2.

The Federal Circuit disagreed. It was not relevant that a particular chair, once constructed, might fit in some cars and not others. The phrase "so dimensioned" was "as accurate as the subject matter permits."[26] "Patent law does not require that all possible lengths corresponding to the spaces in hundreds of different automobiles be listed in the patent, let alone that they be listed in the claims,"[27] the court explained. This would convert a patent into a production specification, which it is not. So long as the PHOSITA could make and use the invention without undue experimentation, the disclosure was enabling,[28] and so long as the PHOSITA could reasonably determine if a particular chair infringed the claim, the claims were sufficiently definite.

The use of adjectives such as "substantially" or "about" to qualify numerical or structural limitations in patent claims does not necessarily render the claims indefinite under 35 U.S.C. §112, ¶2.[29] The patent in *Verve, LLC v. Crane Cams, Inc.*,[30] claimed improved "push rods" for internal combustion engines; the rods actuated "rocker arms" that opened and closed the intake and exhaust valves of engine cylinders. The claimed push rod was made from a single piece of metal in the form of an "elongated hollow tube having . . . *substantially* constant wall thickness throughout the length of the tube. . . ."[31] The district court granted summary judgment to the accused infringer on the ground that, *inter alia*, the patent was invalid as indefinite under §112, ¶2 because the meaning of "substantially" was "unclear" from the intrinsic evidence (i.e., the patent document itself and its prosecution history); the district court also found that liability for infringement depended on whether "substantially" embraced the accused push rods.

[24]*See* U.S. Patent No. 3,891,229 (issued June 24, 1975).

[25]*Orthokinetics*, 806 F.2d at 1575.

[26]*Orthokinetics*, 806 F.2d at 1576.

[27]*Orthokinetics*, 806 F.2d at 1576.

[28]For discussion of the enablement requirement of 35 U.S.C. §112(a) (eff. Sept. 16, 2012), *see* Chapter 3 ("Disclosure Requirements (35 U.S.C. §112(a))"), *infra*.

[29]The America Invents Act of 2011 renamed 35 U.S.C. §112, ¶2 as 35 U.S.C. §112(b) (eff. Sept. 16, 2012).

[30]311 F.3d 1116 (Fed. Cir. 2002).

[31]Verve, LLC v. Crane Cams, Inc., 311 F.3d 1116, 1119 (Fed. Cir. 2002) (emphasis added).

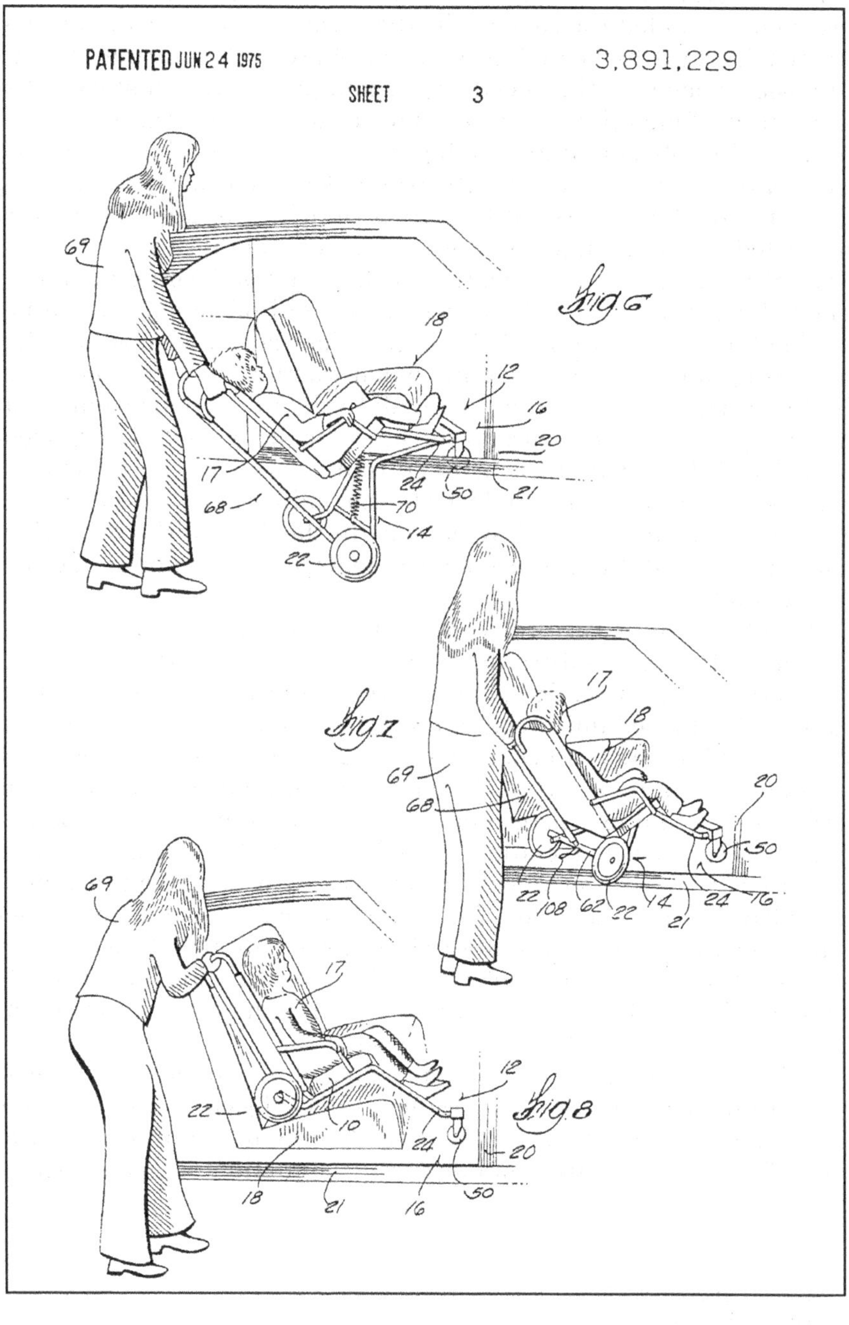

Figure 2.1
***Orthokinetics* U.S. Patent No. 3,891,229**

The Federal Circuit vacated the summary judgment of indefiniteness and remanded the case for further proceedings, concluding that the district court had erred as a matter of law by "requiring that the intrinsic evidence of the specification and prosecution history is the sole source of meaning of words that are used in a technologic context."[32] "[R]esolution of any ambiguity arising from the claims and specification may be aided by extrinsic evidence of usage and meaning of a term in the context of the invention,"[33] the appellate court instructed. A proper analysis would consider whether the word "substantially" as applied to "constant wall thickness" would be understood "by persons experienced in this field of mechanics, upon reading the patent documents."[34] Expressions such as "substantially" are appropriately used in patents when warranted by the nature of the invention, in order to accommodate the minor variations that may be appropriate to secure to the inventor the benefit of her invention. The Federal Circuit concluded that "when the term 'substantially' serves reasonably to describe the subject matter so that its scope would be understood by persons in the field of the invention, and to distinguish the claimed subject matter from the prior art, it is not indefinite."[35]

In contrast to the cases discussed above, the recitation of an "aesthetically pleasing" feature in the claims at issue in *Datamize, LLC v. Plumtree Software, Inc.*,[36] rendered them indefinite under 35 U.S.C. §112, ¶2. Datamize's patent was directed to a software program that allowed a person to customize the user interfaces of electronic kiosks providing information for customers and patrons, such as the kiosk systems that are increasingly seen in museums, airports, banks, hotels, and stores. The claims recited methods for defining custom interface screens for the kiosks in which the screens had an "aesthetically pleasing" look and feel. The Federal Circuit noted at the outset that some ambiguity in a patent claim's wording is not necessarily fatal, and that only claims "not amenable to construction" or "insolubly ambiguous" should be held invalid for indefiniteness (a standard that the Supreme Court in 2014 would revise[37]).

In the case at bar, however, the meaning of "aesthetically pleasing" was entirely dependent on the system user's subjective opinion. Thus the claim language was not sufficiently definite to perform its critical notice function. "A purely subjective construction of 'aesthetically

[32] *Verve*, 311 F.3d at 1119.
[33] *Verve*, 311 F.3d at 1119.
[34] *Verve*, 311 F.3d at 1120.
[35] *Verve*, 311 F.3d at 1120.
[36] 417 F.3d 1342 (Fed. Cir. 2005).
[37] *See infra* Section B.2.b ("Supreme Court Adjusts the Standard (*Nautilus* 2014)").

pleasing' would not notify the public of the patentee's right to exclude since the meaning of the claim language would depend on the unpredictable vagaries of any one person's opinion of the aesthetics of interface screens. While beauty is in the eye of the beholder, a claim term, to be definite, requires an objective anchor."[38] Here, the patentee failed to provide any reasonable, workable, "objective definition identifying a standard for determining when an interface screen [would be] 'aesthetically pleasing.'"

*b. Supreme Court Adjusts the Standard (*Nautilus *(U.S. 2014))*

The Federal Circuit's lenient standard — that claim language was fatally indefinite only if "not amenable to construction" or "insolubly ambiguous," as those formulations were applied in *Datamize* and other Circuit decisions[39]— is no longer good law. The U.S. Supreme Court examined and restated the standard for patent claim definiteness in an important 2014 decision, *Nautilus, Inc. v. Biosig Instruments, Inc.*,[40] detailed below.

As the previous section explained, pre-*Nautilus* Federal Circuit decisions suggested that whether a PHOSITA would understand what was claimed for purposes of assessing definiteness essentially equated to determining whether the patent's claims could be interpreted.[41] The appellate court considered the definiteness requirement of 35

[38]Datamize, LLC v. Plumtree Software, Inc., 417 F.3d 1342, 1350 (Fed. Cir. 2005).

[39]*See* Nautilus, Inc. v. Biosig Instruments, Inc., 134 S. Ct. 2120, 2130 (2014) (observing that "the expressions 'insolubly ambiguous' and 'amenable to construction' permeate the Federal Circuit's recent decisions concerning §112, ¶2's requirement."); *id.* at 2130 n.9, citing:

> [*e*].*g.*, Hearing Components, Inc. v. Shure Inc., 600 F.3d 1357, 1366 (C.A. Fed. 2010) ("the definiteness of claim terms depends on whether those terms can be given any reasonable meaning"); Datamize, LLC v. Plumtree Software, Inc., 417 F.3d 1342, 1347 (C.A. Fed. 2005) ("Only claims 'not amenable to construction' or 'insolubly ambiguous' are indefinite."); Exxon Research & Engineering Co. v. United States, 265 F.3d 1371, 1375 (C.A. Fed. 2001) ("If a claim is insolubly ambiguous, and no narrowing construction can properly be adopted, we have held the claim indefinite."). *See also* Dept. of Commerce, Manual of Patent Examining Procedure §2173.02(I), p. 294 (9th ed. 2014) (PTO manual describing Federal Circuit's test as upholding a claim's validity "if some meaning can be gleaned from the language").

[40]134 S. Ct. 2120 (2014).

[41]*See* Datamize, LLC v. Plumtree Software, Inc., 417 F.3d 1342, 1348 (Fed. Cir. 2005) (stating that "[i]n the face of an allegation of indefiniteness, general principles of claim construction apply") (citing Oakley, Inc. v. Sunglass Hut Int'l, 316 F.3d 1331, 1340-1341 (Fed. Cir. 2003) (noting that a determination of definiteness "requires a construction of the claims according to the familiar canons of claim construction")).

U.S.C. §112, ¶2 (renamed 35 U.S.C. §112(b) by the America Invents Act of 2011) not to have been satisfied only if the claim terms in question were "'not amenable to construction or [we]re insolubly ambiguous. . . ."[42] In the Circuit's view, claim terms were sufficiently definite if they could "be given any reasonable meaning."[43] Even if the claim construction task was difficult, this did not necessarily render the claim language indefinite.[44] Because reasonable persons could frequently disagree over patent claim construction, proof of *in*definiteness had to "'meet an exacting standard.'"[45] In short, the Federal Circuit's standard for claim definiteness was not difficult to satisfy in many cases.[46]

The Supreme Court in 2014 unanimously rejected the Federal Circuit's approach to satisfying the claim definiteness requirement. In *Nautilus, Inc. v. Biosig Instruments, Inc.*,[47] the Supreme Court explained that the Circuit's "not amenable to construction" or "insolubly ambiguous" standards "lack[ed] the precision that §112, ¶2 demands," and had the potential to confuse the lower courts.[48] "To tolerate imprecision just short of that rendering a claim 'insolubly ambiguous' would diminish the definiteness requirement's public-notice function and foster the innovation-discouraging 'zone of uncertainty'... against which this Court has warned."[49]

Rather, the Supreme Court in *Nautilus* "read §112, ¶2 to require that a patent's claims, viewed in light of the specification and prosecution history, *inform those skilled in the art about the scope of the*

[42] *Young*, 492 F.3d at 1346 (quoting Datamize, LLC v. Plumtree Software, Inc., 417 F.3d 1342, 1347 (Fed. Cir. 2005)).

[43] Hearing Components, Inc. v. Shure Inc., 600 F.3d 1357, 1366 (Fed. Cir. 2010).

[44] *Datamize*, 417 F.3d at 1347 (stating that "a difficult issue of claim construction does not *ipso facto* result in a holding of indefiniteness. . . . 'If the meaning of the claim is discernible, even though the task may be formidable and the conclusion may be one over which reasonable persons will disagree, we have held the claim sufficiently clear to avoid invalidity on indefiniteness grounds.'") (quoting Exxon Res. & Eng'g Co. v. United States, 265 F.3d 1371, 1375 (Fed. Cir. 2001)).

[45] Wellman, Inc. v. Eastman Chem. Co., 642 F.3d 1355, 1366 (Fed. Cir. 2011) (quoting Haemonetics Corp. v. Baxter Healthcare Corp., 607 F.3d 776, 783 (Fed. Cir. 2010)).

[46] *Cf. Wellman*, 642 F.3d at 1375; *Datamize*, 417 F.3d at 1347 (observing that "[t]he definiteness requirement . . . does not compel absolute clarity. Only claims 'not amenable to construction' or 'insolubly ambiguous' are indefinite.").

[47] 134 S. Ct. 2120 (2014).

[48] *Nautilus,* 134 S. Ct. at 2130. As an example of district court difficulties, the Court cited *Every Penny Counts, Inc. v. Wells Fargo Bank, N.A.*, 4 F. Supp. 3d 1286, 1291 (M.D. Fla. 2014) (finding that "the account," as used in claim, "lacks definiteness," because it might mean several different things and "no informed and confident choice is available among the contending definitions," but that "the extent of the indefiniteness . . . falls far short of the 'insoluble ambiguity' required to invalidate the claim").

[49] *Nautilus,* 134 S. Ct. at 2130 (quoting United Carbon Co. v. Binney & Smith Co., 317 U.S. 228, 236 (1942)).

invention with reasonable certainty."[50] The Court's new "reasonable certainty" test found its roots in precedent requiring a "reasonable" degree of certainty in patent claims,[51] recognizing that absolute precision in setting forth the boundaries of the patentee's right to exclude is not attainable.[52]

The *Nautilus* Court's "reasonable certainty" test aims to "reconcile concerns that tug in opposite directions."[53] The Supreme Court realized, first, that the definiteness requirement "must take into account the inherent limitations of language."[54] On the other hand, patents must also be precise enough to afford clear notice to the public of what subject matter is encompassed by the claims and what subject matter remains open.[55] The Court additionally observed that without a "meaningful definiteness check," patent applicants faced "powerful incentives to inject ambiguity into their claims."[56] The *Nautilus* Court's new test of "reasonable certainty" about claim scope to those of skill in the art purported to reconcile these opposing policies in a

[50]*Nautilus,* 134 S. Ct. at 2129 (emphasis added).

[51]*See Nautilus,* 134 S. Ct. at 2129-2130 (citing Minerals Separation, Ltd. v. Hyde, 242 U.S. 261, 270 (1916) ("the certainty which the law requires in patents is not greater than is reasonable, having regard to their subject-matter."); *United Carbon*, 317 U.S. at 236 ("claims must be reasonably clear-cut"); Markman v. Westview Instruments, Inc., 517 U.S. 370, 389 (1996) (claim construction calls for "the necessarily sophisticated analysis of the whole document," and may turn on evaluations of expert testimony)).

[52]*Nautilus,* 134 S. Ct. at 2129 (explaining that "[t]he definiteness requirement, so understood, mandates clarity, while recognizing that absolute precision is unattainable").

[53]*Nautilus,* 134 S. Ct. at 2129.

[54]*Nautilus,* 134 S. Ct. at 2128. The Court recognized that "[s]ome modicum of uncertainty" is the "price of ensuring the appropriate incentives for innovation." *Nautilus,* 134 S. Ct. at 2128 (citing Festo Corp. v. Shoketsu Kinzoku Kogyo Kabushiki Co., 535 U.S. 722, 732 (2002)). Moreover, patents are "'not addressed to lawyers, or even to the public generally,' but rather to those skilled in the relevant art." *Nautilus,* 134 S. Ct. at 2128 (quoting Carnegie Steel Co. v. Cambria Iron Co., 185 U.S. 403, 437 (1902) (also stating that "any description which is sufficient to apprise [steel manufacturers] in the language of the art of the definite feature of the invention, and to serve as a warning to others of what the patent claims as a monopoly, is sufficiently definite to sustain the patent").

[55]*See Nautilus,* 134 S. Ct. at 2129. The Court explained that

> a patent must be precise enough to afford clear notice of what is claimed, thereby "'appris[ing] the public of what is still open to them.'" *Markman*, 517 U.S., at 373, 116 S. Ct. 1384 (quoting *McClain v. Ortmayer*, 141 U.S. 419, 424, 12 S. Ct. 76, 35 L. Ed. 800 (1891)).... Otherwise there would be "[a] zone of uncertainty which enterprise and experimentation may enter only at the risk of infringement claims." *United Carbon Co. v. Binney & Smith Co.*, 317 U.S. 228, 236, 63 S. Ct. 165, 87 L. Ed. 232 (1942).

Nautilus, 134 S. Ct. at 2129 (footnote omitted).

[56]*Nautilus,* 134 S. Ct. at 2129 (citing Petitioner's brief and a 2011 Federal Trade Commission study).

manner that "mandates clarity, while recognizing that absolute precision is unattainable."[57]

At issue in the *Nautilus* dispute (captioned *Biosig v. Nautilus, Inc.* at the Federal Circuit[58]) was Biosig Instruments' U.S. Patent No. 5,337,753 ('753 patent), which concerned a heart rate monitor for use with an exercise machine. The monitor improved on the prior art by eliminating certain noise signals during the detection of a user's heart rate. In particular, the claimed monitor eliminated signals given off by the user's skeletal muscles (electromyogram or "EMG" signals) when the user moved her arms or squeezed her fingers. A problem existed because EMG signals are the same frequency as electrocardiograph (ECG) signals generated by the user's heart. Thus EMG signals could mask the ECG signals desired to be measured. The claimed invention provided structure and circuitry that substantially removed the unwanted EMG signals.[59]

Biosig's '753 patent disclosed a heart rate monitor contained in a hollow cylindrical bar (like those typically seen on treadmills or exercise bikes). A user grips the cylindrical bar with both hands, such that each hand comes into contact with two electrodes, one referred to as the "live" electrode and the other the "common" electrode. Importantly, claim 1 of the '753 patent required that on each half of the cylinder, the live and common electrodes be mounted "in a spaced relationship" with each other.[60] This was the disputed claim language. An embodiment of the '753 patent is shown in Figure 2.2 (with the user's hands represented by dotted lines).

[57]*Nautilus,* 134 S. Ct. at 2129.

[58]*See* Biosig Instruments, Inc. v. Nautilus, Inc., 715 F.3d 891 (Fed. Cir. 2013), *vacated*, 134 S. Ct. 2120 (2014).

[59]More specifically, ECG signals detected from a user's left hand have a polarity opposite to that of the signals detected from her right hand (because the heart is not aligned vertically in relation to the center of the body; it tilts leftward). In contrast, EMG signals from each hand have the same polarity. Biosig's patented device worked by measuring equalized EMG signals detected at each hand and then using circuitry to subtract the identical EMG signals from each other, thus filtering out the EMG interference.

[60]The '753 patent's independent claim 1 recited in full:

> 1. A heart rate monitor for use by a user in association with exercise apparatus and/or exercise procedures, comprising;
>
> an elongate member;
>
> electronic circuitry including a difference amplifier having a first input terminal of a first polarity and a second input terminal of a second polarity opposite to said first polarity;
>
> said elongate member comprising a first half and a second half;
>
> a first *live electrode* and a first *common electrode* mounted on said first half *in spaced relationship* with each other;
>
> a second *live electrode* and a second *common electrode* mounted on said second half *in spaced relationship* with each other;
>
> said first and second common electrodes being connected to each other and to a point of common potential;

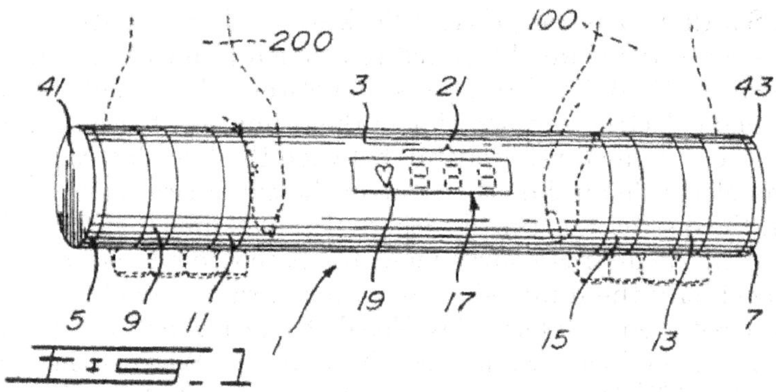

Figure 2.2
Figure 1 of Biosig's U.S. Pat. No. 5,337,753

---

said first live electrode being connected to said first terminal of said difference amplifier and said second live electrode being connected to said second terminal of said difference amplifier;

a display device disposed on said elongate member;

wherein, said elongate member is held by said user with one hand of the user on said first half contacting said first live electrode and said first common electrode, and with the other hand of the user on said second half contacting said second live electrode and said second common electrode;

whereby, a first electromyogram signal will be detected between said first live electrode and said first common electrode, and a second electromyogram signal, of substantially equal magnitude and phase to said first electromyogram signal will be detected between said second live electrode and said second common electrode;

so that, when said first electromyogram signal is applied to said first terminal and said second electromyogram signal is applied to said second terminal, the first and second electromyogram signals will be subtracted from each other to produce a substantially zero electromyogram signal at the output of said difference amplifier;

and whereby a first electrocardiograph signal will be detected between said first live electrode and said first common electrode and a second electrocardiograph signal, of substantially equal magnitude but of opposite phase to said first electrocardiograph signal will be detected between said second live electrode and said second common electrode;

so that, when said first electrocardiograph signal is applied to said first terminal and said second electrocardiograph signal is applied to said second terminal, the first and second electrocardiograph signals will be added to each other to produce a non-zero electrocardiograph signal at the output of said difference amplifier;

means for measuring time intervals between heart pulses on detected electrocardiograph signal;

means for calculating the heart rate of said user using said measure time intervals;

said means for calculating being connected to said display device;

whereby, the heart rate of said user is displayed on said display device.

U.S. Patent No. 5,337,753.

The Southern District of New York was able to construe the '753 patent's contested claim 1 "spaced relationship" phrase to mean that there existed " 'a defined relationship between the live electrode and the common electrode on one side of the cylindrical bar and the same or a different defined relationship between the live electrode and the common electrode on the other side of the cylindrical bar.' "[61] Nevertheless, the district court held Biosig's patent claims invalid for indefiniteness. In the district court's view, the patentee had not articulated with specificity the dimensions or other parameters characterizing the space between the electrodes. The district court asked, " '[i]t [c]ould be half inch, one inch, two inches, three inches. What is the space[d] relationship?' "[62] The district court also charged that the '753 patent failed to disclose the composition of the handle, and whether the electrodes were located " 'between the two middle fingers, the outer first and fourth finger, the thumb underneath and the fingers on top? Where is the spaced relationship?' "[63] The district court questioned whether having "small" hands as opposed to "large" hands would affect the "spaced relationship" between the live and common electrodes. In the district court's view, no evidence explained how a skilled artisan would have determined the appropriate parameters yielding the necessary "spaced relationship." The district court concluded that " 'what [the patentee's expert] says is that through trial and error, which he doesn't describe, one can find a spaced relationship. That may be. But there's no description.' "[64]

The Federal Circuit in *Biosig* reversed. The district court's concerns did not support an indefiniteness holding. The '753 patent's specification did not need to provide the actual measurements for a "spaced relationship." Instead, "the record show[ed] that the variables here, including the spacing, size, shape, and material affecting the 'spaced relationship' between the electrodes, c[ould] be determined by those skilled in the art."[65]

[61]Biosig Instruments, Inc. v. Nautilus, Inc., 715 F.3d 891, 899 (Fed. Cir. 2013) (quoting Summary Judgment Hearing Transcript), *vacated*, 134 S. Ct. 2120 (2014). *See also Biosig*, 715 F.3d at 897 (citing Biosig Instruments, Inc. v. Nautilus, Inc., No. 10CV7722 (S.D.N.Y. Feb. 22, 2012), ECF No. 58 ("Summ. J. Hr'g Tr."), at 51:21-52:1 (granting Nautilus's motion for summary judgment of invalidity, holding that the '753 patent's "spaced relationship" term as recited in claim 1 was indefinite as a matter of law)).

[62]*Biosig*, 715 F.3d at 901 (quoting district court).

[63]*Biosig*, 715 F.3d at 901 (quoting district court).

[64]*Biosig*, 715 F.3d at 901 (quoting district court).

[65]*Biosig*, 715 F.3d at 903. These concerns of the district court addressed enablement rather than claim definiteness:

> [T]he district court's objections to the claims as written do not support imprecision of the claims. Rather, the objections are based on the premise that the '753 patent does not include disclosure sufficiently commensurate with the scope of the claims. These objections, if relevant, provide grounds for invalidity under

B. Claim Definiteness Requirement (35 U.S.C. §112(b))

The central point of the Federal Circuit's reasoning in *Biosig* was that certain "inherent parameters" disclosed in the patent's intrinsic evidence rendered the phrase "spaced relationship" sufficiently definite. First, the appellate court observed that the distance between the live and common electrodes on each side of the cylinder could not be greater than the width of a user's hand. Otherwise, the claim requirement that a user hold each half of the cylinder with one hand so as to make contact with both electrodes would not be satisfied. Second, the distance between the electrodes could not be "infinitesimally small, effectively merging the live and common electrodes" into a single electrode.[66] Given these inherent parameters, a skilled artisan could understand the bounds of claim 1.[67] Applying its existing definiteness standard, the Circuit concluded that the disputed claim language was not "insolubly ambiguous."[68] Accordingly, claim 1 of Biosig's '753 patent was not invalid for failure to satisfy the definiteness requirement of 35 U.S.C. §112, second paragraph.

> §112, ¶1 and not §112, ¶2.... Breadth is not indefiniteness. *SmithKline Beecham Corp. v. Apotex Corp.*, 403 F.3d 1331, 1340-41 (Fed. Cir. 2005). Hence, inquiries as to the size of the users' hands, placement of fingers, and the "composition of the handle" may be relevant, if at all, to issues that relate to enablement under §112, ¶1, not indefiniteness under §112, ¶2, because they are directed to the operability of varying embodiments of the claimed heart rate monitor, not to the precision of the claims at issue. Accordingly, these objections do not address the inherent parameters set forth in the intrinsic evidence.

Biosig, 715 F.3d at 902.

[66]*Biosig,* 715 F.3d at 899.

[67]The Federal Circuit majority also relied on a skilled artisan being able to discern the claim boundaries by testing the invention's functionality:

> In addition, a skilled artisan could apply a test and determine the "spaced relationship" as pertaining to the function of substantially removing EMG signals. Indeed, the test would have included a standard oscilloscope connected to both the inputs and outputs of the differential amplifier to view the signal wave forms and to measure signal characteristics. With this test, configurations could have been determined by analyzing the differential amplifier input and output signals for detecting EMG and ECG signals and observing the substantial removal of EMG signals from ECG signals while simulating an exercise. These parameters constitute the metes and bounds of "spaced relationship" as articulated in the '753 patent. Nothing more rigorous is required under §112, ¶2.

Biosig, 715 F.3d at 901 (Fed. Cir. 2013).

[68]The Circuit majority analogized the case at bar to an earlier decision sustaining claims against an indefiniteness challenge, *Star Scientific, Inc. v. R.J. Reynolds Tobacco Co.*, 655 F.3d 1364 (Fed. Cir. 2011):

> Like *Star Scientific II*, the record shows that the variables here, including the spacing, size, shape, and material affecting the "spaced relationship" between the electrodes, can be determined by those skilled in the art. Thus, "spaced relationship" cannot be said to be insolubly ambiguous.

Biosig, 715 F.3d at 903.

The Supreme Court granted *certiorari* in *Nautilus, Inc. v. Biosig Instruments, Inc.* in January 2014[69] to review the question whether "the Federal Circuit's acceptance of ambiguous patent claims with multiple reasonable interpretations so long as the ambiguity is not 'insoluble'... defeat[s] the statutory requirement of particular and distinct patent claiming."[70]

In an opinion authored for a unanimous Court by Justice Ginsburg, the Supreme Court in June 2014 issued its decision in *Nautilus, Inc. v. Biosig Instruments, Inc.*, vacating the Federal Circuit's judgment and remanding the case to the Circuit.[71] The Supreme Court announced a new standard for claim definiteness that appears intended to raise the bar above the Circuit's too-lenient standard.[72]

At the outset, the Supreme Court in *Nautilus* observed that the Patent Act requires a patent's specification to conclude "'with one or more claims *particularly pointing out and distinctly claiming* the subject matter which the application regards as [the] invention.'"[73] Thus, the case concerned "the proper reading of the statute's clarity and precision demand."[74] That statutory demand has been "largely unaltered" since the Patent Act of 1870 expressly required that an inventor "particularly point out and distinctly claim the part, improvement, or combination which [the inventor] claims as his invention or discovery."[75]

[69]134 S. Ct. 896 (Jan. 10, 2014) (mem.).

[70]Petition for a Writ of Certiorari at *i*, Nautilus, Inc. v. Biosig Instruments, Inc., No. 13-369 (Sept. 19, 2013).

[71]134 S. Ct. 2120, 2124, 2131 (June 2, 2014).

[72]*See Nautilus,* 134 S. Ct. at 2124 (concluding that "the Federal Circuit's formulation, which tolerates some ambiguous claims but not others, does not satisfy the statute's definiteness requirement."). Commentators generally view *Nautilus* as raising the bar for patent claim definiteness. *See, e.g.*, Juliana Kenny, *Patent indefiniteness tightened by Supreme Court in* Nautilus v. Biosig (June 4, 2014) (opining that "[t]he importance of the Supreme Court's decision lies in its tightening of the holds on what definiteness means within patent law, and how accused infringers can potentially bring cases to court on the grounds of 'insolubly ambiguous' tests.... Validity challenges are now more prominently on the table because of this ruling; the definiteness standard for patents has been thusly determined by the Supreme Court, creating the opportunity for more patents to be invalidated."); Ronald Mann, *Opinion analysis: Justices take blue pencil to Federal Circuit opinions on definiteness* (June 3, 2014) (opining that "[t]he Supreme Court in this case decided that the court of appeals should be more critical of patents. Now, a patent should be indefinite, which means invalid, if it does not describe the invention 'with reasonable certainty.' This will mean that the courts will throw out more patents for poor drafting now than they did under the earlier test."), *available at* http://www.scotusblog.com/2014/06/opinion-analysis-justices-take-blue-pencil-to-federal-circuit-opinions-on-definiteness/.

[73]*Nautilus,* 134 S. Ct. at 2124 (quoting 35 U.S.C. §112, ¶2 (2006 ed.)) (emphasis added by Supreme Court).

[74]*Nautilus,* 134 S. Ct. at 2124.

[75]Patent Act of July 8, 1870, §26, 16 Stat. 201; *see also Nautilus,* 134 S. Ct. at 2125.

B. Claim Definiteness Requirement (35 U.S.C. §112(b))

The *Nautilus* Court noted several aspects of the inquiry on which the parties agreed (and with which the Court apparently did not take issue). "First, definiteness it to be evaluated from the perspective of someone skilled in the relevant art."[76] "Second, in assessing definiteness, claims are to be read in light of the patent's specification and prosecution history."[77] "Third, '[d]efiniteness is measured from the viewpoint of a person skilled in [the] art *at the time the patent was filed.*'"[78]

Beyond these three agreed-upon principles, the parties disputed "just how much imprecision §112, ¶2 tolerates."[79] The view of patent validity challenger Nautilus tracked (at least in part) the Federal Circuit's formulation; that is, that "a patent is invalid when a claim is 'ambiguous, such that readers could reasonably interpret the claims scope differently."[80] Patentee Biosig (and the U.S. Solicitor General) "would require only that the patent provide reasonable notice of the scope of the claimed invention."[81]

The Supreme Court in *Nautilus* ultimately adopted a new definiteness standard that sought to balance competing concerns. The Court

[76]*Nautilus,* 134 S. Ct. at 2128 (citing, e.g., General Elec. Co. v. Wabash Appliance Corp., 304 U.S. 364, 371, 58 S. Ct. 899, 82 L. Ed. 1402 (1938); citing also 35 U.S.C. §112, ¶1 (2006) (patent's specification "shall contain a written description of the invention, and of the manner and process of making and using it, in such full, clear, concise, and exact terms as to enable *any person skilled in the art* to which it pertains, or with which it is most nearly connected, to make and use the same") (emphasis added by Supreme Court)).

[77]*Nautilus,* 134 S. Ct. at 2128 (citing, e.g., United States v. Adams, 383 U.S. 39, 48-49 (1966) (specification); Festo Corp. v. Shoketsu Kinzoku Kogyo Kabushiki Co., 535 U.S. 722, 741 (2002) (prosecution history)).

[78]*Nautilus,* 134 S. Ct. at 2128 (quoting Brief for Respondent 55 (emphasis added by Supreme Court); citing generally Sarnoff & Manzo, *An Introduction to, Premises of, and Problems with Patent Claim Construction*, in PATENT CLAIM CONSTRUCTION IN THE FEDERAL CIRCUIT 9 (E. Manzo ed. 2014) ("Patent claims . . . should be construed from an objective perspective of a [skilled artisan], based on what the applicant actually claimed, disclosed, and stated during the application process.")).

In the view of this author, the better date for evaluating the definiteness of language in patent claims would be the patent's *issue* date, at which time the patent is a public document setting forth boundaries that are intended to exclude others from practicing the claimed invention. Prior to issuance, claim language is non-final because it remains subject to change via amendment or cancellation during prosecution in the USPTO. *Cf.* Dennis Crouch, *Supreme Court: To Be Valid, Patent Claims Must Provide Reasonable Certainty Regarding the Claim Scope* (June 2, 2014) (stating that "[t]he Supreme Court indicates [in *Nautilus*] that any ambiguity should be considered 'at the time the patent was filed' and also that the patent's prosecution history are important in the consideration. What is unclear then is whether the court intended to mean that the consideration should be at the *patent issuance*, the application actual filing date, the application's effective filing date (taking into account priority claims to prior filed applications), or the date that the claims in question were filed/amended.") (emphasis in original), http://patentlyo.com/patent/2014/06/reasonable-certainty-regarding.html.

[79]*Nautilus,* 134 S. Ct. at 2128.

[80]*Nautilus,* 134 S. Ct. at 2128.

[81]*Nautilus,* 134 S. Ct. at 2128.

recognized that patent claim drafters confront "inherent limitations of language,"[82] such that absolute precision is not feasible. Contrariwise, the Court understood that patents must be "precise enough to afford clear notice of what is claimed. . . ."[83] Otherwise a " 'zone of uncertainty' " would exist, creating the potential to ward off " 'enterprise and experimentation' " due to risk of infringement liability.[84] In order to reconcile these concerns "that tug[ged] in different directions," the *Nautilus* Court interpreted the mandate of 35 U.S.C. §112, ¶2 as "requir[ing] that a patent's claims, viewed in light of the specification and prosecution history, inform those skilled in the art about the scope of the invention *with reasonable certainty*."[85] Thus understood, the definiteness requirement "mandates clarity, while recognizing that absolute precision is unattainable."[86]

In so holding the Supreme Court rejected the Federal Circuit's prior standard of "amenable to construction" or "insolubly ambiguous." Those formulations lacked the precision demanded by the statute, and could "breed lower court confusion."[87] The Circuit's standard was "more amorphous than the statutory definiteness requirement allows."[88]

The Supreme Court also dismissed patentee Biosig's argument that the Federal Circuit's use of the "insolubly ambiguous" test was merely a shorthand descriptor of an inquiry that, as actually applied, was more probing. Although the appellate court's "fuller explications" of its "insolubly ambiguous" test might "come closer to tracking the statutory prescription,"[89] the Supreme Court noted that that test (as well as the "amenable to construction" test) "permeate[d] the Federal Circuit's recent decisions" on definiteness. Although the Supreme Court would not " 'micromanag[e] the Federal Circuit's particular word choice,' " the claim definiteness inquiry had to be "at least 'probative

[82]*Nautilus,* 134 S. Ct. at 2128.

[83]*Nautilus,* 134 S. Ct. at 2129.

[84]*Nautilus,* 134 S. Ct. at 2129 (quoting United Carbon Co. v. Binney & Smith Co., 317 U.S. 228, 236 (1942)).

[85]*Nautilus,* 134 S. Ct. at 2129 (emphasis added).

[86]*Nautilus,* 134 S. Ct. at 2129.

[87]*Nautilus,* 134 S. Ct. at 2130 n.8 (citing, e.g., Every Penny Counts, Inc. v. Wells Fargo Bank, N.A., 4 F. Supp. 3d 1286, 2014 WL 869092, at *4 (M.D. Fla. Mar. 5, 2014) (finding that "the account," as used in claim, "lacks definiteness," because it might mean several different things and "no informed and confident choice is available among the contending definitions," but that "the extent of the indefiniteness . . . falls far short of the 'insoluble ambiguity' required to invalidate the claim")).

[88]*Nautilus,* 134 S. Ct. at 2131.

[89]*Nautilus,* 134 S. Ct. at 2130 (citing *Biosig,* 715 F.3d at 898 (case below) (stating that "if reasonable efforts at claim construction result in a definition that does not provide sufficient particularity and clarity to inform skilled artisans of the bounds of the claim, the claim is insolubly ambiguous and invalid for indefiniteness" (internal quotation marks omitted))).

of the essential inquiry.' "[90] The Court agreed with validity challenger Nautilus and its *amici* that the Federal Circuit's "insolubly ambiguous" or "amenable to construction" tests "can leave courts and the patent bar at sea without a reliable compass."[91] The Circuit's stated concern for according due weight to the statutory presumption of validity for issued patents did not "alter the degree of clarity that §112, ¶2 demands from patent applicants. . . ."[92]

Notably, the Supreme Court in *Nautilus* acknowledged but chose *not* to address the disputed question "whether factual findings subsidiary to the ultimate issue of definiteness trigger the clear-and-convincing-evidence standard and, relatedly, whether deference is due to the PTO's resolution of disputed issues of fact."[93] In the view of this author, it seems likely that the question will be revisited in the wake of the Supreme Court's equally (if not more) important January 2015 decision in *Teva Pharms. USA, Inc. v. Sandoz, Inc.*[94] The Court in *Teva* held that the task of *patent claim construction* may involve subsidiary fact issues, and that district court findings of fact based on extrinsic evidence should be reviewed by the Federal Circuit with "clear error" deference in accordance with Fed. R. Civ. P. 52 (rather than the zero-deference standard previously applied by the Circuit). Because the task of construing a patent claim seems inextricably connected to understanding whether its terms are definite under §112, ¶2,[95] the claim definiteness inquiry may similarly involve district courts making factual questions that are owed deference if reviewed on appeal.[96]

The Supreme Court in *Nautilus* chose not to assist the patent bar by actually applying its new "reasonable certainty" test to the facts of the case at bar. Despite spending a large portion of its opinion describing the technical facts of the case and the claimed invention, the Court followed its "ordinary practice" of remanding the case to the appellate

[90]*Nautilus,* 134 S. Ct. at 2030 (quoting Warner-Jenkinson Co. v. Hilton Davis Chem. Co., 520 U.S. 17, 40 (1997)).

[91]*Nautilus,* 134 S. Ct. at 2130.

[92]*Nautilus,* 134 S. Ct. at 2130 n.10.

[93]*Nautilus,* 134 S. Ct. at 2130 n.10.

[94]*See* Teva Pharm. USA, Inc. v. Sandoz, Inc., 135 S. Ct. 831 (2015). *Teva* is analyzed *infra* Chapter 9, Section B ("Step One: Patent Claim Interpretation").

[95]*Cf.* Datamize, LLC v. Plumtree Software, Inc., 417 F.3d 1342, 1348 (Fed. Cir. 2005) (stating that "[i]n the face of an allegation of indefiniteness, general principles of claim construction apply") (citing Oakley, Inc. v. Sunglass Hut Int'l, 316 F.3d 1331, 1340-1341 (Fed. Cir. 2003) (noting that a determination of definiteness "requires a construction of the claims according to the familiar canons of claim construction").

[96]The *Nautilus* Court did not mention the Federal Circuit's definiteness decision in *In re Packard*, 751 F.3d 1307 (Fed. Cir. May 6, 2014). There the Circuit upheld the USPTO's practice of rejecting patent application claims as indefinite if the meaning of the words in the claim is "unclear," in accordance with the agency's *Manual of Patent Examining Practice* (MPEP) §2173.05(e).

court, so that the Circuit could "reconsider, under the proper standard, whether the relevant claims in the '753 patent are sufficiently definite."[97] In its April 2015 remand decision,[98] the Federal Circuit maintained its earlier decision sustaining the validity of the '753 patent, concluding that the Supreme Court's new "reasonable certainty" standard for claim definiteness was satisfied.[99]

As with the many other "reasonableness"-based tests found in all areas of U.S. law, the *Nautilus* Court's new test for patent claim definiteness will need to be fleshed out with case-specific examples (one of which is the Federal Circuit's April 2015 remand decision). The Federal Circuit claim definiteness decisions discussed in the previous section that *pre*-date the 2014 Supreme Court decision in *Nautilus* remain relevant as examples,[100] but should be relied on with care,

[97]*Nautilus,* 134 S. Ct. at 2131.

[98]Biosig Instruments, Inc. v. Nautilus, Inc., 783 F.3d 1374 (Fed. Cir. 2015).

[99]The Federal Circuit in the 2015 remand decision in *Biosig* first reviewed the Supreme Court's modification in *Nautilus* (2014) of the indefiniteness standard, commenting dryly that "we may now steer by the bright star of 'reasonable certainty,' rather than the unreliable compass of 'insoluble ambiguity.'" *Biosig,* 783 F.3d at 1379. The Circuit also observed that the notion of "reasonableness" is "the core of much of the common law," and that "reasonable certainty" tests have been applied in "broad spectra" of the law. As evidence, the court provided a page-long footnote citing the "numerous occasions" on which the Supreme Court has discussed "reasonable certainty" in cases ranging from Fifth Amendment takings to employee benefits to criminal law to patent damages determinations to piracy. *Biosig,* 783 F.3d at 1380 n.2.

The Circuit also summarized three 2014 decisions in which it had already applied the new *Nautilus* "reasonable certainty" test. *See* DDR Holdings, LLC v. Hotels.com, 773 F.3d 1245, 1260-1261 (Fed. Cir. 2014) (after analogizing to facts from prior cases and applying a "reasonable certainty" standard, finding the term "look and feel" had an established meaning in the art as demonstrated by the trial record, thus informing those skilled in the art with reasonable certainty); Interval Licensing LLC v. AOL, Inc., 766 F.3d 1364, 1371 (Fed. Cir. 2014) (applying "reasonable certainty" test to determine whether the "wallpaper" embodiment of claimed "method for engaging the peripheral attention of a person in the vicinity of a display device" provided "a reasonably clear and exclusive definition," with a focus on the "relationship" between the embodiments and the claim language, and whether the embodiments created "objective boundaries" for those skilled in the art); *id.* at 1371-1372 (stating that "[t]he [Interval Licensing] patents' 'unobtrusive manner' phrase is highly subjective, and, on its face, provides little guidance to one of skill in the art.... The patents contemplate a variety of stimuli that could impact different users in different ways. As we have explained, a term of degree fails to provide sufficient notice of its scope if it depends on the unpredictable vagaries of any one person's opinion."); Augme Techs. v. Yahoo!, Inc., 755 F.3d 1326, 1340 (Fed. Cir. 2014) (stating that a claim limitation "clear on its face" "unquestionably meets [the *Nautilus II*] standard"). Based on these decisions, the Federal Circuit concluded that "judges have had no problem operating under the reasonable certainty standard." *Biosig,* 783 F.3d at 1381.

On the merits, the Circuit again held that the Biosig '753 patent claims' use of the "spaced relationship" phrase was *not* indefinite and maintained its reversal of the district court's determination to the contrary. *See Biosig*, 783 F.3d at 1382-1384.

[100]*See, e.g.*, Interval Licensing LLC v. AOL, Inc., 766 F.3d 1364 (Fed. Cir. 2014) (post-*Nautilus* decision citing in several instances Circuit's pre-*Nautilus* decision, *Datamize,*

understanding that they may have been decided under a different verbal formulation than the "reasonable certainty" test announced by the Supreme Court in *Nautilus* in 2014.

Many indefiniteness cases challenge "terms of degree" used in drafting patent claims. Such terms or phrases typically include one or more adjectives of facially imprecise scope that allow some room for variation or subjectivity; the patent may or may not provide an explicit mathematical formula or mechanical diagram to define the term. Consider as examples such terms of degree as "spaced relationship" in *Nautilus*; "visually negligible" in *Sonix Tech. Co. v. Publications Int'l, Ltd.*;[101] "unobtrusive manner" in *Interval Licensing LLC v. AOL, Inc.*;[102] and "aesthetically pleasing" in *Datamize, LLC v. Plumtree Software, Inc.*[103]

In order to satisfy the §112, second paragraph definiteness requirement, patents having claims that recite terms of degree "'must provide objective boundaries for those of skill in the art' in the context of the invention."[104] The necessary "objective boundaries" need not be explicit. Rather, they may be derived from the context of a patent; that is, found in the intrinsic evidence (i.e., the claims, figures, and written description of the patent itself as well as its prosecution history in the USPTO).[105]

LLC v. Plumtree Software, Inc., 417 F.3d 1342, 1351 (Fed. Cir. 2005)). *See also* Biosig Instruments, Inc. v. Nautilus, Inc., 783 F.3d 1374, 1381 (Fed. Cir. 2015) (decision after remand from Supreme Court's decision in *Nautilus*, 134 S. Ct. 2120 (2014)) (noting observation of Federal Circuit Judge Bryson, sitting by designation in *Freeny v. Apple Inc.*, No. 2:13-CV-00361-WCB, 2014 WL 4294505, at *5 (E.D. Tex. Aug. 28, 2014), that "[c]ontrary to the defendant's suggestion, [the *Nautilus*] standard does not render all of the prior Federal Circuit and district court cases inapplicable" and "all that is required is that the patent apprise [ordinary-skilled artisans] of the scope of the invention.").

[101] 844 F.3d 1370, 1378 (Fed. Cir. 2017) (Lourie, J.) (holding claim-recited phrase "visually negligible" was a term of degree but not indefinite under §112, second paragraph, or "purely subjective," unlike cases involving purely subjective terms or matters of taste; whether something was "visually negligible" or whether it interfered with a user's perception involved what could be seen by the normal human eye, providing an objective baseline through which to interpret the claims).

[102] 766 F.3d 1364, 1372 (Fed. Cir. 2014) (Chen, J.) (holding claims reciting phrase "unobtrusive manner that does not distract a user" were invalid for indefiniteness where phrase was "highly subjective," specification was "at best muddled," and the "hazy relationship between the claims and the written description fail[ed] to provide the clarity that the subjective claim language needs").

[103] 417 F.3d 1342, 1351 (Fed. Cir. 2005) (analyzed *supra* this section).

[104] Guangdong Alison Hi-Tech Co. v. International Trade Commission, 936 F.3d 1353, 1360 (Fed. Cir. 2019) (Stoll, J.) (hereafter "*Alison*") (quoting One-E-Way, Inc. v. Int'l Trade Comm'n, 859 F.3d 1059, 1062 (Fed. Cir. 2017)).

[105] *Alison*, 936 F.3d at 1360 (citing, e.g., One-E-Way, Inc. v. Int'l Trade Comm'n, 859 F.3d 1059, 1064-1067 (Fed. Cir. 2017) (ruling that consistent use of a disputed term in the claims, specification, and prosecution history informed claim scope); Sonix Tech. Co. v. Publications Int'l, Ltd., 844 F.3d 1370, 1378-1379 (Fed. Cir. 2017) (ruling that specific examples in the written description provided "points of comparison"

Extrinsic evidence such as expert testimony "can also help identify objective boundaries."[106]

The patent challenged in the 2019 Federal Circuit decision *Guangdong Alison Hi-Tech Co. v. International Trade Commission* (hereafter "*Alison*"),[107] contained claims reciting a term of degree. The patent nevertheless survived an indefiniteness challenge under the *Nautilus* "reasonable certainty" framework. The appellate court held that the patent's written description provided sufficient definitions and functional characteristics for the disputed term, as well as multiple examples and test results showing applications and methods of measuring the term in question.

U.S. Patent No. 7,078,359 ('359 patent), owned by U.S. manufacturer Aspen Aerogels, Inc., concerned composite "aerogel" insulation materials. Aerogels are formed by extracting the liquid from a gel and replacing it with a gas, while keeping the remaining gel components intact. Because the resulting aerogels are brittle, they may be combined with fibrous materials to improve flexibility. The '359 patent claimed an insulation product made from combining an aerogel and a "lofty fibrous batting sheet."[108]

The International Trade Commission (ITC) found that Guangdong Alison ("Alison") had violated Section 337 of the Tariff Act of 1930, 19 U.S.C. §1337, by importing into the United States composite aerogel insulation material that infringed the '359 patent. The ITC also rejected Alison's argument that the '359 patent was invalid because the claim-recited phrase "lofty . . . batting" was indefinite.

On appeal, the Federal Circuit affirmed the ITC's judgment that the '359 patent's aerogel insulation claims reciting fibrous "lofty . . . batting" material were *not* indefinite. The Circuit agreed with patent challenger Alison that "lofty . . . batting" was a term of degree; that is, the adjective "lofty," standing alone, was inherently variable in meaning. The appellate court explained that to survive an indefiniteness challenge, patents claiming inventions using terms of degree " 'must

---

informing claim scope); Enzo Biochem, Inc. v. Applera Corp., 599 F.3d 1325, 1332-1336 (Fed. Cir. 2010) (ruling that dependent claims, examples, criteria, and test results in specification and prosecution history informed claim scope)).

[106] *Alison*, 936 F.3d at 1360 (citing, e.g., BASF Corp. v. Johnson Matthey Inc., 875 F.3d 1360, 1368 (Fed. Cir. 2017) (considering expert testimony); *Sonix*, 844 F.3d at 1380 (considering expert testimony and prior litigation positions regarding meaning of disputed term); DDR Holdings, LLC v. Hotels.com, L.P., 773 F.3d 1245, 1260-1261 (Fed. Cir. 2014) (considering advertising for prior art system)).

[107] 936 F.3d 1353 (Fed. Cir. 2019) (Stoll, J.).

[108] Claim 1 of the '359 patent recited (emphasis added):

> 1. A composite article to serve as a flexible, durable, light-weight insulation product, said article comprising a *lofty fibrous batting sheet* and a continuous aerogel through said batting.

provide objective boundaries for those of skill in the art' in the context of the invention."

The '359 patent survived Alison's indefiniteness attack because those objective boundaries were amply present in its written description as well as its prosecution history. First, the patent expressly defined a "lofty" batting as "a fibrous material that shows the properties of *bulk* and *some resilience* (with or without full bulk recovery)."[109] The written description further defined each of the emphasized terms. "Bulk" referred to " 'the air or openness created by the web of fibers in a lofty batting.' "[110] "Sufficiently resilient" batting was that which could " 'be compressed to remove the air (bulk) yet spring back to substantially its original size and shape.' "[111]

Second, the '359 patent provided functional characteristics of the claimed aerogel material. Distinguishing the prior art, the patent's written description contrasted the claim-recited "lofty . . . batting" with the prior art "densely woven or thickly tangled mass" having minimal open space and lacking the resilience of a lofty batting.[112] The '359 patent stated that "the batting useful herein is substantially different" from the prior art "woven mat."[113]

Third, the '359 patent's written description was "replete" with examples and metrics that further identified the meaning of "lofty . . . batting." The '359 patent included a list of nearly 20 "particularly suitable" fibrous materials for forming a "lofty . . . batting," such as the KEVLAR commercial product. Specific commercial products such as "Primaloft" and "Thinsulate Lite Loft" that could qualify as "lofty . . . batting" were identified as examples.[114]

Fourth, the '359 patent's prosecution history also supported the *Alison* Circuit's conclusion that "lofty . . . batting" was not indefinite. The examiner's Statement of Reasons for Allowance quoted and applied the "bulk" and "resilience" definitions, and the patentee had relied on these terms to distinguish prior art. Although not part of the original prosecution, the Federal Circuit also noted that the PTAB had declined to institute an IPR of the '359 patent. The Board's opinion explaining the denial stated that " 'both parties agree[d]' " to the "bulk" and "some resilience" definition.[115]

Lastly, although the intrinsic evidence provided no shortage of guidance, the extrinsic evidence offered further support for the definiteness of "lofty . . . batting." A technical dictionary confirmed that

[109]*Alison,* 936 F.3d at 1360 (emphasis added by Federal Circuit).
[110]*Alison,* 936 F.3d at 1360 (quoting '359 patent).
[111]*Alison,* 936 F.3d at 1360 (quoting '359 patent).
[112]*Alison,* 936 F.3d at 1361.
[113]'359 patent, col. 7, ll. 60-61.
[114]*Alison,* 936 F.3d at 1361.
[115]*Alison,* 936 F.3d at 1361 (quoting *Alison,* 2017 WL 2486089, at *3).

"battings" and "loft" were terms of art that had meanings consistent with their use in the '359 patent. Before the ITC, the experts for both parties could explain the meaning of "bulk" and "some resilience," which were the "two defining characteristics" of "lofty . . . batting."[116]

The Federal Circuit was not persuaded by challenger Alison's argument that the '359 patent claims were indefinite because a competitor would not know when it infringed. Alison contended that the competitor would be unable to draw a line between an infringing lofty batting having "some resilience," and a non-infringing batting having "little [to no] resilience." The appellate court explained that Alison wrongly sought a level of "mathematical precision" that was simply too high.[117] As the Supreme Court in *Nautilus* observed, "[s]ome modicum of uncertainty . . . is the 'price of ensuring the appropriate incentives for innovation.'"[118] Because "'[t]he degree of precision necessary . . . is a function of the nature of the subject matter,'" the *Alison* Circuit agreed with patentee Aspen that a person of ordinary skill in this field "c[ould] tell when a material has zero or a negligible amount of resilience without needing a mathematical definition."[119]

The Federal Circuit also rejected what was likely Alison's best argument — an attempt to equate the claim definiteness analysis with claim construction. Alison reasoned that in order to uphold the definiteness of the '359 claims, the ITC administrative law judge (ALJ) had effectively limited the claim scope to the parameters disclosed in the following example from the '359 patent (using Holofil™ batting):

> Another way of determining if a batting is sufficiently lofty to be within the scope of this invention is to evaluate its compressibility and resilience. In this case a lofty batting is one that (i) is compressible by at least 50% of its natural thickness, preferably at least 65%, and most preferably at least 80%, and (ii) is sufficiently resilient that after compression for a few seconds it will return to at least 70% of its original thickness, preferably at least 75%, and most preferably at least 80%. By this definition a lofty batting is one that can be compressed to remove the air (bulk)

[116] *Alison,* 936 F.3d at 1361-1362 (citing *Sonix*, 844 F.3d at 1380 ("Although . . . application by the examiner and an expert do not, on their own, establish an objective standard, they nevertheless provide evidence that a skilled artisan did understand the scope of this invention with reasonable certainty.").

[117] *Alison,* 936 F.3d at 1362 (citing Enzo Biochem, Inc. v. Applera Corp., 599 F.3d 1325, 1335 (Fed. Cir. 2010); citing also *Nautilus*, 572 U.S. at 909 (quoting *Festo*, 535 U.S. at 732)). *See also* Sonix Tech. Co. v. Publications Int'l, Ltd., 844 F.3d 1370, 1377 (Fed. Cir. 2017) (explaining that "a patentee need not define his invention with mathematical precision in order to comply with the definiteness requirement").

[118] *Nautilus*, 572 U.S. at 909 (quoting *Festo*, 535 U.S. at 732).

[119] *Alison,* 936 F.3d at 1362 (quoting in first quotation Biosig Instruments, Inc. v. Nautilus, Inc., 783 F.3d 1374, 1382 (Fed. Cir. 2015) (on remand from Supreme Court) (first alteration in original) (quoting Miles Labs., Inc. v. Shandon, Inc., 997 F.2d 870, 875 (Fed. Cir. 1993))).

yet spring back to substantially its original size and shape. For example a Holofil™ batting may be compressed from its original 1.5 thickness to a minimum of about 0.2 and spring back to its original thickness once the load is removed. This batting can be considered to contain 1.3 of air (bulk) and 0.2 of fiber. It is compressible by 87% and returns to essentially 100% of its original thickness.[120]

Challenger Alison was correct that when analyzing indefiniteness, the ALJ took note of and quoted portions of Holofil™ example. That example disclosed that bulk is "air" and that a lofty batting is "sufficiently resilient" if "after compression for a few seconds it will return to at least 70% of its original thickness."

But at the claim construction stage, the ALJ specifically declined to limit the scope of the claim to the parameters set forth in the quoted Holofil™ example. Rather, the ALJ simply construed "lofty... batting" by adopting the '359 patent's express definition of "lofty... batting" as "[a] fibrous material that shows the properties of bulk and some resilience (with or without full bulk recovery)."[121] Although the ALJ did not say so, it appears to this author that the judge viewed the Holofil™ example as describing the parameters of one of several potential embodiments of the invention. Absent factors not present in *Alison,* patent claims are not typically construed as limited to single example or to the preferred embodiment.

Accordingly, the Federal Circuit could not accept Alison's argument that the ITC's indefiniteness analysis erroneously rested on an "irreconcilable contradiction" with its claim construction.[122] There was no support for such an argument in the Federal Circuit's case law. Under its precedent, "examples in the specification may be used to inform those skilled in the art of the scope of the invention with reasonable certainty — thus demonstrating the term is not indefinite — without being directly construed into the claims."[123]

The *Alison* Circuit accordingly "conclude[d] that claims 1, 7, and 9 [we]re not indefinite because the '359 patent informs a person of ordinary skill in the art about the scope of 'lofty... batting' with 'reasonable certainty.' "[124]

c. *Judicial Correction of Errors in Patent Claims*

Patent claims are sometimes rendered indefinite under 35 U.S.C. §112(b) by errors introduced into the claim language during patent

[120]'359 patent, col. 7, ll. 40-56.
[121]*Alison,* 936 F.3d at 1357.
[122]*Alison,* 936 F.3d at 1363.
[123]*Alison,* 936 F.3d at 1363 (citing, e.g., *Sonix,* 844 F.3d at 1379; *Enzo,* 599 F.3d at 1334-1335).
[124]*Alison,* 936 F.3d at 1362 (quoting *Nautilus,* 572 U.S. at 901).

prosecution. What appears to be an obvious typographical error can potentially prove fatal to validity, a risk that should reinforce the need for precise, careful drafting and amending of claims. A case in point is *Novo Indus., L.P. v. Micro Molds Corp.*[125] Novo's patent was directed to a carrier assembly that held one of a plurality of vertical slats (or blinds) that covered the interior of a window. The carrier assembly permitted realignment of misaligned slats and included "stop mechanisms" that physically prevented rotation of a support finger when a slat reached an extreme rotational position. During prosecution, the USPTO examiner rejected Novo's application claims 15-17 as obvious under 35 U.S.C. §103.[126] Novo canceled those claims and substituted a new claim 19, which in subparagraphs (a)-(i) incorporated all the limitations of the canceled claims plus one additional limitation; claim 19 was subsequently renumbered and issued as patent claim 13, which read (emphasis added to limitation (g)):

> 13. A carrier assembly for movably supporting one of a plurality of vertical oriented slats in a vertical blind assembly, said carrier assembly comprising:
>
> a) a frame . . . ,
>
> b) a support finger movably mounted to rotate on said frame . . . ,
>
> c) a gear means . . . ,
>
> g) stop means formed on *a rotatable with* said support finger and extending outwardly therefrom into engaging relation with one of two spaced apart stop members formed on said frame,
>
> h) said stop means comprising one outwardly extending protrusion disposed to engage each of said stop members on said frame upon rotation through an arc of substantially 180 degrees, and
>
> i) said drive gear including a substantially round configuration and a plurality of gear teeth formed thereon in spaced relation to one another along an outer periphery of said drive gear to define a circular configuration thereof;. . . .

Notably, the quoted language of limitation (g) of claim 13 was not identical to the wording of the claims Novo had canceled. Rather, it included the additional words "a rotatable with," which did not appear in canceled claim 16. The examiner allowed the claim as written. Novo never sought a certificate of correction from the USPTO.[127]

In subsequent infringement litigation, the parties agreed that issued claim 13 included an error, but disputed whether the error was correctable. While not adopting either party's argument, the

[125] 350 F.3d 1348 (Fed. Cir. 2003).

[126] The nonobviousness requirement of 35 U.S.C. §103 is the subject of Chapter 5, *infra*.

[127] Certificates of correction are discussed *infra* Chapter 8 ("Correcting and Challenging Issued Patents in the USPTO").

district court interpreted the claim so as to correct what it considered "an obvious typographical error." The district court instructed the jury that "a" in limitation (g) of claim 13 should be read as "and." This rendered moot the issue of invalidity for indefiniteness at the district court level. The jury proceeded to find that defendant Micro Molds had literally (and willfully) infringed the patent.

On appeal, the Federal Circuit relied on a 1926 Supreme Court decision, *I.T.S. Rubber Co. v. Essex Rubber Co.,*[128] which held that in a patent infringement suit a court could properly interpret a patent claim to correct an obvious error. In view of subsequent legislative developments codifying the USPTO's certificate of correction procedure, the Federal Circuit concluded that district courts in conjunction with their responsibility to interpret patent claims can correct only *Essex*-type errors. Specifically, a district court can correct a patent "only if (1) the correction is not subject to reasonable debate based on consideration of the claim language and the specification and (2) the prosecution history does not suggest a different interpretation of the claims."[129]

These newly announced criteria were not satisfied in *Novo* because the nature of the error was not evident on the face of the patent. The correct construction had been the subject of considerable debate before the district court. Patentee Novo itself had suggested two different corrections to the district court, which devised a third correction. The correct approach, the Federal Circuit suggested, might be yet a fourth approach, to add a word that was missing, such as "skirt" or "disk." Because the Federal Circuit could not discern "what correction [wa]s necessarily appropriate or how the claim should be interpreted," it held claim 13 invalid for indefiniteness under 35 U.S.C. §112, ¶2. The claim was "insolubly ambiguous" and not "amenable to construction" in its present form.

In contrast with *Novo,* the claim error in *Hoffer v. Microsoft Corp.*[130] was correctable by the district court. Claim 22 of Hoffer's patent as written depended from claim 38. In litigation involving the patent a federal district court held claim 22 invalid for indefiniteness because no claim 38 appeared in the issued patent. The error had been introduced into the patent by the USPTO during prosecution when the claims were renumbered and claim 38 was given a different number; the examiner renumbered all claims in preparation for printing the patent but failed to renumber claim 22's internal reference to claim 38. The Federal Circuit disagreed on appeal that the district court was "powerless" to correct the error. In this case the error in dependency of claim 22 was apparent on the face of the printed patent and the correct antecedent claim was apparent from the prosecution

[128] 272 U.S. 429 (1926).
[129] *Novo*, 350 F.3d at 1354.
[130] 405 F.3d 1326 (Fed. Cir. 2005).

history. Citing *Novo,* the Federal Circuit held that "[w]hen a harmless error in a patent is not subject to reasonable debate, it can be corrected by the court, as for other legal documents."[131] The district court's invalidation of claim 22 for indefiniteness was accordingly reversed.

3. Antecedent Basis

The concept of "antecedent basis" is a common technique that has developed in patent prosecution practice to aid those who draft patent claims in satisfying the definiteness requirement of 35 U.S.C. §112(b).[132] It helps ensure that "terms and phrases used in the claims ... find clear support or antecedent basis in the [the application's] description so that the meaning of the terms in the claims may be ascertainable by reference to the description."[133]

Antecedent basis is implemented as follows. The first time a particular element is introduced in a patent claim, it should be preceded or introduced by the indefinite article "a." Thereafter, each time the claims drafter intends to refer back to that same previously introduced element, it is referred to as "said" element or "the" element.

For example, consider the following claim to a toy football:

> 1. A foam football comprising
>
> (a) a body having a longitudinal axis and an external surface;
>
> (b) said external surface comprising a plurality of grooves aligned with said longitudinal axis;
>
> (c) wherein each of said grooves has a minimum depth of about 0.25 inches and a maximum depth of about 0.5 inches.

The first time that the terms "football," "body," "longitudinal axis," "external surface," and "grooves" are introduced, they are expressed as "*a* foam football," "*a* body," "*a* longitudinal axis," "*an* external surface," and "*a* plurality of grooves."[134] Thereafter, these elements are referred to as "*said* external surface," "*said* longitudinal axis," and "*said* grooves," to indicate that the claims drafter is referring to the same "external surface," the same "longitudinal axis," and the same "grooves" as initially introduced, not some other "longitudinal axis," "external surface," or "grooves."[135]

[131] *Hoffer*, 405 F.3d at 1331.

[132] 35 U.S.C. §112(b) (eff. Sept. 16, 2012).

[133] 37 C.F.R. §1.75(d)(1) (2008).

[134] A **plurality** is a term of art in patent law, meaning a quantity of two or more.

[135] *See generally* United States Patent and Trademark Office, Manual of Patent Examining Procedure (8th ed., 8th rev., 2010), *available at* http://www.uspto.gov/web/offices/pac/mpep/mpep.htm, at §2173.05(e) (discussing basis of rejection for "Lack of Antecedent Basis").

C. Anatomy of a Patent Claim

Every patent claim has three parts: a preamble, a transition, and a body. As the role of each of these parts is described below, consider the following claim as an example:

> 1. A widget comprising:
>
> Part A;
> Part B; and
> Part C, attaching said Part A to said Part B;
>
> wherein said Part A is made of copper and said Part B is made of lead and said Part C is made of gold.

1. Preamble

A preamble is a short and plain expression of what the invention is. In claim 1 above, the words "[a] widget" are the preamble. The preamble need not include an express reference to one of the four statutory classifications of potentially patentable subject matter under 35 U.S.C. §101 (i.e., process, machine, manufacture, or composition of matter), so long as it is clear from the entirety of the claim that the invention fits within one or more of those classifications. In the above example, it is clear that the claimed widget is either a manufacture or a machine.[136]

Claim preambles are sometimes longer than just one or two words. In such cases, the qualifying language in the preamble is sometimes, but not always, treated as a limitation of the claim. For example, consider the following reformulation of the above claim:

> 1. A widget for use in marine applications comprising:
>
> Part A;
> Part B; and
> Part C, attaching said Part A to said Part B;
>
> wherein said Part A is made of copper and said Part B is made of lead and said Part C is made of gold.

The preamble of this claim is the entire phrase "[a] widget for use in marine applications." The issue here is whether the qualifier "for use in marine applications" represents a limitation of the claim, such that an identical widget, if used on land rather than in the water, would not literally infringe the claim.

[136]The categories of potentially patentable subject matter are discussed in further detail *infra* Chapter 7.

The Federal Circuit rule is that, generally, preamble language is considered limiting if the language is necessary to give "life, meaning and vitality" to the claim, or if it recites essential structure or steps.[137] In particular, if the preamble terminology is repeated and referenced in the body of the claim, it is most likely limiting. However, where the body of the claim (i.e., the language following the transition) recites a structurally complete invention and the preamble language only states an intended purpose or use for that invention, the preamble language is generally not limiting.[138]

In the above example, the "marine applications" language is not referred to in the body of the claim, and the body recites a structurally complete invention. The "marine applications" language merely states an intended use for the widget. Thus, it is not likely to be construed as limiting. Unauthorized use of the claimed widget on land would still literally infringe the claim (assuming that all limitations recited in the body of the claim, discussed below, are met).

In contrast with the "marine applications" example, the Federal Circuit construed the preamble term "travel trailer" as a structural limitation, not merely a statement of intended use, in the 2019 decision *In re Fought*.[139] Patent applicant Fought claimed (emphasis added):

> 1. A *travel trailer* having a first and second compartment therein separated by a wall assembly which is movable so as to alter the relative dimensions of the first and second compartments without altering the exterior appearance of *the travel trailer*.

During examination of Fought's application, the USPTO had concluded that "travel trailer" was merely a statement of intended use that did not limit the claim. Accordingly, the agency determined that Fought's application claim 1 was anticipated under 35 U.S.C. §102 by prior art disclosing a conventional truck trailer such as a refrigerated trailer for transporting perishable food products.

The Federal Circuit reversed. Most importantly, Fought's claims relied on the term "travel trailer" for antecedent basis. Specifically, the last line of the claim, reciting "the travel trailer," referred back to the "travel trailer" introduced in the preamble of the claim.

[137]*See* Catalina Marketing Int'l, Inc. v. CoolSavings.com, Inc., 289 F.3d 801, 808 (Fed. Cir. 2002).

[138]*See Catalina Marketing*, 289 F.3d at 810 (reversing summary judgment of noninfringement on basis that preamble phrase "located at predesignated sites such as consumer stores," recited in claim to a selection and distribution system for discount coupons, was not a limitation, because "[t]he applicant did not rely on this phrase to define its invention nor is the phrase essential to understand limitations or terms in the claim body," nor did applicant rely on the phrase to distinguish the prior art).

[139]941 F.3d 1175, (Fed. Cir. Nov. 4, 2019).

The Circuit has "repeatedly held a preamble limiting when it serves as antecedent basis for a term appearing in the body of a claim."[140]

In addition to the language of the claims themselves, two items of extrinsic evidence further supported the *Fought* Circuit's view that "travel trailer" was a structural limitation — specifically, a type of recreational vehicle (RV) that included a living quarters. A published U.S. patent application to Miller disclosed that " '[a] towed recreational vehicle is generally referred to as a "travel trailer." ' "[141] And an RV buyer's guide stated that " '[p]robably the single most-popular class of towable RV is the Travel Trailer.' "[142]

The USPTO Board had further erred by characterizing as merely statements of intended use the distinctions made about travel trailers compared to other recreational vehicles in these extrinsic documents. Contrary to the Board's reading of the evidence, towability was a structural difference rather than an intended use. Likewise, a living area was also a structural requirement.

Having construed the claim's scope in this narrower fashion, the Federal Circuit held in *Fought* that prior art cargo trailers with shipping compartments did *not* anticipate. "Just as one would not confuse a house with a warehouse, no one would confuse a travel trailer with a truck trailer."[143]

2. Transition

The transition of the example claim above is the single word "comprising." The transition is a key code word or term of art that affects the scope of the claim. There are three primary claim transitions used in U.S. patent claiming practice: **comprising**, **consisting of**, and **consisting essentially of.**[144] Each is discussed below.

a. "Comprising" Transition

A "comprising" transition means "including" or "containing" or "having"[145] the elements listed following the transition. Inclusion in a patent claim

[140]*Fought,* 941 F.3d at 1178, 2019 WL 5687699, at *2 (citing, e.g., C.W. Zumbiel Co., Inc. v. Kappos, 702 F.3d 1371, 1385 (Fed. Cir. 2012); Bell Commc'ns Research, Inc. v. Vitalink Commc'ns Corp., 55 F.3d 615, 620-621 (Fed. Cir. 1995); Electro Sci. Indus., Inc. v. Dynamic Details, Inc., 307 F.3d 1343, 1348 (Fed. Cir. 2002); Pacing Techs., LLC v. Garmin Int'l, Inc., 778 F.3d 1021, 1024 (Fed. Cir. 2015)).

[141]*Fought,* 941 F.3d at 1178, (quoting U.S. Patent Application Publication No. 2010/0096873).

[142]*Fought,* 941 F.3d at 1178, (quoting *Woodall's RV Buyer's Guide*).

[143]*Fought,* 941 F.3d at 1179.

[144]*See generally* Ex parte Davis, 80 U.S.P.Q. 448, 450 (Bd. Pat. App. & Int. 1948) (discussing these three "code" terms adopted "to aid uniformity of practice").

[145]In *In re Fought*, 941 F.3d 1175, (Fed. Cir. Nov. 4, 2019), the appellate court treated the word "having" in a claim reciting "a travel trailer having a first and second

of the comprising transition indicates that the claim is open in scope. An "open" claim encompasses or is literally infringed by (or "reads on") another's product that includes each of the explicitly recited elements of the claim, *plus anything else*.

For example, a claim to "a widget comprising A, B, and C" would read on a widget ABC, a widget ABCD, a widget ABCXYZ, and so on.[146] Infringement of a comprising claim cannot be avoided by copying the invention and merely adding on additional elements not recited in the claim.

Use of the "comprising" transition does not broaden a claim to such an extent that it reads on a device containing less (rather than more) than what is expressly recited in the claim, however. In *In re Skvorecz,*[147] a reissue applicant claimed an improved stand for chafing dishes used to keep food warm during serving. The invention's structure allowed multiple stacked stands to be readily separated from one another. The wire legs of the stand included an indent or "offset" located adjacent to the upper ends of the legs, serving to laterally displace each leg relative to its point of attachment to the upper rim of the stand. An embodiment of the claimed invention, including an offset indicated by the number 30 in Fig. 4 of the application drawings, is depicted in Figure 2.3.

Claim 1 of Skvorecz's reissue application recited:

> 1. A wire chafing stand comprising a first rim of wire steel which forms a closed geometrical configuration circumscribing a first surface area, having at least two wire legs with each wire leg having two upright sections interconnected to one another in a configuration forming a base support for the stand to rest upon with each upright section extending upwardly from said base support to from [sic, form] an angle equal to or greater than 90° with respect to a horizontal plane through said base support and being affixed to the first rim adjacent one end thereof and further comprising a plurality of offsets located either in said upright sections of said wire legs or in said first rim for laterally displacing each wire leg relative to said first rim to facilitate the nesting of a multiplicity of stands into one another without significant wedging.[148]

---

compartment therein . . .") as equivalent to a "comprising" transition word. It rejected the USPTO's argument that the claim did not use a transition word, stating "[t]hough this claim does not use the typical claim language (comprising) which denotes the transition between the preamble and the body, the word 'having' performs the same role here." *Fought,* 941 F.3d at 1178.

[146]Every recited element is considered material and must be identically present in the accused device to have **literal infringement**. Another's device that excludes even one element recited in the claim avoids infringement. For example, a widget ACXYZ does not literally infringe the above claim, because it lacks the recited element B.

[147]580 F.3d 1262 (Fed. Cir. 2009).

[148]*Skvorecz,* 580 F.3d at 1265.

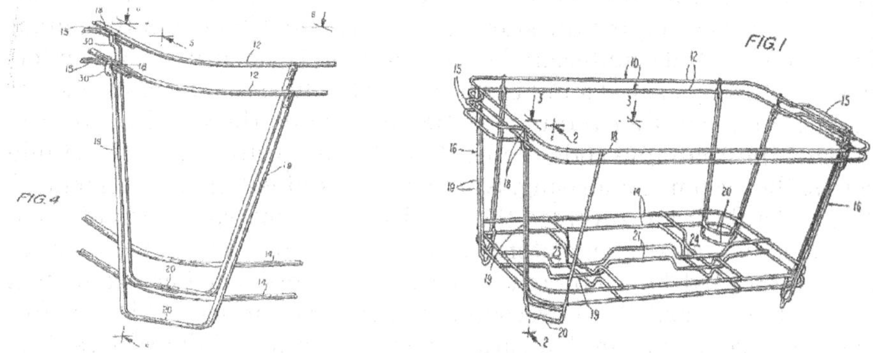

Figure 2.3
Application Drawings from *In re Skvorecz*

The USPTO rejected Skvorecz's claim 1 as anticipated by a prior art structure depicted in a patent to Buff. Notably, the Buff structure did not have an offset located in each wire that served as a leg to support the Buff stand. The USPTO nevertheless took the position that Buff anticipated Skvorecz's claim because of the claim's open-ended "comprising" transition; that is, the claim read on stands having wire legs with offsets, plus anything else — namely, wire legs without such offsets.

The Federal Circuit reversed in *Skvorecz*, concluding that the USPTO had misinterpreted the claim language and therefore had not established anticipation. The USPTO's mandate to give claims their "broadest reasonable interpretation" during examination was not a license to ignore features required by the claims. "The signal 'comprising' does not render a claim anticipated by a device that contains less (rather th[a]n more) than what is claimed," the Federal Circuit explained.[149] In the case at bar, the USPTO had incorrectly applied the "examination expedient" of "broadest reasonable interpretation" when it construed "comprising" to mean that less than all of the wire legs in the claimed invention needed to have offsets.[150] The Federal Circuit read claim 1 to require that "each wire leg" must have an offset. Accordingly, the claim was not anticipated by a prior art structure made up of some legs with offsets and some legs without offsets.

The Federal Circuit considered whether the linguistically similar phrase "comprised of" should be interpreted differently than the

[149]*Skvorecz*, 580 F.3d at 1268.

[150]*See Skvorecz*, 580 F.3d at 1268; *cf.* In re Suitco Surface, Inc., 603 F.3d 1255, 1260 (Fed. Cir. 2010) (stating that "[t]he broadest-construction rubric coupled with the term "comprising" does not give the PTO an unfettered license to interpret claims to embrace anything remotely related to the claimed invention. Rather, claims should always be read in light of the specification and teachings in the underlying patent.").

standard "comprising" transition in *CIAS, Inc. v. Alliance Gaming Corp.,*[151] answering the question in the negative. Claim 1 of the patent in suit recited "[a] counterfeit detection system for identifying a counterfeit object from a set of similar authentic objects, each object in said set having unique authorized information associated therewith *comprised of* machine-readable code elements coded according to a detectable series, the system comprising: [various means-plus-function elements]." The Federal Circuit reversed the district court's interpretation of "comprised of" as a closed-ended term that would exclude any elements other than the recited "machine-readable code elements coded according to a detectable series." While recognizing that "comprised of" is less frequently used as a claim transition than "comprising," the Federal Circuit nevertheless concluded that "[t]he usual and generally consistent meaning of 'comprised of,' when it is used as a transition phrase, is, like 'comprising,' that the ensuing elements or steps are not limiting. The conventional usage of 'comprising' generally also applies to 'comprised of.' "[152] The appellate court found support for its holding in several district court cases that followed the "routine construction" of "comprised of" as open-ended, that is, "not of itself exclud[ing] the possible presence of additional elements or steps." The Federal Circuit's construction of "comprised of" as open-ended meant that the district court in *CIAS* had erred in finding no infringement by Alliance's accused code systems, which included elements coded according to a "secret" series as well as the claim-recited "detectable series."

b. "Consisting of" Transition

Inclusion in a patent claim of the "consisting of" transition indicates that the claim is closed in scope. A "closed" claim encompasses or is literally infringed by (or "reads on") another's product that includes each of the explicitly recited elements of the claim, *but nothing else* (other than impurities normally associated with the recited elements).[153] For example, a claim to "a widget consisting of A, B, and C" would read on a widget ABC, but not on a widget ABCD or on a widget ABCXYZ.

[151]504 F.3d 1356 (Fed. Cir. 2007).

[152]*CIAS*, 504 F.3d at 1360.

[153]A divided panel of the Federal Circuit qualified this understanding of "consisting of" claims. In *Norian Corp. v. Stryker Corp.,* 363 F.3d 1321 (Fed. Cir. 2004), the majority held that a claim to a kit "consisting of" several enumerated chemical components was nevertheless infringed by a kit made up of the same chemical components plus a mechanical component — a spatula. *See id.* at 1331-1332. The dissenting judge charged that the court should not "change the meaning of a well-established phrase to save a patentee from a decision to limit its claims." *Id.* at 1335 (Schall, J., dissenting in part).

Thus, a claim that employs a "consisting of" transition is potentially much narrower in scope than a claim that uses a comprising transition. For this reason, patent applicants generally file their applications with comprising claims, and only narrow the claims by amending to a consisting of transition when absolutely necessary for allowance.

c. *"Consisting Essentially of" Transition*

This type of transition is most commonly used when claiming chemical compositions, and can be thought of as creating a partially closed claim. A "consisting essentially of" transition means that the claim is closed, *except for the addition of any elements that do not change the essential function or properties of the composition.*[154]

For example, a claim that recites "an adhesive consisting essentially of A, B, and C" would read on another's adhesive ABC, as well as on an adhesive ABCD if D was merely a dye that made the adhesive a certain color, not impacting its stickiness. This claim would not read on or encompass an adhesive ABCX if the inclusion of X changed the basic nature of the adhesive from one that forms a very strong, permanent bond like SuperGlue® to one that is very tacky and removable, like the repositionable adhesive used with Post-It® notes.[155]

3. Body

The body of a patent claim lists all elements of the invention and should specify how the elements are related to or interact with each other. For example, consider a claim reciting "the widget comprising A, B, and means for attaching A to B." The body of this claim is all the words after the comprising transition. Thus, the body recites three elements: element A, element B, and a "means" element (explained below) that functions to attach element A to element B.

No minimum or maximum number of elements must be included in the body of a patent claim. But in any case, a sufficient number of elements must be included to recite an invention that is novel, nonobvious, and useful. The device as claimed must be operable; that is, it must work. So long as these conditions are met, it is permissible to claim "subcombination" inventions that are some subset of a larger device. For example, automobile carburetors, tires, and headlights

[154] *See* PPG Indus. v. Guardian Indus. Corp., 156 F.3d 1351, 1354 (Fed. Cir. 1998).

[155] *See* Ex parte Davis, 80 U.S.P.Q. 448, 450 (Bd. Pat. App. & Int. 1948) (holding that where claim to adhesive composition recited three ingredients and prior art reference disclosed four, the claim's "consisting essentially of" transition excluded the fourth ingredient [thus rendering the claim allowable] because that ingredient "materially changes the fundamental characters of the [claimed] three-ingredient composition. . . .").

are subcombination inventions because they consist of major subassemblies of parts and have their own utility.[156]

Deciding how many elements to include in the body of a patent claim requires a trade-off that balances the patent owner's ability to enforce the claim against infringers versus the likelihood that the claim will withstand a challenge to its validity. Both concepts turn on the scope of the claim. It is axiomatic that the more elements included in a claim, the narrower its scope; the fewer elements included, the broader its scope. For example, a claim reciting "a widget comprising elements A, B, and C" is narrower in scope than a claim reciting "a widget comprising elements A and C."

This difference in scope follows from the **all-elements rule**, which we will study in greater depth in Chapter 9 ("Patent Infringement"), *infra*. In summary, the all-elements rule requires that in order to find that an accused device infringes a particular asserted claim of a patent, every element (more properly, every **limitation**) recited in that claim must be met (i.e., matched) either literally or equivalently in the accused device.[157] Thus, as more elements are added to a claim, it will be progressively more difficult to prove infringement of that claim because each recited element must be present or met in the accused device.

Figure 2.4 illustrates the concept of claim scope by way of a Venn diagram. As depicted in Figure 2.4, the claim to "a widget comprising elements A and B," represented by the exterior circle, is literally infringed by (or reads on) an accused widget that has only the two elements AB, or (because of the comprising transition) by an accused widget ABC or by an accused widget ABCXY or by an accused widget ABXYZ. But when an additional element is added so that the claim recites "a widget comprising elements A, B, and C," then in order for the claim to be literally infringed an accused widget must have all three elements ABC (at a minimum). The scope of this claim is represented by the smaller, interior circle. Because the three-element claim uses a comprising transition, it also is infringed by an accused widget ABCXY or by an accused widget ABCXYZ. The accused widgets AB and ABXYZ infringe the former two-element claim but not the latter three-element claim because both accused widgets lack an element C. Because the potential universe of infringing devices is smaller for the three-element claim (as represented by the smaller circular area of the interior circle in Figure 2.4), it is narrower in scope than the two-element claim.

[156]For further examples of subcombinations, *see* ROBERT C. FABER, FABER ON MECHANICS OF PATENT CLAIM DRAFTING §59 (7th ed., Pract. Law Inst. 2015).

[157]The use of "literally or equivalently" here refers to the two theories of infringement we will analyze in Chapter 9, *infra*: (1) literal infringement and (2) infringement under the judicially created doctrine of equivalents.

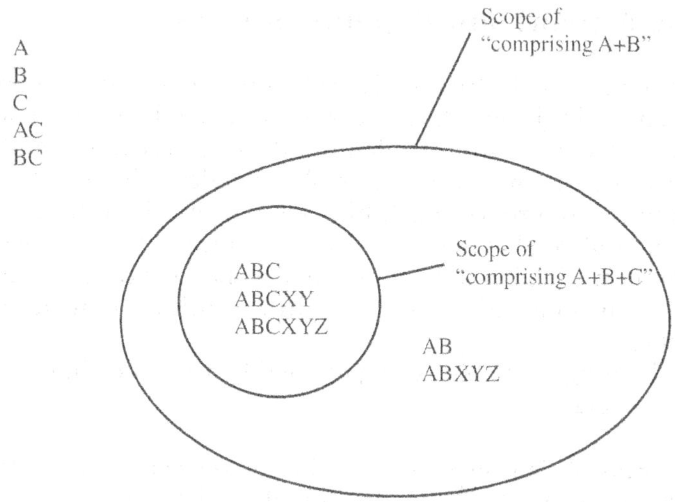

Figure 2.4
Claim Scope

Determining the optimal scope of a claim is a trade-off because its exclusionary scope must be balanced against its sustainable validity. In other words, the scope of a patent claim should not be determined in isolation from consideration of its validity. A claim that is relatively broader in that it is enforceable against a greater number of accused devices is correspondingly easier to invalidate for lack of novelty[158] or for obviousness.[159] For example, the claim to "a widget comprising A and B," represented by the larger circle in Figure 2.4, is more susceptible to invalidation than the claim to "a widget comprising A, B, and C." These relationships lead to the following maxim favored by Judge Giles Rich:

> The strongest claims are the weakest, and the weakest claims the strongest.

This maxim simply means that the claims that are broadest in scope (i.e., the strongest in terms of enforcement against the greatest possible number of accused devices) are also the most vulnerable to invalidation by the prior art, and vice versa.

[158]*See* Chapter 4 ("Novelty, Loss of Right, and Priority Pre- and Post-America Invents Act of 2011 (35 U.S.C. §102)"), *infra*.
[159]*See infra* Chapter 5 ("The Nonobviousness Requirement (35 U.S.C. §103)").

D. Independent and Dependent Claims

Patent claims are drafted in either independent or dependent form. A dependent claim is one that refers to (or depends from) some other, previously presented claim, while an independent claim stands alone without referring to any other claim. A dependent claim includes (i.e., incorporates by reference) all limitations of the claim from which it depends, and also adds some further limitation(s). Thus, use of the dependent form of claiming is merely a shorthand way of repeating the limitations of some other claim while adding some additional limitation(s).

These claiming principles are governed by the following provisions of 35 U.S.C. §112:

> **(c) Form.**— A claim may be written in independent or, if the nature of the case admits, in dependent or multiple dependent form.
>
> **(d) Reference in Dependent Forms.**— Subject to subsection (e) [claims in multiple dependent form], a claim in dependent form shall contain a reference to a claim previously set forth and then specify a further limitation of the subject matter claimed. A claim in dependent form shall be construed to incorporate by reference all the limitations of the claim to which it refers....[160]

The important principle of *claim differentiation* provides that the existence of a dependent claim shows that the independent claim from which it depends is not so (thus) limited. For example, if claim 1 of a hypothetical patent recites "a widget comprising A, B, and C," and claim 2 of the patent recites "the widget of claim 1 wherein A is red," this means that the widget of claim 2 must comprise a red A, a B (of any color), and a C (of any color). The existence of dependent claim 2 shows that the widget of independent claim 1 is *not* limited to having a red A; rather (barring some sort of limiting language in the written description), the A element in claim 1 can be of any color, whether red, or blue, or green, or anything else. The existence of claim 2 differentiates the widget of claim 2 from the widget of claim 1. Claim 2 in this example also can be thought of as a subset or species of claim 1, which recites a genus of widgets.

For purposes of illustration, consider a hypothetical patent having 20 claims, consisting of 2 independent claims and 18 dependent claims, arranged as shown in Figure 2.5.

This typical claiming structure can be visualized as two inverted pyramids that represent the variation in scope of the claims from broadest to narrowest, as depicted in Figure 2.6.

[160]35 U.S.C. §112(c)-(d) (eff. Sept. 16, 2012).

Claim 1. A widget comprising A, B, and C.

[Independent claim (broadest in scope of all 20 claims)]

Claim 2. The widget of claim 1, wherein said A is purple.

[Dependent claim, narrower in scope than claim 1]

Claim 3. The widget of claim 2, wherein said B is green.

[Dependent claim, narrower in scope than claim 2]

Claim 4. The widget of claim 3, wherein said C is brown.

[Dependent claim, narrower in scope than claim 3]

. . .

Claim 10. A widget consisting of A, B, and C.

[Second independent claim, narrower in scope than the first independent claim, claim 1, because "consisting" transition is used]

Claim 11. The widget of claim 10, wherein said A is purple.

Claim 12. The widget of claim 11, wherein said B is green.

Claim 13. The widget of claim 12, wherein said C is brown.

. . .

Claim 20. The widget of claim 19, wherein said A is adjacent to said B.

[Narrowest claim of patent, or "picture" claim — identically covers the product that patentee is selling to the public]

Figure 2.5

Example Claim Groupings

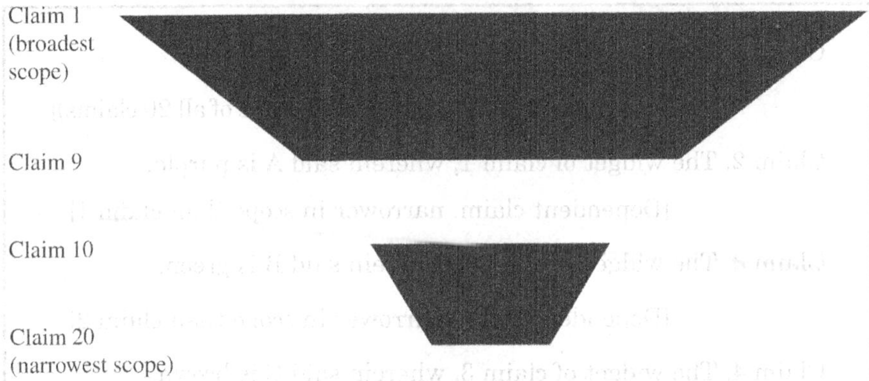

Figure 2.6
Scope Representation for Example Claim Groupings of Figure 2.5

E. Specialized Claiming Formats

In addition to the basic claiming techniques mentioned above, U.S. patent claiming practice uses a number of recognized formats. The use of each specialized format is at the option of the claims drafter. Choice of claiming format can significantly impact the interpretation and scope of the claim in both *ex parte* examination and patent infringement litigation. Some of the most commonly used claiming formats are "means-plus-function" claims, "product-by-process" claims, *Jepson* claims, and *Markush* claims. Each format is discussed below.

1. Means-Plus-Function Claim Elements (35 U.S.C. §112(f))

a. Introduction

Functional claiming refers to the general notion of claiming an invention by what it does, rather than what it is in terms of physical structure. For example, one might functionally claim a "means for fastening part A to part B" rather than reciting a specific structure such as "a nail."

Section 112(f) of the Patent Act governs a particular type of functional claiming.[161] The statute provides that an element in a claim for a combination (of two or more elements) can be claimed in terms of what the element *does,* rather than what its structure is, by

[161] The America Invents Act of 2011 renamed the sixth paragraph of 35 U.S.C. §112 (generally referred to as "35 U.S.C. §112, ¶6") as 35 U.S.C. §112(f) (eff. Sept. 16, 2012) (titled "Element in Claim for a Combination").

expressing the element as a generic "means" that performs a recited function, without reciting its structure. Although this type of means-plus-function claiming is used more frequently for claiming mechanical or electrical inventions than for chemical or biotechnological inventions,[162] all students of patent law need to understand the origins and operation of means-plus-function claiming.

Since the 1980s, the use of means-plus-function claiming has declined precipitously,[163] most probably because the Federal Circuit has made clear that means-plus-function elements operate to narrow (rather than expand) claim scope.[164] Nevertheless, means-plus-function claiming remains a standard technique that is quite commonly encountered.

The historical backdrop of means-plus-function claiming is grounded in judicial disfavor of functional claiming as an instrument of overreaching by inventors. The U.S. Supreme Court in 1946

[162]Patent claims in the chemical or biotechnological arts are often drafted as method or process claims. Such claims may invoke §112(f). This is because, in addition to "means-plus-function" claiming, the Patent Act also contemplates functional claiming in *methods* through the optional use of a "step-plus-function" format. *See generally* O.I. Corp. v. Tekmar Co. Inc., 115 F.3d 1576 (Fed. Cir. 1997), in which the court elaborated:

> The statute [§112, ¶6] of course uses terms that might be viewed as having a similar meaning, namely, steps and acts. It refers to means and steps, which must be supported by structure, material, or acts. It does not state which goes with which. The word "means" clearly refers to the generic description of an apparatus element, and the implementation of such a concept is obviously by structure or material. We interpret the term "steps" to refer to the generic description of elements of a process, and the term "acts" to refer to the implementation of such steps. This interpretation is consistent with the established correlation between means and structure. In this paragraph, structure and material go with means, acts go with steps. Of course, as we have indicated, section 112, ¶6, is implicated only when means *plus function* without definite structure are present, and that is similarly true with respect to steps, that the paragraph is implicated only when steps *plus function* without acts are present. The statute thus in effect provides that an element in a combination method or process claim may be recited as a step for performing a specified function without the recital of acts in support of the function. Being drafted with the permissive "may," the statute does not require that steps in a method claim be drafted in step-plus-function form but rather allows for that form.

115 F.3d at 1582-1583.

[163]*See* Dennis D. Crouch, *The Frequency of Means-Plus-Function Claims*, PATENTLY-O (July 25, 2011), http://www.patentlyo.com/patent/2011/07/the-frequency-of-means-plus-function-claims.html (chart showing percentage of U.S. patents that included at least one "means for" claim limitation declining from almost 50 percent of patents issued in 1980 to about 10 percent of patents issued in 2010).

[164]*See, e.g.*, O.I. Corp. v. Tekmar Co. Inc., 115 F.3d 1576, 1583 (Fed. Cir. 1997) (stating that "[t]he price that must be paid for use of that convenience [of functional claiming by using the means-plus-function format] is limitation of the claim to the means specified in the written description and equivalents thereof."); *see also infra* Section E.1.b ("Interpreting the Scope of Means-Plus-Function Elements").

prohibited functional claiming at the exact point of novelty in *Halliburton Oil Well Cementing Co. v. Walker.*[165] Congress statutorily overruled the *Halliburton* prohibition by enacting then ¶3 of §112 in the 1952 Patent Act. Today, the means-plus-function claiming provision appears as the sixth and final paragraph of 35 U.S.C. §112:

> **(f) Element in Claim for a Combination.**— An element in a claim for a combination may be expressed as a means or step for performing a specified function without the recital of structure, material, or acts in support thereof, and such claim shall be construed to cover the corresponding structure, material, or acts described in the specification and equivalents thereof.[166]

Because the statute speaks of "[a]n element in a claim *for a combination,*" the use of "single means claims" — that is, claims reciting only a single element expressed in means-plus-function terms — is prohibited. However, claims reciting two or more elements are permitted even though each element may be expressed in means-plus-function format. Thus, a claim to a "widget comprising a means for fastening A to B" is not permitted, but a claim to a "widget comprising A, B, and means for fastening A to B" is. Similarly, a claim reciting a "widget comprising a means for [performing function X] and a means for [performing function Y]" is permissible, because this claim includes more than one means-plus-function element.

More commonly, the claims drafter will use the means-plus-function format to express those elements that can be performed by many different types of structures or devices. All such structures or devices need not be explicitly disclosed in the patent application, so long as at least one "corresponding structure" is clearly identified in the written description.[167] In this manner a claim can cover a relatively large number of possible structures without the patent application becoming excessively detailed.

For example, a claim to an athletic shoe might recite

> An athletic shoe comprising:
>
> (i) a left upper portion,
> (ii) a right upper portion,

[165] 329 U.S. 1 (1946).

[166] 35 U.S.C. §112(f) (eff. Sept. 16, 2012).

[167] *See* McGinley v. Franklin Sports, Inc., 262 F.3d 1339, 1347 (Fed. Cir. 2001) (rejecting accused infringer's argument that means-plus-function limitation of asserted claim was not entitled to any range of equivalents as "wholly without merit," and explaining that "[d]rafters of means-plus-function claim limitations are statutorily guaranteed a range of equivalents extending beyond that which is explicitly disclosed in the patent document itself . . .").

(iii) a sole portion integrally connected to said left upper portion and to said right upper portion, and
(iv) means for detachably fastening said left upper portion to said right upper portion.

This claim includes four elements. Elements (i) through (iii) are structural elements — they recite physical items. Element (iv) is expressed in means-plus-function form, because it recites a generic "means" for performing a function, in this case the function of "detachably fastening said left upper portion to said right upper portion," without reciting any structure that could be used to perform the fastening function.

b. Interpreting the Scope of Means-Plus-Function Elements

(i) Scope-Narrowing Operation

If the athletic shoe claim above were construed on its face, without reference to the statutory language of 35 U.S.C. §112(f), one might conclude that the means element would read on (i.e., literally encompass) any and every possible structure in the universe that would perform the recited fastening function. Given the breadth of such a claim, it might be attacked as indefinite under 35 U.S.C. §112(b) (and possibly non-enabled under 35 U.S.C. §112(a)). However, because element (iv) is expressed in means-plus-function form, it must be interpreted in accordance with §112(f). Because this section operates to narrow the scope of the claim, as explained below, paragraph (f) saves the claim from indefiniteness.

The last clause of §112(f) mandates that a means element in a patent claim "shall be construed to cover the corresponding structure, material, or acts described in the specification and equivalents thereof." This is mandatory language, which requires that in order to interpret the scope of a means-plus-function element in a claim, reference to the written description must be made. The written description portion of the patent must disclose the "corresponding structure" (or corresponding material or acts) for the means recited in the claim. Failure to do so renders the claim indefinite under §112(b). As explained in *In re Donaldson Co.*,[168]

> [a]lthough paragraph six [of 35 U.S.C. §112] statutorily provides that one may use means-plus-function language in a claim, one is still subject to the requirement [of 35 U.S.C. §112, ¶2] that a claim "particularly point out and distinctly claim" the invention. Therefore, if one employs means-plus-function language in a claim, one must set forth in the

[168]16 F.3d 1189 (Fed. Cir. 1994) (*en banc*).

> specification an adequate disclosure showing what is meant by that language. If an applicant fails to set forth an adequate disclosure, the applicant has in effect failed to particularly point out and distinctly claim the invention as required by the second paragraph of section 112.[169]

As an example of corresponding structure, assume that the written description of the athletic shoe patent in the above example stated that "a pair of shoe laces can be used to detachably fasten the left upper portion of the shoe to the right upper portion," and that the drawings of the patent depicted the use of shoe laces. The recited means for fastening in element (iv) of the claim would be interpreted in accordance with the last clause of §112(f) as reading on the disclosed structure, that is, a pair of shoe laces, as well as any "equivalents thereof." The equivalents thereof, sometimes also referred to as statutory equivalents, need not be (and usually are not) explicitly disclosed in the patent. Determining just what types of items would qualify as equivalents thereof to the shoe laces would likely need to be resolved in litigation. For example, one might conclude that the statutory equivalents of the disclosed shoe laces are buttons, hooks and eyes, and zippers. This is considered a question of fact.[170]

(ii) Timing of Statutory Equivalents

But suppose that the athletic shoe patent had been granted prior to the invention of Velcro®. Would a later-developed athletic shoe that used a pair of Velcro® tabs as fasteners, instead of shoe laces, literally infringe the patent? The issue raised by this hypothetical is whether the statutory equivalents of a means element must be in existence at the time the patent is granted in order to be considered within the literal scope of the claim.

The Federal Circuit answered in the affirmative in *Al-Site Corp. v. VSI Int'l, Inc.*,[171] holding that "an equivalent structure or act under §112 for literal infringement must have been available at the time of patent issuance. . . ."[172] This rule seems correct from the standpoint of preserving the definiteness of the claim under 35 U.S.C. §112(b); it is difficult to see how a claim that literally encompassed technology not yet in existence could satisfy the statutory requirement for claims that "particularly point out and distinctly claim" the subject matter that the applicant regards as his invention.

[169] *In re Donaldson Co.*, 16 F.3d at 1195.

[170] *See* In re Hayes Microcomputer Prods., Inc. Patent Litig., 982 F.2d 1527, 1541 (Fed. Cir. 1992) (stating that the "determination of literal infringement [of a §112, ¶6 claim element] is a question of fact").

[171] 174 F.3d 1308 (Fed. Cir. 1999).

[172] *Al-Site Corp.*, 174 F.3d at 1320.

(iii) Presumptions

The threshold determination of whether a claim element should be treated as a means-plus-function element begins with examining the words used to draft the element.[173] The Federal Circuit recognizes a presumption that a claim element using the word "means" will be treated as a means-plus-function element under the sixth paragraph of 35 U.S.C. §112.[174] As explained above, such treatment results in limiting the literal scope of the element to the corresponding structure described in the specification and equivalents thereof. The Circuit also recognizes the opposite (or "negative") presumption; i.e., that a claim element lacking the word "means" is presumptively *not* a means-plus-function element.[175]

These presumptions should not be applied mechanically; the presence or absence of the word "means" in a claim element is not the only inquiry to be undertaken. As the Federal Circuit observed in a 2015 partial *en banc* decision, *Williamson v. Citrix Online, LLC*,[176] further addressed below, "the essential inquiry is not merely the presence or absence of the word 'means' but whether the words of the claim are understood by person of ordinary skill in the art to have a sufficiently definitely meaning as the name for structure."[177] In other words, even though the word "means" is used in a claim, the presumption that §112, ¶6 applies may be rebutted "if the claim limitation itself recites sufficient structure to perform the claimed function in its entirety."[178]

For example, the patent in suit in *TI Group Automotive Sys. (N. Am.), Inc. v. VDO N. Am., L.L.C.*,[179] covered an in-tank fuel

[173]The Federal Circuit views the determination of whether certain claim language invokes §112, ¶6 as an exercise in claim construction, and therefore a question of law subject to *de novo* review. Inventio AG v. ThyssenKrupp Elevator Ams. Corp., 649 F.3d 1350, 1356 (Fed. Cir. 2011) (citing Personalized Media Comm., LLC v. ITC, 161 F.3d 696, 702 (Fed. Cir. 1998)).

[174]*See* Rembrandt Data Techs., LP v. AOL, LLC, 641 F.3d 1331, 1340 (Fed. Cir. 2011) (stating that "[a] claim limitation that 'contains the word "means" and recites a function is presumed to be drafted in means-plus-function format under 35 U.S.C. §112, ¶6' ") (quoting Net MoneyIN, Inc. v. VeriSign, Inc., 545 F.3d 1359, 1366 (Fed. Cir. 2008)); TriMed, Inc. v. Stryker Corp., 514 F.3d 1256, 1259 (Fed. Cir. 2008) (stating that "[u]se of the word 'means' in claim language creates a presumption that §112 ¶6 applies") (citing Greenberg v. Ethicon Endo-Surgery, Inc., 91 F.3d 1580, 1583 (Fed. Cir. 1996)).

[175]*See* Personalized Media Comm., LLC v. Int'l Trade Comm'n, 161 F.3d 696, 703-704 (Fed. Cir. 1998) (stating that "the failure to use the word 'means' creates a presumption that §112, ¶6 does not apply") (citing Mas-Hamilton Grp. v. LaGard, Inc., 156 F.3d 1206, 1213 (Fed. Cir. 1998)).

[176]No. 2013-1130, 2015 WL 3687459 (Fed. Cir. June 16, 2015) (*en banc* as to part II.C.1 of opinion).

[177]*Williamson*, 2015 WL 3687459, at *6.

[178]Rembrandt Data Techs., LP v. AOL, LLC, 641 F.3d 1331, 1340 (Fed. Cir. 2011).

[179]375 F.3d 1126 (Fed. Cir. 2004).

assembly for fuel-injected vehicle engines. Independent claim 2 of TI Group's U.S. Patent No. 4,860,714 recited:

> 2. Apparatus for pumping fuel from a fuel tank to an engine comprising: . . . (d) pumping *means* for pumping fuel into the reservoir, said means being located within the reservoir in the region of the opening and including a nozzle and a venturi tube in alignment with the nozzle, the passage of fuel out of the nozzle and through the venturi tube causing fuel to be entrained through the opening into the interior of the reservoir; . . . .[180]

Applying the presumption, a district court interpreted the "pumping means" element as a means-plus-function element under 35 U.S.C. §112, ¶6 (2000).

The Federal Circuit in *TI Group* reversed, because the limitation recited not only the pumping means but also its structure, location, and operation. Specifically, the claim element recited the structure of the pumping means ("including a nozzle and a venturi tube in alignment with the nozzle"), its location ("being located within the reservoir in the region of the opening"), and the manner of its operation ("the passage of fuel out of the nozzle and through the venturi tube causing fuel to be entrained through the opening into the interior of the reservoir"). In this case, the presumption arising from the use of the word "means" was overcome by the recitation in the claim of the structure needed to perform the recited function of "pumping fuel into the reservoir." Moreover, the written description informed and supported the structure recited in the claims by referring to "[j]et pump 30 [which] includes nozzle 54 and venturi tube 58," the numbers corresponding to reference numerals in the patent's drawings.

The appellate court again concluded that a claim using the word "means" should not be read as a mean-plus-function claim in its 2015 decision, *Lighting Ballast Control LLC v. Philips Elecs. N. Am. Corp.* ("*Lighting Ballast III*").[181] On remand from the Supreme Court, the Circuit that the claim-recited phrase "voltage source means" was *not* governed by 35 U.S.C. §112, para. 6.[182] The patent in suit concerned an electronic ballast device used in fluorescent lamp fixtures to shield the fixture from destructive levels of current when the lamp was removed or failed.[183]

[180] *TI Group*, 375 F.3d at 1131.

[181] No. 2012-1014, 2015 WL 3852932 (Fed. Cir. June 23, 2015) ("*Lighting Ballast III*").

[182] *Lighting Ballast III*, 2015 WL 3852932, at *6.

[183] Claim 1 of Lighting Ballast's U.S. Patent No. 5,436,529 recited (emphasis added):

> 1. An energy conversion device employing an oscillating resonant converter producing oscillations, having DC input terminals producing a control signal and adapted to power at least one gas discharge lamp having heatable filaments, the device comprising:

As described elsewhere in this text, the Supreme Court in its landmark 2015 claim construction decision, *Teva Pharms. USA, Inc. v. Sandoz, Inc.*,[184] held that "that while the ultimate question of the proper construction of a claim is a legal question that this court reviews de novo, there may be underlying 'subsidiary' factual findings by the district court related to the extrinsic record that are reviewed for clear error."[185] In *Lighting Ballast,* a district court had relied on extrinsic evidence (i.e., expert and inventor testimony) to determine that "while the 'voltage source means' term does not denote a specific structure, it is nevertheless understood by persons of skill in the lighting ballast design art to connote a class of structures, namely a rectifier, or structure to rectify the AC power line into a DC voltage for the DC input terminals."[186]

After Supreme Court remand for reconsideration of the *Lighting Ballast II* decision in view of *Teva,*[187] the Federal Circuit in *Lighting Ballast III* affirmed the district court's decision concerning "voltage source means."[188] The district court had properly relied on extrinsic evidence, which supported a conclusion that the disputed phrase conveyed a defined structure to one of ordinary skill in the art. The Circuit deferred to the district court's factual findings, absent a showing of clear error, that a skilled artisan would understand that a rectifier was, "at least in common uses, the only structure that would provide 'a constant or variable magnitude voltage.' "[189] The district court was correct to conclude that "voltage source means" was not governed by §112, para. 6. Accordingly, the Circuit affirmed the district court on the "voltage source means" issue (and three other issues).

---

voltage source means providing a constant or variable magnitude DC voltage between the DC input terminals;

output terminals connected to the filaments of the gas discharge lamp;

control means capable of receiving control signals from the DC input terminals and from the resonant converter, and operable to effectively initiate the oscillations, and to effectively stop the oscillations of the converter; and direct current blocking means coupled to the output terminals and operable to stop flow of the control signal from the DC input terminals, whenever at least one gas discharge lamp is removed from the output terminals or is defective.

[184]135 S. Ct. 831 (2015). *Teva* is further addressed *infra* Chapter 9, Section B ("Patent Claim Interpretation").

[185]*Lighting Ballast III*, 2015 WL 3852932, at *3.

[186]*Lighting Ballast III*, 2015 WL 3852932, at *5.

[187]*See* Lighting Ballast Control LLC v. Philips Elecs. N. Am. Corp. ("*Lighting Ballast II*"), 744 F.3d 1272 (Fed. Cir. 2014) (*en banc*) (holding that claim construction is an issue entirely of law that Federal Circuit would review *de novo*), *cert. granted, judgment vacated sub nom.* Lighting Ballast Control LLC v. Universal Lighting Techs., Inc., 135 S. Ct. 1173; *abrogated by* Teva Pharm. USA, Inc. v. Sandoz, Inc., 135 S. Ct. 831 (2015). *Lighting Ballast II* is covered *infra* Chapter 9, Section B.6.a ("Federal Circuit's *De Novo* Standard of Review").

[188]*Lighting Ballast III*, 2015 WL 3852932, at *6. *See also infra* Chapter 9, Section B.6.c ("Federal Circuit Application of the *Teva* Standard").

[189]*Lighting Ballast III*, 2015 WL 3852932, at *5 (quoting district court).

Conversely, the Federal Circuit presumptively does *not* treat a claim element that *lacks* the word "means" as a means-plus-function element.[190] Nevertheless, such "means"-less elements may be interpreted as means-plus-function elements under certain narrow circumstances. For example, the patents in suit in *Welker Bearing Co. v. PHD, Inc.*[191] were directed to pin clamps that held a work piece securely in place during welding and other manufacturing processes. Claim 1 of Welker Bearing's U.S. Patent No. 6,913,254 recited "a locating and clamping assembly . . . characterized by a *mechanism for moving said [clamping] finger along a straight line into and out of said locating pin perpendicular to said axis A in response to said rectilinear movement of said locating pin*."[192] Notably, the quoted claim limitation did not include the word "means" but rather made use of the similarly generic word "mechanism."

Based on the lack of any structural context for "mechanism" in the language of the claim limitation, the Federal Circuit in *Welker Bearing* affirmed a district court's decision to treat it as a means-plus-function limitation. No adjective provided "mechanism" with a physical or structural component; the claim language merely recited the function of the "mechanism" (i.e., moving the clamping finger in response to movement of the locating pin). One of ordinary skill would have had to consult the specification to find any structural connotation for the recited "mechanism." The appellate court concluded that in the case at bar, "the unadorned term 'mechanism' is 'simply a nonce word or a verbal construct [i.e., a word coined for a particular situation] that is not recognized as the name of structure and is simply a substitute for the term "means for.'"[193]

[190]*See* Personalized Media Comm., LLC v. International Trade Comm'n, 161 F.3d 696, 703-704 (Fed. Cir. 1998) (stating that the use of the word "means" in a claim element creates a rebuttable presumption that §112, para. 6 applies, and conversely that the failure to use the word "means" also creates a rebuttable presumption that §112, para. 6 does not apply).

[191]550 F.3d 1090 (Fed. Cir. 2008).

[192]Emphasis added. Claim 1 in its entirety read:

> A locating and clamping assembly comprising:
> a body defining an internal cavity and an opening from said cavity to the exterior of said body;
> a locating pin disposed in said cavity and extending along an axis A out of said opening to a distal end;
> an actuator for moving said locating pin rectilinearly along said axis A into and out of said opening;
> at least one finger supported by said locating pin adjacent said distal end;
> said assembly characterized by a mechanism for moving said finger along a straight line into and out of said locating pin perpendicular to said axis A in response to said rectilinear movement of said locating pin.

Welker Bearing, 550 F.3d at 1093-1094 (emphasis added).

[193]*Welker Bearing*, 550 F.3d at 1096 (quoting Lighting World, Inc. v. Birchwood Lighting, Inc., 382 F.3d 1354, 1360 (Fed. Cir. 2004)). The treatment of "mechanism" as a means-plus-function limitation in *Welker Bearing* resulted in a finding of non-

A similar result obtained in the 2015 decision, *Williamson v. Citrix Online, LLC.*[194] In its second consideration of the case,[195] the Federal Circuit held that the "distributed learning control module" element of claim 8 of Williamson's U.S. Patent No. 6,155,840 ('840 patent), directed to methods and systems that implemented "virtual classroom" environments over the Internet, should be interpreted as a means-plus-function element under 35 U.S.C. §112, para. 6, despite the lack of the word "means" in the element.[196] The appellate court first observed that the entirety of the claim language to be considered was "distributed learning control module for receiving communications transmitted between the presenter and the audience member computer

---

infringement. The structure disclosed in the written description that corresponded to the "mechanism" was a rotating central post. The accused device "propel[led] clamping fingers in and out of the locating pin without any rotational movement." Because the patented rotational mechanism and the accused linear-moving mechanism were "substantially different," the Federal Circuit affirmed a district court's judgment that the latter did not literally infringe.

[194]No. 2013-1130, 2015 WL 3687459 (Fed. Cir. June 16, 2015) (*en banc* as to part II.C.1 of opinion).

[195]In its first review of the case, *Williamson v. Citrix Online, LLC*, 770 F.3d 1371 (Fed. Cir. 2014), the panel majority had concluded that the "module" term *did* recite sufficient structure to remain outside the purview of §112, para. 6. *See Williamson,* 770 F.3d at 1380.

[196]Claim 8 of Williamson's '840 patent recited:

> 8. A system for conducting distributed learning among a plurality of computer systems coupled to a network, the system comprising:
>
> a presenter computer system of the plurality of computer systems coupled to the network and comprising:
> a content selection control for defining at least one remote streaming data source and for selecting one of the remote streaming data sources for viewing; and
> a presenter streaming data viewer for displaying data produced by the selected remote streaming data source;
> an audience member computer system of the plurality of computer systems and coupled to the presenter computer system via the network, the audience member computer system comprising:
> an audience member streaming data viewer for displaying the data produced by the selected remote streaming data source; and
> a distributed learning server remote from the presenter and audience member computer systems of the plurality of computer systems and coupled to the presenter computer system and the audience member computer system via the network and comprising:
> a streaming data module for providing the streaming data from the remote streaming data source selected with the content selection control to the presenter and audience member computer systems; and
> a *distributed learning control module* for receiving communications a *distributed learning control module* for receiving communications transmitted between the presenter and the audience member computer systems and for relaying the communications to an intended receiving computer system and for coordinating the operation of the streaming data module.

Williamson, 2015 WL 3687459, at *2 (emphasis added by Federal Circuit).

systems and for relaying the communications to an intended receiving computer system and for coordinating the operation of the streaming data module." This "lengthy" passage was written "in a format consistent with traditional means-plus-function claim limitations." The claim language simply replaced the term "means" with the term "module" and recited three functions performed by the "distributed learning control module." The Federal Circuit noted that "module" is a "well-known nonce word [or coined word] that can operate as a substitute for 'means' in the context of §112, para. 6." It agreed with the district court that in claim 8, "module" was "simply a generic description for software or hardware that perform[ed] a specified function." The word "module" set forth "the same black box recitation of structure for providing the same specified function as if the term 'means' had been used."[197]

Nor did the prefix "distributed learning control" impart structure to the term "module." The Circuit in *Williamson* found "nothing in the specification or prosecution history that might lead [it] to construe the expression as the name of a sufficiently definition structure as to take the overall claim limitation out of the ambit of §112, para. 6." Nor did the claim recite how the "distributed learning control module" interacted with the other components of the claimed invention in a way that might inform one of the module's structural character.

Lastly, the fact that Williamson's expert Dr. Souri declared that he would know "exactly how to program" a computer to perform the recited functions after reading the '840 patent did not change the court's mind, because "the fact that one of skill in the art could program a computer to perform the recited functions cannot create structure where none otherwise is disclosed."[198]

Having determined that the claim element in question had to be interpreted under the limiting strictures of 35 U.S.C. §112, para. 6, the Federal Circuit looked in the '840 patent's specification for structure corresponding to the recited "coordinating" function of the "distributed learning control module." Finding no disclosure of such structure, the *Williamson* court affirmed the district court's judgment that claims 8-16 of the '840 patent were invalid for indefiniteness under 35 U.S.C. §112, para. 2.[199]

Importantly, although the merits of the 2015 *Williamson* appeal were decided by a three-judge panel,[200] the Federal Circuit also used

[197]*Williamson,* 2015 WL 3687459, at *8 (citing Ranpak Corp. v. Storopack, Inc., 168 F.3d 1316, 1998 WL 513598 (Fed. Cir. 1998) (unpublished decision)).

[198]*Williamson,* 2015 WL 3687459, at *9 (citing Function Media, L.L.C. v. Google, Inc., 708 F.3d 1310, 1319 (Fed. Cir. 2013)).

[199]*Williamson,* 2015 WL 3687459, at *11.

[200]Writing separately, Judge Reyna agreed with his panel colleagues on the merits that the recited "distributed learning control module" term should be construed under 35 U.S.C. §112, para. 6. However, Judge Reyna would have gone further than the *en banc* court; in his view, "we need to revisit our judicially-created §112, para. 6

Williamson as an *en banc* vehicle to lessen the burden of overcoming the "negative" presumption that a claim element that does not use the word "means" is not a means-plus-function element under §112, para. 6. In Part II.C.1 of the *Williamson* opinion, the Circuit went *en banc* to hold that while the negative presumption still existed, it was not to be considered a "strong" presumption as certain earlier Circuit decisions had characterized it.[201] Moreover, the *en banc* court overruled the "strict" language from those earlier opinions that had required that a means-less claim could be construed as a means-plus-function claim only if the claim element in question was "devoid of anything that c[ould] be construed as structure."[202] Judge Newman dissented from the *en banc* ruling.[203]

---

presumptions." *Williamson,* 2015 WL 3687459, at *7 (Reyna, J., concurring-in-part, dissenting-in-part, and offering "additional views").

[201]*See Williamson,* 2015 WL 3687459, at *7 (stating that "[h]enceforth, we will apply the presumption as we have done prior to *Lighting World* ..."), but requiring that the presumption be applied "without requiring any heightened evidentiary showing...." *Williamson,* 2015 WL 3687459, at *7.

[202]*Williamson,* 2015 WL 3687459, at *7 (*en banc*). Providing examples of its earlier cases with overly strict language, the Circuit observed that

> [i]n *Lighting World, Inc. v. Birchwood Lighting, Inc.*, 382 F.3d 1354, 1358 (Fed. Cir. 2004), we applied for the first time a different standard to the presumption flowing from the absence of the word "means" and held that "the presumption flowing from the absence of the term 'means' is a strong one that is not readily overcome" (emphasis added), citing as examples, *Al-Site Corp. v. VSI International, Inc.*, 174 F.3d 1308, 1318-19 (Fed. Cir. 1999) and *Personalized Media Communications*, 161 F.3d at 703-05. A few years later, we reiterated *Lighting World*'s characterization of the presumption as a "strong one that is not readily overcome" in *Inventio AG v. ThyssenKrupp Elevator Americas Corp.*, 649 F.3d 1350, 1358 (Fed. Cir. 2011). In *Flo Healthcare Solutions, LLC v. Kappos*, 697 F.3d 1367, 1374 (Fed. Cir. 2012), decided just a year after *Inventio*, we raised the bar even further, declaring that "[w]hen the claim drafter has not signaled his intent to invoke §112, ¶6 by using the term 'means,' we are unwilling to apply that provision *without a showing that the limitation essentially is devoid of anything that can be construed as structure*" (emphasis added), citing *Masco Corp. v. United States*, 303 F.3d 1316, 1327 (Fed. Cir. 2002), a case involving the different term "step for" and the unusual circumstances in which §112, para. 6 relates to the functional language of a method claim. Recently, in *Apple Inc. v. Motorola, Inc.*, 757 F.3d 1286, 1297 (Fed. Cir. 2014), we yet again observed that this presumption is " 'strong' and 'not readily overcome' " and noted that, as such, we have " 'seldom' held that a limitation without recitation of 'means' is a means-plus-function limitation," citing *Lighting World*, 382 F.3d at 1358, 1362, *Inventio*, 649 F.3d at 1356, and *Flo Healthcare*, 697 F.3d at 1374. Our opinions in *Lighting World, Inventio, Flo Healthcare* and *Apple* have thus established a heightened bar to overcoming the presumption that a limitation expressed in functional language without using the word "means" is not subject to §112, para. 6.

Williamson, 2015 WL 3687459, at *6 (*en banc*).

[203]In her view, the *en banc* ruling in *Williamson* effectively "eliminate[ed] the statutory signal of the word 'means.' " Judge Newman urged her colleagues to recognize that

c. *Distinguishing §112(f) Statutory Equivalents and the Doctrine of Equivalents*

A word of caution is in order here about potentially confusing terminology. The *literal* scope of a means-plus-function claim includes the statutory "equivalents thereof." In that sense, at least, the statutory equivalents of 35 U.S.C. §112(f) are not the same animal as the "equivalents" referred to in application of the judicially created **doctrine of equivalents**, which is addressed in a later chapter of this text.[204] As Professor Chisum has explained, "[u]nlike the doctrine of equivalents, which compares a patent *claim* with an accused product or process, Section 112/6 [post-AIA, §112(f)] entails a comparison of one structure, material or act (that in the specification) to another structure, material or act (that in a product or process alleged to be covered by the patent claim)."[205]

Despite these differences, the Federal Circuit has sanctioned the use of the same insubstantial differences test for equivalency under 35 U.S.C. §112, ¶6 as under the doctrine of equivalents.[206] Because one way of establishing insubstantial differences is to apply the classic tripartite "function, way, and result" test,[207] the Federal Circuit also has held that this test collapses to "way" and "result" when applied to §112, ¶6 claim elements.[208] This is because in order to have **literal infringement** of a means-plus-function claim, the function performed by the accused component must be *identical,* not merely insubstantially different, to the function recited in the claim. Thus, the "substantially identical function" part of the function-way-result test is not applicable when determining literal infringement of a means-plus-function claim.

> it is the applicant's choice during prosecution whether or not to invoke paragraph 6, and the court's job is to hold the patentee to his or her choice. This approach is clear, easy to administer by the USPTO in examination and the courts in litigation, and does no harm, for patent applicants know how to invoke paragraph 6 if they choose.

Williamson, 2015 WL 3687459, at *15 (Newman, J., dissenting). Judge Newman also dissented on the merits and would not have held that the claim-recited "distributed learning control module" fell under §112, para. 6.

[204]*See infra* Chapter 9 ("Patent Infringement"). The doctrine of equivalents permits a finding of patent infringement liability for accused devices that are not encompassed within the literal scope of a claim, but that differ from the claimed invention in merely insubstantial respects.

[205]5A-18A Donald S. Chisum, Chisum on Patents §18.03 (2008) (citations omitted).

[206]*See* Chiuminatta Concrete Concepts, Inc. v. Cardinal Indus. Co., 145 F.3d 1303, 1309 (Fed. Cir. 1998) (stating that "[t]he proper test is whether the differences between the structure in the accused device and any disclosed in the specification are insubstantial").

[207]*See* Graver Tank & Mfg. Co. v. Linde Air Prods., 339 U.S. 605, 608 (1950).

[208]*See* Al-Site Corp. v. VSI Int'l, Inc., 174 F.3d 1308, 1321 n.2.

The previous discussion has focused exclusively on the *literal* scope of a means-plus-function element in a claim. Can there be infringement of a claim drafted in means-plus-function format under the judicially created doctrine of equivalents? This is, in a sense, asking if a statutory equivalent can have a judicial equivalent. Some Federal Circuit judges have answered the question in the negative, objecting to the idea of the patentee getting a "second bite at the apple."[209] On the other hand, other opinions of the Federal Circuit recognize the possibility of infringement under the doctrine of equivalents when the equivalent is after-arising, that is, developed after the patent issued.[210] Yet other opinions recognize that infringement under the doctrine of equivalents also might be possible when the function of the accused component is only insubstantially different, but not identical to, the function recited in the means-plus-function claim element.[211] The case law development in this area is still in flux, and deserves close monitoring by those who draft and/or enforce patents having means-plus-function claims.

2. Product-by-Process Claims

The "product-by-process" claiming format is used primarily in claiming chemical and biotechnological inventions, although it is not limited to that subject matter. The product-by-process claiming technique was developed in Patent Office practice[212] as a way of claiming a product, such as a composition of matter or an article of manufacture, that could not be adequately identified by its structure (e.g., the structure was unknown and could not be determined). Rather, the only way of identifying the product was through a recitation of the process

[209]*See* Dawn Equip. Co. v. Kentucky Farms, Inc., 140 F.3d 1009, 1022 (Fed. Cir. 1998) (Plager, J., expressing "additional views") (asserting that under a proper understanding of 35 U.S.C. §112, ¶6, "the separate judicially-created doctrine of equivalents would have no application to those limitations drawn in means-plus-function form").

[210]*See* NOMOS Corp. v. BrainLAB USA, Inc., 357 F.3d 1364, 1369 (Fed. Cir. 2004) (observing that "[w]hen there is no literal infringement of a means-plus-function claim because the accused device does not use identical or equivalent structure,... the doctrine of equivalents might come into play when after-developed technology is involved"); *Chiuminatta*, 145 F.3d at 1310-1311 (holding that where accused device represents technology that predates claimed invention, "a finding of non-equivalence for §112, ¶6, purposes should preclude a contrary finding under the doctrine of equivalents").

[211]*See* Interactive Pictures Corp. v. Infinite Pictures, Inc., 274 F.3d 1371, 1381-1382 (Fed. Cir. 2001) (distinguishing *Chiuminatta* and explaining that "when a finding of noninfringement under 35 U.S.C. §112, paragraph 6, is premised on an absence of identical *function*, then infringement under the doctrine of equivalents is not thereby automatically precluded").

[212]Product-by-process claiming was permitted by the U.S. Patent Office as early as 1891. *See* In re Bridgeford, 357 F.2d 679, 682 (C.C.P.A. 1966).

by which it was made. The rationale for permitting product-by-process claiming was that "the right to a patent on an invention is not to be denied because of the limitations of the English language, and, in a proper case, a product may be defined by the process of making it. . . . [T]he limitations of known technology concerning the subject matter sought to be patented should not arbitrarily defeat the right to a patent on an invention."[213]

In examining claims for patentability (e.g., for novelty[214] and nonobviousness[215]), the USPTO interprets product-by-process claims as drawn to the product, and not limited by the process steps recited in the claim. The agency effectively ignores the process steps in examining such claims. For example, consider the following product-by-process claim:

A composition of matter X, made by a process comprising the steps of:

(a) obtaining Y,
(b) mixing Y with Z to form a mixture,
(c) heating the mixture to a temperature of 100 degrees C for 30 minutes,
(d) cooling the mixture to form a precipitate,
(e) recovering said precipitate, and
(f) isolating X from said precipitate.

The USPTO's practice in examining this claim for patentability would be to interpret it as a claim to the product X per se, not limited to X made by following the recited process steps (a) through (f). Thus, the USPTO will consider the claim anticipated (i.e., lacking novelty) if the prior art discloses the identical product X made by *any* process, whether that process comprises the steps recited in the claim, uses genetic engineering or nuclear fusion techniques, or employs any other methodology to produce X.

Heated controversy arose within the Federal Circuit in 1992 over the proper interpretation of product-by-process claims in litigation over infringement of issued patents. In 1991, the Federal Circuit held in *Scripps Clinic & Res. Found. v. Genentech, Inc.*[216] that because claims should be treated the same way in determining infringement

[213]*In re Bridgeford,* 357 F.2d at 682.

[214]*See infra* Chapter 4 ("Novelty, Loss of Right, and Priority Pre- and Post-America Invents Act of 2011 (35 U.S.C. §102)").

[215]*See infra* Chapter 5 ("The Nonobviousness Requirement (35 U.S.C. §103)").

[216]927 F.2d 1565 (Fed. Cir. 1991). The *Scripps Clinic* opinion was authored for the court by Judge Newman and joined by then–Chief Judge Markey and a federal district court judge sitting by designation.

or validity, a product-by-process claim in an issued patent in litigation should *not* be considered limited by the recited process steps.[217] In other words, according to *Scripps Clinic,* a federal district court should broadly interpret a product-by-process claim in the same manner as the USPTO would, by ignoring the process limitations.

The following year, however, a different panel of the Federal Circuit concluded that the *Scripps* panel had erred.[218] The panel in *Atlantic Thermoplastics Co. v. Faytex Corp.*[219] held that "process terms in product-by-process claims serve as limitations in determining infringement."[220]

Applying the *Atlantic Thermoplastics* rule to the product-by-process claim in the above example means that the claim has a significantly narrower scope and, hence, economic value. The patent owner seeking to establish literal infringement of the claim would need to prove not only that the accused infringer's product X was the same as that recited in the claim but also that the accused product X was made by the same process as that recited in the claim.[221]

Despite the clear conflict between the *Scripps Clinic* and *Atlantic Thermoplastics* decisions, and over the dissents of then–Chief Judge Nies, Judge Rich, Judge Newman, and Judge Lourie,[222] a majority of Federal Circuit judges refused to rehear the *Atlantic Thermoplastics* case *en banc*. While both decisions stood, they generated confusion and uncertainty for those enforcing patents containing product-by-process claims.[223]

The Federal Circuit eventually resolved the conflict in 2009 by deciding *en banc* a portion of its opinion in *Abbott Labs. v. Sandoz,*

[217]*See Genentech*, 927 F.2d at 1583 (holding that "[s]ince claims must be construed the same way for validity and for infringement, the correct reading of product-by-process claims is that they are not limited to product prepared by the process set forth in the claims").

[218]*See* Atlantic Thermoplastics Co. v. Faytex Corp., 970 F.2d 834, 838 n.2 (Fed. Cir. 1992) (asserting that "[a] decision that fails to consider Supreme Court precedent does not control if the court determines that the prior panel would have reached a different conclusion if it had considered controlling precedent," and concluding that *Scripps Clinic* decision was not controlling on this basis).

[219]*Atlantic Thermoplastics Co.*, 970 F.2d at 834. The *Atlantic Thermoplastics* opinion was authored for the court by Judge Rader and joined by Judge Archer and Judge Michel.

[220]*Atlantic Thermoplastics Co.*, 970 F.2d at 846-847.

[221]Whether an accused product X made by any other process would infringe is a question to be resolved under the doctrine of equivalents. *See infra* Chapter 9 ("Patent Infringement").

[222]*See* Atlantic Thermoplastics Co. v. Faytex Corp., 974 F.2d 1279 (Fed. Cir. 1992) (dissenting opinions from denial of rehearing *en banc*).

[223]*See* Ronald D. Hantman, *Why Not the Statute? Revisited*, 83 J. PAT. & TRADEMARK OFF. SOC'Y 685, 711 (2001) (describing trial courts' difficulties in determining which decision is controlling).

Inc.[224] Following the *Atlantic Thermoplastics* rule, the *en banc* majority in *Abbott Labs.* held that "process terms in product-by-process claims serve as limitations in determining infringement."[225] Because the accused product was made by a process different from that recited in Abbott's product-by-process claims, the Federal Circuit affirmed a district court's summary judgment of noninfringement.

The patent in suit in *Abbott Labs.* was directed to the antibiotic cefdinir in its crystalline form. Claim 1 of Abbott's U.S. Patent No. 4,935,507 recited the composition of matter crystalline cefdinir, characterized by a series of peaks at the diffraction angles in its powder X-ray diffraction pattern. Claims 2-5 of the Abbott patent recited the crystalline cefdinir product without any particular peak limitations, but "obtainable" through a series of process steps.[226] As a threshold matter, the Federal Circuit agreed with the district court that claims 2-5 were properly categorized as product-by-process claims.

The Federal Circuit then rejected patentee Abbott's argument that the district court had erred by following *Atlantic Thermoplastics* rather than *Scripps Clinic.* The Federal Circuit reviewed the "extensive support" it found in Supreme Court precedent for the *Atlantic Thermoplastics* rule that process terms limit product-by-process claims. It also cited pre-1982 regional circuit decisions applying the rule. Notably, the *Abbott Labs.* court also relied on the Supreme Court's 1997 watershed decision in *Warner-Jenkinson Co. v. Hilton Davis Chemical Co.,*[227] rendered several years after the Federal Circuit's conflicting decisions in *Scripps Clinic* and *Atlantic Thermoplastics*:

> [T]he Supreme Court has reiterated the broad principle that "[e]ach element contained in a patent claim is deemed material to defining the scope of the patented invention." *Warner-Jenkinson*, 520 U.S. at 19, 117 S. Ct. 1040. Although *Warner-Jenkinson* specifically addressed the

[224] 566 F.3d 1282 (Fed. Cir. 2009) (addressing Part III.A.2 of opinion *en banc*). Then-Chief Judge Michel and Judges Bryson, Gajarsa, Linn, Dyk, Prost, and Moore joined Part III.A.2, which was authored by Judge Rader. Judges Newman and Lourie dissented in separate opinions, with Judges Mayer and Lourie joining in Judge Newman's dissent. Judge Schall did not participate as a member of the *en banc* court.

[225] *Abbott Labs.*, 566 F.3d at 1293.

[226] For example, claim 5 of Abbott's '507 patent recited:

> 5. Crystalline 7-[2-(2-aminothiazol-4-yl)-2-hydroxyiminoacetamido]-3-vinyl-3-cephem-4-carboxylic acid (syn isomer) which is obtainable by dissolving 7-[2-(2-aminothiazol-4-yl)-2-hydroxyiminoacetamido]-3-vinyl-3-cephem-4-carboxylic acid (syn isomer) in an alcohol, continuing to stir the solution slowly under warming, then cooling the solution to room temperature and allowing the solution to stand.

Abbott Labs., 566 F.3d at 1286.

[227] 520 U.S. 17 (1997).

> doctrine of equivalents, this rule applies to claim construction overall. As applied to product-by-process claims, *Warner-Jenkinson* thus reinforces the basic rule that the process terms limit product-by-process claims. To the extent that *Scripps Clinic* is inconsistent with this rule, this court hereby expressly overrules *Scripps Clinic*.[228]

Responding to the dissenting opinions, the *en banc* majority in *Abbott Labs.* asserted that its decision in no way called into question the right of inventors to include product-by-process claims in their patents.[229] Rather, its decision "merely restate[d] the rule that the defining limitations of a claim — in this case process terms — are also the terms that show infringement."[230] The majority could not "simply ignore as verbiage the only definition supplied by the inventor."[231]

Because patentee Abbott Laboratories had conceded that its claims 2-5 were not literally infringed by the accused product of generic drug manufacturer Lupin Pharmaceuticals "if the product-by-process analysis is performed pursuant to *Atlantic Thermoplastics*,"[232] the Federal Circuit affirmed the district court's finding of no literal infringement. In view of their prosecution history, the product-by-process claims were not infringed under the doctrine of equivalents, either.[233] Nor was equivalency under the doctrine established by the U.S. Food and Drug Administration's decision that Lupin's generic product was bioequivalent to Abbott's approved drug product.[234]

[228] *Abbott Labs.*, 566 F.3d at 1293.

[229] *See Abbott Labs.*, 566 F.3d at 1293 (stating that "[t]his court's *en banc* decision in no way abridges an inventor's right to stake claims in product-by-process terms"). The court further opined that "[i]n the modern context . . . if an inventor invents a product whose structure is either not fully known or too complex to analyze (the subject of this case — a product defined by sophisticated PXRD technology — suggests that these concerns may no longer in reality exist), this court clarifies that the inventor is absolutely free to use process steps to define this product. The patent will issue subject to the ordinary requirements of patentability. The inventor will not be denied protection." *Id.* at 1294.

[230] *Abbott Labs.*, 566 F.3d at 1293.

[231] *Abbott Labs.*, 566 F.3d at 1294.

[232] *Abbott Labs.*, 566 F.3d at 1296.

[233] Claims 2-5 recited "crystalline" cefdinir made by a particular process. In view of the patent's prosecution history, the meaning of "crystalline" was limited to the "Crystal A" form of cefdinir; the patentee had effectively disclaimed the "Crystal B" form. Lupin's accused cefdinir product, the bulk of which comprised the "Crystal B" form, was outside any permissible scope of equivalents. (Whether the accused Lupin product contained some amount of the Crystal A form of cefdinir was not an issue on appeal.)

[234] *See Abbott Labs.*, 566 F.3d at 1298. The Federal Circuit explained that:

> [w]hile bioequivalency may be relevant to the function prong of the function-way-result test, bioequivalency and equivalent infringement are different inquiries. Bioequivalency is a regulatory and medical concern aimed at establishing that

3. Jepson *Claims*

The *Jepson* claiming format, which takes its name from a 1917 Patent Office decision,[235] is most frequently used in the claiming of mechanical inventions, but is not limited to that subject matter. A *Jepson* claim includes a preamble that begins with the word "in" and ends with the phrase, "an improvement comprising" or "the improvement comprising...." For example, the Federal Circuit considered the following claim, written in *Jepson* format, to a double-walled softball bat.

> *In* a hollow bat having a small-diameter handle portion and a large-diameter impact portion, *an improvement comprising* an internal structural insert defining an annular gap with an inside wall of the impact portion of the bat and the impact portion elastically deflectable to close a portion of the annular gap and operably engage the insert.[236]

Jepson claims are understood to impliedly admit that anything recited in the preamble of the claim is in the prior art.[237] Although preamble language in patent claims is not necessarily limiting, the language in a *Jepson* claim's preamble is generally considered to be limiting.[238] This is because the patentee's choice of a *Jepson* format is seen as an indication of intent to use the preamble to define, in part, the structural features of the claimed invention.

Thus in the above example claim, the applicant is impliedly admitting that a "hollow bat having a small-diameter handle portion and a large-diameter impact portion" is in the prior art. What is novel is the "improvement" portion of the claimed invention, in this case, the "internal structural insert." However, the right to exclude for which the patent is granted is defined by the entirety of the claim, that is,

---

> two compounds are effectively the same for pharmaceutical purposes. In contrast, equivalency for purposes of patent infringement requires an element-by-element comparison of the patent claim and the accused product, requiring not only equivalent function but also equivalent way and result. Different attributes of a given product may thus be relevant to bioequivalency but not equivalent infringement, and vice versa.

566 F.3d at 1298.

[235] *See* Ex parte Jepson, 1917 Dec. Comm'r Pat. 62, 243 Off. Gaz. Pat. Office 526 (1917).

[236] DeMarini Sports, Inc. v. Worth, Inc., 239 F.3d 1314, 1319 (Fed. Cir. 2001) (emphasis added to indicate *Jepson* claim format).

[237] An exception to this rule applies when the preamble recites the patentee's own prior work. *See* Reading & Bates Constr. Co. v. Baker Energy Res. Corp., 748 F.2d 645, 649-650 (Fed. Cir. 1984).

[238] *See* Epcon Gas Sys., Inc. v. Bauer Compressors, Inc., 279 F.3d 1022, 1029 (Fed. Cir. 2002).

the improvement in combination with the preamble elements.[239] Thus, in order to find infringement of a *Jepson* claim, every limitation of the claim, including the preamble, must be met in the accused device either literally or equivalently.[240]

4. Markush *Claims*

The *Markush* claiming format, which was officially sanctioned at least as early as a 1925 Patent Office decision,[241] is used primarily in claiming chemical and biotechnological inventions, although it is not limited to that subject matter. "*Markush* groups" are used to claim a class of chemical compounds in terms of a structural formula, where a given substituent of the compound can be selected from among a customized list (i.e., an artificial genus) of alternatives, each of which will result in a compound having the same asserted utility.[242]

For example, a *Markush* claim might read as follows:

> A composition of matter comprising C2H5-R, where R is selected from the group consisting of W, X, Y, and Z.

The *Markush* group recited in this claim lists all possible species of R in the claimed composition: W, X, Y, or Z. There is no set number of species that must be included in a *Markush* grouping. Moreover, it is permissible that the various species recited in a *Markush* group have different chemical or physical properties, so long as each one, when substituted in the claimed composition, results in a product having the same asserted utility.

For example, in *In re Harnisch*[243] the CCPA considered *Markush* claims to a class of dyes known as coumarin compounds. The court reversed the USPTO's rejection of the claims as drawn to "improper *Markush* groups" on the ground that the members of the groups were not "functionally equivalent." All of the enumerated compounds were dyes, the court explained, even though some of them were chemical

[239]*See* Pentec, Inc. v. Graphic Controls Corp., 776 F.2d 309, 315 (Fed. Cir. 1985) (stating that "[a]lthough a preamble is impliedly admitted to be prior art when a *Jepson* claim is used, . . . the claimed invention consists of the preamble in combination with the improvement").

[240]*See Epcon Gas*, 279 F.3d at 1029.

[241]*See* Ex parte Markush, 1925 Dec. Comm'r Pat. 126, 340 Off. Gaz. Pat. Office 839 (1925).

[242]*See* In re Driscoll, 562 F.2d 1245, 1249 (C.C.P.A. 1977) (explaining that "[i]t is generally understood that in thus describing a class of compounds an applicant is, in effect, asserting that the members of the *Markush* group do not fall within any recognized generic class, but are alternatively usable for the purposes of the invention, and therefore, regardless of which of the alternatives is substituted on the basic structure, the compound as a whole will exhibit the disclosed utility").

[243]631 F.2d 716 (C.C.P.A. 1980).

intermediates. The compounds within the *Markush* groups were "not repugnant to scientific classification,"[244] and were all part of a single invention, such that "unity of invention"[245] existed, making the *Markush* groups proper.

In some cases of *Markush* claiming, the USPTO may consider the enumerated members of the *Markush* group to be "independent and distinct" inventions. If this is the case, the agency may require that the applicant provisionally elect a single species for purposes of examination.[246]

5. Beauregard *Claims*

The *Beauregard* claiming format, taking its name from a 1995 Federal Circuit appeal captioned *In re Beauregard*,[247] is typically used to claim computer software-related inventions. Because of ongoing uncertainty concerning the patent-eligibility of software,[248] a *Beauregard* claim recites software embedded in hardware; that is, a tangible,

[244]In re Harnisch, 631 F.2d at 722.

[245]The phrase "unity of invention" has a well-recognized meaning in European patent practice. *See* European Patent Convention (2007), art. 82, *available at* epo.org/law-practice/legal-texts/html/epc/2016/ar82.html (providing that "[t]he European patent application shall relate to one invention only or to a group of inventions so linked as to form a single general inventive concept"). The CCPA in *Harnisch* referred to the "unity of invention" concept because in the court's view, "the term would be more descriptive and more intelligible internationally than is the more esoteric and provincial expression '*Markush* practice.'" *Harnisch*, 631 F.2d at 721.

[246]The MPEP provides in pertinent part:

> [Members of a *Markush* group are considered "independent and distinct"] where two or more of the members are so unrelated and diverse that a prior art reference anticipating the claim with respect to one of the members would not render the claim obvious under 35 U.S.C. 103 with respect to the other member(s). In applications containing a *Markush*-type claim that encompasses at least two independent or distinct inventions, the examiner may require a provisional election of a single species prior to examination on the merits. An examiner should set forth a requirement for election of a single disclosed species in a *Markush*-type claim. . . . Following election, the *Markush*-type claim will be examined fully with respect to the elected species and further to the extent necessary to determine patentability. If the *Markush*-type claim is not allowable, the provisional election will be given effect and examination will be limited to the *Markush*-type claim and claims to the elected species, with claims drawn to species patentably distinct from the elected species held withdrawn from further consideration.

United States Patent and Trademark Office, Manual of Patent Examining Procedure §803.02 (8th ed., 8th rev., 2010), *available at* http://www.uspto.gov/web/offices/pac/mpep/mpep.htm.

[247]53 F.3d 1583 (Fed. Cir. 1995).

[248]*See generally infra* Chapter 7 ("Potentially Patentable Subject Matter (35 U.S.C. §101)").

physical, computer readable medium such as a disk, a hard drive, or other type of data storage device. For example, in *Beauregard*, the patent applicant sought allowance of the following claim to object code embodied in a "computer usable medium" such as a floppy disk:[249]

> 1. An article of manufacture comprising:
> a computer usable medium having computer readable program code means embodied therein for causing a polygon having a boundary definable by a plurality of selectable pels on a graphics display to be filled, the computer readable program code means in said article of manufacture comprising:
> computer readable program code means for causing a computer to effect, with respect to one boundary line at a time, a sequential traverse of said plurality of selectable pels of each respective said boundary line;
> computer readable program code means for causing the computer to store in an array during said traverse a value of an outer pel of said boundary of said plurality of selectable pels for each one of a plurality of scan lines of said polygon; and
> computer readable program code means for causing the computer to draw a fill line, after said traverse, between said outer pels having said stored values, for each said one of said scan lines.

After the USPTO rejected the claim as unpatentable under the printed matter doctrine,[250] Beauregard appealed. Before the Federal Circuit heard oral argument in the case, however, the USPTO changed its policy. The agency withdrew its rejection and informed the Federal Circuit of its new position that "computer programs embodied in a tangible medium, such as floppy diskettes, are patentable subject matter under 35 U.S.C. §101 and must be examined under 35 U.S.C. §102 and 103."[251] The agency agreed with Beauregard that the printed matter doctrine was therefore inapplicable. Because it no longer had a case or controversy before it, the Federal Circuit dismissed the appeal

[249] *See* In re Beauregard, 53 F.3d 1583 (Fed. Cir. 1995) (order granting USPTO's motion to dismiss applicant Beauregard's appeal, vacating USPTO Board's decision that had rejected Beauregard's claims under the printed matter doctrine, and remanding case to USPTO for further proceedings in accordance with USPTO Commissioner's concession that "computer programs embodied in a tangible medium, such as floppy diskettes, are patentable subject matter under 35 U.S.C. §101"); *see also* U.S. Patent No. 5,710,578 (issued Jan. 20, 1998).

[250] The printed matter rejection originated with pre-1952 Act decisions of the CCPA, which declared that "the mere arrangement of printed matter on a sheet or sheets of paper does not constitute patentable subject matter." In re Sterling, 70 F.2d 910, 912 (C.C.P.A. 1934). More recently, the Federal Circuit considered "printed matter" in the context of a §103 obviousness challenge (§101 was not at issue) and stated that "[w]here the printed matter is not functionally related to the substrate, the printed matter will not distinguish the invention from the prior art in terms of patentability." In re Gulack, 703 F.2d 1381, 1385 (Fed. Cir. 1983).

[251] *Beauregard*, 53 F.3d at 1583.

without deciding whether *Beauregard*-type claims were in fact patent-eligible subject matter under §101.

After the Federal Circuit's 1995 dismissal of the *Beauregard* appeal, and in view of the USPTO's approval of such claims, patent claim drafters included *Beauregard*-type claims in software-related patent applications as standard practice.[252] They took the position that claiming software embedded in a tangible medium such as a computer disk made the invention a patent eligible "manufacture" or "machine" under 35 U.S.C. §101. The USPTO supported the practice. The USPTO Board in 2008 issued a decision reaffirming the agency's view that *Beauregard* claims were patent-eligible subject matter.[253] The agency's MANUAL OF PATENT EXAMINING PROCEDURE provided as of 2010 that "[w]hen functional descriptive material [defined as "data structures and computer programs which impart functionality when employed as a computer component"] is recorded on some computer-readable medium, it becomes structurally and functionally interrelated to the medium and will be statutory in most cases since use of technology permits the function of the descriptive material to be realized."[254]

More than 15 years after dismissing the appeal in *In re Beauregard* without deciding its merits, the Federal Circuit in 2011 issued a decision in *Cybersource Corp. v. Retail Decisions, Inc.*[255] that called the legitimacy of some *Beauregard* claims into serious question. In a nutshell, the appellate court reasoned in *Cybersource* that if a claimed method is not patent-eligible because it is merely an abstract idea under the Supreme Court's decision in *Bilski v. Kappos*,[256] then a *Beauregard*-type claim to a "computer-readable medium" containing computer program instructions to carry out the method is likewise not

[252]*See* Dolly Wu, *Joint Infringement and Internet Software Patents: An Uncertain Future?*, 91 J. PAT. & TRADEMARK OFF. SOC'Y 439, 483 (2009) (stating that "many patent prosecution practitioners already draft software claims in the manner of a *Beauregard* claim, referencing to a computer readable medium, which may or may not satisfy the 'machine' threshold").

[253]*See* Ex parte Bo Li, Appeal 2008-1213 (Bd. Pat. App. & Int. Nov. 6, 2008), *available at* https://www.bitlaw.com/source/cases/patent/Bo_Li.html (declining to support USPTO examiner's §101 rejection of applicant's claim 42, a *Beauregard*-type claim reciting "[a] computer program product, comprising a computer usable medium having a computer readable program code embodied therein, said computer readable program code adapted to be executed to implement a method for generating a report, said method comprising: [series of steps]").

[254]UNITED STATES PATANT AND TRADEMARK OFFICE, MANUAL OF PATENT EXAMINING PROCEDURE (MPEP) §2106.01 (8th ed., Rev. 8, July 2010) (citing In re Lowry, 32 F.3d 1579, 1583-1584 (Fed. Cir. 1994) (discussing patentable weight of data structure limitations in the context of a statutory claim to a data structure stored on a computer readable medium that increased computer efficiency)).

[255]654 F.3d 1366 (Fed. Cir. 2011).

[256]130 S. Ct. 3218 (2010). *Bilski* is examined *infra* Chapter 7, Section B.4 ("Business Methods").

patent-eligible. The Federal Circuit in *Cybersource* emphasized that it will look to the nature of the underlying invention, not the literal terminology of the claim at issue.

More particularly, Cybersource's U.S. Patent No. 6,029,154 was directed to a method and system for detecting fraud in a credit card transaction between a consumer and a merchant over the Internet. The invention addressed the specific problem of fraud detection in instances in which a consumer went online to purchase and download content from the Internet. Cybersource's patent disclosed a method of using "Internet address" information (i.e., IP addresses, MAC addresses, e-mail addresses, and so on) to determine whether an Internet address relating to a particular transaction was consistent with other Internet addresses that had been used in previous transactions using the same credit card.

The parties disputed the patentability of two claims of the Cybersource '154 patent. Claim 3 recited a method for verifying the validity of credit card transactions over the Internet.[257] Claim 2, written in *Beauregard* format, recited a computer readable medium containing program instructions for executing the method of claim 3.[258] A district court granted summary judgment of invalidity with respect to both

[257]Claim 3 of the '154 patent recited:

> 3. A method for verifying the validity of a credit card transaction over the Internet comprising the steps of:
>
> obtaining information about other transactions that have utilized an Internet address that is identified with the [ ] credit card transaction;
> constructing a map of credit card numbers based upon the other transactions and;
> utilizing the map of credit card numbers to determine if the credit card transaction is valid.

Cybersource, 654 F.3d at 1368 n.1.

[258]Claim 2 of the '154 patent recited:

> 2. A computer readable medium containing program instructions for detecting fraud in a credit card transaction between a consumer and a merchant over the Internet, wherein execution of the program instructions by one or more processors of a computer system causes the one or more processors to carry out the steps of:
>
> obtaining credit card information relating to the transactions from the consumer; and
> verifying the credit card information based upon values of plurality of parameters, in combination with information that identifies the consumer, and that may provide an indication whether the credit card transaction is fraudulent,
> wherein each value among the plurality of parameters is weighted in the verifying step according to an importance, as determined by the merchant, of that value to the credit card transaction, so as to provide the merchant with a quantifiable indication of whether the credit card transaction is fraudulent,
> wherein execution of the program instructions by one or more processors of a computer system causes that one or more processors to carry out the further steps of;

claims on the ground that they were not drawn to patent-eligible subject matter under 35 U.S.C. §101.

The Federal Circuit in *Cybersource* affirmed. The appellate court characterized the disputed claims as "broad and essentially purport[ing] to encompass any method or system for detecting credit card fraud which utilizes information relating credit card transactions to particular 'Internet address[es].' "[259] First addressing method claim 3, the Federal Circuit concluded that it was drawn to an "unpatentable mental process — a subcategory of unpatentable abstract ideas" that the Supreme Court held were not patent-eligible in *Bilski v. Kappos*. According to the Federal Circuit

> [a]ll of claim 3's method steps can be performed in the human mind, or by a human using a pen and paper. Claim 3 does not limit its scope to any particular fraud detection algorithm, and no algorithms are disclosed in the '154 patent's specification. Rather, the broad scope of claim 3 extends to essentially any method of detecting credit card fraud based on information relating past transactions to a particular "Internet address," even methods that can be performed in the human mind.[260]

Such "computational methods which can be performed entirely in the human mind" are not patent-eligible, the Federal Circuit explained, because they are the types of methods that embody the " 'basic tools of scientific and technological work' that are free to all men and reserved exclusively to none."[261] Moreover, claim 3 failed to meet either prong of the Federal Circuit's "machine or transformation" test, denominated by the Supreme Court in *Bilski v. Kappos* as a "useful and important clue" (although not a dispositive inquiry) for determining a process invention's patent-eligibility under §101.[262]

The *Cybersource* court then turned to the more controversial part of its decision, that which addressed the patent-eligibility of claim 2. The court observed that claim 2 recited "a so-called 'Beauregard claim,' "[263] and explained that a *Beauregard* claim "is a claim to a computer

---

> [a] obtaining information about other transactions that have utilized an Internet address that is identified with the credit card transaction;
>
> [b] constructing a map of credit card numbers based upon the other transactions; and
>
> [c] utilizing the map of credit card numbers to determine if the credit card transaction is valid.

Cybersource, 654 F.3d at 1368 n.1.

[259] *Cybersource*, 654 F.3d at 1368.

[260] *Cybersource*, 654 F.3d at 1372.

[261] *Cybersource*, 654 F.3d at 1373 (quoting Gottschalk v. Benson, 409 U.S. 63, 67 (1972)).

[262] *See Cybersource*, 654 F.3d at 1370-1371.

[263] *Cybersource*, 654 F.3d at 1373.

readable medium (e.g., a disk, hard drive, or other data storage device) containing program instructions for a computer to perform a particular process."[264] In the Federal Circuit's view, claim 2 recited "nothing more than a computer readable medium containing program instructions for executing the method of claim 3."[265] The court eschewed any *per se* rule that a *Beauregard* claim is automatically patent eligible under §101 because it recites hardware, rejecting Cybersource's "main argument . . . that coupling the unpatentable mental process recited in claim 3 with a manufacture or machine renders it patent-eligible."[266] The Federal Circuit stated its intention to look to the invention underlying the claims, rather than the literal terminology of the claims, when determining patent eligibility.[267]

In *Cybersource*, it was "clear" to the Federal Circuit that "the invention underlying both claims 2 and 3 is a method for detecting credit card fraud, not a manufacture for storing computer-readable information."[268] Invoking the CCPA's 1982 decision in *In re Abele*, the *Cybersource* court held it proper to place on the patentee a "burden to demonstrate that claim 2 is 'truly drawn to a specific' computer readable medium, rather than to the underlying method of credit card fraud detection."[269] Concluding that Cybersource did not satisfy that burden, the Federal Circuit treated claim 2 as a process claim for patent-eligibility purposes.

Analyzed as a claim to a process, claim 2 did not satisfy either prong of the Federal Circuit's machine or transformation test for §101 eligibility. Although the recitation in claim 2 of a computer readable medium would admittedly require that the process be performed on a computer, the "incidental use" of a computer to perform the "mental process" recited in claim 3 did not "impose a sufficiently meaningful limit on the claim's scope."[270] In sum, the "computer readable medium" limitation of claim 2 did not make an otherwise unpatentable method patent-eligible under 35 U.S.C. §101.

The import of *Cybersource* is uncertain and awaits further case law development. In the view of this author, the Federal Circuit's focus on an underlying "inventive concept," rather than the words used in the claims, contradicts basic notions of claims defining the scope of a

[264] *Cybersource*, 654 F.3d at 1373.
[265] *Cybersource*, 654 F.3d at 1374.
[266] *Cybersource*, 654 F.3d at 1374.
[267] *See Cybersource*, 654 F.3d at 1374 (stating that "[r]egardless of what statutory category ('process, machine, manufacture, or composition of matter,' 35 U.S.C. §101) a claim's language is crafted to literally invoke, we look to the underlying invention for patent-eligibility purposes").
[268] *Cybersource*, 654 F.3d at 1374.
[269] *Cybersource*, 654 F.3d at 1374-1375 (quoting In re Abele, 684 F.2d 902 (C.C.P.A. 1982)).
[270] *Cybersource*, 654 F.3d at 1375.

patentee's right to exclude and providing notice to the public of that right. Assuming that the USPTO amends its examination practices to incorporate the Federal Circuit's guidance in *Cybersource*, however, future patent applicants presenting *Beauregard* claims will no longer get a "free pass" on the threshold §101 patent-eligibility inquiry. In the language of *Cybersource*, they will have to convince the USPTO that the computer readable medium they claim is a sufficiently "specific" medium to qualify for patent protection.

Chapter 3

Disclosure Requirements (35 U.S.C. §112(a))

A. Introduction

1. The Statutory Framework

The three **disclosure** requirements for a U.S. patent application are found in the first paragraph of 35 U.S.C. §112 (titled "Specification"), which provides

> **(a) In General.** — The specification shall contain a *written description of the invention,* and of the manner and process of making and using it, in such full, clear, concise, and exact terms as to *enable* any person skilled in the art to which it pertains, or with which it is most nearly connected, to make and use the same, and shall set forth the *best mode* contemplated by the inventor or joint inventor of carrying out the invention.[1]

When patent attorneys speak of "the disclosure" or "the teaching" of a patent, they generally are referring to the information provided in the specification other than the claims (i.e., the "written description" portion of the patent, which may include drawings).[2] The italicized terms in the statutory language quoted above are understood as identifying three separate requirements for the disclosure of a patent, each

[1]35 U.S.C. §112(a) (eff. Sept. 16, 2012) (emphases added). Before implementation of the Leahy-Smith America Invents Act of 2011, the individual subparagraphs of 35 U.S.C. §112 were not designated by letter. What is designated as §112(a) after September 15, 2012, was commonly referred to as "§112, ¶1" or "§112, first paragraph" before that date. *See* 35 U.S.C. §112 (2006) (providing that "[t]he specification shall contain a written description of the invention, and of the manner and process of making and using it, in such full, clear, concise, and exact terms as to enable any person skilled in the art to which it pertains, or with which it is most nearly connected, to make and use the same, and shall set forth the best mode contemplated by the inventor of carrying out his invention").

[2]*See* In re Rasmussen, 650 F.2d 1212, 1214 (C.C.P.A. 1981) ("Disclosure is that which is taught, not that which is claimed.").

of which is discussed below: (1) **enablement**, (2) **best mode**, and (3) **written description of the invention**.

These disclosure requirements pertain to the informative quality of the patent *application* rather than the technical merits of the claimed invention. Even assuming that the claimed invention is novel,[3] nonobvious,[4] and useful,[5] if the patent application does not satisfy the disclosure requirements of the first paragraph of 35 U.S.C. §112 with respect to that invention, the applicant will not be granted a patent.

For example, the inventor in *In re Glass*[6] filed a patent application directed to methods and apparatus for artificially growing high-strength crystals used to reinforce refractory materials. Although the USPTO did not challenge the novelty or utility of the claimed invention, the Court of Customs and Patent Appeals (CCPA) affirmed the agency's conclusion that the application's disclosure was fatally deficient under the first paragraph of 35 U.S.C. §112. The application did not disclose essential process parameters such as temperature, pressure, and vapor saturation conditions that the inventor had conceded were necessary to form the crystals, either because the applicant was not himself in possession of that information or simply chose to maintain it as a trade secret. In either case, the inventor was not entitled to a patent on his invention because the application did not satisfy the enablement requirement of the first paragraph of 35 U.S.C. §112.[7]

Likewise, an issued patent, although entitled to a rebuttable presumption of validity that includes a presumption of validity under all three requirements of §112(a), may be invalidated in litigation if the challenger can establish, by clear and convincing evidence, that either the enablement requirement[8] or the written description of the invention requirement[9] was not, in fact, complied with.[10]

[3] *See* Chapter 4 ("Novelty, Loss of Right, and Priority Pre- and Post-America Invents Act of 2011 (35 U.S.C. §102)"), *infra*.

[4] *See* Chapter 5 ("The Nonobviousness Requirement (35 U.S.C. §103)"), *infra*.

[5] *See* Chapter 6 ("The Utility Requirement (35 U.S.C. §101)"), *infra*.

[6] 492 F.2d 1228 (C.C.P.A. 1974).

[7] *See id.* at 1233 (agreeing with USPTO that "the specification leaves too much to conjecture, speculation, and experimentation and is, therefore, insufficient in law to support any of the appealed claims").

[8] *See generally infra* Section B ("The Enablement Requirement").

[9] *See generally infra* Section D ("The Written Description of the Invention Requirement").

[10] *See* 35 U.S.C. §282 ("Presumption of validity; defenses"). The presumption of validity, and the challenger's burden to rebut it, are discussed in further detail in Chapter 10 ("Defenses to Patent Infringement"), *infra*. As discussed later in this chapter, the America Invents Act of 2011 eliminated the possibility of challenging a patent's validity on the ground of failure to satisfy one of the three disclosure requirements, namely, the best mode requirement. *See* 35 U.S.C. §282(b)(3)(A) (eff. Sept. 16, 2011); *see also infra* Section C.1 ("Best Mode Scale-Back by America Invents Act of 2011").

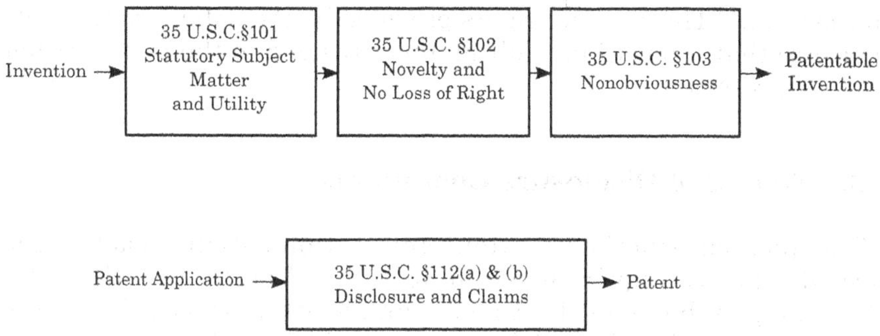

Figure 3.1

Pathway to Patentability

To summarize, obtaining a patent requires not only that the claimed *invention* meets various statutory criteria (detailed in later chapters of this text) but also that the *disclosure* of that invention provided in the patent application satisfies its own statutory criteria. These parallel requirements are depicted in Figure 3.1.

2. Disclosure as *Quid Pro Quo*

The disclosure requirements of 35 U.S.C. §112(a) effectively implement the *quid pro quo* of the patent system. In other words, the statute demands that the applicant's disclosure of her useful, novel, and nonobvious process, machine, manufacture, or composition of matter be of sufficient detail and clarity. In exchange for receiving that disclosure, which will ultimately be disseminated to the public, the U.S. government agrees to convey to the inventor a time-limited right to exclude others from practicing her invention.[11]

Of course, for various strategic and/or economic reasons an inventor may choose not to disclose her invention through patenting and instead maintain it as a trade secret.[12] Trade secret protection is significantly less powerful than patent protection, however, and subject to loss through the inventor's failure to maintain secrecy of the

[11]The nature of the "exclusive right," or right to exclude others, that a patent grants is further examined in Chapter 1 ("Foundations of the U.S. Patent System"), *supra*.

[12]*See* United States v. Dubilier Condenser Corp., 289 U.S. 178, 186 (1933) (recognizing that an inventor "may keep his invention secret and reap its fruits indefinitely," but that "[i]n consideration of its disclosure and the consequent benefit to the community, the patent is granted").

information.[13] The stronger rights provided by the patent system help to ensure that innovation is ultimately divulged to the public rather than suppressed.

3. Timing of Disclosure Compliance

The question whether a patent application satisfies each of the three disclosure requirements of 35 U.S.C. §112(a) (eff. Sept. 16, 2012) (i.e., enablement, best mode, and written description of the invention) is analyzed as of the application's filing date, not at some later date (such as the time of any subsequent infringement litigation in which invalidity under 35 U.S.C. §112(a) might be raised as a counterclaim or affirmative defense[14]). The patent application must comply with the disclosure requirements when it is filed.[15] Its teachings cannot be supplemented with new information (termed **new matter**[16])

[13]*See* Uniform Trade Secrets Act §1(4) (amended 1985) (defining trade secret as "information . . . that . . . is the subject of efforts that are reasonable under the circumstances to maintain its secrecy").

[14]*See* In re Hogan, 559 F.2d 595, 605-607 (C.C.P.A. 1977) (holding that post–filing date development by third party of novel form of generically claimed polymer did not render original disclosure nonenabling; what counts is whether claimed invention *as it was understood at the filing date* was enabled).

[15]*See* In re Glass, 492 F.2d 1228, 1232 (C.C.P.A. 1974) (holding that "application sufficiency under §112, first paragraph, must be judged as of its filing date").

[16]The addition of "new matter" is prohibited by 35 U.S.C. §132. That section "prohibits addition of new matter to the original disclosure. It is properly employed as a basis for objection to amendments to the abstract, specifications, or drawings attempting to add new disclosure to that originally presented." In re Rasmussen, 650 F.2d 1212, 1214-1215 (C.C.P.A. 1981).

The phrase "new matter" is

> a technical legal term in patent law — a term of art. Its meaning has never been clearly defined for it cannot be. The term is on a par with such terms as infringement, obviousness, priority, abandonment, and the like which express ultimate legal conclusions and are in the nature of labels attached to results after they have been reached by processes of reasoning grounded on analyses of factual situations. In other words, the statute gives us no help in determining what is or is not "new matter." We have to decide on a case-by-case basis what changes are prohibited as "new matter" and what changes are not.

In re Oda, 443 F.2d 1200, 1203 (C.C.P.A. 1971) (Rich, J.). The fundamental principle underlying the new matter prohibition is that "the invention described in the original patent [or application] must not be changed." *Id.* at 1204-1205.

The word "new" as used in "new matter" is not interpreted in its most literal extent. The CCPA explained that "[i]n a sense, anything inserted in a specification that was not there before is *new* to the specification but that does not necessarily mean it is prohibited as 'new matter.'" *Id.* at 1203 (emphasis added). For example, the *Oda* court held that the changing of "nitrous" to "nitric" did not introduce new matter. In preparation for filing in the United States, Oda's Japanese language patent application was translated into English. In so doing the phrase "nitric acid," present in several working

after the filing date in order to come into compliance with 35 U.S.C. §112(a).

Nor can the applicant rely on information provided by others, published after the application's filing date, to argue that the application's disclosure, supplemented by such publications, suffices to satisfy the statutory requirements by the time the application issues as a patent.[17] This is true even if the information is included in the disclosure of another's earlier-filed but not yet published patent application.[18] If an applicant cannot supply enabling information at the time when she files her patent application, then she is not yet in a position to file.[19]

The USPTO will allow patent applicants to satisfy the disclosure requirements in the first paragraph of 35 U.S.C. §112 by incorporating by reference (i.e., including a cross-reference to but not reproducing the actual text of) "essential material" from certain sources external to the patent application under examination, that is, either (1) a U.S. patent, or (2) a published U.S. patent application.[20] The applicant cannot incorporate essential material through reference to nonpatent publications or foreign patents or foreign patent applications (whether or not published). The intent in forbidding incorporation by reference through documents other than U.S. patents and published U.S. patent applications is to minimize the burden on the public to "search for and

---

examples of the written description, was mistranslated as "nitrous acid." After the patent had issued, Oda filed an application to reissue it in order to correct the translation error. The CCPA reversed the USPTO's rejection of the reissue claims as being based on a specification that contained prohibited new matter. The evidence of record showed that a skilled chemist would have recognized the error and realized that a translation error had occurred. *See id.* at 1206 (concluding that "one skilled in the art would appreciate not only the existence of error in the specification but what the error is . . . [a]s a corollary, it follows that when the nature of this error is known it is also known how to correct it.").

[17]*See Glass*, 492 F.2d at 1232 (citing "new matter" prohibition of 35 U.S.C. §132 and also noting that, in accordance with practice of treating application's filing date as date of constructive reduction to practice of the invention claimed therein, disclosure in application when filed cannot be said to evidence a completed invention if information to be found only in subsequent publications is needed for enablement).

[18]*See id.* at 1231 (affirming USPTO's refusal to allow Glass to rely on contents of four patents issued to others that were filed prior to Glass's filing date; although these patents would have qualified as prior art under 35 U.S.C. §102(e), as of their filing date they did "not show what is known generally to 'any person skilled in the art,' to quote from §112," because their content was not publicly available as of that date).

[19]*Id.* at 1232.

[20]*See* 37 C.F.R. §1.57(c) (2008). The patent or published application that is referred to must not itself incorporate essential material by reference. *See id.* In other words, there can be only one "layer" of incorporation by reference for essential material. "Essential material" includes material that is necessary to satisfy the enablement, best mode, and/or written description requirements of 35 U.S.C. §112(a) (eff. Sept. 16, 2012). *See id.*

obtain copies of documents incorporated by reference which may not be readily available."[21]

When an invention sought to be patented involves biological material (e.g., bacteria, DNA, plant tissue cultures, and seeds), it is customary for the applicant to deposit a sample of the material with a depository such as the American Type Culture Collection (ATCC).[22] Such a deposit is necessary (not optional) if the biological material cannot be sufficiently described in words to satisfy the disclosure requirements in the first paragraph of §112.[23] In *In re Lundak,*[24] the Federal Circuit held that even though Lundak deposited his sample (of a claimed new human cell line) with the ATCC seven days after the filing date of his patent application, he had not violated the new matter prohibition. The court observed that as of his application filing date, Lundak had already deposited samples of his cell line with colleagues at the University of California and elsewhere. This established a constructive reduction to practice of the invention as of the filing date. Had the USPTO needed to examine the cell line during the pendency of Lundak's application, the agency could have requested a sample from Lundak under 35 U.S.C. §114.[25]

The Federal Circuit held that it was "not material whether this request [would be] filled directly by the applicant, or on the instructions of the applicant by a third person to whom the applicant has entrusted the specimen."[26] In sum, the disclosure requirements of §112, ¶1 do "not require the transfer of a sample of the invention to an independent depository prior to the filing date of the patent

[21]*See* UNITED STATES PATENT AND TRADEMARK OFFICE, MANUAL OF PATENT EXAMINING PROCEDURE §608.01(p) (9th ed., rev. Jan. 2018), *available at* https://www.uspto.gov/web/offices/pac/mpep/index.html. *See also* In re Hawkins, 486 F.2d 569, 572 (C.C.P.A. 1973) (quoting USPTO Board of Appeals' opinion as stating that "[w]hat is available to a foreign patent office is not necessarily available to the United States Patent Office. It may be that such material may never be made available to the United States Patent Office."). The *Hawkins* court ultimately reversed the USPTO's decision that the applicant's post-filing addition to the application of the information originally incorporated by reference from certain British patent applications was a prohibited addition of "new matter" after the filing date. The court found that "at least so much of the British applications as dealt with the contemplated utility for the present products . . . is *not* new matter within the meaning of 35 U.S.C. 132. It was identified and specifically referred to for that information in the U.S. application *as filed*." *Id.* at 575.

[22]For more information on patent deposits with the ATCC, *see Patent Depository*, http://www.atcc.org/DepositServices/PatentDepository/tabid/237/Default.aspx (2014).

[23]The USPTO's rules on biological deposits are extensive and beyond the scope of this book. Interested readers should consult 37 C.F.R. §§1.801-1.809.

[24]773 F.2d 1216 (Fed. Cir. 1985).

[25]Section 114 of 35 U.S.C. provides in part that "[w]hen the invention relates to a composition of matter, the Director may require the applicant to furnish specimens or ingredients for the purpose of inspection or experiment."

[26]*Lundak*, 773 F.2d at 1222.

application."[27] Lundak's initial deposit with university colleagues and later deposit with the ATCC satisfied the requirements of USPTO access to a sample of Lundak's cell line throughout his application's pendency.[28]

Under post-America Invents Act of 2011 (AIA) rules, the date at which an application's compliance with the §112 disclosure requirements is measured is the same date as that used for the determination of novelty and nonobviousness, that is, the effective filing date of the claimed invention.[29] Under pre-AIA rules, however, the date at which compliance with the first paragraph of §112 is evaluated may differ from the date on which novelty and nonobviousness are evaluated. Because our pre-AIA rules are based on the United States' historic first-to-invent priority system,[30] the novelty and nonobviousness of a pre-AIA invention are evaluated as of its "invention date."[31] Although the USPTO initially takes the applicant's filing date as the presumptive invention date under a theory of **constructive reduction to practice**,[32] an earlier actual invention date may be established for pre-AIA inventions by means of appropriate evidentiary submissions.[33]

[27] *Id.*

[28] A second important requirement for deposits of biological materials is that the public be able to access the material after grant of the patent. Lundak's ATCC deposit, properly identified in his specification, met this requirement. More particularly, a biological deposit must be stored under an agreement with a depository which ensures that the material will be "available beyond the enforceable life of the patent for which the deposit was made." 37 C.F.R. §1.806 ("Term of Deposit").

[29] *See* 35 U.S.C. §100(i)(1) (eff. Mar. 16, 2013) (defining term "effective filing date" for a "claimed invention in a patent or application for patent"); *see also* 35 U.S.C. §102 (eff. Mar. 16, 2013) (repeatedly referring to the "effective filing date of the claimed invention"); 35 U.S.C. §103 (eff. Mar. 16, 2013) (referring to the "effective filing date of a claimed invention").

[30] *See generally infra* Chapter 4, Part II ("Novelty, Loss of Right, and Priority Pre- and Post-America Invents Act of 2011").

[31] *See* 35 U.S.C. §§102(a), (e), (g) (2006); 35 U.S.C. §103 (2006). In this sense, "novelty" is distinct from "loss of right" under 35 U.S.C. §102(b) (2006), which evaluates the status of an invention's introduction into the public domain as of a date that is one year before the application filing date. "Invention date" is defined *infra* Chapter 4, Section G.3.

[32] A "constructive reduction to practice" occurs when an inventor files a patent application that discloses his invention in compliance with the first paragraph of 35 U.S.C. §112. The inventor need not have built a prototype or constructed any samples of his invention in order to constructively reduce it to practice, so long as he can provide a sufficient disclosure of the invention in his patent application. In contrast, an **actual reduction to practice** involves constructing a physical embodiment of the invention that works for its intended purpose.

[33] Chapter 4, Section O, *infra*, describes the pre-AIA practice of "antedating" or "swearing behind" a prior art reference by filing an affidavit with the USPTO in accordance with 37 C.F.R. §1.131.

B. The Enablement Requirement

The enablement requirement is grounded in the Patent Act's mandate that

> The specification shall contain a written description of the invention, and of the manner and process of making and using it, in such full, clear, concise, and exact terms as to *enable* any person skilled in the art to which it pertains, or with which it is most nearly connected, to make and use the same. . . .[34]

Thus, the enablement provision specifies that an inventor must disclose both "how to make" the invention as well as "how to use" it. For example, if the claimed invention is a new chemical compound, the application must include an enabling disclosure of how to synthesize the compound, as well as reveal how the compound is used (e.g., in the form of a therapeutic composition to be administered to humans with a certain disease).

The ultimate goal of the enablement requirement is to put the public in effective "possession" of the invention, by providing to persons of ordinary skill in the art a detailed description of how to make and use the invention. Once the patent expires, and with it the patentee's right to exclude others, these persons should be in a position to make and use the invention without "undue experimentation" (discussed below). The enabling disclosure thus provides a type of a blueprint that such persons can follow once the patent expires, and they are free to make and use the invention without liability.

The "how to use" requirement of 35 U.S.C. §112(a) (eff. Sept. 16, 2012) is closely tied to the utility requirement of 35 U.S.C. §101, discussed later in this text.[35] If an inventor does not know what the utility (or usefulness) of her invention is, then logically, she cannot describe how to use the invention.[36]

1. Undue Experimentation

Case law has engrafted an *undue experimentation* qualifier onto the enablement requirement as set forth in 35 U.S.C. §112(a) (eff. Sept. 16, 2012). A patent application will be considered enabling so long as the disclosure permits the hypothetical person skilled in the art to make

[34] 35 U.S.C. §112(a) (eff. Sept. 16, 2012) (emphasis added).

[35] *See* Chapter 6 ("The Utility Requirement (35 U.S.C. §101)"), *infra*.

[36] *See* In re Brana, 51 F.3d 1560, 1564 (Fed. Cir. 1995) (noting that "[o]bviously, if a claimed invention does not have utility, the specification cannot enable one to use it").

and use the invention "without undue experimentation."[37] That the art worker might have to conduct *some* experimentation in order to make and use the invention as broadly as it is claimed is not fatal; only when the degree of experimentation becomes *undue* has the patent application failed to meet the enablement requirement.[38]

For example, the experimentation necessary to carry out a patented numerical control system for machine tools in *White Consol. Indus., Inc. v. Vega Servo-Control, Inc.*,[39] was sufficiently burdensome that the Federal Circuit affirmed a district court's holding of invalidity based on noncompliance with the enablement requirement. The record reflected that the claimed system could be carried out only by obtaining access to software maintained as a trade secret or independently writing software code that would have required 1.5 to 2 person-years of effort.[40]

The Federal Circuit contrasted the undue experimentation required in *White Consol. Indus.* with the "considerable direction and guidance" provided by the specification of the patent in suit in *PPG Indus., Inc. v. Guardian Indus. Corp.*[41] PPG's patent was directed to solar control glass for automobiles. Its specification described "in ample detail" how to make and use the invention with respect to seven specific embodiments set forth in experimental examples. Validity challenger Guardian focused on a software error that PPG had discovered in its glass testing equipment. Due to that error, the computations of ultraviolet transmittance in each of the patent's examples were off by 3 percent. Although the error made it appear that commercial production of a glass composition satisfying certain transmittance limitations of the claims would be difficult, the Federal Circuit concluded that the error did not violate the enablement requirement. The appellate court highlighted a district court's finding that PPG's calculation error was "harmless, inconsequential, and easily detectable by anyone who was skilled in the art of processing solar controlled glass."[42] In light of the guidance provided by PPG's specification, the Federal Circuit concluded that the case before it was "quite different from those in which

[37]*See* In re Wands, 858 F.2d 731, 737 (Fed. Cir. 1988) (recognizing that the phrase "without undue experimentation" is nonstatutory).

[38]*Id.* at 736-737. For example, the quantity of experimentation necessary to carry out the patented numerical control system for machine tools in *White Consol. Indus., Inc. v. Vega Servo-Control, Inc.*, 713 F.2d 788 (Fed. Cir. 1983), was sufficiently high that the Federal Circuit affirmed a district court's holding of invalidity based on noncompliance with the enablement requirement. The record reflected that the claimed system could be carried out only by (1) obtaining access to software maintained as a trade secret, or (2) independently writing software code that would have required 1.5-2 person-years of effort. *See id.* at 790-792.

[39]713 F.2d 788 (Fed. Cir. 1983).

[40]*See White Consol. Indus.*, 713 F.2d at 790-792.

[41]75 F.3d 1558 (Fed. Cir. 1996).

[42]*PPG Indus.*, 75 F.3d at 1564.

enablement has been found lacking because of the need for 'undue experimentation.'"[43]

In a 2013 decision, *Cephalon, Inc. v. Watson Pharms., Inc.*,[44] the Federal Circuit reversed a district court's judgment of invalidity for failure to satisfy the enablement requirement where the proffered evidence of undue experimentation in carrying out a patented method of drug delivery was primarily the accused infringer's expert's "[u]nsubstantiated statements indicating that [the required] experimentation would be 'difficult' and 'complicated.'"[45] Although the district court had accorded credibility to the expert, the Federal Circuit determined that his testimony, particularly his "*ipse dixit* statements,"[46] was "largely unsupported, and therefore, carrie[d] little weight in this analysis."[47] The expert's opinion that carrying out the claimed invention would be "difficult" and "complicated" could not, as a matter of law, be "enough to constitute clear and convincing evidence" required to invalidate an issued patent.[48]

A patent application need not disclose what is well known in the art;[49] otherwise, patent documents would become product manufacturing specifications, which they are not intended to be. For example, "extensive experimentation does not necessarily render the experiments unduly extensive where the experiments involve repetition of known or commonly used techniques."[50] On the other hand, failure to enable the novel aspects or features of an invention can be fatal.[51]

[43]*PPG Indus.*, 75 F.3d at 1565 (citing White Consol. Indus., Inc. v. Vega Servo-Control, Inc., 713 F.2d 788, 790-792 (Fed. Cir. 1983); In re Ghiron, 442 F.2d 985, 992 (C.C.P.A. 1971)).

[44]707 F.3d 1330 (Fed. Cir. 2013).

[45]*Cephalon*, 707 F.3d at 1339.

[46]*Cephalon*, 707 F.3d at 1338.

[47]*Cephalon*, 707 F.3d at 1338.

[48]*Cephalon*, 707 F.3d at 1338.

[49]*Wands*, 858 F.2d at 735.

[50]Cephalon, Inc. v. Watson Pharms., Inc., 707 F.3d 1330, 1338-1339 (Fed. Cir. 2013) (citing Johns Hopkins Univ. v. CellPro, Inc., 152 F.3d 1342, 1360 (Fed. Cir. 1998)). "[T]he focus 'is not merely quantitative, since a considerable amount of experimentation is permissible, if it is merely routine, or if the specification in question provides a reasonable amount of guidance. . . .'" *Cephalon,* 707 F.3d at 1339 (quoting PPG Indus., Inc. v. Guardian Indus., Corp., 75 F.3d 1558, 1564 (Fed. Cir. 1996) (citation and quotation omitted)).

[51]*See* ALZA Corp. v. Andrx Pharms., LLC, 603 F.3d 935, 941 (Fed. Cir. 2010) (affirming district court's judgment invalidating pharmaceutical patent for failure to enable full scope of claimed method of treatment; patentee could not "simply rely on the knowledge of a person of ordinary skill to serve as a substitute for the missing information in the specification."); *cf. ALZA Corp.*, 603 F.3d at 939 (noting accused infringer's argument that "what one of the proper skill in the art knows cannot substitute for disclosure of novel aspects of the invention. . . .").

Whether the degree of experimentation needed to reproduce the claimed invention has become undue, meaning that the enablement requirement has not been satisfied, turns on the application of a number of factors set forth by the Federal Circuit in *In re Wands,*[52] including

(1) the quantity of experimentation necessary;
(2) the amount of direction or guidance presented;
(3) the presence or absence of working examples;
(4) the nature of the invention;
(5) the state of the prior art;
(6) the relative skill of those in the art;
(7) the predictability or unpredictability of the art; and
(8) the breadth of the claims.[53]

Several of these factors are addressed individually below. The *Wands* factors should be analyzed by the USPTO examiner during *ex parte* prosecution of pending patent applications, as well as by the courts in litigation challenging the validity of issued patents on non-enablement grounds. Not every *Wands* factor need be reviewed in every enablement determination, however; the factors are considered "illustrative, not mandatory."[54] Given the facts of a particular case, some factors may be more relevant than others.[55]

The Federal Circuit regards compliance with the enablement requirement, and in turn compliance with the requirement that the experimentation required to make and use an invention not be undue, as questions of law.[56] The Federal Circuit reviews these ultimate questions *de novo.* Because the underlying *Wands* factors are factual in nature, however, the individual factors are reviewed for clear error if found by a district court[57] (rather than a jury, the fact findings of

[52]*Wands,* 858 F.2d at 731.

[53]*Id.* at 737 (citing In re Forman, 230 U.S.P.Q. 546, 547 (Bd. Pat. App. & Int. 1986)).

[54]Amgen, Inc. v. Chugai Pharm. Co., 927 F.2d 1200, 1213 (Fed. Cir. 1991).

[55]The ultimate question of whether a disclosure is enabling under the first paragraph of 35 U.S.C. §112 is a question of law that the Federal Circuit reviews *de novo*; factual findings made on the various underlying *Wands* factors are reviewed in accordance with the "clearly erroneous" standard for bench trials and with the "unsupported by substantial evidence" standard for jury trials (or in the USPTO).

[56]*See* Enzo Biochem, Inc. v. Calgene, Inc., 188 F.3d 1362, 1369 (Fed. Cir. 1999) (stating that "[w]hether undue experimentation would have been required to make and use an invention, and thus whether a disclosure is enabling under 35 U.S.C. §112, ¶1, is a question of law that we review *de novo*").

[57]*See* Cephalon, Inc. v. Watson Pharms., Inc., 707 F.3d 1330, 1336 (Fed. Cir. 2013) (stating on review of bench trial judgment in Hatch-Waxman litigation that "[e]nablement is a question of law that we review without deference, based on underlying factual inquiries that we review for clear error") (citing MagSil Corp. v. Hitachi Global Storage Techs., Inc., 687 F.3d 1377, 1380 (Fed. Cir. 2012)); *Enzo Biochem*, 188 F.3d at

which would be reviewed under the "unsupported by substantial evidence" standard[58]).

2. *Wands* Factor: Predictable Versus Unpredictable Inventions

The enablement analysis is inherently fact-specific and differs in every case. But one *Wands* factor very often central to the inquiry is whether the invention is considered to be within a "predictable" or "unpredictable" technology.[59] In general, inventions in the mechanical and electrical arts are considered to be predictable. Based on generally well-understood laws of physics, thermodynamics, and other basic scientific principles, if one embodiment of the invention is adequately described, then we can predict fairly easily how other embodiments within the scope of the claimed invention could be made and used.[60]

1369 (reviewing district court's judgment, following bench trial, of invalidity for failure to enable patented genetic antisense technology, and stating that "[w]hether undue experimentation would have been required to make and use an invention, and thus whether a disclosure is enabling under 35 U.S.C. §112, ¶1, is a question of law that we review *de novo*, based on underlying factual inquiries that we review for clear error").

[58]*See* Koito Mfg. Co., Ltd. v. Turn-Key-Tech, LLC, 381 F.3d 1142, 1149 (Fed. Cir. 2004) (stating in appeal from jury verdict of invalidity that "[e]nablement is a matter of law that we review without deference; however, this Court reviews the factual underpinnings of enablement for substantial evidence.") (citing BJ Servs. Co. v. Halliburton Energy Servs., Inc., 338 F.3d 1368, 1371-1372 (Fed. Cir. 2003)).

[59]*See* In re Fisher, 427 F.2d 833 (C.C.P.A. 1970). The CCPA, in an oft-quoted passage from *Fisher*, stated that:

> It is apparent that such an inventor should be allowed to dominate the future patentable inventions of others where those inventions were based in some way on his teachings. Such improvements, while unobvious from his teachings, are still within his contribution, since the improvement was made possible by his work. It is equally apparent, however, that he must not be permitted to achieve this dominance by claims which are insufficiently supported and hence not in compliance with the first paragraph of 35 U.S.C. §112. That paragraph requires that the scope of the claims must bear a *reasonable correlation* to the scope of enablement provided by the specification to persons of ordinary skill in the art. In cases involving *predictable* factors, such as mechanical or electrical elements, a single embodiment provides broad enablement in the sense that, once imagined, other embodiments can be made without difficulty and their performance characteristics predicted by resort to known scientific laws. In cases involving *unpredictable* factors, such as most chemical reactions and physiological activity, the scope of enablement obviously varies inversely with the degree of unpredictability of the factors involved.

Id. at 839 (emphases added).

[60]Exceptions to this general rule exist, even in the mechanical arts. For example, the court in *Liebel-Flarsheim Co. v. Medrad, Inc.*, 481 F.3d 1371 (Fed. Cir. 2007), rejected the patentee's argument that its disclosure of a single embodiment enabled a broader mechanical claim. Two of Liebel's patents in suit were directed to power injectors with

For example, consider a mechanical invention claimed as "a widget comprising part A attached to part B by means of a fastener." If the patent application discloses that A can be satisfactorily attached to B by means of a common nail, we can predict that other combinations employing a screw, glue, or Velcro as fasteners would also probably work. At a minimum, a person of ordinary skill in the art of widgets could probably evaluate the feasibility of such alternatives without undue experimentation.

This predictive assumption about alternative embodiments is generally not made in the case of inventions in the chemical and biotechnological arts. In these technologies, at least certain aspects of which are generally considered unpredictable, a minor change in the physical structure of a molecule or compound can result in major changes in properties and functions. In order to be enabling, a patent application directed to these types of inventions must provide a correspondingly greater degree of how-to-make and how-to-use information, in contrast with the disclosure of a simple mechanical device like the widget example above.[61] Exceptions to this rule may be recognized, of course,

---

replaceable syringes capable of withstanding high pressures for delivering a contrast agent to patients. The as-filed claims required a pressure jacket in front of the opening that received the syringe, but the claims were thereafter amended to remove the pressure jacket limitation. During litigation challenging the validity of the patents, Liebel contended that because it had undisputedly provided an enabling disclosure of its preferred embodiment (i.e., an injector with a pressure jacket), it had sufficiently enabled the full scope of its issued claims (i.e., encompassing injectors both with or without a pressure jacket). Affirming the district court, the Federal Circuit rejected Liebel's argument. The appellate court observed that Liebel's patent specifications depicted only jacketed injectors, and in fact "taught away" from jacketless injectors by characterizing them as "impractical." *See id.* at 1379. The Federal Circuit concluded that undue experimentation would have been required of a person of ordinary skill to make the jacketless injectors, based on testimony by the inventors that their own experiments with such injectors failed. As a result, the inventors deemed a jacketless system "too risky" for further development. Noting the irony of invalidation for non-enablement on the heels of Liebel's earlier, successful argument for a broad claim interpretation, the Federal Circuit repeated the well-known warning "beware of what one asks for."

[61]The Federal Circuit confronted an "unpredictable art" in one of the court's watershed biotechnology cases, *Amgen, Inc. v. Chugai Pharm. Co.*, 927 F.2d 1200 (Fed. Cir. 1991). There the Federal Circuit affirmed the trial court's conclusion that Amgen's generic claims, directed to purified and isolated DNA sequences encoding erythropoietin (EPO, a protein that stimulates the production of red blood cells) and host cells transformed or transfected with a DNA sequence, were invalid because the specification did not provide an enabling disclosure commensurate with the broad scope of the claims. The claims "cover[ed] all possible DNA sequences that will encode any polypeptide having an amino acid sequence 'sufficiently duplicative' of EPO to possess the property of increasing production of red blood cells," *id.* at 1212, and thus, "the number of claimed DNA encoding sequences that can produce an EPO-like product is potentially enormous," the Federal Circuit explained. *Id.* at 1213. Noting the trial court's finding that the technology at issue lacked predictability, *id.*, the Federal Circuit concluded its discussion of enablement as follows:

as originally unpredictable technologies mature over time and become better understood and hence more predictable.[62]

Many inventions involve multiple components or factors, some mechanical, some chemical, some physiological, and so on. Consider, for example, the "gene chips" formed by layering DNA nucleotides onto silicon, now being used to screen patients for genetic abnormalities that may indicate a propensity for a certain disease.[63] Certain components of such inventions may be considered within the predictable arts and others not; the inventions do not neatly fall within the mechanical or chemical category. Rather than try to classify the predictability of an invention as a whole, the better approach is to separately consider the nature of each component or factor of the invention. As explained in *In re Cook,*[64] it is preferable to "see [this issue] denominated a dichotomy between predictable and unpredictable factors in any art rather than between 'mechanical cases' and 'chemical cases.'"[65]

3. *Wands* Factor: Scope of the Claims

Another *Wands* factor often of great importance in enablement determinations is the scope of the claims sought by the patent applicant. The degree of enabling disclosure provided by the written description and drawings must bear a "reasonable correlation" to the scope of the claims.[66] In other words, the applicant must seek a right to exclude others from the claimed invention that is reasonably related

---

> Considering the structural complexity of the EPO gene, the manifold possibilities for change in its structure, with attendant uncertainty as to what utility will be possessed by these analogs, we consider that more is needed concerning identifying the various analogs that are within the scope of the claim, methods for making them, and structural requirements for producing compounds with EPO-like activity. It is not sufficient, having made the gene and a handful of analogs whose activity has not been clearly ascertained, to claim all possible genetic sequences that have EPO-like activity.

Id. at 1214.

[62]*See* Enzo Biochem, Inc. v. Calgene, Inc., 188 F.3d 1362, 1375 n.10 (Fed. Cir. 1999) (recognizing that "[i]n view of the rapid advances in science, . . . what may be unpredictable at one point in time may become predictable at a later time").

[63]*See, e.g., Using Gene Chips, Scientists Identify Unique Form of Disease*, GENOMICS & GENETICS WKLY. (News RX, Atlanta, GA), Dec. 21, 2001, at 6.

[64]439 F.2d 730 (C.C.P.A. 1971).

[65]*Id.* at 734.

[66]*See* In re Fisher, 427 F.2d 833, 839 (C.C.P.A. 1970). *See also* In re Angstadt, 537 F.2d 498, 502 (C.C.P.A. 1976) (summarizing the relevant inquiry in enablement cases as "whether the scope of enablement provided to one of ordinary skill in the art by the disclosure is such as to be commensurate with the scope of protection sought by the claims").

in scope to the extent of her inventive contribution as disclosed in the patent application.

Deceptively simple on its face, the task of awarding the "right" claim scope for a particular disclosure of a novel and nonobvious invention actually involves a delicate balancing of policy concerns. If an inventor is awarded claims of scope significantly greater than the scope of her enabling disclosure, the public is harmed because subsequent improvers will be blocked unjustly by the original inventor's patent and disinclined to conduct follow-on research in this area. On the other hand, if the patent protection awarded is no broader in scope than the specific embodiments disclosed in the application, the resulting patent is of little economic value.[67] As succinctly stated by Federal Circuit Judge Newman, "[t]he boundary defining the excludable subject matter must be carefully set: it must protect the inventor, so that commercial development is encouraged; but the claims must be commensurate in scope with the inventor's contribution."[68]

The U.S. Supreme Court grappled with these same policy concerns in the infamous case of Samuel Morse, who invented the telegraph but broadly claimed patent rights in "the use of the motive power of the electric or galvanic current, which I call electro-magnetism, however developed, for making or printing intelligible characters, letters, or signs, at any distances. . . ."[69] The Court held Morse's claim invalid as "too broad,"[70] which modern patent law would interpret as meaning "not supported by an enabling disclosure reasonably commensurate with the scope of the claim."

The problem of balancing claim scope against the extent of the disclosure is particularly challenging when a patent applicant claims his invention "generically" and has disclosed one or more "species" that fall within the genus. How many illustrative species must the application disclose in order to satisfy the enablement requirement? For

[67]In a leading article on patent scope, Professors Merges and Nelson contend that "[a]t first blush it might seem to make sense to limit the rights of a patentee to only those embodiments of the invention she has disclosed in her specification, i.e., those that she has actually created at the time the patent application is filed. But imitators would soon find some minor variation over the disclosed embodiments; with such an ultra-narrow enablement principle, they would then have a nonenablement defense if the patentee tried to enforce the patent. Such a rule would soon render patents useless." Robert P. Merges & Richard R. Nelson, *On the Complex Economics of Patent Scope*, 90 COLUM. L. REV. 839, 845 (1990).

[68]In re Wands, 858 F.2d 731, 741 (Fed. Cir. 1988) (Newman, J., concurring-in-part and dissenting-in-part).

[69]O'Reilly v. Morse, 56 U.S. 62, 112 (1853) (reproducing eighth claim of Morse's patent); *see id.* at 113 (holding that Morse's eighth claim was "too broad, and not warranted by law," because Morse had "claim[ed] an exclusive right to use a manner and process which he has not described and indeed had not invented, and therefore could not describe when he obtained his patent").

[70]*Id.*

example, in a world without furniture (as hypothesized in Chapter 1 of this text), if an inventor was the first to conceive and reduce to practice a four-legged, straight-back chair, should she be allowed to control all later-developed chairs, no matter how designed? Should she be able to prevent others from making and selling rocking chairs, reclining chairs, and bean-bag chairs, which she herself never actually contemplated? Consider also an applicant who discloses that the inert gas argon is useful in her invention — a novel method of depositing silicon on a substrate to make semiconductor chips — but generically claims the method as comprising the step of using any noble gas. To what extent should we allow this inventor to exclude others from using embodiments that she has not in fact made or tested?

There is no one-size-fits-all answer to these questions, but the Federal Circuit has instructed as follows:

> It is well settled that patent applicants are not required to disclose every species encompassed by their claims, even in an unpredictable art. However, there must be sufficient disclosure, either through illustrative examples or terminology, to teach those of ordinary skill how to make and use the invention as broadly as it is claimed....[71] The first paragraph of §112 requires nothing more than *objective* enablement.... How such a teaching is set forth, either by the use of illustrative examples or by broad terminology, is irrelevant.[72]

Federal Circuit decisions have repeatedly emphasized that a patent's disclosure must enable the *full scope* of the invention claimed in the patent.[73] The question whether a disclosure achieves "full scope

[71]In re Vaeck, 947 F.2d 488, 496 & n.23 (Fed. Cir. 1991) (Rich, J.) (citations omitted).

[72]*Id.* at n.23 (citations omitted) (emphasis in original).

[73]*See, e.g.*, Promega Corp. v. Life Techs. Corp., 773 F.3d 1338 (Fed. Cir. 2014) (holding biotechnology patents invalid because full scope of claims as construed was not enabled); *id.* at 1347 (stating that "[t]he enablement requirement ensures that 'the public knowledge is enriched by the patent specification to a degree at least commensurate with the scope of the claims'") (quoting Nat'l Recovery Techs., Inc. v. Magnetic Separation Sys., Inc., 166 F.3d 1190, 1195-1196 (Fed. Cir. 1999)); *id.* at 1347 (stating that "[t]he scope of the claims must be 'less than or equal to the scope of enablement'") (quoting *Nat'l Recovery,* 166 F.3d at 1196); ALZA Corp. v. Andrx Pharms., LLC, 603 F.3d 935, 943 (Fed. Cir. 2010) (affirming district court's judgment of patent invalidity because specification did "not enable the full scope of the claims"); Sitrick v. Dreamworks, LLC, 516 F.3d 993, 1000 (Fed. Cir. 2008) (when asserted claim was interpreted broadly enough to encompass "both movies and video games, the patents must enable both embodiments"); Auto. Tech, Int'l, Inc. v. BMW of N. Am., Inc., 501 F.3d 1274, 1282 (Fed. Cir. 2007) (holding that "district court was correct that the specification did not enable the full scope of the invention because it did not enable electronic side impact sensors" for sensing automobile crashes); Liebel-Flarsheim Co. v. Medrad, Inc., 481 F.3d 1371, 1378-1379 (Fed. Cir. 2007); LizardTech, Inc. v. Earth Res. Mapping, Inc., 424 F.3d 1336, 1344-1345 (Fed. Cir. 2005); Genentech, Inc. v. Novo Nordisk A/S, 108 F.3d 1361, 1365 (Fed. Cir. 1997) (stating that to be enabling, "the specification of a

enablement" often arises when a patent owner succeeded in obtaining a relatively broad claim construction at the *Markman* hearing stage of an infringement litigation.[74] The broader the scope asserted for an allegedly infringed claim, the broader the corresponding disclosure necessary to satisfy the enablement requirement for that claim. The patentee must walk a fine line. Its assertion of a claim interpretation broad enough to ensnare a competitor's accused device can sometimes backfire when a court concludes that that broad scope has not been adequately enabled.

The "full scope" problem arises in both mechanical and chemical/biotechnological arts. An example of the former is the Federal Circuit's 2007 decision in *Liebel-Flarsheim Co. v. Medrad, Inc.*[75] There the court rejected a patentee's argument that its disclosure of a single embodiment enabled a broader mechanical claim. Two of Liebel's patents in suit were directed to power injectors with replaceable syringes capable of withstanding high pressures for delivering a contrast agent to patients. The as-filed claims required a pressure jacket in front of the opening that received the syringe, but the patentee thereafter amended the claims to remove the pressure jacket limitation. During litigation challenging the validity of the patents, Liebel contended that because it had undisputedly provided an enabling disclosure of its preferred embodiment (i.e., an injector with a pressure jacket), it had sufficiently enabled the full scope of the issued claims (i.e., encompassing injectors both with or without a pressure jacket).

Affirming a district court's judgment of invalidity, the Federal Circuit rejected Liebel's argument. The appellate court observed that Liebel's patent specifications depicted only jacketed injectors, and in fact "taught away" from jacketless injectors by characterizing them as "impractical."[76] The Federal Circuit concluded that undue experimentation would have been required of a person of ordinary skill to make the jacketless injectors, based on testimony by the inventors that their own experiments with such injectors failed. As a result, the inventors deemed a jacketless system "too risky" for further development.[77] Noting the irony of invalidation for non-enablement on the heels of Liebel's earlier, successful argument for a broad claim interpretation, the Federal Circuit repeated the familiar warning "beware of what one asks for."[78]

---

patent must teach those skilled in the art how to make and use the full scope of the claimed invention without 'undue experimentation'").

[74] *See generally infra* Chapter 9, Section B.5 ("*Markman* Hearings").

[75] 481 F.3d 1371 (Fed. Cir. 2007).

[76] *Liebel-Flarsheim*, 481 F.3d at 1379.

[77] *Liebel-Flarsheim*, 481 F.3d at 1379.

[78] *Liebel-Flarsheim,* 481 F.3d at 1380. *See also* Auto. Techs. Int'l, Inc. v. BMW of N. Am., Inc., 501 F.3d 1274 (Fed. Cir. 2007) ("*ATI*"), in which the court held that the ATI patent's detailed disclosure of mechanical embodiment of side impact sensor for

Another example of the "full scope enablement" challenge is the Federal Circuit's 2014 decision, *Promega Corp. v. Life Techs. Corp.*,[79] in which the court invalidated four biotechnology patents for want of enablement. Again, the result turned on the failure to enable the full scope of the "broad" claim construction sought by the patentee,[80] which construction neither party contested on appeal.

The Promega patents in suit concerned "multiplex amplification" of "short tandem repeats" (STR) loci. The Federal Circuit explained that in DNA, particular nucleotide sequences are often repeated multiple times in a particular location.[81] The region of the DNA strand in which this occurs is called an "STR locus." The number of repeated sequences within an STR locus varies greatly between individuals; these "alleles," or markers, are responsible for "polymorphisms" (genetic differences) between individuals. Although a single allele is insufficient to differentiate persons, a particular set of alleles at multiple loci within one person's DNA can be used to create a unique DNA "fingerprint" useful in forensic science and genetic testing. Multiple copies of the loci of interest are needed for a detectable sample, which copies are obtained by "amplification" through polymerase chain reaction (PCR).

The Promega patents recognized that it is highly beneficial to amplify multiple STR loci simultaneously, creating a "multiplex" reaction or "co-amplification." However, the greater the number of STR loci sought to be amplified in a single reaction, the more complicated the process of creating a successful multiplex for that loci set.

The four Promega patents in question claimed

> methods or kits for simultaneously determining the alleles present in a set of STR loci from DNA samples, comprising: (a) obtaining a DNA sample; (b) selecting a set of loci of the DNA sample to amplify, including at

---

automobiles but minimal disclosure of electronic embodiment of sensor did not satisfy enablement requirement for broader claim encompassing both mechanical and electronic side impact sensors; analogizing to *Liebel,* the Circuit observed that

> [w]e stated in *Liebel*: "The irony of this situation is that Liebel successfully pressed to have its claims include a jacketless system, but, having won that battle, it then had to show that such a claim was fully enabled, a challenge it could not meet." *Id.* at 1380. ATI sought to have the scope of the claims of the '253 patent include both mechanical and electronic side impact sensors. It succeeded, but then was unable to demonstrate that the claim was fully enabled. Claims must be enabled to correspond to their scope.

ATI, 501 F.3d at 1285.

[79] 773 F.3d 1338 (Fed. Cir. 2014).

[80] *Promega*, 773 F.3d at 1348 (observing that "Promega has chosen broad claim language 'at the peril of losing any claim that cannot be enabled across its full scope of coverage'") (quoting MagSil Corp. v. Hitachi Global Storage Techs., Inc., 687 F.3d 1377, 1381 (Fed. Cir. 2012)).

[81] *See Promega,* 773 F.3d at 1341-1342 ("Background").

least the specific loci recited in the claim; (c) co-amplifying the selected loci in a multiplex amplification reaction; and (d) evaluating the amplified alleles to determine the number of STR that are present at each loci.

Representative claim 23 of Promega's U.S. Patent No. 6,221,598 ('598 patent), one of the asserted "open loci set" claims, recited (emphasis added by Federal Circuit):

> 23. A kit for simultaneously analyzing short tandem repeat sequences in a set of short tandem repeat loci from one or more DNA samples, comprising:
>
> A single container containing oligonucleotide primers for each locus in *a set of* short tandem repeat loci which can be co-amplified, *comprising* HUMCSF1PO, HUMTPOX, and HUMTH01.

In view of the "comprising" transition in the body of representative claim 23,[82] a district court (at Promega's request) broadly construed the claim (and similar claims all four patents owned and asserted by Promega) to cover an STR kit that could successfully co-amplify not only the three recited loci (e.g., as in claim 23, the loci HUMCSF1PO, HUMTPOX, and HUMTH01) but also any other loci combination containing those three recited loci, "whether that combination includes 13, 1,300 or 13,000 STR loci."[83] Rejecting accused infringer LifeTech's enablement and obviousness challenges to Promega's claims, the district court granted Promega summary judgment that the claims were not invalid for lack of enablement (or obviousness). A jury then found the patents willfully infringed by LifeTech's sales of certain STR testing kits.

On appeal, the Federal Circuit reversed on validity, invalidating the Promega-owned patents for lack of enablement under 35 U.S.C. §112, para. 1. Because the district court's claim construction was not disputed on appeal, the Federal Circuit adopted it as the governing construction. Although Promega attempted to characterize the STR loci combinations that were not expressly recited in the "open loci set" limitation of the asserted claims as merely "unrecited elements" that need not be enabled, the Federal Circuit disagreed:

> [U]nder the undisputed claim construction, they are part of the claim scope. In this field of technology, introducing even a single STR locus to an existing loci multiplex significantly alters the chemistry of, and has an unpredictable effect on, whether the resulting multiplex will successfully co-amplify.

[82]The "comprising" claim transition is covered *supra* Chapter 2, Section C ("Anatomy of a Patent Claim").

[83]*Promega,* 773 F.3d at 1343.

> There is no genuine dispute that identifying STR loci multiplexes that will successfully co-amplify is a complex and unpredictable challenge, and as a result, undue experimentation may be required to identify a successfully co-amplifying multiplex that adds even a single new locus to an existing loci combination. . . .[84]

Unfortunately for Promega, the Federal Circuit determined that arguments it had made in attempting to rebut LifeTech's obviousness challenge (an issue the appellate court did not reach[85]) worked against Promega on enablement. For example, the Circuit noted that Promega had "repeatedly describe[ed] the identification of new successfully co-amplifying STR loci combinations as 'unpredictable.'"[86] Without a preexisting teaching, Promega had contended, a skilled artisan "could not predict with any certainty . . . whether a given set of loci would co-amplify successfully together."[87] The Federal Circuit viewed as "overwhelming" the evidence of record that "the addition of a single locus to an existing loci combination can fundamentally transform the character of the resulting multiplex reaction. . . ."[88] Although Promega's claims recited "specific sets of STR loci," they also covered the successful co-amplification of a "virtually unlimited number of STR loci combinations (so long as they include the recited loci) through recitation of the 'open loci set' limitation."[89] Based on Promega's own statements, the Circuit concluded that "the teaching of Promega's patents would not have enabled a skilled artisan at the time of filing to identify significantly more complicated sets of STR loci combinations that would successfully co-amplify — such as those found in LifeTech's [accused] STR kits — without undue experimentation."[90] Thus, Promega's "'difficulty in enabling the asserted claims [wa]s a problem of its own making.'"[91]

The Federal Circuit also rejected Promega's argument that its use of the "comprising" transition in its "open loci set" claim limitations allowed those claims to "encompass a potentially limitless number of primers and multiplex reactions that are not enabled by the specification." The Circuit distinguished the commonplace use of "comprising" in "the preamble of a claim"[92] [*sic*, use of the "comprising" transition

[84]*Promega*, 773 F.3d at 1347.

[85]*Promega*, 773 F.3d at 1350 n.8 (stating that "[b]ecause the asserted claims of the Promega patents are invalid for lack of enablement, adjudication of LifeTech's obviousness challenge under 35 U.S.C. §103 is unnecessary").

[86]*Promega*, 773 F.3d at 1348.

[87]*Promega*, 773 F.3d at 1348.

[88]*Promega*, 773 F.3d at 1348.

[89]*Promega*, 773 F.3d at 1348-1349.

[90]*Promega*, 773 F.3d at 1349.

[91]*Promega*, 773 F.3d at 1348 (quoting MagSil Corp. v. Hitachi Global Storage Techs., Inc., 687 F.3d 1377, 1384 (Fed. Cir. 2012)).

[92]*Promega*, 773 F.3d at 1350.

immediately following the claim's preamble] from Promega's use of "comprising" in the "open loci set" limitation in the body of its claims.[93] The latter usage "expand[ed] the claim at a key limitation in order to cover what are indisputably advances in this unpredictable art."[94] The appellate court refused to regard the "numerous embodiments" covered by Promega's claims as merely "unrecited elements" in a "standard 'open-ended' claim."[95]

Accordingly, the Circuit held that because Promega's patents did "not enable a skilled artisan to practice the full breadth of this claim scope without undue experimentation, the challenged claims . . . are invalid for lack of enablement."[96]

The Federal Circuit declared a semiconductor patent invalid for failure to enable the full scope of the claimed invention in the 2018 decision *Trustees of Boston University v. Everlight Elecs. Co.*[97] As in the case of many other "full scope" cases, the patentee's enablement problem was one of its own making given the broad claim scope it sought for enforcement purposes. The Circuit admonished that "if [the patentee] wanted to exclude others from what it regarded as its invention, its patent needed to teach the public how to make and use that invention. That is 'part of the *quid pro quo* of the patent bargain.'"[98] *Boston U.* also illustrates that the enablement requirement is not satisfied merely by establishing that a claimed invention *could* have been (or was in fact) made as of the challenged patent's filing date. Rather, the correct inquiry is whether the patent's specification taught a hypothetical person of ordinary skill in the art how to make such a device without undue experimentation as of that date.

[93]The Circuit observed:

> It is true that when used in the preamble of a claim, the term "comprising" permits the inclusion of other steps, elements, or materials in addition to the elements or components specified in the claims. *See In re Baxter,* 656 F.2d 679, 686 (CCPA 1981). As we stated in *Gillette Co. v. Energizer Holdings, Inc.,* 405 F.3d 1367, 1371 (Fed. Cir. 2005), open claims "embrace technology that may add features to devices *otherwise within the claim definition*" (emphasis added). But the relevant usage of "comprising" here is not the one recited in the preamble. Rather, it is within the specific claim limitation that lists combinations of successfully co-amplifying STR loci, combinations whose identification and discovery Promega itself asserts is a complex and unpredictable endeavor.

Promega, 773 F.3d at 1350.

[94]*Promega*, 773 F.3d at 1350.

[95]Commentators described *Promega* as "a cautionary tale that says take a second look at claims that stack up too many 'comprises.'" Warren Woessner, *Promega v. Life Technologies — "Too Much of Nothing?,"* patents4life.com (Jan. 20, 2015), http://www.patents4life.com/2015/01/promega-v-life-technologies-too-much-of-nothing.

[96]*Promega*, 773 F.3d at 1350.

[97]896 F.3d 1357 (Fed. Cir. 2019) (Prost, C.J.).

[98]*Boston U.*, 896 F.3d at 1365 (quoting Sitrick v. Dreamworks, LLC, 516 F.3d 993, 999 (Fed. Cir. 2008)).

Boston University's U.S. Patent No. 5,686,738 ('738 patent), having an effective filing date of 1991, concerned semiconductor devices formed from layers or "films" of certain solid-state materials. These materials included gallium nitride ("GaN"), which emits blue light in light-emitting diodes (LEDs) that provide illumination in a variety of products such as printers, phones, and televisions. The prior art faced problems fabricating GaN films because of the material's crystalline lattice structure, which did not match the lattice structure of other semiconductor materials such as sapphire. The claimed invention attempted to solve the "lattice mismatch problem" by providing a two-step method for preparing monocrystalline GaN films via molecular beam epitaxy.[99]

Notably, the potential variations in crystal lattice structures of the claim-recited materials for a substrate, buffer layer, and growth layer meant that the invention encompassed six possible "permutations" or variations.[100]

[99]*Boston U.,* 896 F.3d at 1359. "Monocrystalline" refers to a crystal lattice having "a single-crystalline structure with long-range order." *Boston U.,* 896 F.3d at 1359. "Epitaxy" is

> a process used to fabricate semiconductor layers. During epitaxy, molecules of a semiconductor material are deposited on a substrate, and the deposited layer attempts to mimic the substrate's crystal lattice structure as the layer grows. Ideally, the lattice structures of the substrate and the deposited semiconductor layer will be the same; otherwise, the deposited molecules will strain against their own structure when attempting to mimic the substrate's structure, creating a problem known as lattice mismatch. Such mismatch introduces stress into the growing layer and can create defects in that layer.

Boston U., 896 F.3d at 1359. In a jury trial in the District of Massachusetts, the only claim that Boston U. asserted against accused infringer Everlight recited:

> 19. A semiconductor device comprising:
>
> a substrate, said substrate consisting of a material selected from the group consisting of (100) silicon, (111) silicon, (0001) sapphire, (11-20) sapphire, (1-102) sapphire, (111) gallium aresenide, (100) gallium aresenide, magnesium oxide, zinc oxide and silicon carbide;
> *a non-single crystalline buffer layer*, comprising a first material grown on said substrate, the first material consisting essentially of gallium nitride; and
> a growth layer *grown on* the buffer layer, the growth layer comprising gallium nitride and a first dopant material.

Boston U., 896 F.3d at 1360 (emphasis on "key limitations" added by Federal Circuit).

[100]*Boston U.,* 896 F.3d at 1360 ("Assuming a monocrystalline growth layer, together these constructions raise six permutations for the relationship between claim 19's growth layer and buffer layer: (1) monocrystalline growth layer formed *indirectly* on a polycrystalline buffer layer; (2) monocrystalline growth layer formed *indirectly* on a buffer layer that is a mixture of polycrystalline and amorphous; (3) monocrystalline growth layer formed *indirectly* on an amorphous buffer layer; (4) monocrystalline growth layer formed *directly* on a polycrystalline buffer layer; (5) monocrystalline growth layer formed *directly* on a buffer layer that is a mixture of polycrystalline and

When Boston U. sued Everlight and others for infringement, the accused infringers countered that the '738 patent was invalid for failure to satisfy the enablement requirement. More specifically, they asserted that the patent did not provide an enabling disclosure of what the Federal Circuit referred to as the "sixth permutation" — a semiconductor device comprising a monocrystalline growth layer formed directly on an amorphous buffer layer.[101] A Massachusetts jury heard the case and sided with Boston U., finding the '738 patent infringed and *not* invalid. The district court thereafter denied the accused infringers' motion for JMOL seeking to overturn the jury's verdict.

On appeal, the Federal Circuit reversed, concluding that Boston U.'s patent failed to enable the claimed semiconductor invention in its full scope. The appellate court highlighted the accused infringer's expert's testimony "that it is impossible to epitaxially grow a monocrystalline film directly on an amorphous structure," and the patentee's expert's agreement therewith.[102] The *Boston U.* Circuit was not swayed by the patentee's expert's "entirely conclusory" speculation that by following the "'boundaries within the teachings of the '738 patent, you could realize with not much experimentation . . . the amorphous buffer layer . . . and then a monocrystalline gallium nitride [layer] on top.'"[103] No specific passage of the '738 patent taught how to perform the sixth permutation — that is, how to grow a monocrystalline film directly on an amorphous structure. The expert's musings were insufficient to rectify this failing. The Federal Circuit summarized dryly that it could "safely conclude that the specification does not enable what the experts agree is physically impossible."[104]

Despite the absence of enabling teaching in its patent specification, Boston U. nevertheless sought to rely on testimony of its expert and the named inventor that each of them *had* successfully grown a monocrystalline layer directly on an amorphous buffer layer. Even assuming their accuracy, the Federal Circuit was not persuaded that these results were probative of enablement. It is fundamental that enablement of a claimed invention must be evaluated as of the patent's effective filing date. In the case at bar, the purported successes of the

---

amorphous; and (6) monocrystalline growth layer formed *directly* on an amorphous buffer layer.") (emphasis in original).

[101]In addition to monocrystalline lattice structures and polycrystalline lattice structures, some solid state materials exhibit a third type of lattice structure — "amorphous." An amorphous lattice structure comprises "non-crystal regions with inconsistent spacing among atoms." *Boston U.,* 896 F.3d at 1359.

[102]*Boston U.,* 896 F.3d at 1362.

[103]*Boston U.,* 896 F.3d at 1363.

[104]*Boston U.,* 896 F.3d at 1362.

expert and the inventor were achieved "years after" that date.[105] Moreover, the patentee Boston U. made no showing that the reported results were achieved by following the teaching of the '738 patent's written description. The Circuit highlighted the critical flaw in the patentee's reasoning as follows:

> [T]he inquiry is not whether it was, or is, possible to make the full scope of the claimed device — a scope that here covers a monocrystalline growth layer directly on an amorphous layer. The inquiry is whether the patent's specification taught one of skill in the art how to make such a device without undue experimentation as of the patent's effective filing date. . . . Simply observing that it *could* be done — years after the patent's effective filing date — bears little on the enablement inquiry.[106]

4. *Wands* Factor: Working Examples

The "working examples" referred to in *Wands* are commonly included in patent applications to help satisfy the enablement requirement, although examples are not required by statute.[107] Examples that appear in patents are simply specific, illustrative sets of instructions or "recipes" for how to make and/or use the claimed invention. They are less likely to appear in applications directed to fairly simple inventions. For example, the hot beverage cup–insulating sleeve patent reproduced in Chapter 1 of this treatise does not contain any working examples.[108]

Patent applications may contain two different types of examples.[109] "Working examples" disclose the results of experiments or tests that were actually performed. "Prophetic examples," also referred to as paper examples, suggest how a person of ordinary skill in the art might go about experimenting with or testing the invention in the future.[110] Prophetic examples should be written in the present or future tense, not in the past tense, because they have not actually been conducted.

[105] *Boston U.,* 896 F.3d at 1363.

[106] *Boston U.,* 896 F.3d at 1363-1364 (emphasis added).

[107] *See* In re Borkowski, 422 F.2d 904, 908 (C.C.P.A. 1970) (stating that "a specification need not contain a working example if the invention is otherwise disclosed in such a manner that one skilled in the art will be able to practice it without an undue amount of experimentation").

[108] *See* U.S. Patent No. 5,425,497 (issued June 20, 1995), reproduced in Chapter 1, Section C.5, *supra*.

[109] *See* United States Patent and Trademark Office, Manual of Patent Examining Procedure §2164.02 (9th ed., rev. Jan. 2018) ("Working Example").

[110] *See, e.g.*, In re Strahilevitz, 668 F.2d 1229, 1233 (C.C.P.A. 1982) (describing prophetic example 13 detailing method of preparation of matrix with bound antibodies).

5. Nascent and After-Arising Technology

How should courts determine if a patent application's disclosure is enabling when the patent claims are later asserted to cover embodiments of the invention that were not in existence when the patent application was filed? Courts are increasingly likely to confront this issue of "after-arising" or "later-arising" technology when dealing with rapidly advancing scientific disciplines, as aptly illustrated by *Chiron Corp. v. Genentech, Inc.*[111] The Chiron patent in that case issued from a continuation-in-part (CIP) application filed in 1995; it was the last in a chain of CIPs relating back to a 1984 parent application.[112] The asserted claims of the patent were directed to monoclonal antibodies that bind to human c-erbB-2 antigen (HER2) associated with breast cancer cells. Chiron sued Genentech for infringement based on Genentech's sales of Herceptin, a humanized antibody useful for the long-term treatment of breast cancer. A district court broadly interpreted Chiron's claims as encompassing not only monoclonal antibodies made using traditional hybridoma (murine) technology, but also to include those antibodies made using modern genetic engineering techniques. The latter type of antibodies included "chimeric" antibodies that combine DNA encoding regions from more than one type of species, and "humanized" antibodies that comprise DNA encoding regions primarily from humans (i.e., the type of antibodies used in Genentech's accused product). The district court's interpretation was based in part on an express definition included in written description of the 1995 application (but not in earlier applications in the chain) that the term "antibody . . . encompasses . . . chimeric antibodies and humanized antibodies." On appeal, the Federal Circuit accepted this claim interpretation as correct.

The central dispute before the Federal Circuit was whether Chiron's patent applications filed in the 1980s satisfied the enablement requirement of 35 U.S.C. §112, ¶1 for the claims as broadly interpreted in the litigation. The parties had stipulated before trial that if Chiron could not establish entitlement of the claims of the patent in suit to the filing date of any of the earlier 1984, 1985, or 1986 applications in the chain,[113] then the patent would be invalid based on intervening prior art. The jury found against Chiron on this issue, concluding that none of the 1984, 1985, or 1986 applications satisfied *both* the enablement and written description of the invention

[111] 363 F.3d 1247 (Fed. Cir. 2004).

[112] Continuation-in-part applications are discussed *supra* Chapter 1, Section H.5.

[113] The entitlement of claims in a later-filed patent application to the benefit of the filing date of a related earlier-filed patent application is governed by 35 U.S.C. §120. *See supra* Chapter 1, Section H.5 ("Continuing Application Practice").

requirements. The verdict form did not require the jury to specify whether enablement, written description, or both, were not satisfied.

All three Federal Circuit judges on the *Chiron* panel agreed that the *1985* and *1986* applications did not satisfy the enablement requirement with respect to the monoclonal antibodies as claimed in the Chiron patent in suit. The majority opinion authored by Circuit Judge Rader characterized the genetically engineered antibodies (encompassed by the claims as interpreted by the district court) as "nascent" technology in the 1985 and 1986 time period. For such "nascent" technology, Judge Rader wrote, the enabling disclosure must provide a "specific and useful teaching."[114] Judge Rader would locate nascent technology on a "knowledge continuum" somewhere between "routine" technology, which a patentee "preferably omits from the disclosure," and technology that "arises after" the application's filing date, which a "patent document cannot enable. . . ." An enabling disclosure must be provided for nascent technology "because a person of ordinary skill in the art has little or no knowledge independent from the patentee's instruction."

The scientific literature first reported the successful creation of genetically engineered antibodies in May 1984, after the filing date of Chiron's 1984 application but before the filing date of the 1985 and 1986 applications. Nevertheless, the Federal Circuit concluded, the 1985 and 1986 applications did not provide the required specific and useful teaching of the genetically engineered antibodies. Applying the *Wands* factors discussed above, the court concluded that undue experimentation would have been required to make the antibodies, which were "unpredictable" at that early stage in their development. The 1985 and 1986 applications did not provide any disclosure of how to make and use the genetically engineered antibodies or any working examples thereof, experts testified that making chimeric antibodies was "not routine" in 1985 or 1986, and only a few laboratories possessed the required equipment at that time.

Judges Rader and Bryson disagreed, however, with respect to whether the *1984* application satisfied the enablement requirement for the genetically engineered monoclonal antibodies. Writing for the majority, Judge Rader concluded that (contrary to the jury's verdict) the 1984 application *did* satisfy the enablement requirement with respect to the claimed antibodies of the patent in suit. The chimeric antibodies (a type of antibody within the scope of claim 1 of the patent in suit) were not known as of the filing date of the 1984 application. Under *In re Hogan,*[115] Judge Rader wrote, there can be

[114]*Chiron*, 363 F.3d at 1254 (citing Genentech, Inc. v. Novo Nordisk, A/S, 108 F.3d 1361, 1368 (Fed. Cir. 1997) (on appeal from grant of preliminary injunction, invalidating Genentech patent as non-enabled)).

[115]559 F.2d 595 (C.C.P.A. 1977).

no requirement to provide an enabling disclosure of such later-arising technology. Judge Rader would sustain the jury's verdict on the alternative ground of failure to comply with the written description of the invention requirement of 35 U.S.C. §112, ¶1.[116]

Concurring Judge Bryson disagreed with the majority's application of *Hogan,* and would have upheld the jury's [implied] verdict that the 1984 application did not enable the chimeric antibodies now within claim 1 of the patent in suit. Chiron was arguing that its 1984 application provided support for claims covering technology that was not in existence at that time, Judge Bryson observed. In that setting, where the claims are accorded a scope that exceeds the scope of the enablement, Judge Bryson would hold them not entitled to priority as of 1984 because the disclosure of the 1984 application did not enable the asserted claims. The proper approach in Judge Bryson's view would be "to address cases of new technology by construing claims, where possible, as they would have been understood by one of skill in the art at the time of the invention, and not construing them to reach the as-yet-undeveloped technology that the applicant did not enable."[117]

C. The Best Mode Requirement

1. Best Mode Scale-Back by America Invents Act of 2011

The best mode requirement of 35 U.S.C. §112(a) obliges an inventor to disclose the best way known to her on her patent application filing date of "carrying out the invention."[118] The requirement goes beyond the objective standard of enablement[119] to mandate disclosure of what the inventor believes to be the *best* mode, not just *a* mode, of practicing her invention. Because the best mode is, in part, a subjective inquiry with the potential for significant litigation expenditures to discern what was in the inventor's mind at a particular (sometimes long-past) date,

[116]*See Chiron,* 363 F.3d at 1255 (observing that "[t]he jury may have found that the 1984 application does not provide any support for the new matter, chimeric antibodies, claimed in the [Chiron patent in suit]. Because chimeric antibody technology did not even exist at the time of the 1984 filing, the record conclusively supports that the Chiron scientists did not possess and disclose this technology in the [] 1984 filing.").

[117]*Id.* at 1263 (Bryson, J., concurring).

[118]35 U.S.C. §112(a) (eff. Sept. 16, 2012) (providing that, in addition to an enabling disclosure and a written description of the invention, the specification "shall set forth the best mode contemplated by the inventor or joint inventor of carrying out the invention").

Before enactment of the Leahy-Smith America Invents Act, the individual subparagraphs of 35 U.S.C. §112 were not designated by letter. What is designated as §112(a) after September 15, 2011, was commonly referred to as "§112, ¶1" or "§112, first paragraph" before that date. *See* 35 U.S.C. §112 (2006).

[119]*See generally supra* Section B ("The Enablement Requirement").

some policymakers objected to the continued presence of a best mode disclosure requirement in U.S. patent law.

In response to these concerns, patent reform legislation enacted in 2011 significantly cabined the scope of the best mode disclosure requirement, although it did *not* eliminate it.[120] The Leahy-Smith America Invents Act of 2011 (AIA) prohibits asserting best mode noncompliance as grounds for challenging an issued patent's validity or enforceability either in federal court litigation[121] or as part of a post-grant review proceeding in the U.S. Patent and Trademark Office (USPTO).[122] This important change took effect on the AIA's enactment date of September 16, 2011, and applies "to proceedings commenced on or after that date."[123]

Although best mode noncompliance is no longer a basis for challenging an issued patent, pending patent applications remain subject to compliance with the best mode requirement. The first paragraph of 35 U.S.C. §112 was not amended to remove the best mode requirement; the best mode disclosure obligation remains one of three requirements for patent applications.[124] Despite the AIA's enactment, the USPTO retains the ability to reject a pending patent application for failure to identify the best mode.

Historically, however, "such rejections are reported to be rare."[125] Because of the subjective, inventor-centric nature of the best mode

[120]*See* Leahy-Smith America Invents Act, Pub. L. No. 112-29 (H.R. 1249), §15, 125 Stat. 284, 328 (2011); 35 U.S.C. §282(b)(3)(A) (eff. Sept. 16, 2011).

[121]*See* Leahy-Smith America Invents Act, Pub. L. No. 112-29 (H.R. 1249), §15, 125 Stat. 284, 328 (2011). The legislation provides that Section 282 of title 35, United States Code (2006), which enumerates the defenses available in "any action involving the validity or infringement of a patent," is amended in the second undesignated paragraph by striking paragraph (3) and inserting the following:

> "(3) Invalidity of the patent or any claim in suit for failure to comply with—
>
> (A) any requirement of section 112, except that the failure to disclose the best mode shall not be a basis on which any claim of a patent may be canceled or held invalid or otherwise unenforceable; or
>
> (B) any requirement of section 251."

[122]*See* 35 U.S.C. 321(b) (eff. Sept. 16, 2012) ("Scope") (providing that "[a] petitioner in a post-grant review may request to cancel as unpatentable 1 or more claims of a patent on any ground that could be raised under paragraph (2) or (3) of section 282(b) (relating to invalidity of the patent or any claim)"). *See also infra* Chapter 8, Section E ("AIA-Implemented Procedures for Challenging Issued Patents").

[123]Leahy-Smith America Invents Act, Pub. L. No. 112-29 (H.R. 1249), §15(c), 125 Stat. 284, 328 (2011). This dramatic change means that even if a patent was very likely invalid on September 15, 2011, for failure to satisfy the best mode disclosure requirement, as of September 16, 2011, the patent could no longer be challenged on that basis (so long as litigation was not already underway).

[124]*See* 35 U.S.C. §112(a) (eff. Sept. 16, 2011).

[125]Tony Dutra, *House Approves Patent Reform Bill 304-117; Dissent on PTO Funding Change Quelled*, BNA's Pat., Copyright & Trademark J., June 24, 2011.

disclosure requirement, as well as the USPTO's limited fact-finding resources, a patent applicant's failure to disclose the best mode would be difficult for the agency to discern.[126] On the other hand, patent applicants retain a duty of candor to the agency under 37 C.F.R. §1.56 that the AIA in no way eliminated. Commentators have observed that "[a] violation of the duty of candor under Rule 1.56 . . . may result if a patent attorney or patent agent knows the applicant has a best mode, but fails to disclose it or fails to specifically designate it in response to an RFI [i.e., a "Requirement for Information" under 37 C.F.R. §1.105]. . . . This violation may subject the patent attorney or patent agent to discipline before the Office of Enrollment and Discipline. . . .[127]

Despite the elimination of best mode noncompliance as a basis for contending that an issued patent is invalid, understanding the best mode requirement remains vital. Importantly, the best mode disclosure obligation continues as a statutory requirement for patent applications, as it has since 1870.[128] Moreover, because the AIA's abrogation of the best mode invalidity defense applies to proceedings commenced on or after September 16, 2011,[129] failure to comply with the best mode disclosure obligation remains available as a defense in any proceeding that was already pending on September 16, 2011.

2. Distinguishing Best Mode from Enablement

The best mode requirement of 35 U.S.C. §112(a) can be thought of as a sort of enablement-plus requirement. Under U.S. patent law, it is not enough that an applicant has merely disclosed *one* way of making and using the invention; he bears a further obligation to disclose the *best* way known to him on the application filing date of "carrying out [the] invention."[130] As explained by the Federal Circuit, the difference between the enablement and best mode requirements is that:

> Enablement looks to placing the subject matter of the claims generally in the possession of the public. If, however, the applicant develops specific

[126] *See* Ryan Vacca, *Patent Reform and Best Mode: A Signal to the Patent Office or a Step Toward Elimination?*, 75 Alb. L. Rev. 279, 294 (2012) (observing that "the risk of rejection at the PTO for failure to disclose the best mode is almost nonexistent").

[127] Vacca, 75 Alb. L. Rev. at 300 (footnotes omitted).

[128] *See* An Act to revise, consolidate, and amend the Statutes relating to Patents and Copyrights §26, 16 Stat. 198, 201 (1870) (providing that "in case of a machine, he shall explain the principle thereof, and the best mode in which he has contemplated applying that principle so as to distinguish it from other inventions").

[129] Leahy-Smith America Invents Act, Pub. L. No. 112-29 (H.R. 1249), §15(c), 125 Stat. 284, 328 (2011).

[130] 35 U.S.C. §112(a) (eff. Sept. 16, 2012) provides that, in addition to an enabling disclosure and a written description of the invention, the specification "shall set forth the best mode contemplated by the inventor of carrying out his invention."

instrumentalities or techniques which are recognized at the time of filing as the best way of carrying out the invention, then the best mode requirement imposes an obligation to disclose that information to the public as well.[131]

3. Policy Rationale

Unlike that of the enablement requirement, the policy rationale for the best mode requirement has never been completely transparent. Although the CCPA explained that "the sole purpose of this [best mode] requirement is to restrain inventors from applying for patents while at the same time concealing from the public preferred embodiments of their inventions which they have in fact conceived,"[132] why is such a requirement necessary *in addition to* the enablement requirement?

Some courts have posited that the underlying goal of the best mode requirement is that when a patent expires, members of the public should not only be able to make and use at least one embodiment of the invention, but rather, through the best mode disclosure, should be put in a *commercially competitive position* with the holder of the expired patent.[133] Although this goal seems laudable on its face, it may be more than is required from patent applicants in order to fulfill the constitutional goal of "promot[ing] the Progress of . . . useful Arts." Some experts advocate abolishment of the best mode requirement, which they view as needlessly exacerbating the already extreme cost and complexity of U.S. patent litigation.[134] These concerns motivated

[131]Spectra-Physics, Inc. v. Coherent, Inc., 827 F.2d 1524, 1532 (Fed. Cir. 1987).

[132]In re Gay, 309 F.2d 769, 772 (C.C.P.A. 1962). It is not entirely clear that a violation of the best mode requirement mandates *intentional* concealment of the best mode. *See infra* Section C.5.

[133]*See* Christianson v. Colt Indus. Operating Corp., 870 F.2d 1292, 1303 n.8 (7th Cir. 1989) (stating agreement with proposition that "the best mode requirement is intended to allow the public to compete fairly with the patentee following the expiration of the patents"); *contra* 3-7 Donald S. Chisum, Chisum On Patents §7.05 (2008) (disagreeing with Seventh Circuit's view on ground that it "ignores the realities of the patent system and the commercial marketplace" and explaining that "[r]arely will that disclosure [of the best mode known at the time the application was filed] be of competitive interest when the patent expires").

[134]*See* National Research Council of the National Academies, A Patent System for the 21st Century 82-83 (Stephen A. Merrill et al. eds., 2004), *available at* http://www.nap.edu/html/patentsystem/0309089107.pdf (recommending modification or removal of best mode requirement as a litigation element that depends on a party's state of mind and thus generates high discovery costs and unpredictability of patent infringement litigation outcomes); Advisory Commission on Patent Law Reform: A Report to the Secretary of Commerce 100-103 (1992) (advising under Recommendation V-G(i) that best mode obligation be eliminated).

Congress in 2011 to eliminate best mode noncompliance as an invalidity defense, while retaining it as a patentability requirement.[135]

Another basis for criticizing the U.S. best mode requirement is the fact that most foreign countries do not have a best mode requirement.[136] Indeed, the absence of a best mode requirement in other countries can disadvantage a foreign national who is applying for a U.S. patent. As discussed in Chapter 12 ("International Patenting Issues"), *infra,* the foreign national may need to rely on the earlier filing date of her home country application in order to avoid prior art cited by the USPTO examiner against her U.S. application. She attempts to do this by claiming the benefit of her foreign filing date under 35 U.S.C. §119, the domestic implementation of the Paris Convention's right of priority.[137]

Under pre-AIA rules, the foreign-filed ("priority") application must satisfy all disclosure requirements in the first paragraph of §112, including best mode, as of the earlier foreign filing date on which the applicant is relying, if it is to be entitled to the benefit of that date under 35 U.S.C. §119.[138] Because it was first filed in a foreign country that does not have a best mode requirement, however, the foreign priority application may not adequately disclose the best mode of carrying out the invention claimed in the corresponding later-filed U.S.

[135]*See supra* Section C.1 ("Best Mode Scale-Back by America Invents Act of 2011").

[136]*See* Donald S. Chisum, *Best Mode Concealment and Inequitable Conduct in Patent Procurement: A Nutshell, a Review of Recent Federal Circuit Cases and a Plea for Modest Reform*, 13 SANTA CLARA COMPUTER & HIGH TECH. L.J. 277, 279 (1997) (stating that "[u]nlike other patent law standards, such as novelty and infringement, best mode and inequitable conduct have no counterparts in the major patent systems of Europe, Japan, and elsewhere").

Several developing countries retain a best mode requirement, however, including India and Mexico. *See* India Patents Act 1970 §10(4) (1995) (providing that "[e]very complete specification shall — a. fully and particularly describe the invention and its operation or use and the method by which it is to be performed; b. *disclose the best method of performing the invention which is known to the applicant and for which he is entitled to claim protection*; and c. end with a claim or claims defining the scope of the invention for which protection is claimed") (emphasis added), Mexico — Ley de Protección a la Propiedad Industrial [LPPI] [Industrial Property Protection Law], *as amended*, art. 47, Diario Oficial de la Federación [DO], 27 de junio de 1991 (Mex.). Other countries requiring best mode disclosure include Australia, Canada, Egypt, Sri Lanka, Pakistan, Thailand, and Honduras. *See* Dale L. Carlson, Katarzyna Przychodzen, & Petra Scamborov, *Patent Linchpin for the 21st Century? Best Mode Revisited*, 45 IDEA 267, 284 (2005). For economic policy reasons, the developing countries require a relatively greater degree of disclosure in exchange for the grant of a patent. *See* Carlson et al., 45 IDEA at 287-289 (arguing that best mode disclosures facilitate technology transfer to developing countries and educate the work force).

[137]*See* Paris Convention for the Protection of Industrial Property art. 4, July 14, 1967, 21 U.S.T. 1983, 828 U.N.T.S. 305 ("Right of Priority"). The right of priority and other aspects of the Paris Convention are discussed in further detail in Chapter 12 ("International Patenting Issues"), *infra*.

[138]*See* In re Gosteli, 872 F.2d 1008, 1010-1011 (Fed. Cir. 1989).

application. If this is the case, the applicant will not be able to claim priority back to her home country filing date. The U.S. application filing date will be only the date of actual filing in the United States, and the applicant will not be able to avoid the cited prior art in this fashion.

4. The *Chemcast* Analysis

The Federal Circuit has clearly identified the analysis to be followed when determining whether a patent disclosure satisfies the best mode requirement of the first paragraph of 35 U.S.C. §112. The court outlined a two-step analysis for best mode compliance in *Chemcast Corp. v. Arco Indus. Corp.*,[139] which involved a patent directed to a grommet for sealing openings in sheet metal panels.

a. Step 1: Subjective Inquiry

The first step is a necessarily *subjective* inquiry that focuses on the state of the inventor's mind. Step 1 of the *Chemcast* analysis asks whether, as of the filing date, the inventor considered one particular mode of carrying out his invention to be better than all the others. If so, this mode is the "best mode." For example, the inventor in *Chemcast* considered a certain type of material to be the best mode for making his claimed grommet.[140]

Because of *Chemcast* step 1's focus on the inventor's mind set, it can be said fairly that "the best mode belongs to the inventor."[141] *Glaxo, Inc. v. Novopharm, Ltd.*[142] illustrates this adage. Glaxo's patent claimed a specific crystalline form of ranitidine hydrochloride, a chemical compound useful for treating patients suffering from ulcers; various pharmaceutical compositions and methods of using the compound also were claimed. Unbeknownst to Crookes, the Glaxo scientist who invented the compound, other Glaxo employees subsequently developed a novel azeotroping process that made salts of the compound easier to form into capsules.[143] Glaxo employed this process in the commercial manufacture of its antiulcer product, without any knowledge or further involvement by Crookes. When Glaxo later sued

[139]913 F.2d 923 (Fed. Cir. 1990).

[140]*See id.* at 929 (citing district court findings that inventor "selected the material for the locking portion, a rigid polyvinyl chloride (PVC) plastisol composition; knew that the preferred hardness of this material was 75 +/– 5 Shore D; and purchased all of the grommet material under the trade name R-4467 from Reynosol Corporation (Reynosol), which had spent 750 man-hours developing the compound specifically for Chemcast").

[141]Glaxo, Inc. v. Novopharm, Ltd., 52 F.3d 1043, 1049 (Fed. Cir. 1995).

[142]*Id.* at 1043.

[143]*See id.* at 1046.

Novopharm for patent infringement, Novopharm affirmatively defended by asserting that the patent was invalid for failure to satisfy the best mode obligation because it did not disclose the azeotroping process.

The Federal Circuit majority disagreed, holding that the best mode requirement had been satisfied. The court refused to impute Glaxo's corporate knowledge of the azeotroping process to the inventor, Crookes. Congress chose to use the specific term "inventor" in 35 U.S.C. §112, ¶1 (1994), the court noted; had Congress intended the best mode obligation to be broader, it would have drafted the statute accordingly:

> Congress was aware of the differences between inventors and assignees, see 35 U.S.C. §§100(d) and 152, and it specifically limited the best mode required to that contemplated by the inventor. We have no authority to extend the requirement beyond the limits set by Congress.[144]

b. Step 2: Objective Inquiry

The second step of the *Chemcast* best mode inquiry is completely *objective.* Assuming that a best mode exists, step 2 asks whether the application provides an enabling disclosure of this best mode. The second *Chemcast* step, which really merges the enablement and best mode requirements, addresses the *adequacy* of the best mode disclosure, rather than its *necessity.* In contrast with *Chemcast* step 1, the perspective of the second step is that of the hypothetical person of ordinary skill in the art rather than the inventor himself. In other words, the second *Chemcast* step asks the question, "is the hypothetical person skilled in the art enabled by the patent application's disclosure to make and use the best mode of the invention without undue experimentation?"

In the *Chemcast* case, the answer to this question was negative. The Federal Circuit concluded that in light of the specific material that the inventor considered to be the best mode for making his grommet, the patent specification was "manifestly deficient."[145] The patent neither explicitly nor implicitly disclosed how to make and use the claimed grommet with the proprietary R-4467 material that the inventor preferred. Rather, it merely disclosed an open-ended range for the hardness of the material, broadly stating that "[m]aterials having a

[144]*Id.* at 1052. Dissenting Judge Mayer decried the majority's narrow interpretation of the best mode obligation as strictly limited to the inventor. He contended that "the court blesses corporate shell games resulting from organizational gerrymandering and willful ignorance by which one can secure the monopoly of a patent while hiding the best mode of practicing the invention the law expects to be made public in return for its protection." *Id.* at 1053.

[145]Chemcast Corp. v. Arco Indus. Corp., 913 F.2d 923, 929 (Fed. Cir. 1990).

durometer hardness reading of 70 Shore A or harder are suitable. . . ."[146] The actual hardness reading of the inventor's preferred material, however, was 70 Shore D; materials of Shore A and Shore D hardnesses are recognized as different types of materials with different classes of physical properties. The Federal Circuit also instructed that because the inventor did not know the proprietary formula, composition, or method of manufacture of his preferred material, R-4467, he was obligated to "disclose the specific supplier and trade name" of the material.[147] Having failed to do so, the inventor had not complied with the best mode disclosure obligation of 35 U.S.C. §112, ¶1 (1988).

When the best mode is properly disclosed, in what manner should that disclosure be made? A common convention in drafting patent applications is to refer to the best mode as the "preferred embodiment" of the invention.[148] Case law indicates that no special labeling of the best mode as such is required in a patent application, however; the application need not expressly state "the best mode of carrying out this invention is X." For example, in *Randomex, Inc. v. Scopus Corp.*,[149] the Federal Circuit determined that the indiscriminate listing of the best mode along with a number of other modes did not violate the best mode disclosure obligation.[150] On the other hand, a scenario in which the best mode is indiscriminately listed among so many other possibilities as to result in "burial" or effective concealment might run afoul of the best mode requirement.[151]

5. Scope of the Best Mode Obligation

Although the *Chemcast* analysis is relatively straightforward, it does not address all aspects of best mode compliance. A still-fuzzy area of best mode analysis concerns the scope of the best mode disclosure obligation vis-à-vis the scope of the claims. Because 35 U.S.C. §112(a) uses the seemingly broad phrase "best mode of *carrying out* the

[146]*Id.*

[147]*Id.*

[148]*See* Jeffrey G. Sheldon, How to Write a Patent Application 2d Ed. §14.4.4 (Practising Law Inst. 2009) (explaining that "[t]he best mode may be identified in the specification as a 'particularly preferred," most preferred,' or 'preferred embodiment.'").

[149]849 F.2d 585 (Fed. Cir. 1988).

[150]*See id.* at 589 (holding that "[t]he indiscriminate disclosure in this instance of the preferred cleaning fluid along with one other possible cleaning fluid satisfies the best mode requirement").

[151]*See id.* at 592 (Mayer, J., dissenting) (contending that inventor's "disclosure does not satisfy section 112 because he buried his best mode in a list of less satisfactory ones"). *See also infra* Section C.6 ("Is Intentional Concealment Required?").

invention," some Federal Circuit decisions suggest that the best mode obligation may extend to elements of the invention even if those elements are not recited in the claims.

For example, in *Dana Corp. v. IPC Ltd. Partnership,*[152] the Federal Circuit invalidated the patent in suit, which claimed an elastomeric valve stem seal of the type used in automobile engines, because the patent failed to disclose a fluoride surface treatment that the inventor's test reports indicated was "necessary to [the] satisfactory performance of [the] seal."[153] The court held that the best mode obligation had not been satisfied, despite the fact that this fluoride surface treatment was not recited in the claims of the patent, which were directed to the seal itself.

Reliance on these earlier, more expansive best mode decisions should proceed cautiously. More recently, the Federal Circuit has clarified that "an inventor need not disclose a mode for obtaining unclaimed subject matter unless the subject matter is *novel and essential* for carrying out the best mode of the invention."[154]

This more limited disclosure obligation is illustrated by *Eli Lilly & Co. v. Barr Labs., Inc.,*[155] in which the patent in suit claimed the chemical compound fluoxetine hydrochloride and a method of administering the compound to block the uptake of the monoamine serotonin in patients suffering from anxiety or depression. The written description of the patent identified p-trifluoromethylphenol as a starting material from which the claimed compound could be made, but did not disclose the process by which the patentee synthesized this starting material. The Federal Circuit rejected the accused infringer's contention that the patent did not satisfy the best mode requirement because it did not disclose the patentee's method of synthesizing the starting material, a method that the patentee considered proprietary and commercially advantageous. Although the best mode for developing the claimed compound involved the use of this starting material, the Federal Circuit explained, the patent did not "cover" it.[156]

[152]860 F.2d 415 (Fed. Cir. 1988).

[153]*Id.* at 418.

[154]Eli Lilly & Co. v. Barr Labs., Inc., 251 F.3d 955, 963 (Fed. Cir. 2001) (emphasis added).

[155]*Id.* at 955.

[156]*See id.* at 964, concluding that

> while the best mode for developing fluoxetine hydrochloride involves use of p-trifluoromethylphenol, the claimed inventions do not cover p-trifluoromethylphenol and the patents do not accord Lilly the right to exclude others from practicing Molloy's method for synthesizing p-trifluoromethylphenol. As a result, the best mode requirement does not compel disclosure of Molloy's unclaimed method for synthesizing p-trifluoromethylphenol.

Moreover, the unclaimed starting material was not itself novel and was available from commercial sources other than the patentee.[157]

The Federal Circuit undertook a comprehensive review of its best mode precedent in the 2002 decision *Bayer AG v. Schein Pharms., Inc.*[158] The Bayer patent in suit claimed as a composition of matter the antibiotic ciprofloxacin, sold as CIPRO®. Accused infringer Schein alleged that the patent was invalid for failure to disclose the best mode of carrying out the claimed invention. Schein singled out Bayer's failure to disclose in the patent the inventor's preferred mode of making a certain novel synthetic compound that he had utilized as a chemical intermediate in his synthesis of the claimed invention, ciprofloxacin. The intermediate was not recited in the claims. Thus, the Federal Circuit was again required to grapple with the extent of the best mode disclosure obligation for elements or materials involved in preparation of the invention but not recited in the patent claims.

The *Bayer* panel majority's opinion noted that the Federal Circuit and its predecessor courts had held claims invalid for failure to satisfy the best mode requirement on only seven occasions. The majority concluded that each of these seven decisions could be grouped within one of two categories: either (1) failure to adequately disclose a preferred embodiment of the invention, or (2) failure to disclose aspects of making or using the claimed invention where the undisclosed matter materially affected the properties of the claimed invention. The second type of alleged failure was at issue in this case. Nevertheless, the Federal Circuit held against Schein, the validity challenger. "[N]ot every preference constitutes a best mode of carrying out the invention," the court observed.[159] Notably, Schein had conceded that the inventor's preferred way of making the intermediate had no material effect on the properties of the claimed ciprofloxacin end product. The facts of *Bayer* were thus distinguishable from the four prior cases in which the Federal Circuit had found a best mode violation where an undisclosed preference clearly had a material effect on the properties of the claimed invention.

The *Bayer* majority also rejected Schein's argument that because the intermediate at issue was novel, it did not satisfy the standard

[157]*See id.* at 964-965. The question of the scope of the best mode obligation with respect to unclaimed subject matter, if any, remains unclear. *See* Bayer AG v. Schein Pharms., Inc., 301 F.3d 1306, 1319-1320 (Fed. Cir. 2002) (summarizing Federal Circuit best mode precedent as requiring "that the best mode of making or using the invention need be disclosed if it materially affects the properties of the claimed invention itself," even if such subject matter is unclaimed); *but see id.* at 1324 (Rader, J., concurring) (criticizing *Bayer* majority for "inexplicably and without support in the statute or case law,... widen[ing] its best mode net to capture the properties of the claimed invention and further sweep[ing] in any material effect or impact on those properties").

[158]301 F.3d 1306 (Fed. Cir. 2002).

[159]*Id.* at 1321.

for best mode compliance that the Federal Circuit had set out one year prior in *Eli Lilly v. Barr Labs.* (discussed above). The *Bayer* majority read *Eli Lilly* as requiring a disclosure of unclaimed but novel starting material only to the extent that the best mode must always be *enabled*:

> We merely acknowledged [in *Eli Lilly*] that when a novel compound is necessary to practice the best mode, one of skill in the art must be able to obtain that compound. In other words, our statements regarding "a method for obtaining that subject matter" and "a mode for obtaining unclaimed subject matter" referred only to the requirement that the best mode be enabled. We were not referring to a best mode disclosure itself.[160]

In his concurring opinion, Circuit Judge Rader charged the *Bayer* majority with missing much of the significance of *Eli Lilly*. He viewed *Eli Lilly* as turning on the fact (also present in *Bayer*) that the undisclosed material simply was not covered by the claims, rather than requiring an assessment of the material's effect on the properties of the claimed invention. In Judge Rader's view, the *Bayer* facts "do[] not require creation of a new test for best modes."[161]

6. Is Intentional Concealment Required?

Whether the second step of the two-part *Chemcast* best mode inquiry described *supra*[162] includes an "intent to conceal" component is not completely clear.[163] The Federal Circuit routinely characterizes step 2 as "objective" because it focuses on whether the best mode would be enabled to a hypothetical person of ordinary skill. However, the appellate court also describes step 2 as asking "whether the inventor 'concealed' the preferred mode from the public."[164] To "conceal" is

[160] *Id.* at 1322.
[161] *Id.* at 1323.
[162] *See supra* Section C.4.b ("Step 2: Objective Inquiry").
[163] *See, e.g.*, Ateliers de la Haute-Garonne v. Broetje Automation USA Inc., 717 F.3d 1351 (Fed. Cir. 2013) (divided panel decision disagreeing on whether best mode violation requires intentional concealment); *cf.* Green Edge Enter., LLC v. Rubber Mulch Etc., LLC, 620 F.3d 1287, 1295 (Fed. Cir. 2010) (noting but not reaching accused infringer's contention that the best mode requirement can be violated without a subjective intent to conceal).
[164] *Green Edge*, 620 F.3d at 1296 (citing Chemcast Corp. v. Arco Indus. Corp., 913 F.2d 923, 928 (Fed. Cir. 1990); *see also* Transco Prods. Inc. v. Performance Contracting, Inc., 38 F.3d 551, 560 (Fed. Cir. 1994) (stating that "[a] holding of invalidity for failure to disclose the best mode requires clear and convincing evidence that the inventor both knew of and concealed a better mode of carrying out the claimed invention than was set forth in the specification") (citing Scripps Clinic & Research Found. v. Genentech, Inc., 927 F.2d 1565, 1578 (Fed. Cir. 1991)).

arguably an intentional act, and "concealment" suggests a subjective inquiry focusing on the inventor's conduct.

In 2011, the Federal Circuit stated unequivocally in *Wellman, Inc. v. Eastman Chemical Co.* that "'[i]nvalidation based on a best mode violation requires that the inventor knew of *and intentionally concealed* a better mode than was disclosed.'"[165] Under this view it would be inaccurate to characterize step 2 of the *Chemcast* analysis as completely objective in nature. If intent to conceal is required for a best mode violation, then step 2 should be seen as a largely, but not entirely, objective inquiry.[166]

A 2013 Federal Circuit decision showed that the court remains undecided on the question whether *intentional* concealment is required for a best mode violation (and also illustrates that although the America Invents Act of 2011 "gutted" the best mode requirement, it has not been completely eradicated from U.S. patent law!). Answering in the affirmative, a divided panel of the Circuit in *Ateliers de la Haute-Garonne v. Broetje Automation USA Inc.* ("*AHG*")[167] reversed a district court's grant of summary judgment that Ateliers de la Haute-Garonne's (AHG's) two patents in suit were invalid for failure to satisfy the best mode requirement. In an opinion authored by Judge Newman and joined by Judge Reyna, the *AHG* majority followed a line of cases, represented by the Circuit's 1992 decision in *Brooktree Corp. v. Advanced Micro Devices*,[168] holding that *intentional* concealment of the best mode

[165] 642 F.3d 1355, 1365 (Fed. Cir. 2011) (quoting High Concrete Structures, Inc. v. New Enter. Stone & Lime Co., 377 F.3d 1379, 1384 (Fed. Cir. 2004)) (emphasis added).

[166] *See* Transco Prods. Inc. v. Performance Contracting, Inc., 38 F.3d 551, 560 (Fed. Cir. 1994) (characterizing second step of best mode inquiry as "*largely* an objective inquiry that depends upon the scope of the claimed invention and the level of skill in the art") (emphasis added).

[167] 717 F.3d 1351 (Fed. Cir. 2013).

[168] 977 F.2d 1555, 1575 (Fed. Cir. 1992) (stating that "violation of the best mode requires intentional concealment of a better mode than was disclosed.... That which is included in an issued patent is, *ipso facto,* not concealed"). The *AHG* majority also cited *Wellman, Inc. v. Eastman Chem. Co.*, 642 F.3d 1355, 1365 (Fed. Cir. 2011) ("Invalidation based on a best mode violation requires that the inventor knew of and intentionally concealed a better mode than was disclosed.") (quoting High Concrete Structures, Inc. v. New Enter. Stone & Lime Co., 377 F.3d 1379, 1384 (Fed. Cir. 2004)); *Cardiac Pacemakers, Inc. v. St. Jude Med., Inc.*, 381 F.3d 1371, 1378 (Fed. Cir. 2004) ("The best mode requirement differs from the enablement requirement, for failure to enable an invention will produce invalidity whether or not the omission was deliberate, whereas invalidity for omission of a better mode than was revealed requires knowledge of and concealment of that better mode."); *Engel Indus., Inc. v. Lockformer Co.*, 946 F.2d 1528, 1531 (Fed. Cir. 1991) ("Patent invalidity for failure to set forth the best mode requires that (1) the inventors knew of a better mode of carrying out the claimed invention than they disclosed in the specification, and (2) the inventors concealed that better mode."); *Hybritech Inc. v. Monoclonal Antibodies, Inc.*, 802 F.2d 1367, 1384-1385 (Fed. Cir. 1986) ("Because not complying with the best mode requirement amounts to concealing the preferred mode contemplated by the applicant at the time of filing, in order to find that the best mode requirement is not satisfied, it must be shown that the applicant knew of

is required. The majority determined that the district court had "erred in law" by stating that "any omission need *not* be intentional to invalidate the patent on best mode grounds."[169]

Dissenting Judge Prost disagreed strongly held that the district court had erred on the law. She observed that the Federal Circuit has repeatedly recognized that *Brooktree*'s requirement of intentional concealment for a best mode violation was *dicta*, and that the court has so stated in several cases.[170] According to Judge Prost, the controlling line of Federal Circuit cases has "repeatedly emphasized that 'concealment' need not be intentional."[171]

On the merits, the *AHG* majority determined that the best mode was adequately disclosed. The two AHG patents in suit[172] concerned a process for dispensing objects such as rivets through a pressurized tube with grooves along its inner surface. The grooves provided a rapid and smooth supply of properly positioned rivets for uses such as

---

and concealed a better mode than he disclosed."); *In re Sherwood*, 613 F.2d 809, 816 (C.C.P.A. 1980) ("[E]vidence of concealment (accidental or intentional) is to be considered."); *In re Nelson*, 280 F.2d 172, 184 (C.C.P.A. 1960), *rev'd on other grounds*, *In re Kirk*, 376 F.2d 936 (C.C.P.A. 1967) ("There always exists, on the part of some people, a selfish desire to obtain patent protection without making a full disclosure, which the law, in the public interest, must guard against. Hence . . . the 'best mode' requirement does not permit an inventor to disclose only what he knows to be his second-best embodiment, retaining the best for himself."); *In re Gay*, 309 F.2d 769, 772 (C.C.P.A. 1962) ("Manifestly, the sole purpose of [the best mode requirement] is to restrain inventors from applying for patents while at the same time concealing from the public preferred embodiments of their inventions which they have in fact conceived.").

[169] *AHG*, 717 F.3d at 1358 (emphasis added).

[170] *See AHG*, 717 F.3d at 1360, 1360 n.2 (Prost, J., dissenting) (citing U.S. Gypsum Co. v. Nat'l Gypsum Co., 74 F.3d 1209, 1215-1216 & n.7 (Fed. Cir. 1996) (holding that intent is not required for a best mode violation and noting that the discussion of intent in *Brooktree* was *dicta*)); *id.* (citing also In re Cyclobenzaprine Hydrochloride Extended-Release Capsule Patent Litig., 676 F.3d 1063, 1085 (Fed. Cir. 2012) (holding that "the proper inquiry [in a best mode analysis] focuses on the adequacy of the disclosure rather than motivation for any nondisclosure"), *cert. denied*, 133 S. Ct. 933 (2013); Star Scientific, Inc. v. R.J. Reynolds Tobacco Co., 655 F.3d 1364, 1373 (Fed. Cir. 2011); Graco, Inc. v. Binks Mfg. Co., 60 F.3d 785, 789-790 (Fed. Cir. 1995) (holding that "specific intent to deceive is not a required element of a best mode defense")).

[171] *AHG*, 717 F.3d at 1360, 1360 n.1 (Prost, J., dissenting) (citing, e.g., Spectra-Physics, Inc. v. Coherent, Inc., 827 F.2d 1524, 1535-1536 (Fed. Cir. 1987) (recognizing that "concealment" can be accidental or intentional and that even a deliberate attempt to conform with the best mode requirement can fail if the "quality of the disclosure [is] . . . so poor as to effectively result in concealment"); Dana Corp. v. IPC Ltd. P'ship, 860 F.2d 415, 418 (Fed. Cir. 1988) (recognizing that "concealment" can be accidental or intentional and also finding best mode violation without any reference to "intent"); DeGeorge v. Bernier, 768 F.2d 1318, 1324 (Fed. Cir. 1985) (recognizing that "concealment" can be accidental or intentional); Matter of Application of Sherwood, 613 F.2d 809, 816 (C.C.P.A. 1980) (holding that "evidence of concealment (accidental or intentional) is to be considered")).

[172] U.S. Patent Nos. 5,011,339 ('339 patent); 5,143,216 ('216 patent).

Fig. 2

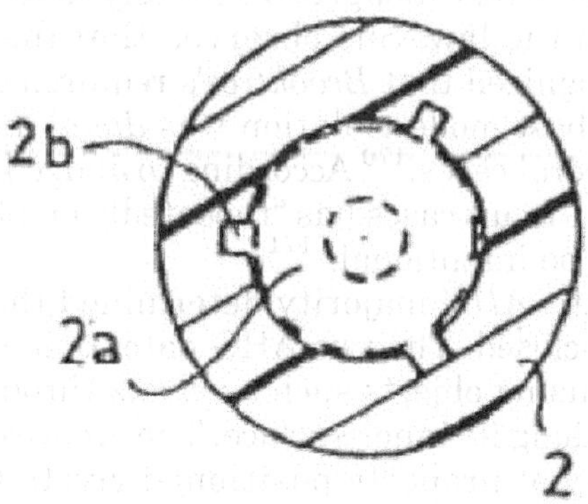

Figure 3.2

Depiction of a Preferred Embodiment in *AHG v. Broetje*

assembling the metal parts of aircraft.[173] The disputed best mode issue was the preferred number of grooves to be included in the tube so that the rivets would not jam or rotate. As depicted in Figure 3.2 herein, a figure described in the '339 patent as among the "preferred embodiments" showed a tube in cross-section featuring *three* grooves.

During the discovery phase of the litigation, co-inventor Jean-Marc Auriol testified in deposition that the figure showed three grooves and volunteered that "[y]ou need an *odd number* ... [t]o avoid that the rivet turns [rotates too easily] on itself."[174] Other embodiments disclosed in the patents under the heading of "preferred embodiments" showed tubes with two grooves and with fifty-five grooves.[175] After several years of post-filing experimentation, AHG ultimately sold a product that had five grooves.[176]

In the *AHG* majority's view, no dispute existed that when the patent application was filed, the three-groove embodiment was the inventor's preferred mode. There was "no evidence that either [of the inventors] possessed and concealed a better embodiment than was

[173]*See AHG*, 717 F.3d at 1353.

[174]*AHG*, 717 F.3d at 1355 (emphasis added). The district court had held the AHG patents invalid because they did not state that an odd number of grooves was preferred over an even number. In the district court's view, "the mere fact that AHG has disclosed an odd number 'at all' does not mean that the specification 'adequately' discloses Mr. Auriol's odd-number best mode." *AGH*, 717 F.3d at 1356 (quoting Ateliers de la Haute-Garonne v. Broetje Automation-USA Inc., 817 F. Supp. 2d 394, 407 (D. Del. 2011)).

[175]*AHG*, 717 F.3d at 1361 (Prost, J., dissenting).

[176]*AHG*, 717 F.3d at 1358.

described in the specification."[177] Moreover, "[t]he general statement that an odd number is better than an even number is not a statement of a better mode than the preferred embodiment [three grooves] shown in the specification."[178] The majority concluded that the disclosure of the three-groove tube was "adequate to enable a person skilled in this art to practice the best mode."[179]

In dissent, Judge Prost contended that even assuming *arguendo* that the three-groove embodiment was the best mode,[180] it had wrongly been included under the heading of "preferred embodiments" along with other embodiments that the inventors "knew did not work."[181] According to Judge Prost, the inventors considered the number of grooves "essential" to the operability of the invention.[182] The inventors "buried the best mode among other embodiments, also falling under the preferred embodiment heading, that did not include the 'essential' feature that the inventors discovered and knew was necessary to successfully implement their invention."[183] In Judge Prost's view, such "burial" of the best mode among several other ineffective modes (wrongly described as "preferred") was not the *quid pro quo* that the best mode requirement demands.

Judge Prost contrasted the case at bar with *Randomex, Inc. v. Scopus Corp.*,[184] relied on by the *AHG* majority and described earlier in this chapter.[185] In *Randomex*, the best mode, a cleaning fluid, was mentioned along with only one other fluid, which the art recognized as a "worst mode" because it caused explosions. The disclosure in *Randomex* did not result in effective concealment because it was "still an adequate guide" by which a skilled artisan could identify which of the two identified modes was best.

[177]*AHG*, 717 F.3d at 1359.
[178]*AHG*, 717 F.3d at 1359.
[179]*AHG*, 717 F.3d at 1359.
[180]She further observed that

> The majority declares that "[i]t is not disputed that [a] three-groove passageway was the best mode." Majority Op. at 1358. The majority also claims that "it is not disputed that the preferred embodiment when the patent application was filed was the three-groove embodiment that the specification describes as preferred." *Id.* The majority cites no support for those conclusions. I do not believe there is any. The identity of the best mode and the preference for the embodiments described in the patents are hotly contested questions in this appeal. And the answer to them formed the basis for the district court's decision that the best mode requirement was violated because the inventors' best mode was an "odd number" of grooves and that preference for that mode was not adequately disclosed in the patents.

AHG, 717 F.3d at 1361 n.4 (Prost, J., dissenting).
[181]*AHG*, 717 F.3d at 1361 (Prost, J., dissenting).
[182]*AHG*, 717 F.3d at 1361 (Prost, J., dissenting).
[183]*AHG*, 717 F.3d at 1361 (Prost, J., dissenting) (quoting Joint Appendix).
[184]849 F.2d 585 (Fed. Cir. 1988).
[185]*Randomex* is described *supra* Section C.4 ("The *Chemcast* Analysis").

In contrast, one of ordinary skill in the case at bar would have had to build and test three, not one, other modes to identify which worked best, and those other embodiments were (unlike *Randomex*) not well known in the prior art. Not only did the inventors in the case at bar leave those of skill without any guide as to which embodiment was the best mode, they "*led them down the wrong path* by disclosing multiple embodiments that only the inventors knew would not work well."[186]

D. The Written Description of the Invention Requirement

The last and most obscure of the three disclosure requirements of 35 U.S.C. §112(a) is the requirement that a patent's specification contain a written description of the invention.[187] Before exploring the details of this requirement, it is helpful to understand that patent law uses the phrase "written description" in two ways. In its more commonly used sense, written description refers to a physical part of the patent document. The written description portion of a patent document encompasses all of the patent specification's content other than the claims[188] (i.e., the written description includes those sections of the patent specification that are typically labeled "Background of the Invention," "Summary of the Invention," and "Detailed Description of the Invention").

In another sense, the phrase "written description" is a shorthand reference to a *disclosure requirement* that the patent's specification must satisfy in accordance with 35 U.S.C. §112(a). As explained below, the traditional view of the written description disclosure requirement was that the language of patent claims presented or amended after the filing date of the application must find adequate "support" in the written description portion of the patent document. In other words, application of the written description of the invention requirement was understood as limited to policing priority — ensuring that the new claims added post–filing date were entitled to the earlier, original filing date of the application.[189] Starting in 1997, a series of Federal

[186]*AHG*, 717 F.3d at 1362 (Prost, J., dissenting) (emphasis in original).

[187]Part of the material in this section is adapted from Janice M. Mueller, *The Evolving Application of the Written Description Requirement to Biotechnological Inventions*, 13 Berkeley Tech. L.J. 615 (1998).

[188]*See* 35 U.S.C. §112(a) (eff. Sept. 16, 2012) (mandating that "[t]he specification shall contain a written description of the invention . . ."); *id.* §112(b) (eff. Sept. 16, 2012) (mandating that "[t]he specification shall conclude with one or more claims . . .").

[189]Or, for example, ensuring that claims in a continuing application filed in accordance with 35 U.S.C. §120 were entitled to the earlier filing date of the corresponding parent application. *See supra* Chapter 1, Section H.5 ("Continuing Application Practice").

Circuit decisions have expanded the scope of the written description of the invention doctrine well beyond this traditional purview.[190]

In attempting to clearly differentiate these two uses of the phrase "written description," this text will generally refer to the legal requirement by its full statutory identifier as the "written description of the invention" requirement.

1. Timing Mechanism

The written description of the invention requirement can best be understood as a timing or "priority policing" mechanism. As detailed in Chapter 4, *infra,* when operating under pre-AIA rules, the USPTO takes the filing date of a patent application as the presumptive or *prima facie* date of invention ("invention date") for the subject matter of the originally filed claims therein.[191] It is quite common for patent applicants to submit amendments to a patent application after it has been filed, for the purpose of modifying the originally filed claims or adding one or more new claims. Are these amended or new claims also entitled to the same *prima facie* invention date as the originally filed claims, or merely to the later date on which the new claims were actually presented?

Similarly, the question when one is operating under post-AIA rules is whether the amended or new claims are entitled to the same effective filing date as the other claims of the application.[192] In either case, the answer may determine whether the amended or new claims are patentable, or rather are rendered anticipated or obvious in view of intervening prior art. This is the domain of the written description of the invention requirement.

Satisfaction of the written description of the invention requirement ensures that such subject matter, claimed *after* an application's filing date, was sufficiently disclosed in the application *at the time of its original filing* so that the *prima facie* date of invention for the later-claimed

[190]The Federal Circuit's expansion of the written description of the invention requirement has its origins in *Regents of the Univ. of Cal. v. Eli Lilly & Co.*, 119 F.3d 1559 (Fed. Cir. 1997), further examined *infra* Section D.5.

[191]*See* Mahurkar v. C.R. Bard, Inc., 79 F.3d 1572 (Fed. Cir. 1996), in which the court explained that

> [i]n *ex parte* patent prosecution, an examiner may refer to a document published within one year before the filing date of a patent application as prior art. However, this label only applies until the inventor comes forward with evidence showing an earlier date of invention. Once the inventor shows an earlier date of invention, the document is no longer prior art under section 102(a).

Id. at 1576. "Invention date" is further defined *infra* Chapter 4, Section G.3.

[192]"Effective filing date" is defined post-AIA at 35 U.S.C. §100(i) (eff. Mar. 16, 2013).

subject matter (or the effective filing date under the AIA) can fairly be held to be the filing date of the application.[193] Without written description of the invention scrutiny, a later-presented or amended claim not truly entitled to the earlier filing date of the application would be improperly examined against a smaller universe of prior art than is legally available. Hence the applicant would unfairly enjoy a windfall vis-à-vis the prior art.

Another way of understanding the written description of the invention requirement is that it functions to ensure that all claims amended or added after the filing date of the application find adequate "support" in the originally filed application. Section 112, first paragraph, requires that claim language be supported in the specification.[194] This can be viewed as a requirement that claim language find "antecedent basis" in the specification. The language added to the claims by amendment or introduced in newly presented claims must have previously appeared in the specification, either explicitly or implicitly.[195]

The policy rationale behind the written description of the invention requirement focuses less on the public than on the patent applicant. While the enablement doctrine is concerned with putting the *public* in possession of the invention so that it can be made and used without undue experimentation once the patent expires, the written description of the invention requirement mandates that the *inventor* must have been "in possession" of the claimed invention as of a particular date, that is, the filing date of the application (which under pre-AIA rules is taken by the USPTO as the presumptive invention date of the claimed subject matter). By ensuring that the later-claimed subject matter was in fact within the inventor's original contribution, the

[193]In re Smith, 481 F.2d 910, 914 (C.C.P.A. 1973). The *Smith* court summarized its precedent on the written description of the invention requirement as follows:

> Acknowledgment of that [written description of the invention] requirement evidences appreciation of an important purpose of §112, first paragraph, which is the definition of the attributes which a patent specification must possess as of the filing date to be entitled to that filing date as a *prima facie* date of invention. Satisfaction of the description requirement insures that subject matter presented in the form of a claim subsequent to the filing date of the application was sufficiently disclosed at the time of filing so that the *prima facie* date of invention can fairly be held to be the filing date of the application. . . . Where the claim is an original claim, the underlying concept of insuring disclosure as of the filing date is satisfied, and the description requirement has likewise been held to be satisfied. . . .

Id. (citations omitted).

[194]In re Rasmussen, 650 F.2d 1212, 1214 (C.C.P.A. 1981).

[195]The support or antecedent basis for the newly added terms need not be verbatim or *in haec verba* (Latin for "in these words"), as the discussion of *In re Smythe, infra*, makes clear.

written description of the invention requirement guards against unfair "overreaching" by inventors.[196]

2. How an Application Conveys Possession of an Invention

To satisfy the legal requirement for an adequate written description of a claimed invention, the application as originally filed must convey with reasonable clarity to persons of ordinary skill in the art that, as of the application's filing date, the inventor was "in possession" of the subject matter subsequently claimed as her invention.[197]

The precise manner in which a claimed invention is described in a patent is not critical, so long as that description is capable of conveying to readers of the patent that the inventor had actually invented the claimed subject matter as of the application filing date. Compliance with the written description of the invention requirement should not be so burdensome as to prohibit an applicant from claiming "undisclosed, but obviously art-recognized equivalent[s]"[198] of expressly disclosed aspects of the invention; these "equivalents" are considered within the inventor's possession.

For example, as the CCPA posited in *In re Smythe,*[199] if the original written description of a patent application directed to the "scales of justice" disclosed only a one-pound "lead weight" as a counterbalance to determine the weight of a pound of flesh, the applicant should not be prevented by the written description of the invention requirement from later more broadly claiming the counterbalance as a "metal weight" or even generically as a one-pound "weight." The broader claims should be permitted because the applicant's disclosure of the use and function of the "lead weight" as a counterbalance would

[196] *See* Vas-Cath, Inc. v. Mahurkar, 935 F.2d 1555, 1561 (Fed. Cir. 1991) (explaining that "[a]dequate description of the invention guards against the inventor's overreaching by insisting that he recount his invention in such detail that his future claims can be determined to be encompassed within his original creation") (quoting Rengo Co. v. Molins Mach. Co., 657 F.2d 535, 551 (3d Cir. 1981)).

[197] Ariad Pharms., Inc. v. Eli Lilly and Co., 598 F.3d 1336, 1351 (Fed. Cir. 2010) (*en banc*) (holding that "the test for sufficiency is whether the disclosure of the application relied upon reasonably conveys to those skilled in the art that the inventor had possession of the claimed subject matter as of the filing date") (citing Vas-Cath Inc. v. Mahurkar, 935 F.2d 1555, 1563 (Fed. Cir. 1991)).

Note the difference between this perspective and that of enablement: the written description inquiry asks whether the *inventor* was in possession at the filing date of the invention she is later claiming, while the enablement inquiry asks whether the patent application would have put the *hypothetical person of ordinary skill in the art* in possession of that invention as of the filing date.

[198] In re Smythe, 480 F.2d 1376, 1384 (C.C.P.A. 1973).

[199] *Smythe*, 480 F.2d at 1376.

immediately convey to others that the applicant had invented a scale with a one-pound counterbalance weight, regardless of the type of material from which the weight was made.[200]

As *Smythe* suggests, the question whether broader claims are adequately supported should consider the criticality (or lack thereof) of the claim limitation in question (in *Smythe*'s hypothetical, the "lead weight" limitation) vis-à-vis the invention as a whole. Similarly, in *In re Global IP Holdings LLC*,[201] the Federal Circuit instructed that the USPTO should have considered whether the use of a "thermoplastic," versus any generic "plastic," was critical (or not) to the claimed invention, which comprised panels for use in automobile floors.

More particularly, Global's original patent concerned composite panels for use in automobile load floors. In one embodiment, the rear side of a car seat operated as the load floor (identified generally by drawing numeral 13), to form trunk space when the car seat was folded down as in Figure 3.3. The composite panels, identified by drawing numerals 10, included hinges 12.

Importantly, Global's patent written description disclosed that the composite panels were made from two "reinforced thermoplastic skins" having a "thermoplastic cellular core" between the skins.[202] Global's U.S. Patent No. 8,690,233 did not refer to any other types of plastic and its issued claims were limited to "thermoplastic" materials.

Global thereafter filed a reissue application[203] seeking to broaden its patent claims by deleting the "thermo-" prefix from each instance of "thermoplastic"; in other words, attempting to expand the coverage of the claims from load floor panels comprising "thermoplastic" skins and cores to panels comprising skins and cores made from *any* type of plastic.[204]

[200]*Smythe*, 480 F.2d at 1384. *See also* All Dental Prodx, LLC v. Advantage Dental Prods., Inc., 309 F.3d 774, 779 (Fed. Cir. 2002) (reversing summary judgment of invalidity for failure to satisfy the written description of the invention requirement where, even though the disputed language was not a "model of clarity" and was added to the claims during prosecution but did not explicitly appear anywhere in the disclosure, the patent did sufficiently identify what the invention was, and what it was not, to satisfy the statutory requirement).

[201]927 F.3d 1373 (Fed. Cir. 2019) (Stoll, J.).

[202]927 F.3d 1373 (Fed. Cir. 2019) (Stoll, J.).

[203]A broadening reissue application must be filed within two years of the grant of the corresponding original patent. 35 U.S.C. §251(d). Reissued patents are examined *infra* Chapter 8, Section C ("Reissue").

[204]Global's representative reissue claim 1, with strikeouts indicating the deletions made to the original claim, recited:

1. A carpeted automotive vehicle load floor comprising:

a composite panel having first and second reinforced thermoplastic skins and a thermoplastic cellular core disposed between and bonded to the skins, the first skin having a top surface;

a cover having top and bottom surfaces and spaced apart from the composite panel; and

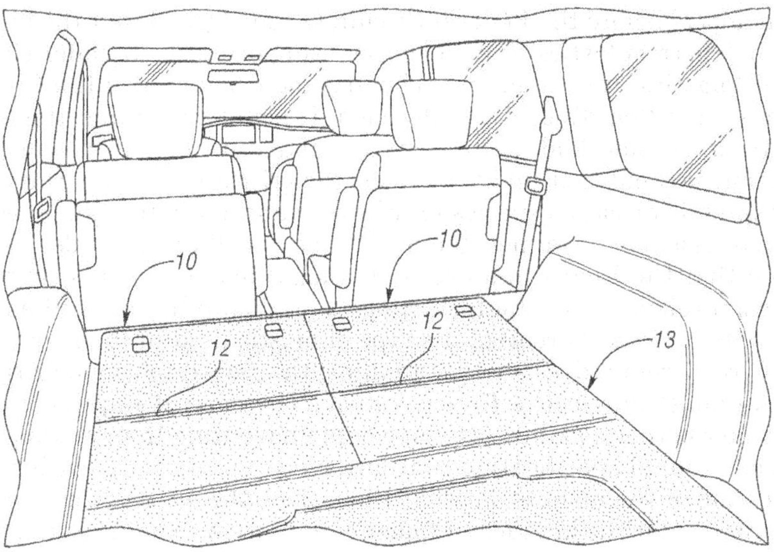

Figure 3.3

Embodiment of Global IP's Patent on Automotive Load Floors

The inventor's declaration accompanied the reissue application. Therein the inventor stated that he was a named inventor on over 50 U.S. patents, and that at the time of the claimed invention, he was aware of the use of plastics other than thermoplastics (e.g., "thermoset plastics") in vehicle load floors. The inventor further asserted that the specific type of plastic (thermoplastic or otherwise) from which the skins and cores of the load floor panels were fabricated was *not* critical or essential to the invention; that is, plastics other than thermoplastics would work. The USPTO Board disagreed, stating that that "'regardless of the predictability of results of substituting alternatives, *or the actual criticality of thermoplastics in the overall invention*, [Global's] [s]pecification, as a whole, indicates to one skilled in the art that the inventors had possession only of the skins and core comprising specifically thermoplastic.'"[205]

---

a substantially continuous top covering layer bonded to the top surface of the panel and the top surface of the cover to at least partially form a carpeted load floor having a carpeted cover, wherein an intermediate portion of the top covering layer between the cover and the panel is not bonded to either the panel or the cover to form a living hinge which allows the carpeted cover to pivot between different use positions relative to the rest of the load floor.

Global IP, 927 F.3d at 1375.

[205]*Global IP,* 927 F.3d at 1376 (quoting PTAB decision) (emphasis added).

On appeal before the Federal Circuit, Global argued that the disclosure of "thermoplastics" (i.e., a species) supported the broader claiming of "plastics" (i.e., a genus). The argument persuaded the Circuit to vacate the Board's contrary decision. It noted firstly that the leading *Ariad* decision "did not present an exhaustive list of relevant factors, and we hold that, in some cases, the criticality or importance of the expressly disclosed species may be relevant to whether an inventor had possession of a claimed genus."[206] The appellate court also determined that the Board had erred as a legal matter by ignoring the potential relevancy of the technology's predictability as well as the criticality (or lack thereof) of the type of plastic used in the invention. The Circuit remanded the case to allow the Board to consider these factual questions in the first instance. The correct inquiry would examine whether a skilled artisan would understand from reading the as-filed original specification that any type of plastic was within the possession of the inventor at that time. If so, the written description requirement for the broadened "plastic" limitations would be satisfied.

A satisfactory written description of the invention need not even be in words. For example, the medical device patent at issue in *Vas-Cath v. Mahurkar*[207] claimed a catheter having double lumens (tubes) of diameters within a specified range of ratios. The Federal Circuit had to decide whether the *drawings* of Mahurkar's earlier-filed *design* patent application[208] could provide adequate written description support for the diameter range limitations later claimed in Mahurkar's *utility* patent.[209] Even though the design patent application drawings showed only one particular ratio of diameters falling within the range recited in the utility patent claims, the Federal Circuit concluded that the drawings provided an adequate written description of the invention: "Under proper circumstances, drawings alone may provide a 'written description' of an invention as required by [section] 112."[210] The fact that the drawings did not (and by their nature could not)

[206]*Global IP*, 927 F.3d at 1377-1378.

[207]935 F.2d 1555 (Fed. Cir. 1991) (Rich, J.).

[208]A design patent is available for "any new, original, and ornamental design for an article of manufacture. . . ." 35 U.S.C. §171. A design patent is directed to the appearance of an article of manufacture. If its design is driven primarily by function (i.e., is essential to the use of the article), it cannot be protected with a design patent. *See* L.A. Gear, Inc. v. Thom McAn Shoe Co., 988 F.2d 1117, 1123 (Fed. Cir. 1993). *See also infra* Chapter 7 ("Potentially Patentable Subject Matter (35 U.S.C. §101)") (discussion of design patents).

[209]In order to overcome an intervening §102(b) (pre-AIA) reference that would otherwise have invalidated his utility patent, Mahurkar sought to claim for that patent the benefit of his earlier design application filing date under 35 U.S.C. §120. Entitlement to an earlier filing date under 35 U.S.C. §120 (eff. Sept. 16, 2012) requires compliance with the enablement and written description requirements 35 U.S.C. §112(a) (eff. Sept. 16, 2012).

[210]*Vas-Cath*, 935 F.2d at 1565.

show every possible embodiment of the claimed catheter within the recited diameter range was not dispositive, in view of expert testimony that persons of skill in the art viewing the drawings would be aware that only certain diameter relationships would produce a physiologically acceptable change in pressure at the transition between catheters.[211]

A Federal Circuit panel in *Enzo Biochem., Inc. v. Gen-Probe, Inc.,*[212] took the extreme view that showing an inventor was in possession of a claimed invention as of the application filing date (e.g., as evidenced by proof of actual reduction to practice) is not necessarily sufficient to satisfy the written description of the invention requirement.[213] The *Enzo* court opined:

> Application of the written description requirement, however, is not subsumed by the "possession" inquiry. A showing of "possession" is ancillary to the *statutory* mandate that "[t]he specification shall contain a written description of the invention," and that requirement is not met if, despite a showing of possession, the specification does not adequately describe the claimed invention.[214]

The court similarly concluded that "proof of a reduction to practice, absent an adequate description in the specification of what is reduced to practice, does not serve to describe or identify the invention for purposes of §112, ¶1."[215]

The *Enzo* court relied solely on its own interpretation of the statutory language and cited no decisional authority for its novel view of the written description of the invention requirement as necessitating more than a showing of possession by the inventor. In the view of this author, the *Enzo* court's elevation of the written description requirement as "the *quid pro quo* of the patent system" confused the requirement with enablement. Moreover, the court's assertion that "[t]he appearance of mere *indistinct* words in a specification or a claim, even an original claim, does not necessarily satisfy"[216] the written description of the invention requirement improperly conflates that requirement with the claim definiteness requirement of 35 U.S.C. §112(b).[217]

[211]*See id.* at 1566-1567.

[212]323 F.3d 956 (Fed. Cir. 2002) (granting petition for rehearing and vacating earlier panel opinion, reported at 285 F.3d 1013 (Fed. Cir. 2002), which erroneously held that biological deposit could not satisfy written description requirement).

[213]*See Enzo Biochem.*, 323 F.3d at 969-970.

[214]*Enzo Biochem.*, 323 F.3d at 969 (emphasis in original).

[215]*Enzo Biochem.*, 323 F.3d at 969.

[216]*Id.* at 968 (emphasis added).

[217]Effective Sept. 16, 2012. At the time of the 2002 *Enzo* decision, the definiteness requirement was referred to as emanating from 35 U.S.C. §112, ¶2 (2000).

The Federal Circuit went *en banc* in 2010 to address and resolve questions concerning the written description of the invention requirement. In *Ariad Pharms., Inc. v. Eli Lilly and Co.,*[218] the Federal Circuit conceded the difficulties with its past articulations of the possession test.[219] The *Ariad* court recharacterized the possession test as "possession shown by the disclosure," stating:

> The term "possession"... has never been very enlightening. It implies that as long as one can produce records documenting a written description of a claimed invention, one can show possession. But the hallmark of written description is disclosure. Thus, "possession as shown in the disclosure" is a more complete formulation. Yet whatever the specific articulation, the test requires an objective inquiry into the four corners of the specification from the perspective of a person of ordinary skill in the art. Based on that inquiry, the specification must describe an invention understandable to that skilled artisan and show that the inventor actually invented the invention claimed.[220]

That the *Ariad* court's reformulation of the possession test clarified anything is unlikely. The *en banc* court also held that various factors are relevant to the written description inquiry, some of which are *external* to the disclosure of the patent — an approach seemingly at odds with the court's quoted "four corners" directive for evidencing possession of an invention. "Specifically, the level of detail required to satisfy the written description requirement varies depending on the nature and scope of the claims and on the complexity and predictability of the relevant technology."[221] When the claims in dispute are generic claims (a situation that often triggers written description scrutiny), the Federal Circuit will apply "a number of factors for evaluating the adequacy of the disclosure, including 'the existing knowledge in the particular field, the extent and content of the prior art, the maturity of the science or technology, [and] the predictability of the aspect at issue.' "[222]

In the view of this author, the Federal Circuit in *Ariad* further complicated the possession test by injecting these external factors into the written description analysis. First, extrinsic evidence going to factors such as predictability or unpredictability of the relevant technology appears inconsistent with a "four corners of the disclosure" rule. More important, the factors identified by the *Ariad* court are also factors traditionally used in the analysis of *enablement* under the first

[218] 598 F.3d 1336 (Fed. Cir. 2010) (*en banc*).

[219] Other aspects of the important *Ariad* decision are examined in further detail *infra* Section C.5 ("Federal Circuit's Expansion of the Written Description Requirement").

[220] *Ariad,* 598 F.3d at 1351.

[221] *Ariad,* 598 F.3d at 1351.

[222] *Ariad,* 598 F.3d at 1351 (quoting Capon v. Eshhar, 418 F.3d 1349, 1357-1358 (Fed. Cir. 2005)).

paragraph of 35 U.S.C. §112.[223] Despite the *Ariad* court's emphasis that the written description of the invention requirement is a separate and independent disclosure requirement from the enablement requirement,[224] the overlap in factors identified by the Federal Circuit contradicts that position. The *en banc* decision in *Ariad* heightened, rather than resolved, doctrinal ambiguity in the standard for showing written description "possession" of an invention.

3. Distinguishing Written Description from Enablement

As interpreted and applied by the Federal Circuit, the written description of the invention requirement stands apart from the enablement requirement considered earlier in this chapter.[225] These two requirements have been recognized in the case law as separate and independent legal notions at least since the CCPA's 1967 foundational decision in *In re Ruschig.*[226]

[223]*See In re Wands*, 858 F.2d 731, 737 (Fed. Cir. 1988) (listing factors for determining whether the degree of experimentation required of an ordinarily skilled person to make and use a claimed invention would be undue) (citing *In re Forman*, No. 602-90, 230 U.S.P.Q. 546, 547 (Bd. Patent App. & Interferences July 2, 1986)). The *Wands* factors include:

1) the quantity of experimentation necessary;
2) the amount of direction or guidance presented;
3) the presence or absence of working examples;
4) the nature of the invention;
5) the state of the prior art;
6) the relative skill of those in the art;
7) the predictability or unpredictability of the art; and
8) the breadth of the claims.

Wands, 858 F.2d at 737.

[224]*See Ariad*, 593 F.3d at 1343 (stating that "[l]ike [Eli] Lilly, we also read Supreme Court precedent as recognizing a written description requirement separate from an enablement requirement even after the introduction of claims"); *id.*, 593 F.3d at 1347 (stating that "[i]n addition to the statutory language and Supreme Court precedent supporting the existence of a written description requirement separate from enablement, *stare decisis* impels us to uphold it now"); *id.*, 593 F.3d at 1351 (stating that "[s]ince its inception, this court has consistently held that §112, first paragraph, contains a written description requirement separate from enablement").

[225]*See Ariad,* 598 F.3d at 1344 (parsing the text of 35 U.S.C. §112, first paragraph, as including a "written description of the invention" separate from the enablement requirement).

[226]379 F.2d 990 (C.C.P.A. 1967). The Federal Circuit's panel opinion in *University of Rochester v. G.D. Searle & Co.*, 358 F.3d 916 (Fed. Cir. 2004) [hereafter *Rochester I*], contends that a written description requirement separate from the enablement requirement was recognized in CCPA decisions even prior to *Ruschig* in 1967. *See Rochester I*, 358 F.3d at 923 (citing Jepson v. Coleman, 314 F.2d 533, 536 (C.C.P.A. 1963); In re Moore, 155 F.2d 379, 382 (C.C.P.A. 1946); In re Sus, 306 F.2d 494, 497 (C.C.P.A. 1962)). *But see* University of Rochester v. G.D. Searle & Co., 375 F.3d 1303, 1311 (Fed. Cir. 2004) [hereafter

The following simple example helps to clarify the difference between the enablement requirement and the written description of the invention requirement. Assume that a patent application as filed discloses and claims a red widget. No other color of widget is mentioned, nor is any suggestion made in the application that the claimed widget could be any color other than red. Although a person of ordinary skill in the art might arguably be *enabled* by this disclosure to make widgets of other colors (such as blue widgets or yellow widgets), a generic claim later presented during the course of the patent application's prosecution that recited "a widget of a primary color" (i.e., "primary color" meaning blue, red, or yellow) would not be valid under the written description of the invention requirement. This is because the as-filed patent application did not provide a written description of "the invention," as later claimed generically; the application showed only that the inventor was in possession of red widgets when she filed. Thus, the later-filed generic claim would not be entitled to the earlier filing date of the application as the *prima facie* date of invention of the claimed genus of primary color widgets (under pre-AIA rules).

Patent law practitioners might say that in such a situation, the patent's disclosure does not "support" the broader, later-presented claim to "a widget of a primary color." In particular, the disclosure does not support a claim encompassing blue widgets, or yellow widgets, or widgets of any non-primary color.[227] Although the disclosure may well *enable* a person having ordinary skill in the art of widgets to make and use widgets of colors other than red, there is no evidence in the application as filed that the inventor was at that time in possession of any invention broader than the red widget.

4. Typical Fact Scenarios Invoking Written Description Scrutiny

The procedural context of the above example, which involves the presentation of a new claim during ongoing prosecution after the patent application had been filed, is a typical one for written description

Rochester II] (Rader, J., dissenting from denial of rehearing *en banc*) (discussing *Jepson, Moore,* and *Sus* and concluding that these cases "shed little light on the modern written description requirement").

[227]The proper basis for rejecting a claim to "a widget of a primary color" in the above hypothetical would be for failure to comply with the written description of the invention requirement of 35 U.S.C. §112(a) (eff. Sept. 16, 2012), *not* as a rejection for new matter under 35 U.S.C. §132(a). The latter section, which states that "[n]o amendment shall introduce new matter into the disclosure of the invention," is "properly employed as a basis for objection to amendments to the abstract, specifications, or drawings attempting to add new disclosure to that originally presented," In re Rasmussen, 650 F.2d 1212, 1214-1215 (C.C.P.A. 1981), but does not apply to amendments made to patent *claims*.

issues. Written description of the invention issues usually arise in "time gap" situations, when (1) new claims are added to a pending patent application, (2) an originally filed claim is substantively amended during prosecution, (3) an applicant claims the benefit of the earlier filing date of a related domestic patent application[228] or a corresponding foreign-origin patent application,[229] or (4) an interference is declared in which the issue is support for a count in the specification of one or more of the parties.[230] These situations have been referred to as involving "priority policing."[231]

Situation (3), involving claims by patent applicants to the benefit of an earlier domestic or foreign filing date, is of central importance in the post-AIA regime. Written description of the invention compliance often will be at issue. In the post-AIA regime, a great deal turns on determining the "effective filing date" of a claimed invention. The AIA-implemented definition of "effective filing date" explicitly contemplates that applicants may assert claims to "a right of priority under section 119," which includes domestic priority under 35 U.S.C. §119(e) to the date of an applicant's §111(b) provisional application. The "effective filing date" also explicitly contemplates claims to "the benefit of an earlier filing date" under 35 U.S.C. §120 that seek the filing date of an applicant's earlier-filed co-pending domestic application.[232] In turn, both of these statutory provisions (i.e., 35 U.S.C. §119(e) and §120) explicitly require that the disclosure in the priority document (i.e., the provisional application or the earlier-filed co-pending application) satisfies not only the enablement requirement but also the written description of the invention requirement of 35 U.S.C. §112(a). The written description of the invention requirement

[228]*See* 35 U.S.C. §119(e) (domestic priority claimed from provisional application); *id.* §120 (domestic priority claimed from parent or earlier-filed continuing application by a later-filed continuing application).

[229]*See* 35 U.S.C. §119(a).

[230]*See* In re Smith, 481 F.2d 910, 914 (C.C.P.A. 1973) (explaining that the written description of the invention "applies whether the case factually arises out of an assertion of entitlement to the filing date of a previously filed application under §120, as was involved, e.g., in *In re Smith* [458 F.2d 1389 (C.C.P.A. 1972)] and *In re Ahlbrecht,* 435 F.2d 908 [(C.C.P.A. 1971)], or arises in the interference context wherein the issue is support for a count in the specification of one or more of the parties, e.g., as was the situation in *Fields v. Conover,* 443 F.2d 1386 [(C.C.P.A. 1971)], and *Snitzer v. Etzel,* 465 F.2d 899 [(C.C.P.A. 1972)], or arises in an *ex parte* case involving a single application, but where the claim at issue was filed subsequent to the filing of the application, e.g. as in *In re Ruschig,* 379 F.2d 990 [(C.C.P.A. 1967)], and *In re Welstead,* 463 F.2d 1110 [(C.C.P.A. 1972)] (which involved a new matter rejection under §132, but which was resolved on the authority of description requirement cases)").

[231]*See* Anascape, Ltd. v. Nintendo Am., Inc., 601 F.3d 1333, 1341 (Fed. Cir. 2010) (Gajarsa, J., concurring) (writing separately to "highlight the majority's best use of the written description requirement as a priority-policing mechanism in contradistinction to an independent basis for invalidity").

[232]*See* 35 U.S.C. §100(i)(1)(B) (eff. Mar. 16, 2013).

must be met for the later-claimed invention as of the earlier effective filing date sought for that invention.[233]

5. Federal Circuit's Expansion of the Written Description Requirement

Beginning in 1997 with its panel decision in *Regents of the Univ. of Cal. v. Eli Lilly & Co.,*[234] the Federal Circuit has expanded written description of the invention analysis to consider the validity of unamended, originally filed claims (i.e., claims presented in a patent application when it was filed and not amended thereafter).[235] In the view of this author, this is an anomalous application of written description principles, contrary to binding precedent.[236] Nevertheless, the Federal Circuit adopted this view *en banc* in its 2010 *Ariad*

[233]*See* Leahy-Smith America Invents Act, Pub. L. No. 112-29 (H.R. 1249), §15(b), 125 Stat. 284, 328 (2011) ("Conforming Amendment. — Sections 119(e)(1) and 120 of title 35, United States Code, are each amended by striking 'the first paragraph of section 112 of this title' and inserting 'section 112(a) (other than the requirement to disclose the best mode)' "); 35 U.S.C. §119(e)(1) (eff. Sept. 16, 2011); 35 U.S.C. §120 (eff. Sept. 16, 2011).

[234]119 F.3d 1559 (Fed. Cir. 1997).

[235]*See* Ariad Pharms., Inc. v. Eli Lilly and Co., 598 F.3d 1336, 1351 (Fed. Cir. 2010) (*en banc*) (holding that "[n]either the statute nor legal precedent limits the written description requirement to cases of priority or distinguishes between original and amended claims"); Enzo Biochem., Inc. v. Gen-Probe, Inc., 323 F.3d 956, 968 (Fed. Cir. 2002) (rejecting patentee's contention that "the written description requirement for the generic claims is necessarily met as a matter of law because the claim language appears in *ipsis verbis* in the specification" and contending that "[i]f a purported description of an invention does not meet the requirements of the statute, the fact that it appears as an original claim or in the specification does not save it"); Regents of the Univ. of Cal. v. Eli Lilly & Co., 119 F.3d 1559 (Fed. Cir. 1997).

[236]The inappropriateness of applying written description of the invention analysis to original claims filed with the application was conclusively established in 1973 with *In re Gardner*, 475 F.2d 1389 (C.C.P.A. 1973). Reversing a USPTO Board of Appeals rejection of an original claim under the written description requirement of 35 U.S.C. §112, ¶1, the *Gardner* court explained that "[c]laim 2, which apparently was an original claim, in itself constituted a description in the original disclosure equivalent in scope and identical in language to the total subject matter now being claimed. . . . Nothing more is necessary for compliance with the description requirement. . . ." *Id.* at 1391 (citation omitted). On petition for rehearing, the CCPA rejected the USPTO's argument that an original application claim should not be considered part of the "written description" unless the specification contained or was amended to contain the subject matter of the claim. Whether such amendment should be made was merely an "administrative matter" for the agency rather than a proper basis for the court's decision on description requirement compliance. In re Gardner, 480 F.2d 879 (C.C.P.A. 1973). The CCPA confirmed *Gardner*'s holding that originally filed claims constitute part of the disclosure in *In re Koller*, 613 F.2d 819, 823 (C.C.P.A. 1980) (citing *Gardner* for the proposition that "original claims constitute their own description"). The *Koller* court held that method claims reciting the term "liquid medium," presented in a continuing application, were supported in accordance with §112 of the Patent Act by a grandparent application's claims

decision, so *Ariad* represents the controlling law unless and until the Supreme Court were to overrule it.

In the author's view, originally filed claims constitute their own disclosure, and by their inclusion in the originally filed application clearly signal that the applicant considered herself to be in possession of the claimed subject matter as of the filing date.[237] There is no "time gap" present by which an applicant could unfairly obtain an advantage in terms of the extent of prior art that would be legally available for citation against her originally filed claim.

Although the question whether the patent application provides an *enabling* disclosure having a scope reasonably commensurate with the scope of the originally filed claims may legitimately be at issue in some cases,[238] this is a completely separate inquiry from that of compliance with the written description of the invention requirement. In the author's view, and contrary to the Federal Circuit's *en banc Ariad* decision, the written description of the invention requirement has no applicability to unamended originally filed claims.

a. Regents of Univ. of Cal. v. Eli Lilly *(1997)*

In its 1997 decision in *Regents of Univ. of Cal. v. Eli Lilly & Co.* (hereafter *Lilly*),[239] the Federal Circuit for the first time relied on the written description requirement as a general-purpose disclosure doctrine to invalidate un-amended, originally filed claims (i.e., claims presented in a patent application on its filing date and not amended thereafter).[240]

that used the same terminology. *See id.* (noting that "the term 'liquid medium' is found in both places [and] the two sets of claims are similar in wording").

[237] *See* Janice M. Mueller, *The Evolving Application of the Written Description Requirement to Biotechnological Inventions*, 13 BERKELEY TECH. L.J. 615, 633-639 (1998) (criticizing Federal Circuit's application of written description scrutiny to originally filed claims in *Regents of the Univ. of Cal. v. Eli Lilly & Co.*, 119 F.3d 1559 (Fed. Cir. 1997)).

[238] For example, Circuit Judge Rader viewed both *Eli Lilly* and *University of Rochester* as invoking enablement issues rather than written description violations. *See* Univ. of Rochester v. G.D. Searle & Co., 375 F.3d 1303, 1312 (Rader, J., dissenting from denial of rehearing *en banc*) (stating that "[i]n both *Eli Lilly* and *Rochester*, for instance, the invention A (rat insulin in *Eli Lilly*; an assay for Cox 1 and 2 in *Rochester*) was enabled and described, but the invention B (human insulin in *Eli Lilly*; a Cox 2 inhibitor in *Rochester*) was not enabled").

[239] 119 F.3d 1559 (Fed. Cir. 1997) (hereafter "*Lilly*").

[240] *See* Enzo Biochem, Inc. v. Gen-Probe Inc., 323 F.3d 956, 968 (Fed. Cir. 2002) (Lourie, J.) (explaining that "[i]n *Eli Lilly*, we were faced with a set of facts in which the words of the claim alone did not convey an adequate description of the invention. . . . In such a situation, regardless whether the claim appears in the original specification and is thus supported by the specification as of the filing date, §112, ¶1 is not necessarily met.") (citing Guidelines for Examination of Patent Applications Under the 35 U.S.C. 112, ¶1 "Written Description" Requirement, 66 FED. REG. 1099, 1100 (Jan. 5, 2001) (noting *Eli Lilly*'s clarification of the "original claim" doctrine in situations

In 1990, the Regents of the University of California (UC) sued Eli Lilly and Company (Lilly) for infringement of UC patents directed to the use of recombinant DNA technology to produce human insulin.[241] The patents were based on UC's successful cloning of the rat insulin gene, a breakthrough development that has been viewed as "open[ing] the way to modern insulin production."[242] Specifically, UC's U.S. Patent No. 4,652,525 ('525 patent) included claims 1, 2, 4, 6, and 7, which were genus claims that recited complementary DNA (cDNA) encoding vertebrate or mammalian insulin.[243] In contrast, claim 5 of UC's '525 patent specifically recited cDNA encoding human insulin. Claim 3 recited "a nucleotide sequence having the structure of and transcribed from the rat gene for insulin."[244]

---

in which the name of the claimed material does not convey sufficient identifying information)); *see also* Christopher M. Holman, *Is* Lilly *Written Description a Paper Tiger? A Comprehensive Assessment of the Impact of* Eli Lilly *and Its Progeny in the Courts and PTO,* 17 ALB. L.J. SCI. & TECH. 1, 14 (2007) (observing that the "biotechnology and patent communities were shocked by *Lilly*, particularly because of the novel manner in which the court applied the written description requirement to originally filed claims, and the stringent disclosure requirements the decision seemed to impose on biotechnology inventors"); Arti K. Rai, *Intellectual Property Rights in Biotechnology: Addressing New Technology*, 34 WAKE FOREST L. REV. 827, 834-835 (1999) (stating that "in [*Lilly*] . . . the CAFC broke new ground by applying the written description requirement not only to later-filed claims but also to claims filed in the original patent"); Janice M. Mueller, *The Evolving Application of the Written Description Requirement to Biotechnological Inventions*, 13 BERKELEY TECH. L.J. 615, 617-618 (1998) (contending that "the *Lilly* court improperly diverged from established description doctrine in two significant aspects: first, by utilizing the description requirement to invalidate original application claims; and second, by requiring that a written description of a claim to DNA must set forth the specific nucleotide sequence of that DNA") (footnote omitted).

[241]*See* Regents of Univ. of Cal. v. Eli Lilly & Co., 119 F.3d 1559, 1562 (Fed. Cir. 1997); *see also A Bitter Battle over Insulin Gene,* 277 SCIENCE 1028, 1028 (1997) (describing suit as a "vicious fight [that] centers on a landmark discovery by [University of California at San Francisco] biologists at the dawn of the biotechnology era: the first successful cloning of the rat insulin gene").

[242]*A Bitter Battle over Insulin Gene,* 277 SCIENCE 1028, 1029 (1997) (remarks of William Rutter, former University of California, San Francisco scientist and chair of Chiron Corporation, Emeryville, California). UC's successful isolation of the rat insulin gene represented "the first time the entire genetic sequence for an insulin gene had been spelled out. . . ." *Id. See also* Christopher M. Holman, *Is* Lilly *Written Description a Paper Tiger? A Comprehensive Assessment of the Impact of* Eli Lilly *and Its Progeny in the Courts and PTO,* 17 ALB. L.J. SCI. & TECH. 1, 13 (2007) (referring to UC's successful cloning of the rat insulin gene as "a technical tour de force").

[243]"Complementary" DNA (cDNA) is a complementary copy or "clone" of messenger RNA (mRNA), made in the laboratory by reverse transcription of mRNA. A cDNA contains only the protein-encoding regions of DNA. *See* In re Deuel, 51 F.3d 1552, 1554 (Fed. Cir. 1995).

[244]The claims of UC's '525 patent read as follows:

1. A recombinant plasmid replicable in procaryotic host containing within its nucleotide sequence a subsequence having the structure of the reverse transcript of an mRNA of a vertebrate, which mRNA encodes insulin.

D. The Written Description of the Invention Requirement

Critical to the *Lilly* saga was that as of the 1977 filing date of the application leading to the '525 patent, UC had determined and isolated the preproinsulin (PPI) and proinsulin (PI) cDNA sequences found in rats, but not those in humans.[245] UC included in its patent application a constructive or "prophetic" example describing a method that could be used to obtain the human insulin–encoding cDNA recited in claim 5, as well as the amino acid sequences of human insulin A and B chains.[246] However, UC did not actually isolate and sequence human cDNA until nearly two years after the application's 1977 filing date.[247]

Accused infringer Lilly did not assert that the '525 patent specification failed to *enable* the human insulin cDNA and vertebrate and mammalian insulin cDNA claims in accordance with §112, ¶1 of the Patent Act.[248] Lilly's decision to forgo a challenge to the '525 patent on enablement grounds was not surprising; UC's isolation of the rat insulin cDNA made the human insulin cDNA "relatively easy" to "fish out" thereafter.[249] Instead, Lilly attacked the validity of the asserted claims on the ground that the '525 patent did not provide an adequate written description of the human, mammalian, and vertebrate cDNA inventions claimed.

---

2. A recombinant procaryotic microorganism modified to contain a nucleotide sequence having the structure of the reverse transcript of an mRNA of a vertebrate, which mRNA encodes insulin.
3. The bacterium Escherichia coli which has been modified to contain a nucleotide sequence having the structure of and transcribed from the rat gene for insulin.
4. A microorganism according to claim 2 wherein the vertebrate is a mammal.
5. A microorganism according to claim 2 wherein the vertebrate is a human.
6. A plasmid according to claim 1 comprising a plasmid containing at least one genetic determinant of col E1.
7. A microorganism according to claim 2 comprising a strain of Escherichia coli.

[245]*See* Regents of Univ. of Cal. v. Eli Lilly & Co., 39 U.S.P.Q.2d (BNA) 1225, 1240 (S.D. Ind. 1995).

[246]*See Lilly*, 119 F.3d at 1567.

[247]*See* Regents of Univ. of Cal. v. Eli Lilly & Co., 39 U.S.P.Q.2d (BNA) 1225, 1240 (S.D. Ind. 1995) (stating that "it was not until nearly two years after the original application for the '525 [patent] was filed that UC inventors actually isolated and characterized human insulin cDNA"); *id.* at 1243 (stating that "UC contends that the [human proinsulin amino acid] sequence was not known until [the September 12, 1979 filing date of UC's U.S. Patent No. 4,431,740 ('740 patent)], at which time inventors of the '740 patent actually isolated and characterized the human source DNA that codes for proinsulin").

[248]*See* Regents of Univ. of Cal. v. Eli Lilly & Co., 39 U.S.P.Q.2d (BNA) 1225, 1239-1241 (S.D. Ind. 1995) (identifying the "written description requirement" as the only issue of invalidity raised with respect to '525 patent); *see also Federal Circuit Rules It Takes More Than One cDNA Sequence to Claim a Genus*, III INTELL. PROP. LAWCAST (Dec. 29, 1997) (audio interview of UC counsel Harold J. McElhinny) (stating that Lilly never raised non-enablement as a defense to UC's '525 patent).

[249]*A Bitter Battle over Insulin Gene,* 277 SCIENCE 1028, 1029 (1997).

The Federal Circuit agreed, affirming a district court's conclusion that all the asserted claims of UC's '525 patent were invalid for failure to comply with the written description of the invention requirement.[250] The appellate court first analyzed species claim 5, which recited human insulin–encoding cDNA, and concluded that the '525 specification was fatally defective for failing to *structurally* describe the claimed cDNA. The human insulin–encoding cDNA of claim 5 was not adequately described, the court held, because the '525 patent's specification lacked a disclosure of that cDNA's "relevant structural or physical characteristics."[251] The court specifically pointed to the absence in the specification of "sequence information indicating which nucleotides constitute human cDNA. . . ."[252] Nor did the '525 specification's provision in Example 6 of a process that could be used to isolate the human cDNA remedy the perceived deficiency of the disclosure; the Federal Circuit concluded that "describing a method of preparing a cDNA or even describing the protein that the cDNA encodes, as the example does, does not necessarily describe the cDNA itself."[253]

The Federal Circuit in *Lilly* then turned to the '525 patent's genus claims 1, 2, 4, 6, and 7, which more broadly recited cDNA encoding vertebrate and mammalian insulin. Like species claim 5, the appellate court held the generic claims invalid as not supported by an adequate written description.[254] The extent of the written description required to support claims 1, 2, 4, 6, and 7 mirrored, on the genus level, the court's earlier pronouncement that a structural description must be provided to support a claim to a species of cDNA:

> [A] cDNA is not defined or described by the mere name "cDNA," even if accompanied by the name of the protein that it encodes, but requires a kind of specificity usually achieved by means of the recitation of the sequence of nucleotides that make up the cDNA. . . . A description of a genus of cDNAs may be achieved by means of a recitation of a representative number of cDNAs, defined by nucleotide sequence, falling within the scope of the genus or of a recitation of structural features common to the members of the genus, which features constitute a substantial portion of the genus.[255]

[250] *See* Regents of Univ. of Cal. v. Eli Lilly & Co., 119 F.3d 1559, 1569 (Fed. Cir. 1997).

[251] *See Lilly,* 119 F.3d at 1567.

[252] *See Lilly,* 119 F.3d at 1567 (contrasting the lack of human cDNA sequence data with UC's provision of rat cDNA sequence data in example 5 of the '525 patent).

[253] *Lilly,* 119 F.3d at 1567.

[254] *Lilly,* 119 F.3d at 1569 (rejecting "UC's argument that the district court clearly erred in finding claims 1, 2, 4, 6 and 7 invalid for failure to provide an adequate written description").

[255] *Lilly,* 119 F.3d at 1568-1569 (citation omitted).

In the Federal Circuit's view, a "functional" definition of cDNA was insufficient because it indicated only "what the gene does, rather than what it is."[256] The *Lilly* court viewed such a functional definition as merely a statement of result and observed that "[m]any such genes may achieve that result."[257] Without more, UC's "generic statement[s]" such as "vertebrate insulin cDNA" and "mammalian insulin cDNA" did not constitute an adequate written description of the generic claims because they did "not distinguish the claimed genus from others, except by function."[258]

b. Univ. of Rochester v. G.D. Searle *(2004)*

In the wake of the 1997 *Lilly* decision, Federal Circuit judges continued to debate the proper role of the written description of the invention requirement. The 2002 *Enzo* decision, discussed *supra* Section D.2, is a prime example. In 2004, the *en banc* appellate court declined to rehear the closely watched case of *University of Rochester v. G.D. Searle & Co.*[259] The university's U.S. Patent No. 6,048,850 ('850 patent) claimed methods "for selectively inhibiting PGHS-2 activity in a human host" by "administering a non-steroidal compound that selectively inhibits activity of the PGHS-2 gene product to [or in] a human host in need of such treatment."[260] This invention provided a screening method for use in determining whether a particular drug selectively inhibited the activity of COX-2 so as to reduce inflammation without the gastrointestinal side effects associated with prior art methods that inhibited not only COX-2 but also COX-1, a distinct cyclooxygenase. The university filed its first application directed to the invention in 1992. After filing a series of continuation, continuation-in-part, and divisional applications relating back to the 1992 parent, it received in 1998 Patent No. 5,837,479 ('479 patent) claiming "methods for identifying a compound that inhibits

[256]*Lilly,* 119 F.3d at 1568 (citing Fiers v. Revel, 984 F.2d 1164, 1169-1171 (Fed. Cir. 1993)).

[257]*Lilly*, 119 F.3d at 1568.

[258]*Lilly*, 119 F.3d at 1568 (stating further that such generic statement "does not specifically define any of the genes that fall within its definition. It does not define any structural features commonly possessed by members of the genus that distinguish them from others. One skilled in the art therefore cannot, as one can do with a fully described genus, visualize or recognize the identity of the members of the genus. A definition by function . . . does not suffice to define the genus because it is only an indication of what the gene does, rather than what it is.").

[259]358 F.3d 916 (Fed. Cir. 2004).

[260]*Rochester,* 358 F.3d at 918. PGHS-2 is a form of prostaglandin H synthase also known as "COX-2." COX-2 is a type of enzyme known as a cyclooxygenase that is expressed (i.e., produced biologically) in response to inflammatory stimuli and is thought to be associated with arthritis.

prostaglandin synthesis catalyzed by [PGHS-2]." Rochester's '850 patent in suit issued in 2000 from a related divisional application.

Rochester sued Pfizer in 2000 for infringement of the '850 patent based on Pfizer's sale of its COX-2 inhibitors Celebrex® and Bextra®. The parties disputed whether Rochester was claiming anything new in its '850 patent that it had not already patented in its '479 patent. A district court granted Pfizer's motion for summary judgment of invalidity based on failure to satisfy the written description requirement (as well as lack of enablement), finding that the university's '850 patent failed to describe any "non-steroidal compound that selectively inhibits activity of the PGHS-2 gene," that the university inventors themselves did not know of any such compounds when they filed their application, and that a skilled artisan would have had to engage in undue experimentation in order to deduce the compounds.

The *Rochester* panel affirmed the district court's grant of summary judgment that the university's '850 patent was invalid on written description grounds. The panel rejected the university's argument that no written description requirement exists independent of enablement, stating that "[a]lthough there is often significant overlap between the three requirements [of written description, enablement, and best mode], they are nonetheless independent of each other."[261] In the Federal Circuit's view, the written-description requirement "serves a teaching function" as a "*quid pro quo*" in which the public is given meaningful disclosure in exchange for being excluded from practice of the invention for a limited time. The court also rejected the university's argument that the written description originally played a public notice function that has been supplanted by the subsequent statutory requirement for claims. "[W]hile the role of the claims is to give public notice of the subject matter that is protected, the role of the specification is to teach, both what the invention is (written description) and how to make and use it (enablement)."[262]

The *Rochester* panel also distinguished earlier cases such as *In re Edwards,*[263] in which the court held that the written description requirement was satisfied by a specification that described a claimed compound by the process by which it was made, rather than by its structure. In that case, the Federal Circuit noted, the CCPA found that the application taken as a whole would reasonably lead persons skilled in the art to the claimed compound. Although there is "some flexibility" in the mode of complying with the written description requirement, the specification must set forth enough detail to allow the person of ordinary skill in the art "to understand what is claimed and to recognize that the inventor invented what is claimed." With

[261] *Rochester,* 358 F.3d at 921.
[262] *Rochester,* 358 F.3d at 922 n.5.
[263] 568 F.2d 1349 (C.C.P.A. 1978).

respect to the Rochester '850 patent in suit, "[t]he only claims that appear to be supported by the specification are claims to assay methods, but those claims were already issued in [Rochester's earlier] '479 patent."[264]

On July 2, 2004, a divided Federal Circuit denied the university's petition for rehearing *en banc*, producing four dissenting votes and five opinions.[265] The lead opinion by Circuit Judge Lourie, author of the *Rochester* panel opinion, concurred in the denial of rehearing largely for the reasons stated in the panel opinion. Circuit Judge Dyk concurred in the decision to deny rehearing *en banc*, but noted that his vote "should not be taken as an endorsement" of the court's existing written description jurisprudence. In Judge Dyk's view, the court "ha[s] yet to articulate satisfactory standards that can be applied to all technologies."

Circuit Judge Newman dissented from the *en banc* court's decision not to resolve the "burgeoning conflict" of the written description requirement, which she characterized as having been "promoted from simple semantics into a fundamental conflict concerning patent scope and the support needed to claim biological products." Dissenting Circuit Judge Linn, joined by Circuit Judges Rader and Gajarsa, contended that there is no written description requirement divorced from enablement. The patent law "requires a written description of the invention, but the measure of the sufficiency of that written description in meeting the conditions of patentability in paragraph 1 [of section 112] depends solely on whether it enables any person skilled in the art to which the invention pertains to make and use the claimed invention and sets forth the best mode of carrying out the invention."[266] "There is simply no reason to interpret section 112 to require applicants for patent to set forth the metes and bounds of the claimed invention in two separate places in the application. That is the exclusive function of the claims."[267] Circuit Judge Rader, joined by Circuit Judges Gajarsa and Linn, provided a lengthy dissenting opinion decrying the court's failure to come to terms with *Lilly* (discussed above), a case in which in 1997 "this court for the first time applied the written description language of 35 U.S.C. §112, ¶1 as a general disclosure requirement in place of enablement, rather than in its traditional role as a doctrine to prevent applicants from adding new inventions to an older disclosure."[268] Judge Rader also noted that "no other patent system in the world has the *Eli Lilly* requirement to this day."[269]

[264]*Rochester,* 358 F.3d at 928.
[265]Univ. of Rochester v. G.D. Searle & Co., 375 F.3d 1303 (Fed. Cir. 2004).
[266]*Rochester*, 375 F.3d at 1325 (Linn, J., dissenting from denial of rehearing *en banc*).
[267]*Id.* at 1326-1327.
[268]*Id.* at 1307 (Rader, J., dissenting from denial of rehearing *en banc*).
[269]*Id.* at 1312.

c. Carnegie Mellon Univ. v. Hoffman-La Roche *(2008)*

Despite some Federal Circuit judges' clear discomfort with *Lilly*'s expansive formulation of the written description of the invention requirement, the court continued to apply it in its 2008 decision *Carnegie Mellon University v. Hoffmann-La Roche Inc.*[270] The CMU patents in suit were directed to, *inter alia*, recombinant plasmids (small, replicating circular loops of DNA) that contained "*polA*" gene coding regions from bacteria for the expression of large quantities of the enzyme "DNA polymerase I." The *CMU* case did not raise the traditional written description question of support for new claims added after the application filing date. Rather, the issue was support for an originally filed genus claim: the CMU patents (as filed for in 1984) disclosed the *polA* gene from only one type of bacteria (*E. coli*), but the claims were not limited to any particular bacterial species. At the time of the invention, the *polA* gene from *E. coli* was one of only three bacterial *polA* genes that scientists had succeeded in cloning, out of thousands of bacterial species. The Federal Circuit observed that "[t]he narrow specifications of the . . . patents only disclose the *polA* gene coding sequence from one bacterial source, *viz., E. coli.* Significantly, the specification fails to disclose or describe the *polA* gene coding sequence for any other bacterial species."[271] Applying *Lilly,* the court held the challenged claims invalid as not supported by an adequate written description. It rejected the patentee's attempt to distinguish *Lilly* on the ground that the case at bar dealt with a "combination of well known elements that create a generic biological tool," whereas *Lilly* involved a specific cDNA sequence. "[N]othing in *Eli Lilly* indicates that [its] holding was limited to inventions involving novel DNA sequences," the Federal Circuit instructed. The *CMU* court also cited as "accurate" and "persuasive" authority the USPTO's "Guidelines for Examination of Patent Applications under the 35 U.S.C. §112, ¶1, 'Written Description' Requirement,"[272] which state that "[f]or inventions in an unpredictable art, adequate written description of a genus which embraces widely variant species *cannot* be achieved by disclosing only one species within the genus."[273] In sum, the CMU patent specifications failed to show that the inventors possessed enough species to show that they had "invented and disclosed the totality of the genus"[274] that they claimed.

[270]541 F.3d 1115 (Fed. Cir. 2008).
[271]*Id.* at 1125.
[272]66 Fed. Reg. 1099 (Jan. 5, 2001).
[273]*Id.* at 1106.
[274]*Carnegie Mellon Univ.,* 541 F.3d at 1126.

d. Ariad Pharms. v. Eli Lilly *(2010) (en banc)*

In 2010, the Federal Circuit went *en banc* to resolve its continuing disagreement over the proper role of the written description of the invention requirement.[275] The prevailing party and validity challenger was again the Eli Lilly Corporation. Unless the Supreme Court decides to take up the issue in some future case, the Federal Circuit's *en banc* decision in *Ariad Pharms., Inc. v. Eli Lilly and Co.*[276] establishes that the expansive form of the written description of the invention requirement, as first applied in the 1997 *Lilly* decision as a general-purpose disclosure requirement, is the controlling law for the U.S. patent system. As a long-awaited response by the *en banc* court to the prolonged uncertainty concerning the requirement's scope, the *Ariad* decision mandates careful study.

The *Ariad* case involved a "high-stakes tussle" over the reach of a pioneering biotechnology patent.[277] In the mid-1980s, 13 scientists collaborating at the Massachusetts Institute of Technology (MIT), the Whitehead Institute for Biomedical Research, and Harvard University were the first to identify a protein known as Nuclear Factor Kappa B (NF-κB).[278] Present in the cytoplasm of various types of cells, the NF-κB protein is a transcription factor, that is, a protein that affects gene expression (the process in which a gene's DNA sequence is converted to a protein in a cell).

The scientists were also first to discover the mechanism by which the NF-κB protein activates gene expression underlying the body's immune responses to infection. They found that the NF-κB protein mediates certain intracellular signaling. The inventors postulated that reducing NF-κB activity could reduce the symptoms of diseases including cancer, AIDS, sepsis, and atherosclerosis. They hypothesized that three classes of molecules were capable of reducing NF-κB

[275]*See Ariad Pharms., Inc. v. Eli Lilly and Co.*, 598 F.3d 1336, 1342 (Fed. Cir. 2010) (*en banc*) (granting Ariad's petition "[i]n light of the controversy concerning the distinctness and proper role of the written description requirement").

[276]598 F.3d 1336 (Fed. Cir. 2010) (*en banc*).

[277]Ken Garber, *Ariad's NF-κB Patent Claims Shot Down on Appeal*, 27 NATURE BIOTECHNOLOGY 494, 494 (2009) (reporting that the *Ariad* case "has embroiled big pharma, several prominent biotech companies and even Nobel Prize winners as courtroom witnesses in a high-stakes tussle over the commercial reach of patents with especially broad claims").

[278]*See* Ariad Pharms., Inc. v. Eli Lilly and Co., 529 F. Supp. 2d 106, 112 (D. Mass. 2007); *see also* Ariad Pharms., Inc. v. Eli Lilly and Co., 598 F.3d 1336, 1340 (Fed. Cir. 2010) (*en banc*). The scientists directing the collaboration were Nobel Laureates Dr. David Baltimore of the Whitehead Institute and Dr. Phillip Sharp of MIT, along with Dr. Thomas Maniatis, the Thomas H. Lee Professor of Molecular and Cellular Biology at Harvard. *See* Complaint at ¶11, Case No. 02 CV 11280RWZ, Ariad Pharms., Inc. et al. v. Eli Lilly & Co., No. 02 CV 11280RWZ, 2002 WL 33027597 (D. Mass. June 25, 2002).

activity: (1) "specific inhibitors," (2) "dominantly interfering molecules," and (3) "decoy molecules."

The 13 collaborating scientists were named as inventors in a U.S. patent application jointly filed by their institutions in 1986. After a lengthy and complex prosecution, U.S. Patent No. 6,410,516 ('516 patent), titled "Nuclear factors associated with transcriptional regulation," issued in 2002 to the original assignees: MIT, Whitehead Institute, and Harvard. Ariad Pharmaceuticals was the exclusive licensee of the '516 patent.[279]

The relevant claims of the '516 patent are genus claims, encompassing the use of all substances that achieve the desired result of reducing the binding of NF-κB to NF-κB recognition sites.[280] Representative claim 80 (rewritten to include the text of the claim from which it depends) recites:

> 80. [A method for modifying effects of external influences on a eukaryotic cell, which external influences induce NF-κB-mediated intracellular signaling, the method comprising altering NF-κB activity in the cells such that NF-κB-mediated effects of external influences are modified, wherein NF-κB activity in the cell is reduced] wherein reducing NF-κB activity comprises reducing binding of NF-κB to NF-κB recognition sites on genes which are transcriptionally regulated by NF-κB.[281]

The language of the asserted claims, although amended during prosecution, corresponds to language in the original ("priority") application.[282] Thus the *Ariad* case is another in the series of decisions, starting with the 1997 *Lilly* decision, in which the Federal Circuit has applied the written description of the invention requirement to originally filed claims despite the absence of any question regarding priority to an earlier filing date.

When the '516 patent issued in 2002, Ariad and the university assignees (collectively "Ariad") sued Eli Lilly and Co. for infringement. A jury found the asserted claims infringed and not invalid, rejecting Lilly's validity challenges on anticipation, written description, and enablement grounds and awarding damages against Lilly of

[279]*See* Complaint at ¶18, Case No. 02 CV 11280RWZ, Ariad Pharms., Inc. et al. v. Eli Lilly & Co., No. 02 CV 11280RWZ, 2002 WL 33027597 (D. Mass. June 25, 2002).

[280]*Ariad,* 598 F.3d at 1341.

[281]*Ariad,* 598 F.3d at 1340. The district court found that "[t]he allowed claims broadly cover a method of inhibiting the expression of a gene whose transcription is regulated by NF-κB in a eukaryotic cell. The only step required to practice the broadest patented method is to 'reduc[e] NF-κB activity in the cell such that the expression of said gene is inhibited.' No particular agent or substance need be used, nor any particular step(s) performed, to reduce NF-κB activity in order to practice the invention." Ariad Pharms., Inc. v. Eli Lilly and Co., 529 F. Supp. 2d 106, 113-114 (D. Mass. 2007) (footnotes omitted).

[282]*Ariad,* 598 F.3d at 1341.

approximately $65 million.[283] In 2009, a panel of the Federal Circuit overturned the jury verdict on the basis that the claims were invalid under the written description of the invention requirement. The panel noted the "vast scope of these generic claims."[284]

The Federal Circuit thereafter granted Ariad's petition for rehearing *en banc* to resolve much-debated questions concerning the nature and scope of the written description of the invention requirement. The *en banc* court requested briefing on the following two issues:

> (1) Whether 35 U.S.C. §112, paragraph 1, contains a written description requirement separate from an enablement requirement?
> (2) If a separate written description requirement is set forth in the statute, what is the scope and purpose of that requirement?[285]

In March of 2010, the *en banc* Federal Circuit decided issue (1) in the affirmative, and answered issue (2) as detailed below. The *en banc* opinion for the court was written by Circuit Judge Lourie, who had previously authored the court's written description opinions in *Lilly, Rochester, Enzo,* and *CMU*. The *en banc* opinion for the court in *Ariad* garnered 9 out of 11 possible votes.[286]

With respect to *en banc* briefing question (1), the Federal Circuit agreed with Eli Lilly that the text of the first paragraph of 35 U.S.C. §112 requires a written description of the invention requirement separate from the enablement requirement. In other words, the court parsed the statute as requiring that

> (1) The specification shall contain a *written description of the invention, and*
> (2) The specification shall contain a written description . . . of the manner and process of making and using it, in such full, clear, concise, and exact terms as to *enable* any person skilled in the art to which it pertains, or with which it is most nearly connected, to make and use the same. . . .[287]

[283]*Ariad Pharms., Inc. v. Eli Lilly and Co.*, 529 F. Supp. 2d 106, 115 (D. Mass. 2007).

[284]*See* Ariad Pharms., Inc. v. Eli Lilly and Co., 560 F.3d 1366, 1376 (Fed. Cir. 2009) (concluding that "[w]hatever thin thread of support a jury might find in the decoy-molecule hypothetical simply cannot bear the weight of the vast scope of these generic claims. . . . Here, the specification at best describes decoy molecule structures and hypothesizes with no accompanying description that they could be used to reduce NF-κB activity. Yet the asserted claims are far broader. We therefore conclude that the jury lacked substantial evidence for its verdict that the asserted claims were supported by adequate written description, and thus hold the asserted claims invalid.").

[285]*Ariad,* 598 F.3d at 1342. In addition to the parties' submissions, the *en banc* court received 25 *amicus curiae* briefs. *Ariad,* 598 F.3d at 1342.

[286]Circuit Judges Rader and Linn each filed dissenting-in-part, concurring-in-part opinions. An "additional views" opinion by Judge Newman and a concurring opinion by Judge Gajarsa meant that in total, the *en banc* rehearing of *Ariad* produced five opinions.

[287]*Ariad,* 598 F.3d at 1344 (citing 35 U.S.C. §112, ¶1 (2006)) (emphasis added).

In the Federal Circuit's view, the contrary reading urged by Ariad — namely, that the written description requirement exists only to identify the invention that must comply with the enablement requirement — would result in a "surplusage" of the statutory language and contravene its "parallelism."[288]

Policy concerns also supported the existence of a separate written description requirement, which the *en banc* court viewed as "part of the *quid pro quo* of a patent."[289] A patent's written description of a claimed invention serves many important purposes: it "allows the United States Patent and Trademark Office ('PTO') to examine applications effectively; courts to understand the invention, determine compliance with the statute, and to construe the claims; and the public to understand and improve upon the invention and to avoid the claimed boundaries of the patentee's exclusive rights."[290]

The Federal Circuit also cited precedent supporting the independence of the written description requirement from enablement. Among Supreme Court decisions, the *Ariad* court highlighted the 1938 decision in *Schriber-Schroth Co. v. Cleveland Trust Co.*[291] Although the Court in *Schriber-Schroth* "did not expressly state" that it was applying a written description requirement separate from enablement, the *Ariad* court concluded that "that is exactly what the Court did."[292]

[288]*Ariad,* 598 F.3d at 1344-1345. Dissenting Judge Linn responded on this point that "there is no justification for reading the statute, beyond the priority context suggested by 35 U.S.C. §120, as requiring anything other than a written description sufficient to enable a skilled artisan to make and use the invention particularly pointed out and distinctly recited in the claims." Ariad Pharms., Inc. v. Eli Lilly and Co., 598 F.3d 1336, 1367 (Fed. Cir. 2010) (*en banc*) (Linn, J., dissenting-in-part and concurring-in-part).

[289]*Ariad,* 598 F.3d at 1345.

[290]*Ariad,* 598 F.3d at 1345.

[291]305 U.S. 47 (1938). *Schriber-Schroth* involved *inter alia* a patent to Gulick on pistons used in internal combustion engines. As filed, Gulick's application disclosed "extremely rigid" web elements in the pistons; five years later, Gulick copied another's claim to provoke an interference and made corresponding additions to his disclosure to include "flexible" webs. The Supreme Court rejected Gulick's argument that flexibility was an inherent property of the disclosed metal from which the webs were fabricated, and concluded that "the Gulick amendments were . . . new matter beyond the scope of the device described in the application as filed." *Schriber-Schroth*, 305 U.S. at 58.

[292]*Ariad,* 598 F.3d at 1346. Judge Rader's dissenting opinion responded that

> *Schriber-Schroth*, as the court acknowledges, dealt with amended claims, as did *MacKay Radio & Tel. Co. v. Radio Corp. of Am.*, 306 U.S. 86, 59 S. Ct. 427, 83 L. Ed. 506 (1939), and *Gill v. Wells*, 89 U.S. (22 Wall.) 1, 22 L. Ed. 699 (1874). These cases stand only for the unremarkable proposition that an applicant cannot add new matter to an original disclosure. Thus Supreme Court precedent is fully consistent with the logical reading of the statute and impeaches this court's *ultra vires* imposition of a new written description requirement for original claims, an imposition that first arose in *Regents of the University of California v. Eli Lilly & Co.*, 119 F.3d 1559, 1566-69 (Fed. Cir. 1997).

D. The Written Description of the Invention Requirement

Identifying what particular purpose or role the written description of the invention requirement serves that is not already addressed by the claims of a patent has always been a conceptual challenge.[293] The *Ariad en banc* court held that a separate written description requirement does not conflict with the function of claims. Claims are principally to provide notice of the boundaries of a patentee's right to exclude, the *en banc* court explained; they do not describe the invention (although their original language contributes to the invention's written description and "in certain cases satisfies" the written description of the invention requirement). Rather, patent claims "define and circumscribe." In contrast, the written description "discloses and teaches."[294]

Another conceptual difficulty with an independent written description of the invention requirement is distinguishing its role from the prohibition on "new matter" in 35 U.S.C. §132.[295] The *en banc* court in *Ariad* explained that improperly adding new matter is distinct from a failure to satisfy the written description of the invention requirement because §132 is merely "an examiner's instruction."[296] "[U]nlike §282 of the Patent Act, which makes the failure to comply with §112 a defense to infringement, §132 provides no statutory penalty for a breach." In contrast, "[e]xpress statutory invalidity defenses carry more weight than examiner's instructions. . . ." In any event, "the prohibition on new matter does not negate the need to provide a written description of one's invention."[297]

In view of the Federal Circuit's 1997 *Lilly* decision and its progeny, it is not surprising that the *Ariad* court firmly rejected the patentee's argument that the written description of the invention requirement should not be applied to original claims, that is, to claims included in an application when it is filed. The argument that such claims should be immune from written description scrutiny is based on the premise that "original claims, as part of the original disclosure, constitute their own written description of the invention."[298] The *Ariad*

Ariad Pharms., Inc. v. Eli Lilly and Co., 598 F.3d 1336, 1363 (Fed. Cir. 2010) (*en banc*) (Rader, J., dissenting-in-part and concurring-in-part).

[293] *See* Vas-Cath, Inc. v. Mahurkar, 935 F.2d 1555, 1560 (Fed. Cir. 1991) (observing that "[o]ne may wonder what purpose a separate 'written description' requirement serves, when the second paragraph of §112 expressly requires that the applicant conclude his specification 'with one or more claims particularly pointing out and distinctly claiming the subject matter which the applicant regards as his invention' ").

[294] *Ariad,* 598 F.3d at 1347.

[295] The Patent Act provides that "[n]o amendment shall introduce new matter into the disclosure of the invention." 35 U.S.C. §132(a) (2006) (last sentence of paragraph).

[296] *Ariad,* 598 F.3d at 1348.

[297] *Ariad,* 598 F.3d at 1348.

[298] *Ariad,* 598 F.3d at 1349. This position is well supported by precedent. *See* In re Gardner, 475 F.2d 1389, 1391 (C.C.P.A. 1973) (reversing Board's rejection of an original claim under the written description requirement of 35 U.S.C. §112, ¶1 and explaining

court rejected this premise, at least in the particular context of genus claims:

> Although many original claims will satisfy the written description requirement, certain claims may not. For example, a generic claim may define the boundaries of a vast genus of chemical compounds, and yet the question may still remain whether the specification, including original claim language, demonstrates that the applicant has invented species sufficient to support a claim to a genus. The problem is especially acute with genus claims that use functional language to define the boundaries of a claimed genus. In such a case, the functional claim may simply claim a desired result, and may do so without describing species that achieve that result. But the specification must demonstrate that the applicant has made a generic invention that achieves the claimed result and do so by showing that the applicant has invented species sufficient to support a claim to the functionally-defined genus.[299]

Repeating the test set forth in its 1997 *Lilly* decision, the *Ariad en banc* court observed that a sufficient description of a claimed genus requires the disclosure of either (1) "a representative number of species falling within the scope of the genus" or (2) "structural features common to the members of the genus so that one of skill in the art can 'visualize or recognize' the members of the genus."[300] Merely "drawing a fence" around the outer limits of a genus is not enough to show "that one has invented a genus and not just a species."[301]

Whether the genus claim in question was an original claim or added by amendment is not relevant. According to the *Ariad* court, "[n]either the statute nor legal precedent limits the written description requirement to cases of priority or distinguishes between original and amended claims."[302]

---

that "[c]laim 2, which apparently was an original claim, in itself constituted a description in the original disclosure equivalent in scope and identical in language to the total subject matter now being claimed.... Nothing more is necessary for compliance with the description requirement....") (citation omitted); In re Koller, 613 F.2d 819, 823 (C.C.P.A. 1980) (citing *Gardner* for the proposition that "original claims constitute their own description"). The *Koller* court held that method claims reciting the phrase "liquid medium," presented in a continuing application, were supported in accordance with §112, ¶1 of the Patent Act by a grandparent application's claims that used the same terminology. *See Koller,* 613 F.2d at 823 (noting that "the term 'liquid medium' is found in both places [and] the two sets of claims are similar in wording").

[299]*Ariad,* 598 F.3d at 1349.

[300]*Ariad,* 598 F.3d at 1350 (quoting *Lilly,* 119 F.3d at 1568-1569).

[301]*Ariad,* 598 F.3d at 1350. As to the number of constituent species that must be described in order to adequately describe a claimed genus, the court declined to "set out any bright-line rules" because "this number necessarily changes with each invention, and it changes with progress in a field." *Ariad,* 598 F.3d at 1351.

[302]*Ariad,* 598 F.3d at 1351.

D. The Written Description of the Invention Requirement

The *en banc Ariad* court then turned to the "possession" test for written description compliance,[303] candidly admitting that the test "has never been very enlightening."[304] Because "the hallmark of written description is disclosure," the *Ariad* court announced that a more complete formulation of the test is "possession as shown in the disclosure."[305] That test requires an "objective inquiry into the four corners of the specification from the perspective of a person of ordinary skill in the art." The description must be such as to show the hypothetical person that the "inventor actually invented the invention claimed."[306]

Because the written description inquiry is a factual one,[307] certain contextual facts are relevant. The level of detail that the specification must supply "varies depending on the nature and scope of the claims and on the complexity and predictability of the relevant technology." For generic claims, relevant contextual factors include (1) "existing knowledge in the particular field"; (2) the "extent and content of the prior art"; (3) the "maturity of the science or technology"; and (4) the "predictability of the aspect at issue."[308]

Although the application of the written description of the invention requirement may vary in accordance with the different facts and arguments presented to the courts in each case, the *Ariad* court explained that there exist "a few broad principles that hold true across all cases."[309] These principles can be summarized as follows:

(1) compliance with the written description of the invention requirement does not require the inclusion of examples in a patent application or proof that the claimed invention has been actually reduced to practice;
(2) a constructive reduction to practice that identifies the claimed invention "in a definite way" can satisfy the requirement;
(3) actual "possession" or reduction to practice outside of the specification is not enough, because the specification itself must demonstrate possession;
(4) compliance with the written description of the invention requirement "does not demand any particular form of disclosure";

[303] *See also supra* Section D.2 ("How an Application Conveys Possession of an Invention").
[304] *Ariad,* 598 F.3d at 1351.
[305] *Ariad,* 598 F.3d at 1351.
[306] *Ariad,* 598 F.3d at 1351.
[307] *See Ariad,* 598 F.3d at 1351 (citing Ralston Purina Co. v. Far-Mar-Co, Inc., 772 F.2d 1570, 1575 (Fed. Cir. 1985)).
[308] *Ariad,* 598 F.3d at 1351.
[309] *Ariad,* 598 F.3d at 1352.

(5) compliance with the written description of the invention requirement does not require "that the specification recite the claimed invention *in haec verba*";[310]
(6) a written description that merely renders obvious the claimed invention does not satisfy the written description of the invention requirement;
(7) the written description requirement is not a "super enablement" standard for chemical and biotechnological inventions;
(8) when genetic material is claimed as a genus, the written description of the invention requirement does not mandate that a specification provide a nucleotide-by-nucleotide recitation of the entire genus; and
(9) one may comply with the written description requirement by disclosing structural features common to the members of a claimed genus.[311]

With these principles in hand, the *en banc* court turned to the merits of the *Ariad* dispute. Judge Lourie's opinion for the court tellingly observed that, like the 1997 *Lilly* decision, the case at bar "illustrate[d] the problem of genus claims."[312] Here the claims were to methods encompassing the use of a genus of molecules to achieve a stated useful result (i.e., reducing binding of NF-κB to NF-κB recognition sites).[313] Although the claims were method claims that did not explicitly recite any molecules, the Federal Circuit interpreted the claims as requiring the use of three particular classes of molecules. These classes of molecules had to be sufficiently disclosed:

> Regardless whether the asserted claims recite a compound, Ariad still must describe some way of performing the claimed methods, and Ariad admits that the specification suggests only the use of the three classes of molecules to achieve NF-κB reduction [i.e., (1) specific inhibitors, (2) dominantly interfering molecules, and (3) decoy molecules]. Thus, to satisfy the written description requirement for the asserted claims, the specification must demonstrate that Ariad possessed the claimed methods by sufficiently disclosing molecules capable of reducing NF-κB activity so as to "satisfy the inventor's obligation to disclose the technologic knowledge upon which the patent is based, and to demonstrate that the patentee was in possession of the invention that is claimed."[314]

[310]Latin for "in these words."
[311]*Ariad,* 598 F.3d at 1352.
[312]*Ariad,* 598 F.3d at 1350.
[313]*Ariad,* 598 F.3d at 1350.
[314]*Ariad,* 598 F.3d at 1355 (quoting Capon v. Eshhar, 418 F.3d 1349, 1357 (Fed. Cir. 2005)).

D. The Written Description of the Invention Requirement

The Federal Circuit treats compliance with the written description of the invention requirement as a question of fact rather than law.[315] Thus the *en banc* court in *Ariad* reviewed the jury's determination that the '516 patent was not invalid for failure to satisfy the written description requirement under the "substantial evidence" standard of review.[316]

To determine whether the jury's verdict upholding validity was supported by substantial evidence, the *en banc* court examined the 1989 patent application's supporting disclosure corresponding to each of three types of molecules.[317] Backdropping the court's examination of the record was its observation that as of 1989, the field of Ariad's invention was "particularly unpredictable," and "existing knowledge and prior art [were] scant."[318]

With respect to category (1) molecules, the specification disclosed that "specific inhibitors" are molecules able to reduce or eliminate NF-κB binding to DNA in the nucleus. The specification provided one example, a naturally occurring molecule known as I-κB that holds NF-κB in an inactive state until the cell receives certain external influences. Ariad's expert testified that I-κB existed in 1989 and that an art

[315]*See Ariad,* 598 F.3d at 1351 (citing Ralston Purina Co. v. Far-Mar-Co, Inc., 772 F.2d 1570, 1575 (Fed. Cir. 1985)).

In this author's view, treating written description as a question of fact while treating enablement as a question of law makes little sense. Admittedly, pre-*Ariad* precedent established written description compliance as a question of fact. *See* In re Ruschig, 379 F.2d 990, 9996 (C.C.P.A. 1967) (Rich, J.) (stating that "[t]he issue here is in no wise a question of [the specification's] compliance with section 112, it is a question of fact: Is the compound of claim 13 described therein?"). The *en banc* court in *Ariad* could have exercised its authority to rationalize the law on this point, but chose not to. In his *Ariad* dissent, Judge Rader observed that

> [t]he court makes the subjective/objective nature of the [written description] test even more confusing by perpetuating the test's status as a question of fact. Other, related objective inquiries that focus on the four corners of the specification, such as claim construction and enablement, are questions of law. If the court is right that the written description of the invention test is objective, then either the court misclassifies written description or claim construction and enablement.

Ariad Pharms., Inc. v. Eli Lilly and Co., 598 F.3d 1336, 1366 (Fed. Cir. 2010) (*en banc*) (Rader, J., dissenting-in-part and concurring-in-part).

[316]*See Ariad,* 598 F.3d at 1355 (stating that " '[a] determination that a patent is invalid for failure to meet the written description requirement of 35 U.S.C. §112, ¶1 is a question of fact, and we review a jury's determinations of facts relating to compliance with the written description requirement for substantial evidence' ") (quoting PIN/NIP, Inc. v. Platte Chem. Co., 304 F.3d 1235, 1243 (Fed. Cir. 2002) (citing Vas-Cath Inc. v. Mahurkar, 935 F.2d 1555, 1563 (Fed. Cir. 1991))).

[317]The jury in *Ariad* found that the priority date of the '516 patent was April 21, 1989, the patent application's filing date, and the parties did not challenge this finding on appeal. *Ariad,* 598 F.3d at 1355.

[318]Ariad Pharms., Inc. v. Eli Lilly and Co., 598 F.3d 1336, 1354 (Fed. Cir. 2010) (*en banc*).

worker could isolate it through experimentation. Nevertheless, the *Ariad* court concluded that the evidence pertaining to specific inhibitor molecules amounted to merely "a vague functional description and an invitation to further research," not an adequate written description of a specific inhibitor.[319]

The disclosure of the 1989 application with respect to category (2) "dominantly interfering molecules" was more scant than that for category (1). A dominantly interfering molecule is a truncated form of the NF-κB molecule that blocks natural NF-κB from inducing the expression of its target genes. In contrast with category (1) molecules, the 1989 application did not disclose any specific examples of dominantly interfering molecules. The Federal Circuit characterized this fact, coupled with testimony of Ariad's expert, as representing "'just . . . a wish, or arguably a plan' for future research."[320]

The closest question regarding written description compliance in *Ariad* centered on the 1989 application's disclosure of category (3) "decoy molecules." Such molecules are "designed to mimic a region of the gene whose expression would normally be induced by NF-κB"; because NF-κB would bind the decoy, it would not be available to bind its natural target.[321] Unlike the other two categories of useful molecules, the 1989 application provided example structures for decoy molecules in the form of specific DNA sequences. But even though the specification adequately described the actual decoy molecules, this did not "answer the question whether the specification adequately describe[d] using those molecules to reduce NF-κB activity."[322]

All that the specification stated with respect to use of the decoy molecules in the claimed methods was that NF-κB "would bind the decoy" and thus "negative regulation can be effected." In the Federal Circuit's view, this disclosure was less a prophetic example than "a mere mention of a desired outcome."[323] The *en banc* court explained that

> [t]he '516 patent discloses no working or even prophetic examples of methods that reduce NF-κB activity, and no completed syntheses of any

[319]*Ariad,* 598 F.3d at 1356. Another significant problem for Ariad was that the bulk of the evidence it relied on concerning I-κB (including DNA sequence data) was not disclosed until 1991, when Ariad filed a continuation-in-part application claiming priority to its parent 1989 application. The jury found that 1989 was the effective filing date of the '516 patent in suit, and "neither party appealed that determination." *Ariad,* 598 F.3d at 1355. Thus, new matter from the 1991 application was "legally irrelevant" to the written description determination. *Ariad,* 598 F.3d at 1355.

[320]*Ariad,* 598 F.3d at 1357 (quoting Fiers v. Revel, 984 F.2d 1164, 1171 (Fed. Cir. 1993) and also citing Regents of Univ. of Cal. v. Eli Lilly & Co., 119 F.3d 1559, 1567 (Fed. Cir. 1997)).

[321]*Ariad,* 598 F.3d at 1357.

[322]*Ariad,* 598 F.3d at 1357.

[323]*Ariad,* 598 F.3d at 1357.

> of the molecules prophesized to be capable of reducing NF-κB activity. The state of the art at the time of filing was primitive and uncertain, leaving Ariad with an insufficient supply of prior art knowledge with which to fill the gaping holes in its disclosure.... Whatever thin thread of support a jury might find in the decoy-molecule hypothetical simply cannot bear the weight of the vast scope of these generic claims.... Here, the specification at best describes decoy molecule structures and hypothesizes with no accompanying description that they could be used to reduce NF-κB activity. Yet the asserted claims are far broader.[324]

Concluding that the record lacked substantial evidence to support the jury's verdict for the patentee, the Federal Circuit held the asserted claims of Ariad's '516 patent invalid for failure to satisfy the written description of the invention requirement.

e. AbbVie Deutschland v. Janssen Biotech *(2014)*

The Federal Circuit's expansion of the written description of the invention requirement continued in the 2014 decision, *AbbVie Deutschland GMH & Co. v. Janssen Biotech, Inc.*[325] ("*AbbVie*" or "*AbbVie v. Centocor*"). The decision extended to antibody technology[326] the reasoning of the Federal Circuit's controversial 1997 decision in *Regents of Univ. of Cal. v. Eli Lilly & Co.* ("*Lilly*"),[327] which concerned claims to genuses of gene sequences. The *AbbVie* decision calls into question the continued viability of antibody claims that recite a genus based on functionality (rather than structure).

In an opinion authored by Judge Lourie (the lead architect of the Federal Circuit's written description jurisprudence), the majority in *AbbVie* affirmed a jury's invalidation based, *inter alia,* on failure to satisfy the written description of the invention requirement with respect to the asserted claims in two AbbVie patents directed to a genus of human antibodies.[328] The claimed antibodies bound to the

[324]*Ariad,* 598 F.3d at 1357-1358 (citations and footnote omitted).

[325]759 F.3d 1285 (Fed. Cir. 2014) (Lourie, J.) (hereafter "*AbbVie*" or "*AbbVie Deutschland*").

[326]Antibodies are proteins that bind to unwanted foreign substances called "antigens" in order to remove them from the body. *AbbVie,* 759 F.3d at 1290.

[327]119 F.3d 1559 (Fed. Cir. 1997). The *Lilly* decision is examined *supra* this section.

[328]Notably, only two of three judges on the *AbbVie* panel supported the written description reasoning. Judge O'Malley concurred in the result (invalidity), but not the written description reasoning, which she considered *dicta*. *See AbbVie,* 759 F.3d at 1305-1307 (O'Malley, J., concurring in judgment). Based on the jury's verdict, the district court had also held AbbVie's claims invalid for obviousness, and AbbVie did not substantively challenge the holding of obviousness on appeal. *AbbVie,* 759 F.3d at 1297 n.5. However, AbbVie did challenge the district court's jury instruction that "new information presented at trial that was not considered by the PTO would make it easier for Centocor to carry its burden of providing invalidity by clear and convincing evidence," *AbbVie,* 759 F.3d at 1303, and asserted that the jury instruction "'infected all

antigen "human IL-12," which is the human interleukin 12 signaling protein. When overproduced in the human body, the IL-12 protein can lead to the diseases psoriasis and rheumatoid arthritis. Because the human body does not produce IL-12 antibodies naturally, AbbVie (formerly Abbott Labs) used genetic engineering techniques to make the antibodies and filed a patent application claiming them in 1999.[329]

Notably, the asserted claims of the AbbVie patents in suit were written in primarily *functional* rather than *structural* terms; i.e., the claims recited a genus of human antibodies achieving a certain degree of "stickiness" or tightness of binding to the IL-12 antigen, as measured by a "k_{off} rate constant." A representative claim of AbbVie's U.S. Patent No. 6,914,128 ('128 patent) recited:

> 29. A neutralizing isolated human antibody, or antigen-binding portion thereof that binds to human IL-12 and dissociates from human IL-12 with a k_{off} rate constant of $1x10^{-2}$ s^{-1} or less, as determined by surface plasmon resonance.[330]

Although the accused antibody marketed by co-defendant Centocor as "Stelara" literally infringed the AbbVie patent claims (satisfying the functional k_{off} rate limitation),[331] the Federal Circuit majority affirmed the district court's judgment of invalidity. In the majority's view, the AbbVie patents failed to adequately describe the *accused* antibody in *structural* terms. More particularly, the Circuit determined that the written description of AbbVie's patents did not sufficiently describe enough representative species (including the species encompassing Centocor's accused antibody) to support the entire

---

of the invalidity verdicts.'" *AbbVie,* 759 F.3d at 1306 (O'Malley, J., concurring in judgment) (quoting Federal Circuit oral argument recording). The *AbbVie* majority asserted that "we need only address whether the challenged instructions constitute reversible error with respect to the jury's written description verdict[, a]nd we conclude that they do not." *AbbVie,* 759 F.3d at 1304. In concurring Judge O'Malley's view, "[i]f we find no prejudicial error in the challenged jury instruction, the finding of *obviousness* stands and the patent is invalid. Alternatively, if we hold that the jury instruction is erroneous, AbbVie is entitled to a new trial on *all* validity issues." *AbbVie,* 759 F.3d at 1306 (O'Malley, J., concurring in judgment) (emphasis added). Judge O'Malley "express[ed] no opinion regarding the thoughtful written description analysis in the majority opinion," but "simply d[id] not think it necessary or dispositive to the outcome of this case." *AbbVie,* 759 F.3d at 1306 (O'Malley, J., concurring in judgment) (citing Nat'l Am. Ins. Co. v. United States, 498 F.3d 1301, 1306 (Fed. Cir. 2007) ("Dicta, as defined by this court, are 'statements made by a court that are unnecessary to the decision in the case, and therefore[,] not precedential. . . .'" (internal quotation marks omitted) (quoting Co-Steel Raritan, Inc. v. Int'l Trade Comm'n, 357 F.3d 1294, 1307 (Fed. Cir. 2004)))).

[329] *AbbVie,* 759 F.3d at 1291.

[330] *AbbVie,* 759 F.3d at 1292. A smaller k_{off} value represents a tighter binding. *AbbVie,* 759 F.3d at 1291.

[331] *See AbbVie,* 759 F.3d at 1300 ("Centocor's Stelara . . . falls within the scope of the claimed genus").

claimed genus. Although the AbbVie patents described 300 antibodies within the claimed functional genus,[332] the patents did not describe any antibodies having the same *structural* features as the accused Stelara antibody. The Federal Circuit determined that those structural features "differ[ed] considerably" from the structure of the species described in AbbVie's patents, which proved fatal to satisfaction of the written description requirement.[333]

The Federal Circuit's written description jurisprudence requires that a sufficient description of a genus requires the disclosure of either (1) a representative number of species falling within the scope of the genus, or (2) structural features common to the members of the genus so that a skilled artisan can visualize or recognize members of the genus.[334] In *AbbVie,* the second method of describing a genus did not apply (as conceded by AbbVie's expert), so "[t]he question therefore is whether the patents sufficiently otherwise describe representative

[332]*AbbVie,* 759 F.3d at 1301 ("The patents describe the amino acid sequence of about 300 antibodies having a range of IL-12 binding affinities.").

[333]With regard to antibody structure, the Federal Circuit explained that each antibody consists of four chains of amino acids, two identical "heavy" chains and two identical "light" chains. *AbbVie,* 759 F.3d at 1290. Comparing the structures of the antibodies disclosed in the AbbVie patents with the structure of the accused product, the court observed:

> All of the antibodies described in AbbVie's patents were derived from Joe-9 [the name given to the "lead" human DNA fragment identified by AbbVie in the course of screening a library for fragments that encoded an antibody fragment with IL-12 antibody affinity] and have V_H3 type heavy chains and Lambda type light chains. Although the described antibodies have different amino acid sequences at the CDRs [complementarity determining regions], they share 90% or more sequence similarity in the variable regions and over 200 of those antibodies differ from Y61 [an improved antibody that AbbVie developed by modifying "Joe-9"] by only one amino acid. The patents describe that other V_H3/Lambda antibodies may be modified to attain IL-12 binding affinity. However, *the patents do not describe any example, or even the possibility, of fully human IL-12 antibodies having heavy and light chains other than the V_H3 and Lambda types.*
>
> In contrast, Centocor's [accused antibody drug marketed as] Stelara, which falls within the scope of the claimed genus, differs considerably from the Joe-9 antibodies described in AbbVie's patents. Stelara has V_H5 type heavy chains and Kappa type light chains. The variable regions of Stelara only share a 50% sequence similarity with the Joe-9 antibodies, which is far lower than the 90% sequence similarity shared among the Joe-9 antibodies described in AbbVie's patents. Centocor's expert testified that antibodies with 80% sequence similarity to J695 [AbbVie's improved version of its Y61 antibody with a significant increase in IL-12 binding and neutralizing activity] could bind to completely different antigens . . . , thus illustrating the *significant structural differences* between Stelara and the Joe-9 antibodies and the *unpredictability* of the field of invention. . . .

AbbVie, 759 F.3d at 1300 (emphasis added) (record citation omitted).

[334]*AbbVie,* 759 F.3d at 1299 (citing Ariad Pharm., Inc. v. Eli Lilly & Co., 598 F.3d 1336, 1350 (Fed. Cir. 2010) (*en banc*)).

species to support the entire genus."[335] In the majority's view, the patents did not do so. Although the number of described species "appear[ed] high *quantitatively*, the described species are all of the similar type and do not *qualitatively* represent other types of antibodies encompassed by the genus."[336]

The Federal Circuit majority held in *AbbVie* that to survive an invalidity challenge for inadequate written description, the patents had to "at least describe some species representative of antibodies that are *structurally* similar to" the accused antibody."[337] Realistically, the AbbVie patents could not have included that structural description because Centocor's accused Stelara antibody (with its dissimilar structure) had not yet been invented when AbbVie filed its patent application in 1999. Commentators have decried the *AbbVie* decision for putting an "unrealistic" and "onerous" burden on patent applicants in the immunological arts to predict all future permutations of their inventions. The burden is particularly heavy in the AIA first-to-file environment with its pressures to file sooner rather than later.[338]

In the view of this author, *AbbVie* contravenes the fundamental patent law tenet that courts should not consider the accused device when determining the validity of the patent in suit; to do so risks confusing the separate analyses for infringement and validity.[339] In this regard, commentators have asserted that the result in *AbbVie* runs counter to the long-established rule of *In re Hogan*.[340] The CCPA's 1977 decision in *Hogan* held that future embodiments of a claimed invention, unknown at the filing date of a patent application, could not be used to hold the Hogan application claims unpatentable for lack of enablement.[341] The CCPA in *Hogan* reasoned that an undue burden would

[335]*AbbVie,* 759 F.3d at 1299.

[336]*AbbVie,* 759 F.3d at 1300.

[337]*AbbVie,* 759 F.3d at 1301 (emphasis added). However, the majority admitted that the patents "need not describe the allegedly infringing [product] in exact terms." *AbbVie,* 759 F.3d at 1301 (citing *Lilly,* 119 F.3d at 1568 ("[E]very species in a genus need not be described in order that a genus meet the written description requirement.")).

[338]*See* Jorge Goldstein, AbbVie Deutschland *and Unknown Embodiments: Has the Written Description Requirement for Antibodies Gone Too Far?*, 9 BNA Life Sciences Law & Industry Report 399 (Apr. 3, 2015).

[339]*Cf.* In re Hogan, 559 F.2d 595, 607 (C.C.P.A. 1977) (Markey, C.J.) (stating that "[t]he courts have consistently considered subsequently existing states of the art as raising questions of infringement, but never of validity").

[340]559 F.2d 595 (C.C.P.A. 1977) (Markey, C.J.). *See* Jorge Goldstein, AbbVie Deutschland *and Unknown Embodiments: Has the Written Description Requirement for Antibodies Gone Too Far?,* 9 BNA Life Sciences Law & Industry Report 399 (Apr. 3, 2015) (stating that *AbbVie* "sheds serious doubt on the continued viability of a fundamental 1977 case, *In re Hogan*. . . . For more than 35 years, *Hogan* has been authority for the proposition that future embodiments, unknown at the filing date, cannot be used to hold claims invalid for lack of enablement.") (citation omitted).

[341]In *Hogan,* the patent applicant (an employee of Phillips Petroleum Company) asserted a 1953 priority date for its 1971 application claim to "[a] normally solid

be placed on inventors to require them to enable embodiments of their invention that no one had yet conceived as of their patent's filing date.[342] The *Hogan* court explained that what must be enabled is the scope of the invention *as it was understood on the patent's filing date,*[343] but future embodiments not yet envisioned or discovered at that time need not be (and realistically cannot be) enabled.[344] *AbbVie*

---

homopolymer of 4-methyl-1-pentene." Hogan had invented and disclosed in the application a "crystalline" form of the claimed solid polymer. In 1962, a third party (Edwards) discovered an "amorphous" form of the solid polymer, unknown in 1953. A USPTO examiner rejected Hogan's claims for, *inter alia,* failure of the application to enable the scope of the claims under 35 U.S.C. §112, first paragraph. The Board agreed, stating that Hogan's disclosure was "restricted to a teaching of how to make *crystalline* polymers," but that the claims were "not limited to a crystalline polymer of 4-methyl-1-pentene" but "encompasses an *amorphous* polymer as well, which is manifestly outside the scope of the enabling teaching present in the case." *Hogan,* 559 F.2d at 601 (emphasis added). The CCPA reversed the rejection, as explained *infra.*

[342]The CCPA in *Hogan* explained:

> The PTO has not challenged appellants' assertion that their 1953 application enabled those skilled in the art in 1953 to make and use "a solid polymer" as described in claim 13. Appellants disclosed, as the only then existing way to make such a polymer, a method of making the crystalline form. To now say that appellants should have disclosed in 1953 the amorphous form which on this record did not exist until 1962, would be to impose an impossible burden on inventors and thus on the patent system. There cannot, in an effective patent system, be such a burden placed on the right to broad claims. To restrict appellants to the crystalline form disclosed, under such circumstances, would be a poor way to stimulate invention, and particularly to encourage its early disclosure. To demand such restriction is merely to state a policy against broad protection for pioneer inventions, a policy both shortsighted and unsound from the standpoint of promoting progress in the useful arts, the constitutional purpose of the patent laws. *See* In re Goffe, 542 F.2d 564, (CCPA 1976). . . .
>
> Consideration of a later existing state of the art in testing for compliance with §112, first paragraph, would not only preclude the grant of broad claims, but would wreak havoc in other ways as well. The use of a subsequently-existing improvement to show lack of enablement in an earlier-filed application on the basic invention would preclude issuance of a patent to the inventor of the thing improved, and in the case of issued patents, would invalidate all claims (even some "picture claims") therein. Patents are and should be granted to later inventors upon unobvious improvements. Indeed, encouragement of improvements on prior inventions is a major contribution of the patent system and the vast majority of patents are issued on improvements. It is quite another thing, however, to utilize the patenting or publication of later existing improvements to "reach back" and preclude or invalidate a patent on the underlying invention.

Hogan, 559 F.2d at 606.

[343]*See Hogan*, 559 F.2d at 605 (stating that "if appellants' 1953 application provided sufficient enablement, considering all available evidence (whenever that evidence became available) of the 1953 state of the art, i.e., of the condition of knowledge about all art-related facts existing in 1953, then the fact of that enablement was established for all time and a later change in the state of the art cannot change it").

[344]*See also* Chiron Corp. v. Genentech, Inc., 363 F.3d 1247, 1254 (Fed. Cir. 2004) (stating that "a patent document cannot enable technology that arises after the date of

appears to use the written description requirement to contravene the enablement rule of *Hogan.*[345]

AbbVie argued to the Federal Circuit that given its patent's functional claims, structural differences were not legally relevant. However, the Federal Circuit rejected AbbVie's attempts to "rely on the k_{off} rates to show representativeness."[346] In the Circuit's view, the k_{off} rate was "merely a desired result, rather than the actual means for achieving that result."[347] The appellate court concluded that "[t]he asserted claims attempt to claim every fully human IL-12 antibody that would achieve a desired result, i.e., high binding affinity and neutralizing activity, and cover an antibody as different as [Centocor's] Stelara, whereas the patents do not describe representative examples to support the full scope of the claims."[348]

In explaining its decision that AbbVie's patents were invalid, the Federal Circuit majority used an analogy to a plot of land to explain the difference between *claiming* an invention and adequately *describing* it:

> One describes a plot of land by its furthest coordinates, in effect drawing a perimeter fence around it. That may be akin to the function of patent claims to particularly point out and distinctly circumscribe the outer boundaries of a claimed invention. With the *written description* of a genus, however, merely drawing a fence around a perceived genus is not a description of the genus. One needs to show that one has truly invented the genus, *i.e.,* that one has conceived and described sufficient representative species encompassing the breadth of the genus.

---

application. The law does not expect an applicant to disclose knowledge invented or developed after the filing date. Such disclosure would be impossible.") (citing In re Hogan, 559 F.2d 595, 605-606 (C.C.P.A. 1977). *But see Chiron,* 363 F.3d at 1262 (Bryson, J., concurring) (stating that "I have no quarrel with the holding of *Hogan*— that enablement must be judged in light of the state of the art at the time of the application. What must be guarded against, in my view, is to interpret *Hogan* to hold that claims that are enabled by the original application may be construed broadly enough to encompass technology that is not developed until later and was not enabled by the original application. Although there is language in *Hogan* that could be read to support such a result, this court has recently (and properly, in my view) expressed reservations about reading Hogan that broadly. *See* Plant Genetic Sys., N.V. v. DeKalb Genetics Corp., 315 F.3d 1335, 1340-1341 (Fed. Cir. 2003)"). The *Chiron v. Genentech* decision is further examined *supra* Section B.5 ("Nascent and After-Arising Technology").

[345]*See* Jorge Goldstein, AbbVie Deutschland *and Unknown Embodiments: Has the Written Description Requirement for Antibodies Gone Too Far?,* 9 BNA Life Sciences Law & Industry Report 399 (Apr. 3, 2015) (stating that "*AbbVie Deutschland* has achieved by failure of written description what *Hogan* warned could not be done by failure of enablement. It has cast serious doubt on the right to broad claims in immunology").

[346]*AbbVie,* 759 F.3d at 1301.

[347]*AbbVie,* 759 F.3d at 1301.

[348]*AbbVie,* 759 F.3d at 1301.

> Otherwise, one has only a research plan, leaving it to others to explore the unknown contours of the claimed genus.[349]

The tenor of this and other language in *AbbVie* shows that in the Circuit majority's view, the AbbVie patents in suit described merely a "desired result" or a "research plan." This was not enough to satisfy the written description of the invention requirement for the asserted genus claims. Elsewhere in *AbbVie*, the court warned ominously that "[f]unctionally defined genus claims can be *inherently vulnerable* to invalidity challenge for lack of written description support, especially in technology fields that are highly unpredictable, where it is difficult to establish a correlation between structure and function for the whole genus or to predict what would be covered by the functionally claimed genus."[350]

The Federal Circuit majority in *AbbVie* concluded that substantial evidence supported the jury's verdict of invalidity for lack of an adequate written description of the claimed genus, and affirmed the district court's denial of JMOL on that issue. In an unusual footnote, the Federal Circuit added that it had been "aided in our consideration of this issue by amicus curiae briefs filed by Eli Lilly and Co. *et al.* and Professor Oskar Liivak."[351]

f. Concluding Thoughts

The written description of the invention requirement as expansively applied by the Federal Circuit since its 1997 decision in *Regents v. Lilly* is a vague and ill-defined doctrine in search of limiting principles. The court wields the doctrine to assuage concerns about patent applicants overreaching, claiming more than they have actually invented, and filing patent applications too soon — before they have finished inventing.[352] These are legitimate concerns, but the Federal Circuit's

[349]*AbbVie,* 759 F.3d at 1300 (citing *Ariad,* 598 F.3d at 1353 (stating that the written description requirement guards against claims that "merely recite a description of the problem to be solved while claiming all solutions to it and . . . cover any compound later actually invented and determined to fall within the claim's functional boundaries")).

[350]*AbbVie,* 759 F.3d at 1301 (citing *Ariad,* 598 F.3d at 1351) (emphasis added).

[351]*AbbVie,* 759 F.3d at 1302 n.6. The cited *amicus curiae* Eli Lilly and Co. was the prevailing party in *Regents of the Univ. of Cal. v. Eli Lilly & Co.*, 119 F.3d 1559 (Fed. Cir. 1997) (Lourie, J.), analyzed *supra* this section. The cited *amicus curiae* Professor Liivak has previously criticized the scope of antibody patents; *see* Oskar Liivak, *Finding Invention*, SSRN version dated August 28, 2012, at 39, 40 Fla. St. U. L. Rev. 57 (2012) (asserting that "antibody patents have scope that far exceeds the inventions disclosed in their patents"), *available at* papers.ssrn.com/sol3/papers.cfm?abstract_id=2137842.

[352]In *Ariad,* for example, the *en banc* court complained that the asserted genus claims, "as in *Eli Lilly* . . . , cover any compound later actually invented and determined to fall within the claim's functional boundaries — leaving it to the pharmaceutical industry to complete an unfinished invention." Ariad Pharms., Inc. v. Eli Lilly and

seeming obsession with the written description doctrine is not the best tool to deal with these issues. Other doctrines such as the enablement and claim definiteness requirements are equally valid approaches.

If the Federal Circuit continues to apply written description in its current, expansive form as a general disclosure requirement separate from enablement, the court should make more explicit the linkage between the "possession" test for written description compliance and the standards for having made an invention.[353] These standards turn on long-established U.S. patent law concepts including conception, diligence, reduction to practice, and evidentiary corroboration.[354]

Ironically, the America Invents Act of 2011 (AIA) made the act and timing of invention far less important by establishing a hybrid first-inventor-to-file system and abrogating the United States' traditional first-to-invent priority framework.[355] Under the AIA-implemented first-to-file system, the pressure to file sooner rather than later only exacerbates the filing of patent applications on inventions that have not yet been completed, plowing fertile ground for written description problems. In the post-AIA world, assertions of written description noncompliance may rival obviousness[356] as the invalidity defense of first choice among accused infringers.

Co., 598 F.3d 1336, 1353 (Fed. Cir. 2010) (*en banc*). *See also* Billups-Rothenberg, Inc. v. Assoc. Regional and Univ. Pathologies, Inc. and Bio-Rad Labs., Inc., 642 F.3d 1031, 1037 (Fed. Cir. 2011) (invalidating patent claiming methods of detecting certain genetic mutations, stating that "[t]he written description requirement exists to ensure that inventors do not 'attempt to preempt the future before it has arrived'") (quoting Fiers v. Revel, 984 F.2d 1164, 1171 (Fed. Cir. 1993)).

[353]In *Ariad,* the *en banc* court effectively tied written description compliance with proving conception (as of the application filing date), stating that "[r]equiring a written description of the invention limits patent protection to those who actually perform the difficult work of "invention" — that is, conceive of the complete and final invention with all its claimed limitations — and disclose the fruits of that effort to the public." Ariad Pharms., Inc. v. Eli Lilly and Co., 598 F.3d 1336, 1353 (Fed. Cir. 2010) (*en banc*).

[354]*See infra* Chapter 4, Part II ("Novelty, Loss of Right, and Priority Pre-America Invents Act of 2011"); Chapter 4, Section M (Derivation and Inventorship Under 35 U.S.C. §102(f) (Pre-AIA)").

[355]*See* Leahy-Smith America Invents Act, Pub. L. No. 112-29 (H.R. 1249), §3 ("First Inventor to File"), 125 Stat. 284, 285-293 (2011).

[356]*See infra* Chapter 5 ("The Nonobviousness Requirement").

Chapter 4

Novelty, Loss of Right, and Priority Pre- and Post-America Invents Act of 2011 (35 U.S.C. §102)

Guide to This Chapter

This chapter is divided into three parts. Its structure has been expanded from earlier editions due to the enactment of the Leahy-Smith America Invents Act (AIA) in late 2011.[1] The AIA fundamentally changed the U.S. Patent Act. The changes are among the most significant since passage of the 1952 Patent Act (which codified the patent laws at Title 35 of the U.S. Code).

This chapter does not cover the entire spectrum of AIA-implemented changes.[2] Rather, the chapter focuses on several fundamental changes relating to novelty and priority of invention, including the switch from the United States' historic first-to-invent priority system to a unique hybrid first-inventor-to-file system. The specific AIA changes covered in this chapter are (1) the determination of novelty and the lack thereof (anticipation) post-AIA, (2) what categories of earlier technology qualify as prior art (and exceptions thereto) under 35 U.S.C. §102 as amended by the AIA, and (3) how the post-AIA patent system handles the question of priority — that is, which of two of more

[1]Leahy-Smith America Invents Act, Pub. L. No. 112-29 (H.R. 1249), 125 Stat. 284 (Sept. 16, 2011).

[2]Perhaps an even more significant change to the U.S. patent system than those discussed in Part III of this chapter are the new AIA-implemented procedures for challenging the validity of issued patents in an adjudicatory proceeding in the USPTO. For more on those procedures; namely, *inter partes* review and post-grant review, *see infra* Chapter 8, Section E. Unsurprisingly, the Federal Circuit has rejected a patentee's challenge to the Constitutionality of AIA-implemented *inter partes* review. *See* MCM Portfolio LLC v. Hewlett-Packard Co., 812 F.3d 1284, 1288-1292 (Fed. Cir. 2015) (rejecting patentee's argument that "any action revoking a patent must be tried in an Article III court with the protections of the Seventh Amendment").

independent inventors who file applications directed to the same invention will receive a patent thereon.

It is important to understand that the AIA changes covered in this chapter generally do *not* impact patents issued or patent applications filed before March 16, 2013. For those patents or applications, the pre-AIA rules will continue to apply throughout their lifespan. Because the AIA is prospective in effect, U.S. patent law will operate on a dual framework of pre- and post-AIA rules for at least 30 years following the AIA's enactment. *Students of patent law now need to understand and apply both sets of rules.*

To facilitate that understanding, Part I of this chapter reviews general concepts of anticipation that remain the same under pre- and post-AIA law. Part II of this chapter explains the long-established pre-AIA framework for novelty, loss of right, and priority based on pre-AIA 35 U.S.C. §102. Part III of this chapter explains the "new" AIA-implemented framework, insofar as it can be illustrated with hypotheticals and understood from the statutory language of post-AIA 35 U.S.C. §102.[3] As of this writing in early 2019, the Federal Circuit has decided only a handful of appeals dealing with patents claiming inventions having effective filing dates on or after March 16, 2013; these cases are still beginning to work their way from examiner to USPTO Board to Federal Circuit (or from USPTO to federal district court to Federal Circuit). Thus we do not yet have a robust body of Federal Circuit case law that interprets Section 3 of the AIA (as newly implemented in the Patent Act) and resolves its many ambiguities. The U.S. Supreme Court decided its first case involving part of post-AIA §102 in January 2019, as detailed in Part III of this chapter. Future editions of this text will analyze more interpretive precedent as the courts develop it.

Part I: General Principles of Anticipation

The general principles covered in this part of the chapter applied before implementation of the America Invents Act of 2011 and remain applicable thereafter.

[3]Although Congress radically amended the substance of 35 U.S.C. §102, it unfortunately did not renumber the section. The work of patent practitioners would be much easier for the next 30 or more years if Congress had enacted a newly numbered statutory section addressing novelty and priority post-AIA—numbering it 35 U.S.C. §1002, for example. Congress did not do so, however, and this text will therefore refer to "§102 (pre-AIA)" (or, alternatively, "§102 (2006)") and to "§102 (post-AIA)." The latter statutory section took effect on March 16, 2013, for applications filed on or after that date and patents issuing therefrom.

A. The Meaning of Anticipation

The statutory requirement of novelty is "patent-speak" for the bedrock principle that to be patented, an invention must be new (as well as nonobvious and useful). When one or more of the novelty provisions of §102 is triggered, patent attorneys say that the invention has been **anticipated**. When an invention has been anticipated, it is old and thus unpatentable. In other words, anticipation is the opposite, absence, or negation of novelty.

B. Burden of Proof

The preamble of 35 U.S.C. §102, in both its pre- and post-AIA forms, places a burden of proof on the Patent and Trademark Office (USPTO) to negate a presumption of novelty: "A person *shall* be entitled to a patent *unless*. . . ." (emphasis added). The statute is drafted to indicate that the initial burden of disproving novelty during examination of a patent application rests with the government—the USPTO.

To reject an applicant's claim(s) under 35 U.S.C. §102, the agency must show that at least one of the statute's novelty-destroying (or, pre-AIA, loss of right) subsections has been triggered. The USPTO examiner typically rejects an applicant's claims based on the citation of one or more prior art **references**, which are documents such as patents, articles from scientific journals, and other technical literature evidencing the applicability of one or more subsections of §102.[4] Claims also may be rejected under certain subsections of §102 based on events, such as the placing of the invention "on sale" or in "public use" within the meaning of §102(b) (pre-AIA) or §102(a) (post-AIA).

It is therefore helpful to consider 35 U.S.C. §102 as the catalog or universe of prior art that potentially can be cited by the USPTO in rejecting a patent applicant's claims. If a patent, journal article, or other document or event is asserted by the USPTO to be prior art, it must qualify under some subsection of 35 U.S.C. §102. If it does not, then the document or event is not legally available for use as prior art to negate the presumed novelty of the applicant's claimed invention. The same is true in a litigation context, where an issued patent's validity is being challenged.

The introductory phrase of 35 U.S.C. §102 is a bit overstated, of course, because to be "entitled to a patent" one must have an invention

[4]*Cf.* In re Hilmer, 359 F.2d 859, 879 (C.C.P.A. 1966) (stating that "[m]uch confused thinking could be avoided by realizing that rejections are based on statutory provisions, not on references, and that the references merely supply the evidence of lack of novelty, obviousness, loss of right or whatever may be the ground of rejection").

that is not only novel, but also in compliance with the Patent Act's additional requirements of statutory subject matter,[5] utility,[6] and nonobviousness,[7] as disclosed and claimed in a patent application that passes muster under the requirements of 35 U.S.C. §112.[8] These additional requirements are detailed elsewhere in this text.

C. The Strict Identity Rule of Anticipation

1. In General

Section 102 uses the word "invention" in two senses: to refer to the anticipatory *prior art invention* and to the *applicant's invention* for which a patent is being sought (or in federal district court litigation challenging validity, the invention of the patent in suit). The relationship between these two inventions in an anticipation analysis must be one of **strict identity**. The strict identity rule states that to evidence anticipation of a claimed invention under 35 U.S.C. §102, a single prior art reference must disclose every element of that invention, arranged as in the claim.[9]

For example, consider a patent claim that recites "a widget comprising part A attached to part B by means of part C." The claim is *not* anticipated by a combination of two prior art references (e.g., earlier printed publications or patents) in which one of the references shows a widget having part A attached to part B by means of a part D, and the other reference shows that part D is considered equivalent to or interchangeable with part C by those of ordinary skill in the art of widgets. This combination of prior art references may very well support the position that the claimed widget would have been *obvious* under 35 U.S.C. §103, assuming some motivation to combine the disclosures of the two references, but the claimed widget has not been *anticipated* in this example because the strict identity rule has not been satisfied. Thus, the claimed widget is novel if not, perhaps, nonobvious.[10]

[5]*See* Chapter 7 ("Potentially Patentable Subject Matter (35 U.S.C. §101)"), *infra*.
[6]*See* Chapter 6 ("The Utility Requirement (35 U.S.C. §101)"), *infra*.
[7]*See* Chapter 5 ("The Nonobviousness Requirement (35 U.S.C. §103)"), *infra*.
[8]*See* Chapter 3 ("Disclosure Requirements (35 U.S.C. §112(a))"), *supra*.
[9]The reference can disclose each element of the invention either explicitly or inherently. For a discussion of anticipation by inherency, *see infra* Section D.
[10]*See* Chapter 5 ("The Nonobviousness Requirement (35 U.S.C. §103)"), *infra*, for further discussion of what is required in order to combine the teachings of multiple prior art references.

2. The Special Case of Species/Genus Anticipation

A *genus* is a grouping or category made up of multiple *species* that share some characteristic. For example, the genus of primary colors encompasses the species red, blue, and yellow. Each of these colors is a primary color.

The operation of anticipation under §102 in a genus/species context requires special mention. Genus/species claiming is often, but not exclusively, encountered in chemical and biotechnological patents. For example, a claim that recites "a composition of matter X comprising a halogen" is a genus (or generic) claim in that it encompasses all possible compositions X that include any member of the halogen family (i.e., those elements listed in column VIIA of the periodic table): fluorine, chlorine, bromine, iodine, and so on.[11] Each such composition X can be considered a species falling within the broader genus of claimed compositions.

A heuristic to keep in mind for anticipation in the species/genus context is that species anticipates genus, but genus does not necessarily anticipate species. To see why this is so, consider a mechanical patent application in which the inventor has claimed "a widget comprising a fastening mechanism." The "fastening mechanism" can be viewed as a generic name for, or genus of, all items that would perform a fastening function. The inventor is therefore claiming a genus of widgets, that is, every widget within the claimed genus of widgets having a fastening mechanism is part of his novel invention.

Now assume that the USPTO examiner finds a prior art reference depicting a widget in which a nail operates as a fastening mechanism. The existence in the prior art of this particular widget species, in which the fastening mechanism is a nail, refutes the inventor's claim that the entirety of his claimed genus of widgets is novel. The genus as a whole cannot be new if one or more of its constituent species is old. Because a species anticipates a genus, the prior art reference is considered anticipatory and prevents the inventor from obtaining his generic claim.[12]

[11]*See* Los Alamos National Laboratory's Chemistry Division, *Periodic Table of the Elements (2016),* http://periodic.lanl.gov.

[12]*See* In re Ruscetta, 255 F.2d 687, 689-690 (C.C.P.A. 1958) (Rich, J.) (stating that "it is axiomatic that the disclosure of a species in a reference is sufficient to prevent a later applicant from obtaining generic claims, unless the reference can be overcome"). Be aware that this "species anticipates genus" rule does not necessarily follow in the §112, ¶1 disclosure context. *See* In re Lukach, 442 F.2d 967, 970 (C.C.P.A. 1971) (explaining that "the description of a single embodiment of broadly claimed subject matter constitutes a description of the invention for anticipation purposes . . . , whereas the same information in a specification might not alone be enough to provide a description of that invention for purposes of adequate disclosure . . .") (citations omitted).

The converse is not necessarily true. Consider a patent application in which the inventor has claimed "a widget comprising a nail," and the USPTO examiner cites against it a prior art reference describing a "widget having a fastening mechanism." So long as the prior art reference does not expressly or inherently[13] disclose that "fastening mechanism" includes "a nail," there is no anticipation. The strict identity rule of anticipation is not met, because each limitation of the claim has not been *identically* disclosed in a single prior art reference, arranged as in the claim.[14]

Although the patent applicant would not receive an *anticipation* rejection in this situation, it is very likely that the USPTO examiner would make an *obviousness* rejection under 35 U.S.C. §103.[15] The examiner would contend that it would have been obvious for a person of ordinary skill in the art to have selected, from the disclosed prior art genus of widgets having a fastening mechanism, the particular species of interest, that is, a widget having a nail as a fastener, in order to make the claimed invention. This type of obviousness rejection will be more easily overcome if the applicant can show some difference in structure or function of the nail versus the other species

[13]To inherently disclose something not expressly stated, a prior art document or event must make clear to the person of ordinary skill that the missing subject matter is "necessarily present" in what is expressly described in or taught by that document or event. Inherency can not be established by mere "probabilities or possibilities." Scaltech, Inc. v. Retec/Tetra, L.L.C., 178 F.3d 1378 (Fed. Cir. 1999). As the court explained:

> The mere fact that a certain thing may result from a given set of circumstances is not sufficient to establish inherency. *See* Continental Can Co. v. Monsanto Co., 948 F.2d 1264, 1269, 20 U.S.P.Q.2d (BNA) 1746, 1749 (Fed. Cir. 1991). However, if the natural result flowing from the operation of the process offered for sale would necessarily result in achievement of each of the claim limitations, then [the] claimed invention was offered for sale. *See id.*

Id. at 1384. For further discussion of anticipation by inherency, *see infra* Section D.

[14]*See* Bristol-Myers Squibb Co. v. Ben Venue Labs., Inc., 246 F.3d 1368, 1380 (Fed. Cir. 2001) (vacating district court's grant of summary judgment of invalidity for anticipation where the "Kris [reference] discloses only the use of premedicants generally, not the specific classes of premedicants in those claims: steroids, antihistamines, and H2-receptor antagonists"). One possible exception to the "genus does not necessarily anticipate species" rule is when the genus disclosed in the reference is so small that it effectively describes the claimed species. *See id.* (noting that "the disclosure of a small genus may anticipate the species of that genus even if the species are not themselves recited") (citing In re Petering, 301 F.2d 676, 682 (C.C.P.A. 1962)).

[15]*See, e.g.*, In re Jones, 958 F.2d 347 (Fed. Cir. 1992), in which the court reversed the USPTO's obviousness rejection of a claim to the 2-(2'-aminoethoxy)ethanol salt of dicamba, a type of acid. *Id.* at 348. The prior art Richter reference, "which all agree is the closest prior art, discloses dicamba in free acid, ester, and salt forms, for use as a herbicide. Among the salt forms disclosed are substituted ammonium salts, a genus that admittedly encompasses the claimed salt. Richter does not specifically disclose the claimed 2-(2'-aminoethoxy) ethanol salt, however." *Id.* at 349.

within the genus, or some kind of criticality or unexpected result that flows from her selection of the nail species.

D. Anticipation by Inherency

The strict identity rule for anticipation, introduced above, provides that in order to anticipate a claimed invention, a single prior art reference must disclose every element of that invention, arranged as in the claim. A reference's disclosure of individual elements is usually explicit, but case law makes clear that the disclosure can also be *inherent.*[16]

For example, suppose that the USPTO is examining for novelty a claim to "a container structure comprising a plurality of plastic ribs that are hollow." The examiner has located a prior art printed publication showing a container with several plastic ribs. The prior art reference does not explicitly state that the ribs are hollow, but it does indicate that the ribs were formed by conventional blow-molding techniques. If other evidence extrinsic to the reference (e.g., other documents or expert testimony) shows that use of the blow-molding process would *necessarily* have resulted in hollow ribs, then the examiner would be justified in concluding that the reference inherently disclosed the "hollow" feature. Stated another way, practice of the prior art reference would *inevitably* have resulted in the claimed invention. A rejection of the claim as anticipated would be justified under these circumstances.[17]

If, however, the extrinsic evidence presents a legitimate question as to whether the blow-molding process would have resulted in hollow ribs, then anticipation by inherency is not established. If it is to be relied upon to destroy novelty, inherency must be certain:

> Inherency . . . may not be established by probabilities or possibilities. The mere fact that a certain thing may result from a given set of circumstances is not sufficient. [Citations omitted.] If, however, the disclosure is sufficient to show that the natural result flowing from the operation

[16]*See* Continental Can Co. USA v. Monsanto Co., 948 F.2d 1264, 1268 (Fed. Cir. 1991) (stating that "[t]o serve as an anticipation when the reference is silent about the asserted inherent characteristic, such gap in the reference may be filled with recourse to extrinsic evidence," and that such evidence "must make clear that the missing descriptive matter is necessarily present in the thing described in the reference, and that it would be so recognized by persons of ordinary skill").

[17]For an argument that reliance on the inherency doctrine should be cabined, and that prior art relied on to show inherent anticipation must satisfy a heightened level of enablement to establish the inevitability of producing the claimed invention, *see* Janice M. Mueller & Donald S. Chisum, *Enabling Patent Law's Inherent Anticipation Doctrine*, 45 Hous. L. Rev. 1101 (2009), *available at* https://papers.ssrn.com/sol3/papers.cfm?abstract_id=1153493.

> as taught would result in the performance of the questioned function, it seems to be well settled that the disclosure should be regarded as sufficient.[18]

The doctrine of anticipation by inherency should be distinguished from situations in which the claimed invention was *accidentally* made or performed previously by others but not appreciated at the time. For example, the plaintiff in *Tilghman v. Proctor*[19] obtained a patent on a process for separating the component parts of fats and oils. These components included a glycerine base and various "fat acids" such as stearic, margaric, and oleic acids, which were useful in the making of candles and soap. Years before Tilghman's invention, one Perkins had used tallow to lubricate the pistons of his steam engine.[20] The Supreme Court rejected the argument that this prior use by Perkins invalidated the patent:

> We do not regard the accidental formation of fat acid in Perkins's steam cylinder from the tallow introduced to lubricate the piston (if the scum which rose on the water issuing from the ejection pipe was fat acid) as of any consequence in this inquiry. What the process was by which it was generated or formed was never fully understood. Those engaged in the art of making candles, or in any other art in which fat acids are desirable, certainly never derived the least hint from this accidental phenomenon in regard to any practicable process for manufacturing such acids.[21]

Although older Supreme Court cases such as *Tilghman* might be read to suggest that inherent anticipation requires *recognition* by prior art workers of the fact of the earlier making or performing of the invention,[22] most judges of the Federal Circuit have rejected any

[18]*Continental Can*, 948 F.2d at 1269 (quoting In re Oelrich, 666 F.2d 578, 581 (C.C.P.A. 1981) (Rich, J.)).

[19]102 U.S. 707 (1880).

[20]For additional background on Perkins' use, *see* Mitchell v. Tilghman, 86 U.S. 287 (1873), *overruled in part by* Tilghman v. Proctor, 102 U.S. 707 (1880).

[21]*Tilghman,* 102 U.S. at 711. The Supreme Court continued in the same vein with respect to other prior art of record:

> The accidental effects produced in Daniell's water barometer and in Walther's process for purifying fats and oils preparatory to soap making, are of the same character. They revealed no process for the manufacture of fat acids. If the acids were accidentally and unwittingly produced, whilst the operators were in pursuit of other and different results, without exciting attention and without its even being known what was done or how it had been done, it would be absurd to say that this was an anticipation of Tilghman's discovery.

Id. at 711-712.

[22]*See also* Eibel Process Co. v. Minnesota & Ontario Paper Co., 261 U.S. 45, 66 (1923) ("[A]ccidental results, not intended and not appreciated, do not constitute anticipation.").

contemporaneous recognition requirement. Applied to the container hypothetical above, the question becomes whether it is necessary in order to establish anticipation by inherency that prior artisans who made or used the container described in the prior art reference actually recognized at that time that the ribs of the container were hollow. In *Schering Corp. v. Geneva Pharms., Inc.,*[23] a panel of the court in 2003 flatly rejected "the contention that inherent anticipation requires recognition in the prior art."[24] It distinguished *Tilghman* on the ground that the record in that case "did not show conclusively that the claimed process occurred in the prior art."[25] Two judges of the Federal Circuit filed dissenting opinions to the subsequent denial of rehearing *en banc* in *Schering,* and a third judge voted to rehear the appeal *en banc.*[26] Nevertheless, the clear weight of current Federal Circuit authority is that proof of recognition in the prior art of an inherent characteristic or quality is not necessary.[27]

E. Enablement Standard for Anticipatory Prior Art

We have already established that anticipation requires the description in a single prior art reference of every element of a claimed invention.[28] We must also consider the *quality* of that description. In order to be anticipatory, the prior art reference must describe the claimed invention in an enabling fashion,[29] that is, with sufficient detail that

[23]339 F.3d 1373 (Fed. Cir. 2003).

[24]*Id.* at 1377.

[25]*Id.* at 1378.

[26]Schering Corp. v. Geneva Pharms., Inc., 348 F.3d 992 (Fed. Cir. 2003) (order denying petition for rehearing *en banc*); *id.* at 993 (Gajarsa, J., voting for rehearing *en banc*); *id.* (Newman, J., dissenting from denial of rehearing *en banc*); *id.* at 995 (Lourie, J., dissenting from denial of rehearing *en banc*).

[27]*See, e.g.*, Leggett & Platt, Inc. v. VUTEk, Inc., 537 F.3d 1349, 1355 (Fed. Cir. 2008) (reaffirming *Schering* panel's rejection of "the contention that inherent anticipation requires recognition in the prior art") (quoting Schering Corp. v. Geneva Pharm., Inc., 339 F.3d 1373, 1377 (Fed. Cir. 2003)); SmithKline Beecham Corp. v. Apotex Corp., 403 F.3d 1331, 1343 (Fed. Cir. 2005) ("inherent anticipation does not require a person of ordinary skill in the art to recognize the inherent disclosure in the prior art at the time the prior art is created"); Toro Co. v. Deere & Co., 355 F.3d 1313, 1321 (Fed. Cir. 2004) ("[T]he fact that a characteristic is a necessary feature or result of a prior art embodiment (that is itself sufficiently described and enabled) is enough for inherent anticipation, even if that fact was unknown at the time of the prior invention.").

[28]*See supra* Section C ("The Strict Identity Rule of Anticipation").

[29]*See* In re Donohue, 766 F.2d 531, 533 (Fed. Cir. 1985) (stating that "[i]t is well settled that prior art under 35 U.S.C. [§102(b)] must sufficiently describe the claimed invention to have placed the public in possession of it. Such possession is effected if one of ordinary skill in the art could have combined the publication's description of the invention with his own knowledge to make the claimed invention. Accordingly, even if the claimed invention is disclosed in a printed publication, that disclosure will not

a person of ordinary skill in the art could make what is described in the prior art reference without undue experimentation. For example, if an inventor files a patent application claiming a new chemical compound X, and a prior art reference describes merely the chemical formula of X but does not describe how to make X, the reference would not be adequate to anticipate because it is not enabling.[30]

In Chapter 3, "Disclosure Requirements," this text discussed the enablement requirement as applied to the *applicant's own disclosure.* Thus the inventor seeking a patent in the above example must provide an enabling disclosure of how to make and use the new chemical compound X that he claims. In parallel fashion, the patent law also applies the enablement requirement to the *description in a prior art reference relied on for anticipation.* In other words, the enablement requirement applies to the inventor seeking a patent as well as to the prior artisan whose description is relied on to defeat patentability. In the above example, the author of the prior art reference did not provide an enabling description of X. Thus, the prior art reference does not anticipate and the claimed invention X is novel.[31]

---

suffice as prior art if it was not enabling. It is not, however, necessary that an invention disclosed in a publication shall have actually been made in order to satisfy the enablement requirement.") (citations omitted).

[30]This assumes that the method of making compound X would not otherwise have been obvious to those of ordinary skill in the art. If it would have been, then the prior art reference would anticipate. *See* In re Le Grice, 301 F.2d 929, 939 (C.C.P.A. 1962) (holding that "the proper test of a description in a publication as a bar to a patent as the clause is used in section 102(b) requires a determination of whether one skilled in the art to which the invention pertains could take the description of the invention in the printed publication and combine it with his own knowledge of the particular art and from this combination be put in possession of the invention on which a patent is sought. Unless this condition prevails, the description in the printed publication is inadequate as a statutory bar to patentability under section 102(b).").

A further twist on the requirement that anticipatory prior art references be enabling is the rule that a disclosure of how to *use* (i.e., the utility of) a prior art chemical compound is *not* required for anticipation. *See* In re Hafner, 410 F.2d 1403, 1405 (C.C.P.A. 1969) (observing that "a disclosure lacking a teaching of how to use a fully disclosed compound for a specific, substantial utility or of how to use for such purpose a compound produced by a fully disclosed process is, under the present state of the law, entirely adequate to anticipate a claim to either the product or the process and, at the same time, entirely inadequate to support the allowance of such a claim"). Thus, in the example in the text, if the inventor claiming compound X asserts in his patent application that X has utility in the treatment of cancer, but the prior art description of X says nothing about potential uses for X (in cancer or otherwise), the prior art reference is nevertheless considered anticipatory so long as it teaches X and how to make X (or so long as the method of making X would have been obvious to a person of ordinary skill in the art).

[31]Whether the claimed invention would have been obvious under 35 U.S.C. §103 in view of the description of X in the prior art reference is a separate question. *See* Chapter 5 ("The Nonobviousness Requirement (35 U.S.C. §103)"), *infra.*

E. Enablement Standard for Anticipatory Prior Art

The Federal Circuit recognizes certain evidentiary *presumptions* about whether various types of prior art are enabling. In *Amgen Inc. v. Hoechst Marion Roussel, Inc.*,[32] the appellate court in 2003 recognized that both claimed and unclaimed information disclosed in a *patent* used as prior art are presumptively enabling:

> In patent prosecution the examiner is entitled to reject application claims as anticipated by a prior art patent without conducting an inquiry into whether or not that patent is enabled or whether or not it is the claimed material (as opposed to the unclaimed disclosures) in that patent that are at issue. *In re Sasse,* 629 F.2d 675, 681, 207 U.S.P.Q. 107, 111 (C.C.P.A. 1980) ("[W]hen the PTO cited a disclosure which expressly anticipated the present invention . . . the burden was shifted to the applicant. He had to rebut the presumption of the operability of [the prior art patent] by a preponderance of the evidence." (citation omitted)). The applicant, however, can then overcome that rejection by proving that the relevant disclosures of the prior art patent are not enabled. *Id.*[33]

The *Amgen* court's rationale for placing the burden on a patent applicant to disprove enablement of a prior art patent was that "the applicant . . . is in a better position to show, by experiment or argument, why the disclosure in question is not enabling or operative. It would be overly cumbersome, perhaps even impossible, to impose on the PTO the burden of showing that a cited piece of prior art is enabling. The PTO does not have laboratories for testing disclosures for enablement."[34]

The *Amgen* court also held that that same presumption of enablement applies in federal district court litigation challenging an issued patent's validity, placing the burden on the patentee to show that unclaimed disclosures in a prior art patent are *not* enabling.[35]

Amgen did not reach the question whether a prior art non-patent *printed publication* (such as a technical paper or journal article), as distinguished from a patent, is presumptively enabling during patent prosecution in the USPTO.[36] The issue squarely confronted the court in the 2012 case, *In re Antor Media Corp.*[37] There the Circuit concluded "that a prior art printed publication cited by an examiner is presumptively enabling barring any showing to the contrary by a

[32]314 F.3d 1313 (Fed. Cir. 2003).

[33]*Amgen,* 314 F.3d at 1355 (footnote omitted).

[34]In re Antor Media Corp., 689 F.3d 1282, 1288 (Fed. Cir. 2012).

[35]*Amgen,* 314 F.3d at 1355.

[36]*See Amgen,* 314 F.3d at 1355 n.22 ("We note that by logical extension, our reasoning here might also apply to prior art printed publications as well, but as [the] Sugimoto [prior art reference] is a patent we need not and do not so decide today.").

[37]689 F.3d 1282 (Fed. Cir. 2012).

patent applicant or patentee."[38] Its rationale built on that of *Amgen*, because under *Amgen*, "unclaimed, unexamined disclosures [of a prior art patent] still receive a presumption of enablement during prosecution of a later patent, there is no reason why printed publications, which of course also lack the scrutiny of examination, should not logically receive the same presumption and for the same reasons."[39]

F. What Is a Printed Publication?

Both §102(a) and §102(b) of 35 U.S.C. (pre-AIA) and §102(a) of 35 U.S.C. (post-AIA) indicate that a claimed invention may be rendered unpatentable if it has previously been described in a "printed publication." What counts as a printed publication for prior art purposes? Consider, for example, whether posting a photograph of an invention on the Internet renders that invention anticipated and/or obvious.

A key policy concern expressed by 35 U.S.C. §102 is that we not permit withdrawal by a patent applicant of technology already in the public's possession. Patent law is fairly liberal about what will suffice to put a technology disclosure into the hands of the public (although U.S. patent law is somewhat less expansive in this respect than the laws of foreign countries[40]). Even a drawing without words can qualify (assuming that it is sufficiently enabling under 35 U.S.C. §112(a)).[41] For example, Judge Learned Hand held in *Jockmus v. Leviton*[42] that a patent claim to a candle-shaped light bulb holder was anticipated by a picture of the holder in a third party's French-language catalog. Hand explained that "printed publication" presupposes enough currency to make the work part of the possessions of the art.[43] In other words, the document or drawing will be considered a printed publication if it is sufficiently accessible to the public interested in this particular technology.

[38]*Antor Media,* 689 F.3d at 1287-1288.

[39]*Antor Media,* 689 F.3d at 1288.

[40]*See infra* Section I.2 ("Grace Period"). The 2011 enactment of the America Invents Act expands the categories of §102 prior art. *See infra* Sections Q and R.

[41]*See supra* Section E ("Enablement Standard for Anticipatory Prior Art"). The America Invents Act of 2011 renamed §112, ¶1 as §112(a), effective Sept. 16, 2012.

[42]28 F.2d 812 (2d Cir. 1928).

[43]*See Jockmus*, 28 F.2d at 813-814, stating:

> While it is true that the phrase, "printed publication," presupposes enough currency to make the work part of the possessions of the art, it demands no more. A single copy in a library, though more permanent, is far less fitted to inform the craft than a catalogue freely circulated, however ephemeral its existence; for the catalogue goes direct to those whose interests make them likely to observe and remember whatever it may contain that is new and useful.

In keeping with Learned Hand's definition, the U.S. Court of Appeals for the Federal Circuit has interpreted printed publication so as to

> give effect to ongoing advances in the technologies of data storage, retrieval, and dissemination. Because there are many ways in which a reference may be disseminated to the interested public, "public accessibility" has been called the touchstone in determining whether a reference constitutes a "printed publication" bar under 35 U.S.C. §102(b).[44]

Just *how* accessible is "sufficiently accessible"? A rather extreme illustration is *In re Hall,*[45] in which the Federal Circuit held that a single copy of a doctoral thesis, properly cataloged in the collection of a German university library, qualified as a novelty-destroying §102(b) "printed publication." Based on the facts of the case, which included competent evidence about routine library practices of cataloging and indexing theses from which an approximate time of accessibility could be determined, the court held that the single cataloged thesis in a foreign university's library "could constitute sufficient accessibility to those interested in the art exercising reasonable diligence."[46] In contrast, three student theses listed alphabetically by their authors' names on index cards, kept among 450 index cards in a shoebox in a college chemistry department's library, and not otherwise cataloged or indexed by subject, were held not sufficiently accessible to count as printed publications in *In re Cronyn.*[47]

A common source of printed publication prior art is a publication authored by the patent's named inventor(s), particularly in the context of inventions made by scientists and professors who dwell in a "publish or perish" environment. In *In re Klopfenstein,*[48] the court concluded that the inventors' academic conference poster presentation, on display for three days but never reproduced or distributed to any of the conference participants, constituted a "printed publication" that resulted in a pre-AIA §102(b) loss of right to a patent.[49] The court

[44]In re Hall, 781 F.2d 897, 898-899 (Fed. Cir. 1986) (citations omitted).

[45]*Id.* at 897.

[46]*Id.* at 900.

[47]890 F.2d 1158, 1161 (Fed. Cir. 1989) (observing that "the only research aid was the student's name, which, of course, bears no relationship to the subject of the student's thesis"). The dissent argued that indexing is only one factor to be considered in the totality of the circumstances that determine whether a work is sufficiently publicly accessible to count as a printed publication. *See id.* (Mayer, J., dissenting).

[48]380 F.3d 1345 (Fed. Cir. 2004).

[49]Although the Federal Circuit in *Klopfenstein* affirmed the USPTO's denial of patentability under 35 U.S.C. §102(b) (on the ground that the claimed invention had been described in a printed publication more than a year before the patent application's filing date), the determination of what counts as a "printed publication" would have equal

rejected the inventors' argument that the poster display could not qualify as a printed publication because it had never been disseminated by the distribution of reproductions or copies, or by indexing in a library or database. Precedents such as *In re Hall*[50] "do not limit this court to finding something to be a 'printed publication' *only* when there is distribution and/or indexing," the Federal Circuit observed.

Rather, the key inquiry for determining if there has been a printed publication is whether or not a reference has been made "publicly accessible." That determination involves a case-by-case inquiry into the facts and circumstances surrounding the reference's disclosure to members of the public. The *Klopfenstein* court considered the following factors relevant:

- The length of time that the display was exhibited
- The expertise of the target audience
- The existence (or lack thereof) of reasonable expectations that the material displayed would not be copied
- The simplicity or ease with which the material displayed could have been copied

Applying these factors, the Federal Circuit cited undisputed facts that the poster presentation (which described methods of preparing foods comprising extruded soy fiber) was "prominently displayed for approximately three cumulative days" to an audience comprising cereal chemists who likely possessed ordinary skill in the art of the invention; that it was displayed "with no stated expectation that the information would not be copied or reproduced by those viewing it"; that the inventors "took no measures to protect the information they displayed," such as by disclaimer discouraging copying; that the professional norms under which the inventors displayed the posters at an academic conference did not entitle them to a reasonable expectation that their display would not be copied; and that the poster display (which comprised four slides of graphs/charts and eight slides of concise bullet points) was relatively simple such that "only a few slides presented would have needed to have been copied by an observer to capture the novel information presented by the slides." Thus, the Federal Circuit concluded, the poster display was made sufficiently accessible to the public to qualify as a "printed publication" under §102(b).

---

relevance in §102(a) situations (i.e., novelty-destroying events, caused by persons other than the inventor, that occurred prior to the invention date of the claimed invention).

[50]781 F.2d 897 (Fed. Cir. 1986) (holding that a single copy of a doctoral thesis, indexed and cataloged in a German university library, was sufficiently publicly accessible to qualify as a §102(b) "printed publication").

The court accordingly affirmed the USPTO's rejection of the Klopfenstein patent application.[51]

New and technology-specific questions of public accessibility arise with regularity in the Internet era. For example, the issue in *SRI Int'l, Inc. v. Internet Sec. Sys., Inc.*[52] was whether an inventor's pre–critical date posting of an otherwise anticipatory paper on the patentee's publicly available FTP ("File Transfer Protocol") server rendered the paper sufficiently accessible to trigger the §102(b) printed publication bar. In response to a call for papers for the 1998 Network and Distributed System Security (NDSS) Symposium, the co-inventor of a network intrusion detection method e-mailed the symposium chair a paper. Titled "Live Traffic Analysis of TCP/IP Gateways," the paper described part of SRI's ongoing "Emerald" research project. Although the call for papers also required a backup submission by postal mail, the inventor opted to post a copy of the paper on SRI's FTP server as the backup copy. The SRI FTP server was publicly accessible and placed no restrictions on access to the "Live Traffic" paper. The inventor also e-mailed the symposium chair the specific FTP address (ftp://ftp.csl.sri.com/pub/emerald/ndss98.ps) of the paper. The "Live Traffic" paper was posted under the "ndss98.ps" file name for seven days in the SRI FTP server's Emerald subdirectory, which the inventor had previously publicized to other members of the cyber security community as a repository of his research on intrusion detection. A district court granted summary judgment of §102(b) invalidity on the ground that "one of ordinary skill would know that the SRI FTP server contained information on the EMERALD 1997 project and therefore would navigate through the folders [i.e., the server's PUB directory and EMERALD subdirectory] to find the Live Traffic paper."[53]

The Federal Circuit majority disagreed, finding genuine issues of material fact on the public accessibility question that precluded summary judgment. The *SRI* majority viewed the inventor's FTP server posting as a prepublication communication for purposes of peer review; intent to publicize the paper was lacking. The majority considered the "ndss98.ps" file name of the "Live Traffic" paper "relatively obscure" and not reasonably likely to be found by a contemporaneous user skilled in the art.[54] Nor did the FTP server provide an index, catalog, or other meaningful research tool to find the paper, a hallmark of

[51]The Federal Circuit observed in a footnote that, in contrast to the facts of the case before it, an entirely *oral* presentation that does not include a display of slides or distribution of copies of the presentation would not constitute a "printed publication" under the statute, and that a merely "transient" display of slides accompanying an oral presentation might not either. *See Klopfenstein*, 380 F.3d at 1349 n.4.

[52]511 F.3d 1186 (Fed. Cir. 2008).

[53]*Id.* at 1195.

[54]*Id.* at 1197.

the Federal Circuit's "library cases" such as *In re Hall.*[55] Distinguishing *In re Klopfenstein,*[56] the majority analogized the "Live Traffic" paper to "a poster at an unpublicized conference without a conference index of the location of the various poster presentations."[57]

The dissenting Federal Circuit judge in *SRI* would have upheld the district court's judgment of invalidity, based on the accused infringer's "mountain of evidence" regarding public accessibility and the patentee's failure to raise more than "some metaphysical doubt" about the material facts.[58] The navigable directory of the FTP server represented a research aid or tool that those skilled in the art of cyber detection could have used easily to locate the "Live Traffic" paper. Far from obscure, the paper's "ndss98.ps" file name comprised the initials of the 1998 NDSS Symposium, then in its fifth year and well known to cyber security workers in government, corporations, and academia. In the dissent's view, the facts created an even stronger case for §102(b) invalidity than those of *Klopfenstein* (in which a pre–critical date conference poster display triggered a §102(b) printed publication bar). The "Live Traffic" paper was continuously available on SRI's FTP server for a longer period of time, to any person located anywhere with Internet access. Unlike the presenters in some academic conferences, patentee SRI could have had no expectation of confidentiality for its FTP server; the inventor had affirmatively advertised the Emerald subdirectory in e-mails and presentations to persons interested in his research. Lastly, ease of copying was extremely high. Rather than transcribing the text or graphics of posters at a conference, in the case at bar the entire "Live Traffic" paper could have been copied through downloading "at the touch of a button."[59]

Insufficient evidence that a document was publicly accessible via the Internet before the critical date avoided a §102(b) printed publication bar in *In re Lister.*[60] Dr. Lister invented a method of playing golf in which players "were permitted to tee up their balls on every shot except for those taken from designated hazard areas or the putting green."[61] Lister first submitted a manuscript describing his method to the U.S. Copyright Office on July 4, 1994, and the Office issued a certificate of copyright registration for the manuscript later that same month. The manuscript was titled "Advanced Handicap Alternatives for Golf." More than a year later, on August 5, 1996, Lister filed a patent application claiming the golfing method described in the

[55]781 F.2d 897 (Fed. Cir. 1986).
[56]380 F.3d 1345 (Fed. Cir. 2004).
[57]*SRI Int'l,* 511 F.3d at 1197-1198.
[58]*Id.* at 1198, 1200 (Moore, J., dissenting) (quoting [at 1198] Matsushita Elec. Indus. Co. v. Zenith Radio Corp., 475 U.S. 574, 586 (1986)).
[59]*Id.* at 1204 (Moore, J., dissenting).
[60]583 F.3d 1307 (Fed. Cir. 2009).
[61]*Lister,* 583 F.3d at 1309.

manuscript. The USPTO Board affirmed an examiner's anticipation rejection citing the manuscript as a §102(b) (pre-AIA) printed publication. The commercial databases Westlaw and Dialog included the titles (but not the full texts) of works registered by the Copyright Office. The USPTO took the position that an interested researcher could have found the Lister manuscript by performing a keyword search of the commercial databases using the word "golf" in combination with "handicap."

The Federal Circuit first agreed that a reasonably diligent researcher with access to Westlaw or Dialog would have located the Lister manuscript by performing key word searches using "golf" in combination with "handicap." The court rejected Lister's argument that the word "handicap," though part of his manuscript's title, was not a good descriptor of the claimed invention. "The question is not whether an individual, selecting terms from the claim language, could execute a single keyword search that would yield all relevant references including the anticipatory reference at issue."[62] Rather, a diligent researcher could be expected to have attempted several searches using a variety of keyword combinations. The Federal Circuit concluded that the Lister manuscript was publicly accessible via the keyword search capability of Westlaw or Dialog, as of the date it was included in those databases.

That conclusion did not end Lister's appeal, however. The USPTO had failed to introduce evidence showing *when* the Lister manuscript was included in the commercial databases, and in particular that such inclusion occurred prior to the §102(b) critical date for Lister's patent application. The Federal Circuit distinguished *In re Hall,*[63] in which the court held that "competent evidence of the general library practice of cataloging and shelving" established that the cited thesis became publicly accessible prior to the applicant's critical date. In the case at bar, the government did not identify any comparable evidence of general practice proving when Westlaw or Dialog would have received and included in their databases the information obtained from the Copyright Office. Absent such evidence, the Federal Circuit in *Lister* had "no basis to conclude that the manuscript was publicly accessible prior to the critical date." Accordingly, the Federal Circuit vacated the USPTO Board's decision that Lister's application claims were barred by a §102(b) printed publication.

In contrast with the *Lister* case, the Federal Circuit in 2018 held in *Acceleration Bay, LLC v. Activision Blizzard Inc.*[64] that a technical report uploaded to a university website before the §102(b) critical date did *not* qualify as a publicly accessible §102 printed publication.

[62]*Lister,* 583 F.3d at 1315.
[63]781 F.2d 897 (Fed. Cir. 1986).
[64]908 F.3d 765 (Fed. Cir. Nov. 6, 2018) (Moore, J.).

Unlike the keyword-searchable titles in *Lister,* the report at issue in *Acceleration Bay* was not indexed in a "meaningful[]" way.[65] Moreover, although the university website had a search functionality, that functionality was not reliable and did not work properly. Hence the Circuit agreed with the USPTO that the report, despite being uploaded to the Internet, was not publicly accessible.

Acceleration Bay's three patents involved a point-to-point communications network with connections between host computers or "nodes." All three patents had a filing date of July 31, 2000.

Activision Blizzard ("Blizzard") challenged those patents in six *inter partes* reviews (IPRs).[66] In considering one of Blizzard's arguments for unpatentability, the Patent Trial and Appeal Board (PTAB or "Board") reviewed a purported prior art technical paper titled Meng-Jang Lin et al. ("Lin"), *Gossip versus Deterministic Flooding: Low Message Overhead and High Reliability for Broadcasting on Small Networks,* Technical Report No. CS1999-0637 (Univ. Cal. San Diego, 1999). Undisputedly, the Lin paper was uploaded to the Technical Report Library's website at the University of California, San Diego's (UCSD's) Computer Science and Engineering (CSE) Department as of November 23, 1999, in the year before the filing date of the Acceleration Bay patents.[67] The website's indexing was minimal, however; it allowed users to view lists of uploaded technical reports indexed only by the author's name or the year of upload, but not by title (as in *Lister*). Moreover, no evidence indicated that the Lin paper was ever disseminated to the public (e.g., no copies were ever handed out at a conference). Mr. Glenn Little, a Systems Administrator for the CSE Department at UCSD, testified to these facts.

The Board concluded that an interested, skilled artisan using reasonable diligence would not have located the Lin report. On appeal, the Federal Circuit agreed. "At best," Blizzard's evidence "'suggest[ed] that an artisan might have located Lin by skimming through potentially hundreds of titles in the same year, with most containing unrelated subject matter, or by viewing all titles in the database listed by author, when the authors were not particularly well known.'"[68]

With respect to the unreliable search functionality of the UCSD's CSE website, Mr. Little admitted during the IPR that that function did not work. Recent searches conducted by the patentee for the IPR proceeding revealed that keyword searching failed to produce any results. The Circuit rejected Blizzard's argument that such recent

[65] *Acceleration Bay,* 908 F.3d at 774.

[66] *Inter partes* review is examined *infra* in Chapter 8, Section E.

[67] Because the upload date for the Lin paper was within the one year preceding the patents' filing date, the Board relied on Lin as a §102(a) (pre-AIA) reference rather than a §102(b) (pre-AIA) reference.

[68] *Acceleration Bay,* 908 F.3d at 773 (quoting Board).

evidence was unauthenticated hearsay conducted years after the critical date because Mr. Little testified that the website presently ran the same software as it had at the critical date. The Circuit found that substantial evidence supported the Board's factual finding that the search function was deficient.[69]

The Circuit in *Acceleration Bay* concluded by noting that the test for public accessibility of materials in a database or catalog is not merely whether a potential prior art reference has been indexed. Instead, whether online or in tangible media, the reference must be *meaningfully* indexed such that an interested artisan exercising reasonable diligence could have found it.[70]

The minimal, non-informative indexing and unreliable search capability in the case at bar did not satisfy that standard. Rather than as the document listed by commercial legal research services in *Lister* or the single thesis catalogued in a German university in *In re Hall,*[71] the *Acceleration Bay* case was closer to the facts of *In re Cronyn.*[72] There the Federal Circuit had concluded that "as in *Application of Bayer*, 568 F.2d 1357 (C.C.P.A. 1978) and unlike *Hall*, the three student theses were not accessible to the public because they had not been either cataloged or indexed in a meaningful way. . . . Here, the only research aid was the student's name, which, of course, bears no relationship to the subject of the student's thesis."[73]

Proof that an asserted prior art reference was actually accessed by particular individuals is not required to establish that the reference is a 35 U.S.C. §102 printed publication; the test is whether a PHOSITA in the field of the claimed invention, by exercising reasonable diligence, could have accessed the reference. Such accessibility may be established by indirect evidence; for example, the testimony of a librarian about the library's cataloging practices. Publication of a reference in a journal or periodical of long standing also supports public accessibility, assuming competent evidence that the issue in question was available to the public before the critical date.

In *Telefoneaktiebolaget LM Ericsonn v. TCL Corp.,*[74] the parties in a 2015-initiated *inter partes* review (IPR) of Ericsonn's U.S. Patent No. 6,029,052 ('052 patent) disputed whether a certain article authored by "Jenschel" and published in a German technical journal had been accessible to the public more than one year before the '052 patent's filing date of July 1997 (that is, whether the article qualified as a §102(b)

[69] *Acceleration Bay,* 908 F.3d at 773.
[70] *Acceleration Bay,* 908 F.3d at 774.
[71] 781 F.2d 897 (Fed. Cir. 1986).
[72] 890 F.2d 1158 (Fed. Cir. 1989).
[73] *Cronyn,* 890 F.2d at 1161.
[74] 941 F.3d 1341, (Fed. Cir. Nov. 7, 2019) (Newman, J.) (hereafter "*Ericsonn*").

printed publication). Lacking evidence of Jenschel's pre–critical date accessibility in the United States,[75] IPR petitioner TCL sought to establish that the article became publicly accessible in June 1996 when an issue of the German journal containing the article was assertedly catalogued and shelved in a German university.

IPR petitioner TCL relied on the testimony of Doris Michel from the Darmstadt University library, who had worked there since at least 1996.[76] As part of the IPR evidence, she was able to retrieve (circa 2015) from the library the actual journal issue containing the Jentschel article. In a sworn declaration given for the IPR, Ms. Michel

> declared that the [German technical] journal Ingenieur der Kommunikationstechnik was in the collection of the [German] Darmstadt Library "since Volume 13, which corresponds to the year 1963." She declared that she worked at this Library in 1996, that Library records show that the journal issue dated Mai/Juni 1996 was catalogued and shelved with the shelf call number Tech Z Fe 57, and the Mai/Juni 1996 issue that she [has] now obtained from the Library bears such call number. She declared that this issue "was inventoried by the Library on June 18, 1996 [and] was openly accessible for use to the public after a processing time of 1-2 days."

[75]The evidence established that the journal issue did not reach the library of the University of California, Los Angeles, until October 1996.

[76]Patentee Ericsonn also challenged the evidentiary admissibility of the Michel Declaration, but did not succeed on that issue. IPR Petitioner TCL submitted the Michel Declaration in July 2016, several months after the PTAB instituted IPR of the '052 patent in a January 2016 written opinion. Title 37 C.F.R. §42.123(b) governs new or supplemental information sought to be admitted to an IPR more than one month after the IPR is instituted. The rule requires that the submitter in such cases

> must show why the supplemental information reasonably could not have been obtained earlier, and that consideration of the supplemental information would be in the interests of justice.

The Board chose to accept the Michel Declaration, finding its admission to be in the interests of justice. It "recognized the possible burden on Ericsson, and assured that Ericsson had the opportunity to depose Ms. Michel [who was willing to travel to the United States for deposition] and to respond to the substance of the Jentschel reference." *Ericsonn,* 941 F.3d at 1345.

The Federal Circuit did not find any abuse of discretion in the Board's evidentiary decision. "[W]hen the challenged evidence is reasonably viewed as material, and the opponent has adequate opportunity to respond and to produce contrary evidence, the interest of justice weighs on the side of admitting the evidence." *Ericsonn,* 941 F.3d at 1345, (citing cf. Genzyme Therapeutic Prods. Ltd. P'ship v. Biomarin Pharm. Inc., 825 F.3d 1360, 1366 (Fed. Cir. 2016) ("[T]he introduction of new evidence in the course of the [PTAB] trial is to be expected in *inter partes* review trial proceedings and, as long as the opposing party is given notice of the evidence and an opportunity to respond to it, the introduction of such evidence is perfectly permissible under the APA.")).

> [Ms.] Michel declared [further] that her testimony was based on her review of the Library register, her personal knowledge of the Library's registration practices, and the current condition of the Mai/Juni 1996 issue that was in the Library. She provided copies of the index card ("Kardex sheet") that recorded the Library's accession of this journal and showed the Library's entry for the issue identified as "Tech Z Fe 57"; she stated that this entry matches the sticker on the Library's copy of the Mai/Juni 1996 issue. Michel Decl. at 4, 6.[77]

Deciding the IPR in favor of petitioner TCL, the USPTO Patent Trial and Appeal Board (PTAB) determined that the Jentschel article qualified as a §102(b) printed publication. Underlying its decision was the Board's finding of fact that the article was received and shelved in the Darmstadt library in May/June 1996. The Board summarized its reasoning in three points: (1) the journal issue in question was housed in a library accessible to the public; (2) the article was published in a journal (i.e., a periodical) that had previously been published for more than 30 years; and (3) articles within an issue of the periodical were treated (the Board assumed) as a public disclosure of the information within them.[78] Having determined that Jentschel was available as prior art, the Board went on to hold that the challenged Ericsonn patent claims would have been obvious in view of Jentschel in combination with other art.

The key threshold issue on appeal to the Federal Circuit was Jentschel's public accessibility. The Federal Circuit held that substantial evidence supported the Board's ruling that Jentschel was publicly accessible in the May/June 1996 period. The appellate court noted that patentee Ericsonn did "not dispute that this journal has been published for at least thirty years and that the library was accessible the public."[79] Indeed, Ericsonn "provided no evidence to counter the Michel Declaration, the date on the face of the journal, and the Library's records showing receipt of the journal and its shelving."[80]

The Federal Circuit in *Ericsonn* distinguished the case before it from those in which a single dissertation or thesis was housed in a library. The Jentschel article published in the long-running German periodical differed from, for example, the uncatalogued, unshelved master's thesis held not publicly accessible in *In re Bayer*.[81] The court also distinguished Jentschel from the undergraduate theses, neither

[77] *Ericsonn,* 941 F.3d at 1346, (citations to record and PTAB opinion omitted).
[78] *Ericsonn,* 941 F.3d at 1346.
[79] *Ericsonn,* 941 F.3d at 1347.
[80] *Ericsonn,* 941 F.3d at 1347.
[81] *Ericsonn,* 941 F.3d at 1347, (citing *Bayer,* 568 F.2d 1357 (C.C.P.A. 1978)).

catalogued or indexed in a "meaningful way," held not publicly accessible in *In re Cronyn.*[82]

Having held that the PTAB did not abuse its discretion in receiving Jentschel as a reference, the Federal Circuit considered the merits of patentability. It affirmed the Board's determination that the teachings of Jentschel, in combination with a Japanese patent application, rendered the '052 patent claims invalid for obviousness.[83]

Part II: Novelty, Loss of Right, and Priority Pre-America Invents Act of 2011

G. Introduction

1. Statutory Basis

This part of the chapter provides readers with a practical understanding of the multifaceted concepts of **novelty** and **loss of right** as defined by §102 of the U.S. Patent Act prior to the AIA's 2011 enactment.[84] Because the AIA is prospective in effect, these concepts remain applicable to the patentability and validity of any U.S. patent or application filed before March 16, 2013, throughout the life of the patent. Given the possibility of validity-challenging litigation during (and beyond) the entire term of a patent, the pre-AIA framework regarding novelty and loss of right will remain relevant for 30 years or more following the AIA's 2011 enactment.

The notion that patents are available only for inventions that are truly novel (i.e., new) is a bedrock concept of all patent systems, and

[82]*Ericsonn,* 941 F.3d at 1347, (citing *Cronyn,* 890 F.2d 1158 (Fed. Cir. 1989)).

[83]*Ericsonn,* 941 F.3d at 1351.

[84]Although the requirement that a patentable invention be "new" is stated in 35 U.S.C. §101, novelty, novelty is analyzed under 35 U.S.C. §102 in accordance with long-standing administrative practice. *See* In re Bergy, 596 F.2d 952 (C.C.P.A. 1979) (Rich, J.), *aff'd sub nom.* Diamond v. Chakrabarty, 447 U.S. 303 (1980), in which the court explained:

> Of the three requirements *stated* in §101, only two, utility and statutory subject matter, are *applied* under §101. As we shall show, in 1952 Congress voiced its intent to consider the novelty of an invention under §102 where it is first made clear what the statute means by "new", notwithstanding the fact that this requirement is first *named* in §101.
>
> The PTO, in administering the patent laws, has, for the most part, consistently applied §102 in making rejections for lack of novelty. To provide the option of making such a rejection under either §101 or §102 is confusing and therefore bad law. . . .

Id. at 961 (emphases in original).

continues to govern under the AIA. What is novel, however, is not uniformly defined around the world. Before the AIA's implementation, the United States analyzed novelty quite differently than other countries, in view of its unique pre-AIA "first to invent" system of priority.[85] The pre-AIA statute provided:

35 U.S.C. §102 (2006). Conditions for patentability; novelty and loss of right to patent

A person shall be entitled to a patent unless —

(a) the invention was known or used by others in this country, or patented or described in a printed publication in this or a foreign country, before the invention thereof by the applicant for patent, or

(b) the invention was patented or described in a printed publication in this or a foreign country or in public use or on sale in this country, more than one year prior to the date of the application for patent in the United States, or

(c) he has abandoned the invention, or

(d) the invention was first patented or caused to be patented, or was the subject of an inventor's certificate, by the applicant or his legal representatives or assigns in a foreign country prior to the date of the application for patent in this country on an application for patent or inventor's certificate filed more than twelve months before the filing of the application in the United States, or

(e) the invention was described in (1) an application for patent, published under section 122(b), by another filed in the United States before the invention by the applicant for patent or (2) a patent granted on an application for patent by another filed in the United States before the invention by the applicant for patent, except that an international application filed under the treaty defined in section 351(a) shall have the effects for the purposes of this subsection of an application filed in the United States only if the international application

[85]The first-to-invent principle is most clearly codified in 35 U.S.C. §102(g), as discussed later in this chapter. *See infra* Section N. The United States' historic first-to-invent system differs from the first-to-file system, under which the rest of the world operates. *See infra* Chapter 12 ("International Patenting Issues").

The United States implemented a first-to-invent priority system as early as the late eighteenth century. *See* Edward C. Walterscheid, *Priority of Invention: How the United States Came to Have a "First-to-Invent" System,* 23 AIPLA Q.J. 263, 264 (1995) (explaining that "the initial impetus came from the titanic struggle between John Fitch and James Rumsey for priority of invention with respect to the steamboat during the late eighteenth century, but the actual creation of a true first-to-invent system took almost fifty years").

After many years of debate, the enactment in 2011 of the AIA changed the United States from first-to-invent to a unique first-inventor-to-file system. This landmark change in priority determination governs applications filed on or after March 16, 2013. *See infra* Part III of this chapter.

designated the United States and was published under Article 21(2) of such treaty in the English language;[86] or

(f) he did not himself invent the subject matter sought to be patented, or

(g) (1) during the course of an interference conducted under section 135 or section 291, another inventor involved therein establishes, to the extent permitted in section 104, that before such person's invention thereof the invention was made by such other inventor and not abandoned, suppressed, or concealed, or (2) before such person's invention thereof, the invention was made in this country by another inventor who had not abandoned, suppressed, or concealed it. In determining priority of invention under this subsection, there shall be considered not only the respective dates of conception and reduction to practice of the invention, but also the reasonable diligence of one who was first to conceive and last to reduce to practice, from a time prior to conception by the other.[87]

Deceptively straightforward at first reading, when applied, the seven subsections (a) through (g) of 35 U.S.C. §102 (2006) may seem a rather bewildering Pandora's box of arcane conventions and obscure terms of art. Many students find that mastering §102 is the most conceptually challenging and time-consuming part of a basic patent law course. Fortunately, the complexities of §102 can be mastered by a careful examination of the statutory provisions, a thorough comprehension of fundamental principles and underlying policy concerns, and the precise use of terminology.

First, here are some general recommendations for readers who seek a better understanding of the intricacies of §102. It is important to become comfortable with the statute. Post a copy of 35 U.S.C. §102 on the wall next to your desk or computer and copy its text into your laptop or smartphone. Read the language over every day until you know it by heart. In the process, you will begin to understand the statute substantively. Another recommended comfort technique is to diagrammatically analyze all §102 problems on a timeline. (These same recommendations apply to the post-AIA version of §102, discussed in Part III *infra.*)

Next, understand that virtually every word in 35 U.S.C. §102 is loaded with meaning. The statute cannot be interpreted in a vacuum; it must be understood in connection with the many judicial decisions and rules of practice that have applied the language of the statute to

[86]This language represents the text of §102(e) as amended by the Twenty-first Century Department of Justice Appropriations Authorization Act, Pub. L. No. 107-273, §13205, 116 Stat. 1758 (2002) (titled "Domestic Publication of Patent Applications Published Abroad") (amending subtitle E of title IV (the American Inventors Protection Act of 1999) of the Intellectual Property and Communications Omnibus Reform Act of 1999, as enacted by Pub. L. No. 106-113, §1000(a)(9), 113 Stat. 1501 (1999).

[87]35 U.S.C. §102 (2006).

a multitude of factual situations. Moreover, much (though not all) of the terminology in pre-AIA §102 was carried over to post-AIA §102. Thus, understanding how the courts have interpreted statutory phrases, such as "printed publication" and "public use," that are present in both the pre- and post-AIA versions of §102 is necessary.

After reviewing some key concepts of general applicability to §102 (pre-AIA), this part of this chapter will individually address each subsection of 35 U.S.C. §102 (pre-AIA).

2. Geographic Distinctions

In starting a journey through 35 U.S.C. §102 (pre-AIA) it is helpful to tackle subsections 102(a) and 102(b) together. A common theme of these subsections is the dichotomy between events that will be recognized as triggering the statute only if they occur in the United States, versus those events that will trigger the statute no matter where in the world they take place. For example, under both subsections an invention is not patentable if it was "patented or described in a printed publication" *anywhere in the world,* either before the invention date (per §102(a)) or more than a year before the filing date (per §102(b)). On the other hand, prior "know[ledge] or use[] by others" under §102(a) and "public use[s]" or placing the invention "on sale" under §102(b) count as anticipations or losses of right only if these events took place *in the United States.*

Why are there geographic distinctions? The statute probably reflects a historical notion, translated into an evidentiary presumption, that "personal" activities (such as an individual's knowledge or use or sale of an invention in a foreign country) require greater effort to disseminate to U.S. citizens than do domestic activities. In contrast, we assume that the content of foreign publications and patents is easily transmitted to and obtainable by U.S. citizens. The geographic distinctions in §102 also may reflect a recognition that the search costs of discovering knowledge and use in a foreign country would be unfairly burdensome if placed on U.S. inventors. Whatever its underpinnings, many have criticized the foreign/domestic dichotomy of patentability-defeating events as antiquated and discriminatory against foreign inventors.[88] Nevertheless, the geographic distinctions will remain in

[88]For example, consider Inventor A, a Japanese national, who made commercial sales of her invention in Japan more than one year before the U.S. patent application filing date of Inventor B, a U.S. national, claiming the same invention (independently developed by B). Under pre-AIA rules, Inventor A cannot rely on her sales activity in Japan in a defensive manner to prevent Inventor B from obtaining a U.S. patent on the invention. In other words, Inventor A's sales of the invention in Japan do not qualify as §102(b) prior art that would destroy Inventor B's claim to the same invention, as they would have had A's sales been made in the United States.

operation for all pre-AIA applications and patents (throughout their lives). The AIA-implemented removal of geographic limitations on patent-defeating events took effect on March 16, 2013, for applications filed on or after that date.

3. Who Is the Actor?

An important distinction between pre-AIA subsections 102(a) and 102(b) of 35 U.S.C. is the identity of the persons who can trigger those subsections and by their actions destroy patentability. Anticipation under 35 U.S.C. §102(a) (pre-AIA) must involve an act by *someone other than the patent applicant,* while loss of right to patent under §102(b) can be the result of acts by *anyone,* including (and in the case of public uses and sales, most often because of) the applicant. The former rule follows from the fact that the novelty-destroying event under §102(a) must have occurred before the applicant's **invention date**.[89] An applicant cannot know, or use, or patent, or describe his invention before he has invented it, so if these events are to anticipate, logically they must have been carried out by others.

Another way of thinking about this is to remember the patent law maxim that "an inventor's own work can only be used against him as prior art if it constitutes a [pre-AIA] §102(b) bar." Thus, if inventor A published a paper describing her invention X on January 1, 2010, and then filed a U.S. patent application claiming X on December 1, 2010, the published paper is *not* §102(a) prior art against the patent application. If the paper had been published on November 1, 2009, however, it would be prior art against the application under §102(b).

[89]The *invention date* of a claimed invention is a central concept under pre-AIA novelty and first-to-invent priority rules. (Post-AIA, however, the significance of invention dates is likely limited to derivation proceedings under 35 U.S.C. §135 (eff. Mar. 16, 2013).) Under pre-AIA rules, the invention date of a claimed invention is, at the earliest, the date of **conception**. The conception date is the date on which the inventor had a complete mental picture of the operative invention, as it was thereafter reduced to practice, *so long as* the inventor displayed reasonable **diligence** in moving from the conception to a reduction to practice. *See* Mahurkar v. C.R. Bard, Inc., 79 F.3d 1572, 1577-1578 (Fed. Cir. 1996). Alternatively, the invention date of a claimed invention may be the date of its **actual reduction to practice**, that is, the date on which the inventor had constructed a physical embodiment of the invention that worked for its intended purpose. There is no set time period in which a patent application must be filed following the invention date, so long as the invention has not been injected into the public domain in some fashion. *See* 35 U.S.C. §102(b) (2006) (providing one-year grace period for application filing following the first patenting or description of the invention in a printed publication anywhere in the world, or the first public use or placement on sale of the invention in the United States).

4. Distinguishing Novelty from Loss of Right

Section 102 of 35 U.S.C. (pre-AIA) is really two provisions in one, as reflected by its title: "Conditions for patentability; novelty and loss of right to patent." Subsections (a), (e), and (g) are true novelty provisions, while subsections (b), (c), and (d) concern loss-of-right situations in which the right to a patent may be lost even though the invention is, technically, novel. (Subsection (f), described below, is *sui generis* and does not comfortably fit in either category.)

One of the fundamental differences between the novelty and loss-of-right provisions lies in their respective triggering dates. Novelty provisions §102(a), (e), and (g) concern (or are triggered by) events taking place "before the invention . . . by the applicant for patent," that is, before the *invention date*.[90] In contrast, the loss-of-right provisions (§102(b) and (d)) key off of the date that is one year prior to the applicant's filing date, sometimes referred to as the §102(b) **critical date**.

To further complicate matters, it should be understood that under the pre-AIA system, the USPTO presumptively treats the applicant's filing date as her invention date (based on a constructive reduction to practice theory[91]) for purposes of applying pre-AIA §102(a), (e), and (g), unless and until the applicant proves an earlier actual invention date. In *ex parte* prosecution, the patent applicant may do this by **antedating** or "swearing behind" a §102(a) or §102(e) prior art reference in accordance with applicable USPTO rules.[92] In litigation challenging the validity of an issued patent, a similar procedure is followed.[93] In a

[90]"Invention date" is defined *supra* Section G.3.

[91]As discussed in greater detail later in this chapter, a reduction to practice of an invention may be an "actual" reduction to practice or a "constructive" reduction to practice. An actual reduction to practice generally involves the construction of a physical embodiment of the invention that works for its intended purpose (testing is often involved to verify whether that purpose is met). A constructive reduction to practice means that a patent application claiming the invention has been filed with the USPTO, which application satisfies the disclosure requirements of 35 U.S.C. §112, ¶1 for the claimed invention. *See* Chapter 3 ("Disclosure Requirements (35 U.S.C. §112(a))"), *supra*.

[92]*See* 37 C.F.R. §1.131 ("Affidavit or Declaration of Prior Invention"). Procedures for antedating a reference are further detailed in Section O of this chapter, *infra*.

[93]*See* Mahurkar v. C.R. Bard, Inc., 79 F.3d 1572 (Fed. Cir. 1996) (affirming district court's grant of patentee's motion for judgment as a matter of law (JMOL) that patent in suit was not anticipated because accused infringer failed to prove that allegedly anticipatory "Cook catalog" was in fact prior art under 35 U.S.C. §102(a)). The court in *Mahurkar* explained that a patentee such as Mahurkar may seek to establish an actual invention date earlier than the application filing date (i.e., constructive reduction to practice date, taken as presumptive invention date) by analogy to the interference rule of priority of invention:

> In the United States, the person who first reduces an invention to practice is "prima facie the first and true inventor." Christie v. Seybold, 55 F. 69, 76 (6th Cir. 1893) (Taft, J.). However, the person "who first conceives, and, in a mental

pre-AIA interference proceeding, an earlier invention date is established under §102(g)(1) and §135.[94]

H. "Known or Used" Under 35 U.S.C. §102(a) (Pre-AIA)

Much controversy and disagreement surrounds the meaning of the statutory phrase "known or used by others" in §102(a). Although some authority exists to support the proposition that prior knowledge or use by even a single person other than the inventor is enough to anticipate, the better view is probably that of Judge Learned Hand, a premier patent jurist.[95] Hand viewed anticipation under §102(a) as requiring that the anticipatory knowledge exist in a manner accessible to the public; that is, it must be "part of the stock of knowledge of the art in question."[96] The current majority rule clearly contemplates that "knowledge and use" under §102(a) must be that which is available to the public.[97]

> sense, first invents . . . may date his patentable invention back to the time of its conception, if he connects the conception with its reduction to practice by reasonable diligence on his part, so that they are substantially one continuous act." *Id.*

Mahurkar, 79 F.3d at 1577. In this validity context, the patentee must essentially establish priority vis-à-vis the effective date of a §102(a) prior art reference (rather than another interference party's invention date). Thus, Mahurkar attempted to show an invention date earlier than the Cook catalog publication date in two ways: (1) through evidence showing that he had conceived and reduced to practice his invention before publication of the catalog; and (2) through evidence that he had conceived his invention prior to the date of publication of the Cook catalog and that he proceeded with reasonable diligence from a date just prior to publication of the catalog to his own filing date. *See id.* at 1578. The accused infringer, Bard, failed to carry its burden to rebut this evidence.

[94] *See infra* Section N.2 ("Interference Proceedings Under §102(g)(1)").

[95] *See generally* PAUL H. BLAUSTEIN, LEARNED HAND ON PATENT LAW (Pineridge Pub. 1983).

[96] Picard v. United Aircraft Corp., 128 F.2d 632, 635 (2d Cir. 1942) (L. Hand, J.).

[97] *See* Woodland Trust v. Flowertree Nursery, Inc., 148 F.3d 1368, 1370 (Fed. Cir. 1998); In re Hilmer, 359 F.2d 859, 878 (C.C.P.A. 1966) (observing that §102(a) patent-defeating "knowledge" of an invention in this country "had been interpreted, long before the [Patent Act of] 1952 codification, to mean public knowledge"); *id.* (quoting from Federico's *Commentary on the 1952 Patent Act*, 35 U.S.C.A. 1, 18 (1954 ed.), that "[t]he Committee Report both in the general part and in the Revision Notes recognizes that the interpretation of this condition is somewhat more restricted than the actual language, stating 'the interpretation by the courts excludes various kinds of private knowledge not known to the public,' and the narrowing interpretations are not changed [in the 1952 Act codification]"); In re Borst, 345 F.2d 851 (C.C.P.A. 1965).

Gayler v. Wilder,[98] the "Salamander safe"[99] case, is an important early illustration of the proper interpretation of "known or used by others" as an anticipatory event. The plaintiff, Wilder, owned a patent directed to a fireproof safe, invented by one Fitzgerald. The safe was constructed of inner and outer iron chests, between which Fitzgerald placed an inflammable material such as gypsum or plaster of paris (mineral-based, cement-like substances that do not burn). Thus, the internal fireproofing construction of the Fitzgerald safe, as claimed in the patent, was not visible from its exterior appearance.

Gayler, having been sued by Wilder for infringement of the patent, defended on the ground that it was invalid as anticipated by the prior knowledge or use of the safe by others, before the date of Fitzgerald's invention.[100] Gayler also asserted that because of this earlier use Fitzgerald could not be the "first and original" inventor of the safe.[101] Gayler's invalidity defenses were based on the independent prior invention of the same safe by one Conner, not a party to the law suit. Conner made the safe for his own business use and kept it in the "counting-room" of his foundry, where his employees passed by it on a daily basis.[102]

Nevertheless, the Supreme Court held, because those persons were not aware of the safe's internal construction, they did not possess "knowledge or use of the invention." The Court sustained the validity of the Fitzgerald patent, despite the fact that Fitzgerald was not, literally, the first inventor of the safe:

> In the case thus provided for, the party who invents [Fitzgerald] is not strictly speaking the first and original inventor. The law assumes that the improvement may have been known and used before his discovery [by Conner]. Yet his patent is valid if he discovered it by the efforts of his own genius, and believed himself to be the original inventor. The clause in question qualifies the words before used, and shows that *by knowledge and use the legislature meant knowledge and use existing in a manner accessible to the public*.... It is the inventor here [Fitzgerald] that brings it to them, and places it in their possession. And as he does

[98]51 U.S. 477 (1850).

[99]*Gayler*, 51 U.S. at 495. In mythology, the salamander was believed capable of surviving fire. *See* AMERICAN HERITAGE DICTIONARY OF THE ENGLISH LANGUAGE (4th ed. 2000) (entry for salamander).

[100]The language of the Patent Act of 1836 at issue in *Gayler v. Wilder* parallels that of 35 U.S.C. §102(a) (2006). *See Gayler,* 51 U.S. at 496 (stating that "[t]he act of 1836, ch. 357, §6, authorizes a patent where the party has discovered or invented a new and useful improvement, 'not known or used by others before his discovery or invention'").

[101]*See Gayler*, 51 U.S. at 496 (quoting from Patent Act of 1836, "the 15th section [of which] provides that, if it appears on the trial of an action brought for the infringement of a patent that the patentee 'was not the original and first inventor or discoverer of the thing patented,' the verdict shall be for the defendant").

[102]*See Gayler*, 51 U.S. at 512.

> this by the effort of his own genius, the law regards him as the first and original inventor, and protects his patent, although the improvement had in fact been invented before, and used by others [Conner].[103]

Thus, to anticipate, prior knowledge or use of an invention by others in this country must have been knowledge or use that was accessible to the public. As between the earlier inventor who maintains his invention in secrecy (e.g., Conner), and a later inventor who is first to put the public in possession of the invention by entering into the patenting process (e.g., Fitzgerald), the patent law rewards the latter. Conner's safe, though literally an earlier invention, did not qualify as prior art that could anticipate Fitzgerald's patent because the knowledge or use of it had never been made accessible to the public.[104]

The Federal Circuit considered the quantum of evidence necessary to establish §102(a) prior knowledge or use in *Woodland Trust v. Flowertree Nursery, Inc.*[105] In that case, several witnesses, all of whom were relatives, friends, or business acquaintances of the owner of the accused infringing company, testified that they had observed or made use of the same system (for protecting foliage plants from freeze damage) as that patented by the plaintiff, some 20 or more years before the patent's filing date. Despite the district court's positive assessment of the witnesses' credibility, the Federal Circuit reversed the lower court's judgment of invalidity based on pre-AIA §102(a) prior public knowledge or use. The appellate court required that the witnesses' entirely oral testimony of prior invention be corroborated, relying on the Supreme Court's *Barbed Wire Patent* case.[106] As applied to the facts of the case at bar, the Supreme Court's guidance in *Barbed Wire Patent* and other cases meant that accused infringer Flowertree Nursery bore a "heavy burden when establishing prior public knowledge and use based on long-past events."[107] Surprisingly, the witnesses for Flowertree were unable to produce a single item of documentary evidence to support their testimony. Given the "ubiquitous paper trail of

[103] *Id.* at 496-497 (emphasis added).

[104] *Gayler v. Wilder* also can be understood as a case in which Conner's earlier making of the safe in this country would not qualify as prior art under 35 U.S.C. §102(g)(2) (2006) (discussed later in this chapter) because Conner had effectively abandoned, suppressed, or concealed his invention after reducing it to practice.

[105] 148 F.3d 1368 (Fed. Cir. 1998).

[106] Washburn & Moen Mfg. Co. v. Beat 'Em All Barbed-Wire Co., 143 U.S. 275 (1892) (hereafter *Barbed Wire Patent*). The Supreme Court in *Barbed Wire Patent* observed that "[i]n view of the unsatisfactory character of testimony, arising from the forgetfulness of witnesses, their liability to mistakes, their proneness to recollect things as the party calling them would have them recollect them, aside from the temptation to actual perjury, courts have not only imposed upon defendants the burden of proving such [earlier-invented] devices, but have required that the proof shall be clear, satisfactory, and beyond a reasonable doubt." *Id.* at 284.

[107] *Woodland Trust*, 148 F.3d at 1373.

virtually all commercial activity," it was notable that "some physical record (e.g., a written document such as notes, letters, invoices, notebooks, or a sketch or drawing or photograph showing the device, a model, or some other contemporaneous record) [did] not exist."[108] In view of this lack of corroboration, the Federal Circuit concluded that defendant Flowertree had failed to carry its burden of establishing invalidity by clear and convincing evidence.[109]

I. The Statutory Bars of 35 U.S.C. §102(b) (Pre-AIA)

1. Introduction

Recall that 35 U.S.C. §102(b) (2006) is a loss-of-right provision rather than a true novelty provision. Section 102(b) (pre-AIA) lists four different ways in which, even though an invention may have been novel as of its invention date, the right to a patent on that invention nevertheless can be lost or forfeited. These four triggering events, also referred to as **statutory bars**, are as follows: more than one year before the application's filing date, the invention was (1) patented anywhere in the world; (2) described in a printed publication anywhere in the world; (3) in public use in the United States; or (4) on sale in the United States. Patent attorneys refer to the date that is one year prior to the application filing date as the **critical date** for §102(b) purposes. Thus, in order to trigger 35 U.S.C. §102(b), a statutory bar event must have occurred prior to the critical date.

The operation of 35 U.S.C. §102(b) is depicted in timeline format in Figure 4.1. As depicted in Figure 4.1, "§102(a) events" are those that occurred prior in time to the invention date,[110] while "§102(b) events" are those that occurred prior in time to the §102(b) critical date. The two relevant time periods overlap for dates prior to the invention date

[108] *Id.*

[109] Other Federal Circuit cases have clarified that corroboration of oral testimony concerning prior invention is to be evaluated under a "rule of reason" standard that considers all pertinent evidence, which is not necessarily limited to documentary evidence. *See* Loral Fairchild Corp. v. Matsushita Elec. Indus. Co., 266 F.3d 1358, 1364 (Fed. Cir. 2001) (stating that "[u]nder the 'rule of reason,' the [alleged prior] inventor's testimony must be sufficiently corroborated by independent evidence, but not necessarily *documentary* evidence") (emphasis in original).

[110] As depicted in Figure 4.1, the invention date before which "§102(a) events" occur is the true or actual invention date. Recall that the USPTO in the first instance will treat an applicant's filing date ("Yr 0" in the figure) as her presumptive or *prima facie* invention date, placing the burden on the applicant to establish the actual date of invention through the antedating procedure detailed in Section O, *infra*. Figure 4.1 depicts a scenario in which the applicant has successfully established her actual invention date ("Yr –X" in the figure), thus antedating any *prima facie* §102(a) prior art having an effective date between "Yr –1" and "Yr 0."

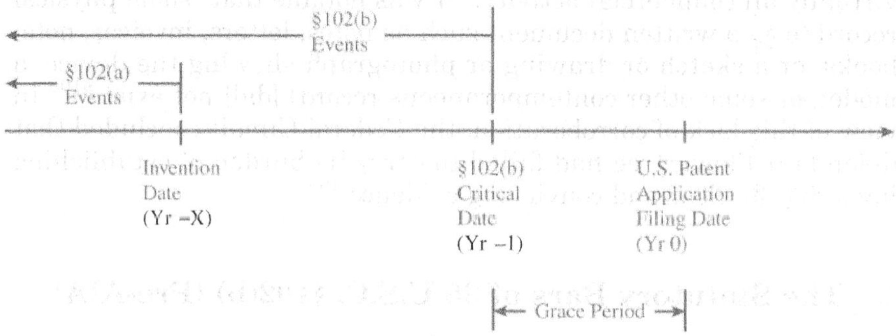

Figure 4.1

35 U.S.C. §102(b) Timeline (Pre-AIA)

as depicted in Figure 4.1. For example, if we assume that a U.S. patent application as illustrated in Figure 4.1 was filed on January 1, 2005, making the §102(b) critical date January 1, 2004, and assume further that the invention date was sometime in 2002, then a technical article published during 2001 (anywhere in the world and authored by someone other than the application inventor) that identically described the invention claimed in the patent application would qualify as "printed publication" prior art under both §102(a) and §102(b).

Understanding *why* our U.S. patent system includes §102(b) is essential to properly applying this important statutory provision.[111] It has often been said that the statutory bars of 35 U.S.C. §102(b) are, in effect, defined by the policies that underlie the bars.[112] Those policies include the following:[113]

1. **Minimize detrimental reliance**— the policy against removing inventions from the public that the public has justifiably come to believe are freely available to all as a consequence of prolonged public use or sales activity.

[111] The historic origin of 35 U.S.C. §102(b) (2006), and why it stands as a patentability requirement separate and independent from 35 U.S.C. §102(a) (2006), can be traced back to *Pennock v. Dialogue*, 27 U.S. 1 (1829).

[112] *See, e.g.*, Western Marine Elecs., Inc. v. Furuno Elec. Co., 764 F.2d 840, 844 (Fed. Cir. 1985) (on sale bar); TP Labs., Inc. v. Professional Positioners, Inc., 724 F.2d 965, 973 (Fed. Cir. 1984) (public use).

[113] *Cf.* Manville Sales Corp. v. Paramount Sys., Inc., 917 F.2d 544, 549-550 (Fed. Cir. 1990) (stating policies as applied to public use bar of §102(b)); UMC Elecs. Co. v. United States, 816 F.2d 647, 652 (Fed. Cir. 1987) (stating policies as applied to on sale bar of §102(b)) (citing Gen. Elec. Co. v. United States, 654 F.2d 55, 60-61 (Ct. Cl. 1981) (*en banc*)). In *In re Caveney*, 761 F.2d 671, 676 n.6 (Fed. Cir. 1985), the court noted that the policies had been identified prior to *General Electric* in Barrett, *New Guidelines for Applying the On Sale Bar to Patentability*, 24 STAN. L. REV. 730, 732-735 (1972).

2. **Encourage prompt dissemination**— the policy favoring prompt and widespread disclosure of new inventions to the public. The inventor is forced to file promptly or risk possible forfeiture of his patent rights due to prior sales or public uses.
3. **Prohibit undue commercial exploitation**— the policy of preventing the inventor from commercially exploiting the exclusivity of his invention substantially beyond the statutorily authorized period (currently about 17-18 years). Section 102(b) forces the inventor to choose between seeking patent protection promptly following sales activity or public use, or taking his chances with his competitors without the benefit of patent protection.
4. **Evaluate marketplace reaction**— the policy of giving the inventor a reasonable amount of time (i.e., the one-year grace period of §102(b)) following sales activity or public uses to determine whether a patent is a worthwhile investment. This benefits the public because it tends to minimize the filing of patent applications of only marginal public interest.

The first three of these four policies primarily benefit the public, while the fourth policy primarily benefits the inventor. Although recent on sale bar decisions of the Federal Circuit eschew the "totality of the circumstances" mantra of the court's earlier §102(b) decisions,[114] in the view of this author the policy underpinnings remain relevant to all §102(b) cases and should not be ignored.[115]

2. Grace Period

Notice in Figure 4.1 that a U.S. patent applicant enjoys a "grace period" or "safe harbor" under 35 U.S.C. §102(b) (2006) comprising the one-year time period between the §102(b) critical date and his

[114]*See* Lacks Indus., Inc. v. McKechnie Vehicle Components USA, Inc., 322 F.3d 1335, 1347 (Fed. Cir. 2003) (defining "totality of the circumstances" test as a flexible analysis in which no single finding or conclusion of law is a *sine qua non* to a holding that a statutory bar has arisen, but characterizing *Pfaff v. Wells Elecs., Inc.*, 525 U.S. 55, 67 (1998), as having "swept away" the totality of the circumstances test); Weatherchem Corp. v. J.L. Clark, Inc., 163 F.3d 1326, 1333 (Fed. Cir. 1998) (stating that Federal Circuit follows the Supreme Court's two-part test [in *Pfaff*] without balancing various policies according to the totality of the circumstances as may have been done in the past").

[115]*Cf.* Bernhardt, L.L.C. v. Collezione Europa USA, Inc., 386 F.3d 1371, 1379 (Fed. Cir. 2004) (applying policies in public use context); Netscape Comm. Corp. v. Konrad, 295 F.3d 1315, 1320 (Fed. Cir. 2002) (same); In re Kollar, 286 F.3d 1326, 1333-1334 (Fed. Cir. 2002) (applying policies in on sale context).

application filing date.[116] During this one-year pre–filing date grace period, an invention may be patented, described in a printed publication, in public use, or on sale, all without triggering a §102(b) loss of right. In other words, the one-year pre–filing date grace period that governed before the AIA's March 16, 2013 implementation of first-to-file is a free pass that allows an inventor to test and refine his invention, make sales of it in the marketplace, and evaluate whether the considerable cost of going forward with the patenting process is justified. So long as the patent application is filed within one year of the first instance of the invention being released into the public domain or commercially exploited by patenting, description in a printed publication, public use, or placement of the invention on sale, either by the patent applicant or a third party, the right to a U.S. patent will not be lost under 35 U.S.C. §102(b).[117]

Importantly, countries other than the United States are generally "absolute novelty" systems that do not recognize any pre–filing date grace period (or when they do, the grace period is only for very limited times and purposes such as particularly defined types of international exhibitions). For example, under the European Patent Convention (EPC) Article 54, any activity that makes an invention part of the "state of the art" at any time prior to the filing date of the European patent application will defeat novelty.[118] Thus, when clients want to obtain patent protection in foreign countries as well as in the United States, they should be advised not to make *any* public disclosure of their inventions at any time prior to filing their priority patent application.[119]

The one-year grace period of the U.S. framework permits us to conceptualize the §102(b) statutory bars in an additional way. The occurrence of any of the four statutory bar events effectively "starts the clock running" against a potential U.S. patent applicant, operating as

[116]Unlike most foreign patent systems, U.S. patent law has long provided patent applicants with a pre-filing grace period. The Patent Act of 1839 instituted a two-year grace period; this was scaled back to one year in 1939.

[117]The America Invents Act of 2011 retained a one-year grace period but only for inventor-generated or inventor-derived disclosures. *See infra* Section S ("Novelty-Preserving Exceptions under Post-AIA 35 U.S.C. §102(b)").

[118]*See* European Patent Convention art. 54(1) (2019) ("An invention shall be considered to be new if it does not form part of the state of the art."), *available at* epo.org/law-practice/legal-texts/html/epc/2016/e/ar54.html; *id.* at art. 54(2) ("The state of the art shall be held to comprise everything made available to the public by means of a written or oral description, by use, or in any other way, before the date of filing of the European patent application.").

[119]*See* Chapter 12 ("International Patenting Issues"), *infra*, for discussion of the right of priority to an earlier foreign filing date under the Paris Convention and the U.S. implementation of the right of priority via 35 U.S.C. §119.

a sort of statute of limitations.[120] In order not to forfeit the right to a U.S. patent on her invention under §102(b), the inventor must file an application claiming that invention within one year of the first occurrence of any of the four statutory bar events. If she waits to file even a single day beyond the one-year grace period, her right to a patent is lost under 35 U.S.C. §102(b).

3. Section 102(b) Public Use

a. Inventor's Control

Because the Patent Act does not define what specific acts will trigger the "public use" or "on sale" statutory bars, we look to the extensive case law on the subject to determine what these terms mean. Broadly speaking, a public use occurs when, prior to the 35 U.S.C. §102(b) critical date, the inventor "releases control" over her invention, effectively dedicating it to the public. The Federal Circuit has defined public use of an invention as any use "by a person other than the inventor who is under no limitation, restriction or obligation of secrecy to the inventor."[121] This definition is overly narrow, because acts by the inventor herself also may (and frequently do) trigger the §102(b) public use bar.

The key criterion of the §102(b) public use bar is whether the inventor kept "control" over the use of her invention. Such "control" does not necessarily require that the inventor kept the invention locked away in secret, however. Rather, the public use bar reflects the traditional case law understanding that patent rights were lost or forfeited when an inventor acted in such a way as to indicate an intent to abandon or otherwise dedicate the invention to the public.[122]

[120]*See* UMC Elecs. v. United States, 816 F.2d 647, 659 (Fed. Cir. 1987) (Smith, J., dissenting) (explaining that "Section 102(b) is in the nature of a statute of limitations, enacted to implement the policy that those who seek the benefits of the patent grant must act promptly after the invention has been placed in possession of the public") (footnote omitted).

[121]In re Smith, 714 F.2d 1127, 1134 (Fed. Cir. 1983).

[122]*See, e.g.*, Pennock v. Dialogue, 27 U.S. 1 (1829), in which the Supreme Court (Story, J.) stated:

> It is admitted that the subject is not wholly free from difficulties; but upon most deliberate consideration we are all of opinion, that the true construction of the [Patent Act of 1793] is, that the first inventor cannot acquire a good title to a patent; if he suffers the thing invented to go into public use, or to be publicly sold for use, before he makes application for a patent. His voluntary act or acquiescence in the public sale and use is an *abandonment* of his right; or rather creates a disability to comply with the terms and conditions on which alone the secretary of state is authorized to grant him a patent.

Pennock, 27 U.S. at 23-24 (emphasis added).

For example, in the oft-cited case of *Egbert v. Lippmann,*[123] the inventor of an improved women's corset[124] gave his "intimate friend," before the critical date, a pair of corset steels that he had made without imposing on his friend any obligation of secrecy or restriction on her use of the steels.[125] The U.S. Supreme Court held that the inventor's acts amounted to a public use that invalidated the corset patent, noting that the inventor's friend "might have exhibited [the steels] to any person, or made other steels of the same kind, and used or sold them without violating any condition or restriction imposed on her by the inventor."[126] The Court concluded that "whether the use of an invention is public or private does not necessarily depend upon the number of persons to whom its use is known. If an inventor, having made his device, gives or sells it to another, to be used by the donee or vendee, without limitation or restriction, or injunction of secrecy, and it is so used, such use is public, even though the use and knowledge of the use may be confined to one person."[127] Figure 4.2 depicts a timeline of events from *Egbert.*

The inventor's relinquishment of control over his invention in *Egbert* is in contrast with the facts of *Moleculon Research Corp. v. CBS, Inc.*[128] Moleculon, assignee of a patent on a three-dimensional, rotating puzzle invented by Nichols, sued CBS (as successor to a toy manufacturer) alleging patent infringement by certain of the well-known Rubik's Cube puzzles. CBS answered by alleging that the

[123]104 U.S. 333 (1881).

[124]*See generally* Valerie Steele, The Corset: A Cultural History (Yale Univ. Press 2001); Kara W. Swanson, *Getting a Grip on the Corset: Gender, Sexuality and Patent Law*, 23 Yale J.L. & Feminism 57 (2011), *available at* https://papers.ssrn.com/sol3/papers.cfm?abstract_id=1753166.

[125]The record also reflected a pre–critical date demonstration of the invention to one Sturgis, a friend of the inventor, without any nondisclosure agreement or obligation of secrecy. *See Egbert*, 104 U.S. at 335.

[126]*Egbert*, 104 U.S. at 337.

[127]*Egbert*, 104 U.S. at 336. This broad statement is in the nature of *dicta*, for the totality of the evidence in *Egbert* showed that many persons besides the inventor had knowledge and use of the corset invention prior to the critical date:

> According to the testimony of the complainant, the invention was completed and put into use in 1855. The inventor slept on his rights for eleven years. Letters-patent were not applied for till March, 1866. In the mean time, the invention had found its way into general, and almost universal, use. A great part of the record is taken up with the testimony of the manufacturers and venders of corset-steels, showing that before he applied for letters the principle of his device was almost universally used in the manufacture of corset-steels. It is fair to presume that having learned from this general use that there was some value in his invention, he attempted to resume, by his application, what by his acts he had clearly dedicated to the public.

Egbert, 104 U.S. at 337.

[128]793 F.2d 1261 (Fed. Cir. 1986).

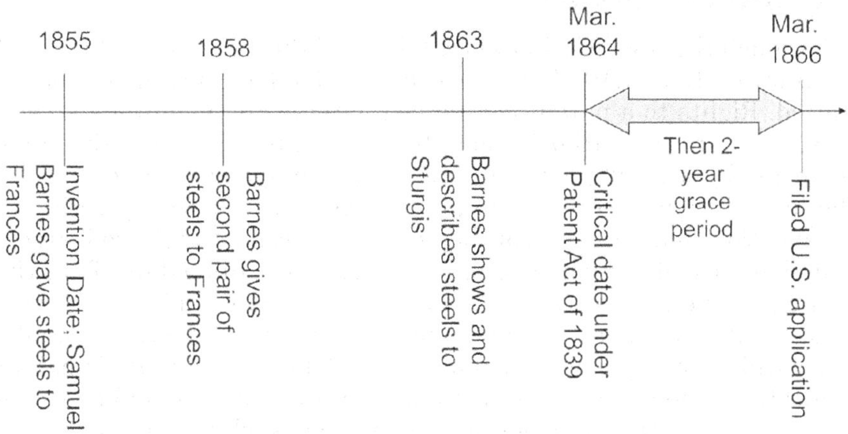

Figure 4.2

Timeline in *Egbert v. Lippmann* (U.S. 1881)

Nichols, patent was invalid for public use of the claimed invention more than a year before the patent application's filing date. The evidence reflected that prior to the §102(b) critical date, Nichols showed paper mockups of the puzzle to his friends at graduate school. When he was later employed by Moleculon as a research scientist, but still prior to the critical date, Nichols brought into his office a working wood-block prototype of the puzzle that he had built at home. Nichols showed the puzzle to Obermayer, the president of Moleculon, and explained its workings. Moleculon thereafter undertook to patent and commercialize the puzzle. The Federal Circuit affirmed the district court's determination that, unlike the inventor in *Egbert,* Nichols had not given over the puzzle invention for free and unrestricted use by others.[129] Rather, based on the personal relationships and surrounding circumstances, Nichols at all times retained control over the puzzle's use and the distribution of information concerning the puzzle. Nichols' use was private and for his own enjoyment; he never used the puzzle or permitted it to be used in a place or time when he did not have a legitimate expectation of privacy and confidentiality. The fact that Nichols allowed Obermayer to briefly use the puzzle without signing a nondisclosure agreement was not determinative, but merely one factor to be considered in the totality of the circumstances.[130]

[129]*See id.* at 1266.
[130]*Id.*

b. Acts by Third Parties

Although the inventor in *Egbert* triggered the loss of right to patent by his own actions, §102(b) public use as understood currently is not so limited. Rights to a patent can be lost without the inventor's knowledge, or intent, or authorization, based on a public use of the same invention by a third party outside of the one-year grace period.[131] The law will not permit an inventor to obtain proprietary rights in an invention that members of the public have come to believe is freely available through prolonged public use before the filing date. Thus the public policy emphasis in statutory bar cases has shifted over time from an "abandonment" rationale to more of a pure "delay" rationale, under which an applicant is penalized for delaying in filing his patent application if he waits more than one year after the first public use of the invention (whether or not he was aware of such public use).

However, even an unauthorized use by third parties will not trigger the public use bar *if* the individuals using the invention maintain it as confidential.[132] In such a case, the public would not understand the invention to be freely available. The Federal Circuit's 2015 decision in *Delano Farms Co. v. California Table Grape Comm'n*,[133] is illustrative.

[131]*See* Lorenz v. Colgate-Palmolive-Peet Co., 167 F.2d 423 (3d Cir. 1948), in which the court held

> [t]he prior public use proviso of R.S. Sec. 4886 [the patent statute then in effect] was enacted by Congress in the public interest. It contains no qualification or exception which limits the nature of the public use. We think that Congress intended that if an inventor does not protect his discovery by an application for a patent within the period prescribed by the Act, and an intervening public use arises from any source whatsoever, the inventor must be barred from a patent or from the fruits of his monopoly, if a patent has issued to him. There is not a single word in the statute which would tend to put an inventor, whose disclosures have been pirated, in any different position from one who has permitted the use of his process.

Id. at 429.

The Federal Circuit subsequently cited *Lorenz* with approval in *Evans Cooling Sys. v. General Motors Corp.*, 125 F.3d 1448, 1452 (Fed. Cir. 1997) (refusing to create third-party exception to on sale bar of §102(b) when, as framed by inventor, "a third party surreptitiously steals an invention while it is a trade secret and then, unbeknownst to the inventor, allegedly puts the invention on sale [more than one year] before the inventor files a patent application covering the stolen invention"). *See also* In re Martin, 74 F.2d 951, 955 (C.C.P.A. 1935) (stating court's opinion that "whatever the correct rule may be with respect to a fraudulent use by another of an invention for more than two years prior to the filing of an application for patent therefor, there is no implied exception in the two-year provision removing the bar of the statute where there is a public use of an invention by an innocent user for more than two years prior to the application for patent").

[132]*See* Delano Farms Co. v. California Table Grape Comm'n, 778 F.3d 1243 (Fed. Cir. 2015).

[133]778 F.3d 1243 (Fed. Cir. 2015).

There the Federal Circuit affirmed a district court's judgment sustaining the validity of two plant patents[134] against a §102(b) (2006) public use invalidity challenge. (The on sale bar applies to plant patents just as it does to utility patents.[135])

In a fact-specific decision, the Federal Circuit sustained the district court's bench trial findings that the actions of two third-party individuals (i.e., not the inventors) who obtained samples of two then-"unreleased" but later-patented table grape varieties from the U.S. government and planted the samples in their own fields did not constitute a §102(b) invalidating public use.[136] More specifically, before the September 2003 critical date of U.S. Patent Nos. PP16,229 (titled "Scarlet Royal") and PP16,284 (titled "Autumn King"), an employee of the U.S. Department of Agriculture (USDA) gave samples of the two then-unreleased grape varieties to California grape grower Jim Ludy and his cousin Larry Ludy after talking with them at an experimental variety open house hosted by a university. The USDA employee was not authorized to give out the samples and the Ludys understood that that their receipt of the material was to be kept confidential and secret.[137]

Thereafter the Ludys grafted the plants and grew a small number of them in their own vineyards, where the plantings were visible from public roads. Nevertheless, the vines were not marked or labeled in any way and their particular varieties could not be ascertained simply by visual inspection. Most of the plantings bore no useable fruit, and the Ludys did not sell any of the grapes before the critical date.

In contrast to the facts of *Egbert v. Lippmann*,[138] the Ludys maintained control over the plant material they received from the USDA employee.[139] The Federal Circuit concluded that "because the evidence

[134]The requirements for patenting a plant are examined *infra* Chapter 7, Section H.1.

[135]The public use bar applies to plant patents. The plant patent statute, 35 U.S.C. §161, mandates that "[t]he provisions of this title relating to patents for inventions shall apply to patents for plants, except as otherwise provided." Such incorporated provisions include the public use bar of 35 U.S.C. §102(b) (2006) for pre-AIA inventions.

[136]*See Delano Farms*, 778 F.3d at 1245.

[137]*See Delano Farms*, 778 F.3d at 1245-1246.

[138]104 U.S. 333 (1881), analyzed *supra*.

[139]*See Delano Farms*, 778 F.3d at 1248-1249. The court elaborated:

> The Supreme Court's decision in *Egbert* turned on the inventor's lack of any effort to maintain control over the use of his invention. The facts of this case, by contrast, show that Jim Ludy sought to maintain control of the plants he obtained from [USDA employee] Mr. Klassen. Although Jim Ludy shared the plants with his cousin, the evidence showed that Larry Ludy was aware of the need to keep the plants secret, and at Jim Ludy's urging, Larry Ludy continued to treat his possession of the unreleased varieties as confidential and non-public. This case is therefore wholly different from the Supreme Court's decision in *Egbert v. Lippmann*, where the inventor himself gave the invention to a third party with no

at trial was sufficient to support the district court's finding that the patented plant varieties were not in public use prior to the critical date, we need not address the question whether use of invention by one who has misappropriated that invention (or obtained it through other improper means) can ever qualify as an invalidating public use."[140] The Ludys' use of the plant varieties at issue in the base at bar was not public, "even apart from the fact that the Ludys obtained the plant material in an unauthorized manner."[141]

Unlike *Delano Farms,* in the case of an unauthorized third-party use that *does* trigger §102(b) (2006), the law will not permit an inventor to obtain proprietary rights in an invention that members of the public have come to believe is freely available through prolonged public use before the filing date. Thus the public policy emphasis in statutory bar cases has shifted over time from an "abandonment" rationale to more of a pure "delay" rationale, under which an applicant is penalized for delaying in filing his patent application if he waits more than one year after the first public use of the invention (whether or not he was aware of such public use).

c. *"Secret" Public Use?*

A patent can be invalidated for §102(b) public use even though the claimed invention was used in secret (at least prior to the America Invents Act of 2011[142]). The common thread of the "non-informing public use" cases is the inventor's secret commercialization of the invention outside of the statutory grace period.[143] A classic example is *Metallizing Engineering Co. v. Kenyon Bearing & Auto Parts Co.*[144] There the inventor Meduna obtained a patent on a process of conditioning metal surfaces, useful for building up worn metal machine parts. Prior to the §102(b) critical date Meduna used his process on jobs for numerous commercial customers but without disclosing any details about the process, which also were not discernible from

---

understanding or expectation that the third party would maintain secrecy as to the invention.

Delano Farms, 778 F.3d at 1248-1249.

[140]*Delano Farms,* 778 F.3d at 1250.

[141]*Delano Farms,* 778 F.3d at 1250.

[142]This is a key question in the interpretation of Section 3 of the AIA as codified in the Patent Act. *See infra* Section Q.3 ("Does the AIA Permit Secret Prior Art?").

[143]*See* Kinzenbaw v. Deere & Co., 741 F.2d 383, 390 (Fed. Cir. 1984) (observing that "[a] commercial use is a public use even if it is kept secret" and citing authority).

In contrast, the America Invents Act of 2011 does not clearly state whether this type of secret information qualifies as post-AIA prior art. *See infra* Section Q.3 ("Does the AIA Permit Secret Prior Art?").

[144]153 F.2d 516 (2d Cir. 1946).

inspecting the finished metal surface.[145] Judge Learned Hand of the Second Circuit reversed a district court decision that had sustained the validity of the patent over a public use challenge; the district court had reasoned that a secret use of a process could never be a public use within the meaning of the statute. In holding that the public use bar can indeed be triggered by secret use that is commercial in nature, Judge Hand overruled his own earlier decision on which the district court had relied:

> [I]t appears that in *Peerless Roll Leaf Co. v. Griffin & Sons,* supra, 2 Cir., 29 F.2d 646, we confused two separate doctrines: (1) The effect upon his right to a patent of the inventor's competitive exploitation of his machine or of his process; (2) the contribution which a prior use by another person makes to the art. Both do indeed come within the phrase, "prior use"; but the first is a defence for quite different reasons from the second. It had its origin — at least in this country — in the passage we have quoted from *Pennock v. Dialogue,* supra, 2 Pet. 1, 7 L. Ed. 327; i.e., that it is a condition upon an inventor's right to a patent that he shall not exploit his discovery competitively after it is ready for patenting; he must content himself with either secrecy, or legal monopoly. It is true that for the limited period of two years he was allowed to do so, possibly in order to give him time to prepare an application; and even that has been recently cut down by half. But if he goes beyond that period of probation, he forfeits his right regardless of how little the public may have learned about the invention....
>
> It is indeed true that an inventor may continue for more than a year to practice his invention for his private purposes of his own enjoyment and later patent it. But that is, properly considered, not an exception to the doctrine, for he is not then making use of his secret to gain a competitive advantage over others; he does not thereby extend the period of his monopoly....[146]

d. Adding a "Ready for Patenting" Requirement for "Public Use"

In an important 2005 decision, *Invitrogen Corp. v. Biocrest Mfg., L.P.*,[147] the Federal Circuit modified the test for triggering the §102(b) public use bar. The test now requires that in addition to being

[145]*See* Metallizing Eng'g Co. v. Kenyon Bearing & Auto Parts Co., 62 F. Supp. 42, 47 (D. Conn. 1945) (finding that "[a]t all times prior to [the critical date of] August 6, 1941, the practice of the process was so guarded as not to come to public knowledge; its nature was disclosed only to a few employees and advisers of the inventor, less than half a dozen in number, in all cases under a promise of confidence which was not abused.... [P]rior to August, 1941, the nature of the process could not have been deduced from inspection or physical tests upon specimens of the processed product in the hands of the public....").

[146]*Metallizing*, 153 F.2d at 519-520.

[147]424 F.3d 1374, 1380 (Fed. Cir. 2005) (Rader, J.).

in "public use," the invention must have been "ready for patenting." The modification followed from the Supreme Court's 1998 analysis of another §102(b) provision, the on sale bar, in the watershed *Pfaff v. Wells Elec., Inc.* case discussed in the next section of this chapter.[148] The *Pfaff* Court considered the degree of development of the invention assertedly on sale and held that, *inter alia,* the invention had to be "ready for patenting" before it could be capable of being placed on sale. Placing a mere "concept" of the invention on sale would not be enough.

The Circuit reasoned in *Invitrogen* that the "ready for patenting" prong of the *Pfaff* on sale bar analysis applies equally in the §102(b) public use context. Under *Invitrogen* and follow-on decisions,[149] the public use bar is triggered when, before the §102(b) critical date,[150] the invention is (1) in public use and (2) ready for patenting. The *Invitrogen* Circuit explained:

> In *Pfaff,* the Court specifically considered the "on sale" portion of the §102(b) statutory bar language, but in so doing, the Court noted that both the "on sale" and "public use" bars were based on the same policy considerations. *Id.* at 64, 119 S. Ct. 304. The Court noted that both the on sale and public use bars of §102 stem from the same "reluctance to allow an inventor to remove existing knowledge from public use." *Id.* In *Pfaff,* the Court applied the separate components of its test to facts raising the "on sale" issue. Nonetheless, *the Court's analysis of the statutory term "invention," or the ready for patenting prong, applies to both of the other parts of section 102(b), "on sale" and "public use."* Thus, the Supreme Court's "ready for patenting test" applies to the public use bar under §102(b). *A bar under §102(b) arises where, before the critical date, the invention is in public use and ready for patenting.*[151]

Accordingly, under the current two-part test for public use that triggers 35 U.S.C. §102(b), prong (1) asks (rather circularly) whether the invention is "in public use." This part of the analysis applies the traditional principles of foundational pre-*Pfaff* public use cases such as *Egbert v. Lippmann,* analyzed earlier in this section.[152] These classic

[148]525 U.S. 55 (1998). The *Pfaff* on sale bar decision is detailed *infra* Section I.4 ("Section 102(b) On Sale Bar").

[149]*See* Barry v. Medtronic, Inc., 914 F.3d 1310, 1320 (Fed. Cir. 2019) (citing *Polara,* 894 F.3d at 1348; citing also *Pfaff,* 525 U.S. at 67; *Invitrogen,* 424 F.3d at 1379); Polara Eng'g Inc. v. Campbell Co., 894 F.3d 1339, 1348 (Fed. Cir. 2018) (citing *Invitrogen,* 424 F.3d at 1379).

[150]That is, the date that is one year before the patent application's filing date. *See supra* Section I.1.

[151]*Invitrogen,* 424 F.3d at 1379-1380 (emphasis added). The Circuit further explained that "in applying the *Pfaff* two-part test in the context of a public use bar, evidence of experimental use may negate either the 'ready for patenting' or 'public use' prong." *Invitrogen,* 424 F.3d at 1380 (citing *EZ Dock,* 276 F.3d at 1352 (recognizing an overlap of the experimental use negation and the ready for patenting standard)).

[152]104 U.S. 333 (1881). *Egbert* was analyzed *supra* Section I.3.a.

cases look at whether the inventor maintained sufficient control over the invention or rather allowed it to go into the public domain without limitation and thereafter delayed filing an application.[153]

Prong (2) of the current two-part test for public use under §102(b), asking whether the invention was "ready for patenting," inquires about the extent of development of "the invention," a phrase included in the text of §102(b).[154] Under *Pfaff,* detailed separately below,[155] the condition that the invention in question is "ready for patenting" "may be satisfied in at least two ways: by proof of reduction to practice before the critical date; or by proof that prior to the critical date the inventor had prepared drawings or other descriptions of the invention that were sufficiently specific to enable a person skilled in the art to practice the invention."[156]

The prong (2), "ready for patenting" aspect of the "public use" (as well as the "on sale") statutory bar frequently invokes the concept of "reduction to practice." As detailed later in this chapter,[157] "reduction to practice" was originally a term of art in patent interference practice — battles over timewise priority between rival inventors.[158] The essential inquiry for a "reduction to practice" is whether an inventor has made a physical embodiment of her invention that works for its intended purpose.[159] Because "reduction to practice" is now implicated in both the §102(b) public use and on sale bars via the case law's mandate that a barred invention must be "ready for patenting," the analysis is admittedly more complex. As we will see, issues turning on the "ready for patenting" (and in turn, "reduction to practice") inquiries are also at the heart of important Federal Circuit disputes concerning the "experimental use" negation of what would otherwise appear to be "public use" or "on sale" activity.[160]

[153]Note that in the §102(b) on sale bar test of *Pfaff,* prong (1) is different — it inquires whether the invention was the subject of a commercial offer for sale before the critical date.

[154]Recall that the statute provides in part that "[a] person shall be entitled to a patent unless — (b) the invention was . . . in public use or on sale in this country, more than one year prior to the date of the application for patent in the United States. . . ." 35 U.S.C. §102 (2006).

[155]*See infra* Section I.4 ("Section 102(b) On Sale Bar").

[156]*Pfaff,* 525 U.S. at 67-68. The *Pfaff* "ready for patenting" inquiry is examined in further detail *infra* Section I.4 ("Section 102(b) On Sale Bar").

[157]*See infra* Section I.4.b ("Is Claimed Invention 'Ready for Patenting'?").

[158]*See infra* Section N.2 ("Interference Proceedings Under §102(g)(1)"); Section N.4 ("Applying the Priority Rule of §102(g)").

[159]This is the definition of an "actual" reduction to practice. A "constructive" reduction to practice involves filing an enabling patent invention that adequately describes the invention in words and pictures. *See infra* Section N.2 ("Interference Proceedings Under §102(g)(1)"); Section N.4 ("Applying the Priority Rule of §102(g)").

[160]*See* Barry v. Medtronic, Inc., 914 F.3d 1310 (Fed. Cir. 2019), examined *infra* Section I.5 ("Experimental Use Negation of the §102(b) Bars").

In the Federal Circuit's important and extensive 2019 split panel opinion in *Barry v. Medtronic, Inc.*,[161] the appellate court considered whether a claimed surgical method invention had been "ready for patenting" before the critical date so as to trigger the §102(b) public use bar. The appeal followed a jury verdict of infringement and non-invalidity (that is, sustaining validity) for patentee Barry in the Eastern District of Texas. The district court in 2017 denied accused infringer Medtronic's post-trial motion challenging the validity of the patent claims under the public use bar (as well as the on sale bar) of §102(b).[162]

Doctor Mark Barry obtained two U.S. patents claiming methods and systems for correcting a patient's spinal cord anomalies, such as those due to scoliosis, by applying force to multiple vertebrae at the same time. Barry filed the applications that led to U.S. Patent Nos. U.S 7,670,358 ('358 patent) and 8,361,121, on December 30, 2004, making December 30, 2003 the §102(b) critical date for the patents.[163]

[161] 914 F.3d 1310 (Fed. Cir. Jan. 24, 2019) (Taranto, J.).

[162] Barry v. Medtronic, Inc., 230 F. Supp. 3d 630 (E.D. Tex. 2017).

[163] Claim 1 of Barry's '358 patent recited:

> 1. A method for aligning vertebrae in the amelioration of aberrant spinal column deviation conditions comprising the steps of:
>
> selecting a first set of pedicle screws, said pedicle screws each having a threaded shank segment and a head segment;
>
> selecting a first pedicle screw cluster derotation tool, said first pedicle screw cluster derotation tool having first handle means and a first group of pedicle screw engagement members which are mechanically linked with said first handle means, each pedicle screw engagement member being configured for engaging with, and transmitting manipulative forces applied to said first handle means to said head segment of each pedicle screw of said first set of pedicle screws,
>
> implanting each pedicle screw in a pedicle region of each of a first group of multiple vertebrae of a spinal column which exhibits an aberrant spinal column deviation condition;
>
> engaging each pedicle screw engagement member respectively with said head segment of each pedicle screw of said first set of pedicle screws; and
>
> applying manipulative force to said first handle means in a manner for simultaneously engaging said first group of pedicle screw engagement members and first set of pedicle screws and thereby in a single motion simultaneously rotating said vertebrae of said first group of multiple vertebrae in which said pedicle screws are implanted to achieve an amelioration of an aberrant spinal column deviation condition;
>
> selecting a first length of a spinal rod member; wherein one or more of said pedicle screws of said first set of pedicle screws each includes:
>
> a spinal rod conduit formed substantially transverse of the length of said pedicle screw and sized and shaped for receiving passage of said spinal rod member therethrough; and
>
> spinal rod engagement means for securing said pedicle screw and said spinal rod member, when extending through said spinal rod conduit, in a substantially fixed relative position and orientation;

The facts of *Barry* were largely undisputed (unlike the legal conclusions to be drawn from them). Before December 30, 2003, Dr. Barry used the claimed method in three surgeries he performed on three different patients, each suffering a different type of spinal abnormality. Barry conducted two of the three surgeries in August 2003 and the third surgery in October 2003. It was undisputed that Barry charged his normal fee for each of the three surgeries and that the method claims of the '358 patent read on the steps Barry performed during the surgeries. Importantly, Barry held post-surgical follow-up appointments with each patient, viewing their spinal x-rays, after they were able to stand up and walk following a three-month acute phase of recovery.[164] Barry conducted the last follow-up appointment in January 2004, a date that fell inside the §102(b) one-year grace period.[165]

The parties' central dispute in *Barry v. Medtronic* was whether (1) as Barry argued and the Texas jury and Federal Circuit majority (in an opinion authored by Circuit Judge Taranto) agreed, the claimed surgical method had not been "ready for patenting" until the January 2004 follow-up appointment for the third surgery, thus falling within the §102(b) grace period and not triggering an invalidating public use bar; or (2) as accused infringer Medtronic and dissenting-in-part Chief Judge Prost countered, the claimed method had been "ready for patenting" no later than the completion of the second surgery in October 2003, more than one year before the December 2004 filing dates of Barry's patents in suit. If Medtronic and Judge Prost were correct, Barry's completion of the second surgery triggered the §102(b) bars, thus invalidating Barry's '358 patent.

Thus, "ready for patenting" was the key point of contention in *Barry*. Under *Pfaff v. Wells Elecs.,* detailed separately below,[166] the Supreme Court instructed in 1998 that the condition that an invention is "ready for patenting" "may be satisfied in at least two ways: [1] by proof of reduction to practice before the critical date; or [2] by proof that prior to the critical date the inventor had prepared drawings or other descriptions of the invention that were sufficiently specific to

---

extending said first length of said spinal rod member through said spinal rod conduits of one or more of said pedicle screws of said first set of pedicle screws; and

after applying said manipulative force to said first handle means, actuating said spinal rod engagement means to secure said vertebrae in their respective and relative positions and orientations as achieved through application of said manipulative force thereto.

[164]*Barry,* 914 F.3d at 1319.
[165]*Barry,* 914 F.3d at 1319.
[166]*See infra* Section I.4 ("Section 102(b) On Sale Bar").

enable a person skilled in the art to practice the invention."[167] In *Barry,* the parties agreed that the pertinent test was the first of the two mentioned in *Pfaff*; that is, whether Barry's surgical method invention had been reduced to practice before the December 2003 critical date.

The classic patent law test for an actual (rather than constructive) reduction to practice comes from interference law;[168] the test has two aspects. An invention is actually reduced to practice when "'the inventor (1) constructed an embodiment or performed a process that met all the limitations [of the disputed claim(s)] and (2) determined that the invention would work for its intended purpose.'"[169] Prong (1) was not disputed in *Barry,* so the "ready for patenting" dispute collapsed to a timing question—when Dr. Barry had determined that his invention "would work for its intended purpose."

The Federal Circuit majority in *Barry* concluded that substantial record evidence adequately supported the jury's verdict that the '358 patent was not invalid; that is, that the §102(b) bars had *not* been triggered. In particular, the majority agreed that "Barry's invention was not ready for patenting until January 2004 because the final follow-up from the October [2003] surgery was reasonably needed for the determination that the invention worked for its intended purpose."[170] This evidence "allow[ed] a reasonable finding that Dr. Barry did not know that his invention would work for its intended purpose until January 2004, when he completed the follow-ups on those surgeries, which were on three patients who fairly reflected the real-world range of application of the inventive method."[171]

Notably, the three patients operated on with the claimed method represented the three most common curve types of scoliosis. The *Barry* majority noted that the invention was "not limited to a particular type of curvature correction." In its view, Dr. Barry was entitled to withhold his judgment about his claimed technique "reliably working until [he had completed] follow-up on a small but representative range of 'deviation conditions' surgeons would normally encounter."[172] Moreover,

[167] *Pfaff,* 525 U.S. at 67-68. The *Pfaff* "ready for patenting" inquiry is examined in further detail *infra* Section I.4.b ("Is Claimed Invention 'Ready for Patenting'?").

[168] An actual reduction to practice means that the inventor has actually constructed a physical embodiment of the claimed invention that works for its intended purpose. A constructive reduction to practice is the filing of a patent application that satisfies the disclosure requirements of 35 U.S.C. §112, first paragraph, with respect to the claimed invention. *See infra* Section N.4 ("Applying the Priority Rule of §102(g)").

[169] *Barry,* 914 F.3d at 1322 (quoting In re Omeprazole Patent Litig., 536 F.3d 1361, 1373 (Fed. Cir. 2008) (internal quotations omitted by Federal Circuit)).

[170] *Barry,* 914 F.3d at 1322.

[171] *Barry,* 914 F.3d at 1323.

[172] *Barry,* 914 F.3d at 1324.

the majority considered it reasonable that Dr. Barry operated on all three primary varieties of spinal curvature conditions before being sure the invention worked for its intended purpose, analogously to the testing under differing weather conditions faced in the court's earlier cases in *Manville Sales Corp. v. Paramount Sys., Inc.*,[173] and *Polara Eng'g Inc v. Campbell Co.*,[174] the different crosswalk dimensions in *Polara*, and the different types of terrain in *Honeywell Int'l Inc. v. Universal Avionics Systems Corp.*[175]

Other evidence further persuaded the *Barry* majority that the jury's verdict sustaining the '358 patent's validity was based on a supported finding that Dr. Barry was unsure his surgical method worked for its intended purpose until after the last follow-up appointment in January 2004 (i.e., after the §102(b) critical date). It was not until after that final appointment that Barry wrote up his work on the development of the method for publication in a professional forum. The jury was also entitled to credit the testimony of Barry's expert, who stated that

> "you know nominally if you have performed a correction of the spine" — agreeing to the "some amelioration" characterization by Medtronic's counsel only to that limited extent — and then immediately explained, starting in the same answer, that what happened afterward was crucial: "when the patient stands up, there are some changes that happen over time." As a result, [Barry's expert] added, although "normally you can see the straightening" at the time of the surgery, "follow-up is absolutely required to determine that it lasts," and the follow-up appointments allowed Dr. Barry to conclude, "'[o]kay, this thing is holding up' and . . .'[n]ow I know I've got a method that works.'"[176]

Moreover, the majority noted, "[b]oth Dr. Barry and his expert indicated that at least that amount of post-surgical follow-up is not just prudent but consistent with standards for peer-reviewed publications reporting new techniques."[177]

The *Barry* majority and dissent disagreed sharply on the weight to be accorded the preamble language in claim 1 of Barry's '358 patent

[173]917 F.2d 544, 549 (Fed. Cir. 1990) (lightpole that needed testing for durability outdoors in various weather environments held not in public use under §102(b)).

[174]894 F.3d 1339, 1348 (Fed. Cir. 2018) (control system for alerting pedestrians when to safely cross streets needed to be tested at actual crosswalks of different sizes and in different weather conditions in order to ensure that invention worked for its intended purpose).

[175]*Barry*, 914 F.3d at 1326 (citing *Honeywell*, 488 F.3d 982 (Fed. Cir. 2007)); *Barry*, 814 F.3d at 1326 (explaining that in *Honeywell*, patentee's determination that claimed terrain warning system for airplanes worked for its intended purpose was reasonably dependent on completion of a range of tests in a variety of real-world situations in which the system would be used; invention held not ready for patenting before critical date).

[176]*Barry*, 914 F.3d at 1323 (Joint Appendix references omitted).

[177]*Barry*, 914 F.3d at 1323-1324.

in suit. Recall that claim 1's preamble recited "[a] method for aligning vertebrae in the amelioration of aberrant spinal column deviation conditions. . . ." Did this language define or limit the scope of the "intended purpose" of the invention for purposes of the reduction to practice variety of "ready for patenting"?

The *Barry* majority answered in the negative, taking the position that the invention's intended purpose was *not* as narrow as the claim language (or the dissent) might suggest. The preamble did not require that the invention's purpose was limited to the successful completion of one or even two surgeries, as the dissent urged, without regard to the correction lasting beyond the surgery so as to improve the patient's health. Rather, the majority took what it termed a "common sense approach" to identifying the intended purpose of Dr. Barry's surgical technique, consistent with the claim preamble language as well as the remainder of the '358 patent's specification. The *Barry* majority's approach "look[ed] past the time of a surgery to evaluate the improvement in patients' conditions and allow[ed] the withholding of judgment about the technique reliable working until follow-up on a small but representative range of 'deviation conditions' surgeons would regularly encounter."[178]

The *Barry* dissenting-in-part opinion, authored by Circuit Chief Judge Prost, took strong issue with the majority's approach on the weight of claim language in establishing intended purpose. Judge Prost charged that for the "ready for patenting" inquiry as applied to the case at bar, "[t]he only question is when Dr. Barry determined that his methods worked for their intended purpose."[179] In her view, the intended purpose of the invention was explicitly stated in the claims' preamble: "the amelioration of aberrant spinal column deviation conditions." Barry's own testimony and that of his expert established that the recited "amelioration" happened during surgery:

> Q. And there is a term that is used in the patent that is not a term that is familiar to me as a lay-person, but it's "amelioration." Does that mean correction?
>
> A. Yes.

[178]*Barry,* 914 F.3d at 1325 (footnote omitted). Indeed, the majority further observed, an invention's intended purpose need not even be stated in a claim preamble or in limitations that define claim scope. This was "hardly surprising" because many process and product claims simply recite physical steps or physical elements "without building functional or purpose language into the claim limitations at all." *Barry,* 914 F.3d at 1325 (citing In re Schreiber, 128 F.3d 1473, 1478 (Fed. Cir. 1997) (explaining that "[a] patent applicant is free to recite features of an apparatus *either* structurally or functionally" but that the latter choice presents distinctive risks) (emphasis added by Federal Circuit)).

[179]*Barry,* 914 F.3d at 1338 (Prost, C.J., dissenting-in-part).

> Q. Okay. So, it happens right there in the operating room, on the spot, true?
>
> A. The surgical correction of the rotated vertebrae back to the midline, yeah, happens with that maneuver. Yes.

Dr. Barry's expert testified similarly ("Q. And at least for the vertebrae, that derotation problem, you'll know if there was at least some amelioration when the surgery is over. A. Fair enough.")

Once this amelioration happened, Dr. Barry secured the derotated vertebrae in place with rods and screws, as the claims require:

> Q. And can you explain for the jury, please, what happens once you get the vertebrae derotated into the proper alignment? How do you hold it there?
>
> A. Well, as mentioned, you have screws up and down throughout that area of that curve. Once those vertebrae are rotated back into the midline and you have the correction that you are happy with, you are comfortable with, you lock down the screws to the two rods. . . . So, that's at the end of the procedure where all of the implants — screws, rods, and the setscrews — are all tightened down, locked down.[180]

Based on this testimony and other evidence, the *Barry* dissent concluded that no later than the completion of his second surgery using the claimed method, Dr. Barry appreciated that his invention worked for its intended purpose. The claim preamble language established that the invention's purpose was "to ameliorate aberrant spinal column deviation conditions." This amelioration occurred in both surgeries. Because Barry appreciated that his invention worked for its intended purpose (and he had performed every step of the claims) before the critical date, the invention was reduced to practice as a matter of law. Hence, the dissent viewed it as "ready for patenting," triggering the §102(b) public use and on sale bars.[181]

The "ready for patenting" issue, prong (2) of the §102(b) public use analysis, was clearly the most hotly disputed issue in *Barry*. But for completeness, the Federal Circuit also considered prong (1), which asks (rather circularly) whether the invention is "in public use." This part of the analysis applies the traditional principles considering whether the inventor maintained sufficient control over the invention or rather allowed it to go into the public domain without limitation.[182]

[180] *Barry,* 914 F.3d at 1339 (Prost, C.J., dissenting-in-part) (citations to Joint Appendix omitted).

[181] *Barry,* 914 F.3d at 1339 (Prost, C.J., dissenting-in-part).

[182] Note that in the §102(b) on sale bar test of *Pfaff,* prong (1) is different — it inquires whether the invention was the subject of a commercial offer for sale before the critical date.

Recall that in the 2005 *Invitrogen* case, the Circuit announced (without citation to authority) that "[t]he proper test for the public use prong of the §102(b) statutory bar is whether the purported use: [i] was accessible to the public; or [ii] was commercially exploited."[183]

The *Barry* majority applied the *Invitrogen* test and determined that neither of subparts [i] or [ii] within the "in public use" prong of the overall §102(b) public use inquiry applied. As to subpart [i], unlike the inventor of the corset in the Supreme Court's foundational *Egbert v. Lippman* decision discussed above,[184] Dr. Barry never relinquished control of his surgical method invention. Barry himself performed the surgery. Although assistant physicians, an anesthesiologist, nurses, and an equipment representative were all present in the operating room, very few of these individuals could see the surgical techniques used because the sterile operating field was draped. More importantly, the jury could have reasonably found that those persons present in the operating room with Dr. Barry owed him an implied duty of confidentiality covering at least the tools and techniques used. In the *Barry* majority's view, the jury's finding of no public accessibility was supported by substantial evidence.[185] Dissenting Judge Prost countered that the "control" factor should not be allotted "much consideration" in the case at bar. When the invention is a surgical method practiced by the inventor surgeon, she reasoned, it is "likely [that the surgeon is] going to retain sole control over the method for as long as he was practicing it."[186]

As to subpart [ii], commercial exploitation, this sub-factor similarly was not triggered in the *Barry* majority's view. Dr. Barry charged his usual rate for each of the three surgeries, not adding any additional fee in recognition of the value added from use of his new surgical technique.[187] The dissent rejoined that the fact of Barry charging his normal fee conclusively established *Pfaff*'s commercial-sale prong for each surgery[188] (absent any experimental use negation, discussed separately below[189]). The dissent "c[ould] not see how charging one's

[183]*Invitrogen,* 424 F.3d at 1380. *See also* Barry v. Medtronic, Inc., 914 F.3d 1310, 1337 n.2 (Fed. Cir. 2019) (Prost, C.J., dissenting-in-part) (stating that "the public-use prong is met if the purported use was accessible to the public or commercially exploited") (citing *Invitrogen,* 424 F.3d at 1379-1380).

[184]104 U.S. 333, 335 (1881). *Egbert* is discussed *supra* Section I.3.a ("Inventor's Control").

[185]*Barry,* 914 F.3d at 1327.

[186]*Barry,* 914 F.3d at 1347-1348 (Prost, C.J., dissenting-in-part).

[187]*Barry,* 914 F.3d at 1327-1328.

[188]*Barry,* 914 F.3d at 1338 (Prost, C.J., dissenting-in-part) (citing Plumtree Software, Inc. v. Datamize, LLC, 473 F.3d 1152, 1163 (Fed. Cir. 2006) ("[P]erforming the patented method for commercial purposes before the critical date constitutes a sale under §102(b)."); In re Kollar, 286 F.3d 1326, 1333 (Fed. Cir. 2002) ("[P]erforming the process itself for consideration would . . . trigger the application of §102(b).")).

[189]*See infra* Section I.5 ("Experimental Use Negation of the §102(b) Bars").

normal fee makes the sale look like anything other than a normal sale."[190]

The *Barry* majority and dissent also sparred over the issue of experimental use negation of the asserted §102(b) public use. This issue is analyzed separately below with other experimental use cases.[191]

4. Section 102(b) On Sale Bar

a. *Introduction*

The "on sale" bar is probably the greatest source of litigation involving 35 U.S.C. §102(b) (2006) challenges to patent validity. Operation of the bar results in a loss of right to a patent when an invention has been sold or offered for sale more than one year before the application filing date (i.e., outside of the one-year pre–filing date grace period). The statutory phrase "on sale" is understood as meaning "placement on sale,"[192] which encompasses offers to sell as well as completed sales. Moreover, a mere offer to sell even a single unit of the invention will trigger the §102(b) clock[193] so long as the offer meets certain "commercialness" requirements established in the on sale bar case law considered below.

The primary public policy rationale underlying the on sale bar is that which prohibits the prolonged commercial exploitation of the invention outside of the statutorily authorized time period of exclusivity.[194]

[190] *Barry,* 914 F.3d at 1346 (Prost, C.J., dissenting-in-part) (citing Electromotive Div. of Gen. Motors Corp. v. Transp. Systems Div. of Gen. Elec. Co., 417 F.3d 1203, 1217 (Fed. Cir. 2005); Sinskey v. Pharmacia Ophthalmics, Inc., 982 F.2d 494, 499 (Fed. Cir. 1992), *overruled on other grounds* by *Pfaff,* 525 U.S. 55 (1998)).

[191] *See infra* Section I.5 ("Experimental Use Negation of the §102(b) Bars").

[192] *See* King Instrument Corp. v. Otari Corp., 767 F.2d 853, 860 (Fed. Cir. 1985) (holding that 35 U.S.C. §102(b) "proscribes not a sale, but a placing 'on sale'") (citing D.L. Auld Co. v. Chroma Graphics Corp., 714 F.2d 1144, 1147 (Fed. Cir. 1983)).

[193] *See* In re Theis, 610 F.2d 786, 791 (C.C.P.A. 1979) (stating that "[e]ven a single, unrestricted sale brings into operation this bar to patentability") (citing Consolidated Fruit-Jar Co. v. Wright, 94 U.S. 92, 94 (1876); In re Blaisdell, 242 F.2d 779, 783 (C.C.P.A. 1957)).

[194] Justice Joseph Story provided the classic expression of this policy rationale:

> If an inventor should be permitted to hold back from the knowledge of the public the secrets of his invention; if he should for a long period of years retain the monopoly, and make, and sell his invention publicly, and thus gather the whole profits of it, relying upon his superior skill and knowledge of the structure; and then, and then only, when the danger of competition should force him to secure the exclusive right, he should be allowed to take out a patent, and thus exclude the public from any farther use than what should be derived under it during his fourteen years [the statutory term at that time]; it would materially retard the progress of science and the useful arts, and give a premium to those who should be least prompt to communicate their discoveries.

Pennock v. Dialogue, 27 U.S. 1, 19 (1829).

Consider a novel and nonobvious invention first put on the market in the United States, for which a patent application is filed within one year. Although the inventor will have no legal right to exclude others from making, using, or selling the invention unless and until her patent issues, she often benefits from a *de facto* exclusivity of sorts during the time period leading up to issuance of her patent (i.e., during the pre-filing grace period plus the patent application's pendency in the USPTO). This *de facto* exclusivity results simply by virtue of her being first to the marketplace with a (presumably) novel and nonobvious product, and may be facilitated by the inventor's right to mark her product as "Patent Pending" once she has filed an application.[195] Because the statute provides the patentee with a very powerful right to exclude others generally lasting 17-18 years (20 years less application pendency in the USPTO), the U.S. patent law construes this time period narrowly. No excess time-wise tacking of *de facto* exclusivity onto the initial part of the patent term will be permitted. Thus, offers to sell or sales of an invention outside of the §102(b) grace period will result in a loss of right to patent (if the information is known to the USPTO), or will invalidate an issued patent if the pre–critical date activity does not come to light until the time of subsequent litigation challenging the patent's validity.[196]

A key issue in many on sale bar cases is what state of development the invention must be in before the inventor possesses an "invention" capable of being placed on sale within the meaning of §102(b). For example, an offer of a mere undeveloped "concept" cannot trigger the §102(b) clock.[197] On the other hand, the invention need not necessarily have been actually reduced to practice (i.e., physically constructed and tested) in order to be capable of placement on sale. In a watershed case, the Supreme Court clarified in *Pfaff v. Wells Elec., Inc.*,[198] that

[195]*See* United States Patent & Trademark Office, *Provisional Application for Patent* (Feb. 2011), http://www.uspto.gov/patents/resources/types/provapp.jsp (noting that filing a provisional patent application "[p]ermits authorized use of 'Patent Pending' notice for 12 months in connection with the description of the invention"). Filing a regular, non-provisional application also permits an applicant to mark products embodying the invention with the words "patent pending." In either case, the words "patent pending" have no enforceable legal effect. They simply provide notice to competitors that the entity marking its products with "patent pending" may eventually obtain a patent on some aspect of the product.

[196]The experimental use doctrine, discussed separately below, may negate what would otherwise appear to be on sale (or public use) activity under 35 U.S.C. §102(b).

[197]*See* UMC Elecs. Co. v. United States, 816 F.2d 647, 656 (Fed. Cir. 1987) (refuting any intention to "sanction attacks on patents on the ground that the inventor or another offered for sale, before the critical date, the mere concept of the invention. Nor should inventors be forced to rush into the Patent and Trademark Office prematurely.").

[198]525 U.S. 55 (1998).

in order to be "on sale" within the meaning of 35 U.S.C. §102(b), two conditions must be satisfied before the critical date:

(1) the invention must be the subject of a commercial offer for sale; and
(2) the invention must be ready for patenting.[199]

Each *Pfaff* prong is examined below (in reverse order).

b. *Is Claimed Invention "Ready for Patenting"?*

With respect to prong (2), the Supreme Court in *Pfaff*[200] held that the "ready for patenting" condition can be satisfied in "at least" two ways:[201] (1) the invention may have already been actually reduced to practice,[202] or (2) the invention may have at least been "reduced to drawings," in the sense that drawings or written descriptions of the invention exist that are sufficiently specific to enable a person having ordinary skill in the art to practice the invention.[203]

The second of these conditions was held satisfied in *Pfaff.* Prior to the critical date, the inventor had offered to sell (and in fact had accepted a purchase order for) 30,100 units of his invention, a simple mechanical socket for holding computer chips during testing, to Texas Instruments for $91,115.[204] Figure 4.3 depicts the socket.

Despite the fact that at the time of the offer, Pfaff had not actually constructed any of the sockets, the Supreme Court considered the invention ready for patenting such that the §102(b) bar was triggered. Detailed mechanical drawings and descriptions of the sockets existed as of the date that Pfaff accepted the purchase order (prior to the critical date), and the Court considered this information to have been enabling.[205] The Court supported its conclusion by noting that Texas

[199]*See Pfaff*, 525 U.S. at 67.

[200]525 U.S. 55 (1998).

[201]*Pfaff*, 525 U.S. at 67. By referring to the "at least" two ways in which an invention can be ready for patenting, the Supreme Court left the door open to additional possibilities for satisfying this condition.

[202]An actual reduction to practice requires the physical construction of an embodiment of the invention that works for its intended purpose, and will usually entail testing. *See Pfaff*, 525 U.S. at 57 n.2 ("A process is reduced to practice when it is successfully performed. A machine is reduced to practice when it is assembled, adjusted and used. A manufacture is reduced to practice when it is completely manufactured. A composition of matter is reduced to practice when it is completely composed.") (quoting Corona Cord Tire Co. v. Dovan Chem. Corp., 276 U.S. 358, 383 (1928)).

[203]*See Pfaff*, 525 U.S. at 67-68.

[204]*See id.* at 58.

[205]*See Pfaff*, 525 U.S at 63. *See also id.* at 68 (stating that "the second condition of the on sale bar is satisfied because the drawings Pfaff sent to the manufacturer before the critical date fully disclosed the invention"). In the view of this author, a significant

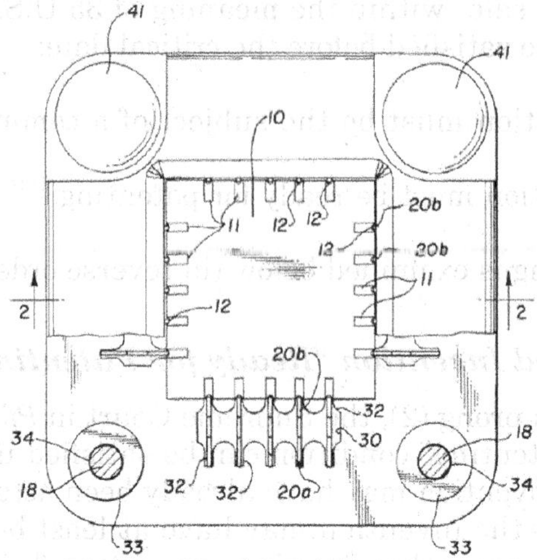

Figure 4.3

Patented Socket from *Pfaff v. Wells* (U.S. 1998)

Instruments was able to produce the sockets using Pfaff's drawings and specifications, and that those sockets contained all the elements of the invention as later claimed in Pfaff's patent.[206]

c. *Is Claimed Invention the Subject of a Commercial Offer for Sale?*

With respect to *Pfaff* prong (1), the Federal Circuit has clarified in decisions subsequent to *Pfaff* that a "commercial offer" is one definite enough to qualify as an "offer" in the general contract law sense, as exemplified by the definition of an "offer" under the Uniform Commercial Code (UCC).[207] "Only an offer which rises to the level of a commercial offer for sale, one which the other party could make into a binding

concern with the *Pfaff* Court's "ready for patenting" analysis is that it effectively places a burden on the inventor of determining whether or not an enabling disclosure of his invention exists, at a time well prior to the filing of a patent application (or in most cases, even prior to consulting a patent attorney). The decision would seem to prejudice independent inventors without previous experience in the patent system, who cannot reasonably be expected to have mastered the finer points of enablement law under 35 U.S.C. §112, ¶1, a subject on which even Federal Circuit judges have been known to disagree.

[206] *See Pfaff*, 525 U.S at 68.

[207] *See* Group One, Ltd. v. Hallmark Cards, Inc., 254 F.3d 1041, 1047-1048 (Fed. Cir. 2001).

contract by simple acceptance (assuming consideration), constitutes an offer for sale under §102(b)," the Federal Circuit has explained.[208]

For example, the claimed invention in *Group One, Ltd. v. Hallmark Cards, Inc.*,[209] concerned machines and methods for producing curled and shredded ribbon. Before the §102(b) critical date, the patentee Group One attempted to generate interest in its invention by sending a letter to Hallmark Cards, Inc. (a leading U.S. and international retailer of greeting cards, wrapping paper, ribbon, and the like). The letter stated in pertinent part:

> We have developed a machine which can curl and shred ribbon so that Hallmark can produce the product you see enclosed — a bag of already curled and shredded ribbon. . . . We could provide the machine and/or the technology and work on a license/royalty basis.[210]

Applying UCC principles, the Federal Circuit in *Group One* held that the quoted language (lacking the hallmarks of a commercial offer such as price and quantity terms) was not specific enough to rise to the level of a commercial offer that would trigger the one-year clock of §102(b). The Circuit's review of the facts led it to "the same conclusion reached [on the commercial offer issue] by the district court — the correspondence and other interactions between Group One and Hallmark prior to the critical date did not add up to a commercial offer to sell the invention, an offer, for example, which Hallmark could have accepted."[211]

A somewhat different and interesting fact pattern involves internal sales between the patentee and third parties that supply the patentee

[208]*Group One*, 254 F.3d at 1048. The *Group One* court did not offer definitive guidelines for determining when a communication rises to the level of a commercial offer sufficient to trigger the §102(b) clock, but did "note in passing" that

> contract law traditionally recognizes that mere advertising and promoting of a product may be nothing more than an invitation for offers, while responding to such an invitation may itself be an offer. Restatement (Second) of Contracts §26 (1981). In any given circumstance, who is the offeror, and what constitutes a definite offer, requires looking closely at the language of the proposal itself. Language suggesting a legal offer, such as "I offer" or "I promise" can be contrasted with language suggesting more preliminary negotiations, such as "I quote" or "are you interested." Differing phrases are evidence of differing intent, but no one phrase is necessarily controlling. *Id.* §§24, 26. Fortunately, as earlier noted, there is a substantial body of general contract law, widely shared by both state and federal courts, to which courts can resort in making these determinations. *See generally, e.g.*, ARTHUR LINTON CORBIN, CORBIN ON CONTRACTS (1964); JOHN D. CALAMARI & JOSEPH M. PERILLO, THE LAW OF CONTRACTS (4th ed. 1998).

Group One, 254 F.3d at 1048.

[209]254 F.3d 1041, 1047-1048 (Fed. Cir. 2001).

[210]*Group One,* 254 F.3d at 1044.

[211]*Group One*, 254 F.3d at 1048.

with services involved in preparing or making the claimed invention, rather than conventional sales (or offers to sell) of the claimed invention by the patentee to its ultimate intended customer. Do such internal sales of services allow the patentee to commercially benefit from the invention too long before filing a patent application? The Federal Circuit has previously rejected the notion of a "supplier" exception to the on sale bar,[212] but the issue is not free from doubt and is subject to a plethora of factual permutations.

In a July 2015 decision in *The Medicines Co. v. Hospira, Inc.*,[213] a panel of the Federal Circuit held that an on sale bar-triggering commercial offer for sale under 35 U.S.C. §102(b) (2006) occurred based on the sale of manufacturing services to a patentee, when the seller's performance of those services resulted in making a pharmaceutical product that met the limitations of the later-obtained patents. This holding followed even though title to the product did not change hands (i.e., title never left the patentee). In November 2015, the appellate court vacated the panel opinion and ordered the *Medicines Co.* case reheard *en banc.*[214] One of the questions for which the court requested *en banc* briefing asked whether the court should "overrule or revise the principle . . . that there is no 'supplier exception' to the on-sale bar of 35 U.S.C. §102(b)."[215]

More specifically, The Medicines Company owned U.S. Patents No. 7,582,727 ('727 patent) and 7,598,343 ('343 patent) directed to the drug bivalirudin,[216] an anti-coagulant synthetic peptide that is typically administered in an aqueous intravenous solution. Medicines Company sold the drug for injection under the brand name Angiomax.® The pH level of the solution is adjusted during compounding to reduce the acidity of bivalirudin in water or saline. The U.S. Food and Drug Administration (FDA) approved a maximum 1.5% permitted level of "Asp^9-bivalirudin impurity" for such solutions.

For almost ten years before seeking its patents, The Medicines Company purchased pharmaceutical batches of a bivalirudin drug for injection from its contract manufacturer, Ben Venue Laboratories ("Ben Venue"). Starting in 2005, some batches produced by Ben Venue did not meet the FDA's purity requirement. To address the problem, The Medicines Company hired a consultant. Dr. Gary Musso discovered that "certain methods of adding a pH-adjusting solution during

[212]*See* Special Devices, Inc. v. OEA, Inc., 270 F.3d 1353, 1357 (Fed. Cir. 2001) (holding, post-*Pfaff*, that "no 'supplier' exception exists for the on-sale bar . . . [and stating that] [i]f such an exception is to be created, Congress, not this court, must create it").

[213]791 F.3d 1368 (Fed. Cir. July 2, 2015), *reh'g en banc granted, opinion vacated*, 805 F.3d 1357 (Fed. Cir. 2015) (*en banc*) (order).

[214]*Medicines Co.,* 805 F.3d 1357 (Nov. 13, 2015) (*en banc*) (order).

[215]*Medicines Co.,* 805 F.3d at 1358 (*en banc*) (order) (requested briefing issue "(b)") (citing *Special Devices*, 270 F.3d at 1353).

[216]*See Medicines Co.,* 791 F.3d at 1370.

the compounding process minimize[d] the Asp^{9}-bivalirudin impurity to less than 0.6%."[217] In July 2008, The Medicines Company filed the applications leading to its '727 and '343 patents, which were directed to Musso's new compounding process. The patents included composition and product-by-process claims[218] that recited the less than 0.6% impurity condition.[219] Dr. Musso was named as a co-inventor.

After the '727 and '343 patents issued, The Medicines Company in 2010 sued generic drug manufacturer Hospira, Inc. in a Hatch-Waxman Act patent suit (i.e., alleging that Hospira's Abbreviated New Drug Applications (ANDAs), if approved by the FDA, would result in infringement of some claims of the '727 and '343 patents).[220] Among other defenses, Hospira alleged that certain transactions between The Medicines Company and Ben Venue had triggered the on sale bar of §102(b) (2006), invalidating the patents.

Hospira emphasized that after Dr. Musso developed the new process for Medicines Company, and more than one year before the applications leading to the '727 and '343 patents were filed in July 2008, Medicines Company hired Ben Venue to prepare three "validation batches" of bivalirudin for an "Optimization Study" of Musso's new

[217] *Medicines Co.,* 791 F.3d at 1369-1370.

[218] Product-by-process claiming is analyzed *supra* Chapter 2, Section E.2.

[219] More specifically, claim 1 of the '727 patent recited:

> Pharmaceutical batches of a drug product comprising bivalirudin (SEQ ID NO: 1) and a pharmaceutically acceptable carrier for use as an anticoagulant in a subject in need thereof, wherein the batches have a pH adjusted by a base, said pH is about 5-6 when reconstituted in an aqueous solution for injection, and wherein the batches have a maximum impurity level of Asp^{9}-bivalirudin that does not exceed about 0.6% as measured by HPLC.

Claim 1 of the '343 patent was written in product-by-process form:

> Pharmaceutical batches of a drug product comprising bivalirudin (SEQ ID NO: 1) and a pharmaceutically acceptable carrier, for use as an anticoagulant in a subject in need thereof, said batches prepared by a compounding process comprising:
>
> (i) dissolving bivalirudin in a solvent to form a first solution;
> (ii) efficiently mixing a pH-adjusting solution with the first solution to form a second solution, wherein the pH adjusting solution comprises a pH-adjusting solution solvent; and
> (iii) removing the solvent and pH-adjusting solution solvent from the second solution;
>
> wherein the batches have a pH adjusted by a base, said pH is about 5-6 when reconstituted in an aqueous solution for injection, and wherein the batches have a maximum impurity level of Asp^{9}-bivalirudin that does not exceed about 0.6% as measured by HPLC.

Medicines Co. v. Hospira, Inc., No. CV 09-750-RGA, 2014 WL 1292802, at *1-*2 (D. Del. Mar. 31, 2014).

[220] Hatch-Waxman Act patent litigation is described *infra* Chapter 9, Section E.3 ("Drug Marketing Application Filings Under [35 U.S.C.] §271(e)").

process. Ben Venue did so, using a process encompassed by the patents' product-by-process claims.

Following a bench trial, a district court held that the patents were not invalid under §102(b) because only one, but not both, *Pfaff* factors had been triggered.[221] Even though the invention was "ready for patenting" before the critical date,[222] the on sale bar had not been triggered because no commercial offer for sale had taken place before the critical date. The district court reasoned that Ben Venue sold Medicines Company only its manufacturing services, not the patented drug itself; title to the pharmaceutical batches Ben Venue made did not transfer away from patentee Medicines Company.[223]

In any event, according to the district court, the batches fell under the experimental use exception to the on sale bar. The three batches Venue Labs made for the Optimization Study were for "validation purposes," not "commercial purposes." Venue Labs made the experimental batches for Medicines Company "in order to verify that the invention worked for its intended purpose."[224]

The July 2015 Federal Circuit panel disagreed, reversing the district court and holding the asserted claims of Medicines Company's '727 and '343 invalid for violating the on sale bar of 35 U.S.C. §102(b) (2006). The appellate court explained that

> the sale of the manufacturing services here provided a commercial benefit to the inventor more than one year before a patent application was filed. Ben Venue's services were performed to prove to the FDA that The Medicines Company's product met the already-approved specifications for finished bivalirudin product. Additionally, Ben Venue marked

[221]*See* Medicines Co. v. Hospira, Inc., No. CV 09-750-RGA, 2014 WL 1292802, at *10 (D. Del. Mar. 31, 2014), *rev'd sub nom.* Medicines Co. v. Hospira, Inc., 791 F.3d 1368 (Fed. Cir. 2015), *reh'g en banc granted, opinion vacated, appeal reinstated sub nom.* The Medicines Co. v. Hospira, Inc., 805 F.3d 1357 (Fed. Cir. 2015) (*en banc*) (order).

[222]The district court determined that the claimed invention was actually reduced to practice prior to the critical date, since batches according to the invention were produced. *Medicines Co.*, 2014 WL 1292802, at *10 (D. Del. Mar. 31, 2014). The Federal Circuit panel in July 2015 affirmed the district court's conclusion that the claimed invention was ready for patenting before the critical date. *See Medicines Co.*, 791 F.3d at 1372.

[223]The district court explained:

> The Medicines Company describes the transaction as a contract manufacturer relationship in which Ben Venue was paid to manufacture Angiomax for The Medicines Company, but wherein title to the Angiomax always resided with The Medicines Company.... The Medicines Company's characterization is the better understanding, as the invoices [from Venue Labs] clearly stated, "Charge to manufacture Bivalirudin lot."

Medicines Co., 2014 WL 1292802, at *11 (D. Del. Mar. 31, 2014) (record citations omitted).

[224]*Medicines Co.*, 2014 WL 1292802, at *11 (D. Del. Mar. 31, 2014).

the batches with commercial product codes and customer lot numbers and sent them to The Medicines Company for commercial and clinical packaging, consistent with the commercial sale of pharmaceutical drugs. This commercial activity was not insignificant; The Medicines Company admits that each batch had a commercial value of over $10 million.

Accordingly, we find that the district court clearly erred in finding the Ben Venue sale of services did not constitute a commercial sale. To find otherwise would allow The Medicines Company to circumvent the on-sale bar simply because its contracts happened to only cover the processes that produced the patented product-by-process. This would be inconsistent with our principle that "no 'supplier' exception exists for the on-sale bar."[225]

The fact that title to the pharmaceutical batches made by Ben Venue did not transfer (i.e., title always resided with Medicines Company[226]) was not dispositive. The Circuit explained that "[t]o ensure the doctrine is not easily circumvented, we have found the on-sale bar to apply where the evidence clearly demonstrated that the inventor commercially exploited the invention before the critical date, even if the inventor did not transfer title to the commercial embodiment of the invention."[227] The case at bar was not one involving a "secret, personal use" of another entity's services in developing products embodying the invention;[228] in the Circuit's view the three batches made by

[225]*Medicines Co.*, 791 F.3d at 1371 (quoting Special Devices, Inc. v. OEA, Inc., 270 F.3d 1353, 1357 (Fed. Cir. 2001)).

[226]*See Medicines Co.*, 2014 WL 1292802, at *11 (D. Del. Mar. 31, 2014).

[227]*Medicines Co.*, 791 F.3d at 1370-1371. As examples of this principle, the Circuit panel cited *D.L. Auld Co. v. Chroma Graphics Corp.*, 714 F.2d 1144 (Fed. Cir. 1983) (holding the on sale bar applied where, before the critical date, an inventor sold products made by the patented method); *W.L. Gore & Assocs., Inc. v. Garlock, Inc.*, 721 F.2d 1540, 1550 (Fed. Cir. 1983); and *Kinzenbaw v. Deere & Co.*, 741 F.2d 383, 390-391 (Fed. Cir. 1984) (finding a third party's testing of the "warrantability, durability, and acceptability" of a commercial embodiment of a patented product before the critical date was an invalidating public use under §102(b) because it "served Deere's commercial purposes").

[228]*Medicines Co.*, 791 F.3d at 1371. The Circuit distinguished the case at bar from *Trading Techs. Int'l, Inc. v. eSpeed, Inc.*, 595 F.3d 1340, 1361-1362 (Fed. Cir. 2010). In *Trading Techs.*, the Federal Circuit had affirmed a district court's judgment that

> ICA2 ["individual consulting agreement #2" between Trading Techs. ("TT") and Brumfield] was not a sales transaction for a product embodying the patented invention. Under ICA2, TT promised to develop trading software for Brumfield because he lacked the technical expertise to do so. ICA2 was a contract for providing hourly programming services to Brumfield — not a computer software license. Brumfield did not sell or offer for sale anything embodying the invention. Therefore, the trial court properly determined that the invention had not been offered for a commercial sale.

Trading Techs., 595 F.3d at 1361.

Ben Venue (having a commercial worth of over $30 million) were prepared for *commercial* exploitation.

The *Medicines Company* panel also held that the district court had clearly erred in finding that the experimental use doctrine barred application of the on sale bar to the pre-critical date Ben Venue batches. The appellate court observed that experimental use cannot occur after a reduction to practice.[229] Even though Medicines Company argued that its invention had not been reduced to practice (i.e., that it had not worked for its intended purpose) when Ben Venue made the three validation batches in question because Medicines Company did not appreciate the maximum impurity level limitation recited in its claims until after 25 batches were manufactured, "[t]he batches sold satisfied the claim limitations," and the inventor was "well aware" that those batches had impurity levels "well below the claimed levels of 0.6%."[230]

In November 2015, the *en banc* Federal Circuit voted to rehear the *Medicines Company* case. In a *per curiam* opinion, the *en banc* court vacated the panel's July 2015 decision described above. It also requested briefing by the parties and *amici* (including the Department of Justice) on the following questions:

> (a) Do the circumstances presented here constitute a commercial sale under the on-sale bar of 35 U.S.C. §102(b)?
>
> (i) Was there a sale for the purposes of §102(b) despite the absence of a transfer of title?
>
> (ii) Was the sale commercial in nature for the purposes of §102(b) or an experimental use?
>
> (b) Should this court overrule or revise the principle in *Special Devices, Inc. v. OEA, Inc.*, 270 F.3d 1353 (Fed. Cir. 2001), that there is no "supplier exception" to the on-sale bar of 35 U.S.C. §102(b)?[231]

In July 2016, the *en banc* Federal Circuit unanimously answered question (a) in the negative in *The Medicines Co. v. Hospira, Inc.*[232] The *en banc* court unanimously held that the pre–critical date transactions between Medicines Company and Ben Venue did *not* constitute commercial sales of the patented product.[233] Thus the full appellate court affirmed the district court's conclusion that the '727 and '343

[229] *Medicines Co.*, 791 F.3d at 1372 (citing In re Cygnus Telecomm. Tech., LLC Patent Litig., 536 F.3d 1343, 1356 (Fed. Cir. 2008)).

[230] *Medicines Co.*, 791 F.3d at 1372 (citing Scaltech, Inc. v. Retec/Tetra, LLC, 269 F.3d 1321, 1331 (Fed. Cir. 2001) (stating that "we have held that where an invention is on sale, conception is not required to establish reduction to practice"); Abbott Labs. v. Geneva Pharms., Inc., 182 F.3d 1315, 1318-1319 (Fed. Cir. 1999) (stating that "[t]he sale of the [invention] in question obviates any need for inquiry into conception")).

[231] *Medicines Co.*, 805 F.3d at 1358 (*en banc*) (order).

[232] 827 F.3d 1363 (Fed. Cir. July 11, 2016) (*en banc*) (O'Malley, J.).

[233] Medicines Co. v. Hospira, Inc., 827 F.3d 1363, 1365 (Fed. Cir. 2016) (*en banc*).

patents were not invalid under the on sale bar of 35 U.S.C. §102(b) (2006). The *en banc* Circuit held that "a contract manufacturer's sale to the inventor of manufacturing services where neither title to the embodiments nor the right to market the same passes to the supplier does not constitute an invalidating sale under §102(b)."[234]

Although patentee Medicines Company likely received a "commercial benefit" through pre–critical date "stockpiling" of the patented drug product made for it via outsourced manufacturing, the receipt of such benefit without more was not enough to trigger the §102(b) on sale bar. The *en banc* court concluded that the claimed product invention was not the subject of a "commercial sale or offer for sale." (*Medicines Company* is also significant for providing a useful *en banc* "brief overview" description of the historical development of the §102(b) on sale bar in U.S. patent law.[235])

The *Medicines Company en banc* court clarified firstly that the mere sale of manufacturing services by Ben Venue to Medicines Company so as to create embodiments of the patented drug product did not constitute a "commercial sale" of the invention. Although *services* were sold, the *claimed invention* was not (as required by the text of §102(b)).[236]

Second, the *en banc* court explained that Medicines Company's pre–critical date "stockpiling" of the patented product, standing alone, was not improper commercialization under §102(b). Stockpiling a patented product via in-house manufacturing prior to the critical date does not trigger the on sale bar, and the court refused to adopt a different rule that would penalize those who outsource manufacturing.

Third, and most importantly, the *en banc* court emphasized that receipt of a "commercial benefit" — even to both parties in a transaction — was not enough to trigger the on sale bar. Rather, an invalidating transaction "must be one in which the product is 'on sale' in the sense that it is 'commercially marketed.'" The *en banc* court concluded that a "'commercial sale' is one that bears the general hallmarks of a sale pursuant to Section 2-106 of the Uniform Commercial Code."[237] That UCC provision defines a "sale" as the passing of title from buyer to seller for a price.[238] Although retention of title is not necessarily dispositive, the *en banc* court observed that Medicines Company "maintained control of the invention, as shown

[234] *Medicines Co.*, 827 F.3d at 1381.
[235] *See Medicines Co.*, 827 F.3d at 1371-1373.
[236] *Medicines Co.*, 827 F.3d at 1375.
[237] *Medicines Co.*, 827 F.3d at 1365.
[238] Section 2-106, a definitional section of the Uniform Commercial Code (UCC) (2002), provides in subsection (1) that "[a] 'sale' consists in the passing of title from the seller to the buyer for a price. . . ."

by the retention of title to the embodiments and the absence of any authorization to Ben Venue to sell the product to others."[239]

Summarizing its analysis, the *en banc* court explained that

> [t]here are, broadly speaking, three reasons for our judgment in this case: (1) only manufacturing services were sold to the inventor — the invention was not; (2) the inventor maintained control of the invention, as shown by the retention of title to the embodiments and the absence of any authorization to Ben Venue to sell the product to others; and (3) "stockpiling," standing alone, does not trigger the on-sale bar.[240]

Each of these three reasons is further examined below.

As to reason (1), that "the invention" was not sold before the critical date, the *Medicines Company en banc* court emphasized that it is "the invention" that §102(b) requires to be "on sale," and "the invention" is that which is defined by the patents' claims. Importantly, all the claims of Medicines Company's patents in suit concerned pharmaceutical *products*, not *processes.* Medicines Company's '727 patent claims recited "pharmaceutical batches"; its '343 patent claims recited those batches prepared by a particular compounding process — i.e., they were product-by-process claims.[241] The court explained that "[f]or validity purposes, the 'invention' in a product-by-process claim is the product."[242] Admittedly, Ben Venue had manufactured, for compensation, embodiments of the patented product. But that, without more, did not put the patented product "on sale" within the meaning of the Patent Act. The *en banc* court observed that it had "never espoused the notion that, where the patent is to a product, the performance of the unclaimed process of creating the product, without an accompanying 'commercial sale' of the product itself, triggers the on-sale bar."[243] Cases suggesting the contrary all involved process or method patents in which inventors sought compensation from the "buying public" for performing the claimed processes or methods.[244]

[239]*Medicines Co.*, 827 F.3d at 1374.

[240]*Medicines Co.*, 827 F.3d at 1373-1374.

[241]Product-by-process claiming is detailed *supra* Chapter 2, Section E.2 ("Product-by-Process Claims").

[242]*Medicines Co.*, 827 F.3d at 1374 (citing Amgen Inc. v. F. Hoffman-La Roche Ltd., 580 F.3d 1340, 1369 (Fed. Cir. 2009) ("In determining validity of a product-by-process claim, the focus is on the product and not on the process of making it."); SmithKline Beecham Corp. v. Apotex Corp., 439 F.3d 1312, 1317 (Fed. Cir. 2006) ("Regardless of how broadly or narrowly one construes a product-by-process claim, it is clear that such claims are always to a product, not a process."); In re Lyons, 364 F.2d 1005, 1016 (C.C.P.A. 1966) ("[A] product-by-process claim is a product, not a process.")).

[243]*Medicines Co.*, 827 F.3d at 1374.

[244]*See, e.g.,* Metallizing Engineering Co. v. Kenyon Bearing, 153 F.2d 516, 517-518 (2d Cir. 1946); D.L. Auld Co. v. Chroma Graphics Corp., 714 F.2d 1144, 1147 (Fed. Cir. 1983)).

The evidence in the case at bar showed that what Ben Venue sold Medicines Company was manufacturing services, not the patented invention. Under Medicines Company's instructions, Ben Venue merely acted as a pair of "laboratory hands" to assist Medicines Company in reducing the claimed invention to practice.[245] Also relevant was the fact that Medicines Company's payment of $347,500 to Ben Venue for its services in making the three validation batches represented only about 1 percent of the total commercial value of the batches — "well over $20 million."[246] Given the relative dollar amounts, the Circuit found it "[u]nsurprising[]" that the district court had described the transaction as payment for manufacture rather than a sale of the validation batches.[247]

Detailing reason (2) supporting its judgment, i.e., patentee Medicines Company's retention of title and control over the patented product, the *en banc* Circuit observed that when title does not transfer in a transaction, it is unlikely that it was sufficiently "commercial" to trigger §102(b). Lacking title, Ben Venue could not use or sell the claimed products it had manufactured for Medicines Company, nor deliver them to anyone but Medicines Company. Although the appellate court declined to "draw a bright line rule making the passage of title dispositive,"[248] it observed that "in most instances" the absence of title transfer "indicates an absence of commercial marketing of the product by the inventor."[249] Contrariwise, passage of title is a "helpful indicator of whether a product is 'on sale,' as it suggests when the inventor gives up its interest and control over the product."[250]

In a similar vein, the confidential nature of the Medicines Company-Ben Venue transactions also weighed against a conclusion that they were commercial in nature. Although a number of Federal Circuit decisions hold that confidential transactions can trigger the on sale bar,[251] the *Medicines Company* court observed that the

[245]*Medicines Co.*, 827 F.3d at 1375.
[246]*Medicines Co.*, 827 F.3d at 1375.
[247]*Medicines Co.*, 827 F.3d at 1375.
[248]*Medicines Co.*, 827 F.3d at 1376.
[249]*Medicines Co.*, 827 F.3d at 1376.
[250]*Medicines Co.*, 827 F.3d at 1375.
[251]*See Medicines Co.*, 827 F.3d at 1376 (citing In re Caveney, 761 F.2d 671, 676 (Fed. Cir. 1985) ("It is well established . . . that a single sale or offer to sell is enough to bar patentability" even if kept secret from the trade.) (citing Gen. Elec. Co. v. United States, 654 F.2d 55, 60 (1981); Mfg. Research Corp. v. Graybar Elec. Corp., 679 F.2d 1355, 1362 (11th Cir. 1982)); Gould, Inc. v. United States, 579 F.2d 571, 580 (Ct. Cl. 1978) ("[A] sale . . . pursuant to a secret military contract . . . was still held to be a sale proscribed by 35 U.S.C. §102(b).") (citing Piet v. United States, 176 F. Supp. 576 (S.D. Cal. 1959), *aff'd*, 283 F.2d 693 (9th Cir. 1960)); Hobbs v. U.S. Atomic Energy Comm'n, 451 F.2d 849, 860 (5th Cir. 1971) (stating that the court "cannot attach any relevance to any conditions of secrecy which may have existed at the time the [invention] was placed 'on sale'")).

confidentiality factor "is not disqualifying in all instances — it . . . is not of talismanic significance."[252] The *en banc* court defended its decision as not "rest[ing] . . . on formalities," but rather "focus[ing] . . . on what makes our on-sale bar jurisprudence coherent: preventing inventors from filing for patents a year or more after the invention has been commercially marketed, whether marketed by the inventor himself or a third party."[253]

With regard to reason (3) supporting its judgment, i.e., that "stockpiling," standing alone, does not trigger the on sale bar, the Federal Circuit characterized stockpiling as "merely a type of preparation for *future* commercial sales";[254] to discourage stockpiling was "not even an identifiable goal of the on-sale bar."[255] The court elaborated:

> *Pfaff* . . . explained that we are not to look to broad policy rationales in assessing whether the on-sale bar applies; we are to apply a straightforward two-step process — one which permits an inventor to "both understand and control the first commercial marketing of his invention." 525 U.S. at 67. For this reason, we find that the mere stockpiling of a patented invention by the purchaser of manufacturing services does not constitute a "commercial sale" under §102(b). Stockpiling — or building inventory — is, when not accompanied by an actual sale or offer for sale of the invention, mere pre-commercial activity in preparation for future sale. This is true regardless of how the stockpiled material is packaged. The on-sale bar is triggered by actual commercial marketing of the invention, not preparation for potential or eventual marketing. Contrary to [validity challenger] Hospira's assertions, not every activity that inures some commercial benefit to the inventor can be considered a commercial sale. . . .[256]

Query whether this confidentiality analysis will change under §102 as amended by the America Invents Act of 2011. *See* 35 U.S.C. §102(a)(1) (eff. Mar. 16, 2013 for patents claiming an invention having an effective filing date on or after that date). The court did not address that question. *Medicines Co.*, 827 F.3d at 1380 n.3 (*en banc*) (stating that "[w]e do not address here whether or to what extent §102(b) may differ post-AIA from the pre-AIA description we now employ"). *But see Helsinn Healthcare S.A. v. Teva Pharm. USA, Inc.* ("*Helsinn III*"), 139 S. Ct. 628 (2019), analyzed *infra* Section Q.3 ("Does the AIA Permit Secret Prior Art?").

[252] *Medicines Co.*, 827 F.3d at 1376.

[253] *Medicines Co.,* 827 F.3d at 1376-1377. In a footnote, the Circuit noted that pre-critical date sales by third parties can trigger the §102(b) bar. The invalidating sale(s) do not have to be made by the inventor. *Medicines Co.,* 827 F.3d at 1377 n.2 (citing, e.g., J.A. La Porte, Inc. v. Norfolk Dredging Co., 787 F.2d 1577, 1581 (Fed. Cir. 1986); Zacharin v. United States, 213 F.3d 1366, 1371 (Fed. Cir. 2000); Evans Cooling Sys., Inc. v. Gen. Motors Corp., 125 F.3d 1448, 1453 (Fed. Cir. 1997)).

[254] *Medicines Co.,* 827 F.3d at 1378 (emphasis in original).

[255] *Medicines Co.,* 827 F.3d at 1378.

[256] *Medicines Co.,* 827 F.3d at 1377.

The Circuit refused to penalize Medicines Company for its need to rely on the confidential services of a contract manufacturer. The court had "never held that stockpiling by an inventor *in-house* triggers the on-sale bar."[257] Stockpiling with the assistance of a contract manufacturer (as in the case at bar) was "no more improper than is stockpiling by an inventor in-house." To conclude to the contrary that stockpiling triggered §102(b) in the case before it would be ineffective to discourage stockpiling because it would not penalize or prevent firms with in-house manufacturing capability from doing so. Section 102(b) provided "no room . . . to apply a different set of on-sale bar rules to inventors depending on whether their business model is to outsource manufacturing or to manufacture in-house."[258]

After concluding the above analyses, the *en banc* court addressed the statement in the Circuit's 2015 *Medicines Company* panel decision recognizing the principle that "no 'supplier' exception exists for the on-sale bar."[259] In other words, the court's earlier cases (specifically including its 2001 decision in *Special Devices, Inc. v. OEA, Inc.*[260]) stood for the proposition that the on sale bar is not escaped merely because a bar-triggering transaction took place between a patentee and its supplier, as opposed to the patentee and its potential or current customer. Whether the *en banc* court should overrule or revise this principle was also a question briefed for *en banc* rehearing in *Medicines Company*.[261]

The *en banc* court concluded that the Circuit's earlier line of cases refusing to apply a "supplier exception" all involved truly commercial transactions,[262] in distinction from the case at bar. The "import of *Special Devices* [wa]s simply that the fact that a sale is made by a supplier is not, *standing alone,* sufficient grounds upon which to characterize a transaction having all the hallmarks of a commercial sale under the UCC as something other than a commercial sale."[263] In contrast, the case before the court did not bear "all the hallmarks of a commercial sale" for the reasons explained above. The *en banc* court emphasized that "[t]he focus must be on the commercial character of the

[257]*Medicines Co.,* 827 F.3d at 1378 (emphasis in original).

[258]*Medicines Co.,* 827 F.3d at 1379.

[259]*Medicines Co.*, 2015 WL 4033143, at 1369-1370 (quoting Special Devices, Inc. v. OEA, Inc., 270 F.3d 1353, 1357 (Fed. Cir. 2001) (emphasis added)).

[260]270 F.3d 1353 (Fed. Cir. 2001).

[261]*See Medicines Co.*, 791 F.3d 1368 (order) (Nov. 13, 2015).

[262]Validity challenger Hospira pointed out that the Circuit had previously invalidated patent claims under §102(b) based on transfers of product by a supplier to an inventor in *Brasseler, U.S.A. I, L.P. v. Stryker Sales Corp.*, 182 F.3d 888, 891 (Fed. Cir. 1999); *Special Devices, Inc. v. OEA, Inc.*, 270 F.3d 1353 (Fed. Cir. 200). Moreover, the Circuit expressly held that no "supplier exception" to the on sale bar exists in *Special Devices*, 270 F.3d at 1357, and reiterated that point in *Hamilton Beach*. *See Medicines Co.*, 827 F.3d at 1380.

[263]*Medicines Co.*, 827 F.3d at 1379 (emphasis in original).

transaction, not solely on the identity of the participants."[264] To the extent that language in the Circuit's earlier cases including *Special Devices* might be viewed as inconsistent with the result in *Medicines Company*, the *en banc* court overruled them.[265]

Lastly, the *en banc Medicines Company* court considered the district court's *"sua sponte"* determination that because the pharmaceutical batches made by Ben Venue for Medicines Company were for "validation" purposes, not for commercial profit, they were made for experimental purposes. The district court had concluded that Medicines Company therefore avoided the on sale bar for that independent reason (despite the district court's additional finding that the claimed invention was "ready for patenting").[266] The *en banc* court observed that in light of its own conclusion that no "commercial sale" of the patented inventions had occurred, it did not need to reach the question of experimental use.[267] It also refused to respond to various *amici*'s "oft-repeated request that [the *en banc* court] make clear that the panel's statement that there can be no experimental use after a reduction to practice is inaccurate."[268] Because the *en banc* court had vacated the panel's opinion, it felt no need to "parse individual statements therein that are not determinative of the question presented."[269] Thus the question whether an actual reduction to practice necessarily ends any period of bar-negating experimental use remains a controversial one.

[264]*Medicines Co.*, 827 F.3d at 1379.

[265]*Medicines Co.*, 827 F.3d at 1380. The *en banc* court stressed, however, that its overruling of the "no supplier exception" line of cases was subject to "one important caveat":

> We still do not recognize a blanket "supplier exception" to what would otherwise constitute a commercial sale as we have characterized it today. While the fact that a transaction is between a supplier and inventor is an important indicator that the transaction is not a commercial sale, understood as such in the commercial marketplace, it is not alone determinative. Where the supplier has title to the patented product or process, the supplier receives blanket authority to market the product or disclose the process for manufacturing the product to others, or the transaction is a sale of product at full market value, even a transfer of product to the inventor may constitute a commercial sale under §102(b). The focus must be on the commercial character of the transaction, not solely on the identity of the participants.

Medicines Co., 827 F.3d at 1380.

[266]*See Medicines Co.*, 827 F.3d at 1368, 1380. The district court determined that the claimed invention was "ready for patenting" under *Pfaff* because Medicines Company had developed two enabling disclosures prior to the critical date or, alternatively, reduced the invention to practice before that date. *See Medicines Co.*, 827 F.3d at 1368.

[267]*Medicines Co.*, 827 F.3d at 1381.

[268]*Medicines Co.*, 827 F.3d at 1381.

[269]*Medicines Co.*, 827 F.3d at 1381.

It is interesting to note that the sale of services by Ben Venue to the Medicines Company was an internal, essentially private transaction (although not, according to the vacated Circuit opinion, a "secret, personal use").[270] Even assuming the sale of Ben Venue's services resulted in a commercial benefit to the Medicines Company so as to trigger the on sale bar, query whether such sale would count as prior art under post-AIA §102(a)(1), which presumptively bars a patent if the "claimed invention was . . . on sale, *or otherwise available to the public* before the effective filing date of the claimed invention."[271] The Supreme Court took up this important question, requiring its interpretation of the AIA prior art provisions for the first time, in its 2019 decision, *Helsinn Healthcare S.A. v. Teva Pharm. USA, Inc.*,[272] examined later in this chapter.[273]

5. Experimental Use Negation of the §102(b) Bars

The public use and on sale bars of §102(b) (2006) are both subject to "negation"[274] under the judicially developed experimental use

[270]*Medicines Co.*, 791 F.3d at 1371.

[271]Emphasis added. *See also infra* Section Q.3 ("Does the AIA Permit Secret Prior Art?").

[272]139 S. Ct. 628 (2019).

[273]*See* Section Q.3 ("Does the AIA Permit Secret Prior Art?").

[274]The experimental use doctrine operates as a negation of, rather than an exception to, the statutory bars of 35 U.S.C. §102(b). *See* TP Labs., Inc. v. Professional Positioners, Inc., 724 F.2d 965 (Fed. Cir. 1984) (Nies, J.), in which the court explained:

> Th[e] difference between "exception" and "negation" is not merely semantic. Under the precedent of this court, the statutory presumption of validity provided in 35 U.S.C. §282 places the burden of proof upon the party attacking the validity of the patent, and that burden of persuasion does not shift at any time to the patent owner. It is constant and remains throughout the suit on the challenger. . . .
>
> Under this analysis, it is incorrect to impose on the patent owner, as the trial court in this case did, the burden of proving that a "public use" was "experimental." These are not two separable issues. It is incorrect to ask: "Was it public use?" and then, "Was it experimental?" Rather, the court is faced with a single issue: Was it public use under §102(b)?
>
> Thus, the [district] court should have looked at all of the evidence put forth by both parties and should have decided whether the entirety of the evidence led to the conclusion that there had been "public use." This does not mean, of course, that the challenger has the burden of proving that the use is not experimental. Nor does it mean that the patent owner is relieved of explanation. It means that if a *prima facie* case is made of public use, the patent owner must be able to point to or must come forward with convincing evidence to counter that showing.

TP Labs., 724 F.2d at 971 (citations omitted).

Thus, the ultimate burden of proof remains on the validity challenger to establish invalidity based on a public use or placement on sale under §102(b). The *TP Labs.* burden-placement framework provides that if the challenger makes a *prima facie* showing of events that appear to trigger a §102(b) bar, the burden of production (i.e., the burden of going forward) shifts to the patentee to produce evidence (such as evidence of experimental use) to counter that showing. But under *TP Labs.*, the ultimate burden of proof (i.e., the burden of persuasion) to establish invalidity remains on the validity challenger. *See* EZ Dock, Inc. v. Schafer Sys., Inc., 276 F.3d 1347, 1354-1355 (Fed. Cir. 2002) (Linn, J., concurring) (stating that "[t]he experimental use exception was, over time, reformulated as experimental use 'negation' of the statutory bar of §102(b), in which the burden of persuasion does not shift at any time to the patentee") (citing *TP Labs.*, 724 F.2d at 971)).

Despite the clear-cut burden assignment established in *TP Labs.* for experimental use, the split-panel decision in *Barry v. Medtronic, Inc.*, 914 F.3d 1310 (Fed. Cir. 2019) (Taranto, J.), suggested that some Federal Circuit judges disagree on the issue. *Barry* also illustrates a fairly rare patentee win on the merits of the experimental use defense. A different aspect of *Barry* (the "ready for patenting" prong of §102(b) public use) was examined *supra* Section I.3.d.

Doctor Mark Barry obtained two U.S. patents claiming methods and systems for surgically correcting a patient's spinal cord anomalies, such as those due to scoliosis, by applying force to multiple vertebrae at the same time. Before the patents' December 30, 2003 critical date for 35 U.S.C. §102(b) (2006), Dr. Barry used his claimed method in three surgeries he performed on three different patients, each suffering a different type of spinal abnormality. Barry conducted two of the three surgeries in August 2003 and the third surgery in October 2003, all before the critical date. It was undisputed that Barry charged his normal fee for each of the surgeries and that the method claims of the patents read on the surgical steps Barry performed.

Importantly, Barry held post-surgical follow-up appointments with each patient, viewing their spinal x-rays, after they were able to stand up and walk following a three-month acute phase of recovery. Barry conducted the last follow-up appointment in January 2004, a date that fell inside the §102(b) one-year grace period. *Barry,* 914 F.3d at 1319. After Barry sued Medtronic for infringement in the Eastern District of Texas, Medtronic countered that Barry's patents were invalid based on the post–critical date activity and that that activity did not qualify as experimental use. Medtronic alleged that Barry had triggered the §102(b) public use and on sale bars because the surgical method was ready for patenting before the critical date and the post–critical date follow-up appointment for the third and final surgery was not necessary to confirm that the method worked as intended. However, a jury found that Medtronic had infringed and had *not* proven Barry's patents invalid (i.e., the jury upheld the patents' validity against Medtronic's public use and on sale challenges). The jury awarded Barry nearly $18 million in damages.

On appeal, the Federal Circuit majority decided multiple issues in Barry's favor, including experimental use. *Barry,* 914 F.3d at 1327-1331. The *Barry* majority concluded that based on the evidence of record, many of the factors enumerated in *Clock Spring, L.P. v. Wrapmaster, Inc.*, 560 F.3d 1317, 1327 (Fed. Cir. 2009), discussed *infra* in the text, "point[ed] toward a conclusion of experimental use." *Barry,* 914 F.3d at 1328. As to the "length of the test period" factor, the majority felt it "reasonable, to truly determine whether a method works, to engage in such testing for a brief time on a small but representative range of expected circumstances and to rely on follow-up." *Barry,* 914 F.3d at 1329. Although "payment was made," Barry charged no more for each of three pre–critical date surgeries than he would have earned for using prior-art methods. Barry's fee was "merely incidental to experimental work — a very limited number of tests, 'reasonably necessary' to the experimental purpose. . . ." *Barry,* 914 F.3d at 1329 (quoting Int'l Tooth Crown Co. v. Gaylord, 140 U.S. 55, 62-63 (1891)).

Importantly, the majority posited that Barry "did not surrender control of the claimed invention before the critical date." Rather, "he kept control through the expectation of secrecy binding the other medical professional present at the surgeries. . . ." *Barry,* 914 F.3d at 1329. Others in the operating room were aware that Barry was experimenting in these surgeries, including one doctor, one nurse, and one medical-device firm representative who helped with instrumentation. *Barry,* 914 F.3d at 1329.

Likely the most difficult counterpoint faced by the *Barry* majority was that Dr. Barry did not tell the three patients he operated on that he would be using an experimental technique. This required that the majority distinguish its 1992 decision, *Sinskey v. Pharmacia Ophthalmics, Inc.*, 982 F.2d 494 (Fed. Cir. 1992), *overruled on other grounds by Pfaff,* 525 U.S. 55 (1998)), a decision rejecting experimental use on which accused infringer Medtronic "heavily relie[d]." *Sinskey* appeared to place great weight on an inventor's communication of experimental purpose to her customers/patients. But the *Barry* majority read the facts of *Sinskey* as differing in "crucial" ways. The *Sinskey* Circuit had held that patentee Dr. Sinskey did *not* engage in experimental use when, before the critical date, he surgically implanted eight intraocular lenses in the eyes of his patients without telling them that the lenses were experimental. Notably, Sinskey's patent recited *product* claims to the intraocular lens itself. The *Barry* majority reasoned that when Sinskey implanted his device in a patient's eye, he had surrendered control of his invention to a third party (i.e., the patient). By contrast in *Barry*, the claimed invention was Dr. Barry's method of straightening the patient's spine. In the *Barry* majority's view, control over that method was not given away by its use in the operating room. Moreover, other persons (e.g., another doctor and a nurse) in the operating room knew that Barry was experimenting. In *Sinskey,* the evidence did not confirm that others understood the eye surgeries to be experimental.

Policy also supported the *Barry* majority's decision. It observed that "[t]he experimental-use exception is properly applied in light of the recognized mix of §102(b) policies — permitting experimental testing, protecting existing public domain knowledge, limiting extension of the statutory period of gaining revenues due to the invention, and encouraging prompt disclosure. . . . Here, on all the facts the jury could properly find, we conclude that the surgeries fall within the experimental-use exception." *Barry,* 914 F.3d at 1331 (citation omitted).

Federal Circuit Chief Judge Prost dissented-in-part in *Barry*. She disagreed on the merits with the majority's experimental use determination in Barry's favor. But as a larger threshold issue, Judge Prost also disagreed with the majority's application of the *TP Labs.* burden-placement framework. *See Barry,* 914 F.3d at 1344 (Part IV of opinion) (Prost, C.J., dissenting-in-part).

Dissenting Judge Prost would have placed a burden of proof (i.e., persuasion) on Barry, the *patentee*, to establish experimental use, contrary to *TP Labs.* In support of this placement she relied primarily on two nineteenth-century Supreme Court cases that required a patentee to provide " 'full, unequivocal, and convincing' " proof of experimental purpose when the public use defense to validity has been raised. *See Barry*, 914 F.3d at 1344 (Prost, C.J., dissenting-in-part) (quoting Smith & Griggs Mfg. Co. v. Sprague, 123 U.S. 249, 264 (1887); citing also Root v. Third Ave. RR Co., 146 U.S. 210, 226 (1892)). She also emphasized that prior to the creation of the Federal Circuit in 1982, the First, Second, Third, and Seventh U.S. Courts of Appeals followed the Supreme Court rule requiring "full, unequivocal, and convincing" proof.

The Federal Circuit in *TP Labs.* had acknowledged *Smith & Griggs* but did not construe it as Judge Prost would in *Barry. See TP Labs.,* 724 F.2d at 972 ("We do not read *Smith & Griggs Mfg. Co. v. Sprague*, 123 U.S. 249, 267, 8 S. Ct. 122, 131, 31 L. Ed. 141 (1887) as contrary to this view [that the burden of persuasion always remains on the validity challenger], as urged by appellees."). But even assuming that the *Smith & Griggs* Court had "intended to impose the ultimate burden of persuasion on the patent holder rather than merely the burden of going forward with countering evidence," the doctrine.[275] This doctrine negates or excuses what would otherwise appear to be statutory bar-triggering activity prior to the §102(b) critical date.[276]

In the classic experimental use case, *City of Elizabeth v. American Nicholson Pavement Co.*,[277] the Supreme Court clarified that "[t]he use of an invention by the inventor himself, or of any other person under his direction, by way of experiment, and in order to bring the invention to perfection, has never been regarded as [public use within the meaning of the statute]."[278] The Court characterized experimental use as use of an invention "only by way of experiment" that is "pursued with a bona fide intent of testing the qualities" of the invention.[279] So long as the inventor "does not voluntarily allow others to make [the invention] and use it, and so long as it is not on sale for general use, he keeps the invention under his own control, and does not lose his title to a patent."[280]

The inventor/patentee Nicholson in the *City of Elizabeth* case developed a method of paving streets using wooden blocks in a checkerboard arrangement, which he tested by paving a well-traveled section of public carriage road in Boston.[281] Despite the fact that

---

TP Labs. court reasoned that that burden-shifting framework was no longer "tenable" in light of the statutory presumption of validity enacted in the 1952 Patent Act; namely, 28 U.S.C. §282 (providing that "[a] patent shall be presumed valid.... The burden of establishing invalidity of a patent or any claim thereof shall rest on the party asserting such invalidity."). *See TP Labs.*, 724 F.2d at 971 n.3.

Judge Prost (along with academic commentators) questioned this reasoning. She responded that even if not statutorily enshrined earlier, the presumption of validity for an issued patent was recognized in the common law long before 1952. *Barry*, 914 F.3d at 1345 (Prost, C.J., dissenting-in-part) (citing 2A Chisum on Patents §6.02[8], p. 6-292 n.41 (2017) (noting that "[t]he court's basis for this holding is questionable" given that "[t]he enactment of [§]282 on the presumption of validity in 1952 was generally thought to have codified prior law")).

For now, the *TP Labs.* framework — maintaining the ultimate burden of proof on the validity challenger and imposing a burden of production on the patentee to come forward with countering evidence only if the challenger establishes a *prima facie* case of public use — remains the majority rule in the Federal Circuit. But the 2019 *Barry* decision suggests that the issue is likely to be revisited.

[275]Experimental use negation of the §102(b) statutory bars is an entirely separate doctrine from the experimental (or research) use exemption from patent infringement. The latter is discussed in Chapter 10 ("Defenses to Patent Infringement"), *infra*.

[276]The experimental use doctrine has no relevance to activity *within* the one-year grace period of 35 U.S.C. §102(b). No negation is necessary for public uses or sales activity in this time period; the activity must occur *prior to* the §102(b) critical date in order to trigger a statutory bar.

[277]97 U.S. 126 (1878).

[278]*Id.* at 134.

[279]*Id.* at 135.

[280]*Id.*

[281]Then known as the "mill dam" or "Mill-Dam Avenue," today this road roughly corresponds to Boston's Beacon Street. *See* Neighborhood Association of the Back Bay, *Back Bay History (2016)*, http://www.nabbonline.com/about_us/back_bay_history.

Nicholson did not file a patent application claiming the pavement invention for six years after commencing this testing,[282] the experimental use doctrine preserved his right to a patent. Because its extended durability while exposed to the elements was essential, Nicholson's pavement invention was of the type that could not be satisfactorily tested anywhere other than a public place like the carriage road.[283] Importantly, Nicholson's intent to test his invention was bona fide, and the evidence of record proved that he kept the invention under his control at all times.[284] On these facts, Nicholson's experimental use of his pavement invention, while in a public place, did not amount to a statutory public use that would have otherwise resulted in the invalidation of his patent.[285]

The experimental use doctrine remains vital for patent owners in the twenty-first century, as illustrated by the Circuit's 2019 decision in *Barry v. Medtronic, Inc.*,[286] detailed, see *supra* fn. 274. In its 2009 decision, *Clock Spring, L.P. v. Wrapmaster, Inc.*,[287] the Federal Circuit catalogued a useful set of factors that in previous cases it had had found "instructive, and in some cases dispositive," for determining whether the experimental use doctrine excused what would otherwise appear to be on sale or public use activity before the critical date:

> (1) the necessity for public testing, (2) the amount of control over the experiment retained by the inventor, (3) the nature of the invention, (4) the length of the test period, (5) whether payment was made, (6) whether there was a secrecy obligation, (7) whether records of the experiment were kept, (8) who conducted the experiment, (9) the degree of commercial exploitation during testing, (10) whether the invention reasonably requires evaluation under actual conditions of use, (11) whether testing was systematically performed, (12) whether the inventor continually monitored the invention during testing, and (13) the nature of contacts made with potential customers.[288]

[282]*See City of Elizabeth*, 97 U.S. at 133 (stating contention of appellants/accused infringers that "the pavement which Nicholson put down by way of experiment, on Mill-Dam Avenue in Boston, in 1848, was publicly used for the space of six years before his application for a patent, and that this was a public use within the meaning of the law").

[283]*See id.* at 134, 136.

[284]*See id.* at 133-134 (describing testimony of toll-collector Lang that inventor Nicholson personally examined the pavement on an "almost daily" basis and characterized it to others as "experimental").

[285]For a contrasting example of an inventor's inability to keep his invention under sufficient control, thereby failing to qualify as experimental use that would have negated §102(b) public use, *see* Lough v. Brunswick Corp., 86 F.3d 1113 (Fed. Cir. 1996).

[286]914 F.3d 1310 (Fed. Cir. 2019) (Taranto, J.).

[287]560 F.3d 1317, 1327 (Fed. Cir. 2009) (Dyk, J.).

[288]*Clock Spring*, 560 F.3d at 1327.

J. Abandonment Under 35 U.S.C. §102(c) (Pre-AIA)

Judicial decisions invalidating a patent under 35 U.S.C. §102(c) (2006) are rarely seen today. This is because subsection (c) is an anachronism — largely a historic holdover from the time when loss of right to a patent was viewed as being triggered by an inventor's own affirmative act of abandonment or dedication of her invention to the public. The on sale and public use bars as encompassed within 35 U.S.C. §102(b) (2006) initially developed as two specific types of conduct giving rise to a general concept of abandonment, which general concept is still reflected today in §102(c) (2006).[289]

The statutory bars of §102(b) are presently understood as reflecting primarily a delay rationale, and may be triggered by persons other than the inventor, as discussed *supra.* Only an affirmative act of the inventor can trigger an abandonment under §102(c), however. The continued existence of §102(c) most likely indicates that patent rights can theoretically be lost at any time, even within the §102(b) grace period, by the relatively unlikely occurrence of an overt, intentional statement of abandonment of patent rights upon which others are entitled to rely.[290]

Note that what is involved in 35 U.S.C. §102(c) (2006) is not an inventor's abandonment of the affirmative right to practice her invention. Rather, statutory abandonment refers to a waiver or forfeiture of the right to patent protection on (i.e., the right to exclude others from practicing) the invention. As the CCPA explained in *In re Gibbs,*[291]

> [w]e are not at all concerned, therefore, with any abandonment of the invention in the sense of the *thing invented* but only, in the words of the §102 heading, with "loss of right to patent," an inability to obtain that incorporeal property right (35 USC 261) which is the right to exclude others from making, using or selling the invention (35 USC 154).[292]

The *Gibbs* court considered whether abandonment of the right to exclude others may be inferred from an inventor's *failure* to act rather than from some affirmative act, but rejected that notion as applied to the facts of *Gibbs.* There the CCPA reviewed a USPTO rejection under

[289] *See, e.g.*, Pennock v. Dialogue, 27 U.S. 1, 24 (1829) (explaining that an inventor's "voluntary act or acquiescence in the public sale and use is an abandonment of his right; or rather creates a disability to comply with the terms and conditions on which alone the secretary of state is authorized to grant him a patent").

[290] *See* City of Elizabeth v. American Nicholson Pavement Co., 97 U.S. 126, 134 (1878) (stating that "[a]n abandonment of an invention to the public may be evinced by the conduct of an inventor at any time, even within the two years named in the law [i.e., the two-year grace period then in effect]").

[291] 437 F.2d 486 (C.C.P.A. 1971) (reversing USPTO rejection under 35 U.S.C. §102(c)).

[292] *Id.* at 489 (emphasis in original).

35 U.S.C. §102(c) based on the agency's argument that the appellant had forfeited his right to patent protection on an invention that was disclosed but not claimed in his own earlier-issued patent.[293] Within one year of the issuance of that patent, however, the appellant filed another application claiming the subject matter that he had failed to claim in the prior application leading to the patent.[294] The CCPA held that the appellant's claiming of the invention in this fashion overcame any presumption of abandonment for failure to claim it in the first application:

> To return to the present case, assuming, *arguendo,* that appellants' patent contains a disclosure of the invention now being claimed, in an application filed less than one year after the patent issued, the claimed subject matter clearly not being the same,[295] was it "abandoned" by the issuance of the patent? We think not. The determination made below that appellants had abandoned their right to patent the subject matter now claimed is a conclusion of law predicated on a mere inference of dedication drawn from the facts of disclosure and failure to claim. This inference may be rebutted in several ways: by an application for reissue of the patent pursuant to statute, §251, last paragraph, which seems to permit a broadening reissue application to be filed up to two years after the patent issues; it can unquestionably be rebutted by claiming in a copending application before the patent issues[296] and possibly even thereafter. We see no logical reason why it cannot also be rebutted in all cases, as has been held, by the filing of an application within the one-year grace period following the issuance of the patent before the patent has become a statutory bar under §102(b). So far as the statutes are concerned, an inventor clearly has that right.[297]

K. Foreign Patenting Bar of 35 U.S.C. §102(d) (Pre-AIA)

As with §102(c), invalidation of patents under 35 U.S.C. §102(d) (2006) is today a relatively rare event.[298] Like 35 U.S.C. §102(b)

[293]*See id.* at 486.

[294]Thus, the patent did not become a §102(b) bar against the subsequent application.

[295]Hence, no rejection was made for **double patenting**. *See generally supra* Chapter 1, Section H.6 ("Double Patenting").

[296]This strategy would involve the filing of a continuing application pursuant to 35 U.S.C. §120.

[297]*Gibbs*, 437 F.2d at 494.

[298]*See* Lisa L. Dolak & Michael L. Goldman, *Responding to Prior Art Rejections: An Analytical Framework*, 83 J. PAT. & TRADEMARK OFF. SOC'Y 5 (2001), explaining that

> [r]ejections under 35 U.S.C. §102(d) are uncommon . . . for several reasons. Patent applicants interested in obtaining the benefit of foreign priority under the Paris Convention or Patent Cooperation Treaty must file foreign patent applications within 12 months of the first filing in a convention or treaty member country,

(2006), §102(d) (2006) is considered a statutory bar provision, but here the right to a patent is lost by a different sort of delay. Rather than being invoked by domestic activity such as sales or public use in the United States, 35 U.S.C. §102(d) is triggered when an inventor files a patent application in a foreign country, files another application on the same invention in the United States more than one year later, and the inventor's foreign patent has already issued before her U.S. filing.[299]

Thus 35 U.S.C. §102(d) seeks to promote prompt entry into the U.S. patent system once an inventor has commenced obtaining protection on the same invention in other countries.[300] The validity of the corresponding foreign patent is not controlling; what matters is that the foreign patent issued with claims directed to the same invention as the U.S. application.[301]

> and only U.S. applications filed more than twelve months after a foreign filing are potentially vulnerable under Section 102(d). Even in those situations where the U.S. application is filed more than 12 months after a corresponding foreign application, Section 102(d) only applies when the foreign patent also issues before the U.S. filing. Finally, for inventions made in the United States, the patent statute prohibits the filing of patent applications in foreign countries until six months have passed since the filing of the corresponding U.S. application, or until the foreign filing is authorized by a foreign filing license (typically obtained by filing a U.S. application). *See* 35 U.S.C. §184. Accordingly, Section 102(d) has little potential application to U.S. patent applications claiming inventions made in this country.

Id. at 11 n.23 (citations omitted).

[299]Problems under 35 U.S.C. §102(d) (2006) also may arise when a foreign country grants patent-*like* rights. For example, Germany grants exclusive rights against imitation of new and original industrial designs, or *Geschmachmusters*. *See* In re Talbott, 443 F.2d 1397, 1398 (C.C.P.A. 1971). In *Talbott*, the court concluded that the grant of a German *Geschmachmuster* registration, directed to an automobile rear-view mirror design, triggered the §102(d) bar against the inventor who delayed in seeking U.S. patent protection. The different nature of the rights granted by the German registration and a U.S. patent (i.e., the former being closer to copyright protection than patent) were not viewed as controlling; the court "agree[d] with the [USPTO] board that 'it is sufficient if the inventor receives from the foreign country the exclusive privilege that its laws provide for.'" *Id.* at 1399.

[300]*See* In re Kathawala, 9 F.3d 942, 946 (Fed. Cir. 1993) (stating that policy and purpose behind §102(d) are "to require applicants for patent in the United States to exercise reasonable promptness in filing their applications after they have filed and obtained foreign patents").

[301]*See id.* at 945, stating:

> Even assuming that Kathawala's compound, composition, and method of use claims are not enforceable in Greece, a matter on which we will not speculate, the controlling fact for purposes of section 102(d) is that the Greek patent issued containing claims directed to the same invention as that of the U.S. application. When a foreign patent issues with claims directed to the same invention as the U.S. application, the invention is "patented" within the meaning of section 102(d); validity of the foreign claims is irrelevant to the section 102(d)

L. Description in Another's Earlier-Filed Patent or Published Patent Application Under 35 U.S.C. §102(e) (Pre-AIA)

1. In General

Subsection (e) of §102 (2006) involves anticipation through the *description* (though not *claiming*[302]) of the applicant's invention in a patent or published patent application of another, where that "other" filed her application in the United States before the applicant's invention date.[303] This subsection was made a part of the 1952 Patent Act in

---

inquiry. This is true irrespective of whether the applicant asserts that the claims in the foreign patent are invalid on grounds of non-statutory subject matter or more conventional patentability reasons such as prior art or inadequate disclosure.... The [US]PTO should be able to accept at face value the grant of the Greek patent claiming subject matter corresponding to that claimed in a U.S. application, without engaging in an extensive exploration of fine points of foreign law. The claims appear in the Greek patent because the applicant put them there. He cannot claim exemption from the consequences of his own actions. The Board thus correctly concluded that the validity of the Greek claims is irrelevant for purposes of section 102(d). Accordingly, the Board properly affirmed the examiner's rejection over the Greek patent.

[302]If the reference patent *claims* the same invention, then an interference may be declared under 35 U.S.C. §102(g) *if* the application claims were presented within one year of the issue date of the reference patent. If more than one year has passed, the USPTO may reject the application under 35 U.S.C. §135(b). *See* In re McGrew, 120 F.3d 1236 (Fed. Cir. 1997) (Rich, J.) (affirming USPTO rejection of application claims under §135(b) where "McGrew [] conceded that the claims at issue in the '280 application [on appeal] are for 'the same or substantially the same subject matter' as the claims of the [reference] Takeuchi patent... [and] that the claims at issue were first presented more than one year after the Takeuchi patent was granted").

It is theoretically possible that the claims of the reference patent, which are part of the reference patent's specification, *describe* the subject matter claimed by the applicant rather than *claim* that subject matter, and therefore could be relied on as §102(e) prior art. This is because the entirety of a reference patent's disclosure is available as prior art under 35 U.S.C. §102(e), but only as of the U.S. filing date of the reference patent, not any earlier date of conception or actual reduction to practice. *See* Sun Studs, Inc. v. ATA Equip. Leasing, Inc., 872 F.2d 978, 983 (Fed. Cir. 1989) (stating that "[w]hen patents are not in interference, the effective date of a reference United States patent as prior art is its filing date in the United States, as stated in §102(e), not the date of conception or actual reduction to practice of the invention claimed or the subject matter disclosed in the reference patent"); *id.* at 983-984 (stating that "[u]nder 35 U.S.C. §102(e) the entire disclosure of Mouat's [the reference patent] specification is effective as a reference, but only as of Mouat's filing date").

[303]Recall that under pre-AIA rules, the USPTO takes the applicant's filing date as her presumptive or *prima facie* invention date based on a constructive reduction to practice theory, and it is up to the applicant to establish an earlier actual invention date if necessary to antedate (i.e., predate or "swear behind") a prior art reference. This may be accomplished through filing an appropriate affidavit or declaration under 37 C.F.R. §1.131 to establish invention of the subject matter of the rejected claim prior to the

order to statutorily codify the rule announced by the U.S. Supreme Court in *Alexander Milburn Co. v. Davis-Bournonville Co.*[304] Distilled to its essence, *Milburn* requires that we treat a prior art U.S. patent as constructively published as soon as it is filed. The patent law engages in the fiction that the contents of the patent's written description instantaneously become available as a printed publication upon filing. Thus, the effective date of the written description portion of a U.S. patent being used as §102(e) prior art is its U.S. filing date.[305]

For example, assume that Andy filed a U.S. patent application claiming a solar-powered toothbrush on January 1, 2005. The USPTO examiner's search of the prior art revealed that Bill had already filed his own U.S. patent application describing (but not claiming) the identical toothbrush on January 1, 2003, and that Bill's application was published 18 months later, on July 1, 2004.[306] The effective date of Bill's application in this example is its U.S. filing date of January 1, 2003, which predates Andy's filing date of January 1, 2005 (i.e., Andy's presumptive invention date). On these facts, the examiner would enter a rejection of Andy's claim under 35 U.S.C. §102(e)(1), one of two prongs of §102(e) (pre-AIA), discussed in further detail below.

Unlike the rest of the world, which operates on a first-to-file system, the United States under pre-AIA rules has long awarded patent rights to the first to invent.[307] The policy rationale underlying the *Milburn*

---

effective date of the reference. Procedures for antedating a reference are detailed in Section O of this chapter, *infra*.

[304]270 U.S. 390 (1926). *See also* P.J. Federico, *Commentary on the New Patent Act*, 35 U.S.C.A. §1 (1954 ed., discontinued in subsequent volumes), *reprinted* at 75 J. PAT. & TRADEMARK OFF. SOC'Y 161, 179 (1993) (explaining that "[p]aragraph (e) is new in the statute and enacts the rule of the decision of the Supreme Court in [*Milburn*] under which a United States patent disclosing an invention dates from the filing of the application for the purpose of anticipating a later inventor, whether or not the invention is claimed in the patent") (citation omitted).

[305]Under the rule of *In re Hilmer*, 359 F.2d 859 (C.C.P.A. 1966), discussed in further detail in Chapter 12 ("International Patenting Issues"), *infra*, the USPTO must ignore any earlier *foreign* filing date, the benefit of which the reference applicant claimed under 35 U.S.C. §119, of a U.S. patent or published application being used as a §102(e) reference. The AIA prospectively eliminated the *Hilmer* rule.

[306]In this hypothetical, for example, Bill might have been claiming a new, compact solar-powered battery and might also have described in his application some specific applications for his invention (e.g., use in a solar-powered toothbrush).

[307]*See* discussion of 35 U.S.C. §102(g), *infra*, and Chapter 12 ("International Patenting Issues"). The United States implemented a first-to-invent priority system as early as the late eighteenth century. *See* Edward C. Walterscheid, *Priority of Invention: How the United States Came to Have a "First-to-Invent" System,* 23 AIPLA Q.J. 263, 264 (1995) (explaining that "the initial impetus came from the titanic struggle between John Fitch and James Rumsey for priority of invention with respect to the steamboat during the late eighteenth century, but the actual creation of a true first-to-invent system took almost fifty years"). The Leahy-Smith America Invents Act of 2011 changed the United States to a first-inventor-to-file priority system. *See infra* Part III of this chapter.

rule is that the presence of a description of the invention that the applicant is claiming in someone else's earlier-filed patent application evidences that the applicant was *not* in fact the first to invent that subject matter. We may not know the actual identity of the prior inventor when the "someone else" (i.e., the statutory "another" or the "reference patentee") has not *claimed* the invention (and thus presumably did not make it). But based on the existence of the earlier-filed description, the law presumes that the first to invent is someone other than our patent applicant.

Prior to the 1999 enactment of the American Inventors Protection Act (AIPA),[308] which introduced 18-month publication of most pending U.S. patent applications, 35 U.S.C. §102(e) required that an earlier-filed application by "another" had to have already *issued* as a patent before it became available for use by a USPTO examiner as a §102(e) prior art reference. This requirement, which is still reflected in the §102(e)(2) prong of 35 U.S.C. §102(e) (2006) form (i.e., as amended by the AIPA and the Twenty-first Century Department of Justice Appropriations Authorization Act (2002)[309]), guaranteed that the contents of the prior art patent ultimately "saw the light of day" through issuance before that patent could be used as a §102(e) reference. The issuance requirement thus ameliorated the concern that 35 U.S.C. §102(e) (pre-AIA) raises about the use of "secret prior art"—that is, prior art that is used at an effective date (in the case of a §102(e) reference patent, its U.S. filing date) when the applicant against whom it is being asserted cannot have known anything about its contents (because of the pre-AIPA secrecy of all pending patent applications until issuance).[310]

Due to enactment of the AIPA in 1999, the contents of most pending U.S. patent applications are now published automatically at 18 months after the application's filing date.[311] This change means that the

[308]Pub. L. No. 106-113, 113 Stat. 1501 (enacted Nov. 29, 1999).

[309]As amended in November 2002, subparagraph (e) of 35 U.S.C. §102 provides that a person shall be entitled to a patent unless

> (e) the invention was described in (1) an application for patent, published under section 122(b), by another filed in the United States before the invention by the applicant for patent or (2) a patent granted on an application for patent by another filed in the United States before the invention by the applicant for patent, except that an international application filed under the treaty defined in section 351(a) shall have the effects for the purposes of this subsection of an application filed in the United States only if the international application designated the United States and was published under Article 21(2) of such treaty in the English language....

[310]*See* Sun Studs, Inc. v. ATA Equip. Leasing, Inc., 872 F.2d 978, 983 n.3 (Fed. Cir. 1989) (defining "secret prior art").

[311]With minor exceptions, an inventor can "opt out" of 18-month publication only if she certifies that she is not seeking patent protection on the invention outside of the

written description of an earlier-filed U.S. patent application is now available for use as a §102(e) prior art reference at an earlier date, that is, at its 18-month publication date rather than at any later issue date. In fact, the §102(e) reference application need never issue as a patent at all, so long as the application is published.[312] An international application filed under the Patent Cooperation Treaty (PCT)[313] also can be relied on by the USPTO as a §102(e)(1) (2006) reference *if* the international application designated the United States *and* was published under the PCT in the English language.[314]

The effective date of a 35 U.S.C. §102(e) reference, whether it is an issued U.S. patent or a published patent application, remains the same in either case, however; the effective date is the U.S. application filing date of the reference patent or application.[315] What has changed is that before the AIPA, the USPTO generally had to wait until the reference application issued as a patent before the agency could rely on its contents as prior art.[316] After the AIPA, that reliance can be made as soon as the reference patent application is published, because at that time it effectively becomes a "printed publication."

United States. *See* 35 U.S.C. §122(b)(2)(B). As of 2004, about 85 percent of U.S. patent applications filed by large entities were published at 18 months after filing. *See* United States General Accounting Office, *Report to Congressional Committees: Patents: Information About the Publication Provisions of the American Inventors Protection Act* 4 (May 2004), *available at* http://www.gao.gov/new.items/d04603.pdf (reporting that for applications received between November 29, 2000 and November 28, 2003, the USPTO "has published or plans to publish applications from about 85 percent of the applicants qualifying as large entities compared with only about 74 percent of those qualifying as small entities").

[312] *See* 35 U.S.C. §102(e)(1) (2006).

[313] The Patent Cooperation Treaty is discussed in greater detail in Chapter 12 ("International Patenting Issues"), *infra*.

[314] *See* 35 U.S.C. §102(e) (2006) (providing in part that "an international application filed under the treaty defined in [35 U.S.C.] section 351(a) [i.e., the Patent Cooperation Treaty] shall have the effects for the purposes of this subsection of an application filed in the United States only if the international application designated the United States and was published under Article 21(2) of such treaty in the English language").

[315] Under the rule of *In re Hilmer*, 359 F.2d 859 (C.C.P.A. 1966), discussed in further detail in Chapter 12 ("International Patenting Issues"), *infra*, the USPTO must ignore any earlier *foreign* filing date, the benefit of which the reference applicant claimed under 35 U.S.C. §119, of a U.S. patent or published application being used as a §102(e) reference. The America Invents Act of 2011 repealed the *Hilmer* rule for applications filed on or after March 16, 2013. *See infra* Section P.3.b ("What Section 3 of the AIA Changed") and *infra* Section R ("Presumptively Novelty-Destroying Events Under Post-AIA 35 U.S.C. §102(a)(2) [First-Inventor-to-File Rule])."

[316] The so-called "provisional" §102(e)-based rejection was an exception to this rule, where the §102(e) reference patent application was commonly owned with the application under examination, and thus could be disclosed to the applicant by the USPTO without violating secrecy obligations. *See* In re Bartfeld, 925 F.2d 1450, 1451 n.5 (Fed. Cir. 1991).

2. Attempted Reliance on Provisional Application Filing Date as Effective Date for §102(e) Reference (Rule of *In re Wertheim*)

The AIA-implemented *inter partes* review (IPR) procedure discussed in Chapter 8 of this text,[317] first available in September 2012, can be used to challenge patents that were filed before the AIA took effect; the pre-AIA law discussed in this Part II of Chapter 4 applies to such patent challenges. As of December 2019, the Federal Circuit had issued many decisions in appeals from USPTO final decisions in IPRs. To the extent those Federal Circuit decisions apply pre-AIA law, they are relevant to this discussion of pre-AIA law and demonstrate the ongoing need to understand both pre- and post-AIA legal frameworks.

In one of its first decisions reviewing the merits of a final written decision by the Patent Trial and Appeal Board (PTAB) in an IPR, the Federal Circuit in the 2015 decision, *Dynamic Drinkware, LLC v. National Graphics, Inc.*,[318] answered important questions about burdens of proof and priority claims in IPRs. The appellate court clarified that the burdens of persuasion and production, and the procedures for establishing a reference patent's priority to earlier related applications, mirror those in federal district court validity litigation.

Importantly for purposes of this chapter, the merits issues in *Dynamic Drinkware* turned on pre-AIA law; the case aptly illustrates that IPR is applicable to pre-AIA patents such as the patent challenged in *Dynamic Drinkware*, the application for which was filed in 2000. More specifically, petitioner Dynamic asserted that the challenged claims of National Graphics' patent were anticipated under the pre-AIA provision, 35 U.S.C. §102(e)(2) (2006),[319] by the teaching of a prior art patent referred to (by the inventor's name) as "Raymond."[320] The dispute turned on whether the petitioner could properly rely on the *provisional* application filing date of the Raymond reference

[317]For more information about IPRs, an important new proceeding implemented by the America Invents Act of 2011, *see generally infra* Chapter 8, Section E ("AIA-Implemented Procedures for Challenging Issued Patents), subsection 1 ("*Inter Partes* Review").

[318]No. 2015-1214, 2015 WL 5166366 (Fed. Cir. Sept. 4, 2015).

[319]Section 102(e)(1), which involves the use of published patent applications as prior art references, was not involved in *Dynamic Drinkware* because the Raymond provisional application was filed in February 2000, and the corresponding non-provisional application filed in May 2000, both filings a few months before the introduction of 18-month publication of pending applications. As explained *supra* Chapter 1, Section H.4 ("Publication of Pending Applications"), publication of pending utility patent applications at eighteen months after their earliest filing date for which a benefit is sought became the default rule for applications filed on or after November 29, 2000. The USPTO began to publish the first such applications on its website around March 2001.

[320]The Raymond patent was assigned to a third party, Travel Tags, Inc.; that is, Travel Tags was not a party to the IPR.

patent under 35 U.S.C. §119(e) (2006) as that patent's effective date for prior art purposes.[321] For the reasons explained below, the PTAB answered in the negative and the Federal Circuit affirmed.

National Graphics' U.S. Patent No. 6,635,196 ('196 patent) concerned methods for making molded articles having a surface comprising a lenticular image, which is a type of three-dimensional image that changes in appearance as the viewer changes her viewing direction. Petitioner Dynamic initially alleged anticipation based on a claim chart that read claims 1 and 12 of National Graphics' patent on the disclosure of the Raymond non-provisional application, which predated by a few weeks the challenged '196 patent's own provisional application filing date. In response, National Graphics argued that it had actually reduced to practice the claimed invention prior to Raymond's non-provisional filing date, and the PTAB agreed.[322] Petitioner Dynamic then countered by asserting that the Raymond reference patent was entitled to its provisional application filing date, which was earlier than National Graphics' invention date (i.e., National Graphics' actual reduction to practice date). Figure 4.4 (not to scale) provides a timeline depicting the pertinent dates.

The Federal Circuit affirmed the PTAB's decision in favor of patentee National Graphics because petitioner Dynamic had not made a proper priority showing for the Raymond reference patent. Although the disclosure of the Raymond provisional application assertedly anticipated the challenged claims of National Graphics' '196 patent, this was not sufficient to establish the otherwise secret Raymond provisional application as prior art. Rather, the rule of an important 1981 Court of Customs and Patent Appeals (CCPA) precedent, *In re Wertheim*,[323] applied.

Wertheim involved the CCPA rejecting a USPTO attempt during *ex parte* prosecution to rely on the parent filing date of a patent that issued from a chain of continuation and continuation-in-part applications, purportedly in accordance with 35 U.S.C. §120. Although provisional applications did not exist in the U.S. patent system when *Wertheim* was decided in 1981, the rule for establishing priority back to an earlier related application similarly applied to the Raymond reference patent in the case at bar. As applied in *Dynamic Drinkware*, the Federal Circuit instructed that *Wertheim* meant that "[a] reference patent is only entitled to claim the benefit of the filing date of its

[321]For further explanation of priority claims to provisional application filing dates in accordance with 35 U.S.C. §119(e)(1), *see supra* Chapter 1, Section H.2 ("Filing the Application").

[322]The PTAB concluded that "Patent Owner has carried successfully its burden of establishing by a preponderance of the evidence an actual reduction to practice of claims 1 and 12 prior to Raymond's effective date." Final Written Decision at 7, Dynamic Drinkware LLC v. National Graphics, Inc., Case IPR2013-00131 (PTAB Sept. 12, 2014).

[323]646 F.2d 527, 537 (C.C.P.A. 1981) (Rich, J.).

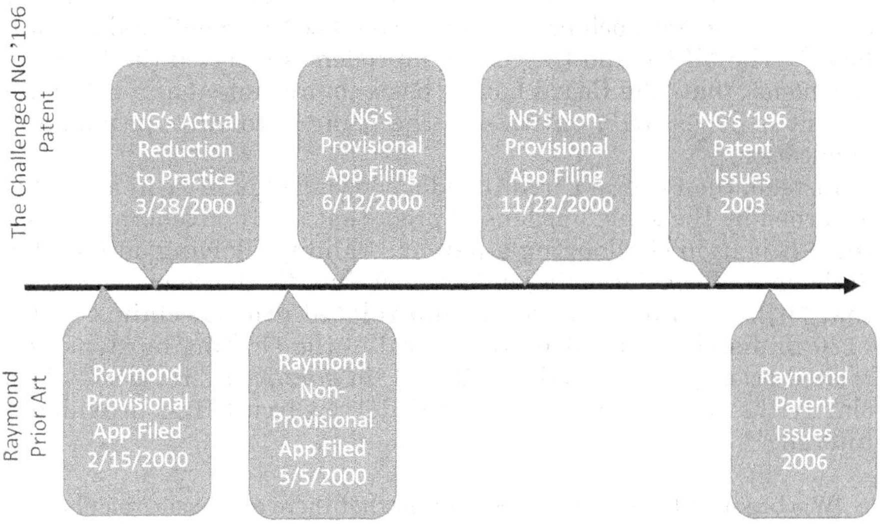

Figure 4.4

Timeline for *Dynamic Drinkware v. National Graphics* (Not to Scale)

provisional application if the disclosure of the provisional application provides support for the claims in the reference patent in compliance with §112, ¶1."[324]

Petitioner Dynamic did not make this showing because it had "failed to compare *the claims* of the Raymond patent to the disclosure in the Raymond provisional application."[325] Instead Dynamic had improperly compared the claims *of the challenged '196 patent* to Raymond's provisional application disclosure. Dynamic's burden was to "demonstrate support in the Raymond provisional application for *the claims of the Raymond patent*,"[326] but it failed to carry that burden. The Circuit emphasized that "[a] provisional application's effectiveness as prior art depends on its written description support for the claims of the issued patent of which it was a provisional."[327] In short, Dynamic made the wrong linkage.

The Federal Circuit adamantly rejected petitioner Dynamic's additional argument that because Raymond was an issued patent, it should benefit from a *presumption* that it was entitled to the benefit of its provisional application filing date. The Circuit observed that

[324]*Dynamic Drinkware,* 2015 WL 5166366, at *6 (citing *Wertheim*, 646 F.2d at 537).
[325]*Dynamic Drinkware,* 2015 WL 5166366, at *6.
[326]*Dynamic Drinkware*, 2015 WL 5166366, at *6.
[327]*Dynamic Drinkware,* 800 F.3d 1375, 2015 WL 5166366, at *6. Presumably, such effectiveness also depends on the provisional application's *enabling* support for the claims of its issued patent.

the USPTO does not routinely examine the merits of such priority claims, and so any such presumption would be "unsound" and unjustified.[328] The MPEP and the court's precedent supported the Circuit's conclusion that "the Board has no basis to presume that a reference patent is necessarily entitled to the filing date of its provisional application."[329]

Instead, the Federal Circuit held a showing of priority in an IPR is governed by the same burdens of proof that apply in federal district court litigation challenging a patent's validity. Relying on its 2008 decision in *Tech. Licensing v. Videotek, Inc.*,[330] the court explained that "[t]he . . . shifting burdens and related priority claims under §120 in district court litigation parallel the shifting burdens and related priority claims under §119(e)(1) in *inter partes* reviews."[331] To clarify the relative burdens, the Federal Circuit first provided a tutorial:

> [W]e begin with the established concept that there are two distinct burdens of proof: a burden of persuasion and a burden of production. *See Tech. Licensing* . . . , 545 F.3d [at] 1326-27. . . . The burden of persuasion "is the ultimate burden assigned to a party who must prove something to a specified degree of certainty," such as by a preponderance of the evidence or by clear and convincing evidence. *Id.* (citations omitted). In an

[328] *Dynamic Drinkware,* 800 F.3d 1375, 2015 WL 5166366, at *4.

[329] *Dynamic Drinkware,* 800 F.3d 1375, 2015 WL 5166366, at *4 (citing MPEP §211.05(I)(A) (2014) and PowerOasis, Inc. v. T-Mobile USA, Inc., 522 F.3d 1299, 1305 (Fed. Cir. 2008)). The USPTO provides in the MPEP that

> *If the filing date of the earlier provisional application is necessary, for example, in the case of an interference or to overcome a reference*, care must be taken to ensure that the disclosure filed as the provisional application adequately provides (1) a written description of the subject matter of the claim(s) at issue in the later filed nonprovisional application, and (2) an enabling disclosure to permit one of ordinary skill in the art to make and use the claimed invention in the later filed nonprovisional application without undue experimentation.

MPEP §211.05(I)(A) (2014) (emphasis added by Federal Circuit). The emphasized language showed that the examination of a provisional application's disclosure for compliance with the written description and enablement requirements of 35 U.S.C. §112, first paragraph is not automatic but rather only carried out when "necessary." *See also PowerOasis*, 522 F.3d at 1305 (stating that "[w]hen neither the PTO nor the Board has previously considered priority, there is simply no reason to presume that claims in a [continuation-in-part] application are entitled to the effective filing date of an earlier-filed application. Since the PTO did not make a determination regarding priority, there is no finding for the district court to defer to.").

[330] 545 F.3d 1316, 1326-1327 (Fed. Cir. 2008).

[331] The issues involved in the cited *Tech. Licensing v. Videotek, Inc.* case — Section 120 ("Benefit of earlier filing date in the United States") of 35 U.S.C., and the corresponding procedures for claiming the benefit of an earlier co-pending application for a later-filed continuation or continuation-in-part application — are examined *supra* Chapter 1, Section H.5 ("Continuing Application Practice").

inter partes review, the burden of persuasion is on the petitioner to prove "unpatentability by a preponderance of the evidence," 35 U.S.C. §316(e), and that burden never shifts to the patentee. "Failure to prove the matter as required by the applicable standard means that the party with the burden of persuasion loses on that point-thus, if the fact trier of the issue is left uncertain, the party with the burden loses." *Tech. Licensing*, 545 F.3d at 1327.

A second and distinct burden, the burden of production, or the burden of going forward with evidence, is a shifting burden, "the allocation of which depends on where in the process of trial the issue arises." *Id.* (citations omitted). The burden of production may entail "producing additional evidence and presenting persuasive argument based on new evidence or evidence already of record." *Id.*[332]

The Federal Circuit then stepped through this procedural framework as applied to the priority claim for the Raymond reference patent involved in the IPR proceeding under review. As in any IPR, petitioner Dynamic bore the ultimate burden of persuasion to prove unpatentability of the '196 patent claims under review by a preponderance of the evidence. That burden never shifted away from Dynamic. Petitioner Dynamic also bore the initial burden of production, or going forward with evidence or argument, which it satisfied by arguing that the disclosure of Raymond anticipated the challenged claims of the '196 patent under 35 U.S.C. §102(e)(2) (2006). Thereafter the burden of production returned to patentee National Graphics. The patentee satisfied that burden by producing evidence (in the form of declarations of its president and an employee) asserting that it had reduced the invention claimed in the '196 patent prior to the Raymond patent's non-provisional application filing date. In pre-AIA parlance, the patentee National Graphics antedated Raymond's filing date by establishing an earlier date of invention (via actual reduction to practice).

The burden of production then shifted back to petitioner Dynamic. The Federal Circuit explained that Dynamic could have satisfied that burden in either of two ways: (1) by establishing that National Graphics did not actually reduce to practice as it had argued, or (2) by establishing that the Raymond reference patent was entitled to an effective date prior to National Graphics' invention date. As to the first option, Dynamic argued that National Graphics' evidence indicated that the patentee still has "a long way to go." The PTAB disagreed, explaining that actual reduction to practice does not require commercial perfection. As to the second option, Dynamic failed to make a proper showing under 35 U.S.C. §119(e) that the Raymond patent was entitled to the benefit of the filing date of its provisional application for the reason explained above — Dynamic filed to satisfy the rule,

[332]*Dynamic Drinkware*, 800 F.3d 1375, 2015 WL 5166366, at *2-*3.

derived from *Wertheim*, that the priority proponent must link the disclosure of the provisional with the claims of the reference patent that issued from that provisional (not with the claims of the patent challenged in the IPR).[333] To summarize, "[a] provisional application's effectiveness as prior art depends on its written description support for the claims of the issued patent of which it was a provisional. Dynamic did not make that showing."[334] The PTAB had properly concluded that Dynamic failed to demonstrate by a preponderance of the evidence that claims 1 and 12 of National Graphics' '196 were unpatentable for anticipation under §102(e)(2). Accordingly, the Federal Circuit affirmed.[335]

M. Derivation and Inventorship Under 35 U.S.C. §102(f) (Pre-AIA)

Subsection 102(f) is neither an anticipation nor a loss-of-right section; it is *sui generis* in the sense that it reflects the central principle of *originality* or proper inventorship. A person cannot simply copy or steal an invention from another and claim it as his own; the claimed invention must be the original creation of the inventor. Although §102(f) (2006) was eliminated by the AIA, the fundamental concept of

[333]It is unclear whether Dynamic was simply unaware of the *Wertheim* rule, or whether the Raymond patent as issued simply lacked any claim that could be supported by the disclosure of Raymond's provisional filing. It is not uncommon for claims in an issued patent to have broader scope than the subject matter disclosed in a corresponding provisional application. *Cf.* New Railhead Mfg., L.L.C. v. Vermeer Mfg. Co., 298 F.3d 1290, 1294 (Fed. Cir. 2002) (stating that "the specification of the *provisional* must 'contain a written description of the invention and the manner and process of making and using it, in such full, clear, concise, and exact terms,' 35 U.S.C. §112 ¶1, to enable an ordinarily skilled artisan to practice the invention *claimed* in the *non-provisional* application") (emphases in original).

[334]*Dynamic Drinkware*, 800 F.3d 1375, 2015 WL 5166366, at *6.

[335]The Federal Circuit also noted, but did not reach, the issue of how the effective date of a reference patent or published patent application will be determined in the future under AIA law. That issue will turn on judicial interpretation of AIA-implemented 35 U.S.C. §102(d). As the Federal Circuit observed in a footnote, "[t]he relevant provision of §102(e)(2) was reorganized into newly designated §102(d)(2) when certain aspects of the Leahy-Smith America Invents Act ("AIA"), Pub. L. No. 112-29, took effect on March 16, 2013." Because the Circuit in *Dynamic Drinkware* "refer[red] to the pre-AIA version of §102," it would "not interpret here the AIA's impact on *Wertheim* in newly designated §102(d)." AIA-implemented §102(d), titled "Patents and published applications effective as prior art," refers to "subject matter described" in a reference patent or application. This phrasing, along with language asking whether the "patent or application for patent is *entitled* to claim a right of priority under section 119," does not make crystal clear whether compliance with the enablement and written description requirements of 35 U.S.C. §112(a) will be required.

originality continues to apply whether one is operating under pre- or post-AIA rules.[336]

Section 102(f) (2006) is implicated in a variety of patent law contexts. For the sake of completeness each is introduced below, although the discussion extends somewhat beyond the scope of this chapter (novelty, loss of right, and priority under 35 U.S.C. §102).

1. Derivation

United States patent law requires that an invention must be the original work of the person(s) named as inventor(s) on the patent application. In other words, Entity A cannot merely copy an invention from Entity B, the true inventor, and claim it as Entity A's own invention.

One particular application of the originality requirement is that an invention is not patentable to an applicant who "derived" it from someone else. **Derivation** in patent law means that another (in the above example, Entity B) conceived the invention and communicated that conception to the person improperly named as the inventor on the patent application at issue (here the "deriver," Entity A).[337]

[336]For reasons that are not particularly clear, the AIA eliminated 35 U.S.C. §102(f) (2006), *see* Leahy-Smith America Invents Act, Pub. L. No. 112-29 (H.R. 1249), §3(b)(1), 125 Stat. 284, 285-286 (2011). However, the AIA did not eliminate the requirement of originality. Specifically, the AIA did not change the requirement that, subject to certain exceptions, patent applications shall be made "by the inventor," 35 U.S.C. §111(a)(1) (2006), and the AIA added a definition of "inventor" as "the individual or, if a joint invention, the individuals collectively who invented or discovered the subject matter of the invention." 35 U.S.C. §100(f) (eff. Mar. 16, 2013); Leahy-Smith America Invents Act, Pub. L. No. 112-29 (H.R. 1249), §3(a)(2), 125 Stat. 284, 285 (2011). The AIA also continued the requirement that a patent applicant's oath include a statement that the applicant believes he is an "original" inventor. *See* 35 U.S.C. §115(b)(2) (eff. Mar. 16, 2013) (providing that "[a]n oath or declaration under subsection (a) shall contain statements that . . . such individual believes himself or herself to be the *original* inventor or an *original* joint inventor of a claimed invention in the application") (emphases added).

[337]*See* Agawan Co. v. Jordan, 74 U.S. 583, 602-603 (1868) (stating that "[s]uggestions from another, made during the progress of such experiments, in order that they may be sufficient to defeat a patent subsequently issued, must have embraced the plan of the improvement, and must have furnished such information to the person to whom the communication was made that it would have enabled an ordinary mechanic, without the exercise of any ingenuity and special skill on his part, to construct and put the improvement in successful operation"); Gambro Lundia AB v. Baxter Healthcare Corp., 110 F.3d 1573, 1576 (Fed. Cir. 1997) (holding that "[t]o show derivation, the party asserting invalidity must prove both prior conception of the invention by another and communication of that conception to the patentee"); Price v. Symsek, 988 F.2d 1187, 1190 (Fed. Cir. 1993) (stating that "[t]o prove derivation in an interference proceeding, the person attacking the patent must establish prior conception of the claimed subject matter and communication of the conception to the adverse claimant"); DeGroff v. Roth, 412 F.2d 1401, 1405 (C.C.P.A. 1969) (noting in appeal from interference proceeding

Derivation under 35 U.S.C. §102(f) (2006) should be contrasted with a priority determination under 35 U.S.C. §102(g) (2006), discussed below. In the latter, it is assumed that both A and B are original, independent inventors of the same invention; the §102(g) dispute is over which inventor, A or B, was the first to invent.[338]

Note that there are no geographic limitations in §102(f), in contrast with other subsections of 35 U.S.C. §102. Only a true inventor of the claimed subject matter is entitled to patent it, and thus the patent law is not concerned about whether the communication of the conception from Entity B to Entity A occurred in the United States or a foreign country.[339]

2. Who Is an Inventor?

The conception of an invention is the mental part of the inventive act (i.e., the formation in the mind of the inventor(s) of the definite and permanent idea of the invention as it is thereafter reduced to practice). Conception is the touchstone of determining inventorship.[340] For a person to be properly named as an inventor on a patent, he must generally contribute to the conception of the invention.[341] One who derived the invention, rather than contributed to its conception, is not properly named as an inventor.[342]

Board's test that "Roth and Hall [junior party in interference], in order to prevail, must prove by a preponderance of the evidence that they 'had a full concept of the invention encompassed by the counts and this concept was transmitted to DeGroff'").

[338]*See Price*, 988 F.2d at 1190 (contrasting claim of derivation with claim of priority of invention).

[339]The America Invents Act of 2011 eliminated interferences (proceedings to determine priority under the traditional first-to-invent system) but added a new derivation proceeding. *See* 35 U.S.C. §135 (eff. Mar. 16, 2013). The AIA derivation proceeding is discussed *infra* Section S.3.a. Interference cases may no longer be filed after March 15, 2013.

[340]*See* Sewall v. Walters, 21 F.3d 411, 415 (Fed. Cir. 1994) (explaining that "[d]etermining 'inventorship' is nothing more than determining who conceived the subject matter at issue, whether that subject matter is recited in a claim in an application or in a count in an interference"). Conception of an invention has occurred "when a definite and permanent idea of an operative invention, including every feature of the subject matter sought to be patented, is known." *Id.*

[341]*See* Burroughs Wellcome Co. v. Barr Labs., Inc., 40 F.3d 1223, 1227-1228 (Fed. Cir. 1994).

[342]The America Invents Act of 2011 added an explicit, though circularly unhelpful, definition of "inventor." *See* 35 U.S.C. §100(f) (eff. Mar. 16, 2013) (providing that "[t]he term 'inventor' means the individual or, if a joint invention, the individuals collectively who invented or discovered the subject matter of the invention").

3. Correction of Inventorship

Section 102(f) is also the pre-AIA vehicle for USPTO rejections on the ground of improper naming of inventors in pending patent applications. In addition, it is the ground on which issued patents may be invalidated based on the improper naming of inventors, whether or not any derivation has occurred.[343] Prior to passage of the 1952 Patent Act, patents were routinely held invalid for failure to correctly name the inventors. Such failures could involve "nonjoinder," which is the failure to name someone who truly is an inventor of the claimed subject matter, or "misjoinder," which is the improper naming of a person as an inventor who is *not* in fact an inventor. For example, assume that both A and B are named as inventors on a patent, but only A invented and B was merely a supervisor or funding source. B is not properly named as a co-inventor (nor, on these facts, is B a deriver).

The risk of invalidation stemming from the improper naming of inventors was significantly lessened with the 1952 Act's enactment of 35 U.S.C. §256, which provides in part that "[t]he error of omitting inventors or naming persons who are not inventors shall not invalidate the patent in which such error occurred if it can be corrected as provided in this section."[344] Under pre-AIA rules, the error to be corrected must be without any deceptive intention on the part of a nonjoined inventor, while the law does not inquire into the intent of a person who was misjoined.[345]

Section 256 further provides that the inventorship of an issued patent may be corrected in two ways. The first paragraph of §256 indicates that if all parties agree on a needed correction, they may apply to the Director of the USPTO for that correction. The second paragraph provides that inventorship disputes in which all parties do not agree may be resolved by "the court before which such matter is called in question,"[346] so long as notice and opportunity for a hearing are provided.[347]

[343]Section 102(f) (2006) should be read in tandem with 35 U.S.C. §111 (2006), which requires that patent applications be made "by the inventor," except in situations otherwise provided for (e.g., an inventor who cannot be located or is deceased).

[344]35 U.S.C. §256, ¶2.

[345]*See* Stark v. Advanced Magnetics, Inc., 119 F.3d 1551, 1554 (Fed. Cir. 1997). The America Invents Act of 2011 eliminated the language "and such error arose without any deceptive intention on his part." *See* 35 U.S.C. §256(a) (eff. Sept. 16, 2012).

[346]Professor Chisum argues that the courts have erred by interpreting the "such matter" language of 35 U.S.C. §256 as creating jurisdiction for an independent cause of action for inventorship correction by omitted inventors. *See* 1-2 DONALD S. CHISUM, CHISUM ON PATENTS §2.04[7] (2008).

[347]Although 35 U.S.C. §256 governs the correction of inventorship for an issued patent, correction of the inventorship on a still-pending patent application takes place within the USPTO, in accordance with the last paragraph of 35 U.S.C. §116.

4. Joint Inventors

When a pending patent application lists multiple inventors, the USPTO examiner may enter a rejection under 35 U.S.C. §102(f) (2006) if evidence exists suggesting that not all of these individuals contributed to the conception of the invention. The law is quite clear, however, that a patented invention may be the work of multiple inventors (and joint invention is routine).[348]

Section 116 of 35 U.S.C. provides the standard for joint inventions made by two or more persons. Prior to 1984, the law required that to be named as a co-inventor, a person must have contributed to every one of the claims of the application or patent at issue. Section 116 was amended in 1984 so that contribution to the conception of the subject matter recited in every claim is not necessary. Under 35 U.S.C. §116 as it now stands, inventors may apply for a patent jointly even though "each did not make a contribution to the subject matter of every claim of the patent."[349] For example, both A and B are properly named inventors on a patent application comprising 20 claims, even though A contributed to the conception of 19 claims and B contributed to the conception of only 1 claim.[350]

N. Prior Invention Under 35 U.S.C. §102(g) (Pre-AIA)

1. Introduction

Section 102(g) of 35 U.S.C. (2006) is the cornerstone of the historic U.S. first-to-invent priority system. The requirement that patents be granted to the first in time to invent is implemented in two different contexts as indicated by the text of the statutory provision, but the basic concept of first-to-invent informs both situations.[351]

Section 102(g) (2006) comprises two prongs. The first prong, §102(g)(1), deals with pre-AIA priority contests called **interferences** between two or more parties who claim to have made the same invention at about the same time. The interference, an *inter partes* proceeding conducted within the USPTO, will determine which party was first

[348]The America Invents Act of 2011 added an explicit, though circular, definition of joint inventorship. *See* 35 U.S.C. §100(g) (eff. Mar. 16, 2013) (providing that "[t]he terms 'joint inventor' and 'coinventor' mean any 1 of the individuals who invented or discovered the subject matter of a joint invention").

[349]35 U.S.C. §116(3).

[350]*See* Ethicon, Inc. v. United States Surgical Corp., 135 F.3d 1456, 1460 (Fed. Cir. 1998) (stating that "[a] contribution to one claim is enough").

[351]The America Invents Act of 2011 prospectively ended the first-to-invent system and changed the United States to a first-inventor-to-file system. *See infra* Part III.

to invent and hence is entitled to the U.S. patent on the invention in question.

The second prong, §102(g)(2), is a basis for proving *anticipation* of the claims of a patent application (in *ex parte* prosecution) or an issued patent (in federal court litigation challenging validity). Anticipation under §102(g)(2) occurs through the act of someone other than the named inventor of the application or patent having made the invention in this country before the invention date of the application or patent.

In both the interference and the anticipation settings, the earlier invention must not have been "abandoned, suppressed, or concealed."[352] The interference and anticipation contexts are discussed separately below, as is the basic rule of time-wise priority that applies in both contexts.

2. Interference Proceedings Under §102(g)(1)

Only one patent can be granted on a particular claimed invention. When two (or more) parties (i.e., inventive entities[353]) apply for a U.S. patent on the same invention, each party having independently made the invention (i.e., not copied it), we cannot award both parties their own patents. Rather, the U.S. patent system devised a procedure that has historically awarded the patent (at least theoretically) to the party who was first in time to invent, regardless of the order in which the parties filed their respective patent applications.

The use of "theoretically" in the previous sentence indicates that the process of determining priority of invention does not occur automatically. The competing claimants must participate in an interference proceeding, a pre-AIA *inter partes* adjudicatory proceeding within the USPTO to determine which party invented first.[354] The party who is the last to file her patent application (the "junior party") bears the

[352] 35 U.S.C. §102(g).

[353] In cases where an invention is made jointly by two or more persons, patent law refers to those persons collectively as the "inventive entity." Consider an invention jointly made by Inventor A and Inventor B. The inventive entity of "A + B" is considered "another" (i.e., a different inventive entity from either A alone or B alone).

[354] The U.S. patent system developed the interference proceeding as a means of determining priority of invention. Adoption of the first-to-invent principle does not necessarily require interferences, however. Historically, England appears to have used the relative order of filing dates as an irrebuttable presumption of the relative dates of invention, thus avoiding protracted factual disputes over first to invent priority. The author thanks Professor Carl Moy for this observation.

The America Invents Act of 2011 eliminated interferences. *See* Leahy-Smith America Invents Act, Pub. L. No. 112-29 (H.R. 1249) (2011), §§3(i) (amending 35 U.S.C. §135 to eliminate interference proceedings and implement derivation proceedings), 3(j) ("Elimination of References to Interferences") (striking the word "interference" from

burden of overcoming a presumption that the first to file (the "senior party") was also the first to invent. Thus, under the historic U.S. priority system the party who was the first to file an application on the invention in question is presumptively entitled to the patent, *unless* the other party can successfully overcome this presumption.

Evidence of earlier invention in an interference proceeding can be based on inventive activity outside the United States in accordance with the pre-AIA version of 35 U.S.C. §104.[355] This section permits the use of evidence of inventive activity (such as conception, diligence, and reduction to practice, as those terms are defined herein) that occurred on or after December 8, 1993, in countries that are signatories to the North American Free Trade Agreement (NAFTA), which currently includes Mexico and Canada in addition to the United States, and on or after January 1, 1996, in countries that are members of the World Trade Organization (WTO).[356] Thus, a person who invented in a NAFTA or WTO member country other than the United States and seeks U.S. patent protection on her invention is placed on a more even footing, from an evidentiary standpoint, with a U.S. inventor of the same invention. However, such a person may also be penalized if she fails to disclose evidence of foreign inventive activity in accordance with U.S. discovery norms.[357]

---

multiple sections of the Patent Act). Interference cases may no longer be filed after March 15, 2013.

[355]35 U.S.C. §104 (2006) provides in part:

> (a) In general
>
> (1) Proceedings. In proceedings in the Patent and Trademark Office, in the courts, and before any other competent authority, an applicant for a patent, or a patentee, may not establish a date of invention by reference to knowledge or use thereof, or other activity with respect thereto, in a foreign country other than a NAFTA country or a WTO member country, except as provided in sections 119 and 365 of this title.

[356]The current membership of the WTO is available at https://www.wto.org/english/thewto_e/whatis_e/tif_e/org6_e.htm (2016). As of January 2020, 164 countries were members of the WTO. Countries that were *not* members as of January 2020 include Bhutan, Bahamas, Iran, and Iraq. *See id.* (listing of "Observer governments").

[357]*See* 35 U.S.C. §104(a)(3) (2006), which provides the following:

> (3) Use of information. To the extent that any information in a NAFTA country or a WTO member country concerning knowledge, use, or other activity relevant to proving or disproving a date of invention has not been made available for use in a proceeding in the Patent and Trademark Office, a court, or any other competent authority to the same extent as such information could be made available in the United States, the Director, court, or such other authority shall draw appropriate inferences, or take other action permitted by statute, rule, or regulation, in favor of the party that requested the information in the proceeding.

This portion of 35 U.S.C. §104 imposes "a type of protection for U.S. companies in the form of penalties against foreign parties that do not provide appropriate discovery."

The procedures for conducting interferences are quite complex and beyond the scope of this text.[358] However, the basic rule of time-wise priority set forth in the last sentence of 35 U.S.C. §102(g) (2006) should be mastered by all students of patent law:

> In determining priority of invention under this subsection, there shall be considered not only the respective dates of conception and reduction to practice of the invention, but also the reasonable diligence of one who was first to conceive and last to reduce to practice, from a time prior to conception by the other.[359]

This rule, which applies in both the interference and the anticipation settings, is examined and applied in several examples below.

3. Anticipation Under §102(g)(2)

a. Introduction

The second subsection of §102(g) (2006) applies not in the interference setting, but rather in either *ex parte* prosecution of a patent application or in federal court litigation challenging the validity of an issued patent. In these settings, unlike interferences, there is no rival party claiming entitlement to a patent on the invention in question. Rather, a USPTO examiner is asserting under §102(g)(2) (2006) that some other inventor's earlier making of the invention in this country is prior art that prevents the grant of a patent on the same invention to a patent applicant. If in the litigation setting, the challenger of validity (typically an accused infringer) is asserting that some other inventor's earlier making of the invention in this country should invalidate the patent in suit.

It is analytically helpful to think of §102(g)(2) (2006) as encompassing or subsuming all other novelty-destroying subsections of §102, and this is why some patent law instructors present §102(g) before covering any other part of the statute. This order of presentation makes a

---

Thomas L. Irving & Stacy D. Lewis, *Proving a Date of Invention and Infringement After GATT/TRIPS*, 22 AIPLA Q.J. 309, 318 (1994).

[358]For further guidance on interference law and practice, *see* Practice Before the Board of Patent Appeals and Interferences, 37 C.F.R. §§41.200-41.208 (eff. May 13, 2015) (titled "Subpart E. Patent Interferences"); United States Patent and Trademark Office, *Interference Proceedings*, Manual of Patent Examining Procedure §§2301-2309 (9th ed., rev. Nov. 2015); Charles W. Rivise & A.D. Caesar, Interference Law and Practice (W.S. Hein 2000); Charles L. Gholz, *Interference Practice*, in 6 Patent Practice 24-1 (Irving Kayton & Karyl S. Kayton eds., 4th ed. 1989). A Federal Circuit judge has described Gholz's work as a "definitive text" on interference practice. *See* Brown v. Barbacid, 276 F.3d 1327, 1340 (Fed. Cir. 2002) (Newman, J., dissenting).

[359]35 U.S.C. §102(g) (2006).

certain amount of logical sense. Viewed on a timeline, a prior art invention must first be "made" before it can be known or used by others or patented or described in a printed publication (per §102(a) (2006)), or put into public use or on sale (per §102(b) (2006)), or described in a U.S. patent or application (per §102(e) (2006)).

b. *Prior Invention Must Not Be "Abandoned, Suppressed, or Concealed"*

An invention is anticipated under 35 U.S.C. §102(g)(2) (2006) if it was "made in this country by another inventor" before the applicant's invention date, and the prior inventor has not subsequently "abandoned, suppressed, or concealed" her invention. Thus, §102(g)(2) is triggered by an earlier "making" of the invention in this country by another inventor, coupled with some sort of introduction of that invention to the U.S. public within a reasonable time period thereafter, whether by patenting, publication, sales, or the like.[360] The prior inventor need not file a patent application on her invention, but she must take other action within a reasonable time after her actual reduction to practice to ensure that the public has obtained knowledge of the invention.[361]

Just how much detail must the prior inventor disclose to adequately convey knowledge of an invention to the public? This issue was disputed in the Federal Circuit's 2012 decision, *Fox Group, Inc. v. Cree, Inc.*[362] The case concerned an infringement action in which the accused infringer Cree successfully asserted a §102(g)(2) invalidity defense based on its own prior making of the invention (i.e., a low-defect silicon carbide ("SiC") crystal used in high-temperature and

[360]*See* Int'l Glass Co. v. United States, 408 F.2d 395, 403 (Ct. Cl. 1969) (stating that "an invention, though completed, is deemed abandoned, suppressed, or concealed if, within a reasonable time after completion, no steps are taken to make the invention publicly known"); *id.* (noting that "failure to file a patent application; to describe the invention in a publicly disseminated document; or to use the invention publicly, have been held to constitute abandonment, suppression, or concealment") (citations omitted). There is no comparable "introduction" requirement for prior knowledge or use of an invention under the text of 35 U.S.C. §102(a), but courts have interpreted 35 U.S.C. §102(a) as requiring that the anticipatory knowledge or use be publicly accessible. *See* Eolas Techs. Inc. v. Microsoft Corp., 399 F.3d 1325, 1334 (Fed. Cir. 2005); Woodland Trust v. Flowertree Nursery, Inc., 148 F.3d 1368, 1370 (Fed. Cir. 1998).

[361]*See* Apotex USA, Inc. v. Merck & Co., 254 F.3d 1031, 1038 (Fed. Cir. 2001). In *Apotex USA*, even though validity challenger Merck likely suppressed or concealed its admittedly prior invention (of a process for making a blood pressure treatment) by maintaining the process as a trade secret for several years after reducing it to practice, the Federal Circuit held that Merck's later publications and trial testimony disclosing the ingredients and other details of the process, all occurring prior to patentee Apotex's alleged conception date, were sufficient to invalidate the Apotex patents in suit under 35 U.S.C. §102(g)(2). *See Apotex USA*, 254 F.3d at 1040.

[362]700 F.3d 1300 (Fed. Cir. 2012).

high-power electronics) prior in time to the plaintiff patentee.[363] On appeal, the *Fox Group* panel divided on whether Cree thereafter had not "abandoned, suppressed, or concealed" its invention within the meaning of §102(g)(2).

Patentee Fox Group contended that Cree had abandoned, suppressed, or concealed by (1) not filing its own patent application on the invention, (2) not presenting proof of commercialization that would allow for reverse-engineering, and (3) not otherwise providing adequate disclosure by failing to reveal details of the growth conditions under which Cree made its crystal. The Federal Circuit majority in *Fox Group* disagreed. Although filing a patent application and commercializing a product are two "convenient" ways of proving an invention has been disclosed to the public, other means exist to prove public disclosure. In the case at bar, Cree "'promptly and publicly disclosed its findings concerning the low defect properties of the SiC . . . through a presentation at the 1995 International Conference and a published paper on the subject.'"[364]

The Circuit majority also rejected Fox Group's argument that Cree's disclosures were not enabling and therefore were not entitled to weight because they did not provide sufficient detail on how Cree "got its results." The *Fox Group* majority distinguished between enablement requirements for disclosures of *product* claim — those of the patent in suit — versus *process* claims. If "the patent claimed a *process*, then a prior inventor would have to prove prior invention *of the process* which had not been abandoned, suppressed, or concealed, to invalidate the patent under §102(g)."[365] In the case at bar, however, "Cree promptly and publicly disclosed its findings concerning the low defect properties" of the *product*— the SiC material — as claimed.

Judge O'Malley dissented in *Fox Group*. In her view, Federal Circuit precedent required that "a prior inventor must show that the public was clearly given the benefit of an invention, via reverse-engineering, a detailed disclosure, or otherwise, if it wants to rely on §102(g) to invalidate a patent."[366] "Despite the majority's finding to

[363]*See Fox Group,* 700 F.3d at 1305 ("There is no genuine issue whether Cree reduced the invention to practice prior to Fox's critical date."). The critical date for the Fox Group patent in suit was 2000; Cree actually reduced the invention to practice in 1995. *Fox Group,* 700 F.3d at 1304.

[364]*Fox Group*, 700 F.3d at 1307 (quoting Fox Group, Inc. v. Cree, Inc., 819 F. Supp. 2d 524, 535 (E.D. Va. 2011)).

[365]*Fox Group*, 700 F.3d at 1306 (emphasis added).

[366]*Fox Group,* 700 F.3d at 1312 (O'Malley, J., dissenting-in-part) (citing Apotex USA, Inc. v. Merck & Co., 254 F.3d 1031, 1038 (Fed. Cir. 2001) (stating that "the spirit and policy of the patent laws encourage an inventor to take steps to ensure that 'the public has gained knowledge of the invention which will insure its preservation in the public domain' or else run the risk of being dominated by the patent of another") (quoting Palmer v. Dudzik, 481 F.2d 1377, 1387 (C.C.P.A. 1973))).

the contrary," Judge O'Malley contended, "simply disclosing the existence of the product, without more, is insufficient to make an invention publicly known. There must be something more."[367]

c. *Geographic Requirements*

In contrast with interferences under 35 U.S.C. §102(g)(1) (2006), the earlier invention that is relied on to anticipate (i.e., destroy novelty) under 35 U.S.C. §102(g)(2) (2006) must have been made in the United States. The provisions of 35 U.S.C. §104 (2006) that speak of events occurring in NAFTA or WTO countries outside the United States do not apply to anticipation under §102(g)(2). In other words, the prior making of an invention relied on to anticipate or invalidate (i.e., defeat patentability) "counts" only if it occurred in the United States. This distinction is reflected in the text of 35 U.S.C. §104, which permits use of evidence of acts abroad only by applicants or patentees who are affirmatively seeking to "establish a date of invention."[368] These persons would include parties in an interference under §102(g)(1) as well as applicants in *ex parte* prosecution who are seeking to antedate §102(a) or §102(e) prior art in accordance with 37 C.F.R. §1.131 by establishing an invention date that predates the effective date of the prior art reference. Both groups of persons are *affirmatively* attempting to establish an invention date, rather than attempting to *defeat* patentability as in §102(g)(2).

What precisely constitutes a §102(g)(2) "making" in the United States? In 2014, a divided panel of the Federal Circuit in *Solvay S.A. v. Honeywell Int'l Inc.* ("*Solvay II*")[369] interpreted the "made in this country" language of 35 U.S.C. §102(g)(2) (2006) as allowing the inventor of the prior art invention to have *conceived* the invention outside the United States. However, the *reduction to practice* of that prior art invention must still have occurred in the United States for the invention to count as §102(g)(2) "made in this country" prior art.

Solvay S.A.'s ("Solvay's") U.S. Patent No. 6,730,817 ('817 patent) was directed to an improved method of making an industrial fluorocarbon known as "HFC-245fa." Because HFC-245fa advantageously does not deplete our ozone layer, it (along with other similar hydrofluorocarbons) has been legislatively mandated to replace ozone-depleting

[367]*Fox Group,* 700 F.3d at 1312 (O'Malley, J., dissenting-in-part). "[T]he evidence at this stage establishes only that the Cree inventors gave a presentation and published a non-enabling article." *Id.* at 1313.

[368]35 U.S.C. §104 (2006).

[369]742 F.3d 998 (Fed. Cir. 2014) (hereafter "*Solvay II*").

alternatives. The only claim on appeal in *Solvay II* recited (in *Jepson* format[370]):

> 1. In a process for the preparation of [HFC-245fa] comprising reaction of [HCC-240fa] with hydrogen fluoride in the presence of a hydrofluorination catalyst, the improvement which comprises carrying out the reaction at a temperature and under a pressure at which [HFC-245fa] is gaseous and isolating... [HFC-245fa] from the reaction mixture by drawing off [HFC-245fa] and hydrogen chloride [HCl] in a gaseous phase as each of said [HFC245fa] and [HCl] is being formed.

The Federal Circuit majority in *Solvay II* affirmed a district court's judgment, based on a jury verdict, that the '817 patent was invalid because the same method invention had been "made" in the United States before the '817 patent's priority date, and that that "making" qualified as invalidating prior art under 35 U.S.C. §102(g)(2).

The result in *Solvay II* turned on the Federal Circuit majority's approval of the *inurement* doctrine. As applied to the case at bar, the inurement doctrine provides that the §102(g)(2) prior art invention's reduction to practice in the United States may be performed by the prior art inventor *or may be performed by another on behalf of* the prior art inventor. That is, the reduction to practice may be carried out by a third party but nevertheless "inure" to the benefit of the prior art inventor. The *Solvay II* majority observed that nothing required that "'the inventor be the one to reduce the invention to practice so long as the reduction to practice was done on his behalf' in the United States."[371]

Moreover, the inurement doctrine "does not require that the [prior art] inventor *expressly* request or direct the non-inventor to perform reductive work."[372] Although inurement cannot arise "from a third party's 'unwarranted and hostile use' of another's invention,"[373] an

[370]The *Jepson* claiming format was covered *supra* Chapter 2, Section E.3.

[371]*Solvay II*, 742 F.3d at 1000 (quoting In re DeBaun, 687 F.2d 459, 463 (C.C.P.A. 1982) (citing Litchfield v. Eigen, 535 F.2d 72, 76 (C.C.P.A. 1976)); citing also 3A Donald S. Chisum, Chisum on Patents §10.06[3] ("[a]cts by others working explicitly or implicitly at the inventor's request will inure to his benefit.")). *See also Solvay II,* 742 F.3d at 1000 n.2 (citing Holmwood v. Sugavanam, 948 F.2d 1236, 1238 (Fed. Cir. 1991) (foreign inventor was "another inventor" under §102(g)(2) when the invention was reduced to practice in the United States on his behalf); Shurie v. Richmond, 699 F.2d 1156, 1158 (Fed. Cir. 1983) (no reduction to practice where the inventive process was carried out in Canada, not the United States); Breuer v. DeMarinis, 558 F.2d 22, 27 (C.C.P.A. 1977) (foreign inventors reduced the invention to practice in this country when reduction to practice was done on their behalf in the United States)).

[372]*Solvay II,* 742 F.3d at 1006 (emphasis added).

[373]*Solvay II*, 742 F.3d at 1006 (quoting Burgess v. Wetmore, 1879 Dec. Comm'r Pat. 237, 240 (no inurement of reduction to practice built by rival applicant)).

"express request or direction is *not* required. The request may be 'implicit[ ].'"[374]

The facts of *Solvay II* suggested that the request for Honeywell to reduce the invention to practice in the United States was, indeed, implicit rather than explicit. After Solvay S.A., a Belgian chemical company, sued Honeywell for infringement of the '817 patent, Honeywell asserted as an invalidity defense that process development work conducted under contract between Honeywell and a Russian entity, carried out primarily in Russia and thereafter re-performed in the United States by Honeywell, amounted to an anticipatory §102(g)(2) prior making of Solvay's claimed process.

The Solvay '817 patent had a priority date of October 23, 1995. Before that date, Honeywell had entered into a research contract with the Russian Scientific Center for Applied Chemistry (RSCAC). Pursuant to that contract, RSCAC engineers conducted process development studies (in Russia) with the goal of commercially producing HFC-245fa. In July 1994, RSCAC sent to Honeywell (in the United States) a report documenting RSCAC's successful development (in Russia) of a continuous process capable of producing high yields of HCC-245fa. In 1995, but before the Solvay '817 patent's October 1995 priority date, Honeywell engineers used the RSCAC report to successfully carry out the same process in the United States.[375]

Honeywell's theories for invalidating Solvay's '817 patent (or perhaps the Federal Circuit's own theories[376]) evolved over time. In an initial appeal to the Federal Circuit ("*Solvay I*"),[377] the court in 2010 rejected Honeywell's argument that Honeywell's own engineers were the §102(g)(2) prior art inventors who reduced the process to practice in the United States. The Circuit in *Solvay I* reasoned that Honeywell's engineers were not "another inventor" under §102(g)(2) because the Honeywell engineers did not *conceive* the '817 patent invention, but rather derived it from the RSCAC engineers.[378]

[374]*Solvay II*, 742 F.3d at 1006 (quoting Cooper v. Goldfarb, 154 F.3d 1321, 1332 (Fed. Cir. 1998)) (emphasis added).

[375]Given the district court's claim construction, which the Federal Circuit affirmed, *see Solvay II*, 742 F.3d at 1004-1005, there was no dispute that the process performed by the Honeywell engineers was the same as that developed by the RSCAC, and that the '817 patent claims read on that process. *See Solvay II,* 742 F.3d at 1002, 1005-1006.

[376]In her dissent, Judge Newman charged that "not even Honeywell made [the] argument" that the Russian invention was "made in this country." *Solvay II*, 742 F.3d at 1010 (Newman, J., dissenting). She contended that Honeywell never stated that its work in the United States was on behalf of the Russian inventors; this was "a postulate of the panel majority." *Solvay II*, 742 F.3d at 1010 (Newman, J., dissenting).

[377]Solvay v. Honeywell Int'l, Inc., 622 F.3d 1367 (Fed. Cir. 2010) ("*Solvay I*").

[378]*See Solvay I*, 622 F.3d at 1378-1379 (explaining that "Honeywell personnel could not qualify as "another inventor" under §102(g)(2) because they "did not conceive the invention of the '817 patent, but derived it from others," specifically, the RSCAC engineers who "first conceived the invention in Russia").

In the second appeal (*Solvay II*), the Federal Circuit majority agreed (as had the District of Delaware) with Honeywell's alternative argument that the RSCAC engineers were the §102(g)(2) "other inventors," and that the Honeywell engineers' performance of the claimed process in the United States, following the RSCAC inventors' instructions, inured to the benefit of the RSCAC inventors. In other words, the Russian inventors effectively made the invention in the United States under §102(g)(2) "by sending instructions to Honeywell personnel who used the instructions to reduce the invention to practice in this country."

The Federal Circuit majority determined that the Honeywell-RSCAC research agreement "confirm[ed] that the RSCAC authorized Honeywell to practice its invention in the United States and contemplated that Honeywell would do so." In exchange for compensation, information, and equipment from Honeywell, the RSCAC had agreed to produce HFC-245fa, develop production processes, and send Honeywell regular progress reports detailing the RSCAC's results. The Federal Circuit found that the Honeywell-RSCAC collaborative research arrangement paralleled that in *Kendall v. Searles*,[379] a 1949 CCPA decision:

> In *Kendall v. Searles*, 36 C.C.P.A. 1045, 173 F.2d 986, 992 (1949), as with Honeywell and the RSCAC, Fafnir and Westinghouse had a "joint program of development." The inventor, an official at Fafnir, conceived the invention and communicated his conception to Westinghouse, which conducted tests necessary to establish the inventor's reduction to practice and the priority of his invention. *Id.* at 991-92. Although it appears that the inventor did not have "anything to do with the tests conducted by Westinghouse," those tests were held to inure to his benefit. *Id.* at 992.[380]

Thus, the Federal Circuit's precedent refuted patentee Solvay's contention that an inventor must make an *express* request or directive to benefit from a third party's reduction to practice. "Authorization" by the inventor is enough, and the *Solvay II* majority considered that via the Honeywell-RSCAC collaborative research agreement, RSCAC had authorized Honeywell "to practice its invention in the United States and contemplated that Honeywell would do so."[381] The *Solvay II* majority observed that "[t]he RSCAC engineers gave Honeywell personnel the information they needed to perform the inventive process in this country in July 1994, and Honeywell relied on that information in so doing."[382]

[379]173 F.3d 986 (C.C.P.A. 1949).

[380]*Solvay II*, 742 F.3d at 1006 (quoting *Kendall*, 173 F.2d 986).

[381]*Solvay II*, 742 F.3d at 1006.

[382]*Solvay II*, 742 F.3d at 1007. *See also Solvay I*, 622 F.3d at 1374 (noting that "in early 1995, Honeywell replicated the Russian process *by following the information*

The fact that Honeywell in July 1996 applied for and later received its own U.S. patent on a "refined version" of the RSCAC process did not change this result.[383] The "mere filing of a related patent application does not in itself preclude inurement," the *Solvay II* majority held. Notably, the RSCAC inventors applied for and received a patent in Russia.[384] "The parties did not view these [patent] applications as rivals, providing that Honeywell was entitled to exclusive rights to inventions resulting from the collaboration while the Russians were entitled only to sublicenses."[385]

---

provided by RSCAC, thereby practicing the invention in the United States before the '817 patent's priority date") (emphasis added by Federal Circuit in *Solvay II*).

[383]*See Solvay II*, 742 F.3d at 1001 n.5 (citing Honeywell's U.S. Patent No. 5,763,706); *id.*, 742 F.3d at 1007.

[384]The RSCAC application ultimately issued as Russian Patent No. RU 2,065,430. Solvay, S.A. v. Honeywell Int'l Inc., 886 F. Supp. 2d 396, 400 (D. Del. 2012). Moreover, the Delaware jury determined that the Russian filing and patent amounted to a disclosure of the invention of claim 1 of the '817 patent such that the Russian inventors did not "abandon, suppress, or conceal" the invention under §102(g)(2). *See Solvay II*, 742 F.3d at 1002.

[385]*Solvay II*, 742 F.3d at 1007. Judge Newman dissented strenuously in *Solvay II*. She charged that the majority had "create[d] a new class of secret prior art, holding that a privately performed experiment, without publication or public knowledge or use or sale or inclusion in a United States patent application, is invalidating 'prior art.'" Judge Newman contended that Honeywell's evaluation of the Russian technology, placed in an unpublished Russian patent application, was "private secret activity." She observed that the issue in the case at bar was "not priority between the Russian invention and the Solvay invention; the issue [wa]s prior art against the world." *Solvay II*, 742 F.3d at 1008 (Newman, J., dissenting). The majority's decision contravened the law and policy that "inventors are charged only with knowledge of what is known or knowable as defined by statute, subject to special limited circumstances." *Solvay II*, 742 F.3d at 1008 (Newman, J., dissenting). In the case at bar, Honeywell's test of the Russian process was merely a "private experiment" which should not have been treated as prior art.

Further, Judge Newman specifically disagreed with the *Solvay II* majority's holding that "§102(g)(2) allows conception to occur in another country, but in such circumstances requires the work constituting the reduction to practice to be performed in the United States by or on behalf of the inventor." She observed, firstly, that the Federal Circuit "has never held than an invention conceived in a foreign country is "made in this country" under §102(g)(2)." *Solvay II*, 742 F.3d at 1010 (Newman, J., dissenting). Second, she disagreed that Honeywell's work was "by or on behalf of" the Russian inventors. "Honeywell never so stated; that is a postulate of the panel majority." *Solvay II*, 742 F.3d at 1010 (Newman, J., dissenting). The inurement cases relied on by the majority were inapplicable in Judge Newman's view, for they concerned priority contests (i.e., interferences) between conflicting U.S. patent applications under §102(g)(1), not whether a making of the invention was prior art against the world under §102(g)(2). Judge Newman charged that "[w]hether activity in the United States can support a foreign inventor's interference priority has no relation to whether that activity is prior art against the world." *Solvay II*, 742 F.3d at 1010 (Newman, J., dissenting).

d. *Section 102(g)(2) as Invalidity Defense*

As *Solvay II* (an appeal from an infringement/invalidity litigation in federal district court) illustrates, §102(g)(2) (2006)-based anticipation challenges are typically asserted in the patent litigation context. Accused infringers in lawsuits are more likely to have the strategic incentives and economic resources to investigate the invention date of potentially invalidating prior art inventions.[386] In contrast, §102(g)(2) rejections are rarely encountered in *ex parte* patent prosecution before the USPTO, because the agency generally does not know (or have the resources to investigate) when the invention *disclosed* in a cited prior art reference was actually *made*.[387]

e. *Expansion of the Role of §102(g)*

Although it was viewed by the drafters of the 1952 Act as a statute to authorize interferences,[388] our understanding of 35 U.S.C. §102(g) has expanded over time. The section was first recognized as a prior art provision for purposes of the USPTO's *ex parte* examination for obviousness in *In re Bass,*[389] an important case discussed in greater detail in Chapter 5 ("The Nonobviousness Requirement") of this text. Use of §102(g) (2006) prior invention in this manner (that is, as §102(g)(2)/§103 prior art) raises the same concerns about the use of "secret prior art" as when a claim is rejected for anticipation by the disclosure of the invention in another's earlier-filed U.S. patent or published application under 35 U.S.C. §102(e) (2006). However, the requirement of §102(g) that the prior invention not be "abandoned, suppressed, or concealed" injects an analogous "publicness" requirement into the statute that ameliorates the secrecy concern, in much the same way as the "issued or published" requirement of §102(e).

[386] *See, e.g.*, Amkor Tech., Inc. v. International Trade Commission, 692 F.3d 1250, 1256 (Fed. Cir. 2012) (holding that an oral communication in the United States of a foreign-made invention can qualify as §102(g)(2) patent-defeating prior art; "[w]hile this court's limited precedent on this issue establishes that writings *can* satisfy the full domestic disclosure requirement, the cases do not establish any per se requirement that such disclosure must be in writing."); Dow Chem. Co. v. Astro-Valcour Inc., 267 F.3d 1334 (Fed. Cir. 2001); Monsanto Co. v. Mycogen Plant Sci., Inc., 261 F.3d 1356 (Fed. Cir. 2001); Apotex USA, Inc. v. Merck & Co., Inc., 254 F.3d 1031 (Fed. Cir. 2001).

[387] *See* In re Bass, 474 F.2d 1276, 1286 n.7 (C.C.P.A. 1973). *Bass* is discussed in further detail under the heading "Section 102/103 Overlap" in Chapter 5 ("The Nonobviousness Requirement (35 U.S.C. §103)"), *infra*.

[388] *See* Paulik v. Rizkalla, 760 F.2d 1270, 1276-1279 (Fed. Cir. 1985) (*en banc*) (Rich, J., concurring) (detailing history of 35 U.S.C. §102(g)).

[389] 474 F.2d 1276 (C.C.P.A. 1973).

4. Applying the Priority Rule of §102(g)

Section 102(g) was amended by the American Inventors Protection Act (AIPA) of 1999 to expressly reflect the modern understanding that the section governs not only interference proceedings, but also anticipation, that is, uses of prior invention as a basis for USPTO rejections in *ex parte* prosecution or as a basis to challenge the validity of an issued patent in federal district court litigation. In all of these settings, the rather cryptic last sentence of §102(g) (2006) applies:

> In determining priority of invention under this subsection, there shall be considered not only the respective dates of conception and reduction to practice of the invention, but also the reasonable diligence of one who was first to conceive and last to reduce to practice, from a time prior to conception by the other.

The quoted statutory provision can be simplified and restated as the following rule for determining time-wise priority of invention:

> ***Generally,* the first to reduce to practice [who thereafter does not abandon, suppress, or conceal] is the first to invent, *unless* the last to reduce to practice is also the first to conceive and sufficiently diligent.**

Application of this rule, whether in *ex parte* prosecution, validity litigation, or a pre-AIA interference proceeding, requires understanding several important terms of art. The date of **conception** is the date at which there is the "formation in the mind of the inventor, of a definite and permanent idea of the complete and operative invention, as it is hereafter to be applied in practice."[390] A **reduction to practice** is either actual or constructive. An *actual* reduction to practice occurs when a physical embodiment of the invention has been constructed that works for its intended purpose.[391] A *constructive* reduction to practice occurs upon the filing of a patent application that satisfies the disclosure requirements of 35 U.S.C. §112, ¶1 (2006) for the invention claimed therein.[392] Reasonable **diligence** is proved by evidence that the inventor was continuously active in working toward a reduction to practice of the invention she conceived, or that a legitimate excuse exists for any inactivity during the relevant time period.[393]

[390] Coleman v. Dines, 754 F.2d 353, 359 (Fed. Cir. 1985).

[391] *See* Great Northern Corp. v. Davis Core & Pad Co., 782 F.2d 159, 165 (Fed. Cir. 1986).

[392] *See* Bigham v. Godtfredsen, 857 F.2d 1415, 1417 (Fed. Cir. 1988).

[393] *See* Griffith v. Kanamaru, 816 F.2d 624, 626 (Fed. Cir. 1987) (explaining that "Griffith must account for the entire period from just before Kanamaru's filing date until his reduction to practice"); *see also* Naber v. Cricchi, 567 F.2d 382, 385 n.5

With these definitions in hand, we can apply the time-wise priority rule to both the §102(g)(1) and the §102(g)(2) contexts. First consider the rule as applied in an interference setting involving Inventor A and Inventor B, both claiming to have made the same invention at about the same time. This is an application of 35 U.S.C. §102(g)(1) (2006).

Figure 4.5 illustrates two different applications of the time-wise priority rule in the pre-AIA interference setting under §102 (g)(1) (2006). Inventor A will be awarded priority in the interference if Inventor A reduced the invention to practice before Inventor B did, and did not thereafter abandon, suppress, or conceal it, as in Case 1 in Figure 4.5, *unless* Inventor B conceived the invention before Inventor A did and was diligent in working toward a reduction to practice during a time period from just before Inventor A's conception through to Inventor B's own reduction to practice (as illustrated in Case 2).

Note that the question whether Inventor A was diligent between her conception and reduction to practice dates is not relevant in Case 2; only B's diligence matters in this example. If we are going to award a patent to the later reducer, which means we are accepting a somewhat delayed completion and dissemination of the invention to the public, we will require that later reducer to have proceeded diligently toward her reduction to practice.

Alternatively, consider the time-wise priority rule as applied in a challenge to the validity of Inventor A's issued patent, raised by accused Infringer X in federal court as an affirmative defense to Inventor A's charge of patent infringement by X. Accused Infringer X may assert that a third party, Inventor B,[394] made the invention in the United States before Inventor A did, and that Inventor A's patent is therefore invalid under 35 U.S.C. §102(g)(2) (2006).[395] To prevail in

(C.C.P.A. 1977) (explaining that reasonable diligence requirement of §102(g) is founded on public policy that favors the early disclosure of inventions, similar to requirement that there be no unreasonable delay in filing patent application following an actual reduction to practice so as to avoid holding of suppression or concealment).

[394]Inventor B in this example is not a party to the validity litigation. Rather, evidence of Inventor B's acts is being relied on by the accused Infringer X as prior art to invalidate the patent in suit. Inventor B need not have obtained a patent on the invention, so long as she took other steps to publicize the invention or otherwise bring knowledge of it to the public (e.g., through commercialization) within a reasonable time after completing it. *See* Apotex USA, Inc. v. Merck & Co., Inc., 254 F.3d 1031 (Fed. Cir. 2001) (unpatented prior invention by accused infringer/validity challenger Merck held not to have been suppressed or concealed under §102(g)); Int'l Glass Co. v. United States, 408 F.2d 395, 403 (Ct. Cl. 1969) (unpatented prior invention by third party McDonnell Douglas held to have been suppressed or concealed under §102(g)).

[395]This theory was successful in *Monsanto Co. v. Mycogen Plant Science, Inc.*, 261 F.3d 1356 (Fed. Cir. 2001). For criticism of the Federal Circuit's refusal in *Monsanto* to adopt a "particularized testimony"/"linking argument" requirement for invalidity

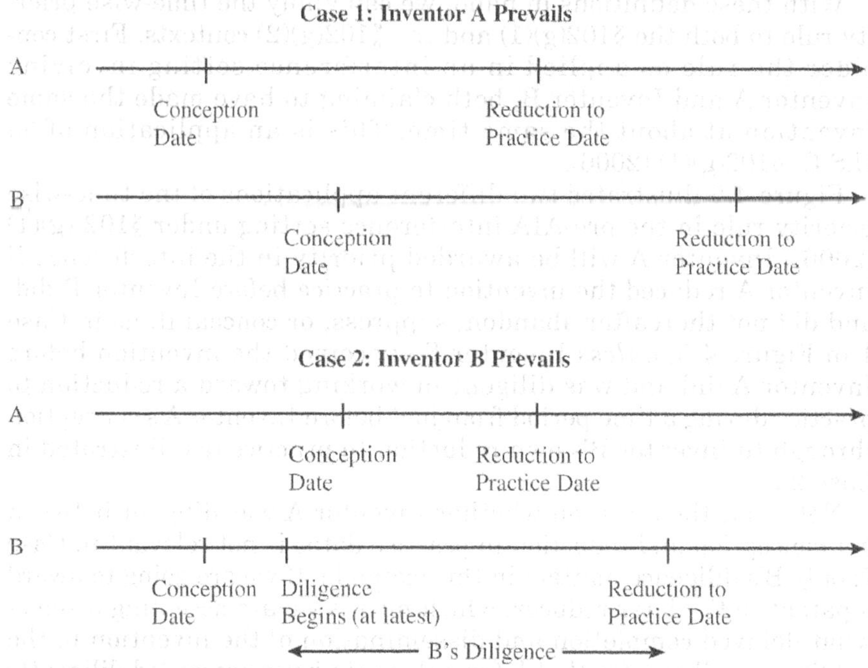

Figure 4.5

Illustrations of the U.S. Traditional Rule of Time-Wise Priority Under 35 U.S.C. §102(g) (2006) in an Interference Setting (Inventor A vs. Inventor B)

this defense, accused Infringer X must establish either (1) that Inventor B reduced the invention to practice before Inventor A and did not thereafter abandon, suppress, or conceal the invention; or (2) that Inventor B conceived the invention before Inventor A and was sufficiently diligent in working toward a reduction to practice of the invention throughout a time period that began just before Inventor A's conception date and ended with Inventor B's own reduction to practice date.[396]

---

defenses litigated in jury trials, *see* Janice M. Mueller, *At Sea in a Black Box: Charting a Clearer Course for Juries Through the Perilous Straits of Patent Invalidity*, 1 J. MARSHALL REV. INTELL. PROP. L. 3 (2001), *available at* repository.jmls.edu/cgl/viewcontent.cgi?article=1001&context=ripl.

[396]See *Monsanto*, 261 F.3d at 1361-1362, 1362-1363; Mahurkar v. C.R. Bard, Inc., 79 F.3d 1572, 1577 (Fed. Cir. 1996).

O. Antedating (or "Swearing Behind") Prior Art (Pre-AIA)

The same traditional first-to-invent principle underlying §102(g) (2006) is the basis for a procedure used in *ex parte* patent prosecution to antedate (i.e., predate or "swear behind") certain categories of prior art references.[397] Recall that the USPTO will assume that an application's filing date is the applicant's invention date, based on the theory that filing an application that satisfies the disclosure requirements of §112 for the subject matter claimed therein represents a constructive reduction to practice of that subject matter. (Moreover, patent applicants do not typically disclose dates of conception and/or actual reduction to practice in their initial application filings.) If the USPTO examiner locates a §102(a) (2006) or §102(e) (2006) reference that describes the identical invention in an enabling manner and has an effective date earlier than the applicant's filing date, such reference is presumptively anticipatory. The existence of the reference's disclosure, prior to the applicant's presumptive invention date, is inconsistent with the idea that the applicant was first to invent it.

In order to eliminate the cited reference as prior art, the patent applicant must show that she invented the subject matter of the rejected claim(s) prior to the effective date of the reference. In other words, the applicant must show that she, rather than the author of the reference, was the first to invent the claimed subject matter. Although the antedating procedure is not an interference (which is a contest between two or more applicants for patent), antedating can be conceptualized as a "quasi-interference" between the patent applicant and the reference she seeks to eliminate as prior art.

The mechanics of antedating a prior art reference are governed by 37 C.F.R. §1.131 (Rule 131). A patent applicant antedates a §102(a) or §102(e) reference by filing an appropriate affidavit or declaration to establish that she invented the subject matter of her rejected claim(s) prior to the effective date of the reference cited by the USPTO examiner.[398] The showing of facts in the affidavit or declaration must establish either (1) an actual reduction to practice of the invention prior to the effective date of the reference, or (2) conception of the invention prior to the effective date of the reference coupled with due diligence from just prior to that effective date until a subsequent

[397]There is no antedating under the first-to-file system of the America Invents Act of 2011 for applications filed on or after March 16, 2013 because the AIA eliminated the concept of invention dates.

[398]*See* 37 C.F.R. §1.131(a).

actual reduction to practice date or to the filing date of the patent application.[399]

The antedating procedure of Rule 131 cannot be used to overcome a statutory bar reference, such as a printed publication under 35 U.S.C. §102(b) (2006).[400] This reflects the policy of encouraging prompt filing of patent applications on novel inventions. Nor can antedating be used where the prior art reference is a U.S. patent or published patent application of another that *claims* the same patentable invention. In such a case the basis of the rejection would be 35 U.S.C. §102(g)(1) (2006), and the applicant may suggest an interference.[401] Lastly,

[399]*See* 37 C.F.R. §1.131(b). The case of *In re Steed*, 802 F.3d 1311 (Fed. Cir. 2015), illustrates an unsuccessful attempt to swear behind a reference (and a Federal Circuit decision reviewing that attempt several years after the fact). Inventors Steed et al. (collectively "Steed") filed an application directed to a "web integrated debt records and debt collection system that can be accessed and operated across the Internet by a variety of users in a variety of user roles." Steed claimed priority to a provisional filing date of November 13, 2003. The USPTO rejected the Steed application claims as obvious in view of the "Evans" reference (either alone or in combination with other references). Evans had an effective date of December 23, 2002. After failing to change the agency's view on the merits of the obviousness rejection, Steed attempted but failed to antedate and thus remove the Evans reference under 37 C.F.R. §1.131. Steed argued both that (1) he had actually reduced his claimed invention to practice prior to Evans' effective date, and that (2) he had conceived his invention prior to Evans' effective date and was thereafter duly diligent in proceeding to his (Steed's) application filing date.

The USPTO rejected Steed's argument based primarily on the inadequacy of Steed's documentary evidence (a declaration and exhibits). For example, as to conception, an examiner found that "the evidence relied on . . . was 'a high level presentation that does not include any specifics of the actual invention, only a broad overview of the idea' and that it 'fail[ed] to disclose any of the key elements of independent claim 37.'" *Steed*, 802 F.3d at 1314 (quoting Office Action).

After the USPTO Board affirmed the examiner, the Federal Circuit affirmed the Board on the Rule 131 issue, observing that

> [t]he Board found that the exhibits did not provide information sufficient to establish that the inventors conceived the claimed invention before the Evans date, or to establish diligence to reduction to practice. *See* MPEP §715.07(a) (Feb. 2003) ("Under 37 C.F.R. §1.131(a), the critical period in which diligence must be shown begins just prior to the effective date of the reference or activity and ends with the date of a reduction to practice, either actual or constructive."). Although the claimed invention is a method conducted by computer software, this does not avoid the need for *sufficient evidentiary specificity*.

Steed, 802 F.3d at 1320 (emphasis added). In short, Steed had failed to "establish possession of the invention described and claimed in [his] Application before the effective date of the Evans reference." *Steed*, 802 F.3d at 1321. Because Steed had failed to remove Evans as a reference under Rule 131, and was also unable to convince the Federal Circuit that the USPTO was wrong in entering its obviousness rejection based on Evans, Steed lost the appeal. The Circuit concluded that "[i]n the absence of a reasonable showing that the Examiner and the Board erred in deeming the Steed system obvious in view of the Evans Rejections, the rejection must be sustained." *Steed*, 802 F.3d at 1321.

[400]*See* 37 C.F.R. §1.131(a)(2).

[401]*See id.* §1.131(a)(1).

although citation by the USPTO of evidence of another's making of the same invention in this country under §102(g)(2) (2006) is rare, if such a rejection was entered the applicant could not overcome it by the Rule 131 antedating procedure. This is because

> subject matter which is available under 35 U.S.C. 102(g) by definition must have been made before the applicant made his or her invention. By contrast, references under 35 U.S.C. 102(a) and (e), for example, merely establish a presumption that their subject matter was made before applicant's invention date. It is this presumption which may be rebutted by evidence submitted under 37 C.F.R. 1.131.[402]

Part III: Novelty and Priority Post-America Invents Act of 2011

P. Introduction

This part of the chapter covers novelty, the definition of prior art, and priority[403] as those topics are defined and analyzed under the Patent Act (35 U.S.C.) as amended by §3 ("First inventor to file") of the Leahy-Smith America Invents Act of 2011 (AIA).[404] As detailed below, §3 of the AIA rewrote 35 U.S.C. §102 in its entirety. Generally speaking, the new rules implemented by the AIA §3 amendments apply to

[402] UNITED STATES PATENT AND TRADEMARK OFFICE, MANUAL OF PATENT EXAMINING PROCEDURE §715(II)(I) (8th ed., rev. July 2010).

[403] The word "priority" in this chapter refers to priority as between two (or more) U.S. patent applicants. If each of multiple inventors independently invents the same invention and files his or her own patent application in the USPTO, which inventor/applicant will be awarded the patent? The AIA generally awards the patent to the first inventor *to file* her patent application. *See* 35 U.S.C. 102(a)(2) (eff. Mar. 16, 2013); *see also infra* Section S.3 ("Post-AIA 35 U.S.C. §102(b)(2): Shields Against Post-AIA §102(a)(2) Presumptively Novelty-Destroying Events").

The AIA recognizes significant exceptions to the first-inventor-to-file rule, however. Notably, a second (i.e., later in time) filer will obtain the patent if the second filer had publicly disclosed the invention before the first filer's effective filing date and thereafter files her own (i.e., the second filer's) application in a timely fashion. *See* 35 U.S.C. §102(b)(2)(B) (eff. Mar. 16, 2013); *see also infra* Section S.3 ("Post-AIA §102(b)(2): Shields Against Post-AIA §102(a)(2) Presumptively Novelty-Destroying Events").

[404] Leahy-Smith America Invents Act, Pub. L. No. 112-29 (H.R. 1249), 125 Stat. 284 (Sept. 16, 2011).

For comprehensive overviews of the entire AIA, *see* Robert A. Armitage, *Understanding the America Invents Act and Its Implications for Patenting*, 40 AM. INTELLECTUAL PROP. L. Q.J. 1, 1-133 (Winter 2012); Donald S. Chisum, *America Invents Act of 2011: Analysis and Cross-References* (Dec. 5, 2011), *available at* http://www.chisum.com/wp-content/uploads/AIAOverview.pdf. *See also* Robert P. Merges, *Priority and Novelty Under the AIA* (Aug. 15, 2012), *available at* papers.ssrn.com/sol3/papers.cfm?abstract_id=2130209.

U.S. patent applications filed on or after March 16, 2013.[405] If patents issuing from such applications are challenged in federal court litigation or in USPTO post-grant review, their validity will be assessed under the post-AIA regime.[406]

Because the AIA §3 ("First inventor to file") changes are just beginning to take effect as of this edition's preparation (2019), few Federal Circuit decisions are yet available to interpret the section's many points of ambiguity. Clarification must wait for disputes to work their way through the courts, although some ambiguities will likely be resolved through the implementation of USPTO rules or, perhaps, congressional "clean-up" amendments to the AIA.[407] Thus, this part of the

[405]*See* Leahy-Smith America Invents Act, Pub. L. No. 112-29 (H.R. 1249), §3(n) ("Effective Date"), 125 Stat. 284, 293 (2011).

[406]Importantly, patents issuing from applications filed *before* the AIA §3 effective date of March 16, 2013, continue to be litigated under pre-AIA rules. *See supra* Part II. As of the March 16, 2013 implementation date of first-to-file, it was highly probable that more than 2 million U.S. patents were already in force. *See* World Intellectual Property Organization, 2011 World Intellectual Property Indicators 197 (Table P2: Patent grants by office and origin, and patents in force, 2010) (reporting 2,017,318 U.S. patents in force as of 2009). The enforceable life of a U.S. patent can (in theory) run as long as 20 years, and a patent's validity can be challenged by an accused infringer in federal court litigation (potentially involving long-running trial and appeal) throughout that period. Thus for 30 years or more following the AIA's enactment, the pre-AIA version of the Patent Act addressed *supra* in Part II of this chapter will continue to be relevant.

[407]In early 2013, Congress passed a "technical corrections" bill to implement certain fixes to the AIA. *See* Leahy-Smith America Invents Technical Corrections Act, Pub. L. No. 112-274, 126 Stat. 2456 (Jan. 14, 2013) (TCA). The TCA was intended to "correct and improve certain provisions of the Leahy-Smith America Invents Act and title 35, United States Code." 126 Stat. at 2456. In December 2012, the USPTO described the proposed legislation (then at the House bill stage) as follows:

> While the 112th Congress will be focusing much of its attention on more prominent issues before it adjourns, a "technical corrections" bill to amend provisions of the Leahy-Smith America Invents Act (AIA) passed the House this past Tuesday and is now being considered by the Senate. Even though the USPTO has not yet completed issuance and implementation of all the various rules mandated by the act, stakeholders and the USPTO have identified corrections, clarifications, and improvements to the law that require congressional action.
>
> The bill, H.R. 6621, makes a number of corrections and improvements to patent law which have been identified as necessary or advisable during the public reviews of proposed rulemaking, as well as discussions and consultations that occurred during the past year. The proposed changes include amendments to specify effective dates where they were omitted; correcting drafting errors and omissions; fixing "dead zones" that inadvertently make it impossible to seek Post Grant Review (PGR) or *Inter Partes* Review (IPR) during certain time periods; clarifying patent term adjustments prospectively; eliminating unnecessary limits on who may file an international application designating the United States; clarifying patent and trademark fee management issues; and clarifying when a derivation proceeding can be instituted. The bill also includes provisions that better coordinate the terms of Patent Public Advisory Committee (PPAC) and

chapter is limited primarily to analyzing the as-enacted text of §3 of the legislation and its legislative history. It offers a number of hypotheticals to illustrate and explore the operation of the statutory text. Later editions of this text will add discussion of new judicial decisions and agency rules that interpret and apply the AIA provisions.[408]

Section 3 of the AIA introduced landmark changes to U.S. patent law.[409] Those changes include redefining what counts as prior art by expanding the 35 U.S.C. §102 categories of novelty-destroying events and removing all prior geographic limitations; altering the date on which novelty is assessed so as to focus on the effective filing date of

---

> Trademark Public Advisory Committee (TPAC) members — to address issues that have been discussed in those bodies in recent years and highlighted due to the additional responsibilities for PPAC required by the AIA related to Section 10 fee setting authority. Finally, the bill also requires the USPTO to report on the handling of pre-1995, pre-Uruguay Round applications that have now been pending for more than a decade and a half.
>
> This bill does not address one issue related to the estoppel standard for possible federal court litigation following the completion of a post-grant review proceeding. Clarity is needed to ensure that the provision functions as Congress intended and I am hopeful it will be addressed in a future bill in the next Congress.

Dana Colarulli, Director, Office of Governmental Affairs, U.S. Patent and Trademark Office, *Congress Acts on AIA Corrections Bill* (Dec. 20, 2012), http://www.uspto.gov/blog/director/entry/congress_acts_on_aia_corrections. *See also* Courtenay C. Brinckerhoff, *A Look at the Technical Amendments to the America Invents Act (AIA) Made by HR 6621* (Feb. 7, 2013), http://www.pharmapatentsblog.com/2013/02/07/a-look-at-the-technical-amendments-to-the-america-invents-act-in-hr-6621 (summarizing (1) changes relating to patent prosecution, including inventor's oath/declaration and U.S. national stage applications; (2) changes relating to patent trials, including IPRs, derivation proceedings, and interference proceedings; (3) changes relating to litigation, including advice of counsel; and (4) changes relating to patent term adjustment); Dennis Crouch, *AIA Technical Amendment Becomes Law* (Jan. 15, 2013), http://patentlyo.com/patent/2013/01/aia-technical-amendment-becomes-law.html.

[408]The USPTO issued proposed rules and proposed examination guidelines for implementing the first-inventor-to-file provisions of the AIA in July 2012. The proposed rules and guidelines also address the agency's interpretation of what qualifies as prior art under the post-AIA versions of 35 U.S.C. §§102 and 103 (eff. Mar. 16, 2013). *See* United States Patent & Trademark Office, *Notice of Proposed Rulemaking: Changes to Implement the First Inventor to File Provisions of the Leahy-Smith America Invents Act*, 77 FED. REG. 43742 (July 26, 2012) (proposed rules), *available at* http://www.uspto.gov/aia_implementation/first-inventor-to-file_proposed_rules.pdf; United States Patent & Trademark Office, *Request for Comments: Examination Guidelines for Implementing the First-Inventor-to-File Provisions of the Leahy-Smith America Invents Act*, 77 FED. REG. 43759 (July 26, 2012) (proposed examination guidelines), *available at* http://www.uspto.gov/aia_implementation/first-inventor-to-file_proposed_examination_guidelines.pdf.

[409]*See generally* Joe Matal, *A Guide to the Legislative History of the America Invents Act: Part I of II*, 21 FED. CIR. B.J. 435, 449 (2012) (stating that "[n]o part of the AIA is more significant, nor has generated more legislative discussion and debate, than the Act's changes to §102").

the application or claim in question rather than the invention date; and switching the United States from its traditional first-to-invent priority system to a unique first-inventor-to-file system (a hybrid of the European first-to-file regime and certain prior art exclusions based on the traditional U.S. pre–filing grace period of 35 U.S.C. §102(b) (pre-AIA).

These §3 AIA changes generally apply to patent applications filed *on or after March 16, 2013*.[410] Critically, the changes do *not* apply to the over two million U.S. patents that were already in force on March 16, 2013,[411] or to pending patent applications filed before March 16, 2013 (or patents issuing therefrom). For decades to come, the pre-AIA version of the Patent Act (as addressed in Part II of this chapter and in other chapters of this text) will continue to apply to millions of U.S. patents and applications. The practical result of the AIA's framework for implementing the first-inventor-to-file system and associated changes to novelty and prior art is that the U.S. patent system will operate under a dual regime (encompassing both "pre-AIA" and "post-AIA" rules) for 30 years or more following the AIA's September 2011 enactment.

To ensure clarity and demarcation between the "old" and "new" systems, this part of the chapter separately analyzes the AIA-implemented changes pertaining to novelty, prior art, and priority. Part II of this chapter addressed the issues of novelty, loss of right (i.e., "statutory bars"), and priority between rival inventors as those issues are determined under the pre-AIA regime. That regime is based on the United States' historic first-to-invent priority system.

A most unfortunate aspect of the AIA is that Congress entirely rewrote key statutory provisions of the Patent Act without renumbering many of the statutory sections in Title 35, U.S.C. To maintain clarity and demarcation between old and new versions, citations by this text to the pre-AIA version of the patent statute (in particular, those analyzed in Part II, *supra*) typically will take the form "35 U.S.C. §102(x) (pre-AIA)" or "35 U.S.C. §102(x) (2006)."[412] In contrast, the

[410]*See* Leahy-Smith America Invents Act, Pub. L. No. 112-29 (H.R. 1249), §3(n) ("Effective Date"), 125 Stat. 284, 293 (2011). *See also infra* Section T ("Effective Date for AIA §3 'First Inventor to File' Amendments").

[411]*See* World Intellectual Property Organization, 2011 World Intellectual Property Indicators 197, tbl. P2 ("Patent grants by office and origin, and patents in force, 2010") (reporting 2,017,318 U.S. patents in force as of 2009).

[412]The America Invents Act (AIA) was signed into law on September 16, 2011. Before that date, the most recent main edition of the official *United States Code*, including the Patent Act at Title 35 U.S.C., was published in 2006. This text will generally follow the citation conventions of *The Bluebook: A Uniform System of Citation* (19th ed. 2010). Bluebook Rule 12.3.2 provides that "[w]hen citing a bound volume of the current official or unofficial code, provide parenthetically the year that appears on the spine of the volume. . . ." At the AIA's enactment in September 2011, the "spine" date of the most

citations by this text to the patent statute, post-AIA implementation (in particular, those analyzed in this part of the chapter) will take the form "35 U.S.C. §102(x) (post-AIA)" or "35 U.S.C. §102(x) (eff. Mar. 16, 2013)." For shorthand purposes, sections of the Patent Act will sometimes be referred to herein as "post-AIA §102," meaning 35 U.S.C. §102 in the form that took effect on March 16, 2013.

1. Statutory Basis

As amended by §3 ("First inventor to file") of the Leahy-Smith America Invents Act of 2011 (AIA),[413] §102 of the U.S. Patent Act (35 U.S.C.) provides:

§102. Conditions for patentability; novelty

(a) NOVELTY; PRIOR ART. — A person shall be entitled to a patent unless —

(1) the claimed invention was patented, described in a printed publication, or in public use, on sale, or otherwise available to the public before the effective filing date of the claimed invention; or

(2) the claimed invention was described in a patent issued under section 151, or in an application for patent published or deemed published under section 122(b), in which the patent or application, as the case may be, names another inventor and was effectively filed before the effective filing date of the claimed invention.

(b) EXCEPTIONS. —

(1) DISCLOSURES MADE 1 YEAR OR LESS BEFORE THE EFFECTIVE FILING DATE OF THE CLAIMED INVENTION. — A disclosure made 1 year or less before the effective filing date of a claimed invention shall not be prior art to the claimed invention under subsection (a)(1) if —

(A) the disclosure was made by the inventor or joint inventor or by another who obtained the subject matter disclosed directly or indirectly from the inventor or a joint inventor; or

(B) the subject matter disclosed had, before such disclosure, been publicly disclosed by the inventor or a joint inventor or another who

---

recent main edition of 35 U.S.C. was 2006. Therefore, pre-AIA code provisions are generally cited herein as "35 U.S.C. §X (2006)."

This citation convention has also been adopted by the Federal Circuit. *See, e.g.*, Kennametal, Inc. v. Ingersoll Cutting Tool Co., 780 F.3d 1376, 1381 (Fed. Cir. 2015) (citing to "35 U.S.C. §102(b) (2006)"); *id.* at 1381 n.3 (explaining that "[t]his provision has since been amended. *See* Leahy-Smith America Invents Act ("AIA"), Pub. L. No. 112-29, §3(c), 125 Stat. 284, 287 (2011). However, because the pending claims have an effective filing date before March 16, 2013, the pre-AIA §102(b) applies. *See* AIA, 125 Stat. at 293; In re Giannelli, 739 F.3d 1375, 1376 n.1 (Fed. Cir. 2014).").

[413]*See* Leahy-Smith America Invents Act, Pub. L. No. 112-29 (H.R. 1249), §3(b)(1), 125 Stat. 284, 285-287 (Sept. 16, 2011) ("First Inventor to File — Conditions for Patentability — In General").

obtained the subject matter disclosed directly or indirectly from the inventor or a joint inventor.

(2) DISCLOSURES APPEARING IN APPLICATIONS AND PATENTS. — A disclosure shall not be prior art to a claimed invention under subsection (a)(2) if—

(A) the subject matter disclosed was obtained directly or indirectly from the inventor or a joint inventor;

(B) the subject matter disclosed had, before such subject matter was effectively filed under subsection (a)(2), been publicly disclosed by the inventor or a joint inventor or another who obtained the subject matter disclosed directly or indirectly from the inventor or a joint inventor; or

(C) the subject matter disclosed and the claimed invention, not later than the effective filing date of the claimed invention, were owned by the same person or subject to an obligation of assignment to the same person.

(c) COMMON OWNERSHIP UNDER JOINT RESEARCH AGREEMENTS. — Subject matter disclosed and a claimed invention shall be deemed to have been owned by the same person or subject to an obligation of assignment to the same person in applying the provisions of subsection (b)(2)(C) if—

(1) the subject matter disclosed was developed and the claimed invention was made by, or on behalf of, 1 or more parties to a joint research agreement that was in effect on or before the effective filing date of the claimed invention;

(2) the claimed invention was made as a result of activities undertaken within the scope of the joint research agreement; and

(3) the application for patent for the claimed invention discloses or is amended to disclose the names of the parties to the joint research agreement.

(d) PATENTS AND PUBLISHED APPLICATIONS EFFECTIVE AS PRIOR ART. — For purposes of determining whether a patent or application for patent is prior art to a claimed invention under subsection (a)(2), such patent or application shall be considered to have been effectively filed, with respect to any subject matter described in the patent or application —

(1) if paragraph (2) does not apply, as of the actual filing date of the patent or the application for patent; or

(2) if the patent or application for patent is entitled to claim a right of priority under section 119, 365(a), 365(b), 386(a), or 386(b), or to claim the benefit of an earlier filing date under section 120, 121, 365(c), or 386(c), based upon 1 or more prior filed applications for patent, as of the filing date of the earliest such application that describes the subject matter.[414]

[414] 35 U.S.C. §102 (effective Mar. 16, 2013) (subparagraph indenting added for clarity). Subsection (d)(2) of 35 U.S.C. as quoted above was further amended post-AIA pursuant to the Patent Law Treaties Implementation Act of 2012, Pub. L. No. 112-211, Title I, §102(2), 126 Stat. 1531 (Dec. 18, 2012) (hereafter PLTIA). The PLTIA implemented the provisions of the Hague Agreement and the Patent Law Treaty. In particular,

Generally speaking, this "post-AIA" version of 35 U.S.C. §102 took effect on March 16, 2013, for patent applications filed on or after that date.[415] Each of the §102 statutory subsections is separately discussed below.

2. Sense of Congress and Legislative History

Relevant to interpretation of the amended 35 U.S.C. §102 are two "sense of Congress" provisions included in §3 of the AIA. These provide:

> (o) SENSE OF CONGRESS. — It is the sense of the Congress that converting the United States patent system from "first to invent" to a system of "first inventor to file" will promote the progress of science and the useful arts by securing for limited times to inventors the exclusive rights to their discoveries and provide inventors with greater certainty regarding the scope of protection provided by the grant of exclusive rights to their discoveries.
>
> (p) SENSE OF CONGRESS. — It is the sense of the Congress that converting the United States patent system from "first to invent" to a system of "first inventor to file" will improve the United States patent system and promote harmonization of the United States patent system with the patent systems commonly used in nearly all other countries throughout the world with whom the United States conducts trade and thereby promote greater international uniformity and certainty in the procedures used for securing the exclusive rights of inventors to their discoveries.[416]

---

the PLTIA added a new Part V to 35 U.S.C. titled "The Hague Agreement Concerning International Registration of Industrial Designs." Section 102 ("Conforming Amendments"), subsection (2) of the PLTIA amended 35 U.S.C. §102 "in section 102(d)(2) (as amended by the Leahy-Smith America Invents Act (Public Law 112-29; 125 Stat. 284)), by striking 'to claim a right of priority under section 119, 365(a), or 365(b), or to claim the benefit of an earlier filing date under section 120, 121, or 365(c)' and inserting 'to claim a right of priority under section 119, 365(a), 365(b), 386(a), or 386(b), or to claim the benefit of an earlier filing date under section 120, 121, 365(c), or 386(c)'"). The amendments made by the PLTIA took effect "on the later of— (1) the date that is 1 year after the date of the enactment of this Act [Dec. 18, 2012]; or (2) the date of entry into force of the treaty with respect to the United States." PLTIA §103(a). "The Hague Agreement Concerning International Registration of Industrial Designs as set forth in Title I of the PLTIA [wa]s effective as of May 13, 2015; the Patent Law Treaty (PLT) Implementation as set forth in Title II of the PLTIA [wa]s effective as of December 13, 2013." U.S. Patent & Trademark Office, *Consolidated Patent Laws — May 2015 Update*, http://www.uspto.gov/web/offices/pac/mpep/consolidated_laws.pdf (Editor's Note).

[415] *See infra* Section T ("Effective Date for AIA §3 'First Inventor to File' Amendments").

[416] Leahy-Smith America Invents Act, Pub. L. No. 112-29 (H.R. 1249), §3(o)-(p), 125 Stat. 284, 293 (2011).

Although Congress's stated intent of "provid[ing] inventors with greater certainty regarding the scope of protection"[417] provided by patents is laudable, it is not clear that the AIA will actually achieve this goal. The post-AIA version of 35 U.S.C. §102, for example, is just as complicated and riddled with ambiguity (if not more so) than its pre-AIA counterpart. The Byzantine wording of post-AIA §102 stands in sharp contrast to the straightforward manner in which other countries define patentable novelty (viz., the European Patent Convention's streamlined Article 54[418]).

Moreover, although Congress speaks of promoting harmonization between the U.S. patent system and foreign patent systems,[419] it is not clear that the AIA achieves this goal either. As described below, §3 of the AIA did not implement a European-style system of first to file with absolute novelty. Rather, the post-AIA version of §102 puts into place a unique hybrid system that preserves many aspects of the pre-AIA grace period found in 35 U.S.C. §102(b) (2006). Instead of a true first-to-file system, the AIA created what is better described (at least in some circumstances) as a "first inventor to disclose" system.[420]

The two "sense of Congress" provisions quoted above are an explicit part of the AIA's text.[421] In addition, a wealth of potentially relevant legislative history exists to inform interpretation of the first-inventor-to-file provisions of the AIA. Such legislative history includes the House Judiciary Committee's report on H.R. 1249,[422] as well as remarks by members of Congress during debates on the floors of the House and Senate.[423]

[417]Leahy-Smith America Invents Act, Pub. L. No. 112-29 (H.R. 1249), §3(o), 125 Stat. 284, 293 (2011).

[418]European Patent Convention art. 54(1), Oct. 5, 1973, *available at* epo.org/law-practice/legal-texts/html/epc/2016/e/ar54:html ("An invention shall be considered to be new if it does not form part of the state of the art."); *id.* at art. 54(2) ("The state of the art shall be held to comprise everything made available to the public by means of a written or oral description, by use, or in any other way, before the date of filing of the European patent application.").

[419]Leahy-Smith America Invents Act, Pub. L. No. 112-29 (H.R. 1249), §3(p), 125 Stat. 284, 293 (2011).

[420]*See* 35 U.S.C. §102(b)(1)(B), 102(b)(2)(B) (eff. Mar. 16, 2013); *see also infra* Section S ("Novelty-Preserving Exceptions Under Post-AIA 35 U.S.C. §102(b)").

[421]As such, they are likely entitled to greater weight than legislative history.

[422]H.R. Rep. No. 112-98 [House Judiciary Comm. Rep. on the America Invents Act] (June 1, 2011).

[423]The U.S. Patent and Trademark Office (USPTO) has compiled a comprehensive collection of AIA legislative history in electronic form. *See* USPTO, *AIA Resources,* www.uspto.gov/patent/laws-and-regulations/america-invents-act-aia/resources (last modified Oct. 17, 2013). *See also* Joe Matal, *A Guide to the Legislative History of the America Invents Act: Part I of II,* 21 Fed. Cir. B.J. 435 (2012) (providing "a guide to legislative materials that may be useful to practitioners who are required to understand and construe the [AIA]," authored by Judiciary Committee Counsel to Senator Jon Kyl).

3. Comparing Pre- and Post-AIA Frameworks

As amended by the AIA, 35 U.S.C. §102(a) (eff. Mar. 16, 2013) (hereafter "post-AIA §102(a)" or simply "§102(a)") enumerates six types of novelty-destroying events. These events make up the catalog or universe of "prior art" for purposes of analyzing an invention's novelty[424] and/or its nonobviousness.[425]

The preamble language of post-AIA §102(a) provides that "[a] person shall be entitled to a patent unless. . . ." This language, carried over from the pre-AIA version of §102, indicates that the initial burden of disproving novelty during examination of a patent application continues to rest with the government — the USPTO.[426]

To establish that novelty of a claimed invention has been destroyed — in other words, that a patent is not available because prior art anticipates the claimed invention — the statute requires that the USPTO establish that before the effective filing date of the claimed invention,[427] the invention was already (1) "patented," (2) "described

[424] *See* 35 U.S.C. §102(a) (eff. Mar. 16, 2013) ("Novelty; Prior Art"); *see also supra* Part I, Section B ("Burden of Proof") (stating that "[i]t is therefore helpful to consider 35 U.S.C. §102 as the catalog or universe of prior art that potentially can be cited by the USPTO in rejecting a patent applicant's claims. If a patent, journal article, or other document or event is indicated by the USPTO to be prior art, it must qualify under some subsection of 35 U.S.C. §102. If it does not, then the document or event is not legally available for use as prior art to negate the presumed novelty of the applicant's claimed invention. The same is true in a litigation context, where an issued patent's validity is being challenged.").

[425] *See* 35 U.S.C. §103 (eff. Mar. 16, 2013) ("Conditions for patentability; non-obvious subject matter"); *see also infra* Chapter 5, Section F.3.a ("Section 102/103 Overlap: Overview") (explaining that §102 can be conceptualized as a catalog of the varieties of information (e.g., documents and events) that may potentially qualify as prior art for §103 purposes). In other words, any reference relied on in determining nonobviousness must first qualify as prior art under one or more subsections of §102 (except that the strict identity rule for anticipation would not be satisfied in the obviousness context). As explained by a co-author of the 1952 Patent Act, "[t]he antecedent of the words 'the prior art'. . . lies in the phrase 'disclosed or described as set forth in Section 102' and hence these words refer to the material specified in Section 102 as the basis for comparison." P.J. Federico, *Commentary on the New Patent Act*, 35 U.S.C.A. §1 (1954 ed., discontinued in subsequent volumes), *reprinted at* 75 J. PAT. & TRADEMARK OFF. SOC'Y 161 (1993). *See also* In re Wertheim, 646 F.2d 527, 532 (C.C.P.A. 1981) (Rich, J.) (quoting Federico's *Commentary* on this point). The requirement that prior art be "analogous" is an additional filter applied to prior art for use in a §103 nonobviousness analysis. *See infra* Chapter 5, Section F.4 ("Analogous Art").

[426] *See supra* Part I, Section B ("Burden of Proof").

[427] Although the phrase has long been used by patent practitioners and the USPTO, the AIA for the first time added to the Patent Act an explicit definition of "effective filing date." Subparagraph (2) of §3(a) ("Definitions") of the AIA adds the following definition to 35 U.S.C. §100:

> (i) (1) The term "effective filing date" for a claimed invention in a patent or application for patent means —

in a printed publication," (3) "in public use," (4) "on sale," (5) "otherwise available to the public," or (6) described in a U.S. patent or published patent application naming another inventor. Each of these six novelty-destroying events is discussed in further detail below.

The AIA is not absolute in its requirement for novelty as of a claimed invention's effective filing date. The occurrence of any of the six §102(a) events before the effective filing date presumptively destroys novelty (i.e., anticipates the invention, assuming that the strict identity standard for anticipation is satisfied[428]). The claimed invention's novelty nevertheless may be preserved (in other words, the presumptively established §102(a) prior art may be removed) if one of the "exceptions" or shields of 35 U.S.C. §102(b) (eff. Mar. 16, 2013) (hereafter "post-AIA §102(b)" or simply "§102(b)") applies.

The post-AIA §102(b) exceptions are discussed separately below.[429] Very generally, the §102(b) exceptions operate in somewhat analogous fashion to "grace period" events under the pre-AIA regime.[430] Hence the post-AIA U.S. Patent Act is not a European-style "absolute novelty" system, despite Congress's stated intent to "promote harmonization of the United States patent system with the patent systems commonly used in nearly all other countries throughout the world with whom the United States conducts trade and thereby promote greater international uniformity and certainty in the procedures used for securing the exclusive rights of inventors to their discoveries."[431] Rather, the post-AIA U.S. Patent Act is a unique hybrid that retains many aspects of the pre-AIA regime but jettisoned many others. The

---

(A) if subparagraph (B) does not apply, the actual filing date of the patent or the application for the patent containing a claim to the invention; or

(B) the filing date of the earliest application for which the patent or application is entitled, as to such invention, to a right of priority under section 119, 365(a), or 365(b) or to the benefit of an earlier filing date under section 120, 121, or 365(c).

(2) The effective filing date for a claimed invention in an application for reissue or reissued patent shall be determined by deeming the claim to the invention to have been contained in the patent for which reissue was sought.

[428] *See supra* Part I, Section C ("The Strict Identity Rule of Anticipation").

[429] *See infra* Section S ("Novelty-Preserving Exceptions Under Post-AIA 35 U.S.C. §102(b)").

[430] *See* H.R. Rep. No. 112-98 [House Judiciary Comm. Rep. on the America Invents Act], at 54 (June 1, 2011) (stating that the AIA "maintains a 1-year grace period for U.S. applicants. Applicants' own publication or disclosure that occurs within 1 year prior to filing will not act as prior art against their applications. Similarly, disclosure by others during that time based on information obtained (directly or indirectly) from the inventor will not constitute prior art. This 1-year grace period should continue to give U.S. applicants the time they need to prepare and file their applications."). *See also supra* Section I.2 ("Grace Period").

[431] Leahy-Smith America Invents Act, Pub. L. No. 112-29 (H.R. 1249), §3(p), 125 Stat. 284, 293 (2011) ("Sense of Congress").

following subsections explore what the AIA kept and what it discarded.

a. *What Section 3 of the AIA Retained*

As amended by the AIA, 35 U.S.C. §102(a) (eff. Mar. 16, 2013) (hereafter "§102(a)" or "post-AIA §102(a)") merges into a single statutory subsection several aspects of the pre-AIA versions of 35 U.S.C. §102(a) and (b). For example, novelty is presumptively destroyed under post-AIA §102(a) if any of the following four events occur before a particular date: the invention was "patented," "described in a printed publication," "in public use," or "on sale." Novelty destruction (i.e., anticipation) based on the invention having previously been "patented" or "described in a printed publication" was recognized in pre-AIA §102(a) and (b).[432] Loss of right to patent based on the invention having previously been "in public use" or "on sale" was recognized in pre-AIA §102(b).[433]

Moreover, each of these four novelty-destroying events (i.e., "patented," "described in a printed publication," "in public use," and "on sale") has a robust history of case law interpretation.[434] Because Congress used well-recognized, common law–defined terms in drafting the AIA, it is reasonable to assume that Congress intended that those same definitions should continue to govern the analysis of novelty under the post-AIA regime.[435]

b. *What Section 3 of the AIA Changed*

Section 3 of the AIA implemented numerous notable changes in U.S. patent law. Probably the most significant is the manner in which the United States will determine priority between two (or more) rival inventors claiming a given invention. The AIA switched the United States from its historic first-to-invent system[436] to a first-inventor-to-file

[432]*See* 35 U.S.C. §102(a), (b) (2006).

[433]*See* 35 U.S.C. §102(b) (2006).

[434]For analysis of the pre-AIA case law interpretation of these terms, *see supra* Section I ("The Statutory Bars of 35 U.S.C. §102(b) (Pre-AIA)").

[435]A contrary argument is that the "or otherwise available to the public" language of 35 U.S.C. §102(a)(1) (eff. Mar. 16, 2013) narrowed the meaning of the public use and on sale bars by excluding "secret" prior art such as confidential commercialization of an invention. For further discussion of this debate, *see infra* Section Q.3 ("Does the AIA Permit Secret Prior Art?").

[436]*See supra* Section N ("Prior Invention under 35 U.S.C. §102(g) (pre-AIA))." The United States implemented a first-to-invent priority system as early as the late eighteenth century. *See* Edward C. Walterscheid, *Priority of Invention: How the United States Came to Have a "First-to-Invent" System,* 23 AIPLA Q.J. 263, 264 (1995) (explaining that "the initial impetus came from the titanic struggle between John Fitch and James Rumsey for priority of invention with respect to the steamboat during the late

system (characterized by Congress as more in keeping with international standards[437]). In implementing the change, the AIA eliminated the statutory bases for interference practice, §102(g)(1) and §135 of the pre-AIA Patent Act, with respect to patent applications filed on or after March 16, 2013.[438]

Somewhat ironically (given the importance of this change), post-AIA §102 does not explicitly set forth a first-inventor-to-file standard. Rather, the first-inventor-to-file standard is implicit in the language of post-AIA §102(a)(2).[439] Nor is the first-inventor-to-file standard absolute; it is subject to three important exceptions under post-AIA §102(b)(2) as detailed *infra.*[440]

Another AIA change of primary import is the timing for determining novelty. Pursuant to the AIA, the novelty of a claimed invention will be assessed under 35 U.S.C. §102 as of the invention's "effective filing date."[441] Under the pre-AIA §102, novelty was assessed at the

---

eighteenth century, but the actual creation of a true first-to-invent system took almost fifty years").

[437]Section 3 of the AIA did not implement a European-style system of first to file with absolute novelty. Rather, the post-AIA version of §102 puts into place a unique hybrid system that preserves many aspects of the pre-AIA grace period in 35 U.S.C. §102(b) (2006). In contrast to a true first-to-file system, the AIA created what is better described (at least in some circumstances) as a "first inventor to disclose" system. *See infra* Section S.3 ("Post-AIA 35 U.S.C. §102(b)(2): Shields Against Post-AIA §102(a)(2) Presumptively Novelty-Destroying Events").

[438]*See supra* Section N.2 ("Interference Proceedings Under §102(g)(1) [2006]"). In *Biogen MA, Inc. v. Japanese Foundation for Cancer Research*, 785 F.3d 648 (Fed. Cir. 2015), the Federal Circuit observed that under the AIA's effective date provision, AIA §3(n)(1), "interference proceedings are to continue with respect to . . . applications filed before March 16, 2013," *Biogen MA,* 785 F.3d at 655, with the single exception of AIA §6(f)(3)(A), which provides that the USPTO Director may dismiss a pending interference in favor of a post-grant review. *Biogen MA,* 875 F.3d at 655 n.8.

[439]*See* 35 U.S.C. §102(a)(2) (eff. Mar. 16, 2013) (providing that "[a] person shall be entitled to a patent unless . . . (2) the claimed invention was described in a patent issued under section 151, or in an application for patent published or deemed published under section 122(b), in which the patent or application, as the case may be, names another inventor and was effectively filed before the effective filing date of the claimed invention"). *Compare* the more explicit European approach, which provides that "[i]f two or more persons have made an invention independently of each other, the right to a European patent therefor shall belong to the person whose European patent application has the earliest date of filing, provided that this first application has been published." European Patent Convention art. 60(2) (14th ed. 2010).

[440]*See infra* Section S.3 ("Post-AIA §102(b)(2): Shields Against Post-AIA §102(a)(2) Presumptively Novelty-Destroying Events").

[441]Although the term has long been used by patent attorneys and the USPTO, the AIA for the first time added to the Patent Act an explicit definition of "effective filing date." Subparagraph (2) of §3(a) ("Definitions") of the AIA adds the following definition to 35 U.S.C. §100:

> (i) (1) The term "effective filing date" for a claimed invention in a patent or application for patent means —

time of the invention's "invention date" rather than as of the corresponding patent application's filing date.[442] Nonobviousness of an invention under pre-AIA §103 was likewise assessed "at the time the invention was made."[443]

Although before the AIA, the USPTO treated an applicant's filing date as her presumptive invention date under a constructive reduction to practice theory, the applicant could potentially antedate (or "swear behind") and thereby remove certain prior art references cited by the agency in anticipation and/or obviousness rejections. Antedating a prior art reference required proving an earlier date of invention than the effective date of the reference. In the USPTO, antedating was accomplished in accordance with Rule 131 (i.e., 37 C.F.R. §1.131);[444] in litigation challenging the validity of an issued patent, a similar procedure was followed.[445] Under the AIA, however, antedating or "swearing behind" a prior art reference is no longer possible. This is because the concepts of "invention date" and priority based on earlier invention date are not part of the post-AIA 35 U.S.C. §102 framework.

A third AIA-implemented change of much importance is the removal of numerous geographic limitations on §102 prior art. Under

---

> (A) if subparagraph (B) does not apply, the actual filing date of the patent or the application for the patent containing a claim to the invention; or
>
> (B) the filing date of the earliest application for which the patent or application is entitled, as to such invention, to a right of priority under section 119, 365(a), or 365(b) or to the benefit of an earlier filing date under section 120, 121, or 365(c).
>
> (2) The effective filing date for a claimed invention in an application for reissue or reissued patent shall be determined by deeming the claim to the invention to have been contained in the patent for which reissue was sought.

35 U.S.C. §100(i) (eff. Mar. 16, 2013) (subparagraph indenting added for clarity).

[442] *See* 35 U.S.C. §102(a) (2006); 35 U.S.C. §102(e) (2006); 35 U.S.C. §102(g) (2006); *see also supra* Section G.4 ("Distinguishing Novelty from Loss of Right").

[443] 35 U.S.C. §103(a) (2006). *See also supra* Chapter 5, Section F.3 ("Section 102/103 Overlap").

[444] *See supra* Section O ("Antedating (or "Swearing Behind") Prior Art (Pre-AIA)").

[445] *See Mahurkar v. C.R. Bard, Inc.*, 79 F.3d 1572 (Fed. Cir. 1996) (affirming district court's grant of patentee's motion for judgment as a matter of law (JMOL) that patent in suit was not anticipated because accused infringer failed to prove that allegedly anticipatory "Cook catalog" was in fact prior art under 35 U.S.C. §102(a)). The court in *Mahurkar* explained that a patentee such as Mahurkar may seek to establish an actual invention date earlier than the application filing date (i.e., constructive reduction to practice date, taken as presumptive invention date) by analogy to the interference rule of priority of invention:

> In the United States, the person who first reduces an invention to practice is "prima facie the first and true inventor." Christie v. Seybold, 55 F. 69, 76 (6th Cir. 1893) (Taft, J.). However, the person "who first conceives, and, in a mental sense, first invents . . . may date his patentable invention back to the time of its conception, if he connects the conception with its reduction to practice by reasonable diligence on his part, so that they are substantially one continuous act." *Id.*

the pre-AIA regime, "know[ledge] or use[] by others" of a claimed invention had to have occurred "in this country" to count as novelty-destroying prior art.[446] Placement of an invention "on sale" or "in public use" created a loss of right to patent only if the activity had occurred "in this country."[447] The prior making of an invention counted as novelty-destroying prior art only if the invention had been "made in this country."[448] In contrast, there are no geographic limitations in the post-AIA §102(a)(1).[449] Thus, for example, pre–effective filing date sales of a claimed invention anywhere in the world will potentially destroy novelty.[450]

[446]35 U.S.C. §102(a) (2006); *see also supra* Section H ("'Known or Used' Under 35 U.S.C. §102(a) (Pre-AIA)").

[447]35 U.S.C. §102(b) (2006); *see also supra* Section I ("The Statutory Bars of 35 U.S.C. §102(b) (Pre-AIA)").

[448]35 U.S.C. §102(g)(2) (2006); *see also supra* Section N.3 ("Anticipation Under §102(g)(2) (Pre-AIA)").

[449]*See infra* Section Q ("Presumptively Novelty-Destroying Events Under Post-AIA §102(a)(1)").

[450]The following hypothetical demonstrates a critical point: that depending on whether a patent application claim being examined in the USPTO (or post-issuance, challenged as invalid in district court litigation) is deemed to have a pre- or post-AIA effective filing date, a particular prior art event may or may not destroy novelty. In other words, the same prior event may or may not be prior art depending on whether the patent or application claim under review has an effective filing date prior to March 16, 2013, or an effective filing date on or after that date.

Consider inventor Alpha, who filed a U.S. patent application claiming invention X on March 1, 2013 (shortly before the AIA §3 changes took effect). Hence, Alpha's application is treated as a "pre-AIA" application. Assume further that inventor Beta independently invented the same invention X and filed a U.S. patent application claiming X on April 1, 2013 (shortly after the AIA §3 changes took effect). Beta's application is accordingly treated as a "post-AIA" application (or simply an "AIA application"). Beta does not claim priority to any earlier filing date.

Now consider the different impacts on Alpha and Beta, respectively, of the act of Zelda, who sold a product embodying invention X to the public in the country of Zimbabwe on February 1, 2012.

Even assuming a USPTO examiner had knowledge of Zelda's sales in Zimbabwe, the sales would not qualify as prior art to prevent Alpha's U.S. patent from issuing. This is because pre-AIA law applies to the examination of Alpha's application. Section 102(b) of 35 U.S.C. (2006) ignores on sale bar events that do not occur "in this country" (i.e., in the United States). In other words, Zelda's foreign sales of X, even though made more than one year before Alpha's U.S. filing date, do not trigger the on sale bar of §102(b) (2006) against Alpha. Nor would the sales have triggered §102(a) (2006), which requires that the invention was "known or used by others *in this country*" before Alpha's invention date (whenever that was).

As noted in the text, the AIA removed most geographic restrictions on prior art. Consider now the examination of Beta's application, the claims of which have an effective filing date after March 15, 2013, thus making Beta's application an "AIA application." Assuming a USPTO examiner gains knowledge of Zelda's sales in Zimbabwe (an assumption that may be more likely in the context of litigation in federal court than prosecution in the USPTO), the foreign sales *will* count against Beta as novelty-destroying prior art. Under 35 U.S.C. §102(a)(1) (eff. Mar. 16, 2013), Beta's claims to X

One geographic limitation is retained by the AIA, however: descriptions of a claimed invention in another's earlier-filed application are prior art only if the "another" ultimately obtains a U.S. patent or the "another's" application is published in accordance with U.S. patent law. Under the pre-AIA regime, descriptions of a claimed invention in another's patent or published application counted as novelty-destroying prior art only if the "another's" patent or published application was "filed in the United States."[451] This domestic connection is effectively retained by the AIA (although stated in different words). Under post-AIA §102, the novelty-destroying description must still appear in "a patent issued under section 151 [of 35 U.S.C.]" or in "an application for patent published or deemed published under section 122(b) [of 35 U.S.C.]."[452]

Although the description being relied on as a prior art reference must ultimately appear in a U.S. patent or application published in accordance with U.S. patent law to qualify as post-AIA §102(a)(2) prior art, there is a different AIA-implemented geographic change of note in this context. Before the AIA's effective date, any earlier foreign filing date to which the U.S. patent or published application being relied on as prior art may have been entitled under the Paris Convention's right of priority was ignored under the judicially created *Hilmer* rule.[453] The AIA repealed the *Hilmer* rule.[454]

---

are anticipated because "the claimed invention was . . . in public use, on sale, or otherwise available to the public [anywhere in the world] before the effective filing date of the claimed invention." (No exception under §102(b)(1) (eff. Mar. 16, 2013) could aid Beta in this hypothetical because Zelda's sales occurred more than one year before Beta's effective filing date; the §102(b)(1) exception is limited to "[d]isclosures made 1 year or less before the effective filing date of the claimed invention.")

The key insight this hypothetical illustrates is that the same event — here, Zelda's sales of invention X in Zimbabwe on February 1, 2012 — may or may not be a novelty-destroying prior art depending on whether pre-AIA or post-AIA rules are applied to the patent application claim at issue. That is, the same event (Zelda's sales) has two different prior art statuses depending on the effective filing date of the claim under review. The author thanks Professor Joseph Miller for emphasizing this important point.

451 35 U.S.C. §102(e) (2006); *see also supra* Section L ("Description in Another's Earlier-Filed Patent or Published Patent Application Under 35 U.S.C. §102(e) (Pre-AIA)").

452 35 U.S.C. §102(a)(2) (eff. Mar. 16, 2013).

453 *See In re Hilmer*, 359 F.2d 859 (C.C.P.A. 1966); *see also supra* Section L ("Description in Another's Earlier-Filed Patent or Published Patent Application Under 35 U.S.C. §102(e) (Pre-AIA)").

454 *See* 35 U.S.C. §102(d) (eff. Mar. 16, 2013), which provides:

> (d) PATENTS AND PUBLISHED APPLICATIONS EFFECTIVE AS PRIOR ART. — For purposes of determining whether a patent or application for patent is prior art to a claimed invention under subsection (a)(2), such patent or application shall be considered to have been effectively filed, with respect to any subject matter described in the patent or application —

To see the impact of abolishing the *Hilmer* rule, consider a hypothetical German inventor who first files a patent application directed to her invention in the German Patent Office in 2014 and within one year files another application for the same invention in the USPTO, properly claiming for her U.S. application the Paris Convention right of foreign priority under 35 U.S.C. §119(a). Assume that the German and U.S. applications are identical in terms of the invention's disclosure (setting aside any language translation issues). The U.S. application is published at 18 months after the 2014 German priority date and thereafter a USPTO examiner cites the U.S. application's description of the invention as prior art against another patent applicant under post-AIA §102(a)(2). The AIA provides that the prior art effective date of the invention's description in the German inventor's published U.S. patent application will be its 2014 German filing date.[455] Pre-AIA, the *Hilmer* rule would have limited the prior art effective date of the published application's description to its later U.S. filing date.[456] Thus, post-AIA, the German inventor of this hypothetical has an enhanced defensive opportunity (sometimes referred to as a "senior right") to prevent others from patenting the invention in the United States.

The AIA removed geographic limitations in yet another way. Evidence relied on pre-AIA by a U.S. patent applicant attempting to swear behind a prior art reference, or relied on by an interference party seeking to establish time-wise priority of invention, was admissible only if the evidence arose from inventive activities in a NAFTA (North American Free Trade Agreement) or WTO (World Trade Organization) member country. Section 104 of 35 U.S.C., the statutory basis for this limitation on evidence relied on to affirmatively establish an earlier date of invention,[457] was eliminated by the AIA.

The AIA made still more changes to 35 U.S.C. §102. It eliminated subsection (c) of 35 U.S.C §102 (2006), which dealt with abandonment;[458] subsection (d) of 35 U.S.C. §102 (2006), which set forth a

---

> (1) if paragraph (2) does not apply, as of the actual filing date of the patent or the application for patent; or
>
> (2) if the patent or application for patent is entitled to claim a right of priority under section 119, 365(a), or 365(b), or to claim the benefit of an earlier filing date under section 120, 121, or 365(c), based upon 1 or more prior filed applications for patent, as of the filing date of the earliest such application that describes the subject matter.

Subparagraph (d)(2) repeals the *Hilmer* rule implicitly by including foreign priority under 35 U.S.C. §119 in its scope.

[455] *See* 35 U.S.C. §102(d) (eff. Mar. 16, 2013) (quoted *infra*).

[456] *See supra* Section L ("Description in Another's Earlier-Filed Patent or Published Patent Application Under 35 U.S.C. §102(e) (Pre-AIA)").

[457] 35 U.S.C. §104 (2006) ("Invention made abroad").

[458] *See supra* Section J.

rarely invoked form of statutory bar based on foreign patenting;[459] and subsection (f) of 35 U.S.C. §102 (2006), the basis for the requirement of originality. Congress's motivation for eliminating §102(f) is unclear, because other portions of the AIA and the post-AIA Patent Act clarify that originality of invention is still a bedrock requirement. In other words, the law remains that one cannot merely copy another's invention and obtain a patent on it.[460]

In addition to its several deletions from 35 U.S.C. §102, the AIA added a new category of novelty-destroying prior art to §102. Post-AIA, a claimed invention is not novel if it was "otherwise available to the public" before the invention's effective filing date. Congress in the AIA text did not define its "otherwise available to the public" language. As further discussed below, a clear understanding of the new language's meaning and scope will likely require interpretation by the courts.[461]

Q. Presumptively Novelty-Destroying Events Under Post-AIA 35 U.S.C. §102(a)(1)

Subsection (a)(1) of post-AIA §102 enumerates five categories of novelty-destroying events. Four of the five categories are identified by terminology well established in numerous interpretative judicial decisions. The fifth category is new to U.S. patent law. The operation of these categories is explained and illustrated by hypotheticals below.[462]

[459] *See supra* Section K.

[460] More specifically, the AIA did not change the requirement that, subject to certain exceptions, patent applications shall be made "by the inventor," 35 U.S.C. §111(a)(1) (2006), and the AIA added a definition of "inventor" as "the individual or, if a joint invention, the individuals collectively who invented or discovered the subject matter of the invention." 35 U.S.C. §100(f) (eff. Mar. 16, 2013); Leahy-Smith America Invents Act, Pub. L. No. 112-29 (H.R. 1249), §3(a)(2), 125 Stat. 284, 285 (2011). The AIA also continued the requirement that a patent applicant's oath include a statement that the applicant believes he is an "original" inventor. *See* 35 U.S.C. §115 (2006) (requiring that "[t]he applicant shall make oath that he believes himself to be the *original* and first inventor of the process, machine, manufacture, or composition of matter, or improvement thereof, for which he solicits a patent") (emphasis added); 35 U.S.C. §115(b)(2) (eff. Mar. 16, 2013) (providing that "[a]n oath or declaration under subsection (a) shall contain statements that . . . such individual believes himself or herself to be the *original* inventor or an *original* joint inventor of a claimed invention in the application") (emphases added).

[461] *See infra* Section Q.3 ("Does the AIA Permit Secret Prior Art?").

[462] In addition to this author's hypotheticals posited in this chapter, readers are encouraged to review the excellent resource, *Prior Art Problems Under AIA and Proposed Solutions* (Mar. 2012), authored by Professors Paul M. Janicke and Lisa M. Dolak, *available at* https://chisum-patent-academy.com/wp-content/uploads/Janicke_Dolak_AIA_Prior_art_problems_and_solutions_3-2012.pdf. Professor Andrew

1. Invention "Patented, Described in a Printed Publication, or in Public Use, [or] on Sale" Before Effective Filing Date

Section §102(a)(1) of 35 U.S.C. (eff. Mar. 16, 2013) provides in part that "[a] person shall be entitled to a patent unless—(1) the claimed invention was patented, described in a printed publication, or in public use, [or] on sale ... before the effective filing date of the claimed invention. . . ." A wealth of pre-AIA case law has interpreted and applied the four novelty-destroying events identified in this portion of the statute.[463] Presumably those judicial interpretations continue to control under the post-AIA regime and will not be revisited here.[464] The following hypothetical and accompanying variations illustrate the operation of the first four novelty-destroying events of post-AIA §102(a)(1).

Hypothetical. Consider U.S. patent applicant Aidan, who invents a widget "X" and thereafter files a non-provisional utility patent application disclosing and claiming widget X in the USPTO on July 1, 2014. Aidan's application is a first-filed application, meaning that it is not entitled to any earlier filing date via a right of foreign or domestic priority under 35 U.S.C. §119, or to the benefit of an earlier-filed copending application under 35 U.S.C. §120. Thus, the effective filing date of the claims in Aidan's application is his application's actual USPTO filing date of July 1, 2014.[465]

Chin offers a succinct summary and additional hypotheticals at Andrew Chin, *The Post-AIA Section 102*, http://andrewchin.com/chin/teaching/patent/aia_handout.pdf (last visited Feb. 26, 2016). Not for the faint of heart, the USPTO offers its take on a number of AIA hypothetical "scenarios" with accompanying timelines at U.S. Patent and Trademark Office, *Welcome: America Invents Act First Inventor to File Roadshow* (Sept. 16-Oct. 9, 2014), http://www.uspto.gov/sites/default/files/aia_implementation/2014_aia_fitf_roadshow_slides.pdf, at 96-131 ("First Inventor to File (FITF) Sample Scenarios"). Readers seeking an even more detailed treatment should consult Alan J. Kasper et al., *Patents After the AIA: Evolving Law and Practice* (Bloomberg BNA 2015) (including "[m]ore than 100 original graphical timeline scenarios [that] provide a myriad of different fact patterns analyzed under the AIA and compared to pre-AIA outcomes").

[463]For discussion of the pre-AIA case law interpretation of these terms, *see supra* Part II.

[464]Some question exists concerning the continued viability of so-called "secret" prior art. For example, long-standing precedent holds that secret offers for sale and "non-informing" public uses count as prior art under 35 U.S.C. §102(b) (2006). Based on certain AIA legislative history, however, a contrary argument can be made that the AIA narrowed the scope of "on sale" and "public use" activity to eliminate secret prior art, and thus limited novelty-destroying "on sale" and "public use" situations to those that are not confidential (i.e., are always "public"). For further discussion of this issue, *see infra* Section Q.3 ("Does the AIA Permit Secret Prior Art?").

[465]*See* 35 U.S.C. §100(i)(1) (eff. Mar. 16, 2013) (defining "effective filing date").

Q. Presumptively Novelty-Destroying Events Under Post-AIA

First Variation. Assume that an identical widget X was patented in Germany on June 30, 2014 (that is, the German patent issued one day before Aidan's effective filing date) by Gertrude, a German national who independently invented widget X.[466] As a result, the novelty of Aidan's claimed widget X has been presumptively destroyed by Gertrude's act of patenting the same widget. In other words, the issuance of Gertrude's patent anticipated Aidan's application claims, and the USPTO will reject them.[467] The date on which Aidan invented his claimed widget X (i.e., his "invention date" in pre-AIA parlance) is not relevant to the analysis, even if earlier in time than Gertrude's invention date.

Second Variation. Alter the facts of the Aidan hypothetical so that the identical widget X was "described in a printed publication" by Eli, a national of Estonia. Assume that Eli independently invented widget X and described it in enabling fashion[468] in an article published in an Estonian newspaper in the Estonian language.[469] The newspaper article was published on June 30, 2014 (one day before Aidan's effective filing date). As a result, the novelty of Aidan's claimed widget X has been presumptively destroyed by Eli's description of the same widget in a printed publication having an effective date before Aidan's effective filing date. Again, the date on which Aidan invented his claimed widget X is not relevant to the analysis, even if earlier in time than Eli's invention date. Nor is the fact that Eli's article was published abroad in a foreign language relevant.[470]

Third Variation. Alter the facts of the Aidan hypothetical so that the identical widget X was in "public use" in Paraguay by independent inventor Pamela on June 30, 2014 (one day before Aidan's effective filing date).[471] Assume that Pamela gave away a dozen widget X's to various persons she encountered on the streets of her Paraguayan hometown, with no restrictions on confidentiality or the recipients' further use of the widgets. As a result, the novelty of Aidan's claimed widget X has been presumptively destroyed by Pamela's act of putting the identical widget into public use before Aidan's effective filing date.

[466]Minimal modern precedent exists regarding the meaning of "patenting" in 35 U.S.C. §102(a) (2006) and 35 U.S.C. §102(b) (2006). In actual practice, Gertrude's patent application would be published by the German Patent Office at 18 months after filing and would be available as "printed publication" prior art on the publication date.

[467]In this hypothetical and its variations, novelty is "presumptively" destroyed in the absence of other facts to suggest that one of the prior art–removing exceptions of 35 U.S.C. §102(b)(1) (eff. Mar. 16, 2013) applies.

[468]*See supra* Section E ("Enablement Standard for Anticipatory Prior Art").

[469]For pre-AIA precedent regarding the meaning of "described in a printed publication," *see supra* Section F ("What Is a Printed Publication?").

[470]This fact would not be relevant under pre-AIA law either.

[471]For pre-AIA precedent regarding the meaning of an invention being in "public use," *see supra* Section I.3.

Again, the date on which Aidan invented his claimed widget X is not relevant to the analysis. The fact that Pamela's public use occurred outside the United States is likewise not relevant.

Fourth Variation. Alter the facts of the Aidan hypothetical so that the identical widget X was placed "on sale" in Hungary by independent inventor Heather on June 30, 2014.[472] On that date Heather sold a dozen widget X's to customers in her retail store in Budapest. As a result, the novelty of Aidan's claimed widget X has been presumptively destroyed by Heather's act of putting the identical widget on sale before Aidan's effective filing date. Again, the date on which Aidan invented his claimed widget X is not relevant to the analysis in this hypothetical. The foreign location of Heather's sales is also not relevant.

2. Invention "Otherwise Available to the Public" Before Effective Filing Date

In addition to the first four presumptively novelty-destroying events discussed in the preceding subsection, §102(a)(1) of 35 U.S.C. (eff. Mar. 16, 2013) provides that "[a] person shall be entitled to a patent unless — the claimed invention was . . . otherwise available to the public before the effective filing date of the claimed invention." This is a newly articulated category of prior art for U.S. patent law. The AIA's text does not provide a definition of "otherwise available to the public."

Examining the meaning of the phrase in the context of the statute suggests that it was intended as catch-all language to cover activity not already falling within the first four §102(a)(1) categories of "patented, described in a printed publication, or in public use, [or] on sale . . . ," so long as the activity is "available to the public." For example, a purely oral disclosure of an invention at a scientific conference of non-restrictive attendance might come within "otherwise available to the public," in a manner analogous to European practice.[473] In contrast, the Federal Circuit observed (in *dicta*) that purely oral divulgations do not qualify as prior art under pre-AIA §102(b).[474]

[472]For pre-AIA precedent regarding the meaning of placing an invention "on sale," *see supra* Section I.4.

[473]*See* European Patent Convention art. 54(1) (14th ed. 2010) (providing that "[a]n invention shall be considered to be new if it does not form part of the state of the art"); *id.* art. 54(2) (providing that "[t]he state of the art shall be held to comprise everything *made available to the public* by means of a written or *oral description*, by use, or in any other way, before the date of filing of the European patent application") (emphasis added).

[474]*See In re Klopfenstein*, 380 F.3d 1345, 1349 n.4 (Fed. Cir. 2004) (observing, in contrast to the facts of the case before it, that an entirely *oral* presentation that does not include a display of slides or distribution of copies of the presentation would not

The primary issue left unanswered by Congress's addition of "otherwise available to the public" as a category of prior art is whether the language works any change to the extant case law–based interpretations of "public use" and "on sale" activity. The next subsection addresses the issue.

3. Does the AIA Permit Secret Prior Art?

For many years before the AIA's enactment, U.S. patent case law recognized that certain "secret" activity can potentially qualify as novelty-destroying prior art. A classic example is a "non-informing public use" involving an inventor's secret commercialization of his invention outside of the pre-AIA statutory grace period.[475] Even though the public was not made aware of the details of the invention (through publication or inspection), the law penalized the inventor for benefiting financially from his invention for a prolonged period of time beyond that allowed by the statute. It did so by treating his secret commercial use as prior art against him.

The leading precedent is *Metallizing Engineering Co. v. Kenyon Bearing & Auto Parts Co.*[476] The inventor in *Metallizing* developed and used an industrial process while working for numerous commercial customers more than one year before filing a U.S. patent application claiming the process. Although commercially exploiting his process for an extended period of time, the inventor did not disclose to others any details about the process. Nor were the details discernible from inspecting the finished product of the process.[477]

The revered jurist Learned Hand of the U.S. Court of Appeals for the Second Circuit reversed a district court decision that sustained

---

constitute a "printed publication" under 35 U.S.C. §102(b) (2006), and that a merely "transient" display of slides accompanying an oral presentation might not either).

[475]*See* Kinzenbaw v. Deere & Co., 741 F.2d 383, 390 (Fed. Cir. 1984) (observing that "[a] commercial use is a public use even if it is kept secret" and citing authority). *See also* Invitrogen Corp. v. Biocrest Mfg., L.P., 424 F.3d 1374, 1381 n.* (Fed. Cir. 2005) (characterizing *Kinzenbaw*'s statement that "[a] commercial use is a public use even if it is kept secret" as *dicta*, because the court in *Kinzenbaw* did not find it necessary to resolve the question whether the use of the invention was secret, but concluding that *Kinzenbaw* "is consistent with the basic principle that a confidential use is not public under §102(b) unless there is commercial exploitation").

[476]153 F.2d 516 (2d Cir. 1946) (L. Hand, J.).

[477]*See* Metallizing Eng'g Co. v. Kenyon Bearing & Auto Parts Co., 62 F. Supp. 42, 47 (D. Conn. 1945) (finding that "[a]t all times prior to [the critical date of] August 6, 1941, the practice of the process was so guarded as not to come to public knowledge; its nature was disclosed only to a few employees and advisers of the inventor, less than half a dozen in number, in all cases under a promise of confidence which was not abused. . . . [P]rior to August, 1941, the nature of the process could not have been deduced from inspection or physical tests upon specimens of the processed product in the hands of the public. . . .").

the validity of the patent over a public use challenge. The district court had reasoned that a secret use of a process could never be a public use within the meaning of the statute. In holding that the public use bar could indeed be triggered by secret use that is commercial in nature, Judge Hand overruled his own earlier decision on which the district court had relied:

> [I]t appears that in *Peerless Roll Leaf Co. v. Griffin & Sons*, supra, 2 Cir., 29 F.2d 646, we confused two separate doctrines: (1) The effect upon his right to a patent of the inventor's competitive exploitation of his machine or of his process; (2) the contribution which a prior use by another person makes to the art. Both do indeed come within the phrase, "prior use"; but the first is a defence for quite different reasons from the second. It had its origin — at least in this country — in the passage we have quoted from *Pennock v. Dialogue*, supra, 2 Pet. 1, 7 L. Ed. 327; i.e., *that it is a condition upon an inventor's right to a patent that he shall not exploit his discovery competitively after it is ready for patenting; he must content himself with either secrecy, or legal monopoly*. It is true that for the limited period of two years he was allowed to do so, possibly in order to give him time to prepare an application; and even that has been recently cut down by half. But if he goes beyond that period of probation, he forfeits his right *regardless of how little the public may have learned about the invention*. . . .[478]

Are such secret uses/commercial exploitations still considered prior art after the enactment of the America Invents Act of 2011? Recall that Congress amended the Patent Act's §102 enumeration of prior art categories by adding the final phrase, "or otherwise available to the public."[479] An argument exists that the addition of the "or otherwise available to the public" language means that *all five* of the listed categories of potentially novelty-destroying prior art must now be "available to the public." In other words, the argument is that §102(a)(1) excludes *any* type of secret prior art that is not available to the public. This interpretation admittedly finds support from (i) the presence of the word "otherwise" in §102(a)(1) as well as (ii) statements in the legislative history of the AIA.[480]

[478] *Metallizing*, 153 F.2d at 519-520 (emphases added).

[479] 35 U.S.C. §102(a)(1) (eff. Mar. 16, 2013).

[480] *See, e.g.*, H.R. Rep. No. 112-98 [House Judiciary Comm. Rep. on the America Invents Act], at 54 (June 1, 2011) (stating that §3 of the AIA "also, and necessarily, modifies the prior-art sections of the patent law. Prior art will be measured from the filing date of the application and will typically include all art that *publicly exists* prior to the filing date, other than disclosures by the inventor within 1 year of filing. Prior art also will no longer have any geographic limitations. Thus, in section 102 the 'in this country' limitation as applied to 'public use' and 'on sale' is removed, *and the phrase* 'available to the public' *is added to clarify the broad scope of relevant prior art, as well as to emphasize the fact that it must be publicly accessible.*") (emphases added).

Q. Presumptively Novelty-Destroying Events Under Post-AIA

But according to Professors Robert Merges and John Duffy, the practical result of accepting this view means that an "inventor's own secret commercial exploitation (possibly for years!) will not bar that inventor from later seeking a patent."[481] In the opinion of this author (agreeing with Merges and Duffy), the better view is that enactment of the AIA did not *sub silentio* overrule the well-established case law interpretations of "public use" and "on sale" as encompassing certain secret or confidential activity. As Professors Merges and Duffy point out, to conclude otherwise would "reverse centuries of U.S. patent law, dating back to the decision in *Pennock v. Dialogue,* 27 U.S. 1 (1829)."[482] Merges and Duffy conclude that the AIA did *not* make "such a dramatic shift in U.S. patent policy" for the following four reasons:

(i) well established rules of statutory construction provide that "reenactment of statutory language with a known legal meaning continues the known meaning";
(ii) although one sentence in a Senate colloquy addressing the grace period supports the contrary view, nothing in that colloquy "suggested that Congress wanted to undo a fundamental principle of patent law";
(iii) in construing statutes it is accepted that Congress does not "hide elephants in mouseholes," and "overturning two centuries of consistent law would be a big elephant to hide in a [Senate] colloquy"; and
(iv) "[r]emarks in legislative history are not the statutory text."[483]

The U.S. Supreme Court considered and resolved this important and much-debated question in its 2019 decision *Helsinn Healthcare S.A. v. Teva Pharm. USA, Inc.* ("*Helsinn III*").[484] In a nutshell, the Court ruled that secret prior art remains prior art even after passage of the AIA.

More specifically, *Helsinn* involved a validity challenge based on the "on sale" bar of post-AIA §102. In a brief and unanimous opinion authored by Justice Thomas, the *Helsinn III* Court held that "an inventor's sale of an invention to a third party who is obligated to keep the invention confidential *can* qualify as prior art" under the AIA-amended §102.[485] In other words, the technical details of an

[481]Robert Merges & John Duffy, *Leahy-Smith America Invents Act of 2011: Overview* 22 (Sept. 16, 2011), *available at* https://chisum-patent-academy.com/wp-content/uploads/Leahy-Smith-AIA-2011-Overview_jfd_v3-Merges-Duffy-16-Sept-2011.pdf.
[482]Robert Merges & John Duffy, *Leahy-Smith America Invents Act of 2011: Overview* 22 (Sept. 16, 2011), *available at* https://chisum-patent-academy.com/wp-content/uploads/Leahy-Smith-AIA-2011-Overview_jfd_v3-Merges-Duffy-16-Sept-2011.pdf.
[483]Robert Merges & John Duffy, *Leahy-Smith America Invents Act of 2011: Overview* 23-24 (Sept. 16, 2011), *available at* https://chisum-patent-academy.com/wp-content/uploads/Leahy-Smith-AIA-2011-Overview_jfd_v3-Merges-Duffy-16-Sept-2011.pdf.
[484]139 S. Ct. 628 (2019).
[485]*Helsinn,* 139 S. Ct. at 634 (emphasis added).

invention need not be disclosed to the public in order to place it "on sale" under the Patent Act — those details can remain secret. The Court determined that Congress's AIA addition to 35 U.S.C. §102 of the broad "catch-all" phrase, "or otherwise available to the public," was "simply not enough of a change . . . to conclude that Congress intended to alter the meaning of the reenacted term 'on sale,'"[486] which has appeared in every U.S. patent statute since the 1836 Act.[487]

The *Helsinn III* decision thus resolved the lingering question whether post-AIA, U.S. patent law still recognized as potentially invalidating prior art a secret event such as a commercial but confidential pre-critical date sale of an invention, or whether the "otherwise available to the public" language of 35 U.S.C. §102(a)(1) (as amended by the AIA) prospectively abrogated the traditional understanding that such secret sales could work a loss to right to patent. The arguments on both sides of the issue are summarized above. This author and most academics took the position that "on sale" had a long-established meaning in the patent case law and that the AIA amendments to §102 did not alter that meaning. In 2019, the Supreme Court agreed. Given the importance of the *Helsinn* case, a thorough background understanding of the facts of the case and its pathway to the Supreme Court are essential.

The *Helsinn* dispute began with Hatch-Waxman litigation venued in the U.S. District Court for the District of New Jersey, then captioned *Helsinn Healthcare S.A. v. Dr. Reddy's Labs. Ltd.* ("*Helsinn I*").[488] At issue was the infringement and validity of Helsinn's U.S. Patent No. 8,598,219 ('219 patent). The '219 patent concerned intravenously-administered formulations that contained the active ingredient palonosetron hydrochloride, useful to reduce the nausea and vomiting that cancer chemotherapy recipients often suffer. More specifically, the '219 patent disclosed and claimed an intravenous formulation using unexpectedly low concentrations of palonosetron compared to the prior art; i.e., 0.25 mg of palonosetron in a 5 ml solution.[489] Helsinn filed

[486]*Helsinn,* 139 S. Ct. at 634.

[487]*Helsinn,* 139 S. Ct. at 633 (citing *Pfaff,* 525 U.S. at 65).

[488]No. CV 11-3962 (MLC), 387 F. Supp. 3d 439 (D.N.J. Mar. 3, 2016) (hereafter "*Helsinn I*").

[489]Representative claim 1 of Helsinn's '219 patent recited:

> 1. A pharmaceutical single-use, unit-dose formulation for intravenous administration to a human to reduce the likelihood of cancer chemotherapy-induced nausea and vomiting, comprising a 5 mL sterile aqueous isotonic solution, said solution comprising:
>
> palonosetron hydrochloride in an amount of 0.25 mg based on the weight of its free base;
>
> from 0.005 mg/mL to 1.0 mg/mL EDTA; and
>
> from 10 mg/mL to 80 mg/mL mannitol,
>
> wherein said formulation is stable at 24 months when stored at room temperature.

the '219 patent application on May 23, 2013, but claimed priority to January 30, 2003.[490]

After a group of generic drug manufacturers including Dr. Reddy's Laboratories and Teva Pharmaceuticals sought USFDA approval to market generic versions of Helsinn's product, Helsinn sued them in the District of New Jersey for technical infringement. In response, the accused infringers identified a confidential "Supply and Purchase Agreement" entered into by Helsinn (a Swiss pharmaceutical company) and MGI Pharma (a Minnesota-based U.S. oncology-focused firm). Signed April 6, 2001 (before the '219 patent's priority date), the Agreement obligated Helsinn to supply MGI's requirements for the 0.25 mg palonosetron formulation, and MGI to exclusively purchase the same from Helsinn, contingent on approval of Helsinn's New Drug Application (NDA) by the FDA. The Helsinn-MGI agreement also specified price, method of payment, and method of delivery.[491]

The generic challengers contended that this pre–critical date transaction rendered Helsinn's '219 patent invalid under the on sale bar—specifically, the on sale bar of §102(a)(1) (AIA version eff. Mar. 16, 2013). The parties in *Helsinn I* did not dispute (and the district court did not question) that Helsinn's patent was an "AIA patent," that is, subject to the AIA-amended definitions of prior art.[492] Thus, the impact of the statute's newly-added "otherwise available to the public" language took center stage.

Following USPTO guidance on interpretation of the new statute,[493] the New Jersey district court concluded that "the post-AIA on-sale

[490]*Helsinn I*, 387 F. Supp. 3d at 449. Under the AIA-amended §102, the "critical date" would be January 30, 2002 for "disclosures" by the inventor or an "obtainer." *See* 35 U.S.C. §102(b)(1) (eff. Mar. 16, 2013) (listing as an "exception" to the pre–effective filing date "on sale" bar of §102(a)(1) "[d]isclosures made 1 year or less before the effective filing date of the claimed invention").

[491]*See Helsinn II*, 855 F.3d at 1362 (noting that "[t]he [Helsinn-MGI] agreement specified price (29% of the gross sales price by MGI with a minimum of $28.50 per vial), method of payment (wire transfer within 30 days of receipt of an invoice), and method of delivery (DDU—which means delivery duty unpaid). *See* Black's Law Dictionary 481, 521 (10th ed. 2014) (defining "DDU" and "delivery duty unpaid").").

[492]*Helsinn I*, 387 F. Supp. 3d at 449. The Helsinn patent application that later issued as the '219 patent was denominated a continuation-in-part of an application filed in April 2011, and referenced a provisional application filed in 2003. Presumably some of the claims of the '219 patent were entitled to a pre-AIA effective filing date but others (drawn to new matter) were not. Hence, the '219 patent would be treated as an AIA patent. *See Examination Guidelines for Implementing the First Inventor to File Provisions of the Leahy-Smith America Invents Act*, 78 Fed. Reg. 11059-01 (Feb. 14, 2013).

[493]*See* United States Patent and Trademark Office, *Examination Guidelines for Implementing the First Inventor to File Provisions of the Leahy-Smith America Invents Act*, 78 Fed. Reg. 11059, 11075 (Feb. 14, 2013).

bar . . . requires that the sale or offer for sale *make the claimed invention available to the public.*"[494] Applying this statutory construction to the evidence of record, the district court concluded that the MGI Supply Agreement "did not make the claimed invention available to the public."[495] The Agreement was admittedly a "contract for sale" that included quantity and price terms. But the record included other relevant evidence. A published "Form 8-K" filed by MGI with the U.S. Securities and Exchange Commission (SEC) was "redacted and indicated only that Helsinn and MGI had entered into an agreement to purchase Helsinn's product." Press releases issued by Helsinn "only disclosed the existence of the agreement between Helsinn and MGI." Notably, the redacted documents did *not* disclose (1) the price terms and (2) the specific 0.25 mg dosage formulation that Helsinn was obligated to supply MGI.[496]

Although these extra-contractual documents publicized *the fact of the sale*, the *Helsinn I* district court concluded that the validity challengers had "failed to show how [the documents] made Helsinn's claimed invention, i.e., its particular palonosetron formulation, available to the public."[497] To be "public" under the AIA, the district court determined, a sale had to publicly disclose *the details of the invention.* The district court found that the MGI Supply and Purchase Agreement did not constitute a public sale or commercial offer for sale because, although it disclosed the sale agreement and substance of the transaction, it failed to publicly disclose the 0.25 mg dose. Because the formulation was not "available to the public," the district court reasoned that its pre–critical date sale did *not* trigger the AIA-amended §102 bars. Thus, the district court held that the '219 patent was *not* invalid under the on sale bar of §102(a)(1) (AIA version eff. Mar. 16, 2013).[498]

An appeal filed in April 2016 in the *Helsinn* case offered the Federal Circuit its first opportunity to determine whether the AIA changed the law of on sale bar as the *Helsinn I* district court had held. Rejecting the

[494]*Helsinn*, 387 F. Supp. 3d at 505, 2016 WL 832089, at *51 (emphasis added) (citing 35 U.S.C. 102(a)(1) (eff. Mar. 16, 2013); United States Patent and Trademark Office, *Examination Guidelines for Implementing the First Inventor to File Provisions of the Leahy-Smith America Invents Act*, 78 Fed. Reg. 11059, 11075 (Feb. 14, 2013).

[495]*Helsinn I*, 387 F. Supp. 3d at 505.

[496]However, the redacted documents did disclose that the covered products were pharmaceutical preparations for human use in intravenous dosage form, containing palonosetron as an active ingredient.

[497]*Helsinn I*, 387 F. Supp. 3d at 505.

[498]The district court also held that the invention of Helsinn's '219 patent was not "ready for patenting" before the critical date, an issue examined *supra* Section I.4.b ("Is Claimed Invention 'Ready for Patenting'?"). On appeal, the Federal Circuit in *Helsinn II* disagreed and held the invention of the '219 patent (and Helsinn's three other pre-AIA patents in suit) was "ready for patenting" by the critical date because it had been reduced to practice.

district court's statutory interpretation, the appellate court answered in the negative.

The Federal Circuit reversed the district court on the on sale issue in its May 2017 panel decision, *Helsinn Healthcare S.A. v. Teva Pharms. USA, Inc.* ("*Helsinn II*").[499] Hewing closely to the facts of the case, the Circuit held that the indisputably publicized transaction between Helsinn and MGI triggered the post-AIA on sale bar of 35 U.S.C. §102(a)(1), even though the information published about the transaction did not reveal key details about the invention itself (specifically, the formulation's dosage). "[T]he AIA did not change the statutory meaning of 'on sale' in the circumstances involved here,"[500] the appellate court concluded.

Before the Federal Circuit, patentee Helsinn (as well as the government and other *amici*) argued that the district court had determined correctly that the AIA had changed "on sale" law by adding the "or otherwise available to the public" concluding phrase in 35 U.S.C. §102(a)(1). They contended both that secret sales can no longer trigger the on sale bar under the AIA and that the AIA requires that an invalidating sale make the invention available to the public.

Deciding this issue of first impression, the Federal Circuit in *Helsinn II* reversed the district court on the "on sale" question. "We conclude that, after the AIA, *if* the existence of the sale is public, *the details of the invention need not be publicly disclosed* in the terms of the sale."[501]

However, the *Helsinn II* Circuit refused to "decide th[e] case more broadly than necessary." It purposefully avoided the question whether a completely secret or confidential sale (i.e., a pre–critical date private sales transaction of which the public has no knowledge whatsoever) can trigger the AIA on sale bar.[502] Rather, the Circuit held that the on sale bar had been triggered in the case before it, where "the existence of the sale [wa]s public,"[503] even though the public documents did not reveal all aspects of the claimed invention.

Patentee Helsinn and the *amici* had based their unsuccessful argument that the on sale bar was not triggered on (1) the addition of the

[499]855 F.3d 1356 (Fed. Cir. May 1, 2017) (Dyk, J.).

[500]*Helsinn II*, 855 F.3d at 1360.

[501]*Helsinn II*, 855 F.3d at 1371 (emphasis added).

[502]The Federal Circuit has held that secret sales can trigger the pre-AIA "on sale" bar. *See* In re Caveney, 761 F.2d 671, 675 (Fed. Cir. 1985) (rejecting argument that a secret sale by a third party was not invalidating because "sales or offers by one person of a claimed invention will bar another party from obtaining a patent").

[503]Professor Dennis Crouch catalogues a number of other questions left unanswered by the *Helsinn* decision in the article *Uncertainty:* Helsinn *Foreshadows Trouble with AIA Patents*, PATENTLY-O (May 10, 2017), https://patentlyo.com/patent/2017/05/uncertainty-helsinn-foreshadows.html?utm_source=feedburner&utm_medium=email&utm_campaign=Feed%3A+PatentlyO.

"otherwise available to the public" statutory language, as well as (2) several statements made on the floor of Congress ("floor statements") by individual legislators. For example, Senator Leahy remarked during congressional deliberation of the AIA in 2011 that "subsection 102(a) [as amended by the AIA] was drafted in part to do away with precedent under current law that *private offers for sale* or private uses or secret processes practiced in the United States that result in a product or service that is then made public may be deemed patent-defeating prior art."[504] Senator Kyl remarked that "[t]here is no reason to fear 'commercialization' that merely consists of a *secret sale or offer for sale* but that does not operate to disclose the invention to the public.... The present bill's new section 102(a) precludes extreme results such as these...."[505]

The *Helsinn II* Circuit was not persuaded by these legislative statements. It observed firstly that "such floor statements are typically not reliable as indicators of congressional intent."[506] In the appellate

[504]157 CONG. REC. S1496 (Mar. 9, 2011) (remarks of Sen. Leahy) (emphasis added), *available at* https://www.congress.gov/112/crec/2011/03/09/CREC-2011-03-09-pt1-PgS1496.pdf.

[505]157 CONG. REC. S1371 (Mar. 8, 2011) (remarks of Sen. Kyl) (emphasis added), *available at* https://www.congress.gov/112/crec/2011/03/08/CREC-2011-03-08-pt1-PgS1360-2.pdf.

[506]*Helsinn II*, 855 F.3d at 1368 (citing, e.g., Exxon Mobil Corp. v. Allapattah Servs., Inc., 545 U.S. 546, 568 (2005) (Kennedy, J.)). The Court in *Exxon Mobil* elaborated:

> As we have repeatedly held, the authoritative statement is the statutory text, not the legislative history or any other extrinsic material. Extrinsic materials have a role in statutory interpretation only to the extent they shed a reliable light on the enacting Legislature's understanding of otherwise ambiguous terms. Not all extrinsic materials are reliable sources of insight into legislative understandings, however, and legislative history in particular is vulnerable to two serious criticisms. First, legislative history is itself often murky, ambiguous, and contradictory. Judicial investigation of legislative history has a tendency to become, to borrow Judge Leventhal's memorable phrase, an exercise in "'looking over a crowd and picking out your friends.'" *See* Wald, *Some Observations on the Use of Legislative History in the 1981 Supreme Court Term*, 68 IOWA L. REV. 195, 214 (1983). Second, judicial reliance on legislative materials like committee reports, which are not themselves subject to the requirements of Article I, may give unrepresentative committee members — or, worse yet, unelected staffers and lobbyists — both the power and the incentive to attempt strategic manipulations of legislative history to secure results they were unable to achieve through the statutory text. We need not comment here on whether these problems are sufficiently prevalent to render legislative history inherently unreliable in all circumstances, a point on which Members of this Court have disagreed.

Exxon Mobil, 545 U.S. at 568-569. *See also* Consumer Prod. Safety Comm'n v. GTE Sylvania, Inc., 447 U.S. 102, 117-118 (1980) (Rehnquist, J.) (stating that "ordinarily even the contemporaneous remarks of a single legislator who sponsors a bill are not controlling in analyzing legislative history") (citing Chrysler Corp. v. Brown, 441 U.S. 281, 311 (1979)); Odow v. United States, 51 Fed. Cl. 425, 432 (2001) (stating that "individual floor statements, by themselves, are not accorded substantial weight as evidence of

court's view, the quoted floor statements of Senators Leahy and Kyl showed "at most" an intent to do away with certain pre-AIA §102 precedent. But importantly, the Leahy and Kyl floor statements cited only cases dealing with secret "public use" cases, not "on sale" cases.[507] The former involved so-called "non-informing public uses," in which the invention was not disclosed to the public as a result of the use (e.g., the corset steels worn under women's clothing in the Supreme Court's 1881 *Egbert v. Lippmann* decision).[508] No §102 "public use" issue was raised in *Helsinn*. Moreover, even assuming *arguendo* that the floor statements evidenced congressional intent to overrule truly secret sale cases such as *In re Caveney*,[509] the Circuit observed that overruling those cases was irrelevant to the case at bar, where the fact of the sale was indisputably public.

The Federal Circuit next rejected Helsinn's argument that in enacting the AIA, Congress intended to require that the details of a claimed invention must be publicly disclosed before the critical date to invoke the on sale bar of AIA §102(a)(1). In the Circuit's view, such a requirement would "work a foundational change in the theory of the statutory on-sale bar."[510]

That theory was first elucidated in the Supreme Court's landmark 1829 decision *Pennock v. Dialogue*,[511] a case that involved patent-invalidating public sales of an item (i.e., riveted leather hose for conveying air, water, or other fluids, formed from joined parts capable of resisting high pressures) but the withholding from "the public the secrets of [the] invention."[512] Over a period of seven years before a patent application for the method of making the hose was filed in 1818, manufacturers sold approximately 13,000 feet of the hose to the

---

legislative intent") (citing *Consumer Prod. Safety Comm'n*, 447 U.S. at 117-118); Bay View, Inc. v. United States, 278 F.3d 1259, 1264 (Fed. Cir. 2001) (Rader, J.) (stating that "[s]ome forms of legislative history supply insights into the meaning of enactments. While statements of a single legislator rarely reflect the will of the entire Congress, a joint statement of a conference committee more often reflects the joint will of each house of Congress.").

[507]*Helsinn II*, 855 F.3d at 1368-1369 (listing public use cases explicitly referred to in floor statements of Senator Kyl as including *Egbert v. Lippman*, 104 U.S. 333 (1881), *Beachcombers Int'l, Inc. v. Wildewood Creative Prods., Inc.*, 31 F.3d 1154 (Fed. Cir. 1994), and *JumpSport, Inc. v. Jumpking, Inc.*, Nos. 05-1182, 05-1196, 05-1197, 2006 WL 2034498 (Fed. Cir. July 21, 2006)); *Helsinn II*, 855 F.3d at 1369 (observing that "[t]he floor statements do not identify any *sale* cases that would be overturned by the [AIA §3] amendments").

[508]The *Egbert* decision and other non-informing public use cases are analyzed *supra* Section I.3 ("Section 102(b) Public Use").

[509]761 F.2d 671, 675 (Fed. Cir. 1985) (rejecting argument that a secret sale by a third party was not invalidating because "sales or offers by one person of a claimed invention will bar another party from obtaining a patent").

[510]*Helsinn II*, 855 F.3d at 1369.

[511]27 U.S. 1, 19 (1829) (Story, J.).

[512]*Pennock*, 27 U.S. at 19.

public. In oft-quoted language, the Supreme Court in *Pennock* explained the policy rationale against permitting this type of prolonged delay in seeking a patent:

> If an inventor should be permitted to *hold back from the knowledge of the public the secrets of his invention*; if he should for a long period of years retain the monopoly, and make, and *sell his invention publicly*, and thus gather the whole profits of it, relying upon his superior skill and knowledge of the structure; and then, and then only, when the danger of competition should force him to secure the exclusive right, he should be allowed to take out a patent, and thus exclude the public from any farther use than what should be derived under it during his fourteen years; *it would materially retard the progress of science and the useful arts, and give a premium to those who should be least prompt to communicate their discoveries.*[513]

This foundational Supreme Court precedent supported the Circuit's position that patentees (like Helsinn) should not be allowed to publicly sell or offer to sell their invention for a prolonged period of time before revealing the nature of the invention by entering the patenting process.

The Federal Circuit's own precedent further supported the position that an invention is placed on sale when it is the subject of a commercial sale or offer before the critical date and that sale is made public. In contrast, the Circuit's earlier decisions had explicitly rejected an "on sale" requirement that the details of the claimed invention be disclosed in the terms of sale.[514]

The *Helsinn II* Circuit identified as "a primary rationale" underlying the on sale bar the concept that publicly offering a product for sale that embodies the claimed invention effectively places that invention in the public domain (in other words, makes it part of the prior art). This result holds whether or not actual delivery occurs. Nor must a pre–critical date sale be consummated or an offer accepted to trigger the bar and place the invention in the public domain. Circuit precedent also established that members of the public need not be aware that the product sold actually embodied the claimed invention.[515] In sum, the Federal Circuit's prior cases "applied the on-sale bar even

[513]*Pennock*, 27 U.S. at 19 (emphasis added).

[514]*Helsinn II*, 855 F.3d at 1370 (citing RCA Corp. v. Data Gen. Corp., 887 F.2d 1056, 1060 (Fed. Cir. 1989) (rejecting argument "that the bid documents themselves must disclose the invention with respect to all claim elements" since that is "clearly not legally correct" and there can be "a definite offer for sale or a sale of a claimed invention even though no details are disclosed"), *overruled in part on other grounds by* Group One, Ltd. v. Hallmark Cards, Inc., 254 F.3d 1041, 1048 (Fed. Cir. 2001)).

[515]*Helsinn II*, 855 F.3d at 1370-1371 (citing Abbott Labs. v. Geneva Pharms., Inc., 182 F.3d 1315, 1317-1318 (Fed. Cir. 1999) ("on sale" bar applied even though at time of sale, neither party to transaction knew whether the product sold embodied the

when there is no delivery, when delivery is set after the critical date, or, even when, upon delivery, members of the public could not ascertain the claimed invention."[516]

Having reviewed the wealth of pertinent Supreme Court and Federal Circuit precedent governing the "on sale" bar, the *Helsinn II* Circuit concluded that the congressional floor statements relied on by Helsinn could not evince a congressional intent to overrule those cases. Rather, "[i]n stating that the invention must be available to the public [Senators Leahy and Kyl] evidently meant that the public sale itself would put the patented product in the hands of the public."[517] By referring to "public sale," the Circuit seemed to suggest that a purely private but pre–critical date sale may not trigger the "on sale" bar under the AIA. But importantly, the Circuit in *Helsinn II* did not decide this key question.[518]

---

claimed invention and had no easy way to determine what the product was)). The *Abbott Labs.* court explained that

> claim 4 is invalid and . . . the parties' ignorance that they were dealing with Form IV [i.e., one of four anhydrous crystalline forms of the compound terazosin hydrochloride, used to treat hypertension] is irrelevant. . . . The invention at issue in this case clearly meets the [Supreme Court's] *Pfaff* test. Even though the parties did not know it at the time, it is undisputed that Form IV was the subject matter of at least three commercial sales in the United States before the critical date. It is also clear that the invention was "ready for patenting" because at least two foreign manufacturers had already reduced it to practice.

Abbott Labs., 182 F.3d at 1318.

[516] *Helsinn II*, 855 F.3d at 1371.

[517] *Helsinn II*, 855 F.3d at 1371 (citing 157 CONG. REC. S1370 (Mar. 8, 2011) (remarks of Sen. Kyl) (stating that "once a product is sold on the market, any invention that is inherent to the product becomes publicly available prior art and cannot be patented")), *available at* https://www.congress.gov/crec/2011/03/08/CREC-2011-03-08-pt1-PgS1360-2.pdf.

[518] In the view of this author, well-established policy dictates that purely private or secret sales or offers by which the *patentee* exploits her invention before the "on sale" bar critical date should continue to count as invalidating under the AIA. Despite being confidential or secret, such sales still violate the policy of prohibiting undue commercial exploitation by the inventor for a period of time beyond the statutorily-allowed period of exclusivity. It is highly unlikely that Congress intended to abrogate this policy concern when it enacted the AIA. *See, e.g.*, Woodland Trust v. Flowertree Nursery, Inc., 148 F.3d 1368, 1370 (Fed. Cir. 1998) (stating that "an inventor's own prior commercial use, albeit kept secret, may constitute a public use or sale under §102(b), barring him from obtaining a patent"); In re Caveney, 761 F.2d 671, 675 (Fed. Cir. 1985) (rejecting argument that a secret sale by a third party was not invalidating because "sales or offers by one person of a claimed invention will bar another party from obtaining a patent"); *Caveney*, 761 F.2d at 675 (stating general rule that "sales or offers by one person of a claimed invention will bar another party from obtaining a patent if the sale or offer to sell is made over a year before the latter's filing date") (citing Pennwalt Corp. v. Akzona Inc., 740 F.2d 1573, 1580 n.14 (Fed. Cir. 1984); General Electric Co. v. United States, 654 F.2d 55, 61-62 (Ct. Cl. 1981)); *Caveney*, 761 F.2d at 675 (stating further that "[a]n exception to this general rule exists where a patented method is kept secret and remains

The Circuit in *Helsinn II* observed lastly that "no floor statements suggest[ed] that the sale or offer documents themselves must publicly disclose the details of the invention before the critical date." If Congress had intended such a "sweeping change" to the court's "on sale" bar case law, so as to overrule the Circuit's prior decisions legislatively, Congress would have done so " 'by clear language.' "[519] Lacking such language in the record of the case at bar, the appellate court concluded that

> after the AIA, if the existence of the sale is public, the details of the invention need not be publicly disclosed in the terms of sale. For the reasons already stated, the Supply and Purchase Agreement between Helsinn and MGI constituted a sale of the claimed invention — the 0.25 mg dose — before the critical date, and therefore both the pre-AIA and AIA on-sale bars apply.[520]

Emphasizing for a final time the limited scope of its decision, the Circuit denied finding that "distribution agreements will always be invalidating" under the on sale bar. Rather, the *Helsinn II* court had "simply f[ou]nd that this particular Supply and Purchase Agreement is."[521]

The U.S. Supreme Court thereafter granted *certiorari* to the Circuit in *Helsinn II*, agreeing to review the following Question Presented:

> Whether, under the Leahy-Smith America Invents Act, an inventor's sale of an invention to a third party that is obligated to keep the

---

secret after a sale of the unpatented product of the method. Such a sale prior to the critical date is a bar *if engaged in by the patentee or patent applicant*, but not if engaged in by another.") (emphasis added) (citing W.L. Gore & Associates, Inc. v. Garlock, Inc., 721 F.2d 1540, 1550 (Fed. Cir. 1983); D.L. Auld Co. v. Chroma Graphics Corp., 714 F.2d 1144, 1147-1148 (Fed. Cir. 1983)); Metallizing Engineering Co. v. Kenyon Bearing & Auto Parts Co., 153 F.2d 516 (2d Cir. 1946) (L. Hand, J.); 2 R. Carl Moy, Moy's Walker on Patents §8:228 (4th ed. 2016) (stating that "even a private sale or offer for sale can be a barring event").

Professor Dennis Crouch also catalogues a number of questions left unanswered by the *Helsinn* decision in the article *Uncertainty:* Helsinn *Foreshadows Trouble with AIA Patents*, Patently-O (May 10, 2017), https://patentlyo.com/patent/2017/05/uncertainty-helsinn-foreshadows.html?utm_source=feedburner&utm_medium=email&utm_campaign=Feed%3A+PatentlyO.

[519] *Helsinn II*, 855 F.3d at 1371 (citing Director, Office of Workers' Comp. Programs, U.S. Dep't of Labor v. Perini N. River Assocs., 459 U.S. 297, 321 (1983) (O'Connor, J.) (stating that "[s]urely, if Congress wished to repeal *Calbeck* [Calbeck v. Travelers Insurance Co., 370 U.S. 114 (1962)] and other cases legislatively, it would do so by clear language . . .")).

[520] *Helsinn II*, 855 F.3d at 1371. Those portions of the Circuit's *Helsinn* decision invalidating the pre-AIA patents under the "on sale" bar of §102(b) (2006) are analyzed *supra* Section I.4 ("Section 102(b) On Sale Bar").

[521] *Helsinn II*, 855 F.3d at 1371.

invention confidential qualifies as prior art for purposes of determining the patentability of the invention.[522]

The Supreme Court answered the question affirmatively in its 2019 decision *Helsinn Healthcare S.A. v. Teva Pharm. USA, Inc.* ("*Helsinn III*"),[523] affirming the Federal Circuit. The *Helsinn III* ruling is particularly significant for patent practitioners because it marks the first Supreme Court decision interpreting the prior art provisions of 35 U.S.C. §102 as amended by the AIA.

In a relatively short and unanimous opinion authored by Justice Thomas, the *Helsinn III* Court held that "an inventor's sale of an invention to a third party who is obligated to keep the invention confidential *can* qualify as prior art" under the AIA-amended §102.[524] In other words, the technical details of an invention need not be disclosed to the public in order to place it "on sale" under the Patent Act. Thus, the Helsinn '219 patent was potentially rendered invalid under the on sale bar even though the Helsinn-MGI documents "failed to . . . ma[k]e Helsinn's claimed invention, i.e., its palonosetron formulation, available to the public."[525]

The *Helsinn III* Court determined that Congress's AIA addition in §102 of the "broad catch-all" phrase, "or otherwise available to the public," was "simply not enough of a change for us to conclude that Congress intended to alter the meaning of the reenacted term 'on sale.'"[526] That term had appeared in every U.S. patent statute since the 1836 Act,[527] and was the subject of numerous common law decisions. The Court noted that "Congress enacted the AIA in 2011 against the backdrop of a substantial body of law interpreting §102's on-sale

[522]Petition for Certiorari, Helsinn Healthcare S.A. v. Teva Pharms. USA, Inc. (Feb. 2018), at (I), *available at* https://www.supremecourt.gov/DocketPDF/17/17-1229/36967/20180228105246621_Helsinn%20cert%20petition.pdf. Notably, the question as stated is not limited to sales activity of which the public is aware, unlike in the Federal Circuit's *Helsinn II* decision.

[523]139 S. Ct. 628 (2019).

[524]*Helsinn III,* 139 S. Ct. at 634 (emphasis added).

[525]*Helsinn I*, 2016 WL 832089, at *52. Note that the Supreme Court decided only the question of law as to the prior art (i.e., by concluding that "such a sale can qualify as prior art," but did not review the merits or factual underpinnings of the potential on sale bar invalidation. Nevertheless, the Supreme Court affirmed the Federal Circuit's decision. *See Helsinn III*, 139 S. Ct. at 632. The Federal Circuit had held that "the asserted claims, . . . claims 1, 2, and 6 of the '219 patent, are invalid under the on-sale bar." *Helsinn II*, 855 F.3d at 1375 (Fed. Cir. 2017). Recall that the Circuit concluded (1) "the Supply and Purchase Agreement between Helsinn and MGI constituted a sale of the claimed invention — the 0.25 mg dose — before the critical date, and therefore . . . the AIA on-sale bar[] appl[ies]," and (2) the "invention here was ready for patenting because it was reduced to practice before the critical date" of January 30, 2002. *Helsinn II*, 855 F.3d at 1371.

[526]*Helsinn III,* 139 S. Ct. at 634.

[527]*Helsinn III,* 139 S. Ct. at 633 (citing *Pfaff*, 525 U.S. at 65).

bar."[528] It further observed that the Federal Circuit, which has "'exclusive jurisdiction' over patent appeals," has "long held that 'secret sales' can invalidate a patent."[529] In light of this "settled pre-AIA precedent," the *Helsinn III* Court "presume[d] that when Congress reenacted the same language in the AIA (that is, the words 'on sale' and 'public use'), it adopted the earlier judicial construction of that phrase."[530]

The *Helsinn III* decision raises some question concerning its scope, because it seems to go well beyond what the Federal Circuit had held in *Helsinn II.* Recall that in *Helsinn II* the Federal Circuit refused to "decide th[e] case more broadly than necessary," avoiding the question whether a completely secret or confidential sale (i.e., a pre–critical date private sales transaction of which the public has no knowledge whatsoever) can trigger the AIA on sale bar.[531] Rather, the *Helsinn II* Circuit held that the on sale bar had been triggered in the case before it, where "the existence of the sale [wa]s public,"[532] even though the publicly-available documents did not disclose all technical aspects of the claimed invention.

Given the Federal Circuit's carefully constrained holding in *Helsinn II,* did the Supreme Court's affirmance in *Helsinn III* resolve the broader question encompassing a truly secret sale, wherein even the fact of the pre–critical date transaction is not publicized? Reasonable arguments exist for both positions. On the affirmative side, the *Helsinn III* Court's language is broad enough to cover both possibilities. The Court framed its task as follows:

> We granted certiorari to determine whether, under the AIA, an inventor's sale of an invention to a third party who is obligated to keep the invention confidential qualifies as prior art for purposes of determining

[528] *Helsinn III,* 139 S. Ct. at 633.

[529] *Helsinn III,* 139 S. Ct. at 633 (citing, e.g., Special Devices, Inc. v. OEA, Inc., 270 F.3d 1353, 1357 (Fed. Cir. 2001) (invalidating patent claims based on "sales for the purpose of the commercial stockpiling of an invention" that "took place in secret"); Woodland Trust v. Flowertree Nursery, Inc., 148 F.3d 1368, 1370 (Fed. Cir. 1998) ("Thus an inventor's own prior commercial use, albeit kept secret, may constitute a public use or sale under §102(b), barring him from obtaining a patent[.]")).

[530] *Helsinn III,* 139 S. Ct. at 633-634.

[531] The Federal Circuit has held that secret sales can trigger the pre-AIA "on sale" bar. *See* In re Caveney, 761 F.2d 671, 675 (Fed. Cir. 1985) (rejecting argument that a secret sale by a third party was not invalidating because "sales or offers by one person of a claimed invention will bar another party from obtaining a patent").

[532] Professor Dennis Crouch catalogues a number of other questions left unanswered by the *Helsinn* decision in the article *Uncertainty:* Helsinn *Foreshadows Trouble with AIA Patents*, PATENTLY-O (May 10, 2017), https://patentlyo.com/patent/2017/05/uncertainty-helsinn-foreshadows.html?utm_source=feedburner&utm_medium=email&utm_campaign=Feed%3A+PatentlyO.

> the patentability of the invention. 585 U.S. ___, 138 S. Ct. 2678, 201 L. Ed. 2d 1070 (2018). We conclude that such a sale can qualify as prior art.[533]

The Court's quoted statement does not include any requirement that the fact of the transaction be public (unlike the facts of *Helsinn*). Moreover, the Court observed that the Federal Circuit's on sale precedent "has made explicit what was implicit in our precedents. [The Circuit] has long held that 'secret sales' can invalidate a patent."[534]

On the negative side, the *Helsinn III* Court affirmed the Circuit's *Helsinn II* decision, which the appellate court had carefully limited to the narrower question. Does such an affirmance have decisional scope beyond the limits of the decision below? Notably in the case at bar, the Question Presented on which *certiorari* was granted is broader in scope than the Circuit's decision in *Helsinn II.*

Although reasonable persons can disagree about the scope of the Supreme Court's *Helsinn III* holding, this author views it as broad enough to mean that an *entirely* secret sale still qualifies as prior art post-AIA. The Question Presented permitted this breadth; the Supreme Court is not bound by the Federal Circuit. This author predicts that the Federal Circuit will eventually confront a completely secret post-AIA on sale bar fact scenario and resolve it under the broader reading of *Helsinn III*. Given the reasoning set forth and the non-limiting statements made by the Supreme Court in *Helsinn III,* this author believes that such a case can give rise to prior art under the AIA-amended §102 (just as the Circuit has held in pre-AIA cases).[535]

[533]*Helsinn III,* 139 S. Ct. at 632. The Court states accurately the Question Presented in Helsinn's Petition for Certiorari. The question asked:

> Whether, under the Leahy-Smith America Invents Act, an inventor's sale of an invention to a third party that is obligated to keep the invention confidential qualifies as prior art for purposes of determining the patentability of the invention.

Petition for Certiorari, Helsinn Healthcare S.A. v. Teva Pharms. USA, Inc. (Feb. 2018), at (I), *available at* https://www.supremecourt.gov/DocketPDF/17/17-1229/36967/20180228105246621_Helsinn%20cert%20petition.pdf. The question as stated is not limited to sales activity of which the public is aware, unlike in *Helsinn II.*

[534]*Helsinn III,* 139 S. Ct. at 633 (citing, e.g., Special Devices, Inc. v. OEA, Inc., 270 F.3d 1353, 1357 (Fed. Cir. 2001) (invalidating patent claims based on "sales for the purpose of the commercial stockpiling of an invention" that "took place in secret"); Woodland Trust v. Flowertree Nursery, Inc., 148 F.3d 1368, 1370 (Fed. Cir. 1998) ("Thus an inventor's own prior commercial use, albeit kept secret, may constitute a public use or sale under §102(b), barring him from obtaining a patent[.]").

[535]*See Helsinn III,* 139 S. Ct. at 633 (observing that "[t]he Federal Circuit — which has 'exclusive jurisdiction' over patent appeals, 28 U.S.C. §1295(a) — has made explicit what was implicit in our precedents. It has long held that 'secret sales' can invalidate a patent.") (citing, e.g., Special Devices, Inc. v. OEA, Inc., 270 F.3d 1353, 1357 (Fed. Cir. 2001) (invalidating patent claims based on "sales for the purpose of the commercial

In this author's view, concluding otherwise would also confusingly co-mingle the two different policy bases underlying the §102 bars. The §102 on sale bar is concerned primarily with preventing an inventor's prolonged commercial exploitation of her invention beyond the grace period, while the public use bar is concerned primarily with preventing withdrawal through patenting of information already understood to be in the public domain. Whether or not the fact of a pre–critical date sales transaction is known to the public is not relevant to the former, although it may be relevant to the latter.

R. Presumptively Novelty-Destroying Events Under Post-AIA 35 U.S.C. §102(a)(2)

Section §102(a)(2) of 35 U.S.C. (eff. Mar. 16, 2013) provides that "[a] person shall be entitled to a patent unless — the claimed invention was described in a patent issued under section 151, or in an application for patent published or deemed published under section 122(b), in which the patent or application, as the case may be, names another inventor and was effectively filed before the effective filing date of the claimed invention."

The language of post-AIA §102(a)(2) is the closest the statute comes to expressing a first-inventor-to-file priority principle, and the principle is only implicitly gleaned from the statutory text. The essence of §102(a)(2) is that the novelty of a claimed invention is presumptively destroyed if the same invention was already described in an earlier-filed U.S. patent or published patent application naming another inventor. In short, the later filer loses the priority contest (barring an exception under §102(b)(2)). The verbal complexity of §102(a)(2) stands in sharp contrast to the first-to-file principle clearly articulated in the European Patent Convention (EPC).[536]

Section 102(a)(2) is the post-AIA counterpart of pre-AIA 35 U.S.C. §102(e).[537] Codified in the 1952 Patent Act, 35 U.S.C. §102(e) implemented the rule announced in the U.S. Supreme Court's landmark

stockpiling of an invention" that "took place in secret"); Woodland Trust v. Flowertree Nursery, Inc., 148 F.3d 1368, 1370 (Fed. Cir. 1998) ("Thus an inventor's own prior commercial use, albeit kept secret, may constitute a public use or sale under §102(b), barring him from obtaining a patent[.]")); *id.* (referring to the Federal Circuit's decisions as "this settled pre-AIA precedent on the meaning of 'on sale'").

[536] Article 60 ("Right to a European Patent") of the EPC provides in pertinent part that "[i]f two or more persons have made an invention independently of each other, the right to a European patent therefor shall belong to the person whose European patent application has the earliest date of filing, provided that this first application has been published." European Patent Convention art. 60(2) (14th ed. 2010).

[537] 35 U.S.C. §102(e) (2006).

decision *Alexander Milburn Co. v. Davis-Bournonville Co.*[538] The policy rationale underlying *Milburn*, a case decided against the backdrop of the United States' historic first-to-invent priority system, was that the presence of a complete description of an invention claimed by a U.S. patent applicant (or patentee), in someone else's earlier-filed U.S. patent, evidences that the applicant or patentee is *not* in fact the first to invent the claimed subject matter and is thus not entitled to patent it. Distilled to its essence, *Milburn* required that the disclosure of a U.S. patent, when used as prior art, must be treated as constructively published on the date that the application for the patent was filed in the USPTO. The *Milburn* Court engaged in the fiction that the contents of the patent's written description became instantaneously available as a printed publication upon filing, although in fact the description would remain secret to the public until some later date (i.e., issuance of the patent or (via later legislative developments) publication of the pending application). Thus, under *Milburn* and pre-AIA law, the effective date of the written description portion of a U.S. patent or published U.S. patent application being used as §102(e) prior art was its U.S. filing date.[539]

The AIA did not change the basic *Milburn* concept of treating an anticipatory description in another's earlier-filed U.S. patent as novelty-destroying prior art. However, the AIA did eliminate the notion of "invention date" from all parts of 35 U.S.C. §102, such that novelty is now assessed as of a claimed invention's effective filing date.[540]

The AIA also added to the Patent Act a new §102(d) defining the effective filing date of §102(a)(2) prior art patents or published applications.[541] In accordance with post-AIA §102(d), a U.S. patent or published (or "deemed published") patent application, the description of which is relied on as prior art under post-AIA §102(a)(2), will be assigned an effective date that is (i) its actual U.S. filing date; (ii) the earlier U.S. filing date of a co-pending application (such as a parent

[538]270 U.S. 390 (1926). *See also* P.J. Federico, *Commentary on the New Patent Act*, 35 U.S.C.A. §1 (1954 ed., discontinued in subsequent volumes), *reprinted at* 75 J. Pat. & Trademark Off. Soc'y 161, 179 (1993) (explaining that "[p]aragraph (e) is new in the statute and enacts the rule of the decision of the Supreme Court in [*Milburn*] under which a United States patent disclosing an invention dates from the filing of the application for the purpose of anticipating a later inventor, whether or not the invention is claimed in the patent") (citation omitted). *See generally supra* Section L ("Description in Another's Earlier-Filed Patent or Published Patent Application Under 35 U.S.C. §102(e) (Pre-AIA)").

[539]*See supra* Section L ("Description in Another's Earlier-Filed Patent or Published Patent Application Under 35 U.S.C. §102(e) (Pre-AIA)").

[540]*See* 35 U.S.C. §102(a) (eff. Mar. 16, 2013); 35 U.S.C. §100(i) (eff. Mar. 16, 2013) (defining "effective filing date" for a claimed invention in a patent or application for patent).

[541]See 35 U.S.C. §102(d) (eff. Mar. 16, 2013) ("Patents and Published Applications Effective as Prior Art").

or provisional) to which the prior art patent or published application may be entitled (for example, under 35 U.S.C. §119(e) or 35 U.S.C. §120); or (iii) the earlier foreign priority date to which the prior art patent or printed publication may be entitled under 35 U.S.C. §119(a) in view of the *Hilmer* rule's repeal.[542] It seems likely (but not yet certain) that the question of entitlement of the prior art patent or printed publication to either effective date (ii) or (iii) will turn on compliance with the enablement and written description of the invention requirements of 35 U.S.C. §112(a).[543]

[542]*See* 35 U.S.C. §102(d) (eff. Mar. 16, 2013), which provides:

> (d) PATENTS AND PUBLISHED APPLICATIONS EFFECTIVE AS PRIOR ART. — For purposes of determining whether a patent or application for patent is prior art to a claimed invention under subsection (a)(2), such patent or application shall be considered to have been effectively filed, with respect to any subject matter described in the patent or application —
>
> (1) if paragraph (2) does not apply, as of the actual filing date of the patent or the application for patent; or
>
> (2) if the patent or application for patent is entitled to claim a right of priority under section 119, 365(a), or 365(b), or to claim the benefit of an earlier filing date under section 120, 121, or 365(c), based upon 1 or more prior filed applications for patent, as of the filing date of the earliest such application that describes the subject matter.

Subparagraph (d)(2) implicitly repeals the rule of *In re Hilmer*, 359 F.2d 859 (C.C.P.A. 1966). *See also supra* Section P.3.b ("What Section 3 of the AIA Changed"); *supra* Section L ("Description in Another's Earlier-Filed Patent or Published Patent Application Under 35 U.S.C. §102(e) (Pre-AIA)").

[543]The enablement and written description disclosure requirements of 35 U.S.C. §112(a) (eff. Sept. 16, 2012) are explicitly incorporated into post-AIA 35 U.S.C. §119(e)(1) (domestic priority) and post-AIA 35 U.S.C. §120 ("Benefit of earlier filing date in the United States"); the AIA deleted the best mode disclosure requirement from these statutory provisions. Case law establishes that the "for the same invention" language of 35 U.S.C. §119(a) implicitly invokes the §112 disclosure requirements for foreign priority claims. *See infra* Chapter 12, Section B.4.

Be aware, however, that as of 2019, the Federal Circuit had not yet resolved this issue. In *Dynamic Drinkware, LLC v. National Graphics, Inc.*, No. 2015-1214, 800 F.3d 1375, 2015 WL 5166366 (Fed. Cir. Sept. 4, 2015), discussed *supra* Section L.2, the Federal Circuit noted, but did not reach, the issue of how the effective date of a reference patent or published patent application will be determined in the future under AIA law. That issue will turn on judicial interpretation of AIA-implemented 35 U.S.C. §102(d). As the Federal Circuit observed in a footnote, "[t]he relevant provision of §102(e)(2) was reorganized into newly designated §102(d)(2) when certain aspects of the Leahy-Smith America Invents Act ("AIA"), Pub. L. No. 112-29, took effect on March 16, 2013." Because the Circuit in *Dynamic Drinkware* "refer[red] to the pre-AIA version of §102," it would "not interpret here the AIA's impact on *Wertheim* in newly designated §102(d)." AIA-implemented §102(d), titled "Patents and published applications effective as prior art," refers to "subject matter described" in a reference patent or application. This phrasing, along with language asking whether the "patent or application for patent is *entitled* to claim a right of priority under section 119," does not make crystal clear whether compliance with the enablement and written description requirements of 35 U.S.C. §112(a) will be required.

R. Presumptively Novelty-Destroying Events Under Post-AIA

The following hypotheticals illustrate the operation of post-AIA §102(a)(2) and §102(d).

Hypothetical. Consider U.S. patent applicant Matthew, who invented a widget "X" and thereafter filed a non-provisional utility patent application disclosing and claiming widget X in the USPTO on July 1, 2014. Unbeknownst to Matthew, on June 30, 2014, one day before Matthew's filing date, Neal filed his own non-provisional utility patent application in the USPTO. Neal's application described widget X in complete detail. When the USPTO publishes Neal's application at 18 months after its filing date (or, if it is not published at 18 months, when Neal's application issues as a U.S. patent), the description of widget X in Neal's application will be available for citation by the USPTO as §102(a)(2) prior art against Matthew's application claims to widget X. Under these facts, the effective date of the description in Neal's application, which is being used by the USPTO as prior art, is Neal's actual U.S. filing date of June 30, 2014, one day before Matthew's filing date. The description in Neal's application is anticipatory, preventing Matthew from obtaining a patent claiming widget X (in the absence of any facts suggesting that Neal's disclosure is removed as prior art under a §102(b)(2) exception[544]). Matthew's invention date is not relevant. In accordance with *Milburn*, whether Neal or some third party actually invented the widget X described in Neal's application is not relevant either. Section 102(a)(2) merely requires that Neal be named as an inventor on his application, which he is.

First Variation. Change the facts of the above hypothetical such that Neal filed a first patent application identically describing widget X in an enabling fashion in the Japanese Patent Office on June 30, 2014. On June 29, 2015 (within the Paris Convention 12-month priority period), Neal filed a non-provisional utility patent application in the USPTO having the same description of widget X that appeared in the Japanese application (translated into English). Neal claimed for his U.S. application the right of priority under 35 U.S.C. §119(a) to his Japanese filing date of June 30, 2014. Neal's U.S. application is entitled to his Japanese filing date because the disclosure of the Japanese application satisfies the requirements of 35 U.S.C. §112, first paragraph (i.e., enablement and written description) for the subject matter claimed in Neal's U.S. application.[545] When the USPTO publishes Neal's application on or after December 30, 2015 (generally 18 months after his foreign filing date), the description in Neal's

[544]*See infra* Section S.3 ("Post-AIA §102(b)(2): Shields Against Post-AIA §102(a)(2) Presumptively Novelty-Destroying Events").

[545]*See infra* Chapter 12, Section B.4. It is presumed that the AIA implicitly removed the best mode requirement from foreign priority claims under 35 U.S.C. §119(a), because it did so explicitly for domestic priority claims under §119(e) and claims to the benefit of an earlier-filed co-pending application under §120.

application will be available for citation as anticipatory §102(a)(2) prior art by the USPTO against Matthew's application claims to widget X. Under these facts, the effective date of Neal's application, which is being used by the USPTO as prior art, is Neal's foreign priority date of June 30, 2014, which is one day before Matthew's filing date. The *Hilmer* rule no longer prevents assigning the foreign priority date as the prior art effective date of Neal's U.S. patent application.[546] The description in Neal's published application is presumptively novelty-destroying prior art under §102(a)(2), preventing Matthew from obtaining a U.S. patent claiming widget X. It is not relevant that as between Matthew and Neal, Matthew was the first to file an application in the USPTO.

S. Novelty-Preserving Exceptions Under Post-AIA 35 U.S.C. §102(b)

1. Introduction

Novelty (or, more precisely, the lack thereof) is not an absolute concept under the AIA. Even though one (or more) of the presumptively novelty-destroying events enumerated in post-AIA §102(a) has occurred, a claimed invention's novelty nevertheless may be preserved (in other words, the presumptively-established §102(a) prior art may be removed) if one of the "exceptions" or shields of 35 U.S.C. §102(b) (eff. Mar. 16, 2013) (hereafter "§102(b)" or "post-AIA §102(b)") applies.

The §102(b) exceptions operate in somewhat analogous fashion to "grace period" events under the pre-AIA regime.[547] Even though significantly amended by the AIA, the resultant U.S. Patent Act does not contain a European-style absolute novelty system. Despite Congress's stated intent to "promote harmonization of the United States patent system with the patent systems commonly used in nearly all other countries throughout the world with whom the United States conducts trade and thereby promote greater international uniformity

[546]Subparagraph (d)(2) of post-AIA §102 implicitly repeals the rule of *In re Hilmer*, 359 F.2d 859 (C.C.P.A. 1966). *See also supra* Section P.3.b ("What Section 3 of the AIA Changed"). *Compare* Section L ("Description in Another's Earlier-Filed Patent or Published Patent Application Under 35 U.S.C. §102(e) (Pre-AIA)").

[547]*See* H.R. Rep. No. 112-98 [House Judiciary Comm. Rep. on the America Invents Act], at 54 (June 1, 2011) (stating that the AIA "maintains a 1-year grace period for U.S. applicants. Applicants' own publication or disclosure that occurs within 1 year prior to filing will not act as prior art against their applications. Similarly, disclosure by others during that time based on information obtained (directly or indirectly) from the inventor will not constitute prior art. This 1-year grace period should continue to give U.S. applicants the time they need to prepare and file their applications."). *See also supra* Section I.2 ("Grace Period").

and certainty in the procedures used for securing the exclusive rights of inventors to their discoveries,"[548] the AIA did not completely (or even largely) harmonize U.S. patent law with international standards. Rather, the AIA created a U.S. patent statute that is a unique hybrid, retaining many aspects of the pre-AIA regime. The "exceptions" of §102(b) are prime examples.

The following subsections separately discuss the exceptions provided for in post-AIA §102(b)(1) and §102(b)(2).

2. Post-AIA §102(b)(1): Shields Against Post-AIA §102(a)(1) Presumptively Novelty-Destroying Events

Post-AIA §102(b)(1) enumerates two categories of exceptions that represent two different ways to remove what would otherwise be novelty-destroying prior art under post-AIA §102(a)(1). The post-AIA version of 35 U.S.C. §102 provides in pertinent part:

> (b) EXCEPTIONS.—
>
> (1) DISCLOSURES MADE 1 YEAR OR LESS BEFORE THE EFFECTIVE FILING DATE OF THE CLAIMED INVENTION.—A disclosure made 1 year or less before the effective filing date of a claimed invention shall not be prior art to the claimed invention under subsection (a)(1) if—
>
> (A) the disclosure was made by the inventor or joint inventor or by another who obtained the subject matter disclosed directly or indirectly from the inventor or a joint inventor; or
>
> (B) the subject matter disclosed had, before such disclosure, been publicly disclosed by the inventor or a joint inventor or another who obtained the subject matter disclosed directly or indirectly from the inventor or a joint inventor.[549]

In the discussion that follows, the two categories of §102(b)(1) exceptions are referred to as "(A)-type" and "(B)-type" exceptions. The (A)-type exceptions are those covered by post-AIA §102(b)(1)(A). The (B)-type exceptions are those covered by post-AIA §102(b)(1)(B).

a. (A)-Type Exceptions

The first, or "(A)-type," exception removes from the prior art certain pre-filing disclosures made by the inventor/patent applicant herself or based on information obtained from the applicant. The pertinent statutory language provides that "[a] disclosure made 1 year or less before the effective filing date of a claimed invention shall not be prior art to

[548] Leahy-Smith America Invents Act, Pub. L. No. 112-29 (H.R. 1249), §3(p), 125 Stat. 284, 293 (2011) ("Sense of Congress").

[549] 35 U.S.C. §102(b)(1) (eff. Mar. 16, 2013).

the claimed invention under subsection (a)(1) if . . . (A) the disclosure was made by the inventor or joint inventor or by another who obtained the subject matter disclosed directly or indirectly from the inventor or a joint inventor."[550] Thus, an (A)-type exception is triggered by the inventor, a joint inventor, or an "obtainer."[551]

For example, consider an inventor who makes a "disclosure" of her invention and then files in the USPTO an application seeking to patent the invention within one year (to use pre-AIA parlance, during the one-year pre-filing "grace period"). On its face, the applicant's pre-filing date disclosure would appear to have destroyed novelty under post-AIA §102(a)(1). However, the statutory text explicitly ties together the §102(a)(1) presumptively novelty-destroying events and the §102(b)(1) exceptions. In view of this explicit statutory link, the applicant's pre-filing "disclosure" of her invention (i.e., "[a] disclosure made 1 year or less before the effective filing date of a claimed invention," as referred to in the preamble of §102(b)(1)) presumably took the form of the applicant having performed one (or more) of the five acts enumerated in §102(a)(1) — that is, having "patented [the claimed invention], described [it] in a printed publication, or [placing the invention] in public use, on sale, or otherwise [making the invention] available to the public." The preamble language of §102(b)(1) provides that the §102(b)(1)(A) "disclosure" (by the inventor, joint inventor, or obtainer, within one year of the invention's effective filing date) "shall not be prior art to the claimed invention under subsection (a)(1)." In other words, the statute removes the inventor's §102(a)(1) disclosure as prior art by means of the (A)-type exception of §102(b)(1). Consider this scenario as applied to facts from the hypothetical in Section Q.1 of this chapter, *supra*.

Hypothetical. Assume that Aidan invents a widget "X." Aidan thereafter discloses the invention by publishing on February 1, 2014, an article in the *International Herald Tribune* newspaper that describes widget X. On July 1, 2014, Aidan files in the USPTO a non-provisional utility patent application disclosing and claiming the identical widget X. Because in this hypothetical Aidan's application is not entitled to any earlier filing date under 35 U.S.C. §§119, 120, or the like, the effective filing date of its claims is Aidan's actual USPTO filing date of July 1, 2014.[552]

Applying post-AIA §102(a)(1) in isolation, the novelty of Aidan's claimed invention was presumptively destroyed (that is, anticipated) by Aidan's February 1, 2014, "descri[ption] [of the claimed invention]

[550] 35 U.S.C. §102(b)(1)(A) (eff. Mar. 16, 2013).

[551] As used herein, "obtainer" refers to the statutory "another who obtained the subject matter disclosed directly or indirectly from the inventor or a joint inventor." *See* 35 U.S.C. §102(b)(1) (eff. Mar. 16, 2013).

[552] *See* 35 U.S.C. §100(i)(1) (eff. Mar. 16, 2013) (defining "effective filing date").

in a printed publication" that occurred "before the effective filing date of the claimed invention." The presumption of anticipation has been overcome, however, because post-AIA §102(b)(1)(A) covers a "disclosure . . . made by the inventor" and post-AIA §102(b)(1)'s preamble provides that Aidan's disclosure "shall not be prior art to the claimed invention." In sum, Aidan will still receive a U.S. patent on widget X despite his disclosure thereof during the one-year grace period before his invention's effective filing date (barring some other ground of non-patentability).[553] The same result would have obtained under the pre-AIA regime.[554] The one-year grace period of U.S. patent law remains in effect for acts during the grace period by the inventor or "obtainer."

First Variation. Section 102(b)(1)(A) removes presumptively novelty-destroying prior art created not only by the inventor/applicant (or a joint inventor) himself but also by an "obtainer"; that is, "by another who obtained the subject matter disclosed directly or indirectly from the inventor. . . ." Vary the facts of the above hypothetical such that Eli, a casual acquaintance of Aidan, stole a notebook that Aidan had created to record information concerning widget X. Using the purloined notebook without Aidan's knowledge or permission, Eli on February 1, 2014, published an article in the *International Herald Tribune* newspaper that described widget X. On July 1, 2014, Aidan filed in the USPTO a non-provisional utility patent application disclosing and claiming the identical widget X. Again, although Eli's published newspaper article presumptively destroyed novelty under §102(a)(1) as a pre–filing date "descri[ption] in a printed publication," the novelty of Aidan's claim to widget X was preserved or restored by means of the §102(b)(1)(A) exception. In this hypothetical, the statutory exception operates to remove the obtainer's (i.e., Eli's) disclosure as prior art against Aidan's application because the inventor (Aidan) filed his patent application within one year or less after the obtainer's disclosure.

Second Variation. The text of §102(b)(1)(A) does not define or explain the limits of the obtainer's act of "obtain[ing] the subject matter disclosed directly or indirectly from the inventor. . . ." At a minimum, it would seem that the obtainer could obtain the subject matter disclosed by misappropriating or stealing information about the subject matter from the inventor/applicant, as in the first variation

[553]If, however, Aidan waits *more than* one year after his February 1, 2014 disclosure to file his application in the USPTO, he will be barred from obtaining a patent. The post-AIA §102(b)(1) exceptions last for only one year. This same result would have followed under the pre-AIA regime; that is, the grace period is one year under both systems.

[554]Aidan should be aware, however, that the patent systems of Europe and most other countries require *absolute* novelty (or offer very limited exceptions thereto). If Aidan desires international patent protection for widget X, he should refrain from making any disclosure of the invention before filing his first patent application on X.

above, or by deriving it (in the patent law sense). Derivation occurs in patent law when the true inventor discloses her invention to another (the "deriver"), and the deriver then falsely patents the invention as his own.[555] More specifically, case law instructs that derivation requires proof of "'prior conception of the invention by another [i.e., the true inventor] and communication of that conception to the patentee [i.e., the deriver].'"[556]

Modifying the previous variation to incorporate derivation (in contrast with trade secret misappropriation or the crime of theft), assume that Aidan invented widget X and communicated his conception in an enabling fashion to Eli. Thereafter, Eli filed a patent application claiming widget X in the Estonian Patent Office. On February 1, 2014, Eli's application issued as an Estonian patent.[557] On July 1, 2014, Aidan filed an application in the USPTO disclosing and claiming the identical widget X. Eli's act of "patent[ing]" widget X before Aidan's effective filing date of July 1, 2014, would presumptively destroy the novelty of Aidan's claim to widget X under §102(a)(1).[558] However, the novelty of Aidan's claim to widget X is preserved by the §102(b)(1)(A) exception. As a deriver, Eli presumably qualifies as "another who obtained the subject matter disclosed directly or indirectly from the inventor . . ." under §102(b)(1)(A), and the preamble of §102(b)(1) operates to remove Eli's disclosure (i.e., the issuance of Eli's Estonian patent during the one-year grace period preceding Aidan's effective filing date) as prior art against Aidan, the true inventor.

b. (B)-Type Exceptions

The second, or "(B)-type," exception under §102(b)(1) involves two "disclosures" of the same invention. Post-AIA §102(b)(1)(B) provides that "[a] disclosure made 1 year or less before the effective filing date of a claimed invention shall not be prior art to the claimed invention under subsection (a)(1) if . . . (B) the subject matter disclosed had, before such disclosure, been publicly disclosed by the inventor or a joint inventor or another who obtained the subject matter disclosed directly or indirectly from the inventor or a joint inventor." To

[555]*See supra* Section M ("Derivation and Inventorship Under 35 U.S.C. §102(f) (Pre-AIA)").

[556]Creative Compounds, LLC v. Starmark Labs., 651 F.3d 1303, 1313 (Fed. Cir. 2011) (quoting Eaton Corp. v. Rockwell Int'l Corp., 323 F.3d 1332, 1334 (Fed. Cir. 2003)).

[557]Assuming that Estonian patent law requires originality, Eli's patent would be invalid, but its issuance rather than its validity is the dispositive event in this hypothetical.

[558]The issuance of the Estonian patent would presumably also qualify as a §102(a)(1) "descri[ption] in a printed publication." The hypothetical does not consider the possibility of 18-month publication of the pending Estonian patent application.

illustrate, if (i) an inventor "publicly disclose[s]" his invention,[559] (ii) another individual (referred to herein as the "third party") thereafter "disclose[s]" the same invention, and (iii) the inventor/first discloser thereafter files his patent application within one year of his (the inventor/first discloser's) public disclosure, the inventor/first discloser will not be prevented by the third party's disclosure (or by the inventor's own public disclosure) from obtaining a patent.[560] Hence, the (B)-type exception illustrates that the AIA implemented what is, at least in part, a "first to disclose" system.

Hypothetical. Consider Aidan and Eli, each of whom independently invents widget X. On February 1, 2014, Aidan publicly discloses widget X by selling hundreds of items, each embodying widget X, to customers at Aidan's retail store located in China.[561] On March 1, 2014, Eli publishes a complete description of widget X in *The New York Times* newspaper. On July 1, 2014, Aidan files an application in the USPTO describing and claiming the identical widget X. Eli's disclosure on March 1, 2014, is removed as prior art under §102(b)(1)(B), because the "subject matter disclosed [by Eli] had, before such disclosure, been publicly disclosed" by Aidan. Aidan's own public disclosure on February 1, 2014, is removed as prior art by operation of §102(b)(1)(A) because Aidan filed his U.S. application within the one-year grace period starting on February 1, 2014.

3. Post-AIA §102(b)(2): Shields Against Post-AIA §102(a)(2) Presumptively Novelty-Destroying Events

The post-AIA §102(b)(2) exceptions remove presumptively novelty-destroying (i.e., anticipatory) §102(a)(2) prior art taking the form of descriptions in earlier-filed patents and patent applications naming

[559]The public disclosure could also have been made by a joint inventor or an "obtainer." *See* §35 U.S.C. §102(b)(1)(B) (eff. Mar. 16, 2013).

[560]Although both terms are used in post-AIA §102(b)(1)(B), the statute does not define or explain the difference between "disclosed" and "publicly disclosed." The use of "disclosed" both with and without the modifier "publicly" suggests that the unqualified "disclosed" could encompass types of "secret" prior art that are traditionally recognized in U.S. case law but probably not "available to the public" under post-AIA §102(a)(1). *See supra* Section Q.3 ("Does the AIA Permit Secret Prior Art?"). Professor Merges analyzes the distinction between "disclosed" and "publicly disclosed" in Robert P. Merges, *Priority and Novelty Under the AIA* (Aug. 15, 2012), *available at* papers.ssrn.com/sol3/papers.cfm?abstract_id=2130209.

[561]The hypothetical assumes that the sale of the item fully and publicly discloses the features of the claimed invention and as such satisfies the "publicly disclosed" language of post-AIA §102(b)(1)(B). This avoids consideration of the *Metallizing*-type "secret prior art" issue discussed *supra* at Section Q.3 ("Does the AIA Permit Secret Prior Art?").

another inventor. The post-AIA version of 35 U.S.C. §102(b) provides in pertinent part:

> (b) EXCEPTIONS.—
>
> . . .
>
> (2) DISCLOSURES APPEARING IN APPLICATIONS AND PATENTS.—A disclosure shall not be prior art to a claimed invention under subsection (a)(2) if—
>
> (A) the subject matter disclosed was obtained directly or indirectly from the inventor or a joint inventor;
>
> (B) the subject matter disclosed had, before such subject matter was effectively filed under subsection (a)(2), been publicly disclosed by the inventor or a joint inventor or another who obtained the subject matter disclosed directly or indirectly from the inventor or a joint inventor; or
>
> (C) the subject matter disclosed and the claimed invention, not later than the effective filing date of the claimed invention, were owned by the same person or subject to an obligation of assignment to the same person.

In similar fashion to the prior art–removing exceptions in post-AIA §102(b)(1), both (A)-type and (B)-type exceptions appear in §102(b)(2). A third exception, dealing with commonly owned prior art and discussed *infra*, also forms part of §102(b)(2).[562]

a. (A)-Type Exceptions

The first, or "(A)-type," exception removes from the prior art a specific type of disclosure—a §102(a)(2) description of the claimed invention in an earlier-filed U.S. patent or published (or "deemed published") patent application naming another inventor—when that disclosure was made by an "obtainer," that is, one who "obtained" the "subject matter disclosed . . . directly or indirectly from the inventor or a joint inventor."[563]

Hypothetical. Consider U.S. patent applicant Alex, who invented a widget X. Alex thereafter communicated his conception of widget X to his friend Mona in an enabling fashion. Unbeknownst to Alex, Mona filed a non-provisional utility patent application disclosing widget X in the USPTO on February 1, 2014. On July 1, 2014, Alex filed in the USPTO his own non-provisional utility patent application disclosing and claiming the identical widget X. Assume that the USPTO

[562] *See infra* Section U ("Common Ownership Under Joint Research Agreements").

[563] 35 U.S.C. §102(b)(2)(A) (eff. Mar. 16, 2013) (providing in full that "[a] disclosure shall not be prior art to a claimed invention under subsection (a)(2) if—(A) the subject matter disclosed was obtained directly or indirectly from the inventor or a joint inventor").

published the contents of Mona's pending application at 18 months after its filing date, that is, on August 1, 2015. A USPTO examiner thereafter cited the description of widget X in Mona's earlier-filed, now published application as anticipatory prior art against the claims of Alex's pending application.

The description in Mona's published application is presumptively novelty-destroying §102(a)(2) prior art because it has an effective date of February 1, 2014, which predates Alex's filing date of July 1, 2014. In other words, the existence of the description of widget X in Mona's earlier-filed patent application presumptively anticipates Alex's application claims to widget X under post-AIA §102(a)(2). The novelty of Alex's claims is preserved, however, by the §102(b)(2)(A) exception. Because Mona derived the widget X invention from Alex, Mona presumably qualifies as one who "obtained" the "subject matter disclosed" in her application "directly or indirectly" from Alex, the true inventor of widget X.[564] The preamble of §102(b)(2) provides that Mona's "disclosure shall not be prior art" to Alex's claimed invention.

As a practical matter, Alex can seek to prove that Mona derived the widget X invention from him by filing a petition to institute a derivation proceeding in accordance with post-AIA 35 U.S.C. §135.[565] That statute provides that the petition must "set forth with particularity the basis for finding that an inventor named in an earlier application [i.e., Mona in this hypothetical] derived the claimed invention from an inventor named in the petitioner's application [i.e., Alex in this hypothetical] and, without authorization, the earlier application claiming such invention was filed."[566]

Alex can file his petition for a derivation proceeding "only within the 1-year period beginning on the date of the first publication of a claim to an invention that is the same or substantially the same as the earlier application's claim to the invention."[567] Although the statute is less than clear, a reasonable interpretation is that Alex, the second filer, must file his derivation petition no later than one year after the publication of the first filer's application, that is, no later than August 1, 2016, in this hypothetical.[568] Alex's petition "shall be made under oath, and shall be supported by substantial evidence."[569] If the USPTO Director determines that a derivation proceeding should be

[564]Mona may or may not be an inventor of some other invention claimed in her own application, although she is a deriver of widget X in this hypothetical. The statute requires only that Mona be named as an inventor on her application.

[565]Derivation proceedings under the AIA-amended 35 U.S.C. §135 become available on March 16, 2013.

[566]35 U.S.C. §135(a) (eff. Mar. 16, 2013) ("Institution of Proceeding").

[567]*See* 35 U.S.C. §135(a) (eff. Mar. 16, 2013) ("Institution of Proceeding").

[568]*See* 35 U.S.C. §135(a) (eff. Mar. 16, 2013) ("Institution of Proceeding").

[569]*See* 35 U.S.C. §135(a) (eff. Mar. 16, 2013) ("Institution of Proceeding").

instituted, the proceeding will be conducted by the Patent Trial and Appeal Board.[570]

b. (B)-Type Exceptions

Like its counterpart in §102(b)(1), the second, or "(B)-type," exception of §102(b)(2) involves two "disclosures" of the same invention. Post-AIA §102(b)(2)(B) provides that "[a] disclosure shall not be prior art to a claimed invention under subsection (a)(2) if . . . (B) the subject matter disclosed had, before such subject matter was effectively filed under subsection (a)(2), been publicly disclosed by the inventor or a joint inventor or another who obtained the subject matter disclosed directly or indirectly from the inventor or a joint inventor."

To illustrate, if (i) an inventor "publicly disclose[s]" his invention, (ii) another individual (referred to hereafter as the "third party") thereafter "disclose[s]" the same subject matter by filing a patent application in the USPTO that names the third party as an inventor and describes the same invention, and (iii) the inventor/first discloser thereafter files his patent application within one year of his (the inventor/first discloser's) public disclosure, then the inventor/first discloser will not be prevented by the third party's description in the third party's application or patent (or by the inventor's own public disclosure) from obtaining a patent.[571] Again, the (B)-type exception of §102(b)(2) illustrates that the AIA implemented what is, at least in part, a "first to disclose" system.

T. Effective Date for AIA §3 First-Inventor-to-File Amendments

A critical threshold issue for patent practitioners, particularly those preparing to file or already prosecuting patent applications in the USPTO during the transition period from pre- to post-AIA regimes, is whether the AIA §3 amendments apply to their applications. Section 3(n) of the AIA controls the issue. Section 3(n) provides that

[570]*See* 35 U.S.C. §135(b) (eff. Mar. 16, 2013) ("Determination by Patent Trial and Appeal Board").

[571]Although both terms are used in post-AIA §102(b)(2)(B), the statute does not define or explain the difference between "disclosed" and "publicly disclosed." Logically, the unqualified "disclosed" must include the initially secret/confidential filing in the USPTO of the third party's patent application. *See supra* Section Q.3 ("Does the AIA Permit Secret Prior Art?"). Professor Merges analyzes the distinction between "disclosed" and "publicly disclosed" in Robert P. Merges, *Priority and Novelty Under the AIA* (Aug. 15, 2012), *available at* https://papers.ssrn.com/sol3/papers.cfm?abstract_id=2130209 (Part II.B).

the first-inventor-to-file system implemented by the AIA (as well as its associated new definitions of "prior art") are strictly prospective.[572]

Notably, the AIA does not incorporate the §3(n) transition provision into the text of the Patent Act. The transition provision reads:

> (n) EFFECTIVE DATE.—
>
> (1) IN GENERAL.—Except as otherwise provided in this section [AIA §3], the amendments made by this section shall take effect upon the expiration of the 18-month period beginning on the date of the enactment of this Act, and shall apply to any application for patent, and to any patent issuing thereon, that contains or contained at any time—
>
> (A) a claim to a claimed invention that has an effective filing date as defined in section 100(i) of title 35, United States Code, that is on or after the effective date described in this paragraph; or
>
> (B) a specific reference under section 120, 121, or 365(c) of title 35, United States Code, to any patent or application that contains or contained at any time such a claim.
>
> (2) INTERFERING PATENTS....[573]

This text interprets the statutory phrase "shall take effect upon the expiration of the 18-month period beginning on the date of the enactment of this Act" to mean that the AIA §3 amendments took effect on March 16, 2013 (i.e., 18 months after the AIA's September 16, 2011,

[572]Professor Chisum observes that "[t]he 2011 Act makes the change to 'first to file' strictly prospective. The trigger date is 18 months after enactment. Enactment was on September 16, 2011, making the trigger date March 16, 2013. The changes on first-to-file do not apply to patent claims that rely on filing dates before the trigger date (March 16, 2013)." Donald S. Chisum, *America Invents Act of 2011: Analysis and Cross-References*, at 10 (Dec. 5, 2011), *available at* https://www.chisum.com/wp-content/uploads/AIAOverview.pdf.

[573]Leahy-Smith America Invents Act, Pub. L. No. 112-29 (H.R. 1249), §3(n), 125 Stat. 284, 293 (2011). The remaining portion of §3(n)(2) reads:

> (2) INTERFERING PATENTS.—The provisions of sections 102(g), 135, and 291 of title 35, United States Code, as in effect on the day before the effective date set forth in paragraph (1) of this subsection, shall apply to each claim of an application for patent, and any patent issued thereon, for which the amendments made by this section also apply, if such application or patent contains or contained at any time—
>
> (A) a claim to an invention having an effective filing date as defined in section 100(i) of title 35, United States Code, that occurs before the effective date set forth in paragraph (1) of this subsection; or
>
> (B) a specific reference under section 120, 121, or 365(c) of title 35, United States Code, to any patent or application that contains or contained at any time such a claim.

enactment date).[574] In accordance with the two prongs of §3(n)(1), the AIA §3 first-inventor-to-file amendments (to §102 and other sections of the Patent Act) apply to a patent or patent application in either of two situations: (1) under §3(n)(1)(A), because the effective filing date of a claim contained (at any time) in the patent or patent application is on or after March 16, 2013; or (2) under §3(n)(1)(B), because the patent or application makes a specific type of reference to another patent or application that contained (at any time) a claim having an effective filing date that is on or after March 16, 2013.

Both prongs of the §3(n)(1) transition provision in turn reference the "effective filing date" of a claimed invention in a patent or patent application. The "effective filing date" phrase is defined in the post-AIA Patent Act. As amended by the AIA, 35 U.S.C. §100 provides in pertinent part:

> (i) (1) The term "effective filing date" for a claimed invention in a patent or application for patent means —
>
> (A) if subparagraph (B) does not apply, the actual filing date of the patent or the application for the patent containing a claim to the invention; or
>
> (B) the filing date of the earliest application for which the patent or application is entitled, as to such invention, to a right of priority under section 119, 365(a), or 365(b) or to the benefit of an earlier filing date under section 120, 121, or 365(c).
>
> (2) The effective filing date for a claimed invention in an application for reissue or reissued patent shall be determined by deeming the claim to the invention to have been contained in the patent for which reissue was sought.[575]

Notably, this "effective filing date" definition is applied to "a claimed invention" in a patent or patent application. It is imprecise to refer to the "effective filing date" of the patent or patent application itself. In other words, "'effective filing date' is defined with respect to each claimed invention, rather than the entire patent application or issued patent."[576]

Although they are worded somewhat similarly, it is important to distinguish AIA §3(n), which governs the *effective date* of the AIA first-to-file *legislation*, from §100(i) of the post-AIA Patent Act, which governs the *effective filing date* for a *claimed invention* in a patent or patent application. Notably, the former is a transition provision that

[574] *See* Biogen MA, Inc. v. Japanese Foundation for Cancer Research, 785 F.3d 648, 655 (Fed. Cir. 2015) (defining the AIA §3(n)(1) phrase "the expiration of the 18-month period beginning on the date of the enactment of this Act" as March 16, 2013).

[575] 35 U.S.C. §100(i) (eff. Mar. 16, 2013).

[576] Joe Matal, *A Guide to the Legislative History of the America Invents Act: Part I of II*, 21 Fed. Cir. B.J. 435, 448 (2012). For example, a single patent application or patent could claim more than one invention. As a practical matter, however, this seems unlikely to occur with much frequency due to restriction requirements under 35 U.S.C. §121.

excludes any mention of priority (domestic or foreign) under 35 U.S.C. §119. In practical terms, this means that when the AIA's §3-implemented first-inventor-to-file system went into effect, it did not have any direct applicability to then-pending U.S. provisional patent applications (dealt with in 35 U.S.C. §119(e)) or foreign priority applications (dealt with in 35 U.S.C. §119(a)). Rather, "[t]he [§3(n)] transition provisions provide that each *nonprovisional* application (and each of that application's *progeny*, defined as any application that at any time made a claim for the benefit of such nonprovisional patent filing) that contained at any time even a single claim with an effective filing date on or after March 16, 2013 (i.e., the effective date for new [post-AIA] §102) is fully subject to new §102."[577]

U. Common Ownership Under Joint Research Agreements

Section 3 of the AIA preserved pre-AIA exclusions or shields of certain commonly owned (or deemed commonly owned) subject matter from being treated as prior art. The AIA expanded the exclusions such that they are applicable to the analysis of novelty under 35 U.S.C. §102 as well as nonobviousness under 35 U.S.C. §103. The AIA's legislative history provides that

> the intent behind the CREATE Act to promote joint research activities is preserved by including a prior art exception for subject matter invented by parties to a joint research agreement. The Act also provides that its enactment of new section 102(c) of title 35 is done with the same intent to promote joint research activities that was expressed in the Cooperative Research and Technology Enhancement Act of 2004 (Public Law 108-453), and that section 102(c) shall be administered in a manner consistent with such intent.[578]

The following background explains the treatment of CREATE Act subject matter in the AIA.

In 1984, Congress amended the patentability requirement of nonobviousness (35 U.S.C. §103) so as to exclude "commonly owned" inventions from the prior art used in nonobviousness analyses.[579] The

[577]Robert A. Armitage, *Understanding the America Invents Act and Its Implications for Patenting*, 40 AM. INTELLECTUAL PROP. L. Q.J. 1, 18 n.62 (Winter 2012) (emphasis added).

[578]H.R. REP. No.112-98, at 54 (June 1, 2011).

[579]The Patent Law Amendments Act of 1984, Pub. L. No. 98-622 (H.R. 6286) (Nov. 8, 1984), amended the then-in-effect version of 35 U.S.C. §103 by appending to the statute the following sentence: "Subject matter developed by another person, which qualifies as prior art only under subsection (f) or (g) of section 102 of this title, shall not preclude

intent of the 1984 legislation was to shield commonly owned inventions from being rendered obvious by the prior work of other inventors in the same company or firm. In essence, Congress gave corporations the right to patent obvious variants of in-house efforts qualifying as prior art under 35 U.S.C. §102(f) (1984) or 35 U.S.C. §102(g) (1984). In the American Inventors Protection Act of 1999, Congress further expanded the nonobviousness prior art shield to encompass commonly owned prior art under 35 U.S.C. §102(e) (1994).[580] These prior art shields became subsection (c) of 35 U.S.C. §103.

The Cooperative Research and Technology Enhancement (CREATE) Act of 2004 expanded the §103(c) exclusions even more broadly to encompass §102(e), (f), and (g) prior art that had been earlier generated by the parties to a "joint research agreement" involving the assignees of inventor(s) named in a patent application.[581] Congress was particularly concerned with removing barriers to patenting for collaborative teams encompassing universities and for-profit corporations of the type encouraged by the Bayh-Dole Act of 1980.[582]

The AIA expanded the concepts underlying the CREATE Act prior art shield to encompass prior art used in the analysis of novelty under 35 U.S.C. §102 as well as nonobviousness under 35 U.S.C. §103. More specifically, the 35 U.S.C. §103(c) (2006) exclusion of commonly owned subject matter was removed from §103 and transferred to post-AIA §102, which defines prior art for anticipation situations as well as obviousness.[583] Post-AIA §102 provides in pertinent part:

> (b)(2) DISCLOSURES APPEARING IN APPLICATIONS AND PATENTS. — A disclosure shall not be prior art to a claimed invention under subsection (a)(2) if...

---

patentability under this section where the subject matter and the claimed invention were, at the time the invention was made, owned by the same person or subject to an obligation of assignment to the same person."

"Commonly owned" means that legal title in both inventions is in the same person (be it a natural person or a firm such as a corporation), or is at least subject to an obligation to assign ownership to the same "person." *See* 35 U.S.C. §102(c) (eff. Mar. 16, 2013).

[580]*See* Pub. L. No. 106-113 (H.R. 3194), §4807 (Nov. 29, 1999) (providing that "section 103(c) of title 35, United States Code, is amended by striking 'subsection (f) or (g)' and inserting 'one or more of subsections (e), (f), and (g)' ").

[581]*See* Pub. L. No. 108-453, §2, 118 Stat. 3596 (2004). The CREATE Act added to the Patent Act a definition of "joint research agreement" as "a written contract, grant, or cooperative agreement entered into by two or more persons or entities for the performance of experimental, developmental, or research work in the field of the claimed invention." 35 U.S.C. §103(c)(3) (2006).

[582]The Bayh-Dole Act is codified at 35 U.S.C. §§200-212 (2006).

[583]*See* Leahy-Smith America Invents Act, Pub. L. No. 112-29 (H.R. 1249), §3(b)(1), 125 Stat. 284, 286 (Sept. 16, 2011) (amending Patent Act to add 35 U.S.C. §102(b)(2)(C) (eff. Mar. 16, 2013)); *see also* AIA §3(c) (deleting subsection (c) from 35 U.S.C. §103 (2006)).

> (C) the subject matter disclosed and the claimed invention, not later than the effective filing date of the claimed invention, were owned by the same person or subject to an obligation of assignment to the same person.[584]

Moreover, the 35 U.S.C. §103(c) (2006) exclusion of joint research work was likewise removed from §103 and transferred to post-AIA §102,[585] which provides in pertinent part:

> (c) COMMON OWNERSHIP UNDER JOINT RESEARCH AGREEMENTS. — Subject matter disclosed and a claimed invention shall be deemed to have been owned by the same person or subject to an obligation of assignment to the same person in applying the provisions of subsection (b)(2)(C) if—
>
> (1) the subject matter disclosed was developed and the claimed invention was made by, or on behalf of, 1 or more parties to a joint research agreement that was in effect on or before the effective filing date of the claimed invention;
>
> (2) the claimed invention was made as a result of activities undertaken within the scope of the joint research agreement; and
>
> (3) the application for patent for the claimed invention discloses or is amended to disclose the names of the parties to the joint research agreement.[586]

In addition to transferring the CREATE Act language to post-AIA §102 of the Patent Act, §3(b) of the AIA also included this subparagraph (in the nature of a "sense of Congress" provision):

> (2) CONTINUITY OF INTENT UNDER THE CREATE ACT. — The enactment of section 102(c) of title 35, United States Code, under paragraph (1) of this subsection is done with the same intent to promote joint research activities that was expressed, including in the legislative history, through the enactment of the Cooperative Research and Technology Enhancement Act of 2004 (Public Law 108-453; the "CREATE Act"), the amendments of which are stricken by subsection (c) of this section. The United States Patent and Trademark Office shall administer section 102(c) of title 35, United States Code, in a manner consistent with the legislative history of the CREATE Act that was relevant to its administration by the United States Patent and Trademark Office.[587]

[584] 35 U.S.C. §102(b)(2)(C) (eff. Mar. 16, 2013).

[585] *See* Leahy-Smith America Invents Act, Pub. L. No. 112-29 (H.R. 1249), §3(b)(1), 125 Stat. 284, 286 (Sept. 16, 2011) (amending Patent Act to add 35 U.S.C. §102(c) (eff. Mar. 16, 2013) ("Common Ownership Under Joint Research Agreements")); *see also* AIA §3(c) (deleting subsection (c) from 35 U.S.C. §103 (2006)).

[586] 35 U.S.C. §102(c) (eff. Mar. 16, 2013).

[587] Leahy-Smith America Invents Act, Pub. L. No. 112-29 (H.R. 1249), §3(b)(2), 125 Stat. 284, 287 (Sept. 16, 2011).

Chapter 5

The Nonobviousness Requirement (35 U.S.C. §103)

A. Introduction

This chapter considers the ultimate condition of patentability: the requirement that the invention be **nonobvious**. Although not statutorily codified until §103 was enacted in 35 U.S.C. as part of the 1952 Patent Act, this final condition has been recognized in U.S. patent case law since at least 1851, when the Supreme Court articulated in the famous "doorknob case," *Hotchkiss v. Greenwood,*[1] that patentability requires "something more" than novelty. An invention may be technically novel, such that none of the novelty-destroying or loss-of-right provisions of 35 U.S.C. §102 are triggered.[2] But to be patentable, the invention also must represent enough of a qualitative advance over earlier technology to justify what Thomas Jefferson called "the

[1] 52 U.S. 248 (1850).

[2] *See* Chapter 4 ("Novelty, Loss of Right, and Priority Pre- and Post-America Invents Act of 2011 (35 U.S.C. §102)"), *supra*. As Chapter 4 describes, §102 of the Patent Act was entirely revised in the America Invents Act of 2011. *See* Leahy-Smith America Invents Act, Pub. L. No. 112-29 (H.R. 1249), §3(b)(1), 125 Stat. 284, 285-286 (2011). The AIA amendments took effect prospectively for patent applications filed on or after March 16, 2013, but applications filed before that date (and patents issuing therefrom) will continue to be assessed under the pre-AIA statutory framework.

An unfortunate aspect of the AIA is that Congress entirely rewrote key provisions of the Patent Act without renumbering many of the statutory sections in Title 35, U.S.C. To maintain clarity and demarcation between old and new, citations in this text to the pre-AIA version of the patent statute (e.g., to §102) typically will take the form "35 U.S.C. §102(x) (pre-AIA)" or "35 U.S.C. §102(x) (2006)." (The 2006 date is used because as of the AIA's enactment in September 2011, the "spine" date of the most recent hard copy main edition of 35 U.S.C. was 2006.) In contrast, citations in this text to the patent statute post-AIA implementation will take the form "35 U.S.C. §102(x) (post-AIA)" or "35 U.S.C. §102(x) (eff. Mar. 16, 2013)." For shorthand purposes, sections of the Patent Act will sometimes be referred to herein as "post-AIA §102," meaning the version of 35 U.S.C. §102 that takes effect on March 16, 2013.

embarrassment of an exclusive patent."[3] This determination is ultimately a question of public policy, based on underlying factual inquiries[4]— namely, which inventions should be patented and which should not.[5] Although the America Invents Act of 2011 (AIA) amended and eliminated certain parts of 35 U.S.C. §103,[6] the AIA did not change the fundamental analysis for determining whether a claimed invention would have been obvious as described in this chapter.

The introductory clause of 35 U.S.C. §103(a) (2006) states that "[a] patent may not be obtained though the invention is not identically disclosed or described as set forth in section 102 of this title, if. . . ." This qualifying language indicates that nonobviousness is an additional condition that must be satisfied for patentability, even if the invention is not anticipated under one or more subsections of §102 (as discussed in Chapter 4 of this text). The America Invents Act of 2011 did not change this basic principle.[7] The "identically disclosed

[3]Graham v. John Deere Co., 383 U.S. 1, 9 (1966) (quoting letter from Thomas Jefferson to Isaac McPherson (Aug. 13, 1813), VI THE WRITINGS OF THOMAS JEFFERSON, at 181 (H.A. Washington ed. 1854)).

[4]Giles S. Rich, *The Vague Concept of "Invention" as Replaced by Section 103 of the 1952 Act* [the "Kettering Speech"] in NONOBVIOUSNESS: THE ULTIMATE CONDITION OF PATENTABILITY 1:401 (John F. Witherspoon ed. 1980).

[5]The determination of nonobviousness has similarly been described as "ultimately one of judgment." In re Lee, 277 F.3d 1338, 1345 (Fed. Cir. 2002).

[6]*See* Leahy-Smith America Invents Act, Pub. L. No. 112-29 (H.R. 1249), §3(c), 125 Stat. 284, 287 (2011) (amending the language of 35 U.S.C. §103(a) (2006) and deleting 35 U.S.C. §103(b) (2006) and 35 U.S.C. §103(c) (2006)). With respect to patent applications filed on or after March 16, 2013 and patents issuing therefrom, the statute will provide as follows:

> **§103. Conditions for patentability; non-obvious subject matter**
>
> A patent for a claimed invention may not be obtained, notwithstanding that the claimed invention is not identically disclosed as set forth in section 102, if the differences between the claimed invention and the prior art are such that the claimed invention as a whole would have been obvious *before the effective filing date of the claimed invention* to a person having ordinary skill in the art to which the claimed invention pertains. Patentability shall not be negated by the manner in which the invention was made.

35 U.S.C. §103 (eff. Mar. 16, 2013) (emphasis added). The emphasized language highlights the primary substantive difference between pre-AIA §103(a) and post-AIA §103. The AIA changed the date for evaluation of an invention's nonobviousness to the date that is "before the effective filing date of the claimed invention," rather than "at the time the invention was made" (i.e., at the invention date, a pre-AIA concept). The AIA also provided a definition of "effective filing date [for a] claimed invention." *See* 35 U.S.C. §100(i) (eff. Mar. 16, 2013). For additional discussion of the AIA and effective filing date, *see supra* Chapter 4, Part III ("Novelty, Loss of Right, and Priority Post-America Invents Act of 2011").

[7]Although the America Invents Act of 2011 amended 35 U.S.C. §103 in several respects, it did not change the substance of the "notwithstanding" phrase of §103. *See* Leahy-Smith America Invents Act, Pub. L. No. 112-29, §3(c), 125 Stat. 284, 287 (2011) (amending 35 U.S.C. §103 to provide that "[a] patent for a claimed invention may not

or described" statutory phrase[8] also reinforces that the test for anticipation under 35 U.S.C. §102 is one of "strict identity"; that is, each and every limitation of the claimed invention must be disclosed in a single prior art reference, in order for it to be considered anticipated under §102.[9]

Analyzing nonobviousness is a challenging but frequently encountered task in U.S. patent law. An understanding of the historical development of the nonobviousness requirement will inform the analysis.

B. Historical Context: The *Hotchkiss* "Ordinary Mechanic" and the Requirement for "Invention"

The patentability requirement for something more than novelty was first recognized by the U.S. Supreme Court in *Hotchkiss v. Greenwood,*[10] which addressed the validity of an issued patent that claimed a mechanical combination of doorknob, shank, and spindle. The novel feature of the device was that the doorknob was formed of clay or porcelain. Prior art doorknobs had been made of wood, which was susceptible to warping and cracking, or of metal, which tended to rust from exposure to the elements. The patentee's substitution of materials resulted in a more attractive doorknob, which also was less expensive to manufacture and more durable than conventional doorknobs.

Despite this seemingly significant and beneficial advance in the manufacture of doorknobs, the *Hotchkiss* majority held the patent invalid on the basis that no patentable "invention" resided in the mere substitution of clay for wood:

> But this [substitution], of itself, can never be the subject of a patent. No one will pretend that a machine, made, in whole or in part, of materials better adapted to the purpose for which it is used than the materials of

---

be obtained, notwithstanding that the claimed invention is not identically disclosed as set forth in section 102, if. . ."). 35 U.S.C. §103 (eff. Mar. 16, 2013). For additional discussion of section 102, *see supra* Chapter 4 ("Novelty, Loss of Right, and Priority Pre- and Post-America Invents Act of 2011 (35 U.S.C. §102)").

[8]For reasons that are unclear, the AIA retained "disclosed" but deleted "described" from the "notwithstanding" phrase. *See* Leahy-Smith America Invents Act, Pub. L. No. 112-29, §3(c), 125 Stat. 284, 287 (2011) (amending 35 U.S.C. §103 to provide that "[a] patent for a claimed invention may not be obtained, notwithstanding that the claimed invention is not identically disclosed as set forth in section 102, if. . ."). 35 U.S.C. §103 (eff. Mar. 16, 2013).

[9]*See supra* Chapter 4, Section C for details of the strict identity standard for anticipation.

[10]52 U.S. 248 (1850).

> which the old one is constructed, and for that reason better and cheaper, can be distinguished from the old one; or, in the sense of the patent law, can entitle the manufacturer to a patent.
>
> The difference is formal, and *destitute of ingenuity or invention.* It may afford evidence of judgment and skill in the selection and adaptation of the materials in the manufacture of the instrument for the purposes intended, but nothing more.[11]

With these words, the Supreme Court's *Hotchkiss* decision gave rise to a vague and ambiguous requirement for "invention," representing some abstract, elusive quality beyond mere novelty. This ill-defined term of art proved incapable of precise application; the Court later observed in circular fashion that "the truth is the word ['invention'] cannot be defined in such manner as to afford any substantial aid in determining whether a particular device involves an exercise of the inventive faculty or not."[12] In short, to be patentable, an invention had to involve invention!

The lower courts, struggling to apply the *Hotchkiss* formulation, devised various tests and rules for what did, and did not, qualify as invention.[13] The nebulous concept of invention became "the plaything of the judiciary."[14] Impractical as the terminology was, it took firm root in the patent law lexicon and was not finally banished for over 100 years following *Hotchkiss.* In the 1952 Act, the notion of invention was finally replaced by the modern concept of nonobviousness, the analysis of which is detailed below.

While the terminology it espoused is now seen as outdated and inaccurate, *Hotchkiss v. Greenwood* nevertheless remains fundamental to our understanding of the *perspective* from which the requirement for nonobviousness is to be judged. The Supreme Court in *Hotchkiss* made clear that an invention created with no more skill or ingenuity than that possessed by an "ordinary mechanic," working in the field of the invention, was not deserving of a patent:

> [U]nless more ingenuity and skill in applying the old method of fastening the shank and the knob were required in the application of it to the clay

[11]*Hotchkiss*, 52 U.S. at 266 (emphasis added).

[12]Graham v. John Deere, 383 U.S. 1, 11-12 (1966) (quoting McClain v. Ortmayer, 141 U.S. 419, 427 (1891); Great Atl. & Pac. Tea Co. v. Supermarket Equip. Corp., 340 U.S. 147, 151 (1950)). The great patent jurist Learned Hand observed that the question whether a patentable "invention" exists is "as fugitive, impalpable, wayward, and vague a phantom as exists in the whole paraphernalia of legal concepts." Harries v. Air King Prods. Co., 183 F.2d 158, 162 (2d Cir. 1950) (Hand, C.J.).

[13]*See* 2-5 DONALD S. CHISUM, CHISUM ON PATENTS §5.02 (2008) (summarizing cases that held that neither a "change in form, proportions, or degree," nor "a mere aggregation of elements," could constitute patentable "invention").

[14]Giles S. Rich, *Why and How Section 103 Came to Be*, in NONOBVIOUSNESS: THE ULTIMATE CONDITION OF PATENTABILITY 1:208 (John F. Witherspoon ed., 1980).

> or porcelain knob than were possessed by *an ordinary mechanic acquainted with the business,* there was an absence of that degree of skill and ingenuity which constitute essential elements of every invention. In other words, the improvement is the work of the skillful mechanic, not that of the inventor.[15]

The *Hotchkiss* "ordinary mechanic" metaphor proved useful as a reference point for determining patentability, and can today be understood as the historic ancestor of the latter-day hypothetical **person having ordinary skill in the art** (PHOSITA) currently reflected in 35 U.S.C. §103. To qualify for a patent under this statutory provision, an invention must not have been obvious to this hypothetical person, possessed of "ordinary skill" in the art (i.e., the technology) of the invention, at a particular past point in time. Under pre-AIA rules, the date in question is the time that the invention was made[16] (i.e., at the "invention date"[17]). Under post-AIA rules, the date in question is "before the effective filing date of the claimed invention."[18]

The PHOSITA perspective ensures that nonobviousness under 35 U.S.C. §103 is not judged from the subjective viewpoint of a judge, jury, patent attorney, USPTO patent examiner, or the named inventor of the patent at issue. Rather, the decision maker must step backward in time, into the shoes (and the mind) of the PHOSITA, and make an objective decision about patentability based on the prior art available at that time. The claims of the patent or application under consideration cannot be used as a blueprint that, in hindsight, may make the solution to the inventor's problem appear trivial. This is an admittedly challenging mental gymnastics exercise, but §103 and the Supreme Court's interpretation thereof in the landmark case of *Graham v. John Deere,*[19] discussed below, provide the analytical roadmap to be followed.

[15]*Hotchkiss*, 52 U.S. at 267 (emphasis added).

[16]*See* 35 U.S.C. §103(a) (2006).

[17]As explained in Part II of Chapter 4 ("Novelty, Loss of Right, and Priority Pre- and Post-America Invents Act of 2011 (35 U.S.C. §102)"), *supra*, under pre-AIA rules a patent's filing date is presumptively the "invention date" of the subject matter claimed therein, under a constructive reduction to practice theory. However, an inventor may establish an invention date earlier than his filing date by establishing either (1) the date of his actual reduction to practice, assuming he did not thereafter abandon, suppress, or conceal his invention; or (2) the date of his conception, if coupled with sufficient diligence in working toward his eventual reduction to practice. *See* 35 U.S.C. §102(g) (2006).

Congress removed the concept of invention dates from the text of the post-AIA Patent Act, although invention date principles such as conception will likely continue to be relevant in post-AIA derivation proceedings under 35 U.S.C. 135 (eff. Mar. 16, 2013).

[18]35 U.S.C. §103 (eff. Mar. 16, 2013).

[19]383 U.S. 1 (1966).

C. Enactment of §103 of the Patent Act of 1952, Incorporating the Requirement of Nonobviousness

In its pre-AIA form, 35 U.S.C. §103 consists of three subsections. Our primary focus is §103(a) (2006), which applies to all types of inventions.[20] Subsection 103(a) provides:

> A patent may not be obtained though the invention is not identically disclosed or described as set forth in section 102 of this title, if the differences between the subject matter sought to be patented and the prior art are such that the subject matter as a whole would have been obvious at the time the invention was made to a person having ordinary skill in the art to which said subject matter pertains. Patentability shall not be negatived by the manner in which the invention was made.[21]

This statutory language was included in the 1952 Patent Act at the behest of its co-authors, Giles Rich and Pasquale Federico. The language reflects the frustration of the patent bar with the traditional invention standard of *Hotchkiss,* which proved so vague and ambiguous as to be unworkable. Judges in different courts around the United

[20]The remaining subsections of 35 U.S.C. §103 (2006) are of more recent vintage, and much more narrow in focus. Subsection 103(b) (2006) concerns biotechnological processes, and §103(c) (2006) addresses the "in-house prior art" problem as well as issues specific to "joint research agreements," both of which are discussed *infra* Section F.3.

[21]35 U.S.C. §103(a) (2006). The America Invents Act of 2011 amended 35 U.S.C. §103 in several respects. *See* Leahy-Smith America Invents Act, Pub. L. No. 112-29, §3(c), 125 Stat. 284, 287 (2011) (amending 35 U.S.C. §103 by, *inter alia*, changing the date on which nonobviousness is evaluated and deleting §103(b) and (c)). Effective for applications filed on or after March 16, 2013 and patents issuing therefrom, the statute will provide as follows:

> **§103. Conditions for patentability; non-obvious subject matter**
>
> A patent for a claimed invention may not be obtained, notwithstanding that the claimed invention is not identically disclosed as set forth in section 102, if the differences between the claimed invention and the prior art are such that the claimed invention as a whole would have been obvious *before the effective filing date of the claimed invention* to a person having ordinary skill in the art to which the claimed invention pertains. Patentability shall not be negated by the manner in which the invention was made.

35 U.S.C. §103 (eff. Mar. 16, 2013) (emphasis added). The italicized language emphasizes the primary difference between pre-AIA §103(a) and post-AIA §103. The AIA changed the evaluation date for nonobviousness to the date that is "before the effective filing date of the claimed invention," rather than evaluating nonobvious "at the time the invention was made" (i.e., at the invention date, a pre-AIA concept). The "effective filing date [for a] claimed invention" is defined at 35 U.S.C. §100(i) (eff. Mar. 16, 2013). For additional discussion, *see supra* Part III of Chapter 4 ("Novelty, Loss of Right, and Priority Pre- and Post-America Invents Act of 2011 (35 U.S.C. §102)").

States came to treat "invention" somewhat like obscenity, by applying an I-know-it-when-I-see-it type of analysis, devoid of common guidelines or uniform analytical framework. After extensive lobbying, Rich, Federico, and others convinced Congress to enact legislation that would effectively abolish invention as a condition of patentability and replace it with a statutory requirement for nonobviousness. Thus, §103 provides the modern-day counterpart to the *Hotchkiss* requirement for invention.

The last sentence of 35 U.S.C. §103(a) (2006) provides that "[p]atentability shall not be negatived by the manner in which the invention was made."[22] This simply means that an invention is no more obvious because it results from painstaking, long-running toil than from a "Eureka!" moment. In other words, the way in which an invention was created cannot negate patentability. The drafters of the 1952 Act included this statutory language with the intent of legislatively overruling earlier statements by the Supreme Court that appeared to require a "flash of genius" for patentability.[23]

D. The *Graham v. John Deere* Framework for Analyzing Nonobviousness

In 1966, almost 15 years after Congress's enactment of 35 U.S.C. §103, the U.S. Supreme Court for the first time had occasion to interpret and apply the statutory language in the course of deciding two companion cases that involved relatively humble technology. The patent in suit in *Graham v. John Deere Co.*[24] was directed to a type of shock-absorber system for a plow shank, while the patent at issue in *Calmar, Inc. v. Cook Chem. Co.*[25] covered a protective cap for shipping spray bottles containing liquids. After surveying the history of the U.S.

[22]For reasons that are unclear, the drafters of the America Invents Act of 2011 changed "negatived" to "negated." *See* Leahy-Smith America Invents Act, Pub. L. No. 112-29, §3(c), 125 Stat. 284, 287 (2011); 35 U.S.C. §103 (eff. Mar. 16, 2013) (stating in last sentence that "[p]atentability shall not be negated by the manner in which the invention was made").

[23]*See* Reviser's Notes, 35 U.S.C.A. §103 (1952) (noting that "[t]he second sentence states that patentability as to this requirement is not to be negatived by the manner in which the invention was made, that is, it is immaterial whether it resulted from long toil and experimentation or from a flash of genius"). The earlier Supreme Court cases of concern to the drafters of the 1952 Act include *Cuno Eng'g Corp. v. Automatic Devices Corp.*, 314 U.S. 84, 91 (1941) (stating that to be patentable, "the new device, however useful it may be, must reveal the flash of creative genius, not merely the skill of the calling"); and *Great Atl. & Pac. Tea Co. v. Supermarket Equip. Corp.*, 340 U.S. 147, 155 n.1 (1950) (citing *Cuno*).

[24]383 U.S. 1 (1966).

[25]*Id.* (companion case).

patent system and its concomitant development of the nonobviousness requirement, the Court held both patents invalid as obvious under §103. The Court's appraisal of the particular technologies involved is ultimately much less important, however, than the *Graham* opinion's generalized analytical guidance for determining the issue of nonobviousness. For this reason *Graham* is a landmark opinion, worthy of close study by all students of patent law.

1. Constitutionality of 35 U.S.C. §103

With respect to the degree of ingenuity or quality of advance (i.e., in the older terminology, the degree of "invention") required for patentability under §103, the Court in *Graham v. John Deere* held that the statutory enactment did not signal any change in substance from the existing standard. Thus, the statute was constitutional as a permissible application of Congress's power to promote the progress of the "useful arts,"[26] and was not a derogation of that responsibility.

Section 103 was merely intended to "codify judicial precedents embracing the principle long ago announced by this Court in *Hotchkiss v. Greenwood,* 11 How. 248 (1851)...,"[27] the Supreme Court explained. The enactment of §103 represented to the *Graham* Court simply a semantic shift in terms of greater focus on nonobviousness, rather than a change in the "general level of innovation necessary to sustain patentability."[28] The fundamental message of *Hotchkiss*—its functional approach to determining patentability—had not changed:

> The *Hotchkiss* formulation... lies not in any label, but in its functional approach to questions of patentability. In practice, *Hotchkiss* has required a comparison between the subject matter of the patent, or patent application, and the background skill of the calling. It has been from this comparison that patentability was in each case determined.[29]

The *Graham* Court concluded that §103's "emphasis on nonobviousness is one of inquiry, not quality, and, as such, comports with the constitutional strictures."[30]

[26]U.S. Const., art. I, §8, cl. 8. The *Graham* Court characterized the Intellectual Property Clause of the Constitution as both a grant of power and a limit thereon. Congress cannot establish a legal system in which patents can be attained for technology that is already in the public domain, or that is a merely obvious extension thereof. *See Graham*, 383 U.S. at 1.

[27]383 U.S. at 3-4.

[28]*Id.* at 4.

[29]*Id.* at 12.

[30]*Id.* at 17.

2. *Graham*'s Analytical Framework for a §103 Analysis

Turning to the details of applying the 35 U.S.C. §103 standard, the Supreme Court in *Graham* explained that nonobviousness is ultimately a question of law, the answer to which depends on several underlying factual inquiries. These factual inquiries, referred to thereafter by patent attorneys as the *Graham* factors, must be answered in any determination of nonobviousness, whether made in the USPTO or by the courts. The classic summation of these factors from the *Graham* decision is as follows:

> While the ultimate question of patent validity is one of law, *Great A. & P. Tea Co. v. Supermarket Equipment Corp.*, . . . the §103 condition, which is but one of three conditions, each of which must be satisfied, lends itself to several basic factual inquiries. Under §103, the scope and content of the prior art are to be determined; differences between the prior art and the claims at issue are to be ascertained; and the level of ordinary skill in the pertinent art resolved. Against this background, the obviousness or nonobviousness of the subject matter is determined. Such secondary considerations as commercial success, long felt but unsolved needs, failure of others, etc., might be utilized to give light to the circumstances surrounding the origin of the subject matter sought to be patented. As indicia of obviousness or nonobviousness, these inquiries may have relevancy. *See* Note, Subtests of "Nonobviousness": A Nontechnical Approach to Patent Validity, 112 U. PA. L. REV. 1169 (1964).[31]

With these words, the Supreme Court gleaned from 35 U.S.C. §103 the following four factors that are essential to every nonobviousness analysis:

(1) level of ordinary skill in the art;
(2) scope and content of the prior art;
(3) differences between the claimed invention and the prior art; and
(4) secondary considerations (i.e., objective indicia of nonobviousness).

Each of these *Graham* factors is discussed separately below.

E. *Graham* Factor: Level of Ordinary Skill in the Art

In litigation challenging a patent's validity under 35 U.S.C. §103, both parties will typically introduce evidence (often in the form of

[31] *Id.* at 17-18 (citation omitted).

expert witness testimony) attempting to establish the level of ordinary skill in the technology of the invention. It is from this perspective and skill set, possessed by the hypothetical PHOSITA, that the question of nonobviousness must be resolved.[32] The proponent of validity usually will attempt to establish as low a level of ordinary skill as possible, such that the invention would have been considered nonobvious by the largest possible number of persons, while the challenger of validity typically will seek to raise that level.[33]

In making a finding on the level of ordinary skill in the art, courts or juries will take into consideration some or all of the following types of evidence:[34]

- education level of the inventor;
- education level of a typical worker in this field (e.g., whether the PHOSITA would have a high school degree, college undergraduate degree, or graduate degree such as a master's or Ph.D.);
- type of problems encountered in this technology and previous solutions to such problems;
- how quickly new innovation occurs in this technology; and
- sophistication of the technology (i.e., is the invention a fishing lure or a method of cloning a gene?).

The educational level and expertise of the *inventor* do not necessarily equate to the level of ordinary skill of a hypothetical PHOSITA, for the inventor may (or may not) be a person of extraordinary skill. Nevertheless, the inventors' qualifications played a central role in the nonobviousness analysis in *Daiichi Sankyo Co. v. Apotex, Inc.*[35] Validity challenger Apotex convinced the Federal Circuit that a district court's

[32]*See* Kloster Speedsteel AB v. Crucible, Inc., 793 F.2d 1565, 1574 (Fed. Cir. 1986) (explaining that "[t]he primary value in the requirement that level of skill be found lies in its tendency to focus the mind of the decisionmaker away from what would presently be obvious to that decisionmaker and toward what would, when the invention was made, have been obvious, as the statute requires, 'to one of ordinary skill in the art' ").

[33]*See, e.g.*, Ryko Mfg. Co. v. Nu-Star, Inc., 950 F.2d 714, 718 (Fed. Cir. 1991) (noting that "[a]ppellee's [accused infringer's] evidence shows that most of the personnel developing the new activation device for [patentee] Ryko had attained an engineering degree at the minimum. However, appellant's [patentee's] expert vaguely described the level of ordinary skill in the art as being 'low to medium.' "); Stratoflex, Inc. v. Aeroquip Corp., 713 F.2d 1530, 1538 (Fed. Cir. 1983) (rejecting patentee's contention that level of ordinary skill was too high).

[34]*See* Envtl. Designs, Ltd. v. Union Oil Co., 713 F.2d 693, 696 (Fed. Cir. 1983).

[35]501 F.3d 1254 (Fed. Cir. 2007). The *Daiichi* court's emphasis on the skill level of the inventors is difficult to square with the Supreme Court's observation that "[t]he question is not whether [an invention] was obvious to the patentee but whether [the invention] was obvious to a person with ordinary skill in the art." KSR Int'l Co. v. Teleflex Inc., 550 U.S. 398 (2007).

determination of the level of ordinary skill was too low, and that this error permeated the lower court's ultimate conclusion of nonobviousness. The Federal Circuit's reversal in *Daiichi* turned on its conclusion that the district court had clearly erred in finding too low a level of ordinary skill in the pertinent art.[36] According to the Federal Circuit, that error tainted the entirety of the district court's nonobviousness analysis.[37]

Daiichi's patent addressed the problem of creating a topical antibiotic compound for treatment of ear infections that would not risk damage to the ear.[38] Claim 1 recited "[a] method for treating otopathy which comprises the topical otic administration of an amount of ofloxacin or a salt thereof effective to treat otopathy in a pharmaceutically acceptable carrier to the area affected with otopathy."[39] The district court found that a hypothetical person of ordinary skill in the art pertinent to this invention would have had a medical degree, experience treating patients with ear infections, and basic knowledge about pharmacology and the use of antibiotics. Such a person would have been a pediatrician or general practitioner, doctors who are often the " 'first line of defense' " in treating ear infections.[40]

The Federal Circuit disagreed, concluding that the person of ordinary skill in the art would have been a specialist in the treatment of ear disease with advanced knowledge of pharmacology. Deeming the district court's contrary finding clearly erroneous, the Federal Circuit found that "[t]he level of ordinary skill in the art of the [ ] patent is that of a person engaged in developing pharmaceutical formulations and treatment methods for the ear or a specialist in ear treatments such as an otologist, otolaryngologist, or otorhinolaryngologist who also has training in pharmaceutical formulations."[41]

[36]The Supreme Court in *Graham v. John Deere,* 383 U.S. 1 (1966), enumerated the "level of ordinary skill in the pertinent art" as one of the four factors underlying an analysis of nonobviousness. *See id.* at 17-18. The Federal Circuit in *Daiichi* initially referred to this factor as "the level of ordinary skill in the *prior* art," 501 F.3d at 1256 (emphasis added), but elsewhere in its opinion referred more generally to "the level of ordinary skill in the art." *See id.* at 1257 (concluding that "the level of ordinary skill in the art of the '741 patent is that of a person engaged in developing pharmaceutical formulations and treatment methods for the ear . . . who also has training in pharmaceutical formulations").

[37]*Id.* at 1257.

[38]*See id. See also* U.S. Patent No. 5,401,741 (issued Mar. 28, 1995).

[39]*Daiichi,* 501 F.3d at 1255-1256. The district court interpreted the claim term "otopathy" as meaning "bacterial ear infection" and the claim phrase "effective to treat" as meaning "safe and efficacious." Daiichi Pharm. Co. v. Apotex, Inc., 441 F. Supp. 2d 672, 677 n.7 (D.N.J. 2006).

[40]*Daiichi,* 501 F.3d at 1256 (quoting district court's Claim Construction Order).

[41]*Id.* at 1257. The Federal Circuit's opinion blurs what should have been a brighter analytical line between inventing a chemical compound and discerning new uses for a known compound. Daiichi's '741 patent in suit claimed a method of treatment using the compound ofloxacin, not the compound itself. Daiichi had previously claimed the

Although the Federal Circuit enumerated several factors relevant to the determination of ordinary level of skill in the art,[42] the dispositive factor in *Daiichi* was the level of skill of the inventors.[43] The patent's inventors were specialists, not generalists: a university professor specializing in otorhinolaryngology plus two Daiichi employees, one a clinical development department manager and another a research scientist.[44] The patent described the inventors' tests of ofloxacin on guinea pigs to ensure that the antibiotic did not cause ear damage; "[s]uch animal testing is traditionally outside the realm of a general practitioner or pediatrician," according to the Federal Circuit.[45]

The Federal Circuit's ultimate conclusion of obviousness in *Daiichi* turned primarily on the disclosure of a prior art reference by Ganz. The Ganz reference was directed to the use of ciprofloxacin, known commercially as Cipro®, in treating ear infections. Ciprofloxacin, like ofloxacin, is a type of gyrase inhibitor.[46] Ganz taught that the use of ciprofloxacin in ear drops was not subject to problems like ototoxicity that normally accompany local treatment of the ear with antibiotics. However, Ganz also referred to gyrase inhibitors (such as ciprofloxacin) as "second choice" antibiotics.[47] According to Ganz, gyrase

---

compound ofloxacin in a separate, already-expired patent. *See* Benzoxazine derivatives, U.S. Patent No. 4,382,892 (issued May 10, 1983). The Federal Circuit's opinion mistakenly refers to the invention of the '741 patent in suit as "the claimed compound." *Daiichi*, 501 F.3d at 1257 (stating that "while a general practitioner or pediatrician could (and would) prescribe the invention of the '741 patent to treat ear infections, he would not have the training or knowledge *to develop the claimed compound* absent some specialty training such as that possessed by the '741 patent's inventors") (emphasis added).

[42]The *Daiichi* court quoted the following passage from *Envtl. Designs, Ltd. v. Union Oil Co.*, 713 F.2d 693 (Fed. Cir. 1983):

> Factors that may be considered in determining level of ordinary skill in the art include: (1) the educational level of the inventor; (2) type of problems encountered in the art; (3) prior art solutions to those problems; (4) rapidity with which innovations are made; (5) sophistication of the technology; and (6) educational level of active workers in the field.

Daiichi, 501 F.3d at 1256 (quoting *Envtl. Designs*, 713 F.2d at 696 (citing Orthopedic Equip. Co. v. All Orthopedic Appliances, Inc., 707 F.2d 1376, 1381-1382 (Fed. Cir. 1983))). The listed factors are "not exhaustive but are merely a guide to determining the level of ordinary skill in the art." *Daiichi,* 501 F.3d at 1256.

[43]The Federal Circuit also stated that "others working in the same field as the inventors of the [] patent were of the same skill level," *Daiichi*, 501 F.3d at 1257, but the court's support for this finding is slim. It cites only a set of Daiichi conference materials, which stated that "there are many voices among medical persons concerned with otorhinolaryngology for demanding development of an otic solution making use of [ofloxacin]." *Id.*

[44]*Id.* at 1257.

[45]*Id.* The Federal Circuit cited no support for this finding.

[46]*Id.* at 1258.

[47]Daiichi Pharm. Co. v. Apotex, Inc., 441 F. Supp. 2d 672, 689 (D.N.J. 2006) (stating that "Ganz also notes, however, that gyrase inhibitors such as [c]iprofloxacin are antibiotics of second choice.").

inhibitors should be "used only in difficult cases and exclusively by the otologist."[48] The district court viewed Ganz as teaching away from the claimed invention, as well as a document directed only to specialists rather than general practitioners.[49]

The Federal Circuit determined that the district court's erroneous finding on the level of ordinary skill led it to improperly discount Ganz. The Federal Circuit also rejected the district court's reliance on the testimony of the patentee's expert that it was not safe to extrapolate the safety profile of one antibiotic to another. The Federal Circuit found this testimony "conclusory" and "unsupported," but did not further explain its negative evaluation.

The Federal Circuit first issued *Daiichi* as a non-precedential decision, but reissued it with precedential status in September 2007.[50] Taken in tandem with the Supreme Court's April 2007 exposition on the nonobviousness requirement in *KSR Int'l Co. v. Teleflex, Inc.*,[51] further discussed *infra*,[52] the elevation of *Daiichi* to precedential status suggests that the "level of ordinary skill in the pertinent art" *Graham* factor may henceforth merit a more detailed analysis. The level-of-skill factor is also likely to provide increased fodder for litigation challenging patents for obviousness.[53]

As demonstrated by *Daiichi*, the "level of ordinary skill" *Graham* factor for assessing nonobviousness is frequently hard-fought when the validity of a patent is litigated in federal court. In contrast, the Federal Circuit holds that in *ex parte* examination of pending patent applications, a USPTO examiner is not ordinarily required to make an explicit finding about the pertinent level of ordinary skill. Instead, the court assumes that the agency determined the correct level of

[48]*Daiichi*, 501 F.3d at 1258.

[49]*Daiichi*, 441 F. Supp. 2d at 689 (stating that "Ganz adds that for local treatment in the ear gyrase inhibitors 'should be used only in difficult cases and exclusively by the otologist.' (*Id.*). Therefore Ganz's disclosure does not support Apotex's argument that a person ordinarily skilled in the art would know that the use of ofloxacin, a gyrase inhibitor, to treat bacterial ear infections topically is both efficacious and safe."). The concept of a prior art reference "teaching away" from a claimed invention is further discussed in Section I.3 of this chapter.

[50]*See Daiichi*, 501 F.3d at 1254 (stating that court's non-precedential opinion issued on July 11, 2007, and its precedential opinion issued on September 12, 2007).

[51]127 S. Ct. 1727 (2007).

[52]*See infra* Section I.2 ("*KSR v. Teleflex*: Combinations, Predictability, and 'Common Sense'").

[53]*See Daiichi*, 501 F.3d at 1257 (describing *Merck & Co. v. Teva Pharm. USA, Inc.*, 347 F.3d 1367 (Fed. Cir. 2003), as a case in which "the level of skill in the art was not disputed by the parties"). The Federal Circuit in *Merck* affirmed a district court's finding that the level of ordinary skill in the art pertinent to a claimed method of treating patients with osteoporosis was that of an M.D. with experience treating such patients. *See Daiichi*, 501 F.3d at 1257. The Federal Circuit faulted the district court in *Daiichi* for relying on *Merck* (the only Federal Circuit decision on point) because "the level of skill in the art was not disputed by the parties in that case." *Id.*

ordinary skill. An explicit finding of fact on the level of ordinary skill in the art of the claimed invention is required only when the applicant affirmatively raises and disputes the matter, and demonstrates that the particular level of skill it advocates would be outcome-changing.[54]

In the Circuit's 2019 decision, *In re Fought*,[55] the USPTO rejected as anticipated a patent applicant's claims reciting a "travel trailer," a type of recreational vehicle. Although it reversed on the merits, the Circuit nevertheless rejected the applicant's argument that the examiner and Board had erred as a legal matter by failing to explicitly define the level of skill in the art for the claimed invention. The appellate court explained that

> [i]t is fundamental that claims are interpreted "in light of the specification as it would be interpreted by one of ordinary skill in the art." Phillips v. AWH Corp., 415 F.3d 1303, 1316 (Fed. Cir. 2005). Unless the patentee places the level of ordinary skill in the art in dispute and explains with particularity how the dispute would alter the outcome, neither the Board nor the examiner need articulate the level of ordinary skill in the art. We assume a proper determination of the level of ordinary skill in the art as required by *Phillips*.[56]

In *Fought*, the patent applicant did not argue or articulate with any specificity the level of ordinary skill in the art, or that that level would change the result. Instead, the applicant raised "a generalized challenge to the Board's decision. . . ."[57] The Federal Circuit found the applicant's non-specific challenge to be "without merit."[58]

F. *Graham* Factor: Scope and Content of the Prior Art

1. Terminology

A term of art in patent law, the phrase **prior art** can be understood at a very basic level as the legally available technology and information with which the claimed invention will be compared in order to determine whether that invention is patentable. Which categories of technology and information are "legally available" for use as prior art in a §103 analysis is governed by the criteria of 35 U.S.C. §102, as well as the notion of **analogous art**. These concepts are detailed below. Prior art documents such as patents and printed publications are typically referred to as **references**.

[54]*See* In re Fought, 941 F.3d 1175, 1179, (Fed. Cir. Nov. 4, 2019).
[55]941 F.3d 1175, (Fed. Cir. Nov. 4, 2019).
[56]*Fought,* 941 F.3d at 1179.
[57]*Fought,* 941 F.3d at 1179.
[58]*Fought,* 941 F.3d at 1179.

2. Sources of Prior Art

In evaluating the "scope and content of the prior art" *Graham* factor, the USPTO and the courts may obtain the prior art from several different sources. In a typical USPTO *ex parte* patent prosecution, the patent applicant will submit relevant prior art of which it is aware in the form of an "Information Disclosure Statement."[59] In addition, the examiner will conduct her own independent search of the prior art accessible to the USPTO. All of this prior art will become part of the official prosecution history file for the patent in question, the contents of which will be publicly available once the patent issues (if not sooner[60]).

If an issued patent's validity is being challenged in federal court, the accused infringer (i.e., the challenger of validity) will introduce into evidence the prior art it seeks to have considered. Typically this prior art will include newly discovered prior art, that is, prior art documents or events that were not known to or considered by the USPTO during the initial examination of the patent application but that have been unearthed through the litigation discovery process. Introduction of such "new" prior art, which may be more pertinent than that considered by the USPTO, does not weaken the patent's presumption of validity. Such introduction can nevertheless facilitate the validity challenger's carrying of its burden to prove invalidity by clear and convincing evidence, for it would require the patentee to come forward with countervailing evidence.[61]

On the other hand, a validity challenger who relies only on prior art that was already known to the USPTO during the initial examination of a patent application bears a somewhat heavier burden to establish obviousness. For example, in *Shire LLC v. Amneal Pharms., LLC*,[62] the "primary" prior art reference relied on by the accused infringers/validity challengers who sought to invalidate the Shire pharmaceutical patents in suit was a published Australian patent application; that application was listed on the face of the Shire patents. The Federal Circuit explained that when a prior art reference is listed on the face of an issued U.S.

[59]*See* 37 C.F.R. §1.98 (2008) ("Content of Information Disclosure Statement"). Under 37 C.F.R. §1.56 ("Rule 56"), the applicant is obligated to disclose to the USPTO all known information that is material to patentability, as defined by the rule. Failure to do so may result in a finding of inequitable conduct and resulting unenforceability of the patent.

[60]The USPTO now makes copies of the prosecution histories of patent applications available to the public via the USPTO's website, on or after the time when the agency publishes the applications under 35 U.S.C. §122(b). *See* portal.uspto.gov/pair/PublicPair (select "Transaction History" for application of interest) (last visited Mar. 11, 2016).

[61]Stratoflex, Inc. v. Aeroquip Corp., 713 F.2d 1530, 1534 (Fed. Cir. 1983).

[62]802 F.3d 1301 (Fed. Cir. 2015).

patent, "the examiner is presumed to have considered it."[63] The validity challengers in *Shire* thus carried "'the added burden of overcoming the deference that is due to a qualified government agency presumed to have properly done its job, which includes one or more examiners who are assumed to have some expertise in interpreting the references and to be familiar from their work with the level of skill in the art and whose duty it is to issue only valid patents.'"[64] For this and other reasons discussed *infra*,[65] the Federal Circuit affirmed a district court's grant of summary judgment to Shire that its challenged patents were not invalid (i.e., sustaining their validity).[66]

3. Section 102/103 Overlap

a. *Overview*

Section 103 of 35 U.S.C. does not define the meaning of prior art as used in that section. Again, case law and legislative history fill the gap. These sources make clear that 35 U.S.C. §102, the statutory provision that governs novelty, loss of right, and priority,[67] is key to determining the scope of the prior art properly available in a *Graham* analysis under §103. Section 102 can be conceptualized as a catalog of the universe of information that may potentially qualify as prior art for purposes of a §103 nonobviousness analysis. In other words, any reference relied on in determining nonobviousness must qualify as prior art under one or more subsections of §102 (except that the strict identity condition for anticipation[68] is relaxed in the §103 obviousness context). As stated by a co-author of the 1952 Act, "[t]he antecedent of the words 'the prior art,' which here appear in a statute [§103] for the first time, lies in the phrase 'disclosed or described as set forth in section 102' and hence these words refer to material specified in section 102 as the basis for comparison."[69] These principles continue to apply whether nonobviousness is being analyzed under pre- or post-America Invents Act of 2011 rules.[70]

[63] *Shire LLC,* 802 F.3d at 1307.

[64] *Shire LLC,* 802 F.3d at 1307 (quoting PowerOasis, Inc. v. T-Mobile USA, Inc., 522 F.3d 1299, 1304 (Fed. Cir. 2008) (citations omitted)).

[65] *See* Section I.4 ("Obvious to Try").

[66] *Shire LLC,* 802 F.3d at 1309.

[67] Section 102 is discussed in greater detail in Chapter 4 ("Novelty, Loss of Right, and Priority Pre- and Post-America Invents Act of 2011 (35 U.S.C. §102)"), *supra*.

[68] *See supra* Chapter 4, Section C ("The Strict Identity Rule of Anticipation").

[69] P.J. Federico, *Commentary on the New Patent Act*, 35 U.S.C.A. §1 (1954 ed., discontinued in subsequent volumes), *reprinted in* 75 J. PAT. & TRADEMARK OFF. SOC'Y 161, 180 (1993).

[70] The post-AIA version of §103 continues to refer to situations in which a claimed invention "is not identically disclosed as set forth in section 102. . . ." 35 U.S.C. §103 (eff. Mar. 16, 2013).

Originally, only §102(a) (2006) prior art (most typically printed publications or patents issued before the applicant's filing date (presumptively the applicant's invention date under pre-AIA rules)) was considered appropriate for use in combination to form §103 obviousness rejections. No concern about the use of "secret" prior art existed because such information would clearly have been published or otherwise available to the PHOSITA on or before her invention date.[71] For example, if a patent application claim recited "a gizmo comprising X and Y," the USPTO examiner might enter a §103 obviousness rejection by contending that the PHOSITA would have been motivated to make the claimed invention in view of the combined disclosures of element X in a gizmo depicted in a first §102(a) (2006) printed publication (having an effective date prior to the applicant's invention date, a pre-AIA concept[72]), with element Y in a gizmo described in a second §102(a) (2006) printed publication (also having an effective date prior to the applicant's invention date).

The categories of §102 prior art that are available for use in a §103 obviousness rejection are no longer so limited, however. A series of judicial decisions subsequently held that other categories of §102 prior art beyond §102(a) (2006)—namely information (i.e., documentation or events) qualifying under subsections §102(b) (2006),[73] §102(e) (2006),[74] §102(f) (2006),[75] and §102(g)

[71]*See* OddzOn Prods., Inc. v. Just Toys, Inc., 122 F.3d 1396, 1402 (Fed. Cir. 1997) (noting that "[i]t has been a basic principle of patent law, subject to minor exceptions, that prior art is 'technology already available to the public' ") (quoting Kimberly-Clark Corp. v. Johnson & Johnson, 745 F.2d 1437, 1453 (Fed. Cir. 1984)).

[72]*See supra* Chapter 4 ("Novelty, Loss of Right, and Priority Pre- and Post-America Invents Act of 2011 (35 U.S.C. §102)") for further discussion of invention dates.

[73]In re Foster, 343 F.2d 980, 988 (C.C.P.A. 1965).

The AIA rewrote §102(b) in its entirety, *see* Leahy-Smith America Invents Act, Pub. L. No. 112-29 (H.R. 1249), §3(b)(1), 125 Stat. 284, 285-286 (2011), but retained "exceptions" that are somewhat similar to the pre-AIA §102(b) grace period. The AIA "exceptions" are limited, however, to disclosures made by the inventor (or one who obtained the disclosed subject matter from the inventor) in the year preceding an invention's effective filing date. *See* 35 U.S.C. §102(b)(1) (eff. Mar. 16, 2013) ("Disclosures Made 1 Year or Less Before the Effective Filing Date of the Claimed Invention"); 35 U.S.C. §102(b)(2) (eff. Mar. 16, 2013) ("Disclosures Appearing in Applications and Patents"). For further discussion, *see infra* Chapter 4, Section S ("Novelty-Preserving Exceptions Under Post-AIA 35 U.S.C. §102(b)").

[74]Hazeltine Research, Inc. v. Brenner, 382 U.S. 252 (1965).

The America Invents Act of 2011 eliminated 35 U.S.C. §102(e) (2006) but retained the concept of prior art including the content of earlier-filed patents or published applications. *See* 35 U.S.C. §102(a)(2) (eff. Mar. 16, 2013). For further discussion, *see supra* Chapter 4, Section R ("Presumptively Novelty-Destroying Events Under Post-AIA 35 U.S.C. §102(a)(2)").

[75]*OddzOn*, 122 F.3d at 1396.

The America Invents Act of 2011 eliminated 35 U.S.C. §102(f) (2006), *see* Leahy-Smith America Invents Act, Pub. L. No. 112-29 (H.R. 1249), §3(b)(1), 125 Stat. 284, 285-286 (2011), but retained the requirement of originality that was reflected by

(2006)[76] of 35 U.S.C.—are legally available as the prior art that can be combined for purposes of making a §103 obviousness rejection.

For example, consider a third party's sale of a product more than one year before the applicant's filing date, which product was similar to but not anticipatory of (i.e., strictly identical to) the claimed invention. The third party's sale of that product would not result in a loss of right to a patent on the claimed invention under §102(b) (2006), because the strict identity rule of anticipation would not be satisfied. However, if the PHOSITA would have been motivated to make the claimed invention by modifying the features of the sold product, in accordance with *other* knowledge available at that time to the PHOSITA (this other knowledge qualifying under some subsection of §102), then the invention would have been unpatentable as obvious under 35 U.S.C. §103. The third party's sale of the product more than a year before the applicant's filing date, even though of something not identical to the claimed invention, effectively added that product to the universe of prior art available to the PHOSITA confronted with the problem addressed by the invention. This can be conceptualized as a "§102(b) (2006)/§103" theory of unpatentability.

b. In re Bass *(C.C.P.A. 1973)*

In re Bass[77] is a seminal case in the development of §102/§103 "overlap" jurisprudence. *Bass* concerned the applicability of pre-AIA 35

---

§102(f). Specifically, the AIA did not change the requirement that, subject to certain exceptions, patent applications shall be made "by the inventor," 35 U.S.C. §111(a)(1) (2006), and the AIA added a definition of "inventor" as "the individual or, if a joint invention, the individuals collectively who inventoried or discovered the subject matter of the invention." 35 U.S.C. §100(f) (eff. Mar. 16, 2013); Leahy-Smith America Invents Act, Pub. L. No. 112-29 (H.R. 1249), §3(a)(2), 125 Stat. 284, 285 (2011). The AIA also continued the requirement that a patent applicant's oath include a statement that the applicant believes he is an "original" inventor. *See* 35 U.S.C. §115 (2006) (requiring that "[t]he applicant shall make oath that he believes himself to be the *original* and first inventor of the process, machine, manufacture, or composition of matter, or improvement thereof, for which he solicits a patent") (emphasis added); 35 U.S.C. §115(b)(2) (eff. Mar. 16, 2013) (providing that "[a]n oath or declaration under subsection (a) shall contain statements that . . . such individual believes himself or herself to be the *original* inventor or an *original* joint inventor of a claimed invention in the application") (emphasis added).

It is not entirely clear whether §102(f) (2006)–type secret prior art will continue to count as prior art for use in nonobviousness determinations post-AIA. This is because the post-AIA version of 35 U.S.C. §102 includes the phrase "or otherwise available to the public. . . ." For further discussion, *see supra* Chapter 4, Section Q.3 ("Does the AIA Permit Secret Prior Art?").

[76]In re Bass, 474 F.2d 1276 (C.C.P.A. 1973). The America Invents Act of 2011 eliminated 35 U.S.C. §102(g) (2006). *See* Leahy-Smith America Invents Act, Pub. L. No. 112-29 (H.R. 1249), §3(b)(1), 125 Stat. 284, 285-286 (2011).

[77]474 F.2d 1276 (C.C.P.A. 1973).

U.S.C. §102(g)[78] as prior art for purposes of nonobviousness analysis under §103. Prior to the *Bass* decision, the courts viewed 35 U.S.C. §102(g) exclusively as a basis for interference proceedings, which are pre-AIA administrative determinations to determine time-wise priority of invention between two rival claimants for the same invention.[79] The USPTO had not had occasion to rely on the prior making of inventions under §102(g) as prior art for the purposes of forming obviousness rejections in *ex parte* prosecution of patent applications.[80] In *Bass,* the CCPA determined that prior invention by another under §102(g) also could be used for that purpose, even though the prior art invention and the invention of the application on appeal were made by employees of the same corporation. The rather complicated facts of *Bass* can be summarized as follows.

The invention of the application on appeal in *Bass,* invented by a group of co-workers consisting of Bass, Jenkins, and Horvat, was a four-element vacuum system for controlling and collecting waste (e.g., dirt and twigs) on carding machines that are used in forming textile fibers. Before the inventive entity of Bass/Jenkins/Horvat filed a

[78]Recall from Chapter 4, *supra*, that under pre-America Invents Act of 2011 rules, 35 U.S.C. §102(g) prohibits a patent when another inventor has made the invention in this country before the invention date of the patent applicant, and has not abandoned, suppressed, or concealed that earlier invention. *See* 35 U.S.C. §102(g)(2) (2006).

[79]*See Bass*, 474 F.2d at 1283 (stating that the case was "the first time we have considered combining §102(g) and §103 in the context of an *ex parte* rejection entirely divorced from the award of priority in an interference which established the prior inventorship relied on in rejecting"). Interferences are explained *supra* Chapter 4, Section N ("Prior Invention Under 35 U.S.C. §102(g) (Pre-AIA)").

[80]In a footnote in the *Bass* majority opinion, Judge Rich recognized that

> [i]t may be wondered why, in the twenty years since §102(g) came into effect, there have not been more adjudicated cases reported relying on it to show "prior art" in support of a §103 rejection. The answer probably is that there are many other defenses much easier to establish and it is a rare case where the effort of going back to the date of invention of a prior inventor is worth the cost. In particular, §102(e) makes patents unquestioned prior art for all purposes as of their United States filing dates and the date of invention is usually not enough earlier to make a difference in the result.

Id. at 1286 n.7.

The *Bass* case presented an exception to this "usual" state of affairs, of course, because the USPTO possessed information concerning the invention date of the Jenkins screen, and that date was "enough earlier" than the date of invention for the Bass/Jenkins/Horvat system "to make a difference in the result." In most cases, the USPTO does not have information concerning the invention date of the subject matter of prior art patents. Such information is more likely to be unearthed in the process of conducting discovery in cases litigating the validity of issued patents. This is why §102(g) prior art is more commonly employed in §103 obviousness challenges to the validity of issued patents rather than in §103-based rejections of pending patent application claims in the USPTO.

patent application claiming their system, however, a separate patent application had been filed that named Jenkins as the sole inventor of one of the four components of the vacuum system (i.e., a main cylinder screen). The USPTO examiner rejected the vacuum system invention as obvious under §103 in view of a combination of prior art references that included the earlier-filed Jenkins patent.[81]

Bass/Jenkins/Horvat were able to antedate the earlier filing date of Jenkins in accordance with 37 C.F.R. §1.131,[82] thus removing the Jenkins patent's disclosure to the extent that it had been relied on by the USPTO as §102(e) (pre-AIA) prior art available for the §103 obviousness rejection. Because Jenkins claimed the main cylinder screen and evidence existed in the prosecution record of Jenkins' dates of conception and actual reduction to practice, however, the USPTO countered that the fact of Jenkins' earlier *invention* nevertheless could be relied on as §102(g) prior art to maintain the obviousness rejection. The CCPA agreed:

> [W]e . . . rule against appellants [Bass/Jenkins/Horvat] and hold that the use of the prior invention of another who had not abandoned, suppressed, or concealed it under the circumstances of this case which include the disclosure of such invention in an issued patent, is available as "prior art" within the meaning of that term in §103 by virtue of §102(g).[83]

The difficulty with the result in *Bass* is that the "another" was Jenkins, the co-worker of Bass and Horvat. Both the Jenkins screen invention, and the Bass/Jenkins/Horvat system invention of which the Jenkins screen was essentially a subcombination, were owned by the same employer. Yet the earlier Jenkins invention theoretically could be used by the USPTO as prior art to prevent the patenting of the later (and arguably more economically important) system invention of Bass/Jenkins/Horvat.[84]

[81]Because the disclosure of Jenkins' patent *described* the "screen" element of the Bass/Jenkins/Horvat combination system invention without claiming the system invention, and because Jenkins was a separate inventive entity from Bass/Jenkins/Horvat, the Jenkins patent was viewed initially by the USPTO as a §102(e) prior art reference, available for combination with other prior art in the §103 obviousness rejection.

[82]The pre-AIA Rule 131 procedure for antedating or "swearing behind" the effective date of a prior art reference by showing earlier invention is covered *supra* in Chapter 4, Section O.

[83]*Bass*, 474 F.2d at 1286-1287.

[84]This did not actually occur in *Bass*. The rejections based on a combination of Jenkins and a patent to Bass and Horvat on a nozzle for use in the system were reversed because the court determined that the Bass/Horvat patent was not prior art. In his concurrence, Judge Baldwin argued that the majority's discussion of §102(g) as prior art for obviousness determinations under §103 was unnecessary to the result in *Bass*. *See Bass*, 474 F.2d at 1291-1292.

c. *1984 Amendments*

Congress addressed this problem in 1984, when it amended 35 U.S.C. §103 to add the following language:

> Subject matter developed by another person, which qualifies as prior art only under subsections (f) or (g) of section 102 of this title, shall not preclude patentability under this section where the subject matter and the claimed invention were, at the time the invention was made, owned by the same person or subject to an obligation of assignment to the same person.[85]

This statutory provision, which patent attorneys refer to as the "*Bass* disqualifier," had the effect of shielding commonly owned inventions[86] from being rendered obvious by the prior work of other inventors in the same company or firm. In order to promote shared research and greater communication between co-workers, Congress effectively gave corporations the right to patents on obvious variants of in-house efforts qualifying as prior invention under 35 U.S.C. §102(f) or (g). Had this statutory provision been in effect at the time of *Bass,* the USPTO examiner could not have cited the commonly owned Jenkins screen invention, which was otherwise §102(g) subject matter, as prior art to establish obviousness of the Bass/Jenkins/Horvat system invention.

d. *AIPA (1999) Amendments*

As part of the American Inventors Protection Act (AIPA) of 1999, the statutory language was further modified to include commonly owned prior art under §102(e) (pre-AIA) (i.e., disclosures in earlier-filed patents or published patent applications of "another") in the list of categories of prior art that "shall not preclude patentability" under §103.[87] This alleviated the problem seen in cases such as *In re Bartfeld.*[88]

[85]35 U.S.C. §103 (1984).

[86]"Commonly owned" means that legal title in both inventions is in the same person (be it a natural person or a firm such as a corporation), or are at least subject to an obligation to assign ownership to the same "person."

[87]*See* 35 U.S.C. §103(c) (2002) (as amended by Pub. L. No. 106-113, §1000(a)(9), based on American Inventors Protection Act of Nov. 29, 1999, S. 1948, 106th Cong, tit. IV, subtit. H, §4807(a)).

[88]925 F.2d 1450 (Fed. Cir. 1991) (affirming §103 rejection of appellant's invention as obvious in view of combination of prior art that included the §102(e) disclosure of a commonly assigned, earlier-filed patent granted to appellant's co-worker). The *Bartfeld* court, deciding the case before it under the pre-1999 version of §103, was compelled to reject the appellant's argument that the rejection on commonly assigned art was contrary to the policy underlying the *Bass* disqualifier amendment of 1984, stating that

e. *CREATE Act (2004) Amendments*

The Cooperative Research and Technology Enhancement (CREATE) Act of 2004[89] expanded the §103(c) (pre-AIA) shield even further. Congress wanted to prevent the use in obviousness determinations of §102(e), (f), and (g) prior art that had been earlier generated not only by an inventor's colleagues in the same corporation, but also §102(e), (f), and (g) prior art that had been earlier generated by the parties to a joint research agreement involving the inventor.[90] In particular, Congress was concerned about the impact of the Federal Circuit's 1997 decision in *OddzOn Prods., Inc. v. Just Toys, Inc.*,[91] on collaborative research agreements between universities and for-profit corporations of the type encouraged by the Bayh-Dole Act of 1980.[92] The Federal Circuit held in *OddzOn* that nonpublic information qualifying under 35 U.S.C. §102(f) (1994) could be relied on as prior art for purposes of assessing obviousness under 35 U.S.C. §103(a).[93] Thus, the CREATE Act's sponsors noted, "some collaborative teams that the Bayh-Dole Act was intended to encourage have been unable to obtain patents for their efforts."[94] In order to fix the problem, the CREATE Act expanded the definition of "owned by the same person or subject to an obligation of assignment to the same person" in 35 U.S.C. §103(c)(1) (2000) as follows:

> (2) For purposes of this subsection [§103(c)], subject matter developed by another person and a claimed invention shall be deemed to have been owned by the same person or subject to an obligation of assignment to the same person if—
>
> (A) the claimed invention was made by or on behalf of parties to a joint research agreement that was in effect on or before the date the claimed invention was made;
>
> (B) the claimed invention was made as a result of activities undertaken within the scope of the joint research agreement; and

---

"[w]e may not disregard the unambiguous exclusion of §102(e) prior art from the statute's purview." *Id.* at 1453.

[89] Pub. L. No. 108-453, §2, 118 Stat. 3596 (2004).

[90] A "joint research agreement" is defined by the CREATE Act amendments to mean "a written contract, grant, or cooperative agreement entered into by two or more persons or entities for the performance of experimental, developmental, or research work in the field of the claimed invention." 35 U.S.C. §103(c)(3).

[91] 122 F.3d 1396 (Fed. Cir. 1997).

[92] The Bayh-Dole Act is codified at 35 U.S.C. §§200-212.

[93] *See OddzOn*, 122 F.3d at 1403-1404 (holding that "subject matter derived from another not only is itself unpatentable to the party who derived it under §102(f), but, when combined with other prior art, may make a resulting obvious invention unpatentable to that party under a combination of §§102(f) and 103").

[94] 150 Cong. Rec. S2559 (Mar. 10, 2004) (remarks of Sen. Leahy).

(C) the application for patent for the claimed invention discloses or is amended to disclose the names of the parties to the joint research agreement.

The CREATE Act amendments to §103 were prospective in effect; they applied only to patents granted on or after the legislation's enactment date of December 10, 2004.[95]

f. AIA (2011) Amendments

In the America Invents Act of 2011 (AIA), Congress expanded the §103(c) (2006) exclusion of commonly owned subject matter, including joint research work, to §102 anticipation situations. That is, Congress deleted the exclusionary provisions from §103 and relocated them in 35 U.S.C. §102.[96]

The current U.S. law is that all types of §102 prior art are available for purposes of establishing obviousness under §103. This rule applies to pre-AIA situations even though some categories of pre-AIA §102 prior art could not have been known to the PHOSITA at the time of her invention, and were thus temporarily "secret" prior art.[97] For example, consider the written description in another's earlier-filed but not yet published or issued U.S. patent application, which qualifies as prior art under 35 U.S.C. §102(e) (2006).[98] As of the PHOSITA's invention date, she could not have known of the contents of a secretly pending patent application. Likewise, earlier inventions of another that qualify as prior art under 35 U.S.C. §102(g) (2006), such as

[95]Pub. L. No. 108-453, §3(a), 118 Stat. 3596 (2004). The USPTO published interim rules implementing the CREATE Act amendments in 37 C.F.R. *See* 70 Fed. Reg. 1818 (Jan. 11, 2005).

[96]The pre-AIA exclusion of commonly owned subject matter found in 35 U.S.C. §103(c)(1) (2006) appears post-AIA at 35 U.S.C. §102(b)(2)(C) (eff. Mar. 16, 2013). The pre-AIA exclusion of joint research agreement work found in 35 U.S.C. §103(c)(2) (2006) appears post-AIA at 35 U.S.C. §102(c) (eff. Mar. 16, 2013) ("Common Ownership Under Joint Research Agreements"). *See* Leahy-Smith America Invents Act, Pub. L. No. 112-29 (H.R. 1249), §3(b)(1), 125 Stat. 284, 285-286 (2011); *id.* at §3(c) (deleting paragraph (c) from 35 U.S.C. §103 (2006)). The evolution of these statutory changes are examined in greater detail *supra* Chapter 4, Section U ("Common Ownership Under Joint Research Agreements").

[97]Although secret information (e.g., a confidential sale of an invention in this country prior to the §102(b) (pre-AIA) critical date) has long been considered available as prior art under pre-AIA rules, as of this writing (in early 2016) it is not clear that such information will qualify as prior art under post-AIA §102, under which the novelty of a claimed invention is presumptively destroyed if the invention was "otherwise available to the public" before the invention's effective filing date. *See* 35 U.S.C. §102(a)(1) (eff. Mar. 16, 2013); *see also supra* Chapter 4, Section Q.3 ("Does the AIA Permit Secret Prior Art?").

[98]*See supra* Chapter 4, Section L ("Description in Another's Earlier-Filed Patent or Published Patent Application Under 35 U.S.C. §102(e) (Pre-AIA)"), for further explanation of 35 U.S.C. §102(e) prior art.

Jenkins' screen in *In re Bass,* would not be known to the PHOSITA in the absence of publication, patenting, or common assignment (as was the case in *Bass*).[99] Even trade secret communications that qualify as prior art under 35 U.S.C. §102(f) (2006) may be cited in a pre-AIA §103 obviousness rejection.[100]

g. European Comparison

European patent law, by contrast, does *not* permit the use of the contents of an earlier-filed European patent application to establish lack of inventive step (i.e., the European counterpart to the U.S. nonobviousness requirement).[101] The content of an earlier-filed European patent application is considered "part of the state of the art" only if it is novelty-destroying, that is, anticipatory.[102]

Unlike the European patent system, in the United States, the prior art referred to by 35 U.S.C. §103 (at least in its pre-AIA version) is not limited to information that was "publicly known" at the time the invention was made.[103] The U.S. approach may seem unfair to inventors, but it substantially reduces the possibility of two separate patents issuing on inventions that are different in only obvious respects.

4. Analogous Art

Although 35 U.S.C. §102 provides a catalog of prior art that may be available for a 35 U.S.C. §103 obviousness rejection, *not all* prior art that otherwise qualifies under some subsection of 35 U.S.C. §102 is properly used in a §103 analysis. There is yet another important filter

[99] *See* In re Bass, 474 F.2d 1276 (C.C.P.A. 1973).

[100] *See* OddzOn Prods., Inc. v. Just Toys, Inc., 122 F.3d 1396 (Fed. Cir. 1997).

[101] *See* European Patent Convention (EPC) art. 56 (16th ed., June 2016) (titled "Inventive Step") (providing in part that "[i]f the state of the art also includes documents within the meaning of Article 54, paragraph 3 [earlier-filed European patent applications], these documents shall not be considered in deciding whether there has been an inventive step").

[102] *See id.* at art. 54(3) (titled "Novelty") (providing that "[a]dditionally, the content of European patent applications as filed, the dates of filing of which are prior to the date referred to in paragraph 2 [the filing date of the European patent application] and which were published on or after that date, shall be considered as comprised in the state of the art").

[103] *See* Hazeltine Research, Inc. v. Brenner, 382 U.S. 252, 255-256 (1965). As of this writing (in early 2016) it is not clear that information that is not available to the public will qualify as prior art under post-AIA §102. Under that provision, the novelty of a claimed invention is presumptively destroyed if the invention was "otherwise available to the public" before the invention's effective filing date. *See* 35 U.S.C. §102(a)(1) (eff. Mar. 16, 2013); *see also supra* Chapter 4, Section Q.3 ("Does the AIA Permit Secret Prior Art?").

or limitation: in order to be considered in a nonobviousness analysis, prior art references also must be what patent attorneys refer to as **analogous art.**[104]

The characteristic of being analogous is a shorthand way of referring to the prior art that courts deem a PHOSITA would reasonably have consulted in solving the problem addressed by the claimed invention. Whether a reference is analogous art is a question of fact.[105] The law recognizes that the PHOSITA cannot know all prior art in every field, and thus "attempt[s] to more closely approximate the reality of the circumstances surrounding the making of an invention by only presuming knowledge by the inventor [sic, PHOSITA] of prior art in the field of his endeavor and in analogous arts."[106]

The Federal Circuit defines analogous art by seeking to recreate the innovation process of a PHOSITA. When faced with a particular problem, it is reasonable to assume that that person would have consulted the following two categories of information:

1. prior art within the same field of endeavor as the invention; and
2. prior art from a different field of endeavor, but reasonably pertinent to the same problem as that addressed by the invention.[107]

Thus, analogous art is the §102 prior art that is legally permissible to use in a §103 analysis, and it must arise from the same technological field as the claimed invention or be directed to the same problem even if in a different technological field. To go beyond analogous art in a §103 analysis runs the risk of hindsight reconstruction of a claimed invention by merely finding each of its constituent elements somewhere in the prior art, without concern for whether a PHOSITA would have reasonably considered that art.[108]

[104]*See* In re Klein, 647 F.3d 1343, 1348 (Fed. Cir. 2011) (stating that "[a] reference qualifies as prior art for an obviousness determination under §103 only when it is analogous to the claimed invention").

[105]Innovention Toys, LLC v. MGA Entertainment, Inc., 637 F.3d 1314, 1321 (Fed. Cir. 2011).

[106]In re Wood, 599 F.2d 1032, 1036 (C.C.P.A. 1979).

[107]*See id.*

[108]*See* Warren D. Woessner, Innovation [sic, Innovention] Toys *and Analogous Art — Defender Against Hindsight?* (Mar. 24, 2011), https://www.patents4life.com/ 2011/03/ innovation-toys-and-analogous-art-%E2%80%93-defender-against-hindsight (explaining that "if a[] [USPTO] Examiner has to reach outside of the relevant art areas to find elements of the claim, the Examiner may be cueing you to argue 'hindsight reconstruction' — the Examiner is using your client's invention like the picture of the finished puzzle on the box, as a guide to locate and assemble widely scattered pieces. In some cases, the Examiner may have reached into such disparate areas of endeavor that the art is not 'logically combinable' to yield the claimed invention.").

Applying the *Wood* formulation, if the invention under consideration is, for example, the shock-absorbing construction of the plow shank in *Graham v. John Deere,* the properly considered analogous art would include:

1. other plow shanks; and
2. shock-absorbing devices, whether part of a plow shank, an automobile, or any other type of mechanical device subjected to physical forces when in motion.

Applying prong 1 of the *Wood* formulation necessarily requires determining the "same field of endeavor" for a given invention. The scope of this phrase is not always self-evident. For example, should a toothbrush be considered within the same field of endeavor as a hair brush? Rather surprisingly, two of three Federal Circuit judges answered affirmatively in *In re Bigio.*[109] The applicant in that case sought to patent an ergonomically designed hair brush. The USPTO rejected his claims as obvious in view of a combination of two prior art patents for toothbrushes, and the Federal Circuit majority affirmed. First, the majority applied the "broadest reasonable interpretation" rule to approve the agency's interpretation of the claim term "hair brush" as encompassing "not only brushes that may be used for human hair on [a] scalp, but also brushes that may be used for hairs [o]n other parts of animal bodies (e.g., human facial hair, human eyebrow hair, or pet hair)." The fact that the "Objects of the Invention" section of Bigio's application referred to an anatomically correct hair brush for brushing scalp hair was not dispositive. Absent claim language carrying a narrow meaning, the majority instructed, the USPTO "should only limit the claim based on the specification or prosecution history when those sources expressly disclaim the broader definition." Second, in view of the broad claim interpretation, toothbrushes fell within the field of endeavor of Bigio's invention — namely, the "field of hand-held brushes having a handle segment and a bristle substrate segment." The Federal Circuit majority disputed Bigio's characterization of the field of endeavor test as wholly subjective and unworkable. Rather, "the examiner and the Board must consider the 'circumstances' of the application — the full disclosure — and weigh those circumstances from the vantage point of the common sense likely to be exerted by one of ordinary skill in the art in assessing the scope of the endeavor."[110] Dissenting Judge Newman found the majority's reasoning lacking in common sense, for "teeth are not bodily hair." According to Judge Newman, the broad claim interpretation in this case simply did not justify "the leap from facial hair to

[109] 381 F.3d 1320 (Fed. Cir. 2004).
[110] *Id.* at 1326.

teeth and thereby render the brushing of teeth analogous to the brushing of hair."[111]

Prong 2 of the *Wood* analysis, asking whether the prior art reference in question concerns the same problem as that addressed by the claimed invention, is an inquiry often applied broadly by the Federal Circuit. Consider *Innovention Toys, LLC v. MGA Entertainment, Inc.*,[112] in which the claimed invention was directed to a physical board game involving "a chess-styled playing surface, laser sources positioned to project light beams over the playing surface when 'fired,' mirrored and non-mirrored playing pieces used to direct the lasers' beams, and non-mirrored 'key playing pieces' equivalent to the king pieces in chess." The prior art included printed publications describing *electronic* versions of similar chess games, that is, computer-based, chess-like strategy games. The Federal Circuit vacated a district court's summary judgment that Innovention's board game patent would not have been obvious, concluding that the lower court had erroneously "failed to consider whether a reference disclosing an *electronic*, laser-based strategy game, even if not in the same field of endeavor, would nonetheless have been reasonably pertinent to the problem facing an inventor of a new, *physical*, laser-based strategy game."[113] Contrary to the district court's reasoning, the electronic game references *were* analogous art because they were directed to the same purpose as the claimed invention: "detailing the specific game elements comprising a chess-like, laser-based strategy game."[114] The references and the claimed invention "relate[d] to the same goal: designing a winnable yet entertaining strategy game." Moreover, the record reflected that inventors on many prior art patents "contemplated the implementation of their strategy games in both physical and electronic formats."[115]

In re Klein provides a contrasting (and relatively rare) illustration of the Federal Circuit reversing a USPTO finding that the prior art cited by the agency was analogous art.[116] The claimed invention in *Klein* involved a mixing device for use in preparing sugar-water nectar for certain bird and butterfly feeders. The claims recited a particular structure having a movable divider that formed compartments for various ratios of sugar and water. In its §103 obviousness rejection, the USPTO cited prior art references pertaining to, *inter alia,* tool trays with movable dividers to hold nuts and bolts as well as a cabinet drawer with removable dividers for separating small household

[111] *Id.* at 1328 (Newman, J., dissenting).
[112] 637 F.3d 1314 (Fed. Cir. 2011).
[113] *Innovention Toys*, 637 F.3d at 1321-1322 (emphasis in original).
[114] *Innovention Toys,* 637 F.3d at 1322.
[115] *Innovention Toys,* 637 F.3d at 1323.
[116] 647 F.3d 1343 (Fed. Cir. 2011).

articles such as cosmetics and paper clips. The Federal Circuit held that the cited references were non-analogous, for they pertained to the problem of *separating* solid objects rather than mixing components of a solution. Specifically, the court agreed

> with [the applicant] Mr. Klein that the Board's conclusory finding that [the] Roberts, O'Connor, and Kirkman [prior art references] are analogous is not supported by substantial evidence. The purpose of each of Roberts, O'Connor, or Kirkman is to separate solid objects. An inventor considering the problem of "making a nectar feeder with a movable divider to prepare different ratios of sugar and water for different animals," would not have been motivated to consider any of these references when making his invention, particularly since none of these three references shows a partitioned container that is adapted to receive water or contain it long enough to be able to prepare different ratios in the different compartments.[117]

The Federal Circuit's 2015 decision in *Circuit Check Inc. v. QXQ Inc.*[118] illustrates a case in which a jury, based on its verdict that the patents in suit would not have been obvious, was deemed to have found that certain prior art references proffered by the accused infringer were *not* analogous art. Circuit Check's patents in suit[119] concerned a device used in testing the circuit boards that are commonly found in electronic devices. As the Federal Circuit explained, many circuit board testers require an "interface plate," which is a plastic grid with holes that permit connections between the tester device and the circuit board. In order to align circuit boards during testing, it is advantageous to mark certain holes on the interface plate.[120] A representative claim of the patents in suit covered "[a]n indicator interface plate" that was "configured to provide readily visible identification of predetermined holes," comprising

> a surface including a plurality of holes having visually discernable markings to allow a user to visually determine which of said plurality of holes are to be populated, wherein a region of the plate said plurality of holes have a first predetermined indicia covering the surface surrounding said plurality of holes, the plate further comprising: *a second removable indicia overlying said first predetermined indicia*, said second indicia being different from said first predetermined indicia, *wherein said second indicia is removed from areas of said plate adjacent each of said predetermined holes*, said predetermined holes are visually identifiable to a user by the appearance of the first indicia.[121]

[117]*Klein*, 647 F.3d at 1350-1351.
[118]795 F.3d 1331 (Fed. Cir. 2015).
[119]U.S. Patent Nos. 7,592,796; 7,695,766; and 7,749,566.
[120]*Circuit Check*, 795 F.3d at 1333.
[121]U.S. Patent No. 7,592,796 (claim 1) (emphasis added by Federal Circuit).

In practice, the recited "indicia" were certain types of paint, the second paint layer being removable from the underlying first paint layer.

At trial, accused infringer/validity challenger QXQ asserted that three prior art references (collectively the "disputed references") — rock carvings, engraved signage, and a machining technique known as "Prussian Blue" — disclosed the critical limitation requiring that the claimed interface plate have "a second removable indicia overlying said first predetermined indicia . . . wherein said second indicia is removed from areas of said plate adjacent each of said predetermined holes." (Other, "nondisputed" references concededly taught the remaining claim limitations.) In the prior art rock carvings, a varnish was applied to rocks and then scraped off to make designs. In the prior art engraved signage, the top layer of a multi-layer product was removed to expose a bottom layer. In the prior art Prussian Blue machining technique, a dye was applied to a workpiece and thereafter removed by a drill or a scribe (a pointed instrument used in metalworking).

Rebuffing QXQ's position, patentee Circuit Check contended before the jury that none of the three disputed references should be considered analogous art. In Circuit Check's view, the references were not relevant or reasonably pertinent to the problem at hand, or simply bore no connection to the claimed invention. Based on the jury's verdict that the claims in suit would not have been obvious, the jury was presumed to agree with Circuit Check that the disputed references were not analogous.[122] Although the district court overrode the jury and granted QXQ's motion for judgment of invalidity as a matter of

[122]Because it was given a general verdict form, the jury only expressly answered the high-level questions whether the claims had been proven invalid (answering no) and whether the claims were infringed (answering yes). In the general verdict context, "[b]y finding the claims nonobvious, the jury presumably found that the disputed prior art is not analogous and therefore not within the scope of the prior art." *Circuit Check*,795 F.3d at 1335 (citing Jurgens v. McKasy, 927 F.2d 1552, 1557 (Fed. Cir. 1991)). The cited *Jurgens* precedent explains that in reviewing a jury's verdict concerning obviousness (or absence thereof), the Federal Circuit

> first presume[s] that the jury resolved the underlying factual disputes in favor of the verdict winner and leave those presumed findings undisturbed if they are supported by substantial evidence. Then we examine the legal conclusion de novo to see whether it is correct in light of the presumed jury fact findings.

Jurgens v. McKasy, 927 F.2d 1552, 1557 (Fed. Cir. 1991) (citations omitted). In an obviousness analysis, one of the "underlying factual disputes" is whether the prior art relied on by the validity challenger is analogous art (analytically one aspect of the "scope and content of the prior art" *Graham* factor). To be considered within the prior art for purposes of the obviousness analysis, a reference must be analogous. *See* Wang Labs., Inc. v. Toshiba Corp., 993 F.2d 858, 864 (Fed. Cir. 1993). The Federal Circuit treats whether a reference is analogous art as a question of fact. *See* Wyers v. Master Lock Co., 616 F.3d 1231, 1237 (Fed. Cir. 2010).

law (JMOL),[123] the Federal Circuit reversed the district court, effectively reinstating the jury's verdict of no invalidity.

With respect to the analogous art issue, the Circuit explained that the disputed prior art references were not in the same field of endeavor as the claimed invention — circuit board testers and test fixtures used in the manufacture of electronics. Thus, the analogous art question turned on whether the disputed references were reasonably pertinent to the problem solved by the invention. In other words, was it reasonable to assume that a person of ordinary skill in the art, attempting to solve the problem of marking circuit board tester interface plates, would have consulted the three disputed references? The Federal Circuit firmly answered "no":

> Just because keying a car, for example, is within the common knowledge of humankind does not mean that keying a car is analogous art. An alleged infringer should not be able to transform all systems and methods within the common knowledge into analogous prior art simply by stating that anyone would have known of such a system or method. The question is not whether simple concepts such as rock carvings, engraved signage, or Prussian Blue dye are within the knowledge of lay people or even within the knowledge of a person of ordinary skill in the art. Rather, the question is whether an inventor would look to this particular art to solve the particular problem at hand. Here, Circuit Check put forward evidence that an inventor would not have considered the disputed prior art when trying to improve marking. It is not hard to arrive at that conclusion. Even though an inventor may be aware of rock carvings, it is not surprising that the inventor would not have looked to rock carvings to improve the process of painting small dots on interface plates for expensive circuit board testers. And, even though an inventor may work in an office with engraved signage, the inventor would not necessarily have considered using the techniques disclosed in engraved signage to solve the problem of marking circuit board tester interface plates. Finally, even though an inventor in this case was aware of Prussian Blue, it is not surprising that one of skill in the art would not consider using a machining technique that employed removable dye on interface plates where such dye could fall into and interfere with the underlying electronics of the circuit board testers.[124]

[123]*See Circuit Check*, 795 F.3d at 1334, observing that (record citations omitted):

> [t]he district court . . . found that although there was no doubt that rock carvings "are not technically pertinent to the 'field' of circuit testers," and "witnesses credibly testified that Prussian Blue dye had not been used on alignment plates," "any layman" would have understood that interface plates could be marked using the techniques described in the disputed prior art. . . . [The district court] further noted that "any vandal who has 'keyed' a car knows that stripping the paint with a key will result in the underlying metal color showing through."

[124]*Circuit Check*, 795 F.3d at 1335-1336.

Accordingly, the Federal Circuit in *Circuit Check* found, supported by substantial evidence the jury's presumed finding that the disputed references were not analogous art. The appellate court similarly upheld the jury's other presumed findings underlying its verdict, i.e., that "significant" differences existed between the claimed invention and the remaining, undisputed references of record (which the parties had stipulated were analogous);[125] and that secondary considerations evidence, namely evidence of copying, long-felt need, commercial success, skepticism, and unexpected results, all supported a conclusion of nonobviousness.[126] The Federal Circuit thus reversed the district court's grant of JMOL and remanded the case for further proceedings.

Because it seeks to mirror the thought process of a person of ordinary skill in the art who is attempting to solve the problem addressed by a claimed invention, an analogous art analysis must consider all record evidence pertinent to that factual determination. The USPTO failed to do so in *Airbus S.A.S. v. Firepass Corporation.*[127]

The claimed invention of Firepass's U.S. Patent No. 6,418,752 ('752 patent) was a system that provided low-oxygen ("hypoxic") but normal-pressure ("normobaric") air in an enclosed area to prevent or extinguish fires.[128] The system advantageously used breathable air instead of water, foam, or toxic chemicals, each of which can carry serious risks to

[125]*See Circuit Check*,795 F.3d at 1336 (explaining that "[t]he stipulated [undisputed] prior art does not disclose what makes the patented claims unique: placing a second removable indicia on top of the interface plate and then selectively removing that layer to identify certain holes on the interface plate"). Moreover, the jury heard testimony that the undisputed prior art actually taught away from the claimed invention. *See id.* (noting that jury heard testimony of "manufacturer specifications [that] contemplated minimizing the amount of paint on interface plates because paint had a tendency to chip off and fall into the tester, which caused serious problems... [and that the jury] also heard testimony that the specifications counselled against covering the entire interface plate with paint") (record citations omitted). Thus, the Circuit concluded, "substantial evidence supports the jury's presumed finding that one of skill would not have been motivated to use more paint to cover the entire surface of the interface plate." *Id.* (footnote omitted).

[126]*See Circuit Check*,795 F.3d at 1336-1337.

[127]941 F.3d 1374, (Fed. Cir. Nov. 8, 2019) (Stoll, J.)

[128]The only independent claim on appeal in *Airbus* recited:

> 91. A system for providing breathable fire-preventive and fire suppressive atmosphere in enclosed human-occupied spaces, said system comprising:
>
> an enclosing structure having an internal environment therein containing a gas mixture which is lower in oxygen content than air outside said structure, and an entry communicating with said internal environment;
>
> an oxygen-extraction device having a filter, an inlet taking in an intake gas mixture and first and second outlets, said oxygen-extraction device being a nitrogen generator, said first outlet transmitting a first gas mixture having a higher oxygen content than the intake gas mixture and said second outlet transmitting a second gas mixture having a lower oxygen content than the intake gas mixture;

humans or electronics. In an *inter partes* reexamination proceeding, the USPTO examiner had rejected the '752 claims at issue. The primary prior art reference, "reference A," disclosed equipment for providing a similar hypoxic but normobaric atmosphere for purposes of athletic training or physical therapy. Notably, reference A said nothing about fire.

On appeal from the examiner's rejection, the Board determined that "reference A" was *not* analogous art to the claimed invention. In the Board's view, reference A was neither (1) in the same field of endeavor as the claimed invention — devices and methods for fire suppression,[129] nor (2) reasonably pertinent to the problem addressed by the claimed invention — how to suppress or prevent fires. As to the latter "reasonably pertinent" inquiry, the Board found "no articulated rational underpinning that sufficiently links the problem of fire suppression/prevention confronting the inventor" to reference A, which was directed to "human therapy, wellness, and physical training."[130]

More specifically, the Board in analyzing whether the disclosure of reference A was "reasonably pertinent" (i.e., prong (2) of the analogous art test) expressly ignored the teachings of four other prior art references ("references B-E") in the record.[131] Notably, the examiner had

---

> said second outlet communicating with said internal environment and transmitting said second mixture into said internal environment so that said second mixture mixes with the atmosphere in said internal environment;
>
> said first outlet transmitting said first mixture to a location where it does not mix with said atmosphere in said internal environment;
>
> said internal environment selectively communicating with the outside atmosphere and emitting excessive internal gas mixture into the outside atmosphere;
>
> said intake gas mixture being ambient air taken in from the external atmosphere outside said internal environment with a reduced humidity; and
>
> a computer control for regulating the oxygen content in said internal environment.

Airbus, 941 F.3d at 1376-1377.

[129]The Federal Circuit affirmed this aspect of the Board's decision, explaining that

> In view of the Board's factual findings that (1) the challenged claims are expressly directed to a fire-preventive and fire-suppressive system, and (2) Kotliar ["reference A"] does not even recite the word "fire" once throughout the entirety of its disclosure, a reasonable mind could conclude that the '752 patent and Kotliar are directed to different fields of endeavor — especially for a "common sense" inquiry like this.

Airbus, 941 F.3d at 1381, (quoting In re Bigio, 381 F.3d 1320, 1326 (Fed. Cir. 2004)).

[130]*Airbus,* 94 F.3d at 1379.

[131]"Reference B" described a study focused on "human performance during [a] prolonged stay in normobaric hypoxia, a so-called 'fire retardant atmosphere.'" It disclosed the results of an experiment in which the human subjects were exposed to different levels of normobaric hypoxia for periods extending up to ten days. "Reference C" disclosed the results of six experiments performed by the U.S. Navy to assess the effect of hypoxia at normobaric pressure on health and mental function over time. The reference

previously considered references B-E when examining claims of the '752 patent *other than* the claims now on appeal.[132] The Board reasoned that because references B-E were not cited or applied in the obviousness rejection of the claims currently on appeal, references B-E were not relevant to the analogous art inquiry. It rejected reexamination petitioner Airbus's contention that references B-E supplied the "missing link" sought by the Board.

Agreeing with Airbus, the Federal Circuit held that the Board had erred as a matter of law and vacated its decision. The appellate court instructed that "an analysis of whether an asserted reference is analogous art should take into account any relevant evidence in the record cited by the parties to demonstrate that knowledge and perspective of a person of ordinary skill in the art."[133] The *Airbus* court explained that the "reasonably pertinent" inquiry is impossible to separate from those characteristics of the PHOSITA:

> Because a "reasonably pertinent" reference is one that an ordinarily skilled artisan would reasonably have consulted in seeking a solution to the problem that the inventor was attempting to solve, the reasonably pertinent inquiry is *inextricably tied* to the knowledge and perspective of a person of ordinary skill in the art at the time of the invention. For example, the reasonably pertinent inquiry may consider *where* an ordinarily skilled artisan would reasonably look, and *what* that person would reasonably search for, in seeking to address the problem confronted by the inventor. In order to determine whether a reference is "reasonably pertinent," then, a reasonable factfinder should consider record evidence cited by the parties to demonstrate the knowledge and perspective of a person of ordinary skill in the art at the time of the invention.[134]

---

endorsed the use of nitrogen dilution to suppress flames aboard patrolling submarines, and also suggested that such dilution could be combined with nitrogen pressurization "at minimal hazard to the crews serving aboard patrolling submarines." "Reference D" reported the effects of experiments with "nitrogen-based, fire-retardant atmospheres" on human performance, particularly visual sensitivity; it concluded that the results supported a strategy of reducing oxygen concentration to suppress fires. Lastly, "Reference E" disclosed "a system and method of adding nitrogen under pressure to a confined area including a habitable atmosphere to suppress a fire without any deleterious effects on humans within the environment in which the fire is suppressed." One object was to "suppress a fire in a closed chamber while maintaining an environment suitable for human activity." Reference E's system could be "used for any controlled habitable environment which is either an enclosed area or an area which may be closed by closing of a door or window." *Airbus,* 941 F.3d at 1378.

[132]The *Airbus* case, challenging the validity of the '752 patent's independent claim 91 (quoted above) came to the Federal Circuit on remand from a prior appeal. In the earlier *Airbus* decision, the Circuit had vacated the Board's decision dismissing Airbus's cross-appeal for lack of jurisdiction and remanded to the Board to consider Airbus's challenge to certain newly presented claims (i.e., including independent claim 91). *See* Airbus S.A.S. v. Firepass Corp., 793 F.3d 1376 (Fed. Cir. 2015).

[133]*Airbus,* 941 F.3d at 1383-1384.

[134]*Airbus,* 941 F.3d at 1382-1383, (emphasis added).

On remand, the Board would have to heed the Circuit's instruction that references B-E "[we]re relevant to the question of whether a person of ordinary skill in the art of fire prevention and suppression would have reasonably consulted references relating to normobaric hypoxic atmospheres to address the problem of preventing and suppressing fires in enclosed environments." In the court's view, References B-E "could lead" a PHOSITA in the field of fire suppression/prevention to consult reference A for its disclosure of a hypoxic enclosure, even though reference A was itself outside the field of endeavor for the claimed invention.[135]

The above discussion and illustrative cases all dealt with the question of prior art "analogousness" in the broader context of analyzing the issue of nonobviousness. In marked contrast, there is no analogousness requirement for prior art to qualify as *anticipatory* under 35 U.S.C. §102.[136] All references that qualify as prior art under some subsection of §102, regardless of their relationship to the field of the claimed invention or the problem addressed thereby, are available for an anticipation rejection, so long as the strict identity rule of anticipation is satisfied.[137]

G. *Graham* Factor: Differences Between Claimed Invention and Prior Art

This factor is the heart of a nonobviousness analysis under 35 U.S.C. §103. There must be some identifiable difference(s) between

[135]*Airbus,* 941 F.3d at 1383.

[136]*See* In re Schreiber, 128 F.3d 1473, 1478 (Fed. Cir. 1997) (stating that "the question whether a reference is analogous art is irrelevant to whether that reference anticipates. . . . A reference may be from an entirely different field of endeavor than that of the claimed invention or may be directed to an entirely different problem from the one addressed by the inventor, yet the reference will still anticipate if it explicitly or inherently discloses every limitation recited in the claims.") (citation omitted).

The broadest claim on appeal in *Schreiber* recited "[a] dispensing top for passing only several kernels of a popped popcorn at a time from an open-ended container filled with popped popcorn, having a generally conical shape and an opening at each end. . . ." In contrast, the prior art reference relied on by the USPTO examiner to show anticipation, a Swiss patent issued to Harz, disclosed "a spout for nozzle-ready canisters," which could be tapered inward in a conical fashion, said to be "useful for purposes such as dispensing oil from an oil can." *Schreiber,*128 F.3d at 1475. The examiner concluded that "the Harz top is clearly capable of dispensing popped popcorn," *id.*, and that the limitations of Schreiber's claim 1 read identically on the structure described in Harz. Because the requirement that prior art references be analogous applied only in the context of obviousness, not anticipation, the Federal Circuit rejected as "irrelevant" applicant Schreiber's argument that Harz did not anticipate because Harz was "non-analogous art to which one of ordinary skill in the art would not have looked in addressing the problem of dispensing tops for popped popcorn containers." *Schreiber,*128 F.3d at 1477.

[137]*See supra* Chapter 4, Section C for details of the strict identity standard for anticipation.

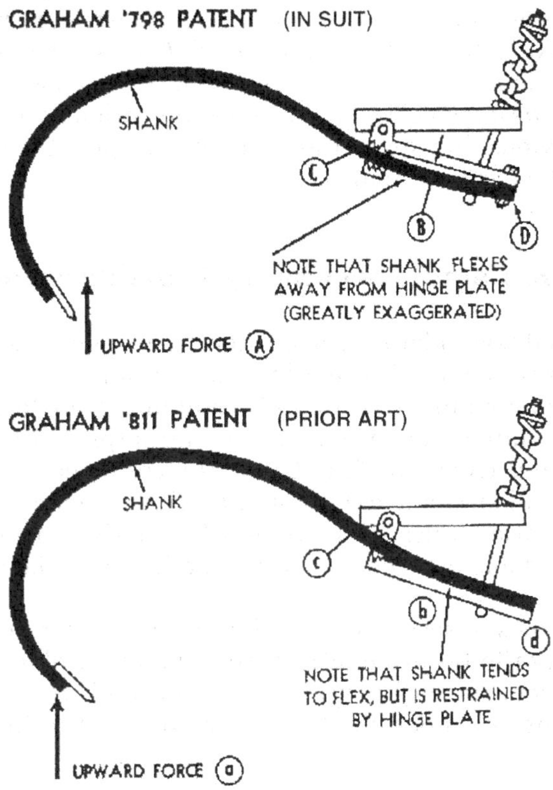

Figure 5.1

Differences Between Claimed Invention and Prior Art in *Graham v. John Deere Co.*, 383 U.S. 1 (1966)

the prior art and the claimed invention; otherwise, the invention would be anticipated under §102. The USPTO should clearly identify these differences in issuing any §103 rejection, as should the courts in evaluating an issued patent for obviousness.

For example, the identifiable differences between the claimed plow shank of the '798 patent at issue in *Graham v. John Deere Co.*[138] and the prior art plow shank (in that case, disclosed in Graham's own earlier '811 patent[139]) included moving the hinge plate from below to above the shank, in order to provide the shank with greater flexing ability. This structural rearrangement is depicted in Figure 5.1.

[138]383 U.S. 1 (1966).

[139]Graham's '811 patent issued on January 10, 1950, more than one year before Graham filed the application (on August 27, 1951) that led to his '798 patent. Thus, the '811 patent was available as a §102(b) reference for use in a §103 challenge by John Deere Co. to the validity of Graham's '798 patent.

This *Graham* "differences" factor should not be confused with the ultimate question of nonobviousness. The question to be answered under 35 U.S.C. §103 is not whether *the differences* themselves would have been obvious to the PHOSITA. Rather, §103 asks whether the *subject matter as a whole* (i.e., the claimed invention as a whole) would have been obvious, in view of those differences plus the other factors required by the *Graham* analysis.

H. *Graham* Factor: Secondary Considerations

The so-called "secondary considerations" pertinent to a nonobviousness analysis under §103, sometimes also referred to as "objective indicia" of nonobviousness, include evidence that focuses on the impact of the claimed invention on the marketplace rather than its technical merits. Thus, this final *Graham* factor is based on economic and motivational facts and data that underlie the making and marketing of the invention. Such evidence may be relatively more accessible and understandable to layperson jurors and judges without a technical background.

Common types of secondary considerations evidence include evidence showing the failure of others to solve the problem addressed by the invention, the commercial success of the invention, the existence of a long-felt need for the invention,[140] the licensing and

[140]The mere fact that no one before the patentee has ever offered the invention in the marketplace is insufficient to establish the existence of a long-felt need for the invention. Absent a showing of long-felt need for the claimed invention, the mere passage of time without the claimed invention does not establish nonobviousness. *See* Iron Grip Barbell Co. v. USA Sports, Inc., 392 F.3d 1317, 1325 (Fed. Cir. 2004). *See also* Nike, Inc. v. Adidas AG, No. 2014-1719, 2016 WL 537609, *8-*9 (Fed. Cir. Feb. 11, 2016) (rejecting patentee's argument that age of prior art references and passage of time between references' public availability and claimed invention should have precluded PTAB's finding that a skilled artisan would have been motivated to combine the references; in case at bar, the references clearly disclosed awareness of problem to be solved and an attempted resolution) (citing *Iron Grip Barbell*, 392 F.3d at 1325; In re Wright, 569 F.2d 1124, 1127 (C.C.P.A. 1977) (stating that "[t]he mere age of the references is not persuasive of the unobviousness of the combination of their teachings, absent evidence that, notwithstanding knowledge of the references, the art tried and failed to solve the problem")).

In contrast, the patentee in *Uniroyal, Inc. v. Rudkin-Wiley Corp.*, 837 F.2d 1044 (Fed. Cir. 1988), successfully established a long-felt need for its invention, an air-deflecting device for reducing wind resistance encountered by tractor-trailer combination vehicles. The invention decreased the effective surface area of the vehicle encountering wind resistance and achieved significant fuel savings because of the reduced resistance or drag. For evidence of a long-felt need for the invention, the patentee successfully relied on an extensive study, published in 1953 (ten years before the patentee's invention) by the University of Maryland, which "show[ed] a significant

acquiescence of others to the patent at issue, and copying of the invention.[141] Be aware that certain inferences must be drawn in order to conclude that evidence such as commercial success is indicative of nonobviousness, and not merely due to a successful advertising campaign, an advantageous price point, or unrelated consumer preferences.[142] As related below, the case law requires a "nexus" between secondary considerations evidence and the features of the claimed invention.

The Federal Circuit has observed that secondary considerations evidence "may often be the most probative and cogent evidence in the record."[143] Despite such positive praise, however, the proper role and

---

interest in drag reduction techniques long before fuel consumption became a critical concern." *Id.* at 1054.

[141]Copying in this context requires proof of replication of a specific product, not just the making of a product that arguably falls within the scope of the patent's claims. Evidence probative of copying includes internal documents, direct evidence such as the disassembly of an invention in order to reverse engineer a virtually identical replica, and access and substantial similarity to the patented product (rather than the patent itself). *See* Iron Grip Barbell Co. v. USA Sports, Inc., 392 F.3d 1317, 1325 (Fed. Cir. 2004).

The proponent of copying as evidence of nonobviousness must also establish a *nexus* between the copying and the novel aspects of the claimed invention. The patentee failed to do so in *Wm. Wrigley Jr. Co. v. Cadbury Adams USA LLC*, 683 F.3d 1356 (Fed. Cir. 2012) (upholding district court's conclusion that, even in light of evidence of secondary considerations, claim 34 of Wrigley's patent would have been obvious in light of two prior art references). The Wrigley patent's claim 34 was directed to a chewing gum that combined menthol and WS-23, a "cooling sensation" agent. Although Wrigley established through internal documents that accused infringer Cadbury had sought to copy Wrigley's invention in some of its products, Wrigley failed to show evidence "suggesting that 'the novel combination of WS-23 and menthol is what led Cadbury to copy Wrigley's chewing gums.'" *Id.* at 1364. Thus the requisite nexus between the copying and the merits of the claimed invention was lacking.

[142]*See* Richard L. Robbins, *Subtests of "Nonobviousness": A Non-Technical Approach to Patent Validity,* 12 U. Pa. L. Rev. 1169, 1176 (1964) (explaining that "[m]arket dominance due to attributes of the product other than those for which the patent was granted, such as the color of the product or the box in which it is packed, should not be used to sustain the inference of validity") (citations omitted); *see also* Robert P. Merges, *Commercial Success and Patent Standards: Economic Perspectives on Innovation*, 76 Cal. L. Rev.805, 838, 866 (1988) (asserting that "[c]ommercial success is a poor indicator of patentability because it is indirect; it depends for its effectiveness on a long chain of inferences, and the links in the chain are often subject to doubt"; suggesting that evidence of the failure of others is much more probative to the nonobviousness inquiry).

[143]Stratoflex, Inc. v. Aeroquip Corp., 713 F.2d 1530, 1538 (Fed. Cir. 1983). For an interesting discussion that supports the use of secondary considerations evidence as less susceptible to hindsight bias than evidence introduced under the other *Graham* factors, *see* Jeffrey J. Rachlinski, *A Positive Psychological Theory of Judging in Hindsight,* 65 U. Chi. L. Rev. 571, 613-615 (1998).

significance of secondary considerations evidence has become fodder for considerable disagreement at the Federal Circuit.

1. The Weight to Be Accorded Secondary Considerations Evidence

a. *Criticality in Federal Circuit Era*

Although the Supreme Court in *Graham v. John Deere* suggested that evidence of secondary considerations "*might* be utilized" and "*may* have relevancy,"[144] this form of evidence took on far greater importance after the Federal Circuit's creation in 1982. Today the phrase "secondary considerations" is a misnomer, because such evidence must not be treated as secondary to the evidence underlying the other *Graham* factors. A long-established line of Federal Circuit decisions considers such evidence "critical . . . in the obviousness analysis."[145] The court has held that where secondary considerations evidence is present in the record, it *must* be considered in determining nonobviousness.[146]

b. *Diverging Views*

Despite the Federal Circuit's elevation of the importance of secondary considerations evidence, some judges of the court began to question this treatment as the Circuit entered its fourth decade. The importance and weight to be given secondary considerations evidence in evaluating nonobviousness lay at the heart of a controversial 2016

[144]*See Graham*, 383 U.S. at 17-18 (emphases added).

[145]Nike, Inc. v. Adidas AG, 812 F.3d 1326, 1339 (Fed. Cir. 2016) (citing In re Kao, 639 F.3d 1057, 1067 (Fed. Cir. 2011) (stating that "when secondary considerations are present . . . it is *error not to consider them*") (emphasis added by *Nike* court); Stratoflex, Inc. v. Aeroquip Corp., 713 F.2d 1530, 1538-1539 (Fed. Cir. 1983) (stating that secondary considerations evidence "may often be the most probative and cogent evidence in the record. It may often establish that an invention appearing to have been obvious in light of the prior art was not."); *Stratoflex*, 713 F.2d at 1538 (deeming it well established that "evidence rising out of the so-called 'secondary considerations' must always when present be considered en route to a determination of obviousness")).

[146]*See* In re Kao, 639 F.3d 1057, 1067 (Fed. Cir. 2011) (stating that "when secondary considerations are present . . . it is *error not to consider them*") (emphasis added); *Stratoflex*, 713 F.2d at 1538. *See also* In re Piasecki, 745 F.2d 1468, 1471 (Fed. Cir. 1984) (reversing §103 rejection based on USPTO's failure to give weight to evidence submitted by applicant in rebuttal of *prima facie* case of obviousness, which was primarily "secondary considerations" evidence). The concept of a *prima facie* case is further detailed *infra* Section J.

en banc decision, *Apple Inc. v. Samsung Elecs. Co. Ltd.*[147] Decided in an unusual procedural posture for *en banc* review,[148] *Apple v. Samsung* revealed burgeoning disagreement on the issue among members of the appellate court.[149]

Somewhat surprisingly (given the high numbers of obviousness cases reviewed by the court), *Apple v. Samsung* marked the first time since the Federal Circuit's 1990 decision in *In re Dillon*[150] that it had considered an obviousness case as an *en banc* court. Hence the facts of *Apple v. Samsung* and the Circuit's statements therein (by both the majority and dissenting judges) merit close attention. The four opinions issued in the *en banc Apple v. Samsung* reveal a significant division of views about the weight to be given secondary considerations evidence, with some dissenting judges advocating a return to (or at least a reconsideration of) the Supreme Court's view that such evidence is not always or necessarily relevant or useful.

The Apple patents in suit concerned now-familiar features of a mobile communication device (such as an iPhone). When Apple sued Samsung (a competing manufacturer of mobile devices) for patent infringement, Samsung challenged the validity of certain claims of Apple's U.S. Patents Nos. 8,046,721 (the '721 or "slide to unlock" patent) and 8,074,172 (the '172 patent concerning text display for word correction) on the basis of obviousness.[151] More particularly, the '721

[147]839 F.3d 1034 (Fed. Cir. Oct. 7, 2016) (*en banc*) (Moore, J.).

[148]*See Apple Inc.,* 839 F.3d at 1063 (Prost, C.J., dissenting) (sharing concerns of fellow dissenting judges Dyk and Reyna as to "the procedural irregularities surrounding this case at the *en banc* stage"); *Apple Inc.,* 839 F.3d at 1074 (Dyk, J., dissenting) (stating that "[r]emarkably, the majority has [taken the case *en banc*] without further briefing and argument from the parties, amici, or the government, as has been our almost uniform practice in this court's *en banc* decisions"); *Apple Inc.,* 839 F.3d at 1074 n.1 (Dyk, J., dissenting) (observing that "[o]ver the last 10 years, the court extended supplemental briefing or argument from parties in 36 *en banc* cases; in only three cases did we not do so"). Some judges questioned whether the case even merited *en banc* consideration. *See Apple Inc.,* 839 F.3d at 1085 (Reyna, J., dissenting) (stating that "[t]he court should not have granted *en banc* review in this case" because it did not meet either requirement for granting *en banc* review: "when necessary to secure or maintain uniformity of the court's decisions or when the proceeding involves a question of exceptional importance") (citing Fed. R. App. Proc. 35(a); Missouri v. Jenkins, 495 U.S. 33, 46 n.14 (1990)); *Apple Inc.,* 839 F.3d at 1063 (Prost, C.J., dissenting) (stating that there "was no need to take this case *en banc*").

[149]839 F.3d 1034 (Fed. Cir. Oct. 7, 2016) (*en banc*) (Moore, J.).

[150]919 F.2d 688 (Fed. Cir. 1990) (*en banc*). *Dillon* is further examined *infra* Section J ("The *Prima Facie* Case of Obviousness").

[151]The case also involved a claim interpretation issue involving Apple's U.S. Patent 5,946,647 and allegations that the panel had improperly relied on extra-record extrinsic evidence to resolve it.

patent concerned the Apple iPhone's "slide to unlock" feature, by which a user could slide a moving digital image (which could include an arrow) across the screen of the phone with her finger to unlock the phone.[152] The feature was intended to avoid accidental activation of mobile devices like the iPhone.

One of the two key prior art references, the "Neonode" device, disclosed continuously sweeping a user's finger across the touchscreen of a mobile phone to unlock it. Unlike Apple's claimed invention, the touchscreen of the Neonode device (depicted in Figure 5.2) did not include a moving image but rather text that instructed the user to "Right sweep to unlock."[153]

The claimed feature missing from Neonode was disclosed in the other prior art reference, referred to as "Plaisant." The Plaisant study compared six different touchscreen-based toggle switches used to control two-state (on/off) devices having wall-mounted controllers (such as "entertainment, security, and climate control systems"). In one of the six toggles, referred to as the "slider toggle," " 'a sliding/dragging movement is required to change the position of the yellow pointer from one side of the toggle to the other. . . . Users can [ ] grab the pointer and slide it to the other side.' "[154] The Plaisant reference is depicted in Figure 5.3.

A jury in the Northern District of California sustained the validity of certain claims of Apple's U.S. Patents Nos. 8,046,721 (the '721 or "slide to unlock" patent) and 8,074,172 (the '172 patent concerning text display for word correction) against Samsung's obviousness challenge.[155] Denying Samsung's request for judgment as a matter of law (JMOL), the federal district court in September 2014 entered judgment in accordance with the jury verdict.[156] In February 2016, a three-judge panel of the Federal Circuit reversed the district court, holding in an opinion authored by Circuit Judge Dyk that the inventions claimed in Apple's '721 and '172 patents would have been obvious.[157] The Circuit panel reasoned that a skilled artisan would have been motivated to combine the teachings of Neonode and Plaisant to

[152]*Apple Inc.*, 816 F.3d at 793-794.

[153]*Apple Inc.*, 816 F.3d at 799-800.

[154]*Apple Inc.*, 816 F.3d at 800 (quoting Joint Appendix).

[155]The case also involved a claim interpretation issue involving Apple's U.S. Patent 5,946,647 and allegations that the panel had improperly relied on extra-record extrinsic evidence to resolve it.

[156]*See* Apple, Inc. v. Samsung Elecs. Co., No. 12-CV-00630-LHK, 2014 WL 4467837, at *7 (N.D. Cal. Sept. 9, 2014) (denying Samsung's motion for judgment as a matter of law that no reasonable jury could find claim 9 of Apple's '721 patent not invalid); *id.* at 2014 WL 4467837, at *15 (denying Samsung's motion for judgment as a matter of law that claim 18 of Apple's '172 patent was invalid).

[157]*See* Apple Inc. v. Samsung Elecs. Co., 816 F.3d 788, 793 (Fed. Cir. Feb. 26, 2016) (Dyk, J.) ("We also reverse the district court's denial of JMOL of invalidity of Apple's '721 and '172 patents, finding that the asserted claims of both patents would have been

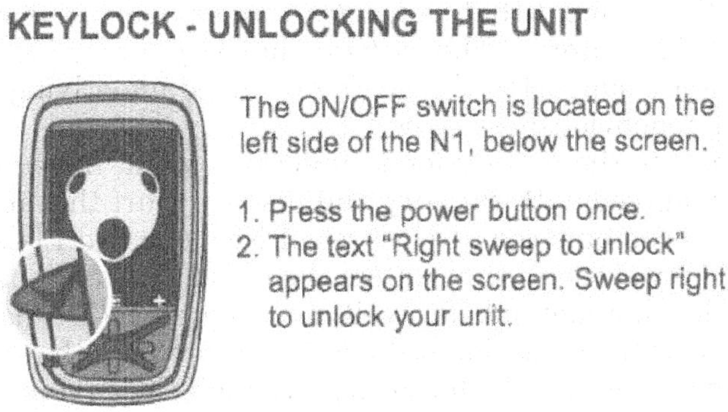

KEYLOCK - UNLOCKING THE UNIT
The ON/OFF switch is located on the left side of the N1, below the screen.
1. Press the power button once.
2. The text "Right sweep to unlock" appears on the screen. Sweep right to unlock your unit.

Figure 5.2

"Neonode" Prior Art Reference in *Apple v. Samsung* (Fed. Cir. Feb. 2016)

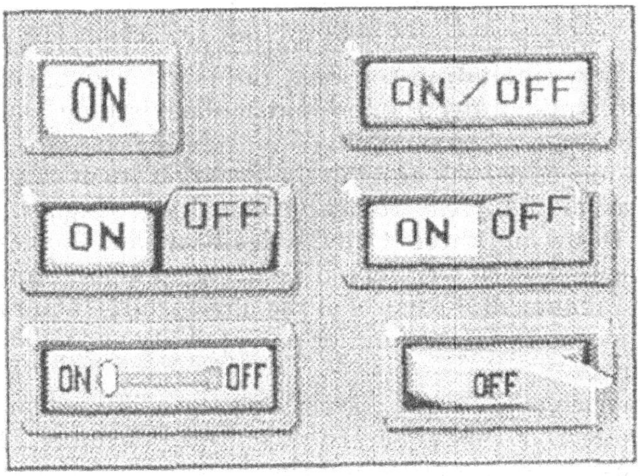

Figure 5.3

"Plaisant" Prior Art Reference in *Apple v. Samsung* (Fed. Cir. Feb. 2016)

achieve the '721 patent's claimed invention, and that no reasonable jury would have found otherwise.

Less than eight months later, the *en banc* Federal Circuit stepped in to reinstate the jury's verdict for patentee Apple. In a majority opinion authored by Circuit Judge Moore, the *en banc* court in October 2016 vacated the Circuit's February 2016 panel opinion and affirmed the

obvious based on the prior art."). The October 2016 panel determined that the Plaisant reference did not "teach away" from Apple's claimed invention.

district court's judgment that had, *inter alia*, sustained the validity of the '721 and '172 patents. The *en banc* majority concluded that substantial evidence supported the jury's presumed underlying fact findings on each nonobviousness issue.[158]

With respect to the '721 ("slide to unlock") patent, the *en banc* Circuit majority agreed with the jury and district court that motivation was lacking to combine the disclosures of Neonode and Plaisant. The *en banc* majority stressed that unlike the claimed invention, Plaisant disclosed unlocking methods for wall-mounted touchscreens and was not concerned with the accidental activation problem that the Apple inventors had targeted.[159] Moreover, although the *en banc* majority did not need to decide the question whether Plaisant "taught away" from the use of sliding a user's finger across a touchscreen by expressing a preference for other methods,[160] it noted that "even if Plaisant does not teach away, its statements regarding users preferring other forms of switches are relevant to a finding regarding whether a skilled artisan would be motivated to combine the slider toggle in Plaisant with the mobile phone in Neonode."[161] Lastly, the *en banc* Circuit majority considered the secondary considerations evidence that was before the jury (including copying, industry praise, commercial success, and long-felt need) to be "particularly strong," such that it " 'tip[ped] the scales of patentability' " in Apple's favor.[162]

Of the 11 judges participating in the Federal Circuit's October 2016 *en banc* decision in *Apple v. Samsung*, one (Judge Hughes) concurred only in the result and three (Chief Judge Prost and Judges Dyk and Reyna) dissented (each writing a dissenting opinion). This degree of division on fundamental aspects of the obviousness inquiry, perhaps the most important requirement for patentability and validity, merits close scrutiny.

Although each of the three dissenting judges touched on the issue, Circuit Judge Dyk (author of the vacated February 2016 panel opinion) most explicitly criticized the *en banc* majority in *Apple v. Samsung* for its treatment of secondary consideration evidence. He advocated strongly a return to the Supreme Court's position that secondary considerations evidence is not always relevant or useful. In Judge Dyk's view, the *en banc Apple v. Samsung* majority had "err[ed] in elevating secondary considerations of nonobviousness beyond their

[158]*See* Apple Inc. v. Samsung Elecs. Co., 839 F.3d 1034, 1039-1040 (Fed. Cir. Oct. 7, 2016) (*en banc*).

[159]*See Apple Inc.*, 839 F.3d at 1051-1052.

[160]The concept of a prior art reference "teaching away" from a claimed invention, such that statements in the reference would discourage or dissuade a skilled art worker from making the claimed invention, is examined *infra* Section I.3.

[161]*Apple Inc.*, 839 F.3d at 1052 n.15.

[162]*Apple Inc.*, 839 F.3d at 1058 (quoting *Graham*, 383 U.S. at 36).

role as articulated by the Supreme Court. Secondary considerations 'without invention[ ] will not make patentability.' "[163]

According to dissenting Judge Dyk, the Supreme Court had "assigned a limited role to secondary considerations"[164] in its two principal recent considerations of the nonobviousness requirement, i.e., the 1966 landmark *Graham v. Deere* decision[165] and the 2007 *KSR v. Teleflex* decision.[166] In *Graham*, the Court referred to secondary considerations as factors that " '*might* be utilized to give light to the circumstances [surrounding the origin of the subject matter sought to be patented].' "[167] Judge Dyk noted that in evaluating the Scoggin insecticide shipper/sprayer patent, the *Graham* Court concluded that despite the presence of "long-felt need in the industry" and "wide commercial success" of the patentee, those factors " 'd[id] not, in the circumstances [of *Graham*], tip the scales of patentability.' "[168] The secondary considerations evidence in *Graham* did not change the result because the Scoggin invention " 'rest[ed] upon exceedingly small and quite non-technical mechanical differences in a device which was old in the art.' "[169] Similarly, in the 2007 *KSR* decision, the Supreme Court required inquiry into secondary considerations only " '*where appropriate*.' "[170] Judge Dyk observed that although the patentee in *KSR* introduced evidence of commercial success,[171] the Supreme Court dismissed it because it " 'conclude[d] [patentee] Teleflex ha[d] shown no secondary factors to dislodge the determination that claim 4 is obvious.' "[172]

[163]*Apple Inc.*, 839 F.3d at 1080 (Dyk, J., dissenting) (quoting Sakraida v. Ag Pro, Inc., 425 U.S. 273, 278 (1976) (internal quotation marks omitted)).

[164]*Apple Inc.*, 839 F.3d at 1081 (Dyk, J., dissenting).

[165]Graham v. John Deere Co., 383 U.S. 1 (1966), examined *supra* Section D ("The *Graham v. John Deere* Framework for Analyzing Nonobviousness").

[166]KSR Int'l Co. v. Teleflex Inc., 550 U.S. 398 (2007), examined *infra* Section I.2 ("*KSR v. Teleflex*: Combinations, Predictability, and 'Common Sense' "). *See also* Dann v. Johnston, 425 U.S. 219 (1976) (reversing CCPA majority's determination that claimed computer program for financial industry was patentable despite USPTO rejections under §§101, 103, and 112; Court's opinion turned on obviousness and declined to discuss §101 patent-eligibility of claimed computerized financial record-keeping system).

[167]*Apple Inc.*, 839 F.3d at 1081 (Dyk, J., dissenting) (quoting *Graham*, 383 U.S. at 17 (emphasis added by Judge Dyk)).

[168]*Apple Inc.*, 839 F.3d at 1081 (Dyk, J., dissenting) (quoting *Graham,* 383 U.S. at 35-36).

[169]*Apple Inc.*, 839 F.3d at 1081 (Dyk, J., dissenting) (quoting *Graham,* 383 U.S. at 36).

[170]*Apple Inc.*, 839 F.3d at 1081 (Dyk, J., dissenting) (citing *KSR,* 550 U.S. at 415) (emphasis added by Judge Dyk).

[171]*Apple Inc.*, 839 F.3d at 1081 (Dyk, J., dissenting) (citing *KSR,* 550 U.S. at 413).

[172]*Apple Inc.*, 839 F.3d at 1081 (Dyk, J., dissenting) (citing *KSR*, 550 U.S. at 426). Judge Dyk's dissent from the *Apple v. Samsung en banc* decision also cited a number of Supreme Court decisions decided before *Graham*. He asserted that in those earlier decisions, the Supreme Court "repeatedly" held that secondary considerations evidence

Judge Dyk concluded that the instant *Apple v. Samsung* case, like the precedent he had cited, was "also . . . not a close one." He characterized as "flimsy" the evidence relied on by the *en banc* majority to support the jury's verdict that Apple's '712 and '172 patents would not have been obvious.[173] In Judge Dyk's view, "[t]he combination of references, the known problem, the predictable results, and the exceedingly small differences from the prior art make the combination evident and *secondary considerations insufficient as a matter of law.*"[174]

Judge Dyk accused the *Apple v. Samsung* majority of turning the ultimately legal question of obviousness into a factual question for the jury to decide. He contended the Supreme Court's holdings in

---

should be assigned "limited weight in the ultimately legal determination of obviousness." *Apple Inc.*, 839 F.3d at 1081 (Dyk, J., dissenting) (footnote omitted), stating that

> [b]efore *Graham*, the Supreme Court repeatedly held that courts should give secondary considerations limited weight in the ultimate legal determination of obviousness and that the courts need not consider them where the claimed invention represents a small advance and there is a strong case for obviousness. For example, *Jungersen v. Ostby & Barton Co.* taught that "[t]he fact that this process has enjoyed considerable commercial success . . . does not render the patent valid. It is true that in cases where the question of patentable invention is a close one, such success has weight in tipping the scales of judgment toward patentability. Where, as here, however, invention is plainly lacking, commercial success cannot fill the void." 335 U.S. 560, 567, 69 S. Ct. 269, 93 L. Ed. 235 (1949) (citations omitted). Similarly, in *Dow Chemical Co. v. Halliburton Oil Well Cementing Co.*, the Court explained that "petitioner claims that the Grebe-Sanford process has filled a long-felt want and has been a commercial success. But these considerations are relevant only in a close case where all other proof leaves the question of invention in doubt. Here the lack of invention is beyond doubt and cannot be outweighed by such factors." 324 U.S. 320, 330, 65 S. Ct. 647, 89 L. Ed. 973 (1945) (citations omitted). *Goodyear Tire & Rubber Co. v. Ray-O-Vac Co.* cautioned that "[t]hese factors [are] entitled to weight in determining whether the improvement amounted to invention and should, in a close case, tip the scales in favor of patentability." 321 U.S. 275, 279, 64 S. Ct. 593, 88 L. Ed. 721 (1944). These pre-*KSR* "decisions remain binding precedent until [the Supreme Court] see[s] fit to reconsider them. . . ." *Hohn v. United States*, 524 U.S. 236, 252-53, 118 S. Ct. 1969, 141 L. Ed. 2d 242 (1998).

In the footnote omitted from the above quotation, Judge Dyk stated that

> *Anderson's-Black Rock* taught that although "[i]t is . . . fervently argued that the combination filled a long felt want and has enjoyed commercial success[,] . . . those matters without invention will not make patentability." 396 U.S. at 61, 90 S. Ct. 305 (internal quotation marks omitted) (citations omitted). *Great Atlantic & Pacific Tea Co. v. Supermarket Equipment Corp.* similarly taught that "[t]he Court of Appeals and the respondent both lean heavily on evidence that this device filled a long-felt want and has enjoyed commercial success. But commercial success without invention will not make patentability." 340 U.S. 147, 153, 71 S. Ct. 127, 95 L. Ed. 162 (1950). These cases are cited with approval in *KSR* or *Graham*. See 550 U.S. at 416-17, 127 S. Ct. 1727; 383 U.S. at 6, 86 S. Ct. 684.

[173]*Apple Inc.*, 839 F.3d at 1075 (Dyk, J., dissenting).

[174]*Apple Inc.*, 839 F.3d at 1081-1082 (Dyk, J., dissenting) (emphasis added).

Graham and *KSR* "demonstrate[d] that both the significance and the weighing of secondary considerations are *legal issues for the court*."[175] Thus, Judge Dyk's dissent presents a decided departure from prior Federal Circuit–era decisions that have treated secondary considerations as one of the four *factual* underpinnings of the obviousness determination (ultimately a legal question).

Although not the primary thrust of her dissenting opinion in the *en banc Apple v. Samsung* case,[176] Circuit Chief Judge Prost wrote that she agreed with Judge Dyk's "concerns regarding the majority's elevation of secondary considerations beyond their historic role." In Judge Prost's view, that role is that "secondary considerations take on less importance when there is little doubt as to obviousness."[177]

In his dissenting opinion in *Apple v. Samsung*, Circuit Judge Reyna stated flatly that the Circuit "should not have granted *en banc* review in this case."[178] Nevertheless, he characterized the disagreement between the majority and dissent over secondary considerations evidence as an "implicit dispute underlying the *en banc* court's reversal of the panel's obviousness determinations, one that might have served as proper grounds for *en banc* review in this case."[179]

In particular, Judge Reyna contended that the February 2016 panel opinion authored by Judge Dyk had advocated what Judge Reyna termed a "burden-shifting analysis"; that is, an analysis in which, once an accused infringer establishes a "strong" *prima facie* case of obviousness based on the first three *Graham* factors, the burden of proof (i.e., persuasion) shifts back to the patentee to rebut the *prima facie* conclusion of obviousness via the fourth factor, evidence of secondary considerations.[180] Judge Reyna observed that in the case at bar, the panel found the patentee's evidence of secondary considerations was "weak"

[175]*Apple Inc.*, 839 F.3d at 1076 (Dyk, J., dissenting) (emphasis added).

[176]The main emphasis of Chief Judge Prost's dissenting opinion was her concern that the *en banc* majority had misapplied the "substantial evidence" standard of review with respect to its nonobviousness analysis, "finding evidence in the record when there is none to support the jury's implicit factual findings." *Apple Inc.*, 839 F.3d at 1064 (Prost, C.J., dissenting).

[177]*Apple Inc.*, 839 F.3d at 1063-1064 (Prost, C.J., dissenting) (citing Dow Chem. Co. v. Halliburton Oil Well Cementing Co., 324 U.S. 320, 330 (1945) ("But these considerations are relevant only in a close case where all other proof leaves the question of invention in doubt."); Goodyear Tire & Rubber Co. v. Ray-O-Vac Co., 321 U.S. 275, 279 (1944) ("These factors were entitled to weight in determining whether the improvement amounted to invention and should, in a close case, tip the scales in favor of patentability.")).

[178]*Apple Inc.*, 839 F.3d at 1085 (Reyna, J., dissenting).

[179]*Apple Inc.*, 839 F.3d at 1088-1089 (Reyna, J., dissenting).

[180]Judge Reyna observed that the Circuit had previously rejected such a burden-shifting analysis for determination of obviousness in federal court litigation in *In re Cyclobenzaprine Hydrochloride Extended-Release Capsule Patent Litig.*, 676 F.3d 1063, 1076-1080 (Fed. Cir. 2012) (O'Malley, J.). In that case the Circuit explained:

and concluded that its patents would have been obvious. On the other hand, the *en banc* majority, which vacated the panel opinion, required that a determination of obviousness mandates consideration of all four *Graham* factors (including secondary considerations), that it is error to reach a conclusion of obviousness before all four of those factors are considered, and that where secondary considerations evidence is present, it *must* be considered.

The important difference in approaches taken by the October 2016 *en banc* majority and the February 2016 panel in *Apple v. Samsung* signaled to Judge Reyna that "the court disagrees over the role objective indicia play in the court's analysis of the ultimate determination of obviousness."[181] Thus, the Circuit in his view "should candidly address this issue *en banc*,"[182] rather than deal with the issue implicitly. Judge Reyna concluded his dissent by calling for *en banc* resolution of two issues: (1) whether an obviousness analysis involving secondary considerations is a one- or two-step process (i.e., whether or not it involves a burden-shifting framework); and (2) how much weight to accord secondary considerations in the obviousness analysis. These were "important issues that should be addressed in the front room of the courthouse, with all stakeholders at the litigation table."[183] Judge Reyna dissented because in his view, the Federal Circuit had failed to act with the necessary transparency in *Apple v. Samsung*.

The strongly-worded opposing opinions resulting from the October 2016 *en banc* decision in *Apple v. Samsung* crystalized a significant division of views among Federal Circuit judges about the weight to be given secondary considerations evidence in a §103 nonobviousness analysis. Whether the Circuit will hew to its own earlier decisions

---

> After the district court found that [defendants/accused infringers] Mylan and Par proved the asserted claims obvious, it considered [the patentee] Cephalon's proof of objective considerations of nonobviousness to determine whether Cephalon's proofs were sufficient to "rebut" that obviousness determination. Specifically, the district court considered Cephalon's evidence of the failure of others to make the patented invention; longfelt but unsolved needs fulfilled by the patented invention; commercial success of the patented invention; and unexpected results produced by the patented invention.... The district court found Cephalon's evidence insufficient to rebut Mylan's and Par's showing. *The district court erred, however, by making its finding that the patents in suit were obvious before it considered the objective considerations and by shifting the burden of persuasion to Cephalon.* In doing so, the district court contravened this court's precedent requiring that a fact finder consider all evidence relating to obviousness before finding a patent invalid on those grounds, and *the court imposed a burden-shifting framework in a context in which none exists.*

Cyclobenzaprine Hydrochloride, 676 F.3d at 1075 (citations omitted) (emphasis added).

[181]*Apple Inc.*, 839 F.3d at 1089 (Reyna, J., dissenting).

[182]*Apple Inc.*, 839 F.3d at 1089 (Reyna, J., dissenting).

[183]*Apple Inc.*, 839 F.3d at 1089 (Reyna, J., dissenting).

(emphasizing the criticality of this evidence) or instead demote its value awaits further decision making by the Circuit (or Supreme Court review[184]).

2. Requirement for Explicit Analysis

Moreover, the factfinder's analysis of such evidence must be *explicit*. In a 2016 decision, the Federal Circuit vacated and remanded a decision of the Patent Trial and Appeal Board (PTAB) in *Nike, Inc. v. Adidas AG*,[185] an appeal from the PTAB's decision in an America Invents Act- (AIA-)implemented *inter partes* review (IPR) proceeding[186] challenging certain Nike shoe patents.[187] The PTAB had determined in the IPR that Nike's proposed substitute claims, directed to a shoe having a unitary flat-knit textile upper, were unpatentable for obviousness. During the course of the IPR, Nike submitted to the PTAB evidence in the form of an expert witness declaration that the problem of reducing material waste during the manufacture of textile footwear uppers was a long-felt need, perhaps recognized by the prior art but not resolved until Nike's invention.[188]

Before the Federal Circuit, neither the USPTO (as intervenor) or Adidas (the IPR petitioner) disputed that the PTAB's decision lacked discussion, or even an acknowledgement, of Nike's secondary considerations evidence. Nevertheless, the USPTO argued that the PTAB had not erred because it *implicitly* considered and rejected Nike's secondary considerations evidence. The PTAB had assertedly done so in the course of discussing why a person of skill in the art would have combined the teachings of the prior art references, thus rendering Nike's proposed substitute claims obvious. The Federal Circuit rejected the USPTO's "implicit consideration" argument:

> Because long-felt need is indisputably a secondary consideration, *see Graham*, 383 U.S. at 17-18, our precedent dictates that the Board

[184]Although the Supreme Court invited the Acting Solicitor General to file an amicus brief expressing the views of the United States in *Apple v. Samsung* on June 26, 2017, *see* https://www.supremecourt.gov/search.aspx?filename=/docketfiles/16-1102.htm, the Court ultimately refused to grant *certiorari*. *See* Samsung Electronics Co., Ltd. v. Apple Inc., 138 S. Ct. 420 (Nov. 6, 2017) (order denying *certiorari*).

[185]No. 2014-1719, 2016 WL 537609 (Fed. Cir. Feb. 11, 2016).

[186]The AIA-implemented *inter partes* review proceeding is examined in further detail *infra* Chapter 8, Section E.1.

[187]*See* U.S. Patent No. 7, 347,011 ('011 patent), directed to an article of footwear having a unitary textile upper. The author believes the commercial embodiment of the invention claimed in the '011 patent is Nike's Flyknit® shoe. *See* http://www.nike.com/us/en_us/c/innovation/flyknit (2016).

[188]*See Nike, Inc.*, 2016 WL 537609, at *9 (Fed. Cir. Feb. 11, 2016) (quoting expert's declaration).

> [PTAB] is bound to fully consider properly presented evidence on the long-felt need for a claimed invention. Recognizing that the Board operates under stringent time constraints, we do not hold that it is obliged to explicitly address conclusory and unsupported arguments raised by a litigant. *Cf. Fresenius USA, Inc. v. Baxter Int'l, Inc.*, 582 F.3d 1288, 1296 (Fed. Cir. 2009) (holding that a party cannot preserve an argument if it presents "only a skeletal or undeveloped argument to the trial court"). Under the particular circumstances presented here, however, we conclude that the Board should have explicitly acknowledged and evaluated Nike's secondary considerations evidence.[189]

When a patentee relies on secondary considerations evidence in the form of commercial success in attempting to establish nonobviousness, a court must consider marketplace realities in determining what weight that evidence should be given. Even though commercial success was successfully proven by the patentee in *Merck & Co. v. Teva Pharms. USA, Inc.*,[190] the Federal Circuit held that under the particular facts of that case the commercial success was only minimally probative of nonobviousness. Merck's patent in suit covered a method for treating osteoporosis through a once-weekly dosing regime of a drug it marketed under the brand name Fosamax®. The Federal Circuit instructed that "[c]ommercial success is relevant because the law presumes an idea would successfully have been brought to market sooner, in response to market forces, had the idea been obvious to persons skilled in the art."[191] But that inference was inappropriate in *Merck* because other firms were legally barred from commercially testing the prior art-provided suggestion of once-weekly dosing. Merck had a right to exclude competitors from practicing the claimed weekly dosing method because of (1) a separate Merck-owned dominant patent covering methods of treating osteoporosis; and (2) Merck's exclusive statutory right, which it had obtained in conjunction with Food and Drug Administration marketing approvals of Fosamax®, to offer Fosamax® at any dosage for a five-year period. The Federal Circuit concluded that "[b]ecause market entry by others was precluded on those bases, the inference of non-obviousness of weekly dosing, from evidence of commercial success, is weak."[192] In view of its minimal weight, the commercial success evidence was not sufficient to establish nonobviousness in view of the prior art of record; the asserted claims of Merck's patent were invalid as obvious. In a subsequent opinion

[189]*Nike, Inc.*,2016 WL 537609, at *10 (Fed. Cir. Feb. 11, 2016).
[190]395 F.3d 1364 (Fed. Cir. 2005).
[191]*Id.* at 1376.
[192]*Id.* at 1377.

dissenting from denial of rehearing *en banc* in *Merck,* three other Federal Circuit judges charged that

> [commercial success] is not negatived by any inability of others to test various formulations because of the existence of another patent. Success is success. The panel's rule is especially unsound in the context of an improvement patent, as here, because it holds in effect that commercial success for an improvement is irrelevant when a prior patent dominates the basic invention.[193]

3. The Nexus Requirement for Evidence of Commercial Success

A patent owner facing a challenge to validity will frequently attempt to introduce into the litigation evidence of the commercial success of the patented invention, such as sales volumes, market share, and similar data of positive marketplace reaction. Such evidence is only probative of the nonobviousness of the invention if a sufficient *nexus,* or causal relationship, exists between the commercial success and features recited in the claims.[194]

For example, suppose that the patentee in *Graham v. John Deere*[195] had introduced evidence showing that the commercial embodiment of his patented invention had captured 50 percent of the U.S. market for plow shanks in each year since the product was introduced into the marketplace. This hypothetical evidence would be probative of nonobviousness only if the patentee could show that his sales success was due to consumer desire for the claimed features of the patented plow shank (i.e., its shock-absorbing design). If farmers bought the patented plow shank only because it was painted purple with green polka dots, the item having become a novelty among farmers for that reason, or because the inventor drastically cut its price to a point far below that of competitors' plow shanks, the alleged commercial success evidence would be rejected as nonprobative of nonobviousness *of the claimed invention.*

In *Iron Grip Barbell Co. v. USA Sports, Inc.*,[196] the owner of a patent on a weight plate for barbells attempted to show commercial success from evidence that three out of six retail competitors selling

[193]Merck & Co. v. Teva Pharms. USA, Inc., 405 F.3d 1338, 1339 (Fed. Cir. 2005) (Lourie, J., dissenting from denial of reh'g *en banc*, joined by Michel, C.J., and Newman, J.).

[194]Professor Robert Merges has challenged the legitimacy of commercial success evidence and suggests that evidence of the failure of others is much more probative to the nonobviousness inquiry. *See* Robert P. Merges, *Commercial Success and Patent Standards: Economic Perspectives on Innovation*, 76 CAL. L. REV. 805 (1988).

[195]383 U.S. 1 (1966).

[196]392 F.3d 1317 (Fed. Cir. 2004).

similar plates had taken licenses under the patent. The Federal Circuit explained that because it is often cheaper to take a license than to defend a patent infringement suit, the court "specifically require[s] affirmative evidence" of nexus in cases where licenses are relied on to establish commercial success.[197] In other words, nexus could not be inferred from the mere existence of the licenses.[198] The patentee in *Iron Grip* did not "explain the terms of the licenses nor the circumstances under which they were granted, except to concede that two were taken in settlement of litigation." Hence, nexus was not established. Without a showing of nexus, whatever "little significance" the licenses might have had was outweighed by the strength of the *prima facie* case of obviousness based on the prior art of record.[199]

The Federal Circuit's January 2016 decision in *Ethicon Endo-Surgery, Inc. v. Covidien LP*,[200] illustrates an unsuccessful attempt by a patentee to rely on the commercial success of an allegedly *infringing* device as evidence supporting nonobvious of the patentee's claimed invention. Siding with the PTAB in an appeal from an *inter partes* review (IPR) proceeding, the Federal Circuit determined that the necessary nexus between commercial success and the claimed invention was lacking.

In simplified terms, the surgical stapling device claimed in Ethicon's U.S. Patent No. 8,317,070 ('070 patent) made use of staples having three characteristics: (1) legs that flared slightly outwardly from the staple base such that the legs were non-parallel with respect to each other; (2) two or more different staple heights *before* the staples were applied to a patient's surgical incision (i.e., different "pre-deformation" heights); and (3) two or more different staple heights *after* the staples were applied to the incision (i.e., different "formed" heights).[201] Ethicon asserted in the IPR that a competing surgical stapling product made and sold by IPR petitioner Covidien (formerly U.S. Surgical Corp.) infringed the '070 patent,[202] and that the considerable

[197] *Id.* at 1324.

[198] Ordinarily, the Federal Circuit noted, nexus may be inferred when the patentee shows both that there is commercial success and that the thing (product or method) that is commercially successful is the invention disclosed and claimed in the patent. *Id.*

[199] When *copying* of the claimed invention is asserted as secondary considerations evidence in support of nonobviousness, a nexus must also exist between the copying and the novel features of the claimed invention. *See* Wm. Wrigley Jr. Co. v. Cadbury Adams USA LLC, 683 F.3d 1356 (Fed. Cir. 2012), discussed *supra* in Section H.1.

[200] 812 F.3d 1023 (Fed. Cir. 2016).

[201] The different heights of the staples beneficially created a "hemostatic barrier" while "cinching" the tissue surrounding an incision, and also facilitated the use of the claimed device to staple a "broader range of tissue thicknesses." *Ethicon*, 812 F.3d at 1027.

[202] Notably, the question whether the accused device infringed Ethicon's '070 patent could not be definitely resolved in the IPR because it was not within the PTAB's jurisdiction. The PTAB in an IPR is limited to assessing patent validity; i.e., whether

commercial success of the Covidien product[203] should inure to Ethicon's benefit in the form of a presumption of nexus between the Covidien product and the features of Ethicon's claimed invention.[204]

While not deciding whether Ethicon would be entitled to a presumption of nexus if infringement had been proven definitively, the Federal Circuit determined (as had the PTAB) that the allegedly infringing Covidien device's commercial success was due either to (1) features of the Covidien product that were *not* recited in the '070 patent claims, or (2) features that were known in the prior art.[205] In other words, Ethicon had failed to sufficiently connect Covidien's commercial success to the *combination* of features claimed in Ethicon's patent. The Circuit reasoned that

> regardless of any presumption of nexus... [a]s the Board [PTAB] recognized, the Covidien products contained numerous unclaimed features, "such as ergonomic design, precise articulation, and reloads that provide simpler selection and reduced inventory," which may instead have been responsible for the commercial success of the products.... Other unclaimed features, such as "[u]ncompromised staple line strength" and "[s]uperior [l]eak [r]esistance," are touted in brochures advertising the Covidien products.... The Board concluded that, in light of these unclaimed features, Ethicon had "not shown sufficient credible evidence that the sales of the [Covidien devices] are the result of the claimed invention."... We agree.
>
> In addition, the Board had substantial evidence before it that the commercial success of the Covidien products was primarily attributable to a *single feature present in the prior art*, varying staple heights, rather than the combination of prior art features that is the alleged invention of the '070 patent. The evidence demonstrates that the Covidien products were successful because of their "graduated compression design and progressive staple heights, which provide less stress on tissue during compression and clamping."... In addition, the varied staple heights allowed for "[b]roader indicated tissue thickness ranges" and "[c]onsistent

---

challenged claims are unpatentable as anticipated or obvious on the basis of prior art patents or printed publications. *See* 35 U.S.C. §§311(b); 318(a).

[203]Ethicon asserted in the IPR that in less than three years on the market, Covidien's competing device achieved sales of over $1 billion and was on track to be Covidien's most successful product ever.

[204]*See Ethicon*, 812 F.3d at 1034 (stating Ethicon's argument that "the Board failed to afford Ethicon a presumption of nexus between the commercial success of an allegedly infringing product made by Covidien and the patented features. It [Ethicon] contends that because it showed that the Covidien devices were infringing, the commercial success of those devices is a strong secondary indication of nonobviousness which the Board ignored.").

[205]*Ethicon*, 812 F.3d at 1034 (citing Ormco Corp. v. Align Tech., Inc., 463 F.3d 1299, 1312 (Fed. Cir. 2006) (stating that "if the commercial success is due to an unclaimed feature of the device" or "if the feature that creates the commercial success was known in the prior art, the success is not pertinent")).

> performance over a broader range of tissue thicknesses." . . . As the Board found and Ethicon concedes, the use of staples of different heights was well known in the prior art at the time of the '070 patent. . . . Nowhere does Ethicon demonstrate, or even argue, that the commercial success of the Covidien products is attributable to the *combination* of the two prior art features — varied staple heights and non-parallel staple legs — that is the purportedly inventive aspect of the '070 patent.[206]

I. Combining the Disclosures of Prior Art References to Establish Obviousness

Frequently, a §103-based rejection of pending application claims in the USPTO (or a §103 challenge to the validity of an issued patent) will be founded on the argument that the respective disclosures of two or more prior art references, in combination, would have rendered the claimed invention obvious. In other words, this argument contends that the PHOSITA, deemed to have had access to such references at the time he made his claimed invention, would have been motivated to combine their teachings, and that these combined teachings would have rendered the claimed invention obvious to the PHOSITA. (This "motivation to combine" is a factual inquiry that can be conceptualized as a subset of the first *Graham* factor, scope and content of the prior art, but other factors also may impact the analysis.[207])

1. Teaching, Suggestion, or Motivation to Combine

a. Generally

In order for a "combination of references" type of obviousness argument to be legitimate, there must exist some teaching, suggestion, or motivation (hereinafter TSM) that would have suggested making the claimed combination. It is legal error to merely combine the discrete disclosures of different references without evidence of some reason or motivation for the PHOSITA to have done so. Rigorous attention to the requirement for a TSM guards against the improper use of hindsight in a nonobviousness analysis,[208] that is, using the claimed invention as a blueprint or plan and merely lumping together multiple prior art references that each disclose some limitation of the claims. Such hindsight reasoning "discount[s] the value of combining various

[206] *Ethicon*, 812 F.3d at 1034-1035 (record citations omitted) (first emphasis added; second emphasis in original).

[207] *See* McGinley v. Franklin Sports, Inc., 262 F.3d 1339, 1351-1352 (Fed. Cir. 2001).

[208] *See id.* at 1351.

existing features or principles in a new way to achieve a new result—often the very definition of invention."[209]

For example, suppose that a patent claim recites "a widget comprising a lever arm A, a pulley B, and a spring C." Suppose further that the USPTO examiner has rejected the claim as obvious, based on the combined teachings of prior art Reference 1, which shows a widget having a lever arm A; Reference 2, which shows another sort of device (e.g., a gizmo) having a pulley B; and Reference 3, which shows yet another type of device (e.g., a whatzit) having a spring C. By extracting the relevant parts from each of the three references and combining those parts, the examiner has effectively re-created the patented invention by using the claim as a blueprint. If the references themselves or other prior art do not suggest the viability of making the combination, it is a legally erroneous analysis.

The law is clear that the record must contain adequate evidence of a suggestion to combine the references. In the above hypothetical, an adequate suggestion to combine might exist if, for example, prior art Reference 1 suggested that a widget can advantageously have multiple parts in addition to a lever arm, and References 2 and 3 showed benefits or advantages to including pulleys and springs in mechanical devices generally.

b. *Nature of Problem*

The Federal Circuit has recognized that motivation to combine the teachings of multiple references may stem from the nature of the problem solved by the invention. The patent in suit in *Ruiz v. A.B. Chance Co.*[210] was directed to a method of underpinning the foundation of a building by use of a screw anchor in conjunction with a metal bracket. One prior art reference disclosed the screw anchor component of the claims while another disclosed the metal bracket component. The Federal Circuit upheld the district court's finding of an implied motivation to combine the teachings of the two references in the nature of the problem itself: how to underpin the unstable foundation of an existing building. Particularly with simpler mechanical technologies, the Federal Circuit observed, motivation may be found in the nature of the problem to be solved; the prior art references themselves need not provide an express, written motivation to combine. The district court in this case properly found the motivation to combine from the fact that the two pertinent prior art references "address[ed] precisely the same problem of underpinning existing structural foundations." Sitting as the finder of fact, the district court correctly "weighed the evidence and found that, because the prior art references address the narrow

[209]Ruiz v. A.B. Chance Co., 357 F.3d 1270, 1275 (Fed. Cir. 2004).
[210]357 F.3d 1270 (Fed. Cir. 2004).

problem of underpinning existing building foundations, a person seeking to solve that exact same problem would consult the references and apply their teachings together."[211]

c. *Reasonable Expectation of Success*

When the teachings of multiple prior art references are combined to support an argument that a claimed invention would have been obvious, it is not enough that there existed some reason or motivation for the PHOSITA to have done so. The challenger of patentability or validity must *also* show that the PHOSITA would have been motivated to make the combination with a reasonable expectation that it would succeed. The Federal Circuit has instructed that "[i]f all elements of the claims are found in a combination of prior art references . . . the factfinder should further consider whether a person of ordinary skill in the art would be motivated to combine those references, and whether in making that combination, a person of ordinary skill would have a reasonable expectation of success."[212]

For example, the patent in suit in *Innovention Toys, LLC v. MGA Entm't, Inc.*,[213] a 2015 non-precedential decision of the Federal Circuit, was directed to a chess-like board game and methods for playing

[211] *Id.* at 1277.

[212] *See* Merck & Cie v. Gnosis S.p.A., 808 F.3d 829, 833 (Fed. Cir. 2015) (citing Medichem, S.A. v. Rolabo, S.L., 437 F.3d 1157, 1164 (Fed. Cir. 2006)). *See also* PAR Pharm., Inc. v. TWI Pharm., Inc., 773 F.3d 1186, 1193 (Fed. Cir. 2014) (stating that "[a] party asserting that a patent is obvious 'must demonstrate by clear and convincing evidence [if in federal court] that a skilled artisan would have had reason to combine the teaching of the prior art references to achieve the claimed invention, and that the skilled artisan would have had a reasonable expectation of success from doing so' ") (quoting In re Cyclobenzaprine Hydrochloride Extended-Release Capsule Patent Litig., 676 F.3d 1063, 1068-1069 (Fed. Cir. 2012)); Velander v. Garner, 348 F.3d 1359, 1363 (Fed. Cir. 2003) (stating that "a proper analysis under §103 requires, inter alia, consideration of two factors: (1) whether the prior art would have suggested to those of ordinary skill in the art that they should make the claimed composition or device, or carry out the claimed process; and (2) whether the prior art would also have revealed that in so making or carrying out, those of ordinary skill would have a reasonable expectation of success").

[213] 611 F. App'x 693, 697-698 (Fed. Cir. 2015) (non-precedential). Although the Federal Appendix reporter does not designate the *Innovention* decision as non-precedential, the slip opinion on the Federal Circuit's website does. *See* http://www.cafc.uscourts.gov/sites/default/files/opinions-orders/14-1731.Opinion.4-24-2015.1.PDF (14-page opinion). "An opinion or order which is designated as nonprecedential is one determined by the panel issuing it as not adding significantly to the body of law." Fed. Cir. R. 32.1(b) (2011). The Federal Circuit "will not give one of its own nonprecedential dispositions the effect of binding precedent." Fed. Cir. R. 32.1(d) (2011).

Although the 2015 *Innovention* decision is designated as non-precedential, this author views the case as a helpful vehicle for understanding the "reasonable expectation of success" requirement (and what type of evidence is necessary to satisfy it).

the game.[214] The board generated laser beams for the players who had various movable board pieces. Some of the board pieces included mirrors that could reflect (and change the direction of) the laser beams. The players took turns moving the pieces from square to square or rotating them in place. Players sought to direct their laser onto the opponent's "key piece."[215]

At trial in federal district court, the accused infringers MGA Entertainment, Inc., Wal-Mart Stores, Inc., and Toys "R" Us, Inc. (collectively "MGA") asserted that Innovention's patent was invalid for obviousness. MGA's argument relied on a combination of two prior art references: (1) a U.S. patent to Swift, which claimed a laser board game with deflecting pieces that players put in place before, but did not move during, the game; and (2) articles from "Laser Chess" magazine that described a computer game in which each player manipulated screen images of a "laser-firing piece and various reflective objects" to try to hit the opponent's "king."[216]

Rejecting MGA's challenge, a jury sustained the Innovention patent (and determined that MGA willfully infringed it). The jury found, *inter alia*, that "it [w]as not highly probable that a skilled artisan would have had both a motivation to combine the prior art and a reasonable expectation of success."[217] A district court entered judgment for Innovention on the jury's verdict, adopting the jury's findings and denying MGA's post-verdict motion for judgment as a matter of law (JMOL) or a new trial on obviousness. Notably, the district court concluded that MGA's obviousness defense was "not objectively reasonable."[218]

When MGA appealed, the Federal Circuit sided with patentee Innovention (affirming the district court's judgment of nonobviousness). Concerning the issue of reasonable expectation of success, the Circuit viewed MGA's evidence as insufficient and conclusory:

> MGA presented little evidence on motivation to combine with a reasonable expectation of success. The only evidence that it has identified, beyond the prior-art documents' own content, is the testimony of its expert, Mr. Phillips. But Mr. Phillips did no more than cursorily identify the conceptual relatedness of Swift and the Laser Chess articles. J.A. 1889 ("Both [are] styles of presentation . . . they're teaching methods. They're ways to get into your mind a concept. And so they're equally valuable, in my view, for teaching you what game elements are. And that's why I think it's [ ] legitimate to combine these. . . ."). This testimony says

[214]*See* U.S. Patent No. 7,264,242 ("Light-Reflecting Board Game"). Innovention marketed the commercial embodiment of the patented game first as "Deflexion" and later as "Khet."

[215]*Innovention,* 611 F. App'x at 695 (non-precedential).

[216]*Innovention*, 611 F. App'x at 696 (non-precedential).

[217]*Innovention*, 611 F. App'x at 696 (non-precedential).

[218]*Innovention*, 611 F. App'x at 696-697 (non-precedential).

> nothing about why an ordinarily skilled artisan would have a reasonable expectation of success in creating the claimed workable physical game, with real lasers and regularly moving and rotating game pieces, based on Swift, which involves pieces fixed during play, and two articles about a computer game involving mere graphical images of lasers.[219]

The Federal Circuit's decision in *Innovention* (albeit non-precedential) aptly demonstrates that a validity challenger will not carry its "clear and convincing" evidence burden in federal court by simply putting on an expert who reiterates the content of the pertinent prior art references and "cursorily identify [the references'] conceptual relatedness." Rather than merely explaining *what* the references taught, the evidence must also explain *why* a PHOSITA would combine the references' teachings and *why* the PHOSITA have a reasonable expectation of success that it could create the claimed invention if it attempted the combination.

2. *KSR v. Teleflex:* Combinations, Predictability, and "Common Sense"

In a highly anticipated decision, the U.S. Supreme Court in 2007 revisited fundamental aspects of the nonobviousness requirement of §103 for the first time since its 1966 foundational decision in *Graham v. Deere.*[220] In *KSR Int'l Co. v. Teleflex, Inc.,*[221] the Court examined what constitutes an adequate TSM to combine prior art disclosures. Expanding the universe of sources from which a TSM may be derived, the Supreme Court reversed the Federal Circuit's holding that an electromechanical device patented by Teleflex would not have been obvious. The Federal Circuit had erred by applying the TSM test too narrowly and rigidly, requiring a more precise and explicit statement of a TSM than the prior art references of record provided.

The Supreme Court's *KSR* decision also stressed the role of "common sense" and "predictability" in determining whether an invention would have been obvious, but did not define those terms or clearly

[219]*Innovention*, 611 F. App'x at 697-698 (non-precedential).

[220]*See generally* Business Law Forum, *Nonobviousness: The Shape of Things to Come*, 12 Lewis & Clark L. Rev. 323-598 (2008) (law review issue compiling multiple articles on the impact of *KSR Int'l v. Teleflex, Inc.*).

After *Graham* but before *KSR,* the Supreme Court applied §103 to hold that the invention at issue in *Dann v. Johnston*, 425 U.S. 219 (1976), would have been obvious. *Dann* primarily dealt with the technical merits of the claimed invention, a computer-implemented system for "provid[ing] bank customers with an individualized and categorized breakdown of their transactions" during particular time periods. The *Dann* Court avoided deciding the §101 patentable subject matter issue that had been the primary focus of the case below.

[221]127 S. Ct. 1727 (2007).

explain how they inform the statutory standard of §103. The net effect of the Supreme Court's *KSR* decision appears to be that the USPTO will more routinely establish a *prima facie* case of obviousness, putting a greater burden on patent applicants to refute or rebut such *prima facie* cases.[222] The *KSR* decision also makes it likely that issued patents will be challenged more frequently as claiming obvious subject matter. The *KSR* Court questioned (without deciding the issue) the rationale for presuming an issued patent valid when the USPTO's examination did not consider a prior art reference later asserted by an accused infringer as evidence of invalidity.[223] In making obviousness easier to establish, at least *prima facie*, the *KSR* decision is consistent with other contemporaneous Supreme Court decisions that signal questions about the balance of power in the patent system. At least some of the Supreme Court Justices (including Justice Kennedy, author of the *KSR* opinion) appeared to be concerned that that balance had shifted too far in favor of patent owners.[224]

[222]The concept of a *prima facie* case of obviousness is further examined *infra* Section J.

[223]*See KSR*, 127 S. Ct. at 1745 (noting that the rationale underlying presumption of validity of issued patent, based on USPTO's expertise when approving the patent's claims, seemed "much diminished" when a prior art reference asserted by accused infringer had not been considered by USPTO).

[224]*See* Mayo Collab. Servs. v. Prometheus Labs., Inc., 132 S. Ct. 1289, 1305 (2012) (Breyer, J., for a unanimous Court) (observing that "[p]atent protection is, after all, a two-edged sword. On the one hand, the promise of exclusive rights provides monetary incentives that lead to creation, invention, and discovery. On the other hand, that very exclusivity can impede the flow of information that might permit, indeed spur, invention, by, for example, raising the price of using the patented ideas once created, requiring potential users to conduct costly and time-consuming searches of existing patents and pending patent applications, and requiring the negotiation of complex licensing arrangements."); Bilski v. Kappos, 130 S. Ct. 3218, 3229 (2010) (Kennedy, J., joined by Roberts, C.J., Thomas, J., and Alito, J.) (observing that "[t]he Information Age empowers people with new capacities to perform statistical analyses and mathematical calculations with a speed and sophistication that enable the design of protocols for more efficient performance of a vast number of business tasks. If a high enough bar is not set when considering patent applications of this sort, patent examiners and courts could be flooded with claims that would put a chill on creative endeavor and dynamic change."); MedImmune, Inc. v. Genentech, Inc., 127 S. Ct. 764, 777 (2007) (effectively expanding opportunities for challenging patents by holding that "petitioner was not required, insofar as Article III is concerned, to break or terminate its . . . license agreement before seeking a declaratory judgment in federal court that the underlying patent is invalid, unenforceable, or not infringed"); eBay Inc. v. MercExchange, L.L.C., 547 U.S. 388, 397 (2006) (Kennedy, J., concurring) (observing that "injunctive relief may have different consequences for the burgeoning number of patents over business methods, which were not of much economic and legal significance in earlier times. The potential vagueness and suspect validity of some of these patents may affect the calculus under the [equitable] four-factor test [for permanent injunctive relief]."); Lab. Corp. of Am. Holdings v. Metabolite Labs., Inc., 548 U.S. 124, 127, 138 (2006) (Breyer, J., dissenting from dismissal of writ of *certiorari* as improvidently granted) (observing that "[t]he problem arises from the fact that patents do not only encourage research by

The patent in suit in *KSR,* owned by Teleflex, was directed to a "vehicle control pedal apparatus" incorporating an electronic sensor in a vehicle's accelerator pedal.[225] The sensor was capable of changing the pedal's position depending on the height of the vehicle's driver. More specifically, the apparatus combined the electronic sensor with an adjustable automobile pedal so that the pedal's position could be transmitted to a computer controlling the throttle in the car's engine.[226] Figure 5.4 depicts the Teleflex invention.

The primary prior art reference relied on by validity challenger KSR was a U.S. patent to Asano.[227] The Asano patent disclosed an adjustable pedal, in a support structure housing the pedal such that even when adjusted relative to a driver's height, one of the pedal's pivot points would remain fixed.[228] The problem addressed by the Asano invention was a "constant ratio" problem — ensuring that the force required to depress the pedal always remain the same, no matter how the pedal was adjusted. Teleflex argued before the Federal Circuit that the problem its own invention solved was different — to design a smaller, less complex, and cheaper electronic pedal assembly. Teleflex contended that Asano's mechanical linkage-based device was complex, expensive to make, and difficult to package.

Reversing a district court's summary judgment of invalidity under 35 U.S.C. §103, the Federal Circuit agreed with Teleflex that its invention would not have been obvious in view of the disclosures of Asano in combination with other prior art references. The appellate court emphasized that "[w]hen obviousness is based on the teachings of multiple prior art references, the movant [validity challenger] must also establish some 'suggestion, teaching, or motivation' that would have led a person of ordinary skill in the art to combine the relevant prior

---

providing monetary incentives for invention. Sometimes their presence can discourage research by impeding the free exchange of information, for example by forcing researchers to avoid the use of potentially patented ideas, by leading them to conduct costly and time-consuming searches of existing or pending patents, by requiring complex licensing arrangements, and by raising the costs of using the patented information, sometimes prohibitively so. . . . [A] decision from this generalist Court could contribute to the important ongoing debate, among both specialists and generalists, as to whether the patent system, as currently administered and enforced, adequately reflects the 'careful balance' that 'the federal patent laws . . . embod[y]' ") (quoting Bonito Boats, Inc. v. Thunder Craft Boats, Inc., 489 U.S. 141, 146 (1989)).

[225] *See* U.S. Patent No. 6,237,565 (issued May 29, 2001).

[226] *KSR*, 127 S. Ct. at 1734.

[227] *See* U.S. Patent No. 5,010,782 (issued Apr. 30, 1991).

[228] Other prior art references taught that the sensor should be located on a fixed part of the pedal assembly rather than the pedal's footpad, and that sensors located on footpads were known to suffer from wire chafing problems when the pedal was depressed and released.

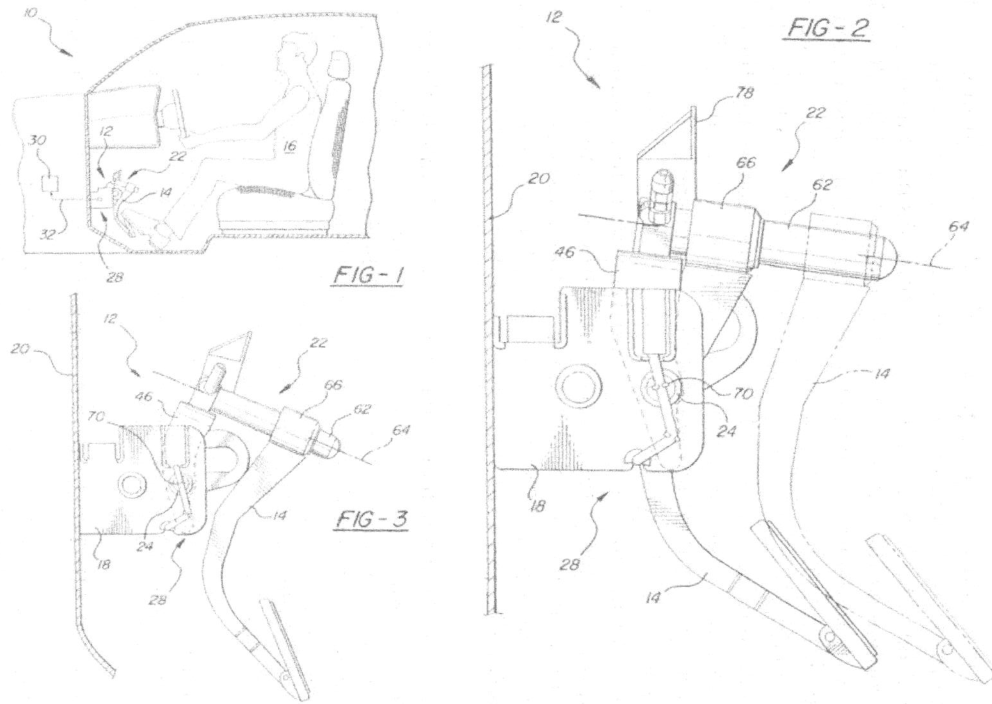

Figure 5.4
Engelgau '565 Patent (Teleflex)

art teachings *in the manner claimed.*"[229] Combining references without such a TSM "simply takes the inventor's disclosure as a blueprint for piecing together the prior art to defeat patentability — the essence of hindsight."[230] The district court correctly held that a TSM may be found from the nature of the problem to be solved, "leading inventors to look to references relating to possible solutions to that problem."[231] However, "the test requires that the nature of the problem to be solved be such that it would have led a person of ordinary skill in the art to combine the prior art teachings in the particular manner claimed."[232] In the case at bar, the Federal Circuit observed, Asano did not address the same problem as the patent in suit. "The objective of the [Teleflex] '565 patent was to design a smaller, less complex, and less expensive electronic pedal assembly. The Asano patent, on the other hand, was directed at solving the 'constant ratio problem.' "[233] The Federal Circuit thus held that the required TSM to combine Asano and the other prior art references was lacking, and accordingly vacated the district court's summary judgment of invalidity for obviousness.[234]

The Supreme Court reversed, concluding that the Federal Circuit had applied too rigid an approach to the TSM test, in a manner contrary to Supreme Court patent precedent. Although the TSM test can serve as a "helpful insight" in analyzing nonobviousness,[235] the Federal Circuit's conception of TSM in the case at bar was simply too narrow.[236] Specifically, the appellate court erred by

> holding that courts and patent examiners should look only to the problem the *patentee* was trying to solve.... The question is not whether the combination was obvious to the patentee but whether the combination was obvious to a person with ordinary skill in the art. Under the correct analysis, *any need or problem known in the field of endeavor at the time of invention and addressed by the patent* can provide a reason for combining the elements in the manner claimed.[237]

The Supreme Court also emphasized the role of "predictability" as well as "common sense," which teaches "that familiar items may have

[229]Teleflex, Inc. v. KSR Int'l Co., 119 F. App'x 282, 285 (Fed. Cir. 2005) (nonprecedential).

[230]*Id.* (quoting In re Dembiczak, 175 F.3d 994, 999 (Fed. Cir. 1999)).

[231]*Id.* (quoting Ruiz v. A.B. Chance Co., 234 F.3d 654, 665 (Fed. Cir. 2000)).

[232]*Id.* at 288.

[233]*Id.*

[234]*See id.* at 286.

[235]KSR Int'l Co. v. Teleflex Inc., 127 S. Ct. 1727, 1741 (2007).

[236]*See id.* at 1741-1742. After reviewing its own earlier cases dealing with the nonobviousness requirement, the *KSR* Court observed that "[h]elpful insights ... need not become rigid and mandatory formulas; and when it is so applied, the TSM test is incompatible with our precedents." *Id.* at 1741.

[237]*Id.* at 1742 (emphases added).

obvious uses beyond their primary purposes, and in many cases, a person of ordinary skill will be able to fit the teachings of multiple patents together like pieces of a puzzle."[238] The Supreme Court rejected Teleflex's contention that a designer hoping to make an adjustable electronic pedal would have ignored the Asano patent because it focused on a different problem; Asano provided an "obvious example" of an adjustable pedal with a fixed pivot point, and other prior art indicated that a fixed pivot point was the ideal location to mount a sensor. "A person of ordinary skill is also a person of ordinary creativity, not an

[238]*Id.* The Supreme Court's emphasis in *KSR* on the use of "common sense" in nonobviousness determinations may require the Federal Circuit to revisit its earlier decisions such as *In re Lee*, 277 F.3d 1338, 1341 (Fed. Cir. 2002). The USPTO Board in *Lee* rejected the patent applicant's argument that the prior art provided no teaching or motivation or suggestion to combine the prior art references cited by the examiner, stating that "[t]he conclusion of obviousness may be made from *common knowledge and common sense* of a person of ordinary skill in the art without any specific hint or suggestion in a particular reference." *Id.* at 1341 (emphasis added). The Federal Circuit in *Lee* vacated the obviousness determination, highlighting the agency's failure to explain the "common knowledge and common sense" on which it relied:

> [W]hen [the Board and examiner] rely on what they assert to be general knowledge to negate patentability, that knowledge must be articulated and placed on the record. The failure to do so is not consistent with either effective administrative procedure or effective judicial review. The board cannot rely on conclusory statements when dealing with particular combinations of prior art and specific claims, but must set forth the rationale on which it relies.

Id. at 1345. One way of rationalizing *Lee* with the Supreme Court's *KSR* decision is to view *Lee* as permitting reliance on "common sense," but nevertheless requiring the government to clearly and precisely explain and "place[] on the record" some evidence of what it asserts to be common sense.

Future Federal Circuit decisions will undoubtedly further explore the meaning and proof of "common sense" in nonobviousness determinations. One example is *Perfect Web Technologies, Inc. v. InfoUSA, Inc.*, 587 F.3d 1324 (Fed. Cir. 2009). Perfect Web's U.S. Patent No. 6,631,400 was directed to methods of distributing bulk e-mail to groups of targeted consumers. The invention involved "comparing the number of successfully delivered e-mail messages in a delivery against a predetermined desired quantity, and if the delivery [did] not reach the desired quantity, repeating the process of selecting and e-mailing a group of customers until the desired number of delivered messages ha[d] been achieved." On motion for summary judgment, a district court invalidated the '400 patent under §103. The district court explained that " '[i]f 100 e-mail deliveries were ordered, and the first transmission delivered only 95, common sense dictates that one should try again. One could do little else.' " *Perfect Web*, 587 F.3d at 1330 (quoting district court's slip opinion). The Federal Circuit affirmed the conclusion of obviousness, holding that "while an analysis of obviousness always depends on evidence that supports the required *Graham* factual findings, it also may include recourse to logic, judgment, and common sense available to the person of ordinary skill that do not necessarily require explication in any reference or expert opinion." *Perfect Web,* 587 F.3d at 1329. In the case at bar, the district court had adequately explained its reliance on "common sense," which was supported by record evidence, "namely the facts that step (D) [of '400 patent claim 1] merely involves repeating earlier steps, and that a marketer could repeat those steps, if desired." *Perfect Web,* 587 F.3d at 1330.

automaton,"[239] the Court observed. Design incentives and market forces can prompt variations of a known item, either in the same field or a different one. "If a person of ordinary skill can implement a *predictable* variation, §103 likely bars its patentability."[240]

The Supreme Court in *KSR* made other important points about the nonobviousness analysis in addition to the TSM test. These include a new interpretation of the "obvious to try" standard, discussed *infra.*

3. Teaching Away

Whether motivation to combine exists also must take into consideration whether any of the references to be combined actually teach away from the claimed invention. To teach away means that a prior art reference's disclosure would discourage or dissuade the PHOSITA from doing what the inventor actually and successfully did.[241] For example, consider

[239] *KSR*, 127 S. Ct. at 1742.

[240] *Id.* at 1740 (emphasis added). Note that the predictability (or nonpredictability) of particular technologies has long been a factor in the analysis of enablement under 35 U.S.C. §112, but before the Supreme Court's *KSR* decision the notion of whether a particular invention would have been "predictable" was not a central inquiry in the determination of nonobviousness under 35 U.S.C. §103. Post-*KSR,* the Federal Circuit has not hesitated to invalidate patents under §103 for involving "predictable" inventions. *See, e.g.,* Rothman v. Target Corp., 556 F.3d 1310, 1319 (Fed. Cir. 2009) (sustaining jury verdict of §103 invalidity of patent directed to a nursing garment having a smooth external appearance that concealed a fully supportive nursing bra, and opining that the claimed invention "falls into a very predictable field . . . [in which] a trial record may more readily show a motivation to combine known elements to yield a predictable result, thus rendering a claimed invention obvious") (citing *KSR*, 127 S. Ct. at 1731, 1740-1741).

[241] *See, e.g.,* DePuy Spine, Inc. v. Medtronic Sofamor Danek, Inc., 567 F.3d 1314, 1327 (Fed. Cir. 2009) (stating that "[a] reference may be said to teach away when a person of ordinary skill, upon reading the reference, would be discouraged from following the path set out in the reference, or would be led in a direction divergent from the path that was taken by the applicant"); In re Gurley, 27 F.3d 551, 553 (Fed. Cir. 1994), stating that

> [a] reference may be said to teach away when a person of ordinary skill, upon reading the reference, would be discouraged from following the path set out in the reference, or would be led in a direction divergent from the path that was taken by the applicant. The degree of teaching away will of course depend on the particular facts; in general, a reference will teach away if it suggests that the line of development flowing from the reference's disclosure is unlikely to be productive of the result sought by the applicant. *See* United States v. Adams, 383 U.S. 39, 52, 86 S. Ct. 708, 714, 15 L. Ed. 2d 572, 148 U.S.P.Q. 479, 484 (1966) ("known disadvantages in old devices which would naturally discourage the search for new inventions may be taken into account in determining obviousness"); W.L. Gore & Assoc., Inc. v. Garlock, Inc., 721 F.2d 1540, 1550-51, 220 U.S.P.Q. 303, 311 (Fed. Cir. 1983) (the totality of a reference's teachings must be considered), cert. denied, 469 U.S. 851, 105 S. Ct. 172, 83 L. Ed. 2d 107 (1984); In re Sponnoble, 405 F.2d 578, 587, 160 U.S.P.Q. 237, 244 (C.C.P.A. 1969) (references taken in combination teach away since they would produce a "seemingly inoperative

again the example of a patent applicant claiming "a widget comprising a lever arm A, a pulley B, and a spring C."[242] The patent applicant faced with the "motivation to combine"–based §103 rejection of that claim might counter with a teaching away argument if prior art Reference 2 stated that a pulley should not be used in combination with a lever arm because of certain harmful effects produced by that combination.

Note that while an argument that a particular prior art reference teaches away from a claimed invention may be relevant to the determination of whether that invention would have been obvious under §103, such a "teaching away" argument is not pertinent to the question of novelty under §102. As discussed in Chapter 4, *supra,* a strict identity test controls anticipation. If a single prior art reference identically discloses every limitation of a claimed invention, arranged as in the claim, then it anticipates, even if the reference disparages the invention or would otherwise discourage a PHOSITA from making the invention.[243]

"Teaching away" must be definite and disparaging. A prior art reference does *not* teach away if it merely expresses a "general preference" for an alternative to the claimed invention, but does not otherwise discourage or criticize investigation into the invention.[244] Merely listing

---

device"); In re Caldwell, 319 F.2d 254, 256, 138 U.S.P.Q. 243, 245 (C.C.P.A. 1963) (reference teaches away if it leaves the impression that the product would not have the property sought by the applicant).

[242]*See* Section I.1, *supra.*

[243]*See* Celeritas Techs. v. Rockwell Int'l Corp., 150 F.3d 1354, 1361 (Fed. Cir. 1998). Celeritas' patent claimed an apparatus that counteracted the adverse effects of the preemphasis and limiter circuits found in conventional analog cellular communications systems, by de-emphasizing the data signal before presenting it to the cellular network. *See id.* at 1356. During prosecution of its patent, Celeritas argued to the USPTO that the agency should not consider a prior art reference referred to as "the Telebit article" because Telebit "describes a modem that uses a large number of simultaneous carriers to transmit data in contrast to single carrier modems for which Applicant's invention is intended, and teaches that the use of de-emphasis would not work for single carrier systems." *Id.* at 1360-1361. Celeritas repeated the argument to a jury during subsequent litigation challenging the validity of its patent. The Federal Circuit held on appeal that Celeritas' teaching away argument was without merit because the Telebit article was anticipatory. It was "beyond dispute that the Telebit article discloses each of the claimed limitations." *Id.* at 1361. The Federal Circuit observed that "[a] reference is no less anticipatory if, after disclosing the invention, the reference then disparages it." *Id.* In this case, "[t]he fact that a modem with a single carrier data signal is shown to be less than optimal does not vitiate the fact that it is disclosed." *Id.* Thus, whether a reference teaches away from a claimed invention is simply "inapplicable to an anticipation analysis." *Id.*

[244]Polaris Indus., Inc. v. Arctic Cat, Inc., 882 F.3d 1056, 1069 (Fed. Cir. 2018) (stating that a prior art reference does not teach away "if it merely expresses a general preference for an alternative invention but does not 'criticize, discredit, or otherwise discourage' investigation into the invention claimed") (quoting DePuy Spine, Inc. v. Medtronic Sofamor Danek, Inc., 567 F.3d 1314, 1327 (Fed. Cir. 2009) (quoting In re Fulton, 391 F.3d 1195, 1201 (Fed. Cir. 2004))).

alternatives to the claimed invention, without criticizing it, does not amount to teaching away.

For example, the applicant in *In re Fulton*[245] sought a utility patent on the structure of an "improved shoe sole for increasing the resistance to slip on a contact surface. . . ."[246] The Federal Circuit rejected Fulton's argument that the prior art, which disclosed numerous structural alternatives to the claimed sole structure, taught away from it. Suggesting alternatives was not the same as affirmatively discouraging a skilled art worker.

More specifically, the claims of Fulton's U.S. Patent Application No. 09/122,198 ('198 application) recited generally a shoe sole having a tiled array of raised or "projected" surfaces. The claims required that (A) the perimeter of the shoe was mostly open; (B) the raised or projected surfaces, also called "studs," were hexagonal (six-sided) in shape; and (C) the hexagonal studs were oriented so that opposite edges of the hexagon "face[d] generally in the directions of said fore-aft axis." Figure 5.5 depicts an embodiment of Fulton's claimed shoe sole, as well as drawings from each of the prior art references of record (i.e., Bowerman, Pope, Davies, and Mastrantuone).

The USPTO Board found that the prior art as a whole suggested or motivated a combination of the teachings of the Bowerman and Pope prior art references. Bowerman disclosed a shoe sole having an open perimeter and orientation, while Pope disclosed a shoe sole surface having hexagonal shapes. The Board also found that none of the prior art references taught away from the combination of Bowerman and Pope; in other words, nothing in Bowerman, Pope, or any other prior art of record would have dissuaded or discouraged the skilled artisan

[245] 391 F.3d 1195 (Fed. Cir. 2004) (Michel, J.).

[246] More specifically, Fulton's application claim 1 recited:

> An improved shoe sole for increasing the resistance to slip on a contact surface, the sole comprising a bottom surface and defining a perimeter bounding a forefoot portion corresponding to the forefoot of the shoe and a heel portion corresponding to the heel of the shoe, wherein the sole extends generally along a fore-aft axis running from said heel portion to said forefoot portion, the sole further comprising a substantially regular tiling array of projections projecting from said bottom surface, said projections terminating in hexagonal shaped projected surfaces spaced from said bottom surface in a direction for making contact with the contact surface, said projections being oriented so that opposite edges of said projected surfaces face generally in the directions of said fore-aft axis, said projected surfaces being substantially flat and parallel to the bottom surface to maximize the area of contact with the contact surface, said projections being spaced from one another to define substantially continuous channels therebetween for conducting liquid, said channels being open over at least most of said perimeter, said forefoot portion and said heel portion of the sole.

In re Fulton, 391 F.3d 1195, 1196-1197 (Fed. Cir. 2004).

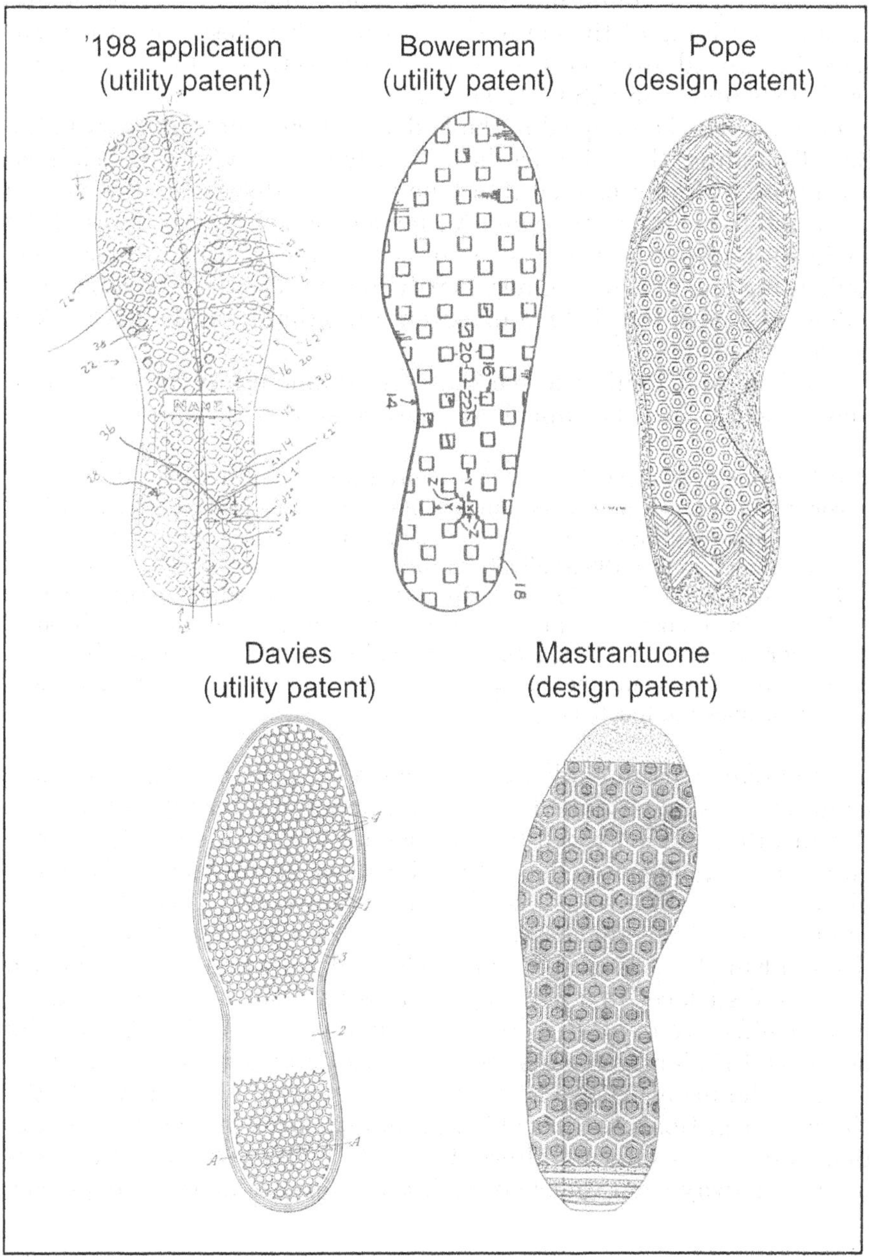

Figure 5.5

Claimed Invention and Prior Art in *In re Fulton* (Fed. Cir. 2004)

from making the combination with a reasonable expectation of successfully arriving at the claimed invention. For these and other reasons, the Board affirmed the examiner's rejection of Fulton's claims as obvious under 35 U.S.C. §103.

Fulton argued on appeal to the Federal Circuit that, contrary to the Board's finding, the prior art did in fact teach away from his claimed invention. Fulton reasoned that "the prior art disclosed alternatives to each of the claimed elements A [the perimeter], B [the shape of the surface], and C [the orientation of the surface]." In Fulton's view, "[c]hoosing one alternative necessarily means rejecting the other, i.e., following a path that is 'in a divergent direction from the path taken by the applicant.'"[247]

The Federal Circuit rejected Fulton's argument and his interpretation of its case law. The appellate court ruled that

> [t]he prior art's mere disclosure of more than one alternative does not constitute a teaching away from any of these alternatives because such disclosure does not criticize, discredit, or otherwise discourage the solution claimed in the '198 application. Indeed, in the case cited by [Fulton], *In re Gurley* [27 F.3d 551 (Fed. Cir. 1994)], we held that the invention claimed in the patent application was unpatentable based primarily on a prior art reference that disclosed two alternatives, one of which was the claimed alternative. Accordingly, mere disclosure of alternative designs does not teach away.[248]

The *Fulton* Circuit explained that while the prior art Pope and Mastrantuone design patents disclosed a number of alternative shoe sole designs, they did not teach that hexagonal projections in a facing orientation (i.e., opposite edges of the hexagon facing "generally in the directions of said fore-aft axis") were *undesirable*. Thus, those two references did not teach away. The prior art Davies utility patent (United Kingdom) disclosed that its claimed invention, which included hexagonal surfaces in a pointing orientation, had "a non-skid characteristic effective in all directions relative to its use." But Davies did not teach that hexagons in a facing orientation would be *ineffective*.

Thus the prior art in *Fulton* disclosed several alternatives to the claimed invention's feature of hexagonal surfaces in a facing orientation. But merely offering alternatives to a claim-recited feature does not teach away from that feature if the reference does not express a

[247]*Fulton,* 391 F.3d at 1201. In support of his position, Fulton quoted the Circuit's decision in *In re Gurley*, 27 F.3d 551, 553 (Fed. Cir. 1994), stating that "[a] reference may be said to teach away when a person of ordinary skill, upon reading the reference, would be discouraged from following the path set out in the reference, or would be led in a direction divergent from the path that was taken by the applicant." *Fulton*, 391 F.3d at 1201.

[248]*Fulton,* 391 F.3d at 1201.

negative view about it. In the absence of such criticism, the prior art alternatives in *Fulton* were not enough to establish that that art taught away from what Fulton had invented. For these and other reasons, the Federal Circuit affirmed the USPTO Board's rejection of Fulton's application claims on the ground that they would have been obvious in view of the combined teachings of Bowerman and Pope.

The disclosures of prior art references must be taken as a whole. A prior art reference's disclosure cannot be cherry-picked. In other words, a prior art reference must be understood and appreciated for all that it discloses — disclosures that would dissuade the skilled artisan from making the claimed invention as well as disclosures that would encourage her to do so.[249] Even if, on balance, a prior art reference cannot be said to "teach away," the Federal Circuit holds that its disclosure is "still relevant to determining whether a skilled artisan would be motivated to combine" the reference with other references in order to achieve the claimed invention.[250]

4. "Obvious to Try"

The Supreme Court's 2007 decision in *KSR Int'l Co. v. Teleflex Inc.*[251] gave new credence to "obvious to try" arguments, which traditionally have been most relevant to chemical obviousness cases. Before *KSR,* the Federal Circuit defined an obvious-to-try situation as one in which a prior art disclosure might have piqued a scientist's curiosity enough to merit further investigation, but the disclosure was too

[249]*See* Polaris Indus., Inc. v. Arctic Cat, Inc., 882 F.3d 1056, 1069 (Fed. Cir. 2018) (O'Malley, J.) (citing Ashland Oil, Inc. v. Delta Resins & Refractories, Inc., 776 F.2d 281, 296 (Fed. Cir. 1985) (holding that a reference "must [be] considered for all it taught, disclosures that diverged and taught away from the invention at hand as well as disclosures that pointed towards and taught the invention at hand") (citation omitted)).

[250]*See, e.g., Polaris,* 882 F.3d at 1070 (advising that on remand, "[e]ven if the Board determines that [the prior art reference] Denney does not teach away because it merely expresses a general preference, the statements in Denney are still relevant to determining whether a skilled artisan would be motivated to combine Denney and [another prior art reference,] Furuhashi") (citing Apple Inc. v. Samsung Elecs. Co., 839 F.3d 1034, 1051 n.15 (Fed. Cir. 2016) (*en banc*). The cited *Apple* case, detailed *supra* Section H.1.b ("Diverging Views"), concerned *inter alia* whether the "slide to unlock" feature of Apple's iPhone smart phone would have been obvious. Although the court did not decide the "teaching away" question, it instructed that the prior art's "preferences" would be relevant to the motivation to combine question. *See Apple*, 839 F.3d at 1051 n.15 (stating that "[b]ecause we find substantial evidence support for the jury's fact finding regarding motivation to combine, we need not reach the issue of whether [prior art reference] Plaisant teaches away from the combination. We note, however, that, even if Plaisant does not teach away, its statements regarding users preferring other forms of switches are relevant to a finding regarding whether a skilled artisan would be motivated to combine the slider toggle in Plaisant with the mobile phone in [prior art reference] Neonode.").

[251]127 S. Ct. 1727 (2007). *See* Section I.2, *supra,* for more discussion of *KSR.*

general to sufficiently teach how to obtain the desired result or that the claimed invention would be obtained if the prior art's directions were pursued.[252] If a validity challenger charged "obvious to try" when arguing that a PHOSITA would have made a particular combination of or modification to prior art teachings with a "reasonable expectation of success," the Federal Circuit tended to reject the argument. Pre-*KSR,* the Federal Circuit repeatedly held that obvious-to-try was *not* the standard for determining the ultimate question of nonobviousness.[253]

The Supreme Court in *KSR* breathed new life into obvious-to-try arguments by redefining obvious-to-try situations as follows:

> When there is a design need or market pressure to solve a problem and there are a finite number of identified, predictable solutions, a person of ordinary skill has good reason to pursue the known options within his or her technical grasp. If this leads to the anticipated success, it is likely the product not of innovation but of ordinary skill and common sense. *In that instance the fact that a combination was obvious to try might show that it was obvious under §103.*[254]

This definition reframed the obvious-to-try inquiry. Post-*KSR*, patent applicants, USPTO examiners and PTAB judges, litigants, federal judges, and juries considering whether a claimed invention would have been obvious must determine whether the prior art identified "predictable" solutions, and whether such solutions were "finite" in number. When these conditions are satisfied, obvious-to-try evidence may indeed establish the ultimate conclusion of obviousness.[255] In

[252]*See* In re Eli Lilly & Co., 902 F.2d 943, 945 (Fed. Cir. 1990) (defining "obvious to try" as when the prior art gives "only general guidance as to the particular form of the claimed invention or how to achieve it") (citing In re O'Farrell, 853 F.2d 894, 903 (Fed. Cir. 1988)).

[253]*See* In re Deuel, 51 F.3d 1552, 1559 (Fed. Cir. 1995) (stating that " '[o]bvious to try' has long been held not to constitute obviousness") (citing In re O'Farrell, 853 F.2d 894, 903 (Fed. Cir. 1988)).

[254]*KSR*, 127 S. Ct. at 1742 (emphasis added).

[255]*See, e.g.*, In re Kubin, 561 F.3d 1351 (Fed. Cir. 2009) (sustaining USPTO rejection of claimed genus of isolated nucleic acid molecules on ground that the claimed invention would have been obvious under §103(a) (2006)). The Federal Circuit concluded that "[i]n light of the concrete, specific teachings of [the] Sambrook and Valiante [prior art references], artisans in this field, as found by the Board in its expertise, had every motivation to seek and every reasonable expectation of success in achieving the sequence of the claimed invention. In that sense, the claimed invention was reasonably expected in light of the prior art and [hence] 'obvious to try.' " *Kubin*, 561 F.3d at 1361. The *Kubin* decision signals that "classical" biotechnology inventions (i.e., claims to isolated genes that encode particular proteins) may now routinely be characterized as "obvious to try" in the *KSR* sense, and thus obvious under 35 U.S.C. §103. *See also* Wm. Wrigley Jr. Co. v. Cadbury Adams USA LLC, 683 F.3d 1356, 1365 (Fed. Cir. 2012) (concluding that "[t]his case is . . . one in which a person of ordinary skill in the art would find it 'obvious to try' " the claimed chewing gum that combined menthol with the "cooling sensation" agent "WS-23"); Pfizer, Inc. v. Apotex, Inc., 488 F.3d 1377, 1384 (Fed. Cir. 2007)

other cases, however, the Federal Circuit has distinguished the Supreme Court's *KSR* definition, emphasizing the latter's narrow confines.[256]

The Federal Circuit's 2015 decision in *Shire LLC v. Amneal Pharms., LLC*,[257] illustrates a patentee prevailing over an accused infringer's argument that the patented invention would have been "obvious to try."[258] The four Shire-owned patents in suit were directed to chemical compounds; specifically, the patents claimed mesylate salts of L-lysine-d-amphetamine ("LDX")[259] and crystalline forms thereof. The patented invention sought to lessen the potential for abuse of amphetamines, a class of drugs used to treat a variety of disorders including attention deficit hyperactivity disorder ("ADHD"). The inventors determined that modifying certain amphetamine drugs with certain amino acids (i.e., L-lysine) and forming certain salts thereof decreased the activity of the amphetamine when administered in high doses, but maintained activity similar to unmodified amphetamine when the modified amphetamine was delivered at lower doses. With approval of the U.S. Food and Drug Administration, Shire marketed LDX dimesylate capsules under the brand name Vyvanse®.

Based on the assertions of several potential generic drug manufacturers of Vyvanse® that Shire's patents were invalid for obviousness, Shire initiated Hatch-Waxman Act patent infringement litigation.[260] After litigation discovery was complete, a district court granted Shire's motion for summary judgment that all the asserted claims of its patents were not invalid (and also would be infringed by the defendants' proposed generic manufacturing).

The Federal Circuit in *Shire LLC* affirmed the district court's summary judgment of no invalidity; for the reasons discussed below, the Circuit concluded that Shire's claimed invention was *not* "obvious to try."[261] The "primary" prior art reference relied on by the accused infringers/validity challengers was a published Australian patent

---

(Rader, J., dissenting from denial of reh'g *en banc*) (stating that obvious to try "appears to be the basis for [the panel's] decision in this case").

[256] *See* Takeda Chem. Indus., Ltd. v. Alphapharm Pty., Ltd., 492 F.3d 1350, 1359 (Fed. Cir. 2007) (concluding that case at bar "fails to present the type of situation contemplated by the [Supreme] Court when it stated [in *KSR*] that an invention may be deemed obvious if it was 'obvious to try.' The evidence showed that [the claimed invention in *Takeda*] was not obvious to try.").

[257] 802 F.3d 1301 (Fed. Cir. 2015).

[258] *Shire LLC*, 802 F.3d at 1308 (concluding that primary prior art reference did not make patented invention obvious to try).

[259] The amino acid lysine has "L" and "D" enantiomers (i.e., mirror-image isomers). *See* Reginald H. Garrett, BIOCHEMISTRY 4TH ED., at 91 (2009).

[260] *See generally infra* Chapter 9, Section E.3 ("Drug Marketing Application Filings Under §271(e)").

[261] *Shire LLC*, 802 F.3d at 1308.

application ("AU '168").[262] They argued that a particular passage of AU '168 identified 18 amino acids by name, including lysine, and stated a preference for L-amino acids and d-amphetamine. Based on this passage, the validity challengers contended that a person of skill in the art "would immediately envisage LDX."[263]

The Federal Circuit disagreed with the validity challengers' reading of the prior art, finding (as had the district court) "no genuine issue of material fact that the prior art did not disclose or make obvious the [claimed] mesylate salt of LDX."[264] The AU '168 reference simply suggested far too many possibilities — "thousands of possible compounds"[265] — and did not provide any direction as to which of the many choices was likely to succeed.[266] Read in its entirety, AU '168 "broadly [taught] combining amphetamine with many amino acids, protected and unprotected, and in different stereochemistries."[267] This was not the "finite" number of possibilities required by *KSR*. Moreover, the reference provided thirty specific examples, "none of which [wa]s LDX."[268] Lacking additional guidance in the reference, the validity challengers could "only come to LDX by 're-trac[ing] the path of the inventor with hindsight.'"[269] The Circuit accordingly rejected the validity challengers' "hindsight claims of obviousness."[270]

5. Unexpected Results

a. *Generally*

When a combination of prior art elements results in an invention with unexpectedly improved performance or properties, such

[262]Australian Patent Application No. 54,168/65 ("AU '168"). The Federal Circuit observed that the AU '168 application was listed on the face of the Shire patents. When a prior art reference is listed on the face of an issued U.S. patent, "the examiner is presumed to have considered it." *Shire LLC*, 802 F.3d at 1307. The validity challengers in *Shire LLC* thus carried " 'the added burden of overcoming the deference that is due to a qualified government agency presumed to have properly done its job, which includes one or more examiners who are assumed to have some expertise in interpreting the references and to be familiar from their work with the level of skill in the art and whose duty it is to issue only valid patents.' " *Shire LLC*, 802 F.3d at 1307 (quoting PowerOasis, Inc. v. T-Mobile USA, Inc., 522 F.3d 1299, 1304 (Fed. Cir. 2008) (citations omitted)).

[263]*Shire LLC*, 802 F.3d at 1307.

[264]*Shire LLC*, 802 F.3d at 1307.

[265]*Shire LLC*, 802 F.3d at 1308.

[266]*Shire LLC*, 802 F.3d at 1308 (citing Unigene Labs, Inc. v. Apotex, Inc., 655 F.3d 1352, 1361 (Fed. Cir. 2011)).

[267]*Shire LLC*, 802 F.3d at 1308.

[268]*Shire LLC*, 802 F.3d at 1308.

[269]*Shire LLC*, 802 F.3d at 1308 (quoting Ortho-McNeil Pharm., Inc. v. Mylan Labs, Inc., 520 F.3d 1358, 1364 (Fed. Cir. 2008).

[270]*Shire LLC*, 802 F.3d at 1308.

"unexpected results" tend to establish that the invention would not have been obvious.[271] If they possess evidence of unexpected results, patent applicants will tend to proffer the evidence in order to rebut a USPTO examiner's (or in the AIA-implemented post-grant proceedings, a Patent Trial and Appeal Board's) *prima facie* case of obviousness, a procedural mechanism discussed below.[272] Patentees in federal district court infringement litigation, faced with a validity challenge brought by the defendants/accused infringers, may also put forth unexpected results evidence.

The patentee succeeded with this strategy in *Eli Lilly and Co. v. Zenith Goldline Pharms.*[273] There the Federal Circuit affirmed a district court's judgment sustaining the validity of a patent claim to a chemical compound although the compound's adjacent homologue was already known in the prior art.[274] The appellate court explained

[271]*See* In re Soni, 54 F.3d 746 (Fed. Cir. 1995) (Lourie, J.), in which the appellate court explained:

> One way for a patent applicant to rebut a *prima facie* case of obviousness [which "may be established by the . . . citation of a reference to a similar composition, the presumption being that similar compositions have similar properties"] is to make a showing of "unexpected results," *i.e.*, to show that the claimed invention exhibits some superior property or advantage that a person of ordinary skill in the relevant art would have found surprising or unexpected. The basic principle behind this rule is straightforward — that which would have been surprising to a person of ordinary skill in a particular art would not have been obvious. The principle applies most often to the less predictable fields, such as chemistry, where minor changes in a product or process may yield substantially different results.

Soni, 54 F.3d at 750. *See also* Procter & Gamble Co. v. Teva Pharm. USA, Inc., 566 F.3d 989, 994 (Fed. Cir. 2009) (stating that "[i]f a patent challenger makes a prima facie showing of obviousness, the owner may rebut based on 'unexpected results' by demonstrating 'that the claimed invention exhibits some superior property or advantage that a person of ordinary skill in the relevant art would have found surprising or unexpected' ") (quoting *Soni*, 54 F.3d at 750).

But see Bristol-Myers Squibb Co. v. Teva Pharms. USA, Inc., 752 F.3d 967, 976 (Fed. Cir. 2014) (Chen, J., joined by Prost, C.J., and Plager, J.) (hereafter "*Bristol-Meyers Squibb II*") (stating that in *In re Dillon*, 919 F.2d 688, 693, 697 (Fed. Cir. 1990) (*en banc*), the Federal Circuit had "explain[ed] that an unexpected result or property does not by itself support a finding of nonobviousness"). In response to that characterization of *Dillon*, Judge Newman, joined by Judges Lourie and Reyna, wrote that "[t]o the contrary, an unexpected result or property is the touchstone of nonobviousness." Bristol-Myers Squibb Co. v. Teva Pharms. USA, Inc., 769 F.3d 1339, 1350 (Fed. Cir. 2014) (hereafter "*Bristol-Myers Squibb III*") (Newman, J., dissenting from Federal Circuit's order denying combined petition for panel rehearing and rehearing *en banc*).

[272]*See infra* Section J ("The *Prima Facie* Case of Obviousness").

[273]471 F.3d 1369 (Fed. Cir. 2006) (hereafter "*Lilly*").

[274]In *In re Dillon*, 919 F.2d 688 (Fed. Cir. 1990), the court explained that "[a] homolog is a chemical compound that differs from another compound only by one or more methylene groups. An 'adjacent' homolog differs by precisely one methylene group." *Id.* at 703.

that "patentability for a chemical compound does not depend only on structural similarity" and noted the "unexpected beneficial properties" of the claimed compound.[275] In the case at bar, these unexpected properties (as well as secondary considerations evidence) "overcame any prima facie case of obviousness."[276]

The result in *Lilly v. Zenith* is consistent with the well-established principle of chemical patent law that unexpected results can overcome a *prima facie* case of obviousness based on structural similarity.[277] In the chemical arts, the subject matter to be assessed for patentability is not only a compound's chemical structure but also the totality of its properties.[278] As the Court of Customs and Patent Appeals, one of the Federal Circuit's two predecessor courts, famously stated,

> *[f]rom the standpoint of patent law, a compound and all of its properties are inseparable; they are one and the same thing.* The graphic formulae, the chemical nomenclature, the systems of classification and study such as the concepts of homology, isomerism, etc., are mere symbols by which compounds can be identified, classified, and compared. But a formula is not a compound and while it may serve in a claim to identify what is being patented, as the metes and bounds of a deed identify a plot of land, the thing that is patented is not the formula but the compound identified by it. And the patentability of the thing does not depend on the similarity of its formula to that of another compound but of the similarity of the former compound to the latter. There is no basis in law for ignoring any property in making such a comparison. An assumed similarity based on a comparison of formulae must give way to evidence that the assumption is erroneous.[279]

[275]*Lilly*, 471 F.3d at 1378. "The trial court . . . discussed the unexpected differences between the closest analog, Compound 222 and [the patented drug] olanzapine, most of which focused on olanzapine not raising cholesterol levels in dogs, and a comparison of some humans tests with other similar drugs that raised CPK [a muscle enzyme called creatine phosphokinase]." *Lilly*, 471 F.3d at 1380.

[276]*Lilly*, 471 F.3d at 1380.

[277]*See* 2-5 Donald S. Chisum, Chisum on Patents §5.06[1][b][i] (2010) (discussing submission to the USPTO of affidavit evidence of " 'unexpectedly superior properties or advantages' of the claimed invention as compared with the prior art products or processes") (quoting In re Peterson, 315 F.3d 1325 (Fed. Cir. 2003)). *See also* Procter & Gamble Co. v. Teva Pharms. USA, Inc., 566 F.3d 989, 996-998 (Fed. Cir. 2009) (crediting expert testimony of unexpected results). The concept of a *prima facie* case of obviousness is further discussed *infra* Section J.

[278]*See* In re Papesch, 315 F.2d 381 (C.C.P.A. 1963) (explaining that "[f]rom the standpoint of patent law, a compound and all of its properties are inseparable; they are one and the same thing."). *See also* Eli Lilly [v. Zenith Goldline], 471 F.3d at 1378 (stating that "[t]his court will not ignore a relevant property of a compound in the obviousness calculus").

[279]In re Papesch, 315 F.2d 381, 391 (C.C.P.A. 1963) (Rich, J.) (emphasis added).

b. *Timing of Evidence*

The Federal Circuit has not yet come to terms with the interesting but difficult question of exactly *when* the evidence of an invention's unexpected results must have been in existence to count as evidence supporting the nonobviousness of the invention. Particularly under the first-inventor-to-file regime of the AIA, patent applicants face significant pressure to file promptly. In many cases, an inventor has a firm belief that her invention will achieve certain superior results, but the inventor does not carry out the experiments and collect the data to definitively establish such results until after filing her patent application. The delay may also be due to a lack of funds to underwrite detailed testing at an early date before the application has been filed and can then be disclosed with less risk to potential investors.

In June 2014, a three-judge panel of the Federal Circuit issued a controversial decision dealing with these issues in *Bristol-Myers Squibb Co. v. Teva Pharms. USA Inc.*,[280] further analyzed below. In October 2014, with four judges dissenting, the *en banc* Circuit denied rehearing *en banc* in *Bristol-Myers Squibb*.[281] Circuit Judges Newman and Taranto (joined by Circuit Judges Lourie and Reyna) issued separate and detailed opinions dissenting from denial.[282] The judges posited important (but as yet unanswered) questions about the timing of unexpected results evidence in the context of evaluating of pharmaceutical patent claims. Specifically, is evidence of unexpected results obtained *after* the invention date (for AIA patents, after the effective filing date) relevant? The Circuit judges' diverging views make the *Bristol-Myers Squibb* decision worthy of close examination. Subsequent Federal Circuit obviousness decisions should be watched with

[280]752 F.3d 967 (Fed. Cir. 2014) (hereafter "*Bristol-Myers Squibb II*") (affirming district court's judgment that claim 8 of Bristol-Myers Squibb's U.S. Patent No. 5,206,244, reciting entecavir, a new drug useful for the treatment of hepatitis B, was invalid for obviousness).

[281]*See* Bristol-Myers Squibb Co. v. Teva Pharms. USA, Inc., 769 F.3d 1339 (Fed. Cir. 2014) (hereafter "*Bristol-Myers Squibb III*") (order denying combined petition for panel rehearing and rehearing *en banc*). The *Bristol-Myers Squibb III* decision to deny rehearing *en banc* generated four dissenting votes and four opinions, each of which is discussed *infra*: (1) Judge Dyk, joined by Judge Wallach, authored an opinion concurring in the denial of the petition for rehearing *en banc*; (2) Judge O'Malley authored an opinion concurring in the denial of the petition for rehearing *en banc*; (3) Judge Neman, joined by Judges Lourie and Reyna, authored an opinion dissenting from the denial of the petition for rehearing *en banc*; and (4) Judge Taranto, joined by Judges Lourie and Reyna, authored an opinion dissenting from the denial of the petition for rehearing *en banc*. *See Bristol-Myers Squibb III*, 769 F.3d at 1340.

[282]752 F.3d 967 (Fed. Cir. 2014) (hereafter "*Bristol-Myers Squibb II*") (affirming district court's judgment that claim 8 of Bristol-Myers Squibb's U.S. Patent No. 5,206,244, reciting entecavir, a new drug useful for the treatment of hepatitis B, was invalid for obviousness).

care as the court irons out this fundamentally important issue of patentability.

The patented invention in *Bristol-Myers Squibb Co. v. Teva Pharms. USA, Inc.*[283] was entecavir, a new drug useful for the treatment of the hepatitis B virus and marketed by Bristol-Myers Squibb (hereafter "Bristol-Myers" or "BMS") as Baraclude.® Following an FDA application by Teva Pharmaceuticals USA to market a generic version of entecavir and ensuing Hatch-Waxman Act litigation under 35 U.S.C. §271(e)(2),[284] a district court held that claim 8 of Bristol-Myers Squibb's U.S. Patent No. 5,206,244, which recited entecavir,[285] was invalid for obviousness. The district court's ruling was based primarily on the close structural similarity of entecavir to the prior art compound 2'-CDG, which BMS had chosen to modify in order to develop entecavir.[286] The district court ruled the entecavir patent invalid despite evidence that shortly after BMS filed its patent application claiming entecavir, the prior art compound 2'-CDG was tested in animals for the first time and found to be highly toxic. The 2'-CDG compound was never used in human testing. In contrast, the patented compound entecavir proved safe and effective and was approved for human administration by the FDA. Whether this distinction, which came to light *after* BMS filed its patent application, was relevant to the unexpected results part of the obviousness analysis was hotly disputed in the *Bristol-Myers Squibb* cases.

In the June 2014 three-judge panel opinion in *Bristol-Myers Squibb* (authored by Judge Chen and joined by Chief Judge Prost and Judge Plager), the Federal Circuit affirmed the district court's invalidation of BMS's patent.[287] With respect to the unexpected results factor of

[283]752 F.3d 967 (Fed. Cir. 2014) (Chen, J., joined by Prost, C.J., and Plager, J.) (hereafter "*Bristol-Meyers Squibb II*") (three-judge panel decision affirming district court's judgment that claim 8 of Bristol-Myers Squibb's U.S. Patent No. 5,206,244, reciting entecavir, a new drug useful for the treatment of hepatitis B, was invalid for obviousness).

[284]*See infra* Chapter 9 ("Patent Infringement"), Section E.3 ("Drug Marketing Application Filings Under §271(e)").

[285]The Federal Circuit explained that entecavir is a "nucleoside analog composed of two regions: a carbocyclic ring and a guanine base." *Bristol-Myers Squibb II*, 752 F.3d at 969. More particularly,

> Entecavir is a modified version of the natural nucleoside 2'-deoxyguanosine (deoxyguanosine). Entecavir is structurally identical to deoxyguanosine except for one difference: it has a carbon-carbon double bond (also known as an exocyclic methylene group) at the 5' position of the carbocyclic ring where deoxyguanosine has an oxygen atom.

Bristol-Myers Squibb II, 752 F.3d at 969.

[286]The district court's opinion is reported at *Bristol-Myers Squibb Co. v. Teva Pharms. USA, Inc.*, 923 F. Supp. 2d 602 (D. Del. 2013) (hereafter "*Bristol-Meyers Squibb I*").

[287]752 F.3d 967 (Fed. Cir. 2014) (Chen, J., joined by Prost, C.J., and Plager, J.) (hereafter "*Bristol-Meyers Squibb II*").

the obviousness analysis, the appellate panel stated that "[t]o be particularly probative, evidence of unexpected results must establish that there is a difference between the results obtained and those of the closest prior art, and that the difference would not have been expected by one of ordinary skill in the art *at the time of the invention*."[288] Moreover, the court asserted that in its earlier *en banc* decision *In re Dillon*,[289] the Federal Circuit had "explain[ed] that an unexpected result or property does not by itself support a finding of nonobviousness."[290] On the merits, the Federal Circuit panel in *Bristol-Myers Squibb* emphasized that "while the district court found that entecavir's *degree* of effectiveness was unexpected, it also noted that entecavir's 'effectiveness against hepatitis B without known toxicity issues' was '*not unexpected*' in light of the structurally similar [prior art lead compound] 2'-CDG."[291]

In requesting that the Federal Circuit rehear the case *en banc*, patentee BMS and supporting *amici* argued that this language in the *Bristol-Myers Squibb II* panel's opinion "foreclose[d] the possibility of reviewing later-discovered differences between the prior art and the claimed invention," and that the panel had erred by failing to consider later-discovered unexpected results (i.e., that entecavir was effective and safe while the prior art lead compound 2'-CDG was highly toxic).[292] The petition for rehearing *en banc* failed to garner the necessary votes, however, and the resulting denial of *en banc* generated a number of diverging opinions, some dissenting from the denial of rehearing and some concurring therein.

In Circuit Judge Taranto's view (dissenting from denial of rehearing *en banc*), in affirming the district court's ruling of invalidity based on obviousness, the June 2014 panel decision in *Bristol-Myers Squibb* "raise[d] questions about core aspects of the widely used approach to obviousness analysis — particularly, the proper meaning of the related elements, 'reasonable expectation of success' and 'unexpected results.'"[293] He believed that "[t]hose questions would benefit from plenary [i.e., *en banc*] consideration." With only four votes for

[288]*Bristol-Myers Squibb II*, 752 F.3d at 977 (emphasis added) (citing Kao Corp. v. Unilever U.S., Inc. 441 F.3d 963, 970 (Fed. Cir. 2006); Pfizer, Inc. v. Apotex, Inc., 480 F.3d 1348, 1371 (Fed. Cir. 2007)).

[289]In re Dillon, 919 F.2d 688, 693, 697 (Fed. Cir. 1990) (*en banc*). *Dillon* is examined in detail *infra* Section J ("The *Prima Facie* Case of Obviousness").

[290]*Bristol-Myers Squibb II*, 752 F.3d at 976.

[291]*Bristol-Myers Squibb II*, 752 F.3d at 978 (emphasis added by Federal Circuit).

[292]Bristol-Myers Squibb Co. v. Teva Pharms. USA, Inc., 769 F.3d 1339 (Fed. Cir. 2014) (hereafter "*Bristol-Myers Squibb III*") (O'Malley, J., concurring in denial of reh'g *en banc*).

[293]*Bristol-Myers Squibb III*, 769 F.3d at 1353 (Taranto, dissenting from denial of rehearing *en banc*).

rehearing *en banc*, however, the questions remain unanswered, but are likely to be encountered again in future appeals.

Concurring in the denial of rehearing *en banc* in *Bristol-Myers Squibb*, Circuit Judge O'Malley disagreed that the June 2014 panel had erred or that rehearing was needed to correct its statements. Judge O'Malley observed that the Federal Circuit's "case law clearly allows the consideration of later-discovered differences between the prior art and the invention."[294] She emphasized the distinction "between limiting the obviousness inquiry to *pre*-invention evidence and finding *post*-invention evidence *unpersuasive*. . . ."[295] In Judge O'Malley's view, the district court *had* in fact considered the later-discovered evidence of 2'-CDG's toxicity, but simply concluded that such evidence was "insufficient to overcome the strong evidence that researchers at the time had a motivation to start with 2'-CDG as the lead compound and modify it in such a way as to make entecavir."[296] Rather than "forg[ing] new ground" by "rewrit[ing] the test for obviousness for pharmaceutical patents" as feared by BMS and the *amici*, the Federal Circuit panel in *Bristol-Myers Squibb* had "simply decide[d] that, on the record before it, the district court did not err in finding the asserted claim of [BMS's] [p]atent invalid as obvious."[297]

Also concurring in the denial of rehearing *en banc* in *Bristol-Myers Squibb*, Circuit Judge Dyk took a much more hard-line approach than Judge O'Malley. In Judge Dyk's view, evidence post-dating an invention's priority date cannot be considered in determining nonobviousness, at least "in the circumstances of this case."[298] According to Judge Dyk, the language of 35 U.S.C. §103 mandates this exclusion because it provides than an invention is not patentable if it "would have been obvious *before the effective filing date* of the claimed

[294]*Bristol-Myers Squibb III*, 769 F.3d at 1342-1343 (O'Malley, J., concurring in denial of reh'g *en banc*) (citing Sanofi-Aventis Deutschland GmbH v. Glenmark Pharm., Inc., 748 F.3d 1354, 1360 (Fed. Cir. 2014) ("Glenmark also argues that later-discovered benefits cannot be considered in an obviousness analysis. . . . That is incorrect; patentability may consider all of the characteristics possessed by the claimed invention, whenever those characteristics become manifest."); Genetics Inst., LLC v. Novartis Vaccines & Diagnostics, Inc., 655 F.3d 1291, 1307 (Fed. Cir. 2011) ("[E]vidence of unexpected results may be [considered] . . . even if that evidence was obtained after the patent's filing or issue date."); Knoll Pharm. Co. v. Teva Pharm. USA, Inc., 367 F.3d 1381, 1385 (Fed. Cir. 2004) ("Evidence developed after the patent grant is not excluded from consideration, for understanding of the full range of an invention is not always achieved at the time of filing the patent application.")).

[295]*Bristol-Myers Squibb III*, 769 F.3d at 1343 (O'Malley, J., concurring in denial of reh'g *en banc*) (emphasis added).

[296]*Bristol-Myers Squibb III*, 769 F.3d at 1343 (O'Malley, J., concurring in denial of reh'g *en banc*).

[297]*Bristol-Myers Squibb III*, 769 F.3d at 1341 (O'Malley, J., concurring in denial of reh'g *en banc*).

[298]*Bristol-Myers Squibb III*, 769 F.3d at 1341 (Dyk, J., concurring in denial of reh'g *en banc*).

invention. . . ."[299] To allow consideration of post-filing date evidence would, in Judge Dyk's view, facilitate hindsight bias.[300] Because the panel's decision correctly did not allow consideration of post-invention evidence, Judge Dyk saw no basis for rehearing *en banc.*

Joined by Judges Lourie and Reyna, Circuit Judge Newman dissented strongly from the denial of rehearing *en banc* in *Bristol-Myers Squibb.* In her view, the panel's opinion created several conflicts with the Circuit's "overwhelming" precedent that clearly permitted consideration of post-invention data to overcome a *prima facie* case of obviousness.[301] The panel's "hindsight decision that Bristol-Myers merely

[299]*Bristol-Myers Squibb III*, 769 F.3d at 1341 (Dyk, J., concurring in denial of reh'g *en banc*) (quoting 35 U.S.C. §103 (emphasis added by Judge Dyk). Although Judge Dyk quoted the AIA version of §103(a) (referring to "effective filing date" rather than the invention date), the pre-AIA version of the statute, 35 U.S.C. §103(a) (2006), was in effect in *Bristol-Myers Squibb.* The distinction makes no substantive difference to Judge Dyk's argument.

[300]Judge Dyk stressed that Supreme Court authority holds that "the pertinent knowledge is that possessed at the time of the invention." *Bristol-Myers Squibb III*, 769 F.3d at 1341 (Dyk, J., concurring in denial of reh'g *en banc*) (citing KSR Int'l Co. v. Teleflex Inc., 550 U.S. 398, 416 (2007) (focusing on "[w]hen Adams designed his battery" and noting that "[t]he fact that the elements worked together in an unexpected and fruitful manner supported the conclusion that Adams' design was not obvious to those skilled in the art") (citing United States v. Adams, 383 U.S. 39 (1966)); Ball & Socket Fastener Co. v. Kraetzer, 150 U.S. 111, 116-117 (1893) (discounting an advantage of a patented invention that "was not originally within the contemplation of the patentee, but is an afterthought")); citing also Genetics Inst., LLC v. Novartis Vaccines and Diagnostics, Inc., 655 F.3d 1291, 1315 (Fed. Cir. 2011) (Dyk, J., dissenting) (disagreeing with the majority's finding "that the later-discovered, undisclosed benefits of retaining the a3 region [i.e., a certain region of a recombinant Factor VIII protein] qualified as unexpected results to help defeat the prima facie case of obviousness, even though the role of the a3 region was not appreciated as of the Novartis patents' priority date. . . . The majority's finding of nonobviousness is based entirely on hindsight and happenstance, and not on what the inventors knew at the time the Novartis patents were filed.")).

[301]*Bristol-Myers Squibb III*, 769 F.3d at 1349 (Newman, J., dissenting in denial of reh'g *en banc*). Precedent cited by Judge Newman included *Sanofi-Aventis Deutschland GmbH v. Glenmark Pharm. Inc., USA*, 748 F.3d 1354, 1360 (Fed. Cir. 2014) (rejecting accused infringer/ANDA filer's argument that "later-discovered benefits cannot be considered in an obviousness analysis . . . referring to the improved kidney and blood vessel function that were observed after the patent application was filed"; holding that "patentability may consider all of the characteristics possessed by the claimed invention, whenever those characteristics become manifest."); *Leo Pharm. Prods., Ltd. v. Rea*, 726 F.3d 1346, 1358 (Fed. Cir. 2013) (in appeal of *inter partes* reexamination during which patentee had conducted tests of the prior art and showed that the reference formulations resulted in significant degradation of vitamin D analog and corticosteroid, stating that these post-invention test results of the prior were "a strong indication that the '013 patent [in suit']s combination of known elements yields more than just predictable results," and reversing Board's obviousness determination); *Genetics Inst., LLC v. Novartis Vaccines & Diagnostics, Inc.*, 655 F.3d 1291, 1307 (Fed. Cir. 2011) (stating that "it would be error to prohibit a patent applicant or patentee from presenting relevant indicia of nonobviousness, whether or not this evidence was available or expressly contemplated at the filing of the patent application."); *Knoll Pharm. Co., Inc. v. Teva*

'ma[de] the minor modification to arrive at entecavir'... while ignoring the unexpected differences in properties between entecavir and the prior art compound, conflicts with the entirety of precedent on the law of obviousness,"[302] Judge Newman declared.

Judge Newman observed that comparative data showing that a newly discovered product (or device or method) has properties not possessed by similar products is often used to demonstrate nonobviousness of the new product (e.g., data submitted in the form of a Rule 132 declaration to the USPTO[303]), and "[s]uch comparative data need not have been previously available or known to the art at the time of the invention."[304] She emphasized that the provision of comparative

---

Pharm. USA, Inc., 367 F.3d 1381, 1385 (Fed. Cir. 2004) (stating that "[t]here is no requirement that an invention's properties and advantages were fully known before the patent application was filed, or that the patent application contains all of the work done in studying the invention, in order for that work to be introduced into evidence in response to litigation attack. Nor is it improper to conduct additional experiments and provide later-obtained data in support of patent validity."); *In re Zenitz*, 333 F.2d 924, 925, 927 (C.C.P.A. 1964) (later discovered hypotensive and tranquilizing properties that were not described in the specification could render claimed compounds nonobvious and thus patentable).

Judge Newman further emphasized that "[t]he provision of comparative data, whether or not the data were available before the patent application was filed, is *long-established practice*." *Bristol-Myers Squibb III*, 769 F.3d at 1348-1349 (Newman, J., dissenting in denial of reh'g *en banc*) (emphasis added), as shown by several CCPA decisions:

> *In re Payne*, 606 F.2d at 315-16 ("A prima facie case of obviousness based on structural similarity is rebuttable by proof that the claimed compounds possess unexpectedly advantageous or superior properties. Direct or indirect comparative testing between the claimed compounds and the closest prior art may be necessary." (citing *In re Papesch*, 50 C.C.P.A. 1084, 315 F.2d 381, 386-87 (1963))); *In re Merchant*, 575 F.2d 865, 869 (C.C.P.A. 1978) ("An applicant relying upon a comparative showing to rebut a prima facie case must compare his claimed invention with the closest prior art."); *In re Miller*, 39 C.C.P.A. 979, 197 F.2d 340, 342 (1952) ("Where, as here, results superior to those produced by the references of the prior art, or public knowledge and use, constitute the basis for the claim of invention, the making of comparative tests and the establishment of the unexpected and superior results never before attained must be established by a proper showing.").

[302] *Bristol-Myers Squibb III*, 769 F.3d at 1347 (Newman, J., dissenting from denial of reh'g *en banc*).

[303] *See* 37 C.F.R. §1.132 ("Affidavits or declarations traversing rejections or objections").

[304] *Bristol-Myers Squibb III*, 769 F.3d at 1347 (Newman, J., dissenting from denial of reh'g *en banc* (citing, *inter alia,* Genetics Inst., LLC v. Novartis Vaccines & Diagnostics, Inc., 655 F.3d 1291, 1307 (Fed. Cir. 2011) ("[I]t would be error to prohibit a patent applicant or patentee from presenting relevant indicia of nonobviousness, whether or not this evidence was available or expressly contemplated at the filing of the patent application."); citing also Knoll Pharm. Co., Inc. v. Teva Pharm. USA, Inc., 367 F.3d 1381, 1385 (Fed. Cir. 2004)). The Federal Circuit in *Knoll Pharm.* stated:

> There is no requirement that an invention's properties and advantages were fully known before the patent application was filed, or that the patent application

data, whether or not available before a patent application was filed, is a "long-established practice."[305] Federal Circuit precedent held that "[i]nformation learned after the patent application was filed may provide evidence of unexpected or unpredicted properties."[306]

Judge Newman flatly rejected the *Bristol-Myers Squibb* panel's assertion that in *In re Dillon*, the Federal Circuit had (*en banc*) "explain[ed] that an unexpected result or property does not be itself support a finding of nonobviousness."[307] Joined by Judge Lourie (the author of *Dillon*) as well as Judge Reyna, Judge Newman responded that "[t]o the contrary, an unexpected result or property is the *touchstone* of nonobviousness."[308] She observed that not only had her colleagues "disregard[ed] the entirety of precedent and practice," but also that the "amici curiae protest the court's changes of law and understanding as confusing, unnecessary, and contrary to the public interest in development of useful and beneficial new products."[309] If, in the wake of the *Bristol-Myers Squibb* panel decision, there is now to be a "major restriction on the evidence that can be adduced in support of

---

> contains all of the work done in studying the invention, in order for that work to be introduced into evidence in response to litigation attack. Nor is it improper to conduct additional experiments and provide later-obtained data in support of patent validity.

Knoll Pharm., 367 F.3d at 1385.

[305] *Bristol-Myers Squibb III*, 769 F.3d at 1348-1349 (Newman, J., dissenting from denial of reh'g *en banc*).

[306] *Bristol-Myers Squibb III*, 769 F.3d at 1347 (Newman, J., dissenting from denial of reh'g *en banc*) (citing Sanofi-Aventis Deutschland GmbH v. Glenmark Pharm. Inc., USA, 748 F.3d 1354, 1360 (Fed. Cir. 2014)). The *Sanofi-Aventis* court stated:

> Glenmark also argues that later-discovered benefits cannot be considered in an obviousness analysis, here referring to the improved kidney and blood vessel function that were observed after the patent application was filed. That is incorrect; patentability may consider all of the characteristics possessed by the claimed invention, whenever those characteristics become manifest.

Sanofi-Aventis, 748 F.3d at 1360. Judge Newman also relied on *In re Zenitz*, 333 F.2d 924, 925, 927 (C.C.P.A. 1964) (later discovered hypotensive and tranquilizing properties that were not described in the specification could render the claimed compounds nonobvious and thus patentable).

[307] *Bristol-Myers Squibb II*, 752 F.3d at 976. *Dillon* is further examined *infra* Section J ("The *Prima Facie* Case of Obviousness").

[308] *Bristol-Myers Squibb III*, 769 F.3d at 1350 (Fed. Cir. 2014) (Newman, J., dissenting from denial of reh'g *en banc*) (emphasis added).

[309] *Bristol-Myers Squibb III*, 769 F.3d at 1349 (Fed. Cir. 2014) (Newman, J., dissenting from denial of reh'g *en banc*) (citing Brief of Amicus Biotechnology Industry Organization in Support of Rehearing *En Banc* at 7) (stating that "[t]he AIA's new first-to-file system puts pressure on companies to file early, lest they lose priority. But, under the panel's approach, innovators might be better off waiting, in case new, unexpected differences between the invention and prior art come to light during clinical testing. There is no reason to put innovators to that difficult choice.")).

patentability of new and improved products," Judge Newman urged that "such change of law should be determined *en banc*."[310]

Also dissenting from denial of rehearing *en banc*, Judge Taranto (joined by Judges Lourie and Reyna) illustrated the potential confusion created by the *Bristol-Myers Squibb* panel's decision:

> Although it is not certain, the panel, in what it actually decided in affirming invalidity for obviousness on the recited facts, may have dismissed postfiling discoveries of prior-art compounds' true properties as *categorically irrelevant* to the statutory inquiry. Or it may have more narrowly deemed *insufficient* the evidence here — that, the first time the prior-art compound was tested in animals, it proved so toxic that it had to be abandoned as a candidate for human-therapeutic use. *Even if the panel merely rejected the particular post-filing evidence here as insufficient, it is significant (for how the decision will be invoked as precedent) that the panel did not give any case-specific reasons for doing so except timing: the discovery of the prior-art compound's toxicity post-dated the invention.* The panel decision seems highly likely to be viewed as addressing the timing-of-evidence question — whether generally or in this context. And that question is worthy of further attention.[311]

With respect to the *Bristol-Myers Squibb* panel's statement about *Dillon* (i.e., that *Dillon* established that "an unexpected result or property does not by itself support a finding of nonobviousness"), Judge Taranto cautioned that the statement not be "read out of context." In his view, the panel did not mean to state or suggest that evidence of unexpected results cannot by itself support an *ultimate* finding that a patent challenger has failed to establish obviousness by clear and convincing evidence.[312] Rather, the panel made its statement about *Dillon* "only in discussing whether to uphold the determination about a key component of the traditional *prima facie* case in an obviousness challenge — that the hypothetical skilled artisan would have had not only a reason to create the new chemical compound (the claimed invention here) but also 'a reasonable expectation of success' concerning its favorable human-therapeutic profile."[313] Moreover, Judge Taranto explained, the Circuit's *en banc* decision in *Dillon* did "not establish that evidence of unexpected results cannot support rejection of an obviousness challenge despite supported findings of the elements

[310]*Bristol-Myers Squibb III*, 769 F.3d at 1349 (Newman, J., dissenting from denial of reh'g *en banc*).

[311]*Bristol-Myers Squibb III*, 769 F.3d at 1353 (Taranto, J., dissenting from denial of reh'g *en banc*) (emphasis added).

[312]*Bristol-Myers Squibb III*, 769 F.3d at 1354 (Taranto, J., dissenting from denial of reh'g *en banc*) (emphasis added).

[313]*Bristol-Myers Squibb III*, 769 F.3d at 1354 (Taranto, J., dissenting from denial of reh'g *en banc*) (citing *Bristol-Myers Squibb II*, 752 F.3d at 976-977).

of a *prima facie* case."[314] This was because in *Dillon*, as well as *Bristol-Myers Squibb*, the Federal Circuit concluded that there were *no* unexpected results; in *Dillon*, the Circuit affirmed the PTO's findings of no unexpected results; in the case at bar, the panel upheld the district court's determination that there were "no appreciable unexpected results." Thus, the *Bristol-Myers Squibb* panel did not need to consider (nor was it making statements about) the doctrinal relationship between a finding of unexpected results (because there were none) and a finding of the *prima facie* case elements.[315]

Judge Taranto emphasized that the *Bristol-Myers Squibb* panel's opinion "ultimately approve[d] the district court's decision to excise from its analysis any consideration of [the prior art compound] 2'-CDG's later-discovered, severe toxicity."[316] This timing-of-evidence question seemed to Judge Taranto to be "at the heart of the obviousness invalidation" and to "warrant further exploration."[317] He acknowledged that Judge Newman, in her opinion dissenting from denial of rehearing *en banc*, had "identifie[d] ways in which the panel's approach to the timing-of-evidence question seems in tension with this court's precedents."[318] And he explained that for practical reasons, determining the properties of a new chemical composition typically requires testing and observation that cannot occur until after the chemical is in hand, and "the statute has always provided an incentive to file early once the chemical is in hand" lest priority be lost.[319] The AIA only enhanced that incentive.

Judge Taranto disputed Judge Dyk's contention (in Judge Dyk's opinion concurring in denial of rehearing *en banc*) that the language of the statute, 35 U.S.C. §103, precluded consideration of post-invention date (or under the AIA, post-effective filing date) evidence. To the contrary, the statute's inquiry as to whether the claimed invention "as a whole" would have been obvious implicated later-discovered properties. As Judge Taranto explained, the doctrine of *In re Papesch* "has long treated all properties, including later discovered ones, as part of the invention 'as a whole.' "[320] Moreover, the "would have been

[314] *Bristol-Myers Squibb III*, 769 F.3d at 1354 (Taranto, J., dissenting from denial of reh'g *en banc*).

[315] *Bristol-Myers Squibb III*, 769 F.3d at 1354-1355 (Taranto, J., dissenting from denial of reh'g *en banc*).

[316] *Bristol-Myers Squibb III*, 769 F.3d at 1356 (Taranto, J., dissenting from denial of reh'g *en banc*).

[317] *Bristol-Myers Squibb III*, 769 F.3d at 1356 (Taranto, J., dissenting from denial of reh'g *en banc*).

[318] *Bristol-Myers Squibb III*, 769 F.3d at 1356 (Taranto, J., dissenting from denial of reh'g *en banc*).

[319] *Bristol-Myers Squibb III*, 769 F.3d at 1356-1357 (Taranto, J., dissenting from denial of reh'g *en banc*).

[320] *Bristol-Myers Squibb III*, 769 F.3d at 1357 (Taranto, J., dissenting from denial of reh'g *en banc*) (citing In re Papesch, 315 F.2d 381 (C.C.P.A. 1963)).

obvious" verb phrase of §103 grammatically invokes a hypothetical situation depending on some "if" condition; that is, "would have been obvious if 'x' had been true." But in §103, there is no "if" clause, Judge Taranto observed; the required condition is not stated. Thus, the statute requires courts to "fill in the conditions for the hypothetical inquiry by an analysis of the provision's history, role in the statute, and purpose, always considering workability of any approach."[321] The proper approach, whatever it may be, "must be developed by looking at more than the effective-date-of-filing (previously, invention-date) phrase in section 103, whose terms as a whole call for a hypothetical inquiry requiring judicial definition."[322]

As the above-described multiple characterizations, explanations, and diverging positions about the import of the panel's June 2014 decision illustrate, the *Bristol-Myers Squibb* decision raised many questions that merit further analysis and exploration. It remains to be seen whether later Federal Circuit panels will rely on the more questionable statements in *Bristol-Myers Squibb* as precedent, or instead simply limit the decision to its facts. Subsequent Federal Circuit decisions confronting the issue of nonobviousness must be closely tracked as the court clarifies this foundational aspect of patentability.

c. *Placement in* Graham *Framework*

Federal Circuit cases occasionally analyze evidence of "unexpected results" within the category of secondary considerations evidence under *Graham* factor (4),[323] which also includes commercial success, long-felt but unresolved need, failure of others, etc. In the view of this author, such categorization is analytically incorrect. Unexpected results relate to the technical nature and properties of the invention, as captured by *Graham* factors (1) through (3), rather than

[321] *Bristol-Myers Squibb III*, 769 F.3d at 1357 (Taranto, J., dissenting from denial of reh'g *en banc*).

[322] *Bristol-Myers Squibb III*, 769 F.3d at 1358 (Taranto, J., dissenting from denial of reh'g *en banc*).

[323] *See, e.g.*, Ethicon Endo-Surgery, Inc. v. Covidien LP, 812 F.3d 1023, 1034 (Fed. Cir. 2016) (stating that "[o]bviousness is a question of law based on underlying factual findings, including. . .(4) *secondary considerations of nonobviousness, such as* commercial success, long-felt but unmet needs, failure of others, and *unexpected results*") (citing KSR Int'l Co. v. Teleflex, Inc., 550 U.S. 398, 406 (2007); Graham v. John Deere Co., 383 U.S. 1, 17-18 (1966)) (emphasis added); In re Sullivan, 498 F.3d 1345, 1353 (Fed. Cir. 2007) (rejecting USPTO's "argument that the applicant for the first time on appeal argues *secondary considerations, such as unexpected results*, and therefore that the argument should be considered waived") (emphasis added); Pfizer, Inc. v. Apotex, Inc., 480 F.3d 1348, 1372 (Fed. Cir. 2007) (holding alternatively that "even if Pfizer showed that [the claimed] amlodipine besylate exhibits *unexpectedly superior results, this secondary consideration* does not overcome the strong showing of obviousness in this case") (emphasis added).

marketplace reaction to the invention as assessed by *Graham* secondary considerations factor (4). *Graham* factors (1)-(3) may be thought of as "direct" evidence on the question of obviousness; secondary considerations factor (4) evidence relies on a series of inferences to make predictions about obviousness (or lack thereof).[324]

More particularly, unexpected results should not be confused with the *Graham* factor (4) secondary consideration of commercial success, which, "even if unexpected, is not part of the 'unexpected results' inquiry."[325] "An unexpected result must arise from combining prior art elements; commercial success is a separate inquiry from unexpected results. . . ."[326]

J. The *Prima Facie* Case of Obviousness

Understanding how the USPTO examines patent application claims for compliance with the nonobviousness requirement mandates familiarity with the concept of a *prima facie* case of obviousness. The *prima facie* case is a rebuttable legal conclusion drawn by the agency that a claimed invention would have been obvious, generally based on the USPTO's findings on the first three *Graham* factors.[327] The *prima facie* case thus represents a rebuttable presumption of obviousness.

In response to the agency's assertion that a *prima facie* case of obviousness has been made out, a patent applicant may attempt to rebut it, for example, by arguing that the examiner has mischaracterized the teaching of the cited references; that the references teach away from the claimed invention;[328] that there is no teaching, suggestion, or motivation for a PHOSITA to have combined the references in the manner claimed;[329] or that the PHOSITA would not have had a reasonable expectation of success in so combining.[330] These types of

[324]Secondary considerations are considered in greater detail *supra* Section H ("*Graham* Factor: Secondary Considerations.")

[325]Media Tech. Licensing, LLC v. Upper Deck Co., 596 F.3d 1334, (Fed. Cir. 2010) (affirming district court's grant of summary judgment that patents in suit, directed to memorabilia cards such as baseball cards to which a piece of a baseball player's bat is adhered, were invalid for obviousness).

[326]*Media Tech.*, 596 F.3d at 1339.

[327]Recall from Section D.2, *supra*, that these factors are (1) the level of ordinary skill in the art; (2) the scope and content of the prior art; and (3) the differences between the claimed invention and the prior art.

[328]For further analysis of when the prior art "teaches away" from a claimed invention, *see supra* Section I.3.

[329]For further analysis of when there exists a reason that would have motived the PHOSITA to combine the teachings of multiple prior art references, *see supra* Section I.1.

[330]The "reasonable expectation of success" prong is part of the "motivation to combine" analysis when the teachings of multiple prior art references assertedly render

arguments directly challenge the establishment of a *prima facie* case by attacking the agency's findings on the "scope and content of the prior art" *Graham* factor. Alternatively, the patent applicant may attempt to rebut the USPTO's assertion of a *prima facie* case by submitting evidence of unexpectedly superior results achieved by the claimed invention, or "secondary considerations" evidence (e.g., commercial success or the failure of others) under the fourth and final *Graham* factor.[331] When the applicant comes forward with relevant rebuttal evidence in response to a *prima facie* case, the USPTO must consider that evidence.[332]

The concept of a *prima facie* case implicates burdens of production (i.e., going forward with evidence) as well as the ultimate burden of proof (i.e., persuasion) on the question of nonobviousness. As the CCPA explained in *In re Rinehart*:[333]

> The concept of rebuttable *prima facie* obviousness is well established.... It is not, however, a segmented concept. When *prima facie* obviousness is established and evidence is submitted in rebuttal, the decision-maker must start over. Though the burden of going forward to rebut the *prima facie* case remains with the applicant, the question of whether that burden has been successfully carried requires that the entire path to decision be retraced. An earlier decision should not, as it was here, be considered as set in concrete, and applicant's rebuttal evidence then be evaluated only on its knockdown ability. Analytical fixation on an earlier decision can tend to provide that decision with an undeservedly broadened umbrella effect. *Prima facie* obviousness is a legal conclusion, not a fact. Facts established by rebuttal evidence must be evaluated along with the facts on which the earlier conclusion was reached, not against the conclusion itself. Though the tribunal must begin anew, a final finding of obviousness may of course be reached, but such finding will rest upon evaluation of all facts

---

obvious a claimed invention. *See* Merck & Cie v. Gnosis S.p.A., 808 F.3d 829, 833 (Fed. Cir. 2015) (stating that "[i]f all elements of the claims are found in a combination of prior art references... the factfinder should further consider whether a person of ordinary skill in the art would be motivated to combine those references, *and whether in making that combination, a person of ordinary skill would have a reasonable expectation of success*") (emphasis added) (citing Medichem, S.A. v. Rolabo, S.L., 437 F.3d 1157, 1164 (Fed. Cir. 2006)). *See also supra* Section I.1.c ("Reasonable Expectation of Success").

[331]*See supra* Section H ("*Graham* Factor: Secondary Considerations").

[332]*See* In re Sullivan, 498 F.3d 1345, 1351-1353 (Fed. Cir. 2007) (agreeing that USPTO had established a *prima facie* case of obviousness, but reversing agency for its failure to consider applicant's rebuttal evidence of teaching away and unexpected results). In *Sullivan*, the unexpected result was the unexpected property and use of the claimed anti-venom composition to neutralize the lethality of rattlesnake venom while also reducing the adverse immune reactions of human patients to whom the composition was administered. *See id.* at 1353.

[333]531 F.2d 1048 (C.C.P.A. 1976).

in evidence, uninfluenced by any earlier conclusion reached by an earlier board upon a different record.[334]

In *In re Piasecki,*[335] the Federal Circuit relied on *Rinehart*'s teaching to criticize the USPTO's evidentiary procedure in a case involving the patentability of a lighter-than-air craft. With controls like a helicopter, the craft was useful for lifting very heavy loads. By giving insufficient or no weight to the patent applicants' "secondary considerations" evidence, the USPTO improperly shifted to the applicants the ultimate burden of proof (rather than merely the burden of production) on the issue of nonobviousness:

> In the case at bar appellants submitted extensive evidence of peer recognition, long-felt need, and commercial interest. Yet the Board's treatment of the rebuttal documents impels us to the conclusion that the Board did exactly that which *Rinehart* warns against: they viewed each piece of rebuttal evidence solely "on its knockdown ability." Under the Board's approach the *prima facie* case took on a life of its own, such that each fact presented in rebuttal, when it was evaluated at all, was evaluated against the conclusion itself rather than against the facts on which the conclusion was based. The *prima facie* case remained "set in concrete."[336]

The USPTO Board's error meant that the conclusion of obviousness flowing from it could not stand. Concluding that the totality of the applicants' rebuttal evidence carried "persuasive weight," the Federal Circuit accordingly reversed the Board's decision that the claimed invention would have been obvious.[337]

Although the invention in *Piasecki* involved an electromechanical device, the concept of a *prima facie* case is more routinely encountered in cases involving chemical and biotechnological inventions. *In re Dillon* is one of the foundational cases for understanding what constitutes a *prima facie* case in the chemical arts.[338] Patent applicant

[334] *Id.* at 1052 (citations omitted).

[335] 745 F.2d 1468 (Fed. Cir. 1984).

[336] *Id.* at 1473.

[337] *See id.* at 1475.

[338] *See* In re Dillon, 919 F.2d 688 (Fed. Cir. 1990) (*en banc*). The Federal Circuit was by no means writing on a clean slate in *Dillon*, however. More than 25 years earlier, the Federal Circuit's predecessor court rejected a more severe position then taken by the USPTO — that a chemical compound's properties and advantages were simply not relevant at all when its chemical structure was similar enough to prior art compounds so as to be considered obvious "beyond doubt" by chemists. *See* In re Papesch, 315 F.2d 381 (C.C.P.A. 1963) (Rich, J.). Rejecting this position, the *Papesch* court explained in a much-quoted passage that

> [f]rom the standpoint of patent law, a compound and all of its properties are inseparable; they are one and the same thing. The graphic formulae, the chemical

Dillon discovered that adding certain *tetra*-orthoester compounds (i.e., compounds having four orthoester groups attached to a central carbon atom) to hydrocarbon fuel compositions would reduce soot emission when the fuel burned. She claimed a composition comprising a hydrocarbon fuel plus a sufficient amount of the tetra-orthoester to reduce soot (i.e., particulate emissions) during combustion. A prior art patent to Sweeney described compositions of hydrocarbon fuels with *tri*-orthoesters, useful for a different purpose — scavenging water from the fuels. Another prior art patent, to Elliot, evidenced the equivalence of tri- and tetra-orthoesters as water scavengers in hydraulic (i.e., non-hydrocarbon) fluids.

The issue before the *en banc* Federal Circuit was whether the USPTO had properly established a *prima facie* case of obviousness when it rejected Dillon's claims in view of the prior art. Although the tetra-orthoesters in Dillon's claimed compositions were structurally similar to the tri-orthoesters in the prior art compositions, the latter compositions had a different use. Dillon's new use of the tetra-orthoesters for

---

> nomenclature, the systems of classification and study such as the concepts of homology, isomerism, etc., are mere symbols by which compounds can be identified, classified, and compared. But a formula is not a compound and while it may serve in a claim to identify what is being patented, as the metes and bounds of a deed identify a plot of land, the thing that is patented is not the formula but the compound identified by it. And the patentability of the thing does not depend on the similarity of its formula to that of another compound but of the similarity of the former compound to the latter. There is no basis in law for ignoring any property in making such a comparison. An assumed similarity based on a comparison of formulae must give way to evidence that the assumption is erroneous.

Id. at 391. In *Papesch*, the USPTO's obviousness rejection of claims to a novel chemical compound was grounded on the agency's finding that the compound was structurally similar to its lower homolog, which was in the prior art (i.e., the claimed and prior art compounds differed "only in that where appellant has three ethyl groups the prior art has three methyl groups"). *Id.* at 383. Although Papesch asserted in his patent application that his claimed compound had unexpectedly potent anti-inflammatory activity, and also submitted during prosecution an affidavit of test results showing that the claimed compound was an "active anti-inflammatory agent" whereas the prior art compound was "completely inactive" in reducing inflammation, the USPTO deemed this evidence irrelevant. According to the agency, evidence of a compound's properties should be considered only in cases where there existed some "doubt" as to obviousness. In the case at bar, the USPTO contended, the claimed compound was obvious "without a shadow of a doubt" based on its structural similarity with the prior art. *Id.* at 385-386.

The CCPA disagreed. Reviewing a long line of chemical patent precedents, the CCPA concluded that "[p]atentability has not been determined on the basis of the obviousness of structure alone." *Id.* at 391. The Board was wrong to conclude that a showing of properties should be used "only to resolve doubt." *Id.* In other words, structural similarity with the prior art creates only a *presumption* of obviousness. *See id.* (observing that "presumption is all we have here"). A chemical compound must be viewed, "realistically and legally, [as] a composite of both structure and properties." *Id.* at 392. The Board's failure to consider Papesch's evidence of the anti-inflammatory property of his claimed compound was "contrary to well established law" and thus justified reversal. *Id.* at 392.

the purpose of reducing soot (i.e., particulate emissions) was not shown or suggested by the prior art.[339]

After a panel of the court reversed the USPTO,[340] the Federal Circuit reheard the case *en banc* and affirmed the USPTO's rejection of Dillon's claims for obviousness. The USPTO had properly established a *prima facie* case of obviousness based on the chemical structural similarity between Dillon's compositions and the prior art compositions. Even though "all evidence of the properties of the claimed compositions and the prior art must be considered in determining the ultimate question of patentability," the *en banc* Federal Circuit emphasized that "the discovery that a claimed composition possesses a property not disclosed for the prior art subject matter [] does not by itself defeat a *prima facie* case."[341] In other words, it was "not necessary in order to establish a *prima facie* case of obviousness that both a structural similarity . . . be shown and that there be a suggestion . . . from the *prior art* that the claimed compound or composition will have the same or a similar utility *as one newly discovered by applicant*."[342] While the prior art did not suggest Dillon's newly discovered use, the Federal Circuit pointed out that her composition claims were not limited to that use.[343]

A *prima facie* case having been properly established by the USPTO, the burden (and opportunity) to rebut it then shifted to applicant Dillon. Such rebuttal might have included, *inter alia*, comparative test data showing that the claimed composition had unexpectedly improved properties compared to the prior art compositions, or that it possessed properties that the prior art lacked.[344] Dillon did not present such data. The Federal Circuit agreed with the Board's finding that Dillon had made "no showing . . . of unexpected results for the claimed compositions compared with the compositions of [the prior art reference] Sweeney."[345] Nor did Dillon "show that the prior art compositions and use were so lacking in significance that there was no motivation for others to make obvious variants."[346] In fact, Dillon's own patent application included data showing that tri- and

[339]*See Dillon*, 919 F.2d at 691.

[340]*See id.* at 690 n.1.

[341]*Id.* at 693.

[342]*Id.* (emphases in original).

[343]*See id.* at 693-694 (stating that the recitation in Dillon's composition claims "that the amount of orthoester must be sufficient to reduce particulate emissions is not a distinguishing limitation of the claims, unless the amount is different from the prior art and critical to the use of the claimed composition"); *id.* at 694 n.4 (pointing out that Dillon's composition claims were "not structurally or physically distinguishable from the prior art compositions by virtue of the recitation of their newly-discovered use").

[344]*See id.* (enumerating the types of evidence and/or arguments that can be used in attempting to rebut a *prima facie* case).

[345]*Id.* at 694.

[346]*Id.*

tetra-orthoesters were equally active in reducing particulate emissions.[347] Having concluded that Dillon had failed to rebut the *prima facie* case of obviousness, the Federal Circuit affirmed the USPTO's rejection of her claims.

As *Dillon* illustrates, the concept of a *prima facie* case is often central to patent disputes involving chemical subject matter (although it is not limited to any particular subject matter, viz., *Piasecki*). A line of Federal Circuit decisions considers whether a *prima facie* case of obviousness has been established when a patentee developed a claimed chemical compound by selecting and then modifying an existing "lead compound" rather than synthesizing the claimed compound "from scratch."

For example, the patent in suit in *Otsuka Pharm. Co., Ltd. v. Sandoz, Inc.*[348] claimed the chemical compound aripiprazole, which is the active ingredient in a very commercially successful drug product for the treatment of the mental disorder schizophrenia. Aripiprazole is a "carbostyril derivative" having a chemical structure different from all other "atypical antipsychotics" approved by the Food and Drug Administration.[349] Affirming a district court, the Federal Circuit sustained the Otsuka patent's validity against an obviousness challenge by applicants to the Food and Drug Administration for approval to market a generic equivalent of Otsuka's drug product. In affirming the district court's judgment that the claimed aripiprazole would not have been obvious under §103, the Federal Circuit explained that whether a new chemical compound would have been *prima facie* obvious over particular prior art chemical compounds "ordinarily follows a two-part inquiry." First, a district court "determines whether a chemist of ordinary skill would have selected the asserted prior art compounds as *lead compounds*, or starting points, for further development efforts."[350] This step of the analysis focuses on the lead compounds proposed by the validity challenger as those that a person

[347]The Federal Circuit rejected Dillon's charge that the USPTO had improperly used her own showing of equivalence against her. Rather, in relying on the data in Dillon's application the USPTO was "simply pointing out that [Dillon] did not or apparently could not make a showing of superiority" for her claimed tetra-ester compositions over the tri-ester compositions of the prior art. *See id.*

[348]678 F.3d 1280 (Fed. Cir. 2012).

[349]*See Otsuka,* 678 F.3d at 1284 (explaining that "[e]very FDA-approved atypical antipsychotic has a chemical structure related either to clozapine or risperidone, with the sole exception of aripiprazole — the compound at issue in the present appeal"). A "typical antipsychotic" treats positive but not negative symptoms and involves a number of problematic side effects, although typical antipsychotics are still administered today. *Id.* In contrast, an "atypical antipsychotic" is useful for treating both positive and negative symptoms of schizophrenia and has a diminished propensity to cause problematic "extrapyramidal symptoms." *Id.* The claimed compound aripiprazole is an atypical antipsychotic. *Id.*

[350]*Otsuka*, 678 F.3d at 1291 (emphasis added).

of ordinary skill in the art "would have had a reason to select from the panoply of known compounds in the prior art." Considerations in the selection of a lead compound include a prior art compound's properties such as activity, potency, and toxicity. Absent a motivation to modify the prior art compound based on this type of evidence, "mere structural similarity between a prior art compound and the claimed compound does not inform the lead compound selection."[351]

In the second step of the two-part inquiry, the district court must analyze "whether the prior art would have supplied one of ordinary skill in the art with a reason or motivation to modify [the] lead compound[s] to make the claimed compound with a reasonable expectation of success."[352] The validity challenger must establish " 'some reason that would have led a chemist to modify a known compound in a particular manner to establish *prima facie* obviousness of a new claimed compound.' "[353] In keeping with the Supreme Court's teachings in *KSR v. Teleflex* (discussed *supra*), "the reason or motivation for modifying a lead compound may come from any number of sources and need not necessarily be explicit in the prior art."[354]

Turning to the merits in *Otsuka*, the Federal Circuit held that the district court correctly rejected the validity challengers' three proposed lead compounds as those that a skilled artisan would have selected for further investigation and modification.[355] Rather, two other prior art compounds (clozapine and risperidone) were the only promising compounds available when the inventors of the claimed compound aripiprazole began their work. But the inventors did not select these two compounds. Importantly, the carbostyril compounds that the inventors actually selected for further research and modification were *not* plausible lead compounds at that time. The selected carbostyril compounds were not marketed as antipsychotics or publicly known to have potent antipsychotic activity with minimal side effects — primary goals of the inventors' effort. Thus, the district court correctly held that the validity challengers failed to prove by clear and convincing evidence that the claims of the Otsuka patent in suit would

[351]*Otsuka*, 678 F.3d at 1292.

[352]*Otsuka*, 678 F.3d at 1292.

[353]*Otsuka*, 678 F.3d at 1292 (quoting Takeda Chem. Indus., Ltd. v. Alphapharm Pty., Ltd., 492 F.3d 1350, 1357 (Fed. Cir. 2007)).

[354]*Otsuka*, 678 F.3d at 1292.

[355]The validity challengers (accused technical infringers) proposed three "lead compounds":

(1) 7-[4-(4-phenylpiperazinyl)-butoxy]-3,4-dihydrocarbostyril, referred to by the parties as the "unsubstituted butoxy";

(2) 7-[3-[4-(2,3-dichlorophenyl)-1-piperazinyl]-propoxy]3,4-dihydrocarbostyril, referred to by the parties as the "2,3-dichloro propoxy"; and (3) a compound termed "OPC-4392," a carbostyril derivative having a 2,3-dimethyl substituted phenyl ring, a propoxy linker, and a carbostyril ring containing a double bond at the 3,4-position. *See Otsuka,* 678 F.3d at 1286-1289.

have been *prima facie* obvious over the prior art compounds asserted by the validity challengers as lead compounds. In unusually frank wording, the Federal Circuit commended the district court's "careful analysis" for "expos[ing] the Defendants' obviousness case for what it was — a poster child for impermissible hindsight reasoning."[356]

K. Federal Circuit Standards of Review in §103 Determinations[357]

The Federal Circuit reviews determinations under 35 U.S.C. §103 made by the USPTO in the context of *ex parte* examination of patent applications; by the USPTO's Patent Trial and Appeal Board (PTAB) in conducting AIA-implemented *inter partes* reviews (IPRs) and post-grant reviews (PGRs) of issued patents;[358] and in federal district court litigation challenging the validity of issued patents. Although ultimately a question of law, the nonobviousness determination of §103 must be based on underlying findings of fact.[359] The Federal Circuit has different standards of review for these factual findings depending on which entity made them.

1. USPTO

The Federal Circuit hears appeals from obviousness rejections of pending patent applications made by the USPTO. The Circuit is required to give the USPTO considerable deference when the agency makes properly supported factual findings on the *Graham* factors.[360]

[356]*Otsuka*, 678 F.3d at 1296.

[357]For a thorough compendium of all Federal Circuit patent-related standards of review, see Lawrence M. Sung, *Echoes of Scientific Truth in the Halls of Justice: The Standards of Review Applied by the U.S. Court of Appeals for the Federal Circuit in Patent-Related Matters,* 48 Am. U. L. Rev. 1233 (1999).

[358]The AIA-implemented *inter partes* review (IPR) proceeding has been available since September 16, 2012 for challenging any issued patent via an adjudicative proceeding within the USPTO. A second AIA-implemented proceeding for challenging issued patents, post-grant review (PGR), is available only for AIA patents (i.e., those having effective filing dates on or after March 16, 2013) and is just coming on line as of this writing in 2019. For more details on IPR and PGR proceedings, both of which can involve the issue of obviousness, *see infra* Chapter 8, Section E.

[359]*See* Graham v. John Deere Co., 383 U.S. 1, 17-18 (1966).

[360]The Federal Circuit similarly gives considerable deference to the agency's findings concerning whether there existed a motivation or reason for a person of ordinary skill to combine the teachings of prior art references. *See* In re Suong-Hyu Hyon, 679 F.3d 1363, 1365-1366 (Fed. Cir. 2012) (affirming rejection of all claims of Hyon's reissue application because USPTO Board's findings concerning motivation to combine were supported by substantial evidence).

In accordance with the judicial review provisions of the Administrative Procedure Act, such USPTO findings may be overturned by the Federal Circuit only if "unsupported by substantial evidence."[361] The *substantial evidence* standard, a term of art in administrative law, asks whether a reasonable fact finder could have arrived at the agency's decision.[362] If he or she could have, then the agency's finding will be upheld. The fact that the record contains evidence going both ways on a particular issue is not sufficient to overturn the agency's finding.[363]

As of 2015-2016, the Federal Circuit began to decide a rapidly growing number of appeals from final written decisions of the PTAB in IPRs. The primary patentability issue in most of these appeals is obviousness. Even though the IPR proceeding is adjudicative rather than examinational, and no jury is involved, the Circuit has determined that findings of fact made by the PTAB in determining the ultimate legal question of obviousness are to be given considerable deference — they stand if supported by "substantial evidence." Thus the PTAB's fact findings in IPRs are given the same, significant degree of deference as are the fact findings made by the USPTO in *ex parte* examination and by juries in court litigation concerning obviousness.[364] Notably, Circuit Judge Newman has challenged as contrary to Congress's intent in enacting the AIA the Circuit's application of the deferential "substantial evidence" standard on review of fact findings in IPR decisions,[365] but as of this writing in 2019, application of

[361]*See* In re Gartside, 203 F.3d 1305, 1315 (Fed. Cir. 2000) (applying substantial evidence standard of review, 5 U.S.C. §706(2)(E), to USPTO patentability fact findings).

[362]*Id.* at 1312.

[363]*See* Consolo v. Fed. Mar. Comm'n, 383 U.S. 607, 620 (1966) (stating that "the possibility of drawing two inconsistent conclusions from the evidence does not prevent an administrative agency's finding from being supported by substantial evidence").

[364]*See, e.g.*, In re Cuozzo Speed Techs., LLC, 793 F.3d 1268, 1280 (Fed. Cir. 2015) (reviewing PTAB's decision in an IPR that held challenged claims unpatentable for obviousness, stating that "[w]e review the Board's factual findings for substantial evidence and review its legal conclusions de novo") (citing In re Baxter Int'l, Inc., 678 F.3d 1357, 1361 (Fed. Cir. 2012)), *cert. granted on other grounds sub nom.* Cuozzo Speed Techs., LLC v. Lee, 136 S. Ct. 890 (2016). "The ultimate determination of obviousness under §103 is a question of law based on underlying factual findings. . . . What a reference teaches and the differences between the claimed invention and the prior art are questions of fact which we review for substantial evidence." *Cuozzo*, 793 F.3d at 1280 (citations omitted).

[365]*See* Merck & Cie v. Gnosis S.p.A., 808 F.3d 829 (Fed. Cir. 2015) (Newman, J., dissenting), stating that

> [a]nother important aspect of the America Invents Act is the provision for finality and estoppel after the PTAB decision and any appeal to the Federal Circuit. The Act does not permit subsequent review of the PTAB's validity/invalidity decision in any other tribunal, whether by appeal or direct review or as a defense or offense in litigation. . . . This change from present law was long-debated, and is directed to the goals of correctness, uniformity, finality, and expedition.

Thus it is incorrect for this court, as the only reviewing tribunal, to review the PTAB decision under the highly deferential "substantial evidence" standard. Our obligation is to assure that the legislative purpose is met, through application of the statute in accordance with its purpose. . . . This court's resort to deferential "substantial evidence" review is at odds with the benefits that Congress intended.

The substantial evidence standard determines whether the decision could reasonably have been made, not whether it was correctly made. . . . The substantial evidence standard originated with appeals of jury verdicts, in recognition of the role of credibility at trial. . . ."Substantial evidence" was incorporated into the Administrative Procedure Act in recognition of the expertise of specialized agencies. . . . Here, however, a new system was created to respond to the belief that the agency was making mistakes. *See, e.g.*, 157 CONG. REC. S1326 (daily ed. Mar. 7, 2011) (statement of Sen. Sessions) ("This will allow invalid patents that were mistakenly issued by the PTO to be fixed early in their life, before they disrupt an entire industry or result in expensive litigation."); 153 Cong. Rec. H10276 (daily ed. Sept. 7, 2007) (statement of Rep. Goodlatte, commenting on a predecessor bill to the AIA) ("The PTO, like any other large government agency, makes mistakes. H.R. 1908 creates a post-grant opposition procedure to allow the private sector to challenge a patent just after it is approved to provide an additional check on the issuance of bogus patents."). This new system is directed at correcting mistakes. Deferential review by the Federal Circuit falls short of the legislative purpose of providing optimum determination of patent validity.

The Federal Circuit is the only review body for these new agency proceedings, for the America Invents Act displaced the alternative path of challenge to PTO decisions in the district court. Thus the PTAB's adjudications must be reviewed for correct application of the standard of proof established by the America Invents Act. In 35 U.S.C. §316(e):

> In an *inter partes* review instituted under this chapter, the petitioner shall have the burden of proving a proposition of unpatentability by a preponderance of the evidence.

On appeal to the Federal Circuit, our assignment is to determine whether the PTAB ruling is correct in law and supported by a preponderance of the evidence. The panel majority errs in importing into these proceedings the Administrative Procedure Act [APA] standard that applies to initial patent examination decisions, Maj. Op. at 833-34, citing *In re Gartside*, 203 F.3d 1305, 1313 (Fed. Cir. 2000) (PTO decisions sustained if supported by substantial evidence).

Appellate review of agency rulings on the preponderance standard, accompanied by finality, is not the general APA rule, but has been adopted by statute in other special situations. For example, under the Service Contract Act, "[i]f supported by a preponderance of the evidence, the [agency's] findings are conclusive in any court of the United States." 41 U.S.C. §6507(e) (formerly 41 U.S.C. §39). The regional circuits have interpreted the preponderance standard to require review for "clear error" on appeal. *See Dantran, Inc. v. U.S. Dep't of Labor*, 171 F.3d 58, 71 (1st Cir. 1999) (rejecting "substantial evidence" review standard); *see also Amcor, Inc. v. Brock*, 780 F.2d 897, 901 (11th Cir. 1986) ("determination by the administrator . . . must be affirmed unless it is not supported by a preponderance of the evidence.").

Such close appellate scrutiny is critical to the legislative balance of the America Invents Act, whose purpose is to reach an expeditious and reliable determination on which inventors and industry innovators and competitors can rely. The Federal Circuit's adoption of deferential "substantial evidence" review strays from this purpose. If Congress intended that deferential review would apply to PTAB determinations in which "substantial evidence" is "something less than

the substantial evidence standard remains the governing Federal Circuit law.

2. Federal District Court

The Federal Circuit also encounters obviousness when it hears appeals from federal district court decisions on the validity of issued patents. When the Circuit reviews patentability fact findings made by a federal district court sitting without a jury, the standard of review is the clearly erroneous standard of Fed. R. Civ. P. 52. The Federal Circuit will overturn a fact finding under the clearly erroneous standard only if on the entire evidence it is left with a "definite and firm conviction that a mistake [was] committed."[366] The clearly erroneous standard of review is seen as somewhat less deferential to the fact finder than the substantial evidence standard discussed above.

Juries can render a verdict on the ultimate legal question of nonobviousness, provided they are properly instructed on the law (i.e., the *Graham* factors).[367] If a post-trial motion for judgment as a matter of law (JMOL) is filed by the losing party, patentability fact findings presumably reached[368] by the jury in the course of determining the ultimate question of nonobviousness must be reviewed under the deferential substantial evidence standard.[369] The jury's factual findings only can be vacated if no reasonable jury could have made the findings based on the evidence of record.[370] "When the jury is supplied with sufficient valid factual information to support the verdict it reaches, that is the end of the matter. In such an instance, the jury's factual conclusions may not be set aside by a JMOL order."[371] Thus, findings of fact by a jury (like those of the PTAB deciding IPRs and PGRs) are (at least in theory) more difficult to set aside than those made by the district court in a bench trial.[372]

---

the weight of the evidence," *Consolo v. Fed. Mar. Comm'n,* 383 U.S. 607, 620, 86 S. Ct. 1018, 16 L. Ed. 2d 131 (1966), explicit assignment of this standard would reasonably have been expected.

Merck & Cie, 808 F.3d at 840-842 (Newman, J., dissenting) (citations omitted).

[366]Ruiz v. A.B. Chance Co., 234 F.3d 654, 663 (Fed. Cir. 2000).

[367]*See* R.R. Dynamics, Inc. v. A. Stucki Co., 727 F.2d 1506, 1514-1515 (Fed. Cir. 1984).

[368]In the absence of specific interrogatories, the jury is presumed to have found disputed factual issues in favor of the verdict winner. Newell Cos. v. Kenney Mfg. Co., 864 F.2d 757, 767 (Fed. Cir. 1988).

[369]*See* Teleflex, Inc. v. Ficosa N. Am. Corp., 299 F.3d 1313, 1333-1335 (Fed. Cir. 2002).

[370]*See id.* at 1335.

[371]McGinley v. Franklin Sports, Inc., 262 F.3d 1339, 1355 (Fed. Cir. 2001).

[372]*See* Structural Rubber Prods. Co. v. Park Rubber Co., 749 F.2d 707, 719 (Fed. Cir. 1984) (noting that "[o]n appeal . . . [f]indings of fact by the jury are more difficult to set aside (being reviewed only for reasonableness under the substantial evidence test) than those of a trial judge (to which the clearly erroneous rule applies)").

Chapter 6

The Utility Requirement (35 U.S.C. §101)

A. Introduction

United States patent law protects inventions that are novel, nonobvious, and *useful*. In "patent-speak," a useful invention is one that possesses **utility**. This chapter explores the utility requirement, which has its genesis in the constitutional goal of promoting the progress of the "*useful* arts."[1] Although the utility requirement is statutorily implemented through the mandate of 35 U.S.C. §101 that patentable inventions must be (among other things) "new and *useful*,"[2] the statute does not define what useful (or utility) means. Case law fills this gap.

In contrast with the novelty[3] and nonobviousness[4] requirements discussed in earlier chapters of this text, the substantive threshold for satisfying the utility requirement is relatively low.[5] The great majority of inventions are never challenged as lacking utility. The utility disputes that do arise tend to involve inventions in the chemical and biotechnological arts. For example, satisfaction of the utility requirement is a central issue in the controversy over patenting of genetic fragments known as ESTs (expressed sequence tags), discussed below.

B. Practical/Real-World Utility

United States patent law requires that patentable inventions possess "practical utility."[6] In other words, to be patentable, an invention

[1]U.S. CONST., art. I, §8, cl. 8 (emphasis added).

[2]35 U.S.C. §101 (2012) (emphasis added).

[3]*See* Chapter 4 ("Novelty, Loss of Right, and Priority Pre- and Post-America Invents Act of 2011 (35 U.S.C. §102)"), *supra*.

[4]*See* Chapter 5 ("The Nonobviousness Requirement (35 U.S.C. §103)"), *supra*.

[5]*See* Juicy Whip, Inc. v. Orange Bang, Inc., 185 F.3d 1364, 1366 (Fed. Cir. 1999) (stating that "[t]he threshold of utility is not high: An invention is useful under section 101 if it is capable of providing some identifiable benefit.").

[6]In re Brana, 51 F.3d 1560, 1564 (Fed. Cir. 1995).

must have some real-world use. "Practical" use does not necessarily mean "significant" or "extensive," however. Even a chemical intermediate, which exists only for an instant of time when it is produced during the course of a chemical reaction, is useful because it is a tool that allows researchers to develop other chemicals that have useful therapeutic properties.[7]

Utility is rarely at issue for mechanical or electrical inventions; even novelty items, games, or toys that might be considered trivial or frivolous can satisfy the utility requirement. For example, the drawings from an issued utility patent directed to a hat in the shape of a fried egg are depicted in Figure 6.1. Perhaps anticipating some question as to its usefulness, the written description of the patent affirms that the hat "finds utility, for example, as an attention-getting item in connection with promotional activities at trade shows, conventions, and the like." This is more than sufficient to satisfy the utility requirement of 35 U.S.C. §101.

Why is the utility threshold relatively low, that is, relatively easy to meet? If an invention does not offer much in the way of usefulness to society, the costs temporarily borne by the public because that invention is protected by patent will not be excessive. Inventions that are

[7] *See* In re Nelson, 280 F.2d 172 (C.C.P.A. 1960) (reversing USPTO's rejection of claimed steroid intermediates as lacking utility under §101). The *Nelson* court considered the practical utility of the chemicals in the following manner:

> The Patent Office position seems to have been that there must be a presently existing "practical" usefulness to some undefined class of persons. We have never received a clear answer to the question "Useful to whom and for what?" Surely a new group of steroid intermediates is *useful to chemists doing research* on steroids, and in a "practical" sense too. Such intermediates are "useful" under section 101. They are often actually placed on the market before much, if anything, is known as to what they are "good" for, other than experimentation and the making of other compounds in the important field of research. *Refusal to protect them at this stage would inhibit their wide dissemination, together with the knowledge of them which a patent disclosure conveys, which disclosure the potential protection encourages. This would tend to retard rather than promote progress.*
>
> The new androstenes, being *useful to research chemists* for the purposes disclosed by appellants, are clearly useful to society and their invention contributes to the progress of an art which is of great potential usefulness to mankind. They are new steroids which in known ways can be made into other steroids, thus furthering the development of this useful art.
>
> We conclude that the claimed compounds are "useful" within the meaning of section 101. . . .

Id. at 180-181 (emphasis added in last sentence of first quoted paragraph; other emphases in original).

The Supreme Court later characterized *Nelson* as the start of a CCPA "trend" toward a more liberal interpretation of patent utility in *Brenner v. Manson*, 383 U.S. 519, 530 (1966), discussed later in this chapter. The Court did not, however, state that it was overruling *Nelson*, and the facts of *Manson* are clearly distinguishable from those of *Nelson*.

US005457821A

United States Patent [19]

Kiefer

[11] **Patent Number: 5,457,821**

[45] **Date of Patent: Oct. 17, 1995**

[54] **HAT SIMULATING A FRIED EGG**

[76] Inventor: **Raymond D. Kiefer**, 105 Shady La., Spring City, Pa. 19475

[21] Appl. No.: **199,950**

[22] Filed: **Feb. 22, 1994**

[51] **Int. Cl.**^{6} **A42B 1/00**

[52] **U.S. Cl.** **2/195.1**; 2/171; 2/195.2; D2/872

[58] **Field of Search** 2/171, 175.1, 195.1, 2/195.2, 195.3, 195.4; D2/865, 869, 872, 873, 874, 876, 879, 882, 884, 886, 893

[56] **References Cited**

U.S. PATENT DOCUMENTS

D. 170,061 7/1953 Maxwell et al. D2/886

D. 267,285 12/1982 Lipschutz D2/872

FOREIGN PATENT DOCUMENTS

292451 6/1928 United Kingdom 2/195.3

Primary Examiner—Diana Biefeld

Attorney, Agent, or Firm—Frederick J. Olsson

[57] **ABSTRACT**

A novelty hat in the form of a baseball cap has a yellow colored dome shaped top and a white colored brim, the outer periphery of which is irregular and part of which projects outwardly to form a visor. On the head of the wearer the hat makes the visual impression of a fried egg.

2 Claims, 2 Drawing Sheets

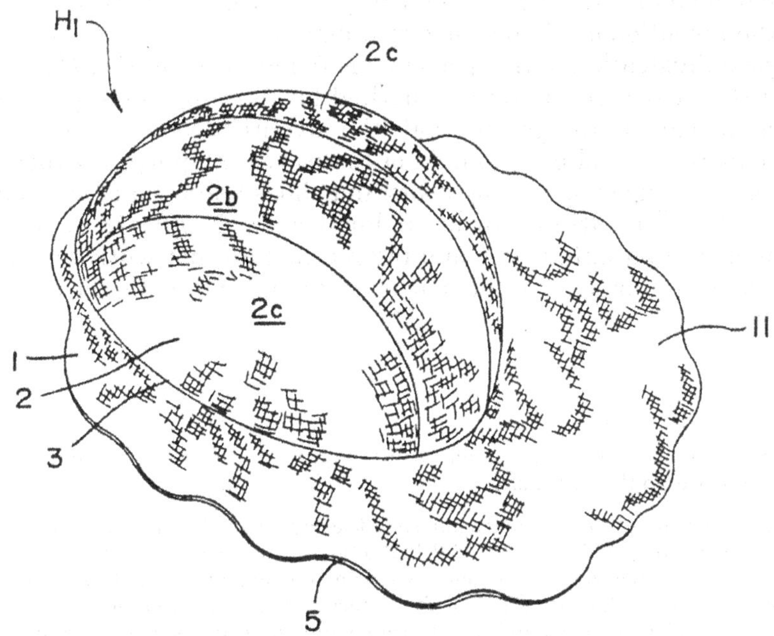

Figure 6.1

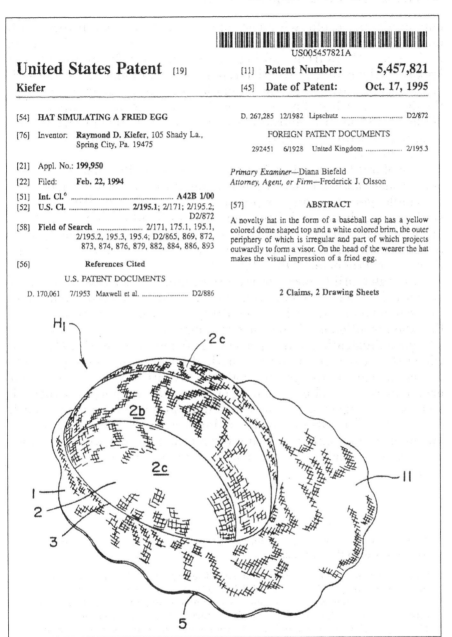

Hat in the Shape of a Fried Egg
U.S. Patent No. 5,457,821 (Issued Oct. 17, 1995)

only minimally useful will most likely be made or sold in very small quantities, either by the patentee or copyists. The patentee's right to exclude all others from making, using, selling, offering to sell, and importing the claimed invention represents a minimal burden on society in this scenario. Thus, the patent law does not attempt to evaluate the degree of utility of an invention, beyond some *de minimis* threshold level. Rather, the marketplace decides which inventions are the most useful, through the price the inventor can command for her patented product.[8]

Lack of utility is rarely raised as a basis for challenging the validity of an issued patent. Practically speaking, if the accused infringer (i.e., the challenger of validity) is producing a copy of an invention that is similar enough to spark litigation, this in itself evidences that the invention has a practical utility. Instead, utility disputes usually arise in the context of *ex parte* patent examination in the United States Patent and Trademark Office (USPTO).

Patentable utility does not require commercial success in the marketplace. Nor does it require that an invention work better than those that came before it. Rather, the utility requirement simply ensures that the invention *works* on some minimal level.

A good illustration of this principle is found in *Bedford v. Hunt,*[9] in which the utility of a patented method for making shoes and boots was challenged on the ground that "the invention was not useful; but upon experience had been found not to answer the purpose expected, and that this mode of making boots and shoes had been of late much laid aside."[10] In other words, at least according to the accused infringer, the patented boot-making method did not work very well and was not being used in the marketplace (other than by the accused infringer!).

[8]This pragmatic view of the patent utility requirement was expressed in a now-classic dissent from the CCPA era:

> It has been pointed out time and again since the days of Justice Story, as fully discussed in *Nelson* [280 F.2d 172 (C.C.P.A. 1960)], that degree of utility is of no public concern whatsoever. This elementary principle appears not to have gotten through to those who still talk of utility in terms of "*quid pro quo*" for a patent. The only *quid pro quo* demanded by statute is full disclosure of a new and unobvious invention which is of some use to someone. If it is of very little use, the patent will correspondingly be of very little value to the patentee, who has never been called on either to know or to explain all potential uses of his invention. The hard fact is he almost never knows the full extent of the utility until years after he makes his invention. Uses evolve after inventions are disclosed.

In re Kirk, 376 F.2d 936, 955 (C.C.P.A. 1967) (Rich, J., dissenting).

[9]3 F. Cas. 37 (C.C. Mass. 1817) (No. 1,217).

[10]*Id.* at 37.

The noted patent jurist Joseph Story refused to invalidate the patent as lacking utility. Story rejected the notion that the patent law is concerned with the *degree* of utility of an invention:

> By useful invention, in the statute, is meant such a one as may be applied to some beneficial use in society, in contradistinction to an invention, which is injurious to the morals, the health, or the good order of society. It is not necessary to establish, that the invention is of such general utility, as to supersede all other inventions now in practice to accomplish the same purpose. It is sufficient, that it has no obnoxious or mischievous tendency, that it may be applied to practical uses, and that so far as it is applied, it is salutary. If its practical utility be very limited, it will follow, that it will be of little or no profit to the inventor; and if it be trifling, it will sink into utter neglect. *The law, however, does not look to the degree of utility; it simply requires, that it shall be capable of use,* and that the use is such as sound morals and policy do not discountenance or prohibit.[11]

Story's view of utility shaped U.S. patent law. We do not look to how useful an invention is, but simply require that it have some practical use to society.

C. The Supreme Court View

1. *Brenner v. Manson* (1966)

The U.S. Supreme Court most recently addressed the requirement of patentable utility in the 1966 decision *Brenner v. Manson.*[12] The controversial *Manson* decision arguably represents the high-water mark for what is required to satisfy 35 U.S.C. §101.[13]

[11] *Id.* (emphasis added).

[12] 383 U.S. 519 (1966).

[13] There is considerable basis for criticism of *Brenner v. Manson*. The Supreme Court's majority opinion evidences a fundamental misconception of the role of patent claims. The opinion's critical reference to the "highly developed art of drafting patent claims so that they disclose as little useful information as possible," *Manson*, 383 U.S. at 534, is misguided because it is not the role of patent claims to "disclose . . . useful information." Patent claims set forth the literal boundaries of the patentee's right to exclude others. Disclosure is found in the written description, which must be enabling and reveal the best mode in accordance with 35 U.S.C. §112(a) (eff. Sept. 16, 2012). The *Manson* majority opinion also mistakenly contends that, until a chemical process has been developed to the point where it produces a product having an identifiable utility, "the metes and bounds of that monopoly are not capable of precise delineation." *Id.* at 534. Determination of whether the claims of a patent, which define the "metes and bounds" of the patentee's right to exclude, are sufficiently definite occurs under 35 U.S.C. §112(b) (eff. Sept. 16, 2012), and is not a function of the utility requirement of

The patent applicant, Manson, claimed a new process for making a known steroid, a type of chemical compound. Manson asserted that his process had utility because the steroid it produced was being screened for tumor-inhibiting effects in mice, and the next adjacent homologue[14] of the steroid had already been shown to work for that purpose.

Reversing the Court of Customs and Patent Appeals (CCPA), the Supreme Court held that the claimed process did not satisfy the utility requirement of 35 U.S.C. §101. It viewed Manson's research in steroid chemistry, which it deemed an unpredictable art, as being at too preliminary a stage to merit patent protection, noting that "a patent is not a hunting license" and "not a reward for the search, but compensation for its successful conclusion."[15] Rather, the Court explained, what is required for patentability is "substantial utility." This substantial utility standard could not be achieved, the Court held, until the process was defined and developed to the point that "specific benefit exists in currently available form."[16]

2. USPTO Implementing Guidelines

The USPTO in 2001 issued examination guidelines that interpret the Supreme Court's *Manson* decision as requiring utility that is "specific, substantial, and credible."[17] Now implemented in the agency's *Manual of Patent Examining Procedure*, the guidelines define "specific and substantial utility" to mean "useful for any particular practical purpose," excluding "throw-away," "insubstantial," or "nonspecific"

---

35 U.S.C. §101. For additional criticism of *Manson, see* In re Kirk, 376 F.2d 936, 947-966 (C.C.P.A. 1967) (Rich, J., dissenting).

[14]Homologues are structurally similar chemical compounds that are members of a series, such as the alkanes (i.e., the straight-chain hydrocarbons methane, ethane, propane, butane, etc.). Adjacent homologues within the alkane family would indicate two member compounds that differ by only one carbon atom, such as ethane (C^2H^6) and propane (C^3H^8).

[15]*Manson*, 383 U.S. at 536.

[16]*Id.* at 534-535.

[17]*See* United States Patent & Trademark Office, *Utility Examination Guidelines*, 66 FED. REG. 1092, 1098 (Jan. 5, 2001), *available at* https://www.uspto.gov/sites/default/files/web/offices/com/sol/notices/utilexmguide.pdf. The *Guidelines* define "specific and substantial utility" to mean "useful for any particular practical purpose," exclusive of "throw-away," "insubstantial," or "nonspecific" utilities, such as the use of a complex DNA sequence as landfill, or genetically transformed mice as food for rats. *See id.* The utility requirement of §101 also is satisfied, according to the *Guidelines*, if the claimed invention has a "well-established" utility, which exists if a "person of ordinary skill in the art would immediately appreciate why the invention is useful based on the characteristics of the invention (e.g., properties or applications of a product or process). . . ." *Id.*

utilities, such as the use of a complex invention as landfill.[18] The credibility of a utility asserted by the patent applicant must be assessed from the perspective of a person "of ordinary skill in the art in view of the disclosure and any other evidence of record (e.g., test data, affidavits or declarations from experts in the art, patents or printed publications) that is probative of the applicant's assertions."[19]

With regard to the credibility assessment, the USPTO "must treat as true a statement of fact made by an applicant in relation to an asserted utility, unless countervailing evidence can be provided that shows that one of ordinary skill in the art would have a legitimate basis to doubt the credibility of such a statement."[20] Likewise, the USPTO "must accept an opinion from a qualified expert that is based upon relevant facts whose accuracy is not being questioned; it is improper to disregard the opinion solely because of a disagreement over the significance or meaning of the facts offered."[21]

When a utility asserted for a claimed invention is self-evident and not controversial, it is generally considered "well-established." According to the USPTO guidelines, a "well-established" utility exists if "(i) a person of ordinary skill in the art would immediately appreciate why the invention is useful based on the characteristics of the invention (e.g., properties or applications of a product or process), and (ii) the utility is specific, substantial, and credible."[22]

A patent applicant need provide only one credible assertion of specific and substantial utility for a claimed invention in order to satisfy the utility requirement.[23] Later-discovered uses of a product invention, even uses discovered by others, will inure to the patentee's benefit. For example, assume that a patent applicant claims a novel and nonobvious composition of matter X that treats disease Y. The asserted utility is specific, substantial, and credible. After the USPTO issues a patent, a third party discovers that composition X is also useful to treat an unrelated disease Z. Even though the patent said nothing about disease Z, the patent claim to composition X will dominate any use of composition X; that is, the claim will cover any use of the composition for treating disease Y, disease Z, or any other disease.[24]

[18]United States Patent and Trademark Office, Manual of Patent Examining Procedure (9th ed., Nov. 2015) (hereafter "MPEP") §2107(II)(B)(1)(i). Examples of so-called "throw-away" utilities include the use of an isolated and purified DNA sequence as landfill or the use of genetically transformed mice as food for rats.

[19]MPEP §2107(II)(B)(1)(ii).

[20]MPEP §2107(D).

[21]MPEP §2107(D).

[22]MPEP §2107(II)(A)(3).

[23]MPEP §2107(II)(B)(1)(ii).

[24]*See* Union Oil Co. of Cal. v. Atl. Richfield Co., 208 F.3d 989, 995 (Fed. Cir. 2000) (explaining that scope of asserted composition of matter claims "cannot, as the appellant refiners argue, embrace only certain uses of that composition. . . . Otherwise these

D. The Federal Circuit View

1. Chemical Compounds

The Federal Circuit for many years gave fairly little attention to the Supreme Court's 1966 *Manson* decision. Decisions such as the Federal Circuit's *In re Brana*[25] appeared to lower the bar back toward the more lenient standards of utility espoused pre-*Manson* by the CCPA, one of the Federal Circuit's two predecessor courts.

In re Brana is an important utility case for several reasons. First, *Brana* clarified the procedural burdens borne by the patent applicant and the USPTO during a utility determination. *Brana* holds that the agency bears the initial burden of challenging an applicant's presumptively correct assertion of utility. Only after the USPTO provides evidence showing that a person having ordinary skill in the art (PHOSITA) would reasonably doubt the asserted utility does the burden shift to the patent applicant to prove that utility. Such proof is typically made through submission of test data, experimental results, affidavits of experts, and the like, although it also may be more qualitative in nature.

Most notably, *Brana* demonstrates that a biomedical invention may possess patentable utility even though it is not yet at the stage of development necessary for sales approval by the U.S. Food & Drug Administration (FDA). Brana's claims were directed to certain novel compounds intended for use in chemotherapy. Brana produced evidence before the USPTO showing that the compounds had cytotoxicity against human tumor cells, *in vitro* (i.e., in a test tube), and an efficacy that favorably compared to that of structurally similar prior art compounds tested in mice. Nevertheless, the USPTO rejected Brana's

---

composition claims would mutate into method claims. The district court correctly applied this principle, refusing to narrow the scope of the claimed compositions to specific uses.") (citation omitted); In re Thuau, 135 F.2d 344, 347 (C.C.P.A. 1943) (stating that "[t]he doctrine is so familiar as not to require citation of authority that a patentee is entitled to every use of which his invention is susceptible, whether such use be known or unknown to him").

Whether one who discovers a new use for a known compound can himself obtain a patent on the new use (as a process or method patent) is a distinct question. *See* In re Gleave, 560 F.3d 1331, 1338 (Fed. Cir. 2009) (affirming USPTO's anticipation rejection and stating that "[a]s we explained in In re Schoenwald, [patent applicant] Gleave's contribution, at best, is 'finding a use for the compound, not discovering the compound itself.' 964 F.2d 1122, 1124 (Fed. Cir. 1992). If the use Gleave discovered is new, he will be able to patent that method of use — 'any more would be a gratuity.' 964 F.2d 1122, 1124.").

[25] 51 F.3d 1560 (Fed. Cir. 1995).

claims on the ground that the claimed compounds had not yet been approved by the FDA for Phase II clinical trials in human subjects.

On appeal, the Federal Circuit held that Brana's evidence satisfied the utility standard and rejected the USPTO's position.[26] Patentable utility can be achieved well before FDA standards are satisfied, the court emphasized:

> FDA approval, however, is not a prerequisite for finding a compound useful within the meaning of the patent laws. Usefulness in patent law, and particularly in the context of pharmaceutical inventions, necessarily includes the expectation of further research and development. The stage at which an invention in this field becomes useful is well before it is ready to be administered to humans.[27]

To support the assertion that Brana's claimed compounds had utility as antitumor substances, Brana supplemented the *in vitro* data included in his application with test data derived *in vivo* (i.e., within a living organism, such as a laboratory mouse). The Federal Circuit permitted Brana to submit the *in vivo* data in a declaration submitted under 37 C.F.R. §1.132 *after* his application filing date. The court explained that "the [] declaration, though dated after applicants' filing date, can be used to substantiate any doubts as to the asserted utility since this pertains to the accuracy of a statement already in the specification.... It does not render an insufficient disclosure enabling, but instead goes to prove that the disclosure was in fact enabling when filed (i.e., demonstrated utility).[28]

Interestingly, the *Brana* opinion did not cite nor even discuss the substantial utility standard previously set forth by the Supreme Court in *Brenner v. Manson*. This silence may have indicated the Federal Circuit's discomfort with some of the more extreme statements in the *Manson* majority opinion.

The Federal Circuit's treatment of the utility requirement has undoubtedly varied in its rigor over time; one reason may be the small number of cases reaching the appellate court that challenge patent validity based on lack of utility. Despite the Circuit's seeming willingness in *Brana* to downplay the Supreme Court's much-criticized *Brenner v. Manson* decision, the Federal Circuit in 2019 seemed to

[26]The USPTO rejected Brana's claims on the basis that the application lacked a "how to use" disclosure under 35 U.S.C. §112, ¶1 (1994), but noted that a rejection for lack of utility under 35 U.S.C. §101 also would have been proper. *See Brana*, 51 F.3d at 1564. The Federal Circuit observed that "the rejection appears to be based on the issue of whether the compounds had a practical utility, a §101 issue...." *Id.*

[27]*Id.* at 1568 (emphasis added) (citations omitted).

[28]*Brana,* 51 F.3d at 1567 n.19.

resurrect *Manson*'s more rigorous utility standard — requiring satisfaction of two prongs: "substantial" as well as "specific" utility.[29]

In *Grunenthal GMBH v. Alkem Labs. Ltd.*,[30] the Circuit reviewed a relatively rare challenge to the utility of an issued (and assertedly infringed) patent in Hatch-Waxman Act litigation. Grunenthal's U.S. Patent No. 7,994,364 ('364 patent) claimed the Form A polymorph (i.e., a chemical compound that exists in different three-dimensional crystalline structures) of the chemical compound tapentadol hydrochloride, assertedly useful for treating pain and/or urinary incontinence. Notably, Grunenthal had previously patented the Form B polymorph of the same drug,[31] but asserted that its more recently patented Form A provided better stability at room temperatures (a substantial advantage for drug manufacturing).

The *Grunenthal* Circuit affirmed the District of New Jersey's judgment that the '364 patent was not invalid for, *inter alia*, failure to comply with the utility requirement of 35 U.S.C. §101.[32] In so holding the Circuit followed its 2005 precedent *In re Fisher* (which in turn had hewed to *Manson*) to require that utility for the claimed invention be

[29]In its 2019 decision *Grunenthal GMBH v. Alkem Labs. Ltd.*, 919 F.3d 1333 (Fed. Cir. Mar. 28, 2019) (Reyna, J.), the Federal Circuit summarized the law of utility, including the "substantial" and "specific" prongs, as follows:

> The bar for utility is not high. *Juicy Whip, Inc. v. Orange Bang, Inc.*, 185 F.3d 1364, 1366 (Fed. Cir. 1999). Nonetheless, a patent must have *specific and substantial utility*. *In re Fisher*, 421 F.3d 1365, 1371 (Fed. Cir. 2005) (citing *Fujikawa v. Wattanasin*, 93 F.3d 1559, 1563 (Fed. Cir. 1996)). The *substantial* requirement, also known as "practical utility," is satisfied when "the claimed invention has a significant and presently available benefit to the public." *Id.* To satisfy the *specific* prong of utility, the claimed invention must show that it can "provide a well-defined and particular benefit to the public." *Id.* In other words, a patent has utility if the alleged invention is capable of providing some identifiable benefit presently available to the public. *Id.* A patent fails to satisfy the utility requirement under 35 U.S.C. §101 only if the invention is "totally incapable of achieving a useful result." *Brooktree Corp. v. Advanced Micro Devices, Inc.*, 977 F.2d 1555, 1571 (Fed. Cir. 1992). For pharmaceutical patents, practical utility may be shown by evidence of "any pharmacological activity." *Fujikawa*, 93 F.3d at 1564.

Grunenthal, 919 F.3d at 1345 (emphasis added).

[30]919 F.3d 1333 (Fed. Cir. Mar. 28, 2019) (Reyna, J.).

[31]U.S. Patent No. 6,248,737 ('737 patent).

[32]The Circuit also affirmed the district court's rejection of the accused infringers' challenge to the '364 patent's nonobviousness over the Form B polymorph of Grunenthal's U.S. Patent No. 6,248,737 in combination with a 1995 article by "Byrn" providing a decision tree for screening chemical compounds for polymorphism. Use of the methods disclosed in the Byrn article would not have provided a skilled artisan with a reasonable expectation of success that she could modify the Form B polymorph to arrive at the Form A polymorph claimed in the '364 patent in suit. Moreover, doing so would not have been "obvious to try." *Grunenthal*, 919 F.3d at 1341-1345.

both "substantial" and "specific."[33] Despite application of this rigorous standard, the appellate court rejected the lack of utility challenge brought by the accused infringers. For the following reasons, it held that both prongs of the utility requirement were satisfied as to the chemical composition claimed in Grunenthal's '364 patent.

First, the appellate court rejected accused infringer/validity challenger Hikma's contention that the invention claimed in the '364 patent lacked *specific* utility. In making that contention, Hikma relied on the '364 patent specification's arguably vague statement that "Crystalline Form A . . . has the same pharmacological activity as Form B but is more stable under ambient conditions. It can be advantageously used as [an] active ingredient in pharmaceutical compositions." Relying on the Circuit's decision in *Fisher,* Hikma argued that this disclosure failed to provide a "well-defined and particular benefit to the public."[34]

The Circuit deemed Hikma's argument "without merit." The '364 patent taught that "[t]he crystalline Form A according to the invention is used for the treatment of pain or the treatment of urinary incontinence." The patent's specification's statements were confirmed by expert testimony given at trial. The prior art also confirmed that tapentadol hydrochloride (of which the '364 invention is a polymorph) was known as an analgesic (i.e., pain reliever) at the time of filing of the '364 patent. The Circuit concluded that "the '364 patent concretely discloses the practical benefit of Form A of tapentadol hydrochloride as an analgesic."[35]

Second, the *Grunenthal* Circuit also rejected Hikma's contention that the claimed Form A lacked *substantial* utility. Hikma argued that the Grunenthal was required not only to prove the asserted superior performance of Form A over Form B at room temperature, but moreover had to prove that superiority by *test data* (which data were not present in the '364 patent or its prosecution history).

Rejecting Hikma's view of utility law, the Federal Circuit emphasized that showing patentable utility did not require Grunenthal to

[33]*Fisher*, 421 F.3d 1365 (Fed. Cir. 2005), is analyzed *infra* Section D.3 ("Genetic Inventions"). This author views *Fisher* as a return by the Federal Circuit in 2005 to the high-water utility criteria ("substantial" plus "specific" as a two-pronged inquiry) announced almost 40 years earlier by the Supreme Court in *Brenner v. Manson*, 383 U.S. 519 (1966), analyzed *supra* Section C.1. When *Fisher* issued in 2005, this author was optimistic that its resurrection and interpretation of *Manson* would be limited to its facts; i.e., to claimed inventions involving genetic materials such as ESTs. However, *Grunenthal* indicates that as of 2019, the Circuit was not limiting the *Manson* framework in this fashion. Rather, *Grunenthal* applied the heightened two-pronged utility formulation of *Fisher* to traditional chemical compound inventions as well as to genetic-based inventions.

[34]*Grunenthal,* 919 F.3d at 1346 (citing Hikma Br. 32 (citing In re Fisher, 421 F.3d 1365, 1371 (Fed. Cir. 2005))).

[35]*Grunenthal*, 919 F.3d at 1345-1346.

prove that Form A worked *better* than Form B at room temperature. Utility requires only that the invention *works*. It was sufficient, the Circuit held, "that Form A is shown to be stable at room temperature and useful for pain relief."[36] The *Grunenthal* court opined that

> Hikma attempts to set too high a bar for purposes of finding a sufficient disclosure of utility. While test results often support claims of utility in patents concerning pharmacological arts, such testing is not always required.[37] . . . Nor do said results need to prove the claimed utility. *E.g., Fujikawa* [Fujikawa v. Wattanasin, 93 F.3d 1559 (Fed. Cir. 1996)], 93 F.3d at 1564 ("[T]est results need not absolutely prove that the compound is pharmacologically active. All that is required is that the tests be *reasonably* indicative of the desired [pharmacological] response." (internal quotations and citations omitted)). All that is necessary is evidence that a POSA [person of ordinary skill in the art] would accept the claimed utility as correct.[38]

The Federal Circuit agreed with Grunenthal and the district court that the disclosure of Example 16 in the '364 patent provided sufficient evidence that a skilled artisan would have accepted Grunenthal's asserted utility as correct. That is, Example 16 was "reasonably indicative" of the stability of Form A at room temperature. Specifically, the example reported a variable temperature XRPD (x-ray powder diffraction) experiment that produced Form B from Form A at temperatures higher than room temperature (i.e., 40-50 degrees Celsius). Example 16 stated that this transition was "reversible with Form B changing over into Form A at lower temperature." Moreover, expert witness testimony at trial confirmed that Example 16 established that "Form A is stable at room temperature and Form B is stable above 50 [degrees] Celsius."[39] Lastly, sufficient evidence established that thermodynamic stability is beneficial for pharmaceutical storage and manufacturing consistency, which in turn can be beneficial characteristics for pharmaceutical compositions.

Accordingly, the Federal Circuit held the district court's finding of utility (a fact question) was not clearly erroneous, and affirmed its judgment sustaining the validity of the '364 patent.

[36] *Grunenthal*, 919 F.3d at 1346.

[37] *Grunenthal*, 919 F.3d at 1346 (citing Rasmusson v. SmithKline Beecham Corp., 413 F.3d 1318, 1323 (Fed. Cir. 2005) ("[I]t is proper for the examiner to ask for substantiating evidence unless one with ordinary skill in the art would accept the allegations as obviously correct." (quoting In re Jolles, 628 F.2d 1322, 1325 (C.C.P.A. 1980))).

[38] *Grunenthal*, 919 F.3d at 1346 (emphasis on "reasonably" in original) (quoting In re Nelson, 626 F.2d at 856).

[39] *Grunenthal*, 919 F.3d at 1346.

2. Methods of Medical Treatment

In contrast to *Brana*, a failure to submit test data to support an asserted utility contributed to the later invalidation of a granted pharmaceutical patent for lack of utility in *In re '318 Patent Litigation.*[40] The patent in that case was directed to a method of treating Alzheimer's disease (rather than a new chemical compound). The Federal Circuit majority in *'318 Patent Litigation* (Judges Dyk and Mayer) observed that "[t]ypically, patent applications claiming new methods of treatment are supported by test results," although the court stopped short of requiring such results in all cases. But their absence in the case at bar proved fatal. Because the *'318 Patent Litigation* decision is decidedly contrary to the tenor of the Federal Circuit's decision in *In re Brana*, it merits close study.

In *'318 Patent Litigation, in vivo* test data from experiments with animal models such as mice were not available to support the inventor's asserted utility until after the USPTO had issued the patent. During prosecution in the USPTO, the applicant supported her assertion of utility by reliance on various prior art teachings, as well as a statement to the examiner that experimental data using animal models would be available within a few months. The USPTO did not reject the application for lack of utility, despite the fact that the applicant never submitted the animal model data to the USPTO.

The claimed invention in *'318 Patent Litigation* was a method of treating Alzheimer's disease by administering an effective amount of the compound galanthamine. Although the USPTO issued the '318 patent in 1987 and the FDA in 2001 approved galanthamine for treatment of moderate Alzheimer's disease, the Federal Circuit in 2009 affirmed a district court's invalidation of the '318 patent[41] for failure to satisfy the enablement requirement on the ground that the patent's application did not establish utility.[42] Citing the Supreme Court's *Brenner v. Manson* decision, the Federal Circuit majority characterized the '318 patent's claimed method of treatment as a "mere

[40]583 F.3d 1317 (Fed. Cir. 2009). The *'318 Patent Litigation*, which resulted from the consolidation of the patentee's several lawsuits against various generic drug manufacturers, has also been cited as *Janssen Pharmaceutica N.V. v. Teva Pharms. USA, Inc.*, 583 F.3d 1317 (Fed. Cir. 2009).

[41]Although the '318 patent issued in 1987, its term was extended on October 22, 2004, pursuant to 35 U.S.C. §156; the '318 patent expired in December 2008. *See* In re '318 Patent Infringement Litigation, 578 F. Supp. 2d 711, 723 n.21 (D. Del. 2008).

[42]*'318 Patent Litigation,* 583 F.3d at 1327. Specifically, the Federal Circuit affirmed a district court's grant of summary judgment that the claims of the '318 patent were invalid for lack of enablement. The Federal Circuit explained that enablement is closely related to utility, in that a claim that fails to meet the utility requirement because it is not useful or inoperative also fails to satisfy the how-to-use prong of the enablement requirement. *'318 Patent Litigation,* 583 F.3d at 1323-1324.

research proposal" or "simply an object of research." Echoing *Manson,* the appellate court observed that "[a]llowing ideas, research proposals, or objects only of research to be patented has the potential to give priority to the wrong party" and to confer power to block entire areas of scientific development.[43]

The results of the animal tests proposed in the '318 patent's application were not available until after the USPTO had already issued the patent. The Federal Circuit held that patentee could not rely on those post-issuance test results to sustain the patent's validity. Nor had the patentee managed to establish utility through "analytic reasoning" based on the prior art results described in the '318 patent application. Although the patentee's expert testified that the application's disclosure "connected the dots" for use of galanthamine as a potential treatment for Alzheimer's disease, the Federal Circuit majority concluded that such testimony fell "far short of demonstrating that a person of ordinary skill in the art would have recognized that the specification conveyed the required assertion of a credible utility."[44] The utility requirement could not be satisfied by filing a patent application that, in the Federal Circuit majority's view, did "no more than state a hypothesis and propose testing to determine the accuracy of that hypothesis."[45]

Dissenting in *'318 Patent Litigation,* Circuit Judge Gajarsa charged that the relevant question on appeal was whether, at the time it was filed, the disclosure of the patent application would have credibly revealed to an ordinarily skilled artisan that galanthamine had utility as a treatment for Alzheimer's disease. In Judge Gajarsa's view, the district court erred by focusing on what the prior art did or did not teach (the focus for determining nonobviousness) while neglecting to determine what the '318 application itself disclosed to a PHOSITA (the focus for determining utility and enablement). The district court's failure to make fact findings about enablement led the Federal Circuit majority to improperly engage in extensive appellate fact finding. According to dissenting Judge Gajarsa, it was "particularly problematic" that the Federal Circuit majority had effectively shifted the burden with respect to validity to the patentee. Because *'318 Patent Litigation* involved an issued patent, the burden should have remained on the accused infringers to disprove utility by clear and convincing evidence. Instead, the Federal Circuit majority improperly

[43]*'318 Patent Litigation,* 583 F.3d at 1324. Priority of invention was not in dispute in *'318 Patent Litigation*; the case did not involve an interference, unlike the Supreme Court's only recent statement on utility, *Brenner v. Manson*, discussed *supra.*

[44]*'318 Patent Litigation,* 583 F.3d at 1327.

[45]*'318 Patent Litigation,* 583 F.3d at 1327.

"focuse[d] almost exclusively on the sufficiency of [the patentee's] showing and the merit of [the patentee's] arguments."[46]

3. Genetic Inventions

In the wake of the USPTO's 2001 promulgation of the *Utility Examination Guidelines* discussed above,[47] a test case was brought to clarify the standards for applying the §101 utility requirement to patent claims reciting ESTs (expressed sequence tags). The result in *In re Fisher*[48] was a return by the Federal Circuit in 2005 to the rigorous utility criteria announced almost 40 years earlier by the Supreme Court in *Brenner v. Manson.*[49] It remains to be seen whether this resurrection of *Manson* signals a heightened utility requirement for *all* inventions, or will instead be limited to those inventions involving genetic materials such as ESTs.

ESTs are short nucleotide sequences that represent a fragment of a cDNA (complementary DNA) clone;[50] they are "typically generated by isolating a cDNA clone and sequencing a small number of nucleotides located at the end of one of the two cDNA strands."[51] In *Fisher,*[52] the USPTO Board of Patent Appeals and Interferences[53] in 2004 affirmed an examiner's rejection of application claims to five ESTs encoding proteins and protein fragments in maize plants[54] as lacking utility under 35 U.S.C. §101.[55] The real party in interest, Monsanto

[46]*'318 Patent Litigation,* 583 F.3d at 1331 (Gajarsa, J., dissenting).

[47]*See* United States Patent & Trademark Office, *Utility Examination Guidelines*, 66 Fed. Reg. 1092, 1098 (Jan. 5, 2001), *available at* https://www.uspto.gov/sites/default/files/web/offices/com/sol/notices/utilexmguide.pdf. The guidelines were discussed *supra* in Section C.2.

[48]421 F.3d 1365 (Fed. Cir. 2005).

[49]383 U.S. 519 (1966).

[50]Complementary DNA (cDNA) is "produced synthetically by reverse transcribing mRNA [messenger ribonucleic acid]. . . . Scientists routinely compile cDNA into libraries to study the kinds of genes expressed in a certain tissue at a particular point in time." *Fisher*, 421 F.3d at 1367. Messenger RNA (mRNA) is what results when a gene, made of deoxyribonucleic acid (DNA), is expressed in a cell. "[T]he relevant double-stranded DNA sequence is transcribed into a single strand of messenger ribonucleic acid ("mRNA")." *Id.* "mRNA is released from the nucleus of a cell and used by ribosomes found in the cytoplasm to produce proteins." *Id.*

[51]*Id.*

[52]Ex parte Fisher, 72 U.S.P.Q.2d 1020 (Bd. Pat. App. & Int. 2004) (non-precedential decision).

[53]Renamed the Patent Trial and Appeal Board by the America Invents Act of 2011.

[54]Claim 1 of the Fisher application recited "[a] substantially purified nucleic acid molecule that encodes a maize protein or fragment thereof comprising a nucleic acid sequence selected from the group consisting of SEQ ID NO:1 through SEQ ID NO:5," where "SEQ ID NO:1 through SEQ ID NO:5 consist of 429, 423, 365, 411, and 331 nucleotides, respectively." In re Fisher, 421 F.3d 1365, 1367-1368 (Fed. Cir. 2005).

[55]*See* Ex parte Fisher, 72 U.S.P.Q.2d 1020, 1021 (Bd. Pat. App. & Int. 2004) (non-precedential decision). The "substantially purified" nucleotide sequences claimed in

Company, contended that the claimed ESTs were useful, *inter alia*, for identifying the presence or absence of polymorphisms (i.e., alternative forms of the recited sequences).[56] According to Monsanto, the ESTs "provide[d] at least one specific benefit to the public, for example the ability to identify the presence or absence of a polymorphism in a population of maize plants." While the Board admitted that using ESTs to determine whether populations share a common genetic heritage may be a "utility," it was not in the agency's view a "substantial utility" as required by *Manson*, that is, one that provides a "specific benefit in currently available form." The Board observed that "[w]ithout knowing any further information in regard to the gene represented by an EST, as here, detection of the presence or absence of a polymorphism provides the barest information in regard to genetic heritage." On the other end of the utility spectrum, the Board suggested, would be "information gleaned from detecting the presence or absence of a polymorphism when it is known what effect the gene from which the EST is derived has in the development and/or phenotype of the plant." The Board concluded that the requisite substantial utility lies somewhere between these two extremes, but had not been approximated in this case of an "insubstantial use."

In the closely watched appeal from the Board's decision, a divided panel of the Federal Circuit affirmed the utility rejection of the *Fisher* EST claims in September 2005.[57] Notably, the *Fisher* majority rejected Justice Story's *de minimis* view of the utility requirement[58] and instead hewed to (and elaborated on) the "specific" and "substantial" utility criteria espoused in *Manson*. The *Fisher* majority held that in order to show a "specific" utility, "an asserted use must . . . show that the claimed invention can be used to provide a well-defined and particular benefit to the public,"[59] and that in order to demonstrate a

---

Fisher are nucleic acid molecules "separated from substantially all other molecules normally associated with [the claimed molecule] in its native state." *Id.* at 1022.

[56]Monsanto asserted at least the following seven uses for the claimed ESTs: "(1) serving as a molecular marker for mapping the entire maize genome, which consists of ten chromosomes that collectively encompass roughly 50,000 genes; (2) measuring the level of mRNA in a tissue sample via microarray technology to provide information about gene expression; (3) providing a source for primers for use in the polymerase chain reaction ('PCR') process to enable rapid and inexpensive duplication of specific genes; (4) identifying the presence or absence of a polymorphism; (5) isolating promoters via chromosome walking; (6) controlling protein expression; and (7) locating genetic molecules of other plants and organisms." *Fisher*, 421 F.3d at 1368.

[57]In re Fisher, 421 F.3d 1365 (Fed. Cir. 2005) (opinion for the court filed by Michel, C.J., and joined by Bryson, J.; dissenting opinion filed by Rader, J.). Eight organizations filed *amicus curiae* briefs in *Fisher*.

[58]*See* Lowell v. Lewis, 15 F. Cas. 1018, 1019 (C.C. Mass. 1817) (No. 8,568) (patentable utility requires only that a claimed invention "not be frivolous, or injurious to the well-being, good policy, or good morals of society").

[59]*Fisher*, 421 F.3d at 1372.

"substantial" utility, "an asserted use must show that [the] claimed invention has a significant and presently available benefit to the public."[60]

In the *Fisher* majority's view, the claimed ESTs failed to satisfy either of these criteria. Each claimed EST uniquely corresponded to the single (or "underlying") gene from which it was transcribed; yet as of the application's filing date, no function was known for the underlying genes. The claimed ESTs were thus no more than "research intermediates" that were "unable to provide any information about the overall structure let alone [] the function of the underlying gene."[61] Such research use was not substantial in the majority's view. Nor were Fisher's asserted uses for the ESTs specific; "[n]othing about Fisher's [] alleged uses set the five claimed ESTs apart from the more than 32,000 ESTs disclosed in the [] application or indeed from any EST derived from any organism."[62]

Granting Fisher a patent on the claimed ESTs would amount to no more than a "hunting license," to use *Manson*'s terminology, because Fisher could not identify the function for the underlying protein-encoding genes. Absent such identification, the *Fisher* majority concluded, "the claimed ESTs have not been researched and understood to the point of providing an immediate, well-defined, real world benefit to the public meriting the grant of a patent."[63]

Federal Circuit Judge Rader vigorously dissented on the basis that the claimed ESTs were patentable research tools of cognizable benefit to society.[64] Much like a microscope, the ESTs take a researcher "one step closer to identifying and understanding a previously unknown and invisible structure." Chiding the *Fisher* majority for being "oblivious to the challenges of complex research," Judge Rader emphasized that science "always advances in small incremental steps." In his view, the USPTO is not capable of knowing which "insubstantial" research step will contribute to a substantial breakthrough in genomic study. According to Judge Rader, the utility requirement of §101 is not the proper tool for rejecting inventions that do not advance the "useful arts" sufficiently to merit a patent; rather, that tool should be the nonobviousness requirement of §103. However, Judge Rader observed, the Federal Circuit's 1995 holding in *In re Deuel*[65] has effectively

[60]*Id.*
[61]*Id.* at 1373.
[62]*Id.* at 1374.
[63]*Id.* at 1376.
[64]*Id.* at 1379 (Rader, J., dissenting).
[65]51 F.3d 1552 (Fed. Cir. 1995) (holding that the combination of a prior art reference teaching a method of gene cloning, together with a reference disclosing a partial amino acid sequence of a protein, does not render DNA and cDNA molecules encoding the protein *prima facie* obvious under 35 U.S.C. §103; and stating that "the existence of a general method of isolating cDNA or DNA molecules is essentially irrelevant to the

"deprived the Patent Office of the obviousness requirement for genomic inventions." Rather than distort the utility requirement, Judge Rader urged, the USPTO should "seek ways to apply the correct test" of nonobviousness.[66]

E. Inoperability

If the utility asserted for an invention contravenes generally accepted scientific principles, the USPTO will reject the inventor's claims under 35 U.S.C. §101 as drawn to inoperable subject matter. Inoperability is a type of rejection for lack of utility. If an invention does not work as claimed, then it is not considered useful in the patent law sense. Moreover, one cannot logically describe how to use an inoperable invention in accordance with 35 U.S.C. §112(a).[67]

1. Examples of Inoperable Inventions

The inventor in *Newman v. Quigg*[68] claimed an "Energy Generation System Having Higher Energy Output Than Input," which the USPTO characterized as a "perpetual motion machine." After the agency's rejection of his claims under §101, Newman brought a civil action against the USPTO Commissioner pursuant to 35 U.S.C. §145 (1988).[69] The Federal Circuit affirmed the federal district court's

---

question whether the specific molecules themselves would have been obvious, in the absence of other prior art that suggests the claimed DNAs").

[66]Following the Supreme Court's watershed decision in *KSR Int'l Co. v. Teleflex Inc.*, 550 U.S. 398 (2007), the Federal Circuit raised the bar significantly for nonobviousness of genetic inventions. *See* In re Kubin, 561 F.3d 1351 (Fed. Cir. 2009) (sustaining USPTO rejection of claimed genus of isolated nucleic acid molecules on ground that the claimed invention would have been obvious under §103(a) (2006)). Consistent with Judge Rader's prediction in *Fisher*, it is unlikely that *Deuel* retains much if any precedential vitality after *KSR* and *Kubin*, both of which are analyzed *supra* Chapter 5 ("The Nonobviousness Requirement (35 U.S.C. §103)").

[67]*See* EMI Group N. Am., Inc. v. Cypress Semiconductor Corp., 268 F.3d 1342, 1348 (Fed. Cir. 2001) (stating that "[a] claimed invention having an inoperable or impossible claim limitation may lack utility under 35 U.S.C. §101 and certainly lacks an enabling disclosure under 35 U.S.C. §112") (citing Raytheon Co. v. Roper Corp., 724 F.2d 951, 956 (Fed. Cir. 1983)).

[68]877 F.2d 1575 (Fed. Cir. 1989).

[69]This §145 procedure authorizes a trial *de novo* in federal court that is not limited to the record evidence that was before the USPTO. *See* Kappos v. Hyatt, 132 S. Ct. 1690 (2012) (holding that in a civil action to obtain a patent under 35 U.S.C. §145, there are no limitations on a patent applicant's ability to introduce new evidence beyond those already present in the Federal Rules of Evidence and the Federal Rules of Civil Procedure, and that if new evidence is presented on a disputed question of fact the district court must make *de novo* factual findings that take account of both the new evidence

conclusion that the invention was "unpatentable under 35 U.S.C. §101 because 'Newman's device lacks utility (in that it does not operate to produce what he claims it does).'" The district court had properly relied on National Bureau of Standards test results proving that Newman's machine did not in fact generate more energy than the amount input, the machine having at most an efficiency of only 77 percent.

The operability of a treatment for hair loss was at issue in *In re Cortright.*[70] There the patent applicant claimed a method of treating baldness by applying Bag Balm® (a commercially available ointment normally used to moisturize the udders of cows) to the head of a human suffering from hair loss. Although the Federal Circuit did not consider the asserted utility of treating baldness to be "inherently suspect" in view of the several hair loss treatments already approved by the FDA, the court nevertheless affirmed the USPTO's rejection of Cortright's claim 15, which recited a method of

> offsetting the effects of lower levels of a male hormone being supplied by arteries to the papilla of scalp hair follicles with the active agent 8-hydroxy-quinoline sulfate to cause hair to grow again on the scalp, comprising rubbing into the scalp the ointment having the active agent 8-hydroxy-quinoline sulfate 0.3% carried in a petrolatum and lanolin base so that the active agent reaches the papilla.[71]

In essence, claim 15 recited the particular way in which Cortright believed that her invention worked. Unfortunately, her patent application lacked any information to substantiate that the method actually operated in this manner; that is, she did not demonstrate that the active ingredient reached the papilla or that it actually offset the effects of lower male hormone levels, as the claims recited. Therefore, the Federal Circuit concluded, Cortright's application did not provide a satisfactory description of how to use the invention of claim 15 in accordance with 35 U.S.C. §112, ¶1 (1994).[72]

2. Inoperable Species Within a Genus

Utility issues sometimes arise in the context of a generic claim that includes within it one or more species that are inoperable.[73] For example, consider a patent claim to a composition of matter comprising

---

and the administrative record before the USPTO). Section 145 actions are further discussed *supra* Chapter 1 ("Foundations of the U.S. Patent System").

[70] 165 F.3d 1353 (Fed. Cir. 1999).

[71] *Id.* at 1355.

[72] The *Cortright* court treated the how-to-use rejection under §112 as essentially equatable to a rejection for inoperability under 35 U.S.C. §101. *See id.* at 1356-1357.

[73] Genus and species claims were introduced in Chapter 2 ("Patent Claims"), *supra.*

component X from 20 to 80 weight percent, for which the inventor asserts the utility of shrinking cancer tumors. If it is established that the embodiment of the invention in which X is present at 30 percent does not have any tumor-shrinking effect on cancer cells, this means that at least that particular species within the genus of all compositions having X present at between 20 to 80 percent is inoperable; that is, the X equals 30 percent species does not possess the utility asserted for the genus. Is the claim in its entirety therefore invalid under 35 U.S.C. §101?

As with so many other patent law questions, the answer depends on the facts of the particular case. Federal Circuit law holds that the presence of *some* inoperative embodiments does not necessarily render a claim invalid as lacking utility.[74] Patent claims need not exclude all possibly inoperative embodiments.[75] However, the presence of too many inoperative species or embodiments may give rise to enablement problems under 35 U.S.C. §112(a).[76] The patent's written description must provide enough information that one of ordinary skill in the art could select or discern which embodiments are operable and which are not, and thus practice the invention, without undue experimentation.[77] If such selection criteria are lacking, the presence of inoperable species in the generic claims could render those claims invalid.[78]

F. Immoral or Deceptive Inventions

Early U.S. judicial decisions recognized a morality component within the utility requirement. For example, Justice Story defined

[74]*See* Atlas Powder Co. v. E.I. du Pont de Nemours & Co., 750 F.2d 1569, 1576-1577 (Fed. Cir. 1984).

[75]*See* In re Anderson, 471 F.2d 1237, 1242 (C.C.P.A. 1973) (noting that "[i]t is always possible to put something into a combination [claim] to render it inoperative," but that "[i]t is not the function of claims to *exclude* all such matters but to point out what the combination is") (emphasis in original).

[76]The America Invents Act of 2011 renamed the first paragraph of 35 U.S.C. §112 (2006) as 35 U.S.C. §112(a) (eff. Sept. 16, 2012).

[77]In re Cook, 439 F.2d 730, 735 (C.C.P.A. 1971).

[78]The inoperability of *some* species or embodiments within a claim should be contrasted with the scenario in which *every* species or embodiment is inoperable. In *EMI Group North America, Inc. v. Cypress Semiconductor Corp.*, 268 F.3d 1342, 1348 (Fed. Cir. 2001), the court confronted a patent in which each asserted claim contained one limitation (among several) that was deemed scientifically "impossible" on the basis of expert testimony. *See id.* at 1346 (citing testimony of accused infringer's expert witness that "explosion mechanism" recited in the asserted claims to metallic fuses for semiconductor chips was "impossible"); *id.* at 1349. This rendered all the claims invalid. *See id.* (stating that "[w]hen a claim itself recites incorrect science in one limitation, the entire claim is invalid, regardless of the combinations of the other limitations recited in the claim").

patentable utility in 1817 as an invention that "may be applied to some beneficial use in society, in contradistinction to an invention, which is injurious to the morals, the health, or the good order of society."[79] Applying this standard, U.S. courts, including the Court of Appeals for the Second Circuit, subsequently invalidated patents directed to artificially spotted tobacco leaves[80] and faux-seamed women's hosiery.[81] These decisions illustrate the difficulty of assigning to judges or USPTO examiners the task of passing judgment on which inventions are moral and which are immoral. Such value-laden judgments are often highly personalized and typically implicate community standards that vary over time.

In 1977, the USPTO issued a decision signaling that the agency would no longer reject inventions on the ground that they might be viewed by some segment of society as immoral. In *Ex parte Murphy,*[82] the agency upheld the patentability of a "one-armed bandit" slot machine. The USPTO Board of Appeals explained that "while some may consider gambling to be injurious to the public morals and the good order of society, we cannot find any basis in 35 U.S.C. 101 or related sections which justify a conclusion that inventions which are useful only for gambling *ipso facto* are void of patentable utility."[83] The Board concluded that "this Office should not be the agency which seeks to enforce a standard of morality with respect to gambling, by refusing, on the ground of lack of patentable utility, to grant a patent on a game of chance if the requirements of the Patent Act otherwise have been met."[84]

In 1999, the Federal Circuit affirmed the rationale of *Murphy* in the oddly named case of *Juicy Whip, Inc. v. Orange Bang, Inc.*[85] The patent in suit was directed to a Slurpee®-like beverage dispenser machine that included a transparent display chamber of the dispensed product, permitting consumers to see in advance the drink they believed they were buying. The patented machine is depicted in Figure 6.2. In actuality the product (syrup and water) was mixed just before dispensing, so that the customer was not given what she had seen in the display chamber.[86] The trial court invalidated the patent in suit under §101

[79]Bedford v. Hunt, 3 F. Cas. 37 (C.C.D. Mass. 1817) (No. 1,217).
[80]*See* Rickard v. Du Bon, 103 F. 868 (2d Cir. 1900).
[81]*See* Scott & Williams, Inc. v. Aristo Hosiery Co., 7 F.2d 1003 (2d Cir. 1925).
[82]200 U.S.P.Q. 801 (Bd. Pat. App. & Int. 1977).
[83]*Id.* at 802.
[84]*Id.* at 803.
[85]185 F.3d 1364 (Fed. Cir. 1999).
[86]In fact, this "deception" benefited consumers because it decreased the risk of contamination.

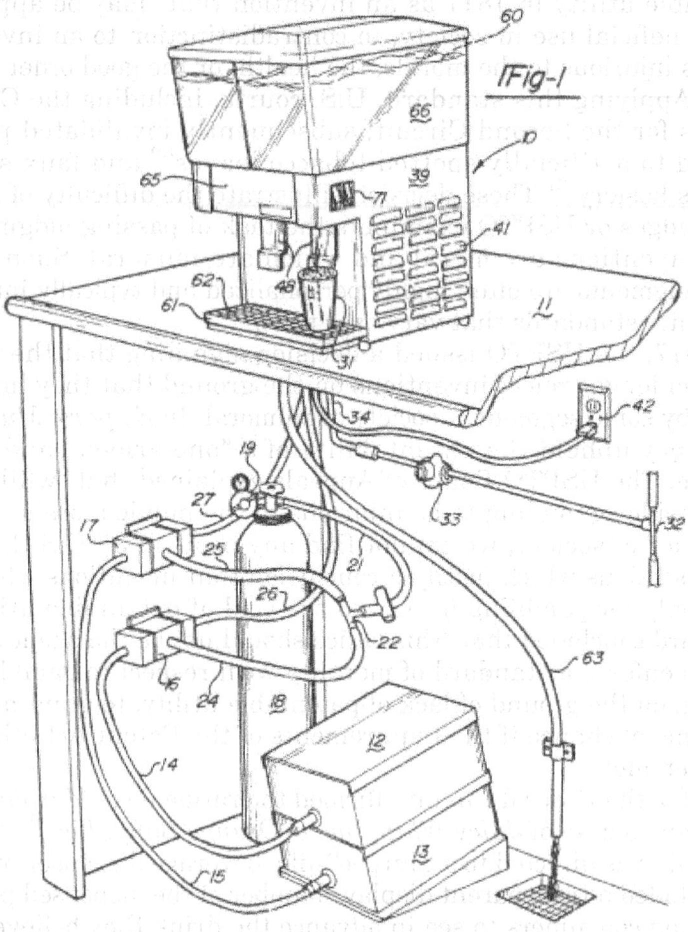

Figure 6.2

Post-Mix Beverage Dispenser with an Associated Simulated Visual Display of Beverage

U.S. Patent No. 5,575,405 (Issued Nov. 19, 1996)

on the ground that the invention was "deceptive," relying on the early Second Circuit morality cases discussed above.

The Federal Circuit reversed, rejecting the relevancy of those decisions. The modern standard for utility as understood post–1952 Patent Act does not attempt to judge the morality of an invention, the court declared; the utility standard only requires some minimal real-world value. The USPTO is not the proper arbiter of whether an invention is moral, or deceptive, or illegal. This is the realm of other agencies (e.g., the FDA or the Federal Trade Commission), or of

Congress if it chooses to legislate that certain subject matter is not patentable.[87] Thus, even an arguably deceptive invention is potentially patentable under the utility requirement of §101.

G. Relationship Between Utility Requirement of §101 and How-to-Use Requirement of §112(a)

If the patent applicant fails to assert a credible utility for her invention, the USPTO will generally make both a §101 rejection for lack of utility of the claimed invention as well as a §112(a) rejection for the failure of the written description of the patent to adequately describe how to use the invention.[88] Both rejections are made because "the how to use prong of section 112 incorporates as a matter of law the requirement of 35 U.S.C. §101 that the specification disclose as a matter of fact a practical utility for the invention."[89] By definition, "if [certain] compositions are in fact useless, appellant's specification cannot have taught how to use them."[90] Thus, a lack of utility can support a rejection both under §101 and under §112(a).

H. Utility Requirement in Foreign Patent Systems

1. Industrial Applicability

In foreign patent systems and multinational patent treaties, the U.S. utility requirement roughly corresponds to a mandate that patentable inventions possess "industrial applicability."[91] The European Patent

[87]In this regard, the decision in *Juicy Whip* harkens back to the Supreme Court's decision in *Diamond v. Chakrabarty*, 447 U.S. 303 (1980), which held that living subject matter such as a genetically engineered bacterium is within the categories of potentially patentable subject matter enumerated in 35 U.S.C. §101. *See* Chapter 7 ("Potentially Patentable Subject Matter (35 U.S.C. §101)"), *infra*. The *Chakrabarty* Court upheld the bacterium's patentability partly because, in its view, the lower courts and the USPTO were not in a position to make such policy judgments by means of cramped interpretations of broad statutory language. Rather, Congress was the proper forum for changing the law.

[88]Prior to the America Invents Act of 2011, 35 U.S.C. §112(a) (eff. Sept. 16, 2012) was commonly referred to as "§112, ¶1."

[89]In re Cortright, 165 F.3d 1353, 1356 (Fed. Cir. 1999) (quoting In re Ziegler, 992 F.2d 1197, 1200 (Fed. Cir. 1993)).

[90]In re Fouche, 439 F.2d 1237, 1243 (C.C.P.A. 1971).

[91]*See* Agreement on Trade-Related Aspects of Intellectual Property Rights (TRIPS) art. 27.1, Dec. 15, 1993, 33 I.L.M. 81 (1994) (requiring that invention be "capable of industrial application"); *id.* at n.5 (stating that for purposes of article, "capable of industrial application" may be deemed by member countries to be synonymous with "useful"); European Patent Convention art. 52(1) (2016), *available at* https://www.epo.org/law-practice/legal-texts/html/epc/2016/e/ar57.html (stating that European patents shall be granted

Convention (EPC) further defines "susceptible of industrial application" as whether an invention "can be made or used in any kind of industry, including agriculture."[92] This language is intended to expressly include agricultural inventions within patentable subject matter, but to exclude methods of medically treating humans and animals.[93]

In its first major patent case on the issue of industrial applicability of biotechnological inventions, the Supreme Court of the United Kingdom (formerly the House of Lords) in *Human Genome Sciences, Inc. v. Eli Lilly & Co.* considered the validity of Human Genome Sciences' (HGS's) European Patent (UK) 0,939,804.[94] The patent claimed *inter alia* the nucleotide sequence of the gene encoding a novel protein called Neutrokine-, a member of the TNF ligand superfamily, which HGS asserted as useful in the diagnosis and treatment of B-cell and T-cell lymphomas. After an exhaustive review of European Patent Office (EPO) Technical Board of Appeal jurisprudence,[95] the UK Supreme Court held that HGS's patent satisfied the industrial applicability requirements of EPC Article 57.[96]

2. Morality Criterion

In contrast with U.S. law, foreign patent codes do speak to the morality of inventions, although they statutorily categorize this as an issue of potentially patentable subject matter rather than of industrial applicability. For example, the EPC provides that European patents shall not be granted in respect of

> (a) inventions the commercial exploitation of which would be contrary to "*ordre public*" or morality; such exploitation shall not be deemed to be so contrary merely because it is prohibited by law or regulation in some or all of the Contracting States. . . .[97]

"for any inventions, in all fields of technology, provided that they are . . . susceptible of industrial application").

[92]European Patent Convention art. 57 (2016), *available at* https://www.epo.org/law-practice/legal-texts/html/epc/2016/e/ar57.html.

[93]*See* W.R. Cornish, Intellectual Property: Patents, Copyright, Trade Marks and Allied Rights §5-53 (4th ed., Sweet & Maxwell 1999).

[94][2012] R.P.C. 6, [2011] U.K.S.C. 51.

[95]Lord Neuberger's opinion helpfully summarizes the EPO Board's approach in relation to the requirements of EPC art. 57 for biological material. *See Human Genome Sci.,* [2012] R.P.C. 6 at para. 107.

[96]*See Human Genome Sci.,* [2012] R.P.C. 6 at para. 129. Lord Neuberger observed that "[j]ust as it would be undesirable to let someone have a monopoly over a particular biological molecule too early, because it risks closing down competition, so it would be wrong to set the hurdle for patentability too high. . . ." *Id.* at para. 130.

[97]European Patent Convention art. 53(a) (2010), *available at* http://www.epo.org/law-practice/legal-texts/html/epc/2010/e/ar53.html.

This provision permits signatory countries to exclude from patenting those inventions whose commercial exploitation is banned in the respective country, if such exclusion is deemed necessary to protect the interests of "*ordre public*"[98] or morality.[99] A handful of decisions from the European Patent Office have not yet ratified a single, succinct test for determining what types of inventions violate this morality criterion.[100] The "*ordre public*" or "morality" language of EPC art. 53(a) is echoed in Article 27.2 of the WTO-administered Agreement on Trade-Related Aspects of Intellectual Property Rights (TRIPS),[101] which gives WTO member countries the option of adopting a similar morality-based exclusion from patenting.[102]

[98]This French phrase most closely translates as "public policy" or "public interest." *See* Donna M. Gitter, *Led Astray by the Moral Compass: Incorporating Morality into European Union Biotechnology Patent Law*, 19 Berkeley J. Int'l L. 1, 3 n.18 (2001).

[99]See Carlos Correa, *The GATT Agreement on Trade-Related Aspects of Intellectual Property Rights: New Standards for Patent Protection*, 16 Eur. Intell. Prop. Rev. 327 (1994).

[100]*See* Donna M. Gitter, *Led Astray by the Moral Compass: Incorporating Morality into European Union Biotechnology Patent Law*, 19 Berkeley J. Int'l L. 1, 17-34 (2001) (discussing four EPO biotechnology decisions that have applied two conflicting morality standards: one a test of "public abhorrence," where patenting is denied when public consensus determines that a patent grant would be abhorrent, and the other test a more stringent criterion of "unacceptability," in which the grant of a patent is deemed unacceptable in view of conventionally accepted standards of European culture). The European debate over the morality of patenting the Harvard University onco-mouse is discussed *infra* Chapter 7, Section D.3 ("Life Forms").

[101]*See* Agreement on Trade-Related Aspects of Intellectual Property Rights, Including Trade in Counterfeit Goods, Dec. 15, 1993, 33 I.L.M. 81 (1994).

[102]The TRIPS Agreement and other multinational intellectual property treaties are discussed in further detail in Chapter 12 ("International Patenting Issues"), *infra*.

Chapter 7

Potentially Patentable Subject Matter (35 U.S.C. §101)

A. Introduction

1. The General Nature of §101

This chapter considers the *types* or *categories* of inventions for which utility patents[1] are potentially available under U.S. law. Patent law practitioners typically refer to these "eligible" types of inventions as comprising **statutory subject matter**, referring to the categories of subject matter recited in 35 U.S.C. §101. That statue provides as follows:

> **§101. Inventions patentable**
>
> Whoever invents or discovers any new and useful *process, machine, manufacture,* or *composition of matter,* or any new and useful improvement thereof, may obtain a patent therefor, subject to the conditions and requirements of this title.[2]

In contrast, this book will generally use the phrase "potentially patentable subject matter" to emphasize that even if an invention is of the proper type or category, it is only "potentially" patentable because it must still satisfy the remaining statutory criteria of utility,[3] novelty,[4] and nonobviousness[5] before a patent will be granted. As Judge Giles Rich explained in *In re Bergy,*[6] "[a] person may have 'invented' a

[1]In addition to utility patents, the subject matter of which is set forth in 35 U.S.C. §101, the U.S. patent system grants *plant patents* and *design patents*. Plant and design patents have separate statutory frameworks. *See infra* Section H ("Patentable Subject Matter Beyond §101: Plant Patents and Design Patents").

[2]35 U.S.C. §101 (2012) (emphases added).

[3]*See* Chapter 6 ("The Utility Requirement (35 U.S.C §101)"), *supra*.

[4]*See* Chapter 4 ("Novelty, Loss of Right, and Priority Pre- and Post-America Invents Act of 2011 (35 U.S.C. §102)"), *supra*.

[5]*See* Chapter 5 ("The Nonobviousness Requirement (35 U.S.C. §103)"), *supra*.

[6]596 F.2d 952 (C.C.P.A. 1979) (Rich, J.), *aff'd sub nom.* Diamond v. Chakrabarty, 447 U.S. 303 (1980).

machine or a manufacture, which may include anything under the sun that is made by man, *but it is not necessarily patentable* under section 101 unless the conditions of the title [35 U.S.C.] are fulfilled."[7]

Satisfying the potentially patentable subject matter threshold of 35 U.S.C. §101 means that an invention has passed through the first of the three doors in Judge Rich's classic "three doors to patentability" metaphor of *Bergy*:

> The first door which must be opened on the difficult path to patentability is §101 (augmented by the §100 definitions).... The person approaching that door is an inventor, whether his invention is patentable or not. There is always an inventor; being an inventor might be regarded as a preliminary legal requirement, for if he has not invented something, if he comes with something he knows was invented by someone else, he has no right even to approach the door. Thus, section 101 begins with the words "Whoever invents or discovers," and since 1790 the patent statutes have always said substantially that. Being an inventor or having an invention, however, is no guarantee of opening even the first door. What *kind* of an invention or discovery is it? In dealing with the question of kind, as distinguished from the qualitative conditions which make the invention patentable, §101 is broad and general; its language is: "any... process, machine, manufacture, or composition of matter, or any... improvement thereof." Section 100(b) further expands "process" to include "art or method, and... a new use of a known process, machine, manufacture, composition of matter, or material." If the invention, as the inventor defines it in his claims (pursuant to §112, second paragraph), falls into any one of the named categories, he is allowed to pass through to the second door, which is §102; "novelty and loss of right to patent" is the sign on it. Notwithstanding the words "new and useful" in §101, the invention is not examined under that statute for novelty because that is not the statutory scheme of things or the long-established administrative practice.[8]

Thus, 35 U.S.C. §101 enumerates the *types* of inventions that can be patented in the United States, in contrast with §102 and §103, which establish *qualitative* conditions for patentability.

The legislative history of the 1952 Patent Act expansively states that U.S. patents are available for "anything under the sun that is made by man."[9] Although the courts have generally construed potentially patentable subject matter quite broadly, in accordance with this legislative direction, the case law interpreting 35 U.S.C. §101 provides important limits on what can be patented. A number of notable judicial decisions have refined our understanding of these limits, as detailed below.

[7] *Id.* at 961.
[8] *Id.* at 960 (footnote omitted).
[9] S. Rep. No. 82-1979, at 5 (1952); H.R. Rep. No. 82-1923, at 6 (1952).

During 2010-2014, the U.S. Supreme Court decided four important cases dealing with §101 patent eligibility; each is discussed further in this chapter.[10] In the latter half of the 2010s, the Federal Circuit issued numerous §101 decisions applying the Supreme Court's guidance, including several important *en banc* cases. Collectively, these Supreme Court and Federal Circuit pronouncements imposed significant new limits on what can be patented in the United States.[11]

Note on Terminology. In the course of deciding its four §101 cases from 2010 to 2014, the Supreme Court adopted the phrase "patent-eligible subject matter" to denote those inventions that *do* qualify under 35 U.S.C. §101. Accordingly, this text will use interchangeably the phrases "patent-eligible subject matter," "statutory subject matter," "§101-eligible," and "potentially patentable subject matter" to refer to inventions that qualify within one (or more) of the statutory categories enumerated in §101. The text will sometimes refer to subject matter that does *not* qualify under §101 as "patent *in*eligible or §101 — ineligible."

2. The Statutory Categories of §101

Each of the four statutory categories of 35 U.S.C. §101 — process, machine, manufacture, and composition of matter — is discussed in detail below, but some working definitions and a few examples are warranted here:

- A **process**, in patent parlance, is synonymous with a method, and is merely a series of steps for carrying out a given task. Process patents have been granted for a method of making a "stuffed-crust" pizza,[12] and to the Internet bookseller

[10] *See* Bilski v. Kappos, 561 U.S. 593 (2010), discussed *infra* Section 4.b; Mayo Collaborative Servs. v. Prometheus Labs., Inc., 132 S. Ct. 1289 (2012), discussed *infra* Section B.5.a; Association for Molecular Pathology v. Myriad Genetics, Inc., 133 S. Ct. 2107 (2013), discussed *infra* Section D.2.b; and Alice Corp. Pty. Ltd. v. CLS Bank Int'l, 134 S. Ct. 2347 (2014), discussed *infra* Section B.4.d.

[11] A former Director of the USPTO has gone so far as to call for the abolition of 35 U.S.C. §101, asserting that the Supreme Court's recent and high-profile Section 101 decisions in *Mayo*, *Myriad* and *Alice* (detailed *infra*) have created a "real mess" and caused "chaos" in the patent system. Ryan Davis, *Kappos Calls for Abolition of Section 101 of the Patent Act*, Law360.com (Apr. 12, 2016) (quoting Kappos' speech at 2016 Federal Circuit Judicial Conference). In the view of David Kappos, who served as USPTO Director from 2009-2013, those Supreme Court decisions and the lower courts' interpretation thereof "have made it too difficult to secure patents on biotechnology and software inventions." *Id.*

[12] *See* "Method for making a stuffed pizza crust," U.S. Patent No. 6,048,556 (issued Apr. 11, 2000).

Amazon.com for its method of "one-click" online ordering of merchandise.[13]

- A **machine** is synonymous with an apparatus, and generally has moving parts, such as an internal combustion engine.
- A **composition of matter** includes chemical compositions and mixtures of substances such as metallic alloys.
- Lastly, a **manufacture** is the "catch-all" category for human-made subject matter without moving parts, such as a helically grooved foam football[14] or the Java Jacket® insulating sleeve for hot drink cups.[15]

These categories of potentially patentable subject matter are examined separately below.

3. Claiming the Inventive Concept Within Different Statutory Categories

The claims of a patent need not explicitly recite the category of potentially patentable subject matter to which the invention belongs (although some patent claims do). The proper categorization is usually clear from the face of the claim. For example, a claim that recites "a programmed computer" is understood as directed to the machine category of §101.[16] So long as the claim is sufficiently definite under the second paragraph of 35 U.S.C. §112,[17] such that the USPTO examiner can determine whether the recited subject matter falls within one or more categories of §101, nothing further is required.

The inventive concept to which a given patent is directed may encompass a number of different manifestations. That is to say, the "invention" may be claimed in many different ways, even within a

[13]*See* "Method and system for placing a purchase order via a communications network," U.S. Patent No. 5,960,411 (issued Sept. 28, 1999). The Federal Circuit questioned the validity of this patent when it refused to uphold a preliminary injunction against accused infringer Barnes & Noble in *Amazon.com, Inc. v. Barnesandnoble.com, Inc.*, 239 F.3d 1343 (Fed. Cir. 2001).

[14]*See* U.S. Patent No. Re. 33,449 (reissued Nov. 20, 1990).

[15]The Java Jacket® patent, U.S. Patent No. 5,425,497 (issued June 20, 1995), is reproduced in Chapter 1, Section C.5 ("The Patent Document and Its Components"), *supra*.

[16]*See* WMS Gaming, Inc. v. Int'l Game Tech., 184 F.3d 1339, 1348 (Fed. Cir. 1999) (stating that "[a] general purpose computer, or microprocessor, programmed to carry out an algorithm creates 'a new machine, because a general purpose computer in effect becomes a special purpose computer once it is programmed to perform particular functions pursuant to instructions from program software'") (quoting In re Alappat, 33 F.3d 1526, 1545 (Fed. Cir. 1994) (*en banc*)).

[17]The claim definiteness requirement of 35 U.S.C. §112(b) (eff. Sept. 16, 2012) is discussed further in Chapter 2 ("Patent Claims"), *supra*.

single patent application, and the claims of that application may be drawn to more than one statutory subject matter category under 35 U.S.C. §101. For example, the inventor of a novel and nonobvious drug may file an application claiming the chemical structure of the drug itself as a composition of matter, as well as a method of synthesizing the drug, as well as a method of treating patients suffering from a certain disease, which method comprises administering an effective amount of the drug. All of these claims would be drawn to various aspects of the same "invention" or "inventive concept," broadly understood.

Claims that recite subject matter falling within different statutory categories, such as those of the preceding new drug example, are often filed in the same patent application because they all stem from the same inventive contribution. In some instances, however, the USPTO will require "restriction" of certain groups of claims into separate patent applications, primarily for the administrative convenience of the agency during the examination process.[18] Restriction is appropriate if the claims are directed to "independent and distinct" inventions.[19] For example, the drug inventor in the above example might be

[18]*See* 35 U.S.C. §121 (providing in part that "[i]f two or more independent and distinct inventions are claimed in one application, the Director [of the USPTO] may require the application to be restricted to one of the inventions"). *See also* Transco Prods., Inc. v. Performance Contracting, Inc., 38 F.3d 551, 558 (Fed. Cir. 1994) (explaining that "when confronted with an application claiming more than one independent and distinct invention, an examiner often will impose a restriction requirement pursuant to 35 U.S.C. §121 to ease the burden of examining that subject matter, thus forcing an applicant to file one or more divisional applications"). *See also* Section H.5 of Chapter 1 ("Foundations of the U.S. Patent System"), *supra*.

[19]35 U.S.C. §121. The USPTO provides the following guidance on the meaning of "independent" and "related but distinct" (i.e., dependent) inventions:

> I. INDEPENDENT
> The term "independent" (i.e., unrelated) means that there is no disclosed relationship between the two or more inventions claimed, that is, they are unconnected in design, operation, and effect. For example, a process and an apparatus incapable of being used in practicing the process are independent inventions....
>
> II. RELATED BUT DISTINCT
> Two or more inventions are related (i.e., not independent) if they are disclosed as connected in at least one of design (e.g., structure or method of manufacture), operation (e.g., function or method of use), or effect. Examples of related inventions include combination and part (subcombination) thereof, process and apparatus for its practice, process and product made, etc. In this definition the term related is used as an alternative for dependent in referring to inventions other than independent inventions.
>
> Related inventions are distinct if the inventions *as claimed* are not connected in at least one of design, operation, or effect (e.g., can be made by, or used in, a materially different process) and wherein at least one invention is PATENTABLE (novel and nonobvious) OVER THE OTHER (though they may each be unpatentable over the prior art)....

required to restrict her original (*parent*) application to only those claims directed to the composition of matter, and to file one or more additional (*divisional*) applications directed to the remaining groups of claims reciting the method of making and the method of treatment.[20]

Sometimes a pioneer invention may represent such an advance over prior innovation as to defy categorization in a single statutory category. For example, the Supreme Court held that the genetically engineered, petroleum-consuming bacterium of *Diamond v. Chakrabarty*[21] could properly be categorized as either a "composition of matter" *or* a "manufacture."[22] For purposes of potential patentability under §101, all that matters is that the invention fall within at least one statutory category. The precise identity of the category is not important, nor need it be explicitly stated in the claim.

The remainder of this chapter addresses the leading judicial decisions interpreting each of the four statutory categories of 35 U.S.C. §101, as well as judicially recognized exceptions from patentability. Patents are not available for certain types of important scientific advances, such as the discovery of a previously unrecognized law of nature or scientific principle such as gravity or Einstein's theory of relativity, despite the obvious significance of these contributions to our society. This chapter concludes by introducing two additional types of non-utility patent protection that are available in the United States: plant patents and design patents.

4. Exceptions to §101

In a landmark 2012 decision, *Mayo Collaborative Servs. v. Prometheus Labs., Inc.*,[23] the Supreme Court observed that it had "long held" that 35 U.S.C. §101 "contains an important implicit exception."[24] That

---

> It is further noted that the terms "independent" and "distinct" are used in decisions with varying meanings. All decisions should be read carefully to determine the meaning intended.

United States Patent and Trademark Office, Manual of Patent Examining Procedure §802.01 (9th ed., last rev. Nov. 2015) (MPEP citations omitted), *available at* http://www.uspto.gov/web/offices/pac/mpep/s802.html#d0e97928.

[20]Divisional applications are discussed in further detail at Section H.5 of Chapter 1 ("Foundations of the U.S. Patent System"), *supra*.

[21]447 U.S. 303 (1980).

[22]*See Chakrabarty*, 447 U.S. at 309-310 (stating that "respondent's . . . claim is not to a hitherto unknown natural phenomenon, but to a nonnaturally occurring manufacture or composition of matter — a product of human ingenuity 'having a distinctive name, character [and] use'") (quoting Hartranft v. Wiegmann, 121 U.S. 609, 615 (1887)).

[23]132 S. Ct. 1289 (2012). *Mayo* is detailed *infra* Section B.4.c and Section B.5.a.

[24]*Mayo*, 132 S. Ct. at 1293. Query whether statutes are logically thought of as creating "implicit exceptions." Generally such exceptions are created by the judiciary.

"implicit exception" (more precisely, three implicit exceptions) provides that "'laws of nature, natural phenomena, and abstract ideas' are not patentable."[25] As examples of these three exceptions or categories of patent-ineligible subject matter, the Court has written that

> a new mineral discovered in the earth or a new plant found in the wild is not patentable subject matter. Likewise, Einstein could not patent his celebrated law that $E = mc^2$; nor could Newton have patented the law of gravity. Such discoveries are "manifestations of... nature, free to all men and reserved exclusively to none."[26]

In 2014, the Court in *Alice Corp. Pty. Ltd. v. CLS Bank Int'l,* discussed below,[27] asserted that "[w]e have interpreted §101 and its predecessors in light of this exception for more than 150 years."

The Supreme Court sometimes uses the concept of "preemption" to describe the policy concerns that support recognition of §101's implicit exception.[28] The Court here uses "preemption" not in the Supremacy Clause sense (under which federal law may preempt or take precedence over certain state laws), but rather in the more common usage of "preempting" as blocking others. Although the Court has not been abundantly clear about the limits of "preemption," the concern is that certain types of fundamental discoveries should not be patentable if such patents would prevent others from innovating.[29] Because the

[25]*Mayo*, 132 S. Ct. at 1293 (quoting Diamond v. Diehr, 450 U.S. 175, 185 (1981); citing also Bilski v. Kappos, 130 S. Ct. 3218, 3233-3234 (2010); Diamond v. Chakrabarty, 447 U.S. 303, 309 (1980); Le Roy v. Tatham, 14 How. 156, 175 (1853); O'Reilly v. Morse, 15 How. 62, 112-120 (1854); citing cf. Neilson v. Harford, Webster's Patent Cases 295, 371 (1841) (English case discussing same)).

[26]*Chakrabarty*, 447 U.S. at 309 (quoting Funk Brothers Seed Co. v. Kalo Inoculant Co., 333 U.S. 127, 130 (1948)).

[27]134 S. Ct. 2347 (2014). *Alice Corp.* is further discussed *infra* Section B.4.d.

[28]*See Alice Corp.*, 134 S. Ct. at 2354 (citing, e.g., Bilski v. Kappos, 561 U.S. 593, 611-612 (2010) (stating that "[t]he concept of hedging, described in claim 1 [of Bilski's patent application] and reduced to a mathematical formula in claim 4, is an unpatentable abstract idea, just like the algorithms at issue in *Benson* and *Flook*. Allowing petitioners to patent risk hedging would pre-empt use of this approach in all fields, and would effectively grant a monopoly over an abstract idea[.]")).

[29]*See, e.g.*, Gottschalk v. Benson, 409 U.S. 63 (1972), stating:

> It is conceded that one may not patent an idea. But in practical effect that would be the result if the formula for converting BCD [binary coded decimal] numerals to pure binary numerals were patented in this case. The mathematical formula involved here has no substantial practical application except in connection with a digital computer, which means that if the judgment below is affirmed, the patent would wholly *pre-empt* the mathematical formula and in practical effect would be a patent on the algorithm itself.

Benson, 409 U.S. at 71-72 (emphasis added). *See also* O'Reilly v. Morse, 56 U.S. 62 (1853), in which the Court explained its rationale for refusing a patent on the eighth claim of telegraph inventor Samuel Morse's patent:

three components of the §101 exception — laws of nature, natural phenomena, and abstract ideas — represent basic tools or building blocks of science and technology, the patent laws must not allow their future use to be improperly tied up. The primary object of the patent laws, promotion of the useful arts,[30] would be thwarted if patenting these basic tools meant that innovation would be impeded more than encouraged.[31]

We perceive no well-founded objection to the description which is given of the whole invention and its separate parts, nor to his right to a patent for the first seven inventions set forth in the specification of his claims. The difficulty arises on the eighth.

It is in the following words:

"Eighth. I do not propose to limit myself to the specific machinery or parts of machinery described in the foregoing specification and claims; the essence of my invention being the use of the motive power of the electric or galvanic current, which I call electro-magnetism, however developed for marking or printing intelligible characters, signs, or letters, at any distances, being a new application of that power of which I claim to be the first inventor or discoverer."

It is impossible to misunderstand the extent of this claim. He claims the exclusive right to every improvement where the motive power is the electric or galvanic current, and the result is the marking or printing intelligible characters, signs, or letters at a distance.

If this claim can be maintained, it matters not by what process or machinery the result is accomplished. For aught that we now know some future inventor, in the onward march of science, may discover a mode of writing or printing at a distance by means of the electric or galvanic current, without using any part of the process or combination set forth in the plaintiff's specification. His invention may be less complicated — less liable to get out of order — less expensive in construction, and in its operation. But yet if it is covered by this patent the inventor could not use it, nor the public have the benefit of it without the permission of this patentee.

Nor is this all, while he shuts the door against inventions of other persons, the patentee would be able to avail himself of new discoveries in the properties and powers of electro-magnetism which scientific men might bring to light. For he says he does not confine his claim to the machinery or parts of machinery, which he specifies; but claims for himself a monopoly in its use, however developed, for the purpose of printing at a distance. New discoveries in physical science may enable him to combine it with new agents and new elements, and by that means attain the object in a manner superior to the present process and altogether different from it. And if he can secure the exclusive use by his present patent he may vary it with every new discovery and development of the science, and need place no description of the new manner, process, or machinery, upon the records of the patent office. And when his patent expires, the public must apply to him to learn what it is. In fine he claims an exclusive right to use a manner and process which he has not described and indeed had not invented, and therefore could not describe when he obtained his patent. The court is of opinion that the claim is too broad, and not warranted by law.

O'Reilly v. Morse, 56 U.S. at 112-113.

[30]*See* U.S. CONST. art. 1, §8, cl. 8.

[31]*See Alice Corp.*, 134 S. Ct. at 2354.

At the same time, the Court has recognized that it must "tread carefully in construing this [§101] exclusionary principle lest it swallow all of patent law."[32] At some level, *all* inventions are based on or make use of laws of nature, natural phenomena, or abstract ideas. Thus, "an invention is not rendered ineligible for patent simply because it involves an abstract concept."[33] The *application* of an abstract concept "'to a new and useful end'... remain[s] eligible for patent protection."[34]

Accordingly, in applying the implicit exception in 35 U.S.C. §101, courts must

> distinguish between patents that claim the "'buildin[g] block[s]'" of human ingenuity and those that integrate the building blocks into something more, *Mayo,* 566 U.S., at ____, 132 S. Ct., at 1303, thereby "transform[ing]" them into a patent-eligible invention, *id.,* at ____, 132 S. Ct., at 1294. The former "would risk disproportionately tying up the use of the underlying" ideas, *id.,* at ____, 132 S. Ct., at 1294, and are therefore ineligible for patent protection. The latter pose no comparable risk of pre-emption, and therefore remain eligible for the monopoly granted under our patent laws.[35]

This text further explores below the three "implicit exception[s]" in 35 U.S.C. §101 — laws of nature, natural phenomena, and abstract ideas — in the context of whether and how they limit the categories of subject matter that *are* explicitly and positively enumerated as potentially patentable under §101 — processes, machines, compositions of matter, and manufactures.

B. Section 101 Processes

1. Basic Principles

The patenting of processes is as old as the patent law itself. The first U.S. patent law, the Patent Act of 1790, referred to a process as an "art."[36] The very first U.S. patent was granted for a process of making

[32]*Alice Corp.*, 134 S. Ct. at 2354 (citing Mayo Collab. Servs. v. Prometheus Labs., Inc., 132 S. Ct. 1289, 1293-1294 (2012)).

[33]*Alice Corp.*, 134 S. Ct. at 2354 (citing Diamond v. Diehr, 450 U.S. 175, 187 (1981)).

[34]*Alice Corp.*, 134 S. Ct. at 2354 (quoting Gottschalk v. Benson, 409 U.S. 63, 67 (1972)).

[35]*Alice Corp.*, 134 S. Ct. at 2354-2355.

[36]Patent Act of April 10, 1790, ch. 7, §1, 1 Stat. 109 (providing that patent grant requires that "he, she, or they, hath or have invented or discovered any useful art, manufacture, engine, machine, or device, or any improvement therein"). *See also* S. Rep. No. 82-1979 (1952), *as reprinted in* 1952 U.S.C.C.A.N. 2394, 2398 (explaining that replacement of "art" by "process" in the enactment of 35 U.S.C. §101 resulted in no substantive change because art had been "interpreted by the courts to be practically synonymous with process or method").

potash, a chemical compound used chiefly in fertilizers.[37] Today, the U.S. Patent Act provides that the term *process* means "process, art, or method."[38]

A process is synonymous with a method, or a series of steps for accomplishing some result. Often, the process is a novel and nonobvious method of making some end product. For example, a typical process claim might recite a method of making a chemical compound X as follows:

1. A process for making compound X, comprising the steps of
   (1) mixing equal parts Y with Z to form a mixture,
   (2) heating the mixture to a temperature of about 100 degrees Celsius,
   (3) cooling the mixture to a temperature of about 20 degrees Celsius, and
   (4) recovering a precipitate of said compound X from the cooled mixture.

Importantly, the end product of the process, in this hypothetical the compound X, need not itself be patentable; in other words, a process claim can be granted for a novel and nonobvious method of making an old product. The Patent Act's definitional section provides that the "term process . . . includes a new use of a known process, machine, manufacture, composition of matter, or material."[39]

The independent patentability of new processes for making known products reflects the importance to society of stimulating new process innovation. Consider, for example, the societal benefit achieved through the invention of new processes to make insulin, a well-known protein needed by people with diabetes. Insulin is now easily obtained in large quantities through DNA cloning techniques. This recombinant process is much more efficient than the conventional method of extracting the insulin from the pancreas of hogs.[40] By providing the incentive of process patent protection, the patent system calls forth new and nonobvious ways to make existing products.

[37] See David W. Maxey & Samuel Hopkins, *The Holder of the First U.S. Patent: A Study of Failure,* 122 Pa. Mag. of Hist. & Biography 3 (1998); David W. Maxey, *Inventing History: The Holder of the First U.S. Patent,* 80 J. Pat. & Trademark Off. Soc'y 155 (1998).

[38] 35 U.S.C. §100(b).

[39] *Id.*

[40] *See* Karl Drlica, Understanding DNA and Gene Cloning: A Guide for the Curious 14 (4th ed. 2003) (describing the method for expression of human insulin genes in bacteria).

2. Process Versus Product

Process claims, as in the example above, should be distinguished from product claims, which are typically drawn to compositions of matter or manufactures, discussed separately below. A process claim is generally considered narrower in scope, and hence of less economic value to the patent owner, than a product claim. Why? Consider the above claim to a process comprising steps (1) to (4), performed in the recited order, (1)-(2)-(3)-(4), which produces a given product, compound X. This process claim is relatively narrow in scope because it is literally infringed only by other processes that make X by repeating the identical series of recited steps, (1) to (4), in that sequence. If a competitor can determine how to make the product X by a different process, for example steps (5) to (8), or by performing steps (1) to (4) in a different order, such as (3)-(4)-(1)-(2), then the process claim has not been literally infringed.[41]

On the other hand, if a patent is obtained with a claim to the product X itself, then the making of X by *any* process, whether it comprises steps (1) to (4), (5) to (8), (3)-(4)-(1)-(2), or any other set of steps, literally infringes the claim. In other words, the scope of protection for the product, claimed as a product, is not limited by the process with which it is made. Nor is it relevant whether the product patent owner knew of or described the processes used by the accused infringer to make product X. "[A] patentee is entitled to every use of which his invention is susceptible, whether such use be known or unknown to him."[42] Accordingly, product claims are generally considered far more economically valuable to a patentee than are process claims.

3. Computer-Implemented Processes

Many patented processes or methods are implemented through the use of computers and software. For example, in 1981, the Supreme Court in *Diamond v. Diehr*[43] upheld the patentability under 35 U.S.C. §101 of a computer-controlled process for curing synthetic rubber. By monitoring the real-time conditions inside the mold, the process control system determined when the mold should be opened by performing calculations based on the well-known Arrhenius equation. Representative claim 1 of the Diehr patent provided:

[41]The process claim might nevertheless be infringed under the doctrine of equivalents if the accused process is insubstantially different. The doctrine of equivalents is examined in Chapter 9 ("Patent Infringement"), *infra*.

[42]In re Thuau, 135 F.2d 344, 347 (C.C.P.A. 1943).

[43]450 U.S. 175 (1981).

1. A method of operating a rubber-molding press for precision molded compounds with the aid of a digital computer, comprising:

providing said computer with a database for said press including at least,

natural logarithm conversion data (ln),

the activation energy constant (c) unique to each batch of said compound being molded, and

a constant (x) dependent upon the geometry of the particular mold of the press,

initiating an interval timer in said computer upon the closure of the press for monitoring the elapsed time of said closure,

constantly determining the temperature (Z) of the mold at a location closely adjacent to the mold cavity in the press during molding,

constantly providing the computer with the temperature (Z),

repetitively calculating in the computer, at frequent intervals during each cure, the Arrhenius equation for reaction time during the cure, which is

$\ln v = CZ + x$

where v is the total required cure time,

repetitively comparing in the computer at said frequent intervals during the cure each said calculation of the total required cure time calculated with the Arrhenius equation and said elapsed time, and

opening the press automatically when a said comparison indicates equivalence.[44]

Although unapplied mathematical algorithms, formulas, and equations are considered unpatentable abstract ideas, the Supreme Court in *Diehr* made clear that the presence of such mathematical subject matter in a patent claim (such as Diehr's claim 1) does not necessarily deprive the claim of potential patentability under 35 U.S.C. §101. Claims must be analyzed as a whole, not dissected into their component parts, for purposes of determining if an invention falls within one or more of the §101 categories. The presence of a mathematical algorithm or formula in a patent claim does not necessarily render it ineligible for patent protection.

The Supreme Court concluded that, in contrast with the inventors in its previous decisions denying patentability to computer-implemented inventions,[45] Diehr did not seek to patent a

[44]*Id.* at 179 n.5.

[45]*Diamond v. Diehr* represents the last of a trilogy of Supreme Court decisions issued between 1972 and 1981 in which the Court struggled with the patentability of computer-implemented inventions. In holding (by a 5-4 margin) that Diehr's claimed process for curing rubber was patentable subject matter within 35 U.S.C. §101, the *Diehr* majority sought to distinguish the two earlier decisions of the trilogy, *Gottschalk v. Benson*, 409 U.S. 63 (1972), and *Parker v. Flook*, 437 U.S. 584 (1978), as follows:

> In *Benson*, we held unpatentable claims for an algorithm used to convert binary code decimal numbers to equivalent pure binary numbers. The sole practical

mathematical formula per se but rather a process of curing synthetic rubber. That process "admittedly employ[ed] a well-known mathematical equation, but [did] not seek to pre-empt the use of that equation."[46] Rather, Diehr sought only to foreclose others from using the Arrhenius equation in conjunction with all of the other steps recited in the claimed process, that is, installing rubber in a press, closing the mold, constantly determining the temperature of the mold, constantly recalculating the appropriate cure time through the use of the Arrhenius equation and a digital computer, and automatically opening the press at the proper time. Although a computer is not necessarily needed to cure natural or synthetic rubber, the Court realized that the computer use incorporated into Diehr's process patent significantly lessened the possibility of overcuring or undercuring the rubber, an important and useful result. The process as claimed represented potentially patentable subject matter under 35 U.S.C. §101.

In the aftermath of *Diehr,* some commentators suggested that in order to come within 35 U.S.C. §101, patent claims to a process (or method) comprising a mathematical algorithm had to involve a "physical transformation" of material into a different state or thing, such as the curing of the synthetic rubber in *Diehr.* The Federal Circuit subsequently rejected a blanket "physical transformation" requirement in *AT&T Corp. v. Excel Communications, Inc.*[47] There the Circuit reversed a district court's summary judgment that AT&T's '184 patent, directed to a method of inserting information called a "primary interexchange carrier (PIC) indicator" into a long-distance telephone call record in order to facilitate differential billing of subscribers (depending on whether the subscriber called someone with the same or different long-distance carrier), was invalid as not falling within §101 subject matter.[48]

> application of the algorithm was in connection with the programming of a general purpose digital computer. We defined "algorithm" as a "procedure for solving a given type of mathematical problem," and we concluded that such an algorithm, or mathematical formula, is like a law of nature, which cannot be the subject of a patent.
>
> *Parker v. Flook* ... presented a similar situation. The claims were drawn to a method for computing an "alarm limit." An "alarm limit" is simply a number and the Court concluded that the application sought to protect a formula for computing this number. Using this formula, the updated alarm limit could be calculated if several other variables were known. The application, however, did not purport to explain how these other variables were to be determined, nor did it purport "to contain any disclosure relating to the chemical processes at work, the monitoring of process variables, or the means of setting off an alarm or adjusting an alarm system. All that it provides is a formula for computing an updated alarm limit."

Diehr, 450 U.S. at 185-187 (footnotes and citations omitted).

[46] *Id.* at 187.

[47] 172 F.3d 1352 (Fed. Cir. 1999).

[48] *Id.* at 1353.

Rejecting defendant Excel's reading of *Diehr* as overly limited, the Federal Circuit interpreted *Diehr* as simply standing for the proposition that a "physical transformation" is "not an invariable requirement, but merely one example of how a mathematical algorithm may bring about a useful application."[49] The Federal Circuit concluded in *AT&T* that, although the claimed process admittedly applied a simple Boolean principle to determine the value of the PIC indicator, this process produced a "useful, concrete, tangible result" without preempting other uses of the mathematical principle.[50] Thus the claimed process "comfortably" fell within the scope of 35 U.S.C. §101.[51]

4. Business Methods

A process or method of doing business or operating a business is potentially patentable, just as is a method for doing anything else, so long as the claimed method is not an unapplied, abstract idea or concept. (Of course, a potentially patentable business method must also be novel, useful, and nonobvious to merit patent protection.) With the rise of the Internet, many individuals and firms sought to patent methods of doing business that involved implementation via computers connected to the Internet (e.g., "one-click" ordering of merchandise from the online purveyor Amazon.com). In many cases, the patents attempted to claim Internet-implemented, "e-commerce" versions of tasks previously performed with pen and paper. Numerous court challenges resulted from the issuance of such patents. From the late 1990s to the present, a series of important Supreme Court and Federal Circuit cases has confronted the question whether such business methods are patent-eligible inventions within 35 U.S.C. §101. The remainder of this section analyzes the progression of the key decisions.

a. State Street Bank *(Fed. Cir. 1998)*

A logical starting point is the Federal Circuit's 1998 watershed case on business method patentability, *State St. Bank & Trust Co. v. Signature Fin. Group, Inc.*[52] The *State Street* dispute concerned the

[49] *Id.* at 1358-1359.
[50] *Id.* at 1358.
[51] *Id.*
[52] 149 F.3d 1368 (Fed. Cir. 1998) (Rich, J.). Judge Rich passed away the year after the Federal Circuit issued *State Street Bank*. *See* Richard A. Oppel Jr., *Giles S. Rich, Oldest Active Federal Judge, Dies at 95*, N.Y. TIMES (June 12, 1999) (stating that "Judge Rich was a towering figure in patent and intellectual-property law for a half-century, playing a leading role in the transformation from a time when patents were enforced unevenly and held in suspicion by many jurists, to a time when not only devices and inventions but also theories and concepts came under protection of the Federal courts").

patentability of Signature's computer-implemented, hub and spoke-configured system for managing a partner-fund financial services configuration. Representative claim 1 of Signature's U.S. Patent No. 5,193,056 ('056 patent) provided as follows, with the bracketed language indicating the structure disclosed in the written description as corresponding to each recited "means" in accordance with 35 U.S.C. §112, ¶6 (1994):

> 1. A data processing system for managing a financial services configuration of a portfolio established as a partnership, each partner being one of a plurality of funds, comprising:
>
> (a) computer processor means [a personal computer including a CPU] for processing data;
>
> (b) storage means [a data disk] for storing data on a storage medium;
>
> (c) first means [an arithmetic logic circuit configured to prepare the data disk to magnetically store selected data] for initializing the storage medium;
>
> (d) second means [an arithmetic logic circuit configured to retrieve information from a specific file, calculate incremental increases or decreases based on specific input, allocate the results on a percentage basis, and store the output in a separate file] for processing data regarding assets in the portfolio and each of the funds from a previous day and data regarding increases or decreases in each of the funds [sic funds'] assets and for allocating the percentage share that each fund holds in the portfolio;
>
> (e) third means [an arithmetic logic circuit configured to retrieve information from a specific file, calculate incremental increases and decreases based on specific input, allocate the results on a percentage basis and store the output in a separate file] for processing data regarding daily incremental income, expenses, and net realized gain or loss for the portfolio and for allocating such data among each fund;
>
> (f) fourth means [an arithmetic logic circuit configured to retrieve information from a specific file, calculate incremental increases and decreases based on specific input, allocate the results on a percentage basis and store the output in a separate file] for processing data regarding daily net unrealized gain or loss for the portfolio and for allocating such data among each fund; and
>
> (g) fifth means [an arithmetic logic circuit configured to retrieve information from specific files, calculate that information on an aggregate basis and store the output in a separate file] for processing data regarding aggregate year-end income, expenses, and capital gain or loss for the portfolio and each of the funds.[53]

[53]*Id.* at 1371-1372. For additional detail on the interpretation of means plus function clauses in patent claims, *see supra* Chapter 2, Section E.1. The America Invents Act of 2011 renamed the sixth paragraph of 35 U.S.C. §112 as 35 U.S.C §112(f) (eff. Sept. 16, 2012).

Figure 7.1 depicts the '056 patent's claimed system in schematic form:

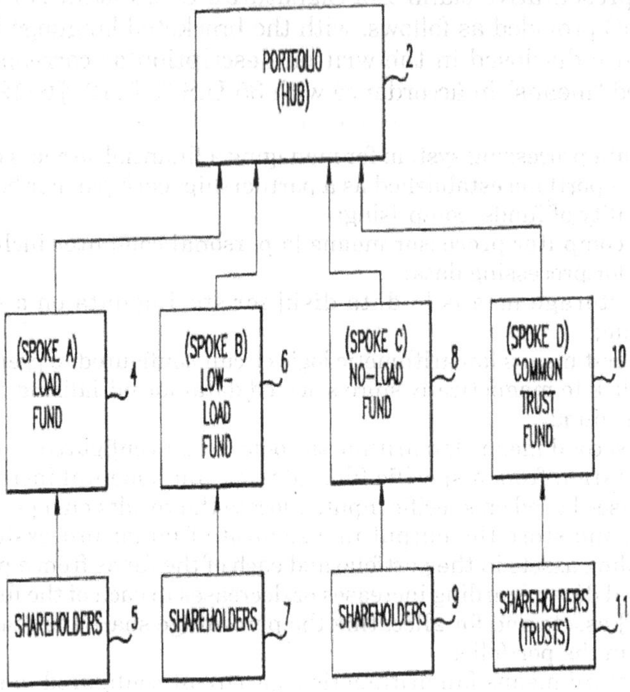

FIG.1

Figure 7.1

Figure from Signature's U.S. Patent No. 5,193,056

On motion for summary judgment by accused infringer State Street, the district court held Signature's patent invalid as claiming subject matter that fell within two judicially recognized exceptions to patentable subject matter under §101: the so-called business method and mathematical algorithm exceptions.

The Federal Circuit reversed, holding the claims at issue were directed to a statutory "machine" under 35 U.S.C. §101, albeit one programmed with "hub and spoke" software. The key question in a §101 determination, the appellate court stressed, is not which of the four statutory categories the claimed invention may fit into (e.g., machine versus process). Rather, attention should focus on the essential characteristics of the invention, namely, its "practical utility."[54] In this case, the Signature system's utility was evidenced by its production of a "useful, concrete, and tangible result,"[55] even though this result was expressed in numerical values (such as a fund share price) rather than something more conventionally physical (e.g., widgets).[56]

The Federal Circuit minced no words in taking the opportunity presented by the *State Street* case "to lay th[e] ill-conceived [business method] exception to rest."[57] A method of doing business should be treated just as any other type of method, the court emphasized. Each of the earlier business method exception cases could have been decided on clearer grounds, the court explained; the results in those cases would have been the same had the inventions been more properly characterized as abstract ideas under the mathematical algorithm exception to patentability.

Following the Federal Circuit's 1998 decision in *State Street,* the USPTO received a flood of business method patent applications.[58] Although the eligibility of business methods as potentially patentable subject matter under §101 is now settled, it remains to be seen whether many of the claimed business methods will meet the exacting novelty and nonobviousness criteria of §102 and §103, as well as the enablement and written description requirements under §112(a). For example, the Federal Circuit raised serious questions about the nonobviousness of the "one-click" product ordering method patented to much fanfare by the Internet retailer Amazon.com.[59]

Is a business method for conducting mandatory arbitration of legal documents such as wills and contracts within §101 patentable subject matter? To the extent that such a method depends entirely on the use of human intelligence, and does not require a computer or other

[54] *State Street*, 149 F.3d at 1375.

[55] *Id.*

[56] In *In re Bilski*, 545 F.3d 943 (Fed. Cir. 2008) (*en banc*), the Federal Circuit characterized *State Street*'s "useful, concrete, and tangible result" language as an inadequate or insufficient test, standing alone, for determining whether claimed subject matter is potentially patentable under 35 U.S.C. §101. *See In re Bilski*, 545 F.3d at 959-960. The Supreme Court thereafter confirmed that "nothing in today's opinion should be read as endorsing interpretations of §101 that the Court of Appeals for the Federal Circuit has used in the past." *Bilski v. Kappos,* 130 S. Ct. 3218, 3231 (citing *State Street*, 149 F.3d at 1373; *AT&T Corp.,* 172 F.3d at 1357). *Bilski* and its treatment of *State Street* are discussed in further detail *infra* Section B.4.b.

[57] *State Street*, 149 F.3d at 1375.

[58] *See generally* United States Patent & Trademark Office, *Whitepaper, Automated Financial or Management Data Processing Methods (Business Methods)* 7, *available at* http://www.uspto.gov/web/menu/busmethp/whitepaper.pdf (last visited Feb. 12, 2016).

[59] *See* Amazon.com, Inc. v. Barnesandnoble.com, Inc., 239 F.3d 1343, 1359-1360 (Fed. Cir. 2001) (vacating district court's grant of preliminary injunction against accused infringer Barnesandnoble.com on ground that it had "mounted a serious challenge to the validity of Amazon's patent" under §103).

machine, the Federal Circuit in 2007 answered in the negative.[60] The claimed invention in *In re Comiskey* encompassed a "method for mandatory arbitration resolution regarding one or more unilateral documents," comprising the steps of enrolling a person and his associated documents (such as a will) in the mandatory arbitration system, incorporating arbitration language in the enrolled document, requiring a complainant to submit a request for binding arbitration resolution when a dispute arises concerning interpretation of the document, conducting arbitration resolution, providing support to the arbitration, and determining a final and binding award or decision in the dispute.[61] Other claims recited using the process to resolve disputes over contracts rather than wills.[62] Applicant Comiskey agreed with the USPTO that these process claims did not require the use of a computer or other mechanical device.

The Federal Circuit affirmed the USPTO's rejection of Comiskey's claims as not within §101 patentable subject matter.[63] Comiskey claimed "the use of mental processes to resolve a dispute"; that is, he sought "to patent the use of human intelligence in and of itself."[64] Even though Comiskey's process arguably performed a useful, practical service (arbitration of legal disputes), "mental processes — or processes of human thinking — standing alone are not patentable even if they have practical application."[65] The Patent Act "does not allow patents to be issued on particular business systems — such as a particular type of arbitration — that depend entirely on the use of mental processes."[66] The *Comiskey* court concluded that such endeavors were intended "both [by] the framers and Congress ... to be beyond the reach of patentable subject matter."[67]

b. Bilski *(U.S. 2010)*

Continued controversy over the patenting of business methods,[68] and a perceived lack of clarity in Federal Circuit law over where to draw the

[60]*See* In re Comiskey, 499 F.3d 1365 (Fed. Cir. 2007).

[61]*See id.* at 1368 n.1 (reproducing text of application claim 1).

[62]*See id.* at 1369 n.2 (reproducing text of application claim 32).

[63]*See id.* at 1381 (affirming rejection of Comiskey's independent claims 1 and 32 and dependent claims 2-14, 16, 33-34, and 45).

[64]*Id.* at 1379.

[65]*Id.* at 1377. *See also* In re Bilski, 545 F.3d 943, 961 n.26 (Fed. Cir. Oct. 30, 2008) (*en banc*) (stating that "a claimed process wherein all of the process steps may be performed entirely in the human mind is obviously not tied to any machine and does not transform any article into a different state or thing. As a result, it would not be patent-eligible under §101.").

[66]*Comiskey*, 499 F.3d at 1378.

[67]*Id.* at 1378-1379.

[68]*See, e.g.*, eBay Inc. v. MercExchange, LLC, 547 U.S. 388, 397 (2006) (Kennedy, J., concurring) (referring to the "potential vagueness and suspect validity" of some business method patents).

line between patentable process inventions within §101 and unpatentable abstract ideas or fundamental principles, led the court in 2007 to grant *en banc* review of these issues in *In re Bilski.*[69] As discussed *infra,* the case would eventually reach the U.S. Supreme Court.[70]

Bilski's claimed invention involved a method of hedging risk in the field of commodities trading.[71] Claim 1 of Bilski's application recited the following:

> 1. A method for managing the consumption risk costs of a commodity sold by a commodity provider at a fixed price comprising the steps of:
>
> (a) initiating a series of transactions between said commodity provider and consumers of said commodity wherein said consumers purchase said commodity at a fixed rate based upon historical averages, said fixed rate corresponding to a risk position of said consumer;
>
> (b) identifying market participants for said commodity having a counter-risk position to said consumers; and
>
> (c) initiating a series of transactions between said commodity provider and said market participants at a second fixed rate such that said series of market participant transactions balances the risk position of said series of consumer transactions.[72]

A USPTO Examiner had rejected Bilski's claims because they were "not implemented on a specific apparatus and merely manipulate[d]

[69]In re Bilski, 545 F.3d 943 (Fed. Cir. 2008) (*en banc*). As discussed *infra,* the Supreme Court subsequently granted *certiorari* and reviewed the Federal Circuit in *Bilski v. Kappos*, 130 S. Ct. 3218 (2010), a splintered decision that sustained the Federal Circuit on the merits but rejected much of the appellate court's reasoning.

[70]Bilski v. Kappos, 130 S. Ct. 3218 (2010).

[71]The Federal Circuit provided the following example of one implementation of Bilski's invention:

> [C]oal power plants (i.e., the "consumers" [of claim 1]) purchase coal to produce electricity and are averse to the risk of a spike in demand for coal since such a spike would increase the price and their costs. Conversely, coal mining companies (i.e., the "market participants") are averse to the risk of a sudden drop in demand for coal since such a drop would reduce their sales and depress prices. The claimed method envisions an intermediary, the "commodity provider," that sells coal to the power plants at a fixed price, thus isolating the power plants from the possibility of a spike in demand increasing the price of coal above the fixed price. The same provider buys coal from mining companies at a second fixed price, thereby isolating the mining companies from the possibility that a drop in demand would lower prices below that fixed price. And the provider has thus hedged its risk; if demand and prices skyrocket, it has sold coal at a disadvantageous price but has bought coal at an advantageous price, and vice versa if demand and prices fall.

In re Bilski, 545 F.3d at 950. Notably, Bilski's claim 1 was "not limited to transactions involving actual commodities." *Id.* Bilski's application disclosed that the recited transactions might "simply involve options, i.e., rights to purchase or sell the commodity at a particular price within a particular timeframe." *Id.*

[72]*Id.* at 949.

[an] abstract idea and solve[d] a purely mathematical problem without any limitation to a practical application."[73] The USPTO Board agreed that the claims were not patentable, but on the grounds that their "transformation of non-physical financial risks and legal liabilities" was not patentable subject matter, that they pre-empted every possible way of performing the claimed process "by human or by any kind of machine," and that they were directed only to an abstract idea.[74]

The Federal Circuit affirmed the USPTO's rejection of Bilski's claims as not being within §101 patentable processes.[75] In reaching its conclusion, the appellate court undertook an extensive review of Supreme Court, CCPA, and Federal Circuit case law addressing the meaning of "process" under 35 U.S.C. §101. The key issues for the Federal Circuit were whether Bilski was "seeking to claim a fundamental principle (such as an abstract idea) or a mental process,"[76] and if so, whether Bilski's claim "would pre-empt substantially all uses of that fundamental principle if allowed."[77]

Admitting that these issues are "hardly straightforward,"[78] the Federal Circuit devised a new test to govern determinations by the USPTO or the courts "as to whether a claim to a process is patentable under §101, or, conversely, is drawn to unpatentable subject matter because it claims only a fundamental principle."[79] The Federal Circuit drew its test primarily from two Supreme Court decisions, *Gottschalk v. Benson*[80] and *Diamond v. Diehr*[81] (the latter, 1981

[73]*Id.* at 950.

[74]*See id.*

[75]*Id.* at 965.

[76]*Id.* at 952. The court defined the phrase "fundamental principles" as used in its *Bilski* opinion to encompass "laws of nature, natural phenomena, and abstract ideas." *Id.* at 952 n.5.

[77]*Id.* at 954. Elaborating on how a claim might "pre-empt" all uses of a fundamental principle, the *Bilski* court explained that "pre-emption is merely an indication that a claim seeks to cover a fundamental principle itself rather than only a specific application of that principle." *Id.* at 957. However, "a claim that is tied to a particular machine or brings about a particular transformation of a particular article does not pre-empt all uses of a fundamental principle in any field but rather is limited to a particular use, a specific application. Therefore, [such a claim] is not drawn to the principle in the abstract." *Id.* For example, recall that even though the synthetic rubber-curing process in *Diamond v. Diehr*, 450 U.S. 175 (1981), involved the use of the well-known Arrhenius equation, the process did not pre-empt all uses of that equation. Instead, Diehr's patent only prevented competitors from using the equation in conjunction with performing all the other steps recited in Diehr's process of operating a rubber-molding press with the aid of a digital computer. For further discussion of *Diehr, see supra* Section B.3 ("Computer-Implemented Processes").

[78]*Bilski*, 545 F.3d at 953.

[79]*Id.*

[80]409 U.S. 63 (1972).

[81]450 U.S. 175 (1981).

decision representing the Supreme Court's then-most recent consideration of the patentability of a process under §101).[82] The *Bilski* court concluded that

> [a] claimed process is surely patent-eligible under §101 if (1) it is tied to a particular machine or apparatus, *or* (2) it transforms a particular article into a different state or thing.... A claimed process involving a fundamental principle that uses a particular machine or apparatus would not pre-empt uses of the principle that do not also use the specified machine or apparatus in the manner claimed. And a claimed process that transforms a particular article to a specified different state or thing by applying a fundamental principle would not pre-empt the use of the principle to transform any other article, to transform the same article but not in a manner not covered by the claim, or to do anything other than transform the specified article.[83]

The "machine or transformation" test announced by the Federal Circuit in *Bilski* left a number of questions unanswered. For example, because Bilski's claim 1 did not require a machine, the Federal Circuit did not elaborate on issues specific to the "process tied to a machine or apparatus" prong (1) of its machine or transformation test. The court explicitly left open the question whether reciting a computer in a process claim will necessarily satisfy prong (1) and thus render that claim potentially patentable subject matter under §101.[84]

More relevant to the case at bar was whether Bilski's claim 1 satisfied the "transform[ation] of a particular article into a different state or thing" prong (2) of the Federal Circuit's new test. Satisfaction of prong (2) in turn depends on what qualifies as an "article." The court explained that "article" in the sense of its transformation test need not be limited to a tangible, physical substance such as the rubber cured in *Diehr*. It recognized that "[t]he raw materials of many information-age processes... are electronic signals and electronically-manipulated data."[85]

Rather than set forth an explicit definition of "article," the Federal Circuit in *Bilski* adopted a "measured approach"[86] and provided examples from precedent. Based on its predecessor court's decision in *In re Abele*,[87] the Federal Circuit concluded that "transformation of... raw data into a particular visual depiction of a physical object" will result in a §101 patentable process.[88] For example, Abele's invention as recited in certain dependent claims involved the transformation of

[82] *Diehr* is discussed *supra* Section B.3 ("Computer-Implemented Processes").
[83] *Bilski*, 545 F.3d at 954 (citations omitted).
[84] *See id.* at 951.
[85] *Id.* at 961.
[86] *Id.* at 962.
[87] 684 F.2d 902 (C.C.P.A. 1982).
[88] *Bilski*, 545 F.3d at 962.

x-ray attenuation data to represent physical, tangible objects such as the body's bones, organs, and tissues. These dependent claims were allowable,[89] in contrast to Abele's broader (and not allowable) independent claim that recited a process of graphically displaying variances of data from average values.[90] The Federal Circuit in *Bilski* clarified that transformation of data into a visual depiction (as in *Abele*'s dependent claims) is sufficient; §101 process claims are "not required to involve any transformation of the underlying physical object that the data represented."[91] In sum, a process will satisfy the "transformation" prong (2) of the Federal Circuit's *Bilski* test "[s]o long as the claimed process is limited to a practical application of a fundamental principle to transform specific data, and the claim is limited to a visual depiction that represents specific physical objects or substances...."[92] If a process claim is thus limited, "there is no danger that its scope would wholly pre-empt all uses of the principle."[93]

With this understanding of "transformation" in hand, the Federal Circuit returned to an analysis of Bilski's claim 1 and concluded that it did not satisfy the "transformation" prong of the machine or transformation test. Bilski's claimed process for hedging risk in commodities trading involved the "[p]urported transformations or manipulations simply of public or private legal obligations relationships, business risks, or other such abstractions."[94] Such "abstractions" cannot satisfy the transformation test "because they are not physical objects or substances [like the rubber cured in *Diehr*], and they are not representative of physical objects or substances [as were the data in the dependent claims of *Abele*]."[95]

The Federal Circuit in *Bilski* admitted that its new machine or transformation test might present "difficult challenges" for "future developments in technology and the sciences."[96] The Supreme Court apparently agreed. As discussed below, the Supreme Court granted *certiorari* and held in its 2010 *Bilski v. Kappos* decision that while the Federal Circuit's machine or transformation (MORT) test may signify an "important clue" to patent eligibility, it is not a satisfactory stand-alone test.[97]

While the weight to be afforded the Federal Circuit's machine or transformation test remains uncertain, it is important to keep in mind

[89]*See id.* at 963; *Abele*, 684 F.2d at 908-909.
[90]*See Bilski*, 545 F.3d at 962; *Abele*, 684 F.2d at 909.
[91]*Bilski*, 545 F.3d at 963.
[92]*Bilski*, 545 F.3d at 963.
[93]*Bilski*, 545 F.3d at 963.
[94]*Bilski*, 545 F.3d at 963.
[95]*Bilski*, 545 F.3d at 945.
[96]*Bilski*, 545 F.3d at 956.
[97]*See Bilski v. Kappos,* 130 S. Ct. 3218 (2010).

those §101 basic principles that the Federal Circuit in *Bilski* did not alter. The appellate court reaffirmed that the question whether subject matter is potentially patentable under §101 is entirely separate from the analysis of whether that subject matter is novel and nonobvious under §102 and §103, respectively.[98] Moreover, identifying the §101 eligibility of a process claim requires analyzing the claim as a whole, rather than dissecting it to consider whether individual process steps or limitations would be unpatentable under §101.[99]

Notably, the Federal Circuit in *Bilski* did not overrule the core holding of *State St. Bank & Trust Co. v. Signature Fin. Group, Inc.*,[100] discussed *supra*: that business methods are potentially patentable subject matter under §101 just like any other type of method or process.[101] Nor did the Federal Circuit adopt a "broad exclusion over software," as some *amici* had urged.[102] Nevertheless, the Federal Circuit in *Bilski* rejected *State Street*'s "useful, concrete, and tangible result" inquiry as an adequate stand-alone test for determining §101 patentability.[103] While the *State Street* inquiry may still be useful in many cases, it is no longer a controlling legal inquiry for patent eligibility of business methods.

Much as the Federal Circuit rejected the "useful, concrete, and tangible result" test it had previously adopted in *State Street*, so too did the Supreme Court reject the "machine or transformation" test announced by the Federal Circuit in *In re Bilski* as *the* controlling test for determining whether a process claim is eligible for patenting under §101. After the Federal Circuit's decision in *In re Bilski*, the Supreme Court in June 2009 granted a petition for *certiorari* filed by patent applicants Bilski and Warsaw.[104] More than a year later, the Court issued its much-anticipated decision in *Bilski v. Kappos*.[105] The Supreme Court produced a complex, fragmented opinion, but ultimately affirmed the Federal Circuit's holding on the merits that Bilski's claimed method was not a patent-eligible "process" within the meaning of 35 U.S.C. §101. Five Justices joined some (but not all) parts of the "opinion of the Court" authored by Justice Kennedy

[98]*See Bilski*, 545 F.3d at 958.

[99]*See Bilski*, 545 F.3d at 958.

[100]149 F.3d 1368 (Fed. Cir. 1998).

[101]*See Bilski*, 545 F.3d at 960 (citing *State Street*, 149 F.3d at 1375-1376).

[102]*See id.* at n.23.

[103]*See id.* at 959 (explaining that "while looking for 'a useful, concrete and tangible result' may in many instances provide useful indications of whether a claim is drawn to a fundamental principle or a practical application of such a principle, that inquiry is insufficient to determine whether a claim is patent-eligible under §101").

[104]*See* 129 S. Ct. 2735 (2009).

[105]130 S. Ct. 3218 (2010). The June 28, 2010, date of the decision was significant; it marked both the final day for issuance of opinions in cases argued during the October 2009 term and the last day of Justice John Paul Stevens' 34-year tenure on the Supreme Court.

(hereafter "Kennedy majority").[106] The four other Supreme Court Justices concurred only in the judgment of the Court, in a separate opinion authored by retiring Justice Stevens (hereafter "Stevens minority").

Most importantly, the Supreme Court's decision in *Bilski v. Kappos* confirmed (by a one-vote margin) that business methods are still potentially patentable as processes under §101. The Kennedy majority did not categorically exclude business methods from §101 as the Stevens minority would have.

But what are the criteria or indicia required for a claimed process or method, particularly a business method, to qualify as potentially patentable under §101? Unhelpfully, the Supreme Court in *Bilski v. Kappos* clarified what would *not* suffice as an acceptable test, but offered little new or illuminating explanation of what *would*.

The Kennedy majority began by describing §101 patent eligibility principles as "broad," but constrained by three "specific exceptions": (1) laws of nature, (2) physical phenomena, and (3) abstract ideas.[107] The last of these exceptions, "abstract ideas," applied to the case before the Court.

The Kennedy majority took pains to avoid defining the precise parameters of an "abstract idea." Indeed, the Stevens minority aptly complained that "[t]he Court . . . never provides a satisfying account of what constitutes an unpatentable abstract idea."[108] Rather, the Kennedy majority clung to the facts of a trilogy of 1970s/1980s decisions in which the Supreme Court for the first time had confronted the patent eligibility of computer-implemented processes. "Rather than adopting categorical rules that might have wide-ranging and unforeseen impacts," the Kennedy majority in *Bilski v. Kappos* chose to

[106]Justice Scalia did not join Parts II.B.2 and II.C.2 of Justice Kennedy's opinion. Thus Parts II.B.2 and II.C.2 of the Kennedy opinion, while of considerable interest, have only "plurality" or four-vote status and do not constitute binding precedent or a judgment of the Court.

Part II.B.2 of the Kennedy plurality opinion can be summarized by quoting Justice Kennedy's own phrase: "times change." Although the Federal Circuit's MORT test may have worked well for evaluating process patent eligibility in the Industrial Age, application of MORT to "Information Age" technologies such as software and advanced medical diagnostic techniques would create unacceptable uncertainty. Bilski v. Kappos, 130 S. Ct. at 3227.

Part II.C.2 of the Kennedy plurality opinion reiterates Justice Kennedy's concerns about business method patents, some of which he believes "raise special problems in terms of vagueness and suspect validity." Bilski v. Kappos, 130 S. Ct. at 3229 (quoting eBay Inc. v. MercExchange, LLC, 547 U.S. 388, 397 (2006) (Kennedy, J., concurring)).

[107]Bilski v. Kappos, 130 S. Ct. at 3227.

[108]Bilski v. Kappos, 130 S. Ct. at 3236 (Stevens, J., concurring in the result). The concurring Justices agreed that the majority's "mode of analysis (or lack thereof) may have led to the correct outcome in this case, but it also means that the Court's musings on this issue stand for very little." 130 S. Ct. at 3236.

resolve the case before it "narrowly on the basis of [the Supreme Court's prior] decisions in *Benson, Flook,* and *Diehr*, which show that petitioners' claims are not patentable processes because they are attempts to patent abstract ideas."

In denying §101 eligibility to Bilski's application claims, the Kennedy majority relied primarily on the first case of the trilogy, the Supreme Court's 1972 decision in *Gottschalk v. Benson.*[109] Justice Kennedy summarized the *Benson* decision as follows:

> In *Benson*, the Court considered whether a patent application for an algorithm to convert binary-coded decimal numerals into pure binary code was a "process" under §101. . . . The Court first explained that " '[a] principle, in the abstract, is a fundamental truth; an original cause; a motive; these cannot be patented, as no one can claim in either of them an exclusive right.' " . . . The Court then held the application at issue was not a "process," but an unpatentable abstract idea. "It is conceded that one may not patent an idea. But in practical effect that would be the result if the formula for converting . . . numerals to pure binary numerals were patented in this case." . . . A contrary holding "would wholly pre-empt the mathematical formula and in practical effect would be a patent on the algorithm itself."[110]

The Kennedy majority summarily concluded that Bilski's process was an "unpatentable abstract idea, just like the algorithm[] at issue in *Benson,*"[111] but did not explain how or why Bilski's method was at the same level of abstractness as Benson's.[112]

Also relevant as illustrating an unpatentable "abstract idea" was the Supreme Court's 1978 decision in *Parker v. Flook,*[113] the Court's "next logical step after *Benson.*"[114] As in *Benson,* the Court in *Flook* denied §101 eligibility for a process. Flook claimed a process control method for use in connection with catalytic conversion in the oil industry. According to the Kennedy majority in *Bilski v. Kappos*, the *Flook* invention's only point of novelty was its "reliance on a mathematical algorithm."

Admittedly, Flook's process was more narrowly claimed than the *Benson* process because the claims in *Flook* were limited to use of the recited process in the petrochemical and oil refining contexts. Thus

[109]409 U.S. 63 (1972) (denying §101 eligibility to a claimed process that utilized an algorithm to convert binary-coded decimal numerals into pure binary code).

[110]Bilski v. Kappos, 130 S. Ct. at 3230 (citations omitted).

[111]Bilski v. Kappos, 130 S. Ct. at 3231.

[112]Professor Chisum critiques the *Bilski* Court's reliance on *Benson,* a decision he views as driven not by sound policy but rather by the anti-patent bias prevalent in the 1960s and 1970s. Donald S. Chisum, *Patenting Intangible Methods: Revisiting* Benson *(1972) After* Bilski *(2010)* (Oct. 27, 2010), *available at* papers.ssrn.com/sol3/papers.cfm?abstract_id=1698724.

[113]437 U.S. 584 (1978).

[114]Bilski v. Kappos, 130 S. Ct. at 3230.

the *Flook* process would not "pre-empt" the use of the recited mathematical algorithm in *all* fields of endeavor. Nevertheless, the *Flook* process did not qualify within §101 because it added only conventional "postsolution activity" to the algorithm or formula recited in the claims. The Supreme Court in *Flook* instructed that "the prohibition against patenting abstract ideas 'cannot be circumvented by attempting to limit the use of the formula to a particular technological environment' or adding 'insignificant postsolution activity.'"[115]

Based on this summary of its precedent, the Kennedy majority analogized the process claimed in *Bilski v. Kappos* to the processes at issue in *Benson* and *Flook,* and declared Bilski's claims similarly outside the scope of §101 patent-eligible subject matter. In the Kennedy majority's view, claims 1 and 4 of Bilski's patent application "explain[ed] the basic concept of hedging, or protecting against risk," which the majority considered a "fundamental economic practice long prevalent in our system of commerce."[116] The Kennedy majority held that "the concept of hedging, described in claim 1 [of Bilski's application] and reduced to a mathematical formula in claim 4, is an unpatentable abstract idea, just like the algorithms at issue in *Benson* and *Flook.*"[117] To allow Bilski to patent what the majority deemed "risk hedging" would "pre-empt use of this approach in all fields, and would effectively grant a monopoly over an abstract idea."[118]

Thus the Supreme Court in *Bilski v. Kappos* affirmed the Federal Circuit's holding on the merits that Bilski's claimed method was not a patent-eligible "process" within the meaning of 35 U.S.C. §101. All nine Supreme Court Justices agreed on this point; the Kennedy majority opinion confirmed that "all members of the Court agree that the patent application at issue here falls outside of §101 because it claims an abstract idea."[119]

Although Bilski's claimed process would not satisfy §101, the Kennedy majority did not go so far as to categorically exclude *all* business methods from patenting. The Patent Act specifically enumerates a process as potentially patentable subject matter,[120] and nothing in the statute excludes processes used to conduct a business (i.e., "business methods") from the conventional definition of "process." The Kennedy majority explained that the "term 'method,' which is within §100(b)'s definition of 'process,' at least as a textual matter and before

[115]Bilski v. Kappos, 130 S. Ct. at 3230 (quoting Diamond v. Diehr, 450 U.S. 175, 191-192 (1981)).

[116]Bilski v. Kappos, 130 S. Ct. at 3231.

[117]Bilski v. Kappos, 130 S. Ct. at 3231.

[118]Bilski v. Kappos, 130 S. Ct. at 3231.

[119]Bilski v. Kappos, 130 S. Ct. at 3230.

[120]35 U.S.C. §101.

consulting other limitations in the Patent Act and this Court's precedents, may include at least some methods of doing business."[121]

Other provisions of the Patent Act supported the Kennedy majority's reluctance to bar all business methods from eligibility under §101. In the version then in effect, §273 of the patent statute provided a limited prior user defense to charges of infringement of a patent claim that recited a method of doing or conducting business.[122] When Congress enacted §273, it explicitly referred to (and thus implicitly acknowledged) the existence of patent claims for business methods. Thus, the Kennedy majority felt it ill advised to interpret §101 in a manner that would categorically exclude all such methods from patentability. In other words, interpreting §101 to bar all business methods would contravene the statutory construction canon that prohibits interpreting one statutory provision in a manner that would render superfluous another provision of the statute.

The four concurring Justices in *Bilski v. Kappos* would have gone considerably beyond the Kennedy majority in restraining the patenting of business methods. Concurring Justice Stevens (writing for himself and Justices Ginsburg, Breyer, and Sotomayor) would have categorically held that business methods are not patentable.[123] Emphasizing policy concerns, the Stevens minority expressed "serious doubts about whether patents are necessary to encourage business innovation," citing as an example Federal Express's unpatented development of overnight delivery.[124] The Stevens minority also offered a detailed historical justification, focusing on the development of English and American patent law, to conclude that a method of doing business should not be considered a "process" within §101.

Nor was the Stevens minority persuaded by the Kennedy majority's reliance on the enactment of 35 U.S.C. §273 as part of the 1999 First Inventor Defense Act. The opinion in 1999 of some members of

[121]Bilski v. Kappos, 130 S. Ct. at 3228. The Court also reasoned that "[n]or is it clear how far a prohibition on business method patents would reach, and whether it would exclude technologies for conducting a business more efficiently." 130 S. Ct. at 3228 (citing Bronwyn H. Hall, *Business and Financial Method Patents, Innovation, and Policy*, 56 Scottish J. Pol. Econ. 443, 445 (2009) ("There is no precise definition of... business method patents.")).

[122]*See* 35 U.S.C. §273(a)(3), (b) (2006). The America Invents Act of 2011 significantly broadened the potential applicability of prior user rights to alleged infringements involving much more than business methods. *See* Leahy-Smith America Invents Act, Pub. L. No. 112-29 (H.R. 1249), §5, 125 Stat. 284, 297 (2011) ("Defense to infringement based on prior commercial use"); 35 U.S.C. §273(a) (effective Sept. 16, 2011, for patents issued on or after that date) (providing that prior use defense is potentially available for otherwise infringing acts involving "subject matter consisting of a process, or consisting of a machine, manufacture, or composition of matter used in a manufacturing or other commercial process").

[123]*See* Bilski v. Kappos, 130 S. Ct. at 3232 (Stevens, J., concurring in the judgment).

[124]*See* Bilski v. Kappos, 130 S. Ct. at 3254 (Stevens, J., concurring in the judgment).

Congress that patents were potentially available for business methods should not trump the narrower interpretation of earlier Congresses as evidenced by the historical record. In the Stevens minority's view, the §273 argument was simply a "red herring." Rather than affirmatively *endorsing* the grant of business method patents, the 1999 First Inventor Defense Act focused on providing a *defense* to charges of business method patent infringement, "reflect[ing] surprise and perhaps even dismay that business methods might be patented" in the wake of the Federal Circuit's 1998 decision in *State Street Bank*.[125]

Although affirming the Federal Circuit on the merits, holding that Bilski's claim was not a "process" within §101, the Kennedy majority certainly did not embrace all doctrinal aspects of the Federal Circuit's decision. Consistent with its desire to avoid defining any exact parameters of the "abstract idea" exception to patentable subject matter, the Kennedy majority declined to adopt the Federal Circuit's narrow conceptualization of the machine or transformation test as the *sole* test for §101 eligibility of a process. While the Kennedy majority described the machine or transformation test as a "useful and important clue, an investigative tool" for determining what constitutes a statutory process, it rejected the test as the exclusive or exhaustive test.[126] Although the Supreme Court had admittedly adopted a MORT-style test in its nineteenth-century decisions,[127] more recent precedent such as *Gottschalk v. Benson* "rejected the broad implications of this dictum" and demonstrated that a machine or transformation inquiry "was not intended to be an exhaustive or exclusive test."[128]

Thus, the Supreme Court in its 2010 *Bilski v. Kappos* decision held the claimed business method unpatentable under §101 as an "abstract idea," while providing minimal substantive guidance to aid future identification of unpatentable abstract ideas.[129]

[125]*See* Bilski v. Kappos, 130 S. Ct. at 3251 (Stevens, J., concurring in the judgment).

[126]Bilski v. Kappos, 130 S. Ct. at 3227.

[127]*See* Bilski v. Kappos, 130 S. Ct. at 3226 (citing Cochrane v. Deener, 94 U.S. 780, 788 (1877) (explaining that a "process" is "an act, or a series of acts, performed upon the subject-matter to be transformed and reduced to a different state or thing")).

[128]Bilski v. Kappos, 130 S. Ct. at 3227 (holding that "[t]he machine-or-transformation test is not the sole test for deciding whether an invention is a patent-eligible 'process' ").

[129]The USPTO issued guidance to its examining corps that characterized *Bilski v. Kappos* as having "refined the abstract idea exception to subject matter that is eligible for patenting." *See* United States Patent & Trademark Office, *Interim Guidance for Determining Subject Matter Eligibility for Process Claims in View of* Bilski v. Kappos, 75 Fed. Reg. 43922 (July 27, 2010) (stating that "[t]he Office is especially interested in receiving comments regarding the scope and extent of the holding in *Bilski*").

c. Mayo *(U.S. 2012)*

In 2012, the Supreme Court decided another §101 case, this time with a more specific (and potentially wider-reaching) refutation of patent eligibility. On the merits, *Mayo Collaborative Servs. v. Prometheus Labs. Inc.*[130] held that patent claims directed to certain diagnostic methods used in health care were not patent eligible under 35 U.S.C. §101. The *Mayo* Court set forth a two-step framework for applying the "implicit exception" of §101, applicable to all three components or "concepts" of that exception — laws of nature, natural phenomena, and abstract ideas.[131]

Step one of the *Mayo* framework asks "whether the claims at issue are directed to one of those patent-ineligible concepts."[132] As in *Bilski,* the Supreme Court in *Mayo* did not attempt to provide a definition of the "abstract idea" concept; rather than a business method, the facts of *Mayo* involved a claimed method in the medical arts that the Court held was a patent-ineligible "law of nature."[133] Nevertheless, the *Mayo* framework applies for all three of the §101 exceptions, including "abstract ideas."[134]

If the answer to the first *Mayo* question is yes, then step two of the *Mayo* framework asks " '[w]hat else is there in the claims before us?' "[135] To answer the second *Mayo* question, courts should "consider the elements of each claim both individually and 'as an ordered combination' to determine whether the additional elements 'transform the nature of the claim' into a patent-eligible application."[136] The Court has described the second step of the *Mayo* framework as "a search for an 'inventive concept' — i.e., an element or combination of elements that is 'sufficient to ensure that the patent in practice amounts to significantly more than a patent upon the [ineligible concept] itself.' "[137]

[130] 132 S. Ct. 1289 (2012).

[131] *See* Alice Corp. Pty. v. CLS Bank Int'l, 134 S. Ct. 2347, 2355 (2014) (observing that "[i]n *Mayo Collaborative Services v. Prometheus Laboratories, Inc.*, 566 U.S. ____, 132 S. Ct. 1289, 182 L. Ed. 2d 321 (2012), we set forth a framework for distinguishing patents that claim laws of nature, natural phenomena, and abstract ideas from those that claim patent-eligible applications of those concepts").

[132] *Alice Corp.*, 134 S. Ct. at 2355 (citing *Mayo*, 132 S. Ct. at 1296-1297).

[133] *Mayo*, 132 S. Ct. at 1296 (stating that "Prometheus' patents set forth laws of nature — namely, relationships between concentrations of certain metabolites in the blood and the likelihood that a dosage of a thiopurine drug will prove ineffective or cause harm").

[134] *See Alice Corp.*, 134 S. Ct. at 2355 (stating that "[i]n *Mayo* . . . , we set forth a framework for distinguishing patents that claim laws of nature, natural phenomena, and abstract ideas from those that claim patent-eligible applications of those concepts") (citation omitted).

[135] *Alice Corp.*, 134 S. Ct. at 2355 (quoting *Mayo*, 132 S. Ct. at 1297).

[136] *Alice Corp.*, 134 S. Ct. at 2355 (quoting *Mayo*, 132 S. Ct. at 1298, 1297).

[137] *Alice Corp.*, 134 S. Ct. at 2355 (quoting *Mayo*, 132 S. Ct. at 1294).

The Court's use of the word "inventive" as a characteristic of patent eligibility is unfortunate and circular, harkening back to the nineteenth-century notion that "to be patentable, an invention had to involve invention."[138]

On the merits, the *Mayo* decision did not turn on the "abstract idea" exception to §101, in contrast with *Bilski*.[139] The issue in *Mayo* concerned whether the claimed invention, processes that involved the use of thiopurine drugs in the treatment of autoimmune diseases, fell within the "law of nature" exception to §101.[140] For this reason, the application of *Mayo*'s two-step framework to the facts of the *Mayo* case is detailed in a later section of this chapter.[141] Nevertheless, *Mayo* is critical to any discussion of business method patent eligibility because *Mayo* provided the analytical foundation for the Supreme Court's landmark 2014 decision dealing with business methods and the "abstract idea" exception, *Alice Corp. Pty. Ltd. v. CLS Bank Int'l*.[142]

d. Alice Corp. *(U.S. 2014)*

The Supreme Court's 2014 decision in *Alice Corp. Pty. Ltd. v. CLS Bank Int'l* was its next decision after *Bilski* to apply the "abstract idea" exception of §101 to an invention in the realm of business methods.[143] Closely following *Mayo*'s two-step framework described above, the

[138] *See* Chapter 5[B] ("Historical Context: The *Hotchkiss* 'Ordinary Mechanic' and the Requirement for 'Invention'").

[139] *Bilski* is examined *supra* Section B.4.b.

[140] *See Mayo*, 132 S. Ct. at 1296 (stating that "Prometheus' patents set forth laws of nature — namely, relationships between concentrations of certain metabolites in the blood and the likelihood that a dosage of a thiopurine drug will prove ineffective or cause harm"); *Mayo*, 132 S. Ct. at 1297 (issue for decision was whether "the patent claims add *enough* to their statements of the correlations to allow the processes they describe to qualify as patent-eligible process that *apply* natural laws"). As detailed *infra*, the *Mayo* Court answered in the negative. *See Mayo*, 132 S. Ct. at 1305 (concluding that "the patent claims at issue here effectively claim the underlying laws of nature themselves [and] are consequently invalid").

[141] *See infra* Section B.5 ("Methods of Medical Treatment").

[142] 134 S. Ct. 2347 (2014).

[143] Justice Thomas's opinion in *Alice Corp.* for a unanimous Supreme Court did not expressly refer to the invention claimed therein as a "business method," but did summarize it as a "scheme[] to manage certain forms of financial risk." *Alice Corp.*, 134 S. Ct. at 2352. However, three Justices joined a short concurring opinion that treated the invention as non-patent eligible because it recited a business method. *See Alice Corp.*, 134 S. Ct. at 2360 (Sotomayor, J., concurring, joined by Ginsburg, J., and Breyer, J.) (stating that "I adhere to the view that any 'claim that merely describes a method of doing business does not qualify as a 'process' under §101'") (quoting Bilski v. Kappos, 561 U.S. 593, 614 (2010) (Stevens, J., concurring in judgment)); *Id.* (citing also In re Bilski, 545 F.3d 943, 972 (Fed. Cir. 2008) (Dyk, J., concurring) ("There is no suggestion in any of th[e] early [English] consideration of process patents that processes for organizing human activity were or ever had been patentable")).

Court in *Alice Corp.* concluded that claims drawn to a method using computers to minimize settlement risk in financial transactions were attempts to patent an abstract idea and thus not patent-eligible under 35 U.S.C. §101.

More particularly, the patented invention in *Alice Corp.* concerned computer-implemented methods, systems, and media for mitigating "settlement risk," which the Court defined as "the risk that only one party to a financial transaction will pay what it owes."[144] The claims of Alice Corporation's U.S. Patents Nos. 5,970,479; 6,912,510; 7,149,720; and 7,725,375 recited methods (as well as systems and media) for facilitating the exchange of financial obligations between two parties by using a computer system as a third-party intermediary.[145] As the Court explained, the computer intermediary

> creates "shadow" credit and debit records (i.e., account ledgers) that mirror the balances in the parties' real-world accounts at "exchange institutions" (e.g., banks). The intermediary updates the shadow records in real time as transactions are entered, allowing "only those transactions for which the parties' updated shadow records indicate sufficient resources to satisfy their mutual obligations." . . . At the end of the day, the intermediary instructs the relevant financial institutions to carry out the "permitted" transactions in accordance with the updated shadow records, . . . thus mitigating the risk that only one party will perform the agreed-upon exchange.[146]

The patents in suit claimed this method in the form of (1) claims reciting the method itself;[147] (2) system claims reciting a computer system

[144]*Alice Corp.*, 134 S. Ct. at 2351-2352.
[145]*Alice Corp.*, 134 S. Ct. at 2352.
[146]*Alice Corp.*, 134 S. Ct. at 2352 (citations omitted).
[147]A representative method claim of Alice Corp.'s '479 patent recited:

> 33. A method of exchanging obligations as between parties, each party holding a credit record and a debit record with an exchange institution, the credit records and debit records for exchange of predetermined obligations, the method comprising the steps of:
>
> (a) creating a shadow credit record and a shadow debit record for each stakeholder party to be held independently by a supervisory institution from the exchange institutions;
> (b) obtaining from each exchange institution a start-of-day balance for each shadow credit record and shadow debit record;
> (c) for every transaction resulting in an exchange obligation, the supervisory institution adjusting each respective party's shadow credit record or shadow debit record, allowing only these transactions that do not result in the value of the shadow debit record being less than the value of the shadow credit record at any time, each said adjustment taking place in chronological order; and
> (d) at the end-of-day, the supervisory institution instructing ones of the exchange institutions to exchange credits or debits to the credit record and debit record of the respective parties in accordance with the adjustments of the said

configured to carry out the method;[148] and (3) computer-readable medium claims requiring program code for performing the method.[149]

Applying step one of the *Mayo* framework (i.e., determining whether the claims at issue were directed to a patent-ineligible

---

permitted transactions, the credits and debits being irrevocable, time invariant obligations placed on the exchange institutions.

U.S. Patent No. 5,970,479.

[148]A representative system claim of Alice Corp.'s '720 patent read:

1. A data processing system to enable the exchange of an obligation between parties, the system comprising:

a data storage unit having stored therein information about a shadow credit record and shadow debit record for a party, independent from a credit record and debit record maintained by an exchange institution; and

a computer, coupled to said data storage unit, that is configured to (a) receive a transaction; (b) electronically adjust said shadow credit record and/ or said shadow debit record in order to effect an exchange obligation arising from said transaction, allowing only those transactions that do not result in a value of said shadow debit record being less than a value of said shadow credit record; and (c) generate an instruction to said exchange institution at the end of a period of time to adjust said credit record and/or said debit record in accordance with the adjustment of said shadow credit record and/or said shadow debit record, wherein said instruction being an irrevocable, time invariant obligation placed on said exchange institution.

U.S. Patent No. 7,149,720.

[149]A representative media claim of Alice Corp.'s '375 patent read:

39. A computer program product comprising a computer readable storage medium having computer readable program code embodied in the medium for use by a party to exchange an obligation between a first party and a second party, the computer program product comprising:

program code for causing a computer to send a transaction from said first party relating to an exchange obligation arising from a currency exchange transaction between said first party and said second party; and

program code for causing a computer to allow viewing of information relating to processing, by a supervisory institution, of said exchange obligation, wherein said processing includes (1) maintaining information about a first account for the first party, independent from a second account maintained by a first exchange institution, and information about a third account for the second party, independent from a fourth account maintained by a second exchange institution; (2) electronically adjusting said first account and said third account, in order to effect an exchange obligation arising from said transaction between said first party and said second party, after ensuring that said first party and/or said second party have adequate value in said first account and/or said third account, respectively; and (3) generating an instruction to said first exchange institution and/or said second exchange institution to adjust said second account and/or said fourth account in accordance with the adjustment of said first account and/or said third account, wherein said instruction being an irrevocable, time invariant obligation placed on said first exchange institution and/or said second exchange institution.

U.S. Patent No. 7,725,375.

concept), the Court in *Alice Corp.* did not need to "labor to delimit the precise contours of the 'abstract ideas' category" in the case at bar.[150] Based primarily on analogies to its earlier decisions concerning unpatentable "ideas,"[151] the Court in *Alice Corp.* easily concluded that the challenged claims of the patents in suit recited an abstract idea, thus satisfying step one of the *Mayo* framework. The claims "[o]n their face" were drawn to the concept of intermediated settlement.[152] The Court found "no meaningful distinction" between that concept and the concept of risk hedging as claimed in *Bilski*.[153]

Moreover, both concepts were "'fundamental economic practice[s] long prevalent in our system of commerce.'"[154] Echoing preemption concerns, the Court viewed the concept of intermediated settlement (or "clearing house") as a "building block of the modern economy."[155]

[150] *Alice Corp.*, 134 S. Ct. at 2357.

[151] This precedent included *Gottschalk v. Benson*, 409 U.S. 63, 67 (1972); *Parker v. Flook*, 437 U.S. 584, 594-595 (1978); and *Bilski*, 561 U.S. at 611 ("The concept of hedging, described in claim 1 and reduced to a mathematical formula in claim 4, is an unpatentable abstract idea, just like the algorithms at issue in *Benson* and *Flook*").

[152] *Alice Corp.*, 134 S. Ct. at 2356.

[153] *Alice Corp.*, 134 S. Ct. at 2357.

[154] *Alice Corp.*, 134 S. Ct. at 2356 (quoting *Bilski*, 561 U.S. at 611; also citing Emery, *Speculation on the Stock and Produce Exchanges of the United States*, in 7 Studies in History, Economics and Public Law 283, 346-356 (1896) (discussing the use of a "clearinghouse" as an intermediary to reduce settlement risk)); *id.* (stating that "[t]he use of a third-party intermediary (or 'clearinghouse') is also a building block of the modern economy") (citing, e.g., Yadav, *The Problematic Case of Clearinghouses in Complex Markets*, 101 Geo. L.J. 387, 406-412 (2013); J. Hull, Risk Management and Financial Institutions 103-104 (3d ed. 2012)).

[155] *Alice Corp.*, 134 S. Ct. at 2356 (citing Yadav, *The Problematic Case of Clearinghouses in Complex Markets*, 101 Geo. L.J. 387, 406-412 (2013); J. Hull, Risk Management and Financial Institutions 103-104 (3d ed. 2012)). The Court explained that "preemption" is the "concern that drives this exclusionary principle [i.e., that abstract ideas, as well as laws of nature and natural phenomena, are not patent-eligible]":

> See, *e.g., Bilski, supra,* at 611-612, 130 S. Ct. 3218 (upholding the patent "would pre-empt use of this approach in all fields, and would effectively grant a monopoly over an abstract idea"). Laws of nature, natural phenomena, and abstract ideas are "'"the basic tools of scientific and technological work."'" *Myriad, supra,* at ____, 133 S. Ct., at 2116. "[M]onopolization of those tools through the grant of a patent might tend to impede innovation more than it would tend to promote it," thereby thwarting the primary object of the patent laws. *Mayo, supra,* at ____, 132 S. Ct., at 1923; see U.S. Const., Art. I, §8, cl. 8 (Congress "shall have Power... To promote the Progress of Science and useful Arts"). We have "repeatedly emphasized this... concern that patent law not inhibit further discovery by improperly tying up the future use of" these building blocks of human ingenuity. *Mayo, supra,* at ____, 132 S. Ct., at 1301 (citing *Morse, supra,* at 113).
>
> At the same time, we tread carefully in construing this exclusionary principle lest it swallow all of patent law. *Mayo,* 566 U.S., at ____, 132 S. Ct., at 1293-1294. At some level, "all inventions... embody, use, reflect, rest upon, or apply laws of nature, natural phenomena, or abstract ideas." *Id.,* at ____, 132 S. Ct., at 1293. Thus, an invention is not rendered ineligible for patent simply

In the view of this author, this part of the *Alice Corp.* analysis is particularly troubling because it intermingles §101 patent eligibility with novelty (35 U.S.C. §102[156]) and nonobviousness (35 U.S.C. §103[157]). These are three entirely separate statutory provisions with longstanding independent pedigrees and analytical frameworks; the §101 patent eligibility analysis should not be used as a shortcut to bypass the work of assessing the technical merits of a claimed invention against the relevant prior art in accordance with §§102 and 103.

The *Alice Corp.* Court rejected the patentee's argument that its invention was not a patent-ineligible abstract idea because the category of abstract ideas should be limited to "'preexisting, fundamental truth[s]' that 'exis[t] in principle apart from any human action,'"[158] such as mathematical formulas. The Court observed that although longstanding, the concept of risk hedging in *Bilski* was not a fundamental truth about the natural world that had always existed. Instead, Bilski's invention was "a *method of organizing human activity*,"[159] and the Court found no meaningful distinction between the concepts sought to be patented in *Bilski* and in the case at bar. Hence, *Alice Corp.* held that "[m]ethods of organizing human activity" such as Alice Corp.'s method of intermediated settlement are also included within the category of unpatentable abstract ideas. Here, the Court gives us some assistance in understanding the scope of patent-ineligible "abstract ideas"—they include at least "preexisting fundamental truths" and "methods of organizing human activity."

The *Alice Corp.* Court next addressed the second step of the *Mayo* framework; i.e., asking what else is there in the claims besides an unpatentable abstract idea, law of nature, or natural phenomenon? The Court concluded that the challenged method claims' "mere[] require[ment]" for "generic computer implementation" was not enough

---

because it involves an abstract concept. See Diamond v. Diehr, 450 U.S. 175, 187, 101 S. Ct. 1048, 67 L. Ed. 2d 155 (1981). "[A]pplication[s]" of such concepts "'to a new and useful end,'" we have said, remain eligible for patent protection. Gottschalk v. Benson, 409 U.S. 63, 67, 93 S. Ct. 253, 34 L. Ed. 2d 273 (1972).

Accordingly, in applying the §101 exception, we must distinguish between patents that claim the "'buildin[g] block[s]'" of human ingenuity and those that integrate the building blocks into something more, *Mayo,* 566 U.S., at ____, 132 S. Ct., at 1303, thereby "transform[ing]" them into a patent-eligible invention, *id.,* at ____, 132 S. Ct., at 1294. The former "would risk disproportionately tying up the use of the underlying" ideas, *id.,* at ____, 132 S. Ct., at 1294, and are therefore ineligible for patent protection. The latter pose no comparable risk of pre-emption, and therefore remain eligible for the monopoly granted under our patent laws.

Alice Corp., 134 S. Ct. at 2354-2355.

[156]*See supra* Chapter 4.

[157]*See supra* Chapter 5.

[158]*Alice Corp.*, 134 S. Ct. at 2356 (quoting Brief for Petitioner (quoting *Mayo,* 132 S. Ct. at 1297)).

[159]*Alice Corp.*, 134 S. Ct. at 2356.

to transform the abstract idea of intermediated settlement into a patent-eligible invention.[160]

The Court first explained that step two of *Mayo* looks for the presence of an "inventive concept" sufficient to transform the abstract idea into a patent-eligible invention. "Additional features" must be recited in the claim to ensure that it is "more than a drafting effort" intended to monopolize the abstract idea.[161] That "transformation" must be "'more than simply stat[ing] the [abstract idea]' while adding the words 'apply it.'"[162]

The parties in *Alice Corp.* had stipulated that all of the challenged patent claims required computer implementation.[163] But using a computer was not enough to accomplish the required transformation of the abstract idea of intermediated settlement into §101 subject matter. The Court explained by analogy that computer implementation did not render patent-eligible the abstract ideas involved in the Court's earlier decisions in *Gottschalk v. Benson* (1972)[164] and *Parker v. Flook* (1978).[165]

[160]*See Alice Corp.*, 134 S. Ct. at 2357.

[161]*See Alice Corp.*, 134 S. Ct. at 2357.

[162]*See Alice Corp.*, 134 S. Ct. at 2357 (quoting *Mayo*, 132 S. Ct. at 1294).

[163]*See Alice Corp.*, 134 S. Ct. at 2353 (explaining that "[a]ll of the claims are implemented using a computer; the system and media claims expressly recite a computer, and the parties have stipulated that the method claims require a computer as well").

[164]The Court summarized its decision in *Gottschalk v. Benson*, 409 U.S. 63 (1972), as follows:

> In *Benson* . . . we considered a patent that claimed an algorithm implemented on "a general-purpose digital computer." 409 U.S., at 64, 93 S. Ct. 253. Because the algorithm was an abstract idea, see *supra*, at 2355, the claim had to supply a "'new and useful'" application of the idea in order to be patent eligible. 409 U.S., at 67, 93 S. Ct. 253. But the computer implementation did not supply the necessary inventive concept; the process could be "carried out in existing computers long in use." *Ibid*. We accordingly "held that simply implementing a mathematical principle on a physical machine, namely a computer, [i]s not a patentable application of that principle." *Mayo*, *supra*, at _____, 132 S. Ct., at 1301 (citing *Benson*, *supra*, at 64, 93 S. Ct. 253).

Alice Corp., 134 S. Ct. at 2357-2358.

[165]The Court summarized its decision in *Parker v. Flook*, 437 U.S. 584 (1978), as follows:

> *Flook* is to the same effect [as *Benson*]. There, we examined a computerized method for using a mathematical formula to adjust alarm limits for certain operating conditions (*e.g.*, temperature and pressure) that could signal inefficiency or danger in a catalytic conversion process. 437 U.S., at 585-586, 98 S. Ct. 2522. Once again, the formula itself was an abstract idea, see *supra*, at 2355, and the computer implementation was purely conventional. 437 U.S., at 594, 98 S. Ct. 2522 (noting that the "use of computers for 'automatic monitoring-alarming'" was "well known"). In holding that the process was patent ineligible, we rejected the argument that "implement[ing] a principle in some specific fashion" will "automatically fal[l] within the patentable subject matter of §101." *Id.*, at 593, 98 S. Ct. 2522. Thus, "*Flook* stands for the proposition that the prohibition

The most interesting and helpful aspect of *Alice Corp.* is the Supreme Court's characterization of patent-eligible inventions as those that seek to solve "technological problems."[166] It explained that in contrast with the inventions of *Benson* and *Flook*, the computer-implemented process for curing rubber in the Court's 1981 decision *Diamond v. Diehr*[167] was patent-eligible, but not because it involved using a computer. Rather, the claims in *Diehr* used a "well-known" mathematical equation (i.e., the Arrhenius equation, "long used to calculate the cure time in rubber-molding presses"[168]) in a process "designed to *solve a technological problem* in 'conventional industry practice.'"[169] The *Alice Corp.* Court explained that the *Diehr* process used thermocouples to record constant temperature measurements inside a rubber mold, which the rubber curing industry had not previously been able to accomplish. A computer repeatedly recalculated the remaining rubber cure time by using the temperature measurements and the Arrhenius equation. These additional steps (beyond using the mathematical formula itself) sufficiently transformed the rubber curing process into an "'inventive application of the formula.'"[170] Thus, *Alice Corp.* clarified that the claims in *Diehr* "were patent eligible because they *improved an existing technological process*,"[171] not because they required the use of a computer.

To emphasize the point, the *Alice Corp.* Court observed that "mere recitation of a generic computer cannot transform a patent-ineligible abstract idea into a patent-eligible invention."[172] This would amount to no more than reciting an abstract idea and adding the words "apply it on a computer." The Court noted that computers are now ubiquitous, such that generic computer implementation of an abstract idea is not the sort of "additional feature" that practically assures that a claimed invention is more than a mere drafting effort to monopolize the abstract idea.[173] The fact that a computer is a physical, tangible system (a "machine" in the language of §101) was "beside the point."[174] If a computer's physicality was determinative, patent applicants could

---

against patenting abstract ideas cannot be circumvented by attempting to limit the use of [the idea] to a particular technological environment." *Bilski*, 561 U.S., at 610-611, 130 S. Ct. 3218 (internal quotation marks omitted).

Alice Corp., 134 S. Ct. at 2358.

[166] *See Alice Corp.*, 134 S. Ct. at 2358.

[167] 450 U.S. 175 (1981).

[168] Diamond v. Diehr, 450 U.S. 175, 220 (1981). *Diehr* is further examined *supra* Section B.3 ("Computer-Implemented Processes").

[169] *Alice Corp.*, 134 S. Ct. at 2358 (quoting *Diehr*, 450 U.S. at 177) (emphasis added).

[170] *Alice Corp.*, 134 S. Ct. at 2358 (quoting *Mayo*, 132 S. Ct. at 1299).

[171] *Alice Corp.*, 134 S. Ct. at 2358 (emphasis added).

[172] *Alice Corp.*, 134 S. Ct. at 2358.

[173] *Alice Corp.*, 134 S. Ct. at 2358 (citing *Mayo*, 132 S. Ct. at 1297).

[174] *Alice Corp.*, 134 S. Ct. at 2358.

simply claim "any principle of the physical or social sciences by reciting a computer system configured to implement the relevant concept."[175]

Under step two of the *Mayo* framework, in order to determine whether the "something more" recited in addition to the abstract idea is enough to transform the patent claim to patent-eligible subject matter, the elements of the claim must be considered both individually and as an " 'ordered combination.' "[176] In the view of this author, this part of the *Alice Corp.* analysis is also troubling. It seems to condone analyzing individual limitations of patent claims divorced from the claims in their entirety. Patent law fundamentals make clear that the "invention" is the *entire* claim — all the limitations or elements *in combination*. An individual limitation or element is not what is claimed. It is wrong to identify a particular subset of a patent claim as the "heart" or "gist" of an invention.

Whether considered either individually or in combination, the elements of the claims in *Alice Corp.* did not satisfy *Mayo*'s second step. Firstly considering the method steps individually, the Court summarized them as using a computer to create electronic records, track multiple transactions, and issue simultaneous instructions; in short, employing the computer itself as the intermediary.[177] In the Court's view, "the function performed by the computer at each step of the process [wa]s 'purely conventional.' "[178] Each step was a "basic" or "generic" computer function and represented a " 'well-understood, routine, conventional activit[y]' previously known to the industry."[179] (Here again the Court unfortunately conflates §101 patent eligibility with §102 novelty and §103 nonobviousness.)

Viewed in combination, the method steps recited in the challenged claims fared no better. "Viewed as a whole, petitioner's method claims simply recite the concept of intermediated settlement as performed by a generic computer."[180] Notably, the claims did not "purport to improve the functioning of the computer itself" or "effect an improvement in any other technology or technical field."[181] The claims merely instructed users to apply the abstract idea of intermediated settlement using a generic computer. This was simply not "enough" to transform that idea into a patent-eligible invention under §101.

[175]*Alice Corp.*, 134 S. Ct. at 2359.

[176]*See Alice Corp.*, 134 S. Ct. at 2355 (quoting *Mayo*, 132 S. Ct. at 1298 (citing *Diehr*, 450 U.S. at 188 ("[A] new combination of steps in a process may be patentable even though all the constituents of the combination were well known and in common use before the combination was made"))).

[177]*Alice Corp.*, 134 S. Ct. at 2359.

[178]*Alice Corp.*, 134 S. Ct. at 2359 (quoting *Mayo*, 132 S. Ct. at 1298).

[179]*Alice Corp.*, 134 S. Ct. at 2359 (quoting *Mayo*, 132 S. Ct. at 1294).

[180]*Alice Corp.*, 134 S. Ct. at 2359.

[181]*Alice Corp.*, 134 S. Ct. at 2359.

Like its process claims, Alice Corporation's system and media claims also failed to recite patent-eligible subject matter. The *Alice Corp.* Court concluded that the system claims were "no different from the method claims in substance."[182] In other words, "[t]he method claims recite[d] the abstract idea implemented on a generic computer; the system claims recite[d] a handful of generic computer components configured to implement the same idea."[183] Holding the system claims patent-eligible while denying patent eligibility to the method claims would make dispositive exercise of "the draftsman's art," and would improperly treat the concept of §101 patent-eligibility "like a nose of wax which may be turned and twisted in any direction."[184] Moreover, the patentee had previously conceded that the patent-eligibility of its media claims rose or fell with its method claims.[185] Accordingly, because the system and media claims "add[ed] nothing of substance to the underlying abstract idea," the *Alice Corp.* Court held that they too were patent-ineligible under §101.[186]

e. *Federal Circuit "Abstract Idea" Cases After* Alice Corp.

Following the Supreme Court's 2014 decision in *Alice Corp.*, the Federal Circuit confronted a plethora of appeals challenging patent claims directed to processes and methods on the ground that they sought to protect patent-ineligible abstract ideas. As of late 2019, §101 cases continued to demand a substantial amount of the court's resources; the influx of appeals challenging eligibility showed no sign of slowing. Patent challengers and accused infringers succeeded in invalidating numerous patents for claiming non-eligible subject matter, as illustrated by the cases cited in the margin.[187] In fact, as of

[182]*Alice Corp.*, 134 S. Ct. at 2360.

[183]*Alice Corp.*, 134 S. Ct. at 2360.

[184]Alice Corp., 134 S. Ct. at 2360 (quoting *Flook*, 437 U.S. at 590).

[185]*Alice Corp.*, 134 S. Ct. at 2360.

[186]*Alice Corp.*, 134 S. Ct. at 2360.

[187]*See, e.g.*, Solutran, Inc. v. Elavon, Inc., 931 F.3d 1161 (Fed. Cir. 2019) (Chen, J.) (reversing D. Minn.'s denial of summary judgment that asserted claims of Solutran's U.S. Patent No. 8,311,945, concerning systems and methods for processing paper checks, were invalid under 35 U.S.C. §101 for failing to recite patent-eligible subject matter; written at a "distinctly high level of generality," the claims were directed to the abstract idea of "crediting a merchant's account as early as possible while electronically processing a check"; the claims were not "directed to a specific improvement to the way computers operate" as in *Enfish, LLC v. Microsoft Corp.*, 822 F.3d 1327, 1336 (Fed. Cir. 2016), nor were they "limited to rules with specific characteristics" to create a technical effect as in *McRO, Inc. v. Bandai Namco Games America Inc.*, 837 F.3d 1299, 1313 (Fed. Cir. 2016)); Trading Techs. Int'l, Inc. v. IBG LLC, 921 F.3d 1378 (Fed. Cir. 2019) (Moore, J.) (affirming PTAB in Covered Business Method review that claims of U.S. Patent No. 7,783,556, related to displaying market information on a screen, were unpatentable because §101 patent-ineligible; claims directed to abstract idea of providing a trader with additional financial information to facilitate market trades; nothing in the

non-abstract elements, taken individually or in combination, supplied an inventive concept); ChargePoint, Inc. v. SemaConnect, Inc., 920 F.3d 759 (Fed. Cir. 2019) (Prost, C.J.) (affirming D. Md.'s dismissal under Fed. R. Civ. P. 12(b)(6) of lawsuit alleging infringement of claims in four patents concerning electric vehicle charging stations connected to a network; claimed invention was "nothing more than the abstract idea of communication over a network for interacting with a device, applied to the context of electric vehicle charging stations"; association of the abstract idea with a charging station — a physical, tangible machine — was not dispositive; problematically, "the broad claim language would cover any mechanism for implementing network communication on a charging station, thus preempting the entire industry's ability to use networked charging stations"); Univ. of Fla. Research Found., Inc. v. Gen. Elec. Co., 916 F.3d 1363 (Fed. Cir. 2019) (Moore, J.) (affirming district court's dismissal on accused infringer's Rule 12(b)(6) motion because university's U.S. Patent No. 7,062,251, which concerned method and system for "integrat[ing] physiologic data from at least one bedside machine," was not §101 patent-eligible; claims were directed to abstract idea of collecting, analyzing, manipulating, and displaying data; patent in suit was "a quintessential 'do it on a computer' patent [that] acknowledge[d] that data from bedside machines was previously collected, analyzed, manipulated, and displayed manually, and it simply propose[d] doing so with a computer"; patent did not claim or otherwise identify any "specific improvement to the way computers operate"); In re Marco Guldenaar Holding B.V., 911 F.3d 1157 (Fed. Cir. 2018) (Chen, J.) (affirming USPTO's *ex parte* examination rejection under §101 of patent application claims directed to the abstract idea of rules for playing a dice game, in which "the only arguable inventive concept relate[d] to the dice markings, which constitute printed matter"); *id.,* 911 F.3d at 1162 (Mayer, J., concurring) (stating that "claims directed to dice, card, and board games can never meet the section 101 threshold because they endeavor to influence human behavior rather than effect technological change"); Data Engine Techs. LLC v. Google LLC, 906 F.3d 999 (Fed. Cir. 2018) (Stoll, J.) (affirming district court's entry of judgment on the pleadings that, *inter alia,* claim 1 of DET's U.S. Patent No. 5,303,146, which concerned methods that allowed electronic spreadsheet users to track their changes, was invalid as §101 patent-ineligible; under *Alice* step one claim 1 was directed to the abstract idea of collecting, recognizing, and storing changed information; claim-recited limitations of partitioning cells to be presented as a spreadsheet, referencing in one cell of a page a formula referencing a second page, and saving the pages such that they appeared as being stored as one file, merely "recite[d] the method of implementing the abstract idea itself and thus fail[ed] under *Alice* step two"); BSG Tech LLC v. Buyseasons, Inc., 899 F.3d 1281 (Fed. Cir. 2018) (Hughes, J.) (affirming E.D. Tex.'s summary judgment of §101 ineligibility because asserted software indexing method claims were directed to "the abstract idea of considering historical usage information while inputting data"; the claims did "not recite any improvement to the way in which such databases store or organize information analogous to the self-referential table in *Enfish* or the adaptable memory caches in *Visual Memory*"; and under *Alice* step two, the claims lacked an inventive concept because no evidence suggested that the other, non-abstract claim limitations, alone or in combination, were not well understood, routine and conventional database structures and activities); Interval Licensing LLC v. AOL, Inc., 896 F.3d 1335 (Fed. Cir. 2018) (Chen, J.) (panel majority affirming W.D. Wash.'s judgment that claims invalid because §101 ineligible; claims directed to abstract idea of the presentation of two sets of information, in a non-overlapping way, on a display screen; properly construed claim-recited "attention manager" not limited to a means of locating space on the screen unused by a first set of displayed information and then displaying a second set of information in that space; claim limitations for "accessing," "scheduling," and then "displaying" second information set are conventional functions stated in general terms that do not further define how attention manager segregates display of two sets of data on a display screen; considered as a whole, the claims "lack any arguable technical advance over conventional computer and network technology for performing the recited functions of acquiring and displaying information"); SAP Am., Inc. v. Investpic, LLC, 890 F.3d 1016 (Fed. Cir. 2018) (Taranto, J.) (affirming N.D. Tex.'s judgment on the pleadings that all claims of U.S. Pat. No. 6,349,291 were patent-ineligible and thus invalid under 35 U.S.C. §101; claims were directed to the abstract idea of an improved statistical analysis of financial information, no matter how "groundbreaking" the advance; under *Alice* step two, although some claims required physical components such as databases and processors, these limitations did not mandate any "improved computer resources" but rather only "off-the-shelf computer technology, and did not involve anything "inventive"); *id.*, 733 F. App'x 554 (Fed. Cir. Aug. 2, 2018) (withdrawing May 15, 2018 opinion and granting panel reh'g, replacing original with "modified precedential opinion accompanying this order," which modified opinion is available at http://www.cafc.uscourts.gov/sites/default/files/opinions-orders/17-2081.Opinion.8-2-2018.pdf); Voter Verified, Inc. v. Election Sys. & Software LLC, 887 F.3d 1376 (Fed. Cir. 2018) (Lourie, J.) (affirming N.D. Fla.'s dismissal under Fed. R. Civ. P. 12(b)(6) based on judgment that U.S. Reissue Patent No. RE40,449, concerning method and systems for "auto-verification" of a voter's ballot, was not patent-eligible under 35 U.S.C. §101; patent's claims were directed to the steps of voting, verifying the vote, and tabulating — all abstract ideas, and generic computer implementation of those steps was not an inventive concept sufficient to transform the claims to patent-eligible subject matter); Two-Way Media Ltd. v. Comcast Cable Comm'ns, 874 F.3d 1329 (Fed. Cir. 2017) (Reyna, J.) (affirming district court's judgment on the pleadings of patent-ineligibility of four Internet streaming patents, generally relating to a system for streaming audio/visual data over a communications system such as the Internet; district court properly excluded evidence from earlier litigations determining claims' novelty and nonobviousness, because they are "separate inquiries" from patent eligibility); Smart Sys. Innovations, LLC v. Chicago Transit Authority, 873 F.3d 1364 (Fed. Cir. 2017) (Wallach, J.) (Circuit majority affirmed district court's grant of motion for judgment on the pleadings that asserted claims were not patent-eligible under §101; the claims were directed to the abstract idea of the collection, storage, and recognition of data in the formation of financial transactions and related data collection in the mass transit field; the recitation of various computer hardware components enabling validation on-site rather than remotely did not provide an inventive concept under *Alice* step two; in substance, the claims were still directed to "nothing more than running a bank-card sale"; dissenting Judge Linn disagreed that the claims were directed to an abstract idea and charged majority with engaging in the "reductionist exercise of ignoring the limitations of the claims in question . . ."); Secured Mail Solutions LLC v. Universal Wilde, Inc., 873 F.3d 905 (Fed. Cir. 2017) (Reyna, J.) (affirming C.D. Cal.'s dismissal under Rule 12(b)(6) of infringement suit asserting seven patents concerning bar codes on mailed items because they did not claim patent-eligible subject matter under 35 U.S.C. §101; under *Alice* step one the claims embraced the abstract idea of using a marker affixed to the outside of a mail object to communicate information about the object; i.e., its sender, recipient, and contents; the non-specific claims lacked technical detail and recited well-known and conventional ways of allowing senders and recipients to communicate using "generic computer technology"); Credit Acceptance Corp. v. Westlake Services, 859 F.3d 1044 (Fed. Cir. 2017) (Dyk, J.) (affirming PTAB's Covered Business Method (CBM) review decision that challenged claims were unpatentable because (1) directed to abstract idea of "processing an application for financing a purchase," such as the purchase of an automobile; "no meaningful distinction" seen between claimed type of financial industry practice and "the concept of intermediated settlement" held to be abstract in *Alice* or the "basic concept of hedging" held to be abstract in *Bilski*; and (2) under *Alice* step two, no inventive concept evidenced by challenged claims that recited "merely "configur[ing]" generic computers in order to "supplant and enhance" an otherwise abstract manual process"; significantly, the claims "d[id] not provide details as to any non-conventional software for enhancing the financing process"); Recognicorp, LLC v. Nintendo Co., Ltd., 855 F.3d 1322 (Fed. Cir. 2017) (Reyna, J.) (affirming district court's judgment on the pleadings that patent in suit, concerning method and apparatus for building a composite facial image using constituent parts, was not patent-eligible under 35 U.S.C. §101; patent's claims were directed to the "abstract idea of encoding and decoding image data" and under *Alice* step two did not contain an inventive concept sufficient to render the patent eligible); Apple, Inc. v. Ameranth, Inc., 842 F.3d 1229 (Fed. Cir. 2016) (Reyna, J.) (affirming PTAB's Covered Business Method (CBM) review determination that challenged claims were directed to abstract idea of generating menus with certain features, but not to a "particular way of programming or designing the software to create menus that have these features"; claims were "not directed to a specific improvement in the way computers operate"; holding under *Alice* step two that claims' limitations were "insignificant post-solution activities that d[id] not support the invention having an 'an inventive concept'"); Synopsys, Inc. v. Mentor Graphics Corp., 839 F.3d 1138 (Fed. Cir. 2016) (affirming district court's summary judgement that claims of U.S. Patents Nos. 5,530,841; 5,680,318; and 5,748,488, concerning generally the process of logic circuit design, were not patent-eligible; determining that claims were directed to abstract idea of "translating a functional description of a logic circuit into a hardware component description of the logic circuit," and process recited in claims, which did not require any form of computer implementation, could be performed "mentally or with pencil and paper"; and concluding under *Alice* step two that, although "the contours of what constitutes an inventive concept are far from precise," the claims at bar did not contain any inventive concept, for they did not introduce a technical advance or improvement nor contain anything that "amount[ed] to significantly more than a patent upon the [abstract idea] itself," in contrast with claims at issue in *DDR Holdings*, 773 F.3d 1245 (Fed. Cir. 2014) and *Bascom*, 827 F.3d 1341 (Fed. Cir. 2016)); FairWarning IP, LLC v. Iatric Sys., Inc., 839 F.3d 1089 (Fed. Cir. 2016) (Stoll, J.) (affirming district court's dismissal of infringement complaint under Fed. R. Civ. P. 12(b)(6) because claims of U.S. Patent No. 8,578,500, which concerned ways to detect fraud and misuse by identifying unusual patterns in users' access of sensitive patient health information, were not patent-eligible under 35 U.S.C. §101; claims were directed to abstract idea of collecting and analyzing information to detect misuse and notifying a user when misuse was detected and claims' limitations, analyzed alone and in combination, failed to add "something more" to transform the abstract idea into a patent-eligible application); Intellectual Ventures I LLC v. Symantec Corp., 838 F.3d 1307 (Fed. Cir. 2016) (Dyk, J.) (holding asserted claims of Intellectual Ventures' U.S. Patents Nos. 6,460,050; 6,073,142; and 5,987,610 were not patent-eligible; determining that (1) claims of '050 patent were directed to abstract idea of "receiving e-mail (and other data file) identifiers, characterizing e-mail based on the identifiers, and communicating the characterization — in other words, filtering files/e-mail," and under *Alice* step two, the claim steps did not "improve the functioning of the computer itself" but rather "use[d] generic computers to perform generic computer functions"; (2) claims of '142 patent, concerning a type of "electronic post office," were directed to abstract ideas of screening messages, which were "'fundamental... practice[s] long prevalent in our system' and 'method[s] of organizing human activity'" (quoting *Alice*); under *Alice* step two, '142 patent's specification confirmed that implementation of the abstract idea was routine and conventional, and did not "improve the functioning of the computer itself" (as in *Alice*) or solve a "challenge particular to the Internet" (as in *DDR Holdings*, 773 F.3d 1245 (Fed. Cir. 2014)); and (3) the only asserted claim of the '610 patent was directed to abstract idea of computer virus screening, an idea well known at time of '610 patent's application filing date; under *Alice* step two, the claim recited "no more than generic computers that use generic virus screening technology"); claim limitation requiring delivery of content only to cellular telephones merely confined the abstract idea to a particular technological environment; Affinity Labs of Texas, LLC v. Amazon.com Inc., 838 F.3d 1266 (Fed. Cir. 2016) (Bryson, J.) (affirming district court's grant of motion to dismiss infringement complaint under Fed. R. Civ. P. 12(b)(6) on ground that claims of U.S. Patent No. 8,688,085, concerning a "method for targeted advertising" in which an advertisement is selected for delivery to the user of a portable device based on at least one piece of demographic information about the user, were patent-ineligible; claims were directed to abstract idea of delivering user-selected media content to portable devices, and merely "add[ed] conventional computer components to well-known business practices" rather than facilitating "an improvement in the functioning of a computer"; under *Alice* step two, features such as network streaming and a customized user interface did not convert the abstract idea into a concrete solution to a problem; the features were claimed "generically rather than with the specificity necessary to show how those components provide a concrete solution to the problem addressed by the patent"); Affinity Labs of Texas, LLC v. DIRECTV, LLC, 838 F.3d 1253 (Fed. Cir. 2016) (Bryson, J.) (holding patent-ineligible U.S. Patent No. 7,970,379, which concerned a system for streaming regional broadcast signals to cellular telephones located outside the region served by the regional broadcaster; holding under *Alice* step one that asserted claims were directed to the abstract idea of "providing out-of-region access to regional broadcast content"; the patent claimed "the function of wirelessly communicating regional broadcast content to an out-of-region recipient [but] not a particular way of performing that function," nor did it solve a "technological problem" or improve computer or network functionality; under *Alice* step two court found no "inventive concept" that transformed the abstract idea of out-of-region delivery of regional broadcasting into a patent-eligible application of that abstract idea, observing that "[t]he claim simply recites the use of generic features of cellular telephones, such as a storage medium and a graphical user interface, as well as routine functions, such as transmitting and receiving signals, to implement the underlying idea"); Elec. Power Grp., LLC v. Alstom S.A., 830 F.3d 1350 (Fed. Cir. 2016) (Taranto, J.) (affirming district court's grant of summary judgment that EPG's U.S. Patents Nos. 7,233,843; 8,060,259; and 8,401,710, which concerned systems and methods for performing real-time performance monitoring of an electric power grid by collecting data from multiple data sources, analyzing the data, and displaying the results, were invalid under §101 for claiming patent-ineligible subject matter; concluding that the "lengthy and numerous" claims did "not go beyond requiring the collection, analysis, and display of available information in a particular field, stating those functions in general terms, without limiting them to technical means for performing the functions that are arguably an advance over conventional computer and network technology"; and determining that because the claims "defined a desirable information-based result" and were "not limited to inventive means of achieving the result," they failed under §101); In re TLI Commc'ns LLC Patent Litig., 823 F.3d 607 (Fed. Cir. 2016) (Hughes, J.) (affirming district court's judgment that asserted patents claimed "no more than the abstract idea of classifying and storing digital images in an organized manner"; claim-recited components, described in "vague, functional" terms, represented well-understood, routine, conventional activities previously known in the industry); Mortgage Grader, Inc. v. First Choice Loan Servs. Inc., 811 F.3d 1314 (Fed. Cir. 2016) (holding that claims attaching generic computer components to perform "anonymous loan shopping" were not patent eligible); Versata Dev. Grp. v. SAP America, 793 F.3d 1306 (Fed. Cir. 2015) (holding that computer performed "purely conventional" steps to carry out patent claims directed to the "abstract idea of determining a price using organization and product group hierarchies"); Intellectual Ventures I LLC v. Capital One Bank (USA), 792 F.3d 1363 (Fed. Cir. 2015) (affirming district court's judgment that Intellectual Ventures' U.S. Patent No. 8,083,137, directed

August 2015, the Federal Circuit had *upheld* patent eligibility in only one of nine post-*Alice* business method cases.

The cases examined in the remainder of this subsection demonstrate a gradual increase in the number of successful appeals from §101 invalidations. Some of the cases were resolved at step one of *Mayo/Alice,* by the Circuit concluding that the challenged claims were not directed to abstract ideas. Others required inquiry into step two, the search for an "inventive concept" in the non-abstract portion of the claims.

---

to "methods of tracking and storing information relating to a user's purchases and expenses and presenting that information to the user vis-à-vis the user's pre-established, self-imposed spending limits," and its U.S. Patent No. 7,603,382, directed to "methods and systems for providing customized web page content to the user as a function of user-specific information and the user's navigation history," were invalid as drawn to patent-ineligible subject matter under 35 U.S.C. §101; determining that the patents claimed abstract ideas without otherwise claiming inventive concepts); OIP Techs., Inc. v. Amazon.com, Inc., 788 F.3d 1359 (Fed. Cir. 2015) (affirming district court's grant of accused infringer Amazon.com's motion to dismiss for failure to state a claim because U.S. Patent No. 7,970,713 merely used a general purpose computer to implement the abstract idea of "offer-based price optimization," which "any business owner or economist does in calculating a demand curve for a given product"); *id.*, 788 F.3d at 1364 (stating that "we must read [*Diamond v.*] *Diehr* [450 U.S. 175 (1981)] in light of *Alice*, which emphasized that *Diehr* does not stand for the general proposition that a claim implemented on a computer elevates an otherwise ineligible claim into a patent-eligible improvement") (citing *Alice Corp.*, 134 S. Ct. at 2358)); Content Extraction & Transmission LLC v. Wells Fargo Bank, Nat'l Ass'n, 776 F.3d 1343 (Fed. Cir. 2014) (affirming district court's dismissal of infringement lawsuit under Fed. R. Civ. P. 12(b)(6) because claims of U.S. Patent Nos. 5,258,855; 5,369,508; 5,625,465; and 5,768,416, generally directed to a method of (1) extracting data from hard copy documents using an automated digitizing unit such as a scanner, (2) recognizing specific information from the extracted data, and (3) storing that information in a memory (which method could be performed by software on an automated teller machine), were not patent eligible under 35 U.S.C. §101 as directed to "the abstract idea of extracting and storing data from hard copy documents using generic scanning and processing technology"); Ultramercial, Inc. v. Hulu, LLC, 772 F.3d 709 (Fed. Cir. 2014) (affirming district court's judgment that claims of U.S. Patent No. 7,346,545, directed to a method for distributing copyrighted media products over the Internet in which a consumer received a copyrighted media product at no cost in exchange for viewing an advertisement and the advertiser paid for the copyrighted content, were not patent eligible under 35 U.S.C. §101 because claims were "directed to no more than a patent-ineligible abstract idea"), *cert. denied*, Ultramercial, LLC v. WildTangent, Inc., No. 14-1392, 2015 WL 2457913 (U.S. June 29, 2015); buySAFE, Inc. v. Google, Inc., 765 F.3d 1350 (Fed. Cir. 2014) (affirming district court's judgment that claims of U.S. Patent No. 7,644,019, reciting methods and machine-readable media encoded to perform steps for guaranteeing a party's performance of its online transaction, were invalid under 35 U.S.C. §101 as directed to an abstract idea); Digitech Image Techs., LLC v. Electronics for Imaging, Inc., 758 F.3d 1344 (Fed. Cir. 2014) (affirming district court's judgment that claims of U.S. Patent No. 6,128,415, directed to a device profile and a method for creating a device profile within a digital image processing system, were invalid because not patent eligible under 35 U.S.C. §101).

(i) Decisions Sustaining Patent Eligibility at Step One

The Federal Circuit's December 2014 decision in *DDR Holdings, LLC v. Hotels.com, L.P.*[188] was a then-rare case in which patent claims to an e-commerce system and method *survived* a post-*Alice Corp.* §101 challenge. Nonetheless, the Circuit panel in *DDR Holdings* split 2-1, illustrating the continuing controversy and difficulty in separating patent-ineligible abstract ideas from patent-eligible applications of those ideas.

DDR Holdings, LLC ("DDR"), a non-practicing entity, sued National Leisure Group, Inc. and a number of other defendants in the travel industry (collectively "NLG") for allegedly infringing, *inter alia*, certain claims of DDR's U.S. Patent No. 7,818,399 ('399 patent), titled "Methods of expanding commercial opportunities for internet websites through coordinated offsite marketing." The '399 patent addressed the problem of maintaining a website's "stickiness"; that is, the problem of visitors to a host website being "lured away" to other sites when they clicked on links for third-party merchants' advertisements. The '399 patent disclosed systems for generating a "composite" web page that combined certain visual elements of the host website (e.g., its logo, background color, and fonts) with the content of the third-party merchant. Thus, the composite website retained the "look and feel" of the host site. The composite site displayed the third-party merchant's products, but retained the host site's visitor traffic by displaying the third-party product information in a manner that gave the viewer the impression she was still "viewing pages served by the host" website.[189]

[188] 773 F.3d 1245 (Fed. Cir. 2014).

[189] *DDR Holdings*, 773 F.3d at 1249. Representative claim 19 of the '399 patent recited:

> 19. A system useful in an outsource provider serving web pages offering commercial opportunities, the system comprising:
>
> (a) a computer store containing data, for each of a plurality of first web pages, defining a plurality of visually perceptible elements, which visually perceptible elements correspond to the plurality of first web pages;
>
> (i) wherein each of the first web pages belongs to one of a plurality of web page owners;
>
> (ii) wherein each of the first web pages displays at least one active link associated with a commerce object associated with a buying opportunity of a selected one of a plurality of merchants; and
>
> (iii) wherein the selected merchant, the outsource provider, and the owner of the first web page displaying the associated link are each third parties with respect to one other;
>
> (b) a computer server at the outsource provider, which computer server is coupled to the computer store and programmed to:
>
> (i) receive from the web browser of a computer user a signal indicating activation of one of the links displayed by one of the first web pages;

Following trial in the Eastern District of Texas in October 2012, a jury found that NLG directly infringed the asserted claims of the '399 patent and that the claims were not invalid. The district court denied NLG's post-trial motions for judgement as a matter of law (JMOL), including one contending that the '399 patent claims were invalid under 35 U.S.C. §101 as directed to patent-ineligible subject matter.[190]

In December 2014, a divided panel of the Federal Circuit in *DDR Holdings* affirmed the district court's denial of JMOL, concluding that "though used by businesses, [the claimed system] is patent-eligible under §101."[191] The *DDR Holdings* majority conceded that drawing the line between claims that recite a patent-eligible invention and those that merely add too little to an abstract concept to cross the §101 threshold into the "technological realm" can be "difficult," because the line "is not always clear."[192] Although the Supreme Court in *Alice Corp.* did not identify the precise contours of the "abstract idea" exception to §101, the *DDR Holdings* majority summarized "some important principles" that the Supreme Court had provided. "[M]athematical algorithms, including those executed on a generic computer, are abstract ideas,"[193] as are "some fundamental economic and conventional business practices."[194]

Although admittedly directed to solving the "business challenge" of retaining visitors to a website, the claims of DDR's '399 patent did *not* recite a mathematical algorithm or a fundamental economic or longstanding commercial practice. In the Federal Circuit majority's view, DDR's claims were different because they addressed a challenge "*particular to the Internet*."[195] Although implemented on a computer (like the claims in *Bilski* and *Alice Corp.*, held to be patent ineligible),

---

(ii) automatically identify as the source page the one of the first web pages on which the link has been activated;

(iii) in response to identification of the source page, automatically retrieve the stored data corresponding to the source page; and

(iv) using the data retrieved, automatically generate and transmit to the web browser a second web page that displays: (A) information associated with the commerce object associated with the link that has been activated, and (B) the plurality of visually perceptible elements visually corresponding to the source page.

[190] *DDR Holdings*, 773 F.3d at 1251.

[191] *DDR Holdings*, 773 F.3d at 1259. Circuit Judge Chen, former Solicitor of the USPTO, authored the majority opinion, which was joined by Circuit Judge Wallach. Circuit Judge Mayer filed a dissenting opinion, discussed *infra*.

[192] *DDR Holdings*, 773 F.3d at 1255.

[193] *DDR Holdings*, 773 F.3d at 1256 (citing Gottschalk v. Benson, 409 U.S. 63, 64 (1972)).

[194] *DDR Holdings*, 773 F.3d at 1256 (citing Bilski v. Kappos, 561 U.S. 593, 130 S. Ct. 3218, 3231 (2010) (finding the "fundamental economic practice" of hedging to be patent ineligible); *Alice Corp.*, 134 S. Ct. at 2356 (same for intermediated settlement)).

[195] *DDR Holdings*, 773 F.3d at 1257 (emphasis added).

> these claims stand apart because they do not merely recite the performance of some business practice known from the pre-Internet world along with the requirement to perform it on the Internet. Instead, the claimed solution is necessarily rooted in computer technology in order to overcome a problem specifically arising in the realm of computer networks.[196]

While concluding that DDR's challenged claims "st[oo]d apart," the majority also cautioned that "not all claims purporting to address Internet-centric challenges are eligible for patent." For example, the claimed invention in *Ultramercial, Inc. v. Hulu, LLC,*[197] a case decided by the Circuit three weeks earlier, did *not* fall within §101. The *Ultramercial* claims merely recited "the abstract idea of using advertising as a currency as applied to the particular technological environment of the Internet."[198]

In contrast with those of *Ultramercial*, DDR's claims did not "broadly and generically" claim the use of the Internet to perform an abstract business practice. Rather, DDR's claims "specif[ied] how interactions with the Internet are manipulated — to yield a desired result — a result that overrides the routine and conventional sequence of events ordinarily triggered by the click of a hyperlink."[199] This was "not merely the routine or conventional use of the Internet."[200]

As to public policy, the Federal Circuit majority was not concerned that the claims were "drafting effort[s]" designed to preempt all applications of an abstract idea. It observed that DDR's claims did "not attempt to preempt every application of the idea of increasing sales by making two web pages look the same, or of any other variant suggested by [the accused infringers]."[201] Rather, the claims recited "a specific way" to address a "particular" problem faced by websites on the Internet. DDR's solution to the problem amounted to an "inventive concept," as required for patent eligibility by *Alice Corp.*[202] Though used by businesses, DDR's claimed system was nevertheless patent eligible.

Circuit Judge Mayer dissented. In his view, DDR's claims were not within §101 because they "simply describe[d] an abstract concept — that an online merchant's sales can be increased if two web pages have the same 'look and feel' — and appl[ied] that concept using a generic computer."[203] The claimed invention was merely an "Internet

[196]*DDR Holdings*, 773 F.3d at 1257.
[197]772 F.3d 709 (Fed. Cir. Nov. 14, 2014).
[198]*DDR Holdings*, 773 F.3d at 1256.
[199]*DDR Holdings*, 773 F.3d at 1258.
[200]*DDR Holdings*, 773 F.3d at 1259.
[201]*DDR Holdings*, 773 F.3d at 1259.
[202]*DDR Holdings*, 773 F.3d at 1259.
[203]*DDR Holdings*, 773 F.3d at 1263 (Mayer, J., dissenting).

iteration" of the "well-known and widely-applied" idea of having a "store within a store."[204] For example, defendant NLG previously sold vacations to customers shopping at brick-and-mortar BJ's Wholesale Clubs. Just as the customers could purchase travel products from NLG without leaving BJ's warehouse, DDR's claimed system permitted a host website user to purchase goods from a third-party vendor without seeming to have left the host's site. DDR's invention was not rooted in any new computer technology, and the solution it offered to the problem of retaining website traffic was an "entrepreneurial, rather than a technological, one."[205] Lastly, Judge Mayer observed that the potential scope of DDR's claims as "staggering," and that their "broad and sweeping" reach was "vastly disproportionate to their minimal technological disclosure."[206]

As of 2019, the Federal Circuit had scrutinized many more patents that ultimately survived §101 eligibility challenges.

For example, the Federal Circuit's 2016 decision in *Enfish, LLC v. Microsoft Corp.*[207] is a frequently-cited cornerstone case in the appellate court's post-*Alice* jurisprudence. *Enfish* marked only the second time after the Supreme Court's 2014 decision in *Alice* that the appellate court sustained the §101 validity of patent claims challenged as merely directed to abstract ideas. The *Enfish* Circuit reversed a district court's determination that claims directed to a self-referential model for a computer database were *not* §101-eligible under the *Alice* framework. The appellate court concluded that Enfish's patent claims focused on "an improvement to computer functionality itself, not on economic or other tasks for which a computer is used in its ordinary capacity."[208] Critically, the claims were "*directed to a specific improvement to the way computers operate*, embodied in the self-referential table."[209] This was a "specific implementation" to solve of a software problem, not merely a case in which "general-purpose computer components [we]re added post-hoc to a fundamental economic practice or mathematical equation."[210]

In sustaining the Enfish patent against the §101 challenge, the *Enfish* Circuit provided important guidance about the proper interpretation of the *Mayo/Alice* step one inquiry, i.e., "whether the claims at issue are directed to a patent-ineligible concept."[211] First, it observed that the Supreme Court had not yet "established a definitive rule to determine what constitutes an 'abstract idea' sufficient to satisfy the

[204]*DDR Holdings*, 773 F.3d at 1264-1265 (Mayer, J., dissenting).
[205]*DDR Holdings*, 773 F.3d at 1265 (Mayer, J., dissenting).
[206]*DDR Holdings*, 773 F.3d at 1266 (Mayer, J., dissenting).
[207]822 F.3d 1327 (Fed. Cir. May 12, 2016) (Hughes, J.).
[208]*Enfish*, 822 F.3d at 1336.
[209]*Enfish*, 822 F.3d at 1336 (emphasis added).
[210]*Enfish,* 822 F.3d at 1339.
[211]*Alice,* 134 S. Ct. at 2355.

first step of the *Mayo/Alice* inquiry"; rather, "both [the Circuit] and the Supreme Court have found it sufficient to compare claims at issue to those claims already found to be directed to an abstract idea in previous cases."[212] (In the view of this author, the courts' failure to establish a substantive identification for an "abstract idea" has enshrined an unsatisfactory "I know it when I see it" approach.)

The Circuit next explained that step one of the *Alice* formulation, which it termed the "'directed to' inquiry," should look at the challenged claims' "character as a whole." The analysis

> plainly contemplates that the first step of the inquiry is a meaningful one, i.e., that a substantial class of claims are *not* directed to a patent-ineligible concept. The "directed to" inquiry, therefore, cannot simply ask whether the claims *involve* a patent-ineligible concept, because essentially every routinely patent-eligible claim involving physical products and actions *involves* a law of nature and/or natural phenomenon — after all, they take place in the physical world.... Rather, the "directed to" inquiry applies a stage-one filter to claims, considered in light of the specification, based on whether "their character as a whole is directed to excluded subject matter."[213]

Although the Supreme Court had considered whether patent claims improve "technological process[es]" or "the functioning of the computer itself" as part of the *second* step of the *Alice* framework,[214] the Federal Circuit in *Enfish* did not consider dispositive the *Alice* step-one-versus-step-two question. It refused to read *Alice* as broadly holding that all improvement in computer-related technology, or all improvements in software versus hardware,[215] were inherently abstract; if that were

[212]*Enfish,* 822 F.3d at 1334.

[213]*Enfish,* 822 F.3d at 1335 (citations omitted).

[214]*Alice,* 134 S. Ct. at 2358-2359.

[215]The court noted further with respect to software-implemented inventions that Enfish's improvement was

> not defined by reference to "physical" components does not doom the claims. To hold otherwise risks resurrecting a bright-line machine-or-transformation test, *cf. Bilski v. Kappos*, 561 U.S. 593, 604, 130 S. Ct. 3218, 177 L. Ed. 2d 792 (2010) ("The machine-or-transformation test is not the sole test for deciding whether an invention is a patent-eligible 'process.'"), or creating a categorical ban on software patents, *cf. id.* at 603, 130 S. Ct. 3218 ("This Court has not indicated that the existence of these well-established exceptions gives the Judiciary *carte blanche* to impose other limitations that are inconsistent with the text and the statute's purpose and design."). Much of the advancement made in computer technology consists of improvements to software that, by their very nature, may not be defined by particular physical features but rather by logical structures and processes. We do not see in *Bilski* or *Alice*, or our cases, an exclusion to patenting this large field of technological progress.

Enfish, 822 F.3d at 1339.

the case, it would mean they could be analyzed *only* under *Alice* step two.[216] Instead, the appellate court asked "whether the claims are directed to an improvement to computer functionality versus being directed to an abstract idea, even at the first step of the *Alice* analysis."[217] If the former was true, then the second step of *Alice* need not be considered.

The *Enfish* Circuit applied its reasoning to the invention before it to conclude that the claims *were* directed to an improvement in computer functionality. Enfish's U.S. Patents Nos. 6,151,604 ('604 patent) and 6,163,775 ('775 patent), claiming priority to 1995, involved an "innovative logical model for a computer database."[218] As explained by the court, a logical model creates particular tables of data in a database, but does not describe how the bits and bytes of those tables are arranged. "Conventional" or "standard" logical models, also known as "relational" models, store data about each separate type of entity (e.g., create separate tables of data for documents, persons, and companies employing them as part of a particular project).

In contrast, the claimed invention of Enfish's patents involved databases with "self-referential" properties. The patented logical model included all data entities in a single table, with column definitions provided by rows in that same table.[219] Specifically, Enfish's representative patent claims were directed to a "data storage and retrieval system for a computer memory" comprising, *inter alia*, "means for configuring said memory according to a logical table."[220] The patent

216The court further observed that

> some improvements in computer-related technology when appropriately claimed are undoubtedly not abstract, such as a chip architecture, an LED display, and the like. Nor do we think that claims directed to software, as opposed to hardware, are inherently abstract and therefore only properly analyzed at the second step of the *Alice* analysis. Software can make non-abstract improvements to computer technology just as hardware improvements can, and sometimes the improvements can be accomplished through either route. We thus see no reason to conclude that all claims directed to improvements in computer-related technology, including those directed to software, are abstract and necessarily analyzed at the second step of *Alice*, nor do we believe that *Alice* so directs.

Enfish, 822 F.3d at 1335.

217*Enfish,* 822 F.3d at 1335.

218*Enfish,* 822 F.3d at 1329.

219*Enfish,* 822 F.3d at 1330.

220Claim 17 of Enfish's '604 patent recited:

> A data storage and retrieval system for a computer memory, comprising:
> means for configuring said memory according to a logical table, said logical table including:
> a plurality of logical rows, each said logical row including an object identification number (OID) to identify each said logical row, each said logical row corresponding to a record of information;

specification supplied a four-step algorithm corresponding to the means element that required a "self-referential" table.[221]

A district court had concluded on summary judgment that Enfish's patent claims were invalid under §101 as simply directed to the abstract idea of "organizing information in tabular formats."[222] Accused infringer Microsoft similarly asserted that the claims were directed to unpatentable "concepts of organizing data into a logical table with identified columns and rows where one or more rows are used to store an index or information defining columns."[223]

The Circuit rejected these interpretations of Enfish's claims; they were "at such a high level of abstraction and untethered from the language of the claims" as to "all but ensure[] that the exceptions to §101 swallow the rule."[224] Enfish's claims were not "simply directed to *any* form of storing tabular data, but instead [we]re specifically directed to a *self-referential* table for a computer database."[225]

To support this distinction, the Circuit looked to the Enfish patents' specifications. Representative claim 17 of the '604 patent included a "means for configuring" element.[226] The structure corresponding to

---

a plurality of logical columns intersecting said plurality of logical rows to define a plurality of logical cells, each said logical column including an OID to identify each said logical column; and

means for indexing data stored in said table.

Enfish, 822 F.3d at 1336.

[221]The district court construed the "means for configuring" language of representative claim 17 as requiring this algorithm:

1. Create, in a computer memory, a logical table that need not be stored contiguously in the computer memory, the logical table being comprised of rows and columns, the rows corresponding to records, the columns corresponding to fields or attributes, the logical table being capable of storing different kinds of records.

2. Assign each row and column an object identification number (OID) that, when stored as data, can act as a pointer to the associated row or column and that can be of variable length between databases.

3. For each column, store information about that column in one or more rows, rendering the table self-referential, the appending, to the logical table, of new columns that are available for immediate use being possible through the creation of new column definition records.

4. In one or more cells defined by the intersection of the rows and columns, store and access data, which can include structured data, unstructured data, or a pointer to another row.

Enfish, 822 F.3d at 1336-1337.

[222]*Enfish,* 822 F.3d at 1337 (quoting J.A. at 321).

[223]*Enfish,* 822 F.3d at 1337 (quoting Appellee's Br. at 17).

[224]*Enfish,* 822 F.3d at 1337.

[225]*Enfish,* 822 F.3d at 1337.

[226]Claim elements drafted in "means plus function" format are analyzed *supra* Chapter 2, Section E.1.

the claimed means was a four-step algorithm. In particular, step three of the algorithm required:

> For each column, store information about that column in one or more rows, rendering the table self-referential, the appending, to the logical table, of new columns that are available for immediate use being possible through the creation of new column definition records.[227]

This language established that Enfish's claims did not cover *any* form of storing tabular data, but rather a *self-referential* table for a database. In particular, step three explained "that the table stores information related to each column in rows of that very same table, such that new columns can be added by creating new rows in the table." Moreover, the specification emphasized that "the present invention comprises a flexible, self-referential table that stores data."

In the Circuit's view, the district court's interpretation of Enfish's claims did not sufficiently credit the advantages of the claimed self-referential table. It "function[ed] differently" than conventional database structures, which the specification described as "inferior." Enfish's invention did "not require a programmer to preconfigure a structure to which a user must adapt data entry."[228] The invention "improve[d] an existing technology" by achieving "increased flexibility, faster search times, and smaller memory requirements."[229] In disregarding these advantages the district court had improperly "downplayed the invention's benefits."

The Circuit distinguished the *Enfish* case before it from the Supreme Court's 2014 *Alice* decision and from the Circuit's own 2015 decision in *Versata Dev. Grp. v. SAP America.*[230] The claims in those cases "simply add[ed] conventional computer components to well-known business practices." They did not pass §101 muster in other cases either because they "recited use of an abstract mathematical formula on any general purpose computer," "recited a purely conventional computer implementation of a mathematical formula," or "recited generalized steps to be performed on a computer using conventional computer activity."[231] In contrast, Enfish's claims were "directed to an improvement in the functioning of a computer."[232]

The *Enfish* Circuit concluded that

> the self-referential table recited in the claims on appeal is a specific type of data structure designed to improve the way a computer stores and

[227]*Enfish,* 822 F.3d at 1336-1337.
[228]*Enfish,* 822 F.3d at 1337.
[229]*Enfish,* 822 F.3d at 1337.
[230]793 F.3d 1306 (Fed. Cir. 2015).
[231]*Enfish,* 822 F.3d at 1338.
[232]*Enfish,* 822 F.3d at 1338.

> retrieves data in memory. The specification's disparagement of conventional data structures, combined with language describing the "present invention" as including the features that make up a self-referential table, confirm that our characterization of the "invention" for purposes of the §101 analysis has not been deceived by the "draftsman's art." *Cf. Alice*, 134 S. Ct. at 2360. In other words, we are not faced with a situation where general-purpose computer components are added post-hoc to a fundamental economic practice or mathematical equation. Rather, the claims are directed to a specific implementation of a solution to a problem in the software arts. Accordingly, we find the claims at issue are not directed to an abstract idea.[233]

Because step one of the *Alice* framework was not met, the *Enfish* court "d[id] not need to proceed to step two of that analysis."[234] The case at bar did not present a "close call[]" that might justify an *Alice* step two analysis.[235]

Patent owners concerned about the eligibility-limiting impact of the Supreme Court's *Mayo/Alice* decisions were also encouraged by the Federal Circuit's 2017 decision in *Thales Visionix Inc. v. United States*.[236] As in the *Enfish* decision analyzed above, the Circuit in *Thales Visionix* declined to find that patent claims concerning an inertial tracking system were directed to an abstract idea under step one of the *Mayo/Alice* framework. Rather, the challenged claims recited a "particular" and "unconventional" arrangement of sensors that improved prior art tracking systems. The invention's use of certain mathematical equations necessary for operation of the system did "not doom the claims to abstraction."[237]

Patentee Thales Visionix, Inc. ("TVI") sued the United States government under 28 U.S.C. §1498 for unauthorized use by or for the federal government of the invention claimed in TVI's U.S. Patent No.

[233] *Enfish*, 822 F.3d at 1339.

[234] *Enfish*, 822 F.3d at 1339.

[235] *Enfish*, 822 F.3d at 1339.

The USPTO soon issued a memorandum to its examining corps pertaining to *Enfish*. *See* Robert W. Bahr, Deputy Commissioner for Patent Examination Policy, *Recent Subject Matter Eligibility Decisions (Enfish, LLC v. Microsoft Corp.* and *TLI Communications LLC v. A.V. Automotive, LLC)* (May 19, 2016), *available at* http://www.uspto.gov/sites/default/files/documents/ieg-may-2016_enfish_memo.pdf (stating that "[w]hile the [*Enfish*] decision does not change the subject matter eligibility framework, it provides additional information and clarification on the inquiry for identifying abstract ideas.... [W]hen performing an analysis of whether a claim is directed to an abstract idea..., examiners are to continue to determine if the claim recites (i.e., sets forth or describes) a concept that is similar to concepts previously found abstract by the courts. The fact that a claim is directed to an improvement in computer-related technology can demonstrate that the claim does not recite a concept similar to previously identified abstract ideas.").

[236] 850 F.3d 1343 (Fed. Cir. 2017) (Moore, J.).

[237] *Thales Visionix*, 850 F.3d at 1349.

6,474,159 ('159 patent).[238] As detailed below, TVI alleged that a helmet-mounted display system used by pilots flying the government's F-35 Joint Strike Fighter aircraft infringed the patent.[239]

The Court of Federal Claims ("trial court") granted the government's motion for judgment on the pleadings that the asserted claims of the '159 patent were invalid for reciting patent-ineligible subject matter under §101. Rejecting the trial court's determination that the claims were directed to an abstract idea, the Federal Circuit reversed on appeal.

TVI's '159 patent related generally to motion-tracking relative to a moving platform instead of relative to the earth; it disclosed an inertial tracking system for tracking the motion of an object relative to a moving reference frame (such as an aircraft). Prior art inertial sensors included accelerometers (i.e., motion sensors) and gyroscopes (i.e., rotation sensors), which measured the specific forces associated with changes in a sensor's position and orientation relative to a known starting position. These sensors are used in various applications including aircraft navigation and virtual reality simulations. TVI's patented system addressed a problem with these prior art "conventional" approaches to tracking inertial motion of an object on a moving platform. According to the '159 patent, the flaw in the conventional systems was that both object- and platform-based inertial sensors measured motion relative to earth, but the error-correcting optical or magnetic sensors that are typically added to such inertial sensing systems measured position relative to a moving platform.

TVI's '159 patent addressed this problem by adopting what the Federal Circuit termed an "unconventional" approach of measuring inertial changes with respect to the earth. In the patented system, platform-mounted sensors (e.g., sensors mounted on a vehicle such as an aircraft) directly measured the gravitational field in the platform's frame. In addition, object-mounted sensors (e.g., sensors mounted on the aircraft pilot's helmet) then calculated position information relative to the frame of the moving platform. By changing the reference frame, the patented system allowed tracking the position and orientation of the object (e.g., the helmet) within the moving vehicle (e.g., the

[238]In contrast with *state* governments that enjoy Eleventh Amendment immunity, the U.S. *federal* government has expressly waived its sovereign immunity from suit for patent infringement. Such lawsuits against the United States are brought exclusively in the U.S. Court of Federal Claims, a specialized trial court that sits in Washington, D.C. The federal government retains the power to use any patented invention without injunction, but must pay just compensation for the taking if infringement is proved. 28 U.S.C. §1498(a). The Federal Circuit has exclusive jurisdiction over appeals from Court of Federal Claims' decisions under §1498.

[239]*See* Thales Visionix, Inc. v. United States, 122 Fed. Cl. 245, 248 (2015), *rev'd and remanded*, 850 F.3d 1343 (Fed. Cir. 2017). The helmet-mounted display system was manufactured for the U.S. government by subcontractor Elbit Systems of America, which joined the lawsuit as a third-party defendant.

aircraft) without input from a vehicle attitude reference system or without having to calculate the orientation or position of the moving platform itself.[240] In its §1498 action against the government, TVI alleged that its '159 patent was infringed by the helmet-mounted display system used by pilots flying the government's F-35 Joint Strike Fighter aircraft.[241]

The trial court determined that the asserted claims of the '159 patent (1) were directed to the abstract idea of using laws of nature governing motion to track to objects, and (2) provided no inventive concept beyond that abstract idea.[242] Accordingly, the trial court granted the government's motion for judgment on the pleadings and held that all claims of the '159 patent were patent-ineligible under 35 U.S.C. §101.

The Federal Circuit reversed in *Thales Visionix*. First, the appellate court noted multiple advantages of TVI's claimed invention over the prior art: increased accuracy in measuring the tracked object on the moving platform; independent operation without requiring other hardware on the moving platform; and simpler installation because the entire system was installed on the inside of the moving platform.[243]

Turning to the *Alice* step one analysis, the Circuit in *Thales Visionix* found parallels between the case before it and precedent concluding that claimed inventions were patent-eligible, citing *Rapid Litigation Management Ltd. v. CellzDirect, Inc.*,[244] *Enfish LLC v. Microsoft Corp.*,[245] and most importantly, the Supreme Court's 1981 decision in *Diamond v. Diehr*.[246] The Circuit observed that the '159 patent

[240]The two independent claims of TVI's '159 patent recited:

1. A system for tracking the motion of an object relative to a moving reference frame, comprising:
a first inertial sensor mounted on the tracked object;
a second inertial sensor mounted on the moving reference frame; and
an element adapted to receive signals from said first and second inertial sensors and configured to determine an orientation of the object relative to the moving reference frame based on the signals received from the first and second inertial sensors.

22. A method comprising determining an orientation of an object relative to a moving reference frame based on signals from two inertial sensors mounted respectively on the object and on the moving reference frame.

[241]*See* Thales Visionix, Inc. v. United States, 122 Fed. Cl. 245, 248 (2015), *rev'd and remanded*, 850 F.3d 1343 (Fed. Cir. 2017). The helmet-mounted display system was manufactured for the U.S. government by subcontractor Elbit Systems of America, which joined the lawsuit as a third-party defendant.

[242]*Thales Visionix,* 850 F.3d at 1346.

[243]*Thales Visionix,* 850 F.3d at 1345.

[244]827 F.3d 1042, 1045 (Fed. Cir. 2016), analyzed *infra* Section B.5.b ("Federal Circuit Applications of *Mayo*").

[245]822 F.3d 1327 (Fed. Cir. 2016), analyzed *infra* this section.

[246]450 U.S. 175 (1981), analyzed *supra* Section B.3 ("Computer-Implemented Processes").

claims at bar were "nearly indistinguishable" from those in *Diehr,* which were "directed to an improvement in a rubber curing process, not a mathematical formula."[247] Although the '159 patent claims used mathematical equations to determine the orientation of the object (e.g., helmet) relative to the moving reference platform (e.g., aircraft), the equations were derived from the arrangement of sensors that the claims required and served only to tabulate the position and orientation information in the required configuration. The claims were thus analogous to those in *Diehr,* which required temperature measurement at a "'location closely adjacent to the [rubber] mold cavity in the press during molding.'"[248] The appellate court observed that "[j]ust as the claims in *Diehr* reduced the likelihood that the rubber molding process would result in "overcuring" or "undercuring," . . . the claims here result in a system that reduces errors in an inertial system that tracks an object on a moving platform."[249]

The *Thales Visionix* Circuit thus determined that TVI's '159 patent claims were *not* merely directed to abstract idea of using "mathematical equations for determining the relative position of a moving object to a moving reference frame," as the trial court had concluded. Rather, "the claims are directed to systems and methods that use inertial sensors in a non-conventional manner to reduce errors in measuring the relative position and orientation of a moving object on a moving reference frame."[250] The appellate court cautioned, with respect to *Alice* step one, that the patent-eligibility analysis is not limited to determining whether claims simply "identify" a patent-ineligible concept; courts must determine whether the claims are "directed to" that concept. The challenged claims were not "directed to" mathematical equations. "That a mathematical equation is required to complete the claimed method and system does not doom the claims to abstraction."[251]

The *Thales Visionix* court concluded by holding that the patent claims at issue recited a "particular" and "unconventional" arrangement of sensors; the mathematical equations utilized were *a result* of that arrangement:

> The '159 patent claims at issue in this appeal are not directed to an abstract idea. The claims specify a particular configuration of inertial sensors and a particular method of using the raw data from the sensors in order to more accurately calculate the position and orientation of an object on a moving platform. The mathematical equations are a consequence of the arrangement of the sensors and the unconventional choice of reference frame in order to calculate position and orientation. Far from

[247] *Thales Visionix,* 850 F.3d at 1348.
[248] *Thales Visionix,* 850 F.3d at 1348 (quoting *Diehr*, 450 U.S. at 179 n.5).
[249] *Thales Visionix,* 850 F.3d at 1348.
[250] *Thales Visionix,* 850 F.3d at 1348-1349.
[251] *Thales Visionix,* 850 F.3d at 1349.

> claiming the equations themselves, the claims seek to protect only the application of physics to the unconventional configuration of sensors as disclosed. As such, these claims are not directed to an abstract idea and thus the claims survive *Alice* step one.[252]

Because it had concluded that the '159 patent claims were not directed to an abstract idea, the Circuit did not proceed to further analyze them under *Alice* step two.

(ii) Decisions Sustaining Patent Eligibility at Step Two

In February 2018, the Federal Circuit issued two important companion decisions exploring the *Mayo/Alice* step two analysis and the "well-understood, routine, conventional" ("WURC") inquiry in particular. *Berkheimer v. HP Inc.*[253] and *Aatrix Software, Inc. v. Green Shades Software, Inc.*[254] considered whether and when the existence of genuine questions of underlying fact may preclude the ultimately legal determination of §101 patent eligibility. In emphasizing the procedural and evidentiary aspects of a patent-eligibility determination rather than its merits,[255] *Berkheimer* and *Aatrix* stand out in the post-*Alice* §101 milieu. Because the Circuit decided not to rehear either decision *en banc*,[256] *Berkheimer* and *Aatrix* represent controlling law unless and until the Supreme Court intervenes.[257]

[252] *Thales Visionix,* 850 F.3d at 1349.

[253] 881 F.3d 1360, 1368 (Fed. Cir. Feb. 8, 2018) (Moore, J.), reh'g *en banc* denied, 890 F.3d 1369 (Fed. Cir. May 31, 2018) (*en banc*) (Moore, J.).

[254] 882 F.3d 1121, 1125 (Fed. Cir. Feb. 14, 2018) (Moore, J.), reh'g *en banc* denied, 890 F.3d 1354 (Fed. Cir. May 31, 2018) (*en banc*) (Moore, J.).

[255] *See* Berkheimer v. HP Inc., 2018 WL 2437140, at *4 (Fed. Cir. May 31, 2018) (Moore, J.) (denying reh'g *en banc*), explaining that

> [w]hether a claim element is well-understood, routine and conventional to a skilled artisan in the relevant field at a particular time is a fact question, and *Berkheimer* and *Aatrix* merely hold that it must be answered under the normal procedural standards, including the Federal Rules of Civil Procedure standards for motions to dismiss or summary judgment and the Federal Rules of Evidence standards for admissions and judicial notice.

[256] The Circuit denied rehearing *en banc* in both cases in May 2018. *See* Berkheimer v. HP Inc., 890 F.3d 1369 (Fed. Cir. May 31, 2018) (Moore, J.) (denying petition for rehearing *en banc*); Aatrix Software, Inc. v. Green Shades Software, Inc., 890 F.3d 1354 (Fed. Cir. May 31, 2018) (denying petition for rehearing *en banc*). As detailed below, both denial decisions occasioned dissents from Judge Reyna and concurrences from Judge Lourie.

[257] Accused infringer Hewlett Packard, Inc. (HP) in the *Berkheimer* case filed a petition for *certiorari* in the Supreme Court in September 2018. *See* HP Inc. v. Steven E. Berkheimer, No. 18-415, _____ S. Ct. _____ (order docketing petition Oct. 3, 2019). HP stated the Question Presented as follows:

To fully understand the context of *Berkheimer* and *Aatrix,* recall the Supreme Court's instruction in *Alice* that for the second step of the §101 patent-eligibility inquiry first elaborated in *Mayo*, courts

> must examine the elements of the claim to determine whether it contains an " 'inventive concept' " sufficient to "transform" the claimed abstract idea into a patent-eligible application. [*Mayo*,] 566 U.S., at ____, ____, 132 S. Ct., at 1294, 1298. A claim that recites an abstract idea must include "additional features" to ensure "that the [claim] is more than a drafting effort designed to monopolize the [abstract idea]." *Id.*, at ____, 132 S. Ct., at 1297. *Mayo* made clear that transformation into a patent-eligible application requires "more than simply stat[ing] the [abstract idea] while adding the words 'apply it.' " *Id.*, at ____, 132 S. Ct., at 1294.[258]

Later in the *Alice* opinion, the Supreme Court applied the above-quoted step two "inventive concept" or "transformation" inquiry to first consider separately the elements of the method claims at issue in that case (concerning a computer-implemented scheme for mitigating "settlement risk" by using a third-party intermediary). Ultimately concluding the claims before it were not patent-eligible, the *Alice* Court determined in step two that the "generic" computer components used to carry out the claimed method performed functions that were merely "well-understood, routine, conventional activit[ies]" previously known to the industry:

> Taking the claim elements separately, the function performed by the computer at each step of the process is "[p]urely conventional." *Mayo*, supra, at ____, 132 S. Ct., at 1298 (internal quotation marks omitted). Using a computer to create and maintain "shadow" accounts amounts to electronic recordkeeping — one of the most basic functions of a computer. *See, e.g., Benson*, 409 U.S., at 65, 93 S. Ct. 253 (noting that a computer "operates . . . upon both new and previously stored data"). The same is true with respect to the use of a computer to obtain data, adjust account balances, and issue automated instructions; *all of these computer functions are "well-understood, routine, conventional activit*[*ies*]" *previously known to the industry*. *Mayo*, 566 U.S., at ____, 132 S. Ct., at

---

> [W]hether patent eligibility is a question of law for the court based on the scope of the claims or a question of fact for the jury based on the state of the art at the time of the patent.

Petition for a Writ of Certiorari at i, HP Inc. v. Steven E. Berkheimer (Sept. 28, 2018), *available at* https://www.supremecourt.gov/DocketPDF/18/18-415/65216/20180928162630738_36823%20pdf%20Hong%20I%20br.pdf. The Supreme Court in January 2019 invited the Solicitor General to file a brief in the case expressing the views of the United States, *see* https://www.supremecourt.gov/docket/docketfiles/html/public/18-415.html, but as of the writing of this edition in October 2019, the Court had not yet received the Solicitor General's submission.

[258] Alice Corp. Pty. v. CLS Bank Int'l, 134 S. Ct. 2347, 2357 (2014).

1294. In short, each step does no more than require a generic computer to perform generic computer functions.[259]

The Circuit's February 2018 panel opinions in *Berkheimer* and *Aatrix* emphasized the "well-understood, routine, conventional" ("WURC") inquiry announced in *Mayo*. The most notable aspect of the decisions is the holding that the WURC inquiry is a question of fact, which in some cases may preclude summary disposition (i.e., through grant of a motion for summary judgment or a motion to dismiss) of §101 eligibility challenges.

Based on the Supreme Court's reliance on the WURC inquiry in step two of the *Mayo/Alice* framework, the Circuit declared in *Berkheimer* that WURC was the sum and substance of step two:

> The second step of the *Alice* test is satisfied when the claim limitations "involve more than performance of 'well-understood, routine, [and] conventional activities previously known to the industry.'"[260]

[259] *Alice Corp.*, 134 S. Ct. at 2359 (emphasis added). Although the *Alice* Court uses it only once, the *Mayo* Court used the "well-understood, routine, conventional" phrase at several points in its discussion. *See, e.g.,* Mayo Collaborative Servs. v. Prometheus Labs., Inc., 566 U.S. 66, 73 (2012) ("the steps in the claimed processes (apart from the natural laws themselves) involve well-understood, routine, conventional activity previously engaged in by researchers in the field"); *Mayo*, 566 U.S. at 79 ("this step tells doctors to engage in well-understood, routine, conventional activity previously engaged in by scientists who work in the field. Purely 'conventional or obvious' '[pre]-solution activity' is normally not sufficient to transform an unpatentable law of nature into a patent-eligible application of such a law") (quoting *Flook*, 437 U.S. at 590; *Bilski*, 130 S. Ct. at 3230); *Mayo*, 566 U.S. at 79-80 ("[T]he claims inform a relevant audience about certain laws of nature; any additional steps consist of well-understood, routine, conventional activity already engaged in by the scientific community; and those steps, when viewed as a whole, add nothing significant beyond the sum of their parts taken separately."); *Mayo*, 566 U.S. at 82 ("These instructions add nothing specific to the laws of nature other than what is well-understood, routine, conventional activity, previously engaged in by those in the field[.]").

[260] *Berkheimer,* 881 F.3d at 1367 (quoting Content Extraction & Transmission LLC v. Wells Fargo Bank, 776 F.3d 1343, 1347-1348 (Fed. Cir. 2014) (Chen, J.) (quoting *Alice*, 134 S. Ct. at 2359)).

This author agrees with Judge Reyna, who dissented from the denial of rehearing *en banc* in *Berkheimer,* that the *Berkheimer* treatment of WURC as entirely dispositive of the step two inquiry improperly collapses the step two analysis. *See* Berkheimer v. HP Inc., 890 F.3d 1369, 1377 (Fed. Cir. May 31, 2018) (Reyna, J., dissenting from denial of reh'g *en banc*) (charging that "[a]fter declaring [the WURC question] to be a question of fact, the panels found this question dispositive of the step two analysis. This action has the effect of reducing the entire step two inquiry into what is routine and conventional, rather than determining if an inventive concept expressed in the claims transforms the nature of the claims into a patent-eligible application. Step two is thus divorced from the claims."). Moreover, the *Berkheimer* approach of exclusively focusing on the WURC question does not address the preemption concerns as part of the step two "transformational" analysis. *Cf.* Alice Corp.,134 S. Ct. at 2354-2355 (stating that "in applying the §101 exception, we must distinguish between patents that claim

In other words, "[i]f the elements involve 'well-understood, routine, [and] conventional activity previously engaged in by researchers in the field,' *Mayo*, 566 U.S. at 73, 132 S. Ct. 1289, they do not constitute an 'inventive concept.'"[261]

The Circuit in *Berkheimer*[262] and *Aatrix*[263] elaborated that if genuine issues of material fact existed about whether disputed claim limitations recited activities that would be considered WURC to an art worker, it would be improper for a district court to summarily invalidate the claims as patent-ineligible on a motion on the pleadings (i.e., under Fed. R. Civ. P. 12) or at the summary judgment stage of a litigation (i.e., under Fed. R. Civ. P. 56). Patent eligibility, like claim definiteness, enablement, and nonobviousness, is ultimately a question of law based on underlying facts.[264] If those facts are genuinely disputed, granting a dismissal on the pleadings or summary judgment based on patent ineligibility is error as a matter of federal civil procedure.

---

the "'buildin[g] block[s]'" of human ingenuity and those that integrate the building blocks into something more, *Mayo*, 566 U.S., at _____, 132 S. Ct., at 1303, thereby "transform[ing]" them into a patent-eligible invention, *id.*, at _____, 132 S. Ct., at 1294. The former "would risk disproportionately tying up the use of the underlying" ideas, *id.*, at _____, 132 S. Ct., at 1294, and are therefore ineligible for patent protection. The latter pose no comparable risk of pre-emption, and therefore remain eligible for the monopoly granted under our patent laws.").

[261]*Aatrix,* 882 F.3d at 1128. The Circuit cited its own precedent in further support:

> We have explained that the second step of the *Alice / Mayo* test is satisfied when the claim limitations "involve more than performance of 'well-understood, routine, [and] conventional activities previously known to the industry.'" *Content Extraction*, 776 F.3d at 1347-48 (quoting *Alice*, 134 S. Ct. at 2359); *see also* Affinity Labs of Tex., LLC v. DIRECTV, LLC, 838 F.3d 1253, 1262 (Fed. Cir. 2016) (holding that the features constituting the inventive concept in step two of *Alice / Mayo* "must be more than 'well-understood, routine, conventional activity'" (quoting *Mayo*, 566 U.S. at 79-80, 132 S. Ct. 1289)); Intellectual Ventures I LLC v. Erie Indem. Co., 850 F.3d 1315, 1328 (Fed. Cir. 2017) (same); *BASCOM*, 827 F.3d at 1350 ("[I]t is of course now standard for a §101 inquiry to consider whether various claim elements simply recite 'well-understood, routine, conventional activit[ies].'" (quoting *Alice*, 134 S. Ct. at 2359)).

Aatrix, 882 F.3d at 1128.

[262]881 F.3d 1360, 1368 (Fed. Cir. Feb. 8, 2018) (Moore, J.), reh'g *en banc* denied, 890 F.3d 1369 (Fed. Cir. May 31, 2018) (*en banc*) (Moore, J.).

[263]882 F.3d 1121, 1125 (Fed. Cir. Feb. 14, 2018) (Moore, J.), reh'g *en banc* denied, 890 F.3d 1354 (Fed. Cir. May 31, 2018) (*en banc*) (Moore, J.).

[264]*Berkheimer,* 881 F.3d at 1368, stating that

> [w]e have previously stated that "[t]he §101 inquiry '*may* contain underlying factual issues.'" Mortg. Grader, [Inc. v. First Choice Loan Servs. Inc., 811 F.3d 1314 (Fed. Cir. 2016)], 811 F.3d at 1325 (emphasis in original) (quoting Accenture Global Servs., GmbH v. Guidewire Software, Inc., 728 F.3d 1336, 1341 (Fed. Cir. 2013)). And the Supreme Court recognized that in making the §101 determination, the inquiry "might sometimes overlap" with other fact-intensive inquiries like novelty under §102. *Mayo*, 566 U.S. at 90, 132 S. Ct. 1289.

The Circuit explained further in *Berkheimer* that the question whether a particular technology is WURC "goes beyond what was simply known in the art. The mere fact that something is disclosed in a piece of prior art, for example, does not mean it was well-understood, routine, and conventional."[265] The Circuit cited no authority for this assertion, however, nor did it offer a test or standard for determining what evidence beyond inclusion in the prior art would indicate that a claim element is WURC to a skilled artisan. The WURC inquiry seems similar to the question whether the invention would have been obvious under 35 U.S.C. §103, but the Circuit did not equate the two analyses.[266]

Importantly, the existence of fact questions about §101 patent eligibility does not prevent dismissal of a patent lawsuit if the factual disputes are not genuine. And some patent-eligibility cases may not raise any fact questions whatsoever. The Federal Circuit was quick to acknowledge in *Berkheimer* that in prior decisions, it had frequently affirmed the invalidation of patents as §101-ineligible upon review of a district court's grant of a motion to dismiss on the pleadings (Fed. R. Civ. P. 12(c)), or for failure to state a claim for which relief may be granted (Fed. R. Civ. P. 12(b)(6)), or for summary judgment (Fed. R. Civ. P. 56). Nothing in *Berkheimer* or *Aatrix* was intended to cast aspersions or doubt on those decisions. "When there is no genuine issue of material fact regarding whether the claim element or claimed combination is well-understood, routine, conventional to a skilled artisan in the relevant field, this issue can be decided on summary judgment as a matter of law."[267]

But the records in *Berkheimer* and *Aatrix* were different. In the Circuit's view, unresolved genuine factual disputes existed that made dismissal on the pleadings premature in those cases. The facts of each of these important cases are analyzed below.

Firstly, *Berkheimer v. HP Inc.*[268] involved the assertion of Berkheimer's U.S. Patent No. 7,447,713 ('713 patent). The '713 patent related to digitally processing and archiving files in a digital asset management system. The system parsed files into multiple objects and tagged the objects to create relationships between them.[269] These relationships allowed a user to carry out a "one-to-many" editing process of

[265] *Berkheimer,* 881 F.3d at 1369.

[266] *Cf.* Berkheimer v. HP Inc., 890 F.3d 1369, 1376 (May 31, 2019) (Lourie, J., concurring in denial of reh'g *en banc*) (asserting that *Alice/Mayo* step two's prohibition on identifying the inventive "something more" from computer functions [that] are "'well-understood, routine, conventional activit[ies]' previously known to the industry" is "essentially a §§102 and 103 inquiry") (quoting *Alice*, 134 S. Ct. at 2359).

[267] *Berkheimer,* 881 F.3d at 1368.

[268] 881 F.3d 1360, 1368 (Fed. Cir. Feb. 8, 2018) (Moore, J.), reh'g *en banc* denied, 890 F.3d 1369 (Fed. Cir. May 31, 2018) (*en banc*) (Moore, J.).

[269] *Berkheimer,* 881 F.3d at 1362.

object-oriented data, in which a change to one object carried over to all other archived documents having the same object. According to the specification of Berkheimer's '713 patent, the claimed system advantageously eliminated redundant storage of common text and graphical elements, which improved the system's operating efficiency and reduced storage costs.

Following a *Markman* patent claim construction hearing, the Northern District of Illinois had held on summary judgment that claims 1-7 and 9 of Berkheimer's '713 patent were invalid as patent-ineligible under 35 U.S.C. §101.[270] More specifically, the district court determined that the patent claims did not contain an inventive concept under *Alice* step two because they recited "steps that employ[ed] only 'well-understood, routine, and conventional' computer functions" and were claimed "at a relatively high level of generality."[271]

The Federal Circuit agreed with the district court's view as to some of Berkheimer's patent claims but not others. The appellate court cited the '713 patent specification's references to the invention's purported advantages of reducing redundancy and enabling one-to-many editing. If these concepts were captured in the claims, the Circuit reasoned, a genuine issue of fact existed concerning whether the claims recited WURC activities (contrary to the district court's finding).

The Circuit agreed with the district court that claims 1-3 and 9 of the '713 patent did *not* capture the purported inventive concepts disclosed in the specification; i.e., they did not recite eliminating redundancy of stored object structures or effecting a one-to-many change to the linked documents within an archive.[272] Accordingly, the Circuit affirmed that portion of the district court's summary judgment declaring claims 1-3 and 9 invalid as patent-ineligible under §101.

The Circuit reached a contrary result when considering Berkheimer's claims 4-7, however; the appellate court vacated the summary judgment of ineligibility for those claims. It concluded that claims 4-7

[270]*See* Berkheimer v. Hewlett-Packard Co., 224 F. Supp. 3d 635 (N.D. Ill. 2016).

[271]*Berkheimer*, 224 F. Supp. 3d at 647-648 (quoting *Content Extraction*, 776 F.3d at 1348). The Circuit also noted that whether the claimed invention was well understood, routine, and conventional presented an underlying fact question "for which [accused infringer/validity challenger] HP offered no evidence." *Berkheimer*, 881 F.3d at 1368.

[272]Representative claim 1 of the '713 patent recited:

> 1. A method of archiving an item in a computer processing system comprising:
> presenting the item to a parser;
> parsing the item into a plurality of multi-part object structures wherein portions of the structures have searchable information tags associated therewith;
> evaluating the object structures in accordance with object structures previously stored in an archive;
> presenting an evaluated object structure for manual reconciliation at least where there is a predetermined variance between the object and at least one of a predetermined standard and a user defined rule.

"recite[d] a specific method of archiving that, according to the specification, provides benefits that improve computer functionality."[273]

Unlike claims 1-3 and 9, the purported inventive concepts disclosed in the patent's specification were captured or recited in claims 4-7. First, the Circuit explained that claim 4 recited "storing a reconciled object structure in the archive without substantial redundancy." This limitation captured statements in the '713 patent specification that storing object structures in the archive without substantial redundancy improved system operating efficiency and reduced storage costs. The specification also stated that known asset management systems did not archive documents in this manner.

Claim 5, depending from claim 4, further recited "selectively editing an object structure, linked to other structures to thereby effect a one-to-many change in a plurality of archived items." This limitation reflected the specification's statements that one-to-many editing substantially reduced effort needed to update files because a single edit could update every document in the archive linked to that object structure. Contrary to the district court's finding, the one-to-many functionality was more than simply "editing data in a straightforward copy-and-paste fashion."[274] The '713 specification asserted that conventional digital asset management systems could not perform one-to-many editing because they stored documents with numerous instances of redundant elements, rather than eliminating redundancies through the storage of linked object structures.[275]

The Circuit panel in *Berkheimer* did not reach the ultimate issue whether claims 4-7 were patent-eligible under §101. Rather, it "only decide[d] that on this record summary judgment was improper, given the fact questions created by the specification's disclosure."[276]

One week later, the Circuit decided *Aatrix Software, Inc. v. Green Shades Software, Inc.*,[277] again emphasizing the existence of disputed fact questions in the WURC inquiry of *Mayo/Alice* step two. As in *Berkheimer*, Judge Moore (with whom Judge Taranto joined) authored the majority opinion for the panel. Judge Reyna dissented in *Aatrix*, however, as discussed below.

The key issue in *Aatrix* was the same as that in *Berkheimer*— the role of factual questions about whether claims recite more than "well understood, routine, conventional" ("WURC") technology in step two of the *Mayo/Alice* analysis for §101 patent eligibility. The two cases differed

[273] *Berkheimer*, 881 F.3d at 1370.

[274] *Berkheimer,* 881 F.3d at 1370 (quoting *Berkheimer,* 224 F. Supp. 3d at 645).

[275] Lastly, claims 6-7 depended from claim 5 and thus contained the same limitations.

[276] *Berkheimer*, 881 F.3d at 1370.

[277] 882 F.3d 1121, 1125 (Fed. Cir. Feb. 14, 2018) (Moore, J.), reh'g *en banc* denied, 890 F.3d 1354 (Fed. Cir. May 31, 2018) (*en banc*) (Moore, J.).

procedurally, however. While the Circuit in *Berkheimer* was reviewing a district court's grant of summary judgment of non-eligibility, the Circuit in *Aatrix* considered the propriety of a Rule 12(b)(6) dismissal for failure to state a claim based on non-eligibility. The result reached by the Circuit in both cases was the same: it overturned (at least in part) the district courts' summary dispositions based on non-eligibility because of unresolved fact questions concerning the WURC inquiry.

Aatrix Software's U.S. Patent Nos. 7,171,615 ('615 patent) and 8,984,393 ('393 patent) concerned methods and systems for designing, creating, and importing data into a viewable form (such as a tax form) on a computer so that a user could manipulate the form data and create viewable forms and reports. The data processing system comprised a form file, a data file, and a viewer.[278] The "form file" was particularly important. Aatrix asserted that the claimed inventions advantageously allowed data to be imported from an end user application without needing to know proprietary database schemas, and without having to custom-program the form files to work with each outside application.[279]

The Middle District of Florida dismissed Aatrix's infringement complaint upon granting defendant Green Shades' motion under Fed. R. Civ. P. 12(b)(6). The district court held that the patent claims were directed to the abstract idea of "'collecting, organizing, and performing calculations on data to fill out forms: a fundamental human activity that can be performed using a pen and paper.'"[280] It found no inventive concepts in the claim elements, taken individually or as a group. Rather, the district court found that the claimed data file described a "well understood and routine" component and function of a computer.[281]

[278]Representative claim 1 of the '615 patent recited:

> 1. A data processing system for designing, creating, and importing data into, a viewable form viewable by the user of the data processing system, comprising:
>
> (a) a form file that models the physical representation of an original paper form and establishes the calculations and rule conditions required to fill in the viewable form;
>
> (b) a form file creation program that imports a background image from an original form, allows a user to adjust and test-print the background image and compare the alignment of the original form to the background test-print, and creates the form file;
>
> (c) a data file containing data from a user application for populating the viewable form; and
>
> (d) a form viewer program operating on the form file and the data file, to perform calculations, allow the user of the data processing system to review and change the data, and create viewable forms and reports.

[279]*Aatrix,* 882 F.3d at 1127 (proposed Second Amended Complaint).
[280]*Aatrix,* 882 F.3d at 1124 (quoting Joint Appendix).
[281]*Aatrix,* 882 F.3d at 1129.

Importantly, the district court also denied patentee Aatrix's motion for leave to file a second amended complaint. Aatrix had argued that the amended complaint would have supplied additional allegations and evidence raising genuine factual issues precluding a dismissal under §101 at the Rule 12(b)(6) stage, but the district court was not persuaded.

On appeal in *Aatrix*, the Federal Circuit vacated the Florida district court's dismissal. First, the appellate court held that the district court had abused its discretion in denying Aatrix leave to file the proposed second amended complaint. Leave to amend is to be granted freely. The district court had given no reason or explanation for its denial. Allowing Aatrix to file the second amended complaint would not have been futile, for it contained "allegations that, taken as true, would directly affect the district court's eligibility analysis."[282] These allegation, if true, would contradict the district court's conclusion that the claimed combination was conventional and routine.[283]

In particular, the *Aatrix* Circuit quoted portions of the proposed second amended complaint that "at a minimum" raised factual questions as to whether the claim-recited "data file" constituted an inventive concept under *Alice* step two. "Numerous" allegations in the second amended complaint related to the inventive concepts present in the claimed form file technology.[284] The allegations of the proposed second amended complaint also demonstrated that the claimed system improved the functioning and operation of the computer running it. For example, the complaint alleged that the invention saved storage space both in short-term and permanent, slower computer storage; used less memory; processed at a faster speed; and reduced the risk of "thrashing," a problem that had slowed down prior art systems.[285]

Accordingly, the Federal Circuit *Aatrix* majority vacated the district court's dismissal under Rule 12(b)(6), and reversed its denial of patentee Aatrix's motion for leave to file its proposed second amended complaint.[286]

Circuit Judge Reyna dissented in *Aatrix* (as he would when the Circuit later denied rehearing *en banc* in *Aatrix* and *Berkheimer*, discussed below). He disagreed with the majority's fundamental premise that the §101 inquiry involves underlying questions of fact. Judge Reyna contended that the Circuit's precedent "is clear that the §101 inquiry is a legal question."[287] He criticized the *Aatrix* majority

[282] *Aatrix,* 882 F.3d at 1126.
[283] *Aatrix,* 882 F.3d at 1128.
[284] *Aatrix,* 882 F.3d at 1127.
[285] *Aatrix,* 882 F.3d at 1127.
[286] *Aatrix,* 882 F.3d at 1130.
[287] *Aatrix,* 882 F.3d at 1130 (Reyna, J., dissenting-in-part) (citing Intellectual Ventures I LLC v. Capital One Fin. Corp., 850 F.3d 1332, 1338 (Fed. Cir. 2017)).

for "attempt[ing] to shoehorn a significant factual component into the *Alice* §101 analysis."[288] In Judge Reyna's view, the majority's approach created significant practical problems of trial management, reducing the benefits of Rule 12(b)(6). He charged that the majority had "opened the door" to patentees introducing an "inexhaustible array of extrinsic evidence, such as prior art, publications, other patents, and expert opinion," in both steps of the *Alice* inquiry.[289]

In late May 2018, the Federal Circuit denied rehearing *en banc* in both *Berkheimer* and *Aatrix*,[290] with Judge Reyna dissenting from denial in each case and Judge Lourie writing a concurring opinion in each case. The opposing views expressed in those opinions (plus the majority opinion denying rehearing) signal that the issues raised in *Berkheimer* and *Aatrix* are subject to ongoing debate and discussion at the Federal Circuit. It is worthwhile to explore the judges' disparate views as the Circuit's §101 jurisprudence continues to evolve.

The *en banc* majority (in an opinion authored by Judge Moore) downplayed its decisions in *Berkheimer* and *Aatrix* as "narrow" and "unremarkable." The two cases held merely that the *Mayo*/*Alice* step two question, whether a patent claim element or combination of elements would have been well understood, routine, and conventional ("WURC") to a skilled artisan in the relevant field at a particular point in time, is a question of fact. It should "not [be] surprising" that the ultimately legal question of §101 patent eligibility contains underlying fact questions, the majority observed; every other type of patent validity challenge is either entirely or at least partially factual.[291]

The *en banc* majority in *Berkheimer* and *Aatrix* noted that the procedural and evidentiary standards for federal court litigation apply to patent cases as they do to any other type of dispute. Accordingly, factual questions about patent eligibility "must be answered under the normal procedural standards," including the standards of the Federal Rules of Civil Procedure for motions to dismiss or for summary judgment and the standards of the Federal Rules of Evidence for admissions and judicial notice.[292] For example, a court considering a defendant's Fed. R. Civ. P. 12(b)(6) motion to dismiss for failure to state a claim (as in *Aatrix*) must

[288] *Aatrix,* 882 F.3d at 1130 (Reyna, J., dissenting-in-part).

[289] *Aatrix,* 882 F.3d at 1130 (Reyna, J., dissenting-in-part).

[290] Berkheimer v. HP Inc., 890 F.3d 1369 (Fed. Cir. May 31, 2018) (Moore, J.) (denying petition for rehearing *en banc*); Aatrix Software, Inc. v. Green Shades Software, Inc., 890 F.3d 1354 (Fed. Cir. May 31, 2018) (denying petition for rehearing *en banc*).

[291] *Berkheimer*, 890 F.3d at 1370 (denying reh'g *en banc*) (stating that the invalidity defenses of anticipation, written description, and utility are "entirely factual"; that obviousness and enablement are "question[s] of law with underlying facts"; and that indefiniteness is a question of law that "may contain underlying facts").

[292] *Berkheimer*, 890 F.3d at 1371 (*en banc*).

treat the allegations of the plaintiff's complaint as true, and indeed construe them in the light most favorable to the plaintiff.[293] Fed. R. Civ. P. 56(a) (at issue in *Berkheimer*) mandates that the existence of genuinely disputed fact questions precludes summary judgment.[294] The Federal Rules of Evidence would allow a court, for example, to take judicial notice in cases when a patent's specification effectively admitted that certain claims elements were WURC rather than "inventive concepts."[295]

Joined by Judge Newman, Judge Lourie authored separate opinions concurring in the majority's decisions not to rehear *en banc* the *Berkheimer* and *Aatrix* cases (Judge Lourie's concurring opinion in each case was the same). He found "plausib[le]" the panel holdings that fact issues were potentially involved in the panels' consideration of the abstract idea exception to patent eligibility,[296] and he "doubt[ed]" that the two cases were "decided wrongly." Nevertheless, Judge Lourie viewed the *Berkheimer* and *Aatrix* panel decisions as making an

[293]*Berkheimer,* 890 F.3d at 1372 (*en banc*), stating:

> A motion to dismiss for failure to state a claim must be denied if "in the light most favorable to the plaintiff and with every doubt resolved in the pleader's favor — but disregarding mere conclusory statements — the complaint states any legally cognizable claim for relief." 5B Charles Alan Wright & Arthur R. Miller, Federal Practice and Procedure §1357 (3d ed. 2018). In the Eleventh Circuit [where Aatrix's lawsuit was filed], the Rule 12(b)(6) standard requires accepting as true the complaint's factual allegations and construing them in the light most favorable to the plaintiff. *Aatrix Software, Inc. v. Green Shades Software, Inc.*, 882 F.3d 1121, 1124 (Fed. Cir. 2018) (citing *Speaker v. U.S. Dep't of Health & Human Servs. Ctrs. for Disease Control & Prevention*, 623 F.3d 1371, 1379 (11th Cir. 2010)).

[294]"The court shall grant summary judgment if the movant shows that there is no genuine dispute as to any material fact and the movant is entitled to judgment as a matter of law." Fed. R. Civ. P. 56(a).

[295]As an example, the *en banc* court observed that

> [b]ecause the patent challenger bears the burden of demonstrating that the claims lack patent eligibility, 35 U.S.C. §282(a), there must be evidence supporting a finding that the additional elements were well-understood, routine, and conventional. Relying on the specification alone may be appropriate where, as in *Mayo*, the specification admits as much. 566 U.S. at 79, 132 S. Ct. 1289; *see also id.* at 73-74, 132 S. Ct. 1289. In *Mayo*, the Court considered disclosures in the specification of the patent about the claimed techniques being "routinely" used and "well known in the art." *Id.* at 73-74, 79, 132 S. Ct. 1289. Based on these disclosures, the Court held that "any additional steps [beyond the law of nature] consist of well-understood, routine, conventional activity already engaged in by the scientific community" that "add nothing significant beyond the sum of their parts taken separately." *Id.* at 79-80, 132 S. Ct. 1289. In a situation where the specification admits the additional claim elements are well-understood, routine, and conventional, it will be difficult, if not impossible, for a patentee to show a genuine dispute. . . .

Berkheimer, 890 F.3d at 1371 (Fed. Cir. May 31, 2018) (*en banc*) (citation omitted).

[296]*Berkheimer*, 890 F.3d at 1374 (Fed. Cir. May 31, 2018) (Lourie, J., concurring in denial of reh'g *en banc*).

unfortunately complicated §101 analysis even more complicated; the two cases "dig[] the hole deeper. . . ."[297]

Judge Reyna was the sole dissenter from the denial of rehearing *en banc* in both *Berkheimer* and *Aatrix*, entering an identical opinion in each case.[298] He echoed and amplified the position earlier stated in his panel dissent in *Aatrix* that the Circuit's precedents made the §101 eligibility determination entirely a question of law. Indeed, he charged, "there is no precedent that the §101 inquiry is a question of fact."[299]

Rather than accept the "nothing has changed" tenor of the panel opinions, Judge Reyna characterized the import of *Berkheimer* and

[297]*Berkheimer*, 890 F.3d at 1376 (Fed. Cir. May 31, 2018) (Lourie, J., concurring in denial of reh'g *en banc*). He called for "clarification by higher authority, perhaps Congress," of what "so many in the innovation field consider [to be] §101 problems." Traditionally, Judge Lourie explained, courts determined patent eligibility in a relatively straightforward manner, considering the text of §101 and the "statutory gloss" of the implicit exceptions thereto (i.e., laws of nature, natural phenomena, and abstract ideas). But "problems and uncertainties" arose in carrying out that analysis once the Supreme Court in *Mayo* began to "whittle[] away" at the §101 statute by adopting its two-step test. Judge Lourie protested that "[w]e now are interpreting what began, when it rarely arose, as a simple §101 analysis, as a complicated multiple-step consideration of inventiveness ("something more"), with the result that an increasing amount of inventive research is no longer subject to patent." *Berkheimer*, 890 F.3d at 1375 (Fed. Cir. May 31, 2018) (Lourie, J., concurring in denial of reh'g *en banc*).

Judge Lourie agreed with the fundamental premise that abstract ideas (or any ideas) should not be the subject of patents because they are free for all to use and build on. But he questioned "why [there] should be a step two in an abstract idea analysis at all." In Judge Lourie's view, the *Mayo/Alice* step two prohibition on finding the "something more" from WURC claim elements was redundant because it is "essentially a §§102 and 103 inquiry." *Berkheimer*, 890 F.3d at 1376 (Fed. Cir. May 31, 2018) (Lourie, J., concurring in denial of reh'g *en banc*).

Judge Lourie concluded his concurrence with a plea for "higher intervention, hopefully with ideas reflective of the best thinking that can be brought to bear on the subject." *Berkheimer*, 890 F.3d at 1376 (Fed. Cir. May 31, 2018) (Lourie, J., concurring in denial of reh'g *en banc*). But he conceded that the two cases at bar were not the appropriate vehicles for that intervention. They did not raise the larger policy issues Judge Lourie focused on; namely, the need for patent protection to incentivize much-needed inventive research. And individual cases, "whether heard by [the Circuit] or the Supreme Court, are imperfect vehicles for enunciating broad principles because they are limited to the facts presented." It was clear to Judge Lourie that the problems and uncertainties attendant to the current §101 eligibility analysis, arising from the "script" written by the Supreme Court, "require attention beyond the power of this court." *Berkheimer*, 890 F.3d at 1374 (Fed. Cir. May 31, 2018) (Lourie, J., concurring in denial of reh'g *en banc*).

[298]*See Berkheimer*, 890 F.3d at 1376 (Fed. Cir. May 31, 2018) (Reyna, J., dissenting from denial of reh'g *en banc*); *Aatrix*, 890 F.3d 1354 (Fed. Cir. May 31, 2018) (dissenting from denial of reh'g *en banc*).

[299]*Berkheimer*, 890 F.3d at 1377 (Fed. Cir. May 31, 2018) (Reyna, J., dissenting from denial of reh'g *en banc*).

Aatrix as a "profound change" with "staggering" consequences.[300] In his view the decisions collapsed the entire step two inquiry into the WURC question, divorcing the step two analysis from the patent claims. The panel decisions

> alter the §101 analysis in a significant and fundamental manner by presenting patent eligibility under §101 as predominately a question of fact. For example, in addressing *Alice* step two, the *Aatrix* and *Berkheimer* panels raised and considered the same, exact question of "whether the invention describes well-understood, routine, and conventional activities." *Aatrix*, 882 F.3d at 1129; *see also Berkheimer*, 881 F.3d at 1369. After declaring this to be a question of fact, the panels found this question dispositive of the step two analysis. This action has the effect of reducing the entire step two inquiry into what is routine and conventional, rather than determining if an inventive concept expressed in the claims transforms the nature of the claims into a patent-eligible application. Step two is thus divorced from the claims.[301]

Moreover, Judge Reyna observed, the *Berkheimer* and *Aatrix* panels offered "no meaningful guidance" to the courts, the USPTO, or the public on how to determine the WURC fact question, creating a host of unanswered issues that the district courts must deal with in the first instance. Judge Reyna queried,

> [f]or example, to what extent will discovery be allowed to prove or disprove a fact that has been placed in contention? Does this new factual inquiry extend to other aspects of the §101 inquiry, such as whether a claim is directed to an abstract idea or a natural phenomenon? Can expert opinion supplant the written description? Does the court or jury determine this factual issue? What deference is due to the fact finder? These and similar questions will have to be addressed and resolved by the district courts. Instead of creating a period of uncertainty with the expectation of addressing these issues sometime in the future, this court should address them now.[302]

Judge Reyna characterized as "staggering" the consequences of the *Berkheimer* and *Aatrix* holding, removing the "inventive concept" inquiry from the claims and specification and instead placing it "firmly in the realm of extrinsic evidence." This shift had negative practical implications for patent litigation, "almost guarantee[ing] that §101

[300]*Berkheimer*, 890 F.3d at 1380 (Fed. Cir. May 31, 2018) (Reyna, J., dissenting from denial of reh'g *en banc*).

[301]*Berkheimer*, 890 F.3d at 1377 (Fed. Cir. May 31, 2018) (Reyna, J., dissenting from denial of reh'g *en banc*).

[302]*Berkheimer*, 890 F.3d at 1377-1378 (Fed. Cir. May 31, 2018) (Reyna, J., dissenting from denial of reh'g *en banc*).

issues will be carried through to trial rather than resolved early in a case.[303] He predicted, contrary to Circuit precedent, that juries will henceforth decide whether patent claims include an "inventive concept" sufficient to survive *Mayo/Alice* step two. And in his view, there was no principled reason why the same factual analysis should not enter into the step one "abstract idea" inquiry.

Contrary to the panel decisions, Judge Reyna took the position that the §101 analysis should proceed in analogous fashion to contract interpretation or patent claim interpretation.[304] In those contexts, looking beyond the four corners of the document (here, the patent) "should only occur in exceptional circumstances."[305] And for practical reasons, the ability to address patent eligibility at the outset of a case is significant, not only because it conserves scarce judicial resources and saves litigants the "staggering" costs of discovery and claim construction, but also because it " 'works to stem the tide of vexatious suits brought by the owners of vague and overbroad business method patents.' "[306]

As of the writing of this edition in late 2019, it is too soon to judge whether the differing opinions and viewpoints expressed in *Berkheimer* and *Aatrix* represent a real change in litigation procedure for §101 challenges or relatively narrow blips. In the aftermath of *Berkheimer* and *Aatrix,* the Circuit has continued to issue precedential decisions affirming that claims were not patent-eligible at the early stage of a motion to dismiss or a motion for summary judgement.[307] On the other hand, the Circuit has also relied on its *Berkheimer* and *Aatrix* decisions as precedent for vacating district court case dismissals based on asserted §101 ineligibility.

The Circuit's 2019 decision in *Cellspin Soft, Inc. v. Fitbit, Inc.*[308] illustrates the latter scenario. In *Cellspin,* the Federal Circuit determined that even though a challenged patent claim was directed to an abstract idea under the first step of the *Mayo/Alice* framework, it was nevertheless patent-eligible under the second step. The claim

[303]*Berkheimer*, 890 F.3d at 1380 (Fed. Cir. May 31, 2018) (Reyna, J., dissenting from denial of reh'g *en banc*).

[304]*Berkheimer*, 890 F.3d at 1381-1382 (Fed. Cir. May 31, 2018) (Reyna, J., dissenting from denial of reh'g *en banc*).

[305]*Berkheimer*, 890 F.3d at 1383 (Fed. Cir. May 31, 2018) (Reyna, J., dissenting from denial of reh'g *en banc*).

[306]*Berkheimer*, 890 F.3d at 1383 (Fed. Cir. May 31, 2018) (Reyna, J., dissenting from denial of reh'g *en banc*) (quoting OIP Techs., Inc. v. Amazon.com, Inc., 788 F.3d 1359,1364-1365 (Fed. Cir. 2015) (Mayer, J., concurring)).

[307]*See, e.g.,* SAP Am., Inc. v. InvestPic LLC, 890 F.3d 1016 (Fed. Cir. May 15, 2018) (Taranto, J.) (holding claims patent-ineligible at Rule 12(c) stage); Voter Verified, Inc. v. Election Sys. & Software LLC, 887 F.3d 1376 (Fed. Cir. Apr. 20, 2018) (same at Rule 12(b)(6) stage)).

[308]927 F.3d 1306 (Fed. Cir. 2019) (O'Malley, J.).

survived because its non-abstract portion provided an "inventive concept." In other words, the patent claims in *Cellspin* were "saved" under the *Mayo/Alice* step two inquiry, at least at a preliminary stage in litigation. In the Circuit's view, the complaint's "plausible and specific factual allegations that aspects of the claims [we]re inventive [i.e., unconventional]" were sufficient to survive the accused infringers' motion to dismiss.[309]

Cellspin Soft, Inc. ("Cellspin") owned four patents that related generally to easily and quickly connecting a "data capture device" (such as a digital camera, video camera, digital modular camera system, or other digital data capturing system) to a "mobile device" (such as a cell phone). By means of this connection, a user could automatically publish content (e.g., text or multimedia data) from the data capture device to a website. The data capture device and the mobile device communicated via short-range wireless communication protocols such as Bluetooth.[310] Cellspin's patents shared a common specification and claimed priority to a 2007 provisional application.

More specifically, a "client application" on the claim-recited mobile device detected and received content from the data capture device over the short-range communication connection. The mobile device then published the content on one or more websites. Unlike prior art processes, the claimed process assertedly worked "automatically or with minimal user intervention."[311] Moreover, the Cellspin patent claims recited a timing limitation; they required that a paired connection be established between the data capture device and the mobile device *before* content was transmitted between the two.[312]

[309] *Cellspin,* 927 F.3d at 1317-1318.

[310] Bluetooth is

> a wireless technology standard for exchanging data between fixed and mobile devices over short distances using short-wavelength UHF radio waves in the industrial, scientific and medical radio bands, from 2.400 to 2.485 GHz, and building personal area networks (PANs). It was originally conceived as a wireless alternative to RS-232 data cables.

Bluetooth, Wikipedia.org, https://en.wikipedia.org/wiki/Bluetooth (Sept. 30, 2019).

[311] Cellspin's patents explained that the conventional (prior art) method for publishing data and multimedia content on a website was time-consuming and required manual user intervention:

> Typically, the user would capture an image using a digital camera or a video camera, store the image on a memory device of the digital camera, and transfer the image to a computing device such as a personal computer (PC). In order to transfer the image to the PC, the user would transfer the image off-line to the PC, use a cable such as a universal serial bus (USB) or a memory stick and plug the cable into the PC. The user would then manually upload the image onto a website which takes time and may be inconvenient for the user.

U.S. Patent No. 8,738,794 ('794 patent).

[312] Claim 1 of the '794 patent recited (emphasis added):

Cellspin sued 14 companies for infringing various claims of its patents, including well-known defendants Fitbit, Nike, Fossil, Cannon, GoPro, and Panasonic. The accused infringers responded by filing an omnibus motion to dismiss Cellspin's lawsuits pursuant to Fed. R. Civ. P. 12(b)(6) for failure to state a claim on which relief could be granted. In their view, the asserted claims were not patent-eligible under 35 U.S.C. §101. The Northern District of California agreed, granting the motion to dismiss.

---

1. A method for acquiring and transferring data from a Bluetooth enabled data capture device to one or more web services via a Bluetooth enabled mobile device, the method comprising:

providing a software module on the Bluetooth enabled data capture device;

providing a software module on the Bluetooth enabled mobile device;

establishing a paired connection between the Bluetooth enabled data capture device and the Bluetooth enabled mobile device;

acquiring new data in the Bluetooth enabled data capture device, wherein new data is data acquired *after* the paired connection is established;

detecting and signaling the new data for transfer to the Bluetooth enabled mobile device, wherein detecting and signaling the new data for transfer comprises:

determining the existence of new data for transfer, by the software module on the Bluetooth enabled data capture device; and

sending a data signal to the Bluetooth enabled mobile device, corresponding to existence of new data, by the software module on the Bluetooth enabled data capture device automatically, over the established paired Bluetooth connection, wherein the software module on the Bluetooth enabled mobile device listens for the data signal sent from the Bluetooth enabled data capture device, wherein if permitted by the software module on the Bluetooth enabled data capture device, the data signal sent to the Bluetooth enabled mobile device comprises a data signal and one or more portions of the new data;

transferring the new data from the Bluetooth enabled data capture device to the Bluetooth enabled mobile device automatically over the paired Bluetooth connection by the software module on the Bluetooth enabled data capture device;

receiving, at the Bluetooth enabled mobile device, the new data from the Bluetooth enabled data capture device;

applying, using the software module on the Bluetooth enabled mobile device, a user identifier to the new data for each destination web service, wherein each user identifier uniquely identifies a particular user of the web service;

transferring the new data received by the Bluetooth enabled mobile device along with a user identifier to the one or more web services, using the software module on the Bluetooth enabled mobile device;

receiving, at the one or more web services, the new data and user identifier from the Bluetooth enabled mobile device, wherein the one or more web services receive the transferred new data corresponding to a user identifier; and

making available, at the one or more web services, the new data received from the Bluetooth enabled mobile device for public or private consumption over the internet, wherein one or more portions of the new data correspond to a particular user identifier.

On appeal, the Federal Circuit concurred with the district court that under step one of the *Mayo/Alice* framework, Cellspin's patent claims were directed to the abstract idea of capturing and transmitting data from one device to another.[313] This view was consistent with other Circuit cases holding that "similar claims reciting the collection, transfer, and publishing of data [we]re directed to an abstract idea."[314]

The *Cellspin* Circuit and the district court parted ways on *Mayo/Alice* step two, however — the search for an "inventive concept." Importantly, the Circuit relied on its *Aatrix Software* decision, analyzed above in conjunction with *Berkheimer*. The appellate court in those two decisions recognized that the step two analysis *may* involve fact questions concerning whether the claimed invention reflects "something more than the application of [the] abstract idea using 'well-understood, routine, and conventional activities previously known to the industry.'"[315] Both *Aatrix* and *Cellspin* were appeals from a district court's dismissal under Fed. R. Civ. P. 12. Under the courts' implementation of that rule, the factual allegations of a plaintiff's complaint must be taken as true.[316] In the case at bar, Cellspin's

[313]*Cellspin,* 927 F.3d at 1315.

[314]*Cellspin,* 927 F.3d at 1315 (citing, e.g., Elec. Power Grp., LLC v. Alstom S.A., 830 F.3d 1350, 1353 (Fed. Cir. 2016); In re TLI Comm'ns LLC Patent Litigation, 823 F.3d 607, 610-612 (Fed. Cir. 2016)).

[315]*Cellspin,* 927 F.3d at 1316 (quoting *Aatrix,* 882 F.3d at 1128).

[316]*See, e.g.*, Neitzke v. Williams, 490 U.S. 319, 326-327 (1989) (citations omitted), explaining that

> Rule 12(b)(6) authorizes a court to dismiss a claim on the basis of a dispositive issue of law.... This procedure, operating on the assumption that the factual allegations in the complaint are true, streamlines litigation by dispensing with needless discovery and factfinding.... What Rule 12(b)(6) does not countenance are dismissals based on a judge's disbelief of a complaint's factual allegations.

See also Bell Atl. Corp. v. Twombly, 550 U.S. 544, 555 (2007) (citations and footnote omitted), cautioning that

> [w]hile a complaint attacked by a Rule 12(b)(6) motion to dismiss does not need detailed factual allegations... a plaintiff's obligation to provide the "grounds" of his "entitle[ment] to relief" requires more than labels and conclusions, and a formulaic recitation of the elements of a cause of action will not do.... Factual allegations must be enough to raise a right to relief above the speculative level, see 5 C. Wright & A. Miller, Federal Practice and Procedure §1216, pp. 235-236 (3d ed. 2004) (hereinafter Wright & Miller) ("[T]he pleading must contain something more... than... a statement of facts that merely creates a suspicion [of] a legally cognizable right of action"), on the assumption that all the allegations in the complaint are true (even if doubtful in fact).")

Considering whether an antitrust plaintiff's complaint survived a Rule 12(b)(6) dismissal, the Supreme Court in *Twombly* set forth a "plausibility" standard (rather than a "probability" standard) for the factual allegations of complaints:

complaint stated "specific, plausible factual allegations" of nonconventionality. The district court had erred by failing to accept those allegations as true. Because the allegations had to be accepted as true at this procedural stage of the case, the Circuit could "not conclude that the asserted claims lack[ed] an inventive concept."[317]

The Circuit noted that Cellspin's complaint "identified several ways in which its [claimed] application of capturing, transferring, and publishing data was *un*conventional."[318] For example, prior art devices that featured a capture device with built-in mobile wireless Internet were bulky and expensive. In contrast, the claimed method separated the steps of capturing and publishing data so that each step would be performed by a different device linked via a wireless, paired connection — a "two-step, two-device structure."[319] Advantageously, the data capture device of the claimed invention needed to serve only one core function — capturing data — and did not need to incorporate other hardware and software components to store or publish that data. Because that device could leverage the hardware and software on the user's paired mobile device, the manufacture of smaller and cheaper data capture devices was made possible. Additionally, the claimed method provided that the data could be uploaded to the Internet via the paired mobile device even if the data capture device was physically inaccessible to the user.[320]

Cellspin's complaint further alleged that the "specific ordered combination" of elements in its patent claims was inventive. Prior art systems forwarded data from their data capture devices to mobile devices "as captured." In contrast, the claimed invention required establishing a paired connection between the two devices *before* any data could be transmitted. Thus, the claimed invention transmitted data only if the mobile device was capable of receiving it.

Yet another assertedly inventive aspect of the claimed method was Cellspin's use of HTTP (hypertext transfer protocol) by an "intermediary device" and while the data was "in transit." Certain of Cellspin's patent claims required that the mobile device transmit data from the mobile device to an "internet service" according to HTTP. Prior to its

---

> In applying these general standards to a [Sherman Act] §1 claim, we hold that stating such a claim requires a complaint with enough factual matter (taken as true) to suggest that an [illegal] agreement was made. Asking for plausible grounds to infer an agreement does not impose a probability requirement at the pleading stage; it simply calls for enough fact to raise a reasonable expectation that discovery will reveal evidence of illegal agreement.

Twombly, 550 U.S. at 556 (footnote omitted).

[317] *Cellspin,* 927 F.3d at 1318.

[318] *Cellspin,* 927 F.3d at 1316 (emphasis added).

[319] *Cellspin,* 927 F.3d at 1316.

[320] *Cellspin,* 927 F.3d at 1317.

claimed invention, Cellspin asserted, " 'HTTP transfers of data received over [a] paired wireless connection to web services [were] non-existent.' "[321] Cellspin pointed to evidence that its data sharing and HTTP use techniques had not previously been implemented in a similar way, stating in its complaint that " 'it was not until 2009 or later when the leading tech companies, such as Facebook and Google, started releasing HTTP APIs [application program interfaces] for developers to utilize a HTTP transfer protocol for mobile devices.' "[322]

Because Cellspin's complaint enumerated these "specific, plausible factual allegations" of non-conventionality, and because they had to be taken as true at a motion-to-dismiss stage, the Circuit could "not conclude that the asserted claims lack an inventive concept."[323] Accordingly, it vacated the district court's dismissal (as well as the district court's subsequent award of attorney fees to the accused infringers).[324]

As *Cellspin* illustrates, when addressing the second step of the *Mayo/Alice* framework the Federal Circuit considers whether the non-abstract portion of the claimed invention adds an "inventive concept" sufficient to confer patent eligibility, or instead is merely drawn to "well understood, routine, conventional" ("WURC") technology. In *Cellspin,* the allegations of the complaint, which had to be accepted as true for purposes of deciding a motion to dismiss, were sufficient to persuade the Circuit that Cellspin had achieved an "inventive concept." In this regard the outcome in *Cellspin* echoed that of *Aatrix Software*:

> In *Aatrix*,... we repeatedly cited allegations in the complaint to conclude that the disputed claims were potentially inventive. *See, e.g.*, 882 F.3d at 1128 ("There are concrete allegations in the second amended complaint that individual elements and the claimed combination are not well-understood, routine, or conventional activity."). While we do not read *Aatrix* to say that any allegation about inventiveness, wholly divorced from the claims or the specification, defeats a motion to dismiss, plausible and specific factual allegations that aspects of the claims are inventive are sufficient. *Id.* As long as what makes the claims inventive is recited by the claims, the specification need not expressly list all the reasons why this claimed structure is unconventional. In this case, Cellspin made specific, plausible factual allegations about why aspects of its claimed inventions were not conventional, *e.g.*, its two-step, two-device structure requiring a connection *before* data is transmitted. The district court erred by not accepting those allegations as true.[325]

[321] *Cellspin,* 927 F.3d at 1317.
[322] *Cellspin,* 927 F.3d at 1318-1319.
[323] *Cellspin,* 927 F.3d at 1318.
[324] *Cellspin,* 927 F.3d at 1320.
[325] *Cellspin,* 927 F.3d at 1317-1318.

5. Methods of Medical Treatment

a. Mayo v. Prometheus *(U.S. 2012)*

The Supreme Court's watershed 2012 decision in *Mayo Collaborative Servs. v. Prometheus Labs. Inc.*, introduced above,[326] held that patent claims directed to certain diagnostic methods used in health care were not patent-eligible under 35 U.S.C. §101.[327] The Supreme Court's *Mayo* decision refutes the idea that methods of medical treatment claims are fundamentally different and inherently more likely to fit comfortably within §101 than business method claims of the type at issue in *Bilski v. Kappos.*[328] The *Mayo* decision has potentially sweeping negative repercussions for the medical research community. But the language of *Mayo* is not limited to medical diagnostic methods. In the long term, *Mayo* will likely have a far greater impact than *Alice* and *Bilski* on patent eligibility across the board. Hence, a detailed understanding of the facts and procedure of *Mayo* is essential.

The patents at issue in *Mayo,* owned by plaintiff Prometheus Laboratories, Inc., claimed methods for calibrating the proper dosage of a drug for treating autoimmune diseases such as Crohn's disease and ulcerative colitis.[329] The goal of the methods was to determine a therapeutically optimal drug dosage while minimizing toxic side effects to the patients taking the drug. More particularly, certain of the claimed methods involved the steps of (1) administering to a patient a drug that, in the patient's body, would metabolize to 6-thioguanine ("6-TG"); then (2) determining the level of 6-TG metabolite in a blood sample taken from the patient; and finally, (3) comparing the level determined from the sample against particular pre-determined levels, to warn the patient or indicate a need to adjust the drug dosage administered thereafter. A representative claim recited:

> 1. A method of optimizing therapeutic efficacy for treatment of an immune-mediated gastrointestinal disorder, comprising:
>
> (a) *administering* a drug providing 6-thioguanine to a subject having said immune-mediated gastrointestinal disorder; and
>
> (b) *determining* the level of 6-thioguanine in said subject having said immune-mediated gastrointestinal disorder,
>
> wherein the level of 6-thioguanine less than about 230 pmol per 8×10^8 red blood cells *indicates a need* to increase the amount of said drug subsequently administered to said subject and

[326] *See supra* Section B.4.c.

[327] 132 S. Ct. 1289 (2012).

[328] The Federal Circuit felt differently, *see* Prometheus Labs., Inc. v. Mayo Collaborative Servs., 628 F.3d 1347, 1356 n.2 (Fed. Cir. 2010) (pointing out that "this case does not involve business method patents"), but the Supreme Court nonetheless reversed.

[329] *See* U.S. Pat. Nos. 6,355,623 and 6,680,302.

> wherein the level of 6-thioguanine greater than about 400 pmol per 8×10^8 red blood cells indicates a need to decrease the amount of said drug subsequently administered to said subject.[330]

A federal district court held that Prometheus's claims were not patentable under 35 U.S.C. §101 because the claims were drawn to correlations between metabolite levels and therapeutic efficacy and toxicity. According to the district court, such correlations were unpatentable natural phenomena resulting from a natural body process and hence outside of §101.

The Federal Circuit reversed.[331] The Circuit interpreted Prometheus's patent claims as directed not to a natural phenomenon, but rather to a particular *application* of that phenomenon. Allowing patents on the former would admittedly and entirely pre-empt the use of the correlation, which would contravene the Supreme Court's teachings in *Gottschalk v. Benson*[332] and *Parker v. Flook*.[333] In the case at bar, however, the claims passed muster under the Supreme Court's preemption test because the correlation was put to practical use in a method of medical treatment. According to the Federal Circuit, such particular applications of natural phenomena are patentable in accordance with the Supreme Court's decision in *Diamond v. Diehr*.[334]

Prometheus's claimed methods of medical treatment were also patent-eligible under §101, in the Federal Circuit's view, because the claims satisfied the "transformation" prong of the Federal Circuit's machine or transformation (MORT) test. Although the Supreme Court in *Bilski v. Kappos* held that the MORT test was not a dispositive inquiry for §101 eligibility, the Court nevertheless described the MORT test as a "useful and important clue, an investigative tool" for determining whether some claimed inventions are processes under §101.[335] Relying on the continued vitality of the MORT test (at least as an "important clue"), the Federal Circuit in *Prometheus* reaffirmed that the claimed treatment methods transform a human body.[336] In particular, "[t]he asserted claims are in effect claims to methods of treatment, which are *always* transformative when one of a defined

[330] *Prometheus,* 628 F.3d at 1350 (quoting '623 patent claim 1) (emphases added by Federal Circuit).

[331] Prometheus Labs., Inc. v. Mayo Collaborative Servs., 628 F.3d 1347 (Fed. Cir. 2010).

[332] 409 U.S. 63 (1972), discussed *supra* Section B.4.

[333] 437 U.S. 584 (1978), discussed *supra* Section B.4.

[334] *See Prometheus,* 628 F.3d at 1354, 1355 (citing *Diehr,* 450 U.S. 175 (1981)). *Diehr* is discussed *supra* Section B.4.

[335] *Prometheus,* 628 F.3d at 1352-1353.

[336] *Prometheus,* 628 F.3d at 1355.

group of drugs is administered to the body to ameliorate the effects of an undesired condition."[337] That the claimed methods treated the human body was made clear by the patents' disclosure as well as the preambles of the asserted claims. These claims recited, for example, a method of optimizing therapeutic efficacy to treat certain gastrointestinal disorders and a method of reducing the toxicity associated with such treatment.[338]

The Federal Circuit in *Prometheus* conceded that, as the district court had ruled, the final "wherein" clauses of the asserted claims were merely "mental steps." These claim clauses required a comparison of the level of 6-TG determined from sampling the patient against a pre-determined level of 6-TG, so as to provide an indication or warning that the drug dosage thereafter administered would need to be adjusted up or down. Such a mental step, *in isolation*, would not be patent-eligible under §101. But Prometheus's claimed invention was the *entire* recited method, comprising the administering and determining steps as well as the final indicating step. "[W]hen viewed in the proper context, the final step of providing a warning based on the results of the prior steps does not detract from the patentability of Prometheus's claimed methods as a whole."[339] Although the claimed methods did not require a physician to make any adjustment in a patient's drug dosage, the administering and determining steps provided useful information for such adjustments using particular drugs for a particular patient/subject. Hence, the Federal Circuit concluded, the claims satisfied the transformation prong of the MORT test, as well as the Supreme Court's *Bilski* pre-emption test.[340]

In a unanimous decision with potentially vast ramifications for patent eligibility, the Supreme Court in March 2012 roundly rejected the

[337] *Prometheus,* 628 F.3d at 1356 (emphasis added).

[338] Contrary to validity challenger Mayo's arguments, the Federal Circuit took the position that the "administering" and "determining" steps of Prometheus's claimed methods did not merely involve data gathering for use in the recited correlations. Although these first two steps did gather data, they were part of a larger treatment protocol. The "administering" step provided a drug for treating a disease, and the "determining" step measured the drug's metabolite levels to assess the drug's dosage level during the course of treatment.

[339] *Prometheus,* 628 F.3d at 1358. This is because all asserted claims required all three steps, and contrary to defendant Mayo's assertion, "a physician who only evaluates the result of the claimed methods, without carrying out the administering and/or determining steps that are present in all the claims, cannot infringe any claim that requires such steps." *Id.*

In the author's view, this statement by the *Prometheus* court would seem to ignore the possibility of inducing infringement liability on the part of the physician, as well as the possibility of "joint" infringement by the physician and other actors who are under the common control of a single "mastermind" entity. *See infra* Chapter 9 ("Patent Infringement").

[340] *Prometheus,* 628 F.3d at 1359.

Federal Circuit's reasoning in *Prometheus* and reversed the appellate court's 2010 judgment.[341] In the Supreme Court's view, Prometheus's claims did not recite patentable subject matter under 35 U.S.C. §101 because they expressed unpatentable "laws of nature" accompanied merely by "additional steps consist[ing] of well-understood, routine, conventional activity already engaged in by the scientific community."[342] The additional steps "add[ed] nothing significant beyond the sum of their parts taken separately" and were "not sufficient to transform unpatentable natural correlations into patentable applications of those regularities."[343]

The Supreme Court in *Mayo* initially observed that §101 contains "an important implicit exception" providing that " '[l]aws of nature, natural phenomena, and abstract ideas' are not patentable."[344] In the case at bar, the first of these categories — "laws of nature" — encompassed Prometheus's newly discovered "precise correlations" between metabolite levels in a patient's blood[345] and the "likelihood that a particular dosage of a thiopurine drug could cause harm or prove ineffective."[346] The correlations (recited in the "wherein" clauses of representative claim 1 quoted above[347]) were "relationships" that, although triggered by human action in the administration of a thiopurine drug, nevertheless "exist[ed] in principle apart from any human action."[348] The correlation or relation was a "consequence of the ways in which [the drugs] are metabolized by the body — entirely natural processes."[349] A patent such as Prometheus's that "simply describes that relation sets forth a natural law,"[350] the Court concluded, even though the "laws of nature" at issue were admittedly "narrow" and likely had "limited applications."[351]

[341]Mayo Collaborative Servs. v. Prometheus Labs., Inc., 132 S. Ct. 1289 (2012).
[342]*Mayo,* 132 S. Ct. at 1298.
[343]*Mayo,* 132 S. Ct. at 1298.
[344]*Mayo,* 132 S. Ct. at 1293 (quoting Diamond v. Diehr, 450 U.S. 175, 185 (1981)).
[345]*Mayo,* 132 S. Ct. at 1295.
[346]*Mayo,* 132 S. Ct. at 1296.
[347]*See supra* (quoting representative claim 1 of Prometheus's U.S. Patent No. 6,355,623). The "wherein" clauses of claim 1 recited as follows:

> wherein the level of 6-thioguanine less than about 230 pmol per 8×10^8 red blood cells indicates a need to increase the amount of said drug subsequently administered to said subject and
>
> wherein the level of 6-thioguanine greater than about 400 pmol per 8×10^8 red blood cells indicates a need to decrease the amount of said drug subsequently administered to said subject.

[348]*Mayo,* 132 S. Ct. at 1297.
[349]*Mayo,* 132 S. Ct. at 1297.
[350]*Mayo,* 132 S. Ct. at 1297.
[351]*Mayo,* 132 S. Ct. at 1302.

The additional recitation of the "administering" and "determining" steps in Prometheus's method claims was not enough to "transform an unpatentable law of nature into a patent-eligible *application* of such a law."[352] The *Mayo* Court decreed that

> [i]f a law of nature is not patentable, then neither is a process reciting a law of nature, unless that process has additional features that provide practical assurance that the process is more than a drafting effort designed to monopolize the law of nature itself. A patent, for example, could not simply recite a law of nature and then add the instruction "apply the law."[353]

In the case at bar, the "administering" and "determining" steps did not themselves recite laws of nature, but "neither [were] they sufficient to transform the nature of the claim."[354] Both steps were known in the art and represented "well-understood, routine, conventional activity" to scientists in the relevant technology.[355] Taken together with the "wherein" clauses, all the method steps in combination "add[ed] nothing to the laws of nature that is not already present when the steps are considered separately."[356] In the Court's view, the claimed series of steps "simply tell doctors to gather data from which they may draw an inference in light of the correlations."[357]

The Supreme Court supported its decision denying patent eligibility in *Mayo* with citation to precedent and policy. It identified the precedent "most directly on point" as its earlier decisions in *Diamond v. Diehr*[358] and *Parker v. Flook*.[359] As detailed elsewhere in this chapter, *Diehr* and *Flook* both involved the application of mathematical formulae in computer programs used to control industrial processes. The *Mayo* court characterized Prometheus's method claims as

[352]*Mayo,* 132 S. Ct. at 1294.
[353]*Mayo,* 132 S. Ct. at 1297.
[354]*Mayo,* 132 S. Ct. at 1297.
[355]*Mayo,* 132 S. Ct. at 1298.
[356]*Mayo,* 132 S. Ct. at 1298.
[357]*Mayo,* 132 S. Ct. at 1298. The Court summarized that

> the claims inform a relevant audience about certain laws of nature; any additional steps consist of well-understood, routine, conventional activity already engaged in by the scientific community; and those steps, when viewed as a whole, add nothing significant beyond the sum of their parts taken separately. For these reasons we believe that the steps are not sufficient to transform unpatentable natural correlations into patentable applications of those regularities.

Mayo, 132 S. Ct. at 1298.

[358]450 U.S. 175 (1981). *Diehr* is discussed *supra* at Section B.3 ("Computer-Implemented Processes").

[359]437 U.S. 584 (1978). *Flook* is discussed *supra* at Section B.3 ("Computer-Implemented Processes").

"present[ing] a case for patentability that is weaker than the (patent-eligible) claim in *Diehr* and no stronger than the (unpatentable) claim in *Flook*."[360] The *Mayo* Court's characterization of the claimed inventions in *Diehr* and *Flook* as "processes that embodied *the equivalent of natural laws*"[361] demonstrates the wide-ranging applicability of the *Mayo* holding, potentially reaching far beyond medical diagnostic subject matter.

The Supreme Court's *Mayo* opinion observed that in *Diamond v. Diehr,* the Court had previously held that "the basic mathematical equation, like a law of nature, was not patentable."[362] The overall process claimed in *Diehr* was patent-eligible, however, because the combination of process steps in addition to the recited mathematical formula were not "in context obvious, already in use, or purely conventional." Rather, the additional steps in *Diehr* "apparently added to the formula something that in terms of patent law's objectives had significance — they transformed the process into an inventive application of the formula."[363] In contrast, the process steps in *Parker v. Flook* that supplemented the recitation of a mathematical formula for updating alarm limits were "well known," such that there "was no 'inventive concept' in the claimed application of the formula."[364]

The *Mayo* Court also supported its disqualification of Prometheus's method claims from patent eligibility as furthering the public policy that "patent law [should] not inhibit further discovery by improperly tying up the future use of laws of nature."[365] Although the "laws of nature" encompassing Prometheus's correlations were "narrow" and of "limited application[]," the method claims at issue nevertheless implicated this policy concern. By "tell[ing] a treating doctor to

[360]*Mayo,* 132 S. Ct. at 1299. The *Mayo* opinion also distinguished the patent-ineligible claims of Prometheus with the patentable process claimed in the English case *Neilson v. Harford*, Webster's Patent Cases 295 (1841). The *Neilson* process for operating a blast furnace applied the "law of nature" that "hot air promotes ignition better than cold air," *Mayo,* 132 S. Ct. at 1300, but added to that principle "several unconventional steps (such as inserting the receptacle, applying heat to the receptacle externally, and blowing the air into the furnace) that confined the claims to a particular, useful application of the principle." *Mayo,* 132 S. Ct. at 1300.

[361]*Mayo,* 132 S. Ct. at 1298 (emphasis added).

[362]*Mayo,* 132 S. Ct. at 1298.

[363]*Mayo,* 132 S. Ct. at 1299. The *Mayo* Court's use of the qualifying adjective "inventive" is a troubling regression to pre-1952 Patent Act terminology that circularly required that patentable inventions involve an ill-defined quality of "invention." *See infra* Chapter 5, Section B ("Historical Context: The *Hotchkiss* 'Ordinary Mechanic' and the Requirement for 'Invention'").

[364]*Mayo,* 132 S. Ct. at 1299 (quoting *Flook*, 437 U.S. at 594). Again, the Court's reliance on the quotation from *Flook* referring to an "inventive concept" as a criterion of §101 patent eligibility is alarming. *See infra* Chapter 5, Section B ("Historical Context: The *Hotchkiss* 'Ordinary Mechanic' and the Requirement for 'Invention'").

[365]*Mayo,* 132 S. Ct. at 1301.

measure metabolite levels and to consider the resulting measurements in light of the statistical relationships they describe, [Prometheus's claims] tie up the doctor's subsequent treatment decision whether that treatment does, or does not, change in light of the inference he has drawn using the correlations."[366] Moreover, the claims "threaten to inhibit the development of more refined treatment recommendations (like that embodied in [accused infringer] Mayo's test), that combine Prometheus' correlations with later discovered features of metabolites, human physiology or individual patient characteristics."[367]

The *Mayo* Court skirted arguments of Prometheus and several *amici* that treating the claimed processes as unpatentable "laws of nature" would significantly chill further medical diagnostic research, responding that it would defer to Congress on such issues.[368] The 2015 *Ariosa Diagnostics* decision by the Federal Circuit, discussed below, suggests that the predictions of further limits on diagnostic research had merit.[369] Beyond diagnostic research, *Mayo* has also significantly limited the patent eligibility of Internet-based methods, as demonstrated by the Supreme Court's 2014 decision in *Alice Corp. Pty. Ltd. v. CLS Bank Int'l,*[370] discussed above, and its progeny.[371]

b. Federal Circuit Applications of Mayo

The Supreme Court's sweeping 2012 decision in *Mayo Collaborative Servs. v. Prometheus Labs., Inc.*[372] was soon to further impact the

[366]*Mayo,* 132 S. Ct. at 1302.

[367]*Mayo,* 132 S. Ct. at 1302.

[368]*See Mayo,* 132 S. Ct. at 1305 (recognizing "the role of Congress in crafting more finely tailored rules where necessary [citing Plant Patent Act, 35 U.S.C. §§161-164]" and declining to "determine here whether, from a policy perspective, increased protection for discoveries of diagnostic laws of nature is desirable").

The Court also rejected the argument of *amicus* United States that the novelty, nonobviousness, and disclosure requirements of 35 U.S.C. §§102, 103, and 112 act as the primary screening tools for patentability. According to the Court, "[t]his approach . . . would make the 'law of nature' exception to §101 patentability a dead letter." *Mayo,* 132 S. Ct. at 1303. The Court opined, without citation to authority, that "to shift the patent-eligibility inquiry entirely to these later sections risks creating significantly greater legal uncertainty, while assuming that those sections can do work that they are not equipped to do." *Mayo,* 132 S. Ct. at 1304. The Court "decline[d] the Government's invitation to substitute §§102, 103, and 112 inquiries for the better established inquiry under §101." *Mayo,* 132 S. Ct. at 1304. The Court did not explain why, in its view, the §101 inquiry is "better established" than the analysis under §§102, 103, and 112.

[369]*See infra* Section B.5.b.

[370]134 S. Ct. 2347 (2014). *Alice Corp.* is further discussed *supra* Section B.4.d.

[371]*See supra* Section B.4.e.

[372]132 S. Ct. 1289 (2012).

medical diagnostics research community. In the view of this author, the *Mayo* framework has resulted in (presumably) unintended negative consequences that will chill future medical diagnostic research (an issue raised by Prometheus and various *amici* in *Mayo*).

The Federal Circuit's June 2015 decision in *Ariosa Diagnostics, Inc. v. Sequenom, Inc.*,[373] aptly illustrates the problem. Compelled by the Supreme Court's broad language defining the second step of the *Mayo* framework, the Federal Circuit in *Ariosa* affirmed the invalidation under §101 of a groundbreaking patent on prenatal testing. Following in the footsteps of *Ariosa,* the Circuit's 2019 panel decision in *Athena Diagnostics, Inc. v. Mayo Collab. Servs., LLC* ("*Athena I*"),[374] and the full court's subsequent denial of rehearing *en banc* in *Athena II,*[375] confirmed that post-*Mayo*, most medical diagnostics inventions are no longer patentable. The remainder of this subsection analyzes the *Ariosa* and *Athena* decisions, as well as the small number of decisions in which the Circuit has determined that the claimed invention was a patent-eligible method of treatment rather than directed to a patent-ineligible law of nature.

In *Ariosa,* declaratory judgment defendant Sequenom's U.S. Patent No. 6,258,540 ('540 patent) was directed to certain non-invasive methods of prenatal diagnosis of fetal DNA. Advantageously, the new methods avoided the risks of prior methods involving sampling from the fetus or placenta. In 1997, Drs. Dennis Lo and James Wainscoat discovered the presence in maternal plasma and serum of cell-free fetal DNA ("cffDNA"), a non-cellular fetal DNA that circulates freely in the blood stream of pregnant women. Previously, other researchers had discarded the plasma and serum in maternal blood samples as medical waste. Drs. Lo and Wainscoat developed a method for detecting the small fraction of *paternally* inherited cffDNA in the maternal plasma or serum that could be used to determine fetal characteristics such as gender and genetic defects. The '540 patent owner, Sequenom, commercialized the invention as the MaterniT21 test, which was the first marketed non-invasive prenatal diagnostic test for fetal aneuploidies (i.e., an abnormal number of chromosomes) such as Down's syndrome.[376] The Lo and Wainscoat invention was lauded as a "paradigm shift in non-invasive prenatal diagnosis" and the inventors' article describing the invention was cited more than a thousand times.[377]

[373]Nos. 2014-1139, 2014-1144, 2015 WL 3634649 (Fed. Cir. June 12, 2015).
[374]915 F.3d 743 (Fed. Cir. Feb. 6, 2019) (Lourie, J.).
[375]927 F.3d 1333 (Fed. Cir. July 3, 2019) (*en banc* order plus eight opinions) ("*Athena II*").
[376]*See Ariosa,* 2015 WL 3634649, at *9 (Linn, J., concurring).
[377]*Ariosa*, 2015 WL 3634649, at *9 (Linn, J., concurring).

Although the Federal Circuit in *Ariosa* agreed that the Lo and Wainscoat invention "revolutionized prenatal care,"[378] the court nevertheless held the asserted claims of the '540 patent invalid as directed to a patent-ineligible method under 35 U.S.C. §101 of using a natural phenomenon. While the court did "not disagree that detecting cffDNA in maternal plasma or serum that before was discarded as waste material is a positive and valuable contribution to science," it ominously concluded that "even such valuable contributions can fall short of statutory patentable subject matter, as it does here."[379]

Applying step one of the *Mayo* framework (i.e., determining whether the claims at issue are directed to a patent-ineligible concept), the Federal Circuit in *Ariosa* first noted that Sequenom's asserted claims "begin[] and end[]" with natural phenomena. Representative claim 1 of the '540 patent recited:

> 1. A method for detecting a paternally inherited nucleic acid of fetal origin performed on a maternal serum or plasma sample from a pregnant female, which method comprises
>
> amplifying a paternally inherited nucleic acid from the serum or plasma sample and
>
> detecting the presence of a paternally inherited nucleic acid of fetal origin in the sample.

As elaborated in the written description of the '540 patent, the claimed method started with obtaining the cffDNA in maternal blood, and then used known amplification tools such as polymerase chain reaction (PCR) to provide a usable sample of paternally inherited cffDNA. According, the Federal Circuit concluded that the claims were directed to naturally occurring subject matter or phenomena, satisfying step one of the *Mayo* framework.

The Federal Circuit in *Ariosa* next explained that the second step of the *Mayo* framework considers whether "additional elements 'transform the nature of the claim' into a patent-eligible application."[380] The Supreme Court described the second *Mayo* step as a "search for an 'inventive concept'—i.e., an element or combination of elements that is 'sufficient to ensure that the patent in practice amounts to significantly more than a patent upon the [ineligible concept] itself.' "[381] A claim that recites a natural phenomenon "must include 'additional features' to ensure 'that the [claim] is more than a drafting effort designed to monopolize the [natural phenomenon].' "[382]

[378] *See Ariosa*, 2015 WL 3634649, at *8.
[379] *Ariosa*, 2015 WL 3634649, at *8.
[380] *Ariosa*, 2015 WL 3634649, at *3 (quoting *Mayo,* 132 S. Ct. at 1298).
[381] *Ariosa*, 2015 WL 3634649, at *3 (quoting *Mayo,* 132 S. Ct. at 1294).
[382] *Ariosa*, 2015 WL 3634649, at *5 (quoting *Mayo,* 132 S. Ct. at 1297).

Critically to the case at bar, the Federal Circuit read the Supreme Court's guidance regarding *Mayo* step two to mean that "[f]or process claims that encompass natural phenomenon, *the process steps are the additional features that must be new and useful.*"[383] The Circuit determined that, like those in *Mayo*, the process steps in Sequenom's claims were *not* new and useful:

> Using methods like PCR to amplify and detect cffDNA was well-understood, routine, and conventional activity in 1997. The method at issue here amounts to a general instruction to doctors to apply routine, conventional techniques when seeking to detect cffDNA. *Because the method steps were well-understood, conventional and routine, the method of detecting paternally inherited cffDNA is not new and useful.* The only subject matter new and useful as of the date of the application was the discovery of the presence of cffDNA in maternal plasma or serum.[384]

In the view of this author, the Federal Circuit's conclusion in *Ariosa* that Sequenom's patent claims were not patent eligible was fundamentally flawed. The Circuit erroneously dissected the '540 patent claims rather than considering the patent eligibility of the method *as a whole*. The heart of the court's error was to narrowly view the novelty of the individual "detection" and "amplification" process steps divorced from the subject matter on which they operated, cffDNA. As convincingly explained in a concurring opinion by Judge Linn, before the claimed invention "*no one* was amplifying and detecting paternally-inherited cffDNA using the plasma or serum of pregnant mothers."[385] In contrast, the process steps of *Mayo* "were the very steps that doctors were already doing — administering the [thiopurine] drug at issue, measuring metabolite levels, and adjusting dosing based on the metabolite levels. . . ."

In his concurring opinion, Judge Linn grudgingly joined the *Ariosa* court's opinion (invalidating the asserted '540 patent claims under §101) because he felt "bound" to do so "by the sweeping language of the test set out in *Mayo*. . . ." In Judge Linn's view, "the breadth of the second part of the test was unnecessary to the decision reached in *Mayo*." The *Mayo* Court "discounted, *seemingly without qualification*, any 'post-solution activity that is purely conventional or obvious.'"[386] To do so effectively ignored the Supreme Court's earlier instruction

[383] *Ariosa*, 2015 WL 3634649, at *5 (citing Parker v. Flook, 437 U.S. 584, 591 (1978) ("The process itself, not merely the mathematical algorithm, must be new and useful.")).

[384] *Ariosa*, 2015 WL 3634649, at *5 (emphasis added).

[385] *Ariosa*, 2015 WL 3634649, at *9 (Linn, J., concurring) (emphasis in original).

[386] *Ariosa*, 2015 WL 3634649, at *9 (Linn, J., concurring) (quoting *Mayo*, 132 S. Ct. at 1299 (original alterations omitted)) (emphasis added).

in its landmark 1981 decision *Diamond v. Diehr*[387] that "'a new combination of steps in a process may be patentable even though *all* the constituents of the combination were well-known and in common use before the combination was made.'"[388]

Judge Linn convincingly contrasted the facts of *Mayo* with those of *Ariosa*. In *Mayo*, the "conventional activity" recited in the process steps (i.e., administering a readily available drug, measuring metabolite levels, and adjusting dosage accordingly) was already well known at the time of the invention. In contrast, in *Ariosa* "the amplification and detection of cffDNA had never before been done."[389] In Judge Linn's view, Sequenom's '540 patent claimed "a new method that should be patent eligible."[390] Its invention was "nothing like the invention at issue in *Mayo*."[391] Sequenom had "'effecuate[d] a practical result and benefit not previously attained,'" such that under traditional principles its patent should have been upheld.[392] Unfortunately,

[387]450 U.S. 175 (1981). *Diehr* is further examined *supra* Section B.3 ("Computer-Implemented Processes").

[388]*Ariosa*, 2015 WL 3634649, at *9 (Linn, J., concurring) (quoting Diamond v. Diehr, 450 U.S. 175, 188 (1981)) (emphasis added).

[389]*Ariosa*, 2015 WL 3634649, at *9 (Linn, J., concurring) (emphasis added).

[390]*Ariosa*, 2015 WL 3634649, at *9 (Linn, J., concurring).

[391]*Ariosa*, 2015 WL 3634649, at *10 (Linn, J., concurring).

[392]*Ariosa*, 2015 WL 3634649, at *10 (Linn, J., concurring) (quoting Le Roy v. Tatham, 63 U.S. 132, 135-136 (1859); citing generally Jeffrey A. Lefstin, *Inventive Application: A History,* 67 Fla. L. Rev. 565 (2015), *available at* SSRN: http://ssrn.com/abstract=2398696 or http://dx.doi.org/10.2139/ssrn.2398696) (analyzing traditional notions of patent eligibility of newly discovered laws of nature). Professor Lefstin, author of the law review article cited by Judge Linn in his concurrence, also commented:

> [T]he *Ariosa* opinion appears to endorse dissection of the claim to a degree not only contrary to *Diehr*, but beyond that suggested by *Flook* itself. While *Flook* explained that "the process itself" must be new and useful, *Ariosa* suggests that the individual steps of the process must be new and useful, and identifies the discovery of cffDNA as "[t]he only subject matter new and useful as of the date of the application." Given that most inventions consist of rearrangements of old elements, it is difficult to understand how the court can refrain from addressing the claim steps as an ordered whole, as mandated by *Mayo* itself.
>
> And that highlights what is perhaps the most puzzling (or disturbing) aspect of *Ariosa*. According to Judge Linn's concurrence, the steps of the method *were* new: at the time of the invention, no one was amplifying paternally-inherited sequences from maternal serum or plasma, because no one thought that those fractions contained significant amounts of fetal DNA. That contrasts with *Mayo*, where the acts recited in the method were identical to those performed in the prior art. . . .
>
> If the step of amplifying paternally inherited DNA from serum or plasma was new, by what analysis could the court could regard it as "well-understood, routine, and conventional activity"? One way would be to sub-dissect that step into the conventional step of obtaining a cell-free fraction, and the conventional step of amplifying a sample containing DNA. That approach seems to lead to the *reductio ad absurdum* that most biotechnology processes are patent-ineligible,

Judge Linn concluded, the Supreme Court's "blanket dismissal of conventional post-solution steps leaves no room to distinguish *Mayo* from this case."[393]

Another troubling aspect of the Federal Circuit's decision in *Ariosa* is its cramped and conclusory analysis of the role of preemption concerns in the §101 patent eligibility inquiry. The appellate court observed that "[t]he Supreme Court has made clear that the principle of preemption is the basis for the judicial exceptions to patentability."[394] Thus, in the Circuit's view, "questions on preemption are *inherent* in and resolved by the §101 analysis."[395] When a patent's claims are deemed to recite patent-ineligible subject matter under *Mayo,* "as they are in this case, preemption concerns are *fully addressed and made moot*."[396] The Circuit also refused to distinguish between partial and complete preemption, rejecting Sequenom's arguments that its '540 patent claimed a narrow and specific application of using cffDNA that did not encompass numerous other uses of cffDNA. In the court's view, "[w]hile preemption may signal patent ineligible subject matter, *the absence of complete preemption does not demonstrate patent eligibility*."[397]

---

because they consist of the conventional steps of transferring drops of fluid from one tube to another. . . .

Jeffrey A. Lefstin, *Ariosa v. Sequenom and the Path Ahead for Subject-Matter Eligibility*, PATENTLY-O (June 14, 2015), https://patentlyo.com/patent/2015/06/sequenom-subject-eligibility.html. Another excellent and thoughtful analysis of *Ariosa* and the "natural products" debate is Leslie Fischer, *Guest Post — On* Ariosa *and Natural Products*, PATENT DOCS (Sept. 27, 2015), https://www.patentdocs.org/2015/09/guest-post-on-ariosa-and-natural-products.html.

393 *Ariosa*, 2015 WL 3634649, at *9 (Linn, J., concurring).

394 *Ariosa*, 2015 WL 3634649, at *7 (citing Alice Corp. v. CLS Bank Int'l, 134 S. Ct. 2347, 2354 (2014) ("We have described the concern that drives this exclusionary principal as one of pre-emption")).

395 *Ariosa*, 2015 WL 3634649, at *7 (emphasis added).

396 *Ariosa*, 2015 WL 3634649, at *7 (emphasis added).

397 *Ariosa*, 2015 WL 3634649, at *7 (emphasis added). *See also* Jeffrey A. Lefstin, *Ariosa v. Sequenom and the Path Ahead for Subject-Matter Eligibility*, PATENTLY-O (June 14, 2015), http://patentlyo.com/patent/2015/06/sequenom-subject-eligibility.html (commenting that "the Federal Circuit seems to be suggesting that arguments regarding preemption can be taxed against the patentee in the §101 inquiry, but not counted in the patentee's favor").

The Federal Circuit denied rehearing *en banc* in December 2015. *See* Ariosa Diagnostics, Inc. v. Sequenom, Inc., No. 2014-1139, 2015 WL 9914886 (Fed. Cir. Dec. 2, 2015) (*en banc*) (order). With 12 judges participating, only one appeared to vote against the denial. *See Ariosa Diagnostics*, 2015 WL 9914886, at *10 (Fed. Cir. Dec. 2, 2015) (Newman, J., dissenting from denial of petition for rehearing *en banc*) (stating that she "agree[d] with my colleagues that this case is wrongly decided" but "not shar[ing] their view that this incorrect decision is required by Supreme Court precedent"). In Judge Newman's view, the facts of *Ariosa* "diverge significantly from the facts and rulings in *Mayo Collaborative Services v. Prometheus Laboratories, Inc.*, [566 U.S. 66], 132 S. Ct. 1289 (2012), and in *Association for Molecular Pathology v. Myriad Genetics,*

B. Section 101 Processes

A 2019 Federal Circuit panel decision, *Athena Diagnostics, Inc. v. Mayo Collab. Servs., LLC* ("*Athena I*"),[398] and the full court's subsequent denial of rehearing *en banc* in *Athena II*,[399] confirmed the near-impossibility of medical diagnostics patenting after the Supreme Court's *Mayo* decision.

[569 U.S. 576], 133 S. Ct. 2107, 186 L. Ed. 2d 124 (2013)." *Id.* Three other judges joined opinions supporting the denial. *See Ariosa Diagnostics*, 2015 WL 9914886, at *1 (Lourie, J., joined by Moore, J.) (concurring in denial of petition for rehearing *en banc*) (finding "no principled basis to distinguish this case from *Mayo*, by which we are bound," but writing separately to "express some thoughts concerning laws of nature and abstract ideas, which seem to be at the heart of patent-eligibility issues in the medical sciences"); *id.* at *4 (concluding that "it is unsound to have a rule that takes inventions of this nature out of the realm of patent eligibility on grounds that they only claim a natural phenomenon plus conventional steps, or that they claim abstract concepts"); *see also Ariosa Diagnostics*, 2015 WL 9914886, at *4 (Dyk, J., concurring in denial of petition for rehearing *en banc*), stating that

> I share the concerns of some of my colleagues that a too restrictive test for patent eligibility under 35 U.S.C. §101 with respect to laws of nature (reflected in some of the language in *Mayo*) may discourage development and disclosure of new diagnostic and therapeutic methods in the life sciences, which are often driven by discovery of new natural laws and phenomena. This leads me to think that some further illumination as to the scope of *Mayo* would be beneficial in one limited aspect. At the same time I think that we are bound by the language of *Mayo*, and any further guidance must come from the Supreme Court, not this court.

The discontented tenor of the Newman, Lourie/Moore, and Dyk opinions, plus the decision of the eight other judges not to join any of those opinions, suggests continued disagreement and uncertainty within the Federal Circuit about the seemingly broad scope of *Mayo*.

Post-*Ariosa* decisions of the Federal Circuit continue to demonstrate *Mayo*'s constrictive impact on patenting in the medical biotechnology space. *See* Athena Diagnostics, Inc. v. Mayo Collab. Servs., LLC ("*Athena I*"), 915 F.3d 743 (Fed. Cir. Feb. 6, 2019) (Lourie, J.), reh'g *en banc* denied, 927 F.3d 1333 (Fed. Cir. July 3, 2019) (*en banc* order plus eight opinions) ("*Athena II*"), detailed *infra* in text; Cleveland Clinic Found. v. True Health Diagnostics LLC, 859 F.3d 1352 (Fed. Cir. 2017) (Reyna, J.) (affirming district court's dismissal of infringement lawsuit under Fed. R. Civ. P. 12(b)(6) because asserted patent claims, reciting methods for characterizing a test subject's risk for cardiovascular disease by determining levels of the enzyme myeloperoxidase (MPO) in a bodily sample and comparing that with the MPO levels in persons not having cardiovascular disease, were directed to a patent-ineligible law of nature under 35 U.S.C. §101; as in *PerkinElmer, Inc. v. Intema Ltd.*, 496 F. App'x 65 (Fed. Cir. 2012), the Cleveland Clinic patent claims did "not require that a doctor act on any risk . . . [r]ather, the steps in combination simply instruct a user to apply a natural law, i.e., that an increase in MPO mass or MPO activity in a blood sample correlates to an increase in CVD risk"); Genetic Techs. Ltd. v. Merial LLC, 818 F.3d 1369 (Fed. Cir. 2016) (Dyk, J.) (affirming district court's dismissal of patentee's infringement suit for failure to state a claim under Fed. R. Civ. P. 12(b)(b) on ground that claimed method for detecting a coding region of an individual's genome by analyzing a linked non-coding ("junk" DNA) region was a patent-ineligible law of nature under 35 U.S.C. §101; characterizing challenged claims as similar to those of *Mayo* and *Ariosa*).

[398] 915 F.3d 743 (Fed. Cir. Feb. 6, 2019) (Lourie, J.).

[399] 927 F.3d 1333 (Fed. Cir. July 3, 2019) (*en banc* order plus eight opinions) ("*Athena II*").

In February 2019, a divided panel of the Federal Circuit affirmed the District of Massachusetts's holding that claims 6-9 of Athena Diagnostic's U.S. Patent 7,267,820 ('820 patent) were invalid because patent-ineligible under 35 U.S.C. §101. The '820 patent concerned methods for diagnosing neurological disorders by detecting antibodies to a protein called muscle specific tyrosine kinase ("MuSK"). In the *Athena I* majority's view, the Supreme Court's 2012 *Mayo* decision dictated that the district court had properly dismissed Athena's complaint on a Fed. R. Civ. P. 12(b)(6) motion; the medical diagnostic claims at issue were directed to a natural law and lacked an inventive concept.

More broadly (and problematically), *Athena* illustrates the virtual impossibility of obtaining patent protection in the field of medical diagnostics given the Supreme Court's expansive statements in *Mayo* about the patent-ineligibility of laws of nature.[400] The full Federal Circuit (that is, all 12 active-status judges) weighed in on the issue in July 2019. In *Athena II*, the Circuit voted 7-5 to deny rehearing *en banc* in *Athena I*.[401] The *en banc* majority was resigned that because the Circuit (and lower courts) are bound by *Mayo*, most medical diagnostics inventions are no longer patentable.[402]

[400]Mayo Collaborative Servs. v. Prometheus Labs., Inc., 132 S. Ct. 1289 (2012).

[401]927 F.3d 1333 (Fed. Cir. July 3, 2019) (*en banc* order plus eight opinions) ("*Athena II*").

[402]*See, e.g., Athena II*, 927 F.3d at 1337 (Hughes, J., concurring in denial of rehearing *en banc*) ("The multiple concurring and dissenting opinions regarding the denial of *en banc* rehearing in this case are illustrative of how fraught the issue of §101 eligibility, especially as applied to medical diagnostics patents, is."); *id.*, 927 F.3d at 1339 (Dyk, J., concurring in denial of rehearing *en banc*) ("Although the Supreme Court's decision in *Mayo* did not make all diagnostic claims patent ineligible, as we previously held in *Ariosa*, 788 F.3d at 1376-77, *Mayo* left no room for us to find typical diagnostic claims patent eligible, absent some inventive concept at *Mayo* step two."); *id.*, 927 F.3d at 1349 (Chen, J., concurring in denial of rehearing *en banc*) ("Relying on the *Diehr* framework, the Patent Office examined and granted many patents for medical diagnostic methods, establishing settled expectations in those granted property rights, and prompted companies and research institutions to organize their conduct and choices accordingly. Many of these diagnostic claims, including the ones at issue here, do not hold up well against *Mayo*'s more searching, claim dissection scrutiny."); *see also id.*, 927 F.3d at 1352 (Moore, J., dissenting from denial of rehearing *en banc*) ("Since *Mayo*, we have held every single diagnostic claim in every case before us ineligible.") (citing Cleveland Clinic Found. v. True Health Diagnostics LLC, 760 F. App'x 1013 (Fed. Cir. 2019) ("*Cleveland Clinic II*"); Athena Diagnostics, Inc. v. Mayo Collaborative Servs., LLC, 915 F.3d 743 (Fed. Cir. 2019); Roche Molecular Sys., Inc. v. CEPHEID, 905 F.3d 1363 (Fed. Cir. 2018); Cleveland Clinic Found. v. True Health Diagnostics LLC, 859 F.3d 1352 (Fed. Cir. 2017) ("*Cleveland Clinic I*"); Genetic Techs. Ltd. v. Merial L.L.C., 818 F.3d 1369 (Fed. Cir. 2016); Ariosa Diagnostics, Inc. v. Sequenom, Inc., 788 F.3d 1371 (Fed. Cir. 2015); In re BRCA1- and BRCA2-Based Hereditary Cancer Test Patent Litig., 774 F.3d 755 (Fed. Cir. 2014); PerkinElmer, Inc. v. Intema Ltd., 496 F. App'x 65 (Fed. Cir. 2012)) (footnote omitted); *id.*, 927 F.3d at 1369 (Newman, J., dissenting from denial of rehearing *en banc*) ("Our holdings on medical diagnostics contravene the admonition that courts 'should not read into the patent laws limitations and conditions

Eight separate opinions totaling about 82 pages of text accompanied the *Athena II* order denying rehearing *en banc*. Given *Mayo*'s strictures and the Circuit's refusal to disregard them, the *Athena II* court deferred to the legislative branch to amend the patent law to accommodate medical diagnostics. Circuit Judges Lourie, Hughes, Dyk, and Chen each wrote an opinion concurring in the denial of rehearing *en banc*; the four concurring opinions were joined variously by Judges Reyna, Prost, and Taranto. Authoring opinions dissenting from the denial were Judges Moore, Newman, Stoll, and O'Malley; Judge Wallach joined three of the four dissenting opinions. Unless and until the Supreme Court should decide to review *Athena* or Congress amends the patent laws, *Athena I* remains the "law of the land" for medical diagnostics. They are generally *not* patent-eligible.

The remainder of this subsection analyzes the February 2019 *Athena I* panel majority and dissenting opinions. Athena's '820 patent claims recited methods of diagnosing serious neurological disorders such as myasthenia gravis ("MG")[403] by detecting "autoantibodies" that bind to an "epitope" of MuSK.[404] An epitope, also known as an

---

which the legislature has not expressed.'") (quoting *Chakrabarty*, 447 U.S. at 308); *id.*, 927 F.3d at 1370 (Newman, J., dissenting from denial of rehearing *en banc*) ("As summarized by Senators Chris Coons and Thom Tillis, co-chairs of the [U.S.] Senate Subcommittee that is conducting hearings on proposed remedial legislation, 'courts have clouded the line to exclude critical medical advances like life-saving precision medicine and diagnostics,' and 'studies showed that investors familiar with the current lack of clarity invest less in critical research and development in areas like medical diagnostics.'") (quoting Report available at https://www.law360.com/articles/1171672/what-coons-and-tillis-learned-at-patent-reform-hearings (June 21, 2019)); *id.*, 927 F.3d at 1370 (Stoll, J., dissenting from denial of rehearing *en banc*) ("In a series of cases since the Supreme Court's decision in *Mayo Collaborative Services v. Prometheus Laboratories, Inc.*, 566 U.S. 66 (2012), we have established a bright-line rule of ineligibility for all diagnostic claims.") (citing, e.g., Ariosa Diagnostics, Inc. v. Sequenom, Inc., 788 F.3d 1371, 1377 (Fed. Cir. 2015) (rejecting a diagnostic claim because the "only subject matter new and useful as of the date of the application was the discovery of the presence of cffDNA in maternal plasma or serum")).

[403]Patients with MG experience muscle weakness and symptoms including drooping eyelids, double vision, and slurred speech. *Athena I,* 915 F.3d at 747.

[404]The district court invalidated claims 6-9 of the '820 patent. Claim 1, not at issue before the Federal Circuit, was the only independent claim and recited:

> 1. A method for diagnosing neurotransmission or developmental disorders related to [MuSK] in a mammal comprising the step of detecting in a bodily fluid of said mammal autoantibodies to an epitope of [MuSK].
>
> Depended claim 7 (at issue) recited:
>
> 7. A method according to claim 1, comprising
>
> contacting MuSK or an epitope or antigenic determinant thereof having a suitable label thereon, with said bodily fluid,
>
> immunoprecipitating any antibody/MuSK complex or antibody/MuSK epitope or antigenic determinant complex from said bodily fluid and
>
> monitoring for said label on any of said antibody/MuSK complex or antibody/MuSK epitope or antigen determinant complex,

"antigenic determinant," is a segment of a protein recognized by an antibody.

Before Athena's invention, others had discovered that MG is an autoimmune disease caused by a patient generating antibodies against her own acetylcholine receptors. Such antibodies that recognize a person's own proteins as foreign antigens are known as "autoantibodies."

Importantly, about 80 percent of patients with MG produced acetylcholine receptor autoantibodies, but the other 20 percent did not. Thus it was not possible to diagnose MG in the 20 percent segment.

The '820 patent inventors discovered that many of the 20 percent of MG patients without acetylcholine receptor autoantibodies instead generated autoantibodies to the membrane protein called MuSK. Prior to that discovery, no disease had been associated with MuSK. Athena developed and marketed a diagnostic test called "FMUSK" that functioned by evaluating the antibodies to MuSK. Mayo Collaborative Services, LLC ("Mayo") sold two competing tests, leading to litigation between the parties.

Athena sued Mayo in 2015 in the District of Massachusetts for infringement based on Mayo's competing tests. In response, Mayo filed a Rule 12(b)(6) motion for dismissal, arguing that the asserted claims were §101 patent-ineligible. Applying *Mayo Collaborative Services v. Prometheus Laboratories, Inc.* (U.S. 2012),[405] and *Alice Corp. v. CLS Bank International* (U.S. 2014),[406] the district court agreed. It concluded that the claims were directed to a law of nature, focusing on the interaction of 125I-labeled[407] MuSK with MuSK autoantibodies in bodily fluid, an interaction that occurs naturally. The district court also determined that the claims lacked an inventive concept because the recited non-natural-law steps involved only standard techniques in the art.

On appeal, the *Athena I* Circuit (like the district court) directed its primary attention to claims 7-9 of the '820 patent (claim 6 was somewhat different in that it labeled MuSK with a "reporter molecule" rather than a radioisotope). Claim 9, the most specific of the claims on appeal, recited the method of detecting MuSK autoantibodies by (1) mixing MuSK or an epitope thereof having a 125I radioactive label with bodily fluid; (2) immunoprecipitating any resulting antibody/MuSK complex; and (3) monitoring for the label on the complex. Claim

---

wherein the presence of said label is indicative of said mammal is suffering from said neurotransmission or developmental disorder related to [MuSK].

Id. col. 12 l. 62-col. 13 l. 5 (spacing added).

[405] 566 U.S. 66 (2012).

[406] 573 U.S. 208 (2014).

[407] 125I is a radioactive isotope of iodine. *Athena I,* 915 F.3d at 747.

9 concluded in its "wherein" clause with a statement of the natural law, i.e., the discovery that MuSK autoantibodies naturally present in a patient sample, detected with the 125I label bound to the MuSK/antibody complex, indicated that the patient was suffering from a MuSK-related neurological disorder.[408]

Athena argued firstly that its claims 6-9 were *not* directed to a natural law at *Mayo/Alice* step one because they recited innovative, specific, and concrete steps that did not preempt a natural law. Rather, the claims were directed to a new laboratory technique that made use of human-made molecules.

The Circuit majority in *Athena I* agreed with the district court and accused infringer Mayo that the '820 patent claims in dispute were directed to a law of nature; namely, "the *correlation* between the presence of naturally-occurring MuSK autoantibodies in bodily fluid and MuSK-related neurological diseases like MG."[409] This correlation existed in nature apart from any human action. Accordingly, "[t]here [was] no dispute that it is an ineligible natural law."[410]

The *Athena I* majority observed that unlike step two, the *Mayo/Alice* step one "directed to" inquiry should focus on the claims "as a whole" rather than their individual elements. The Circuit's *Mayo/Alice* step one analysis in previous cases had "frequently considered whether the claimed advance improve[d] upon a technological process or merely an ineligible concept, based on both the written description and the claims."[411] In *Athena I,* the patent claims in dispute involved not only the discovery of a natural law but also admittedly "concrete" steps to observe its operation.

The concreteness or specificity of the '820 patent's claim-recited observation steps did not save their patent eligibility, however. As with the claims in the Federal Circuit's *Cleveland Clinic* and *Ariosa* decisions and unlike those in *CellzDirect,*[412] the *Athena I* majority concluded that claims 7-9 were "directed to a natural law because the claimed advance was only in the discovery of a natural law, and [] the additional recited steps only appl[ied] conventional techniques to

[408] *Athena I,* 915 F.3d at 751 (patent citations omitted).

[409] *Athena I,* 915 F.3d at 750 (footnote omitted) (emphasis added).

[410] *Athena I,* 915 F.3d at 750.

[411] *Athena I,* 915 F.3d at 750 (citing Cleveland Clinic Found. v. True Health Diagnostics LLC, 859 F.3d 1352, 1361 (Fed. Cir. 2017); Rapid Litig. Mgmt. Ltd. v. CellzDirect, Inc., 827 F.3d 1042, 1047-1049 (Fed. Cir. 2016); Ariosa Diagnostics, Inc. v. Sequenom, Inc., 788 F.3d 1371, 1376 (Fed. Cir. 2015); citing also McRO, Inc. v. Bandai Namco Games Am. Inc., 837 F.3d 1299, 1314-1315 (Fed. Cir. 2016); Elec. Power Grp., LLC v. Alstom S.A., 830 F.3d 1350, 1354 (Fed. Cir. 2016)).

[412] *See* Cleveland Clinic Found. v. True Health Diagnostics LLC, 859 F.3d 1352 (Fed. Cir. 2017); Rapid Litig. Mgmt. Ltd. v. CellzDirect, Inc., 827 F.3d 1042 (Fed. Cir. 2016); Ariosa Diagnostics, Inc. v. Sequenom, Inc., 788 F.3d 1371 (Fed. Cir. 2015).

detect that natural law."[413] No technological improvements or innovative laboratory techniques were involved, other than Athena's discovery of the correlation — a natural law.

The *Athena I* majority agreed with patentee Athena that preemption, a concern raised in *Mayo*, was not problematic in the case at bar. The specificity of the '820 patent's claim-recited steps ensured that they did not cut off the public from "other ways of interrogating the correlation between MuSK autoantiboeis and MuSK-related disorders. . . ."[414] But a preemption-free claim did not automatically equate to a §101-eligible claim. "Preemption is sufficient to render a claim *in*eligible under §101, but it is not necessary."[415]

Athena also argued that its claims were different in kind from other diagnostic claims that the Federal Circuit had previously held ineligible. Athena's claims required labeling MuSK with a human-made substance (e.g., 125I). The Circuit was not persuaded, responding that "the use of a man-made molecule is not decisive if it amounts to only a routine step in a conventional method for observing a natural law." In other words, "use of a man-made molecule in a method claim employing standard techniques to detect or observe a natural law may still leave the claim directed to a natural law."[416] The appellate court noted that *Mayo* had involved administering to patients a human-made substance, i.e., a drug "providing" 6-thioguanine; that some of the claims in *Ariosa* required amplification through polymerase chain reaction (PCR), which made use of human-made reagents; and that *BRCA1* involved hybridizing a synthetic DNA probe to a DNA strand.[417] All of these claims were held directed to natural laws and not §101 eligible.

Turning to step two of the *Mayo/Alice* framework, Athena argued that claims 6-9 satisfied the "inventive concept" requirement because they provided an innovative sequence of steps involving human-made molecules. Before its inventors' discovery, no one had previously disclosed a method to detect MuSK autoantibodies.

Again siding with accused infringer Mayo, the *Athena I* majority determined that the limitations of Athena's claims, other than those drawn to the natural law, only required "standard techniques to be

[413]*Athena I*, 915 F.3d at 751.
[414]*Athena I*, 915 F.3d at 752.
[415]*Athena I*, 915 F.3d at 752 (emphasis added) (citing Gottschalk v. Benson, 409 U.S. 63, 71-72 (1972) (holding claim involving mathematical formula invalid under §101 that did not preempt a mathematical formula); *Ariosa*, 788 F.3d at 1379; In re BRCA1- & BRCA2-Based Hereditary Cancer Test Patent Litig., 774 F.3d 755, 764 n.4 (Fed. Cir. 2014)).
[416]*Athena I*, 915 F.3d at 752.
[417]*Athena I*, 915 F.3d at 752.

applied in a standard way."[418] This result obtained whether the claim steps were viewed, as directed by *Mayo*, either individually or as an "ordered combination." The '820 patent's specification clearly identified the techniques of iodination and immunoprecipitation as standard, as well as the overall radioimmunoassay technique. The district court was justified in giving no weight to a contrary affidavit from Athena's expert arguing that the iodination and immunoprecipitation steps were "not routine as applied to the claimed invention."[419] The expert's assertion was simply not consistent with Athena's complaint read in light of its '820 patent. As the Circuit majority explained,

> [t]hese technical allegations [by Athena's expert] include[d]: (1) that detecting MuSK autoantibodies required the "creative step" of breaking up MuSK into smaller fragments; (2) that identifying a specific site on MuSK to label would not have been routine because many factors contribute to whether a binding site for a label is adequate; and (3) that immunoprecipitation is generally uncertain and not routine. None of these details are recited in the claims of the '820 patent: no claim requires breaking MuSK into fragments as opposed to using the entire MuSK protein; no claim is limited to a particular MuSK binding site; and no claim recites any detail with respect to immunoprecipitation. Those omissions are consistent with the specification's description of iodination, immunoprecipitation, and the overall radioimmunoassay as standard techniques. Because Athena's expert declaration made allegations inconsistent with the '820 patent, the district court was not obliged to accept them as true.[420]

Because the district court had not erred in ignoring the expert's declaration, no disputed fact issues precluded its dismissal of Athena's complaint under Rule 12(b)(6).[421]

Circuit Judge Newman penned a forceful dissent in *Athena I*.[422] She emphasized the importance of the patented invention — before Athena's discovery, 20 percent of patients suffering from MG could not be diagnosed. Athena claimed a new and nonobvious multi-step diagnostic method that exemplified the type of innovation that the patent laws were intended to promote. Judge Newman charged that her colleagues in the majority (Judges Lourie and Stoll) had "enlarge[d] the inconsistencies and exacerbate[d] the judge-made disincentives to development of new diagnostic methods, with no public benefit."[423]

[418] *Athena I*, 915 F.3d at 753.
[419] *Athena I*, 915 F.3d at 755.
[420] *Athena I*, 915 F.3d at 755-756 (record citations omitted).
[421] *Athena I*, 915 F.3d at 755-756.
[422] *Athena I*, 915 F.3d at 757.
[423] *Athena I*, 915 F.3d at 757 (Newman, J., dissenting).

The *Athena I* majority candidly agreed with much of what Judge Newman wrote in her dissent, but considered itself bound by the Supreme Court's *Mayo* decision. *Mayo* meant that correlations between a biological material in a patient's bodily sample and the patient's disease are simply not patentable, even when the method techniques applied are "somewhat specific" but nevertheless "conventional":

> The dissent states much that one can agree with from the standpoint of policy, and history, including that "the public interest is poorly served by adding disincentive to the development of new diagnostic methods." We would add further that, in our view, providing patent protection to novel and non-obvious diagnostic methods would promote the progress of science and useful arts. But, whether or not we as individual judges might agree or not that these claims only recite a natural law, *cf.* Berkheimer v. HP Inc., 890 F.3d 1369, 1374 (Fed. Cir. 2018) (Lourie, J., concurring in the denial of rehearing *en banc*) (discussing traditional laws of nature such as "Ohm's Law, Boyle's Law, [and] the equivalence of matter and energy"), the Supreme Court has effectively told us in *Mayo* that correlations between the presence of a biological material and a disease are laws of nature, see 566 U.S. at 77, and "[p]urely 'conventional or obvious' '[pre]-solution activity' is normally not sufficient to transform an unpatentable law of nature into a patent-eligible application of such a law," *id.* at 79 (second alteration in original) (quoting *Flook*, 437 U.S. at 590). We have since confirmed that applying somewhat specific yet conventional techniques (such as the polymerase chain reaction) to detect a newly discovered natural law does not confer eligibility under §101. *Ariosa*, 788 F.3d at 1377; *see also Cleveland Clinic*, 859 F.3d at 1356, 1362 (addressing other conventional techniques such as flow cytometry). Our precedent leaves no room for a different outcome here.[424]

As related above, the *en banc* Federal Circuit grappled with the issue of medical diagnostics patenting in July 2019. In *Athena II*, the Circuit voted 7-5 to *deny* rehearing *en banc* in *Athena I*.[425] The *en banc* opinions concurring in the denial made clear that because the Circuit (and lower courts) are bound by *Mayo*, most medical diagnostics inventions are no longer patentable.[426] This unfortunate outcome remains

[424] *Athena I,* 915 F.3d at 753 n.4 (citation omitted).

[425] 927 F.3d 1333 (Fed. Cir. July 3, 2019) (*en banc* order plus eight opinions).

[426] *See, e.g., Athena II*, 927 F.3d at 1337 (Hughes, J., concurring in denial of rehearing *en banc*) ("The multiple concurring and dissenting opinions regarding the denial of *en banc* rehearing in this case are illustrative of how fraught the issue of §101 eligibility, especially as applied to medical diagnostics patents, is."); *id.*, 927 F.3d at 1339 (Dyk, J., concurring in denial of rehearing *en banc*) ("Although the Supreme Court's decision in *Mayo* did not make all diagnostic claims patent ineligible, as we previously held in *Ariosa*, 788 F.3d at 1376-77, *Mayo* left no room for us to find typical diagnostic claims patent eligible, absent some inventive concept at *Mayo* step two."); *id.*, 927 F.3d at

the controlling law unless and until the Supreme Court or Congress intercede.

In a small number of post-*Mayo* appeals, the Federal Circuit has determined that a claimed invention is a patent-eligible method of treatment or medical process rather than being drawn to a patent-ineligible law of nature.[427] An important example of the former is the

---

1349 (Chen, J., concurring in denial of rehearing *en banc*) ("Relying on the *Diehr* framework, the Patent Office examined and granted many patents for medical diagnostic methods, establishing settled expectations in those granted property rights, and prompted companies and research institutions to organize their conduct and choices accordingly. Many of these diagnostic claims, including the ones at issue here, do not hold up well against *Mayo*'s more searching, claim dissection scrutiny."); *see also id.*, 927 F.3d at 1352 (Moore, J., dissenting from denial of rehearing *en banc*) ("Since *Mayo*, we have held every single diagnostic claim in every case before us ineligible.") (citing Cleveland Clinic Found. v. True Health Diagnostics LLC, 760 F. App'x 1013 (Fed. Cir. 2019) ("*Cleveland Clinic II*"); Athena Diagnostics, Inc. v. Mayo Collaborative Servs., LLC, 915 F.3d 743 (Fed. Cir. 2019); Roche Molecular Sys., Inc. v. CEPHEID, 905 F.3d 1363 (Fed. Cir. 2018); Cleveland Clinic Found. v. True Health Diagnostics LLC, 859 F.3d 1352 (Fed. Cir. 2017) ("*Cleveland Clinic I*"); Genetic Techs. Ltd. v. Merial L.L.C., 818 F.3d 1369 (Fed. Cir. 2016); Ariosa Diagnostics, Inc. v. Sequenom, Inc., 788 F.3d 1371 (Fed. Cir. 2015); In re BRCA1- and BRCA2-Based Hereditary Cancer Test Patent Litig., 774 F.3d 755 (Fed. Cir. 2014); PerkinElmer, Inc. v. Intema Ltd., 496 F. App'x 65 (Fed. Cir. 2012)) (footnote omitted); *id.,* 927 F.3d at 1369 (Newman, J., dissenting from denial of rehearing *en banc*) ("Our holdings on medical diagnostics contravene the admonition that courts 'should not read into the patent laws limitations and conditions which the legislature has not expressed.'") (quoting *Chakrabarty*, 447 U.S. at 308); *id.,* 927 F.3d at 1370 (Newman, J., dissenting from denial of rehearing *en banc*) ("As summarized by Senators Chris Coons and Thom Tillis, co-chairs of the [U.S.] Senate Subcommittee that is conducting hearings on proposed remedial legislation, 'courts have clouded the line to exclude critical medical advances like life-saving precision medicine and diagnostics,' and 'studies showed that investors familiar with the current lack of clarity invest less in critical research and development in areas like medical diagnostics.'") (quoting Report available at https://www.law360.com/articles/1171672/what-coons-and-tillis-learned-at-patent-reform-hearings (June 21, 2019)); *id.*, 927 F.3d at 1370 (Stoll, J., dissenting from denial of rehearing *en banc*) ("In a series of cases since the Supreme Court's decision in *Mayo Collaborative Services v. Prometheus Laboratories, Inc.*, 566 U.S. 66 (2012), we have established a bright-line rule of ineligibility for all diagnostic claims.") (citing, e.g., Ariosa Diagnostics, Inc. v. Sequenom, Inc., 788 F.3d 1371, 1377 (Fed. Cir. 2015) (rejecting a diagnostic claim because the "only subject matter new and useful as of the date of the application was the discovery of the presence of cffDNA in maternal plasma or serum")).

[427]Other §101 patent-eligible life sciences process or method of treatment cases include:

Rapid Litig. Mgmt. Ltd. v. CellzDirect, Inc., 827 F.3d 1042 (Fed. Cir. July 5, 2016) ("*IVT* decision," because after various corporate transactions, the patentee/plaintiffs are now identified as Rapid Litigation Management Ltd. and In Vitro, Inc. (collectively, "IVT")). The *IVT* decision marked the first significant "win" for life sciences patenting in the aftermath of *Mayo Collaborative Servs. v. Prometheus Labs., Inc.*, 132 S. Ct. 1289 (2012). *IVT* illustrates the Federal Circuit finding a way through the constraints of *Mayo* to find patent eligibility for what the court termed a "constructive process," *IVT,* 827 F.3d at 1048, one that provided a "significant" improvement and "notable advance" over the prior art. *IVT,* 827 F.3d at 1047. The appellate court "immediately distinguish[ed]" the

2018 decision in *Vanda Pharms. Inc. v. West-Ward Pharms. Int'l Ltd.*[428] In an opinion authored by Judge Lourie (who, along with Judge Newman, worked as a Ph.D. chemist before practicing patent law), the *Vanda* panel majority affirmed the District of Delaware's holding that the claimed method of treating patients suffering from schizophrenia *was* patent-eligible under 35 U.S.C. §101. Unlike the claims held patent-ineligible by the Supreme Court in *Mayo Collaborative Services v. Prometheus Laboratories, Inc.*,[429] the claims in *Vanda* concerned a specific method of treating a specific disease, not merely a diagnostic method based on natural relationships. Chief Judge Prost dissented, rejecting the majority's attempt to distinguish *Vanda* from *Mayo*.

IVT case before it from *Mayo*; *Ariosa Diagnostics, Inc. v. Sequenom, Inc.*, 788 F.3d 1371 (Fed. Cir. 2015); Genetic Techs., Ltd. v. Merial L.L.C., 818 F.3d 1369 (Fed. Cir. 2016); and *In re BRCA1- & BRCA2-Based Hereditary Cancer Test Patent Litig.*, 774 F.3d 755 (Fed. Cir. 2014), as not involving simply an observation, detection, or identification of a law of nature. *See IVT,* 827 F.3d at 1048. Rather, IVT's claimed process was a method of *producing useful things*— in this case, an improved method of preserving a type of liver cell called a "hepatocyte." Such cells have attributes useful for testing, diagnostic, and medical treatment purposes.

Like the court's 2018 *Vanda* and 2016 *CellzDirect* decisions, the Federal Circuit's March 2019 decision in *Endo Pharm. Inc. v. Teva Pharm. USA, Inc.*, 919 F.3d 1347 (Fed. Cir. Mar. 28, 2019) (Stoll, J.) found patent-eligible subject matter rather than an ineligible law of nature. Endo's U.S. Patent No. 8,808,737 ('737 patent) concerned the treatment of pain suffered by patients with impaired kidney ("renal") function. The inventor discovered that patients with moderate-to-severe renal impairment could be treated with a lesser amount of the pain drug oxymorphone than usual (i.e., the "usual" case being a healthy patient with normal kidney function) and still achieve a similar level of pain management. More specifically, the inventor determined that a statistically significant correlation existed between a patient's degree of renal impairment and her "plasma AUC" for oxymorphone, an indication of the amount of the drug in the body over time.

The *Endo* Circuit rejected a district court's determination that the '737 patent claims were directed to an ineligible natural law, i.e., " 'the reaction of the human body of a renally impaired individual to oxymorphone.' " Rather, the '737 patent's claims were directed to a patent-eligible method of treatment. The claims admittedly *applied* a natural law, which almost any invention does, but in a novel and specific way to treat patients' pain. Although preemption had concerned the Supreme Court in *Mayo,* because the patent claim in that case could " 'tie up the doctor's subsequent treatment decision,' " *Endo,* 919 F.3d at 1355 (quoting *Mayo*, 566 U.S. at 86), the same preemption concern was not valid in *Endo* given the specificity of the recited specific dosage range based on a particular patient's kidney performance. Importantly, the claims of Endo's patent "prescribe[d] a specific dosage regimen through the wherein clause, under which the physician administers oxymorphone to achieve a specific range of AUC of oxymorphone based on the patient's creatinine clearance rate." *Endo,* 919 F.3d at 1355. The combination of the "wherein" clause with the "administering" step made Endo's patent claims "as specific as those in *Vanda*" in a manner that avoided the preemption/"tying up" concerns expressed in *Mayo*.

[428] 887 F.3d 1117 (Fed. Cir. Apr. 13, 2018) (Lourie, J.).

[429] 566 U.S. 66 (2012).

Vanda's U.S. Patent No. 8,586,610 ('610 patent) disclosed a novel method of treating patients suffering from schizophrenia, a serious mental disorder, with the drug iloperidone. The claims required optimizing the dosage range of iloperidone based on a patient's genotype (i.e., genetic identity). The '610 patent disclosed that a particular human gene, the cytochrome P450 2D6 gene ("CYP2D6"), encodes an enzyme known to metabolize a large number of drugs, including iloperidone. The '610 patent targeted patients with a lower-than-normal CYP2D6 activity (i.e., a lower-than-normal ability to metabolize the enzyme). Such patients are at risk for heart disease caused by "QTc prolongation," an extended time between the Q wave[430] and the T wave[431] of the patient's heart rhythm (corrected for the patient's heart rate). The '610 patent referred to the patients as "CYP2D6 poor metabolizers." Because QT prolongation can lead to serious cardiac problems, the '610 patent disclosed dose reductions of iloperidone for poor metabolizers to reduce that risk and to more safely administer iloperidone.

As summarized by the *Vanda* majority, the claims of the '610 patent required specific steps: (1) determining the patient's CYP2D6 metabolizer genotype by (a) obtaining a biological sample and (b) performing a genotyping assay (test); and (2) administering specific dose ranges of iloperidone depending on the patient's CYP2D6 genotype. Representative claim 1 of the '610 patent recited:

> A method for treating a patient with iloperidone, wherein the patient is suffering from schizophrenia, the method comprising the steps of:
>
> determining whether the patient is a CYP2D6 poor metabolizer by:
>
> obtaining or having obtained a biological sample from the patient; and
>
> performing or having performed a genotyping assay on the biological sample to determine if the patient has a CYP2D6 poor metabolizer genotype; and
>
> if the patient has a CYP2D6 poor metabolizer genotype, then internally administering iloperidone to the patient in an amount of 12 mg/day or less, and
>
> if the patient does not have a CYP2D6 poor metabolizer genotype, then internally administering iloperidone to the patient in an amount that is greater than 12 mg/day, up to 24 mg/day,
>
> wherein a risk of QTc prolongation for a patient having a CYP2D6 poor metabolizer genotype is lower following the internal administration of 12 mg/day or less than it would be if the iloperidone were administered in an amount of greater than 12 mg/day, up to 24 mg/day.

[430] *See* https://www.healio.com/cardiology/learn-the-heart/ecg-review/ecg-interpretation-tutorial/q-wave.

[431] *See* https://www.healio.com/cardiology/learn-the-heart/ecg-review/ecg-interpretation-tutorial/t-wave.

The *Vanda* Circuit majority rejected accused infringer West-Ward's argument that, similarly to the claims at issue in *Mayo*, Vanda's claims were not patent-eligible because they recited simply a method of optimizing the dosage of iloperidone in accordance with a natural law. In the majority's view, the '610 patent claims were not like those of *Mayo* because the *Mayo* claims were "not directed to a novel method of treating a disease."[432] Rather, the *Mayo* claims were directed to a diagnostic method based on relationships between concentrations of certain metabolites in a patient's blood and the likelihood that a dosage of the drug thiopurine would prove ineffective or cause harm.

Moreover, although both the claims at issue in *Vanda* and those in *Mayo* required an "administering" method step, the *Mayo* claims "as a whole w[ere] not directed to the application of a drug to treat a particular disease."[433] The Supreme Court in *Mayo* had noted that "'[u]nlike, say, a typical patent on a new drug or a new way of using an existing drug, the patent claims do not confine their reach to particular applications of those laws.'"[434] In contrast, the '610 patent claims at bar were a "particular application" of a natural law and a "new way of using an existing drug." Admittedly, the Vanda inventors recognized (importantly) the relationships between iloperidone, CYP2D6 metabolism, and QTc prolongation. But their '610 patent claimed an *application* of those relationships, not the relationships themselves.

Notably, the *Vanda* claims *required* a treating doctor to administer iloperidone in a dosage dependent on the result of a genotyping assay. In contrast, the claims in *Mayo* merely spoke of what the metabolite levels "indicated" in terms of dosage but did not require that a doctor administer the recommended dosage.[435] The claims at bar were a

[432]*Vanda*, 887 F.3d at 1134.
[433]*Vanda*, 887 F.3d at 1134.
[434]*Vanda*, 887 F.3d at 1135 (quoting *Mayo,* 132 S. Ct. at 1289).
[435]Recall that representative claim 1 in *Mayo* recited:

A method of optimizing therapeutic efficacy for treatment of an immune-mediated gastrointestinal disorder, comprising:

(a) administering a drug providing 6-thioguanine to a subject having said immune-mediated gastrointestinal disorder; and

(b) determining the level of 6-thioguanine in said subject having said immune-mediated gastrointestinal disorder,

wherein the level of 6-thioguanine less than about 230 pmol per $8x10^8$ red blood cells *indicates a need* to increase the amount of said drug subsequently administered to said subject and

wherein the level of 6-thioguanine greater than about 400 pmol per $8x10^8$ red blood cells *indicates a need* to decrease the amount of said drug subsequently administered to said subject.

Mayo, 566 U.S. at 74-75 (emphasis added).

"new way of using an existing drug" that was safer for patients because the claimed regime reduced the risk of QTc prolongation.

In addition, the majority asserted, the preemption concerns present in *Mayo* did not apply in *Vanda*. The treatment claims of the '610 patent did not "'tie up the doctor's subsequent treatment decision.'"[436] The claims in *Mayo* were not treatment claims and, more broadly than those in *Vanda*, did not require the doctor to actually administer a particular dosage indicated by testing as advisable. In contrast, the '610 patent claims more narrowly *required* the doctor to carry out a particular dosage regimen dependent on the results of genetic testing.[437]

The *Vanda* majority concluded that

> [a]t bottom, the claims here are directed to a specific method of treatment for specific patients using a specific compound at specific doses to achieve a specific outcome. They are different from *Mayo*. They recite more than the natural relationship between CYP2D6 metabolizer genotype and the risk of QTc prolongation. Instead, they recite a method of treating patients based on this relationship that makes iloperidone safer by lowering the risk of QTc prolongation. Accordingly, the claims are patent eligible.[438]

In dissent, Chief Judge Prost charged the *Vanda* majority with improperly conflating the *Mayo* step one analysis with *Mayo* step two. In accordance with *Mayo*, the "administering" step of the '610 claims and the specific dosages relied on by the majority should have been analyzed as part of the *Mayo* framework's step two, the search for an "inventive concept." In the dissent's view, these elements were not sufficient to provide that concept.

Addressing *Mayo* step one, dissenting Judge Prost characterized the '610 patent claims as directed to a law of nature or a "natural relationship"; i.e., the relationship between the CYP2D6 genotype and the likelihood that a dosage of iloperidone would cause QTc prolongation.[439] In her view, the claims were directed to no more than an "optimization" of an existing treatment for schizophrenia, just as the *Mayo* claims involved optimizing therapeutic efficacy of the thiopurine drugs involved in that case.

Applying *Mayo* step two, Judge Prost did not find that the claim-recited steps added an inventive concept sufficient to transform them into patent-eligible subject matter. The recited "administering" step

[436] *Vanda*, 887 F.3d at 1135 (quoting *Mayo*, 132 S. Ct. at 1289).
[437] *Vanda*, 887 F.3d at 1135.
[438] *Vanda*, 887 F.3d at 1136.
[439] *Vanda*, 887 F.3d at 1141 (Prost, C.J., dissenting).

should have been analyzed as part of step two rather than step one. In Judge Prost's view, the "specific dosage add[ed] nothing inventive to the claims beyond the natural law."[440] In addition, the fact that the claims required rather than merely "indicated" a specific dosage administration was a difference of "no moment."[441] Lastly, the claim-recited genetic assay was "purely conventional pre-solution activity" that could not elevate the claims to §101 eligibility.

In the view of this author, the patent-eligibility issue in *Vanda* is a close call. Judge Lourie makes a valiant attempt to distinguish *Mayo* that is not entirely convincing in light of the dissent's rejoinder. But Judge Lourie's arguments were sufficient to cause the third judge on the panel (Judge Hughes) to join his opinion. Thus, *Vanda* stands as a victory for the patentability of methods of medical treatment and as a template for claim drafting in that art.[442]

C. Section 101 Machines

A machine (or apparatus) is a human-made device that has moving parts. The only real area of controversy involving the machine category of potentially patentable subject matter is whether programmed computers (i.e., computers operating under the control of computer software programs) qualify as machines within the meaning of §101. Recent case law generally answers this question in the affirmative.

The *en banc* Federal Circuit considered whether a computer-implemented device qualifies as a machine under 35 U.S.C. §101 in *In re Alappat.*[443] Alappat's patent application was directed to a "rasterizer," a device for creating a smooth waveform display in a digital oscilloscope (analogous to creating a clearer picture on a television screen). The only independent claim at issue in the application recited the following:

> A rasterizer for converting vector list data representing sample magnitudes of an input waveform into anti-aliased pixel illumination intensity data to be displayed on a display means comprising:

[440]*Vanda*, 887 F.3d at 1142 (Prost, C.J., dissenting).

[441]*Vanda*, 887 F.3d at 1142 (Prost, C.J., dissenting).

[442]*See also* Endo Pharm. Inc. v. Teva Pharm. USA, Inc., 919 F.3d 1347 (Fed. Cir. 2019) (Stoll, J.), which followed in the same vein as the Circuit's 2018 *Vanda* and 2016 *CellzDirect* ("*IVT*") decisions (all three finding patent-eligible subject matter rather than ineligible laws of nature). The presence of an "administering" step coupled with a "wherein" clause that recited specific dosage limitations saved the patent eligibility of the challenged Endo patent claims.

[443]33 F.3d 1526 (Fed. Cir. 1994) (*en banc*).

(a) means for determining the vertical distance between the endpoints of each of the vectors in the data list;
(b) means for determining the elevation of a row of pixels that is spanned by the vector;
(c) means for normalizing the vertical distance and elevation; and
(d) means for outputting illumination intensity data as a predetermined function of the normalized vertical distance and elevation.[444]

In an unconventional procedure, an "expanded" panel of the USPTO Board of Patent Appeals and Interferences rejected this claim as failing to recite potentially patentable subject matter under §101. The Board refused to construe the recited "means" limitations in accordance with 35 U.S.C. §112, ¶6 (1988), which would have limited the claim's reach to the "corresponding structure" that the application disclosed as performing each function, and any "equivalents thereof."[445] Rather, the Board interpreted each means limitation as encompassing any and every means for performing the recited function. The Board concluded that the rasterizer claim, thus interpreted, was in reality a claim to a process, and each means clause merely a disguised step in that process. In the Board's view, the resulting process was nothing more than an unpatentable "mathematical algorithm" for computing pixel information, and thus not patentable because unapplied mathematical algorithms are outside the purview of §101.[446]

The *en banc* Federal Circuit majority reversed, admonishing the USPTO that the agency was not exempt from interpreting patent application claims in accordance with 35 U.S.C. §112, ¶6.[447] Properly applying the statute yielded the following claim construction, with

[444]*Id.* at 1538-1539.

[445]*See* Chapter 2 ("Patent Claims"), *supra*, for further discussion of means-plus-function claims and statutory equivalents under 35 U.S.C. §112, ¶6. The America Invents Act of 2011 renamed this statutory provision 35 U.S.C. §112(f) (eff. Sept. 16, 2012).

[446]*See* Diamond v. Diehr, 450 U.S. 175, 187 (1981) ("It is now commonplace that an *application* of a law of nature or mathematical formula to a known structure or process may well be deserving of patent protection."); Gottschalk v. Benson, 409 U.S. 63, 71-72 (1972) (concluding that "[t]he mathematical formula involved here [for converting binary-coded decimal (BCD) numerals to pure binary numerals] has no substantial practical application except in connection with a digital computer, which means that if the judgment below is affirmed, the patent would wholly pre-empt the mathematical formula and in practical effect would be a patent on the algorithm itself").

[447]This ongoing interpretational battle between the Federal Circuit and USPTO seemingly had been resolved in *In re Donaldson Co.*, 16 F.3d 1189, 1194-1195 (Fed. Cir. 1994) (*en banc*) (holding that the "broadest reasonable interpretation" that an examiner may give means-plus-function language when interpreting patent application claims is that statutorily mandated in 35 U.S.C. §112, ¶6 (1988), and that "the PTO may not disregard the structure disclosed in the specification corresponding to such language when rendering a patentability determination").

the structure disclosed in the written description as corresponding to each recited "means" appearing in brackets:

> A rasterizer [a "machine"] for converting vector list data representing sample magnitudes of an input waveform into anti-aliased pixel illumination intensity data to be displayed on a display means comprising:
> (a) [an arithmetic logic circuit configured to perform an absolute value function, or an equivalent thereof] for determining the vertical distance between the endpoints of each of the vectors in the data list;
> (b) [an arithmetic logic circuit configured to perform an absolute value function, or an equivalent thereof] for determining the elevation of a row of pixels that is spanned by the vector;
> (c) [a pair of barrel shifters, or equivalents thereof] for normalizing the vertical distance and elevation; and
> (d) [a read only memory (ROM) containing illumination intensity data, or an equivalent thereof] for outputting illumination intensity data as a predetermined function of the normalized vertical distance and elevation.[448]

Thus understood, this claim "unquestionably recite[d] a machine, or apparatus, made up of a combination of known electronic circuitry elements,"[449] the Federal Circuit concluded. Although each means element represented circuitry that performed mathematical calculations (essentially true of all digital electrical circuits), the claimed invention as a whole was not a "disembodied mathematical concept." Rather, the claim recited a "specific machine to produce a useful, concrete, and tangible result,"[450] and was thus within §101. The Federal Circuit would later echo the "useful, concrete, and tangible" criteria in the *State Street* case, discussed earlier in this chapter.[451]

D. Section 101 Compositions of Matter

A composition of matter is a mixture of substances such as a chemical composition or metallic alloy. The Supreme Court in *Diamond v. Chakrabarty*[452] summarized its earlier decisions defining the phrase "composition of matter" as "consistent with its common usage to include 'all compositions of two or more substances and . . . all composite articles,

[448]*Alappat*, 33 F.3d at 1541.
[449]*Id.*
[450]*Id.* at 1544.
[451]State St. Bank & Trust Co. v. Signature Fin. Group, Inc., 149 F.3d 1368, 1373-1375 (Fed. Cir. 1998). For further discussion of *State Street*, *see supra* Section B.4.a.
[452]447 U.S. 303 (1980).

whether they be the results of chemical union, or of mechanical mixture, or whether they be gases, fluids, powders or solids.' "[453]

1. Structure Versus Properties

If a composition of matter is claimed as such, it is the physical structure of the composition that must be novel, not merely its properties. The discovery or recognition of a composition's previously unappreciated property (e.g., the ability of aspirin to lessen the risk of heart attacks) will not impart patentability to that composition if its structure is already known. Such a discovery might merit patentability if claimed as a process, but not as a product.

For example, the inventors in *Titanium Metals Corp. v. Banner*[454] discovered that a titanium alloy made up of certain amounts of titanium, nickel, molybdenum, and iron exhibited exceptionally good corrosion resistance. They claimed the alloy as follows:

> 1. A titanium base alloy consisting essentially by weight of about 0.6% to 0.9% nickel, 0.2% to 0.4% molybdenum, up to 0.2% maximum iron, balance titanium, said alloy being characterized by good corrosion resistance in hot brine environments.[455]

The prior art was a Russian printed publication that disclosed a particular alloy falling within the ranges recited in claim 1, but made no mention of any corrosion resistance property.

The Federal Circuit held that the Russian reference anticipated (i.e., negated the novelty of) the claimed alloy, despite the claim's inclusion of the corrosion resistance limitation. Whether or not the corrosion resistance property was inherent in the Russian alloy, and regardless of whether the authors of the Russian reference recognized this property, its recitation in the claim could not impart novelty to what was an otherwise old composition of matter. The applicants might have obtained a patent by claiming a *process* for preventing corrosion in titanium alloys, but as discussed earlier in this chapter such a claim would be much narrower in scope and thus of less economic value than the product claim they sought (i.e., to the alloy itself). Nevertheless, the more limited scope of a process claim more closely corresponds to the inventors' contribution — the recognition of a previously unrecognized property of a known alloy.

[453] *Id.* at 308 (quoting Shell Dev. Co. v. Watson, 149 F. Supp. 279, 280 (D.D.C. 1957)).
[454] 778 F.2d 775 (Fed. Cir. 1985).
[455] *Id.* at 776.

2. Products of Nature

a. *Purified Forms of Natural Products*

The "product of nature" doctrine recognizes that potentially patentable subject matter must be created through human intervention. Patents are not available for the handiwork of nature. Thus, a newly discovered mineral or a plant found in the wild is not patentable subject matter under 35 U.S.C. §101. Those who make such discoveries or findings have certainly made an important contribution to society, but public policy demands that such advances remain freely available for all to use and build upon.

In contrast, so-called purified forms of natural products may be patentable if sufficiently different from the nonpurified (i.e., natural) forms so as to be novel and nonobvious. In fact, the USPTO has a long history of granting patents on purified forms of natural products; for example, the famous scientist Louis Pasteur was awarded a U.S. patent for purified yeast in 1873.[456]

Judge Learned Hand set forth the modern understanding of the patentability of purified forms of natural products in *Parke-Davis & Co. v. H.K. Mulford Co.*[457] The patent in suit in that case was directed to a purified form of adrenaline, a naturally occurring hormone secreted by the suprarenal glands of animals and released into the bloodstream in situations of fear or stress. The inventor Takamine claimed "[a] substance possessing the herein-described physiological characteristics and reactions of the suprarenal glands in a stable and concentrated form, and practically free from inert and associated gland-tissue."[458] Judge Hand rejected the accused infringer's challenge to the claim's validity. "Nor is the patent only for a degree of purity, and therefore not for a new 'composition of matter,' " he observed. Takamine was "the first to make it available for any use by removing it from the other gland-tissue in which it was found."[459] While Hand conceded that it was "of course possible logically to call this a purification of the principle," the claimed composition "became for every practical purpose a new thing commercially and therapeutically." Hand considered that fact "a good ground for a patent."[460]

[456]*See Chakrabarty*, 447 U.S. at 314 n.9 (noting that Louis Pasteur in 1873 obtained U.S. Pat. No. 141,072, which contained the following claim: "[Y]east, free from organic germs of disease, as an article of manufacture").

[457]189 F. 95 (S.D.N.Y. 1911) (L. Hand, J.).

[458]U.S. Pat. No. 730,176 (issued June 2, 1903) (claim 1).

[459]*Parke-Davis*, 189 F. at 103.

[460]For a historical investigation concluding that "Hand's now-famous *Parke-Davis* pronouncements on the patentability of isolated products of nature were underinformed *dicta*, which conflicted with existing patent law," *see* Jon M. Harkness, *Dicta on Adrenalin(e): Myriad Problems with Learned Hand's Product-of-Nature*

In re Bergy further illustrates this principle. The patent applicant, Bergy, claimed a biologically pure culture of a microorganism that produced the antibiotic lincomycin.[461] The CCPA reversed the USPTO's rejection of the claim as, among other grounds, a mere product of nature. The court stressed that "[t]he biologically pure culture of claim 5 clearly does not exist in, is not found in, and is not a product of, 'nature.' It is man-made and can be produced only under carefully controlled laboratory conditions."[462] Indeed, "[t]he nature and commercial uses of biologically pure cultures of microorganisms like the one defined in claim 5 are much more akin to inanimate chemical compositions such as reactants, reagents, and catalysts than they are to horses and honeybees or raspberries and roses."[463]

b. Genetic Materials

Realizing the limits on the product of nature doctrine helps us understand why some human-based genetic materials have been patented, a point often discounted by persons opposed to the granting of such patents. First, understand that genes[464] *as they exist in the human body* would, indeed, be considered products of nature outside the purview of 35 U.S.C. §101.[465]

But starting in the 1980s, the USPTO granted thousands of gene patents,[466] taking the position that the discovery of a gene could be

---

Pronouncements in Parke-Davis v. Mulford, 93 J. PAT. & TRADEMARK OFF. SOC'Y 363 (2011).

[461]*See* In re Bergy, 596 F.2d 952, 967 (C.C.P.A. 1979) (quoting claim 5 of Bergy's application).

[462]In re Bergy, 563 F.2d 1031, 1035 (C.C.P.A. 1977).

[463]*Id.* at 1038.

[464]Genes are chemicals, the "instruction sets" from which the human body produces proteins. More precisely, a gene is "[t]he region of DNA on the chromosome that codes for the sequence of a single polypeptide." In re O'Farrell, 853 F.2d 894, 897 (Fed. Cir. 1988). Proteins, also called polypeptides, are "biological molecules of enormous importance... [that] include enzymes that catalyze biochemical reactions, major structural materials of the animal body, and many hormones." *Id.* at 895-896.

[465]Approximately 95 percent of the human genome is considered "junk DNA" that does not code for proteins. *See* AMERICAN HERITAGE DICTIONARY OF THE ENGLISH LANGUAGE (4th ed. 2000) (defining *junk DNA* as "DNA that does not code for proteins or their regulation but constitutes approximately 95 percent of the human genome" and noting that junk DNA is "postulated to be involved in the evolution of new genes and possibly in gene repair").

[466]Since the 1980s, the USPTO has granted more than 20,000 patents claiming isolated DNA molecules, almost 4,000 of which claim isolated human DNA encoding proteins. *See* Remarks of David Kappos, Under Secretary of Commerce for Intellectual Property and Director of the United States Patent and Trademark Office, BIO International Convention (May 3-6, 2010), *available at* https://www.ipwatchdog.com/2010/05/04/kappos-talks-patent-reform-and-gene-patents-at-bio-convention/ id=10382 (May 4, 2010); *see also* Statement of Q. Todd Dickinson, Under Secretary of Commerce for Intellectual Property & Director of the U.S. Patent & Trademark Office before the

the basis for a patent on the gene as "isolated from its natural state and processed through purifying steps that separated the gene from other molecules naturally associated with it."[467] Patent claims directed to such modified genes and gene fragments typically recite "a purified and isolated nucleic acid" comprising a particular nucleic acid sequence set forth in the patent application.[468] The sequence of nucleotides[469] encompassed by this type of claim arguably represented

---

Subcommittee on Courts and Intellectual Property, Committee on the Judiciary, U.S. House of Representatives (July 13, 2000), at 3:

> Over the past twenty years, many patent applications have been filed that are drawn to subject matter relating to genes. The filing rate of applications relating to genes has dramatically increased in the past few years. Currently, over 20,000 applications relating to genes are pending before the USPTO. Since the first gene related applications were filed, approximately 6,000 patents have issued which are drawn to full-length genes from human, animal, plant, bacterial and viral sources. Of these 6,000 patents, over 1,000 are specifically drawn to human genes and human gene variations that distinguish individuals.

See also Ass'n for Molecular Pathology v. U.S. Patent & Trademark Office, 689 F.3d 1303, 1333 (Fed. Cir. 2012) (Lourie, J.), *aff'd in part, rev'd in part sub nom.* Ass'n for Molecular Pathology v. Myriad Genetics, Inc., 133 S. Ct. 2107 (2013), observing that

> the PTO has issued patents relating to DNA molecules for almost thirty years. In the early 1980s, the Office granted the first human gene patents. *See* Eric J. Rogers, *Can You Patent Genes? Yes and No, 93 J. Pat. & Trademark Off. Soc'y* 19 (2010). It is estimated that the PTO has issued 2,645 patents claiming "isolated DNA" over the past twenty-nine years, J.A. 3710, and that by 2005, had granted 40,000 DNA-related patents relating to, in non-native form, genes in the human genome, Rogers, *supra* at 40. In 2001, the PTO issued *Utility Examination Guidelines*, which reaffirmed the agency's position that isolated DNA molecules are patent eligible, 66 FED. REG. 1092-94 (Jan. 5, 2001). . . .

[467] *See* USPTO, *Utility Examination Guidelines*, 66 FED. REG. 1092, 1093 (Jan. 5, 2001), *available at* https://www.uspto.gov/sites/default/files/web/offices/com/sol/notices/utilexmguide.pdf.

[468] *See, e.g.*, *In re Deuel*, 51 F.3d 1552, 1555 (Fed. Cir. 1995) (addressing patentability of claim to "[a] purified and isolated DNA sequence consisting of a sequence encoding human heparin binding growth factor of 168 amino acids having the following amino acid sequence: Met Gln Ala . . . [remainder of 168 amino acid sequence]"); *cf.* Prostate Cancer Gene, U.S. Patent No. 5,945,522 (issued Aug. 31, 1999) (claiming "[a] purified *or* isolated nucleic acid comprising the sequence of SEQ ID NO: 1 or the sequence complementary thereto") (emphasis added).

[469] As the Federal Circuit explained in *In re O'Farrell*, 853 F.2d 894 (Fed. Cir. 1988),

> [t]he subunits of the DNA chain are called *nucleotides*. A nucleotide consists of a nitrogen-containing ring compound (called a *base*) linked to a 5-carbon sugar that has a phosphate group attached. DNA is composed of only four nucleotides. They differ from each other in the base region of the molecule. The four bases of these subunits are adenine, guanine, cytosine, and thymine (abbreviated respectively as A, G, C and T). The sequence of these bases along the DNA molecule specifies which amino acids will be inserted in sequence into the polypeptide chain of a protein.

O'Farrell, 853 F.2d at 896 (footnotes omitted).

a significantly different composition or manufacture from the unpurified and unisolated DNA as it existed in the human body.[470]

(i) *Myriad Genetics* (U.S. 2013)

In the twenty-first century, the topic of gene patents has increasingly attracted heated public debate,[471] eventually drawing the scrutiny of the U.S. Supreme Court. In 2013, the Court significantly limited the patentability of certain genetic materials in *Ass'n for Molecular Pathology v. Myriad Genetics, Inc.* ("*Myriad IV*"),[472] as detailed *infra*. Prior to the Court's decision in *Myriad*, the consensus view had been that "purified and isolated" DNA was not necessarily excluded from patentability under §101 as a "product of nature." The Supreme Court's *Myriad IV* decision rewrote the law and severely contracted the gene patenting landscape.[473]

[470]*See generally* Anna E. Morrison, *The U.S. PTO's New Utility Guidelines: Will They Be Enough to Secure Gene Patent Rights?*, 1 J. Marshall Rev. Intell. Prop. L. 142 (2001), http://www.jmripl.com/Publications/Vol1/Issue1/morrison.pdf.

[471]*See generally* Julia Carbone et al., *DNA Patents and Diagnostics: Not a Pretty Picture,* 28 Nature Biotechnology 784 (2010) (observing that "[f]our decades after the U.S. Supreme Court first held that an artificially created bacterium had the potential to be patented in the United States . . . , biotech patents continue to generate controversy — particularly human gene patents used in diagnostic testing") (citation to Diamond v. Chakrabarty (U.S. 1980) omitted), *available at* http://www.nature.com/nbt/journal/v28/n8/full/nbt0810-784.html; *cf.* Ass'n for Molecular Pathology v. U.S. Patent & Trademark Office, 689 F.3d 1303, 1348 (Fed. Cir. 2012) ("*Myriad III*") (Bryson, J., concurring-in-part and dissenting-in-part), *aff'd in part, rev'd in part sub nom.* Ass'n for Molecular Pathology v. Myriad Genetics, Inc., 133 S. Ct. 2107, 186 L. Ed. 2d 124 (2013), observing that

> [i]n its simplest form, the question in this case is whether an individual can obtain patent rights to a human gene. From a common-sense point of view, most observers would answer, "Of course not. Patents are for inventions. A human gene is not an invention." The essence of Myriad's argument in this case is to say that it has not patented a human gene, but something quite different — an *isolated* human gene, which differs from a native gene because the process of extracting it results in changes in its molecular structure (although not in its genetic code). We are therefore required to decide whether the process of isolating genetic material from a human DNA molecule makes the isolated genetic material a patentable invention. The court concludes that it does; I conclude that it does not.

[472]Ass'n for Molecular Pathology v. Myriad Genetics, Inc., 133 S. Ct. 2107, 2111, 2113, 2117 (2013) ("*Myriad IV*") (holding that "a naturally occurring DNA segment is a product of nature and not patent eligible merely because it has been isolated," such that patentee Myriad's claim reciting "[a]n isolated DNA coding for a BRCA1 polypeptide" having the "amino acid sequent set forth in SEQ ID NO:2" was not patent-eligible under 35 U.S.C. §101; stating that patentee Myriad "found an important and useful gene, but separating that gene from its surrounding genetic material is not an act of invention").

[473]*See, e.g.*, Andrew Pollack, *New Genetic Tests for Breast Cancer Hold Promise,* N.Y. Times, Apr. 21, 2015, at A1 (referring to "surge in competition in genetic risk screening

The *Myriad* saga entered the public consciousness when a New York federal district court in March 2010 granted summary judgment invalidating a number of biotechnology patents directed to the "BRCA1" and "BRCA2" human breast cancer genes.[474] One of the most highly publicized patent disputes in recent memory, *Association for Molecular Pathology (AMP) v. United States Patent and Trademark Office (USPTO) and Myriad Genetics, Inc.* ("*Myriad I*")[475] pitted patient care advocates against the patent-owning biotechnology industry.[476] The several patents in suit, owned by Myriad Genetics, Inc., included, *inter alia*,[477] numerous composition of matter claims directed to two human genes, known as BRCA1 and BRCA2. Myriad had identified the precise location and sequences of the BRCA genes in the 1990s, including certain mutations of the genes that correlated with an increased likelihood of developing breast or ovarian cancer. By testing for the presence of the mutations, doctors could determine whether a patient was at risk of developing these cancers.[478]

The composition of matter claims in Myriad's patents were of two types: (1) claims to "isolated DNA" coding for the BRCA1 and BRCA2 breast cancer genes, the location and nucleotide sequence of which Myriad had identified;[479] and (2) claims to complementary DNA ("cDNA"), which recited only the cDNA exons (i.e., those DNA nucleotides that code for amino acids) in the BRCA genes rather than their full DNA sequence containing both exons and introns (i.e., those

---

for cancer since 2013, when the Supreme Court invalidated the gene patents that gave Myriad Genetic a monopoly on BRCA testing").

[474]*See* Ass'n for Molecular Pathology v. U.S. Patent and Trademark Office and Myriad Genetics, Inc., 702 F. Supp. 2d 181, 185-186 (S.D.N.Y. 2010) (as amended Apr. 5, 2010) ("[T]he challenged patent claims are directed to (1) isolated DNA containing all or portions of the BRCA1 and BRCA2 gene sequence and (2) methods for 'comparing' or 'analyzing' BRCA1 [sic] and BRCA2 gene sequences to identify the presence of mutations correlating with a predisposition to breast or ovarian cancer.").

[475]*Myriad*, 702 F. Supp. 2d at 181.

[476]*See* Timothy Caulfield, *Human Gene Patents: Proof or Problems?*, 84 Chi.-Kent L. Rev. 133, 139-140 (2009) (discussing "social trade-off inherent in the patent system" in the biotechnology context and public concern over patient access to clinically useful technologies).

[477]The Myriad patents also included certain method claims.

[478]*See* In re BRCA1- and BRCA2-Based Hereditary Cancer Test Patent Litigation, 774 F.3d 755, 758 (Fed. Cir. 2014).

[479]Representative claim 1 of Myriad's U.S. Patent No. 5,747,282 recited:

> 1. An isolated DNA coding for a BRCA1 polypeptide, said polypeptide having the amino acid sequence set forth in SEQ ID NO:2.

The recited "SEQ ID NO:2" listed the 1,863 amino acids that a typical BRCA1 gene encodes. *See Myriad IV*, 133 S. Ct. at 2113. "Put differently, claim 1 asserts a patent claim on the DNA code that tells a cell to produce the strong of BRCA1 amino acids listed in SEQ ID NO:2." *Myriad IV*, 133 S. Ct. at 2113. The human body uses strings of amino acids to build proteins. *Myriad IV*, 133 S. Ct. at 2111.

DNA nucleotides that do not code for amino acids).[480] After the district court held that the challenged composition claims (both the isolated DNA claims and the cDNA claims) were invalid because they covered patent-ineligible products of nature, Myriad appealed.

Prior to the appeal in *Myriad* in 2011, the Federal Circuit had upheld the validity of gene patents, but those challenges had been based on issues of compliance with the nonobviousness requirement of 35 U.S.C. §103 and the disclosure requirements of 35 U.S.C. §112 rather than §101 patent-eligibility grounds.[481] Thus the appellate court's decisions in the *Myriad* dispute were closely watched by the scientific and investment communities. The Federal Circuit issued its first of two merits decisions in *Myriad* on July 29, 2011 ("*Myriad II*"), generating three separate opinions.[482] In the opinion "for the court" authored by Judge Lourie, the Federal Circuit majority reversed the

[480]Representative claim 2 of Myriad's U.S. Patent No. 5,747,282 recited:

> 2. The isolated DNA of claim 1, wherein said DNA has the nucleotide sequence set forth in SEQ ID NO:1.

The recited "SEQ ID NO:1" "lists only the cDNA exons in the BRCA1 gene, rather than a full DNA sequence containing both exons and introns." *Myriad IV*, 133 S. Ct. at 2113. The Court explained that "[o]nly some DNA nucleotides... code for amino acids; these nucleotides are known as 'exons.' Nucleotides that do not code for amino acids, in contrast, are known as 'introns.'" *Myriad IV*, 133 S. Ct. at 2111. Complementary DNA ("cDNA") is synthetic DNA created in the laboratory from messenger RNA ("mRNA"). *Myriad IV*, 133 S. Ct. at 2112.

[481]The Federal Circuit has previously upheld the validity of gene patents. *See, e.g.*, In re Deuel, 51 F.3d 1552, 1560 (Fed. Cir. 1995); *See also* In re Bell, 991 F.2d 781 (Fed. Cir. 1993); Amgen, Inc. v. Chugai Pharm. Co., 927 F.2d 1200 (Fed. Cir. 1991). These decisions applied qualitative patentability criteria such as nonobviousness under 35 U.S.C. §103 and disclosure compliance under 35 U.S.C. §112. However, the Federal Circuit has not previously confronted a *Myriad*-type challenge to the patent-eligibility of gene patents under 35 U.S.C. §101, most likely because §101 qualification was taken as a given by the parties and not raised as an issue on appeal in the court's earlier cases.

One judge of the Federal Circuit has suggested that the Supreme Court's decision in *Bilski v. Kappos, see* Section B.4.b, has potential applicability to the *Myriad* dispute. "Just as the patentability of abstract ideas would preempt others from using ideas that are in the public domain..., so too would allowing the patenting of naturally occurring substances preempt the use by others of substances that should be freely available to the public." Intervet Inc. v. Merial Ltd., 617 F.3d 1282, 1294 (Fed. Cir. 2010) (Dyk, J., concurring-in-part and dissenting-in-part).

For further discussion of the *Myriad* dispute, *see* Janice M. Mueller, *Facilitating Patient Access to Patent-Protected Genetic Testing*, 6 J. Bus. & Tech. L. 81, 81-93 (2011).

[482]Ass'n for Molecular Pathology v. U.S. Patent & Trademark Office, 653 F.3d 1329 (Fed. Cir. 2011) ("*Myriad II*"), *cert. granted, judgment vacated sub nom.* Ass'n for Molecular Pathology v. Myriad Genetics, Inc., 132 S. Ct. 1794 (2012), *opinion vacated, appeal reinstated sub nom.* Ass'n for Molecular Pathology v. U.S. Patent & Trademark Office, 467 F. App'x 890 (Fed. Cir. 2012). In *Myriad II*, Judge Lourie authored the opinion "for the court," Judge Moore concurred-in-part, and Judge Bryson concurred-in-part and dissented-in-part.

district court's decision that the claimed isolated DNA molecules were patent-ineligible products of nature under 35 U.S.C. §101. Rather, the *Myriad II* majority held, the molecules qualified as §101 compositions of matter because "the molecules as claimed do not exist in nature."[483] The Federal Circuit also reversed the district court with regard to Myriad's claim to a method of screening potential cancer therapeutics via changes in cell growth rates; in the court's view, this claim recited a patent-eligible method within §101 rather than a patent-ineligible scientific principle. The Federal Circuit affirmed only one aspect of the district court's decision, agreeing with the lower court that "Myriad's method claims directed to 'comparing' or 'analyzing' DNA sequences are patent ineligible [because] such claims include no transformative steps and cover only patent-ineligible abstract, mental steps."[484]

On March 26, 2012, one week after deciding *Mayo v. Prometheus*,[485] the Supreme Court vacated the Federal Circuit's *Myriad II* decision and directed the Circuit to reconsider that decision in view of *Mayo*.[486] As analyzed *supra*,[487] the Supreme Court had held in *Mayo* that certain methods of optimizing therapeutic efficacy for treatment of an immune-mediated gastrointestinal disorder were not patent-eligible subject matter under 35 U.S.C. §101 because the claims at issue merely recited "laws of nature" plus additional steps consisting of "well-understood, routine, conventional activity already engaged in by the scientific community."[488] The subject matter at issue in *Mayo* — methods of treatment — was fundamentally different from the composition of matter claims at the heart

[483]*Myriad*, 653 F.3d at 1334; *See also id.* at 1350 (stating that "we conclude that the challenged claims to isolated DNAs, *whether limited to cDNAs or not*, are directed to patent-eligible subject matter under §101") (emphasis added). Judge Bryson disagreed on this point. *See Myriad*, 653 F.3d at 1373 (Bryson, J., dissenting-in-part) (contending that although the cDNA claims were patent-eligible within §101, Myriad's BRCA gene claims and its claims to gene fragments were not). In Judge Bryson's view, "those [BRCA gene claims and gene fragment] claims are not directed to patentable subject matter, and if sustained the court's decision will likely have broad consequences, such as preempting methods for whole-genome sequencing, even though Myriad's contribution to the field is not remotely consonant with such effects." *Myriad*, 653 F.3d at 1373. Judge Moore joined the majority "with respect to claims to isolated cDNA sequences [] and concur[red] in the judgment with respect to the remaining sequences." *Myriad*, 653 F.3d at 1358 (Moore, J., concurring-in-part).

[484]*Myriad*, 653 F.3d at 1334.

[485]*See* Mayo Collab. Serv. v. Prometheus Labs., Inc., 132 S. Ct. 1289 (Mar. 20, 2012) (hereafter "*Mayo*"), discussed *supra* Section B.4.c and Section B.5.a.

[486]*See* Ass'n for Molecular Pathology v. Myriad Genetics, Inc., 132 S. Ct. 1794 (Mar. 26, 2012) (granting petition for writ of *certiorari* in *Myriad II*, vacating Fed. Cir. judgment, and remanding case to Fed. Cir. for further consideration in light of *Mayo*).

[487]*See supra* Section B.5 ("Methods of Medical Treatment") (discussing Supreme Court's decision in *Mayo*, 132 S. Ct. 1289 (2012)).

[488]*See Mayo*, 132 S. Ct. at 1298.

of the *Myriad* dispute. Nevertheless, vacating and remanding the Federal Circuit's *Myriad II* decision suggested that the Supreme Court did not readily agree with the Circuit that gene patents were §101 patent-eligible subject matter. Rather, the remand indicated that the Supreme Court might consider isolated genes to be another type of patent-ineligible "law of nature" or "natural phenomenon."

On remand, the Federal Circuit panel in August 2012 issued its decision in "*Myriad III*."[489] The same 2-1 panel majority in *Myriad III* upheld its earlier decision in *Myriad II* that both the isolated DNA claims and the cDNA claims of Myriad's patents *were* patent-eligible subject matter. As in *Myriad II*, the Circuit's *Myriad III* decision generated three separate opinions. All three Circuit judges agreed that the challenged claims reciting complementary DNA ("cDNA") were patent eligible under §101. With respect to the isolated DNA claims, however, each judge held a different view on the central question whether "the act of *isolating* DNA — separating a specific gene or sequence of nucleotides from the rest of the chromosome — is an inventive act that entitles the individual who first isolates it to a patent."[490] Two of three Circuit judges answered that question affirmatively.[491]

[489]Ass'n for Molecular Pathology v. U.S. Patent & Trademark Office, 689 F.3d 1303 (Fed. Cir. Aug. 16, 2012) ("*Myriad III*"), *aff'd in part, rev'd in part sub nom.* Ass'n for Molecular Pathology v. Myriad Genetics, Inc., 133 S. Ct. 2107 (2013). In *Myriad III*, Judge Lourie authored the "Opinion for the court," Judge Moore filed an opinion concurring-in-part, and Judge Bryson filed an opinion concurring-in-part and dissenting-in-part). *See Myriad III*, 689 F.3d at 1308.

[490]*Myriad IV*, 133 S. Ct. at 2114.

[491]As summarized by the Supreme Court,

> Judges Lourie and Moore agreed that Myriad's claims were patent eligible under §101 but disagreed on the rationale. Judge Lourie relied on the fact that the entire DNA molecule is held together by chemical bonds and that the covalent bonds at both ends of the segment must be severed in order to isolate segments of DNA. This process technically creates new molecules with unique chemical compositions. See *id.* [*Myriad III*, 689 F.3d], at 1328 ("Isolated DNA... is a free-standing portion of a larger, natural DNA molecule. Isolated DNA has been cleaved (*i.e.*, had covalent bonds in its backbone chemically severed) or synthesized to consist of just a fraction of a naturally occurring DNA molecule"). Judge Lourie found this chemical alteration to be dispositive, because isolating a particular strand of DNA creates a nonnaturally occurring molecule, even though the chemical alteration does not change the information-transmitting quality of the DNA. See *id.*, at 1330 ("The claimed isolated DNA molecules are distinct from their natural existence as portions of larger entities, and their informational content is irrelevant to that fact. We recognize that biologists may think of molecules in terms of their uses, but genes are in fact materials having a chemical nature"). Accordingly, he rejected petitioners' argument that isolated DNA was ineligible for patent protection as a product of nature.
>
> Judge Moore concurred in part but did not rely exclusively on Judge Lourie's conclusion that chemically breaking covalent bonds was sufficient to render isolated DNA patent eligible. *Id.*, at 1341 ("To the extent the majority rests its conclusion on the chemical differences between [naturally occurring] and isolated

The Supreme Court granted *certiorari* in *Myriad III*, heard argument, and issued its decision in *Ass'n for Molecular Pathology v. Myriad Genetics* (hereafter "*Myriad IV*") on June 13, 2013. The Court affirmed-in-part and reversed-in-part the Federal Circuit's *Myriad III* decision. Most significantly, the Supreme Court in *Myriad IV* held, contrary to the Federal Circuit's view, that Myriad's patent claims to isolated DNA recited naturally-occurring subject matter that was *not* patent eligible under §101; rather, the claims were directed to a "natural phenomenon," a "law of nature," or a "product of nature" (unhelpfully, the Supreme Court used all three terms interchangeably).[492] Agreeing with the Federal Circuit, however, the Supreme Court also held that Myriad's claims to complementary DNA ("cDNA") *were* patent-eligible subject matter under §101. In the Court's view, the cDNA claims were within §101 because they were drawn to synthetic

---

DNA (breaking the covalent bonds), I cannot agree that this is sufficient to hold that the claims to human genes are directed to patentable subject matter"). Instead, Judge Moore also relied on the United States Patent and Trademark Office's (PTO) practice of granting such patents and on the reliance interests of patent holders. *Id.*, at 1343. However, she acknowledged that her vote might have come out differently if she "were deciding this case on a blank canvas." *Ibid.*

Finally, Judge Bryson concurred in part and dissented in part, concluding that isolated DNA is not patent eligible. As an initial matter, he emphasized that the breaking of chemical bonds was not dispositive: "[T]here is no magic to a chemical bond that requires us to recognize a new product when a chemical bond is created or broken." *Id.*, at 1351. Instead, he relied on the fact that "[t]he nucleotide sequences of the claimed molecules are the same as the nucleotide sequences found in naturally occurring human genes." *Id.*, at 1355. Judge Bryson then concluded that genetic "structural similarity dwarfs the significance of the structural differences between isolated DNA and naturally occurring DNA, especially where the structural differences are merely ancillary to the breaking of covalent bonds, a process that is itself not inventive." *Ibid.* Moreover, Judge Bryson gave no weight to the PTO's position on patentability because of the Federal Circuit's position that "the PTO lacks substantive rulemaking authority as to issues such as patentability." *Id.*, at 1357.

Myriad IV, 133 S. Ct. at 2114-2115.

[492]The Court did not distinguish between "product of nature," "natural phenomenon," and "law of nature," but rather used the terms interchangeably to describe non-eligible subject matter. *See Myriad IV*, 133 S. Ct. at 211 (holding that "a naturally occurring DNA segment is a *product of nature* and not patent eligible merely because it has been isolated") (emphasis added); *Myriad IV*, 133 S. Ct. at 2116 (stating that "[w]e must apply this well-established standard to determine whether Myriad's patents claim any 'new and useful . . . composition of matter,' §101, or instead claim *naturally occurring phenomena*") (emphasis added); *Myriad IV*, 133 S. Ct. at 2117 (stating that "[h]is [the patentee's in *Funk Brothers Seed Co. v. Kalo Inoculant Co.*, 333 U.S. 127 (1948)] patent claim . . . fell squarely within the *law of nature* exception. So do Myriad's. Myriad found the location of the BRCA1 and BRCA2 genes, but that discovery, by itself, does not render the BRCA genes 'new . . . composition[s] of matter,' §101, that are patent eligible.") (emphasis added).

DNA created in the laboratory. These two key holdings are examined below.

The Supreme Court's first and most significant holding in *Myriad IV*, that Myriad's isolated DNA claims were *not* potentially patentable compositions of matter within 35 U.S.C. §101, largely turned on the Court's distinction between the acts of "discovery" and "invention." Myriad had admittedly made an important "breakthrough" in discovering the precise location and sequence of the BRCA1 and BRCA2 genes.[493] But "Myriad did not create or alter any of the genetic information encoded in the BRCA1 and BRCA2 genes. The location and order of the nucleotides existed in nature before Myriad found them."[494] In short, Myriad "did not create anything."[495] Although Myriad had found "an important and useful gene, the Court determined that separating that gene from its surrounding genetic material [wa]s not an act of invention."[496] Myriad's research efforts were surely extensive,[497] but "extensive research effort alone is insufficient to satisfy the demands of §101."[498]

The *Myriad IV* Court contrasted its earlier decisions in *Diamond v. Chakrabarty* (1980)[499] and *Funk Bros. Seed Co. v. Kalo Inoculant Co.* (1948)[500] to illustrate the point. In *Chakrabarty*, four plasmids had been inserted into an existing, live bacterium, allowing the resulting genetically modified bacterium to break down various components of crude oil. The modified bacterium was not "naturally occurring" or a

[493]The Court observed that

> Myriad identified the exact location of the BRCA1 and BRCA2 genes on chromosomes 17 and 13. Chromosome 17 has approximately 80 million nucleotides, and chromosome 13 has approximately 114 million. *Association for Molecular Pathology v. United States Patent and Trademark Office,* 689 F.3d 1303, 1328 (C.A. Fed. 2012). Within those chromosomes, the BRCA1 and BRCA2 genes are each about 80,000 nucleotides long. If just exons are counted, the BRCA1 gene is only about 5,500 nucleotides long; for the BRCA2 gene, that number is about 10,200. *Ibid.* Knowledge of the location of the BRCA1 and BRCA2 genes allowed Myriad to determine their typical nucleotide sequence.... That information, in turn, enabled Myriad to develop medical tests that are useful for detecting mutations in a patient's BRCA1 and BRCA2 genes and thereby assessing whether the patient has an increased risk of cancer.

Myriad IV, 133 S. Ct. at 2112-2113 (footnote omitted).

[494]*Myriad IV*, 133 S. Ct. at 2116.

[495]*Myriad IV*, 133 S. Ct. at 2117.

[496]*Myriad IV*, 133 S. Ct. at 2117.

[497]The Court observed that the Myriad patents in suit "detail[ed] the 'iterative process' of discovery by which Myriad narrowed the possible locations for the gene sequences that it sought." *Myriad IV*, 133 S. Ct. at 2118.

[498]*Myriad IV*, 133 S. Ct. at 2118.

[499]447 U.S. 303 (1980).

[500]333 U.S. 127 (1948).

"natural phenomenon"; instead the bacterium possessed "'markedly different characteristics from any [other bacterium] found in nature.'"[501] In contrast, the patent in *Funk Bros.* concerned a mixture of naturally occurring strains of bacteria that helped leguminous plants take nitrogen from the air and fix it in the soil. After learning that certain nitrogen-fixing bacteria did not deleteriously inhibit each other, the patent applicant in *Funk Bros.* combined them into a single inoculant. The Court held that the resulting claimed composition of matter was not patent eligible because the patent holder "did not alter the bacteria in any way."[502] Rather, the claim in *Funk Bros.* "fell squarely within the law of nature exception."[503]

The Supreme Court in *Myriad IV* concluded that Myriad's efforts were analogous to those in *Funk Bros.*, not *Chakrabarty*. Although Myriad had found an "important and useful gene," it did not create or invent anything by separating that gene from its surrounding genetic material.[504] Like the inoculant in *Funk Bros.*, Myriad's isolated DNA fell "squarely within the law of nature exception." Discovering the location of the BRCA genes did not render the genes patent-eligible "'new . . . composition[s] of matter.'"[505]

Notably, the *Myriad IV* Court also rejected the view espoused below by Federal Circuit Judge Lourie that because its terminal covalent bonds were severed in the isolation process, isolated DNA was a new and non-naturally occurring molecule and thus a patent-eligible composition of matter within §101. In the Supreme Court's view, Myriad's isolated DNA claims were "concerned primarily with the information contained in the genetic *sequence,* not with the specific chemical composition of the particular molecule."[506] The Court elaborated:

> Myriad's claims [are not] saved by the fact that isolating DNA from the human genome severs chemical bonds and thereby creates a nonnaturally occurring molecule. Myriad's claims are simply not expressed in terms of chemical composition, nor do they rely in any way on the chemical changes that result from the isolation of a particular section of DNA. Instead, the claims understandably focus on the genetic information encoded in the BRCA1 and BRCA2 genes. If the patents depended upon the creation of a unique molecule, then a would-be infringer could arguably avoid at least Myriad's patent claims on entire genes (such as claims 1 and 2 of the '282 patent) by isolating a DNA sequence that included both the BRCA1 or BRCA2 gene and one additional nucleotide pair. Such

[501]*Myriad IV*, 133 S. Ct. at 2117 (quoting *Chakrabarty*, 447 U.S. at 310).
[502]*Myriad IV*, 133 S. Ct. at 2117 (citing *Funk Bros.*, 333 U.S. at 132).
[503]*Myriad IV*, 133 S. Ct. at 217.
[504]*Myriad IV*, 133 S. Ct. at 217.
[505]*Myriad IV*, 133 S. Ct. at 2117 (quoting 35 U.S.C. §101).
[506]*Myriad IV*, 133 S. Ct. at 2118 (emphasis in original).

> a molecule would not be chemically identical to the molecule "invented" by Myriad. But Myriad obviously would resist that outcome because its claim is concerned primarily with the information contained in the genetic *sequence,* not with the specific chemical composition of a particular molecule.[507]

Nor was the *Myriad IV* Court persuaded that the USPTO's longstanding practice of granting patents on isolated DNA[508] justified the continued recognition of that subject matter as patent eligible. The Court contrasted the case at bar with its 2001 decision in *J.E.M. Ag Supply, Inc. v. Pioneer Hi-Bred Int'l, Inc.,*[509] in which it had held that new sexually reproduced plants and seeds were potentially eligible for utility patent protection under 35 U.S.C. §101 despite the existence of a separate statutory scheme for plant patents under 35 U.S.C. §§161-164. In its opinion in *J.E.M.*, the Supreme Court had mentioned that Congress had recognized and endorsed the USPTO's position that new plant breeds were within §101 in a subsequent Patent Act amendment.[510] In contrast, "Congress has not endorsed the views of the PTO in subsequent legislation" concerning isolated DNA.[511] Moreover, the argument of the U.S. Solicitor General in the case at bar that isolated DNA was *not* within §101 was a "concession[] [that] weigh[ed] against

[507]*Myriad IV*, 133 S. Ct. at 2118.

[508]*See* Ass'n for Molecular Pathology v. U.S. Patent & Trademark Office, 689 F.3d 1303, 1333 (Fed. Cir. 2012) (Lourie, J.), *aff'd in part, rev'd in part sub nom.* Ass'n for Molecular Pathology v. Myriad Genetics, Inc., 133 S. Ct. 2107 (2013), observing that

> the PTO has issued patents relating to DNA molecules for almost thirty years. In the early 1980s, the Office granted the first human gene patents. *See* Eric J. Rogers, *Can You Patent Genes? Yes and No, 93 J. Pat. & Trademark Off. Soc'y* 19 (2010). It is estimated that the PTO has issued 2,645 patents claiming "isolated DNA" over the past twenty-nine years, J.A. 3710, and that by 2005, had granted 40,000 DNA-related patents relating to, in non-native form, genes in the human genome, Rogers, *supra* at 40. In 2001, the PTO issued *Utility Examination Guidelines*, which reaffirmed the agency's position that isolated DNA molecules are patent eligible, 66 FED. REG. 1092-94 (Jan. 5, 2001)....

[509]534 U.S. 124 (2001). The *J.E.M.* decision is further discussed *infra* Section H.1.

[510]*Myriad IV*, 133 S. Ct. at 2118 (citing *J.E.M.,* 534 U.S. at 144-145 (citing In re Hibberd, 227 U.S.P.Q. 443 (Bd. Pat. App. & Interf. 1985) and 35 U.S.C. §119(f)). Section 119 of the Patent Act provided in pertinent part:

> (f) Applications for plant breeder's rights filed in a WTO member country (or in a foreign UPOV Contracting Party) shall have the same effect for the purpose of the right of priority under subsections (a) through (c) of this section as applications for patents, subject to the same conditions and requirements of this section as apply to applications for patents.

35 U.S.C. §119 (as amended 1999).

[511]*Myriad IV*, 133 S. Ct. at 2118.

deferring to the PTO's determination."[512] Lastly, the *Myriad IV* Court rejected Myriad's argument that it should recognize and respect the reliance interests of owners of already-granted patents on isolated DNA. Rather, "insofar as they are relevant," "[c]oncerns about reliance interests arising from PTO determinations . . . are better directed to Congress."[513]

The Supreme Court's second primary holding in *Myriad IV* was that Myriad's complementary DNA ("cDNA") claims *were* potentially patentable compositions of matter within 35 U.S.C. §101.[514] The patent eligibility of cDNA largely turned on the Court's characterization of cDNA as "synthetically created" DNA that was "not naturally occurring."[515] Although the Court appeared to agree with the patent challengers' position that the nucleotide sequence of cDNA is dictated by nature rather than a laboratory technician, "the lab technician unquestionably creates something new when cDNA is made."[516] As the Court explained,

> cDNA does not present the same obstacles to patentability as naturally occurring, isolated DNA segments. As already explained, creation of a cDNA sequence from mRNA [messenger RNA] results in an exons-only [i.e., only coding for amino acids] molecule that is not naturally occurring. . . . Petitioners concede that cDNA differs from natural DNA in that "the non-coding regions have been removed." . . . cDNA retains the naturally occurring exons of DNA, but it is distinct from the DNA from which it was derived. As a result, cDNA is not a "product of nature" and is patent eligible under §101. . . .[517]

[512]*Myriad IV*, 133 S. Ct. at 2119.

[513]*Myriad IV*, 133 S. Ct. at 2119 n.7 (citing Mayo Collab. Servs. v. Prometheus Labs., Inc., 132 S. Ct. at 1304-1305).

[514]*Myriad IV*, 133 S. Ct. at 2111, 2119.

[515]*Myriad IV*, 133 S. Ct. at 2111.

[516]*Myriad IV*, 133 S. Ct. at 2119. Earlier in its opinion, the Court had explained how cDNA is created in the laboratory:

> It is . . . possible to create DNA synthetically through processes . . . well known in the field of genetics. One such method begins with an mRNA molecule and uses the natural bonding properties of nucleotides to create a new, synthetic DNA molecule. The result is the inverse of the mRNA's inverse image of the original DNA, with one important distinction: Because the natural creation of mRNA involves splicing that removes introns, the synthetic DNA created from mRNA also contains only the exon sequences. This synthetic DNA created in the laboratory from mRNA is known as complementary DNA (cDNA).

Myriad IV, 133 S. Ct. at 2112.

[517]*Myriad IV*, 133 S. Ct. at 2119 (footnotes, text, and citations omitted). The Court recognized an exception to its holding that cDNA is different from natural DNA in the instance when a "very short series of DNA may have no intervening introns to remove when creating cDNA. In that situation, a short strand of cDNA may be indistinguishable from natural DNA." *Myriad IV*, 133 S. Ct. at 2119, 2119 n.8.

The Supreme Court concluded its opinion in *Myriad IV* by stressing three points that were *not* implicated by its decision. First, although the *method* claims of Myriad's patents were not under review in the instant case, the Court suggested that if Myriad "[h]ad . . . created an innovative method of manipulating genes while searching for the BRCA1 and BRCA2 genes, it could possibly have sought a method patent."[518] Nevertheless, the Court observed that "the processes used by Myriad to isolate DNA were well understood by geneticists at the time of Myriad's patents [and] 'were well understood, widely used, and fairly uniform insofar as any scientist engaged in the search for a gene would likely have utilized a similar approach. . . .' "[519] (The Federal Circuit would address the patent eligibility of certain of Myriad's process claims in a December 2014 decision, *In re BRCA1- and BRCA2-Based Hereditary Cancer Test Patent Litigation*, examined below.[520])

Second, the *Myriad IV* Court emphasized that "this case does not involve patents on new *applications* of knowledge about the BRCA1 and BRCA2 genes."[521] It noted with approval Federal Circuit Judge Bryson's "apt[]" observation that " '[a]s the first party with knowledge of the [breast cancer gene] sequences, Myriad was in an excellent position to claim applications of that knowledge. Many of its unchallenged claims are limited to such applications.' "[522]

Lastly, the *Myriad IV* Court stated that it had not considered "the patentability of DNA in which the order of the naturally occurring nucleotides has been altered." Such alterations presented "a different inquiry" about which the Court would not express any opinion. Rather, in *Myriad IV*, the Court had "merely h[e]ld that genes and the information they encode are not patent eligible under §101 simply because they have been isolated from the surrounding genetic material."[523]

[518]*Myriad IV*, 133 S. Ct. at 2119.

[519]*Myriad IV*, 133 S. Ct. at 2119-2120 (quoting Ass'n for Molecular Pathology v. United States Patent and Trademark Office, 702 F. Supp. 2d 181, 202-203 (S.D.N.Y. 2010)).

[520]774 F.3d 755 (Fed. Cir. Dec. 17, 2014). *See infra* Section D.2.b.ii ("Post-*Myriad* Federal Circuit Decisions").

[521]*Myriad IV*, 133 S. Ct. at 2120 (emphasis in original).

[522]*Myriad IV*, 133 S. Ct. at 2120 (quoting Ass'n for Molecular Pathology v. U.S. Patent & Trademark Office, 689 F.3d 1303, 1349 (Fed. Cir. 2012) (Bryson, J., concurring-in-part and dissenting-in-part)).

[523]*Myriad IV*, 133 S. Ct. at 2120. In addition to Justice Thomas's opinion of the Court, Justice Scalia offered a peculiar one-paragraph opinion:

> I join the judgment of the Court, and all of its opinion except Part I-A [explaining the science of genes and DNA] and some portions of the rest of the opinion going into fine details of molecular biology. I am unable to affirm those details on my own knowledge or even my own belief. It suffices for me to affirm, having studied the opinions below and the expert briefs presented here, that the portion of DNA isolated from its natural state sought to be patented is identical to that portion of

(ii) Post-*Myriad* (U.S. 2013) Federal Circuit Decisions

The *Myriad* gene patent battle was not yet over; the Federal Circuit in 2014 further limited the patent eligibility of certain genetic materials. One year after the Supreme Court's 2013 decision in *Myriad IV*, patentee Myriad and its co-plaintiffs (collectively "Myriad") sued Ambry Genetics Corp. ("Ambry") in the U.S. District Court for the District of Utah. Ambry sold medical test kits designed to test for the presence of gene mutations linked to breast and ovarian cancer.[524] Myriad asserted that Ambry infringed several method and composition claims of Myriad's breast cancer gene patents, which claims the Supreme Court had not previously considered in *Myriad IV*. After the district court denied Myriad's motion for a preliminary injunction,[525] Myriad appealed to the Federal Circuit.

In *In re BRCA1- and BRCA2-Based Hereditary Cancer Test Patent Litigation* ("*Myriad VI*"),[526] the Federal Circuit in December 2014 affirmed the denial of Myriad's preliminary injunction motion. As detailed below, the Circuit agreed with the district court that neither the appealed composition of matter claims or the method claims qualified as patent-eligible subject matter within 35 U.S.C. §101.

The Federal Circuit in *Myriad VI* first considered Myriad's four appealed composition of matter claims. The composition claims were directed to primers, "which are 'short, synthetic, single-stranded DNA molecule[s] that bind [ ] specifically to . . . intended target nucleotide sequence[s].' "[527] Claim 16 of Myriad's U.S. Patent No. 5,747,282 ('282 patent), a claim not considered by the Supreme Court in *Myriad IV*, was representative of the primer claims:

> 16. A pair of single-stranded DNA primers for determination of a nucleotide sequence of a BRCA1 gene by a polymerase chain reaction,

---

> the DNA in its natural state; and that complementary DNA (cDNA) is a synthetic creation not normally present in nature.

Myriad IV, 133 S. Ct. at 2120 (Scalia, J., concurring-in-part and concurring in the judgment).

[524] In re BRCA1- and BRCA2-Based Hereditary Cancer Test Patent Litigation, 774 F.3d 755, 757 (Fed. Cir. 2014). The district court observed that "[w]ithin days of the Supreme Court's *AMP* [*Myriad IV*] decision, Defendant Ambry Genetics Corporation (Defendant) announced plans to sell tests less expensive than Myriad's to screen BRCA1 and BRCA2 genes. Since then, other companies have followed suit — publicly offering such tests or announcing plans to do so. . . ." In re BRCA1-, BRCA2-Based Hereditary Cancer Test Patent Litig., 3 F. Supp. 3d 1213, 1218 (D. Utah Mar. 10, 2014) (footnote omitted).

[525] In re BRCA1-, BRCA2-Based Hereditary Cancer Test Patent Litig., 3 F. Supp. 3d 1213 (D. Utah Mar. 10, 2014) ("*Myriad V*").

[526] 774 F.3d 755 (Fed. Cir. Dec. 17, 2014) ("*Myriad VI*") (opinion authored by Dyk, J., joined by Prost, C.J., and Clevenger, J).

[527] *Myriad VI*, 774 F.3d at 758 (quoting Joint Appendix 13).

> the sequence of said primers being derived from human chromosome 17q, wherein the use of said primers in a polymerase chain reaction results in the synthesis of DNA having all or part of the sequence of the BRCA1 gene.[528]

In denying Myriad's preliminary injunction motion, the Utah district court had held the primer claims were likely patent-ineligible under §101 because they recited "so-called products of nature — that is, they claim[ed] the same nucleotide sequence as naturally occurring DNA."[529]

The Federal Circuit in *Myriad VI* agreed. The appellate court gave short shrift to Myriad's arguments that primers should be treated differently because they were single-stranded DNA that cannot be found in nature. Contrary to Myriad's position, the Supreme Court had made clear in *Myriad IV* that "neither naturally occurring compositions of matter, *nor synthetically created compositions that are structurally identical to the naturally occurring compositions*, are patent eligible."[530] The Circuit observed that in addition to holding patent ineligible the isolated DNA recited in claim 1 of Myriad's '282 patent, the Supreme Court in *Myriad IV* had also found patent ineligible the subject matter of dependent claim 5 of the '282 patent. Claim 5 recited "[a]n isolated DNA having at least 15 nucleotides of the DNA of claim 1."[531] The primer claims on appeal before the Federal Circuit in *Myriad VI* were the same length as the isolated DNA of claim 5 that had been considered and rejected by the Supreme Court.[532] In the Circuit's view, this similarity "suggest[ed] that even short strands identical to those found in nature are not patent eligible."[533] Moreover, the Supreme Court in *Myriad IV* had made clear that " 'separating [DNA] from its surrounding genetic material is not an act of invention.' "[534]

Nor was the Federal Circuit persuaded by Myriad's argument that the primer sequences, once extracted from a DNA strand, performed

[528] U.S. Pat. No. 5,747,282.

[529] *Myriad VI*, 774 F.3d at 758-759.

[530] *Myriad VI*, 774 F.3d at 760 (emphasis added).

[531] *Myriad IV*, 133 S. Ct. at 2113.

[532] *See Myriad VI*, 774 F.3d at 760.

[533] *Myriad VI*, 774 F.3d at 760.

[534] *Myriad VI*, 774 F.3d at 760 (quoting *Myriad IV*, 133 S. Ct. at 2117). The Circuit also supported its holding that Myriad's primer claims were not patent eligible by analogy to its decision in *In re Roslin Institute (Edinburgh)*, 750 F.3d 1333 (Fed. Cir. 2014):

> This situation is similar to [*Roslin Institute*]. There, we held unpatentable a genetic copy of a naturally occurring organism — Dolly, a cloned sheep — because she "is an exact genetic replica of another sheep and does not possess 'markedly different characteristics from any farm animals found in nature.' " *Id.* (quoting Diamond v. Chakrabarty, 447 U.S. 303, 310, 100 S. Ct. 2204, 65 L. Ed. 2d 144 (1980)) (punctuation omitted).

a "fundamentally different function" than their function when still part of the strand. Extraction did not facilitate the performance of a "significantly new function." Rather,

> the naturally occurring material is used to form the first step in a chain reaction — a function that is performed because the primer maintains the exact same nucleotide sequence as the relevant portion of the naturally occurring sequence. One of the primary functions of DNA's structure in nature is that complementary nucleotide sequences bind to each other. It is this same function that is exploited here — the primer binds to its complementary nucleotide sequence. *Thus, just as in nature, primers utilize the innate ability of DNA to bind to itself.*[535]

In the Federal Circuit's view, the Supreme Court's decision in *Myriad IV* meant that a "DNA structure with a function similar to that found in nature can only be patent eligible as a composition of matter if it has a *unique* structure, different from anything found in nature."[536] Because primers "do not have such a different structure," the appellate court concluded that they are not patent-eligible compositions of matter under 35 U.S.C. §101.[537]

The second part of the Federal Circuit's opinion in *Myriad VI* addressed Myriad's two asserted method claims, which the Supreme Court likewise had not considered in *Myriad IV* (although the Circuit had considered parts of the method claims in its 2012 decision in *Myriad III*[538]). Affirming the district court, the Federal Circuit in *Myriad VI* held that the asserted method claims were not patent eligible because they were directed to abstract ideas under the Supreme Court's 2014 decision in *Alice Corp. v. CLS Bank*,[539] discussed *supra*.[540]

More particularly, Myriad's asserted method claims were directed to comparisons between "wild-type" BRCA sequences (i.e., the typical sequences of the BRCA genes most often found in humans) and a particular patient's BRCA gene sequences. Representative claim 7 of

---

Myriad VI, 774 F.3d at 760 (quoting *Roslin Institute*, 750 F.3d at 1337). *Roslin Institute* is further examined *infra* Section D.3.c ("Clones").

[535] *Myriad VI*, 774 F.3d at 761 (emphasis added).

[536] *Myriad VI*, 774 F.3d at 761 (citing *Myriad IV*, 133 S. Ct. at 2116-2117) (emphasis added).

[537] *Myriad VI*, 774 F.3d at 761.

[538] *See* Ass'n for Molecular Pathology v. U.S. Patent & Trademark Office, 689 F.3d 1303, 1333-1335 (Fed. Cir. Aug. 16, 2012) ("*Myriad III*") (holding claims 1 of Myriad's '999 patent, '001 patent, and '441 patent and claims 1 and 2 of Myriad's '857 patent invalid under 35 U.S.C. §101 for claiming patent-ineligible processes), *aff'd in part, rev'd in part sub nom.* Ass'n for Molecular Pathology v. Myriad Genetics, Inc., 133 S. Ct. 2107 (2013).

[539] 134 S. Ct. 2347 (2014).

[540] *See supra* Section B.4.d ("*Alice Corp.* (U.S. 2014)").

Myriad's U.S. Patent No. 5,753,441 ('441 patent), revised to include the language of claim 1 from which it depended, recited:

> 7. A method for screening germline of a human subject for an alteration of a BRCA1 gene which comprises comparing germline sequence of a BRCA1 gene or BRCA1 RNA from a tissue sample from said subject or a sequence of BRCA1 cDNA made from mRNA from said sample with germline sequences of wild-type BRCA1 gene, wild-type BRCA1 RNA or wild-type BRCA1 cDNA, wherein a difference in the sequence of the BRCA1 gene, BRCA1 RNA or BRCA1 cDNA of the subject from wild-type indicates an alteration in the BRCA1 gene in said subject[,]
>
> wherein a germline nucleic acid sequence is compared by hybridizing a BRCA1 gene probe which specifically hybridizes to a BRCA1 allele to genomic DNA isolated from said sample and detecting the presence of a hybridization product wherein a presence of said product indicates the presence of said allele in the subject.[541]

Accused infringer Ambry had argued that the Federal Circuit should apply the Supreme Court's 2012 decision in *Mayo Collab. Servs. v. Prometheus Labs., Inc.*,[542] discussed *supra*,[543] to resolve the case at bar. Ambry contended that *Mayo* was directly on point because Myriad's method claims simply identified "laws of nature"—here, the precise sequence of the BRCA genes and comparisons of the wild-type BRCA genes and certain mutations of the gene sequences found in the patient—and applied conventional techniques.[544] The

[541]*Myriad VI*, 774 F.3d at 761. The "allele"s recited in Myriad's process claim 7 refer to "alternative possibilities for the size and frequency" of repeated DNA sequences scattered throughout the human genome, known in turn as "short tandem repeats" (STRs), which are shared among all people. *See* Maryland v. King, 133 S. Ct. 1958, 1967 (2013). "Alleles are responsible for 'polymorphism,' or genetic differences between individuals." Promega Corp. v. Life Techs. Corp., 773 F.3d 1338, 1341 (Fed. Cir. 2014).

Myriad's other method claim on appeal recited:

> 8. A method for screening germline of a human subject for an alteration of a BRCA1 gene which comprises comparing germline sequence of a BRCA1 gene or BRCA1 RNA from a tissue sample from said subject or a sequence of BRCA1 cDNA made from mRNA from said sample with germline sequences of wild-type BRCA1 gene, wild-type BRCA1 RNA or wild-type BRCA1 cDNA, wherein a difference in the sequence of the BRCA1 gene, BRCA1 RNA or BRCA1 cDNA of the subject from wild-type indicates an alteration in the BRCA1 gene in said subject[,]
>
> wherein a germline nucleic acid sequence is compared by amplifying all or part of a BRCA1 gene from said sample using a set of primers to produce amplified nucleic acids and sequencing the amplified nucleic acids.

Myriad VI, 774 F.3d at 761-762 (revised to include the language of claim 1, from which claim 8 depended).

[542]132 S. Ct. 1289 (2012).

[543]*See supra* Section B.4.c and Section B.5.a.

[544]*Myriad VI*, 774 F.3d at 762.

Federal Circuit in *Myriad VI* chose not to decide whether *Mayo* was directly on point, however, because Myriad's method claims "suffer[ed] from a separate infirmity: they recite[d] abstract ideas."[545] Thus, the appellate court resolved the method claim part of *Myriad VI* by applying the "abstract idea" analysis of the Supreme Court's 2014 decision in *Alice Corp. v. CLS Bank,* discussed *supra,*[546] rather than by determining whether Myriad's method claims were directed to unpatentable "laws of nature" under *Mayo.*

The Federal Circuit first observed that the above-quoted method claims 7 and 8 depended from claim 1 of Myriad's '441 patent. The first paragraph of each of claims 7 and 8 repeated the language of independent claim 1, describing a step of comparing wild-type genetic sequences with a test subject's genetic sequence. The Circuit explained that the first paragraph comparison step of claims 7 and 8 should be analyzed in accordance with the first step of the Supreme Court's two-step analysis in *Alice Corp.*[547]

Step one of the *Alice Corp.* analysis determines whether the claims at issue are directed to a patent-ineligible concept such as an abstract idea. In its 2012 *Myriad III* decision, the Circuit had already determined that claim 1 of the '441 patent (i.e., repeated as the first paragraphs of dependent claims 7 and 8 of the '441 patent in *Myriad VI*) was directed to a patent-ineligible abstract idea.[548] Accordingly,

[545]*Myriad VI*, 774 F.3d at 762.

[546]134 S. Ct. 2347 (2014). *Alice Corp.* is analyzed *supra* Section B.4.d. In summary, the *Alice Corp.* Court identified the following two-step framework for determining patent eligible subject matter, based on its 2012 decision in *Mayo*:

> In *Mayo Collaborative Services v. Prometheus Laboratories, Inc.*, 566 U.S. _____, 132 S. Ct. 1289, 182 L. Ed. 2d 321 (2012), we set forth a framework for distinguishing patents that claim laws of nature, natural phenomena, and abstract ideas from those that claim patent-eligible applications of those concepts. First, we determine whether the claims at issue are directed to one of those patent-ineligible concepts. *Id.*, at _____, 132 S. Ct., at 1296-1297. If so, we then ask, "[w]hat else is there in the claims before us?" *Id.*, at _____, 132 S. Ct., at 1297. To answer that question, we consider the elements of each claim both individually and "as an ordered combination" to determine whether the additional elements "transform the nature of the claim" into a patent-eligible application. *Id.*, at _____, 132 S. Ct., at 1298, 1297. We have described step two of this analysis as a search for an "'inventive concept'"—i.e., an element or combination of elements that is "sufficient to ensure that the patent in practice amounts to significantly more than a patent upon the [ineligible concept] itself." *Id.*, at _____, 132 S. Ct., at 1294. . . .

Alice Corp., 134 S. Ct. at 2355 (closing footnote omitted).

[547]*Myriad VI*, 774 F.3d at 763 (stating that "the first paragraphs of claims 7 and 8, which describe the comparison of wild-type genetic sequences with the subject's genetic sequence[,] correspond to the first step of *Alice* . . .").

[548]*See* Ass'n for Molecular Pathology v. U.S. Patent & Trademark Office, 689 F.3d 1303, 1333-1335 (Fed. Cir. Aug. 16, 2012) ("*Myriad III*") (holding claims 1 of Myriad's '999 patent, '001 patent, and '441 patent and claims 1 and 2 of Myriad's '857 patent

the Circuit now held that the "comparisons described in the first paragraphs of claim 7 and 8 are directed to the patent-ineligible abstract idea of comparing BRCA sequences and determining the existence of alterations."[549] Such determinations merely "compar[ed] the patient's gene with the wild-type and identifying any differences that arise."[550]

As a policy matter, the first paragraphs of claims 7 and 8 of Myriad's '441 patent raised the same "preemption" concerns identified by the Supreme Court in *Myriad IV*. Namely, because the number of covered comparisons included in the claims' scope was "unlimited,"[551] was not limited to the detection of risk of breast or ovarian cancer,[552] and covered "detection of yet-undiscovered alterations,"[553] "allowing a patent on the comparison step could impede a great swath of research relating to the BRCA genes. . . ."[554] In short, the first paragraphs of claims 7 and 8 of Myriad's '441 patent were directed to "basic building blocks of scientific research" that should not be monopolized.[555]

Turning to application of the second step in the *Alice Corp.* analysis, the Federal Circuit in *Myriad VI* asked what more was recited in Myriad's method claims 7 and 8 beyond the patent-ineligible abstract idea of comparing BRCA sequences and determining the existence of alterations. The *Alice Corp.* decision required that to take claims reciting an abstract idea into the realm of patent eligibility, the remainder of the claims has to provide a "further inventive concept."[556] In Myriad's method claims 7 and 8, the second paragraph of each claim (i.e., the "wherein" clause of each claim) recited the particular mechanism for the comparisons required in the first paragraph. As the Circuit explained, the second paragraph of each claim "describes the way in which the [gene] sequences are compared."[557] In claim 7, the "wherein" clause mandated that the sequences are compared by

---

invalid under 35 U.S.C. §101 for claiming patent-ineligible processes), *aff'd in part, rev'd in part sub nom.* Ass'n for Molecular Pathology v. Myriad Genetics, Inc., 133 S. Ct. 2107 (2013).

[549] *Myriad VI*, 774 F.3d at 763.

[550] *Myriad VI*, 774 F.3d at 763.

[551] *Myriad VI*, 774 F.3d at 763.

[552] *Myriad VI*, 774 F.3d at 764.

[553] *Myriad VI*, 774 F.3d at 763.

[554] *Myriad VI*, 774 F.3d at 764. Of course, the issue before the Circuit in *Myriad VI* was not whether "allowing a patent on the comparison step" was proper; rather, the issue was whether method claims 7 and 8 *as a whole* recited patent-eligible inventions.

[555] *Myriad VI*, 774 F.3d at 764 (citing *Myriad IV*, 133 S. Ct. at 2116; Gottschalk v. Benson, 409 U.S. 63, 64 (1972)).

[556] *Alice Corp.*, 134 S. Ct. at 2355 (stating that "[w]e have described step two of this analysis as a search for an " 'inventive concept' " — i.e., an element or combination of elements that is " 'sufficient to ensure that the patent in practice amounts to significantly more than a patent upon the [ineligible concept] itself' ") (quoting *Mayo*, 132 S. Ct. at 1294).

[557] *Myriad VI*, 774 F.3d at 764.

(1) hybridizing a BRCA gene probe and (2) detecting the presence of a hybridization product. In claim 8, the "wherein" clause required (1) amplification of the BRCA1 gene and (2) sequencing of the amplified nucleic acids.[558]

The Federal Circuit concluded that these second-paragraph "non-patent-ineligible" elements of claims 7 and 8, viewed either in isolation or combination, did not add "enough" to make the claims patent eligible as a whole.[559] Rather, these elements were merely well understood, routine, and conventional activities when Myriad filed its patent applications. The second-paragraph "wherein" clauses simply "spell[ed] out what practitioners already knew — how to compare gene sequences using routine, ordinary techniques."[560] Accordingly, the Federal Circuit in *Myriad VI* held that the appealed claims were "directed to ineligible subject matter in violation of 35 U.S.C. §101," affirmed the district court's denial of Myriad's motion for a preliminary injunction, and remanded the case to the district court.[561]

c. *Spontaneously-Generated Compositions*

Is an otherwise patentable composition of matter an unpatentable product of nature when it is capable of being generated by the spontaneous transformation of a different chemical composition? Although there is no binding precedent on the question, at least one member of the Federal Circuit would answer affirmatively. Claim 1 of the patent in suit in *SmithKline Beecham Corp. v. Apotex Corp.*[562] recited in its entirety "crystalline paroxetine hydrochloride hemihydrate." Accused

[558]*Myriad VI*, 774 F.3d at 764.

[559]*Myriad VI*, 774 F.3d at 764.

[560]*Myriad VI*, 774 F.3d at 764. Nor was the appellate court persuaded by Myriad's argument that its claims 7 and 8 were similar to claim 21 of the '441 patent, which Circuit Judge Bryson had suggested was patent eligible in his separate opinion in the Circuit's 2012 *Myriad III* decision. *See Myriad VI,* 774 F.3d at 765 (citing *Myriad III*, 689 F.3d at 1349). First, claim 21 was not on appeal in *Myriad VI*. Second, even assuming *arguendo* the patent eligibility of claim 21, it was "qualitatively different" from the claims 7 and 8 on appeal:

> Claim 21 claims a method of detecting alterations in which the alterations being detected are expressly identified in the specification by tables 11 and 12.... These tables expressly identify ten predisposing mutations of the BRCA1 gene sequence discovered by the patentees.... Thus, the detection in claim 21 is limited to the particular mutations the inventors discovered: detecting ten specific mutations from the wild-type, identified as "[p]redisposing [m]utations," for the specific purpose of identifying increased susceptibility to specific cancers.... Claims 7 and 8 are significantly broader and more abstract, as they claim all comparisons between the patient's BRCA genes and the wild-type BRCA genes....

Myriad VI, 774 F.3d at 765 (footnote and citations omitted).

[561]*Myriad VI*, 774 F.3d at 765.

[562]403 F.3d 1331 (Fed. Cir. 2005).

infringer Apotex's manufacture of the prior art product paroxetine hydrochloride (PHC) *anhydrate* resulted in the spontaneous production of trace amounts of the PHC *hemihydrate* patented by SmithKline.[563] Because the Federal Circuit interpreted claim 1 to embrace PHC hemihydrate without further limitation (i.e., to cover PHC hemihydrate in any amount, whether or not commercially significant), Apotex infringed whether it intended to or not. Apotex escaped infringement liability, however, because the Federal Circuit majority invalidated claim 1 of SmithKline's patent on grounds of inherent anticipation under 35 U.S.C. §102(b) (2000).[564]

In a concurring opinion, Federal Circuit Judge Gajarsa wrote that claim 1 should instead have been invalidated for failure to recite statutory subject matter within 35 U.S.C. §101. He took the position that "patent claims drawn broadly enough to encompass products that spread, appear, and 'reproduce' through natural processes cover subject matter unpatentable under Section 101 — and are therefore invalid."[565] The patent law does not sanction the notion of "inevitable infringement," Judge Gajarsa noted. In future cases of this sort, "[i]nventors wishing to claim products that can either be synthesized in laboratories or generated by natural processes may protect themselves by incorporating negative limitation terms like 'non-natural' or 'non-human' into the claims that they submit for examination."[566]

3. Life Forms

a. *Foundation:* Diamond v. Chakrabarty *(U.S. 1980)*

In *Diamond v. Chakrabarty,*[567] the U.S. Supreme Court confronted what was probably the most controversial issue of patent law to ever reach it: whether living subject matter, such as a genetically engineered organism, is patentable subject matter under 35 U.S.C. §101. Ananda Chakrabarty, then a researcher for General Electric, developed a bacterium that was intended to consume petroleum spills. Chakrabarty

[563]As explained by the *SmithKline* court, "PHC anhydrate comprises crystals of PHC without bound water molecules. PHC hemihydrate comprises PHC crystals with one bound water molecule for every two PHC molecules. PHC hemihydrate proved more stable, and thus more easily packaged and preserved, than PHC anhydrate." *Id.* at 1334.

[564]*See id.* at 1342-1346. Inherent anticipation is further discussed in Section D of Chapter 4 ("Novelty, Loss of Right, and Priority Pre- and Post-America Invents Act of 2011 (35 U.S.C. §102)"), *supra.*

[565]*Id.* at 1361 (Gajarsa, J., concurring in the judgment).

[566]*Id.* at 1363.

[567]447 U.S. 303 (1980).

custom-designed its genetic material such that the bacterium would digest a variety of different petroleum components, a property that unmodified bacteria found in nature did not possess. The USPTO rejected certain of Chakrabarty's claims as directed to subject matter that was living, which the agency viewed as something that §101 was not intended to cover.

The Federal Circuit's predecessor court, the Court of Customs and Patent Appeals (CCPA) reversed the agency's rejection, emphasizing that the issue was not whether the claimed bacterium was living or inanimate, but whether it constituted an invention made by human intervention. In the court's view, the fact that Chakrabarty's bacterium was alive was "without legal significance."[568]

In a landmark 5-4 decision, the U.S. Supreme Court affirmed the CCPA's decision in *Chakrabarty*. Chakrabarty's bacterium was "not nature's handiwork," the Court reasoned, "but his own."[569] The Court relied on the choice by the drafters of the first U.S. patent statute, the Act of 1790, to use very broad, general terminology (i.e., "any," "composition of matter," or "manufacture"), which had scarcely changed in the ensuing 200 years. This selection of broad language suggested that the drafters' goal was to stimulate innovation in a wide variety of then-unknown technologies and scientific fields, a goal that would be frustrated if Congress were repeatedly required to amend the statute so as to explicitly delineate new categories of patentable inventions. Moreover, the Court observed, the legislative history of the 1952 Patent Act states that patentable subject matter includes "anything under the sun that is made by man."[570] To place a narrow interpretation on §101 would be diametrically opposed to this expansive legislative history and to the general notion that the patent system encourages the creation of new, previously unforeseen inventions.

Rather than directly responding to the many ethical and moral criticisms of "patenting life" that the case invoked from many corners, the Supreme Court in *Chakrabarty* refused to engage in speculation about the "gruesome parade of horribles" presented by various *amici*.[571] The Court insisted that it lacked the institutional competence required to take on the complex, public policy-based issues raised by the patenting

[568]*Id.* at 306.

[569]*Id.* at 310.

[570]*Id.* at 309 (quoting S. REP. No. 82-1979, at 5 (1952); H.R. REP. No. 82-1923, at 6 (1952)).

[571]*See id.* at 316 (noting arguments by Nobel laureate scientists and others that "genetic research may pose a serious threat to the human race, or, at the very least, that the dangers are far too substantial to permit such research to proceed apace at this time" and that "genetic research and related technological developments may spread pollution and disease, that it may result in a loss of genetic diversity, and that its practice may tend to depreciate the value of human life").

of life forms; this was the realm of Congress and the legislative branch, not the judiciary.

b. Multicellular Organisms

In the aftermath of the Supreme Court's *Chakrabarty* decision, the U.S. biotechnology industry flourished. Today, the United States is a world leader in biotechnology-based research, development, and product introduction, and the availability of patent protection has much to do with this.[572] Numerous U.S. patents have been granted on human-made higher life forms such as transgenic mice, fish, and cows.[573]

[572]*See generally* Jasemine Chambers, *Patent Eligibility of Biotechnological Inventions in the United States, Europe, and Japan: How Much Patent Policy Is Public Policy?*, 34 GEO. WASH. INT'L L. REV. 223 (2002) (emphasizing importance of patenting to U.S. biotechnology industry).

[573]Europe has been far less welcoming toward the patenting of life forms. For example, the transgenic "onco-mouse" developed by Harvard University researchers to have susceptibility to cancer was granted patent protection in the United States in 1988. *See* Transgenic Non-Human Mammals, U.S. Pat. No. 4,736,866. The counterpart application in Europe was not allowed until 1992. *See* In Re President and Fellows of Harvard College, 1992 O.J. EUR. PAT. OFF. 588, *available at* http://archive.epo.org/epo/pubs/oj1992/p557_615.pdf (decision of Examining Division granting European Pat. No. 0 169 672) [hereinafter *Onco-mouse / Harvard*]. Numerous opposition proceedings were thereafter instituted in the European Patent Office (EPO) against the onco-mouse patent. *See generally* Cynthia M. Ho, *Splicing Morality and Patent Law: Issues Arising from Mixing Mice and Men*, 2 WASH. U. J.L. & POL'Y 247, 257-261 (2000).

A central aspect of the debate concerned whether the granting of a European patent on the Harvard onco-mouse would violate Art. 53(a) of the European Patent Convention. That provision states that European patents shall not be granted in respect of "inventions the commercial exploitation of which would be contrary to '*ordre public*' or morality; such exploitation shall not be deemed to be so contrary merely because it is prohibited by law or regulation in some or all of the Contracting States." European Patent Convention art. 53(a) (14th ed. 2010), *available at* http://www.epo.org/law-practice/legal-texts/html/epc/2010/e/ar53.html. (The French phrase *ordre public* loosely translates as public policy or public interest.)

In its deliberations the EPO Examining Division considered whether the societal benefit of the invention as a new and improved human anticancer treatment justified the suffering that would be inflicted on the transgenically manipulated mice and the potential risk to the environment in terms of uncontrolled dissemination of unwanted genes. The Examining Division determined that the potential benefits of the invention outweighed the costs, concluding that

> the present invention cannot be considered immoral or contrary to public order. The provision of a type of test animal useful in cancer research and giving rise to a reduction in the amount of testing on animals together with a low risk connected with the handling of the animals by qualified staff can generally be regarded as beneficial to mankind. A patent should therefore not be denied for the present invention on the ground of Article 53(a) EPC.

Onco-mouse / Harvard, at 593 §(v).

Although the USPTO views multicellular organisms as potentially patentable subject matter,[574] it has set one important limit: the agency will not grant patents on human beings per se. The USPTO takes the position that "[i]f the broadest reasonable interpretation of the claimed invention as a whole encompasses a human organism, then a rejection under 35 U.S.C. 101 and AIA sec. 33(a) must be made indicating that the claimed invention is directed to a human organism and is therefore nonstatutory subject matter. . . ."[575]

c. Clones

In 1996, researchers Campbell and Wilmut of the Roslin Institute of Edinburgh, Scotland ("Roslin") successfully produced the famous sheep Dolly,[576] the first mammal ever cloned from an adult somatic cell.[577] Campbell and Wilmut obtained a U.S. patent on their somatic method of cloning mammals.[578] They also filed a patent application claiming the clones themselves — U.S. Patent Application No. 09/225,233 ('233 application).[579] Representative claims of the '233 application recited:

> 155. A live-born clone of a pre-existing, non-embryonic, donor mammal, wherein the mammal is selected from cattle, sheep, pigs, and goats.
>
> 164. The clone of any of claims 155-159, wherein the donor mammal is non-foetal.

The USPTO Patent Trial and Appeal Board (PTAB) in 2013 affirmed an examiner's rejection that the '233 application claims were

[574]*See* Animal Legal Defense Fund v. Quigg, 932 F.2d 920, 923 (Fed. Cir. 1991) (announcing that "the Patent and Trademark Office is now examining claims directed to multicellular living organisms, including animals" and that "[t]o the extent that the claimed subject matter is directed to a non-human 'nonnaturally occurring manufacture or composition of matter — a product of human ingenuity' (*Diamond v. Chakrabarty*), such claims will not be rejected under 35 U.S.C. §101 as being directed to nonstatutory subject matter") (quoting USPTO, 1077 Off. Gaz. Pat. & Trademark Office 24 (1987)).

[575]United States Patent and Trademark Office, Manual of Patent Examining Procedure §2105 (9th ed., rev. Jan. 2018) referenced "AIA sec. 33(a)" is Leahy-Smith America Invents Act (AIA), Public Law 112-29, §33(a), 125 Stat. 284 (providing that "[n]otwithstanding any other provision of law, no patent may issue on a claim directed to or encompassing a human organism").

[576]*See generally* University of Edinburgh, Roslin Institute, *Dolly the Sheep* (Apr. 7, 2015), http://www.roslin.ed.ac.uk/public-interest/dolly-the-sheep.

[577]In re Roslin Institute (Edinburgh), 750 F.3d 1333, 1334 (Fed. Cir. 2014) (hereafter "*Roslin*"). A somatic cell is any body cell other than gametes (egg or sperm).

[578]*See* U.S. Patent No. 7,514,258 (issued Apr. 7, 2009), assigned to the Roslin Institute.

[579]The '233 application was filed Jan. 4, 1999, claiming priority as a division of application Ser. No. 08/802,282, filed Feb. 19, 1997 (now U.S. Pat. No. 6,147,276), which is a continuation of PCT/GB 96/02099, filed Aug. 30, 1996. *See* U.S. Pat. No. 7,514,258.

ineligible for patent protection under 35 U.S.C. §101 because the claimed invention constituted "a natural phenomenon that did not possess 'markedly different characteristics than any found in nature.'"[580]

In 2014, the Federal Circuit affirmed the USPTO's §101 rejection in *In re Roslin Institute (Edinburgh)* ("*Roslin*").[581] The appellate court first observed that "discoveries that possess 'markedly different characteristics from any found in nature,'... are eligible for patent protection[, but] [i]n contrast, any existing organism or newly discovered plant found in the wild is not patentable."[582] It then rejected Roslin's arguments that the claimed clones were eligible for patenting as §101 compositions of matter or manufactures because they were the handiwork of humans rather than nature. The Circuit explained in *Roslin* that "Dolly herself is an exact genetic replica of another sheep and does not possess 'markedly different characteristics from any [farm animals] found in nature.'"[583] In short, "Dolly's genetic identity to her donor parent renders her unpatentable."[584]

The Federal Circuit also rejected the remainder of Roslin's arguments. First, the "phenotypic differences" (e.g., observable characteristics such as shape, size, color, and behavior) stemming from "environmental factors" that distinguished the clones from their donor mammals did not confer patent eligibility. These differences were not claimed (or recited in the claims), and any such differences were admittedly not the result of any effort by the Roslin inventors.[585] Nor did differences in mitochondrial DNA, which originates from the donor oocyte (i.e., a female egg cell prior to maturation) rather than the donor nucleus, confer patentability. Again, the Circuit observed that any such differences in mitochondrial DNA were unclaimed; rather, the clones were "defined in terms of the identity of their nuclear DNA to that of the donor mammals."[586] Nor had Roslin "identif[ied]

[580]*Roslin*, 750 F.3d at 1335 (quoting PTAB decision). The PTAB also affirmed the examiner's finding that the claimed subject matter was anticipated by and obvious in light of the relevant prior art under 35 U.S.C. §102 and §103. The Federal Circuit in *Roslin* did not reach these grounds.

[581]750 F.3d 1333 (Fed. Cir. 2014). Judge Dyk authored the opinion in *Roslin*, joined by Judge Moore and Judge Wallach.

[582]*Roslin*, 750 F.3d at 1336 (quoting Diamond v. Chakrabarty, 447 U.S. 303, 309 (1980); citing also In re Beineke, 690 F.3d 1344, 1352 (Fed. Cir. 2012) (Dyk, J.) (holding that a newly discovered type of plant is not eligible for plant patent protection, in part, because such a plant was not "in any way the result of [the patent applicant's] creative efforts or indeed anyone's creative efforts")).

[583]*Roslin*, 750 F.3d at 1337 (quoting *Chakrabarty*, 447 U.S. at 310; citing also Applicants' Reply Br. 13 (stating that "the clones are genetic copies")).

[584]*Roslin*, 750 F.3d at 1337.

[585]*Roslin*, 750 F.3d at 1338.

[586]*Roslin*, 750 F.3d at 1339. The Circuit included the proviso that "[t]o be clear, having the same nuclear DNA as the donor mammal may not necessarily result in patent

how differences in mitochondrial DNA influence or could influence the characteristics of cloned mammals."[587] Lastly, Roslin's argument that the claimed clones were different from their donors because they were "time delayed versions" of the donors "cannot confer patentability."[588] As the PTAB had noted, the time-delayed characteristic would be true to any copy of an original.[589]

E. Section 101 Manufactures

A manufacture in patent law parlance is something of a catch-all category for those inventions that are human-made but do not neatly fall into the other three categories of 35 U.S.C. §101. A manufacture is generally thought of as a human-made item without moving parts, in contrast to a machine. In *Chakrabarty,* the Supreme Court "read the term 'manufacture' in §101 in accordance with its dictionary definition to mean 'the production of articles for use from raw or prepared materials by giving to these materials new forms, qualities, properties, or combinations, whether by hand-labor or by machinery.'"[590]

Recent attempts to obtain patent protection for claims in the electronic arts that recite software on a storage medium, electrical signals, and "device profiles" generally have not succeeded. Not surprisingly, a great deal depends on the manner in which such claims are drafted. The Federal Circuit's treatment of each of these controversial categories is examined below.

1. Computer Media Claims

When claiming software-implemented inventions, patent drafters at one time routinely attempted to satisfy §101 by claiming the software embodied in a particular "computer usable medium" such as a disk. The intent was to recite a potentially patentable manufacture within the meaning of 35 U.S.C. §101. Such claims were referred to

---

ineligibility in every case," but concluded that in the case at bar, "the claims do not describe [sic, recite] clones that have markedly different characteristics from the donor animals of which they are copies." *Roslin*, 750 F.3d at 1339.

[587]*Roslin*, 750 F.3d at 1338.

[588]*Roslin*, 750 F.3d at 1339.

[589]*Roslin*, 750 F.3d at 1339.

[590]Diamond v. Chakrabarty, 447 U.S. 303, 308 (1980) (quoting Am. Fruit Growers, Inc. v. Brogdex Co., 283 U.S. 1, 11 (1931)).

as "*Beauregard* claims." In *In re Beauregard,* the applicant sought allowance of the following claim to object code on a floppy disk:[591]

> 1. An article of manufacture comprising:
> a computer usable medium having computer readable program code means embodied therein for causing a polygon having a boundary definable by a plurality of selectable pels on a graphics display to be filled, the computer readable program code means in said article of manufacture comprising:
> computer readable program code means for causing a computer to effect, with respect to one boundary line at a time, a sequential traverse of said plurality of selectable pels of each respective said boundary line;
> computer readable program code means for causing the computer to store in an array during said traverse a value of an outer pel of said boundary of said plurality of selectable pels for each one of a plurality of scan lines of said polygon; and
> computer readable program code means for causing the computer to draw a fill line, after said traverse, between said outer pels having said stored values, for each said one of said scan lines.

After the USPTO initially rejected this claim as unpatentable under the "printed matter doctrine,"[592] Beauregard appealed. Before the Federal Circuit heard oral argument in the case, however, the USPTO changed its policy. The agency withdrew its rejection and told the court that "computer programs embodied in a tangible medium, such as floppy diskettes, are patentable subject matter under 35 U.S.C. §101 and must be examined under 35 U.S.C. §§102 and 103."[593] The agency agreed with Beauregard that the printed matter doctrine was therefore inapplicable.

[591]*See* In re Beauregard, 53 F.3d 1583 (Fed. Cir. 1995); U.S. Patent No. 5,710,578 (issued Jan. 20, 1998). For background on the now largely obsolete floppy disk, *see* IBM100, *Icons of Progress: The Floppy Disk* (2011), http://www-03.ibm.com/ibm/ history/ibm100/us/en/icons/floppy (explaining that "The floppy disk was once ubiquitous. More than five billion were sold per year worldwide at its peak in the mid-1990s. Now, the little plastic packages are a fast-fading memory. It has been widely reported that Sony, the last major floppy disk maker, will stop producing them in major markets this year. Today, the disks can be found mainly in the dusty bottoms of desk drawers and filing cabinets. Yet the floppy disk will go down as a singular advance in computing history. Floppies helped enable the PC revolution and the emergence of an independent software industry that now includes more than 10,000 companies.").

[592]The printed matter rejection originated with pre-1952 Act decisions of the CCPA, which declared that "the mere arrangement of printed matter on a sheet or sheets of paper does not constitute patentable subject matter." In re Sterling, 70 F.2d 910, 912 (C.C.P.A. 1934). More recently, the Federal Circuit considered "printed matter" in the context of a §103 obviousness challenge (§101 was not at issue) and stated that "[w]here the printed matter is not functionally related to the substrate, the printed matter will not distinguish the invention from the prior art in terms of patentability." In re Gulack, 703 F.2d 1381, 1385 (Fed. Cir. 1983).

[593]*Beauregard*, 53 F.3d at 1583.

Because it no longer had a case or controversy before it, the Federal Circuit did not decide the issue. It appeared that the Circuit approved these types of claims, however, for it had sustained the patentability (albeit under §103) of related types of manufactures such as a computer "memory" that stored a "data structure."[594]

More than 15 years after dismissing the appeal in *In re Beauregard* without deciding its merits, the Federal Circuit in 2011 issued a decision in *Cybersource Corp. v. Retail Decisions, Inc.*[595] that called the legitimacy of some *Beauregard* claims into serious question. The appellate court reasoned in *Cybersource* that if a claimed method was not patent eligible because it was merely an abstract idea under the Supreme Court's decision in *Bilski v. Kappos*,[596] then a *Beauregard*-type claim to a "computer-readable medium" containing computer program instructions to carry out the method was likewise not patent eligible. The Federal Circuit in *Cybersource* emphasized that courts should look to the nature of the underlying invention, not the literal terminology of the claim at issue.

Despite the Circuit's ruling in *Cybersource*, any notion that software is not patentable is no longer accurate, at least in the United

[594]*See* In re Lowry, 32 F.3d 1579, 1581 (Fed. Cir. 1994). The applicant in *Lowry* presented the following claim, which the Federal Circuit upheld as patentable in the face of a §103 obviousness challenge:

> 1. A memory for storing data for access by an application program being executed on a data processing system, comprising:
>
> a data structure stored in said memory, said data structure including information resident in a database used by said application program and including: a plurality of attribute data objects stored in said memory, each of said attribute data objects containing different information from said database; a single holder attribute data object for each of said attribute data objects, each of said holder attribute data objects being one of said plurality of attribute data objects, a being-held relationship existing between each attribute data object and its holder attribute data object, and each of said attribute data objects having a being-held relationship with only a single other attribute data object, thereby establishing a hierarchy of said plurality of attribute data objects; a referent attribute data object for at least one of said attribute data objects, said referent attribute data object being nonhierarchically related to a holder attribute data object for the same at least one of said attribute data objects and also being one of said plurality of attribute data objects, attribute data objects for which there exist only holder attribute data objects being called element data objects, and attribute data objects for which there also exist referent attribute data objects being called relation data objects; and an apex data object stored in said memory and having no being-held relationship with any of said attribute data objects, however, at least one of said attribute data objects having a being-held relationship with said apex data object.

[595]654 F.3d 1366 (Fed. Cir. 2011).
[596]130 S. Ct. 3218 (2010).

States.[597] An unapplied mathematical algorithm is not potentially patentable subject matter within §101, but the physical embodiment of that algorithm on a floppy disk, claimed as a manufacture, is considered potentially patentable by the USPTO. As is the case with claims to business methods discussed above, the most difficult challenge for such patents is whether the claimed software inventions are novel and nonobvious, rather than their threshold qualification within 35 U.S.C. §101.

2. Electrical Signals

Does an electronic signal qualify as a potentially patentable "manufacture" under §101? The Federal Circuit held (by 2-1 vote) in *In re Nuijten* that claims covering "transitory electrical and electromagnetic signals propagating through some medium, such as wires,

[597]European attitudes toward the patentability of computer software have not been as welcoming as those of the United States. The European Patent Convention (EPC) excludes from patentability "programs for computers... as such." EPC arts. 52(2)(c), 52(3).

Patentability of software-related inventions in the EPO turns on whether the invention supplies a "technical effect." As explained in the EPO's *How to Get* a *European Patent: Guide for Applicants* 3.2.002 (April 2019), *available at* http://documents.epo.org/projects/babylon/eponet.nsf/0/8266ED0366190630C12575E10051F40E/$File/how_to_get_a_european_patent_2019_en.pdf,

> programs for computers... are not regarded as inventions if claimed as such. However, a computer program is not excluded from patentability under Article 52 if, when running on a computer, it causes a further technical effect going beyond the "normal" physical interaction between the program (software) and the computer (hardware). An example of a further technical effect is where the program serves to control a technical process or governs the operation of a technical device. The internal functioning of the computer itself under the influence of the program could also bring about such an effect.
>
> If the computer program itself is not excluded, it is immaterial whether the program is claimed by itself, as a data medium storing the program, as a method or as part of a computer system.
>
> Thus computer programs are not automatically excluded from patentability....

A leading case on software patentability in Europe is *In re Vicom*, 1987 O.J. Eur. Pat. Off. 14 (EPO Decision T0208/84-3.5.1). In *Vicom* the EPO Board of Appeals upheld the patentability of "[a] method of digitally processing images in the form of a two-dimensional data array...," which made use of a mathematical method incorporated in a computer program run on a computer to do the processing. The claimed method was held not to be excluded from patentability because it constituted a technical process that was carried out on a physical entity. This entity could include an image stored as an electric signal. Thus the method was neither a mathematical method as such nor a computer program as such under EPC art. 52. *See* In re International Business Machines Corp., 1999 O.J. Eur. Pat. Off. 609 (EPO Decision T 1173/97-3.5.1) (discussing *Vicom*).

air, or a vacuum" are *not* §101 patentable subject matter.[598] More particularly, Nuijten's electronic signal claims did not qualify as §101 "manufacture[s]."[599]

When a signal such as a digital audio file is watermarked to protect the file against unauthorized copying, encoding the additional watermark data into the signal introduces some degree of distortion. Nuijten's patent application disclosed a technique for reducing this distortion. In addition to claiming his invention as a process, Nuijten claimed the watermarked signal itself. Claim 14 of Nuijten's application recited:

> A signal with embedded supplemental data, the signal being encoded in accordance with a given encoding process and selected samples of the signal representing the supplemental data, and at least one of the samples preceding the selected samples is different from the sample corresponding to the given encoding process.[600]

The claimed signal was admittedly human-made subject matter, because it was "encoded, generated, and transmitted by artificial means."[601] However, such artificiality is not alone sufficient to render something a §101 manufacture, the Federal Circuit held. The *Nuijten* majority specified that a manufacture must be a "tangible article[] or commodit[y]."[602] In the majority's view, an electronic signal or transmission that is transient does not qualify as a manufacture. "[E]nergy embodying the claimed signal is fleeting and is devoid of any semblance of permanence during transmission."[603] Moreover, the fact that electronic signals, which involve photons traveling at the speed of light, behave in some ways like particles, "does not make them tangible articles."[604]

Dissenting Judge Linn contended that "manufacture" should not be limited to tangible or nontransitory inventions. He observed that an invention should qualify if it lasts long enough to be useful, citing precedent holding that " 'transitory, unstable, and non-isolatable' "

[598] 500 F.3d 1346, 1352 (Fed. Cir. 2007).

[599] *See Nuijten*, 500 F.3d at 1357 (holding that Nuijten's signals, standing alone, were not "manufacture[s]" within the meaning of §101). *See also* In re Bilski, 545 F.3d 943, 951 n.2 (Fed. Cir. 2008) (*en banc*) (declining to discuss *Nuijten* because primary issue in that case was whether an electronic signal qualified as a §101 "manufacture," whereas issue facing *en banc* court in *Bilski* was the scope of a §101 "process").

[600] *Nuijten*, 500 F.3d at 1351.

[601] *Id.* at 1356.

[602] *Id.*

[603] *Id.* The court noted that, in contrast, a signal stored for later use would result in a "storage medium" containing the signal. Because the USPTO had allowed another of Nuijten's claims drawn to a storage medium, the §101 patentability of the storage medium claim was not before the Federal Circuit. *Id.* at 1356 n.6.

[604] *Id.* at 1357 n.8.

chemical intermediates are patentable.[605] Among other arguments for patentability of Nuijten's signal, Judge Linn pointed to the Supreme Court's venerable decision in *O'Reilly v. Morse,* which addressed the validity of a patent issued to the inventor of Morse code.[606] Although the Court in that case held invalid Morse's claim 8, for the use of "electromagnetism, however developed for marking or printing intelligible characters, signs, or letters, at any distances,"[607] it upheld the validity of Morse's claim 5. The latter claim, which covered the use of telegraphy to convey Morse code, recited a " 'system of signs, consisting of dots and spaces, and of dots, spaces, and horizontal lines, for numerals, letters, words, or sentences, substantially as herein set forth and illustrated, for telegraphic purposes.' "[608] Judge Linn concluded that Morse's claim 5 was "directed to a signal — a particular way of encoding information so that it can be conveyed . . . in a useful manner at a distance."[609] Both Morse's and Nuijten's signals were new and useful, in Judge Linn's view; both should be patentable.

3. Device Profiles

The Federal Circuit in 2014 relied on its earlier decision in *Nuijten* to hold in *Digitech Image Techs., LLC v. Elecs. for Imaging, Inc.*[610] that certain "device profile" claims did not recite patent-eligible subject matter within 35 U.S.C. §101. As explained below, the court interpreted the claims at issue as simply reciting non-tangible data. The Circuit concluded that "[d]ata in its ethereal, non-physical form is simply information that does not fall under any of the categories of eligible subject matter under section 101."[611]

Digitech's U.S. Patent No. 6,128,415 ('415 patent) was directed to the generation and use of an "improved device profile" that described spatial and color properties of a device within a digital image processing system.[612] The independent claims of the '415 patent recited:

[605] *See id.* at 1359 (Linn, J., dissenting-in-part) (quoting In re Breslow, 616 F.2d 516, 519, 521-522 (C.C.P.A. 1980)).

[606] 56 U.S. (15 How.) 62 (1853).

[607] *Nuijten*, 500 F.3d at 1368 (quoting *Morse*, 56 U.S. (15 How.) at 112).

[608] *Id.* at 1368-1369 (quoting *Morse*, 56 U.S. (15 How.) at 86).

[609] *Id.* at 1369.

[610] 758 F.3d 1344 (Fed. Cir. 2014) (Reyna, J.).

[611] *Digitech Image Techs.*, 758 F.3d at 1350.

[612] The Central District of California further explained the technology:

> A device profile describes the color and spatial properties of a device so that a processed image can be more accurately captured, transformed, or rendered, minimizing color and spatial distortions produced by an imaging device. Although past attempts to correct these image distortions are not new, they have been device dependent. The '415 Patent seeks to improve digital-imaging

> 1. A device profile for describing properties of a device in a digital image reproduction system to capture, transform or render an image, said device profile comprising:
>
> first data for describing a device dependent transformation of color information content of the image to a device independent color space; and
>
> second data for describing a device dependent transformation of spatial information content of the image in said device independent color space.
>
> * * *
>
> 26. A device profile for describing properties of a device in a digital image reproduction system to capture, transform or render an image, said device profile comprising data for describing a device dependent transformation of spatial information content of the image to a device independent color space, wherein through use of spatial stimuli and device response for said device, said data is represented by spatial characteristic functions.

Before the Federal Circuit, patentee Digitech argued that its claims were within §101 because the recited device profile was a tangible object. According to Digitech, that object represented an " 'integral part of the design and calibration of a processor device within a digital image processing system.' "[613]

The Federal Circuit disagreed, affirming a district court's grant of summary judgment of invalidity under §101. In the view of the district court and the Circuit, the claimed device profile was "not a tangible or physical thing and thus does not fall within any of the categories of eligible subject matter."[614] The Circuit explained that the device profile as claimed comprised two sets of data. These data described a device dependent transformation — one set of data for color information and the other set of data for spatial information. "The asserted claims are not directed to any tangible embodiment of this information (i.e., in physical memory or other medium) or claim any tangible part of the digital processing system." Rather, "[t]he claims [were] directed to information in its non-tangible form."[615]

The Circuit's 2007 decision in *Nuijten* supported its holding in *Digitech Image Techs.* The court in *Nuijten* had acknowledged that an electrical signal had physical properties with " 'tangible causes and effects.' " Nevertheless, it had concluded that " 'such transitory

---

> processing through use of device-independent device profiles by applying a device[-]independent paradigm for the spatial characterization.

Digitech Image Techs., LLC v. Elecs. for Imaging, Inc., No. 8:12-CV-1324-ODW, 2013 WL 3946579, at *1 (C.D. Cal. July 31, 2013) (citations to '415 patent omitted).

[613] *Digitech Image Techs.*, 758 F.3d at 1348 (quoting Digitech's brief on appeal).

[614] *Digitech Image Techs.*, 758 F.3d at 1349.

[615] *Digitech Image Techs.*, 758 F.3d at 1349.

embodiments are not directed to statutory subject matter.' "[616] The Circuit thus held in *Nuijten* that the physical embodiment of the supplemental data — the claimed "signal" — was not patent eligible.

The Circuit observed that the device profile claims before it in *Digitech Image Techs.* were even broader in scope than those in *Nuijten.* "While the claim in *Nuijten* require[d] supplemental data in the form of a [physical] transitory embodiment, the device profile claims of the '415 patent do not require any physical embodiment, much less a non-transitory one."[617] As claimed, Digitech's device profile was simply a patent-ineligible "collection of intangible color and spatial information."[618]

F. Nonpatentable Subject Matter

Unlike that of other countries,[619] U.S. patent law defines patentable subject matter *positively*, meaning that 35 U.S.C. §101 expresses what *is* patentable, but does not state what is *not.* In the U.S. patent framework, case law establishes the categories of subject matter that are excluded from patenting. These are categories form the "implicit exception" to §101 that the Supreme Court recognized in its 2012 *Mayo* decision.[620]

As elaborated previously in this chapter, judicial decisions have established that the following are *not* potentially patentable subject matter in the United States:

- laws of nature;[621]
- natural phenomena;[622]
- abstract ideas;
- unapplied mathematical algorithms;[623] and

[616] *Digitech Image Techs.*, 758 F.3d at 1350 (quoting *Nuijten*, 500 F.3d at 1353, 1357).

[617] *Digitech Image Techs.*, 758 F.3d at 1350.

[618] *Digitech Image Techs.*, 758 F.3d at 1350.

[619] *See, e.g.*, European Patent Convention art. 52(2) (16th ed. 2016), (stating that the following shall not be regarded as patentable inventions: "(a) discoveries, scientific theories and mathematical methods; (b) aesthetic creations; (c) schemes, rules and methods for performing mental acts, playing games or doing business, and programs for computers; and (d) presentations of information").

[620] *Mayo* is analyzed *supra* Section B.4.c and Section B.5.a.

[621] *See supra* Section B.5.a, discussing the Supreme Court's treatment of the "laws of nature" exception to §101 in *Mayo Collaborative Serv. v. Prometheus Labs., Inc.*, 132 S. Ct. 1289 (2012).

[622] *See supra* Section D.2.b.i, discussing the Supreme Court's treatment of the "product of nature" exception (which the Court interchangeably referred to as the "natural phenomena" or "naturally occurring phenomena" exception) as applied to genetic materials in *Ass'n for Molecular Pathology v. Myriad Genetics, Inc.*, 133 S. Ct. 2107 (2013).

[623] *See supra* Section B.3 ("Computer-Implemented Processes").

- products of nature.[624]

For example, the law of gravity, or fundamental laws of motion such as F (force) = M (mass) × A (acceleration), or the value of pi (approximately 3.14159), or the Pythagorean Theorem ($a^2 + b^2 = c^2$), or Einstein's special theory of relativity (expressed by the relationship $E = mc^2$), are not considered patentable. *Applications* of these fundamental laws and principles may be patentable if useful, novel, and nonobvious, but the underlying scientific truths are not. As the Supreme Court has explained, "[h]e who discovers a hitherto unknown phenomenon of nature has no claim to a monopoly of it which the law recognizes. If there is to be invention from such a discovery, it must come from the application of the law of nature to a new and useful end."[625]

Clearly the discovery of previously unrecognized scientific principles and fundamental laws of nature potentially bestows a great benefit on society. So why not reward the discoverers with patent protection, as an incentive for the discovery of even greater numbers of scientific principles and laws of nature? As a matter of public policy, U.S. law on this point reflects the determination that such fundamental building blocks of science and technology must be left in the public domain, free for all to use and build upon.

European patent lawyers view this as a dividing line between "discovering" and "inventing" and do not consider discoveries to be patentable.[626] This position is at least facially inconsistent with the Intellectual Property Clause of the U.S. Constitution, however. Recall that the Constitution speaks of giving inventors exclusive rights for limited times to "their discoveries."[627] Moreover, the U.S. Patent Act expressly defines "invention" as meaning "invention or discovery."[628]

G. Medical/Surgical Procedures

Medical and surgical procedures *are* patentable subject matter in the United States as "processes" within 35 U.S.C. §101.[629] In 1996,

[624]*See supra* Section D.2.b.i, discussing the Supreme Court's treatment of the "product of nature" exception as applied to genetic materials in *Ass'n for Molecular Pathology v. Myriad Genetics, Inc.*, 133 S. Ct. 2107 (2013).

[625]Funk Bros. Seed Co. v. Kalo Inoculant Co., 333 U.S. 127, 130 (1948).

[626]*See* European Patent Convention art. 52(2)(a) (16th ed. 2016), (stating that discoveries are not to be regarded as inventions).

[627]U.S. Const., art. I, §8, cl. 8.

[628]35 U.S.C. §100(a).

[629]This contrasts the views of many foreign countries, which categorically exclude methods of treatment of the human or animal body by surgery or therapy and diagnostic

however, Congress added an obscure provision to the Patent Act that renders some of these patents essentially null and void. The legislation created a remedies exclusion. Under 35 U.S.C. §287(c), a patent on certain medical or surgical procedures, as narrowly defined by the statute, cannot be enforced. The patentee has no remedy against direct or inducing infringement of such a patent because the provisions of 35 U.S.C. §281 (civil action for infringement), §283 (injunction), §284 (damages), and §285 (attorney fees) are not applicable.

This remedies exclusion came about when one U.S. medical doctor sued another for infringement of a patent on a surgical technique for a method of incision of the eye to implant an intraocular lens.[630] Chagrined members of the medical community lobbied Congress for an exclusion from patentability for medical and surgical procedures. In an eleventh-hour compromise, Congress passed a watered-down version of the legislation, codified at 35 U.S.C. §287(c), which does not prevent such procedures from being patented but deprives the patent owner of any remedy for infringement.[631] In practice, the "medical procedures" encompassed by the statute are so narrowly defined[632] that the legislation has had little more than a symbolic impact.

H. Patentable Subject Matter Beyond §101: Plant Patents and Design Patents

The large majority of all issued U.S. patents are utility patents,[633] which are available for the categories of subject matter enumerated

---

methods from patenting. *See, e.g.*, European Patent Convention art. 52(3) (16th ed. 2016), Agreement on Trade-Related Aspects of Intellectual Property Rights, including Trade in Counterfeit Goods, art. 27.3(a), Dec. 15, 1993, 33 I.L.M. 81 (1994) (giving member countries the option to deny such patents).

[630]*See* Method of making self-sealing episcleral incision, U.S. Patent No. 5,080,111 (issued Jan. 14, 1992).

[631]*See generally* Cynthia M. Ho, *Patents, Patients, and Public Policy: An Incomplete Intersection at 35 U.S.C. §287(c)*, 33 U.C. Davis L. Rev. 601 (2000); Richard P. Burgoon, Jr., *Silk Purses, Sows Ears, and Other Nuances Regarding 35 U.S.C. §287(c)*, 4 U. Balt. Intell. Prop. J. 69 (1996).

[632]*See* 35 U.S.C. §287(c)(2)(A) (narrowly defining "medical activity" as "the performance of a medical or surgical procedure on a body, but . . . not . . . (i) the use of a patented machine, manufacture, or composition of matter in violation of such patent, (ii) the practice of a patented use of a composition of matter in violation of such patent, or (iii) the practice of a process in violation of a biotechnology patent").

[633]For example, in the calendar year 2018, the USPTO granted the following numbers and types of patents:

Utility: 307,759;
Design: 30,497;

within 35 U.S.C. §101. In addition to utility patents, however, the United States also grants plant patents and design patents. Each is discussed below.

1. Plant Patents

The subject matter of U.S. plant patents is governed not by 35 U.S.C. §101 but rather by 35 U.S.C. §161. That section provides that plant patents are available for those who

> invent[ ] or discover[ ] and asexually reproduce[] any distinct and new variety of plant, including cultivated sports, mutants, hybrids, and newly found seedlings, other than a tuber propagated plant or a plant found in an uncultivated state....[634]

The hallmark of a plant patent is the "asexual" reproduction of the new plant "variety."[635] To asexually reproduce a plant means to grow a genetically identical copy through budding, grafting, or cutting. In contrast, the reproduction of plants from seed is considered sexual reproduction and is not covered by plant patents under §161. However, a *sui generis* form of protection for sexually reproduced plant varieties, as well as tuber-propagated plants such as potatoes, is available in the United States under the Plant Variety Protection Act (PVPA).[636]

Why are there separate provisions of the Patent Act for plants? The answer is primarily historical. Prior to 1930, the general consensus was that plants could not qualify for patent protection because even those plants bred by humans were believed to be "products of nature." Moreover, plants were thought not amenable to the written description requirement as set forth in the statutory predecessor of what is today 35 U.S.C. §112(a).[637]

Plant: 1,208; and
Reissue: 528

See United States Patent & Trademark Office, *U.S. Patent Statistics Chart, Calendar Years 1963-2018, available at* uspto.gov/web/offices/ac/ido/oeip/taf/us_stat.htm.

[634]35 U.S.C. §161.

[635]A variety is a taxonomic rank beneath subspecies. For example, well-known varieties of grapes from which wine is produced include Chardonnay, Pinot Grigio, Cabernet Sauvignon, Merlot, and so on. As a result of selective breeding, each member of a variety possesses certain common characteristics or traits.

[636]*See* 7 U.S.C. §§2401 *et seq.* (Plant Variety Protection Act). The PVPA is administered by the U.S. Department of Agriculture. Certain plant-related inventions that are protectable under the PVPA may also be eligible for protection under 35 U.S.C. §101 as the subject matter of a utility patent, if they meet the substantive requirements of utility, novelty, and nonobviousness. *See* J.E.M. Ag. Supply, Inc. v. Pioneer Hi-Bred Int'l, Inc., 534 U.S. 124 (2001).

[637]*See* Imazio Nursery, Inc. v. Dana Greenhouses, 69 F.3d 1560, 1563 (Fed. Cir. 1995).

As a means of encouraging greater innovation in plant breeding, Congress, in 1930, enacted a special statute, the Plant Patent Act, which addressed these concerns. Congress's action represents an acceptance of the modern view that asexually reproduced, distinct, and new plant varieties are not unprotectable "products of nature," but rather exist only through the intervention of humans. The Plant Patent Act also relaxes the written description requirement for plants.[638] The term of a plant patent is the same as that of a utility patent.[639]

Importantly, plant patent protection is available only for plants resulting from human creative efforts by the patent applicant, and not for plants merely found by the applicant. The "invents or discovers" language of 35 U.S.C. §161 means that the plant must result from the applicant's own work, rather than resulting from "a 'chance find' or discovery of a plant explorer."[640] This requirement was not satisfied in *In re Beineke*.[641] In that case Walter Beineke noticed desirable genetic traits in two white oak trees, each over 100 years in age, growing in another person's front yard. Thereafter Beineke planted acorns from the oak trees on his own property, observed that the desirable traits were retained by the progeny trees, asexually reproduced the trees, and sought to patent them as new and distinct tree varieties.

The Federal Circuit affirmed the USPTO's rejection of Beineke's plant patent applications. After reviewing the legislative history of the 1930 Plant Patent Act, the court explained that protection under §161 requires, *inter alia*, that "(1) the plant must have been created in its inception by human activity, i.e., it must be the result of plant breeding or other agricultural or horticultural efforts; and (2) the plant must have been created by the 'inventor,' i.e., the person seeking the patent must have contributed to the creation of the plant in addition to having appreciated its uniqueness and asexually reproduced it."[642] Beineke did not satisfy either of these requirements. The oak trees he sought to patent were not in any way the result of Beineke's creative efforts, or of anyone else's efforts for that matter. Thus the court

[638]*See* 35 U.S.C. §162 (providing that "[n]o plant patent shall be declared invalid for noncompliance with section 112 of this title if the description is as complete as is reasonably possible. The claim in the specification shall be in formal terms to the plant shown and described."). In practice, many plant patent applications include color photographs showing the features of the plant. *See, e.g.*, Chrysanthemum Plant Named Maroon Pride, U.S. Patent No. PP7,269 (issued July 10, 1990, to the Regents of the University of Minnesota).

[639]*See* 35 U.S.C. §161 (stating that "[t]he provisions of this title relating to patents for inventions shall apply to patents for plants, except as otherwise provided").

[640]*See* In re Beineke, 690 F.3d 1344, 1351 (Fed. Cir. 2012) (quoting S. Rep. No. 71-315 (1930), at 3-4)).

[641]690 F.3d 1344 (Fed. Cir. 2012).

[642]*Beineke*, 690 F.3d at 1348.

held that the trees did "not fall within the scope of those plants protected by the 1930 Act."[643]

The scope of exclusionary rights afforded by a plant patent is quite narrow. In the leading case of *Imazio Nursery v. Dana Greenhouses,*[644] the Federal Circuit interpreted the Plant Patent Act to conclude that "the scope of a plant patent is the asexual progeny of the patented plant variety."[645] In order to establish infringement of her plant patent, the patentee must therefore establish that the defendant's allegedly infringing plant is the asexually reproduced progeny of the original patented parent plant.[646] An independently developed plant, even if genetically identical to the patented plant, does not infringe.[647]

Although Congress created two specific types of intellectual property protection for plants (i.e., plant patents and Plant Variety Protection Act certificates as discussed above), the existence of these separate statutory schemes does not prevent plant-related subject matter from being claimed in utility patents. Plant-related subject matter can qualify for protection in a utility patent under 35 U.S.C. §101 *if* the claimed subject matter satisfies all other requirements of utility patentability (e.g., novelty and nonobviousness).

In *J.E.M. Ag Supply, Inc. v. Pioneer Hi-Bred Int'l, Inc.*[648] the Supreme Court considered the validity of multiple U.S. utility patents obtained by Pioneer Hi-Bred Int'l (Pioneer) to protect the company's inbred and hybrid corn seed products.[649] An accused infringer contended that Pioneer's utility patents were invalid because the Plant Patent Act and the Plant Variety Protection Act set forth the exclusive statutory means for the protection of plant life. The Supreme Court disagreed, holding that neither of these acts foreclosed utility patent protection for plants. "Whatever Congress may have believed about the state of patent law and the science of plant breeding in 1930 [when it passed the Plant Patent Act], plants have always had the *potential* to fall within the general subject matter of §101, which is a dynamic provision designed to encompass new and unforeseen inventions."[650] Denying utility patent protection to plant life under §101 simply because such coverage was thought "technologically

[643]*Beineke*, 690 F.3d at 1352.
[644]69 F.3d 1560 (Fed. Cir. 1995).
[645]*Id.* at 1568.
[646]*See id.* at 1569.
[647]*See id.* at 1570.
[648]534 U.S. 124 (2001).
[649]Pioneer's utility patents for inbred corn lines claimed both the seeds and plants of the inbred line and the hybrids produced by crossing the protected inbred line with another corn line. The patents for corn hybrid plants claimed the plant, its seeds, variants, mutants, and trivial modifications of the hybrid. *See id.* at 127.
[650]*Id.* at 135 (emphasis in original).

infeasible" when Congress passed the Plant Patent Act "would be inconsistent with the forward-looking perspective of the utility patent statute."[651] The Supreme Court observed that it had taken a broad view of §101 subject matter in its landmark 1980 *Chakrabarty* decision,[652] and thus interpreted §101 "clearly includes plants within its subject matter."[653]

Of course, obtaining utility patent protection on plant-related subject matter requires that the claimed matter satisfy the rigorous §102 novelty and §103 nonobviousness requirements and that it be disclosed in accordance with the requirements of §112. But if these statutory criteria are met, §101 does not stand as a threshold bar.

2. Design Patents

In addition to utility patents and plant patents, the United States also grants a third type of patent: design patents. Design patent protection is an increasingly important form of intellectual property protection because judicial decisions have made it more difficult to attain trademark protection for product design.[654] Moreover, design patents recently have become the subject of high-profile litigation, a new battleground for high-tech companies that also invest heavily in the external appearance of their products.[655]

Like plant patents, the subject matter of design patents is defined not in 35 U.S.C. §101. Rather, the criteria for patentable designs are set forth in a separate section of the Patent Act, 35 U.S.C. §171.

[651] *Id.*

[652] *See supra* Section D.3 ("Life Forms").

[653] *J.E.M. Ag Supply*, 534 U.S. at 144.

[654] *See* Wal-Mart Stores, Inc. v. Samara Bros., Inc., 529 U.S. 205, 212 (2000) (concluding that product design, like color, cannot be inherently distinctive); *id.* at 214 (holding that product design cannot be protected under §43(a) of the Lanham [Trademark] Act without a showing of secondary meaning [i.e., a showing that consumers have come to identify a particular design primarily as an indicator of product source]); *id.* (stating that the "availability of [design patent or copyright] protections greatly reduces any harm to the producer that might ensue from our conclusion that a product design cannot be protected under §43(a) without a showing of secondary meaning").

[655] *See* Brian X. Chien, *Jury to Decide How Much More Samsung Must Pay Apple in Patent Case*, N.Y. TIMES, Nov. 12, 2013, at B3 (describing November 2013 retrial of August 2012 jury verdict finding Samsung liable for more than $1 billion in damages for infringement of five Apple patents including one patent covering design of mobile device face); Christopher V. Carani, *Apple v. Samsung: Design Patents Take Center Stage*, LANDSLIDE, Jan./Feb. 2013, at 25-32 (describing "epic battle" centered on design rights between Apple, Inc. and Samsung Elecs. Co., touted as the "Patent Trial of the Century" by the *Wall Street Journal*).

a. *Criteria for Obtaining Design Patents*

A design patent protects the "new, original and ornamental design for an article of manufacture,"[656] for example, the unique external appearance of a digital music player,[657] a line of furniture,[658] an automobile fender, or even a roofing shingle. Patentable designs must also satisfy the nonobviousness requirement of 35 U.S.C. §103.[659] Unlike utility and plant patents, design patents have a term of only 14 years from date of grant,[660] and their content is not published until grant.[661]

The protection afforded by a design patent is limited to the *ornamental* features of a design and cannot encompass features that are primarily functional (i.e., in which the nature of the design contributes to the operation or performance of the article).[662] For example, the existence of a design patent on a golf club would not prevent others from copying features such as the streamlined shape of the club head, if this shape (although pleasing to look at, especially for golf aficionados) also increased the loft and distance of the golf ball. In this respect, design patent law adopts a nonfunctionality criterion analogous to the useful article doctrine of copyright law.[663]

[656]35 U.S.C. §171.

[657]*See, e.g.*, U.S. Patent No. D497,618 (issued Oct. 26, 2004). The '618 patent, owned by Apple Computer, Inc., claims the "ornamental design for a media device." *Id.* The media device in question is the 3G model of Apple's well-known iPod music player.

[658]Furniture designs are common subject matter of U.S. design patents. See Daniel H. Brean, *Enough Is Enough: Time to Eliminate Design Patents and Rely on More Appropriate Copyright and Trademark Protection for Product Designs,* 16 Tex. Intell. Prop. L.J. 325, 361 (2008); *id.* at 355 (tbl. 1) (reporting that since 1976, more design patents have issued in the USPTO's "Furnishings" design classification than in any other classification).

[659]*See* 35 U.S.C. §171 (providing in part that "[t]he provisions of this title relating to patents for inventions shall apply to patents for designs, except as otherwise provided"); Avia Group Int'l, Inc. v. L.A. Gear Cal., Inc., 853 F.2d 1557, 1563 (Fed. Cir. 1988) ("Design patents must meet a nonobviousness requirement identical to that applicable to utility patents."). Whether a design would have been nonobvious is determined in accordance with the *Graham* factors, as applied from the perspective of a " 'designer of ordinary capability who designs articles of the type presented in the [design patent] application.' " *Id.* at 1564 (quoting In re Nalbandian, 661 F.2d 1214, 1216 (C.C.P.A. 1981)).

For more on reconceptualizing the nonobviousness requirement in design patents, *see* Janice M. Mueller & Daniel H. Brean, *Overcoming the "Impossible Issue" of Nonobviousness in Design Patents*, 99 Ky. L.J. 419 (2011).

[660]*See* 35 U.S.C. §173.

[661]35 U.S.C. §122(b)(2)(A)(iv).

[662]*See* Lee v. Dayton-Hudson Corp., 838 F.2d 1186 (Fed. Cir. 1988).

[663]*See* 17 U.S.C. §101 (2006) (providing that "the design of a useful article, as defined in this section, shall be considered a [copyrightable] pictorial, graphic, or sculptural work only if, and only to the extent that, such design incorporates pictorial, graphic, or sculptural features that can be identified separately from, and are capable of existing independently of, the utilitarian aspects of the article").

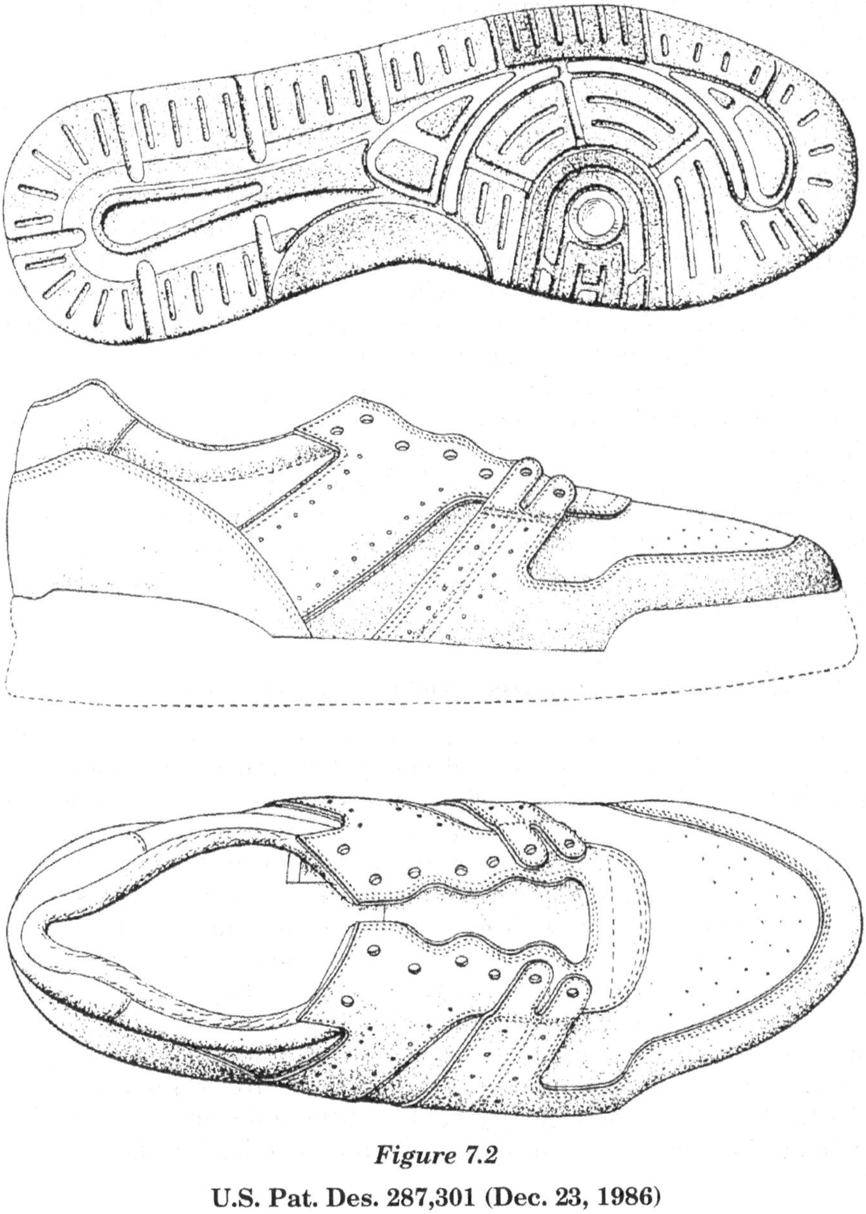

Figure 7.2

U.S. Pat. Des. 287,301 (Dec. 23, 1986)

Care must be taken to distinguish the functionality of the underlying article of manufacture from the alleged functionality of its external design. For example, in *Avia Group Int'l, Inc. v. L.A. Gear Cal.,*

Inc.[664] the Federal Circuit upheld the validity of two athletic-shoe design patents over the arguments of the accused infringer that the designs were primarily functional rather than ornamental as required by 35 U.S.C. §171. The court did not dispute that "shoes are functional and that certain features of the shoe designs in issue perform functions."[665] However, if functionality of the underlying article is not separable from the alleged functionality of its design, "it would not be possible to obtain a design patent on a utilitarian article of manufacture . . . or to obtain both design and utility patents on the same article."[666] Moreover, the patentability of a claimed design must be considered as a whole. The Federal Circuit agreed with the district court that the patented designs in question, directed to the aesthetic aspects of an athletic shoe's outer sole and its upper, were primarily ornamental. The designs encompassed features such as the location and arrangement of perforations and stitching in the shoe upper, and a "swirl effect" around the pivot point on the sole of the shoe, as depicted in Figure 7.2.[667] Moreover, to the extent that the design features performed the functions suggested by the defendants, the Federal Circuit found persuasive the district court's reasoning that all such functions could have been performed by many other possible design choices.[668]

b. Establishing Infringement of Design Patents

The leading U.S. Supreme Court case on design patents, *Gorham Co. v. White,*[669] established that design patent infringement must be assessed from the perspective of an "ordinary observer." The ordinary observer is not an expert in the manufacture of designs but rather is a hypothetical purchaser or observer "of ordinary acuteness, bringing to the examination of the article upon which the design has been placed that degree of observation which men of ordinary intelligence give. It is persons of the latter class who are the principal purchasers of the articles to which designs have given novel appearances, and if they are misled, and induced to purchase what is not the article they supposed it to be . . . the patentees are injured, and that advantage of a market which the patent was granted to secure is destroyed."[670] The *Gorham* Court accordingly held that the following test governs in determining whether a design patent has been infringed:

[664]853 F.2d 1557 (Fed. Cir. 1988).
[665]*Id.* at 1563.
[666]*Id.* (citations omitted).
[667]*See id.*
[668]*See id.*
[669]81 U.S. 511 (1871).
[670]*See id.* at 527-528.

> [I]f, in the eye of an ordinary observer, giving such attention as a purchaser usually gives, two designs are substantially the same, if the resemblance is such as to deceive such an observer, inducing him to purchase one supposing it to be the other, the first one patented is infringed by the other.[671]

After the Federal Circuit's creation in 1982, the court expanded the test for design patent infringement by adding a second prong to the *Gorham* test. In addition to satisfying substantial similarity of the claimed and accused designs, the design patent holder also had to establish that the accused design appropriated the novel feature(s) of the patented design.[672] As evolved by a series of Federal Circuit decisions, this additional "point of novelty" component to the design patent infringement analysis was problematic because it mixed concepts of design patent validity with infringement. The point of novelty inquiry effectively required a patentee to affirmatively establish the novelty of its presumptively valid design.

The Federal Circuit in 2008 went *en banc* in *Egyptian Goddess, Inc. v. Swisa, Inc.* to clarify the standard for infringement of design patents.[673] The court in *Egyptian Goddess* rejected a freestanding point of novelty inquiry as a separate part of the standard. Rather, the infringement test should be applied as a single inquiry, that is, whether the *Gorham* ordinary observer would find the claimed and accused designs substantially similar. The Federal Circuit emphasized that the "ordinary observer" test is "the sole test for determining whether a design patent has been infringed."[674] Under that test, "infringement will not be found unless the accused article 'embod[ies] the patented design or any colorable imitation thereof.'"[675]

The *Egyptian Goddess* court explained further that the "ordinary observer" may sometimes be informed by knowledge of the prior art. For example, in cases where the claimed and accused designs do not appear "plainly dissimilar," the question whether an ordinary observer would determine that the two designs are substantially the same will benefit from comparing both designs with the prior art.

[671] *Id.* at 528.

[672] *See* Litton Sys., Inc. v. Whirlpool Corp., 728 F.2d 1423, 1444 (Fed. Cir. 1984) (stating that no matter how similar two designs look, the patented design is not infringed unless "the accused device . . . appropriate[s] the novelty in the patented device which distinguishes it from the prior art"). Federal Circuit decisions following *Litton Sys.* interpreted that decision's language as requiring that design patent infringement "consider both the perspective of the ordinary observer and the particular novelty in the claimed design." Egyptian Goddess, Inc. v. Swisa, Inc., 543 F.3d 665, 671 (Fed. Cir. 2008) (*en banc*) (citing Circuit's design patent infringement decisions issued in the time period from 1988 to 2004).

[673] Egyptian Goddess, Inc. v. Swisa, Inc., 543 F.3d 665 (Fed. Cir. 2008) (*en banc*).

[674] *Id.* at 678.

[675] *Id.* (quoting Goodyear Tire & Rubber Co. v. Hercules Tire & Rubber Co., 162 F.3d 1113, 1116-1117 (Fed. Cir. 1998)).

The Federal Circuit observed that "[w]here there are many examples of similar prior art designs . . . , differences between the claimed and accused designs that might not be noticeable in the abstract can become significant to the hypothetical ordinary observer who is conversant with the prior art."[676] In short, the prior art may provide an important context or frame of reference for assessing how similar the claimed and accused designs truly are.

Although the Federal Circuit's characterization of the "ordinary observer" to include a person aware of the prior art may suggest that the *Egyptian Goddess* test is not so very different from the rejected two-pronged test that included a point of novelty component, an important practical difference exists. Under the test for design patent infringement as formulated in *Egyptian Goddess,* the burden of proof to introduce any prior art that may have relevance to the infringement inquiry is placed on the accused infringer rather than the patentee.[677] This result is consistent with the principle that a design patent, like a utility patent, is presumed novel,[678] and the burden of invalidating the patent (e.g., on the basis of prior art that would render the claimed design anticipated or obvious) always remains on the accused infringer/validity challenger.

The patented design in *Egyptian Goddess* was that of a four-sided fingernail file or buffer, having a hollow, square cross-section plus raised strips of nail buffing material on three of its four sides. The accused design incorporated buffing material on all four sides of a nail buffer. The prior art buffers (of square and triangular cross-sections) also included buffing material on all sides. Figure 7.3 depicts the claimed and accused buffers along with the closest prior art nail buffer designs.

The infringement question for the Federal Circuit was "whether an ordinary observer, familiar with the prior art Falley and Nailco designs, would be deceived into believing the Swisa buffer is the same as the patented buffer."[679] Answering that question in the negative, the Federal Circuit affirmed the district court's entry of summary judgment of no infringement. Although the patented and accused buffers had the same general shape (hollow and square in cross-section), the absence of buffer material on the fourth side of the claimed design could not be considered a minor feature in view of the closest prior art, which featured buffer material on all sides. An ordinary observer would likely regard the accused design as being closer to the prior art than the patented design.[680]

[676]*Id.*

[677]*See id.* (stating that "if the accused infringer elects to rely on the comparison prior art as part of its defense against the claim of infringement, the burden of production of that prior art is on the accused infringer").

[678]*See* 35 U.S.C. §282; Avia Group Int'l, Inc. v. L.A. Gear Cal., Inc., 853 F.2d 1557, 1562 (Fed. Cir. 1988) (stating, in a case in which validity of a design patent was challenged by accused infringer, that "[a] patent is presumed valid").

[679]*Egyptian Goddess*, 543 F.3d at 681.

[680]*See id.* at 682 (discussing "problem with" declaration of patentee's expert Eaton).

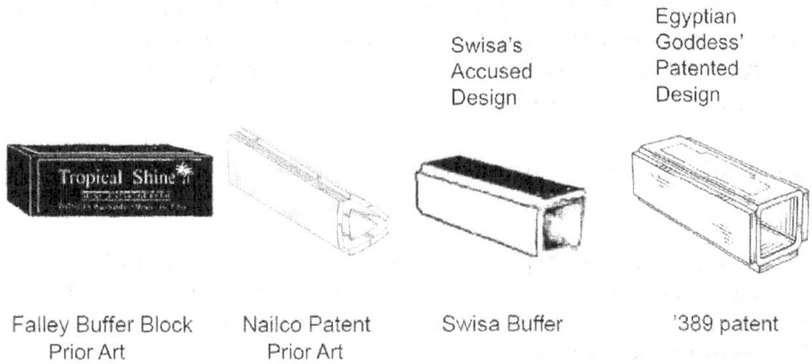

Figure 7.3

The Federal Circuit concluded that "[i]n light of the similarity of the prior art buffers to the accused buffer . . . no reasonable fact-finder could find that [the patentee, Egyptian Goddess] met its burden of showing . . . that an ordinary observer, taking into account the prior art, would believe the accused design to be the same as the patented design."[681]

c. *Unique Remedy for Design Patent Infringement*

(i) Statutory Basis: 35 U.S.C. §289

The potential remedies for infringement of a design patent differ significantly from those available for infringement of a utility patent. "A design patentee may recover damages under 35 U.S.C. §284 *or* [the infringer's profits] under 35 U.S.C. §289, entitled 'Additional remedy for infringement of design patent.' "[682]

Since 1946, the general damages provision for utility patent infringement (today set forth at 35 U.S.C. §284[683]) has not included

[681] *Id.*

[682] Catalina Lighting, Inc. v. Lamps Plus, Inc., 295 F.3d 1277, 1290 (Fed. Cir. 2002) (emphasis added). *See also* Nike, Inc. v. Wal-Mart Stores, Inc., 138 F.3d 1437, 1442 (Fed. Cir. 1998) (explaining that "[w]ith the 1952 codification of the patent law into Title 35, the general damages provision appears at §284 and the additional provision for design patents appears at §289").

[683] Section 284 of the Patent Act provides:

> Upon finding for the claimant the court shall award the claimant damages adequate to compensate for the infringement, but in no event less than a reasonable royalty for the use made of the invention by the infringer, together with interest and costs as fixed by the court.
>
> When the damages are not found by a jury, the court shall assess them. In either event the court may increase the damages up to three times the amount found or assessed. Increased damages under this paragraph shall not apply to provisional rights under section 154(d).

the remedy of an accounting of the profits of an adjudged infringer,[684] sometimes referred to as "disgorgement."[685] However, the current Patent Act still provides for recovery of the infringer's profits when a *design* patent has been infringed:

> **§289. Additional remedy for infringement of a design patent**
>
> Whoever during the term of a patent for a design, without license of the owner, (1) applies the patented design, or any colorable imitation thereof, to any article of manufacture for the purpose of sale, or (2) sells or exposes for sale any article of manufacture to which such design or colorable imitation has been applied shall be liable to the owner to the extent of *his total profit*, but not less than $250, recoverable in any United States district court having jurisdiction of the parties.

> The court may receive expert testimony as an aid to the determination of damages or of what royalty would be reasonable under the circumstances.

35 U.S.C. §284 (eff. Sept. 16, 2012).

[684]*See* SCA Hygiene Prods. Aktiebolag v. First Quality Baby Prods., LLC, 807 F.3d 1311, 1326 (Fed. Cir. 2015) (*en banc*) (explaining that "in the Patent Act of 1946, Congress eliminated accounting of profits as a remedy for patent infringement (except for design patents)") (citing Act of Aug. 1, 1946, Pub. L. No. 79-587, 60 Stat. 778; citing also Kori Corp. v. Wilco Marsh Buggies & Draglines, Inc., 761 F.2d 649, 654 (Fed. Cir. 1985) ("The 1946 amendment to the damages provisions effectively eliminated this double recovery.")). *See also Nike, Inc.*, 138 F.3d at 1442, explaining:

> Section 284 as written [i.e., enacted in the 1952 Patent Act] did not state the 1946 Act's concept of recovering profits as an element of general damages, a purported ambiguity that was clarified in *Aro Mfg. Co. v. Convertible Top Replacement Co.*, 377 U.S. 476, 507, 84 S. Ct. 1526, 1543, 12 L. Ed. 2d 457, 141 U.S.P.Q. 681, 694 (1964). The Court interpreted §284 as meaning that only the patentee's losses can be recovered, "without regard to the question whether the defendant has gained or lost by his unlawful acts," thus removing the equitable remedy of the infringer's profits from recovery under §284.

See also Rite-Hite Corp. v. Kelley Co., Inc., 56 F.3d 1538, 1557 (Fed. Cir. 1995) (Nies, J., dissenting-in-part) (emphasis added):

> Under precedent in 1946, a patentee was entitled to recover, either at law or in equity, only the profits attributable to the invention. A patentee's property rights were limited to its exclusivity in the market for the patented goods in suit. "Damages" were awardable only for injury to that trade, and only to the extent of the contribution of the invention to profits. . . . *In 1946, Congress eliminated the remedy of an equitable accounting for a defendant's profits* and reenacted the provision for "damages" in 1946 and 1952. Congress made no change in the precedential law of "damages" except for prejudgment interest.

[685]*See* Nike, Inc. v. Wal-Mart Stores, Inc., 138 F.3d 1437, 1448 (Fed. Cir. 1998) (explaining that §289 "requires the disgorgement of the infringers' profits to the patent holder, such that the infringers retain no profit from their wrong").

> Nothing in this section shall prevent, lessen, or impeach any other remedy which an owner of an infringed patent has under the provisions of this title [35 U.S.C.], but he shall not twice recover the profit made from the infringement.[686]

In *Nike, Inc. v. Wal-Mart Stores, Inc.*,[687] the Federal Circuit thoroughly reviewed the history of 35 U.S.C. §289. Congress in 1887 enacted the predecessor provision of §289 in order to legislatively overrule a series of Supreme Court decisions that had effectively denied any recovery to the owners of infringed patents covering the designs of carpets. In the *Dobson* cases,[688] the Supreme Court had applied a rule of *apportionment* that required the design patentees to show "what portion of their losses or the infringers' profits was due to the patented design and what portion was due to the unpatented carpet."[689] Because the patentees in the *Dobson* cases were unable to make that showing, the Supreme Court held that the infringers were liable for "only nominal damages" of six cents.[690]

Congress responded promptly to the *Dobson* decisions. The Design Patent Act of 1887 removed the apportionment requirement when a design patent owner sought to recover an infringer's profits.[691] Thereafter, Congress in the 1952 Patent Act codified the Act of 1887

[686] 35 U.S.C. §289 (2012) (emphasis added).

[687] 138 F.3d 1437 (Fed. Cir. 1998).

[688] *See* Dobson v. Dornan, 118 U.S. 10 (1886); Dobson v. Hartford Carpet Co., 114 U.S. 439 (1885); Dobson v. Bigelow Carpet Co., 114 U.S. 439 (1885).

[689] *Nike, Inc.*, 138 F.3d at 1441.

[690] *See* Dobson v. Dornan, 118 U.S. 10, 18 (1886) (concluding that "[t]he final decree of the [C]ircuit [C]ourt is reversed, and the case is remanded to that court, with direction to disallow the award of damages, and to award six cents damages . . .").

[691] *See Nike, Inc.*, 138 F.3d at 1441. The 1887 Act, which was specific to design patents, provided:

> §1. Hereafter, during the term of letters patent for a design, it shall be unlawful for any person other than the owner of said letters patent, without the license of such owner, to apply the design secured by such letters patent, or any colorable imitation thereof, to any article of manufacture for the purpose of sale, or to sell or expose for sale any article of manufacture to which such design or colorable imitation shall, without the license of the owner, have been applied, knowing that the same has been so applied. *Any person violating the provisions, or either of them, of this section, shall be liable in the amount of two hundred and fifty dollars, he shall be further liable for the excess of such profit over and above [that sum, the full amount recoverable] either by action at law or upon a bill in equity for an injunction to restrain such infringement.*
>
> §2. That nothing in this Act contained shall prevent, lessen, impeach, or avoid any remedy at law or in equity which any owner of letters patent for a design, aggrieved by the infringement of the same might have had if this act had not been passed; but such owner shall not twice recover the profit made from the infringement.

provisions for design patent remedies in 35 U.S.C. §289 but deleted the requirement that the infringement be "knowing."[692]

(ii) No Apportionment

In a 2015 decision, the Federal Circuit relied on the *Nike v. Walmart* exposition of §289's history in affirming a jury verdict that awarded a design patentee the infringer's entire profits. *Apple Inc. v. Samsung Elecs. Co., Ltd.*,[693] in which the Circuit refused to apportion the infringer Samsung's total smartphone profits between infringing and non-infringing features, is one of many court decisions in a much-publicized, long-running battle between two electronics giants over utility- and design-patented features of smartphones and tablets.[694]

After substantial reduction by the district court, the total jury award to Apple for infringement of its asserted design and utility

---

Nike, Inc., 138 F.3d at 1441-1442 (quoting Act of 1887, 24 Stat. 387) (emphasis added). *See also* Frederick H. Betts, *Some Questions Under the Design Patent Act of 1887,* 1 YALE L.J. 181 (1892).

[692]Notably, the 1887 Act required that the infringement be "knowing," *see Nike, Inc.*, 138 F.3d at 1442 (stating that "[t]he Act of 1887 thus authorized recovery by the patentee of the infringer's profit when the infringer appropriated the patented design 'knowing that the same has been so applied.'"). Courts interpreted this as imposing a "willfulness" requirement. *See* Graeme B. Dinwoodie & Mark D. Janis, TRADE DRESS AND DESIGN LAW 429 (Wolters Kluwer 2010) (note 1).

When Congress enacted §289 in 1952, however, no willfulness requirement was included. Graeme B. Dinwoodie & Mark D. Janis, TRADE DRESS AND DESIGN LAW at 429. The Federal Circuit does not interpret §289 as permitting an infringer's profits to be awarded only when its design patent infringement is willful. *See* Graeme B. Dinwoodie & Mark D. Janis, TRADE DRESS AND DESIGN LAW at 429 (citing Catalina Lighting, Inc. v. Lamps Plus, Inc., 295 F.3d 1277, 1290 (Fed. Cir. 2002) (stating that "[t]he present version of §289, which has been in effect since 1952, has no . . . 'knowing' requirement. Lamps Plus is therefore entitled to damages for Catalina's infringement regardless of whether the infringement was willful.")). *See also Nike, Inc.*, 138 F.3d at 1442 (explaining that "[w]ith the 1952 codification of the patent law into Title 35, the general damages provision appears at §284 and the additional provision for design patents appears at §289").

On the other hand, even if infringement of a design patent *is* willful, the patentee that elects to obtain the infringer's profits under §289 cannot receive enhanced damages for willfulness (in contrast with the enhanced damages potentially available under §284). *See* Braun Inc. v. Dynamics Corp. of Am., 975 F.2d 815 (Fed. Cir. 1992).

[693]786 F.3d 983 (Fed. Cir. 2015).

[694]*See also infra* Chapter 11, Section B ("Injunctions") (examining a series of 2012-2015 Federal Circuit decisions concerning motions for preliminary and permanent injunctions in the *Apple-Samsung* litigation).

The infringed design patents in *Apple v. Samsung,* 786 F.3d 983 (Fed. Cir. 2015), were U.S. Design Patent Nos. D618,677, D593,087, and D604,305, which claimed certain design elements embodied in Apple's iPhone. The jury also found that certain of Apple's utility patents and trade dress were infringed and diluted.

patents and trade dress amounted to approximately $600 million.[695] On appeal, infringer Samsung argued that the district court had legally erred in allowing the jury to award Samsung's entire profits on its infringing smartphones as damages. According to Samsung, the damages for design patent infringement should have been limited to the profit attributable to the infringement because of " 'basic causation principles. . . .' "[696] Samsung contended that " 'Apple failed to establish that infringement of its limited design patents . . . caused any Samsung sales or profits.' "[697]

The Federal Circuit rejected Samsung's "causation" arguments because they advocated "the same 'apportionment' requirement that Congress rejected."[698] The appellate court quoted its 1998 *Nike v. Walmart* decision: "Apportionment . . . required [the patentee] to show what portion of the infringer's profit, or of his own lost profit, was due to the design and what portion was due to the article itself. . . . The Act of 1887, specific to design patents, removed the apportionment requirement. . . ."[699] Congress thereafter codified the design patent infringement damages provisions of the Act of 1887 in Section 289 of Title 35.[700]

The *Apple* court concluded that the "clear statutory language" and legislative history of 35 U.S.C. §289 necessarily defeated Samsung's proposed "causation" rule.[701] The court confirmed that "[i]n reciting that an infringer 'shall be liable to the owner to the extent of [the infringer's] total profit,' Section 289 explicitly authorizes the award of total profit from the article of manufacture bearing the patented design."[702] Although the Circuit noted policy arguments of *amici* who contended that awarding a design patent infringer's total profits "ma[de] no sense in the modern world,"[703] those arguments needed to be addressed to Congress rather the Federal Circuit.[704]

[695]The jury initially awarded Apple a total of $1,049,343,540.00 in damages (for infringement of utility and design patents and trade dress), and provided a breakdown of the award by Samsung product. Apple, Inc. v. Samsung Elecs. Co., 926 F. Supp. 2d 1100, 1103 (N.D. Cal. 2013). After considering various post-trial motions, the district court struck $450,514,650 from the jury's award but sustained it in the amount of $598,908,892 for infringement by 14 specified Samsung products. *See Apple, Inc.*, 926 F. Supp. 2d at 1120.

[696]*Apple, Inc.*, 786 F.3d at 1001 (quoting Appellants' Brief at 36-37).

[697]*Apple, Inc.*, 786 F.3d at 1001 (quoting Appellants' Brief at 40).

[698]*Apple, Inc.*, 786 F.3d at 1001 (citing Nike, Inc. v. Wal-Mart Stores, Inc., 138 F.3d 1437, 1441 (Fed. Cir. 1998)).

[699]*Apple, Inc.*, 786 F.3d at 1001 (quoting *Nike*, 138 F.3d at 1441).

[700]*Apple, Inc.*, 786 F.3d at 1001 (citing *Nike*, 138 F.3d at 1440-1443, as "containing a detailed and thorough discussion of the legislative history").

[701]*Apple, Inc.*, 786 F.3d at 1002.

[702]*Apple, Inc.*, 786 F.3d at 1001-1002 (footnote omitted).

[703]*Apple, Inc.*, 786 F.3d at 1002 n.1 (quoting amicus brief of "27 Law Professors").

[704]The Circuit further supported its rejection of Samsung's causation argument by observing that several other courts, including pre-1982 regional circuit decisions, had

In December 2015, Samsung filed a petition for *certiorari* with the U.S. Supreme Court that challenged, *inter alia*, the total profits award.[705] The Supreme Court granted Samsung's request for review in March 2016, limited to the second (i.e., total profits) question of Samsung's petition: "[w]here a design patent is applied to only a component of a product, should an award of infringer's profits be limited to those profits attributable to the component.[706] Given the growing attention paid to design patents and litigation thereof, it is not surprising that the proper interpretation of 35 U.S.C. §289 attracted the Court's attention.

The Supreme Court issued its decision in late 2016. In *Samsung Elecs. Co. v. Apple Inc.*,[707] the unanimous Court reversed the Federal Circuit and held that an "article of manufacture" to which a patented design is applied for purpose of computing a design patent infringet's "total profit" under 35 U.S.C. §289 "encompasses *both* a product sold to a cinsumer and a component of that product."[708] The Court rejected the Federal Circuit's reasoning that the only permissible "article of manufacture" for calculating §289 profits was the entire accused smartphone as available for purchase by consumers.

---

previously concluded that §289 authorizes an award of the infringer's total profit. *See Apple, Inc.*, 786 F.3d at 1002 (citing Schnadig Corp. v. Gaines Mfg. Co., 620 F.2d 1166, 1171 (6th Cir. 1980); Henry Hanger & Display Fixture Corp. of Am. v. Sel-O-Rak Corp., 270 F.2d 635, 643-644 (5th Cir. 1959); Bergstrom v. Sears, Roebuck & Co., 496 F. Supp. 476, 495 (D. Minn. 1980)).

[705]Petition for Certiorari, No. 15-777, Samsung Elecs. Co., Ltd. v. Apple Inc. (docketed Dec. 16, 2015), http://www.supremecourt.gov/search.aspx?filename=/docketfiles/15-777.htm. The petition presents two questions, the second going directly to the apportionment issue:

> 1. Where a design patent includes unprotected non-ornamental features, should a district court be required to limit that patent to its protected ornamental scope?
> 2. Where a design patent is applied to only a component of a product, should an award of infringer's profits be limited to those profits attributable to the component?

Petition for Certiorari, No. 15-777, Samsung Elecs. Co., Ltd. v. Apple Inc. (docketed Dec. 16, 2015), at (i), *text available at* Scotusblog.com/wp-content/uploads/2016/01/15-777_PetitionForAWritOfCertiorari.pdf. For additional commentary on Samsung's petition, *see* Lyle Denniston, *Smartphone design feud reaches the Court*, Lyle Denniston Law News (Dec. 14, 2015), https://lyldenlawnews.com/2015/12/14/smartphone-design-feud-reaches-the-court/; Steve Lohr, *Samsung's Patent Loss to Apple Is Appealed to Supreme Court*, N.Y. Times, Dec. 14, 2015, http://www.nytimes.com/2015/12/15/technology/apple-samsung-supreme-court-patent-case.html?src=busln&_r=0 (noting that Supreme Court is not expected to take up Samsung's petition before February 2016).

[706]*See* Samsung Elecs. Co. v. Apple Inc., No. 15-777, 2016 WL 1078934 (U.S. Mar. 21, 2016).

[707]137 S. Ct. 429 (Dec. 6, 2016) (Sotomayor, J.).

[708]*Samsung*, 137 S. Ct. at 434 (emphasis added).

Chapter 8

Correcting and Challenging Issued Patents in the USPTO

A. Introduction

Even though it has been granted by the USPTO, an issued patent may suffer from certain defects. The defects may be so severe that, at the conclusion of litigation, a federal court will hold the patent invalid and/or unenforceable.[1] In other cases, however, the patent's defects are of a more minor nature and can be corrected through procedures conducted within the USPTO that are generally less expensive and of shorter duration than federal court litigation. This chapter describes several methods by which issued patents can be returned to the USPTO for correction: certificates of correction, reissue, and reexamination.[2]

This chapter also describes two procedures, newly implemented via the America Invents Act of 2011, by which persons other than patent owners can challenge the validity of issued patents in the USPTO: *inter partes* review and post-grant review. As further detailed below,[3] these post-grant, adjudicatory (litigation-like) procedures represent a

[1]The presumption of validity for issued patents, *see* 35 U.S.C. §282 (2012), is rebuttable. Based on clear and convincing evidence, a federal court may hold a patent invalid for failure to comply with the statutory requirements for patentability, 35 U.S.C. §101, §102, or §103; or for failure to satisfy the disclosure and/or claim definiteness requirements of 35 U.S.C. §112(a), (b). Alternatively, the patent may be held unenforceable for inequitable conduct or patent misuse.

[2]Yet another method of correcting an issued patent is by filing a disclaimer of a particular claim or claims of the patent. After obtaining his patent, a patent owner may determine that certain of its claims are invalid. Claims stand or fall independently as far as their validity. If certain claims of the patent are invalid without any deceptive invention, the remaining claims are not thereby rendered invalid. 35 U.S.C. §253, ¶1. The patentee may disclaim the invalid claims by filing a written disclaimer and paying the appropriate fee to the USPTO. The Patent Act provides an incentive to do so. The patentee can bring an action for infringement in which he asserts only the valid claims of a patent, even though he believes other claims in the patent to be invalid. However, the patentee will forfeit any potential recovery of costs from the infringement lawsuit *unless* he filed a disclaimer of the invalid claims before commencing the suit. 35 U.S.C. §288.

[3]*See infra* Section E ("AIA-Implemented Procedures for Challenging Issued Patents").

groundbreaking new system for attacking and testing issued patents. Notably, patent validity challenges no longer require the expensive and time-consuming venue of federal district court. Challengers can now make use of the new framework for assessing patent validity inside the USPTO, and enjoy a lessened burden of proof. Indeed, they have flocked to *inter partes* review, which became available in September 2012. As of July 2019, patent challengers have filed a total of almost 9,600 petitions seeking to institute *inter partes* review in the USPTO, and the agency's Patent Trial and Appeal Board has conducted trials and issued over 2,790 final written decisions in post-issuance reviews.[4] The Federal Circuit is grappling with a flood of appeals from those decisions.

B. Certificates of Correction

In some cases, minor mistakes in a patent such as misspellings can be corrected by use of a certificate of correction. The opportunity to seek a certificate of correction arises once the patent applicant (or her patent attorney or agent) receives the official "ribbon copy" of her U.S. patent. The patent should be reviewed carefully for typographical accuracy, and the document maintained in a safe place. If mistakes are found, steps should be taken promptly to correct them.[5] The manner in which any minor mistakes in the patent can be remedied

[4] *See* United States Patent and Trademark Office, Trial Statistics: IPR, P6R, CBM (June 2019), https://www.ustpo.gov/sites/default/files/documents/Trials_Statistics_2019-06-03.pdf.

[5] The patentee in *Southwest Software, Inc. v. Harlequin, Inc.*, 226 F.3d 1280 (Fed. Cir. 2000), learned this lesson the hard way. Not noticing a USPTO-caused mistake in its patent until after the matter was raised by the opposing party in a lawsuit alleging infringement of the patent, the patentee obtained a certificate of correction from the USPTO during the pendency of the infringement action. Although the Federal Circuit determined that the USPTO had validly issued the certificate under 35 U.S.C. §254, it nevertheless held as a matter of statutory interpretation that the certificate was not effective for causes of action, such as the case at bar, that arose prior to the issuance of the certificate. *See id.* at 1295. Thus, the certificate of correction was not effective for the patent in suit, and the case had to be remanded for consideration of whether the patent was valid under 35 U.S.C. §112, ¶1 absent the disclosure in an appendix that the USPTO had neglected to include in the issued patent. *See id.* at 1297. The fault was not entirely that of the agency, however; the Federal Circuit further remarked that

> it does not seem to us to be asking too much to expect a patentee to check a patent when it is issued in order to determine whether it contains any errors that require the issuance of a certificate of correction. In this case, the omission of the Program Printout Appendix from the '257 patent resulted in the absence of approximately 330 pages of text from the specification. It would seem that such an error would be readily apparent.

Id. at 1296.

depends on the party responsible for the mistake: the USPTO or the applicant.

If minor mistakes in the issued patent are the fault of the USPTO, they can be corrected by seeking a certificate of correction in accordance with 35 U.S.C. §254. Because the mistake in the patent is the fault of the agency, there is no charge to the applicant for certificates of correction issued under 35 U.S.C. §254. This statutory section requires that the mistake in the patent was "incurred through the fault of the Patent and Trademark Office," and was "clearly disclosed by the records of the Office."[6] For example, in *Southwest Software, Inc. v. Harlequin, Inc.*[7] the patent in suit was twice corrected under 35 U.S.C. §254: once to correct the agency's omission of a comma,[8] and a second time to add to the issued patent a missing "Program Printout Appendix" that disclosed software code arguably necessary for enablement and best mode of the claimed method and apparatus for calibrating digital images in desktop publishing.[9] This appendix was submitted by the patent applicant with the originally filed application but was inadvertently excluded from the patent specification when issued by the USPTO.[10]

If the mistake in the patent is the fault of the applicant rather than the USPTO, it may be remediable with a certificate of correction issued in accordance with 35 U.S.C. §255. To qualify under this section, the mistake must have occurred "in good faith," and be of "a clerical or typographical nature, or of minor character."[11] For example, correction under §255 might be appropriate where a patent's written description referred to a certain process temperature in "degrees Celsius," but the claims as presented by the applicant merely recited "degrees."[12] Because the mistake is not the fault of the USPTO, the patent owner will be required to pay a fee for this type of correction.

New matter cannot be added through the certificate of correction procedure, and the correction cannot be of such magnitude as would be addressed in reexamination or reissue proceedings (discussed

[6]35 U.S.C. §254.

[7]226 F.3d 1280 (Fed. Cir. 2000).

[8]*See id.* at 1287 n.6.

[9]*See id.* at 1287.

[10]*Id.* at 1291 (stating that "[t]he PTO determined that the appendix had been filed with the application for the '257 patent and that the separation and loss of the appendix, as well as the failure to print the appendix in the issued patent, were the result of an error on its part"). The Federal Circuit rejected the accused infringer's argument that the omission of the appendix was the fault of the patentee rather than the USPTO and thus that the certificate of correction should not have been issued under §254; the court stated that it "discern[ed] no clear error in the district court's findings and therefore affirm[ed] the ruling that the certificate of correction was not issued in violation of §254." *Id.* at 1293.

[11]35 U.S.C. §255.

[12]*See* In re Arnott, 19 U.S.P.Q.2d 1049, 1053 (Comm'r Pat. 1991).

below). In particular, the proposed correction cannot be one that would change the scope of the patent claims.[13] For example, the patentee in *In re Arnott*[14] was granted a reissue patent directed to an intraocular lens implant. As reissued, a particular dependent claim (claim 8) depended from another claim of the patent (claim 1). The patentee contended that claim 8 should have depended from claim 7, and that his patent counsel's assistant had simply made a typographical error when typing the application from a handwritten draft in which the number 7 looked like the number 1. The USPTO Commissioner denied the patentee's request for correction because changing the claim dependency under these circumstances would have meant changing the scope of claim 8. When claim 8 depended from claim 7, it incorporated a limitation requiring the implant to be made from a particular material, polymethyl methacrylate, which did not appear in claim 1. Therefore changing the claim dependency as requested by the patentee would have changed the scope of claim 8 and could not be permitted via the certificate of correction procedure.[15]

Whether a certificate of correction is sought under 35 U.S.C. §254 or §255, the USPTO will issue a separate document titled "Certificate of Correction" that operates much like an errata sheet for the patent. The certificate will list specific corrections by the patent's line and column numbers. The certificate is made a part of the official patent documentation, and the patent is treated as if the corrections had been part of the original patent as issued.[16]

C. Reissue

1. Overview

For errors not remediable by a certificate of correction as discussed above, the patentee may need to consider whether to seek reissuance of his patent. Reissue is an administrative procedure conducted within the USPTO for correcting an issued patent that suffers from certain enumerated errors that must have occurred "without any deceptive intention."[17] Reissue involves an offer by the patentee to surrender

[13] *Id.* at 1052.

[14] 19 U.S.P.Q.2d 1049 (Comm'r Pat. 1991).

[15] An applicant in this scenario would need to attempt correction by filing an application to reissue the patent, as discussed below.

[16] *But see* Southwest Software, Inc. v. Harlequin, Inc., 226 F.3d 1280 (Fed. Cir. 2000), in which the Federal Circuit held that a certificate of correction issued under 35 U.S.C. §254 was *not* effective for an infringement cause of action that arose prior to the issuance of the certificate.

[17] 35 U.S.C. §251 (2006).

the original patent,[18] submission of a reissue application with an oath setting forth the asserted errors, and a reprosecution of the patent's claims. During the reprosecution, all claims of the reissue application are subject to rejection on any statutory ground.[19] The possible results of this procedure are to reissue the patent in original or amended form for the remaining term of the original patent, or if no error is found, a refusal by the agency to reissue the patent. Unless and until a reissued patent is granted, the original patent remains in effect.[20]

The USPTO assigns reissued patents a new patent number that begins with the abbreviation "Re."—for example, "U.S. Patent No. Re. 40,000." The specification of the reissued patent will be printed by the agency "in such a manner as to show the changes over the original patent text by enclosing any material omitted by the reissue in heavy brackets [ ] and printing material added by the reissue in *italics*."[21] Although it has been corrected in the USPTO, a reissued patent nevertheless remains subject to the possibility of invalidation in federal court litigation, just as an original patent.

2. Historical Development

The practice of reissuing defective patents was first approved by the U.S. Supreme Court in 1832[22] and legislatively codified in the Patent Act of 1836.[23] Reissue was conceived as a validity-saving mechanism, available when by an innocent mistake, "the instrument introduced to secure this privilege [the patentee's right to exclude] fails in its

[18]*See* 37 C.F.R. §1.178(a) (providing that "[t]he application for reissue of a patent shall constitute an offer to surrender that patent, and the surrender shall take effect upon reissue of the patent").

[19]*See* Hewlett-Packard Co. v. Bausch & Lomb Inc., 882 F.2d 1556, 1563 (Fed. Cir. 1989) (explaining that "[r]eissue is essentially a reprosecution of all claims. For example, original claims which a patentee wants to maintain unchanged may nevertheless be rejected on any statutory ground.").

[20]*See* 37 C.F.R. §1.178(a) (providing that "[u]ntil a reissue application is granted, the original patent shall remain in effect.").

[21]United States Patent and Trademark Office, Manual of Patent Examining Procedure §1455 (9th ed., last rev. Jan, 2018), *available at* https://www.uspto.gov/web/offices/pac/mpep/s1455.html.

[22]*See* Grant v. Raymond, 31 U.S. (6 Pet.) 218 (1832).

[23]*See* Festo Corp. v. Shoketsu Kinzoku Kogyo Kabushiki Co., 234 F.3d 558, 602 n.3 (Fed. Cir. 2000) (*en banc*) (Michel, J., dissenting) (noting that "[t]he Patent Act of 1836 authorized a patentee to surrender the claims of his original patent and to obtain a reissue patent whenever the patent was 'inoperative, or invalid, by reason of a defective or insufficient description or specification, or by reason of the patentee claiming in his specification as his own invention, more than he had or shall have a right to claim as new.' Patent Act of 1836, Ch. 357, 5 Stat. 117, at §13 (July 4, 1836)."), *vacated on other grounds*, 535 U.S. 722 (2002).

object. . . ."[24] In other words, reissue was available when the patentee had innocently made an inadequate exchange.

The possibility of reissue recognizes the need for fairness to inventors, given the difficulty of drafting patents.[25] As a remedial provision based on fundamental notions of equity and fairness, reissue is intended to "bail applicants out of difficult situations into which they got 'without any deceptive intention.'"[26] Accordingly, the reissue statute "should be construed liberally."[27]

The nineteenth century saw extensive abuses of the reissue procedure.[28] For example, in *Miller v. Brass Co.*,[29] the Supreme Court held that an application for reissue should be denied because the patent owner delayed in seeking to broaden its claims for 15 years after issuance of the original patent. The Court recognized that reissue might be permitted to broaden claims, even though the statute at that time did not expressly provide for broadening reissues, if the reissue was sought within two years of the original grant (two years being the prefiling grace period at that time). But in this case, the patentee's prolonged delay was unreasonable, and permitting reissue would have had unjust consequences: "Every independent inventor, every mechanic, every citizen, is affected by such delay, and by the issue of a new patent with a broader and more comprehensive claim. The

[24]*Grant*, 31 U.S. (6 Pet.) at 244.

[25]*See* Topliff v. Topliff, 145 U.S. 156 (1892), in which the Court observed the following:

> To hold that a patent can never be reissued for an enlarged claim would be not only to override the obvious intent of the statute, but would operate in many cases with great hardship upon the patentee. The specification and claims of a patent, particularly if the invention be at all complicated, constitute one of the most difficult legal instruments to draw with accuracy; and, in view of the fact that valuable inventions are often placed in the hands of inexperienced persons to prepare such specifications and claims, it is no matter of surprise that the latter frequently fail to describe with requisite certainty the exact invention of the patentee, and err either in claiming that which the patentee had not in fact invented, or in omitting some element which was a valuable or essential part of his actual invention. Under such circumstances, it would be manifestly unjust to deny him the benefit of a reissue to secure to him his actual invention, provided it is evident that there has been a mistake, and he has been guilty of no want of reasonable diligence in discovering it, and no third persons have in the meantime acquired the right to manufacture or sell what he had failed to claim. The object of the patent law is to secure to inventors a monopoly of what they have actually invented or discovered, and it ought not to be defeated by a too strict and technical adherence to the letter of the statute, or by the application of artificial rules of interpretation.

Id. at 171.

[26]In re Oda, 443 F.2d 1200, 1203 (C.C.P.A. 1971) (Rich, J.).

[27]In re Weiler, 790 F.2d 1576, 1579 (Fed. Cir. 1986).

[28]*See generally* Kendall J. Dood, *Pursuing the Essence of Inventions: Reissuing Patents in the 19th Century*, 32 TECH. & CULTURE 999, 999-1017 (1991).

[29]104 U.S. 350 (1881).

granting of a reissue for such a purpose, after an unreasonable delay, is clearly an abuse of the power to grant reissues, and may justly be declared illegal and void."[30]

The reissue provisions of the Patent Act were subsequently amended in the 1952 Act to make explicit that broadening reissues must be sought within a two-year window after the grant of the original patent. This and other amendments, as well as a series of Supreme Court decisions on reissue patents, curbed the earlier abuses. Today, less than 1 percent of the U.S. patents granted annually are reissue patents.[31] However, those patents that do go into reissue are often very valuable; many reissued patents are involved in pending or contemplated litigation over infringement and/or validity.

3. Statutory Basis

The statutory provision governing patent reissues is 35 U.S.C. §251, which provides in part that:

> **(a) In general** — Whenever any patent is, through error, deemed wholly or partly inoperative or invalid, by reason of a defective specification or drawing, or by reason of the patentee claiming more or less than he had a right to claim in the patent, the Director shall, on the surrender of such patent and the payment of the fee required by law, reissue the patent for the invention disclosed in the original patent, and in accordance with a new and amended application, for the unexpired part of the term of the original patent. No new matter shall be introduced into the application for reissue. . . .
>
> **(d) Reissue patent enlarging scope of claims** — No reissued patent shall be granted enlarging the scope of the claims of the original patent unless applied for within two years from the grant of the original patent.[32]

[30] *Id.* at 355.

[31] For example, in the calendar year 2018 the USPTO granted the following numbers and types of patents:

> Utility: 307,759;
> Design: 30,497;
> Plant: 1,208; and
> Reissue: 528.

United States Patent and Trademark Office, *U.S. Patent Statistics Chart, Calendar Years 1963-2018*, *available at* see URL at Chapter 7, footnote 633. Thus, only about 0.16 percent of all U.S. patents granted in calendar year 2014 were reissued patents.

[32] 35 U.S.C. §251 (eff. Sept. 16, 2012) (as amended by the AIA). The pre-AIA version of the first paragraph of 35 U.S.C. §251 required that the error be "without any deceptive intention." The AIA deleted the intent language. *See* Leahy-Smith America Invents Act, Pub. L. No. 112-29 (H.R. 1249), §20(d)(1)(B),125 Stat. 284, 334 (Sept. 16, 2011). This amendment to §251 is effective Sept. 16, 2012, and applies prospectively to "proceedings commenced on or after that effective date." AIA §20(l).

The basic criteria for reissue are identified by parsing this statutory text. In order to qualify for reissue, a patent must be "wholly or partly inoperative or invalid," meaning that the patent is "ineffective to protect the invention adequately or it is a nullity. . . ."[33] Importantly, this inoperativeness or invalidity must have been caused by "error." Thus, reissue *cannot* be used to rehabilitate a patent that was procured through inequitable conduct,[34] which by definition involves intent to deceive the USPTO. Types of reissue error specifically mentioned in the statute are "a defective specification or drawing,"[35] or "the patentee claiming more or less than he had a right to claim in the patent."[36]

If the patent is reissued, the reissued patent will expire on the same date that the original patent would have, so that reissue in no way extends the term of the patent. Moreover, no new matter can be introduced in a reissue application.[37] Thus, although the scope of claims may be broadened in reissue, this is only possible to the extent that the broadening is supported by the original specification in accordance with 35 U.S.C. §112(a). The reissue must be "for the invention disclosed in the original patent."[38]

4. Broadening Reissues

A "broadening reissue" is sought when the patentee erred by "claiming less than he had a right to claim in the patent," and wants to obtain claims of broader scope than those that appear in the issued patent. Such broadened claims must nevertheless be supported by the patent's disclosure in accordance with 35 U.S.C. §112(a), because the reissue must be "for the invention disclosed in the original patent."[39] If a broadening reissue is desired, the patentee must file an application to reissue "within two years from the grant of the original patent."[40] This two-year statute of limitations for broadening reissues is based on the two-year prefiling grace period provided by the Patent Act between 1839 and 1939. Courts construed any delay longer than

[33]In re Oda, 443 F.2d 1200, 1206 (C.C.P.A. 1971) (Rich, J.).

[34]*See* Hewlett-Packard Co. v. Bausch & Lomb, Inc., 882 F.2d 1556, 1563 n.7 (Fed. Cir. 1989).

[35]35 U.S.C. §251(a) (eff. Sept. 16, 2012).

[36]35 U.S.C. §251(a) (eff. Sept. 16, 2012).

[37]In interpreting the reissue statutes the Supreme Court has explained that "by 'new matter' we suppose to be meant new substantive matter, such as would have the effect of changing the invention, or of introducing what might be the subject of another application for a patent." Powder Co. v. Powder Works, 98 U.S. 126, 138 (1878).

[38]35 U.S.C. §251(a) (eff. Sept. 16, 2012).

[39]*Id.*

[40]*Id.*

the two-year period as a presumptive abandonment of any described but nonclaimed subject matter.[41]

Case law on what constitutes a broadening reissue applies a "broader in any respect" rule; in other words, if the scope of even a single limitation of a claim is broadened, although other limitations remain unchanged or are even narrowed in scope, this counts as a broadening reissue that must be initiated within the two-year statute of limitations.[42] For example, consider the following claim of an issued patent:

> 1. A ceiling fan comprising a plurality of hollow blades, attached to a rod, attached to a motor.

Assume that the written description supports the modification of claim 1 to read as follows:

> 1. A ceiling fan comprising a plurality of blades, attached to a solid rod, attached to a motor.

If the patentee seeks to reissue the patent so as to obtain the modified version of claim 1, he must file his reissue application within two years of the issuance of the original patent. The proposed modification of claim 1 satisfies the "broader in any respect" rule. Even though the rod limitation is now narrower in scope because the qualifier "solid" has been added, the blades limitation has been broadened because the "hollow" qualification for the blade configuration has been removed (i.e., the blades can be hollow or solid or of any other construction).

When considering whether to seek broadening reissue, the patentee should keep in mind that this strategy may give rise to intervening rights in third parties who relied on the narrower version of the claims that issued in the original patent, as discussed further in Section C.7 below.

5. Reissue Error

A number of types of errors in an issued patent may qualify it for reissue. The Patent Act of 1946, which defined reissue error in terms of "inadvertence, accident, mistake," was generally construed rather liberally. Although the 1952 Act implementation of reissue required that the error be committed "without any deceptive intention,"[43] the

[41] *See* Topliff v. Topliff, 145 U.S. 156, 170-171 (1892); Miller v. Brass Co., 104 U.S. 350, 352 (1881).

[42] *See* Ball Corp. v. United States, 729 F.2d 1429, 1437-1438 (Fed. Cir. 1984).

[43] 35 U.S.C. §251 (2006).

America Invents Act of 2011 deleted the "without any deceptive intention" language.[44] Post-AIA, reissues must still correct "error" in patents, but the statutory amendment indicates that intent of the entity responsible for the error is no longer relevant.

A representative type of reissue error is a translation error in the patent specification that is more severe than the type of typographical error correctable by a certificate of correction. For example, in *In re Oda,*[45] the translating of a Japanese priority application into English resulted in the mistranslation of "nitric acid" as "nitrous acid," two different chemical entities. These mistranslations occurred in several places in the written description of the patent, including a working example, but not in the claims. The USPTO rejected the reissue application as drawn to new matter. The Court of Customs and Patent Appeals (CCPA), one of the Federal Circuit's two predecessor courts, disagreed. The CCPA concluded, based on all evidence of record, that one skilled in the art "would appreciate not only the existence of error in the specification but what the error is,"[46] and that from this it followed that "when the nature of this error is known it is also known how to correct it."[47] Thus, the reissue was permissible to change nitrous to nitric in the written description and did not constitute prohibited new matter.

Another type of reissue error occurs when the patentee claimed more or less than she had a right to claim. In *Scripps Clinic & Research Foundation v. Genentech, Inc.,*[48] the inventors asserted that they had erred in claiming less than they had a right to claim. In the original patent, which was directed to highly purified Factor VIII:C protein product, a substance involved in the clotting of blood, the invention was claimed only by means of process and product-by-process claims. The patent did not include product claims (i.e., to Factor VIII:C itself as a composition of matter) because the patent attorney at the time of the original prosecution did not believe that such claims were legally available.

The Federal Circuit held in *Scripps Clinic* that the patent attorney's misunderstanding of the law was the type of error that could be corrected by reissue. "Although attorney error is not an open invitation to reissue in every case in which it may appear,"[49] the court cautioned,

[44]*See* Leahy-Smith America Invents Act, Pub. L. No. 112-29 (H.R. 1249), §20(d)(1)(B), 125 Stat. 284, 334 (Sept. 16, 2011). This amendment, made to what is now designated 35 U.S.C. §251(a), is effective Sept. 16, 2012, and applies prospectively to "proceedings commenced on or after that effective date." AIA §20(l).

[45]443 F.2d 1200 (C.C.P.A. 1971).

[46]*Id.* at 1206.

[47]*Id.*

[48]927 F.2d 1565 (Fed. Cir. 1991).

[49]*Id.* at 1575.

here the error was made without deceptive intent, and the reissue application complied with all pertinent statutory and regulatory requirements. Contrary to the district court's view, the reissue applicant need not prove that "no competent attorney or alert inventor could have avoided the error sought to be corrected by reissue."[50]

A reissue applicant must be truthful about the cause of the error(s) sought to be corrected, as illustrated by *Hewlett-Packard Co. v. Bausch & Lomb, Inc.*,[51] a case that highlights the risks involved in attempting to reissue a patent purchased from a third party. After Bausch & Lomb (B&L) purchased a patent directed to an X-Y plotter in an attempt to gain negotiating leverage in an ongoing infringement lawsuit against Hewlett-Packard (HP), B&L filed an application to reissue the patent. The reissue application added new dependent claims specifically targeted at the device being sold by HP, and the accompanying oath asserted reissue error in the failure to include dependent claims of narrower scope. When B&L amended its complaint to assert the reissue patent, HP defended on the ground that the reissue patent was invalid and the district court so held.

On appeal the Federal Circuit agreed, holding that B&L's reissue application was defective and the reissue patent claims invalid. The statutorily required "error" of §251 has two parts, the court explained, both of which the reissue applicant must establish: (1) error (or defect) in the patent, and (2) inadvertent error in conduct.[52] With respect to error (or defect) in the patent, the court did not need to decide whether as a legal matter a failure to file dependent claims constitutes reissue error.[53] With respect to the asserted error in conduct, however, the court concluded that the affidavits of a former B&L patent agent, purporting to explain why narrower claims were not previously included in the patent, were "blatantly inaccurate"[54] and "factually untrue,"[55] and therefore did not support reissue. The patent agent had averred that the failure to include more specific claims was based on his inability to contact the inventor, coupled with his misunderstanding of the invention, when in fact the agent's records, produced in discovery, established that the patent agent and inventor had met and communicated repeatedly and extensively.[56]

[50]*Id.*
[51]882 F.2d 1556 (Fed. Cir. 1989).
[52]*See id.* at 1564 (citing In re Clark, 522 F.2d 623, 626 (C.C.P.A. 1975)).
[53]*See id.* at 1565.
[54]*Id.* at 1558.
[55]*Id.* at 1566.
[56]*See id.* at 1561.

6. The Recapture Rule

The recapture rule, which can be thought of as analogous to the doctrine of prosecution history estoppel,[57] provides that a patentee cannot use reissuance of his patent as a means to "recapture" subject matter that he earlier surrendered during prosecution of the original patent in order to gain issuance thereof. Such surrenders are not the kind of error that reissue was intended to correct. The Federal Circuit has explained that "[u]nder the rule against recapture, a patentee's reissue claims are invalid when the patentee broadens the scope of a claim in reissue to cover subject matter that he surrendered during prosecution of the original claims."[58]

For example, the Federal Circuit held in *Mentor Corp. v. Coloplast, Inc.*,[59] that claims 6 to 9 of the reissue patent in suit, directed to a male condom catheter for patients suffering from incontinence, were invalid because they were broader than the corresponding claims of the original patent in a manner directly pertinent to subject matter that had been surrendered during prosecution of the original patent. In order to overcome a §103 obviousness rejection of the claims in its original patent application, Mentor distinguished prior art catheters by arguing to the USPTO examiner that none of them showed transfer of the adhesive from the catheter's outer surface to its inner surface as the sheath is rolled up and then unrolled. After Mentor amended the claims to recite this transfer feature, the patent issued.

Within two years of issuance, Mentor filed an application seeking broadening reissuance of the patent, adding new claims 6 to 9 that deleted the adhesive transfer limitation. Mentor asserted reissuable error in claiming less than it had a right to claim, admitting in its oath that the claims of the original patent did not literally read on a type of catheter (made by Mentor's competitors) in which the adhesive is applied to the inner surface of the sheath before the device is rolled up. Mentor's patent attorney had assumed, incorrectly, that this method of manufacture was too impractical to be commercially feasible.

The Federal Circuit agreed with accused infringer Coloplast that Mentor's "deliberate and intentional" amendment of its claims to recite the adhesive transfer feature, made in order to overcome a §103 obviousness rejection, was not the kind of error that the reissue procedure is intended to correct. The court distinguished cases in which "there is no evidence that amendment of the originally filed

[57]The doctrine of prosecution history estoppel, which operates as a legal limitation on the availability of the doctrine of equivalents theory of infringement, is detailed in Chapter 9 ("Patent Infringement"), *infra*.

[58]MBO Labs., Inc. v. Becton, Dickinson & Co., 602 F.3d 1306, 1313 (Fed. Cir. 2010).

[59]998 F.2d 992 (Fed. Cir. 1993).

claims was in any sense an admission that the scope of that claim was not in fact patentable."[60] As the court explained,

> [e]rror under the reissue statute does not include a deliberate decision to surrender specific subject matter in order to overcome prior art, a decision which in light of subsequent developments in the marketplace might be regretted. It is precisely because the patentee amended his claims to overcome prior art that a member of the public is entitled to occupy the space abandoned by the patent applicant. Thus, the reissue statute cannot be construed in such a way that competitors, properly relying on prosecution history, become patent infringers when they do so. In this case, Mentor narrowed its claims for the purpose of obtaining allowance in the original prosecution and it is now precluded from recapturing what it earlier conceded.[61]

The impact of invoking the recapture rule, as in *Mentor*, should be contrasted with an assertion of intervening rights, discussed in the following section. In *Mentor,* application of the recapture rule resulted in invalidation of claims 6 to 9 of the reissue patent. This protected not only the accused infringer Coloplast, but also the public at large — anyone who might have otherwise infringed those claims. In contrast, application of intervening rights would not have invalidated the patent, and would merely have provided Coloplast (but no others) with a defense to infringement.

In *MBO Labs., Inc. v. Becton, Dickinson & Co.*,[62] the Federal Circuit explained that it follows a three-step test in determining whether the rule against recapture has been violated when reissued patents broaden claim scope:

> First, the court construes the reissued claims to "determine whether and in what 'aspect' the reissue claims are broader than the [original] patent claims." . . . Second, if the reissue claims are broader, the court determines whether the patentee surrendered subject matter [in the prosecution of the original patent] and "whether the broader aspects of the reissued claim relate to [the] surrendered subject matter." . . . To determine whether a patentee surrendered subject matter [in the prosecution of the original patent], we ask "whether an objective observer viewing the prosecution history would conclude that the purpose of the patentee's amendment or argument was to overcome prior art and secure the [original] patent." . . . If the patentee surrendered by argument [rather than by explicitly amending the claims], he must clearly and unmistakably argue that his invention does not cover certain subject matter to overcome an

[60] *Id.* at 995 (citing Seattle Box Co. v. Indus. Crating & Packing, Inc., 731 F.2d 818, 826 (Fed. Cir. 1984)).

[61] *Id.* at 996.

[62] 602 F.3d 1306 (Fed. Cir. 2010).

examiner's rejection based on prior art. . . . Third, a court must "determine whether the reissued claims were materially narrowed in other respects to avoid the recapture rule."[63]

The parties in *MBO Labs.* disputed the validity of MBO's reissue patent and specifically whether the second step of the above test was met. MBO's patents were directed to hypodermic safety syringes intended to protect health care workers from accidental needle sticks following patient injections. During original prosecution, MBO twice overcame USPTO obviousness rejections by emphasizing that although the prior art disclosed a type of guard that moved relative to a fixed needle, MBO's needle instead moved relative to the guard by "slidably retracting." MBO thereafter obtained a broadening reissue patent in order to "claim a system having 'any relative movement between the needle and the body,' not just a 'system wherein the needle must be bodily moved toward the safety device.'"[64] Affirming a district court's invalidation of four claims in MBO's reissue patent, the Federal Circuit concluded that MBO had violated the rule against recapture. During original prosecution, MBO "clearly and unmistakably" surrendered a guard body that moved forward to cover a fixed needle, but then sought to reclaim relative movement in its reissue claims.[65] In so doing, MBO had violated the rule against recapture, rendering the challenged reissue patent claims invalid.[66]

[63]*MBO Labs.,* 602 F.3d at 1314 (citations omitted).

[64]*MBO Labs.,* 602 F.3d at 1311.

[65]*MBO Labs.,* 602 F.3d at 1313, 1314-1315.

[66]For a decision analyzing the third and final prong of the three-step recapture test, *see* In re Mostafazadeh, 643 F.3d 1353 (Fed. Cir. 2011) (affirming USPTO rejection of reissue application claims that impermissibly attempted to recapture subject matter surrendered during prosecution of the original patent application). The *Mostafazadeh* court explained that in analyzing the third step of the recapture test, one must distinguish between the original claims (i.e., the claims before the surrender), the patented claims (i.e., the claims allowed after surrender), and the reissue claims. Violation of the rule against recapture may be avoided under step 3 of the recapture test "if the reissue claims 'materially narrow' the claims relative to the original claims such that full or substantial recapture of the subject matter surrendered during prosecution is avoided." *Id.* at 1358-1359. The narrowing "must relate to the subject matter surrendered during the original prosecution (i.e., the applicant cannot recapture the full scope of what was surrendered)." *Id.* at 1359. More specifically, a claim limitation that was added during prosecution to distinguish the prior art cannot be entirely eliminated on reissue; doing so would constitute recapture of the surrendered subject matter. *Id.* at 1359. The added claim limitation may be modified, however, "so long as it continues to materially narrow the claim scope relative to the surrendered subject matter such that the surrendered subject matter is not entirely or substantially recaptured." *Id.* at 1359.

The *Mostafazadeh* court rejected the reissue patentee's argument that its recapture was only "partial." The claims (directed to packaging for semiconductors) retained an "attachment pad" limitation that was related to the surrendered subject matter. The claim scope was not *materially* narrowed, however, because the use of an attachment pad was well known in the prior art. *See id.* at 1361. The reissue application claims also

7. Effect of Reissue: Intervening Rights

When a patent owner obtains reissue of her patent from the USPTO, her right to exclude under the original patent continues after reissue, for the remainder of the term of the original patent, insofar as the claims of the original and reissue patents are "substantially identical."[67] Thus, although the original patent no longer exists once the reissue patent has been granted (because the original patent has been surrendered upon reissue), the claims of the reissue patent "reach back" to the date that the original patent issued if the claims are "substantially identical."[68]

With respect to claims in the reissue patent that are *not* substantially identical, particularly those that have been broadened, the patentee's right to exclude may be limited by the intervening rights of third parties. Recognition of intervening rights represents the patent system's attempt to protect the third party who relied on the notice provided by the claims of the original patent as signalling what subject matter was within the patentee's exclusive right and what was in the public domain, available to all. If the third party commences the manufacture and sale of a product that does not infringe the claims of the original patent, only to later find that the patent has been broadened through reissue such that the same product now infringes the reissue claims, the third party will be permitted to use or sell those already-manufactured items, and may be permitted to continue manufacturing

---

included "bus bar" limitations. Although the bus bar limitations narrowed the reissue claims relative to the original claims, that narrowing was related only to the bus bar and not to the circular attachment pad limitation. "In other words, the narrowing limitations [were] unrelated to the surrendered subject matter and thus insufficient to avoid recapture." *Id.* at 1361.

[67] 35 U.S.C. §252, ¶1.

[68] *See* 35 U.S.C. §252 ("Effect of Reissue"), ¶1 (emphasis added):

> The surrender of the original patent shall take effect upon the issue of the reissued patent, and every reissued patent shall have the same effect and operation in law, on the trial of actions for causes thereafter arising, as if the same had been originally granted in such amended form, but in so far as the claims of the original and reissued patents are substantially identical, such surrender shall not affect any action then pending nor abate any cause of action then existing, and the reissued patent, to the extent that its claims are *substantially identical* with the original patent, shall constitute a continuation thereof and have effect continuously from the date of the original patent.

Federal Circuit case law has interpreted "identical" as used in §252 to require that the claims of the reissue patent not be substantively changed in scope from those of the original patent; the reissue claim language need not be literally identical to that of the original claims, however. *See* Slimfold Mfg. Co. v. Kinkead Indus., Inc., 810 F.2d 1113, 1115-1116 (Fed. Cir. 1987).

more of the same under certain circumstances.[69] "Recapture through a reissue patent of what is dedicated to the public by omission in the original patent is permissible under specific conditions, but not at the expense of innocent parties."[70]

Intervening rights are governed by the second paragraph of 35 U.S.C. §252. The text of this rather long-winded paragraph is

[69]To be clear, intervening rights are not necessarily limited to reissues or to situation in which a patentee has broadened the scope of its claims. Intervening rights may also arise as a result of reexamination, another USPTO procedure examined *infra* Section D, in which the scope of the claims cannot be broadened. *See* 35 U.S.C. §305 (2012) (claim scope cannot be enlarged via reexamination); 35 U.S.C. §307(b) (2012) (providing that "[a]ny proposed amended or new claim determined to be patentable and incorporated into a patent following [an *ex parte*] reexamination proceeding will have the same effect as that specified in section 252 of this title for reissued patents on the right of any person who made, purchased, or used within the United States, or imported into the United States, anything patented by such proposed amended or new claim, or who made substantial preparation for the same, prior to issuance of a [reexamination] certificate under the provisions of subsection (a) of this section"); 35 U.S.C. §316(b) (2012) (providing same for pre-AIA *inter partes* reexamination). *See also* Marine Polymer Techs., Inc. v. Hemcon, Inc., 672 F.3d 1350, 1362 (Fed. Cir. 2012) (*en banc*) (explaining that although intervening rights doctrine originated as a defense against patents modified through reissue, the doctrine has been extended to the reexamination context); R & L Carriers, Inc. v. Qualcomm, Inc., 801 F.3d 1346, 1351 (Fed. Cir. 2015) (stating that "[a] patentee of a patent that survives reexamination is only entitled to infringement damages for the time period between the date of issuance of the original claims and the date of the reexamined claims if the original and the reexamined claims are 'substantially identical'") (quoting 35 U.S.C. §252 (2012)).

In *Convolve, Inc. v. Compaq Computer Corp.*, No. 2014-1732, 2016 WL 520247 (Fed. Cir. Feb. 10, 2016), the appellate court emphasized that it is the scope of the claims (as interpreted under the *Phillips* framework), not the precise words used in the claims, that must be "substantially identical" to avoid an accused infringer's defense of intervening rights. "[A]mendments made during reexamination do not necessarily compel a conclusion that the scope of the claims has been substantively changed." *Convolve, Inc.*, 2016 WL 520247, at *7. Even though patentee Convolve had amended certain claims during reexamination after a USPTO rejection based on prior art, that amendment (which added the modifier "seek" in front of the phrase "acoustic noise" in a claim to a method for controlling the operation of a computer hard drive) did not substantively change the scope of those claims. Considering all the intrinsic evidence, the Circuit determined that the original claims (i.e., before the addition of "seek") were nevertheless limited in meaning to controlling "seek acoustic noise," i.e., acoustic noise generated by the movement of the hard drive's arm and read/write head during the seek process, and excluded noise generated by spindle rotation. Because the reexamination amendment did not alter the scope of the claims, intervening rights on the part of accused infringer Compaq were not triggered. The Circuit accordingly reversed the district court's grant of summary judgment that intervening rights precluded Compaq's infringement liability. *Convolve, Inc.*, 2016 WL 520247, at *11.

[70]Seattle Box Co. v. Indus. Crating & Packing, 756 F.2d 1574, 1579 (Fed. Cir. 1985).

reproduced below, with the addition of bracketed labels for each sentence and a space between them for readability:

> [A] A reissued patent shall not abridge or affect the right of any person or that person's successors in business who, prior to the grant of a reissue, made, purchased, offered to sell, or used within the United States, or imported into the United States, anything patented by the reissued patent, to continue the use of, to offer to sell, or to sell to others to be used, offered for sale, or sold, the specific thing so made, purchased, offered for sale, used, or imported unless the making, using, offering for sale, or selling of such thing infringes a valid claim of the reissued patent which was in the original patent.
>
> [B] The court before which such matter is in question may provide for the continued manufacture, use, offer for sale, or sale of the thing made, purchased, offered for sale, used, or imported as specified, or for the manufacture, use, offer for sale, or sale in the United States of which substantial preparation was made before the grant of the reissue, and the court may also provide for the continued practice of any process patented by the reissue that is practiced, or for the practice of which substantial preparation was made, before the grant of the reissue, to the extent and under such terms as the court deems equitable for the protection of investments made or business commenced before the grant of the reissue.[71]

Sentence [A] of §252, ¶2 gives the third party who made a non-infringing "specific thing" prior to the grant of the reissue, which now infringes the reissue patent, an absolute right to continue to use or to sell that "specific thing."[72] Note that this is an *absolute* right to continue to use or sell, but not to manufacture more of, the "specific thing."[73]

Sentence [B] of §252, ¶2 involves *equitable* rights.[74] The text of sentence [B] gives a federal district court the discretion, to the extent that

[71] 35 U.S.C. §252, ¶2.

[72] *See* Pasquale J. Federico, *Commentary on the New Patent Act*, 35 U.S.C.A. 1 (1954 ed.), *reprinted in* 75 J. Pat. & Trademark Off. Soc'y 161, 207 (1993) (noting that "[t]his absolute protection extends only to the specific objects actually made before the grant of the reissued patent and does not extend to the making of additional objects of identical or like kind. With respect to the latter the court is given discretion to act.").

[73] *See* Marine Polymer Techs., Inc. v. Hemcon, Inc., 672 F.3d 1350, 1361-1362 (Fed. Cir. 2012) (*en banc*) (explaining that "absolute intervening rights" are those that "abrogate liability for infringing claims added to or modified from the original patent if the accused products were made or used before the reissue").

[74] *See* Marine Polymer Techs., Inc. v. Hemcon, Inc., 672 F.3d 1350, 1362 (Fed. Cir. 2012) (*en banc*) (explaining that "equitable intervening rights" are those that "apply as a matter of judicial discretion to mitigate liability for infringing such claims even as to products made or used after the reissue if the accused infringer made substantial preparations for the infringing activities prior to reissue").

the court deems necessary to protect business investments made before the reissue, to permit the third party to *continue* to manufacture more of "the thing" made before the grant of the reissue (which "thing" did not infringe the original patent but now infringes the reissue), or to continue the manufacture of that which the patentee made "substantial preparation" to manufacture before the grant of the reissue.[75] This is an exercise of the district court's equitable powers, reviewable by the Federal Circuit for abuse of discretion.

Seattle Box Co. v. Industrial Crating & Packing, Inc.[76] illustrates the application of sentence [B] of 35 U.S.C. §252, ¶2. The original patent of plaintiff Seattle Box, directed to an arrangement for separating oil pipes stacked in a pipe bundle, claimed a double-concave wooden "spacer block" having a height "greater than the diameter of the pipe."[77] After commencing an infringement action against Industrial Crating, Seattle Box applied to reissue the patent, asserting error in claiming less than it had a right to, and broadening the claims to recite a spacer block with height "substantially equal to or greater than" the pipe diameter.[78] Industrial Crating's accused spacer blocks did not literally infringe (and most likely did not equivalently infringe) the claims of the original patent because the blocks were of a height 1/16 of an inch less than the pipe height.[79] The accused blocks did arguably infringe the broadened claims of the reissue patent, however, which the Federal Circuit held to be "substantively different" from the original claims. As of the date that the reissue patent was granted, defendant Industrial Crating had in its inventory the materials necessary to make 224 bundles. The bundles were assembled after the grant of the reissue, however.[80] A district court denied Industrial Crating the defense of intervening rights for the 224 bundles.

The Federal Circuit held on appeal that sentence [B] of §252, ¶2 applied. Concluding that the district court had abused its discretion in denying intervening rights, the Federal Circuit ruled that defendant Industrial Crating should have been allowed to dispose of the old inventory on hand at the date of reissue, without liability to the

[75]*See* Pasquale J. Federico, *Commentary on the New Patent Act*, 35 U.S.C.A. 1 (1954 ed.), *reprinted in* 75 J. PAT. & TRADEMARK OFF. SOC'Y 161, 207 (1993) (stating that "[w]hen the specified conditions obtain, the court has the power to permit (1) continuation of the manufacture of things made before the grant of the reissue (that is, the manufacture of additional objects), and their use or sale, (2) the continued manufacture, use or sale when substantial preparation was made before the grant of the reissue, and (3) the continued practice of a process patented by the reissue practiced, or for the practice of which substantial preparation was made, before the grant of the reissue").

[76]756 F.2d 1574 (Fed. Cir. 1985).

[77]*Id.* at 1576.

[78]*Id.*

[79]*See id.* at 1580.

[80]*See id.* at 1577.

patentee.[81] The equities favored Industrial Crating, the Federal Circuit found, because it relied on the advice of counsel in attempting to design around the original patent, and because at the time that the reissue patent was granted it already had pending orders for the 224 spacer blocks in its inventory.[82] The court concluded that "[i]n these circumstances, the new reissue claims in this case present a compelling case for the application of the doctrine of intervening rights because a person should be able to make business decisions secure in the knowledge that those actions which fall outside the original patent claims are protected.... Here, the spacer blocks involved were made or acquired, before the reissue, so as not to infringe the then existing [original] patent."[83]

8. Strategic Considerations for Reissue

The decision to reissue a patent deserves careful consideration. As with most actions taken in regard to an issued patent, substantial risks may be encountered. Various strategic aspects of the reissue procedure will affect the decision.

First, reissue differs from reexamination (discussed in Section D, *infra*) in that only the patentee can seek reissuance of his patent. There is no means of third-party involvement in reissue.[84] An accused infringer does not have standing to seek reissuance of a patent (unless the accused infringer becomes the owner thereof).

The AIA-implemented post-grant review procedure became available to patent challengers on March 16, 2013, but only for patents issued under the new AIA §3 rules. As of July 2019, the USPTO had received only 172 petitions for post-grant review,[85] so the procedure is still in its infancy as of this writing. Nevertheless, such patents will be open to attack in the USPTO by any person on a wide variety of grounds during the nine-month window following the patent's

[81]*See id.* at 1581.

[82]*See id.* at 1580.

[83]*Id.* (citations omitted).

[84]However, a reissue application may be subject to a third party's protest under 37 C.F.R. §1.291 ("Protests by the public against pending applications"), as occurred in *In re Hall*, 781 F.2d 897, 897 (Fed. Cir. 1986). *Hall* is better known for its analysis of whether a single copy of a thesis catalogued in a German library qualified as a "printed publication" under 35 U.S.C. §102(b) (1982). This latter aspect of *Hall* is discussed in Chapter 4 ("Novelty, Loss of Right, and Priority Pre- and Post-America Invents Act of 2011 (35 U.S.C. §102)"), *supra*.

[85]*See* United States Patent and Trademark Office, https://www.ustpo.gov/sites/default/files/documents/Trials_Statistics_2019-06-03.pdf.

issuance.[86] Patent owners will likely have only a single opportunity to amend their claims during the post-grant review (if the USPTO allows amendment at all).[87] As a result, patentees may increasingly turn to reissue as a means to circumvent the restrictions of post-grant review and gain greater opportunities to control the revision of their claim scope.[88]

Reissue can be highly advantageous to the patent owner because it is generally a far less expensive alternative than litigation for correcting patent defects. Moreover, reissue is conducted in the USPTO, the forum that previously issued the patent and that is presumed to have technical expertise in the subject matter of the invention.

The patentee may use reissue to add new claims to her patent that specifically target a competitor's product, so long as the specification supports these claims in accordance with 35 U.S.C. §112(a). The patentee in some cases also may seek to reissue the patent with claims narrower than those that issued in the original patent, with the intent of avoiding newly discovered prior art that was not before the USPTO during its examination of the original patent.

Reissue also can involve considerable risks for the patent owner. Applying for reissue requires an offer to surrender the original patent, with no guarantee that the patent will be reissued. The presumption of validity that accompanies an issued patent does not continue once an application to reissue the patent has been filed.[89] This makes logical sense because in filing to reissue, the patentee is admitting that its patent may be "wholly or partly inoperative or invalid. . . ."[90] All claims of the reissue application, even claims of the original patent that the patentee wants to carry over unchanged, are subject to examination and rejection on any statutory ground.[91]

[86]*See infra* Section E.2 ("Post-Grant Review").

[87]*See* 35 U.S.C. §326(d)(1) (eff. Sept. 16, 2013, for patents having claims with an effective filing date on or after Mar. 16, 2013) (providing that "IN GENERAL.—During a post-grant review instituted under this chapter, the patent owner may file 1 motion to amend the patent in 1 or more of the following ways: (A) Cancel any challenged patent claim. (B) For each challenged claim, propose a reasonable number of substitute claims."). Section 326(d)(2) provides that additional motions to amend a challenged patent may be permitted when they are jointly requested by the post-grant review petitioner and the patentee to materially advance a settlement of the post-grant review, or when requested by the patentee "for good cause shown."

[88]*See* DONALD S. CHISUM, REISSUE: RECENT FEDERAL CIRCUIT DECISIONS (2012).

[89]*See* In re Sneed, 710 F.2d 1544, 1550 n.4 (Fed. Cir. 1983) (noting that "contrary to appellants' argument, claims in a reissue *application* enjoy no presumption of 'validity' ") (emphasis in original).

[90]35 U.S.C. §251(a) (eff. Sept. 16, 2012).

[91]*See* Hewlett-Packard v. Bausch & Lomb, 882 F.2d 1556, 1563 (Fed. Cir. 1989) (characterizing reissue as "essentially a reprosecution of all claims").

D. Reexamination

1. Introduction

Reexamination is a much newer administrative procedure in the U.S. patent system than reissue, having been established by legislation enacted in 1980.[92] Reexamination's purpose was to provide a lower-cost alternative to federal court litigation in which to resolve certain questions of validity. Congress was influenced by studies showing that in the 1950s and 1960s, a large portion of the U.S. patents adjudicated invalid by federal courts were invalidated based on newly discovered prior art that had never been considered by the USPTO.[93] Reexamination was seen as creating a relatively low-cost method of obtaining a USPTO examination on this newly discovered prior art. Reexamination represented, if not a copy of, at least the closest parallel in U.S. practice to the well-regarded post-grant opposition procedure of the European patent system.[94]

In practice, reexamination did not prove to be the panacea its proponents hoped for. The reexamination system was criticized as biased in favor of patent owners because of the extremely limited opportunities for third-party participation. Responding to these and other concerns, Congress as part of the American Inventors Protection Act of 1999 enacted a second, *inter partes* form of reexamination (renaming the original form *ex parte* reexamination). Although it offered greater participation for third parties, *inter partes* reexamination suffered from its own shortcomings in terms of a severe estoppel provision and procedural delays.[95] In the America Invents Act of 2011, Congress phased

[92]*See* Act of Dec. 12, 1980, Pub. L. No. 96-517, 94 Stat. 3015 (codified as amended in scattered sections of 35 U.S.C.).

[93]*See* In re Portola Packaging, Inc., 110 F.3d 786 (Fed. Cir. 1997), stating that

> Congress recognized that holdings of patent invalidity by courts were mostly based on prior art that was not before the PTO. *Patent Reexamination: Hearings on S. 1679 Before the Senate Comm. on the Judiciary*, 96th Cong. 2 (1980) (opening statement of Senator Birch Bayh) ("All too often, patent holders find themselves in lengthy court proceedings where valuable patents are challenged on the grounds that the patent examiner missed pertinent data during the initial patent search."); *id.* at 14 (testimony of Sydney Diamond, Commissioner, U.S. Patent and Trademark Office) (referring to Gloria K. Koenig, *Patent Validity: A Statistical and Substantive Analysis* §5.05[4] (1974), in which the author found that from 1953 through 1967 "the proportion of invalid patents wherein uncited prior art [i.e., prior art not before the PTO] figured into the result is between 66 and 80 percent").

Id. at 789 (italics added).

[94]*See* European Patent Convention arts. 99-105 (16th ed. 2016).

[95]USPTO officials admit that "*[i]nter partes* reexamination has not proven as efficient as was originally intended. It has taken an average of 32 to 38 months to move

out *inter partes* reexamination and replaced it with a new proceeding called "*inter partes* review" (eff. Sept. 16, 2012).[96]

Both *ex parte* and *inter partes* reexamination are detailed below. The statutes governing *ex parte* reexamination are found at 35 U.S.C. §§301-307 and continue in effect post-AIA. The statutes dealing with *inter partes* reexamination are found at 35 U.S.C. §§311-318 (2006), and will no longer be in effect after September 16, 2012. In order to initiate either type of reexamination, the USPTO must be convinced that a "substantial new question of patentability"[97] arises from the prior art on which the request is based, as discussed below. If a substantial new question of patentability exists, the USPTO will issue an order for reexamination.[98] The reexamination of a patent proceeds in essentially the same manner as an original examination.[99] Reexaminations are decided in the first instance by individual examiners, as in the examination of original applications. The presumption of validity that applies to an issued patent under 35 U.S.C. §282 is no longer applicable once a patent is in reexamination; in rejecting claims during reexamination the USPTO examiner is not required to satisfy the rigorous "clear and convincing" standard that applies in federal court litigation challenging the validity of issued patents.[100]

At the completion of either type of reexamination proceeding, the USPTO will issue a "Reexamination Certificate" that becomes part of the official patent document. The certificate will operate to (1) cancel any claim of the issued patent that is determined to be unpatentable, (2) confirm any claim of the issued patent that is determined to be patentable, and/or (3) incorporate into the issued patent any proposed amended claims or new claims that have been determined to be patentable.[101]

---

from filing to issuance of a final reexamination certificate. The time to a final determination within the USPTO is even longer, when you factor in appeals." Teresa Stanek Rea, Deputy Under Secretary of Commerce for Intellectual Property and Deputy Director of the USPTO, *Building a Better Post Grant* (May 15, 2012), *available at* http://www.uspto.gov/blog/director/entry/building_a_better_post_grant.

[96]*See infra* Section E.1 ("*Inter Partes* Review").

[97]35 U.S.C. §§303(a), 304 (*ex parte*); 35 U.S.C. §312(a) (2006) (*inter partes*).

[98]*See* 35 U.S.C. §304 (*ex parte* reexamination order); 35 U.S.C. §313 (2006) (*inter partes* reexamination order).

[99]*See* 35 U.S.C. §305 (conduct of *ex parte* reexamination proceedings); 35 U.S.C. §314 (2006) (conduct of *inter partes* reexamination proceedings). Reexamination proceedings are to be conducted with "special dispatch" within the USPTO. 35 U.S.C. §305; 35 U.S.C. §314(c) (2006).

[100]*See* In re Etter, 756 F.2d 852, 855-859 (Fed. Cir. 1985) (*en banc*).

[101]35 U.S.C. §307(a).

2. *Ex Parte* Reexamination

a. Who Can Request

The *ex parte* reexamination procedure, the "older" form of reexamination, is governed by 35 U.S.C. §§301-307 and continues to be available post-America Invents Act of 2011. Although the name "ex parte" might suggest otherwise, this form of reexamination can be requested by anyone, not just the patent owner.[102] Even the Director of the USPTO has requested reexamination of patents issued by his own agency.[103] When someone other than the patent owner requests that a patent be reexamined, that person or entity is generally referred to as the "third-party requester." A third-party requester may be anonymous.[104]

The *ex parte* nature of this form of reexamination reflects the very limited opportunities for participation by the third-party requester after it files the request for reexamination. If the USPTO orders reexamination, the patent owner will be permitted to file a responsive statement, which may include a proposed amendment to his claims, or new claims.[105] The third-party requester will receive a copy of this statement and can file a response to it.[106] From that point on, however, the reexamination proceeds much like the initial examination of an original application; the prosecution is conducted entirely between the patent owner and the USPTO, and the administrative records are maintained in secrecy (until application publication or patent issuance).[107]

It is commonly thought that because it has so little opportunity to participate, a third party (who is often in the position of accused or potential infringer of the patent) should request *ex parte* reexamination only if it has "dead-on" prior art that is virtually sure to invalidate the claims. If the third party's attempt does not succeed and the reexamination certificate confirms the patentability of all the claims, the patent may take on a "gold-plated" hue to judges and juries who will understand that the USPTO has twice confirmed its validity.

[102]*See* 35 U.S.C. §302 (providing that "[a]ny person at any time may file a request for reexamination").

[103]*See* Peter J. Ayers, *Interpreting* In re Alappat *with an Eye Towards Prosecution*, 76 J. PAT. & TRADEMARK OFF. SOC'Y 741, 744 n.18 (1994).

[104]*See* 35 U.S.C. §301 (providing in part that "[a]t the written request of the person citing the prior art, his or her identity will be excluded from the patent file and kept confidential").

[105]35 U.S.C. §304.

[106]*Id.*

[107]35 U.S.C. §305.

b. *Statutory Grounds for Reexamination*

Sections 301 and 302 of the Patent Act significantly limit the grounds on which reexamination of a patent can be sought. A request for reexamination can be based only on prior art consisting of patents or printed publications,[108] and patentability can be challenged in reexamination only under an appropriate portion of 35 U.S.C. §102 (lack of novelty) or under 35 U.S.C. §103 (obviousness).[109] Reexamination cannot be sought to challenge inventorship, or to assert nonstatutory subject matter or lack of utility under 35 U.S.C. §101, or non-enablement or noncompliance with the written description of the invention requirement under 35 U.S.C. §112(a). Reexamination cannot be used to inquire into potentially invalidating on sale or public use bars under 35 U.S.C. §102(b) (2006).

c. *Substantial New Question of Patentability*

Before it will issue an order for reexamination, the USPTO must find that the request raises a "substantial new question of patentability."[110] The purpose of incorporating this threshold requirement into the statute was to prevent abuse of the system and harassment of patentees by third parties making multiple requests for reexamination without a substantial basis.[111] The standard applied by the USPTO for identifying a substantial new question sufficient to support an order for reexamination is that the prior art identified in the request would be considered "important" in deciding patentability to

[108]*Id.* at §302 (providing that request for reexamination may be filed "on the basis of any prior art cited under the provisions of section 301 of this title").

[109]*See* In re Recreative Techs. Corp., 83 F.3d 1394, 1397 (Fed. Cir. 1996) (stating with respect to reexamination as enacted by Congress in 1980, "[n]o grounds of reexamination were to be permitted other than based on new prior art and sections 102 and 103"); United States Patent and Trademark Office, Manual of Patent Examining Procedure §2217 (9th ed., last rev. Nov. 2015) (identifying appropriate portions of §102 on which substantial new question of patentability can be based), *available at* http://www.uspto.gov/web/offices/pac/mpep/s2217.html.

[110]35 U.S.C. §§303, 304. As discussed *infra,* the threshold standard for the AIA-implemented *inter partes* review is different: whether "the information presented in the request shows that there is a reasonable likelihood that the requester would prevail with respect to at least 1 of the claims challenged in the request." 35 U.S.C. §312(a) (eff. Sept. 16, 2012). The threshold standard for granting the AIA-implemented post-grant review is also different: whether the information in the petition, "if such information is not rebutted, would demonstrate that it is more likely than not that at least 1 of the claims challenged in the petition is unpatentable." 35 U.S.C. §324(a) (eff. Mar. 16, 2013)).

[111]*See* In re Portola Packaging, Inc., 110 F.3d 786, 790 (Fed. Cir. 1997).

a reasonable examiner, but need not necessarily render the claims *prima facie* unpatentable.[112]

Can a substantial new question of patentability be based on prior art that was known to the USPTO during examination of the original application? The Federal Circuit's 1997 decision in *In re Portola Packaging, Inc.*[113] temporarily eliminated this possibility.[114] The *Portola* court held that the agency cannot make rejections in reexamination based on any combination of prior art references that were previously considered by the USPTO in the prosecution of the original application, even where the claims had been amended during reexamination such that they were not the same as those considered in the original examination.

The facts of *Portola* are these: during examination of the original application, a number of prior art references were cited by the examiner, including the "Hunter" patent and the "Faulstich" patent. Specifically, the examiner rejected certain claims of the original application as anticipated under §102 by Hunter, and other claims as obvious under §103 in view of Faulstich in combination with two other references.[115] The applicant amended the claims in response to the rejections, added new claims, and was ultimately granted a patent, which was assigned to Portola.

A third party subsequently requested reexamination of the Portola patent, and the USPTO so ordered. Following amendments to the claims, the agency rejected them as obvious under §103 in view of the combined teachings of the Hunter and Faulstich patents. On appeal to the Federal Circuit, the patentee Portola contended that the reexamination statute does not permit the USPTO to issue rejections in a reexamination based solely on the same prior art that was previously before the agency. The USPTO responded that because the claims of the original application were never rejected under §103 in view of the combination of Hunter and Faulstich, the rejection was a "new" one that was permitted by statute.

The Federal Circuit sided with Portola. The court expressed great concern about the potential for abuse of the reexamination process based on subjecting a patentee to repeated reexaminations based on the same prior art previously considered by the USPTO.[116] The agency cannot use reexamination as a mechanism to correct an examiner's

[112]*See* United States Patent and Trademark Office, Manual of Patent Examining Procedure §2242 (9th ed., last rev. Nov. 2015), *available at* http://www.uspto.gov/web/offices/pac/mpep/s2242.html.

[113]110 F.3d 786 (Fed. Cir. 1997).

[114]In November 2002 the holding of *Portola* was legislatively overruled, as discussed below.

[115]*Portola*, 110 F.3d at 787.

[116]*See id.* at 789-790.

mistakes, such as a failure to make all proper rejections in the initial examination, the court cautioned. Examiners are presumed to have considered all combinations of the cited prior art. The court would not allow the USPTO to use reexamination to second guess itself.[117]

The *Portola* requester's best argument for a substantial new question of patentability was that the patentee had amended the claims during reexamination, such that they were not the same as the claims examined in the original prosecution. By definition, the requester contended, this must present a substantial new question of patentability. The Federal Circuit again disagreed. Claims amended in a reexamination must be narrower in scope than the original claims; unlike reissue, no broadening of claims is permitted in reexamination.[118] Therefore, the court explained, any question of patentability for the narrower reexamination claims was "necessarily" considered by examiner during the original examination.[119]

d. *Legislative Changes in Response to* Portola

On November 2, 2002, then-President George W. Bush signed into law new legislation that, *inter alia*, overruled the Federal Circuit's holding in *Portola.*[120] The legislation amended the language of 35 U.S.C. §303(a) (2000) ("Determination of issue by Director" in *ex parte* reexamination proceedings) and 312(a) (2000) ("Determination of issue by Director" in *inter partes* reexamination proceedings) by adding the following sentence to each section: "The existence of a substantial new question of patentability is not precluded by the fact that a patent or printed publication was previously cited by or to the [U.S. Patent and Trademark] Office or considered by the Office."[121] This change was not retroactive; that is, it was effective only for determinations of a "substantial new question of patentability" made by the USPTO on or after the date of enactment of the Act (i.e., Nov. 2, 2002). The Act also modified the appeal procedures for *inter partes* reexamination to give enhanced appeal rights to third-party requesters.[122]

[117]*See id.* at 791 (citing In re Etter, 756 F.2d 852, 865 (Fed. Cir. 1985) (Nies, Smith & Bissell, JJ., concurring) ("Clearly, reexamination was not designed to allow the PTO simply to reconsider and second guess what it has already done.")).

[118]Reexamination is further compared to reissue *infra*.

[119]*See Portola*, at 791 (Fed. Cir. 1997).

[120]*See* Twenty-First Century Department of Justice Appropriations Authorization Act, H.R. 2215, 107th Cong. §13105 (2002) ("Determination of Substantial New Question of Patentability in Reexamination Proceedings") (amending 35 U.S.C. §§303(a), 312(a)).

[121]*Id.*

[122]*See id.* §13106 ("Appeals in *inter partes* reexamination proceedings") (amending 35 U.S.C. §§315(b), 134(c), 141).

e. Reexamination Compared to Reissue

The reexamination and reissue procedures differ in fundamental respects. Reexamination is narrower than reissue in the sense that reexamination cannot be used to correct defects other than anticipation and obviousness based exclusively on the content of the prior art references.[123] Reexamination is broader than reissue, however, in the sense that anyone can request reexamination,[124] while only the owner of the patent in question can seek to reissue it.[125]

The most important difference between the two procedures is probably the fact that, unlike reissue, reexamination cannot be used to broaden the claims of an issued patent.[126] There is no broadening reexamination. For example, in *Quantum Corp. v. Rodime, PLC*,[127] the accused infringer brought a declaratory judgment action seeking a declaration that a previously reexamined patent, directed to a micro hard-disk drive system suitable for use in personal computers, was invalid and not infringed. The validity challenge was based on the facts that as originally issued, the claims of the patent recited a track density of "at least 600 concentric tracks per inch," but that during reexamination, the patentee amended the claims to recite "at least *approximately* 600 concentric tracks per inch," and the USPTO issued a reexamination certificate confirming the patentability of these amended claims. The accused infringer thus contended that the amendments made by the patentee during the reexamination

[123]*See* 35 U.S.C. §§301, 302.

[124]*See* 35 U.S.C. §302 (providing that "[a]ny person at any time may file a request for reexamination by the Office of any claim of a patent on the basis of any prior art cited under the provisions of section 301 of this title").

[125]*See* 35 U.S.C. §251(a) (eff. Sept. 16, 2012) (requiring "surrender" of the patent to the USPTO in order to reissue it); *id.* (stating that the "provisions of this title relating to applications for patent shall be applicable to applications for reissue of a patent, except that application for reissue may be made and sworn to by the assignee of the entire interest if the application does not seek to enlarge the scope of the claims of the original patent"); 37 C.F.R. §1.172(a) (providing that "[a] reissue oath must be signed and sworn to or declaration made by the inventor or inventors except as otherwise provided (see §§1.42, 1.43, 1.47), and must be accompanied by the written consent of all assignees, if any, owning an undivided interest in the patent, but a reissue oath may be made and sworn to or declaration made by the assignee of the entire interest if the application does not seek to enlarge the scope of the claims of the original patent"). *See also* Baker Hughes, Inc. v. Kirk, 921 F. Supp. 801, 809-810 (D.D.C. 1995) (in case where Baker Hughes and Hydril were both assignees of original patent, holding that USPTO did not have authority under 35 U.S.C. §251 to consider reissue application filed by Hydril only and to which Baker Hughes did not consent, and concluding that "a reissue application, if made by an assignee, must be made by the assignee of the entire interest in the patent").

[126]*See* 35 U.S.C. §305 (providing in part that "[n]o proposed amended or new claim enlarging the scope of a claim of the patent will be permitted in a reexamination proceeding under this chapter").

[127]65 F.3d 1577 (Fed. Cir. 1995).

amounted to an impermissible broadening of the claims, as prohibited by 35 U.S.C. §305.

The Federal Circuit agreed, pointing to dictionary definitions of "at least" as meaning "as the minimum," and thus interpreted the original claim language as meaning "600 tpi on up." The addition of the *approximately* qualifier during reexamination eliminated the precise lower limit of the range, the court concluded, and therefore defined an open-ended range starting slightly below 600 tpi. This constituted an impermissible broadening of claim scope in reexamination. The Federal Circuit refused to rewrite the claims back to their original scope. Because the patentee violated the terms of §305, the claims of the reexamined patent could not stand. The reexamined patent was therefore invalid.

Another difference between reexamination and reissue concerns timing. Reexamination may be requested at any time during the life of a patent.[128] In contrast, when a reissue application is filed that seeks to *broaden* the scope of a patent's claims, such application must be filed "within two years from the grant of the original patent."[129]

3. *Inter Partes* Reexamination (Pre-AIA)

The newer, *inter partes* form of reexamination[130] became available for U.S. patents granted on original applications filed in the USPTO on or after November 29, 1999.[131] Due to dissatisfaction with the

[128]*See* 35 U.S.C. §302 (providing that "[a]ny person at any time may file a request for reexamination . . .").

[129]35 U.S.C. §251(d) (eff. Sept. 16, 2012).

[130]*See generally* Tun-Jen Chiang, *The Advantages of* Inter Partes *Reexamination*, 90 J. PAT. & TRADEMARK OFF. SOC'Y 579 (2008); Sherry M. Knowles et al., Inter Partes *Patent Reexamination in the United States*, 86 J. PAT. & TRADEMARK OFF. SOC'Y 611 (2004); Kenneth L. Cage & Lawrence T. Cullen, *An Overview of* Inter Partes *Reexamination Procedures*, 85 J. PAT. & TRADEMARK OFF. SOC'Y 931 (2003); Michael L. Goldman & Alice Y. Choi, *The New Optional* Inter Partes *Reexamination Procedure and Its Strategic Use*, 28 AIPLA Q.J. 307 (2000).

[131]*See* Cooper Techs. Co. v. Dudas, 536 F.3d 1330, 1331 (Fed. Cir. 2008) (stating that "Congress established the *inter partes* reexamination procedure as part of the American Inventors Protection Act of 1999. . . . ('AIPA'). Pursuant to section 4608 of the AIPA, the *inter partes* reexamination procedure is available for 'any patent that issues from an original application filed in the United States on or after' November 29, 1999 — the date of the enactment of the AIPA.") (citations omitted). The court in *Cooper* interpreted "original application" to include, *inter alia*, continuation applications. *See id.* at 1343. Thus, *inter partes* reexamination can be sought for patents issuing from applications actually filed on or after November 29, 1999, but claiming priority to a pre-November 29, 1999, filing date. Affirming the USPTO's statutory interpretation, the Federal Circuit concluded that "original application" broadly encompasses "utility, plant and design applications, including first filed applications, continuations, divisionals,

proceeding,[132] the America Invents Act of 2011 phased out *inter partes* reexamination and replaced it with a new proceeding called "*inter partes* review," discussed separately below. For clarity, this chapter refers to *inter partes* reexamination as "*inter partes* reexamination (pre-AIA)." Petitions for *inter partes* reexamination (pre-AIA) could no longer be filed after September 15, 2012.

The procedures for *inter partes* reexamination (pre-AIA) were governed by 35 U.S.C. §§311-318 (2006). *Inter partes* reexamination (pre-AIA) supplemented, but did not replace, the older *ex parte* reexamination process (discussed above). *Ex parte* reexamination is governed by 35 U.S.C. §§301-307 and continues to be available post-AIA.

As the name "*inter partes*" suggests, the purpose of creating an alternative form of reexamination was to permit greater participation by third-party requesters. Indeed, only "third party requesters" (i.e., entities other than the patent owner) could file a request for *inter partes* reexamination.[133] Additionally, the third-party requester in *inter partes* reexamination was permitted to file a response to each statement filed by the patentee throughout the entire reexamination process.

When *inter partes* reexamination (pre-AIA) was implemented in late 1999, the atypical appeal provisions of the procedure were subject to much criticism. Although a patent owner could appeal an adverse decision by the examiner in *inter partes* reexamination to the USPTO Board of Patent Appeals and Interferences (BPAI) and, if unsuccessful there, to the Federal Circuit, the third-party requester in *inter partes* reexamination could appeal an adverse decision only as far as the BPAI;[134] no appeal by the third-party requester to the Federal Circuit was permitted. Moreover, if the patentee appealed to the Federal Circuit, the third-party requester was not permitted to participate. Commentators questioned whether these limitations on the third-party requester's appeal rights comported with the Due Process, Takings, or other clauses of the U.S. Constitution.

---

continuations-in-part, continued prosecution applications and the national stage phase of international applications." *Id.* at 1331.

[132]*See* Teresa Stanek Rea, Deputy Under Secretary of Commerce for Intellectual Property and Deputy Director of the USPTO, *Building a Better Post Grant* (May 15, 2012), *available at* http://www.uspto.gov/blog/director/entry/building_a_better_post_grant (admitting that "[i]nter partes reexamination has not proven as efficient as was originally intended. It has taken an average of 32 to 38 months to move from filing to issuance of a final reexamination certificate. The time to a final determination within the USPTO is even longer, when you factor in appeals.").

[133]35 U.S.C. §311(a) (2006) (providing that "[a]ny third party requester at any time may file a request for *inter partes* reexamination by the Office of a patent on the basis of any prior art cited under the provisions of section 301 [35 U.S.C. §301]").

[134]*See* 35 U.S.C. §315(b). The America Invents Act of 2011 renamed and expanded the jurisdiction of the Board of Patent Appeals and Interferences (BPAI). The post-AIA administrative tribunal is named the Patent Trial and Appeal Board (PTAB).

The issue became moot when the *inter partes* reexamination statutes were amended, effective November 2, 2002, to alleviate the disparity of appeal options between patent owners and third-party requesters.[135] Thereafter, both the patentee and the third-party requester had equal rights to appeal unfavorable decisions to the Federal Circuit and to participate in appeals filed there by the other party.[136]

Although they obtained the same appeal rights as patent owners, third-party requesters remained subject to a rather draconian estoppel provision that operated to prevent them from raising the same validity issues in any subsequent litigation of the patent in federal court.[137] Section 315(c) (2006) of the Patent Act prohibited the third-party requester from

> asserting at a later time, in any civil action arising in whole or in part under section 1338 of title 28 [United States Code], the invalidity of any claim finally determined to be valid and patentable on any ground which the third-party requester *raised or could have raised* during the *inter partes* reexamination proceedings. This subsection does not prevent the assertion of invalidity based on newly discovered prior art unavailable to the third-party requester and the Patent and Trademark Office at the time of the *inter partes* reexamination proceedings.[138]

Because of the relative severity of this estoppel provision, some commentators predicted that the *inter partes* reexamination procedure would not be used extensively.[139] The predictions were fairly accurate. A study published in 2005 reported that only 65 requests for *inter partes* reexamination had been filed with the USPTO through the

[135]*See* Twenty-First Century Department of Justice Appropriations Authorization Act, Pub. L. No. 107-273, div. C, tit. III ("Intellectual Property"), subtit. A ("Patent and Trademark Office Authorization"), §13106, subtit. B ("Intellectual Property and High Technology Technical Amendments"), §13202(a)(4), (c)(1), 116 Stat. 1900, 1901, 1902 (Nov. 2, 2002).

[136]*See* 35 U.S.C. §315(a) (2006) (patent owner's appeal rights), 315(b) (2006) (third-party requester's appeal rights).

[137]*See* Mark D. Janis, Inter Partes *Reexamination*, 10 Fordham Intell. Prop. Media & Ent. L.J. 481, 492 (2000) (characterizing the *inter partes* reexamination estoppel provisions as "draconian").

[138]35 U.S.C. §315(c) (2006) (emphasis added).

[139]*See* Mark D. Janis, *Inter Partes Reexamination*, 10 Fordham Intell. Prop. Media & Ent. L.J. 481, 498 (2000) (characterizing *inter partes* reexamination as "a dog . . . [of] a proceeding that is likely to confuse and annoy its participants, few though they may be"); Robert P. Merges, *One Hundred Years of Solicitude: Intellectual Property Law, 1900-2000,* 88 Cal. L. Rev. 2187, 2232 n.209 (2000) (predicting that "[f]ew patent lawyers will be willing to risk a reexamination request for a client, knowing the client will be precluded from arguing the same factual issues in a patent case in district court").

end of 2004.[140] Although 374 *inter partes* reexamination requests were filed in fiscal year 2011, this number is considerably lower than the 759 *ex parte* reexamination requests filed in the same time period.[141] The legislative history hints that even the statute's drafters had mixed feelings about the propriety of the estoppel provision.[142]

The *inter partes* reexamination statutes provided an important strategic benefit, however, for the owner of a patent whose validity was concurrently being litigated in federal court. Under 35 U.S.C. §318 (2006), the patentee in *inter partes* reexamination could request a stay of the federal court litigation, which could be denied only if the court "determines that a stay would not serve the interests of justice." The *ex parte* reexamination statutes do not speak of the possibility of a stay of concurrent validity litigation; in such a case, the grant or denial of a stay is entirely at the discretion of the federal district court.[143]

E. AIA-Implemented Procedures for Challenging Issued Patents

Although a great deal of attention focused on our patent system's change from its historic first-to-invent priority system to a first-inventor-to-file priority system as implemented by Section 3 of the America Invents Act of 2011 (AIA),[144] other changes wrought by the AIA are likely to have a far more significant long-term impact on U.S. patent law practice. Specifically, the AIA implemented two new primary procedures for challenging the validity of issued patents in the USPTO rather than the federal courts, both of which are referred

[140]*See* Joseph D. Cohen, *What's Really Happening in* Inter Partes *Reexamination,* 87 J. Pat. & Trademark Off. Soc'y 207, 213 (2005) (stating that "[r]equesters filed 65 *inter partes* requests through December 23, 2004"); *id.* at 207 n.3 (noting that the first request for *inter partes* reexamination was filed with the USPTO on July 27, 2001); *id.* at 218 (stating that "[o]nly 65 *inter partes* requests have been filed in the last three years").

[141]*See* USPTO, *2011 Performance and Accountability Report, Fiscal Year 2011 USPTO Workload Tables*, tbl. 14A ("Ex Parte Reexamination"), *available at* https://www.uspto.gov/sites/default/files/about/stratplan/ar/USPTOFY2011PAR.pdf; *id.* at tbl. 14B ("*Inter Partes* Reexamination").

[142]The Intellectual Property and Communications Omnibus Reform Act of 1999 provided with regard to the estoppel provision of 35 U.S.C. §315 that "if this section is held to be unenforceable, the enforceability of the remainder of this subtitle or of this title shall not be denied as a result." S. 1948, 106th Cong. §4607 (1999) (enacted by Act of Nov. 29, 1999, Pub. L. No. 106-113, §1000(a)(9), 113 Stat. 1536, and effective as provided by S. 1948, §4608, which is set out in 35 U.S.C. §41).

[143]*See* Ethicon, Inc. v. Quigg, 849 F.2d 1422, 1426-1427 (Fed. Cir. 1988); 4-11 Donald S. Chisum, Chisum on Patents §11.07[4][b][iv][B] (2008).

[144]*See supra* Chapter 4, Part III ("Novelty and Priority Post-America Invents Act of 2011").

to under the "umbrella" of "post-issuance review": (1) *inter partes* review ("IPR"), which replaces *inter partes* reexamination, and (2) post-grant review ("PGR"), which is similar (but not identical) to European-style opposition practice.[145] These new procedures were intended to provide for challenging potentially invalid patents in proceedings conducted before specialist administrative patent judges in the USPTO, in a more expeditious and inexpensive fashion than federal district court litigation challenging patent validity. According to one Federal Circuit judge, the new post-grant proceedings "have become the new frontier of patent litigation."[146]

Patent challengers have flocked to the new AIA procedures, and with good reason — the first six-plus years of results from the USPTO are decidedly in favor of the challengers. From September 16, 2012, the first date on which *inter partes* review petitions could be filed, through June 30, 2019, the USPTO received a total of 9,545 petition filings seeking *inter partes* review, which amounted to 93 percent of

[145]*See* European Patent Convention arts. 99-105 (14th ed. 2010), *available at* http://www.epo.org/law-practice/legal-texts/html/epc/2010/e/ma1.html.

In addition to *inter partes* review and post-grant review, a third adjudicative proceeding implemented by the AIA is the "Transitional Program for Covered Business Method Patents" (TPCBM). The TPCBM review proceeding operates similarly in many respects to post-grant review, but applies only to certain business method patents related to financial products or services. Moreover, only entities already sued or charged with infringement of a covered business method patent may petition for TPCBM review. The TPCBM took effect on September 16, 2012, and is scheduled to sunset on September 16, 2020. *See* Leahy-Smith America Invents Act, Pub. L. No. 112-29 (H.R. 1249), §18, 125 Stat. 284, 329 (Sept. 16, 2011).

The Supreme Court has summarized:

> the "covered-business-method review" (CBM review) provision provides for changes to a patent that claims a method for performing data processing or other operations used in the practice or management of a financial product or service. AIA §18(a)(1), (d)(1), 125 Stat. 329, note following 35 U.S.C. §321, p. 1442. CBM review tracks the "standards and procedures of" post-grant review [PGR] with two notable exceptions: CBM review is not limited to the nine months following issuance of a patent, and "[a] person" may file for CBM review only as a defense against a charge or suit for infringement. §18(a)(1)(B), 125 Stat. 330.1.

Return Mail, Inc. v. United States Postal Serv., 139 S. Ct. 1853, 1860 (2019) (Sotomayor, J.).

Notably, the AIA did not codify the TPCBM review provisions in the Patent Act; thus the proceeding's contours are set forth by the implementing legislation (AIA §18) and USPTO implementing regulations. *See* United States Patent & Trademark Office, *Final Rule: Changes to Implement* Inter Partes *Review Proceedings, Post-Grant Review Proceedings, and Transitional Program for Covered Business Method Patents*, 77 FED. REG. 48680 (Aug. 14, 2012), *available at* http://www.uspto.gov/aia_implementation/fr_specific_trial.pdf (adding 37 C.F.R. Chapter I, Part 42 ("Trial Practice Before the Patent Trial and Appeal Board"), Subpart D ("Transitional Program for Covered Business Methods"), 37 C.F.R. §§42.300-42.304).

[146]Ethicon Endo-Surgery, Inc. v. Covidien LP, 812 F.3d 1023, 1037 (Fed. Cir. 2016) (Newman, J., dissenting).

the 10,299 total petitions filed for all types of AIA-implemented post-grant review (including the Transitional Program for Covered Business Methods Reviews (CBMs) reviews and Post-Grant Reviews (PGRs) as well as IPRs).[147] By the end of June 2019, the PTAB had issued final written decisions in 2,796 completed IPR, PGR, and CBM proceedings.[148] The AIA post-issuance reviews have strongly favored petitioners (i.e., validity challengers). In the cumulative period of September 16, 2012 through June 30, 2019, the PTAB held *all* instituted claims unpatentable in 1,753 (or 63 percent) of the 2,796 completed AIA reviews (IPRs, PGRs, and CBMs) in which the Board issued final written decisions.[149] An additional 18 percent of the completed AIA reviews held at least *some* instituted claims unpatentable.[150] After less than seven years of the AIA post-issuance review regime, it is too soon to say whether this high "kill rate" will remain constant or whether it simply represents the results of early challenges to "low-hanging fruit."

Appeals from AIA-implemented post-issuance reviews have taken over the Federal Circuit's patent docket. The number of appeals to the Federal Circuit from the USPTO (presumably primarily IPR decisions) now far surpasses the number of appeals from federal district court patent decisions).[151]

Significantly, Congress termed the AIA-implemented post-issuance review proceedings *adjudicative* rather than *examinational*.[152] They are decidedly adversarial proceedings with some of the characteristics of in-court litigation, such as the ability to cross-examine an

[147]*See* United States Patent and Trademark Office, *Trial Statistics: IPR, PGR, CBM* (June 2019), at 3, https://www.uspto.gov/sites/default/files/documents/Trial_Statistics_2019-06-30.pdf.

[148]*See* United States Patent and Trademark Office, *Trial Statistics: IPR, PGR, CBM* (June 2019), at 10, https://www.uspto.gov/sites/default/files/documents/Trial_Statistics_2019-06-30.pdf. Note that the USPTO does not provide a breakdown of the total number of 2,796 final written decisions by type of proceeding; i.e., whether the decision issued in an IPR, PGR, or CBM review. But 93 percent of the total petitions filed were petitions for IPR. *Id.* at 3.

[149]*See* United States Patent and Trademark Office, *Trial Statistics: IPR, PGR, CBM* (June 2019), at 10, https://www.uspto.gov/sites/default/files/documents/Trial_Statistics_2019-06-30.pdf.

[150]*See* United States Patent and Trademark Office, *Trial Statistics: IPR, PGR, CBM* (June 2019), at 10, https://www.uspto.gov/sites/default/files/documents/Trial_Statistics_2019-06-30.pdf.

[151]*See* United States Court of Appeals for the Federal Circuit, *Year-to-Date Activity as of July 31, 2019*, http://www.cafc.uscourts.gov/sites/default/files/the-court/statistics/YTD-Activity-July-2019.pdf (listing number of appeals pending from USPTO on July 31, 2019 as 641 compared to 332 appeals pending from federal district courts).

[152]*See* H.R. Rep. No. 112-98 [House Judiciary Comm. Rep. on the America Invents Act] (June 1, 2011), at 57 (stating that the AIA "converts *inter partes* reexamination from an examinational to an adjudicative proceeding, and renames the proceeding '*inter partes* review' ").

opponent's expert witness (although via deposition rather than live testimony).[153]

Standing requirements to participate at the USPTO level are null — the proceedings can be initiated by anyone who is not an owner of the challenged patent.[154] The petitioner need not have been accused of infringing the patent it challenges.[155] The petitioner may also be the new employer of the inventor named on the challenged patent; the Federal Circuit has held that the assignor estoppel defense does not apply in IPR proceedings.[156]

[153]The Supreme Court has summarized:

> The AIA's three post-issuance review proceedings are adjudicatory in nature. Review is conducted by a three-member panel of the Patent Trial and Appeal Board, 35 U.S.C. §6(c), and the patent owner and challenger may seek discovery, file affidavits and other written memoranda, and request an oral hearing, see §§316, 326; AIA §18(a)(1), 125 Stat. 329; Oil States Energy Services, LLC v. Greene's Energy Group, LLC, 584 U.S. ____, ____-____, 138 S. Ct. 1365, 1371-72, 200 L. Ed. 2d 671 (2018). The petitioner has the burden of proving unpatentability by a preponderance of the evidence. §§282, 316(e), 326(e). The Board then either confirms the patent claims or cancels some or all of the claims. §§318(b), 328(b). Any party "dissatisfied" with the Board's final decision may seek judicial review in the Court of Appeals for the Federal Circuit, §§319, 329; see §141(c), and the Director of the Patent Office may intervene, §143.

Return Mail, Inc. v. United States Postal Serv., 139 S. Ct. 1853, 1860 (June 10, 2019) (Sotomayor, J.).

[154]35 U.S.C. §311(a).

[155]This is *not* necessarily the case if a party wishes to appeal an unfavorable final decision by the USPTO Patent Trial and Appeal Board (PTAB) in a post-issuance review to the U.S. Court of Appeals for the Federal Circuit. Because the Federal Circuit is an Article III court under the U.S. Constitution, any party to an appeal before the Circuit must have constitutional "standing." *See, e.g.,* Consumer Watchdog v. Wisconsin Alumni Research Found., 753 F.3d 1258, 1261 (Fed. Cir. 2014) (Rader, J.) (dismissing appeal from USPTO because Consumer Watchdog "ha[d] not established an injury in fact sufficient to confer Article III standing," and explaining that "although Article III standing is not necessarily a requirement to appear before an administrative agency, once a party seeks review in a federal court, 'the constitutional requirement that it have standing kicks in' ") (quoting Sierra Club v. E.P.A., 292 F.3d 895, 899 (D.C. Cir. 2002)). Three requirements form the constitutional minimum for standing:

> First, the party must show that it has suffered an "injury in fact" that is both concrete and particularized, and actual or imminent (as opposed to conjectural or hypothetical).... Second, it must show that the injury is fairly traceable to the challenged action.... Third, the party must show that it is likely, rather than merely speculative, that a favorable judicial decision will redress the injury.

Consumer Watchdog, 753 F.3d at 1260-1261 (citations omitted to Lujan v. Defenders of Wildlife, 504 U.S. 555, 560-561 (1992)).

[156]In *Arista Networks, Inc. v. Cisco Sys., Inc.*, 908 F.3d 792 (Fed. Cir. 2018) (Prost, C.J.), the Circuit held that the defense of assignor estoppel cannot be asserted to prevent one's patent from undergoing a post-grant patentability challenge in the USPTO such as *inter partes* review (IPR). In *Arista,* the inventor of Cisco's challenged network device security patent, Dr. Cheriton, was employed by Cisco at the time of the invention

E. AIA-Implemented Procedures for Challenging Issued Patents

One exception to the broad potential availability of post-issuance review should be noted, however; although the statute says that any "person" (other than the patentee) may seek it,[157] the Supreme Court ruled in 2019 that federal government agencies do *not* qualify as "person[s]" who can do so.[158]

When Congress enacted the AIA statutory framework for post-issuance review in 2011, some questioned the constitutionality of the new procedures. For example, does a proceeding such as IPR violate the Constitution because it is conducted in the USPTO (a non-Article III forum) without a jury? Does an IPR violate the Fifth Amendment Takings Clause because it potentially results in the loss of a valuable private property right without compensation?

---

and assigned all his rights therein to Cisco. Later in time, Cheriton and fellow Cisco employees left the company in order to found Arista, which became a competitor of Cisco. Arista thereafter filed a petition for IPR seeking to invalidate the Cisco patent on the grounds of anticipation or obviousness. The Federal Circuit affirmed the USPTO PTAB's holding that the defense of assignor estoppel is not validly raised to preclude IPR. The appellate court construed 35 U.S.C. §311(a), which allows "a person who is not the owner of a patent" to file a petition to institute IPR, and concluded that the statute "unambiguously dictates that assignor estoppel has no place in IPR proceedings," even when the person filing the petition to cancel the patent is the current employer of the patent's inventor. *See Arista,* 908 F.3d at 804. In the Circuit's view, the statutory language was not ambiguous and left "no room for assignor estoppel in the IPR context." *Arista,* 908 F.3d at 803.

[157]*See, e.g.,* 35 U.S.C. §35 U.S.C. §311(a) (providing that "(a) . . . Subject to the provisions of this chapter, a person who is not the owner of a patent may file with the Office a petition to institute an *inter partes* review of the patent").

[158]*See* Return Mail, Inc. v. United States Postal Serv., 139 S. Ct. 1853 (June 10, 2019) (Sotomayor, J.) (holding that a federal agency is not a "person" entitled to challenge the validity of a patent post-issuance in the USPTO via an *inter partes* review (IPR), post-grant review (PGR) or covered business method (CBM) proceeding). The *Return Mail* Court relied chiefly on the "presumption that the Government is not a 'person' authorized to initiate these proceedings absent an affirmative showing to the contrary." *Return Mail,* 139 S. Ct. at 1863. It concluded that the Postal Service had not made a satisfactory contrary showing, because nothing in the "text or context of the statute [AIA] . . . affirmatively show[ed that] Congress intended to include the Government." *Return Mail,* 139 S. Ct. at 1863. More particularly, the Court rejected each of the Postal Service's three arguments for displacing the presumption:

> First, the Postal Service argues that the statutory text and context offer sufficient evidence that the Government is a "person" with the power to petition for AIA review proceedings. Second, the Postal Service contends that federal agencies' long history of participation in the patent system suggests that Congress intended for the Government to participate in AIA review proceedings as well. Third, the Postal Service maintains that the statute must permit it to petition for AIA review because [28 U.S.C.] §1498 subjects the Government to liability for infringement.

Return Mail, 139 S. Ct. at 1863. For the reasons elaborated in its opinion, the Court concluded drolly that none of the Postal Service's arguments "deliver[ed]." *Return Mail,* 139 S. Ct. at 1863.

In June 2017, almost six years after the AIA's enactment, the U.S. Supreme Court agreed to review the first of those constitutional queries in *Oil States Energy Services, LLC v. Greene's Energy Group, LLC.*[159] The Court granted *certiorari* on the following Question Presented:

> Whether *inter partes* review — an adversarial process used by the Patent and Trademark Office (PTO) to analyze the validity of existing patents — violates the Constitution by extinguishing private property rights through a non-Article III forum without a jury.[160]

The Supreme Court issued its decision in *Oil States* in April 2018.[161] In view of the Court's 2016 *Cuozzo* decision analyzed elsewhere in this chapter,[162] which appeared to strongly approve IPRs and the USPTO's power to conduct and regulate them, the result in *Oil States* was not surprising. By a 7-2 vote, the *Oil States* majority held that the AIA-implemented post-grant procedures do *not* violate either Article III or the Seventh Amendment of the U.S. Constitution.

The *Oil States* majority reached this conclusion easily. Its decision that the Constitution was not violated by IPRs flowed almost entirely from characterizing the IPR review process as existing within the "public rights" doctrine (as does the process for initially granting a patent).[163] Public rights determinations may be susceptible of judicial interpretation but do not require it;[164] hence Article III of the Constitution was not violated.

Although the Supreme Court admittedly has not explained the distinction between a "public right" and a "private right" in a consistent

[159]137 S. Ct. 2239 (June 12, 2017) (mem.) (granting petition limited to Question 1).

[160]Petition for a Writ of Certiorari at i, No. No. 16-712, Oil States Energy Services, LLC v. Greene's Energy Group, LLC, *available at* https://www.scotusblog.com/wp-content/uploads/2017/06/16-712-petition.pdf.

[161]Oil States Energy Servs., LLC v. Greene's Energy Grp., LLC, 138 S. Ct. 1365 (Apr. 24, 2018) (Thomas, J.).

[162]*Cuozzo* is analyzed *infra* Section E.1.d ("Standard to Initiate") and Section E.3 ("'Broadest Reasonable Construction' Rule for Claims").

[163]Scholars agree about the centrality (though not the correctness) of the rights classification to the *Oil States* majority's decision. *See* Adam Mossoff, *Statutes, Common-Law Rights, and the Mistaken Classification of Patents as Public Rights* (Nov. 9, 2018) (forthcoming Iowa L. Rev.), at 2 (stating that "Foundations matter. *Oil States* proves this. A venerable and fundamental classification of legal rights — public rights or private rights — determined the result in a significant case at the intersection of administrative law, constitutional law, and patent law."), *available at* SSRN: https://ssrn.com/abstract=3289338.

[164]*Oil States,* 138 S. Ct. at 1373 (citing Crowell v. Benson, 285 U.S. 22, 50 (1932); Ex parte Bakelite Corp., 279 U.S. 428, 451 (1929)).

manner,[165] that distinction did not make a difference for the case at bar. What was clear to the *Oil States* majority is that the Court's precedents

> have recognized that the doctrine covers matters "which arise between the Government and persons subject to its authority in connection with the performance of the constitutional functions of the executive or legislative departments.'" Crowell v. Benson, 285 U.S. 22, 50, 52 S. Ct. 285, 76 L. Ed. 598 (1932). In other words, the public-rights doctrine applies to matters "'arising between the government and others, which from their nature do not require judicial determination and yet are susceptible of it.'" *Ibid.* (quoting Ex parte Bakelite Corp., 279 U.S. 438, 451, 49 S. Ct. 411, 73 L. Ed. 789 (1929)).[166]

At the threshold, no dispute existed in *Oil States* that the initial *grant* of a patent is a matter involving public rights — "specifically, the grant of a 'public franchise.'"[167] The process of granting a patent involves the "key features" that fall within the Court's public rights doctrine. First, the grant of a patent involves a matter arising between the government and others — that is, a matter between "'the public, who are the grantors, and . . . the patentee.'"[168] When it issues a patent, the USPTO takes away from the public rights of "immense value," and transfers them (temporarily) to the patentee.[169] Moreover, granting patents is one of the "constitutional functions" that can be carried out by the executive or legislative branches without "judicial determination."[170] Although Congress can itself grant patents,[171] it has authorized the executive branch to do so since the founding of the United States.

The *Oil States* majority further characterized patents as "public franchises" granted by the government to inventors of "new and useful improvements."[172] The patent "franchise" conveys to the patent owner the right to exclude others from practicing the patented invention

[165] *Oil States,* 138 S. Ct. at 1373 (citing Northern Pipeline Constr. Co. v. Marathon Pipe Line Co., 458 U.S. 50, 69 (1982); Stern v. Marshall, 564 U.S. 462, 488 (2011)).

[166] *Oil States,* 138 S. Ct. at 1373.

[167] *Oil States,* 138 S. Ct. at 1373 (quoting United States v. Duell, 172 U.S. 576, 582-583 (1899)).

[168] *Oil States,* 138 S. Ct. at 1373 (quoting *Duell,* 172 U.S. at 586).

[169] *Oil States,* 138 S. Ct. at 1373 (quoting United States v. Am. Bell Tel., 128 U.S. 315, 370 (1888).

[170] *Oil States,* 138 S. Ct. at 1373 (quoting Crowell v. Benson, 285 U.S. 22, 50-51 (1932)).

[171] *Oil States,* 138 S. Ct. at 1374 (citing Bloomer v. McQuewan, 14 How. 539, 548-550 (1853)).

[172] *Oil States,* 138 S. Ct. at 1373 (quoting Seymour v. Osborne, 11 Wall. 516, 533, 20 L. Ed. 2d 33 (1871); citing also Pfaff v. Wells Elecs., 525 U.S. 55, 63-64 (1998)).

during the term of the patent,[173] which right did not exist at common law.[174] Patents are entirely "creature[s] of statute law."[175]

Turning to the AIA-implemented *inter partes* review procedure at issue, the *Oil States* majority viewed IPR as a "second look" at the original USPTO decision to grant a patent.[176] Because IPR determines patentability under the same statutory requirements as initial examination, it "involves the same interests as the determination to grant a patent in the first instance."[177] Admittedly, IPR occurs *after* the issuance of a patent, but that distinction did not make a difference to the majority. Granted patents remain subject to the qualification that the USPTO can reexamine, and perhaps cancel, them. Thus, patents remain subject to the agency's authority to cancel, outside the confines of an Article III court.

The *Oil States* majority noted that other types of public franchise grants have been qualified in a similar manner, citing examples of permits to private companies to build toll bridges, railroads, or telegraph lines. "Thus, the public-rights doctrine covers the matter resolved in *inter partes* review. The Constitution does not prohibit the Board from resolving it outside of an Article III court."[178]

Precedent also refuted patentee Oil States' other contention, that conducting IPRs in the USPTO violated the Constitution's Seventh Amendment right to a jury trial. The *Oil States* majority observed that "when Congress properly assigns a matter to adjudication in a non-Article III tribunal, 'the Seventh Amendment poses no independent bar to the adjudication of that action by a nonjury factfinder.' "[179] Neither party attempted to rebut or dispute this precedent. Hence, the *Oil States* Court's rejection of the patentee's Article III challenge also resolved its Seventh Amendment challenge. Congress can properly assign IPRs to the USPTO. Hence, a jury is not necessary in IPR proceedings.

The remainder of this subsection further explores the procedures for AIA-implemented post-issuance reviews. *Inter partes* review (IPR) and

[173] *See* 35 U.S.C. §154(a)(1).

[174] *Oil States,* 138 S. Ct. at 1374 (quoting Gayler v. Wilder, 10 How. 477, 494, 13 L. Ed. 504 (1851)).

[175] *Oil States,* 138 S. Ct. at 1374 (quoting Crown Die & Tool Co. v. Nye Tool & Mach. Works, 281 U.S. 24, 40 (1923)). Some scholars disagree, strongly. *See* Adam Mossoff, *Statutes, Common-Law Rights, and the Mistaken Classification of Patents as Public Rights* (Nov. 9, 2018) (forthcoming Iowa L. Rev.), at 2 (asserting that the "reduction of the distinction between public rights and private rights to a distinction between statutes and judge-made doctrines is deeply mistaken, both on historical and legal grounds"), *available at* SSRN: https://ssrn.com/abstract=3289338.

[176] *Oil States,* 138 S. Ct. at 1374 (quoting *Cuozzo,* 136 S. Ct. at 2144).

[177] *Oil States,* 138 S. Ct. at 1374 (citing *Duell,* 172 U.S. at 586).

[178] *Oil States,* 138 S. Ct. at 1375.

[179] *Oil States,* 138 S. Ct. at 1379 (quoting Granfinanciera, S.A. v. Nordberg, 492 U.S. 33, 53-54 (1989)).

post-grant review (PGR) proceedings are decided in the first instance before panels of three administrative patent judges from the AIA-implemented Patent Trial and Appeal Board (PTAB) rather than a single examiner (as in conventional *ex parte* patent prosecution). Certain forms of pre-trial discovery, including depositions, are available. Appeal from final written decisions of the PTAB is directly to the Federal Circuit;[180] there is no option of an intermediate civil action in federal district court under 35 U.S.C. §145, in contrast with *ex parte* examinations or reexaminations.

In the view of this author, it would not be precisely accurate to say that patents reviewed under IPR or PGR completely lose the presumption of validity conveyed by 28 U.S.C. §282.[181] Rather, the quantum of the challenger's evidentiary burden is lessened. In federal district court litigation, the challenger of validity must establish invalidity of an issued patent by "clear and convincing evidence."[182] In an IPR, in contrast, the IPR challenger/petitioner bears a somewhat lower burden of persuasion — it must prove "unpatentability by a preponderance of the evidence."[183] However, that burden never shifts to the patentee.[184]

Inter partes review and post-grant review share a great many procedural and administrative aspects,[185] although substantively the scope

[180]35 U.S.C. §319.

[181]*Compare* Patlex Corp. v. Mossinghoff, 758 F.2d 594, 605 (Fed. Cir. 1985) (stating that "section 282 is not applicable in *reexamination* proceedings") (citing In re Etter, 756 F.2d 852, 855-859 (Fed. Cir. 1985) (emphasis added)), *on reh'g*, 771 F.2d 480 (Fed. Cir. 1985). "Nor does it meet the statutory purpose of section 282, whose origin is the presumption of administrative correctness, to apply this presumption to a procedure whose purpose is the remedy of administrative error." *Patlex Corp.*, 758 F.2d at 605.

[182]Microsoft Corp. v. i4i Ltd. P'ship, 131 S. Ct. 2238 (2011), examined *infra* Chapter 10, Section E.1.

[183]35 U.S.C. §316(e) ("Evidentiary Standards") (providing that "[i]n an *inter partes* review instituted under this chapter, the petitioner shall have the burden of proving a proposition of unpatentability by a preponderance of the evidence").

[184]Dynamic Drinkware, LLC v. Nat'l Graphics, Inc., 800 F.3d 1375, 1378 (Fed. Cir. 2015).

[185]The USPTO has issued a helpful trial practice guide setting forth the procedural aspects for the new AIA-implemented proceedings, including *inter partes* review and post-grant review. *See* United States Patent & Trademark Office, *Office Patent Trial Practice Guide*, 77 FED. REG. 48756 (Aug. 14, 2012), *available at* http://www.uspto.gov/aia_implementation/trial_practice_guide_48756.pdf (providing "a practice guide for the trial final rules to advise the public on the general framework of the regulations, including the structure and times for taking action in each of the new proceedings [i.e., *inter partes* review, post-grant review, the transitional program for covered business method patents, and derivation proceedings]"). The trial rules themselves are set forth in United States Patent & Trademark Office, *Final Rule: Rules of Practice for Trials Before the Patent Trial and Appeal Board and Judicial Review of Patent Trial and Appeal Board Decisions*, 77 FED. REG. 48612 (Aug. 14, 2012), *available at* http://www.uspto.gov/aia_implementation/fr_general_trial.pdf (providing a "consolidated set of rules relating to Board trial practice for *inter partes* review, post-grant review, the

of post-grant review is far broader than that of *inter partes* review. On the other hand, post-grant review is available only during the nine months following a patent's issuance, while *inter partes* review can be sought once the nine-month window has closed and then throughout the remaining life of a patent. Each proceeding is discussed separately below.

1. *Inter Partes* Review

a. Introduction

The AIA-implemented *inter partes* review proceeding replaced and expanded *inter partes* reexamination. Sections 311 through 319 of the Patent Act, 35 U.S.C., as amended by the AIA govern *inter partes* review.[186] Petitions for *inter partes* review could be filed with the USPTO beginning on September 16, 2012, and such petitions could challenge existing (i.e., pre-AIA) patents.[187]

b. Time Limits

Many (but not all) IPRs are conducted in parallel (or serially) with federal district court litigation challenging the same patent. The AIA imposed several time limitations that impact this interaction. For example, if an accused infringer (or real party in interest) has already filed in federal district court a civil action such as a declaratory judgment action challenging a patent's validity,[188] a petition for IPR of

---

transitional program for covered business method patents, and derivation proceedings[, as well as] a consolidated set of rules to implement the provisions of the AIA related to seeking judicial review of Board decisions"). Another useful resource is Alan J. Kasper et al., PATENTS AFTER THE AIA: EVOLVING LAW AND PRACTICE (Bloomberg BNA 2015).

[186]*See* 35 U.S.C. §§311-319 (eff. Sept. 16, 2012).

[187]A panel of the Federal Circuit held in 2019 that permitting retroactive application of IPR to invalidate (without compensation) patents having an effective filing date before the AIA's September 16, 2012 effective date does *not* amount to an unconstitutional taking under the Fifth Amendment of the U.S. Constitution. Celgene Corp. v. Peter, 931 F.3d 1342, 1362 (Fed. Cir. July 30, 2019) (Prost, C.J.). The Circuit reasoned that

> [p]atent owners have always had the expectation that the validity of patents could be challenged in [federal] district court. For forty years, patent owners have also had the expectation that the PTO could reconsider the validity of issued patents on particular grounds, applying a preponderance of the evidence standard [as in *ex parte* reexamination proceedings governed by 35 U.S.C. §§301-307]. Although differences exist between IPRs and their reexamination predecessors, those differences do not outweigh the similarities of purpose and substance and, at least for that reason, do not effectuate a taking of Celgene's patents.

Celgene, 931 F.3d at 1362-1363.

[188]Patent declaratory judgment actions are discussed *infra* Chapter 10, Section G.

the same patent cannot be instituted.[189] On the other hand, if the accused infringer (or real party in interest) first files a petition for IPR and thereafter files a declaratory judgment action in federal district court challenging the validity of the disputed patent, the action in court will be automatically stayed.[190] If a patent owner first files a lawsuit in federal district court alleging patent infringement, the accused infringer has only one year thereafter to file a petition seeking IPR.[191] If the petitioner files an IPR in this situation, a stay of the district court litigation is not mandatory but rather at the discretion of the district court.[192]

For newly granted patents, a petition for *inter partes* review cannot be filed until nine months after the grant (i.e., not during the nine-month window for filing a petition for post-grant review[193]). If a petition for post-grant review is filed and granted, the post-grant review must be terminated before *inter partes* review can be sought.[194]

c. *Scope of Review*

Like reexamination, *inter partes* review is limited with respect to the scope of issues that the petitioner can raise. The *inter partes* review petitioner can request to cancel as unpatentable one or more claims of a patent "only on a ground that could be raised under

[189] *See* 35 U.S.C. §315(a)(1) ("*Inter partes* review barred by civil action").

[190] *See* 35 U.S.C. §315(a)(2) ("Stay of civil action").

[191] *See* 35 U.S.C. §315(b) ("Patent owner's action"). More specifically, the one-year time bar runs from the date on which "the petitioner, real party in interest, or privy of the petitioner" is served with the infringement complaint. *Id.* The meaning and significance of "real party in interest" and "privy of the petitioner" are examined *infra* Section E.1.d ("Standard to Institute Review and Non-Reviewability of the Institution Decision").

[192] *See, e.g.*, Cypress Semiconductor Corp. v. GSI Tech., Inc., No. 13-CV-02013-JST, 2014 WL 5021100, at *1 (N.D. Cal. Oct. 7, 2014) (granting defendant GSI Technology's motion for partial stay pending *inter partes* relief). *Cf.* Ethicon, Inc. v. Quigg, 849 F.2d 1422, 1426-1427 (Fed. Cir. 1988) (stating that "[c]ourts have inherent power to manage their dockets and stay proceedings, . . . including the authority to order a stay pending conclusion of a PTO reexamination") (citations omitted). The Federal Circuit also reversed district court denials of patent litigation stay requests in two 2014 cases involving patents challenged under the AIA-implemented Transitional Program for Covered Business Method Patents (CBM). *See* Versata Software, Inc. v. Callidus Software, Inc., 771 F.3d 1368 (Fed. Cir. Nov. 20, 2014); VirtualAgility Inc. v. Salesforce.com, Inc., 759 F.3d 1307, 1308 (Fed. Cir. 2014).

[193] Filing deadlines for post-grant review are discussed *infra* at Section E.2.

[194] More specifically, 35 U.S.C. §311 (eff. Jan. 14, 2013) provides in part:

> (c) Filing deadline. — A petition for *inter partes* review shall be filed after the later of either —
>
> (1) the date that is 9 months after the grant of a patent; or
>
> (2) if a post-grant review is instituted under chapter 32 [35 U.S.C. §§321-329], the date of the termination of such post-grant review.

section 102 [novelty] or 103 [nonobviousness] and only on the basis of prior art consisting of patents or printed publications."[195] This significant limitation on the scope of review is a carryover from reexamination,[196] and also represents one of the major distinctions between *inter partes* review and post-grant review, discussed *below*.[197]

d. Standard to Institute Review and Non-Reviewability of Institution Decision

The threshold standard for institution of *inter partes* review is no longer a "substantial new question of patentability" as in reexamination. Rather, the USPTO will not institute *inter partes* review unless the petitioner's petition and any response thereto by the patentee "show[] that there is a reasonable likelihood that the petitioner would prevail with respect to at least 1 of the claims challenged in the petition."[198]

Whether this new threshold was intended to be a lower or higher threshold than "substantial new question of patentability" is unclear. Given that the AIA provides new ways to challenge the validity of issued patents, however, it is reasonable to interpret the statutory text as lowering the threshold. As of July 2019, the USPTO had instituted PTAB trials in about 52 percent of the post-issuance petitions (over 90 percent seeking IPR) that have been completed to date.[199]

Following the 2011 enactment of the AIA-implemented post-issuance procedures, another vigorous debate ensued — could the Federal Circuit review the USPTO's decision not to institute (or, to affirmatively institute) an IPR proceeding? The newly enacted statutory provisions appeared to answer firmly in the negative, stating in

[195] 35 U.S.C. §311(b) (eff. Sept. 16, 2012) ("Scope").

[196] *See* In re Recreative Techs. Corp., 83 F.3d 1394, 1397 (Fed. Cir. 1996) (stating with respect to reexamination as enacted by Congress in 1980, "No grounds of reexamination were to be permitted other than based on new prior art and sections 102 and 103."); UNITED STATES PATENT AND TRADEMARK OFFICE, MANUAL OF PATENT EXAMINING PROCEDURE §2217 (8th ed., rev. July 2010) (identifying appropriate portions of 35 U.S.C. §102 (pre-AIA version) on which substantial new question of patentability can be based), *available at* http://www.uspto.gov/web/offices/pac/mpep/documents/2200_2217.htm#sect2217.

[197] As explained *infra,* a petition for post-grant review can raise "any ground that could be raised under paragraph (2) or (3) of [35 U.S.C.] section 282(b) (relating to invalidity of the patent or any claim)." 35 U.S.C. §321(b) (eff. Sept. 16, 2012, for patents having an effective filing date on or after Mar. 16, 2013) ("Scope").

[198] 35 U.S.C. §314(a) (eff. Sept. 16, 2012) ("Threshold").

[199] *See* United States Patent and Trademark Office, *Trial Statistics: IPR, PGR, CBM* (June 2019), at 10 (cumulative data for the period of September 16, 2012 through June 30, 2019, reporting that 5,330 trials have been instituted out of the 10,299 total post-issuance review petitions completed to date), https://www.uspto.gov/sites/default/files/documents/Trial_Statistics_2019-06-30.pdf.

a section titled "No Appeal" that "[t]he determination by the Director [of the USPTO] whether to institute an *inter partes* review under this section shall be final and nonappealable."[200]

That statutory language (found in AIA-enacted 35 U.S.C. §314(d)) did not completely resolve the judicial reviewability question, however, because the statutory prohibition ran counter to a strong public policy. That policy provides that statutory interpretation (e.g., by a government agency such as the USPTO interpreting the statutory requirements for instituting IPRs) should be reviewable by the judiciary, and includes the presumptive reviewability of statutes that may limit or preclude judicial review (such as §314(d)).[201]

The Supreme Court ultimately took up the reviewability question. In June 2016, the Court issued *Cuozzo Speed Techs., LLC v. Lee*,[202] an important decision marking the Court's first occasion to review the AIA. In a 7-2 majority opinion authored by Justice Breyer, the Court affirmed the USPTO's positions in virtually all respects. As detailed below, this included affirming a Federal Circuit panel's holding[203] (and the USPTO's position) that the PTAB's decision to institute an IPR is final and not judicially reviewable (absent limited exceptions such as pervasive constitutional problems or agency "shenanigans").[204] Hence the *Cuozzo* decision appeared to signal strongly the Supreme Court's approval of the new post-issuance review procedures and the USPTO's power to conduct and regulate them.[205]

[200]35 U.S.C. §314(d) (eff. Sept. 16, 2012).

[201]*See* Cuozzo Speed Techs., LLC v. Lee, 136 S. Ct. 2131, 2140 (2016) (majority recognizing "the 'strong presumption' in favor of judicial review that we apply when we interpret statutes, including statutes that may limit or preclude review") (citing Mach Mining, LLC v. EEOC, 135 S. Ct. 1645, 1650-1651 (2015) (internal quotation marks omitted)).

[202]136 S. Ct. 2131 (June 20, 2016) (Breyer, J.).

[203]*See* In re Cuozzo Speed Techs., LLC, 793 F.3d 1268 (Fed. Cir. July 8, 2015) (Dyk, J.) (superseding on rehearing and withdrawing original *Cuozzo* panel opinion published at 778 F.3d 1271 (Fed. Cir. Feb. 4, 2015)).

[204]The Supreme Court also affirmed the position of the USPTO and the Federal Circuit that the USPTO had the authority to require use of the broadest reasonable construction ("BRC") rule for interpretation of claims challenged in IPRs. *See Cuozzo,* 136 S. Ct. at 2142 (stating that "[t]he [AIA-amended Patent Act] statute, however, contains a provision that grants the Patent Office authority to issue 'regulations . . . establishing and governing *inter partes* review under this chapter.' 35 U.S.C. §316(a)(4). The Court of Appeals held that this statute gives the Patent Office the legal authority to issue its broadest reasonable construction regulation. We agree."). The BRC issue of *Cuozzo* is discussed separately *infra* Section E.3.

[205]The Supreme Court in *Cuozzo* did not consider any constitutional challenges to the new post-issuance review regime, however. Those issues would be addressed later by the Court in *Oil States Energy Servs., LLC v. Greene's Energy Group, LLC*, 138 S. Ct. 1365 (2018), examined *supra* Section E.

Cuozzo's U.S. Patent No. 6,778,074 ('074 patent) concerned a speedometer with an indicator to alert a driver when she was driving above the speed limit.[206] Garmin, a manufacturer of GPS navigational devices for automobiles, filed a petition for IPR in 2012 that challenged the patentability of claims 10, 14, and 17 of Cuozzo's '074 patent. In response, the PTAB instituted IPR of claims 10, 14, and 1 based on a reasonable likelihood of obviousness in view of a combination of three prior art patent references – "Aumeyer," "Evans," and "Wendt."[207] Notably, patentability challenger Garmin had *not* identified the Evans and Wendt patents in its petition as grounds for IPR of claims 10 and 14, but rather only as a ground for IPR of claim 17. But the PTAB, observing that claim 17 depended from claim 14, which in turn depended from claim 10, reasoned that Garmin had "implicitly" challenged the broader claims 10 and 14 on the basis of the same prior art as the narrowest challenged claim, claim 17.[208] After further

[206]Independent claim 10 of Cuozzo's '074 patent recited:

A speed limit indicator comprising:
a global positioning system receiver;
a display controller connected to said global positioning system receiver, wherein said display controller adjusts a colored display in response to signals from said global positioning system receiver to continuously update the delineation of which speed readings are in violation of the speed limit at a vehicle's present location; and
a speedometer integrally attached to said colored display.

Claim 14 of the '074 patent depended from claim 10 and recited "[t]he speed limit indicator as defined in claim 10, wherein said colored display is a colored filter." Dependent claim 17 (the most narrow claim challenged) recited: "[t]he speed limit indicator as defined in claim 14, wherein said display controller rotates said colored filter independently of said speedometer to continuously update the delineation of which speed readings are in violation of the speed limit at a vehicle's present location."

[207]The three references relied on to support Garmin's obviousness challenge were U.S. Patent Nos. 6,633,811 ("Aumayer"); 3,980,041 ("Evans"); and 2,711,153 ("Wendt"). The Federal Circuit has observed that "[o]bviousness is the most common invalidity issue in both district court and post-grant proceedings before the PTO." Apple Inc. v. Samsung Elecs. Co., Ltd., 839 F.3d 1034, 1074 (Fed. Cir. 2016) (Dyk, J., dissenting from *en banc* majority) (citing 2-5 Chisum on Patents §5.06 (2015)). The PTAB's decision to institute IPR of Cuozzo's patent is reported at *Garmin Int'l, Inc. et al. v. Patent of Cuozzo Speed Techs. LLC,* No. IPR2012-00001 (JL), 2013 WL 5947691, at *1 (PTAB Jan. 9, 2013).

[208]*Cuozzo,* 136 S. Ct. at 2138. The PTAB urged that instituting IPR was proper because "[a]ny grounds which would invalidate claim 17 would by necessary implication also invalidate claims 10 and 14." *Cuozzo,* 793 F.3d at 1275 (citing Callaway Golf Co. v. Acushnet Co., 576 F.3d 1331, 1344 (Fed. Cir. 2009) ("A broader independent claim cannot be nonobvious where a dependent claim stemming from that independent claim is invalid for obviousness.")).

proceedings, the Board held in a final written decision that all three claims were unpatentable.[209]

After losing the IPR on the merits, Cuozzo appealed to the Federal Circuit. One of Cuozzo's primary contentions was that the Board had erred in instituting IPR of claims 10 and 14 because it wrongly relied on prior art not cited in Garmin's petition as grounds for instituting IPR of those two claims. In Cuozzo's view, this violated the requirement of 35 U.S.C. §312 that a petition for IPR must identify "*with particularity*, each claim challenged, the grounds on which the challenge to each claim is based, and the evidence [e.g., the prior art references] that supports the grounds for the challenge to each claim. . . ."[210] "Particularity" was not satisfied, Cuozzo contended, because Garmin's petition did not identify Wendt or Evans as evidence supporting the obviousness challenge to claim 10 or identify Wendt as evidence supporting the obviousness challenge to claim 14.[211]

A divided panel of the Federal Circuit rejected Cuozzo's argument.[212] In the *Cuozzo* majority's view, the fact that the petition was defective was not relevant because "a proper petition could have been drafted."[213] As in the Circuit's 1998 decision in the reexamination case *In re Hiniker Co.*,[214] any defect in the petition was effectively "washed clean" during the IPR proceeding.

[209]*See* Garmin Int'l, Inc. v. Cuozzo Speed Techs., 108 U.S.P.Q.2d 1852, 2013 WL 6355081 (PTAB 2013). The Board explained that

> the Aumayer patent "makes use of a GPS receiver to determine . . . the applicable speed limit at that location for display," the Evans patent "describes a colored plate for indicating the speed limit," and the Wendt patent "describes us[ing] a rotatable pointer for indicating the applicable speed limit." . . . Anyone, the Board reasoned, who is "not an automaton" — anyone with "ordinary skill" and "ordinary creativity" — could have taken the automated approach suggested by the Aumayer patent and applied it to the manually adjustable signals described in the Evans and Wendt patents.

Cuozzo, 136 S. Ct. at 2138-2139 (citations to Board's decision omitted).

[210]35 U.S.C. §312(a)(3).

[211]*See* Garmin Int'l, Inc. et al. v. Patent of Cuozzo Speed Techs. LLC, No. IPR2012-00001 (JL), 2013 WL 5947691, at *2 (PTAB Jan. 9, 2013) (listing grounds for, and prior art relied on in, challenge to each claim).

[212]*See* In re Cuozzo Speed Techs., LLC, 793 F.3d 1268, 1271 (Fed. Cir. July 8, 2015) (Dyk, J.) (superseding on rehearing and withdrawing original *Cuozzo* panel opinion published at 778 F.3d 1271 (Fed. Cir. Feb. 4, 2015).

[213]*Cuozzo,* 793 F.3d at 1274.

[214]150 F.3d 1362 (Fed. Cir. 1998). At the time that *Hiniker* was decided, the PTO was forbidden by statute (35 U.S.C. §303(a) (1994)) from instituting reexamination based on prior art already considered in the original patent examination. The PTO nevertheless relied on such "old" prior art in deciding to institute reexamination in *Hiniker*, but its final decision relied on different prior art that had never been before the examiner in the original examination. The Circuit held that its jurisdiction extended only over the Board's final decision. While that decision would have been subject to reversal had it relied on the old art, "any error in instituting reexamination based on the [old] reference

On the threshold matter of its jurisdiction, the *Cuozzo* Circuit majority held that under the "no appeal" provision of 35 U.S.C. §314(d), the Circuit did *not* have jurisdiction to review the PTAB's decision to institute IPR (even as part of reviewing the PTAB's later-issued final written decision).[215] Judge Newman dissented.[216] Thereafter a fractured Federal Circuit denied rehearing *en banc* by a 6-5 vote.[217]

The Supreme Court thereafter granted Cuozzo's petition for *certiorari* and issued its decision in June 2016.[218] Agreeing with the Federal Circuit panel majority, the Supreme Court majority held that the propriety of the Board's institution decision could not be judicially reviewed. Justice Breyer's reasoning hewed closely to the plain language of the statute. He opined that "[l]ike the Court of Appeals, we believe that Cuozzo's contention that the Patent Office unlawfully initiated its agency review is not appealable. For one thing, that is what §314(d) says."[219] This forceful language, and other evidence, made clear that at least in this case, the general presumption in favor of judicial review had been rebutted.[220]

As further framed by the Supreme Court in *Cuozzo*, the particular issue for its consideration was the precise scope of the "no appeal" provision set forth in 35 U.S.C. §314(d).[221] Did that statute "bar[] a court from considering whether the Patent Office wrongly 'determin[ed] . . . to

---

was 'washed clean during the reexamination proceeding,' which relied on new art." *Cuozzo,* 793 F.3d at 1274 (quoting *Hiniker,* 150 F.3d at 1367).

215 *See* In re Cuozzo Speed Techs., LLC, 793 F.3d 1268, 1271 (Fed. Cir. July 8, 2015) (Dyk, J.) (superseding on rehearing and withdrawing original *Cuozzo* panel opinion published at 778 F.3d 1271 (Fed. Cir. Feb. 4, 2015); panel majority holding that it lacked jurisdiction to review the PTAB's decision to institute IPR; affirming the PTAB's final determination that Cuozzo's patent claims 10, 14, and 17 would have been obvious; finding no error in the Board's construction of the patent claims under the "broadest reasonable interpretation" standard; and affirming the PTAB's denial of Cuozzo's motion to amend the patent claims).

216 *Cuozzo,* 793 F.3d at 1291 (Newman, J., dissenting) (asserting that "[t]he statute does not preclude judicial review of whether the statute was applied in accordance with its legislated scope").

217 In re Cuozzo Speed Techs., LLC, 793 F.3d 1297 (Fed. Cir. July 8, 2015) (denying *en banc* rehearing).

218 Cuozzo Speed Techs., LLC v. Lee, 136 S. Ct. 2131 (June 20, 2016) (Breyer, J.).

219 *Cuozzo,* 136 S. Ct. at 2139.

220 *Cuozzo,* 136 S. Ct. at 2131 (explaining that the "presumption [favoring judicial reviewability] . . . may be overcome by 'clear and convincing' indications, drawn from 'specific language,' 'specific legislative history,' and 'inferences of intent drawn from the statutory scheme as a whole,' that Congress intended to bar review") (quoting Block v. Community Nutrition Institute, 467 U.S. 340, 349-350 (1984)).

221 35 U.S.C. §314(d) (eff. Sept. 16, 2012), titled "No Appeal," provides that "[t]he determination by the Director whether to institute an *inter partes* review under this section [i.e., 35 U.S.C. §314, titled "Institution of *inter partes* review"] shall be final and nonappealable."

institute an *inter partes* review,'... when it did so on grounds not specifically mentioned in a third party's review request?"[222]

The *Cuozzo* Supreme Court majority answered that question in the affirmative, while hinting at some exceptions. It concluded that "though [§314(d)] may not bar consideration of a constitutional question, for example, [it] does bar judicial review of the kind of mine-run [i.e., common, "run of the mill"] claim at issue here, involving the Patent Office's decision to institute *inter partes* review."[223]

Accordingly, patentee Cuozzo's contention that the agency unlawfully initiated the IPR challenging (and ultimately invalidating) his U.S. Patent No. 6,778,074 was "not appealable."[224] The Supreme Court majority identified several reasons supporting its decision. In addition to the plain language of §314(d), the *Cuozzo* majority characterized the dispute below as an "ordinary" one, involving "the application of certain relevant patent statutes concerning the Patent [and Trademark] Office's decision to institute *inter partes* review."[225] Unhelpfully, the Supreme Court majority did not specify the precise scope of such "relevant... statutes," but did mention §312 in connection with §314. Section 312 (titled "Petitions"), subsection (a)(3), provides that a petition for IPR "may be considered only if... the petition identifies, in writing and *with particularity,* each claim challenged, the grounds on which the challenge to each claim is based, and the evidence that supports the grounds for the challenge to each claim...." (emphasis added). As described above, Cuozzo's argument turned on this failure of "particularity"; he asserted that the PTAB erred in instituting the IPR because challenger Garmin's petition was not sufficiently "particular" in its identification of the prior art on which IPR was justified.

In the *Cuozzo* Supreme Court majority's view, this was a type of issue that the "no appeal" provision, §314(d), was plainly intended to cover. Section 314(d) "must, at the least, forbid an appeal that attacks a 'determination... whether to institute' review by raising *this kind of legal question and little more.*"[226] Thus, the *Cuozzo* majority appeared to conclude that appeal cannot be taken when the PTAB's determination to institute (or not) is based on an argument that the petition requirements enumerated in §312 were not (or were) satisfied. Such "minor statutory technicalit[ies] related to [the Board's] preliminary decision to institute *inter partes* review," as the Court characterized them, are not sufficient to ground an appeal.[227] A contrary holding

[222] *Cuozzo,* 136 S. Ct. at 2136 (citation omitted).
[223] *Cuozzo,* 136 S. Ct. at 2136.
[224] *Cuozzo,* 136 S. Ct. at 2139.
[225] *Cuozzo,* 136 S. Ct. at 2139.
[226] *Cuozzo,* 136 S. Ct. at 2139 (emphasis added).
[227] *Cuozzo,* 136 S. Ct. at 2140.

would undercut the "important congressional objective" of "giving the Patent [and Trademark] Office significant power to revisit and revise earlier patent grants."[228]

To further support its holding, the *Cuozzo* majority pointed to "similar provisions in this, and related, patent statutes" that reinforced its conclusion that no appeal was available. It cited

> [35 U.S.C.] §319 (limiting appellate review to the "final written decision"); §312(c) (2006 ed.) (repealed) (the "determination" that a petition for *inter partes* reexamination "raise[s]" a "substantial new question of patentability" is "final and non-appealable"); see also §303(c) (2012 ed.); In re Hiniker Co., 150 F.3d 1362, 1367 (C.A. Fed. 1998) ("Section 303 . . . is directed toward the [Patent Office's] authority to institute a reexamination, and there is no provision granting us direct review of that decision").[229]

Joined by Justice Sotomayor, Justice Alito authored a compelling dissent in *Cuozzo*.[230] Although he agreed with the Supreme Court majority that no immediate or interlocutory appeal exists from the grant (or denial) of a PTAB institution decision, Justice Alito urged that, "consistent with the strong presumption favoring judicial review [of agency action], Congress required only that judicial review, including of issues bearing on the institution of patent review proceedings, *be channeled through an appeal from the agency's final decision*."[231] In other words, institution-related issues should at least be reviewable by the Federal Circuit in the course of reviewing the PTAB's final written decision, once the IPR proceeding is final at the agency level. In Justice Alito's view, the USPTO should not be completely shielded from judicial scrutiny of its compliance, or noncompliance, with the "significant conditions" that Congress imposed on the agency's institution of patent review proceedings.[232]

In *Cuozzo*, the Supreme Court clarified that "run-of-the-mill" issues pertaining to patentability-related questions decided by the USPTO in determining whether to institute an IPR (like the particularity of the grounds stated in Garmin's IPR petition) are *not* judicially reviewable. Nevertheless, *Cuozzo* left open more difficult questions about the reviewability of other issues that may arise in the PTAB's analysis of

[228] *Cuozzo,* 136 S. Ct. at 2139-2140.

[229] *Cuozzo,* 136 S. Ct. at 2140.

[230] *See Cuozzo*, 136 S. Ct. at 2148-2153 (Alito, J., dissenting-in-part, joined by Sotomayor, J.). Justices Alito and Sotomayor did not dissent, however, from the other portion of the Court's decision, concerning the propriety of the "broadest reasonable construction" rule for claims in IPRs. *See Cuozzo*, 136 S. Ct. at 2149 n.1. The BRC issue from *Cuozzo* is further detailed *infra* Section E.3.

[231] *Cuozzo*, 136 S. Ct. at 2149 (Alito, J., dissenting-in-part) (emphasis added).

[232] *See Cuozzo*, 136 S. Ct. at 2149 (Alito, J., dissenting-in-part).

whether to institute. These issues are arguably less central to the patentability determination.

For example, 35 U.S.C. §315 provides in part that if an accused infringer, its privy,[233] or its real party in interest[234] are sued by a patent owner for infringement in federal district court, any petition requesting IPR of the same patent by any of those entities must be filed within one year.[235] Patent attorneys refer to this time limit for IPRs as the "section 315(b) time bar."

To better understand how §315 might operate, consider a hypothetical in which Corporation A assembles and sells semiconductor chips using certain components manufactured and supplied by Corporation B. Corporation B has signed an agreement with Corporation A stating that the supplied components do not infringe any patent *and* providing that Corporation B will indemnify (that is, reimburse) Corporation A for any patent infringement liability Corporation A may incur as a result of using Corporation B's components.

Patentee thereafter sues Corporation A in federal district court alleging that Corporation A's chip products infringe Patentee's patent on a certain semiconductor. At 13 months after the service of Patentee's complaint on Corporation A, Corporation B files a petition in the USPTO seeking IPR of the semiconductor patent. Is Corporation B's attempt to obtain IPR of the patent time-barred by 35 U.S.C. §315(b) because Corporation A and Corporation B are in "privity," or one is the "real party in interest" of the other? In other words, is the

[233]"Privity" (or "privy") and "real party in interest" are terms developed in the common law, but not defined in the AIA or the Patent Act. *See* WesternGeco LLC v. ION Geophysical Corp., 889 F.3d 1308, 1317 (Fed. Cir. 2018). A "privy" refers to a person who is in "privity" with another person. In turn, "privity" traditionally meant a "mutual or successive relationship to the same rights of property." TheLawDictionary.org (featuring Black's Law Dictionary Free Online Legal Dictionary 2d ed.), https://thelawdictionary.org/privity (last visited Aug. 21, 2019). As applied in the context of contract law, "privity" refers to the "connection or relationship which exists between two or more contracting parties." *Id.*

The Federal Circuit follows the common law–based understanding of "privity" set forth in the USPTO's *Trial Practice Guide,* 77 FED. REG. 48756, 48759 (Aug. 14, 2012). *See WesternGeco*, 889 F.3d at 1318. That analysis asks "whether the relationship between the purported 'privy' and the relevant other party is sufficiently close such that both should be bound by the trial outcome and related estoppels." *Trial Practice Guide,* 77 FED. REG. at 48759. Determining whether two parties are in privity is typically a fact-intensive exercise, so the USPTO and the Circuit treat the analysis on a flexible, case-by-case basis. *Id.*

[234]For an explanation of "real party in interest," *see* Applications in Internet Time, LLC v. RPX Corp., 897 F.3d 1336, 1347 (Fed. Cir. 2018).

[235]*See* 35 U.S.C. §315 ("Relation to other proceedings or actions") provides in relevant part that "[a]n inter partes review may not be instituted if the petition requesting the proceeding is filed more than 1 year after the date on which the petitioner, real party in interest, or privy of the petitioner is served with a complaint alleging infringement of the patent. . . ." 35 U.S.C. §315(b) (eff. Sept. 16, 2012).

nature of the relationship created by the indemnification agreement between Corporation A and Corporation B such that it is fair to treat Corporation A as Corporation B's privy and bar Corporation B from seeking IPR? This is likely a fact-intensive question. Assume further that based on the terms of the indemnification agreement, the PTAB determines that Corporation A and Corporation B *are* in privity. The PTAB accordingly refuses to institute IPR based on Corporation B's petition because the PTAB believes the petition is time-barred under §315(b). Under the reasoning of *Cuozzo,* could Corporation B appeal the PTAB's decision not to institute an IPR to the Federal Circuit?

In the 2018 decision *Wi-Fi One, LLC v. Broadcom Corp.,*[236] the Federal Circuit held as an *en banc* court that the PTAB's §315 IPR time bar determinations *are* reviewable by Federal Circuit, in contrast to the more patentability-related determination of *Cuozzo.* In so holding, the *en banc* Circuit overruled its 2015 contrary decision, *Achates Reference Publishing, Inc. v. Apple Inc.*[237]

Later in 2018, the Circuit again went *en banc,* but only for a single footnote, in *Click-to-Call Techs., LP v. Ingenio, Inc.,*[238] to rule on a specific application of the §315(b) time bar. The *en banc* court in *Click-to-Call* held that under §315(b), the USPTO cannot institute an IPR in cases where the petitioner was served with an infringement complaint more than one year before filing its petition, but the federal district court in the litigation voluntarily dismissed the lawsuit without prejudice.[239]

In 2019, the Supreme Court announced that it would review one part of the *Click-to-Call* decision, now captioned *Dex Media, Inc. v. Click-to-Call Techs., LP.*[240] Not surprisingly in light of *Cuozzo,* the

[236] 878 F.3d 1364 (Fed. Cir. Jan. 8, 2018) (*en banc*) (Reyna, J.).

[237] 803 F.3d 652 (Fed. Cir. 2015).

[238] 899 F.3d 1321 (Fed. Cir. Aug. 16, 2018) (*en banc* as to footnote 3 only).

[239] *Click-to-Call,* 899 F.3d at 1328 n.3 (stating that "[t]he *en banc* court formed of Prost, Chief Judge, Newman, Lourie, Dyk, Moore, O'Malley, Reyna, Wallach, Taranto, Chen, Hughes, and Stoll, Circuit Judges, considered whether 35 U.S.C. §315(b)'s time bar applies to bar institution when an IPR petitioner was served with a complaint for patent infringement more than one year before filing its petition, but the district court action in which the petitioner was so served was voluntarily dismissed without prejudice. The *en banc* court holds that §315(b)'s time bar applies in such a scenario.").

The PTAB in *Click-to-Call* had held to the contrary that the §315(b) time bar did *not* apply; it instituted the IPR. The PTAB reasoned that " '[t]he Federal Circuit consistently has interpreted the effect of such [voluntary] dismissals as leaving the parties as though the action had never been brought.' " *Click-to-Call,* 899 F.3d at 1326-1327 (quoting PTAB's Institution Decision). The Board also "relied on Wright & Miller's FEDERAL PRACTICE AND PROCEDURE treatise for the proposition that, 'as numerous federal courts have made clear, a voluntary dismissal without prejudice under [Fed. R. Civ. P.] Rule 41(a) leaves the situation as if the action never had been filed.' " *Click-to-Call,* 899 F.3d at 1327 (quoting PTAB's Institution Decision).

[240] 139 S. Ct. 2742 (June 24, 2019) (order granting writ of *certiorari,* limited to Question Presented 1).

aspect of *Dex Media* that the Court agreed to consider is the threshold judicial reviewability issue; that is, "[w]hether 35 U.S.C. §314(d) [the "no-appeal" provision earlier considered in *Cuozzo*] permits appeal of the PTAB's decision to institute an *inter partes* review upon finding that §315(b)'s time bar did not apply."[241] The Court's decision in *Dex Media* will be analyzed in a future edition of this treatise.

As evidenced by its 2019 grant of *certiorari* in *Click-to-Call* and its decisions in *Oil States* (2018) and *Cuozzo* (2016), the Supreme Court has signalled a keen interest in the AIA-implemented post-issuance review framework. During 2018, the Court scrutinized yet another aspect of the agency's operation of the reviews, again focusing on the USPTO's decision to institute review. Prior to the Court's decision in *SAS Instit., Inc. v. Iancu*,[242] the USPTO had routinely granted IPR on less than all grounds asserted by a petitioner, or on less than all the patent claims challenged in the petition. The agency justified its "partial institution practice" on the basis of efficiency — " 'it permits the Board to focus on the most promising challenges and avoid spending time and resources on others.' "[243] The Court was not persuaded. In an opinion authored by Justice Gorsuch, a 5-4 majority in *SAS Instit.* forbade the USPTO practice of partial institution.[244]

In determining whether partial institution would be permitted, the *SAS Inst.* majority determined that the relevant statute supplied a clear, negative answer. AIA-implemented Section 318(a) of 35 U.S.C. mandates that the USPTO must "issue a final written decision with respect to the patentability of *any* patent claim challenged by the petitioner."[245] The *SAS Inst.* majority reasoned that "[i]n this context, as in so many others, 'any' means 'every.' The agency cannot curate the claims at issue but must decide them all."[246] Rejecting the agency's efficiency-based policy argument for partial institution, the *SAS Inst.* majority countered that

> [p]olicy arguments are properly addressed to Congress, not this Court. It is Congress's job to enact policy and it is this Court's job to follow the policy Congress has prescribed. And whatever its virtues or vices,

[241]Petition for a Writ of Certiorari, Dex Media, Inc. v. Click-To-Call Techs., LP, No. 18-916, at i (Jan. 11, 2019), *available at* https://www.supremecourt.gov/DocketPDF/18/18-916/80221/20190111121331953_Dex%20Medix%20Inc.%20Petition.pdf.

[242]138 S. Ct. 1348 (Apr. 24, 2018) (Gorsuch, J.).

[243]*SAS Inst.*, 138 S. Ct. at 1357 (quoting Brief for Federal Respondent 35-36).

[244]*SAS Inst.*, 138 S. Ct. at 1359-1360 (concluding that "[b]ecause everything in the statute before us confirms that SAS is entitled to a final written decision addressing all of the claims it has challenged and nothing suggests we lack the power to say so, the judgment of the Federal Circuit is reversed and the case is remanded for further proceedings consistent with this opinion").

[245]35 U.S.C. §318(a) (emphasis added).

[246]*SAS Inst.*, 138 S. Ct. at 1353.

Congress's prescribed policy here is clear: the petitioner in an *inter partes* review is entitled to a decision on *all* the claims it has challenged.[247]

Currently, the USPTO must issue a final written decision in any IPR it institutes within one year.[248] Whether the *SAS Inst.* decision will significantly dampen the USPTO's ability to handle its post-issuance review docket in the timely fashion required by statute remains to be seen.

e. PTAB as Adjudicator

Unlike reexaminations, *inter partes* reviews are decided in the first instance by a three-member panel of the Patent Trial and Appeal Board (PTAB) rather than a single patent examiner. Moreover, the same PTAB panel that makes the initial decision whether to institute review[249] also conducts the IPR trial, decides the case, and issues a final written decision on the merits.[250] The PTAB's final

[247]*SAS Inst.,* 138 S. Ct. at 1358 (emphasis added).

[248]35 U.S.C. §316 ("Conduct of *inter partes* review") provides in pertinent part that "[t]he Director shall prescribe regulations . . . requiring that the final determination in an *inter partes* review be issued not later than 1 year after the date on which the Director notices the institution of a review under this chapter, except that the Director may, for good cause shown, extend the 1-year period by not more than 6 months. . . ." 35 U.S.C. §316(a)(11) (eff. Sept. 16, 2012).

[249]*See* 35 U.S.C. §314 ("Institution of *inter partes* review").

[250]Under current practice, the same decision maker within the USPTO — the Patent Trial and Appeal Board — makes the threshold decision whether to institute IPR and thereafter (barring some alternative disposition such as settlement) conducts the IPR trial, decides the case, and issues the final written decision. A patentee unsuccessfully challenged this practice as violating Due Process under the Constitution as well as the statutory provisions of the AIA. In *Ethicon Endo-Surgery, Inc. v. Covidien LP*, No. 2014-1771, 2016 WL 145576 (Fed. Cir. Jan. 13, 2016), the patentee Ethicon Endo-Surgery Inc. ("Ethicon") argued that the Board's impartiality in reaching its final determination in an IPR could be tainted by first seeing an incomplete and preliminary record in deciding whether to institute that IPR.

A divided panel of the Federal Circuit rejected the Ethicon's arguments. The *Ethicon* majority concluded that "neither the statute nor the Constitution precludes the same panel of the Board that made the decision to institute *inter partes* review from making the final determination." *Ethicon*, 2016 WL 145576, at *1. The majority relied firstly on *Withrow v. Larkin,* 421 U.S. 35 (1975), "the leading case involving due process and the combination of functions. . . ." *Ethicon,* 2016 WL 145576, at *1. In *Withrow*, which involved a state medical board's suspension of a physician's license when the same board both investigated, and later adjudicated, the issue, the Court held that combining investigative and adjudicatory functions in a single body did not raise Due Process or other constitutional concerns. *See Withrow*, 421 U.S. at 58. At the USPTO, the "combined functions" issue was even less problematic because the Board's institution decision and its final decision are both adjudicatory and do not involve combining investigative and/or prosecutorial functions. *Ethicon*, 2016 WL 145576, at *5. Moreover, written decisions in IPRs are appealable directly to the Federal Circuit.[251]

Notably, the review proceeding must be conducted expeditiously; the Patent Act requires a final determination within one year of the institution of *inter partes* review, absent a showing of good cause for a six-month extension.[252] The Patent Act also requires the USPTO to issue regulations concerning the conduct of *inter partes* review, including issues such as discovery standards and procedures, protective orders, patent owner response and amendment of claims, and oral hearings.[253] The USPTO issued final regulations on these issues in August 2012.[254]

Withrow afforded adjudicators a "'presumption of honesty and integrity.'" *Ethicon*, 2016 WL 145576, at *5 (quoting *Withrow*, 421 U.S. at 47).

Second, the *Ethicon* majority observed, the AIA specifically gave the Director of the USPTO the power to decide whether to institute an IPR, *see* 35 U.S.C. §314(a), and the USPTO promulgated a regulation under that statute that allows the Board to institute IPR "on behalf of the Director." 37 C.F.R. §42.4(a). The *Ethicon* majority held that in enacting the AIA, Congress had given the Director "inherent authority" (though not explicit authority) to delegate the institution decision to the Board. *Ethicon*, 2016 WL 145576, at *7. Moreover, the Director's "broad rulemaking power" as the head of the USPTO further supported her delegation to the Board as a permissible interpretation of the AIA statutes under *Chevron, U.S.A., Inc. v. Nat. Res. Def. Council, Inc.,* 467 U.S. 837, 842-843 (1984). *See Ethicon*, 2016 WL 145576, at *8.

The dissent in *Ethicon* noted that practitioners have criticized the practice of having the same PTAB panel that decides to institute an IPR thereafter decide it on the merits, citing an "'actual or perceived bias'" against the patent owner because the PTAB judges are "'put in the position of defending their prior decision to institute the trial.'" *Ethicon,* 2016 WL 145576, at *12 (Newman, J., dissenting) (quoting American Intellectual Property Law Association, *Comments on PTAB Trial Proceedings,* at 20 (Oct. 16, 2014), *available at* http://www.uspto.gov/ip/boards/bpai/aipla_20141016.pdf). The dissent concluded that the "transfer to the Board of the Director's statutory assignment violates the text, structure, and purpose of the America Invents Act." *Ethicon,* 2016 WL 145576, at *13 (Newman, J., dissenting). In Judge Newman's view, the AIA-implemented post-grant proceedings must be above reproach, for they

> are a pioneering measure to shift several aspects of patent validity from the district courts to the PTO. The legislative purpose is to provide optimum decisional objectivity, in order to restore public confidence in the reliability of patents as investment incentives; this requires that the PTO proceedings conform to the statute.

Ethicon, 2016 WL 145576, at *15 (Newman, J., dissenting).

[251] *See* 35 U.S.C. §319.

[252] 35 U.S.C. §316(a)(11) (eff. Sept. 16, 2012).

[253] 35 U.S.C. §316(a)(1)-(13) (eff. Sept. 16, 2012).

[254] *See* United States Patent & Trademark Office, *Final Rule: Changes to Implement* Inter Partes *Review Proceedings, Post-Grant Review Proceedings, and Transitional Program for Covered Business Method Patents*, 77 Fed. Reg. 48680 (Aug. 14, 2012), *available at* http://www.uspto.gov/aia_implementation/fr_specific_trial.pdf (adding 37 C.F.R. Chapter I, Part 42 ("Trial Practice Before the Patent Trial and Appeal Board"), Subpart B ("*Inter Partes* Review"), 37 C.F.R. §§42.100-42.123).

f. Estoppel

As discussed *supra,* the estoppel provision for *inter partes* reexamination may have dissuaded some patent challengers from using that form of reexamination.[255] An estoppel provision remains in the statute for *inter partes* review, but its impact may be relatively less draconian. The Patent Act provides that

> [t]he petitioner in an *inter partes* review of a claim in a patent under this chapter that results in a final written decision under section 318(a), or the real party in interest or privy of the petitioner, may not assert either in a civil action arising in whole or in part under section 1338 of title 28 or in a proceeding before the International Trade Commission under section 337 of the Tariff Act of 1930 that the claim is invalid *on any ground that the petitioner raised or reasonably could have raised during that* inter partes *review.*[256]

In other words, if the petitioner in an *inter partes* review that goes to final determination is thereafter involved in federal court or ITC litigation challenging the patent's validity, the petitioner (and those in privity with the petitioner) are estopped from asserting that the patent is invalid on the same ground(s) that the petitioner raised (or reasonably could have raised) during the *inter partes* review in the USPTO. This statutory language differs from the pre-AIA estoppel provision for *inter partes* reexamination by adding the qualifier "reasonably" to the phrase "could have raised."[257] Moreover, the grounds on which the petitioner will be estopped are only those that were raised (or reasonably could have been raised) *during* the *inter partes* review, and not (apparently) any and all invalidity grounds that might have been considered at a time before the USPTO instituted the *inter partes* review.[258]

2. Post-Grant Review

Responding to high-level calls for a less expensive and more widely available system to challenge the validity of issued patents,[259]

[255] *See supra* Section D.3.

[256] 35 U.S.C. §315(e)(2) (eff. Sept. 16, 2012) ("Civil Actions and Other Proceedings").

[257] *Compare* 35 U.S.C. §315(e)(2) (eff. Sept. 16, 2012) *with* 35 U.S.C. §315(c)(2006).

[258] *Inter partes* review is not "instituted" until the USPTO Director determines that the petition satisfies the threshold standard set out in 35 U.S.C. §314(a) (eff. Sept. 16, 2012). This suggests that the statutory phrase "during that *inter partes* review" refers only to the time period after the Director granted the petition.

[259] For example, the Federal Trade Commission's 2003 comprehensive study of the patent system recommended the enactment of post-grant opposition in the U.S. patent system. *See* Federal Trade Commission, To Promote Innovation: The Proper Balance

E. AIA-Implemented Procedures for Challenging Issued Patents

Congress in the America Invents Act of 2011 also implemented a new adjudicative proceeding termed "post-grant review" (PGR), in addition to IPR. The PGR procedure is similar, but not identical, to the opposition system that has successfully operated for a number of years under the European Patent Convention.[260] Sections 321 through 329 of the Patent Act as implemented by the AIA govern post-grant review.[261] Section 326 of the Patent Act requires the USPTO Director to prescribe regulations for the conduct of post-grant review; the agency issued its final rules in August 2012.[262] The AIA-implemented post-grant review proceeding does not replace *ex parte* reexamination but rather exists in addition thereto.[263]

Any person who is not the patent owner can petition the USPTO to authorize post-grant review, with the petitioner's goal being to invalidate the patent by persuading the USPTO to cancel its claims. The petitioner need not be practicing the patented invention (in other words, need not be a potential infringer). This is a significant difference from the pre-AIA framework under which patent validity challenges were largely limited to expensive, long-running federal court

---

OF COMPETITION AND PATENT LAW AND POLICY 7 (2003), *available at* http://www.ftc.gov/os/2003/10/innovationrpt.pdf [hereinafter FTC Report] (recommending the enactment of legislation to allow post-grant review and opposition to patents). The FTC Report explained that "[e]xisting means for challenging questionable patents are inadequate." *Id.* (discussing limitations of reexamination and high costs and lengthy duration of federal court litigation). Given these drawbacks with the existing methods of challenging issued patents, the FTC Report recommended the creation of "an administrative procedure for post-grant review and opposition that allows for meaningful challenges to patent validity short of federal court litigation." *Id.*

[260]*See* European Patent Convention arts. 99-105 (16th ed. 2016).

[261]*See* 35 U.S.C. §§321-329 (eff. Sept. 16, 2012, for patent claims having an effective filing date that is on or after Mar. 16, 2013).

[262]*See* United States Patent & Trademark Office, *Final Rule: Changes to Implement* Inter Partes *Review Proceedings, Post-Grant Review Proceedings, and Transitional Program for Covered Business Method Patents*, 77 FED. REG. 48680 (Aug. 14, 2012), *available at* http://www.uspto.gov/aia_implementation/fr_specific_trial.pdf (adding 37 C.F.R. Chapter I, Part 42 ("Trial Practice Before the Patent Trial and Appeal Board"), Subpart C ("Post-Grant Review"), 37 C.F.R. §§42.200-42.224).

[263]After the AIA-implemented *inter partes* review proceeding became effective on September 16, 2012, reexamination is limited to the *ex parte* form of reexamination. *Ex parte* reexamination was analyzed at Section D.2, *supra*. *Ex parte* reexamination can be requested by anyone, including the patent owner, throughout the life of a patent. The scope of issues and evidence that can be relied on in *ex parte* reexamination is limited, however, and a "substantial new question of patentability" must be involved. Reexaminations are decided in the first instance by USPTO examiners rather than by the Patent Trial and Appeal Board (PTAB). Reexaminations are a more examinational proceeding than an adjudicative one, *see* H.R. REP. No. 112-98 [House Judiciary Comm. Rep. on the America Invents Act] (June 1, 2011), at 57 (stating that the AIA "converts *inter partes* reexamination from an examinational to an adjudicative proceeding, and renames the proceeding "*inter partes* review"), and do not involve litigation-type procedures such as discovery depositions.

proceedings involving parties who were accused of infringing the patent (or at least in legitimate danger of being sued therefor).[264]

Perhaps the most important *procedural* aspect of post-grant review to understand is that such review may be sought only during the nine-month "window" following the issuance of a patent.[265] Post-grant review is *not* available throughout the life of the patent, in contrast with *ex parte* reexamination and the AIA-implemented *inter partes* review. Other procedural aspects of post-grant review largely track those specified for *inter partes* review.[266]

The most important *substantive* aspect of post-grant review is the broad scope of the review; that is, a petitioner can assert a relatively large number of grounds to establish patent invalidity (in contrast with *ex parte* reexamination and *inter partes* review). Specifically, a petition for post-grant review can raise "any ground that could be raised under paragraph (2) or (3) of [35 U.S.C.] section 282(b) (relating to invalidity of the patent or any claim)."[267] Such grounds include patent-ineligible subject matter or lack of utility under 35 U.S.C. §101; anticipation (i.e., lack of novelty) under 35 U.S.C. §102;

[264]The Supreme Court clarified the jurisdictional prerequisites for actions seeking a declaratory judgment of patent invalidity in *MedImmune, Inc. v. Genentech, Inc.*, 549 U.S. 118 (2007) (holding that subject-matter jurisdiction existed over licensee's Declaratory Judgment Act lawsuit challenging validity, enforceability, and infringement of licensed patent; justiciable case or controversy under U.S. Constitution Art. III existed despite licensee's payment of royalties under protest). *MedImmune* is further analyzed *infra* Chapter 10, Section G.

Even prior to the AIA, federal court litigation such as declaratory judgment actions and invalidity defenses or counterclaims in infringement actions was not the sole means of challenging the validity of issued patents. As discussed *supra, ex parte* reexamination has been available since 1980 and remains available post-AIA, but is limited in scope as outlined above in Section D. Reexamination is considered an "examinatory" proceeding rather than an "adjudicative" one.

[265]*See* 35 U.S.C. §321(c) (eff. Sept. 16, 2012, for patent claims having an effective filing date on or after Mar. 16, 2013).

[266]*See* United States Patent & Trademark Office, *Final Rule: Rules of Practice for Trials Before the Patent Trial and Appeal Board and Judicial Review of Patent Trial and Appeal Board Decisions*, 77 FED. REG. 48612 (Aug. 14, 2012), *available at* http://www.uspto.gov/aia_implementation/fr_general_trial.pdf (providing a "consolidated set of rules relating to Board trial practice for *inter partes* review, post-grant review, the transitional program for covered business method patents, and derivation proceedings [, as well as] a consolidated set of rules to implement the provisions of the AIA related to seeking judicial review of Board decisions"); United States Patent & Trademark Office, *Office Patent Trial Practice Guide*, 77 FED. REG. 48756 (Aug. 14, 2012), *available at* http://www.uspto.gov/aia_implementation/trial_practice_guide_48756.pdf (providing "a practice guide for the trial final rules to advise the public on the general framework of the regulations, including the structure and times for taking action in each of the new proceedings [i.e., *inter partes* review, post-grant review, the transitional program for covered business method patents, and derivation proceedings]").

[267]35 U.S.C. §321(b) (eff. Sept. 16, 2012, for patent claims having an effective filing date on or after Mar. 16, 2013) ("Scope").

obviousness under 35 U.S.C. §103; and non-enablement, failure to satisfy the written description of the invention requirement, and claim indefiniteness under 35 U.S.C. §112. Presumably double patenting can also be asserted as a ground relating to invalidity.[268] Post-grant review *cannot* be used to assert a failure to satisfy the best mode requirement of 35 U.S.C. §112,[269] or the defenses of noninfringement and unenforceability (the latter traditionally viewed as including inequitable conduct and patent misuse).[270]

The threshold standard for the USPTO Director to grant a petition for post-grant review is whether "the information presented in the petition . . . , if not rebutted, would demonstrate that it is more likely than not that at least 1 of the claims challenged in the petition is unpatentable."[271] The USPTO Director may also grant the petition if it "raises a novel or unsettled legal question that is important to other patents or patent applications."[272] These two threshold tests are different from the "reasonable likelihood that the petitioner would prevail" threshold for *inter partes* review. At least the first threshold test, "more likely than not," arguably sets a somewhat higher bar, but the Federal Circuit has not yet addressed that question.

With regard to the interaction of post-grant review and civil actions (e.g., federal court litigation) involving patent invalidity, the automatic stay and estoppel provisions for post-grant review operate in the same manner as those described above for *inter partes* review.[273]

Any ambiguities in the procedural or substantive aspects of post-grant review will not be resolved with finality for some time. As of July 2019, the USPTO had received only 172 petitions for post-grant

[268]Same invention-type double patenting is viewed as based on the language of 35 U.S.C. §101, although obviousness-type double patenting is a judicially created doctrine and not analytically the same as obviousness under 35 U.S.C. §103. Double patenting is further discussed *supra* Chapter 1, Section H.6.

[269]*See* 35 U.S.C. §282(b)(3) (eff. Sept. 16, 2012) (providing that "[t]he following shall be defenses in any action involving the validity . . . of a patent . . .: any requirement of section 112, *except that the failure to disclose the best mode shall not be a basis on which any claim of a patent may be cancelled . . .*") (emphasis added).

[270]*See* 35 U.S.C. 282(b)(1) (eff. Sept. 16, 2012). Unenforceability (including inequitable conduct and patent misuse) is analyzed *infra* Chapter 10, Section D.

[271]35 U.S.C. §324(a) (eff. Sept. 16, 2012, for patent claims having an effective filing date on or after Mar. 16, 2013) ("Threshold"). The statutes permit the patent owner to attempt to rebut the information in the petition for post-grant review by filing a "preliminary response" thereto. *See* 35 U.S.C. §323 (eff. Sept. 16, 2012, for patent claims having an effective filing date on or after Mar. 16, 2013) ("Preliminary response to petition").

[272]35 U.S.C. §324(b) (eff. Sept. 16, 2012, for patent claims having an effective filing date on or after Mar. 16, 2013) ("Additional Grounds").

[273]*See* 35 U.S.C. §325 (eff. Sept. 16, 2012, for patent claims having an effective filing date on or after Mar. 16, 2013) ("Relation to other proceedings or actions). Subsection 325(a)(2) deals with stays of civil actions; subsection 325(e) deals with estoppel. *See also supra* Section E.1 ("*Inter Partes* Review").

review.[274] This means that the Federal Circuit likely will not be hearing many appeals from USPTO decisions in post-grant reviews before 2021 or beyond. Although the new sections 321 to 329 of the Patent Act that govern post-grant review took effect on September 16, 2012, they "shall apply only to patents described in section 3(n)(1)" of the America Invents Act of 2011.[275] In other words, a patent subject to post-grant review must by an "AIA patent"; that is, it must contain a claim to a claimed invention having an effective filing date on or after March 16, 2013; or, alternatively, the patent must contain a specific reference under 35 U.S.C. §120 (continuation or continuation-in-part application), 35 U.S.C. §121 (divisional application), or 35 U.S.C. §365(c) (international application designating the United States and entitled to benefit of earlier-filed application) to a patent that contains such a claim.[276] With U.S. patent application pendency averaging over

[274]*See* United States Patent and Trademark Office, *Patent Trial and Appeal Board Statistics* (June 2019) (cumulative data for the period of September 16, 2012 through June 30, 2019), https://www.uspto.gov/sites/default/files/documents/Trial_Statistics_2019-06-30.pdf.

[275]Leahy-Smith America Invents Act, Pub. L. No. 112-29 (H.R. 1249), §6(f)(2)(A), 125 Stat. 284, 311 (Sept. 16, 2011).

[276]*See* Leahy-Smith America Invents Act, Pub. L. No. 112-29 (H.R. 1249), §3(n)(1), 125 Stat. 284, 293 (Sept. 16, 2011), which provides that

> IN GENERAL. — Except as otherwise provided in this section, the amendments made by this section shall take effect upon the expiration of the 18-month period beginning on the date of the enactment of this Act, and shall apply to any application for patent, and to any patent issuing thereon, that contains or contained at any time —
>
> (A) a claim to a claimed invention that has an effective filing date as defined in section 100(i) of title 35, United States Code, that is on or after the effective date described in this paragraph; or
>
> (B) a specific reference under section 120, 121, or 365(c) of title 35, United States Code, to any patent or application that contains or contained at any time such a claim.

The AIA-amended version of 35 U.S.C. §100 in turn defines "effective filing date" as follows:

> (i) (1) The term "effective filing date" for a claimed invention in a patent or application for patent means —
>
> (A) if subparagraph (B) does not apply, the actual filing date of the patent or the application for the patent containing a claim to the invention; or
>
> (B) the filing date of the earliest application for which the patent or application is entitled, as to such invention, to a right of priority under section 119, 365(a), or 365(b) or to the benefit of an earlier filing date under section 120, 121, or 365(c).
>
> (2) The effective filing date for a claimed invention in an application for reissue or reissued patent shall be determined by deeming the claim to the invention to have been contained in the patent for which reissue was sought.

35 U.S.C. §100 (eff. Mar. 16, 2013).

two years, few patents subject to challenge via post-grant review issued before 2015.

3. "Broadest Reasonable Construction" Rule for Claims

Before late 2018, one of the most hotly debated issues in the conduct of the AIA-implemented patent review procedures (e.g., IPR) was whether the Patent Trial and Appeal Board (PTAB) should use the "broadest reasonable construction" (BRC) rule to interpret the patent claims (thereby determining the scope of those claims) being challenged by an IPR petitioner. The BRC rule, which the USPTO implemented by regulation for IPRs,[277] is generally understood as resulting in claim interpretations broader in scope than those that a federal district court would reach under the guidance of the Federal Circuit's landmark 2005 *en banc* decision, *Phillips v. AWH Corp.*[278] As a result, patent owners targeted in IPRs assert that their patents were relatively more vulnerable to having claims cancelled when prior art is applied in an obviousness or anticipation challenge (i.e., because their claims will tend to be more broadly construed by the PTAB).

Although the USPTO has long used the BRC standard in *ex parte* examination and in reexamination and reissue, the patent applicants and owners in those procedures have opportunities to amend their claims *as of right*; they are often able to iteratively negotiate a claim scope that satisfies the USPTO as well as the patent owner by distinguishing the prior art of record. In contrast, the opportunity to amend claims in the AIA-implemented post-issue review procedures such as IPR is *not* available as of right;[279] the Federal Circuit has described

[277] *See* 37 C.F.R. §42.100(b) (eff. Sept. 16, 2012) (providing that "[a] claim in an unexpired patent shall be given its broadest reasonable construction in light of the specification of the patent in which it appears").

[278] 415 F.3d 1303 (Fed. Cir. 2005) (*en banc*), discussed *infra* Chapter 9, Section B.4.

[279] *See* 35 U.S.C. §316(d)(1) (eff. Sept. 16, 2012) (providing that "[d]uring an *inter partes* review instituted under this chapter, the patent owner *may* file 1 motion to amend the patent in 1 or more of the following ways: (A) cancel any challenged patent claim. (B) For each challenged claim, propose a reasonable number of substitute claims.") (emphasis added).

In *Nike, Inc. v. Adidas AG*, No. 2014-1719, 2016 WL 537609 (Fed. Cir. Feb. 11, 2016), patentee Nike argued that when the patentee moves to amend its patent by proposing substitute claims, the burden of proof should be on the IPR petitioner/challenger, rather than the patent owner, to show that the proposed substitute claims are *not* patentable over the prior art. Nike relied on the language of 35 U.S.C. §316(e), which provides that in an IPR "*the petitioner shall have the burden* of proving a proposition of unpatentability by a preponderance of the evidence." *Nike,* 2016 WL 537609, at *4 (emphasis added). Although the Circuit found Nike's position "not without some merit," *id.,* the court disagreed that §316 made "such a broad command." Although it was correct that the IPR petitioner bears the burden of proof to show the unpatentability of the challenged claims in the form that they issued in the patent, it is the patent owner who must bear

it as "cabined." Accordingly, patent owners question the fundamental fairness of applying the BRC standard when their claims under review cannot routinely be amended. The BRC debate as applied to IPRs has thus far played out in a series of Federal Circuit decisions captioned *In re Cuozzo.*

In a February 2015 decision, *In re Cuozzo,*[280] the first Federal Circuit review on the merits of an IPR final written decision, a two-judge panel majority of the Circuit seemed to bend over backwards to

---

the burden of proof to show patentability of any claims it newly proposes as substitute claims during the IPR. Notably, unlike the original claims, the patentee's proposed substitute claims have never previously been evaluated by the USPTO. *Id.* The court concluded that the Board's decision in the case at bar to place the burden of showing patentability on patentee Nike was consistent with the language of the USPTO's regulation on motions practice, 37 C.F.R. §42.20 (providing in part (c) that "[t]he moving party has the burden of proof to establish that it is entitled to the requested relief") and with the Circuit's earlier decision in *Microsoft Corp. v. Proxyconn, Inc.,* 789 F.3d 1292, 1306-1308 (Fed. Cir. 2015) (holding that Board's interpretation of its regulation 37 C.F.R. §42.20(c) was permissible in light of the text of 35 U.S.C. §316(a)(9) and the language of the regulation). *See Nike,* 2016 WL 537609, at *4-*5.

Another important part of the Federal Circuit's February 2016 *Nike* decision concerned precisely what universe of prior art a patentee must distinguish when proposing substitute claims in an IPR. In the PTAB's decision, *Idle Free Sys., Inc. v. Bergstrom,* IPR 2012-00027, 2013 WL 5947697 (PTAB June 11, 2013) (designated "informative"), the Board held that an IPR motion to amend will only succeed if the patentee "persuade[s] the Board that the proposed substitute claim is patentable over the prior art of record, *and over prior art not of record but known to the patent owner.*" *Idle Free,* 2013 WL 5947697, at *4 (emphasis added). In *Nike,* the Board had also denied Nike's motion to amend because it simply stated that Nike's proposed substitute claims were "patentable over prior art known to Nike, but not part of the record of the proceedings." *Nike,* 2016 WL 537609, at *19. In the Board's view, this statement was "conclusory" and "facially inadequate" under *Idle Free.*

The Federal Circuit in *Nike* disagreed. The court noted that in a more recent Board decision, *MasterImage 3D, Inc. v. RealD Inc.,* IPR2015-00040, 2015 WL 4383224 (PTAB July 15, 2015) (designated as a "Representative Decision on Motions to Amend"), the Board made certain "clarifications" about its earlier statements in *Idle Free.* In particular, the Board explained that "prior art known to the patent owner" should be understood as "no more than the material prior art that Patent Owner makes of record in the current proceeding pursuant to its duty of candor and good faith to the Office under 37 C.F.R. §42.11, in light of the Motion to Amend." *MasterImage 3D,* 2015 WL 4383224, Slip. Op. at 3. The Circuit observed that the heart of the issue was the "question of whether the patent owner has submitted the necessary information to comply with its duty of candor. . . ." *Nike,* 2016 WL 537609, at *20. In the case at bar, there had never been any allegation that Nike violated its duty of candor. Moreover, the PTO had acknowledged at oral argument before the Federal Circuit that Nike's statement about its substitute claims' patentability over the prior art not of record but known to Nike *would* satisfy the patentee's obligation as explained in *MasterImage 3D.* Accordingly, the Federal Circuit could "not see how the statement used by Nike would be inadequate, absent an allegation of conduct violating the duty of candor." *Nike,* 2016 WL 537609, at *20. Thus the Board had erred in denying Nike's motion to amend on this ground.

[280] 2015 WL 448667 (Feb. 4, 2015) (Dyk, J.) (copy on file with author), withdrawn and superseded by *In re Cuozzo,* 793 F.3d 1268 (Fed. Cir. July 8, 2015) (Dyk, J.).

approve the USPTO's use of the BRC rule for interpreting patent claims in IPRs, despite admitting that opportunities to amend claims in IPRs are "cabined."[281] Although dissenting Judge Newman observed that as of January 2015, the PTAB had granted motions to amend claims in only *two* IPR cases, the *Cuozzo* majority countered that an opportunity to amend was "nonetheless available." The majority asserted that the facts that the patent owner's presumptively single amendment had to address the grounds of unpatentability "involved in the trial" and could not enlarge claim scope were not "material difference[s]" from pre-AIA proceedings (such as reexaminations and reissues) that also applied the BRC. Moreover, the BRC rule was used in interferences, another type of adjudicatory proceeding.

In the *Cuozzo* majority's view, Congress was aware of the BRC rule when it passed the AIA and thus legislatively ratified it. And even if the AIA did not explicitly incorporate a BRC standard for IPR claim constructions, the agency's regulation mandating BRC in IPRs[282] was properly adopted under the test of the Supreme Court's watershed administrative law decision, *Chevron USA, Inc. v. Nat'l Res. Def. Council.*[283] Given its approval of the PTAB's broad construction of the claim phrase "integrally attached" in Cuozzo's patent claim directed to a speed limit indicator,[284] the *Cuozzo* majority had no difficulty affirming the PTAB's obviousness determination on the merits.[285]

[281]In re Cuozzo Speed Techs., LLC, 793 F.3d 1268, 1278 (Fed. Cir. July 8, 2015) (stating that "[a]lthough the opportunity to amend is cabined in the IPR setting, it is thus nonetheless available"), *cert. granted sub nom.* Cuozzo Speed Techs., LLC v. Lee, 136 S. Ct. 890 (2016) (mem.).

[282]*See* 37 C.F.R. §42.100(b) (eff. Sept. 16, 2012) (providing that "[a] claim in an unexpired patent shall be given its broadest reasonable construction in light of the specification of the patent in which it appears").

[283]467 U.S. 837 (1984).

[284]*See* U.S. Patent No. 6,778,074 (titled "Speed Limit Indicator and Method for Displaying Speed and the Relevant Limit") (filed 2002). Claim 10 of the '074 patent required (emphasis added) "[a] speed limit indicator comprising . . . a global positioning system receiver; a display controller connected to said global positioning system receiver, wherein said display controller adjusts a colored display in response to signals from said global positioning system receiver to continuously update the delineation of which speed readings are in violation of the speed limit at a vehicle's present location; and a speedometer *integrally attached* to said colored display."

Applying the broadest reasonable construction rule, the Board interpreted the claim phrase "integrally attached" to mean "discrete parts physically joined together as a unit without each part losing its own separate identity." *Cuozzo,* 793 F.3d at 1272 (Fed. Cir. July 8, 2015). The Federal Circuit affirmed the Board's determination that claim 10 was unpatentable for obviousness given this construction. *Cuozzo,* 793 F.3d at 1282 (Fed. Cir. July 8, 2015) (concluding that "Claim 10 would have been obvious over [prior art references] Aumayer, Evans, and Wendt because it encompasses the analog embodiment of the invention discussed in the specification").

[285]*Cuozzo,* 2015 WL 448667 (Feb. 4, 2015) (copy on file with author), withdrawn and superseded by *In re Cuozzo,* 793 F.3d 1268 (Fed. Cir. July 8, 2015); *see Cuozzo,* 793 F.3d

In July 2015, the Federal Circuit (in a badly fractured 6-5 decision) denied rehearing *en banc* in *Cuozzo*.[286] At the same time, the court issued a revised panel opinion that superseded the February panel opinion (with no reference to the withdrawn February opinion and no introductory explanation of how or why the majority's reasoning had changed).[287] The July panel majority in *Cuozzo* maintained its prior position that application of BRC was proper in the case at bar, but significantly narrowed its reasoning (most likely to appease the other Circuit judges who desired *en banc* rehearing).

The PTAB had denied Cuozzo's motion to amend his claims on the ground that the proposed amendment would have improperly enlarged the scope of the claims (a conclusion with which Cuozzo strenuously disagreed).[288] The pre-AIA procedures, reexamination and reissue, likewise prohibited amendments that enlarged claim scope. Because both reexamination and reissue used the BRC rule, it

---

at 1282 (concluding that "Claim 10 would have been obvious over Aumayer, Evans, and Wendt because it encompasses the analog embodiment of the invention discussed in the specification").

[286]793 F.3d 1297 (Fed. Cir. July 8, 2015) (order denying rehearing *en banc*). Eleven judges participated in the *en banc* vote. Four judges (Dyk, Lourie, Chen, and Hughes) joined opinions concurring in the denial. Five judges (Prost, Newman, Moore, O'Malley, and Reyna) joined opinions dissenting from denial of rehearing *en banc*. Two judges (Taranto and Wallach) apparently voted not to rehear the case *en banc* but did not join any opinion.

[287]In re Cuozzo, 793 F.3d 1268 (Fed. Cir. July 8, 2015) (Dyk, J.).

[288]In his motion to amend, Cuozzo proposed to substitute for existing claim 10 a new claim 21, which recited "a speed limit indicator comprising . . . a speedometer integrally attached to said colored display, wherein the speedometer comprises a liquid crystal display, and wherein the colored display is the liquid crystal display." *Cuozzo,* 793 F.3d at 1283. Cuozzo argued that the proposed claim could not be broadening because it merely copied limitations from two dependent claims of his patent.

In reviewing the PTAB's determination to deny Cuozzo's motion because proposed new claim 21 would have enlarged the scope of original claim 10, the Federal Circuit applied the rule from reexamination that a claim "is broader in scope than the original claims if it contains within its scope any conceivable apparatus or process which would not have infringed the original patent." *Cuozzo,* 793 F.3d at 1283. The Circuit agreed with the Board's finding that "claim 21 was broadening because it would encompass a single-LCD embodiment wherein both the speedometer and the colored display are LCDs, which was not within the original claims." More specifically, the Circuit explained that

> Proposed claim 21 recites "a speedometer integrally attached to said colored display, wherein the speedometer comprises a liquid crystal display, and wherein the colored display is *the* liquid crystal display." J.A. 358 (emphasis added). The word "the," emphasized in the quoted language above, requires a single-LCD embodiment that includes both the speedometer and the colored display in one LCD. Because proposed claim 21 would encompass an embodiment not encompassed by claim 10, it is broadening, and the motion to amend was properly denied.

Cuozzo, 793 F.3d at 1283.

was also proper to apply it in the case at bar. Limiting its holding to the facts before it, the July panel majority in the Circuit's *Cuozzo* decision observed that "[i]f there are challenges to be brought against other restrictions on amendment opportunities as incompatible with using the broadest reasonable interpretation standard, they must await another case."[289]

In the view of this author, what began (in February 2015) as an across-the-board approval of the USPTO's application of the BRC rule for IPRs was limited by the July 2015 *Cuozzo* result — that BRC is correctly applied so long as an IPR involves an attempt by the patent owner to *enlarge* its claim scope. Even if the Federal Circuit correctly determined that Cuozzo was seeking to broaden his claims, the broadening scenario will be relatively rare. Most patent owners being challenged in IPRs will seek a *narrower* claim scope that avoids the prior art, not a broader claim scope that renders the claim more susceptible to anticipation or obviousness. Because the holding of the July 2015 *Cuozzo* panel decision was so confined, and given that five of eleven judges voted to rehear *Cuozzo en banc*,[290] it appeared that the debate over the propriety of applying BRC in IPRs was not resolved.

On January 15, 2016, the Supreme Court granted Cuozzo's petition for *certiorari* to review the Federal Circuit's July 2015 panel decision.[291] The Court agreed to review both questions presented in Cuozzo's petition:

> 1. Whether the court of appeals erred in holding that, in IPR proceedings, the Board may construe claims in an issued patent according to their broadest reasonable interpretation rather than their plain and ordinary meaning.
>
> 2. Whether the court of appeals erred in holding that, even if the Board exceeds its statutory authority in instituting an IPR proceeding, the Board's decision whether to institute an IPR proceeding is judicially unreviewable.[292]

The Supreme Court issued its decision in June 2016. *Cuozzo Speed Techs., LLC v. Lee*[293] marked the Court's first occasion to review the America Invents Act of 2011. In an opinion authored by Justice Breyer, the Court affirmed the USPTO's positions in virtually all respects. On Question Presented (1), the Court affirmed the Federal

[289] *Cuozzo,* 793 F.3d at 1278.

[290] 793 F.3d 1297 (Fed. Cir. July 8, 2015) (order denying rehearing *en banc* by 6-5 vote).

[291] *See* Cuozzo Speed Techs., LLC v. Lee, 136 S. Ct. 890 (2016) (mem.).

[292] Petition for a Writ of Certiorari, No. 15-446, Cuozzo Speed Techs., LLC v. Lee (Oct. 6, 2015), at II, *available at* https://www.scotusblog.com/wp-content/uploads/2015/10/Cuozzo-Petition-Final.pdf.

[293] 136 S. Ct. 2131 (June 20, 2016) (Breyer, J.).

Circuit panel's (and USPTO's) determination that claims considered in an IPR were to be interpreted under the "broadest reasonable interpretation" rule.[294]

This treatise will not devote significantly more coverage to the BRC aspect of the *Cuozzo* decision, because it was effectively mooted (at least prospectively) by a subsequent USPTO rule change.[295] As of November 2018, claims considered in post-issuance reviews must be interpreted under the same standard used by federal district courts, which is set forth in the Federal Circuit's 2005 landmark *en banc* decision, *Phillips v. AWH Corp.* (discussed elsewhere in this treatise).[296] The *Phillips* standard is generally thought to result in a narrower claim scope than the BRC standard.

[294]*Cuozzo,* 136 S. Ct. at 2142.

[295]United States Patent and Trademark Office, *Final Rule: Changes to the Claim Construction Standard for Interpreting Claims in Trial Proceedings Before the Patent Trial and Appeal Board*, 83 FED. REG. 51340 (Oct. 11, 2018; effective Nov. 13, 2018), *available at* https://www.federalregister.gov/documents/2018/10/11/2018-22006/changes-to-the-claim-construction-standard-for-interpreting-claims-in-trial-proceedings-before-the. The new rule prospectively applies to "all IPR, PGR and CBM petitions filed on or after the effective date [of Nov. 13, 2018]." *Id.*

[296]415 F.3d 1303 (Fed. Cir. 2005) (*en banc*), examined *infra* Chapter 9 ("Patent Infringement"), Section B.4.

Chapter 9

Patent Infringement

A. Introduction

Equipped with an understanding of the process for obtaining a U.S. patent, we are now ready to consider how a patent owner enforces her statutory right to exclude others from unauthorized making, using, selling, offering to sell, or importing of the patented invention.[1] Analysis of patent **infringement** in the United States involves the application of governing statutory provisions as well as judicial decisions. Briefly, the U.S. courts recognize two basic forms of infringement, each discussed in detail below: (1) **literal infringement** and (2) infringement under the judicially created **doctrine of equivalents**. Literal infringement means that an accused product or process comes precisely within the terms of an asserted patent claim, while infringement under the doctrine of equivalents recognizes that, in order to adequately protect a patentee, we may sometimes extend the scope of her right to exclude beyond the literal boundaries of the claim. This chapter surveys the essential authority.[2]

1. Statutory Framework

The sections of the U.S. Patent Act, 35 U.S.C., most pertinent to an analysis of patent infringement are these:

§271. Infringement of patent

(a) Except as otherwise provided in this title [35 U.S.C. §§1 *et seq.*], whoever without authority makes, uses, offers to sell, or sells any

[1]*See* 35 U.S.C. §271(a) (2012).

[2]For more detailed treatments of patent enforcement, *see* AM. BAR ASS'N: SECTION OF INTELLECTUAL PROPERTY LAW, PATENT LITIGATION STRATEGIES HANDBOOK (William P. Atkins & Deborah E. Fishman, eds., BNA Books 4th ed. 2015); PAUL M. JANICKE, MODERN PATENT LITIGATION (Carolina Acad. Press 3d ed. 2012); KIMBERLY A. MOORE, TIMOTHY HOLBROOK & JOHN F. MURPHY, PATENT LITIGATION AND STRATEGY (Thomson Reuters 4th ed. 2013).

patented invention, within the United States or imports into the United States any patented invention during the term of the patent therefor, infringes the patent.

(b) Whoever actively induces infringement of a patent shall be liable as an infringer.

(c) Whoever offers to sell or sells within the United States or imports into the United States a component of a patented machine, manufacture, combination or composition, or a material or apparatus for use in practicing a patented process, constituting a material part of the invention, knowing the same to be especially made or especially adapted for use in an infringement of such patent, and not a staple article or commodity of commerce suitable for substantial noninfringing use, shall be liable as a contributory infringer.

(d)...(i)....[3]

§281. Remedy for infringement of patent

A patentee shall have remedy by civil action for infringement of his patent.[4]

Section 271 of 35 U.S.C. does not so much define what constitutes infringement as set forth the categories of acts (i.e., "mak[ing]," "us[ing]," "sell[ing]," and so on) that can create liability for infringement. Case law, discussed below, fleshes out the elements of these acts.

As provided by §281, patent infringement actions are brought in the United States as civil actions. No criminal proceeding is recognized for patent infringement in the United States.

a. Direct Versus Indirect Infringement Under 35 U.S.C. §271

Section 271 of the Patent Act (35 U.S.C.) distinguishes between acts of *direct* infringement and acts of *indirect* infringement. Subsection 271(a) governs *direct* infringement — the unauthorized making, using, selling, offering to sell, or importing[5] of the *entire*

[3]35 U.S.C. §271 (2012). Subsection (d) of §271 is discussed in Chapter 10, Section D.2, *infra*. Subsections (e) through (g) of §271 are quoted and discussed in Section E of this chapter, *infra*.

[4]35 U.S.C. §281 (2012).

[5]The "offers to sell" and "imports" provisions of 35 U.S.C. §271(a) became effective January 1, 1996. They were added to the statute by the Uruguay Round Agreements Act, which brought U.S. patent law into compliance with certain provisions of the World Trade Organization–administered Agreement on Trade-Related Aspects of Intellectual Property Rights (TRIPS). For further discussion of TRIPS, *see* Chapter 12, Section D, *infra*. A good resource on the meaning of §271(a)'s "offers to sell" infringement provision is Timothy R. Holbrook, *Liability for the "Threat of a Sale": Assessing Patent*

claimed invention. By application of the **all-limitations rule**, derived from case law as discussed below, the act of "making" the claimed invention under 35 U.S.C. §271(a) requires that an accused infringer has manufactured a device that meets each and every **limitation** of the asserted claim. Generally speaking, this means that if the claimed invention is a combination of elements, the **accused device** must be fully assembled and ready for use.[6]

Notably, 35 U.S.C. §271(a) enumerates the various directly infringing acts in the disjunctive (i.e., using "or"). Thus the act of merely making the claimed invention without authority creates infringement liability, even if the accused infringer thereafter does not sell the infringing device. Likewise, a mere "using" of the claimed invention without authority creates liability even where the accused infringer did not make the infringing device. To see this, consider a scenario in which Accused Infringer 1 manufactures an infringing machine for sowing seeds and sells it to Accused Infringer 2, a farmer who merely uses the infringing machine to plant his crop. Accused Infringer 1 and Accused Infringer 2 are considered jointly and severally liable for patent infringement.[7]

Indirect infringement concerns activity involving *less than* a making of the entire invention, such as assisting one who does or supplying certain required components of the invention. Nevertheless, such indirect activity is considered infringing because it assists or supports another party's direct infringement. The direct infringer and the indirect infringer are considered jointly and severally liable for the infringement under a theory of joint tortfeasance.[8] Another distinction between indirect and direct infringement is that indirect infringement liability requires proof of intent, or *scienter*, while "a direct infringer's knowledge or intent is irrelevant."[9] Forms of indirect infringement under 35 U.S.C. §271(b), which governs inducing infringement, and §271(c), which governs contributory infringement, are discussed later in this chapter.[10]

Infringement for Offering to Sell an Invention and Implications for the On-Sale Patentability Bar and Other Forms of Infringement, 43 SANTA CLARA L. REV. 751 (2003).

[6]*But see* Paper Converting Machine Co. v. Magna-Graphics Corp., 745 F.2d 11, 19 (Fed. Cir. 1984) (finding infringement where "significant, unpatented assemblies of elements [were] tested during the patent term, enabling the infringer to deliver the patented combination in parts to the buyer"), *aff'd after remand,* 785 F.2d 1013 (Fed. Cir. 1986).

[7]*See* Birdsell v. Shaliol, 112 U.S. 485, 489 (1884). In practice, a consumer purchaser of an infringing product may be entitled to sue her seller for breach of warranty under the Uniform Commercial Code. *See* U.C.C. §2-312.

[8]*See* Hewlett-Packard Co. v. Bausch & Lomb, Inc., 909 F.2d 1464, 1469 (Fed. Cir. 1990).

[9]Global-Tech Appliances, Inc. v. SEB S.A., 131 S. Ct. 2060, 2065 n.2 (2011).

[10]*See* Section E, *infra.*

b. *"Divided" Infringement by Multiple Parties Under §271(a)*

Consider the increasingly common scenario of a patent claiming a business method comprising a number of steps. Depending on the manner in which the method claim is drafted, no single entity may perform all the steps of the method. In other words, a "use" of the patented method would involve acts by multiple entities. These entities may be completely unrelated or nominally related only at arm's length. Is there direct infringement in this scenario? The question has been addressed in a line of Federal Circuit decisions and went to the U.S. Supreme Court in 2014. The following section traces the evolution of the courts' thinking on the issue of "divided" patent infringement.

The patents in suit in *BMC Resources, Inc. v. Paymentech, L.P.*[11] claimed a method for processing debit or credit card transactions without having to enter a personal identification number (PIN). The method allowed a customer to pay her bills by accessing an interface between a standard touch-tone telephone and a debit or credit card network. Performance of the method as claimed required acts by four different entities, each of whom participated in carrying out and authorizing the transaction, that is, the merchant whom the customer sought to pay, an agent of the merchant (such as the patentee BMC Resources), a remote payment network such as an ATM network, and the financial institution that issued the debit or credit card.[12] BMC Resources sued Paymentech, a payment services processor, alleging that Paymentech's PIN-less debit bill payment service directly infringed BMC's patented method claims.[13] Paymentech responded that it could not be a direct infringer because it did not perform all the steps of the claimed process, nor did it perform all the steps "in coordination with its customers and financial institutions."[14]

Recall that §271(a) creates direct infringement liability for "whoever" without authority "uses" a patented invention within the United States during the term of the patent. Thus, the precise issue raised by *BMC Resources* is this: who qualifies as the statutory "whoever"? Must "whoever" be limited to a single entity that performs each and every method step, or can a single entity (e.g., Paymentech, the sole named defendant in *BMC Resources*) be liable for direct infringement based

[11]498 F.3d 1373 (Fed. Cir. 2007).

[12]*See id.* at 1375 (describing claimed method); *id.* at 1376-1377 (quoting allegedly infringed claim 7 of BMC's U.S. Patent No. 5,870,456, and allegedly infringed claim 2 of BMC's U.S. Patent No. 5,718,298).

[13]Patentee BMC also asserted that Paymentech was liable for inducing infringement under 35 U.S.C. §271(b). *See id.* at 1376.

[14]*Id.* at 1377.

on its participation in the combined acts of multiple entities under a theory of "joint" or "divided" infringement?[15]

In 2007, the Federal Circuit in *BMC Resources* rejected a mere "participation and combined action" standard,[16] holding instead that direct liability exists in a joint infringement scenario only when the accused infringer is the effective "mastermind" who "controls or directs" all the other entities performing the method steps.[17] For example, if an accused infringer entered into contracts with other entities requiring them to perform steps of a patented process, the accused infringer presumably would be "in control" and liable as a direct infringer; "[a] party cannot avoid infringement . . . simply by contracting out steps of a patented process to another entity."[18] In the case at bar, however, the various entities that carried out the multiple steps of the claimed process were related merely at "arm's length,"[19] and not by contract.[20] The evidence proffered by BMC to establish "some relationship" between Paymentech and the other entities was not sufficient to create a genuine issue of material fact as to whether Paymentech controlled or directed the activity of the other entities. Accordingly, the Federal Circuit affirmed the district court's grant of summary judgment of no infringement.[21] The appellate court concluded that "[i]n this situation, neither the financial institutions, the debit networks, nor the payment services provider, Paymentech, bears responsibility for the actions of the other."[22]

[15]This theory has also been referred to as "distributed" infringement.

[16]A "participation and combined action" standard for joint infringement was set forth in jury instructions that the Federal Circuit had previously approved in *On Demand Machine Corp. v. Ingram Indus., Inc.*, 442 F.3d 1331 (Fed. Cir. 2006). *See BMC Resources*, 498 F.3d at 1379 (quoting instructions from *On Demand*). However, the Federal Circuit in *BMC Resources* agreed with the district court that that aspect of *On Demand* was merely dictum, not relied on by the *On Demand* court in reaching its decision. *See id.* at 1380 (stating that "*On Demand* did not change this court's precedent with regard to joint infringement").

[17]*See id.* at 1381.

[18]*Id.*

[19]*Id.* at 1380 (quoting with approval statement of district court that "[n]o court has ever found direct infringement based on the type of arms-length business transaction presented here").

[20]*See id.* at 1382 (noting district court's observance that "the record contained no evidence even of a contractual relationship between Paymentech and the financial institutions").

[21]Nor could Paymentech be liable for inducing infringement under 35 U.S.C. §271(b), because the patentee BMC had not established a predicate act of direct infringement. *See id.* at 1379 (stating that "[i]ndirect infringement requires, as a predicate, a finding that some party amongst the accused actors has committed the entire act of direct infringement").

[22]*Id.* at 1382. *Compare* Centillion Data Sys., LLC v. Qwest Comm. Int'l, Inc., 631 F.3d 1279, 1285 (Fed. Cir. 2011) (holding that the customer of accused infringer Qwest "is a single 'user' of the [on-demand operation of the patented] system [for processing call data and delivering it to customers in a format appropriate for a personal computer]

The Federal Circuit soon reconfirmed the *BMC Resources* "control or direction" standard in *Muniauction, Inc. v. Thomson Corp.*, reversing a district court's post-jury trial judgment that had awarded a patentee $77 million in damages.[23] Like *BMC Resources, Muniauction* involved a business method patent. Specifically, Muniauction's patent covered methods for conducting original issuer municipal bond auctions over an electronic network such as the Internet. Advantageously, bond issuers (e.g., municipalities) could run an auction and bidders (e.g., underwriters) could submit bids using a conventional Web browser without requiring other separate, preinstalled software. The *Muniauction* court summarized the standards enunciated in *BMC Resources* as follows:

> [W]here the actions of multiple parties combine to perform every step of a claimed method, the claim is directly infringed only if one party exercises "control or direction" over the entire process such that every step is attributable to the controlling party, i.e., the "mastermind." At the other end of this multi-party spectrum, mere "arms-length cooperation" will not give rise to direct infringement by any party.[24]

Applying the *BMC Resources* standard, the *Muniauction* court concluded that even though accused infringer Thomson "control[led] access to its system and instruct[ed] bidders on its use," these acts were not sufficient to incur liability for direct infringement.[25] Rather, the requisite "control or direction" standard is satisfied "in situations where the law would traditionally hold the accused direct infringer vicariously liable for the acts committed by another party that are required to complete performance of a claimed method."[26] In the case at bar, accused infringer Thomson did not perform all the claim steps when it conducted auctions using its accused BidComp/Parity® system, nor did others (e.g., the bidders) perform those steps on Thomson's behalf. The Federal Circuit concluded that Thomson was not vicariously liable for the actions of the auction bidders.

The take-away message of these joint infringement cases is that those who draft business method claims should strive whenever possible to craft single-user claims. For example, the *BMC Resources* court suggested that the method claims in that case could have been drafted to "feature[] references to a single party's supplying or receiving each

---

and because there is a single user, there is no need for the vicarious liability analysis from *BMC* [*Resources*] . . .").

[23]532 F.3d 1318 (Fed. Cir. 2008).

[24]*Id.* at 1329 (citations omitted).

[25]*Id.* at 1330.

[26]*Id.* (citing, *inter alia*, BMC Resources, Inc. v. Paymentech, L.P., 498 F.3d 1373, 1379 (Fed. Cir. 2007)).

element of the claimed process."[27] In cases where such drafting strategies are not a feasible way to capture the invention, the patentee will be required to show that the accused infringer satisfies the rigorous "direction and control" standard with respect to the other entities performing the method steps.

Attempting to clarify continued uncertainty about the standard for divided infringement liability, the Federal Circuit in 2012 took two additional distributed infringement cases under *en banc* review.[28] In *Akamai Techs., Inc. v. Limelight Networks, Inc.* (hereafter *Akamai II*),[29] the *en banc* court avoided answering the question "whether direct infringement can be found when no single entity performs all of the claimed steps of the patent."[30] By a 6-5 vote, the *Akamai II* majority instead resolved the joint infringement issue in the cases before it under the theory of induced infringement under 35 U.S.C. §271(b).[31] The majority rejected the single entity rule of *BMC Resources* insofar as the rule applied to induced infringement liability.[32] Although "all the steps of a claimed method must be performed in order to find induced infringement," the majority held, "it is not necessary to prove that all the steps were committed by a single entity."[33] As a policy matter, resolving the joint **infringement** question under the doctrine of induced infringement advantageously protected unsuspecting innocent parties. Because liability for induced infringement (unlike direct infringement) requires "specific intent to cause infringement," "using inducement to reach joint infringement does not present

[27]*BMC Resources*, 498 F.3d at 1381.

[28]*See* Akamai Techs., Inc. v. MIT, 419 F. App'x 989 (Fed. Cir. 2011) (*en banc*) (order granting rehearing *en banc* and vacating panel's opinion in Akamai Techs., Inc. v. Limelight Networks, Inc., 629 F.3d 1311 (Fed. Cir. 2010)); McKesson Techs., Inc. v. Epic Sys. Corp., 463 F. App'x 906 (Fed. Cir. 2011) (*en banc*) (order granting rehearing *en banc* and vacating panel's opinion in McKesson Techs., Inc. v. Epic Sys. Corp., No. 2010-1291 (Fed. Cir. Apr. 12, 2011).

[29]692 F.3d 1301 (Fed. Cir. 2012) (*en banc*) (*Akamai II*), *rev'd*, 134 S. Ct. 2111 (2014). The original Federal Circuit panel decision was *Akamai Techs., Inc. v. Limelight Networks, Inc.*, 629 F.3d 1311 (Fed. Cir. 2010) (*"Akamai I"*), *reh'g en banc granted, opinion vacated sub nom.* Akamai Techs., Inc. v. MIT, 419 F. App'x 989 (Fed. Cir. 2011).

[30]*Akamai II,* 692 F.3d at 1306. The majority explained that "[b]ecause the reasoning of our decision today is not predicated on the doctrine of direct infringement, we have no occasion at this time to revisit any of those principles regarding the law of divided infringement as it applies to liability for direct infringement under 35 U.S.C. §271(a)." *Id.,* 692 F.3d at 1307.

[31]Indirect infringement liability under the theory of induced infringement is analyzed *infra* Section E.1.

[32]*Akamai II,* 692 F.3d at 1306 ("[W]e reconsider and overrule the 2007 decision of this court in which we held that in order for a party to be liable for induced infringement, some other single entity must be liable for direct infringement. *BMC Resources, Inc. v. Paymentech, L.P.*, 498 F.3d 1373 (Fed. Cir. 2007).").

[33]*Akamai II,* 692 F.3d at 1306.

the risk of extending liability to persons who may be unaware of the existence of a patent or even unaware that others are practicing some of the steps claimed in the patent."[34]

In June 2014, the Supreme Court adamantly rejected the *en banc* Federal Circuit's *Akamai II* expansion of inducing infringement liability. In a unanimous opinion authored by Justice Alito, the Supreme Court's decision in *Limelight Networks, Inc. v. Akamai Techs.* (hereafter "*Akamai III*" or "*Limelight*")[35] renounced the *Akamai II* majority's reasoning "that a defendant can be liable for inducing infringement under §271(b) even if no one has committed direct infringement within the terms of §271(a) (or any other provision of the patent laws), because direct infringement can exist independently of a violation of these statutory provisions."[36]

In the Supreme Court's view, the *en banc* Federal Circuit majority's analysis in *Akamai II* "fundamentally misunderst[ood] what it means to infringe a method patent."[37] Direct infringement never occurred in the case at bar because "performance of all the claimed steps [could] not be attributed to a single person. . . ."[38] Neither the parties nor the Federal Circuit disputed the proposition that inducing infringement liability cannot exist without underlying direct infringement.[39] Accordingly, "[accused infringer] Limelight [could] not be liable for inducing infringement that never came to pass."[40] The majority's decision in *Akamai II* had erroneously created a definition of inducing infringement with "serious and problematic consequences, namely, creating for §271(b) purposes some free-floating concept of 'infringement' both untethered to the statutory text and difficult for the lower courts to apply consistently."[41]

[34]*Akamai II,* 692 F.3d at 1308 n.1. The Supreme Court granted *certiorari* in *Akamai II* in January 2014. *See* Limelight Networks, Inc. v. Akamai Techs., Inc., 134 S. Ct. 895 (2014) (mem.).

[35]134 S. Ct. 2111 (2014).

[36]*Akamai III,* 134 S. Ct. at 2117 (citing Akamai Techs., Inc. v. Limelight Networks, Inc., 692 F.3d 1301, 1314 (Fed. Cir. 2012) (*en banc*) ("*Akamai II*")).

[37]*Akamai III,* 134 S. Ct. at 2117.

[38]*Akamai III,* 134 S. Ct. at 2118.

[39]*See Akamai III,* 134 S. Ct. at 2117 ("Neither the Federal Circuit, see 692 F.3d, at 1308, nor respondents, see Tr. of Oral Arg. 44, dispute the proposition that liability for inducement must be predicated on direct infringement."). The Supreme Court considered this proposition unassailable. *See Akamai III,* 134 S. Ct. at 2117 (stating that "our case law leaves no doubt that inducement liability may arise 'if, but only if, [there is] . . . direct infringement.' ") (quoting Aro Mfg. Co. v. Convertible Top Replacement Co., 365 U.S. 336, 341 (1961) (emphasis deleted)). The Court explained in a footnote that while *Aro* addressed contributory infringement under §271(c) rather than inducing infringement under §271(b), it saw "no basis to distinguish for these purposes between the two, which after all spring from common stock." *Akamai III,* 134 S. Ct. at 2117 n.3 (citing Global-Tech Appliances, Inc. v. SEB S.A., 131 S. Ct. 2060, 2067-2068 (2011)).

[40]*Akamai III,* 134 S. Ct. at 2118.

[41]*Akamai III,* 134 S. Ct. at 2120.

The Supreme Court's reversal in *Akamai III* turned on its decision to "[a]ssum[e] without deciding that the Federal Circuit's holding in *Muniauction* [i.e., that the performance of all method steps must be attributable to a single entity, either acting alone or as a "mastermind" exercising direction or control over all other actors[42]] [wa]s correct. . . ."[43] In other words, "*Muniauction* (which, again, we assume to be correct) instructs that a method patent is not directly infringed — and the patentee's interest is thus not violated — unless a single actor can be held responsible for the performance of all steps of the patent."[44] In view of its dependence on the *Muniauction* rule, the Supreme Court concluded that "there has simply been no infringement of the method in which respondents [Akamai Techs. et al.] have staked out an interest, because the performance of all the patent's steps is not attributable to any one person."[45]

The Supreme Court refused to tackle the merits of the Circuit's *Muniauction* "direction and control" standard for direct infringement liability because that aspect of the case was beyond the scope of the question presented in the petition for *certiorari*.[46] The Court acknowledged the concerns of Akamai et al. and the *Akamai II en banc* majority about the *Muniauction* rule; the Supreme Court's determination to hew to the narrow *Muniauction* "direction and control" test (without deciding its merits) admittedly approved an "interpretation of

[42]*See* Muniauction, Inc. v. Thomson Corp., 532 F.3d 1318, 1329 (Fed. Cir. 2008) (holding that "where the actions of multiple parties combine to perform every step of a claimed method, the claim is directly infringed only if one party exercises 'control or direction' over the entire process such that every step is attributable to the controlling party, i.e., the 'mastermind.' [*BMC Resources, Inc. v. Paymentech, L.P.*, 498 F.3d 1373 (Fed. Cir. 2007)] at 1380-81. At the other end of this multi-party spectrum, mere 'arms-length cooperation' will not give rise to direct infringement by any party. *Id.* at 1371.").

[43]*Akamai III,* 134 S. Ct. at 2117.

[44]*Akamai III,* 134 S. Ct. at 2119.

[45]*Akamai III,* 134 S. Ct. at 2117.

[46]The Court explained:

> Respondents ask us to review the merits of the Federal Circuit's *Muniauction* rule for direct infringement under §271(a). We decline to do so today.
>
> In the first place, the question presented is clearly focused on §271(b), not §271(a). We granted certiorari on the following question: "Whether the Federal Circuit erred in holding that a defendant may be held liable for inducing patent infringement under 35 U.S.C. §271(b) even though no one has committed direct infringement under §271(a)." Pet. for Cert. i. *The question presupposes that Limelight has not committed direct infringement under §271(a).* And since the question on which we granted certiorari did not involve §271(a), petitioner did not address that important issue in its opening brief. Our decision on the §271(b) question necessitates a remand to the Federal Circuit, and on remand, the Federal Circuit will have the opportunity to revisit the §271(a) question if it so chooses.

Akamai III, 134 S. Ct. at 2120 (emphasis added).

§271(b) as permitting a would-be infringer to evade liability by dividing performance of a method patent's steps with another whom the defendant neither directs nor controls."[47] However, such evasion would be of the Federal Circuit's own making—"[a]ny such anomaly... would result from the Federal Circuit's interpretation of §271(a) in *Muniauction*."[48] The Court conspicuously invited the Federal Circuit to revisit the "direction and control" rule of *Muniauction* by remanding *Akamai III* so that "the Federal Circuit will have the opportunity to revisit the §271(a) question if it so chooses."[49] The Circuit would soon take up that invitation.

In the following month (on July 24, 2014), the *en banc* Federal Circuit issued *sua sponte* an order vacating its earlier *en banc* judgment in *Akamai II*, dissolving the case's *en banc* status, and ordering it returned to a three-judge panel for further consideration.[50] At least in the view of this author, it appeared that the Circuit's narrow standard for direct infringement liability under §271(a) in divided or distributed infringement scenarios would likely be relaxed to ameliorate the concerns voiced by the *en banc* Circuit in *Akamai II* and acknowledged by the Supreme Court in *Akamai III*. After a panel majority chose not to do so, the Circuit again took the *Akamai* case *en banc* as described below and expanded the standard.

The Federal Circuit issued a short-lived, divided panel decision in May 2015. In an opinion authored by Judge Linn and joined by Chief Judge Prost, the panel majority held that direct infringement liability of a method claim under 35 U.S.C. §271(a) was limited to "a principal-agent relationship,... a contractual arrangement, or... a joint enterprise."[51] Because the case at bar did not involve any of those

[47]*Akamai III,* 134 S. Ct. at 2120.

[48]*Akamai III,* 134 S. Ct. at 2120.

[49]*Akamai III,* 134 S. Ct. at 2120.

[50]Akamai Techs., Inc. v. Limelight Networks, Inc., 571 F. App'x 958 (Fed. Cir. 2014). The three Circuit judges deciding the court's original 2010 panel decision in *Akamai* were Chief Judge Rader and Circuit Judges Linn and Prost. *See* Akamai Techs., Inc. v. Limelight Networks, Inc., 629 F.3d 1311 (Fed. Cir. 2010), *reh'g en banc granted, opinion vacated sub nom.* Akamai Techs., Inc. v. MIT, 419 F. App'x 989 (Fed. Cir. 2011). In its July 2014 order sending the case back to the panel, the *en banc* Federal Circuit directed that *Akamai* would be referred to "the two remaining panel members and a newly-selected judge," Judge Rader having retired from the Federal Circuit effective June 30, 2014. Akamai Techs., Inc. v. Limelight Networks, Inc., 571 F. App'x 958 (Fed. Cir. 2014).

[51]Akamai Techs., Inc. v. Limelight Networks, Inc., 786 F.3d 899, 904 (Fed. Cir. May 13, 2015), *reh'g en banc granted, opinion vacated sub nom.* Akamai Techs., Inc. v. Limelight Networks, Inc., 612 F. App'x 617 (Fed. Cir. Aug. 13, 2015) (order (1) granting Akamai's petition for rehearing *en banc;* (2) vacating court's panel opinion of May 13, 2015; (3) simultaneously issuing court's *en banc* opinion reported at 797 F.3d 1020 (Fed. Cir. 2015) (*en banc*) ("*Akamai IV*"); and (4) returning case to merits panel for further proceedings).

three arrangements, the panel majority found that accused infringer Limelight was not liable for direct infringement.[52] Judge Moore dissented.[53]

Exactly two months later, without prior notice, the Federal Circuit vacated the May 2015 panel opinion in *Akamai* and issued a new *en banc* opinion, *Akamai Techs., Inc. v. Limelight Networks, Inc.* (hereafter "*Akamai IV*").[54] Not unexpectedly, the *Akamai IV* court accepted the Supreme Court's suggestion in *Akamai III* to broaden the standard for divided infringement liability under 35 U.S.C. §271(a).

In an unusually brief, succinct, and unanimous opinion designated "*per curiam*," the *Akamai IV en banc* Circuit "set forth the law of divided infringement under 35 U.S.C. §271(a)" and applied it to the facts at bar. Under the new, broader definition for divided infringement announced by the *en banc* court, the jury's 2008 verdict was reinstated;[55] substantial evidence supported the jury's finding that

[52]Akamai Techs., Inc v. Limelight Networks, Inc., 786 F.3d 899 (Fed. Cir. May 13, 2015), *reh'g en banc granted, opinion vacated sub nom.* Akamai Techs., Inc. v. Limelight Networks, Inc., 612 F. App'x 617 (Fed. Cir. Aug. 13, 2015).

[53]Judge Moore wrote:

> Today the majority holds that the actions of multiple parties can only result in direct infringement of a method claim in three circumstances: in a principal-agent relationship, in a contractual arrangement, or in a joint enterprise functioning as a form of mutual agency. It divorces patent law from mainstream legal principles by refusing to accept that §271(a) includes joint tortfeasor liability. The majority's rule creates a gaping hole in what for centuries has been recognized as an actionable form of infringement. It claims that this result is mandated by the statute. I do not agree. The single entity rule promulgated in *BMC* and *Muniauction* is a recent judicial creation inconsistent with statute, common law, and common sense. For centuries, the concerted actions of multiple parties to infringe a patent gave rise to liability. The plain language of §271(a) codified this joint infringement. To construe that language otherwise would permit identical language in the statute to have inconsistent meanings. Congress meant to and did codify liability for joint infringement. It did not, as the majority suggests, purposefully do away with a broad swath of recognized forms of liability for infringement. I respectfully *dissent* from the majority's decision to interpret §271(a) in a manner that condones the infringing conduct in this case.

Akamai Techs., Inc v. Limelight Networks, Inc., 786 F.3d 899, 915-916 (Fed. Cir. May 13, 2015) (Moore, J., dissenting), *reh'g en banc granted, opinion vacated sub nom.* Akamai Techs., Inc. v. Limelight Networks, Inc., 612 F. App'x 617 (Fed. Cir. Aug. 13, 2015) (order (1) granting Akamai's petition for rehearing *en banc*; (2) vacating court's panel opinion of May 13, 2015; (3) simultaneously issuing court's *en banc* opinion reported at 797 F.3d 1020 (Fed. Cir. 2015) ("*Akamai IV*"); and (4) returning case to merits panel for further proceedings).

[54]797 F.3d 1020 (Fed. Cir. Aug. 13, 2015) (*en banc*) (hereafter "*Akamai IV*").

[55]*See* Akamai Techs., Inc. v. Limelight Networks, Inc., 614 F. Supp. 2d 90, 119 (D. Mass. 2009) (stating that "the jury returned a finding of infringement" at end of trial in 2008).

Limelight Networks directly infringed Akamai's '703 patent under §271(a).[56]

The *Akamai IV* court explained firstly:

> Direct infringement under §271(a) occurs where all steps of a claimed method are performed by or attributable to a single entity. *See BMC Res., Inc. v. Paymentech, L.P.*, 498 F.3d 1373, 1379-81 (Fed. Cir. 2007). Where more than one actor is involved in practicing the steps, a court must determine whether the acts of one are attributable to the other such that a single entity is responsible for the infringement. We will hold an entity responsible for others' performance of method steps in two sets of circumstances: (1) where that entity directs or controls others' performance, and (2) where the actors form a joint enterprise.[57]

Contrary to the vacated May 2015 panel majority opinion, the *Akamai IV* court clarified that liability under §271(a) is "not limited solely to principal-agent relationships, contractual arrangements, and joint enterprise. . . ."[58] The overarching test to determine whether direct infringement liability attaches in a divided or distributed infringement situation is "whether all method steps can be attributed to a single entity."[59]

The *Akamai IV* court then elaborated on two sets of circumstances under which such attribution may occur: (1) where the entity responsible for others' performance of method steps directs or controls the others' performance, and (2) where the actors form a joint enterprise. Each of the "directs or controls" and "joint enterprise" scenarios are further examined below. However, the *Akamai IV* court cautioned that "[i]n the future, other factual scenarios may arise which warrant attributing others' performance of method steps to a single actor. Going forward, principles of attribution are to be considered in the context of the particular facts presented."[60]

[56]*Akamai IV*, 797 F.3d at 1022 (therefore reversing district court's grant of judgment of noninfringement as a matter of law). In November 2015, a Federal Circuit panel tasked by the *en banc* court with resolving "all residual issues" in the appeal reinstated the jury's 2008 award to Akamai of $45.5 million in damages. *See* Akamai Techs., Inc. v. Limelight Networks, Inc., 805 F.3d 1368 (Fed. Cir. 2015).

[57]*Akamai IV*, 797 F.3d at 1022 (footnote omitted). In the omitted footnote, the *en banc* court overruled its decision in *Golden Hour Data Sys., Inc. v. emsCharts, Inc.*, 614 F.3d 1367 (Fed. Cir. 2010), "[t]o the extent that [that decision] is inconsistent with this conclusion [i.e., that an entity is responsible for others' performance of method steps in two situations: (1) where the entity directs or controls the others' performance, and (2) where the actors form a joint enterprise]." *Akamai IV*, 797 F.3d at 1022 n.1. Elsewhere in the opinion, the *en banc* court also held that "[t]o the extent our prior cases formed the predicate for the vacated panel decision [786 F.3d 899 (Fed. Cir. May 13, 2015)], those decisions are also overruled." *Akamai IV*, 797 F.3d at 1023 n.3.

[58]*Akamai IV*, 797 F.3d at 1023.

[59]*Akamai IV*, 797 F.3d at 1023.

[60]*Akamai IV*, 797 F.3d at 1023.

Most significantly, the *Akamai IV en banc* court held that in addition to the previously recognized "directs or controls" scenarios for divided infringement liability when multiple actors are in a principal/agent or contractual relationship (as enumerated in *BMC Resources* and *Muniauction*, analyzed above), liability under 35 U.S.C. §271(a) "can also be found when an alleged infringer conditions participation in an activity or receipt of a benefit upon performance of a step or steps of a patented method and establishes the manner or timing of that performance."[61] The *Akamai IV* court's expansion of the "directs or controls" category followed from "general principles of vicarious liability."[62] These principles operated in a manner that "the third party's actions are attributed to the alleged infringer such that the alleged infringer becomes the single actor chargeable with direct infringement."[63] The *en banc* court also clarified that the question whether the single actor directed or controlled the acts of the third party is one of fact, reviewed on appeal for substantial evidence when a case has been tried to a jury.[64]

In applying its newly expanded "directs or controls" category of direct infringement liability to the case at bar, the *en banc* court first summarized the "basic facts":

> In 2006, Akamai Technologies, Inc. ("Akamai") filed a patent infringement action against Limelight alleging infringement of several patents, including the '703 patent, which claims methods for delivering content over the Internet. The case proceeded to trial, at which the parties agreed that Limelight's customers — not Limelight — perform the "tagging" and "serving" steps in the claimed methods. For example, as for claim 34 of

[61]*Akamai IV,* 797 F.3d at 1023 (citing *cf.* Metro-Goldwyn-Mayer Studios Inc. v. Grokster, Ltd., 545 U.S. 913, 930 (2005) (stating that an actor "infringes vicariously by profiting from direct infringement" if that actor has the right and ability to stop or limit the infringement)).

[62]*Akamai IV,* 797 F.3d at 1023. In a footnote, the court explained that while the "vicarious liability" construct was not a "perfect analog" for the divided patent infringement scenario, it was satisfactory as a legal basis for attributing the acts of one party to another:

> We note that previous cases' use of the term "vicarious liability" is a misnomer. Restatement (Third) of Torts: Apportionment of Liability §13 (2000). In the context of joint patent infringement, an alleged infringer is not liable for a third party's commission of infringement — rather, an alleged infringer is responsible for method steps performed by a third party. Accordingly, we recognize that vicarious liability is not a perfect analog. Nevertheless, as both vicarious liability and joint patent infringement discern when the activities of one entity are attributable to another, we derive our direction or control standard from vicarious liability law. *See BMC,* 498 F.3d at 1379.

Akamai IV, 797 F.3d at 1023 n.2.

[63]*Akamai IV,* 797 F.3d at 1023.

[64]*Akamai IV,* 797 F.3d at 1023.

> the '703 patent, Limelight performs every step save the "tagging" step, in which Limelight's customers tag the content to be hosted and delivered by Limelight's content delivery network. After the close of evidence, the district judge instructed the jury that Limelight is responsible for its customers' performance of the tagging and serving method steps if Limelight directs or controls its customers' activities. The jury found that Limelight infringed claims 19, 20, 21, and 34 of the '703 patent. Following post-trial motions, the district court first denied Limelight's motion for judgment of noninfringement as a matter of law, ruling that Akamai had presented substantial evidence that Limelight directed or controlled its customers. After we decided *Muniauction, Inc. v. Thomson Corp.*, 532 F.3d 1318 (Fed. Cir. 2008), the district court granted Limelight's motion for reconsideration, holding as a matter of law that there could be no liability.[65]

Given these and other facts of record, the *Akamai IV* court had no difficulty finding direct infringement liability. It concluded that "Limelight directs or controls its customers' performance of each remaining method step, such that all steps of the method are attributable to Limelight."[66] More specifically, the *en banc* court determined that Limelight had (1) conditioned its customers' use of its content delivery system on the customers' performance of the "tagging" and "serving" method steps,[67] and (2) established the manner or timing of its customers' performance.

[65]*Akamai IV,* 797 F.3d at 1024.

[66]*Akamai IV,* 797 F.3d at 1024.

[67]Akamai Technology's U.S. Patent No. 6,108,703 ('703 patent) claimed a method of more efficiently delivering website content by placing some of a content provider's content elements (such as graphics) on a set of replicated servers and modifying the content provider's web page to instruct web browsers to retrieve that content from those servers. A representative claim of the '703 patent recited:

> 34. A content delivery method, comprising:
>
> distributing a set of page objects across a network of content servers managed by a domain other than a content provider domain, wherein the network of content servers are organized into a set of regions;
>
> for a given page normally served from the content provider domain, tagging at least some of the embedded objects of the page so that requests for the objects resolve to the domain instead of the content provider domain;
>
> in response to a client request for an embedded object of the page:
>
> resolving the client request as a function of a location of the client machine making the request and current Internet traffic conditions to identify a given region; and
>
> returning to the client an IP address of a given one of the content servers within the given region that is likely to host the embedded object and that is not overloaded.

Accused infringer Limelight Networks maintained a network of servers that, as in the patented method, allowed for efficient content delivery by placing some content elements on its own servers. Rather than modify the content providers' web pages itself, however, Limelight instructed its customers on the steps needed to do that

With respect to determination (1), the Circuit noted that all of Limelight's customers had to sign a standard contract. The contract required that if the customers wished to use Limelight's service, the customers had to perform the steps of tagging and serving content. This amounted to substantial evidence that Limelight had conditioned the use of its content delivery network on its customers' performance of the tagging and serving method steps.[68]

With respect to determination (2), Limelight sent each of its customers an instruction letter informing them that a Limelight employee had been assigned as Technical Account Manager to lead the implementation of Limelight's services for that customer. Limelight's engineers continually engaged the customers during installation and thereafter in quality assurance testing. Limelight's instruction letter also provided a hostname that the customers were responsible for integrating into their own Web pages (thus performing the tagging step). The *Akamai IV* court concluded that "Limelight's customers do not merely take Limelight's guidance and act independently on their own. Rather, Limelight establishes the manner and timing of its customers' performance so that customers can only avail themselves of the service upon their performance of the method steps."[69]

The *Akamai IV* court found direct infringement liability on Limelight's part based on the "directs or controls" category of attribution. Nevertheless, the court also held that in other cases presenting different facts,[70] attribution could be based on a theory of joint enterprise liability. The *Akamai IV* court elaborated:

> [W]here two or more actors form a joint enterprise, all can be charged with the acts of the other, rendering each liable for the steps performed by the other as if each is a single actor. *See* Restatement (Second) of Torts §491 cmt. *b* ("The law . . . considers that each is the agent or servant of the others, and that the act of any one within the scope of the enterprise is to be charged vicariously against the rest."). A joint enterprise requires proof of four elements:

---

modification. Thus, Limelight's customers performed one of the recited steps of the claimed method and Limelight performed the remaining steps. Accordingly, the alleged infringement was "divided." *See Akamai II*, 692 F.3d at 1306-1307 ("because Limelight's customers (and not Limelight itself) performed one of the steps of the claimed method, the district court granted Limelight's motion for judgment as a matter of law based on this court's opinions in *BMC* and *Muniauction, Inc. v. Thomson Corp.*, 532 F.3d 1318 (Fed. Cir. 2008)").

[68] *See Akamai IV,* 797 F.3d at 1024.

[69] *Akamai IV,* 797 F.3d at 1025.

[70] *Cf.* Akamai Techs., Inc v. Limelight Networks, Inc., 786 F.3d 899, 931 (Fed. Cir. May 13, 2015) (panel opinion) (stating that "[b]ecause this case does not implicate joint enterprise liability, this case is not the appropriate vehicle to adopt joint enterprise liability"), *reh'g en banc granted, opinion vacated sub nom.* Akamai Techs., Inc. v. Limelight Networks, Inc., 612 F. App'x 617 (Fed. Cir. 2015).

(1) an agreement, express or implied, among the members of the group;
(2) a common purpose to be carried out by the group;
(3) a community of pecuniary interest in that purpose, among the members; and
(4) an equal right to a voice in the direction of the enterprise, which gives an equal right of control.

Id. §491 cmt. c. As with direction or control, whether actors entered into a joint enterprise is a question of fact, reviewable on appeal for substantial evidence. *Id.* ("Whether these elements exist is frequently a question for the jury, under proper direction from the court.").[71]

2. Two-Step Analysis for Patent Infringement

Numerous judicial decisions provide that analyzing patent infringement is a two-step process comprising:

1. interpretation of the patent claims; and
2. comparison of the properly interpreted claims with the accused device.[72]

These steps are considered separately in Sections B and C below.

A few words on terminology are appropriate here. Step One of the infringement analysis, interpreting the claims, is sometimes also referred to by patent attorneys as claim construction or as the task of construing the claims. This author prefers to speak of claim interpretation rather than construction, because the notion of construction is somewhat confusingly similar to claim drafting, a related but conceptually distinct task. Step Two of the analysis, comparing the properly interpreted claims with the accused device, is sometimes referred to by patent attorneys as "reading the claims onto the accused device."[73]

[71]*Akamai IV*, 797 F.3d at 1023 (citing RESTATEMENT (SECOND) OF TORTS §491).

[72]*See, e.g.*, Cybor Corp. v. FAS Techs., Inc., 138 F.3d 1448, 1454 (Fed. Cir. 1998) (*en banc*) ("First, the court determines the scope and meaning of the patent claims asserted.... [Second,] the properly construed claims are compared to the allegedly infringing device.") (citations omitted); Caterpillar Tractor Co. v. Berco, S.p.A., 714 F.2d 1110, 1114 (Fed. Cir. 1983) (citing Autogiro Co. of America v. United States, 384 F.2d 391, 401 (Ct. Cl. 1967)).

In the comparison step (Step Two of the process for analyzing infringement), infringement will be found only if each and every limitation of the claim is met in the accused device, either literally or under the doctrine of equivalents. Infringement cannot be determined by comparing the claimed and accused devices as a whole; the analysis must be performed on a limitation-by-limitation level. This "all-limitations rule," and the meaning of "limitation," are discussed in further detail below.

[73]Patent claims are said to "read on" an accused device when the device would literally infringe the claimed invention (likewise, patent claims are said to "read on" the

B. Step One: Patent Claim Interpretation

It cannot be overstated that, in patent law, "the name of the game is the claim."[74] This maxim reflects the prominence of claims in patent litigation. Federal Circuit judges observe that "[c]laim construction is the single most important event in the course of a patent litigation."[75] The manner in which the claims are interpreted is, in many cases, dispositive of literal infringement. In a smaller but growing number of cases, claim interpretation also may effectively decide whether infringement is found under the doctrine of equivalents.[76]

After a review of the central function played by the claims of a patent, the remainder of this section considers three key questions pertaining to patent claim interpretation: Who interprets patent claims? What evidentiary sources are used to interpret patent claims? And last, what are the primary rules (or "canons") of claim interpretation?

1. The Central Role of Claims

Chapter 2 of this text addressed patent claims in detail, and the reader is encouraged to review Chapter 2 prior to consulting this chapter. Some key aspects of patent claims as they impact patent enforcement are repeated here for emphasis.

The claims are the most important part of a patent. A patent claim is a single-sentence definition of the literal boundary of the patent

---

prior art when that subject matter would anticipate the claimed invention). It is improper to say that a device "reads on" a patent claim, however. Claims "read on" accused or prior art devices, not the other way around.

[74]Giles S. Rich, *The Extent of the Protection and Interpretation of Claims: American Perspectives,* 21 Int'l Rev. Indus. Prop. & Copyright L. 497, 499, 501 (1990).

[75]Retractable Techs., Inc. v. Becton, Dickinson and Co., 659 F.3d 1369, 1373 (Fed. Cir. 2011) (Moore, J., joined by Rader, C.J., dissenting from denial of rehearing *en banc*).

[76]Disposing of the doctrine of equivalents infringement question at the completion of the claim interpretation stage is increasingly common as the Federal Circuit develops its jurisprudence concerning "vitiation" of claim limitations. Recall the Supreme Court's guidance in *Warner-Jenkinson Co. v. Hilton Davis Chem. Co.*, 520 U.S. 17 (1997), that various legal limitations on a patentee's ability to rely on the doctrine of equivalents should be decided by the trial court, possibly on pre-trial motion. *See id.* at 39 n.8. For example, "if a theory of equivalence would entirely vitiate a particular claim element, partial or complete judgment should be rendered by the court, as there would be no further material issue for the jury to resolve." *Id.* By "vitiation" the *Warner-Jenkinson* Court referred to a situation in which finding a particular claim limitation infringed under the doctrine of equivalents would be tantamount to ignoring or eliminating that limitation. *See, e.g.,* Asyst Techs., Inc. v. Emtrak, Inc., 402 F.3d 1188, 1195 (Fed. Cir. 2005) (stating that "[t]o hold that 'unmounted' is equivalent to 'mounted' would effectively read the 'mounted on' limitation out of the patent"). Section D.5, *infra*, addresses in greater detail the Federal Circuit's unsettled jurisprudence concerning vitiation as a legal limit on the doctrine of equivalents.

owner's right to exclude. Acting as a sort of verbal fence, the patent claim is intended to provide reasonably clear notice, in advance of litigation, of just how far the patentee's competitors can proceed in imitating the patented invention without infringing the patent owner's right to exclude.[77]

In emphasizing to students the importance of patent claims, the patent law professor's classic analogy compares a patent claim with a deed to real property. The deed very specifically defines the boundaries of a plot of land, but does not describe what may be located in the interior — buildings, trees, water, and the like. Similarly, a patent claim does not describe the invention to which the patent is directed. Rather, it defines the extent of the patent owner's right to prevent others from exploiting that invention.[78]

The role of describing the patented invention is played not by the patent's claims, but rather by its written description and drawings. In accordance with 35 U.S.C. §112(a) (eff. Sept. 16, 2012), these parts of the patent specification must provide an enabling disclosure of how to make and use the invention without undue experimentation, and also must disclose the best mode of carrying out the invention if such a mode was known to the inventor on the application filing date.[79] Thus, it is legally erroneous to refer to patent claims as *describing* an invention.

During the process of applying for a patent, the claims may be amended (frequently by narrowing) such that their final scope varies from the scope of the inventive concept as described to its fullest extent in the written description and drawings. Thus, what is described in the patent as "the invention" may (and often does) differ in scope from the claims that ultimately issue.

[77]As the Supreme Court has observed,

> The patent laws "promote the Progress of Science and useful Arts" by rewarding innovation with a temporary monopoly. U.S. Const., Art. I, §8, cl. 8. The monopoly is a property right; and like any property right, its boundaries should be clear. This clarity is essential to promote progress, because it enables efficient investment in innovation. A patent holder should know what he owns, and the public should know what he does not.

Festo Corp. v. Shoketsu Kinzoku Kogyo Kabushiki Co., 535 U.S. 722, 730-731 (2002).

[78]As mentioned in the introduction to this chapter, U.S. patent law recognizes two forms of infringement: (1) literal infringement, and (2) infringement under the doctrine of equivalents. A patent claim recites the boundaries of the patentee's right to exclude others from making, using, selling, offering to sell, or importing products or processes that *literally* infringe the claim. Under the judicially created doctrine of equivalents, however, a patentee's right to exclude may be extended beyond the literal scope of the claims when circumstances warrant.

[79]The requirements of 35 U.S.C. §112(a) are detailed *supra* Chapter 3 ("Disclosure Requirements (35 U.S.C. §112(a))").

The claims are found at the end of each patent's specification; a patent must conclude with at least one claim,[80] and a utility patent usually includes 10, 20, or more claims. The only limits on the number of claims included in a utility patent are the applicant's willingness to pay additional filing fees, which increase as claims are added,[81] and human resource limitations on the USPTO's ability to examine large numbers of claims, particularly in complex technologies such as biotechnology.

2. Judge or Jury as Interpreter? The *Markman* Revolution

The first question of the three posed above, who interprets patent claims, is particularly important in the context of jury trials. In recent years, slightly more patent infringement cases are being tried to juries than to the courts.[82] In *Markman v. Westview Instruments,*[83] the Supreme Court held that the Seventh Amendment of the U.S. Constitution[84] does not provide a right to a jury trial for the interpretation of patent claims. Rather, policy concerns dictate that the role of claim interpretation is to be performed by the judge instead of the jury in a jury trial. *Markman* was a watershed event in the history of U.S. patent litigation, and thus the details of the case merit considerable attention.

[80]35 U.S.C. §112(b) (eff. Sept. 16, 2012).

[81]The USPTO currently charges additional fees for independent claims in excess of 3, and for a total number of claims in excess of 20. *See* United States Patent & Trademark Office, *USPTO Fee Schedule* (last rev. Jan. 1, 2020), https://www.uspto.gov/learning-and-resources/fees-and-payment/uspto-fee-schedule. *See also* 37 C.F.R. §1.16(h) (2015) (independent claims in excess of 3); 37 C.F.R. §1.16(i) (2015) (claims in excess of 20).

[82]*See* Administrative Office of the U.S. Courts, *U.S. District Courts — Civil Statistical Tables for the Federal Judiciary* (June 30, 2015), tbl. C4, http://www.uscourts.gov/statistics/table/c-4/statistical-tables-federal-judiciary/2015/06/30 (reporting for 12-month period ending June 30, 2015, that out of 98 patent cases terminated during or after trial in the U.S. District Courts, 61 of the cases (or 62 percent) were tried before juries). This percentage has remained fairly constant in recent years. *See id.*; Kimberly A. Moore, *Judges, Juries, and Patent Cases: An Empirical Peek Inside the Black Box,* 99 MICH. L. REV. 365, 366 n.7 (2000) (reporting that in 1998, 60 percent of all patent trials (62 out of 103) were tried before juries) (citing ADMIN. OFF. U.S. CTS., JUD. BUS. U.S. CTS. 167 tbl. C4 (1998)). For 1999, the percentage of patent jury trials rose to 62 percent (61 out of 98). *See id.* (citing ADMIN. OFF. U.S. CTS., JUD. BUS. U.S. CTS. 161 tbl. C4 (1999)).

[83]517 U.S. 370 (1996).

[84]The Seventh Amendment provides that "[i]n Suits at common law, where the value in controversy shall exceed twenty dollars, the right of trial by jury shall be preserved. . . ." U.S. CONST., amend. VII.

Markman, the plaintiff, owned a patent on a system for tracking articles of clothing in a dry-cleaning process.[85] The claims of Markman's patent required that the system include means to maintain an inventory total, and that the system be able to "detect and localize spurious additions to inventory as well as spurious deletions therefrom."[86] The key claim interpretation dispute concerned the meaning of "inventory." Because the defendant's accused system tracked only cash invoices, not articles of clothing, Markman introduced expert testimony to support his position that "inventory" meant cash invoices. After the jury found for Markman, the district court granted the defendant's motion for judgment of noninfringement as a matter of law. The district court concluded that the intrinsic evidence (the patent itself and its prosecution history) made clear that "inventory" as used in Markman's patent had to include "items of clothing." Because the accused system did not track clothing, there could be no literal infringement.[87]

On appeal, Markman's primary argument was that the Seventh Amendment of the U.S. Constitution guarantees a right to a jury trial on claim interpretation, and that the district court had erred by effectively taking that role away from the jury through the grant of judgment as a matter of law (JMOL). The Federal Circuit rejected this argument, and the Supreme Court affirmed. Applying the "historical" test, the Supreme Court explained that although it is clear that English juries were hearing patent infringement cases in 1791 (when the Seventh Amendment was ratified), there was no clear historical antecedent at that time for the practice of claim interpretation. In fact, patent claims were not mentioned by statute in the United States until the Patent Act of 1836, and were not statutorily required until the Patent Act of 1870.

Because the historical test does not answer the question of whether judge or jury should construe patent claims in a jury trial of patent infringement, the Supreme Court's decision in *Markman* ultimately turned on functional (i.e., public policy) considerations. The Court concluded that judges are simply better equipped than jurors to construe the meaning of claim terms based on documentary evidence, because

[85]*See* U.S. Pat. No. Re. 33,054.

[86]Markman v. Westview Instruments, Inc., 772 F. Supp. 1535, 1537 (E.D. Pa. 1991).

[87]In *Markman*, a federal district court construed the patent claims in the context of a post-trial motion for judgment as a matter of law (JMOL). The Federal Circuit and the Supreme Court ostensibly blessed this practice by affirming the trial court's decision in *Markman*; at least those decisions did *not* hold that claim interpretation at the JMOL stage was reversible error. Although many federal district courts now construe the claims of a patent relatively early in the course of a patent litigation (sometimes before the close of discovery), the Federal Circuit has not yet held in any case following *Markman* that it is reversible error to proceed as the *Markman* district court did and postpone claim interpretation until after trial.

the bread-and-butter work of the judiciary is to construe the meaning of language in legal documents (e.g., contracts and statutes) upon receipt of evidence. Judges understand that this role must be performed in a manner that comports with a "whole contents" approach, that is, the fundamental interpretive canon that a term or phrase in a document must be construed in such a way as to comport with the document as a whole. In this manner a patent's internal coherence is best preserved. Although some cases may arise in which competing interpretations of patent terms by opposing experts would require that judges make credibility determinations, a traditional province of the jury, "in the main" the Court expects that these determinations will be "subsumed within the necessarily sophisticated analysis of the whole document, required by the standard construction rule that a term can be defined only in a way that comports with the instrument as a whole." [88]

The Supreme Court in *Markman* also cited the importance of the uniform interpretation of a given patent as another policy reason why judges are better suited than juries to interpret patent claims. In the Court's view, "[u]niformity would . . . be ill served by submitting issues of document construction to juries."[89] The treatment of claim interpretation as a "purely legal" issue for the court will promote certainty through *stare decisis* principles, the Court declared.[90] Consistent with the common law system's fundamental principle of "standing by the decision," courts should give due weight and consideration to the decisions of other courts who have previously ruled on the same issues, even in cases where the Federal Circuit has not yet blessed a particular claim interpretation or where collateral estoppel would not apply because a defendant did not have a full and fair opportunity to litigate a particular claim interpretation issue in an earlier proceeding involving the same patent.[91]

[88]*Markman,* 517 U.S. at 389.

[89]*Id.* at 391.

[90]*Id.*

[91]In order for collateral estoppel to apply against a party, the following elements are required:

(1) The issues raised in both proceedings must be identical;
(2) The relevant issue must have actually been litigated and decided in prior proceeding;
(3) The party to be estopped must have had a full/fair opportunity to litigate the issue in prior proceeding; and
(4) Resolution of the issue must have been necessary to support a valid and final judgment on the merits.

TM Patents, L.P. v. Int'l Bus. Machs. Corp., 72 F. Supp. 2d 370, 375, 377 (S.D.N.Y. 1999) (holding patent owner estopped from asserting a different claim interpretation in second action asserting infringement of same patent against new defendant, where patentee had full and fair opportunity to litigate claim construction in first proceeding and

3. Evidentiary Sources for Claim Interpretation

In the aftermath of *Markman,* the Federal Circuit has developed a robust jurisprudence addressing what evidentiary sources should be relied on to interpret patent claims. The foundational case here is *Vitronics Corp. v. Conceptronic, Inc.*[92] The Federal Circuit in *Vitronics* established a hierarchy of claim interpretational tools that distinguishes between "intrinsic" and "extrinsic" evidence. *Intrinsic* evidence is that which is part of the public record associated with a patent's issuance: the patent itself and its prosecution history,[93] including the prior art cited therein.[94] Competitors have access to this

---

claim construction decision in first case, rendered following a *Markman* hearing, was sufficiently "final" to satisfy collateral estoppel rule). *See also* Jet, Inc. v. Sewage Aeration Sys., 223 F.3d 1360, 1365-1366 (Fed. Cir. 2000) (identifying four prerequisites to the application of issue preclusion).

Note that the *TM Patents* case cited above held that the *patent owner* was collaterally estopped. In contrast, under any traditional definition of collateral estoppel an *accused infringer* who was not a party to an earlier infringement litigation concerning the same patent should not be estopped in a later, separate infringement proceeding from challenging the claim interpretation reached in the earlier proceeding. *Cf.* In re Trans Texas Holdings Corp., 498 F.3d 1290, 1297 (Fed. Cir. 2007) (stating that "[w]e have never applied issue preclusion *against* a non-party to the first action"). The Federal Circuit rejected reexamination applicant Trans Texas's argument that the USPTO should be bound by a federal district court's earlier (and narrower) interpretation of the same disputed claim limitations. Issue preclusion (also known as collateral estoppel) did not apply against the USPTO, which was not a party in the earlier district court proceeding. *See id.* Rather, the USPTO correctly applied a "broadest reasonable interpretation, consistent with the specification" rule in the reexamination proceeding. *See id.* at 1298.

Should it make any difference, in a later proceeding in which a party seeks to apply the claim interpretation from an earlier proceeding against a non-party to that earlier proceeding, if the Federal Circuit has "blessed" (i.e., reviewed and affirmed) the district court's claim interpretation in the earlier proceeding? In other words, should "law of the case" principles be expanded into "law of the patent" rules for patent litigation?

[92] 90 F.3d 1576 (Fed. Cir. 1996) (reversing district court's summary judgment of noninfringement, based on an erroneous claim construction that improperly relied on extrinsic evidence to determine meaning of claim term "solder reflow temperature").

[93] The Federal Circuit for the first time as an *en banc* court expressed some reservation about reliance on a patent's prosecution history for claim interpretation purposes in *Phillips v. AWH Corp.*, 415 F.3d 1303 (Fed. Cir. 2005) (*en banc*):

> [B]ecause the prosecution history represents an ongoing negotiation between the PTO and the applicant, rather than the final product of that negotiation, it often lacks the clarity of the specification and thus is less useful for claim construction purposes. Nonetheless, the prosecution history can often inform the meaning of the claim language by demonstrating how the inventor understood the invention and whether the inventor limited the invention in the course of prosecution, making the claim scope narrower than it would otherwise be.

Id. at 1317 (citations omitted).

[94] *Vitronics* is somewhat ambiguous with respect to the status of prior art not cited in the prosecution history. *See* Hon. Paul R. Michel & Lisa A. Schneider, *Side Bar:*

information as soon as the patent issues, if not before,[95] and it is not considered "litigation-influenced." *Extrinsic* evidence is evidence outside the official administrative record of the patent's procurement, such as expert testimony.

Although literally extrinsic to the official administrative record, some Federal Circuit judges questioned whether *dictionaries* are properly classified as extrinsic evidence. The Federal Circuit opined in a 2001 decision that dictionaries hold a "special place" and "may sometimes be considered along with the intrinsic evidence when determining the ordinary meaning of claim terms."[96] In a 2002 decision the court went further, expressing the following view:

> As resources and references to inform and aid courts and judges in the understanding of technology and terminology, it is entirely proper for both trial and appellate judges to consult these materials at any stage of a litigation, regardless of whether they have been offered by a party in evidence or not. Thus, categorizing them as "extrinsic evidence" or even a "special form of extrinsic evidence" is misplaced and does not inform the analysis.[97]

Despite the tenor of these Federal Circuit decisions that dictionaries, encyclopedias, and treatises that were available at the time a patent was procured should be treated as intrinsic evidence, the *en banc* court clarified in 2005 that dictionaries are extrinsic evidence.[98] As such, they may be useful construction tools, but they are not assigned primary importance in the evidentiary hierarchy for patent claim interpretation.

Vitronics instructs that, in most cases, the intrinsic evidence alone will be sufficient to resolve any claim interpretation issues. Only when the disputed patent claim terminology is still genuinely ambiguous following review of the public record of the patent may a district court rely on the extrinsic evidence.[99] Although a district court may always admit and use extrinsic evidence for the purpose of *understanding*

Vitronics — Some Unanswered Questions, in Donald S. Chisum et al., Principles of Patent Law, Cases and Materials 870, 871 (2d ed. 2001).

[95]Most pending patent applications are now published 18 months after their earliest effective filing date, in accordance with 35 U.S.C. §122(b).

[96]Bell Atl. Network Servs., Inc. v. Covad Commc'ns Group, Inc., 262 F.3d 1258, 1267 (Fed. Cir. 2001).

[97]Texas Digital Sys., Inc. v. Telegenix, Inc., 308 F.3d 1193, 1203 (Fed. Cir. 2002).

[98]*See* Phillips v. AWH Corp., 415 F.3d 1303, 1318 (Fed. Cir. 2005) (*en banc*) (characterizing dictionaries and treatises as "[w]ithin the class of extrinsic evidence" that "can be useful in claim construction"). *See also* Section B.4 *infra* for further discussion of the use of dictionaries.

[99]*See* Vitronics Corp. v. Conceptronic, Inc., 90 F.3d 1576, 1583 (Fed. Cir. 1996) (stating that "[i]n those cases where the public record unambiguously describes the scope of the patented invention, reliance on any extrinsic evidence is improper").

the invention, it may not rely on the extrinsic evidence to arrive at a claim interpretation that is contrary to that provided by the intrinsic evidence.[100]

4. The *Phillips* Debate: "Contextualist" Versus "Literalist" Approaches

Decisions of the Federal Circuit issued between 2002 and 2005 demonstrated a sharp divergence in approaches to patent claim interpretation. The Circuit judges appeared to have aligned themselves in two schools of thought on the issue: the "contextualist" and "literalist" viewpoints.[101] This divergence of interpretational methodologies led the court in 2004 to issue an *en banc* referendum on patent claim interpretation.[102] The basis of the dispute can be summarized as follows.

Federal Circuit judges who espoused the contextualist approach[103] seek the "felt meaning" of patent claim terms in the context of the

[100]*See id.* at 1584 (stating that "extrinsic evidence in general, and expert testimony in particular, may be used only to help the court come to the proper understanding of the claims; it may not be used to vary or contradict the claim language"). Federal Circuit Judge Rader has commented that the line between understanding and interpreting is a blurred one in the real world of patent litigation:

> As a matter of logic, this instruction is difficult to grasp. What is the distinction between a trial judge's understanding of the claims and a trial judge's interpretation of the claims to the jury? Don't judges instruct the jury in accordance with their understanding of the claims? In practice, how does this court's lofty appellate logic work? As this court acknowledges, a trial court must often resort to experts to learn complex new technologies. *See, e.g., Markman I,* 52 F.3d at 986. What happens when that learning influences a trial judge's interpretation of the claim terms? Are trial judges supposed to disguise the real reasons for their interpretation? How will this perverse incentive to "hide the ball" improve appellate review?

Cybor Corp. v. FAS Techs., 138 F.3d 1448, 1474-1475 (Fed. Cir. 1998) (*en banc*) (Rader, J., dissenting).

[101]Commentators charged during this era that outcomes in claim interpretation decisions were statistically predictable depending upon the composition of the panel of judges deciding the case. *See* Professor Polk Wagner's claim construction predictor tool ("If you know the panel, we'll predict the result!"), http://predictor.claimconstruction.com (last visited Oct. 15, 2015). Due to the subsequent effect of the Federal Circuit's decision in *Phillips v. AWH Corp.*, 415 F.3d 1303 (Fed. Cir. 2005) (*en banc*), discussed *infra*, Professor Wagner cautions that his claim construction predictor tool no longer reliably indicates the court's approach to claim construction. Nevertheless, he maintains the Web site for historical purposes. *See* http://predictor.claimconstruction.com (last visited Oct. 15, 2015).

[102]Phillips v. AWH Corp., 376 F.3d 1382 (Fed. Cir. July 21, 2004) (order) (*en banc*).

[103]Judges following the contextualist approach have also been referred to as "holistics" or "pragmatic textualists." *See* R. Polk Wagner & Lee Petherbridge, *Is the Federal*

invention described in the patent specification. They view the written description and drawings of the patent as the primary tool for discerning what terms in the patent's claims mean. Contextualist judges "look to the specification 'to ascertain the meaning of a claim term as it is used by the inventor in the context of the entirety of his invention.' "[104] The ordinary meaning of a term in a claim "must be considered in view of the intrinsic evidence: the claims, the specification, and the prosecution history."[105] This is the traditional approach to patent claim interpretation generally followed by the Federal Circuit in its decisions prior to 2002.

In contrast, Federal Circuit judges in the literalist school[106] took as their lodestar the court's 2002 decision in *Texas Digital Sys. v. Telegenix, Inc.*[107] In accordance with that decision, the literalist judges engage in a "heavy presumption" that claim terms carry the "ordinary and customary" meaning that a person having ordinary skill in the art (PHOSITA) would attribute to them. To discern this meaning, the literalist judges typically consult definitions in dictionaries, technical treatises, and other evidentiary sources extrinsic to the patent itself.[108] Indeed, *Texas Digital* instructed that in construing patent claims, courts should consult the dictionary before turning to a patent's written description and drawings.[109] The ordinary and customary meaning as gleaned from dictionaries would be trumped only when a patent's written description or its prosecution history showed that the patentee was her "own lexicographer" in providing an explicit definition for a claim term, or had

---

Circuit Succeeding? An Empirical Assessment of Judicial Performance, 152 U. PA. L. REV. 1105, 1111 (2004) (dividing Federal Circuit into "holistic" and "proceduralist" methodological approaches for patent claim interpretation); Craig Allen Nard, *A Theory of Claim Interpretation*, 14 HARV. J.L. & TECH. 1, 4-6 (2000) (dividing court into "hypertextualists" and "pragmatic textualists").

[104] *See* Phillips v. AWH Corp., 363 F.3d 1207, 1213 (Fed. Cir. 2004) (Lourie, J.) (quoting Comark Commc'ns v. Harris Corp., 156 F.3d 1182, 1187 (Fed. Cir. 1998)), *vacated*, 376 F.3d 1382 (Fed. Cir. 2004) (order granting rehearing *en banc*).

[105] *See id.* (citing Rexnord Corp. v. Laitram Corp., 274 F.3d 1336, 1342-1343 (Fed. Cir. 2001)).

[106] Literalist judges have also been referred to as "proceduralists" or "hypertextualists." *See* R. Polk Wagner & Lee Petherbridge, *Is the Federal Circuit Succeeding? An Empirical Assessment of Judicial Performance*,152 U. PA. L. REV. 1105 (2004); Craig Allen Nard, *A Theory of Claim Interpretation*, 14 HARV. J.L. & TECH. 1 (2000).

[107] 308 F.3d 1193 (Fed. Cir. 2002).

[108] Most often the literalist judges rely on general-usage dictionaries such as WEBSTER'S THIRD NEW INTERNATIONAL DICTIONARY. *See* Joseph Scott Miller & James A. Hilsenteger, *The Proven Key: Roles and Rules for Dictionaries at the Patent Office and the Courts*, 54 AM. U. L. REV. 829 (2005).

[109] The *Texas Digital* court concluded that it is improper to consult "the written description and prosecution history as a threshold step in the claim construction process, before any effort is made to discern the ordinary and customary meanings attributed to the words themselves." *Texas Digital*, 308 F.3d at 1204.

otherwise clearly disclaimed or disavowed the ordinary and customary meaning.

The April 2004 decision of a Federal Circuit panel in *Phillips v. AWH Corp.*[110] exemplifies the burgeoning conflict between the "literalist" and "contextualist" claim interpretation approaches. Phillips' patent was directed to modular, vandalism-resistant wall panels useful in building prisons and security institutions.[111] The parties disputed the meaning of "baffle" in the asserted patent claim, which recited in part, "means disposed inside the [outer] shell for increasing its load bearing capacity comprising internal steel *baffles* extending inwardly from the steel shell walls." The *Phillips* panel majority affirmed the district court's reading of "baffle" as limited by the patent's specification to baffles that are oriented at acute or obtuse angles other than 90 degrees from the wall face. Such angles were necessary to the invention's purpose of providing impact or projectile-resistant panels and constituted the only embodiment of the invention depicted in the patent's figures as shown in Figure 9.1. Because the accused infringer used only 90 degree-angled baffles in its panels, the *Phillips* majority affirmed the district court's grant of summary judgment of noninfringement.

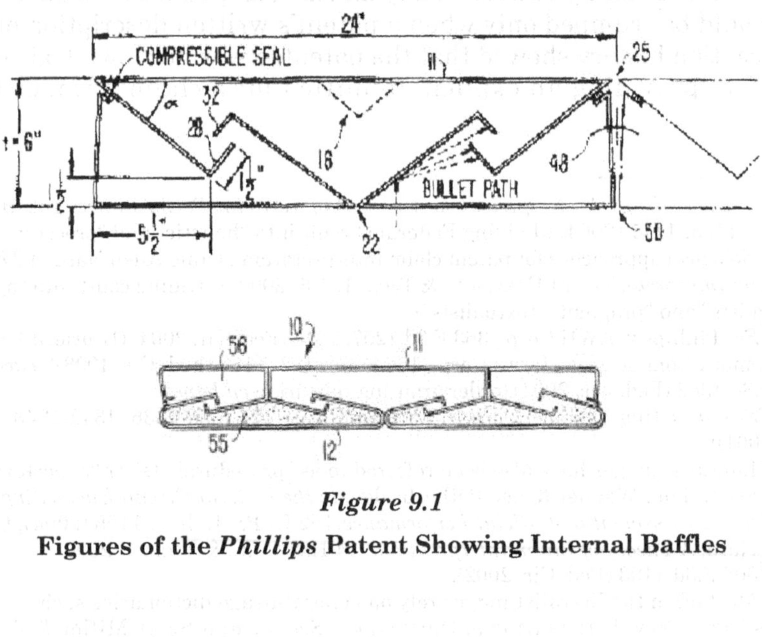

Figure 9.1

Figures of the *Phillips* Patent Showing Internal Baffles

[110]363 F.3d 1207 (Fed. Cir. Apr. 8, 2004), *vacated*, 376 F.3d 1382 (Fed. Cir. July 21, 2004) (order granting rehearing *en banc*).

[111]*See* Steel shell modules for prisoner detention facilities, U.S. Pat. No. 4,677,798 (issued July 7, 1987).

The dissenting Federal Circuit judge on the *Phillips* panel criticized the majority for effectively limiting the claim to the preferred embodiment of the invention. The majority's reading was "contrary to the plain meaning" of "baffle" in the absence of any "suggestion that the patentee, acting as his own lexicographer, gave a special meaning to the term baffles."[112] According to the dissent, the ordinary meaning as set out in the dictionary should control, that is, "baffle" defined as "a means for obstructing, impeding, or checking the flow of something." Limiting the claim to nonperpendicular (i.e., acute- or obtuse-angled) baffles was not required, because impact resistance/bullet deflection was only one of several objectives identified for the invention. Other objectives included structural stability and sound dampening. In the dissent's view, the assertion that an invention achieves several objectives did not require that the claims be limited to structures capable of achieving all of them.

On July 21, 2004, the *en banc* Federal Circuit vacated the panel decision in *Phillips* and ordered that the case be reheard.[113] One year later, the Federal Circuit announced its *en banc* decision on the merits in *Phillips.*[114] The *en banc* court decreed a return to the traditional contextualist analysis and downgraded the use of dictionaries in interpreting patent claims. Observing that excessive reliance on dictionaries risks claim interpretations that are abstract and divorced from the context of the invention, the *en banc* court explained that

> [t]he main problem with elevating the dictionary to such prominence is that it focuses the inquiry on the abstract meaning of words rather than on the meaning of claim terms within the context of the patent. Properly viewed, the "ordinary meaning" of a claim term is its meaning to the ordinary artisan after reading the entire patent. Yet heavy reliance on the dictionary divorced from the intrinsic evidence risks transforming the meaning of the claim term to the artisan into the meaning of the term in the abstract, out of its particular context, which is the specification.[115]

Thus, the *en banc Phillips* court reaffirmed, a patent's specification, rather than extrinsic evidence such as a dictionary, is " 'the primary basis for construing the claims.' "[116]

[112]*Phillips*, 363 F.3d at 1217 (Dyk, J., dissenting-in-part).

[113]*See* Phillips v. AWH Corp., 376 F.3d 1382 (Fed. Cir. 2004) (order granting rehearing *en banc*). The Federal Circuit sought briefing from the parties and *amici* with respect to an extensive series of questions. *See id.* at 1383. Federal Circuit Judge H. Robert Mayer dissented in a separate opinion, charging that "any attempt to refine the process is futile" so long as the court refuses to reconsider "the fiction that claim construction is a matter of law." *Id.* at 1384.

[114]Phillips v. AWH Corp., 415 F.3d 1303 (Fed. Cir. 2005) (*en banc*).

[115]*Id.* at 1321.

[116]*Id.* at 1315 (quoting Standard Oil Co. v. Am. Cyanamid Co., 774 F.2d 448, 452 (Fed. Cir. 1985) (Rich, J.)). Although the *Phillips en banc* decision downgraded reliance

Despite its strong affirmance of the contextualist rationale, the *Phillips en banc* court disagreed with the panel majority on the merits and ultimately adopted the broader definition of a "baffle" as not limited to any particular angle and thus encompassing baffles perpendicular to the shell wall. The *en banc* court relied first on the principle of claim differentiation, noting for example that dependent claim 2 of Phillips' patent recited baffles that were "oriented with the panel sections disposed at angles for deflecting projectiles such as bullets able to penetrate the steel plates." The inclusion of such a specific limitation on the term "baffles" in claim 2 made it likely that the patentee did not contemplate that "baffles" as recited in independent claim 1 already incorporated that limitation.[117] Second, the *en banc* court observed (as the panel dissent had also noted) that the Phillips patent disclosed several functions for the baffles besides that of deflecting bullets, and concluded that claim 1 did not have to be interpreted narrowly so as to encompass each such function: "Although deflecting projectiles is one of the advantages of the baffles of the '798 patent, the patent does not require that the inward extending structures always be capable of performing that function."[118]

Answering some of the other questions posed by the July 2004 order for rehearing *en banc*, the *Phillips en banc* decision also held that the appropriate temporal perspective for assessing the words in a patent claim is their ordinary and customary meaning to a person having ordinary skill in the art in question "at the time of the invention, i.e., as of the effective filing date of the patent application."[119] Moreover, the maxim that claims should be interpreted so as to preserve their validity is of "limited utility" in general, and in any event is not applicable to the facts of *Phillips*.[120] The *en banc* decision did not address

---

on dictionaries for patent claim interpretation, it did not preclude their use in appropriate circumstances. The *en banc* court reaffirmed the Federal Circuit's earlier pronouncement in *Vitronics Corp. v. Conceptronic, Inc.*, 90 F.3d 1576 (Fed. Cir. 1996), that "judges are free to consult dictionaries and technical treatises 'at any time in order to better understand the underlying technology and may also rely on dictionary definitions when construing claim terms, so long as the dictionary definition does not contradict any definition found in or ascertained by a reading of the patent documents.'" *Phillips*, 415 F.3d at 1322-1323 (quoting *Vitronics*, 90 F.3d at 1584 n.6).

[117]*Phillips*, 415 F.3d at 1324.

[118]*Id.* at 1327.

[119]*Id.* at 1313. This statement apparently refers to the concept of a *prima facie* invention date based on construing the patent application's filing date as the invention's constructive reduction to practice date. *See* Chapter 4, Section J, *supra*. The *Phillips en banc* decision does not explain the correct time frame for claim interpretation when the inventor can (under pre-AIA rules) backdate her invention date from the filing date to her earlier conception date or actual reduction to practice date (assuming that the difference in dates would be material to the meaning of disputed claim terms).

[120]*See Phillips*, 415 F.3d at 1328. Although acknowledging the maxim of construing claims so as to preserve their validity, the *Phillips* court observed that in earlier decisions it had "not applied that principle broadly, and [had] certainly not endorsed a

the controversial question of the appropriate standard of appellate review of claim interpretation decisions by district courts, leaving that dispute for another day.[121]

5. *Markman* Hearings

Most district courts now carry out their claim interpretation responsibilities in the context of a separate pre-trial hearing variously referred to as a "claim interpretation hearing" or a "*Markman* hearing." District courts around the country vary widely in their approach to *Markman* hearings, and no uniform procedure exists.[122] Some district courts conduct the *Markman* hearing relatively early in a case, perhaps even before the close of discovery. Other courts conduct the *Markman* hearing in the context of a motion for summary judgment of infringement or noninfringement. A 1997 American Bar Association report indicated that 85 percent of *Markman* hearings are conducted

---

regime in which validity analysis is a regular component of claim construction." *Id.* at 1327. Rather, the relevancy of the doctrine should be limited to cases "in which 'the court concludes, after applying all the available tools of claim construction, that the claim is still ambiguous.'" *Id.* (quoting Liebel-Flarsheim Co. v. Medrad, Inc., 358 F.3d 898, 911 (Fed. Cir. 2004)). In such cases, courts should discern "whether it is reasonable to infer that the PTO would not have issued an invalid patent, and that the ambiguity in the claim language should therefore be resolved in a manner that would preserve the patent's validity." *Id.* In *Phillips*, however, the term "baffle" was "not ambiguous" and could therefore "be construed without the need to consider whether one possible construction would render the claim invalid while the other would not." *Id.* at 1328.

[121]*See* Section B.6 ("Appellate Review of Claim Interpretation"), *infra*, for more background on this issue. Federal Circuit (and former Chief) Judge H. Robert Mayer, joined by Judge Pauline Newman, wrote a stinging dissent to the *Phillips en banc* majority's failure to address the standard of review question, emphasizing the "futility, indeed the absurdity, of [the] court's persistence in adhering to the falsehood that claim construction is a matter of law devoid of any factual component." *Id.* at 1330.

[122]*See* Committee No. 601 — Federal Practice and Procedure, *Reports Considered (Annual Report 2000-01),* in ABA Section of Intellectual Property Law, Annual Reports 1996-2001, *available at* http://www.abanet.org/intelprop/intelprop.pdf, which provides, in part:

> As a consequence, *Markman* hearings (as claim construction hearings are known) "run the gamut from mid-trial sidebar conferences that undergird relevance rulings . . . to virtual mini-trials extending over several days and generating extensive evidentiary records." Some courts prefer an early decision, with others warning that claim construction at too early a stage in a case may constitute an unconstitutional advisory opinion. Other courts address the question following discovery. Some favor the combination of claim construction with summary judgment motions, while others warn against it, citing the risk of "erodi[ng] . . . the role of the fact finder in patent litigation." Still other courts defer claim construction until after the close of evidence at trial.

Id. at 615 (footnotes and citations omitted).

prior to trial but after the close of discovery.[123] The federal district court for the Northern District of California, San Jose, was the first U.S. court to adopt a set of local rules that provide a very detailed procedure and timetable for claim interpretation and other pre-trial patent matters.[124]

Following a claim interpretation hearing, a district court will typically issue an order setting forth the manner in which the claims will be construed in the remainder of the case.[125] Although a number of parties have attempted to obtain immediate Federal Circuit review of district court claim interpretations through the vehicle of a certified question for interlocutory appeal under 28 U.S.C. §1292(b), thus far, the Federal Circuit has denied all such appeals. Thus, a litigant's chance of getting an early Federal Circuit review of a claim interpretation depends on the grant of a motion for summary judgment on the infringement issue that permits an immediate appeal.[126] Absent the district court granting such a summary judgment, claim interpretations generally will not be reviewed by the Federal Circuit until appeal is taken from a final judgment rendered after the completion of trial.

6. Appellate Review of Claim Interpretation: From *Cybor* (Fed. Cir. 1998) to *Teva* (U.S. 2015)

What standard of review should the Federal Circuit apply to a district court's interpretation of disputed language in patent claims? Given the centrality of claim interpretation to almost all patent disputes, the answer significantly impacts the balance of power in patent

[123]*See* Committee No. 601 — Federal Practice and Procedure, *Reports Considered (Annual Report 1997-98),* in ABA Section of Intellectual Property Law, Annual Reports 1996-2001, at 2716, *available at* http://www.abanet.org/intelprop/intelprop.pdf (summarizing survey results).

[124]The U.S. District Court for the Northern District of California first promulgated a set of Patent Local Rules effective January 1, 2001. Revised rules are now in effect. *See* Northern Dist. of Cal., *Patent Local Rules* (last rev. Nov. 1, 2014), *available at* http://www.cand.uscourts.gov/localrules/patent.

[125]For a helpful example of a district court's *Markman* order, *see* Neomagic Corp. v. Trident Microsystems, Inc., 98 F. Supp. 2d 538 (D. Del. 2000) (McKelvie, J.) (construing claim terms), *later proceeding,* 129 F. Supp. 2d 689 (D. Del. 2001) (granting defendant's motion for summary judgment of no infringement), *aff'd-in-part, vacated-in-part, and remanded,* 287 F.3d 1062 (Fed. Cir. 2002).

[126]"A substantial majority of patent cases decided by the Federal Circuit are on appeals from summary judgment." University of Houston Law Center, *Patstats: U.S. Patent Litigation Statistics*, http://www.patstats.org/editors_page.rev5.html (last visited Oct. 12, 2015). *See also* Nystrom v. TREX Co., 339 F.3d 1347 (Fed. Cir. 2003) (dismissing appeal for lack of jurisdiction where district court granted summary judgment of noninfringement based on its claim construction rulings but stayed counterclaim on invalidity and unenforceability, thereby violating the final judgment rule of 28 U.S.C. §1295).

cases as between the federal district courts, which try the cases, and the Federal Circuit, which hears them on appeal.

a. *Federal Circuit's* De Novo *Standard of Review*

Until 2015, the controlling authority on this question was the Federal Circuit's 1998 *en banc* decision in *Cybor Corp. v. FAS Techs., Inc.*[127] Recall that in *Markman v. Westview,*[128] the Supreme Court clearly held that patent claim interpretation is for the court rather than the jury.[129] But by referring to claim interpretation as a "mongrel practice,"[130] the Court left some question as to whether a district court in carrying out its interpretational responsibilities is making an entirely legal determination or instead may be finding facts.

Because of continued disagreement among Federal Circuit judges over this fact-versus-law question, the appellate court went *en banc* in 1998 to resolve the issue. In *Cybor,* a majority of Federal Circuit judges agreed that claim interpretation was entirely a legal determination.[131] In their view, no findings of fact are made by a district court in the construction of claims. Thus, the Federal Circuit reviewed a district court's claim interpretation under the *de novo* (i.e., no deference) standard of review.

Supporters of the *Cybor* decision contended that it promoted greater uniformity in the treatment of a given patent. For example, consider a hypothetical in which two different district courts construed the same patent claim, and one court interpreted the disputed language in a manner that rendered the patent invalid while the other court reached a contrary decision and sustained validity. If the Federal Circuit were required to defer to each of these opposing interpretations as factual findings, an unacceptable level of inconsistency would result.

Detractors of *Cybor* pointed to the dissent of Circuit Judge Rader, who cited a study indicating that approximately 40 percent of the claim interpretation decisions reviewed on appeal by the Federal Circuit are reversed.[132] In Judge Rader's view, shared by many patent litigators, this level of uncertainty renders the patent litigation process little better than a coin toss in terms of predictability of outcome. Circuit Judge Mayer charged that the Federal Circuit's continued treatment of claim interpretation as lacking any factual component

[127]138 F.3d 1448 (Fed. Cir. 1998) (*en banc*).

[128]Markman v. Westview Instruments, Inc., 517 U.S. 370 (1996).

[129]*Markman* is analyzed *supra* Section B.2 ("Judge or Jury as Interpreter? The *Markman* Revolution").

[130]*Markman*, 517 U.S. at 378.

[131]*See Cybor,* 138 F.3d at 1456 (holding that "as a purely legal question, we review claim construction *de novo* on appeal including any allegedly fact-based questions relating to claim construction").

[132]*See id.* at 1476 (Rader, J., dissenting).

has resulted in "mayhem," which "seriously undermine[s] the legitimacy of the process, if not the integrity of the institution."[133]

Despite the rather strident tone of the *Cybor* majority opinion that district courts deserved no deference in their claim interpretations because these determinations were entirely legal rather than factual, some members of the Federal Circuit appeared to take a more pragmatic, common-sense position. These judges suggested that, despite the "no deference" absolutism of the *Cybor* majority opinion, in practice the Federal Circuit would give weight to a district court's claim interpretation commensurate with the degree of care taken by the district court in its analysis and the informational value of the record that the district court considered.[134]

This pragmatic approach could be taken only so far given the strict edicts of *Cybor*. Federal Circuit judges continued to disagree sharply on the proper appellate standard of review for district court claim interpretation decisions. A significant number of Federal Circuit judges repeatedly called for reevaluation of the 1998 *en banc* decision in *Cybor*.

For example, in her 2011 dissent from denial of rehearing *en banc* in *Retractable Techs., Inc. v. Becton, Dickinson and Co.*,[135] Judge Moore observed that the Federal Circuit had "waited five years (since *Amgen Inc. v. Hoechst Marion Roussel, Inc.*, 469 F.3d 1039 (Fed. Cir. 2006), where six judges claimed a willingness to review *Cybor*) for that ever-elusive perfect vehicle to review the issue of deference to the district court's claim construction." She urged that it "is time to rethink the deference we give to district court claim constructions and the fallacy that the entire process is one of law."[136] Also dissenting from denial of rehearing *en banc* in *Retractable Techs.*, Judge O'Malley stated adamantly that "[i]t is time to revisit and reverse our decision in *Cybor*. . . . That decision was ill considered thirteen years ago and has not proven 'beneficial' to patent jurisprudence 'in the long run.' "[137] Judge O'Malley (the only former federal district court judge serving on the Federal Circuit as of 2015) noted that since the Supreme

[133]Phillips v. AWH Corp., 415 F.3d 1303, 1330 (Fed. Cir. 2005) (Mayer, J., dissenting).

[134]*See Cybor*, 138 F.3d at 1462 (Plager, J., concurring); *id.* at 1463 (Bryson, J., concurring).

[135]659 F.3d 1369, 1373 (Fed. Cir. 2011) (Moore, J., joined by Rader, C.J., dissenting from denial of rehearing *en banc*).

[136]*Retractable Techs.*, 659 F.3d at 1373 (Moore, J., joined by Rader, C.J., dissenting from denial of rehearing *en banc*).

[137]*Retractable Techs.*, 659 F.3d at 1373-1374 (O'Malley, J., dissenting from denial of rehearing *en banc*) (quoting Cybor Corp. v. FAS Techs., Inc., 138 F.3d 1448, 1463 (Fed. Cir. 1998) (Plager, J., concurring) ("Whether this approach to patent litigation will in the long run prove beneficial remains to be seen.")).

Court's 1996 *Markman* decision that assigned them the task of patent claim construction,

> district judges have been trained to — and do — engage in detailed and thoughtful analysis of the claim construction issues presented to them. They conduct live hearings with argument and testimony, sometimes covering several days, and certainly always extending beyond the mere minutes that courts of appeals have to devote to live exchanges with counsel. Simply, "the trial court has tools to acquire and evaluate evidence that this court lacks." *Cybor*, 138 F.3d at 1477 (Rader, J., dissenting).[138]

Related to the standard of review issue, another matter of concern is the Circuit's consistent refusal to accept any interlocutory appeals of claim interpretation determinations under 28 U.S.C. §1292(b). Although a number of district courts have certified their claim interpretation determinations as "involv[ing] a controlling question of law as to which there is substantial ground for difference of opinion and that an immediate appeal from the order may materially advance the ultimate termination of the litigation,"[139] the Federal Circuit has thus far exercised its discretion to refuse all such appeals.[140] One could legitimately question whether the Federal Circuit should "have it both ways" in applying a *de novo* standard of review for claim interpretations while refusing to accept any interlocutory appeals from those determinations.[141]

In 2014, the Federal Circuit once again considered — and reaffirmed — the *de novo* standard of review for patent claim interpretation. On February 21, 2014, the Circuit issued its *en banc* decision in *Lighting Ballast Control LLC v. Philips Elecs. N. Am. Corp.*[142] The ten judges deciding the case split 6-4.[143] To the surprise of many in the

[138]*Retractable Techs.*, 659 F.3d at 1374 (O'Malley, J., dissenting from denial of rehearing *en banc*).

[139]28 U.S.C. §1292(b).

[140]*See Cybor*, 138 F.3d at 1479 (Newman, J., stating "additional views") (observing that "[a]lthough the district courts have extended themselves, and so-called '*Markman* hearings' are common, this has not been accompanied by interlocutory review of the trial judge's claim interpretation. The Federal Circuit has thus far declined all such certified questions.").

[141]See Craig Allen Nard, *Intellectual Property Challenges in the Next Century: Process Considerations in the Age of* Markman *and Mantras*, 2001 U. Ill. L. Rev. 355, 357.

[142]744 F.3d 1272 (Fed. Cir. 2014) (*en banc*).

[143]Circuit Judges Chen and Hughes did not participate. The *en banc* court generated three opinions totaling 88 pages in *Lighting Ballast*: a majority opinion authored by Judge Newman, a dissenting opinion authored by Judge O'Malley, and a concurring opinion by Judge Lourie in which he fully joined in the majority's opinion and offered additional justifications for retaining the *Cybor* regime.

patent community,[144] the *en banc* majority reaffirmed that the *de novo* standard of review for patent claim construction, previously adopted in *Cybor Corp. v. FAS Techs., Inc.*,[145] would continue to control. Thus, the Federal Circuit again refused to cede any meaningful interpretational power to the district courts. In an opinion authored by Circuit Judge Newman and joined by Circuit Judges Lourie, Dyk, Prost, Moore, and Taranto, the *Lighting Ballast* majority applied

> the principles of *stare decisis* [to] confirm the *Cybor* standard of *de novo* review of claim construction, whereby the scope of the patent grant is reviewed as a matter of law. After fifteen years of experience with *Cybor*, we conclude that the court should retain plenary [i.e., absolute or unconditional] review of claim construction, thereby providing national uniformity, consistency, and finality to the meaning and scope of patent claims. The totality of experience has confirmed that *Cybor* is an effective implementation of *Markman II*, and that the criteria for departure from *stare decisis* are not met.[146]

b. *Supreme Court Requires Deference for Fact Finding:* Teva *(2015)*

Less than six weeks after the Circuit's *Lighting Ballast* decision, the Supreme Court stepped into the fray. On March 31, 2014, the Court granted *certiorari* to review the deference issue in a different claim construction case captioned *Teva Pharm. USA, Inc. v. Sandoz, Inc.*[147] In January 2015, the Supreme Court issued its decision in *Teva v. Sandoz*,[148]

[144]Judge O'Malley began her dissenting opinion as follows:

> District judges, both parties in this case, and the majority of intellectual property lawyers and academics around the country will no doubt be surprised by today's majority opinion — and for good reason. The majority opinion is surprising because it refuses to acknowledge what experience has shown us and what even a cursory reading of the Supreme Court's decision in *Markman v. Westview Instruments, Inc.*, 517 U.S. 370 (1996), confirms: construing the claims of a patent at times requires district courts to resolve questions of fact. And, it puts itself at odds with binding congressional and Supreme Court authority when it refuses to abide by the requirements of Rule 52(a)(6) of the Federal Rules of Civil Procedure, which expressly instructs that, on appeal, *all* "findings of fact . . . must not be set aside unless clearly erroneous."

Lighting Ballast, 744 F.3d at 1296 (O'Malley, J., dissenting).

[145]138 F.3d 1448 (Fed. Cir. 1998) (*en banc*).

[146]*Lighting Ballast,* 744 F.3d at 1276-1277 (citing Markman v. Westview Instruments, Inc., 517 U.S. 370 (1996) ("*Markman II*")).

[147]134 S. Ct. 1761 (Mar. 31, 2014) (order granting petition for writ of *certiorari* to the Federal Circuit in Teva Pharm. USA, Inc. v. Sandoz, Inc., 723 F.3d 1363 (Fed. Cir. 2013)).

[148]Teva Pharms. USA, Inc. v. Sandoz, Inc., 135 S. Ct. 831 (2015).

its most significant patent claim construction case since the 1996 blockbuster *Markman v. Westview.*[149]

The importance of the Supreme Court's 2015 decision in *Teva* should not be underestimated. In the view of this author, for the first time in the Federal Circuit's history, the Supreme Court clearly and explicitly recognized (and instructed the Federal Circuit) that patent claim construction *can* involve questions of fact. Moreover, the Supreme Court ruled in *Teva* that when a district court relies on extrinsic evidence (e.g., a technical treatise or expert testimony concerning what a disputed claim term would mean to a PHOSITA) in order to find facts during the claim construction process, the Federal Circuit *must* give those findings "clear error" deference (rather than zero deference). In other words, the district court's findings of fact stand and cannot be ignored or wiped away unless the appellate court concludes that the findings were clearly erroneous pursuant to Fed. R. Civ. P. 52.[150] This represents a potentially significant shift of power back to the federal district courts hearing patent cases.

In a 7-2 opinion authored by Justice Breyer, the Supreme Court in *Teva* started from the important (and to this author, unremarkable) premise that patent claim construction *does* sometimes involve underlying factual disputes.[151] It thus rejected the Federal Circuit's

[149]Markman v. Westview Instruments, Inc., 517 U.S. 370 (1996).

[150]Federal Rules of Civil Procedure Rule 52 ("Findings and Conclusions by the Court; Judgment on Partial Findings") (2015) provides in pertinent part (emphasis added):

> (a) Findings and Conclusions.
>
> . . .
>
> (6) Setting Aside the Findings. Findings of fact, whether based on oral or other evidence, must not be set aside unless *clearly erroneous*, and the reviewing court must give due regard to the trial court's opportunity to judge the witnesses' credibility.

[151]*See Teva,* 135 S. Ct. at 840, stating:

> The dissent argues that claim construction does not involve any "factfinding," or, if it does, claim construction factfinding is akin to the factfinding that underlies our interpretation of statutes. *Post,* at 844, 846-848 (opinion of Thomas, J.). Its first, broader contention runs contrary to our recognition in *Markman* that claim construction has "evidentiary underpinnings" and that courts construing patent claims must sometimes make "credibility judgments" about witnesses. 517 U.S., at 389-390, 116 S. Ct. 1384. Indeed, as discussed in Part III, *infra,* this case provides a perfect example of the factfinding that sometimes underlies claim construction: The parties here presented the District Court with competing fact-related claims by different experts, and the District Court resolved the issues of fact that divided those experts.
>
> The dissent's contention also runs contrary to Sandoz's concession at oral argument that claim construction will sometimes require subsidiary factfinding. Tr. of Oral Arg. 33-34, 38-40. It is in tension with our interpretation of related

contrary protestations dating from at least the appellate court's 1998 *Cybor en banc* decision.[152] In claim construction disputes involving "evidentiary underpinnings" (an unhelpful characterization, because *all* claim construction involves intrinsic evidence and sometimes extrinsic evidence[153]), district courts will sometimes find it helpful to consult the extrinsic evidence (such as an expert's testimony concerning what a term of art meant to a skilled artisan as of the invention's effective filing date). When district court findings of fact result, the Federal Circuit *must* review them under the clear error standard of Fed. R. Civ. P. 52.

The Supreme Court explained that, as with determinations of the "usage of trade or locality" in interpreting contracts, district courts may consult extrinsic evidence that is helpful to determine patent claim meaning.[154] When district courts make findings of fact, those findings are subject to Rule 52 review like any other type of finding of fact. Notably, the *Teva* Court relied in part on a 1950 Second Circuit

---

> areas of patent law, such as the interpretation of "obviousness," which we have said involves subsidiary factfinding subject to Rule 52(a)'s clear error review. See *Dennison,* 475 U.S., at 811, 106 S. Ct. 1578. And it fights the question presented in this case, which *assumes* the existence of such factfinding. See Pet. for Cert. i (whether "a district court's factual finding in support of its construction of a patent claim term may be reviewed *de novo,* . . . or only for clear error").

[152]Cybor Corp. v. FAS Techs., Inc., 138 F.3d 1448 (Fed. Cir. 1998) (*en banc*).

[153]The concepts of intrinsic and extrinsic evidence in patent claim construction are analyzed *supra* Section B.3 ("Evidentiary Sources for Claim Interpretation").

[154]Responding to the dissent, the *Teva* majority determined that the construction of terms in patent claims is analogous to the interpretation of contracts and deeds, but unlike the interpretation of language in statutes:

> Neither do we find factfinding in this context sufficiently similar to the factfinding that underlies statutory interpretation. Statutes, in general, address themselves to the general public; patent claims concern a small portion of that public. Statutes typically (though not always) rest upon congressional consideration of general facts related to a reasonably broad set of social circumstances; patents typically (though not always) rest upon consideration by a few private parties, experts, and administrators of more narrowly circumscribed facts related to specific technical matters. The public, and often an adversarial public, typically considers and discusses the relevant general facts before Congress enacts a statute; only private parties, experts, and administrators likely consider the relevant technical facts before the award of a patent. Given these differences, it is not surprising that this Court has never previously compared patent claim construction in any here relevant way to statutory construction. As discussed *supra,* at 837, however, the Court has repeatedly compared patent claim construction to the construction of other written instruments such as deeds and contracts. See, *e.g., Markman, supra,* at 384, 386, 388, 389, 116 S. Ct. 1384; *Motion Picture Patents Co.,* 243 U.S., at 510, 37 S. Ct. 416; *Goodyear,* 102 U.S., at 227.

Teva, 135 S. Ct. at 840.

opinion by Judge Learned Hand that mandated deference to fact finding in patent claim construction.[155]

Nevertheless, the Court clarified that findings of fact are "subsidiary" to the "ultimate question" of patent claim interpretation. The ultimate, overall question of a patent claim's interpretation remains a legal conclusion subject to *de novo* (i.e., no deference) review by the Federal Circuit:

> Accordingly, the question we have answered here concerns review of the district court's resolution of a subsidiary factual dispute that helps that court determine the proper interpretation of the written patent claim. The district judge, after deciding the factual dispute, will then interpret the patent claim in light of the facts as he has found them. *This ultimate interpretation is a legal conclusion. The appellate court can still review the district court's ultimate construction of the claim de novo.* But, to overturn the judge's resolution of an underlying factual dispute, the Court of Appeals must find that the judge, in respect to those factual findings, has made a clear error. Fed. Rule Civ. Proc. 52(a)(6).[156]

As a practical matter, the *Teva* majority doubted that fact findings based on extrinsic evidence would be required in many claim construction disputes.[157] When they are, courts will be capable of disentangling fact from law. Various doctrines and procedures such as collateral estoppel and case consolidation will help maintain uniformity in the construction of particular patents.[158]

Having announced the correct law, the Supreme Court in *Teva* applied it to the merits of the case. The claim construction dispute in *Teva* concerned the meaning of the phrase "molecular weight" as used

[155]*See Teva*, 135 S. Ct. at 838 (observing that "[b]efore the creation of the Federal Circuit, the Second Circuit explained that in claim construction, the subsidiary 'question... of how the art understood the term... was plainly a question of fact; and unless the [district court's] finding was "clearly erroneous," we are to take' [sic] it 'as controlling.' Harries v. Air King Products, Co., 183 F.2d 158, 164 (C.A.2 1950) (L. Hand, C.J.).").

Judge Learned Hand was a highly respected jurist in numerous legal fields including patent law, and his patent decisions have been cited many times by the Supreme Court, Federal Circuit, and CCPA. *See generally* Gerald Gunther, Learned Hand: The Man and the Judge, 2d Edition (Oxford Univ. Press 2010); Paul H. Blaustein, Learned Hand on Patent Law (Pineridge Pub. House 1983). *See also* Application of Benner, 174 F.2d 938, 943 (C.C.P.A. 1949) (referring to Learned Hand as "justly esteemed a high authority on patent law").

[156]*Teva*, 135 S. Ct. at 841 (emphasis added).

[157]*See Teva,* 135 S. Ct. at 840-841, stating:

> We recognize that a district court's construction of a patent claim, like a district court's interpretation of a written instrument, often requires the judge only to examine and to construe the document's words without requiring the judge to resolve any underlying factual disputes. As all parties agree, when the district court reviews only evidence intrinsic to the patent (the patent claims and specifications, along with the patent's prosecution history), the judge's determination will amount solely to a determination of law, and the Court of Appeals will review that construction *de novo*.

[158]*See Teva,* 135 S. Ct. at 839-840.

in the claims of several asserted Teva patents, including representative U.S. Patent No. 5,981,589 ('589 patent).[159] Teva's patents were directed to a drug product (and methods of making the drug) for the treatment of multiple sclerosis marketed by Teva as Copaxone®.[160] The patented drug comprised a mixture of polymers, each having a different molecular weight. The patent claims required a particular "molecular weight" range for the composite polymer mixture.

The claim construction problem arose in *Teva* because there existed at least three different methods for measuring "molecular weight," and the Teva patents did not clearly specify which of three applied. The prosecution history of the patents also muddied the waters (as further described below). The three statistical measures under consideration were:

— peak average molecular weight (M_p);
— number average molecular weight (M_n); and
— weight average molecular weight (M_w).[161]

At trial, opposing experts debated the proper meaning of "molecular weight" as used in Teva's patent claims. A district court credited the testimony of Teva's expert that "molecular weight" as used in the claims meant the first of the three methods listed above, peak average molecular weight (M_p). The district court rejected Sandoz's counter-argument that the term "molecular weight" was insolubly ambiguous (and thus Teva's patent claims fatally indefinite) because "molecular weight" could refer to M_p, M_n, M_w, or some other molecular weight measure.

[159]Claim 1 of Teva's '589 patent recited (emphasis added):

> Copolymer-1 having a *molecular weight* of about 5 to 9 kilodaltons, made by a process comprising the steps of:
> reacting protected copolymer-1 . . . ; and
> purifying said copolymer-1, to result in copolymer1 having a *molecular weight* of about 5 to 9 kilodaltons.

[160]More specifically, the Teva patent claims recited a polymer mixture called "copolymer-1" having four different component polymer molecules of different weights. The issue was how to determine the "molecular weight" for the composite mixture of polymer molecules.

[161]The Supreme Court provided a helpful hypothetical to explain the difference between the three measurements:

> To illustrate, imagine we have a sample of copolymer-1 (the active ingredient) made up of 10 molecules: 4 weigh 6 kilodaltons each, 3 weigh 8 kilodaltons each, and 3 weigh 9 kilodaltons each. Using the first method of calculation, the "molecular weight" [M_p] would be 6 kilodaltons, the weight of the most prevalent molecule. Using the second method, the molecular weight [M_n] would be 7.5 (total weight, 75, divided by the number of molecules, 10). Using the third method, the molecular weight [M_w] would be more than 8, depending upon how much extra weight we gave to the heavier molecules.

Teva, 135 S. Ct. at 842.

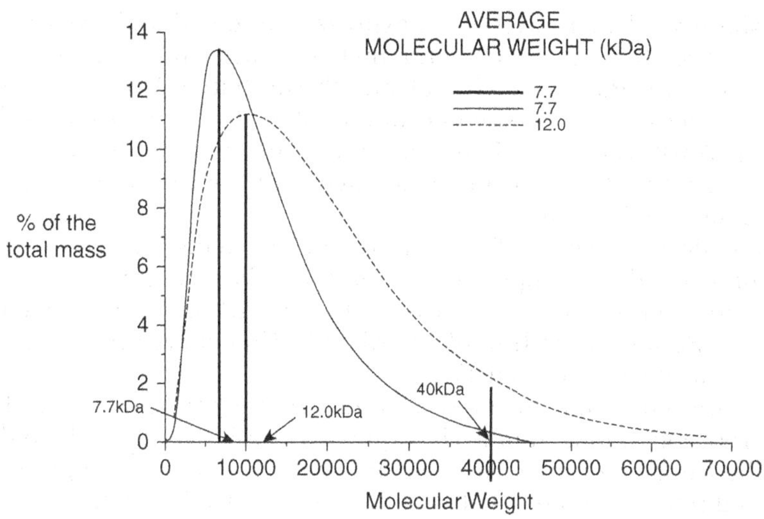

FIG. 1

Figure 9.2

Molecular Weight Distribution in *Teva v. Sandoz* (vertical lines added by accused infringer Sandoz)

The key battle of the experts in *Teva* involved dueling explanations of a molecular weight distribution diagram appearing as the first figure of the Teva '589 patent, shown below in Figure 9.2.

Patentee Teva's expert testified that "molecular weight" as used in the patent claims referred to the "average molecular weight" shown in the distribution of Figure 9.2. He explained that "molecular weight" and "average molecular weight" had to mean peak average molecular weight (M_p), because only M_p could be derived directly by looking at the distribution (i.e., "molecular weight" was simply the peak value of the curves). Accused infringer Sandoz inserted the vertical lines depicted in Figure 9.2 to show that the peaks of the curves in the figure did not correspond exactly to the values denoted as "average molecular weight" in the figure's legend, and thus could not be M_p.

Teva's expert responded that the molecular weight distributions shown in the figure were produced by a process known as size exclusion chromatography (SEC), as explained in the patent's examples. He testified that a person of ordinary skill in the art would understand that the distributions in Figure 9.2 were created by transforming data from a chromatogram to the curves depicted. Importantly, the skilled artisan would understand "that the process of transferring the data from the chromatogram would likely cause the peak on each curve to shift slightly." The district court expressly accepted and credited the Teva expert's testimony. Thus the district court found, "the fact that the peaks in Figure [9.2] do not match the listed AMWs precisely would not dissuade a person of ordinary skill in the art from concluding that AMW refers to M_p in the context of the patents-in-suit."[162] Accordingly the district court concluded that Teva's claims were *not* invalid for indefiniteness.

The Federal Circuit in 2013 had reversed the district court's judgment of no invalidity, applying a *de novo* standard of review to the district court's claim interpretation. The Circuit sided with accused infringer Sandoz's reading of the distribution curves in Figure 9.2 rather than the district court's.[163]

The Supreme Court granted *certiorari* in *Teva* to resolve the claim interpretation standard of review question. In its January 2015 decision the Supreme Court vacated the Federal Circuit's judgment in *Teva* and remanded the case to the appellate court for further proceedings.[164] The Circuit had erred in overturning the district court's

[162]Teva Pharm. USA, Inc. v. Sandoz Inc., 810 F. Supp. 2d 578, 591 (S.D.N.Y. 2011). The district court rejected Sandoz's contrary arguments, stating:

> Sandoz, for its part, devotes substantial energy to discrediting [Teva expert] Dr. Grant and his explanation regarding how one of ordinary skill in the art would understand Figure [9.2]. Sandoz relies almost exclusively, however, on unsubstantiated attorney-argument. The Court finds that Sandoz's unsubstantiated attorney-argument is insufficient to cast doubt on Dr. Grant's opinions, which, as explained above, the Court credits and accepts. *See Invitrogen Corp. v. Clontech Labs., Inc.*, 429 F.3d 1052, 1068 (Fed. Cir. 2005) ("Unsubstantiated attorney argument regarding the meaning of technical evidence is no substitute for competent, substantiated expert testimony.").

Teva, 810 F. Supp. 2d at 591.

[163]*See* Teva Pharm. USA, Inc. v. Sandoz, Inc., 723 F.3d 1363, 1369 (Fed. Cir. 2013), *cert. granted*, 134 S. Ct. 1761 (2014) *and vacated*, 135 S. Ct. 831 (2015), stating:

> On *de novo* review of the district court's indefiniteness holding, we conclude that [Teva expert] Dr. Grant's testimony does not save Group I claims from indefiniteness. As Dr. Grant himself opined, SEC does not exclusively provide M_p—both M_n and M_w can also be obtained from the data generated by the SEC method after some calculations. J.A. 1005. His testimony is consistent with that of one of [Sandoz's] experts, who opined that SEC "can give at least peak average, number average, and weight average 'molecular weights.'" J.A. 1229. Furthermore, as illustrated in the figure [9.2], the peaks of the curves in [the figure] do not correspond to the values denoted as "average molecular weight" in the figure's legend ([Sandoz's] additions in color [shown *supra* Fig. 9.2 as vertical lines]). In fact, the 7.7 kDa value is closer to the M_w than to the M_p of the corresponding batch, which makes it difficult to conclude that M_p is the intended measure. J.A. 5285. Thus, we hold that Group I claims are indefinite.

[164]Teva Pharms. USA, Inc. v. Sandoz, Inc., 135 S. Ct. 831 (2015).

finding of fact that Teva's proposed definition of the claim phrase "molecular weight" (i.e., meaning M_p) was correct. In particular, the appellate court had improperly reviewed without deference the district court's decision to credit the Teva expert's explanation of why the discrepancies in the molecular weight distribution curves shown in Figure 9.2 did not undermine Teva's position. This was a finding of fact that should have been reviewed under the "clearly erroneous" standard of review.[165]

Writing for himself and Justice Alito in dissent, Justice Thomas doubted the *Teva* majority's prediction that "subsidiary factfinding" is unlikely to loom large in future patent claim constructions. Rather, he charged that the majority's holding would spawn costly and meritless collateral litigation on the law/fact distinction, as parties prevailing at the district court will be incentivized to argue on appeal that the claim construction below involved findings of fact owed Rule 52 deference.[166]

[165]*See Teva,* 135 S. Ct. at 843, stating:

> Teva's expert testified that a skilled artisan would understand that converting data from a chromatogram to molecular weight distribution curves like those in figure [9.2] would cause the peak on each curve to shift slightly; this could explain the difference between the value indicated by the peak of the curve (about 6.8) and the value in the figure's legend (7.7). App. 138a-139a. Sandoz's expert testified that no such shift would occur. App. 375a-376a. The District Court credited Teva's expert's account, thereby rejecting Sandoz's expert's explanation. 810 F. Supp. 2d, at 589; Brief for Respondents 61. The District Court's finding about this matter was a factual finding — about how a skilled artisan would understand the way in which a curve created from chromatogram data reflects molecular weights. Based on that factual finding, the District Court reached the legal conclusion that figure [9.2] did not undermine Teva's argument that molecular weight referred to the first method of calculation (peak average molecular weight). 810 F. Supp. 2d, at 590-591.
>
> When the Federal Circuit reviewed the District Court's decision, it recognized that the peak of the curve did not match the 7.7 kilodaltons listed in the legend of figure [9.2]. 723 F.3d, at 1369. But the Federal Circuit did not accept Teva's expert's explanation as to how a skilled artisan would expect the peaks of the curves to shift. And it failed to accept that explanation without finding that the District Court's contrary determination was "clearly erroneous." See *ibid.* The Federal Circuit should have accepted the District Court's finding unless it was "clearly erroneous." Our holding today makes clear that, in failing to do so, the Federal Circuit was wrong.

[166]*See Teva,* 135 S. Ct. at 852 (Thomas, J., dissenting) (stating that "[i]f this case proves anything, it is that the line between fact and law is an uncertain one — made all the more uncertain by the majority's failure to identify sound principles for the lines it draws").

c. *Federal Circuit Application of the* Teva *Standard*

As of the writing of this edition in 2019, the Federal Circuit had decided many precedential patent claim construction cases post-*Teva*. In most, the district court construed the claims relying only on intrinsic evidence. Hence, the Federal Circuit applied *de novo* review and the Supreme Court's decision in *Teva* had no impact.

The Federal Circuit's June 2015 decision on remand from the Supreme Court in *Lighting Ballast v. Philips Elecs.*[167] represents a rare post-*Teva* Federal Circuit decision in which the Circuit has specifically relied on and deferred to a district court's findings of fact in affirming the court's claim interpretation.[168] Expert testimony in *Lighting Ballast* convinced the district court (and on appeal, the Federal Circuit) that the claim-recited "voltage source means" conveyed a class of structures known to skilled artisans.[169] Thus the claim element in dispute was *not* a means-plus-function element under 35 U.S.C. §112(f) and was not indefinite for lack of supporting

[167]Lighting Ballast Control LLC v. Philips Elecs. N. Am. Corp., 790 F.3d 1329 (Fed. Cir. June 23, 2015). A week after the Supreme Court decided *Teva* on January 20, 2015, it granted *certiorari* in the *en banc* decision in *Lighting Ballast,* described *supra* Section B.6.a. The Supreme Court vacated the Circuit's *en banc* judgment in *Lighting Ballast* and remanded the case to the Federal Circuit for further consideration in light of *Teva*. *See* Lighting Ballast Control LLC v. Universal Lighting Technologies, Inc., 135 S. Ct. 1173 (2015) (order).

[168]*See Lighting Ballast*, 790 F.3d at 1338 (recognizing that district court's claim interpretation involved findings of fact; explaining that "[t]he district court made findings of fact based on extrinsic evidence. *See Teva*, 574 U.S. at ___, 135 S. Ct. at 842. Under the circumstances, it was not legal error for the district court to rely on extrinsic evidence, because the extrinsic evidence was 'not used to contradict claim meaning that is unambiguous in light of the intrinsic evidence.' Phillips v. AWH Corp., 415 F.3d 1303, 1324 (Fed. Cir. 2005).").

[169]*See Lighting Ballast*, 790 F.3d at 1338-1339, stating that

> the district court determined that "while the 'voltage source means' term does not denote a specific structure, it is nevertheless understood by persons of skill in the lighting ballast design art to connote a class of structures, namely a rectifier, or structure to rectify the AC power line into a DC voltage for the DC input terminals." J.A. 22. The district court went on to note that the language following "voltage source means" in the claim — "providing a constant or variable magnitude DC voltage between the DC input terminals" — "when read by one familiar with the use and function of a lighting ballast, such as the one disclosed by the 529 Patent, [sic] would understand a rectifier is, at least in common uses, the only structure that would provide 'a constant or variable magnitude DC voltage.'" *Id.* at 23. The district court further noted that "[i]t is clear to one skilled in the art that to provide a DC voltage when the source is a power line, which provides an AC voltage, a structure to rectify the line is required and is clear from the language of the 'voltage source means' term." *Id. We defer to these factual findings, absent a showing that they are clearly erroneous.*

(emphasis added).

structure.[170] The Federal Circuit reversed course from its original, pre-*Teva*, non-precedential panel opinion in which it had held the Lighting Ballast patent claims indefinite.[171] In short, *Teva* made all the difference in *Lighting Ballast*.

In marked contrast, the Federal Circuit's June 18, 2015 decision on remand from the Supreme Court in *Teva* itself[172] produced a 2-1 panel decision in which the Circuit majority clung tenaciously to its original position that the Teva patent claims were invalid for indefiniteness, but cited new reasons in support. The *Teva* remand majority, in an opinion authored by Judge Moore, relied on an aspect of the case not specifically dealt with by the Supreme Court — inconsistent statements in the prosecution histories of related Teva patents. Despite expert testimony that had convinced the district court in *Teva* that skilled artisans would not have relied on a plainly scientifically erroneous statement in the prosecution history,[173] the Federal Circuit majority held that the patentee was bound by its inaccurate statement. In the majority's view, the matter presented a legal question of interpreting the prosecution history rather than a question of fact about what a skilled artisan would understand from that history.[174]

[170]Means-plus-function claim elements were examined *supra* Chapter 2, Section E.1.

[171]*See* Lighting Ballast Control LLC v. Philips Elecs. N. Am. Corp., 498 F. App'x 986 (Fed. Cir. 2013) (non-precedential) (holding that the term "voltage source means" in the claims of the '529 patent in suit was a means-plus-function limitation under §112, ¶6; finding in the specification no corresponding structure, holding the claims invalid for indefiniteness and reversing district court's judgment).

[172]Teva Pharms. USA, Inc. v. Sandoz, Inc., 789 F.3d 1335 (Fed. Cir. 2015).

[173]*See* Teva Pharm. USA, Inc. v. Sandoz Inc., 810 F. Supp. 2d 578, 592 (S.D.N.Y. 2011), stating:

> [W]ith respect to the statement made during the prosecution of the '847 patent, Teva admits its statement — "kilodalton units implies a weight average molecular weight" — was incorrect. Because the statement was incorrect, a person of ordinary skill in the art would not rely on it. As Sandoz's expert, Dr. Frantisek Svec, explained, "each type of 'average molecular weight' can use the dalton." (Svec Decl. ¶33.) Understanding that the statement is wrong (see Grant Decl. ¶64 (Teva v. Sandoz claim construction), a person of ordinary skill in the art would not conclude that AMW, in the context of the patents-in-suit, "implies . . . weight average molecular weight." (Kramer Decl. Ex. 7 at p. 3 (Amendment).)

[174]In its divided remand decision, the Federal Circuit maintained its earlier position that the Group I claims of Teva's U.S. Patent No. 5,800,808 ('808 patent), directed to a method of making the drug marketed as Copaxone®, were invalid for indefiniteness. *See* Teva Pharm. USA, Inc. v. Sandoz, Inc., 789 F.3d 1335 (Fed. Cir. June 18, 2015). The split decision illustrates that a fundamental philosophical split remains at the Federal Circuit concerning deference to district court fact finding in the wake of the Supreme Court's decisions in *Teva* (2015) and *Nautilus* (2014).

The Federal Circuit's *Teva* remand decision turned primarily on the majority's treatment of the prosecution history of two patents related (as continuations) to the '808

Dissenting in the *Teva* remand decision, Circuit Judge Mayer charged that the relied-upon prosecution statement was "nonsensical, and a skilled artisan would not rely upon any part of it."[175] In deciding otherwise, the majority had erroneously ignored the district court's extensive fact finding about the background science involved, including the consideration of competing expert declarations, deposition testimony, and two hearings.

As of this writing in 2019, it appears that future claim interpretation cases will not routinely present underlying fact questions to which Federal Circuit panels will defer. Typically, the appellate court considers such findings unnecessary because (in its view) the intrinsic evidence resolves any ambiguities. Given the current trend and tone of its decisions such as the *Teva* remand decision, it seems likely that the Federal Circuit will continue to rely heavily on the Supreme Court's statement in *Teva* that the "ultimate" question of patent claim construction remains one of law, not fact, and thus not subject to any deference.

---

patent in suit. Although the majority found no clear error in the district court's fact finding that the applicant's statement during prosecution of the '847 continuation patent was scientifically erroneous (i.e., that the use of kilodalton units necessarily implied that the disputed term "molecular weight" meant "weight average molecular weight" ("M_W")), the majority nevertheless held that the applicant was bound as a matter of law by its definition of "molecular weight" as M_w:

> Regardless of the scientific accuracy of the statement, a person of ordinary skill in the art would have understood that the applicants defined the term "molecular weight" as M_w to gain allowance of the claims. This is a legal conclusion unaffected by the scientific error made during prosecution. To the extent that the dissent claims that the significance to be given to the patentee's express definition of molecular weight as M_w, made to overcome a rejection, is a question of fact, the dissent is wrong. *The determination of the significance of statements made during prosecution to the claim construction is a question of law.*

Teva, 789 F.3d at 1344 (emphasis added). The majority concluded that claim 1 of the '808 patent was invalid for indefiniteness by clear and convincing evidence because "read in light of the specification and the prosecution history, the patentee has failed to inform with *reasonable certainty* those skilled in the art about the scope of the invention." *Teva,* 789 F.3d at 1345 (emphasis in original).

[175]*Teva*, 789 F.3d at 1347 (Mayer, J., dissenting). Judge Mayer further observed that "[t]his is particularly true given that Teva confirmed, when subsequently prosecuting the '539 patent, that — consistent with the use of the SEC method disclosed in the specification — the term "molecular weight" meant peak average molecular weight. *See* Elbex Video, Ltd. v. Sensormatic Elecs. Corp., 508 F.3d 1366, 1372-1373 (Fed. Cir. 2007) (concluding that an earlier, incorrect statement in the prosecution history did not override a later, correct statement as to claim scope)." *Teva*, 789 F.3d at 1347 (Mayer, J., dissenting).

7. Claim Interpretation Canons

A number of rules or "canons" exist for interpreting patent claims, developed primarily through case law. Some of the most important rules to keep in mind are:

- Claim terms are interpreted from the perspective of the hypothetical person having ordinary skill in the art (the PHOSITA), rather than a judge, jury, or technical expert.
- The general rule is that claim terms are assigned their ordinary and customary meaning to the PHOSITA.[176]
- An important exception to the general rule is that a patentee "may be her own lexicographer." In other words, a patentee may choose to redefine a claim term away from its common, ordinary meaning. Most typically, this will be accomplished through an *express* redefinition, as where a patent's written description expressly states that "as used herein, the term 'primary color' means brown, black, or purple." Less typically, a patentee may be her own lexicographer and redefine a term *implicitly,* by a consistent use of a term in a particular way throughout the written description, even without an express definitional statement of what the term means.[177]
- A fine line often must be drawn between properly interpreting claims in light of the written description, and improperly

[176] *See* Phillips v. AWH Corp., 415 F.3d 1303, 1312 (Fed. Cir. 2005) (*en banc*) ("We have frequently stated that the words of a claim 'are generally given their ordinary and customary meaning.' ") (quoting *Vitronics Corp. v. Conceptronic, Inc.*, 90 F.3d 1576, 1582 (Fed. Cir. 1996)); Bell Atl. Network Servs., Inc. v. Covad Commc'ns Group, Inc., 262 F.3d 1258, 1267 (Fed. Cir. 2001).

A line of Federal Circuit decisions admits only narrow exceptions to the "general" rule. *See, e.g.,* Thorner v. Sony Computer Ent. Am. LLC, 669 F.3d 1362, 1365 (Fed. Cir. 2012), stating:

> The words of a claim are generally given their ordinary and customary meaning as understood by a person of ordinary skill in the art when read in the context of the specification and prosecution history. *See Phillips v. AWH Corp.*, 415 F.3d 1303, 1313 (Fed. Cir. 2005) (*en banc*). There are only two exceptions to this general rule: 1) when a patentee sets out a definition and acts as his own lexicographer, or 2) when the patentee disavows the full scope of a claim term either in the specification or during prosecution. *Vitronics Corp. v. Conceptronic, Inc.*, 90 F.3d 1576, 1580 (Fed. Cir. 1996).

See also Aventis Pharma S.A. v. Hospira, Inc., 675 F.3d 1324, 1330 (Fed. Cir. 2012) (reiterating *Thorner*'s "stringent standard for narrowing a claim term beyond its plain and ordinary meaning").

[177] *See* Bell Atl. Network Servs., Inc. v. Covad Commc'ns Group., Inc., 262 F.3d 1258, 1273 (Fed. Cir. 2001) (concluding that patentee "defined the [claim] term 'mode' by implication, through the term's consistent use throughout the [] patent specification").

narrowing the claims by reading in limitations from the written description.[178]

- Courts generally should not adopt a claim interpretation that would exclude the preferred embodiment of an invention, although rare exceptions have been recognized in which a patentee amended the claims during prosecution in such a manner as to exclude the preferred embodiment.[179]
- The principle of *claim differentiation* provides that the existence of a narrower dependent claim shows that the broader claim from which it depends is not so limited.[180] For example, consider the following example in which the patent's written description refers to widgets of a "primary color":

  Claim 1. A widget of a primary color.
  Claim 2. The widget of claim 1 wherein said primary color is blue.

The existence of dependent claim 2 shows that independent claim 1 includes blue widgets but is not limited to blue widgets — claim 1 also literally reads on red widgets and yellow widgets (based on the "ordinary meaning" of "primary color" as encompassing the colors blue, red, and yellow).[181]

[178] *See* Unique Concepts, Inc. v. Brown, 939 F.2d 1558, 1561-1563 (Fed. Cir. 1991).

[179] *See, e.g.,* Elekta Instrument S.A. v. O.U.R. Scientific Int'l, Inc., 214 F.3d 1302 (Fed. Cir. 2000).

[180] More broadly stated, the claim differentiation principle means that when a claim of a patent "does not contain a certain limitation and another claim [of that patent] does, that limitation cannot be read into the former claim in determining either validity or infringement." SRI Int'l v. Matsushita Elec. Corp., 775 F.2d 1107, 1122 (Fed. Cir. 1985) (*en banc*). There are limits, however. *See* O.I. Corp. v. Tekmar Co., 115 F.3d 1576, 1582 (Fed. Cir. 1997) (stating that "the doctrine [of claim differentiation] cannot alter a definition that is otherwise clear from the claim language, description, and prosecution history").

[181] A series of Federal Circuit decisions evidenced strong disagreement within the court concerning the relative persuasive weight due the claim differentiation principle as compared with disclosure set forth in a patent's written description and drawings. These decisions suggest that, despite the *en banc* resolution of other claim interpretation issues in the 2005 *Phillips* decision, a claim interpretation schism continues post-*Phillips*. *Compare* Arlington Indus., Inc. v. Bridgeport Fittings, Inc., 632 F.3d 1246, 1253-1256 (Fed. Cir. 2011) (Rader, C.J., joined by Moore, J.) (broadly interpreting "spring metal adaptor" of claimed electrical junction box fitting as simply formed from spring metal and not requiring a split or opening; relying *inter alia* on claim differentiation principle because the limitation "less than a complete circle" was added to independent claim 1 of parent application during its prosecution but not added to independent claim 22 of continuation application that issued as '050 patent in suit) *with* Retractable Techs., Inc. v. Becton, Dickinson and Co., 653 F.3d 1296, 1305 (Fed. Cir. 2011) (Lourie, J., joined by Plager, J.) (narrowly interpreting "body" of safety syringe as limited to one-piece construction because that construction was "required to tether the claims to what the specifications indicate the inventor actually invented"; stating that despite

presence of a "one-piece" limitation in dependent claims of patent in suit but not in its independent claims, "any presumption created by the doctrine of claim differentiation [is] 'overcome by a contrary construction dictated by the written description or prosecution history'") (quoting Seachange Int'l, Inc. v. C-COR, Inc., 413 F.3d 1361, 1369 (Fed. Cir. 2005)).

Notably, Judge Lourie, author of the majority opinion in *Retractable Techs.,* dissented in *Arlington Indus.,* and Judge Rader, author of the majority opinion in *Arlington Indus.,* dissented in *Retractable Techs. See Arlington Indus.,* 632 F.3d at 1258 (Lourie, J., concurring-in-part and dissenting-in-part) (stating that "[t]he bottom line of claim construction should be that the claims should not mean more than what the specification indicates, one way or another, the inventors invented"); *id.* at 1257 (stating that "[i]n colloquial terms, 'you should get what you disclose'"); *Retractable Techs.,* 653 F.3d at 1312 (Rader, C.J., dissenting-in-part) (stating that in *Phillips v. AWH Corp.,* 415 F.3d 1303, 1312 (Fed. Cir. 2005) (*en banc*), Federal Circuit recognized as "bedrock principle" that "the claims themselves, not the written description portion of the specification, define the invention"); *id.* (stating that claim differentiation principle is "'especially strong when the limitation in dispute is the only meaningful difference between an independent and dependent claim, and one party is urging that the limitation in the dependent claim should be read into the independent claim'") (quoting SunRace Roots Enter. Co., Ltd. v. SRAM Corp., 336 F.3d 1298, 1303 (Fed. Cir. 2003)).

The debate concerning the proper weight to be given the claim differentiation principle continued (without resolution) in *Marine Polymer Techs., Inc. v. HemCon, Inc.,* 672 F.3d 1350 (Fed. Cir. 2012) (*en banc*). The Federal Circuit in *Marine Polymer* split 5-5 on the claim interpretation issue, thus affirming the district court's interpretation. The claim interpretation dispute concerned the meaning of "biocompatible" for certain claimed "biocompatible" purified compositions of a naturally occurring polymer used to treat traumatic bleeding. Writing for a five-judge plurality, Judge Lourie admitted that accused infringer HemCon's claim construction arguments were "not baseless." *Marine Polymer,* 672 F.3d at 1359. Hemcon's arguments highlighted the inconsistency between the district court's narrow construction of "biocompatible" as permitting "*no* detectable biological reactivity as determined by biocompatibility tests," *id.* at 1356 (emphasis added), and dependent claims of the patent in suit that required non-zero scores on "elution" tests, one of four types of tests disclosed for testing biocompatibility. Even if "not baseless," however, Hemcon's arguments "essentially amount[ed] to a conflict between teachings in the specification and the doctrine of claim differentiation. As we have held, claim differentiation is 'not a hard and fast rule and will be overcome by a contrary construction dictated by the written description or prosecution history.'" *Marine Polymer,* 672 F.3d at 1359 (quoting Seachange Int'l, Inc. v. C-COR, Inc., 413 F.3d 1361, 1369 (Fed. Cir. 2005); citing also Laitram Corp. v. Rexnord, Inc., 939 F.2d 1533, 1538 (Fed. Cir. 1991) ("Claim differentiation is a guide, not a rigid rule.")).

Writing for the other five judges on the claim interpretation issue, Judge Dyk countered that "[i]f 'biocompatible' [as present in six independent claims] requires that there be no reactivity, but [six] dependent claims require slight or mild reactivity, they are nullified and become utterly meaningless.... Where a particular construction of an independent claim would nullify claims that depend from it, the doctrine of claim differentiation creates a presumption that such a construction is improper." *Marine Polymer,* 672 F.3d at 1368 (citing Liebel-Flarsheim Co. v. Medrad, Inc., 358 F.3d 898, 910 (Fed. Cir. 2004)).

C. Step Two: Comparing the Properly Interpreted Claims to the Accused Device

The second step of the patent infringement analysis requires that each limitation of the properly interpreted claim be met in the accused device, either literally or equivalently. Although referred to in some earlier decisions as the all-elements rule, this doctrine is more properly termed the all-limitations rule.[182] Infringement cannot be determined by comparing the claimed and accused devices as a whole; the analysis must be performed on a limitation-by-limitation level. Each limitation of a patent claim is material. If even a single limitation is not met in the accused device, there cannot be infringement. For example, if a patent claims "a widget comprising parts A, B, C, D, and E," and an accused widget incorporates parts A, B, C, and E, but lacks a part D (or an equivalent of part D), then the accused widget cannot infringe.

The all-limitations rule incorporates the two basic types of infringement recognized in U.S. patent law: (1) literal infringement and (2) infringement under the judicially created doctrine of equivalents. Each is discussed below.

1. Literal Infringement

Literal infringement is found where the accused subject matter falls precisely within the express boundaries of the claim. For example, if a claim recites

> 1. A composition of matter comprising 20-30 percent component X by weight.

and the accused composition includes 25 percent component X, then claim 1 is literally infringed.[183] If the accused composition includes only 15 percent X, however, claim 1 is not literally infringed.[184]

[182]Patent attorneys and Federal Circuit judges sometimes use the words "element" and "limitation" interchangeably. The preferred usage is to speak of limitations of a patent claim and elements of an accused device. *See* Dawn Equip. Co. v. Kentucky Farms Inc., 140 F.3d 1009, 1014 n.1 (Fed. Cir. 1998); Perkin-Elmer Corp. v. Westinghouse Elec. Corp., 822 F.2d 1528, 1533 n.9 (Fed. Cir. 1987).

[183]Note here that because the claim uses an open "comprising" transition, the accused composition may include anything else besides component X but nevertheless still literally infringe.

[184]One might still consider whether the accused composition having 15 percent X infringes under the doctrine of equivalents, although some Federal Circuit decisions applying a theory of "vitiation" of claim limitations would answer in the negative. The court's vitiation jurisprudence remains unsettled. *See* Section D.5, *infra*.

One might expect instances of literal infringement to be relatively rare, assuming that patent claims provide clear, advance notice to competitors of what is and is not permissible imitation. Competitors could reasonably be expected to read the claims and plan their activities accordingly so as to avoid literal infringement. As the Supreme Court has recognized, "[o]utright and forthright duplication is a dull and very rare type of infringement."[185]

In practice, instances of literal infringement are quite common. This follows from the uncertainty of claim interpretation, that is, the prelitigation ambiguity of the literal scope of the claims. Despite the aspirational goal that patent claims should provide clear, advance notice of the literal scope of the patentee's exclusionary right, as well as the statutory presumption that the claims of an issued patent comply with the definiteness requirement of 35 U.S.C. §112(b) (eff. Sept. 16, 2012), the meaning of one or more terms in the allegedly infringed claim(s) is hotly disputed in practically every patent infringement litigation. An accused infringer may be held to literally infringe a claim that it intended to avoid when that claim is interpreted broadly enough in later litigation to literally read on the accused device. Even technology arising after the patent in suit may literally infringe, if the claims are construed broadly enough (and, of course, are still valid under that broad construction).[186]

2. Infringement Under the Doctrine of Equivalents

United States patent law also recognizes the possibility of "nonliteral" or "nontextual" infringement under the doctrine of equivalents.[187] Notably, the doctrine of equivalents is entirely judge-made

[185]Graver Tank & Mfg. Co. v. Linde Air Prods. Co., 339 U.S. 605, 607 (1950).

[186]*See* Innogenetics, N.V. v. Abbott Labs., 512 F.3d 1363, 1371-1372 (Fed. Cir. 2008). The *Innogenetics* court rejected Abbott's argument that it did not literally infringe because the "Realtime PCR" utilized in Abbott's accused genotyping assay kits was not known to the ordinary artisan when Innogenetics filed the application leading to its '704 patent in suit. *See id.* In so holding the court relied on its earlier decision in *SuperGuide Corp. v. DirecTV Enters., Inc.*, 358 F.3d 870 (Fed. Cir. 2004), in which it found that the claim limitation "regularly received television signals" was broad enough to literally encompass digital signals, even though no televisions capable of receiving digital signals existed at the time that SuperGuide filed its patent application. *See id.* at 878-880; *Innogenetics*, 512 F.3d at 1371-1372. Note, however, that functional claim limitations drafted in the means-plus-function (MPF) format of 35 U.S.C. §112(f) (eff. Sept. 16, 2012) are treated more narrowly than the non-MPF claim limitations at issue in *Innogenetics* and *SuperGuide*. *See* Al-Site Corp. v. VSI Int'l, Inc., 174 F.3d 1308, 1320 (Fed. Cir. 1999) (holding that "[a]n equivalent structure or act under §112 cannot embrace technology developed after the issuance of the patent because the literal meaning of a claim is fixed upon its issuance").

[187]The proper name of this doctrine is the doctrine of *equivalents,* not the doctrine of *equivalence.*

law; it does not appear in the Patent Act.[188] The doctrine is of long standing, however; "[f]ew propositions of patent law have been so consistently sustained by the Supreme Court as the doctrine of equivalents."[189] Although the Supreme Court has repeatedly reaffirmed the doctrine's viability, it has also pointedly recognized that "Congress can legislate the doctrine of equivalents out of existence any time it chooses."[190]

a. Historical Origins

The doctrine of equivalents has its U.S. genesis in early Supreme Court patent cases such as *Winans v. Denmead.*[191] There the Court found that a patent claiming the configuration of a railroad coal car having a cylindrical, cone-like shape was infringed by an accused car shaped in cross-section like an octagon. *Winans* does not expressly refer to a doctrine of equivalents, but such a doctrine is implied in the result of the case.

Claiming practice at the time of *Winans* (i.e., prior to the Patent Act of 1870) was much more of a **central claiming** regime than the **peripheral claiming** system used today in the United States. Under the central claiming regime, a claim recited the "preferred embodiment" of the invention but was deemed as a matter of law to include all equivalents to (i.e., substantially similar copies of) that preferred embodiment.[192] The *Winans* Court recognized that

[188] The doctrine of equivalents should not be confused with the related but separate notion of *statutory* equivalency under 35 U.S.C. §112(f) (eff. Sept. 16, 2012) (referred to pre-America Invents Act of 2011 as "§112, ¶6"). These statutory equivalents are part of the *literal* scope of an MPF claim. *See supra* Chapter 2 ("Patent Claims"); Pennwalt Corp. v. Durand-Wayland, Inc., 833 F.2d 931, 934 (Fed. Cir. 1987) (*en banc*) (explaining that "[s]ection 112, paragraph 6, plays no role in determining whether an equivalent function is performed by the accused device under the doctrine of equivalents").

[189] Eli Lilly and Co. v. Hospira, Inc., 933 F.3d 1320, 1329 (Fed. Cir. 2019) (Lourie, J.) (citing Festo Corp. v. Shoketsu Kinzoku Kogyo Kabushiki Co., 535 U.S. 722, 733 (2002) ("[E]quivalents remain a firmly entrenched part of the settled rights protected by the patent."); Warner-Jenkinson Co. v. Hilton Davis Chem. Co., 520 U.S. 17, 40 (1997) ("[W]e adhere to the doctrine of equivalents."); Graver Tank & Mfg. Co. v. Linde Air Prods. Co., 339 U.S. 605, 608 (1950) ("Originating almost a century ago in the case of *Winans v. Denmead*, [56 U.S. 330, 15 How. 330, 14 L. Ed. 717 (1853)] . . . [the doctrine of equivalents] has been consistently applied by this Court and the lower federal courts, and continues today ready and available for utilization when the proper circumstances for its application arise.")).

[190] Warner-Jenkinson Co. v. Hilton Davis Chem. Co., 520 U.S. 17, 28 (1997).

[191] 56 U.S. 330 (1853).

[192] *Cf. Warner-Jenkinson,* 520 U.S. at 27 n.4 (characterizing central claiming as "describing the core principles of the invention" and peripheral claiming as "describing the outer boundaries of the invention").

> [t]he exclusive right to the thing patented is not secured, if the public are at liberty to make substantial copies of it, varying its form or proportions. And, therefore, the patentee, having described his invention, and shown its principles, and claimed it in that form which most perfectly embodies it, is, in contemplation of law, deemed to claim every form in which his invention may be copied, unless he manifests an intention to disclaim some of those forms.[193]

Thus, the central claiming regime in effect at the time of *Winans* recognized that the patentee's invention was not truly protected unless the patent prohibited not only the unauthorized making of *identical* copies, but also the making of "substantial" copies thereof. As the U.S. patent system eventually transitioned from central claiming to the peripheral claiming system used today, the underlying goal of protecting the patentee to the full extent of her contribution has been maintained and resurrected, so to speak, in the guise of the judicially recognized doctrine of equivalents.

b. Policy Rationales

As the Court in *Graver Tank & Mfg. Co. v. Linde Air Prods. Co.*[194] characterized it, the essential thrust of the doctrine of equivalents is that "one may not practice a fraud on a patent."[195] The doctrine of equivalents is a judicial response to the practical reality that if a patent can be avoided by copying the claimed invention while making a minor, insubstantial change of just enough scope to take the copied matter outside of the literal boundaries of the claim, the right to exclude that the patent bestows will not be worth very much. If the value of a patent is lessened by an inability to stop nonliteral copyists, the economic incentive to innovate that the patent represents is likewise diminished and society suffers a resulting impoverishment of new inventions.

In addition to this economic/fairness rationale, the doctrine of equivalents also serves as an important linguistic safety valve. Judicial recognition of the doctrine of equivalents reflects that words are not always the optimal medium for conveying inventive concepts. Many inventions are best embodied in physical prototypes, mechanical drawings, molecular modeling, or other nonlingual scientific and technical media. Particularly when dealing with "pioneer" inventions involving state-of-the-art technology for which there may not yet exist a recognized, well-established vocabulary, the doctrine of equivalents

[193] *Winans,* 56 U.S. at 343.
[194] 339 U.S. 605 (1950).
[195] *Id.* at 608.

is an essential tool for conveying to the patent owner the full benefit of her invention.[196]

c. *Tension with the Notice Function of Claims*

These rationales in support of the doctrine of equivalents admittedly conflict with the principle that claims are intended to provide clear, advance notice to competitors of the scope of the patentee's right to exclude.[197] As the Supreme Court summed it up, "[a] patent holder should know what he owns, and the public should know what he does not."[198] A certain tension arises when courts find liability under the doctrine of equivalents, because they are extending the right to exclude beyond that denoted by the literal boundaries of the patent's claims.[199] How useful is the advance "notice" provided by patent claims if we essentially ignore it for equitable reasons in applying the doctrine of equivalents? This undeniable tension has been succinctly described as the "fair protection–certainty conundrum."[200]

[196]As expressed in a classic passage from *Autogiro Co. of Am. v. United States,* 384 F.2d 391, 397 (Ct. Cl. 1967):

> An invention exists most importantly as a tangible structure or a series of drawings. A verbal portrayal is usually an afterthought written to satisfy the requirements of patent law. This conversion of machine to words allows for unintended idea gaps which cannot be satisfactorily filled. Often the invention is novel and words do not exist to describe it. The dictionary does not always keep abreast of the inventor. It cannot. Things are not made for the sake of words, but words for things.

[197]*See* Festo Corp. v. Shoketsu Kinzoku Kogyo Kabushiki Co., 535 U.S. 722, 727 (2002) (stating that "we appreciate[ ] that by extending protection beyond the literal terms in a patent the doctrine of equivalents can create substantial uncertainty about where the patent monopoly ends. If the range of equivalents is unclear, competitors may be unable to determine what is a permitted alternative to a patented invention and what is an infringing equivalent.") (citations omitted).

[198]*Id.* at 731.

[199]*See* Wilson Sporting Goods Co. v. David Geoffrey & Assocs., 904 F.2d 677 (Fed. Cir. 1990) (Rich, J.):

> To say that the doctrine of equivalents extends or enlarges the *claims* is a contradiction in terms. The claims — i.e., the scope of patent protection as *defined* by the claims — remain the same and application of the doctrine *expands the right to exclude* to "equivalents" of what is claimed. The doctrine of equivalents, by definition, involves going beyond any permissible interpretation of the claim language; i.e., it involves determining whether the accused product is "equivalent" to what is described by the claim language.

Id. at 684 (emphases in original).

[200]Donald S. Chisum, *The Scope of Protection for Patents After the Supreme Court's* Warner-Jenkinson *Decision: The Fair Protection–Certainty Conundrum,* 14 SANTA CLARA COMPUTER & HIGH TECH. L.J. 1, 6 (1998).

d. All-Limitations Rule

In *Warner-Jenkinson Co. v. Hilton Davis Chem. Co.,*[201] the Supreme Court instructed that we can minimize the fair protection–certainty conundrum by vigilant application of the all-elements rule, which requires that the doctrine of equivalents be applied on a claim limitation-by-limitation basis rather than to the "invention as a whole."[202] The Court stated:

> Each element contained in a patent claim is deemed material to defining the scope of the patented invention, and thus the doctrine of equivalents must be applied to individual elements of the claim, not to the invention as a whole. It is important to ensure that the application of the doctrine, even as to an individual element, is not allowed such broad play as to effectively eliminate that element in its entirety.[203]

For example, if a patent claim recites "a widget comprising lever A, pulley B, and spring C," the doctrine of equivalents must be separately applied to determine if (1) lever A of the claimed invention is equivalently met in the accused device; (2) if pulley B of the claimed invention is equivalently met in the accused device; and (3) if spring C of the claimed invention is equivalently met in the accused device. If any of these three limitations is not met equivalently (or literally), there can be no infringement.

e. What Is a Limitation?

Applying the all-limitations rule requires that we first identify each limitation of a claim. Often the task of determining what portion of a patent claim represents a discrete limitation (also sometimes referred to as an element)[204] is not so straightforward. The answer will depend on the level of generality that the court reviewing the matter chooses to adopt.

For example, consider the interpretation of a patent claim to a widget "having a plastic tube." The district court may consider "plastic" and "tube" to be two separate limitations, such that each limitation would separately need to be met in the accused device in order to find infringement. Thus, if the accused device was a widget that used a steel pipe rather than a plastic tube, the fact finder in the second step

[201]520 U.S. 17 (1997).

[202]*See id.* at 29.

[203]*Id.*

[204]The preferred usage is to speak of limitations of a patent claim and elements of an accused device. *See* Dawn Equip. Co. v. Kentucky Farms Inc., 140 F.3d 1009, 1014 n.1 (Fed. Cir. 1998); Perkin-Elmer Corp. v. Westinghouse Elec. Corp., 822 F.2d 1528, 1533 n.9 (Fed. Cir. 1987).

of the infringement analysis (whether judge or jury) would need to separately determine (1) whether the steel used in the accused widget's pipe is insubstantially different from the plastic of the claimed tube, and (2) whether the pipe of the accused widget is insubstantially different from the claimed tube. With respect to question (1) the fact finder might evaluate the insubstantiality of the differences by asking whether steel performs the same function in the accused widget's pipe as plastic does in the claimed tube, in substantially the same way, to achieve substantially the same result. Known interchangeability of steel and plastic in widgets also might be relevant to the analysis. For question (2) the fact finder might evaluate the insubstantiality of the differences by asking whether a pipe performs the same function in the accused widget as a tube does in the claimed widget, in substantially the same way, to achieve substantially the same result. Known interchangeability of pipes and tubes in widgets also might be relevant.

Alternatively, the district court interpreting the claim of this example may adopt a higher level of generality and choose to treat the phrase "plastic tube" as one single limitation, rather than two separate limitations. In that case the fact finder would need to determine whether the accused widget's steel pipe is insubstantially different from the claimed widget's plastic tube. In order to analyze the extent of that difference, the fact finder might ask whether the steel pipe performs the same function in the accused widget as the plastic tube does in the claimed widget, in substantially the same way, to achieve substantially the same result. Known interchangeability of steel pipes and plastic tubes in widgets also might be relevant.

As this example attempts to illustrate, the level of generality versus specificity that the district court applies when enumerating the individual limitations of a claim can have a very real impact on the determination of technologic equivalency in the second step of the infringement analysis. Generally speaking, an accused infringer will attempt to establish the greatest possible number of limitations, making more burdensome the patentee's job of having to establish insubstantial differences with respect to each such limitation. In contrast, a patentee generally will seek to minimize the number of limitations so as to lessen her burden.

Determining what the limitations are in a patent claim to biotechnological subject matter may represent an even greater challenge. For example, consider a claim reciting

> a purified, isolated DNA molecule comprising the nucleotide sequence AAGGTCAGGTCA.[205]

[205]For explanation of basic biotechnological terminology, *see supra* Chapter 7 ("Potentially Patentable Subject Matter (35 U.S.C. §101)") at Section D.2 ("Purified Forms of Natural Products").

What are the pertinent limitations of this claim? Is a single nucleotide, A (the base adenine), the relevant limitation to be met in the accused molecule? Or is the pertinent limitation in this example a codon of three nucleotides, AAG (which together form the amino acid lysine)? Or is it an even longer stretch of the recited nucleotide sequence (perhaps the entirety of AAGGTCAGGTCA)? Federal Circuit decisions have not yet clearly answered these questions; the answers are likely to be case-specific.

A foundational Federal Circuit decision dealing with the identification of claim limitations is *Corning Glass Works v. Sumitomo Elec. USA Inc.*[206] Corning's patent in suit was directed to an optical waveguide fiber useful for long-distance telephone transmissions. The fiber was formed from an inner core of fused silica surrounded by an outer cladding; the invention required that the refractive index (RI) of the core be greater than the RI of the cladding. The Corning inventors achieved this RI differential by adding a positive dopant to the core material to increase its RI. Claim 1 recited:

> 1. An optical waveguide comprising
> (a) a cladding layer formed of a material selected from the group consisting of pure fused silica and fused silica to which a dopant material on at least an elemental basis has been added, and
> (b) a core formed of fused silica to which a dopant material on at least an elemental basis has been added to a degree in excess of that of the cladding layer so that the index of refraction thereof is of a value greater than the index of refraction of said cladding layer, said core being formed of at least 85 percent by weight of fused silica and an effective amount up to 15 percent by weight of said dopant material.

In the accused Sumitomo fiber, the RI differential was achieved not by adding a positive dopant to the core but rather by adding a negative dopant to the cladding. Thus, the parties' dispute centered on whether the language of paragraph (b) of claim 1 was met by the accused device (there being no dispute that the language of paragraph (a) was literally met). The Federal Circuit parsed the language of paragraph (b) into discrete limitations. The accused Sumitomo fibers literally met the limitation that the fiber be composed of "a core formed of fused silica," as well as the limitation that "the index of refraction [of the core] is of a value greater than the index of refraction of said cladding layer."

The infringement dispute thus centered on the words of the claim following the initial "core" limitation, namely, the limitation "to which a dopant material . . . has been added to a degree in excess of that of the cladding layer." Sumitomo argued that its fibers did not meet this

[206]868 F.2d 1251 (Fed. Cir. 1989).

language either literally or equivalently because it did not add any dopant to the core, nor did it add to the core anything equivalent to a dopant.

The Federal Circuit rejected Sumitomo's approach, distinguishing between "components" and "limitations":

> Sumitomo's analysis is faulty in that it would require equivalency in components, that is, the substitution of something in the core for the absent dopant. However, the determination of equivalency is not subject to such a rigid formula. *An equivalent must be found for every limitation of the claim somewhere in an accused device, but not necessarily in a corresponding component, although that is generally the case.*[207]

The Federal Circuit accordingly upheld the district court's finding of infringement under the doctrine of equivalents. Analyzing the equivalency of the disputed limitation, the district court had properly found that "the use of . . . a [negative] dopant in the cladding . . . performs substantially the same function in substantially the same way as the use of a [positive] dopant in the core to produce the same result of creating the refractive index differential between the core and cladding of the fiber which is necessary for the fiber to function as an optical waveguide."[208]

f. Determining Technologic Equivalence

If the doctrine of equivalents applies in a given case to a particular claim limitation, what rules are used to determine whether the limitation is equivalently met in the accused device? This determination is considered a question of fact rather than law.[209] Accordingly, how does the fact finder (whether judge or jury) decide whether an element of the accused device is technologically equivalent to the pertinent claim limitation?

[207] *Id.* at 1259 (emphasis added).

[208] *Id.* at 1260.

[209] *See* Graver Tank & Mfg. Co. v. Linde Air Prods. Co., 339 U.S. 605 (1950):

> A finding of equivalence is a determination of fact. Proof can be made in any form: through testimony of experts or others versed in the technology; by documents, including texts and treatises; and, of course, by the disclosures of the prior art. Like any other issue of fact, final determination requires a balancing of credibility, persuasiveness and weight of evidence. It is to be decided by the trial court and that court's decision, under general principles of appellate review, should not be disturbed unless clearly erroneous. Particularly is this so in a field where so much depends upon familiarity with specific scientific problems and principles not usually contained in the general storehouse of knowledge and experience.

Id. at 609-610.

C. Step Two: Comparing the Properly Interpreted Claims

The Supreme Court in *Sanitary Refrigerator Co. v. Winters*[210] indicated that an accused device infringes under the doctrine of equivalents "if it performs substantially the same function in substantially the same way to obtain the same result."[211] This statement sets forth the classic test for infringement under the doctrine of equivalents, which patent attorneys variously refer to as the "function/way/result," "FWR," "triple identity," or "tripartite" test.[212] More recently, the Federal Circuit explained that function/way/result is merely one way of determining the ultimate equivalency question: are the differences between the claimed invention and the accused device merely "insubstantial"?[213] If so, the accused device may be found to infringe under the doctrine of equivalents.

While under current law the degree of substantiality of the differences is the overarching test for infringement under the doctrine of equivalents, it is possible that the Federal Circuit will further refine the inquiry as the court gains experience in applying it to particular technologies. As the Supreme Court in *Warner-Jenkinson* recognized, "[d]ifferent linguistic frameworks may be more suitable to different

[210]280 U.S. 30 (1929).

[211]*Id.* at 42 (citation omitted).

[212]The Supreme Court in *Graver Tank* gave this further guidance on how to apply the function/way/result inquiry:

> What constitutes equivalency must be determined against the context of the patent, the prior art, and the particular circumstances of the case. Equivalence, in the patent law, is not the prisoner of a formula and is not an absolute to be considered in a vacuum. It does not require complete identity for every purpose and in every respect. In determining equivalents, things equal to the same thing may not be equal to each other and, by the same token, things for most purposes different may sometimes be equivalents. Consideration must be given to the purpose for which an ingredient is used in a patent, the qualities it has when combined with the other ingredients, and the function which it is intended to perform. An important factor is whether persons reasonably skilled in the art would have known of the interchangeability of an ingredient not contained in the patent with one that was.

Graver Tank, 339 U.S. at 609. The Federal Circuit has emphasized the "known interchangeability" factor of *Graver* as particularly important. *See* Vulcan Eng'g Co. v. FATA Aluminum, Inc., 278 F.3d 1366, 1374 (Fed. Cir. 2002); Interactive Pictures Corp. v. Infinite Pictures, Inc., 274 F.3d 1371, 1383 (Fed. Cir. 2001); Overhead Door Corp. v. Chamberlain Group, Inc., 194 F.3d 1261, 1270 (Fed. Cir. 1999).

[213]Hilton Davis Chem. Co. v. Warner-Jenkinson Co., 62 F.3d 1512, 1517-1518 (Fed. Cir. 1995) (*en banc*). *See also Graver Tank,* 339 U.S. at 610 (characterizing inquiry as to whether the accused infringer's variation, "under the circumstances of this case, and in view of the technology and the prior art, is a change of such substance as to make the doctrine of equivalents inapplicable; or conversely, whether under the circumstances the change was so *insubstantial* that the trial court's invocation of the doctrine of equivalents was justified") (emphasis added).

cases, depending on their particular facts."[214] For example, the classic function/way/result inquiry seems best suited for mechanical inventions but often is not very helpful with respect to biotechnological subject matter.[215] The *Warner-Jenkinson* Court refused to engage in "micromanaging the Federal Circuit's particular word choice for analyzing equivalence,"[216] and chose to leave such decisions up to the Circuit's "sound judgment in this area of its special expertise."[217]

[214]Warner-Jenkinson Co. v. Hilton Davis Chem. Co., 520 U.S. 17, 40 (1997).

[215]To see why this is so, consider a claim to "an isolated and purified DNA molecule comprising the nucleotide sequence AAGTCTGGTCCA." Even if we assume that the single nucleotide A is the pertinent limitation, what is the function of that limitation? In what way is that function performed? What is the result?

[216]*Warner-Jenkinson,* 520 U.S. at 40.

[217]*Id.* Despite the Supreme Court's suggestion that the Federal Circuit might customize different linguistic frameworks to determine the equivalency of different types of technology, the Circuit generally has not departed from the classic "function"/ "way"/"result" test. In most cases, the "way" prong is dispositive. For example, the Circuit in *Akzo Nobel Coatings, Inc. v. Dow Chem. Co.,* No. 2015-1331, 2016 WL 363443 (Fed. Cir. Jan. 29, 2016) affirmed a district court's grant of summary judgment that Dow Chemical did not infringe the claims of Akzo Nobel Coatings' U.S. Patent 6,767,956 ('956 patent") either literally or under the doctrine of equivalents. Akzo's '956 patent was directed to directed to a chemical process — an extrusion process that generated low viscosity aqueous polymer dispersions. The appellate court concluded that patentee Akzo failed to establish a genuine issue of material fact as to whether Dow's accused process operated in substantially the same "way," based primarily on the inadequacy of the testimony of the patentee's expert, Dr. Mount:

> Akzo introduced Dr. Mount's declaration as support [of equivalency]. In the last paragraph of a fifty-one paragraph declaration, Dr. Mount states:
>
> > Dow's . . . piping and heat exchangers perform the same function (maintain the pressure) and achieve the same result (maintaining sufficient pressure to prevent boiling of the aqueous medium) in substantially the same way (by collecting the dispersed material in a contained volume) as the vessel used by the inventors in Examples 2 and 3 of the ['956] patent. . . .
>
> Dr. Mount's discussion of the doctrine of equivalents is broad and scant. Telemac *Cellular Corp. v. Topp Telecom, Inc.,* 247 F.3d 1316, 1329 (Fed. Cir. 2001) ("Broad conclusory statements offered by Telemac's expert are not evidence and are not sufficient to establish a genuine issue of material fact."). Nevertheless, what truly undermines Akzo's reliance on the above-quoted statement is the statement's *failure to articulate how Dow's accused process operates in substantially the same way.* Dr. Mount states that Dow's process operates "in substantially the same way (by collecting the disperse material in a contained volume)," yet he fails to articulate which construction of "collecting" he invokes, much less articulate how the differences between the two processes are insubstantial. Such ambiguity and generality cannot create a genuine issue of material fact.

Akzo Nobel Coatings, 2016 WL 363443, at *7 (record citations omitted) (emphasis added).

g. *Reverse Doctrine of Equivalents*

The "wholesome realism"[218] of the doctrine of equivalents, as the Supreme Court in *Graver Tank* rather euphemistically termed it, is that the doctrine, which is almost always asserted in its conventional (or "forward") formulation to benefit a patent owner by expanding the scope of exclusive rights beyond those literally encompassed by the patent claims, also can operate (at least theoretically) in "reverse" to assist an accused infringer.

The reverse doctrine of equivalents acts as a defense to a charge of literal infringement. The doctrine absolves an accused infringer from infringement liability where the accused device, although literally falling within the scope of the asserted patent claim, is so far changed in principle from the claimed invention that a finding of liability cannot be justified as a policy matter.[219] The reverse doctrine of equivalents is "equitably applied based upon underlying questions of fact."[220] The doctrine applies "when the accused infringer proves that, despite the asserted claims literally reading on the accused device, 'it has been so changed that it is no longer the same invention.' "[221]

Despite being the topic of favorable academic attention,[222] the reverse doctrine of equivalents has rarely been applied by the courts

[218] *Graver Tank,* 339 U.S. at 608 (stating that "[t]he wholesome realism of this doctrine is not always applied in favor of a patentee but is sometimes used against him").

[219] *See id.* at 608-609; Westinghouse v. Boyden Power Brake Co., 170 U.S. 537, 568 (1898).

[220] *See* Amgen, Inc. v. Hoechst Marion Roussel, Inc., 314 F.3d 1313, 1351 (Fed. Cir. 2003) (citing Scripps Clinic & Res. Found. v. Genentech, Inc., 927 F.2d 1565, 1581 (Fed. Cir. 1991)).

[221] *Id.* (quoting Del Mar Avionics, Inc. v. Quinton Instrument Co., 836 F.2d 1320, 1325 (Fed. Cir. 1987)).

[222] *See* Robert P. Merges & Richard R. Nelson, *On the Complex Economics of Patent Scope,* 90 Colum. L. Rev. 839, 862-868 (1990) (advocating reverse doctrine of equivalents as mechanism to limit patent scope in face of significant technological improvement by accused infringer). For more recent commentary, *see* Samuel F. Ernst, *The Lost Precedent of the Reverse Doctrine of Equivalents*, 18 Vand. J. Ent. & Tech. L. 467 (2016). The abstract of Ernst's article states in part:

> [T]here is a common law tool to protect innovation from the patent thicket lying right under our noses: the reverse doctrine of equivalents. Properly applied, this judge-made doctrine can be used to excuse infringement on a case-by-case basis if the court determines that the accused product is substantially superior to the patented invention, despite proof of literal infringement. Unfortunately, the reverse doctrine is disfavored by the Court of Appeals for the Federal Circuit and therefore rarely applied. It was not always so. This article is the first comprehensive study of published opinions applying the reverse doctrine of equivalents to excuse infringement between 1898, when the Supreme Court established the doctrine, and the 1982 creation of the Federal Circuit. This "lost precedent" reveals a flexible doctrine that takes into account the technological and commercial superiority of the accused product to any embodiment of the patented invention made by the patent-holder. An invigorated reverse doctrine of equivalents

to excuse liability.[223] For example, in *Roche Palo Alto LLC v. Apotex, Inc.*, the Federal Circuit observed that application of the doctrine is "rare[]" and emphasized that the Federal Circuit "has never affirmed a finding of non-infringement under the reverse doctrine of equivalents."[224]

D. Legal Limitations on the Doctrine of Equivalents

1. Overview

The Supreme Court pointed out in the very important footnote 8 of its 1997 *Warner-Jenkinson* decision that a patentee may not avail itself of the doctrine of equivalents if certain legal limitations preclude it from doing so.[225] If these limitations are triggered, an infringement

---

could therefore serve to protect true innovations from uncommercialized patents on a case-by-case basis, without the potential harm to the innovation incentive that prospective patent legislation might cause.

[223]*See* Mark A. Lemley, *The Economics of Improvement in Intellectual Property Law,* 75 Tex. L. Rev. 989, 1011 (1997). *See also Amgen,* 314 F.3d at 1351-1352 (rejecting defense of noninfringement based on reverse doctrine of equivalents where court was "not persuaded by [accused infringer] TKT that this is a case where equity commands a determination of non-infringement despite its product literally falling within the scope of the asserted claims").

[224]531 F.3d 1372, 1378 (Fed. Cir. 2008). The Federal Circuit has relied on the reverse doctrine of equivalents, however, to vacate a district court's grant of summary judgment of infringement. *See* Scripps Clinic & Res. Found. v. Genentech, Inc., 927 F.2d 1565, 1581 (Fed. Cir. 1991) (finding that accused infringer Genentech had raised genuine issues of scientific and evidentiary fact requiring trial to determine whether Genentech's recombinantly produced version of Factor VIII:C blood-clotting protein literally infringed Scripps' broadly interpreted product patent claim to Factor VIII:C, or instead was so far changed in principle from claimed invention as to be excused from liability under the reverse doctrine of equivalents).

[225]*See* Warner-Jenkinson Co. v. Hilton Davis Chem. Co., 520 U.S. 17, 39 n.8 (1997). The Federal Circuit has enumerated the judicially-recognized limitations on the doctrine of equivalents as follows:

> [C]ourts have placed important limitations on a patentee's ability to assert infringement under the doctrine of equivalents. *See, e.g., Festo VIII* [Festo Corp. v. Shoketsu Kinzoku Kogyo Kabushiki Co., 535 U.S. 722 (2002)], 535 U.S. at 737-41, 122 S. Ct. 1831 (prosecution history estoppel); *Warner-Jenkinson* [Warner-Jenkinson Co. v. Hilton Davis Chem. Co., 520 U.S. 17 (1997)], 520 U.S. at 39 n.8, 117 S. Ct. 1040 ("[A] theory of equivalence [cannot] entirely vitiate a particular claim element. . . ."); Graver Tank [Graver Tank & Mfg. Co. v. Linde Air Prods. Co., 339 U.S. 605 (1950)], 339 U.S. at 608, 70 S. Ct. 854 (accused equivalent cannot differ substantially from the claimed invention); Johnson & Johnston Assocs. Inc. v. R.E. Serv. Co., 285 F.3d 1046, 1054 (Fed. Cir. 2002) (*en banc*) (subject matter disclosed but not claimed is dedicated to the public) (citing

case may be resolved on summary judgment and the fact question of technologic equivalency may never reach the fact finder.

The primary legal limitations on the doctrine of equivalents that Federal Circuit case law has identified thus far include the following:

- **Prosecution history estoppel:** The doctrine of prosecution history estoppel (PHE) provides that a patentee may not seek to ensnare under the doctrine of equivalents any subject matter that it surrendered in order to obtain the patent from the USPTO. Prosecution history estoppel is the most frequently encountered legal limitation on the doctrine of equivalents.[226]
- **All-limitations rule:** If even a single claim limitation is not met, either literally or equivalently, in the accused device, there is no infringement. Every limitation of a claim is considered material and must be met in the accused device in order to have infringement.
- **Vitiation of a claim limitation:** The doctrine of equivalents must not be applied so broadly as to entirely vitiate or effectively eliminate a particular claim limitation.[227]
- **Prior art:** A patentee cannot obtain coverage through the doctrine of equivalents over subject matter that it could not have obtained from the USPTO in the first instance. In short, one who merely "practices the prior art" does not infringe under the doctrine of equivalents.[228]
- **Dedication to the public:** The patentee may not attempt to cover through the doctrine of equivalents any subject matter that it disclosed but did not claim in its patent application, thereby avoiding USPTO examination of that subject matter.[229]
- **Foreseeability:** A patentee may not encompass through the doctrine of equivalents reasonably foreseeable alterations to claimed structure, when it had an opportunity to negotiate broader claim coverage in the USPTO but did not do so.[230]

Maxwell v. J. Baker, Inc., 86 F.3d 1098 (Fed. Cir. 1996)); Wilson Sporting Goods Co. v. David Geoffrey & Assocs., 904 F.2d 677, 683 (Fed. Cir. 1990) ("[T]he asserted scope of equivalency [cannot] encompass the prior art. . . ." (Rich, J.) (citations omitted)).

Eli Lilly and Co. v. Hospira, Inc., 933 F.3d 1320, 1330 (Fed. Cir. 2019) (Lourie, J.).

[226]*See* Section D.2, *infra*.

[227]*See* Section D.5, *infra*.

[228]The leading case here is *Wilson Sporting Goods Co. v. David Geoffrey & Assocs.*, 904 F.2d 677, 683 (Fed. Cir. 1990). For further discussion, *see* Section D.3, *infra*. Note, however, that the Federal Circuit has rejected the applicability of a "practicing the prior art" defense to allegations of *literal* infringement. *See* Tate Access Floors, Inc. v. Interface Arch. Res., Inc., 279 F.3d 1357, 1365-1366 (Fed. Cir. 2002).

[229]*See* Section D.4, *infra*.

[230]*See* Sage Prods., Inc. v. Devon Indus., Inc., 126 F.3d 1420, 1425 (Fed. Cir. 1997).

The most frequently encountered of these limitations are discussed in further detail below.

2. Prosecution History Estoppel

a. Definition

Like the doctrine of equivalents, the doctrine of prosecution history estoppel is judge-made law. The most commonly asserted legal limitation on the doctrine of equivalents, prosecution history estoppel is based on the notion that if a patent applicant surrendered certain subject matter in the USPTO in order to obtain its patent (e.g., by narrowing the scope of a claim through amendment in order to distinguish subject matter disclosed in a cited prior art reference), it cannot thereafter rely on the doctrine of equivalents to obtain exclusionary rights over that same subject matter. By reading the patent and its prosecution history in order to determine what the patentee surrendered, competitors should be provided a reasonable degree of certainty that so long as they operate within the confines of the surrendered subject matter, they will not be found to infringe under the doctrine of equivalents.

The most common form of prosecution history estoppel results from narrowing amendments made to the patent application claims during prosecution. For example, the patent allegedly infringed in *Dixie USA, Inc. v. Infab Corp.*[231] was directed to a type of plastic "stretcher" for use in transporting hospital patients. Claim 1 of the issued patent recited the following:

> A patient shifting aid comprising:
>
> a plastic slab having rounded corners forming a rectangular support surface upon which a patient is adapted [sic] to be placed and having sufficient thickness to support the weight of a patient placed thereon while enabling the obtaining of x-rays through the plastic slab to determine the extent of patient injury without the necessity of additional shifting of the patient;
>
> a plurality of openings in said slab and disposed adjacent the periphery of said support surface providing means for gripping the plastic slab to effect sliding movement of the plastic slab and the patient support [sic, supported] thereon;
>
> *said plurality of openings comprising generally rectangular openings having rounded corners and rounded openings for grasping the slab for moving a patient....*[232]

[231] 927 F.2d 584 (Fed. Cir. 1991).
[232] *Id.* at 585-586 (emphasis added).

Notably, the corresponding claims of the patent application as originally filed did *not* limit the nature of the openings. Rather, the claims merely required that the stretcher comprise "a plurality of openings in said slab and disposed adjacent the periphery of said support surface providing means for gripping the plastic slab to effect sliding movement of the plastic slab and the patient support [sic, supported] thereon."[233]

In due course the USPTO rejected the claims as obvious under 35 U.S.C. §103 in view of several prior art references. The patent applicant responded by amending the claims to add the "rectangular openings" and "rounded openings" limitation (emphasized above). In remarks accompanying this amendment, the applicant contended that what distinguished the claimed invention from the relevant prior art was the presence of both round *and* rectangular openings, emphasizing to the examiner that "regarding [the amended] claim . . . , none of the cited patents discloses the specific shape and location of the claimed rectangular *and* round openings."[234]

The defendant's accused stretcher did not literally infringe the patent because its handhold openings were all rectangular, not a mixture of rectangular and rounded openings. Because of the described prosecution history, the district court held that prosecution history estoppel precluded the patentee's reliance on the doctrine of equivalents and granted the accused infringer's motion for summary judgment of no infringement.

The Federal Circuit affirmed the district court in *Dixie USA*. Regardless of whether the accused stretcher performed the same function as the claimed invention, in substantially the same way, to achieve substantially the same result (i.e., was technologically equivalent), the patentee in this case was estopped from relying on the doctrine of equivalents to establish infringement liability. The court concluded that "when a patentee, during the prosecution of his application, adds a limitation to rectangular and round openings in response to a rejection based on prior art references describing rectangular openings in an effort to overcome that rejection, the patentee cannot later successfully argue that an accused device that lacks the rectangular and round limitation infringes the patent."[235]

Prosecution history estoppel resulted in *Dixie USA* from the combined effect of the patent applicant's amendment of his claims as well as his legal arguments made to the USPTO in the form of written remarks accompanying the amendment. However, the claims need not be amended at all in order to create prosecution history estoppel. In some cases, the applicant's arguments alone, generally made in

[233] *Id.* at 585-586.
[234] *Id.* at 588 (emphasis in original).
[235] *Id.* at 587-588.

the form of the applicant's written "remarks" filed in response to the examiner's rejections, can create estoppel. These arguments may involve characterizations of the claimed invention and/or the prior art, and will typically assert differences between the two that support patentability. Because this type of estoppel, referred to by the Federal Circuit as "argument-based prosecution history estoppel," is not founded on any explicit changes being made to the claims, a "clear and unmistakable surrender of subject matter" is necessary to invoke it.[236]

b. *Scope of Estoppel*

Assuming that a patentee's actions during prosecution (in the form of claim amendments and/or arguments) triggered prosecution history estoppel, the next step of the analysis is to determine the proper scope of that estoppel. In other words, may the patentee narrow its claim via amendment in response to USPTO rejections and yet still retain some scope of equivalents beyond the literal scope of the amended claim? Consider, for example, a claim reciting "a composition of matter comprising less than 50 percent X by weight." In response to a USPTO rejection based on prior art that taught a composition having 40 percent X, assume that the patent applicant narrowed its claim to recite that the patented composition must comprise "less than 20 percent X by weight."[237] If an accused infringer manufactures and sells a composition having 25 percent X, there is no literal infringement. Nevertheless, could the accused composition still infringe under the doctrine of equivalents?

In its early decisions the Federal Circuit adopted a "flexible" or "spectrum" approach to this question concerning the proper scope of prosecution history estoppel. In frequently quoted language, the court stated in *Hughes Aircraft Co. v. United States*[238] that prosecution history estoppel "may have a limiting effect" on the doctrine of equivalents "within a spectrum ranging from great to small to zero."[239] As discussed below, the Federal Circuit later rejected the flexible

[236]*See* Conoco, Inc. v. Energy & Env. Int'l, L.C., 460 F.3d 1349, 1364 (Fed. Cir. 2006); Pharmacia & Upjohn Co. v. Mylan Pharms., Inc., 170 F.3d 1373, 1377 (Fed. Cir. 1999). The Federal Circuit has explained that, in contrast with amendment-based estoppel, the court will "not presume a patentee's arguments to surrender an entire field of equivalents through simple arguments and explanations to the patent examiner. Though arguments to the examiner may have the same effect, they do not always evidence the same clear disavowal of scope that a formal amendment to the claim would have." *Conoco*, 460 F.3d at 1364.

[237]This assumes that the originally filed patent application provided adequate support for the 20 percent limitation in accordance with 35 U.S.C. §112(a) (eff. Sept. 16, 2012).

[238]717 F.2d 1351 (Fed. Cir. 1983).

[239]*Id.* at 1363.

approach in favor of an absolute, "complete bar" rule of prosecution history estoppel in its 2000 *en banc* decision in *Festo Corp. v. Shoketsu Kinzoku Kogyo Kabushiki Co.*[240] In 2002, the U.S. Supreme Court vacated the Federal Circuit's decision in *Festo* and announced a "presumptive bar" rule that lies somewhere between the flexible and complete bar rules. The evolution of the Supreme Court's view of prosecution history estoppel is demonstrated by its 1997 decision in *Warner-Jenkinson* and its 2002 follow-up decision in *Festo,* as discussed in the following section.

c. *Presumption of Estoppel Under* Warner-Jenkinson

The Supreme Court in *Warner-Jenkinson Co. v. Hilton Davis Chem., Co.*[241] announced a presumption with respect to prosecution history estoppel in the case of a silent or unexplained record, where the prosecution history does not reveal the reason for amending the claims.[242] The Court held that in this situation, fairness requires that the burden of establishing a reason for the amendment be placed on the patent owner. Where no explanation is established, a court should "presume that the patent applicant had a substantial reason related to patentability"[243] for making the amendment.

If the patent owner is unable to rebut the presumption that the change was made to the claims for a reason related to patentability, "prosecution history estoppel would bar the application of the doctrine of equivalents as to that element."[244] In other words, an unrebutted presumption of prosecution history estoppel results in a complete bar to the application of the doctrine of equivalents with respect to the disputed claim limitation.

[240] 234 F.3d 558 (Fed. Cir. 2000) (*en banc*).

[241] 520 U.S. 17 (1997).

[242] *See id.* at 33-34. The patent application claims as filed in *Warner-Jenkinson* did not place any limits on the pH range at which the claimed dye purification process operated. The USPTO examiner cited against the claims a prior art reference showing a similar process operating at a pH of above nine (9). *See id.* at 22. In response, the applicant amended its claims to require that the pH parameter of the claimed process fall within a range of "approximately 6.0-9.0." *See id.* Although the reason for the inclusion of pH 9 as the upper limit of this range is obvious (i.e., to distinguish the cited prior art process), the prosecution record was unclear as to why the applicant included pH 6 as a lower limit. *See id.* at 32. Because the prosecution record in *Warner-Jenkinson* did not explain the reason for this aspect of the narrowing claim amendment, a presumption of complete estoppel was triggered as to that limitation of the claim. *See id.* at 33-34.

[243] *Id.* at 33. The Supreme Court did not expressly define what it meant by "reason[s] related to patentability," but provided a number of case law examples that all involved changes made to claims in response to prior art rejections (i.e., based on anticipation under 35 U.S.C. §102 or obviousness under 35 U.S.C. §103). *See id.*

[244] *Id.*

d. Federal Circuit's Complete Bar Rule of Festo I

In 2000, the Federal Circuit drastically strengthened the limiting impact of prosecution history estoppel beyond that enunciated in *Warner-Jenkinson* when the *en banc* appellate court decided the long-awaited *Festo Corp. v. Shoketsu Kinzoku Kogyo Kabushiki Co.* [hereinafter "*Festo I*"].[245] Although the U.S. Supreme Court subsequently overturned the *Festo I* decision as described below, a summary of the Federal Circuit's thinking on the matter is important to understanding the current framework for determining prosecution history estoppel.

In *Festo I*, a majority of the *en banc* Federal Circuit announced an absolute "bar by amendment" rule that went considerably further than the limited "silent record" presumption announced in *Warner-Jenkinson.* Under the Federal Circuit's *Festo I* rule, *no* scope of equivalents survived for any claim limitation that was narrowed during patent prosecution for any reason related to patentability; such limitations could only be literally infringed. (Thus, the accused composition having 25 percent X from the previous hypothetical would not infringe, either literally or under the doctrine of equivalents.) "Reasons related to patentability" included anything related to the Patent Act, 35 U.S.C., including changes made in response to indefiniteness rejections under the second paragraph of 35 U.S.C. §112. Because at least before *Festo I,* the narrowing of claims by amendment was commonplace practice in the iterative process of patent prosecution, almost all issued patents were impacted and their value significantly reduced by the Federal Circuit's *Festo I* decision.

The *Festo I* majority's policy argument that contracting the doctrine of equivalents would promote innovation by encouraging design-arounds and improvements was certainly valid with respect to follow-on enterprises, but it ignored the dramatic reduction in incentives for "pioneer" innovation and basic research. In *Festo I* the Federal Circuit slashed incentives for the breakthrough inventor because the scope of protection that a patent grant provides had in many cases been narrowed to easily avoided literal infringement.

An especially troubling aspect of the Federal Circuit's decision was the apparently retrospective application of *Festo I*'s absolutism on the approximately 1.2 million U.S. patents then in force. Unlike the

[245] 234 F.3d 558 (Fed. Cir. 2000) (*en banc*) (*Festo I*), *vacated and remanded,* Festo Corp. v. Shoketsu Kinzoku Kogyo Kabushiki Co., 535 U.S. 722 (2002) (*Festo II*). The shorthand descriptor "*Festo I*" is used herein for convenience, but is not literally correct; the Federal Circuit first encountered the long-running dispute over infringement of Festo's magnetic rodless cylinder patents five years earlier. *See* Festo Corp. v. Shoketsu Kinzoku Kogyo Kabushiki Co., 72 F.3d 857 (Fed. Cir. 1995) (affirming district court's grant of summary judgment of infringement of Festo's Carroll patent and affirming judgment of infringement of Festo's Stoll patent following jury trial).

Supreme Court in *Warner-Jenkinson,* the Federal Circuit *Festo I* majority showed no sensitivity to reliance interests of patent owners or concern for "chang[ing] so substantially the rules of the game";[246] that is, it did not protect the expectations of those who had procured patents before the Supreme Court in *Warner-Jenkinson* announced its rebuttable presumption of estoppel in certain instances where claim amendments were unexplained. The *Festo I* majority announced a new estoppel framework much more severe than that of *Warner-Jenkinson,* with nonrebuttable, uniform application to all narrowing amendments made for any reason related to the statutory requirements for obtaining a patent, yet provided no grandfathering for existing patents.

e. *Supreme Court's Presumptive Bar Rule of* Festo II

In a landmark decision issued May 28, 2002, the U.S. Supreme Court vacated the Federal Circuit's decision in *Festo I* and remanded the case to the appellate court.[247] The Supreme Court flatly rejected the Federal Circuit's *per se* rule of complete estoppel (i.e., the "complete bar" approach). The Court agreed that narrowing amendments[248] made for any reason based on the Patent Act, including amendments made in response to rejections under 35 U.S.C. §112, can give rise to estoppel.[249] Rather than apply a *per se* rule that

[246]*Warner-Jenkinson,* 520 U.S. at 32 n.6.

[247]Festo Corp. v. Shoketsu Kinzoku Kogyo Kabushiki Co., 535 U.S. 722 (2002) (hereafter "*Festo II*").

[248]Not every amendment made to patent claims during the prosecution history narrows the scope of the claim. For example, the Federal Circuit held in *Interactive Pictures Corp. v. Infinite Pictures, Inc.,* 274 F.3d 1371 (Fed. Cir. 2001), that a patent applicant's amendment of the phrase "output signals" to read "output transform calculation signals" in a claim directed to an image viewing system was *not* a narrowing amendment that triggered prosecution history estoppel. *See id.* at 1377. The court agreed with the patentee that the amendment was not narrowing because it "merely clarified [the claim] by relabeling the signals without changing their identity or qualities." *Id.* In *Primos, Inc. v. Hunter's Specialties, Inc.*, 451 F.3d 841 (Fed. Cir. 2006), the patentee's amendment of the claim phrase "a plate" to "a plate having a length" did not narrow the scope of the claim because "every physical object has a length." *Id.* at 849.

[249]*See Festo II,* 535 U.S. at 736-737:

> Estoppel arises when an amendment is made to secure the patent and the amendment narrows the patent's scope. If a §112 amendment is truly cosmetic, then it would not narrow the patent's scope or raise an estoppel. On the other hand, if a §112 amendment is necessary and narrows the patent's scope — even if only for the purpose of better description — estoppel may apply. A patentee who narrows a claim as a condition for obtaining a patent disavows his claim to the broader subject matter, whether the amendment was made to avoid the prior art or to comply with §112. We must regard the patentee as having conceded an inability to claim the broader subject matter or at least as having abandoned his right to appeal a rejection. In either case estoppel may apply.

narrowing amendments automatically destroy all possible scope of equivalents, however, an examination of the subject matter surrendered by the narrowing amendment is required.[250]

The Supreme Court in *Festo II* adopted a *rebuttable* presumption that a narrowing amendment surrenders the particular equivalent in question. This can be seen both as an expansion of the "silent record" presumption that the Court had previously announced in *Warner-Jenkinson,*[251] but also as a significant relaxation of the complete bar rule announced in the Federal Circuit's *Festo I* decision. Under the Supreme Court's *Festo II* decision, a patentee can potentially overcome the presumption of estoppel in the following settings:

> There are some cases, however, where the amendment cannot reasonably be viewed as surrendering a particular equivalent. The equivalent may have been *unforeseeable at the time of the application; the rationale underlying the amendment may bear no more than a tangential relation to the equivalent in question; or there may be some other reason suggesting that the patentee could not reasonably be expected to have described the insubstantial substitute in question.* In those cases the patentee can overcome the presumption that prosecution history estoppel bars a finding of equivalence.

[250]*See id.* at 737 (explaining that, "[t]hough prosecution history estoppel can bar a patentee from challenging a wide range of alleged equivalents made or distributed by competitors, its reach requires an examination of the subject matter surrendered by the narrowing amendment").

[251]The presumption of estoppel announced in *Warner-Jenkinson* appeared to be limited to those amendments made with no explanation in the record of the reasons for the amendments. *See Warner-Jenkinson Co. v. Hilton Davis Chem., Co.*, 520 U.S. 17, 33 (1997) (holding that "[w]here no explanation is established, however, the court should presume that the patent applicant had a substantial reason related to patentability for including the limiting element added by amendment"). Under the Supreme Court's subsequent decision in *Festo II,* the presumption of estoppel applies across the board whenever a "narrowing" amendment has been made, without limitation to amendments made without any accompanying explanation of the reasons therefor:

> When the patentee is unable to explain the reason for amendment, estoppel not only applies but also "bar[s] the application of the doctrine of equivalents as to that element." *Ibid.* These words do not mandate a complete bar; they are limited to the circumstance where "no explanation is established." They do provide, however, that when the court is unable to determine the purpose underlying a narrowing amendment — and hence a rationale for limiting the estoppel to the surrender of particular equivalents — the court should presume that the patentee surrendered all subject matter between the broader and the narrower language.
>
> Just as *Warner-Jenkinson* held that the patentee bears the burden of proving that an amendment was not made for a reason that would give rise to estoppel, we hold here that the patentee should bear the burden of showing that the amendment does not surrender the particular equivalent in question.

Festo II, 535 U.S. at 740.

> This presumption is not, then, just the complete bar by another name. Rather, it reflects the fact that the interpretation of the patent must begin with its literal claims, and the prosecution history is relevant to construing those claims. When the patentee has chosen to narrow a claim, courts may presume the amended text was composed with awareness of this rule and that the territory surrendered is not an equivalent of the territory claimed. In those instances, however, the patentee still might rebut the presumption that estoppel bars a claim of equivalence. *The patentee must show that at the time of the amendment one skilled in the art could not reasonably be expected to have drafted a claim that would have literally encompassed the alleged equivalent.*[252]

The Supreme Court's formulation of the prosecution history estoppel test in *Festo II* left a number of important questions unanswered. For example, what will be required to show satisfaction of the "unforeseeability" criterion? Under what circumstances does an amendment bear "no more than a tangential relation" to a particular equivalent that a patentee seeks to encompass through reliance on the doctrine of equivalents? What types of "other reason[s]" would suggest that a "patentee could not reasonably have been expected to have described [sic, claimed] the insubstantial substitute in question"?[253] What is the proper timing for these showings — at the time the application was filed, at the time the amendment in question was made, or the time the patent issued? Who is the "one skilled in the art" for purposes of answering the question whether the claim's author "could not reasonably be expected to have drafted a claim that would have literally encompassed the alleged equivalent"? More specifically, is he/she a person of ordinary skill in the art of the invention in question, or a person of ordinary skill in the art of drafting patent claims?[254] Are each of the above questions to be considered an issue of law or fact? Is there a right to a jury trial on any of these questions?

Before the Federal Circuit could address these questions, some federal district courts began the task, with divergent results.[255]

[252]*Id.* at 740-741 (emphases added).

[253]For example, what if the patentee did not literally claim the alleged insubstantial substitute because of a lack of written description support in the specification? *See* Donald S. Chisum, *The Supreme Court's* Festo *Decision: Implications for Patent Claim Scope and Other Issues* (June 2002), at 16, *available at* https://www.lexisnexis.com/practiceareas/ip/pdfs/chisumfesto.pdf.

[254]Although some inventors are quite sophisticated about the patenting process, in many cases an inventor requires the services of a patent attorney or patent agent who is trained in the law (and lore) of claim drafting.

[255]For example, the following three district court decisions all involved the same patent but reached different conclusions concerning the effect of prosecution history estoppel as resolved in accordance with the Supreme Court's decision in *Festo II*. *See* Glaxo Wellcome, Inc. v. IMPAX Labs., Inc., 220 F. Supp. 2d 1089 (N.D. Cal. 2002); Glaxo Wellcome, Inc. v. Eon Labs Mfg., Inc., No. 00 Civ. 9089, 2002 U.S. Dist. LEXIS 14923

f. Federal Circuit's Remand Decision in Festo III

The Federal Circuit on September 26, 2003, issued an *en banc* decision[256] from the Supreme Court's remand in *Festo II*. The *Festo III* decision set forth a framework for implementing the new presumptive bar regime and answered many, if not all, of the questions raised by *Festo II*. The *Festo III* decision specifically addressed the following four questions on which the Federal Circuit had requested briefing from the parties and *amici*:

1. Whether rebuttal of the presumption of surrender, including issues of foreseeability, tangentialness, or reasonable expectations of those skilled in the art, is a question of law or one of fact; and what role a jury should play in determining whether a patent owner can rebut the presumption.
2. What factors are encompassed by the criteria set forth by the Supreme Court.
3. If a rebuttal determination requires factual findings, then whether, in this case, remand to the district court is necessary to determine whether Festo can rebut the presumption that any narrowing amendment surrendered the equivalent now asserted, or whether the record as it now stands is sufficient to make those determinations.
4. If remand to the district court is not necessary, then whether Festo can rebut the presumption that any narrowing amendment surrendered the equivalent now asserted.[257]

With respect to the first question, concerning the proper role of judge and jury, the *Festo III* court held that whether a patentee has rebutted the presumption that any equivalents to a narrowed claim limitation have been surrendered is a question of law. As such, the question is to be determined by the district court, not a jury, in light of the traditional view of prosecution history estoppel as an equitable determination. Although rebuttal of the presumption may be subject to underlying facts, a district court is to make these factual findings in the course of determining the ultimate issue of law.[258]

The second question addressed by the *Festo III* court was intended to flesh out the three criteria identified by the Supreme Court in *Festo II* for overcoming the presumption of complete estoppel. As discussed

(S.D.N.Y. 2002); Smithkline Beecham Corp. v. Excel Pharms., Inc., 214 F. Supp. 2d 581 (E.D. Va. 2002).

[256]Festo Corp. v. Shoketsu Kinzoku Kogyo Kabushiki Co., 344 F.3d 1359 (Fed. Cir. 2003) (*en banc*) (hereinafter "*Festo III*").

[257]Festo Corp. v. Shoketsu Kinzoku Kogyo Kabushiki Co., 304 F.3d 1289, 1290-1291 (Fed. Cir. 2002) (order).

[258]*See Festo III*, 344 F.3d at 1368-1369.

in the previous section, those three rebuttal criteria are (1) that the patentee demonstrates that the alleged equivalent would have been unforeseeable at the time of the narrowing amendment, (2) that the rationale underlying the narrowing amendment bears no more than a tangential relation to the equivalent in question, or (3) that there is "some other reason" suggesting that the patentee could not reasonably have been expected to have drafted a claim encompassing the alleged equivalent at the time the patentee narrowed its claim.

The Federal Circuit in *Festo III* announced that rebuttal criterion (1), "unforeseeability," is an "objective inquiry, asking whether the alleged equivalent would have been unforeseeable to one of ordinary skill in the art at the time of the amendment."[259] Later-developed technology (e.g., transistors in relation to vacuum tubes, or Velcro® in relation to nails or screws) generally would not have been foreseeable, while technology known in the art at the time of the patentee's amendment would more likely have been foreseeable. Objective unforeseeability depends on underlying factual issues such as the state of the art and the understanding of a hypothetical person of ordinary skill in the art at the time of the amendment. Thus, district courts may hear expert testimony on these questions and consider other relevant extrinsic evidence.

Rebuttal criterion (2), "mere tangentialness," asks whether the reason for a narrowing amendment was peripheral, not directly relevant, tenuous, or in other words, unrelated to the alleged equivalent. *See* Eli Lilly and Co. v. Hospira, Inc., 933 F.3d 1320, 1331 (Fed. Cir. 2019) (Lourie, J.) (stating that "[t]angential means 'touching lightly or in the most tenuous was.' ") (quoting WEBSTER'S THIRD NEW INTERNATIONAL DICTIONARY (2002)). If a narrowing amendment surrendered the accused equivalent, it cannot be merely tangential: "an amendment made to avoid prior art that contains the equivalent in question is not tangential; it is central to allowance of the claim."[260] The inquiry must focus on the patentee's objectively apparent reason for the narrowing amendment; thus, a district court is limited in answering this question to consideration of the intrinsic evidence. Whether the reason for the amendment was merely tangential to the accused equivalent "is for the court to determine from the prosecution history record without the introduction of additional evidence, except, when necessary, testimony from those skilled in the art as to the interpretation of that record."[261]

Rebuttal criterion (3), that "some other reason" suggests that a patentee could not reasonably have been expected to have claimed the insubstantial substitute in question, is a "narrow" inquiry, but may

[259] *Id.* at 1369.
[260] *Festo III*, 344 F.3d at 1369.
[261] *Id.* at 1370.

at least include "the shortcomings of language." Although not definitely ruling out the possibility that extrinsic evidence might be relevant on this point, the *Festo III* court instructed that "[w]hen at all possible, determination of the third rebuttal criterion should also be limited to the prosecution history record,"[262] as is the case with rebuttal criterion (2), mere tangentialness.

Applying the above framework to the parties' arguments and the prosecution history of the Stoll and Carroll patents in suit, the *Festo III* court determined that patentee Festo could not show that the "magnetizable" and "sealing ring" amendments to the Stoll and Carroll patents were merely "tangential" or were made for "some other reason." However, factual issues relating to the objective unforeseeability of the accused equivalents existed; for example, Festo argued that SMC's accused two-way sealing ring was an inferior and unforeseeable equivalent of the one-way sealing rings located at each end of the piston in the claimed invention. The existence of these fact questions necessitated a remand to the district court to determine whether Festo could successfully rebut the presumption of surrender by demonstrating that the accused elements would have been unforeseeable to a person of ordinary skill in the art at the time of the amendments.[263]

g. *Federal Circuit Decisions Applying the* Festo *Rebuttal Criteria*

Federal Circuit decisions following *Festo III* provide further guidance on application of the three rebuttal criteria. For example, a patentee successfully rebutted the *Festo* presumption of complete estoppel under rebuttal criterion (2), "mere tangentialness," in *Insituform Techs., Inc. v. Cat Contracting, Inc.*[264] Patentee Insituform

[262] *Id.*

[263] Festo did not prevail on remand on the unforeseeability question. *See* Festo Corp. v. Shoketsu Kinzoku Kogyo Kabushiki Co., No. Civ.A. 88-1814-PBS, 2006 WL 47695, *1 (D. Mass. Jan. 10, 2006) (denying Festo's motion under Fed. R. Civ. P. 59(e) to alter or amend the district court's earlier judgment for Shoketsu of noninfringement, finding that "in the context of the very small [magnetic] leakage fields [resulting from Festo's design], the use of an aluminum alloy sleeve (an old technology) instead of a magnetizable one was foreseeable to a person of ordinary skill in the art at the time of the 1981 amendments"). The district court further found that "in the context of the invention, . . . it was objectively foreseeable to one of ordinary skill in the art in 1981 to use one two-way sealing ring, which existed in the prior art, in combination with the guide rings as an equivalent of a sealing ring/guide ring combination at each end of the piston [as recited in Festo's claims]"). *Id.* at *3. As discussed in Section D.2.g, *infra*, the Federal Circuit subsequently affirmed the district court's decision that Festo had not satisfied the unforeseeability rebuttal criterion. *See* Festo Corp. v. Shoketsu Kinzoku Kogyo Kabushiki Co., 493 F.3d 1368 (Fed. Cir. 2007).

[264] 385 F.3d 1360 (Fed. Cir. 2004).

claimed a process for repairing a broken underground pipe by installing a resin-impregnated liner within the pipe. Although Insituform narrowed its claim during prosecution to recite *inter alia* that the process employed only a single cup for creating a vacuum inside the liner, the Federal Circuit concluded that the rationale underlying that amendment bore "no more than a tangential relation to the equivalent in question," the accused Cat process utilizing multiple vacuum cups. The prosecution history showed that the reason for Insituform's narrowing amendment, which added other limitations to the claim besides the single cup limitation, was to distinguish a prior art process that disadvantageously employed a large compressor at the end of the liner; limiting the number of vacuum cups was not related to this reason. In other words, Insituform's amendment distinguishing the prior art was based on *where* the vacuum source was located; this was "only tangentially related to an equivalent directed at the *number* of vacuum sources."[265]

The patentee in *Primos, Inc. v. Hunter's Specialties, Inc.* likewise managed to rebut the *Festo* presumption by reliance on rebuttal criterion (2).[266] The patented invention was a game call device used by hunters to emulate the sounds of animals such as turkeys. It featured a moderately curved plate that rose above a flat membrane; the membrane vibrated to produce sound when a hunter used the game call. In response to a USPTO rejection of claim 2 of Primos's '578 patent[267] based on a prior art game call device featuring a shelf-like structure with *no* spacing above the membrane, Primos narrowed the claim to require that its plate be "differentially spaced" above the membrane. Hunter's Specialties' accused product (the "Tone Trough") included a domed structure raised above the membrane, rather than a plate. The Federal Circuit concluded that "[b]ecause the accused device's dome includes the spacing, the amendment was merely tangential to the contested element in the accused device, and thus prosecution history estoppel does not apply to prevent the application of the doctrine of equivalents."[268]

The pharmaceutical patentee in *Eli Lilly and Co. v. Hospira, Inc.*[269] also rebutted the *Festo* presumption by reliance on rebuttal criterion

[265]Cross Med. Prods., Inc. v. Medtronic Sofamor Danek, Inc., 480 F.3d 1335, 1342 (Fed. Cir. 2007) (citing Biagro W. Sales, Inc. v. Grow More, Inc., 423 F.3d 1296, 1306 (Fed. Cir. 2005)). The amendment and the alleged equivalent in *Insituform* involved "different aspects of the invention — the location of the vacuum source relative to the resin versus the number of vacuum cups." *Biagro*, 423 F.3d at 1306.

[266]*See* Primos, Inc. v. Hunter's Specialties, Inc., 451 F.3d 841, 848-850 (Fed. Cir. 2006).

[267]*See* Game Call Apparatus, U.S. Patent No. 5,415,578 (issued May 16, 1995).

[268]*Primos,* 451 F.3d at 849.

[269]933 F.3d 1320 (Fed. Cir. 2019) (Lourie, J.).

(2), "mere tangentialness."[270] Lilly marketed the chemotherapy medicine pemetrexed in the form of a disodium salt (i.e., "pemetrexed disodium"); its ALIMTA product was used to treat patients with non–small cell lung cancer. Importantly, pemetrexed is a type or species of "antifolate," a well-studied class of molecules that can inhibit or slow down cancer cell growth and division.

When clinical trials revealed severe side effects from the administration of pemetrexed disodium, Lilly invented (in 2001) and patented an improved method of treatment that supplemented the administration of pemetrexed disodium with a methylmalonic acid lowering agent (e.g., vitamin B12) as well as folic acid. These additions "substantially reduced pemetrexed-induced toxicity and deaths while delivering a superior chemotherapeutic response rate."[271] Claims of Lilly's U.S. Patent No. 7,772,209 ('209 patent), reciting a "method for administering pemetrexed disodium to a patient in need of chemotherapeutic treatment," required the sequential steps of (1) administering certain recited dosages of folic acid and vitamin B12, and then (2) administering pemetrexed disodium.[272]

Particularly relevant to the prosecution history estoppel defense it would later face when asserting the '209 patent, Lilly significantly narrowed its claims during prosecution in the USPTO in order to obtain the '209 patent. Although the issued claims of the '209 patent (summarized above) were limited to a method for administering "pemetrexed disodium," Lilly's originally-filed claims (in a parent application) were much broader. The claims first submitted to the USPTO recited a method of administering an "antifolate," which is a class or species of molecules of which pemetrexed is but one member or species. The USPTO issued a 35 U.S.C. §102 anticipation rejection against Lilly's "antifolate" claims based on the 1978 "Arsenyan" reference. Arsenyan disclosed the experimental treatment of mice having tumors with a combination of another type of antifolate, methotrexate, plus methylcobalamin, a vitamin B12 derivative. In order to overcome the rejections,[273] Lilly amended its claims to narrow "antifolate" to

[270]*See Lilly,* 933 F.3d at 1330-1334 (section titled "Prosecution History Estoppel").
[271]*Lilly,* 933 F.3d at 1325.
[272]Representative claim 12 of Lilly's '209 patent recited:

> 12. An improved method for administering pemetrexed disodium to a patient in need of chemotherapeutic treatment, wherein the improvement comprises:
> a) administration of between about 350 g and about 1000 g of folic acid prior to the first administration of pemetrexed disodium;
> b) administration of about 500 g to about 1500 g of vitamin B12, prior to the first administration of pemetrexed disodium; and
> c) administration of pemetrexed disodium.

[273]The USPTO rejected other claims of Lilly's parent application as obvious over a combination of Arsenyan and other references.

"pemetrexed disodium." Its accompanying remarks asserted that the amendment overcame the anticipation rejection because Arsenyan did not disclose pemetrexed disodium. The USPTO examiner agreed and withdrew the rejection, and Lilly's '209 patent eventually issued.

Lilly in 2016 sued generic pharmaceutical manufacturers Hospira and Dr. Reddy's Labs. ("DRL") for infringement of the '209 patent in Hatch-Waxman litigation venued in the Southern District of Indiana. Notably, the accused infringers sought USFDA approval to market pemetrexed ditromethamine, a different salt of pemetrexed than Lilly's pemetrexed disodium. Lilly asserted literal infringement as well as infringement under the doctrine of equivalents.

In response to the latter equivalency assertion, the accused infringers countered with prosecution history estoppel. The parties did not dispute that Lilly's claim amendment during prosecution was (1) narrowing and (2) made for a substantial reason related to patentability (i.e., to overcome the anticipation rejection). So the baseline requirements for a presumption of prosecution history estoppel under *Festo* were satisfied.

However, Lilly responded that it was entitled to the "merely tangential" exception of *Festo*, which precluded application against it of prosecution history estoppel. In Lilly's view, the reason for its claim amendment was to distinguish antifolates other than pemetrexed, not to distinguish *all* pemetrexed salts other than the claim-recited pemetrexed disodium. In other words, Lilly argued that it did not intend to surrender pemetrexed ditromethamine (the accused compound) from the scope of equivalents of its patent claims. Because Lilly's amendment was made to distinguish other antifolates, not all other pemetrexed salts, the amendment was therefore only "tangential" to the accused equivalent, pemetrexed ditromethamine.

The district court agreed with Lilly, as did the Federal Circuit when the accused infringers later appealed. Notably, the appellate court in *Lilly* appeared to signal a more magnanimous view of the "tangentialness" exception to prosecution history estoppel. Although the accused infringers attempted to rely on earlier Circuit cases asserting that the "tangential" exception was " 'very narrow,' "[274] the *Lilly* Circuit rejected the defendants' view as "too rigid."[275]

[274]*Lilly,* 933 F.3d at 1331 (observing that accused infringers emphasize Circuit's statement that the tangential exception is "very narrow") (quoting Integrated Tech. Corp. v. Rudolph Techs., Inc., 734 F.3d 1352, 1358 (Fed. Cir. 2013) (Moore, J.) (quoting Cross Med. Prods., Inc. v. Medtronic Sofamor Danek, Inc., 480 F.3d 1335, 1342 (Fed. Cir. 2007) (per curiam; Rader, Schall, Prost) (stating that "[t]his court reaffirms the principle that the tangential relation criterion for overcoming the *Festo* presumption is very narrow"))).

[275]*Lilly,* 933 F.3d at 1331.

The Circuit clarified that "tangential" means " 'touching lightly or in the most tenuous way.' "[276] In the case at bar, Lilly's claim amendment related only in the "most tenuous" way (if at all) to the accused equivalent, pemetrexed ditromethamine. The prosecution record made clear that Lilly's reason for its amendment was to avoid the prior art Arsenyan reference, "which only discloses treatments using methotrexate, a different antifolate."[277] Lilly narrowed its claim "to more accurately define what it actually invented" — a better way to administer pemetrexed. "[T]he particular type of salt to which pemetrexed is complexed [i.e., ditromethamine, as in the accused compound, or disodium, as in the claimed compound] relates only tenuously to the reason for the narrowing amendment, which was to avoid Arsenyan."[278]

The Circuit thus held that the amendment was "merely tangential" to the accused pemetrexed ditromethamine. The record "strongly" indicated that Lilly did not intend by its amendment to give us "other, functionally identical, pemetrexed salts."[279] Hence, prosecution history estoppel did not bar Lilly's reliance on the doctrine of equivalents to argue that the accused pemetrexed ditromethamine worked in substantially the same way as the pemetrexed disodium of the claimed invention. Lilly ultimately prevailed on its equivalency theory, with the Circuit declaring that the case was "eminently suitable" for application of the doctrine.[280]

Other Federal Circuit decisions in the wake of *Festo III* illustrate patentee failures to establish any of the three rebuttal criteria and thereby invoke the doctrine of equivalents. For example, the patentee in *Glaxo Wellcome, Inc. v. Impax Labs., Inc.*[281] was unable to rebut the *Festo* presumption under the "unforeseeability" criterion (1). Glaxo's patent was directed to controlled sustained-release tablets containing the antidepressant bupropion hydrochloride, which Glaxo sold commercially under the brand name Wellbutrin® SR for treatment of depression. Specifically, Glaxo's patent claimed a sustained-release tablet containing an admixture of bupropion hydrochloride

[276]*Lilly,* 933 F.3d at 1331 (quoting WEBSTER'S THIRD NEW INTERNATIONAL DICTIONARY (2002)).

[277]*Lilly,* 933 F.3d at 1331.

[278]*Lilly,* 933 F.3d at 1331.

[279]*Lilly,* 933 F.3d at 1331.

[280]*Lilly,* 933 F.3d at 1336. The Circuit affirmed the district court's determination on the merits that the accused product infringed under the doctrine of equivalents. It agreed with the district court's findings that "DRL's product will accomplish an identical aim, furnishing the same amount of pemetrexed to active sites in the body; in exactly the same way, by diluting a pemetrexed salt in a aqueous solution for intravenous administration." *Lilly,* 933 F.3d at 1335-1336.

[281]356 F.3d 1348 (Fed. Cir. 2004).

and hydroxypropyl methylcellulose (HPMC), which extends drug release by transforming into a gel that swells upon ingestion. Rather than HPMC, the release agent used in the accused product was hydroxypropyl cellulose (HPC), a hydrogel-forming compound. The parties did not dispute that HPMC and HPC were technologically equivalent sustained-release agents; nevertheless, accused infringer Impax contended that Glaxo was barred by prosecution history estoppel from recourse to the doctrine of equivalents because Glaxo had narrowed its claims by adding a specific recitation of HPMC (as filed, Glaxo's claim did not recite any particular release agent). Glaxo countered that HPC was unforeseeable at the time of its amendment of the disputed claims. Glaxo could not have amended the claims broadly enough to include the accused HPC, it contended, because to do so would have drawn a new matter rejection;[282] its patent application did not reference HPC or any other sustained-release agents beyond HPMC. The Federal Circuit rejected this argument, observing that the "Supreme Court's [discussion of unforeseeability in *Festo II*] addresses the time of amendment only and does not address the instance where the applicant could not properly claim a known equivalent because it had purposely left that known substitute out of its disclosure at the time of filing." The Federal Circuit admitted that at the time Glaxo amended its claims, no known hydrogels other than HPMC had been tested with bupropion hydrochloride to achieve sustained release. Nevertheless, the record contained "considerable evidence" that Glaxo could have described the sustained release compound HPC at the time the '798 patent claims were amended, if not earlier. HPC was then known to Glaxo, the Federal Circuit concluded, at least in view of Glaxo's submission during prosecution of an Information Disclosure Statement that "describe[d] HPC, HPMC, and numerous other polymeric compounds as extended release drug formulations."[283]

In its most recent (and last) decision in the long-running *Festo v. Shoketsu* battle, the Federal Circuit affirmed in 2007 a district court's conclusion that Festo could not rely on "unforeseeability" rebuttal criterion (1) to overcome the presumption of complete estoppel and ensnare Shoketsu's magnetically coupled rodless cylinder having a

[282]The prohibition on adding new matter to the disclosure of a pending patent application is found in 35 U.S.C. §132(a) (stating that "[n]o amendment shall introduce new matter into the disclosure of the invention"). Patent claims and amendments thereto must be supported by the as-filed disclosure (i.e., written description and drawings). *See* UNITED STATES PATENT AND TRADEMARK OFFICE, MANUAL OF PATENT EXAMINING PROCEDURE (9th ed., Jan. 2018) §608.01(o) ("Basis for Claim Terminology in Description").

[283]*Glaxo Wellcome*, 356 F.3d at 1355.

nonmagnetizable outer sleeve.[284] Reviewing its precedent on application of the unforeseeability criterion, the court observed that "we have consistently held that an equivalent is foreseeable when the equivalent is known in the pertinent prior art at the time of amendment."[285] The court rejected Festo's proposed alternative test, which contended that in order to be considered foreseeable an accused equivalent must have satisfied the "function/way/result" or "insubstantial differences" test as of the time of the claim amendment, looking only at information available at that date.[286] The court instructed that the purpose of the function/way/result or insubstantial differences test is to determine whether an accused equivalent is sufficiently close to a claimed feature that the patentee should be able to capture it under the doctrine of equivalents; that test is not designed for the "entirely different context" of determining whether prosecution history estoppel applies because of a patentee's limiting amendment of its claims.[287] In short, the function/way/result or insubstantial differences inquiry is not applicable to the question of foreseeability.[288]

Additionally, the timing of Festo's proposed test for unforeseeability was incorrect. The Federal Circuit explained that "[t]he question is not whether *after* the narrowing amendment the [accused] alternative was a known equivalent, but rather whether it was a known equivalent *before* the narrowing amendment."[289] Applying this understanding, an "equivalent is foreseeable if one skilled in the art would have known that the alternative existed in the field of art as defined by the original claim scope, even if the suitability of the alternative for the particular purposes defined by the amended claim scope were unknown."[290] The Federal Circuit illustrated its rule by positing that "if a claim before amendment broadly claimed a metal filament for a light bulb but was later amended to avoid prior art and to specify metal A because of its longevity, the equivalent metal B, known in the prior art to function as a bulb filament, is not unforeseeable even though its longevity was unknown at the time of amendment."[291]

[284]*See* Festo Corp. v. Shoketsu Kinzoku Kogyo Kabushiki Co., 493 F.3d 1368 (Fed. Cir. 2007), *cert. denied*, 553 U.S. 1093 (2008).

[285]*Id.* at 1378.

[286]*See id.* at 1378-1379.

[287]*See id.* at 1380.

[288]*See id.* at 1382.

[289]*Id.* at 1381 (emphasis in original).

[290]*Id.* In other words, "an alternative is foreseeable if it is known in the field of the invention as reflected in the claim scope before amendment." *Id.* at 1379. The court did not rule out the possibility of additional formulations for foreseeability, but stated that it had "no occasion here to determine in what other circumstances an equivalent might be foreseeable." *Id.*

[291]*Id.* at 1381.

Other post-*Festo III* decisions have addressed the nature of the amendments that will trigger the *Festo* presumption in the first instance. For example, the Federal Circuit went *en banc* in *Honeywell Int'l Inc. v. Hamilton Sundstrand Corp.*[292] to clarify that "the rewriting of dependent claims into independent form coupled with the cancellation of the original independent claims creates a presumption of prosecution history estoppel."[293] This is true even when, as in *Honeywell,* the dependent claim included an additional claim limitation not found in the cancelled independent claim. Honeywell contended that although it had surrendered its broader originally filed independent claims by cancellation, there was no presumption of surrender because the scope of the rewritten claims themselves was not narrowed; they had simply been rewritten in independent form.[294] The Federal Circuit disagreed, because "the proper focus is whether the amendment narrow[ed] the *overall* scope of the claimed subject matter."[295] "[T]he fact that the scope of the rewritten claim has remained unchanged will not preclude the application of prosecution history estoppel if, by canceling the original independent claim and rewriting the dependent claims into independent form, the scope of subject matter claimed in the [original] independent claim has been narrowed to secure the patent."[296]

3. Prior Art (Hypothetical Claim Analysis)

The prior art represents another important legal limitation on a patentee's ability to rely on the doctrine of equivalents to establish infringement. This prior art limitation may be applicable even when no prosecution history estoppel exists, for example, when the patent in suit was allowed on a first Office Action without any claims having been rejected by the USPTO, as was the case in *Wilson Sporting Goods v. David Geoffrey & Associates,*[297] the foundational case in this area.

The distilled essence of the prior art limitation on the doctrine of equivalents is that an accused infringer cannot be liable for infringement under the doctrine if by making the accused device it is merely "practicing the prior art"; that is, the accused infringer is making a device that is already in the public domain.[298] The underlying policy

[292]370 F.3d 1131 (Fed. Cir. 2004) (*en banc*).

[293]*Id.* at 1134.

[294]Independent and dependent claims were introduced *supra* Chapter 2, Section D.

[295]*Honeywell*, 370 F.3d at 1141 (emphasis added).

[296]*Id.* at 1142.

[297]904 F.2d 677, 680 (Fed. Cir. 1990) (Rich, J.).

[298]*See Wilson,* 904 F.2d at 683 (explaining that accused infringer Dunlop "contends that there is no principled difference between the balls which the jury found to infringe and the prior art Uniroyal ball; thus to allow the patent to reach Dunlop's balls under

concern is that a patentee should not be able to use the doctrine of equivalents to encompass subject matter over which the patentee could not have obtained exclusionary rights in the first instance from the USPTO by applying for patent protection of that scope.[299] The *Wilson* court observed the following:

> [A] patentee should not be able to obtain, under the doctrine of equivalents, coverage which he could not lawfully have obtained from the PTO by literal claims. The doctrine of equivalents exists to prevent a fraud on a patent, *Graver Tank & Mfg. Co. v. Linde Air Prods. Co.,* 339 U.S. 605, 608, 94 L. Ed. 1097, 70 S. Ct. 854 (1950), *not* to give a patentee something which he could not lawfully have obtained from the PTO had he tried. Thus, since prior art always limits what an inventor could have claimed, it limits the range of permissible equivalents of a claim.[300]

In order to determine whether the prior art operates as a limitation (or defense) to the doctrine of equivalents, it is analytically helpful to construct a "hypothetical claim." The hypothetical claim analysis follows the steps listed in Figure 9.3.[301]

Having performed that analysis, one may ask why, when trying to determine the question of *infringement,* we should expend the analytical effort to construct and evaluate the *patentability* of a hypothetical claim. This task seems all the more unlikely because the patentee does not bear the burden of establishing the *validity* of its issued patent.[302] Simply stated, the hypothetical claim exercise is an effort to put the analysis of whether prior art limits the scope of equivalents on more familiar turf. We understand how to evaluate patent claims for patentability under §102 and §103, because this is what USPTO examiners and patent attorneys do on a regular basis.[303] It is not so easy, however, to determine the patentability of an accused device, for which

---

the doctrine of equivalents would improperly ensnare the prior art Uniroyal ball as well"); *id.* (stating that "there can be no infringement if the asserted scope of equivalency of what is literally claimed would encompass the prior art"). Note that although the "practicing the prior art" defense is available against a charge of infringement under the doctrine of equivalents, the Federal Circuit has rejected its applicability to allegations of *literal* infringement. *See* Tate Access Floors, Inc. v. Interface Arch. Res., Inc., 279 F.3d 1357, 1365-1366 (Fed. Cir. 2002).

[299]*See Wilson*, 904 F.2d at 684.

[300]*Id.* (emphasis in original).

[301]A straightforward example of the above approach is the hypothetical claim analysis applied by the Federal Circuit in *Abbott Labs. v. Dey, L.P.,* 287 F.3d 1097, 1105 (Fed. Cir. 2002) (stating that "[t]o determine the scope of the doctrine of equivalents in light of the prior art, a court can consider a 'hypothetical claim' that literally recites the range of equivalents asserted to infringe").

[302]*See* 35 U.S.C. §282 (providing that "[a] patent shall be presumed valid").

[303]The analysis is described in detail *supra* Chapter 4 ("Novelty, Loss of Right, and Priority Pre- and Post-America Invents Act of 2011 (35 U.S.C. §102)") and *supra* Chapter 5 ("The Nonobviousness Requirement (35 U.S.C. §103)").

1. Begin with the properly interpreted language of the patent claim that is allegedly infringed under the doctrine of equivalents.

↓

2. Amend the claim so that it is just broad enough to literally read on the accused device. This may require broadening only a single limitation, or multiple limitations, depending upon the differences between the claimed invention and the accused device. The claim you have rewritten in this manner is the hypothetical claim.

↓

3. Analyze the patentability of the hypothetical claim for novelty under 35 U.S.C. §102 and nonobviousness under 35 U.S.C. §103 in view of the prior art of record in the litigation. If the hypothetical claim *would* have been allowable (*i.e.*, is not anticipated or rendered obvious by the pertinent prior art), then the prior art does *not* operate as a legal limitation on the doctrine of equivalents. If the hypothetical claim would *not* have been allowable, then the patentee cannot rely on the doctrine of equivalents.

Figure 9.3

Procedure for Analyzing Whether Prior Art Limits the Availability of the Doctrine of Equivalents by Means of a Hypothetical Claim

(in most cases[304]) no "claim" exists. This is why we construct a hypothetical claim, based on the claim assertedly infringed, but amended so as to literally encompass the accused device. As explained by the *Wilson* court, the hypothetical claim analysis "allows use of traditional patentability rules and permits a more precise analysis than determining whether an *accused product* (which has no claim limitations on which to focus) would have been obvious in view of the prior art."[305]

4. Dedication to the Public

A patentee may not rely on the doctrine of equivalents to recapture subject matter that it clearly disclosed in its patent application but failed to claim. Allowing access to the doctrine of equivalents in such circumstances would encourage patent applicants to avoid USPTO examination of disclosed but unclaimed embodiments.[306] The Federal

[304]In some cases the accused device may itself be the subject of a patent.

[305]*Wilson,* 904 F.2d at 684 (emphasis in original).

[306]In such situations a patentee may attempt to reissue the patent in order to enlarge the scope of the claims to include the disclosed but previously unclaimed subject matter. A broadening reissue of this nature must be sought within two years from the grant of the original patent, however. *See* 35 U.S.C. §251.

Circuit sometimes refers to this principle by the shorthand phrase the "disclosure-dedication rule."[307]

For example, the patentee in *Maxwell v. J. Baker, Inc.*[308] disclosed in her application two different embodiments of her inventive concept (a system for securing together the mates of a pair of shoes sold in retail stores), but claimed only one of the disclosed embodiments. By failing to claim the second embodiment, the USPTO did not have an opportunity to assess its patentability. As a matter of law, the Federal Circuit held, the accused infringer Baker could not infringe "by using an alternate shoe attachment system that Maxwell dedicated to the public."[309]

A later decision, *YBM Magnex, Inc. v. Int'l Trade Comm'n,*[310] appeared to conflict with the holding of *Maxwell.* The Federal Circuit went *en banc* in 2002 to resolve the conflict by deciding *Johnson & Johnston Assocs. v. R.E. Serv. Co.*[311] The J&J patent in suit claimed an assembly that lessened possible handling damage to fragile copper foil layers of printed circuit boards by temporarily adhering the layers to a substrate of aluminum. The patent's written description provided that although aluminum was the preferred substrate material, other metals such as stainless steel could be used. Claim 1 of the patent was limited to aluminum substrates, however; it required "a laminate constructed of a sheet of copper foil which, in a finished printed circuit board, constitutes a functional element and a sheet of *aluminum*

[307] *See, e.g.,* Eli Lilly and Co. v. Hospira, Inc., 933 F.3d 1320, 1334 (Fed. Cir. 2019) (Lourie, J.). The *Lilly* court explained that

> [u]nder the disclosure-dedication rule, subject matter disclosed by a patentee, but not claimed, is considered dedicated to the public. *See Johnson & Johnston*, 285 F.3d at 1054. The reason for the doctrine is that members of the public reading a disclosure of particular subject matter are entitled, absent a claim to it, to assume that it is not patented and therefore dedicated to the public (unless, for example, claimed in a continuation or other application based on the disclosure). *Cf. Maxwell*, 86 F.3d at 1107 (failure to claim inventive subject matter "is clearly contrary to 35 U.S.C. §112 which requires that a patent applicant 'particularly point[ ] out and distinctly claim[ ] the subject matter which the applicant regards as his invention'"). Subject matter is considered disclosed when a skilled artisan "can understand the unclaimed disclosed teaching upon reading the written description," but not "any generic reference . . . necessarily dedicates all members of that particular genus." PSC Comput. Prod., Inc. v. Foxconn Int'l, Inc., 355 F.3d 1353, 1360 (Fed. Cir. 2004).

Lilly, 933 F.3d at 1334.

[308] 86 F.3d 1098 (Fed. Cir. 1996).

[309] *Id.* at 1108.

[310] 145 F.3d 1317 (Fed. Cir. 1998).

[311] 285 F.3d 1046, 1054 (Fed. Cir. 2002) (*en banc*).

which constitutes a discardable element."[312] The laminate made by accused infringer RES joined a layer of *steel* to the copper foil. Reaffirming the rule of *Maxwell v. J. Baker, Inc.*, the *Johnson & Johnston en banc* majority concluded that "when a patent drafter discloses but declines to claim subject matter, . . . this action dedicates that unclaimed subject matter to the public."[313] Because J&J had disclosed the steel substrates without claiming them, the court would not allow it to invoke the doctrine of equivalents to extend its aluminum claim limitation to encompass the accused steel substrate. To the extent that the court's earlier decision in *YBM Magnex* was in conflict, the *en banc* court overruled it.[314]

In *PSC Computer Prods., Inc. v. Foxconn Int'l, Inc.*,[315] the Federal Circuit addressed the level of specificity required of a patentee's disclosure of unclaimed material in order to work a dedication to the public under the *Johnson & Johnston* doctrine. PSC's patent was directed to a heat-sink assembly and retainer clip used to dissipate heat from an electronic package or semiconductor device. The patent's broadest claim recited clips containing "an elongated, resilient *metal* strap."[316] In discussing the background of the invention, the written description of PSC's patent disclosed that certain "prior art devices use molded *plastic* and/or metal parts that must be cast or forged which again are more expensive metal forming operations."[317] Rejecting PSC's argument that this disclosure was merely "oblique and incidental," the Federal Circuit held it specific enough to have dedicated the unclaimed embodiment, plastic clips, to the public, and therefore to have placed plastic clips beyond any permissible scope of equivalents to the claimed metal clips. The test is whether one of ordinary skill in the art can understand the unclaimed disclosed teaching upon reading the written description, the Federal Circuit instructed. In this case, a reader of ordinary skill in the art "could reasonably conclude from th[e] language in the written description that plastic clip parts could be substituted for metal clip parts."[318] PSC was thus "obliged either to claim plastic parts in addition to metal parts and to submit this broader claim for examination, or to not claim them and dedicate

[312] *Id.* at 1050 (emphasis added).

[313] *Id.* at 1054.

[314] *See id.* at 1055. A dissenting judge contended that J&J's filing of broader claims reciting "metal" substrate sheets in continuation applications was objective evidence that J&J did not intend to dedicate that broader subject matter to the public. *See id.* at 1067 (Newman, J., dissenting) (citing In re Gibbs, 437 F.2d 486 (C.C.P.A. 1971) (holding that claiming subject matter in a continuing application rebuts any inference that the disclosed but unclaimed subject matter was abandoned)).

[315] 355 F.3d 1353 (Fed. Cir. 2004).

[316] *Id.* at 1355 (emphasis added).

[317] *Id.* at 1356 (emphasis added).

[318] *Id.* at 1360.

the use of plastic parts to the public."[319] Because PSC chose the latter option, it had thereby dedicated plastic clips to the public.

The accused infringers' "dedication to the public" defense did *not* succeed in the 2019 pharmaceutical case *Eli Lilly and Co. v. Hospira, Inc.* (also analyzed above in connection with the accused infringers' separate and unsuccessful prosecution history estoppel defense[320]). The *Lilly* case makes a good contrast to *PSC Prods.*, discussed in the preceding paragraph, which was a straightforward mechanical case. Recall that the patent specification in *PSC Prods.* explicitly disclosed the unclaimed embodiment. In *Lilly,* however, a generic disclosure in the chemical arts that potentially encompassed thousands of member species did not necessarily disclose each species so as to dedicate each to the public.

More specifically, Eli Lilly and Co. ("Lilly") marketed the chemotherapy medicine pemetrexed in the form of a disodium salt (i.e., "pemetrexed disodium"). Importantly, pemetrexed is a type or species of "antifolate," a well-studied class of molecules that can inhibit or slow down cancer cell growth and division. In response to severe side effects observed from the administration of pemetrexed disodium, Lilly invented (in 2001) and obtained U.S. Patent No. 7,772,209 ('209 patent). The '209 patent claimed an improved method of treatment that supplemented the administration of pemetrexed disodium with a methylmalonic acid lowering agent (e.g., vitamin B12) as well as folic acid.

Lilly thereafter sued two generic drug manufacturers in Hatch Waxman Act litigation, asserting that their proposed product, which used pemetrexed ditromethamine, a different salt of pemetrexed, infringed the '209 patent claims under the doctrine of equivalents. The accused infringers countered by asserting *inter alia* that Lilly was not entitled to capture their product by a theory of equivalents infringement because Lilly had dedicated it to the public. They took the position that Lilly had disclosed pemetrexed ditromethamine in the application that ultimately issued as the '209 patent, but failed to include any claim to pemetrexed ditromethamine. Under the disclosure-dedication rule, the accused infringers argued, subject matter that Lilly disclosed but failed to claimed is considered surrendered to the public and not within any scope of equivalency for the '209 patent.

[319] *Id.*

[320] 933 F.3d 1320 (Fed. Cir. 2019) (Lourie, J.). *Lilly*'s application of the "mere tangentialness" exception to the *Festo* presumption of prosecution history estoppel for a narrowing amendment made for a reason substantially related to patentability is examined *supra* Section D.2.g ("Federal Circuit Decisions Applying the *Festo* Rebuttal Criteria").

The parties' dispute about potential dedication to the public centered on the level of specificity in the disclosure of U.S. Patent No. 4,997,838 ("Akimoto"), prior art to Lilly's '209 patent.[321] Lilly's patent application specifically identified and relied on Akimoto as disclosing "preferred examples of antifolates,"[322] one of which (pemetrexed) was required in Lilly's claimed method. Akimoto admittedly disclosed a "large genus" of compounds that generically encompassed pemetrexed. Akimoto explicitly enumerated 50 "exemplary compounds," but none of these was pemetrexed.[323]

The accused infringers argued that Lilly's reliance on Akimoto was effectively a disclosure of their proposed compound, pemetrexed ditromethamine, albeit a generic disclosure rather than an explicit one (because pemetrexed was not explicitly listed by Akimoto, nor any of its salts). According to the accused infringers, "a skilled artisan reading the '209 patent would both look for a disclosure of pemetrexed in Akimoto, and also seek to use a well-known cation like tromethamine, which . . . is generically disclosed in Akimoto in the form of [a disclosure of the suitability of] 'substituted ammonium' base salts."[324]

The Federal Circuit was not persuaded, citing *PSC Comput. Prod., Inc. v. Foxconn Int'l, Inc.* for its statement that "not 'any generic reference . . . necessarily dedicates all members of that particular genus.' "[325] At best, Akimoto provided only a "generic description," and certainly not an express one, of the accused compound pemetrexed ditromethamine. The appellate court observed that

> Akimoto's formula . . . includes seven functional group variables and encompasses thousands of compounds, and while Akimoto discloses about fifty exemplary compounds, none of them is pemetrexed. Moreover, Akimoto does not even disclose tromethamine expressly but only generically among dozens of other salts. At most, Akimoto discloses ammonium salts generally, which is far from a description of tromethamine.[326]

The law is settled concerning the level of specificity required of a disclosure in order to dedicate subject matter therein to the public. The Circuit has previously held that a "sufficient description of a genus" requires that a skilled artisan be able to "'visualize or

[321]Lilly also took a license under the Akimoto patent. *Lilly,* 933 F.3d at 1324.
[322]*Lilly,* 933 F.3d at 1334.
[323]*Lilly,* 933 F.3d at 1324.
[324]*Lilly,* 933 F.3d at 1334-1335.
[325]*Lilly,* 933 F.3d at 1334 (quoting *PSC Comput.,* 355 F.3d 1353, 1360 (Fed. Cir. 2004)). *PSC Comput.* is examined *supra* this subsection.
[326]*Lilly,* 933 F.3d at 1335 (citation omitted).

recognize' the members of the genus."[327] In the *Lilly* Circuit's view, Akimoto did not so describe pemetrexed ditromethamine. The appellate court saw "no reason why a skilled artisan would set out on [the accused infringers'] winding path to cobble together pemetrexed ditromethamine." Although Lilly's '209 patent taught that pemetrexed disodium (the claim-recited compound) was the "most preferred" antifolate for use in its method, "that knowledge would not change the skilled artisan's understanding of what Akimoto discloses."[328]

Because Akimoto contained only a " 'generic reference' " to the accused pemetrexed ditromethamine, the Circuit concluded that Lilly had not dedicated it to the public.[329] Thus, the disclosure-dedication rule did not preclude Lilly's reliance on the doctrine of equivalents.

5. Vitiation of Claim Limitations

The concept of "vitiation" is yet another legal limitation on a patentee's ability to use the doctrine of equivalents. The doctrine of equivalents should not be applied to a particular claim limitation if doing so would eliminate or vitiate that limitation, that is, would effectively read the limitation out of the claim. For example, the court in *Asyst Techs., Inc. v. Emtrak, Inc.* contended that "[t]o hold that 'unmounted' is equivalent to 'mounted' would effectively read the 'mounted on' limitation out of the patent."[330]

[327] *Lilly,* 933 F.3d at 1335 (citing Ariad Pharm., Inc. v. Eli Lilly & Co., 598 F.3d 1336, 1350 (Fed. Cir. 2010) (quoting Regents of the Univ. of Cal. v. Eli Lilly & Co., 119 F.3d 1559, 1568-1569 (Fed. Cir. 1997))).

[328] *Lilly,* 933 F.3d at 1335.

[329] *Lilly,* 933 F.3d at 1335 (quoting *PSC Comput.*, 355 F.3d at 1360).

[330] 402 F.3d 1188, 1195 (Fed. Cir. 2005). The Asyst patent in suit claimed an information processing system having *inter alia* a "second microcomputer means for receiving and processing digital information communicated with said respective second two-way communication means *mounted on* the respective work station therewith." *Id.* at 1190 (quoting claim 1) (emphasis added). The Federal Circuit agreed with the district court's interpretation of "mounted" as literally limited to securely attached or affixed. The accused IridNet system was unmounted such that it did not literally infringe. Moreover, the Federal Circuit held, "[i]n this case . . . the district court was correct in ruling that the doctrine of equivalents cannot be extended to reach an 'unmounted' system such as the IridNet system without vitiating the 'mounted on' limitation altogether." *Id.* at 1195. Doing so would have violated the "all elements rule" as well as its corollary, the "specific exclusion" principle, "since the term 'mounted' can fairly be said to specifically exclude objects that are 'unmounted.' " *Id.* (citing SciMed Life Sys. v. Advanced Cardiovascular Sys., 242 F.3d 1337, 1346 (Fed. Cir. 2001) (noting close kinship of the "all elements rule" and the "specific exclusion" principle); Moore U.S.A., Inc. v. Standard Register Co., 229 F.3d 1091, 1106 (Fed. Cir. 2000); Athletic Alternatives, Inc. v. Prince Mfg., Inc., 73 F.3d 1573, 1582 (Fed. Cir. 1996) ("specific exclusion" principle is "a corollary to the 'all limitations' rule")).

D. Legal Limitations on the Doctrine of Equivalents

The vitiation doctrine finds its genesis in *Warner-Jenkinson Co. v. Hilton Davis Chem. Co.,*[331] discussed *supra.* Recall the Supreme Court's caution that in order to reduce the uncertainty inherent in applying the doctrine of equivalents, equivalency must be evaluated between each limitation of a claim and its corresponding element in the accused device, rather than comparing the claimed invention as a whole to the accused device as a whole. The Court emphasized the importance of "ensur[ing] that the application of the doctrine [of equivalents], even as to an individual element, is not allowed such broad play as to effectively eliminate that element in its entirety."[332] If applied within appropriate limits, the Court explained, the doctrine of equivalents will not "vitiate the central functions of the patent claims themselves."[333] The *Warner-Jenkinson* Court further instructed that "under the particular facts of a case, if... a theory of equivalence would entirely vitiate a particular claim element, partial or complete judgment should be rendered by the [district] court, as there would be no further material issue for the jury to resolve."[334]

In the view of this author, the conceptual difficulty with the vitiation doctrine is that it lacks workable limits. If taken to an extreme, application of the vitiation doctrine itself vitiates the doctrine of equivalents. By definition, application of the doctrine of equivalents contemplates finding infringement liability for accused subject matter that falls outside the literal scope of the claims as construed in step (1) of an infringement analysis. In other words, applying the doctrine of equivalents has always involved a type of "vitiation" of claim limitations. Yet the Supreme Court has consistently reaffirmed the viability of the doctrine of equivalents, despite the uncertainty it creates for those seeking to avoid infringement.[335] Even in *Warner-Jenkinson,* despite the Court's cautionary remarks about vitiating claim limitations, the Court remanded the case to permit further consideration of whether the accused process, operating at a pH of 5, equivalently infringed the patentee's claimed process operating at a pH range of "approximately 6.0-9.0."[336]

Federal Circuit jurisprudence has not developed a consistent framework for identifying when the vitiation doctrine applies, or when it should be rejected. For example, one of the first cases in which the court applied vitiation is *Moore U.S.A., Inc. v. Standard Register*

[331] 520 U.S. 17 (1997).
[332] *Id.* at 29.
[333] *Id.* at 30-31.
[334] *Id.* at 39 n.8.
[335] *See* Eli Lilly and Co. v. Hospira, Inc., 933 F.3d 1320, 1329 (Fed. Cir. 2019) (Lourie, J.) ("Few propositions of patent law have been so consistently sustained by the Supreme Court as the doctrine of equivalents.").
[336] *See Warner-Jenkinson*, 520 U.S. at 41 (reversing and remanding case for further proceedings).

Co.[337] There the court refused to find infringement under the doctrine of equivalents by an accused envelope having adhesive on 47.8 percent of its length. Recognizing equivalency would have "vitiate[d]" the patent claim limitation that required the adhesive to be applied to a "majority" (50.0 percent or more) of the envelope's length.

Although the *Moore U.S.A.* case arguably involved claims reciting numerical ranges (i.e., if one interprets the word "majority" as meaning from 50 to 100 percent of a given length), other Federal Circuit cases reject application of the vitiation doctrine to numerical limitations. For example, in *Abbott Labs. v. Dey, L.P.*,[338] Abbott's asserted claims required that the overall phospholipid component of a lung surfactant composition be present by dry weight in the range of 68.6-90.7 percent. The Federal Circuit vacated a district court's grant of summary judgment of noninfringement and refused to "preclud[e] Abbott from relying on the doctrine of equivalents simply because [its] claim recites numeric ranges for the components of the claimed surfactant."[339] The Federal Circuit concluded that "[t]he fact that a claim recites numeric ranges does not, by itself, preclude Abbott from relying on the doctrine of equivalents."[340]

E. Aspects of Infringement Beyond 35 U.S.C. §271(a)

The majority of patent infringement lawsuits center on allegations that the accused infringer directly infringed under 35 U.S.C. §271(a) by making, using, or selling the claimed invention without authority, as detailed above. These are not the only acts that constitute patent infringement, however. The following section analyzes liability under each of remaining subsections (b) through (g) of 35 U.S.C. §271.

1. Inducing Infringement Under §271(b)

a. Overview

Section 271(b) pertains to the act of inducing infringement, which is analogous to the act of aiding and abetting a crime. Inducing infringement requires that the alleged inducer actively and knowingly aid and

[337] 229 F.3d 1091, 1106 (Fed. Cir. 2000).
[338] 287 F.3d 1097 (Fed. Cir. 2002).
[339] *Id.* at 1108.
[340] *Id.* at 1107-1108 (relying on Jeneric/Pentron, Inc. v. Dillon Co., 205 F.3d 1377, 1381, 1384 (Fed. Cir. 2000); and Forest Labs., Inc. v. Abbott Labs., 239 F.3d 1305, 1313 (Fed. Cir. 2001)).

abet another's direct infringement.[341] While proof of intent is necessary,[342] direct evidence of that intent is not required; rather, circumstantial evidence may suffice.[343] The inducer must have actual or constructive knowledge of the patent.[344]

Inducement cases under 35 U.S.C. §271(b) typically involve one actor (the inducing infringer) providing another (the direct infringer) with instructions and information about how to make or use the accused device or carry out the accused process.[345] A good example of inducing infringement is presented by *Water Techs. Corp. v. Calco, Ltd.*[346] Water Technologies' patent in suit was directed to improved bactericidal resins used as disinfectants for purifying water; the company incorporated the resins into a drinking cup and other products useful to campers, backpackers, and travelers. Calco, a competitor of Water Technologies, directly infringed by making and selling products

[341]*See* Water Techs. Corp. v. Calco, Ltd., 850 F.2d 660, 668 (Fed. Cir. 1998) (explaining that "[a]lthough [35 U.S.C.] section 271(b) does not use the word 'knowing,' the case law and legislative history uniformly assert such a requirement") (citing 4 DONALD S. CHISUM, CHISUM ON PATENTS §17.04[2], [3] (1984) and cases cited therein).

[342]*See Hewlett-Packard Co.,* 909 F.2d at 1469 (noting that although §271(b) does not speak of any intent requirement to actively induce infringement, "we are of the opinion that proof of actual intent to cause the acts which constitute the infringement is a necessary prerequisite to finding active inducement"). For more on the intent standard, *see infra* section E.1.d ("*Global-Tech* (U.S. 2011): 'Willful Blindness' Standard").

[343]*Id.* In *Metro-Goldwyn-Mayer Studios Inc. v. Grokster, Ltd.*, 545 U.S. 913 (2005), the Supreme Court considered whether a software company could face liability for copyright infringement under a theory of inducement when it supplied customers with software that could be used for legitimate noninfringing as well as infringing use (to download copyrighted digital music files). In answering the question affirmatively, the Court adopted and applied the patent law doctrine of inducing infringement under 35 U.S.C. §271(b) to the copyright setting. With respect to proving the intent element of inducing infringement, the Court observed that "[e]vidence of 'active steps . . . taken to encourage direct infringement,' *Oak Industries, Inc. v. Zenith Electronics Corp.*, 697 F. Supp. 988, 992 (N.D. Ill. 1988), such as advertising an infringing use or instructing how to engage in an infringing use, show an affirmative intent that the [dual use] product be used to infringe, and a showing that infringement was encouraged overcomes the law's reluctance to find liability when a defendant merely sells a commercial product suitable for some lawful use" (citations omitted). *Grokster*, 545 U.S. at 936.

[344]*See* Insituform Techs., Inc. v. CAT Contracting, Inc., 161 F.3d 688, 695 (Fed. Cir. 1998). In 2011, the Supreme Court clarified in *Global-Tech Appliances, Inc. v. SEB S.A.*, 131 S. Ct. 2060 (2011) (further analyzed below), that "knowledge of the patent" can be had by one who is "willfully blind" to its existence. A "willfully blind" defendant (more egregious than a "reckless" or "negligent" defendant) "is one who takes deliberate actions to avoid confirming a high probability of wrongdoing and who can almost be said to have actually known the critical facts." *Global-Tech*, 131 S. Ct. at 2070.

[345]Inducing infringement is sometimes also found on the part of corporate officers who actively assist their corporation's direct infringement. Such officers "may be personally liable for inducing infringement regardless of whether the circumstances are such that a court should disregard the corporate entity and pierce the corporate veil." Manville Sales Corp. v. Paramount Sys., Inc., 917 F.2d 544, 553 (Fed. Cir. 1990).

[346]850 F.2d 660 (Fed. Cir. 1988).

formed from the claimed resins. Gartner, a consultant to Calco, provided formulas to Calco, helped the company make the infringing resins, and prepared consumer use instructions. Gartner also owned the trademark Pocket Purifier under which Calco's accused products were sold, which gave him a contractual right to approve the construction of the product. The Federal Circuit found that the totality of these acts and circumstances made Gartner liable for inducing infringement under §271(b).[347] Gartner's activities provided sufficient circumstantial evidence to sustain the district court's finding that his inducement was intentional. As a result, Gartner was held jointly and severally liable with Calco for all damages attributable to Calco's direct infringement.[348]

b. Direct Infringement Predicate

It is well settled that holding an accused infringer liable for inducement under §271(b) also requires proving direct infringement under §271(a). In other words, the activity being induced must itself be infringing; direct infringement is a necessary predicate for the existence of inducing infringement liability.[349] In some cases, the accused direct infringer may be a consumer who allegedly directly infringed by following instructions provided by the alleged inducing infringer. Must the patentee in such scenarios proffer an actual consumer who will testify that he or she directly infringed?

Not necessarily. In appropriate cases, the Federal Circuit has allowed patent owners to establish a consumer's direct infringement by circumstantial (as opposed to direct) evidence. For example, in *Symantec Corp. v. Computer Assocs. Int'l, Inc.,*[350] the patentee Symantec's method claims required that its antivirus program run in conjunction with a consumer/end-user's downloading program (such as an Internet browser). Accused infringer Computer Associates (CA) marketed its own antivirus program. Symantec contended that CA induced its customers to directly infringe because CA's software product manual promoted use of the CA program in an infringing manner, that is, in conjunction with a downloading (browser) program. Symantec further contended that the CA program had no utility other than to

[347]*See id.* at 668-669.

[348]*Id.* at 669.

[349]*See* Akamai Techs., Inc. v. Limelight Networks, Inc., 692 F.3d 1301, 1308 (Fed. Cir. 2012) (*en banc*) ("*Akamai II*") (explaining that "inducement gives rise to liability only if the inducement leads to actual infringement. That principle, that there can be no indirect infringement without direct infringement, is well settled. . . . The reason for that rule is simple: There is no such thing as attempted patent infringement, so if there is no infringement, there can be no indirect liability for infringement.") (citations omitted), *rev'd on other grounds,* 134 S. Ct. 2111 (2014).

[350]522 F.3d 1279 (Fed. Cir. 2008).

work in conjunction with a browser. Although a district court granted CA summary judgment of no inducing infringement based on Symantec's failure to prove that any CA customer directly infringed by actually performing the claimed method, the Federal Circuit reversed. The appellate court concluded that CA's customers could have only used CA's program in an infringing manner; this was "not a case where the customers may be using the product in either an infringing way or a non-infringing way."[351] Symantec had "produced sufficient *circumstantial* evidence of direct infringement to create a genuine issue of material fact, even though Symantec has not produced evidence that *any particular customer* has directly infringed the patent."[352] Circumstantial evidence, as opposed to direct evidence, was adequate to establish the direct infringement predicate for inducing infringement liability in this case.

c. *Intent Requirement*

Federal Circuit case law on inducing infringement under §271(b) has arguably lacked clarity as to whether an accused inducer must merely intend to cause the *acts* that induce another's direct infringement, or whether the accused inducer must also know that its acts would induce what amounts to direct *infringement of a patent.* For example, would Jack be liable for inducing Jill's direct infringement if Jack provided Jill with instructions for making device X, but was not aware that device X was patented or that Jill would infringe the patent if she followed Jack's directions? In light of a perceived conflict in its precedent,[353] the Federal Circuit went *en banc* for a portion of its 2006 opinion in *DSU Med. Corp. v. JMS Co., Ltd.* to clarify the requisite level of intent required for inducing infringement under 35 U.S.C. §271(b).[354]

[351] *Id.* at 1293.

[352] *Id.* (emphasis added).

[353] In *Hewlett-Packard Co. v. Bausch & Lomb*, 909 F.2d 1464 (Fed. Cir. 1990), the court stated that "proof of actual intent to cause the acts which constitute the infringement is a necessary prerequisite to finding active inducement." *Id.* at 1469. Some read *Hewlett-Packard* as signalling that such "intent to cause the acts" is the *only* component of the intent standard for §271(b). This interpretation of *Hewlett-Packard* rendered the case in conflict with the Federal Circuit's decision in *Manville Sales Corp. v. Paramount Sys., Inc.*, 917 F.2d 544 (Fed. Cir. 1990). The court in *Manville Sales* held that "[t]he plaintiff has the burden of showing that the alleged infringer's actions induced infringing acts *and* that he knew or should have known his actions would induce actual infringements." *Id.* at 553 (emphasis added). Not all judges of the Federal Circuit agreed with the restricted reading of *Hewlett-Packard. See* DSU Med. Corp. v. JMS Co., Ltd., 471 F.3d 1293, 1311 (Michel, C.J., and Mayer, J., concurring) (stating that patentee DSU "misreads *Hewlett-Packard*" and that "[t]here is no actual conflict between *Hewlett-Packard* and *Manville* . . .").

[354] 471 F.3d 1293 (Fed. Cir. 2006) (Part III.B of opinion issued by court *en banc*).

The DSU patent in suit was directed to a guarded, winged-needle assembly intended to reduce the risk of accidental needle-stick injuries to health care workers.[355] Accused infringer JMS (Japanese Medical Supply) purchased the guards in Malaysia from co-defendant ITL Corp., an Australian manufacturer, then closed the guards around needles and imported the completed assemblies into the United States. A jury found importer JMS and its U.S. distributor/subsidiary, JMS U.S.A., liable for direct (as well as inducing and contributory) infringement, but declined to find ITL liable for either contributory or inducing infringement. Rejecting patentee DSU's appeal, the Federal Circuit sustained the jury verdicts. With respect to ITL's alleged inducement by selling its needle guards to JMS, the fact that this act occurred outside the United States did not itself shield ITL from liability, because "'induced infringement does not require any activity by the indirect infringer in this country, as long as the direct infringement occurs [in the United States].'"[356] The primary issue, therefore, was whether ITL possessed the requisite *intent* required for liability as an inducer.

The Federal Circuit clarified the intent standard for inducement in an *en banc* portion of the *DSU Med.* decision, instructing that

> as was stated in *Manville Sales Corp. v. Paramount Systems, Inc.*, 917 F.2d 544, 554 (Fed. Cir. 1990), "[t]he plaintiff has the burden of showing that the alleged infringer's actions induced infringing acts and that he knew or should have known his actions would induce actual infringements." The requirement that the alleged infringer knew or should have known his actions would induce actual infringement necessarily includes the requirement that he or she knew of the patent.[357]

In the case at bar, sufficient evidence existed to support the finding implied from the jury's noninfringement verdict that ITL lacked the requisite intent insofar as knowing that its acts would induce actual infringement.[358] Although ITL unquestionably was aware of the DSU patent, ITL's Australian attorney concluded that ITL's needle guard would not infringe. ITL thereafter obtained a written opinion of noninfringement from U.S. counsel. A co-owner of ITL who had participated in designing ITL's guard testified before the jury that ITL had no intent to infringe DSU's patent. This record "support[ed] the jury's

[355] *See* Guarded Winged Needle Assembly, U.S. Patent No. 5,112,311 (issued May 12, 1992).

[356] *DSU Med.*, 471 F.3d at 1305 (quoting district court's jury instruction with approval).

[357] *Id.* at 1304 (*en banc*).

[358] *See id.* at 1306-1307 (describing evidence).

verdict based on the evidence showing a lack of the necessary specific intent," the Federal Circuit concluded.[359]

The Federal Circuit in 2010 applied its *DSU Med.* standard for intent in a case involving knockoffs of "cool touch" deep fat fryers for home use. *SEB S.A. v. Montgomery Ward & Co.*[360] involved an accused inducing infringer, Pentalpha (a wholly owned subsidiary of Global-Tech Appliances, Inc.), which manufactured home appliances in Hong Kong. Pentalpha obtained and copied "all but the cosmetic features" of a deep fryer sold in Hong Kong by SEB S.A. (a French appliance manufacturer). SEB's fryer was protected in the United States by SEB's U.S. patent, but the Hong Kong product bore no U.S. patent marking. Pentalpha obtained an attorney opinion letter that its fryer was non-infringing, but did not bother to tell the attorney that its fryer was a copy of SEB's fryer. Nor did the attorney locate SEB's U.S. patent. When Pentalpha thereafter supplied its copied fryers in the United States to SEB's competitors Sunbeam Products, Fingerhut Corp., and Montgomery Ward & Co., SEB sued for infringement. A jury found Pentalpha liable for inducing infringement under §271(b) (as well as direct infringement under §271(a)), and found that the infringement was willful.

On appeal, the Federal Circuit sustained the jury's verdict. Although the record contained no direct evidence that Pentalpha knew of SEB's patent before SEB filed its lawsuit, the Federal Circuit found adequate evidence to satisfy the circuit's *DSU Med.* "knew of the patent" standard. The Federal Circuit found that "Pentalpha deliberately disregarded a known risk that SEB had a protective patent," and concluded that such "deliberate disregard" was "a form of actual knowledge."[361]

d. Global-Tech *(U.S. 2011): "Willful Blindness" Standard*

The Supreme Court thereafter granted *certiorari* to consider the Federal Circuit's intent standard for inducing infringement under 35 U.S.C. §271(b). In its 2011 decision in *Global-Tech Appliances, Inc. v. SEB S.A.*,[362] the Supreme Court affirmed the Federal Circuit on the merits but rejected the appellate court's "deliberate disregard"

[359]*Id.* at 1307. Questions left open by the *DSU Med.* decision include the scope of the "should have known" component of the inducing intent standard, as well as how the "knowledge of the patent" requirement can be constructively satisfied (a question not at issue in *DSU Med.* because accused inducer ITL had actual knowledge of the patent in suit). In 2011, the Supreme Court addressed the Federal Circuit's "knowledge of the patent" requirement in *Global-Tech Appliances, Inc. v. SEB S.A.*, 131 S. Ct. 2060 (2011). The *Global-Tech* decision is discussed *infra* Section E.1.d.

[360]594 F.3d 1360 (Fed. Cir. 2010).

[361]*See* Global-Tech Appliances, Inc. v. SEB S.A., 131 S. Ct. 2060, 2065 (2011).

[362]131 S. Ct. 2060 (2011).

standard. As a threshold matter, and consistent with its 1964 contributory infringement decision in *Aro Mfg. Co. v. Convertible Top Replacement Co.*,[363] the Supreme Court in *Global-Tech* first held that "induced infringement under §271(b) requires knowledge that the induced acts constitute patent infringement."[364]

Turning to the Federal Circuit's standard for knowledge of the patent, the *Global-Tech* Court agreed with accused infringer Pentalpha that "deliberate indifference to a known risk that a patent exists is not the appropriate standard under §271(b)." Rather, the Court held that the "willful blindness" doctrine of criminal law should apply in civil lawsuits for induced patent infringement under 35 U.S.C. §271(b).[365] The willful blindness doctrine has two basic requirements: "(1) the defendant must subjectively believe that there is a high probability that a fact exists, and (2) the defendant must take deliberate actions to avoid learning of that fact."[366] More egregious than a "reckless" or "negligent" defendant, a "willfully blind" defendant "is one who takes deliberate actions to avoid confirming a high probability of wrongdoing and who can almost be said to have actually known the critical facts."[367]

Applying these standards to the case at bar, the *Global-Tech* Court concluded that the evidence before it "was more than sufficient for a jury to find that Pentalpha subjectively believed there was a high probability that SEB's fryer was patented, that Pentalpha took deliberate steps to avoid knowing that fact, and that it therefore willfully blinded itself to the infringing nature of Sunbeam's sales [i.e., the direct infringement]."[368] The jury "could have easily found" that before the lawsuit was filed, Pentalpha had willfully blinded itself to the infringing nature of the sales it induced Sunbeam to make. Pentalpha's CEO, John Sham, himself an inventor, was "well aware that products made for overseas markets usually do not bear U.S. patent markings."[369] Sham admittedly conducted market research and gathered as much information as he could about SEB's fryer. Most telling was Sham's decision not to inform the attorney from whom he requested a right-to-use opinion that Pentalpha's fryer "was simply a knockoff" of SEB's product. Although the Federal Circuit had applied an incorrect standard, this evidence was more than enough to affirm the circuit's judgment sustaining the jury's verdict of Pentalpha's inducing infringement liability under a correct "willfully blind" standard.

[363]377 U.S. 476 (1964) ("*Aro II*").
[364]*Global-Tech,* 131 S. Ct. at 2068.
[365]*See Global-Tech,* 131 S. Ct. at 2069.
[366]*Global-Tech,* 131 S. Ct. at 2070.
[367]*Global-Tech,* 131 S. Ct. at 2070.
[368]*Global-Tech,* 131 S. Ct. at 2072.
[369]*Global-Tech,* 131 S. Ct. at 2071.

e. Commil USA *(U.S. 2015): Rejecting Belief of Invalidity as Inducement Defense*

In the wake of the Supreme Court's 2011 *Global-Tech* decision, a line of Federal Circuit and district court decisions addressed the separate question whether an accused infringer could avoid inducing infringement liability if it held a good faith belief in the *invalidity* of the asserted patent (regardless of its allegedly infringing acts).[370] The proponents of this theory contended that such belief would negate knowledge that the induced acts were infringing, under the axiom that there can be no infringement of an invalid patent.

In May 2015, the Supreme Court in *Commil USA, LLC v. Cisco Sys., Inc.* (hereafter "*Commil III*") repudiated this position and clarified that a belief as to invalidity is *not* a defense to inducing infringement liability.[371] With eight Justices participating,[372] a majority of six vacated the Federal Circuit's 2013 decision in *Commil I* and held that, as a matter of first impression, an accused infringer's belief regarding patent validity is not a credible defense to a claim of induced infringement under §271(b).[373]

As a threshold matter, five Justices in the *Commil III* majority reaffirmed that the Court's 2011 decision in *Global-Tech Appliances, Inc. v. SEB S.A.*,[374] discussed above, meant that the intent requirement for inducing infringement has two prongs: (1) the alleged inducer must know of the patent in question, and (2) the alleged inducer must know

[370]*See* Commil USA, LLC v. Cisco Sys., Inc., 720 F.3d 1361, 1368 (Fed. Cir. 2013) ("*Commil I*") (majority holding that "evidence of a good-faith belief of invalidity may [also] negate the requisite intent for induced infringement"); *id.* (citing VNUS Med. Techs., Inc. v. Diomed Holdings, Inc., 2007 WL 2900532, at *1 (N.D. Cal. Oct. 2, 2007) ("denying plaintiff's motion for summary judgment on induced infringement based, in part, on an opinion of counsel that the patents-in-suit were invalid"); Kolmes v. World Elastic Corp., 1995 WL 918081, at *10 (M.D.N.C. Sept. 18, 1995) (finding, after a bench trial, no intent to induce infringement where defendants "had a good faith belief in the invalidity" of the patent-in-suit); DataQuill Ltd. v. High Tech Computer Corp., 2011 WL 6013022, at *10 (S.D. Cal. Dec. 1, 2011) (indicating that a belief of invalidity may present a triable issue of fact as to intent to induce infringement); Mark Lemley, *Inducing Patent Infringement*, 39 U.C. Davis L. Rev. 225, 243 (2005) ("[I]t is not reasonable to assume that merely because a defendant is aware of the existence of a patent, he intended to infringe it. He may believe the patent invalid")).

In October 2013, a sharply divided Federal Circuit denied rehearing *en banc* in *Commil I*. *See* Commil USA, LLC v. Cisco Sys., Inc., 737 F.3d 699 (Fed. Cir. Oct. 25, 2013) (*en banc*) (order) (*Commil II*). Circuit Judges Reyna and Newman each authored opinions dissenting from the denial, with a total of 5 out of 11 Circuit judges voting to dissent.

[371]*See* 135 S. Ct. 1920, 1928 (2015) (hereafter *Commil III*).

[372]Justice Breyer did not take part in the case.

[373]*Commil III,* 135 S. Ct. at 1928.

[374]131 S. Ct. 2060 (2011).

that the induced acts infringed the patent.[375] Contrary to this reading, Commil USA and the United States as *amicus* had argued that the *Global-Tech* decision should be understood to require only the first prong (i.e., knowledge of the patent); they contended that the facts of *Global-Tech* did not require the Court to decide in that case whether knowledge of infringement (prong (2)) was required for inducement liability.[376]

The *Commil III* majority rejected the interpretation of *Global-Tech* urged by Commil USA and *amicus* United States. The *Global-Tech* Court's description of the facts before it in that case "suggest[ed] otherwise." In particular, the *Global-Tech* Court had

> concluded there was enough evidence to support a finding that Pentalpha knew "the infringing nature of the sales it encouraged Sunbeam to make." 563 U.S., at ____, 131 S. Ct., at 2071. It was not only knowledge of the existence of SEB's patent that led the Court to affirm the liability finding but also it was the fact that Pentalpha copied "all but the cosmetic features of SEB's fryer," demonstrating Pentalpha knew it would be causing customers to infringe SEB's patent. *Id.*, at ____, 131 S. Ct., at 2071.[377]

The *Commil III* majority thus approved *Global-Tech*'s two-pronged standard for intent as "sound." A more qualified or limited intent standard, as proposed by Commil USA and the United States, would have negative consequences:

> [It] would lead to the conclusion, both in inducement and contributory infringement cases, that a person, or entity, could be liable even though he did not know the acts were infringing. In other words, even if the defendant reads the patent's claims differently from the plaintiff, and that reading is reasonable, he would still be liable because he knew the acts *might* infringe. *Global-Tech* requires more. It requires proof the defendant *knew* the acts were infringing. And the Court's opinion was clear in rejecting any lesser mental state as the standard.[378]

Having thus reaffirmed that under *Global-Tech,* knowledge that the induced acts infringe is required to meet the intent standard for inducement liability, the *Commil III* majority turned to the primary issue before it — whether a good faith belief of a patent's *invalidity* would mean that an alleged inducer could not have such knowledge

[375] *See Commil III,* 135 S. Ct. at 1926-1928. For reasons unstated, Justice Thomas did not join this part of the *Commil III* majority opinion.

[376] *Commil III,* 135 S. Ct. at 1927.

[377] *Commil III,* 135 S. Ct. at 1927.

[378] *Commil III,* 135 S. Ct. at 1928 (citing *Global-Tech,* 131 S. Ct. at 2070-2071) (emphases added).

that the acts it induced were infringing (the theory being that an invalid patent cannot be infringed).

The *Commil III* six-judge majority flatly rejected the notion of an accused inducer's belief in patent invalidity as negating the intent requirement for inducing infringement liability.[379] The majority summarized:

> The question the Court confronts today concerns whether a defendant's belief regarding patent validity is a defense to a claim of induced infringement. It is not. The scienter element for induced infringement concerns infringement; that is a different issue than validity. Section 271(b) requires that the defendant "actively induce[d] infringement." That language requires intent to "bring about the desired result," which is infringement. [*Global-Tech*], 131 S. Ct., at 2065. And because infringement and validity are separate issues under the Act, belief regarding validity cannot negate the scienter required under §271(b).[380]

As further support for its conclusion that infringement and validity should be treated separately, the Court first cited its precedent. Its earlier decisions were "in accord with the long-accepted truth — perhaps the axiom — that infringement and invalidity are separate matters under patent law." [381] Specifically, in its 1993 decision, *Cardinal Chem. Co. v. Morton Int'l, Inc.,*[382] the Court had explained that when a party seeks a declaratory judgment of invalidity, it is "present[ing] a claim independent of the patentee's charge of infringement."[383] Noninfringement and invalidity were "alternative grounds" for dismissing the suit in *Cardinal Chem.*[384] To the same effect, the Court in its 1980 decision, *Deposit Guaranty Nat'l Bank v. Roper,*[385] had explained that an accused infringer "may prevail either by

[379]*See Commil III,* 135 S. Ct. at 1928. Justice Thomas joined this part of the Court's opinion.

[380]*Commil III,* 135 S. Ct. at 1928.

[381]*See Commil III,* 135 S. Ct. at 1928 (citing Pandrol USA, LP v. Airboss R. Prods., Inc., 320 F.3d 1354, 1365 (Fed. Cir. 2003)). In *Pandrol USA,* a district court had entered summary judgment of patent infringement and found that the defendants had waived their affirmative defenses and counterclaims by not raising them during briefing of cross-motions for summary judgment. The Circuit held that the district court did not err in construing the claims; in granting summary judgment of patent infringement against all defendants; or in determining the amount of plaintiffs' lost profits. However, it also held that the defendants did not waive their defense of patent invalidity; nor did they waive their invalidity counterclaim. Accordingly, the Circuit vacated the district court's decision and remanded for further proceedings. *Pandrol USA,* 320 F.3d at 1357.

[382]508 U.S. 83 (1993).

[383]*Cardinal Chem.,* 508 U.S. at 96.

[384]*Cardinal Chem.,* 508 U.S. at 98.

[385]445 U.S. 326 (1980).

successfully attacking the validity of the patent *or* by successfully defending the charge of infringement."[386]

Moreover, the Patent Act (35 U.S.C.) separately locates infringement and validity. The former is dealt with in Part III of the Act (titled "Patents and Protection of Patent Rights"), including the right to be free of infringement.[387] Validity is covered in Part II of the Act (titled "Patentability of Inventions and Grants of Patents").[388] In addition, noninfringement and invalidity are enumerated as two separate defenses under 35 U.S.C. §282(b). The *Commil III* Court accordingly refused to "conflate the issues of infringement and validity" by interpreting §271(b) as permitting a defense of belief in invalidity.

Accepting belief of invalidity as a defense to inducing infringement liability would also undermine the patent law's long-held presumption of validity.[389] "If belief in invalidity were a defense to induced infringement," the *Commil III* Court explained, "the force of that presumption would be lessened to a drastic degree, for a defendant could prevail if he proved he reasonably believed the patent was invalid."[390] That result would contravene the high "clear and convincing evidence" bar that Congress "is presumed to have chosen."[391]

The patent statute treats invalidity as an affirmative defense that " 'can preclude enforcement of a patent against otherwise infringing conduct.' "[392] If a patent is properly shown to be invalid, an accused infringer is not liable for infringing it. That is "because invalidity is not a defense to *infringement*, it is a defense to *liability*," the Court explained, "[a]nd because of that fact, a belief as to invalidity cannot negate the scienter required for induced infringement."[393]

[386] *Deposit Guaranty,* 445 U.S. at 334 (emphasis added).
The Court also noted that determining validity and infringement under the Patent Act's framework requires different procedures and sequences, allocations of burden of proof, and timing. *See Commil III,* 135 S. Ct. at 1929 (citing *Commil I,* 720 F.3d at 1374 (Newman, J., dissenting) (stating that "[v]alidity and infringement are distinct issues, bearing different burdens, different presumptions, and different evidence")).

[387] *Commil III,* 135 S. Ct. at 1928 (citing 35 U.S.C. §§251-329).

[388] *Commil III,* 135 S. Ct. at 1928 (citing 35 U.S.C. §§100-212).

[389] *See* 35 U.S.C. §282(a) (providing in part that "[a] patent shall be presumed valid").

[390] *Commil III,* 135 S. Ct. at 1929. The dissent flatly rejected this reasoning:

> Th[e] presumption [of validity] is not weakened by treating a good-faith belief in invalidity as a defense to induced infringement. An alleged inducer who succeeds in this defense does not thereby call a patent's validity into question. He merely avoids liability for a third party's infringement of a *valid* patent, in no way undermining that patent's presumed validity.

Commil III, 135 S. Ct. at 1931-1932 (Scalia, J., dissenting) (citations omitted).

[391] *Commil III,* 135 S. Ct. at 1929 (citing Microsoft Corp. v. i4i Ltd. Partnership, 131 S. Ct. 2238, 2245-2247 (2011)). *Microsoft v. i4i* is further examined *infra* Chapter 10, Section E.1 ("Burden of Proof").

[392] *Commil III,* 135 S. Ct. at 1929 (quoting 6A Chisum on Patents §19.02 (2015)).

[393] *Commil III,* 135 S. Ct. at 1929 (emphases added).

Practical concerns also counseled against creating a defense based on a good faith belief in invalidity. Firstly, accused infringers who believe the patent they have been charged with infringing is invalid have a number of existing options to obtain a ruling of invalidity; i.e., a declaratory judgment action in federal court or *inter partes* review (as implemented by the America Invents Act of 2011) or reexamination in the USPTO. Accused infringers in federal court may also raise the affirmative defense of invalidity under 35 U.S.C. §282(b)(2); if successful, they will be immune from liability.

As another practical matter, treating a defense to inducement liability based on a good faith belief in patent invalidity would make litigation more burdensome and expensive; "[e]very accused inducer would have an incentive to put forth a theory of invalidity and could likely come up with myriad arguments."[394] Discovery costs would increase, and juries would be challenged to separate an accused inducer's belief regarding validity from the actual issue of validity.

Lastly, the *Commil III* majority responded to the concern that its holding would not make life easier for companies, such as respondent Cisco Systems, targeted by patent assertion entities (pejoratively referred to as patent "trolls").[395] Observing that other avenues exist for dealing with the problem, the Court reminded district courts of their power to impose Fed. R. Civ. P. 11 sanctions in frivolous infringement lawsuits and to shift attorney fees when cases are "exceptional" under §285 of the Patent Act:

> The Court is well aware that an "industry has developed in which firms use patents not as a basis for producing and selling goods but, instead, primarily for obtaining licensing fees." *eBay Inc. v. MercExchange, L.L.C.*, 547 U.S. 388, 396, 126 S. Ct. 1837, 164 L. Ed. 2d 641 (2006) (Kennedy, J., concurring). Some companies may use patents as a sword to go after defendants for money, even when their claims are frivolous. This tactic is often pursued through demand letters, which "may be sent very broadly and without prior investigation, may assert vague claims of infringement, and may be designed to obtain payments that are based more on the costs of defending litigation than on the merit of the patent claims." L. Greisman, Prepared Statement of the Federal Trade Commission on Discussion Draft of Patent Demand Letter Legislation before the Subcommittee on Commerce, Manufacturing, and

[394]*Commil III*, 135 S. Ct. at 1929-1930 (citing Nathan A. Sloan, *Think It Is Invalid? A New Defense to Negate Intent for Induced Infringement*, 23 FED. CIR. B.J. 613, 618 (2013)).

[395]Cisco described patentee Commil to the Court as "a patent assertion entity that does not develop or sell any products but merely holds and monetizes intellectual property. . . ." Brief for Respondent, No. 13-896, Commil USA, LLC v. Cisco Sys., Inc. (Feb. 2015), at 4, *available at* http://www.americanbar.org/content/dam/aba/publications/supreme_court_preview/BriefsV5/13-896_resp.authcheckdam.pdf.

> Trade of the House Committee on Energy and Commerce 2 (2014). This behavior can impose a "harmful tax on innovation." *Ibid.*
>
> No issue of frivolity has been raised by the parties in this case, nor does it arise on the facts presented to this Court. Nonetheless, it is still necessary and proper to stress that district courts have the authority and responsibility to ensure frivolous cases are dissuaded. If frivolous cases are filed in federal court, it is within the power of the court to sanction attorneys for bringing such suits. Fed. Rule Civ. Proc. 11. It is also within the district court's discretion to award attorney's fees to prevailing parties in "exceptional cases." 35 U.S.C. §285; see also *Octane Fitness, LLC v. ICON Health & Fitness, Inc.,* 572 U.S. ___, ___ ___, 134 S. Ct. 1749, 1755-1756, 188 L. Ed. 2d 816 (2014)....[396]

The *Commil III* majority concluded that these safeguards, when added to the several different avenues that accused inducers already possess to obtain rulings on patent invalidity, militated in favor of maintaining "the separation expressed throughout the Patent Act between infringement and validity. This dichotomy means that belief in invalidity is no defense to a claim of induced infringement."[397]

2. Contributory Infringement Under §271(c)

Section 271(c) governs contributory infringement, which involves one entity (the contributory infringer) supplying a "nonstaple" component of a claimed invention to another entity (the direct infringer), who makes, uses, or sells the entire invention. A nonstaple component is a component or part of an invention that is not suitable for any substantial use other than in the patented invention.[398] Determining that a supplied component is a nonstaple allows courts to "identify instances in which it may be presumed from distribution of an article in commerce that the distributor intended the article to be used to infringe another's patent, and so may justly be held liable for that infringement."[399] Where an article is " 'good for nothing else' but infringement, there is no legitimate public interest in its unlicensed availability, and there is no injustice in presuming or imputing an intent to infringe."[400]

[396] *Commil III,* 135 S. Ct. at 1930-1931. The dissent charged that in including this discussion, the majority had "seemingly acknowledge[d]" that its decision "increases the *in terrorem* power of patent trolls." *Commil,* 135 S. Ct. at 1932 (Scalia, J., dissenting).

[397] *Commil III,* 135 S. Ct. at 1931.

[398] *See* Dawson Chem. Co. v. Rohm & Haas Co., 448 U.S. 176, 184 (1980) (citing Fifth Circuit's definition of a nonstaple article as "one that has no commercial use except in connection with respondent's patented invention").

[399] Metro-Goldwyn-Mayer Studios Inc. v. Grokster, Ltd., 545 U.S. 913, 932 (2005).

[400] *Id.* (citations omitted).

For example, the accused contributory infringer in *Dawson Chemical Co. v. Rohm & Haas Co.*[401] supplied the herbicide propanil to farmers. By using the propanil to control weeds in their rice crops in accordance with the process claimed in the patent in suit, the farmers became liable as direct infringers (presumably for "using" the patented process without authorization). While not covered by a patent, the herbicide propanil was a qualifying nonstaple commodity that had no use other than in the claimed method.[402]

The staple/nonstaple distinction is the key to contributory infringement. Section 271(c) provides a patent owner with "a limited power to exclude others from competition in nonstaple goods,"[403] but does not permit her to control the supply of staple goods, which could have many noninfringing uses.[404] For example, consider a patented process for making cookies that comprises (among other steps) a step of adding salt to a dough mixture. A party who supplies salt to the accused cookie maker cannot be liable for contributory infringement because salt is a staple that has many uses other than in the claimed cookie-making process.[405]

As is the case for inducing infringement under §271(b), there cannot be contributory infringement liability under §271(c) unless direct infringement is proven under §271(a). In the absence of direct infringement, there is no improper act to which an accused contributory infringer can be said to have contributed. When a patentee seeks to establish the §271(a) predicate for §271(c) contributory liability by a component supplier, attention must be given to patent law's distinction between permissible "repair" versus infringing "reconstruction." For example, in *Aro Mfg. Co. v. Convertible Top Replacement Co.*,[406] the patent in suit was directed to a top assembly for convertible cars. The claimed assembly required several different components, one of

[401] 448 U.S. 176 (1980).

[402] *Id.* at 199.

[403] *Id.* at 201.

[404] The staple article of commerce doctrine "absolves the equivocal conduct of selling an item with substantial lawful as well as unlawful uses, and limits liability to instances of more acute fault than the mere understanding that some of one's products will be misused. It leaves breathing room for innovation and a vigorous commerce." *Grokster*, 545 U.S. at 932-933 (citations omitted).

[405] *See* Carbice Corp. of Am. v. Am. Patents Dev. Corp., 283 U.S. 27 (1931) (reversing finding that patent directed to "transportation packages" in which solid carbon dioxide was used as a refrigerant was contributorily infringed by defendant supplier of solid carbon dioxide ("dry ice")). It was not relevant that the defendant sold its product "with knowledge that the dioxide is to be used by the purchaser in transportation packages like those described in the patent," *id.* at 30, or that "the unpatented refrigerant [was] one of the necessary elements of the patented product." *Id.* at 33.

[406] 365 U.S. 336 (1961) ("*Aro I*").

which was a fabric top.[407] These tops tended to wear out much more rapidly than the other components of the assembly,[408] and consumers purchased replacement fabric tops directly from the defendant supplier. When the patentee sued the supplier for contributory infringement, the Supreme Court held that no such liability existed because no direct infringement had occurred. The replacement of the fabric top was within the consumers' implied right to repair their property; a purchaser is deemed to have obtained an implied license to use the patented device she has purchased, which includes a right to repair it.[409] Replacement of the fabric top did not amount to an infringing reconstruction (i.e., a new making) of the entire claimed assembly.[410] Because the consumer purchasers were not direct infringers, the defendant supplier of the replacement tops could not be liable as a contributory infringer.

Infringement actions asserting contributory liability under 35 U.S.C. §271(c) will sometimes trigger an affirmative defense of patent misuse, as in the *Dawson* case described above and further considered in Chapter 10 ("Defenses to Patent Infringement"), *infra.* In such cases §271(c) must be read in conjunction with 35 U.S.C. §271(d). Rather than affirmatively defining patent misuse, §271(d) enumerates acts that are *not* misuse by listing five specific exceptions or "safe harbors" to patent misuse on which a patentee may rely. Chapter 10 considers in further detail the §271(d) statutory exceptions to patent misuse as well as judicially recognized acts that *will* constitute patent misuse.

3. Drug Marketing Application Filings Under §271(e)

Section 271(e) is particularly pertinent to allegations of infringement in the pharmaceutical industry. In recent years, an increasing number of firms that manufacture generic equivalent drugs have sought entry onto the market before the expiration of the patents covering those drugs, which are owned by brand-name pharmaceutical

[407] *See id.* at 337 (noting that patent in suit "covers the combination, in an automobile body, of a flexible top fabric, supporting structures, and a mechanism for sealing the fabric against the side of the automobile body in order to keep out the rain").

[408] *See id.* at 337-338 (explaining that "[t]he components of the patented combination, other than the fabric, normally are usable for the lifetime of the car, but the fabric . . . usually so suffers from wear and tear, or so deteriorates in appearance, as to become 'spent,' and normally is replaced, after about three years of use").

[409] *See* Aro Mfg. Co. v. Convertible Top Replacement Co., 377 U.S. 476, 484 (1964) ("*Aro II*") (stating that "it is fundamental that sale of a patented article by the patentee or under his authority carries with it an 'implied license to use' ") (citing Adams v. Burke, 84 U.S. (17 Wall.) 453, 456 (1873)).

[410] *See* Hewlett-Packard Co. v. Repeat-O-Type Stencil Mfg. Corp., 123 F.3d 1445, 1451-1452 (Fed. Cir. 1997).

manufacturers.[411] These efforts frequently lead to patent infringement/validity litigation between the brand-name and generic firms, as described below. Such litigation activity has spawned a growing demand for attorneys trained both in patent law and regulatory food and drug law.

Section 271(e) was enacted in 1984 pursuant to the Drug Price Competition and Patent Term Restoration Act of 1984,[412] popularly known as the Hatch-Waxman Act. The legislation added, *inter alia*, §271(e)(1) to the Patent Act, which provides in pertinent part that the use of a patented invention solely for purposes reasonably related to gathering data in support of an application seeking Food and Drug Administration (FDA) approval for the manufacture and sale of a generic version of a previously FDA-approved drug (i.e., an "Abbreviated New Drug Application," or ANDA) is *not* patent infringement.[413] Without such a provision, generic drug manufacturers would have to wait to begin testing of an equivalent drug until after the relevant patent had expired, and the patentee of the branded drug would receive a *de facto* extension of the patent term.[414]

The §271(e)(1) safe harbor is not limited to testing conducted by generic drug manufacturers, however. The Supreme Court interpreted the scope of §271(e)(1) in *Merck KgaA v. Integra Lifesciences I, Ltd.*,[415] and held it broad enough to encompass clinical (human) trials as well as pre-clinical (test tube and laboratory animal) testing activity associated with the development of new (or "pioneer") drugs. The Federal Circuit had erred in excluding Merck KgaA–sponsored testing at the Scripps Research Institute of patented peptides with potential cancer-fighting activity from the statutory safe harbor on the ground that its purpose was to identify the best drug candidate for future clinical testing and was thus too remote from the safe harbor's purview. According to the Supreme Court, the facts that not all data developed

[411]*See* Federal Trade Commission, *Generic Drug Entry Prior to Patent Expiration: An FTC Study*, at ii (July 2002), *available at* https://www.ftc.gov/sites/default/files/documents/reports/generic-drug-entry-prior-patent-expiration-ftc-study/genericdrugstudy_0.pdf.

[412]Pub. L. No. 98-417, 98 Stat. 1585 (1984).

[413]Section 271(e)(1) of 35 U.S.C. provides:

> It shall not be an act of infringement to make, use, offer to sell, or sell within the United States or import into the United States a patented invention . . . solely for uses reasonably related to the development and submission of information under a Federal law which regulates the manufacture, use, or sale of drugs or veterinary biological products.

[414]The U.S. Supreme Court subsequently interpreted 35 U.S.C. §271(e)(1) as broad enough to encompass not only regulatory data gathering on pharmaceuticals but also the comparable testing of medical devices. *See* Eli Lilly & Co. v. Medtronic, Inc., 496 U.S. 661, 679 (1990) (affirming Federal Circuit's interpretation).

[415]545 U.S. 193 (2005).

during pre-clinical and clinical testing are ultimately submitted to the FDA, and that some testing involves drugs not ultimately the subject of an FDA application, are not determinative of eligibility for the liability shield. Rather, "[p]roperly construed, §271(e)(1) leaves adequate space for experimentation and failure on the road to regulatory approval: At least where a drugmaker has a reasonable basis for believing that a patented compound may work, through a particular biological process, to produce a particular physiological effect, and uses the compound in research that, if successful, would be appropriate to include in a submission to the FDA, that use is 'reasonably related' to the 'development and submission of information under... Federal law.' §271(e)(1)."[416] Although broad enough to encompass testing of new drugs as well as generic equivalents, the *Merck KgaA* Court made clear that the statutory safe harbor does have limits; §271(e)(1) is not broad enough to reach back in time to shield "[b]asic scientific research on a particular compound, performed without the intent to develop a particular drug or a reasonable belief that the compound will cause the sort of physiological effect the researcher intends to induce."[417]

Federal Circuit decisions in the wake of *Merck KgaA* continue to explore permutations of the §271(e)(1) safe harbor. For example, the appellate court held in *Amgen, Inc. v. Int'l Trade Comm'n* that the safe harbor shielded imports of the biopharmaceutical erythropoiten (EPO) by intervenor Hoffman-La Roche, because the safe harbor applies to §337 actions at the International Trade Commission (ITC).[418] In contrast, the Federal Circuit distinguished *Merck KgaA* and narrowly interpreted the §271(e)(1) safe harbor in *Proveris Sci. Corp. v. Innovasystems, Inc.*[419] so as to uphold a district court's finding of infringement by Innova's optical spray "Analyzer" device. The Analyzer was not itself subject to FDA approval, but rather was a laboratory tool used exclusively by those preparing FDA regulatory submissions to measure and calibrate physical parameters of aerosol sprays used in devices such as inhalers. The Federal Circuit was persuaded that because Innova was not itself seeking FDA approval for the Analyzer device and did not face regulatory barriers to market entry after the expiration of competitors' patents (unlike the typical case with drug manufacturers), Innova was not within the scope of intended beneficiaries of the §271(e)(1) safe harbor and did not need that statutory protection.

The Hatch-Waxman Act also added §271(e)(2) to the Patent Act. This subsection provides that it *is* an act of patent infringement to submit an

[416] *Id.* at 207.
[417] *Id.* at 205-206.
[418] 519 F.3d 1343 (Fed. Cir. 2008).
[419] 536 F.3d 1256 (Fed. Cir. 2008).

ANDA to the FDA if the generic applicant is seeking approval to engage in the commercial manufacture, use, or sale of a patented drug before the expiration of the patent.[420] The mere act of filing the ANDA is considered an act of infringement, even though the generic firm has not yet engaged in any commercial manufacture or sale of the drug (because it does not yet have FDA approval to do so).[421]

Generic drug manufacturers submitting an ANDA must certify one of four things: (1) that the drug for which the ANDA is submitted has not been patented (a "paragraph I" certification); (2) that any patent on such drug has expired (a "paragraph II" certification); (3) the date on which the patent on such drug will expire, if it has not yet expired (a "paragraph III" certification); or (4) that the patent on such drug "is invalid or that it will not be infringed by the manufacture, use, or sale of the new drug" for which the ANDA is submitted (a "paragraph IV" certification).[422]

Paragraph IV certifications are of the greatest interest here, because they generally trigger patent infringement litigation. A generic firm that submits a paragraph IV certification to the FDA also must give notice to the owner of the relevant patent.[423] This notice triggers a 45-day period in which the patentee can initiate an action against the generic firm for infringement under 35 U.S.C. §271(e)(2). If the patentee does not sue within this period, then approval of the ANDA "shall be made effective immediately" (assuming that the ANDA meets all applicable scientific and regulatory requirements).[424]

If, however, the patent owner brings an infringement action under §271(e)(2) within the required time period, the FDA must suspend approval of the ANDA.[425] The suspension continues — and the FDA cannot approve the ANDA — until the earliest of three dates: (1) if the district court hearing the lawsuit decides that the patent is invalid or not infringed, the date of the court's decision; (2) if the court decides

[420]Subsection 271(e)(2) of 35 U.S.C. provides:

> It shall be an act of infringement to submit —
>
> (A) an application under section 505(j) of the Federal Food, Drug, and Cosmetic Act [21 U.S.C. §355(j)] or described in section 505(b)(2) of such Act [21 U.S.C. §355(b)(2)] for a drug claimed in a patent or the use of which is claimed in a patent,
>
> . . . if the purpose of such submission is to obtain approval under such Act to engage in the commercial manufacture, use, or sale of a drug or veterinary biological product claimed in a patent or the use of which is claimed in a patent before the expiration of such patent.

[421]*See* Yamanouchi Pharm. Co. v. Danbury Pharmacal, Inc., 231 F3d 1339, 1346 (Fed. Cir. 2000). Courts sometimes refer to the ANDA filing as "technical infringement."

[422]*See* 21 U.S.C. §355(j)(2)(A)(vii)(I)-(IV).

[423]*See id.* §355(j)(2)(B)(i)(I).

[424]*See id.* §355(j)(5)(B)(iii).

[425]*See id.*

that the patent has been infringed, the date that the patent expires; or (3) subject to modification by the court, the date that is 30 months from the date on which the patent owner received notice of the generic firm's paragraph IV certification.[426]

Summarizing the above statutory scheme, the Federal Circuit concluded that

> the Hatch-Waxman Act strikes a balance between the interests of a party seeking approval of an ANDA and the owner of a drug patent. On the one hand, the manufacture, use, or sale of a patented drug is not an act of infringement, to the extent it is necessary for the preparation and submission of an ANDA. On the other hand, once it is clear that a party seeking approval of an ANDA wants to market a patented drug prior to the expiration of the patent, the patent owner can seek to prevent approval of the ANDA by bringing a patent infringement suit. While it is pending, such a suit can have the effect of barring ANDA approval for two and a half years [i.e., 30 months].[427]

Some pharmaceutical industry observers question whether the current statutory framework correctly balances the interests of patent owners, generic drug manufacturers, and consumers. They contend that the regulatory framework permits patent owners to postpone competition from generic manufacturers for too long, to the detriment of the consumers who would otherwise benefit from lower drug prices.

In October 2002, then-President George W. Bush announced proposed changes to the FDA's rules for approval of ANDAs, targeting patent owners whom the government contends have improperly delayed market entry of generic drugs for up to 40 additional months by obtaining multiple 30-month stays of FDA approval of a given ANDA.[428] The proposed rules limited patent owners to only one 30-month automatic

[426]*See id.* §355(j)(5)(B)(iii)(I)-(III); 35 U.S.C. §271(e)(4)(A).

[427]Bristol-Myers Squibb Co. v. Royce Labs., Inc., 69 F.3d 1130, 1132 (Fed. Cir. 1995).

[428]*See* Office of the White House Press Secretary, *President Takes Action to Lower Prescription Drug Prices by Improving Access to Generic Drugs* (Oct. 21, 2002), https://georgewbush-whitehouse.archives.gov/news/releases/2002/10/20021021-4.html; Federal Trade Commission, *Generic Drug Entry Prior to Patent Expiration: An FTC Study* (July 2002), *available at* https://www.ftc.gov/sites/default/files/documents/reports/generic-drug-entry-prior-patent-expiration-ftc-study/genericdrugstudy_0.pdf. The *FTC Study* explains how patent owners may generate multiple 30-month stays by listing additional patents in the FDA's Orange Book after a given ANDA is filed by a generic firm. The generic firm is required to recertify as to those additionally listed patents, which may trigger the patentee to seek additional 30-month stays by adding those patents to its infringement complaint. *See id.* at iii. The "Orange Book" is the colloquial term for an FDA publication officially titled *Approved Drug Products with Therapeutic Equivalents. Id.* at 5. When a brand-name company seeks FDA approval to market a new drug product, it must list in the Orange Book the patents relevant to that product, including not only any patents on the active ingredient(s) of the drug product but also patents on specific formulations (e.g., a tablet form) and methods of use (e.g., use to

stay per a given ANDA, which the government contended is an appropriate time period for resolution of the infringement case.[429] The proposed rule was made final and effective as of August 2003.[430]

4. Component Exports Under §271(f)

a. Overview

Subsection (f) of 35 U.S.C. §271 is a hybrid statutory provision that concerns acts of infringement that are completed outside the geographic borders of the United States, but were begun by inducing or contributory activity within the United States. Thus, §271(f) involves certain extraterritorial activities, but those activities must have a nexus to acts occurring in the United States. When that nexus is adequately established, §271(f) creates liability as an exception to the "general rule under United States patent law that no infringement occurs when a patented product is made and sold in another country."[431] Section 271(f) provides:

> (f) (1) Whoever without authority supplies or causes to be supplied in or from the United States all or a substantial portion of the components of a patented invention, where such components are uncombined in whole or in part, in such manner as to actively induce the combination of such components outside of the United States in a manner that would infringe the patent if such combination occurred within the United States, shall be liable as an infringer.
>
> (2) Whoever without authority supplies or causes to be supplied in or from the United States any component of a patented invention that is especially made or especially adapted for use in the invention and not a staple article or commodity of commerce suitable for substantial noninfringing use, where such component is uncombined in whole or in part, knowing that such component is so made or adapted and intending that such component will be combined outside of the United States in a manner that would infringe the patent if such combination occurred within the United States, shall be liable as an infringer.

Section 271(f) can be more easily understood if one is familiar with its history. Congress enacted the section in 1984 to close a loophole in 35 U.S.C. §271 that came to light with the U.S. Supreme Court's

---

treat heartburn in mammals). *See id. See also* U.S. FOOD & DRUG ADMINISTRATION, ELECTRONIC ORANGE BOOK (Sept. 2008), http://www.fda.gov/cder/ob.

[429]*See* Federal Trade Commission, *Generic Drug Entry Prior to Patent Expiration: An FTC Study* 6-7 (July 2002), *available at* https://www.ftc.gov/sites/default/files/documents/reports/generic-drug-entry-prior-patent-expiration-ftc-study/genericdrugstudy_0.pdf.

[430]68 FED. REG. 36676 (June 18, 2003).

[431]Microsoft Corp. v. AT&T Corp., 550 U.S. 437, 127 S. Ct. 1746, 1750 (2007).

1972 decision in *Deepsouth Packing Co. v. Laitram Corp.*[432] There the Court was confronted with a case of alleged patent infringement in which the various component parts of a patented shrimp deveining machine were separately sold by a U.S. manufacturer to foreign buyers, who then assembled the deveining machine beyond U.S. borders in countries such as Brazil.[433] Was this offshore assembly actionable as a making of the patented invention under §271(a)? The Court concluded that it was not, because it interpreted "making" to require final assembly or combination of the "operable whole,"[434] and the assembly in question did not occur within U.S. borders.[435] The Court moreover refused to apply U.S. patent laws extraterritorially to make the foreign assembly an act of infringement in the United States.[436]

[432]406 U.S. 518 (1972). *See also* Rotec Indus., Inc. v. Mitsubishi Corp., 215 F.3d 1246, 1258 (Fed. Cir. 2000) (Newman, J., concurring) (explaining that "Congress enacted 35 U.S.C. §271(f), 'respond[ing] to the United States Supreme Court decision in [*Deepsouth*], concerning the need for a legislative solution to close a loophole in patent law.' 130 Cong. Rec. 28,069 (1984). *See also* S. Rep. No. 98-663 at 2 (1984) (describing the legislation as 'reversal of *Deepsouth* decision').").

[433]*Deepsouth,* 406 U.S. at 523 n.5.

[434]*See id.* at 528 (stating that "[w]e cannot endorse the view that the 'substantial manufacture of the constituent parts of [a] machine' constitutes direct infringement when we have so often held that a combination patent protects only against the operable assembly of the whole and not the manufacture of its parts").

[435]The Federal Circuit distinguished *Deepsouth* in a case involving alleged infringement by the Blackberry wireless e-mail device. In *NTP, Inc. v. Research in Motion, Ltd.*, 392 F.3d 1336 (Fed. Cir. 2004), the patent in suit was directed to a system for sending e-mail messages between two subscribers; transmissions were made between an originating processor and a destination processor but passed through an "interface switch." In the accused Blackberry system, the interface switch claim limitation was met by a relay physically housed in Canada; on this basis the alleged infringer argued that under *Deepsouth*, there was no actionable infringement within the United States. The Federal Circuit disagreed, concluding that the location of infringement in this case was within U.S. territory, in contrast with *Deepsouth.* All components of the accused Blackberry system except the relay were located in the United States, and the location of the beneficial use and function of the whole operable system assembly was the United States. Therefore, the situs of the "use" of the accused system for purposes of 35 U.S.C. §271(a) was the United States. *See NTP*, 392 F.3d at 1366-1370 (analogizing case to *Decca Ltd. v. United States*, 544 F.2d 1070 (Ct. Cl. 1976)).

[436]*See Deepsouth*, 406 U.S. at 531, stating:

> In conclusion, we note that what is at stake here is the right of American companies to compete with an American patent holder in foreign markets. Our patent system makes no claim to extraterritorial effect; "these acts of Congress do not, and were not intended to, operate beyond the limits of the United States," *Brown v. Duchesne,* 19 How., at 195; and we correspondingly reject the claims of others to such control over our markets. *Cf.* Boesch v. Graff, 133 U.S. 697, 703 (1890). To the degree that the inventor needs protection in markets other than those of this country, the wording of 35 U.S.C. §§154 and 271 reveals a congressional intent to have him seek it abroad through patents secured in countries where his goods are being used. Respondent holds foreign patents; it does not adequately explain why it does not avail itself of them.

Because in the *Deepsouth* Court's view there was no act of direct infringement, the component supplier could not be held liable for contributory infringement under 35 U.S.C. §271(c).[437]

Section 271(f) represents a legislative overruling of the *Deepsouth* decision. The two subparagraphs of §271(f) are structured so as to parallel the inducing and contributory infringement provisions of 35 U.S.C. §271(b) and (c). More specifically, §271(f)(1) echoes the inducing infringement provisions of §271(b) to render infringing the act of supplying "in or from the United States all or a substantial portion of the components of a patented invention" in such a manner as to "actively induce the combination of such components outside of the United States." Similarly, §271(f)(2) echoes the contributory infringement provisions of §271(c) to render infringing the act of supplying "in or from the United States" a nonstaple component of a patented invention "intending that such component will be combined outside of the United States."[438]

b. Liability

Federal Circuit decisions continue to grapple with the limits of extraterritoriality under 35 U.S.C. §271(f). For example, the potential infringement liability of one who "supplies or causes to be supplied in or from the United States all or a substantial portion of the components of a patented invention" under §271(f)(1) does not extend to the mere supply of instructions or authorization from the United States, according to the Federal Circuit's decision in *Pellegrini v. Analog Devices, Inc.*[439] Pellegrini's patent was directed to brushless motor drive circuits that incorporated integrated circuit chips. The chips fabricated and sold by accused infringer Analog Devices were manufactured entirely outside the United States and shipped only to customers outside the United States. Nevertheless, Pellegrini argued that because Analog's corporate headquarters was located in the United States and instructions for the production and disposition of the chips emanated there, the chips should have been regarded as "supplied or caused to be supplied in or from the United States." The Federal Circuit disagreed, holding that the plain meaning of §271(f)(1) makes it applicable only where components of a patent

[437]*See id.* at 526.

[438]The patentee asserting infringement under 35 U.S.C. §271(f)(2) need not show that the final assembly in the foreign country actually occurred, only that the nonstaple component was supplied from the United States with the intent that the final assembly would take place. *See* Waymark Corp. v. Porta Sys. Corp., 245 F.3d 1364 (Fed. Cir. 2001).

[439]375 F.3d 1113 (Fed. Cir. 2004).

invention are physically present in the United States and then either sold or exported "in such a manner as to actively induce the combination of such components outside the United States in a manner that would infringe the patent if such combination occurred within the United States." Here, the components (i.e., circuit chips) were not present in the United States prior to their combination offshore. The language "supplying or causing to be supplied" in §271(f)(1) "clearly refers to physical supply of components, not simply to the supply of instructions or corporate oversight," the *Pellegrini* court concluded. "[A]lthough Analog may be giving instructions from the United States that cause the components of the patented invention to be supplied, it is undisputed that those components are not being supplied in or from the United States."[440]

The Federal Circuit distinguished *Pellegrini* in *Eolas Techs., Inc. v. Microsoft Corp.*[441] The patent in suit in *Eolas* claimed a "computer program product" comprising *inter alia* a "computer usable medium having computer readable program code physically embodied therein." The claimed invention allowed a user to employ a Web browser in a fully interactive environment, for example, viewing news clips or playing games across the Internet. Eolas, the exclusive licensee of the patent, alleged that certain aspects of Microsoft's Internet Explorer (IE) browser incorporated the claimed invention. Eolas further contended that under 35 U.S.C. §271(f)(1), Microsoft's foreign sales of its IE browser should have been included in the damages base. The legal dispute centered on whether Microsoft's export to foreign manufacturers of certain "golden master" disks containing software code for the Microsoft Windows operating system (including code for the IE browser) constituted the supply of "components" under the statute. The foreign manufacturers used the golden master disks to replicate the software code onto computer hard drives for sale outside of the United States, but the golden master disks themselves did not become a physical part of any infringing product.

The Federal Circuit rejected accused infringer Microsoft's argument that "components of a patented invention" under §271(f)(1) must be limited to physical or tangible components, as suggested by *Pellegrini*. Rather, the *Eolas* court concluded, "every form of invention eligible for patenting falls within the protection of section 271(f)," and "software code claimed in conjunction with a physical structure, such as a disk, fits within . . . the broad statutory label of 'patented invention.'" Exact

[440] *Id.* at 1118.
[441] 399 F.3d 1325 (Fed. Cir. 2005).

duplicates of the software code on the golden master disks were incorporated into the ultimate products, and that code was "probably the key part" of the patented invention. The *Eolas* court distinguished *Pellegrini* as requiring only that components be "physically *supplied* from the United States,"[442] not that the components themselves *be* physical. *Pellegrini* did "not impose on section 271(f) a tangibility requirement that does not appear anywhere in the language of that section."[443]

Eolas was not the only patent owner to allege a violation of §271(f) based on Microsoft's distribution of its Windows operating system software to foreign computer manufacturers. When the AT&T Corporation sued Microsoft for infringement under §271(f), the case eventually made its way to the Supreme Court. In *Microsoft Corp. v. AT&T Corp.,*[444] the Court held that Microsoft's export of the golden master disks (or counterpart electronic transmissions) containing Windows software for copying and installation on foreign-made computers did *not* trigger infringement liability under §271(f).

AT&T's patent in suit was directed to apparatus for digitally encoding and compressing recorded speech. Microsoft's Windows operating system admittedly included code that enabled a computer to process speech per AT&T's patent claims. Importantly, however, the AT&T claims were infringed only when the relevant Windows code was *installed* on a computer; infringement of the claims occurred "only when a computer is loaded with Windows and is thereby rendered capable of performing as the patented speech processor."[445] The key facet of Microsoft's distribution scheme that avoided infringement liability was that while Microsoft exported the disks (or sent electronic transmissions) containing the code capable of infringing AT&T's patent, those disks or e-mails were not *themselves* installed on the foreign-made computers. Instead, the foreign computer manufacturers first made *copies* of the Windows software, and then used those foreign-made software copies for installation outside the United States. The Supreme Court held that Microsoft's liability did *not* extend to "computers made in another country when loaded with Windows software *copied abroad* from a master disk or electronic transmission

[442] *Id.* at 1341 (emphasis in original).
[443] *Id.*
[444] 550 U.S. 437, 127 S. Ct. 1746 (2007).
[445] *Id.*, 127 S. Ct. at 1750.

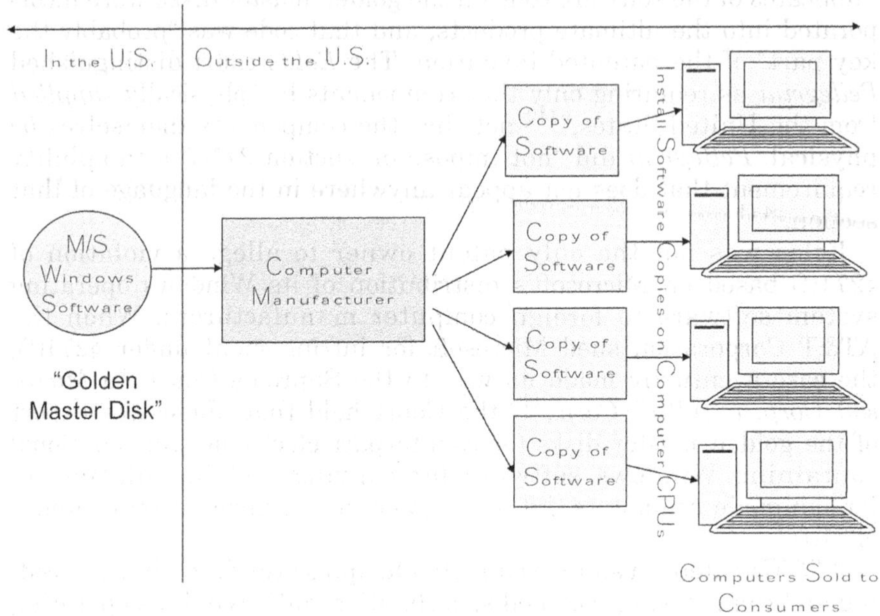

Figure 9.4

Software Distribution Scheme in *AT&T v. Microsoft*

dispatched by Microsoft from the United States."[446] Figure 9.4 depicts Microsoft's distribution scheme.

Because Microsoft did not export the software copies actually installed on the foreign-made computers, the *AT&T* Court concluded, Microsoft had not supplied "components" of the claimed invention from the United States "under §271(f) as currently written."[447] The relevant components were the software copies, and those components were supplied from places outside the United States. In its ruling the Supreme Court emphasized the general presumption against extraterritorial application of U.S. laws. The presumption that United States law "does not rule the world" applies "with particular force" in patent law.[448] The Court accordingly "resist[ed] giving the language in which Congress cast §271(f) an expansive interpretation," deferring to "Congress' informed judgment [whether] any adjustment of §271(f) [is] necessary or proper."[449]

[446]*Id.* at 1750-1751 (emphasis added).

[447]*Id.* at 1750.

[448]*Id.* at 1758 (citing 35 U.S.C. §154(a)(1) and Deepsouth Packing Co. v. Laitram Corp., 406 U.S. 518, 531 (1972)).

[449]*Id.* at 1751. Responding to AT&T's argument that denying §271(f) liability in this case creates an easily exploited loophole for software makers, the Supreme Court observed that "Congress is doubtless aware of the ease with which software (and other

c. *Remedy*

As commerce and trade in patented technology become increasingly global, the importance of 35 U.S.C. §271(f) continues to expand. A 2018 Supreme Court decision concerning the damages available when §271(f) infringement is proved will likely further enhance the statutory provision's significance.

The Supreme Court in *WesternGeco LLC v. ION Geophysical Corp.* ("*WesternGeco IV*")[450] approved a Southern District of Texas jury's award of substantial lost profits damages[451] accrued for a patentee's loss of contract services performed by the accused infringer *outside* the United States. The infringer ION had exported the invention's key components for foreign assembly so as to violate §271(f)(2). It manufactured the components of its competing system (including component(s) specially adapted for the claimed invention) in the United States, then shipped them abroad for offshore combination (hence, §271(a) liability was not triggered because a complete "making" did not occur in United States territory.)

At trial, patentee WesternGeco proved that due to ION's infringement, it had lost ten contracts for surveying various ocean floor locations outside U.S. waters. Upon finding liability, the jury awarded WesternGeco damages of $12.5 million in reasonable royalties plus, central to the parties' dispute, $93.4 million in lost profits for the value of the ten lost overseas contracts.

It is well settled that if patent infringement involves "using" or "selling" an entire patented invention under *subsection (a)* of 35 U.S.C. §271, the direct infringement provision, damages are recoverable only for those uses or sales that occur within U.S. borders, *not* for any extraterritorial uses or sales.[452] That is, the reach of §271*(a)* is purely domestic.

---

electronic media) can be copied." *Id.* at 1760 (citing Congress's 1998 enactment of the Digital Millennium Copyright Act, 17 U.S.C. §§1201 *et seq.*). If patent law should be adjusted to better account for the realities of software distribution, such alteration "should be made after focused legislative consideration, and not by the Judiciary forecasting Congress' likely disposition." *Id.*

[450] 138 S. Ct. 2129 (June 22, 2018) (Thomas, J.) ("*WesternGeco IV*").

[451] The remedy of lost profits damages seeks to put a patentee back in the position it would have been in but for the infringement. This includes profits the patentee would have made had the infringer not infringed. Lost profits damages are examined in further detail *infra* Chapter 11, Section D.2.a.

[452] *See* Power Integrations, Inc. v. Fairchild Semiconductor Int'l, Inc., 711 F.3d 1348, 1371 (Fed. Cir. 2013) (agreeing with district court that jury's award of "worldwide damages" for infringer's making or selling the patented invention in the United States under §271(a) was contrary to law; accordingly rejecting patentee's argument that "it was foreseeable that Fairchild's infringement in the United States would cause Power Integrations to lose sales in foreign markets"); *id.*, stating:

> Our patent laws allow specifically "damages adequate to compensate *for the infringement.*" 35 U.S.C. §284 (emphasis added). They do not thereby provide compensation for a defendant's foreign exploitation of a patented invention, which is not infringement at all. *Brown* [Brown v. Duchesne, 60 U.S. (19 How.)

WesternGeco IV seemingly departs from that principle for violations of §271*(f)*. Although it acknowledged the strong presumption against extraterritorial application of U.S. statutes, the *WesternGeco IV* Court rationalized its holding by emphasizing that §271(f) must be considered in tandem with §284, which provides a general damages remedy for patent infringement. The Court explained that the primary focus of these two statutory provisions, considered "in concert," is *domestic* infringement. The patentee's loss of overseas contracts to the infringer was "merely incidental" to the domestic act of infringement (i.e., the export of key components from the United States), and did not have "primacy" for purposes of the extraterritoriality analysis.[453]

More specifically, the Court in *WesternGeco IV* held that the infringer's domestic act of exporting specially-adapted components of a patented undersea survey system in violation of §271(f)(2) was "the infringement" to be compensated for under the general patent damages statute, 35 U.S.C. §284.[454] In the Court's view, that *domestic* act of infringement was the focus or "solicitude" of §284. Thus, the Texas jury's award of $93.4 million in profits lost on ten foreign services contracts that the patentee would have made but for the infringement was a proper "domestic application of §284."

In contrast to the 2007 *Microsoft v. AT&T* decision examined earlier in this chapter,[455] the Court in *WesternGeco IV* exercised its discretion *not* to decide the "difficult question[]" whether the presumption against extraterritorial application of U.S. statutes had been rebutted in the case at bar. Bypassing that threshold inquiry, the Court explained that "'[i]f the conduct relevant to the statute's focus occurred in the United States, then the case involves a permissible domestic application 'of the statute' even if other conduct occurred abroad.'"[456] Given the nature of the defendant's violation of §271(f)(2), i.e., the domestic act of exporting the claimed invention's

183 (1856)], 60 U.S. at 195 ("And the use of it outside of the jurisdiction of the United States is not an infringement of his rights, and he has no claim to any compensation for the profit or advantage the party may derive from it.")....

Power Integrations' "foreseeability" theory of worldwide damages sets the presumption against extraterritoriality in interesting juxtaposition with the principle of full compensation. Nevertheless, Power Integrations' argument is not novel, and in the end, it is not persuasive. Regardless of how the argument is framed under the facts of this case, the underlying question here remains whether Power Integrations is entitled to compensatory damages for injury caused by infringing activity that occurred outside the territory of the United States. The answer is no.

[453] *WesternGeco IV,* 138 S. Ct. at 2138.

[454] Section 284 authorizes in relevant part "damages adequate to compensate for *the infringement* ..." (emphasis added).

[455] 550 U.S. 437 (2007). *Microsoft* is examined *supra* Section E.4.b.

[456] *WesternGeco IV,* 138 S. Ct. at 2137 (quoting *RJR Nabisco,* 579 U.S. at _____, 136 S. Ct. at 2101).

key components from the United States, the conduct relevant to "the focus" of the general damages statute §284 — "the infringement" — occurred in U.S. territory.[457] Hence, the Court found justified the jury's award to the patentee of its foreign lost profits.

Lastly (and potentially significantly), the *WesternGeco IV* Court noted that in reaching its holding that foreign lost profits were available in the case at bar, it had not considered general tort law principles that might limit or exclude the possibility of foreign lost profits. "[W]e do not address the extent to which other doctrines, such as proximate cause, could limit or preclude damages in particular cases."[458]

Writing in dissent for himself and Justice Breyer, Justice Gorsuch responded in *WesternGeco IV* that the use of U.S.-patented invention abroad is simply not actionable. "WesternGeco is not entitled to lost profits caused by the use of its invention *outside* the United States."[459] In his view, territoriality was not the dispositive question. Justice Gorsuch observed that "while the Federal Circuit may have relied in part on a mistaken extraterritoriality analysis, ... it reached the right result in concluding that the Patent Act forecloses WesternGeco's claim for lost profits."[460]

In the view of this author, the majority in *WesternGeco IV* provided a rather cramped, conclusory justification for rejecting the presumption against extraterritorial application of U.S. statutes; in this case, 35 U.S.C. §284. However, the dissent's focus on the definition in 35 U.S.C. §154(a)(1) of a patentee's right to exclude,[461] which parallels

[457]The Court explained that its jurisprudence has established a two-step framework for deciding whether U.S. statutes should be applied extraterritorially (that is, for deciding when the general presumption against such application has been rebutted). The Court annunciated this framework in its 2016 RICO (Racketeer Influenced and Corrupt Organizations Act) decision, *RJR Nabisco, Inc. v. European Community*, 579 U.S. _____, _____, 136 S. Ct. 2090, 2101 (2016). Under *RJR Nabisco*, a court asks in step one "whether the presumption against extraterritoriality has been rebutted." Rebuttal occurs only if the statutory text provides a "'clear indication of an extraterritorial application.'" *WesternGeco IV*, 138 S. Ct. at 2136 (quoting Morrison v. National Australia Bank Ltd., 561 U.S. 247, 255 (2010)). If the presumption against extraterritoriality has *not* been rebutted, the second step of the *RJR Nabisco* framework asks "whether the case involves a domestic application of the statute." Courts determine whether the statute is being applied domestically by identifying "'the statute's "focus" and asking whether the conduct relevant to that focus occurred in United States territory.'" *WesternGeco IV*, 138 S. Ct. at 2136 (quoting *RJR Nabisco*, 136 S. Ct. at 2101). If it did, then the case involves a "permissible domestic application of the statute."

[458]*WesternGeco IV*, 138 S. Ct. at 2139 n.3.

[459]*WesternGeco IV*, 138 S. Ct. at 2140 (emphasis in original).

[460]*WesternGeco IV*, 138 S. Ct. at 2139 (Gorsuch, J., dissenting).

[461]35 U.S.C. §154(a) grants the patentee "the right to exclude others from making, using, offering for sale, or selling the invention throughout the United States or importing the invention into the United States. . . ."). Section 154 does not explicitly incorporate or parallel the other types of infringement set forth in §271, such as component exports under §271(f).

the definition of direct infringement in §271(a), also missed the mark. Following the majority's analysis, the act of infringement in *WesternGecoIV* was not §271(a) "use" outside the United States (which is clearly not actionable under U.S. patent law[462]). Rather, the infringing use was the §271(f)(2) act of exporting the specially-made components, which took place in (or from) the United States. This domestic "hook," one of primary importance in the majority's view, allowed for the award of foreign lost profits.

5. Importation Under §271(g)

Like §271(f), 35 U.S.C. §271(g) is concerned with acts that take place, in part, outside the geographic borders of the United States. Section 271(g) provides as follows:

> (g) Whoever without authority imports into the United States or offers to sell, sells, or uses within the United States a product which is made by a process patented in the United States shall be liable as an infringer, if the importation, offer to sell, sale, or use of the product occurs during the term of such process patent. In an action for infringement of a process patent, no remedy may be granted for infringement on account of the noncommercial use or retail sale of a product unless there is no adequate remedy under this title for infringement on account of the importation or other use, offer to sell, or sale of that product. A product which is made by a patented process will, for purposes of this title, not be considered to be so made after —
>
> (1) it is materially changed by subsequent processes; or
>
> (2) it becomes a trivial and nonessential component of another product.

Section 271(g) is particularly important for biotechnology firms that own process patents. In many cases such firms may obtain patents on innovative biotech processes for making known products, such as a novel recombinant method for obtaining insulin needed by patients suffering from diabetes. Prior to the enactment of §271(g) in 1988, a U.S. process patent owner had no recourse under the Patent Act[463] against a competitor who carried out the process abroad (where it

[462] *See* Power Integrations, Inc. v. Fairchild Semiconductor Int'l, Inc., 711 F.3d 1348, 1371 (Fed. Cir. 2013).

[463] Prior to 1988, the process patent owner's only option was to seek an exclusion order for the imported products from the International Trade Commission under Section 337a of the Tariff Act of 1930, 19 U.S.C. §1337a (1982). *See* Eli Lilly & Co. v. Am. Cyanamid Co., 82 F.3d 1568, 1571-1572 (Fed. Cir. 1996).

would not violate the U.S. process patent) and imported the product (which was not protected by U.S. patent) into the United States. By enacting §271(g) in 1988 as part of the Process Patent Amendments Act,[464] Congress closed the loophole and brought this aspect of U.S. patent law into conformity with that of other nations.[465]

Section 271(g) contains certain safeguards. Subsection 271(g)(1) provides that there is no infringement if the imported product of the patented process is "materially changed by subsequent processes" before the product was imported.[466] The Federal Circuit interpreted the meaning of §271(g)'s "materially changed" clause in *Eli Lilly v. American Cyanamid Co.*[467] Although acknowledging its "considerable appeal," the court ultimately rejected patentee Eli Lilly's argument that "materially changed" must be construed in light of the statute's underlying purpose, which is to protect the economic value of U.S. process patents to their owners. The statutory language focuses on changes to the *product,* the Federal Circuit pointed out, not to the economic value of the process patent to its owner. "In the chemical context," the court noted, "a 'material' change in a compound is most naturally viewed as a significant change in the compound's structure and properties."[468]

In *Eli Lilly,* the compound being imported by the accused infringer was different in four important structural respects from the compound produced by the patented process; these structural differences corresponded to four additional process steps performed abroad by the accused infringer that were not part of the patented process. Although it did not attempt "to define with precision what classes of changes would be material and what would not," the Federal Circuit shared the view of the district court that the changes in chemical structure and properties in the case at bar could not be dismissed as "immaterial."[469] Thus the Federal Circuit concluded that Eli Lilly, which had sought a preliminary injunction below, was not likely to succeed on the merits of its infringement claim under 35 U.S.C. §271(g).

[464]Pub. L. No. 100-418, §§9001-9007, 102 Stat. 1107 (Aug. 23, 1988).

[465]*See* Ajinomoto Co. v. Archer-Daniels-Midland Co., 228 F.3d 1338, 1347 (Fed. Cir. 2000).

[466]*See* Eli Lilly & Co. v. Am. Cyanamid Co., 82 F.3d 1568, 1571 (Fed. Cir. 1996).

[467]*Id.* at 1568.

[468]*Id.* at 1573.

[469]*Id.*

Chapter 10

Defenses to Patent Infringement

A. Introduction

As a practical matter, when sued for patent infringement an **accused infringer** will almost always assert the following two defenses: (1) "my product/process does not infringe"; and (2) "even if my product/process does infringe, your patent is invalid, so I cannot be liable for infringement." In many cases, the accused infringer will add a third defense: "The court should refuse to enforce your patent because you acted inequitably in procuring it."[1]

The statutory basis for these and other defenses is paragraph (b) of 35 U.S.C. §282 (eff. Sept. 16, 2012), which provides that the following defenses can be pleaded in a lawsuit concerning the validity or infringement of a U.S. patent:

> (1) Noninfringement, absence of liability for infringement or unenforceability.
> (2) Invalidity of the patent or any claim in suit on any ground specified in part II [35 U.S.C. §§100 et seq.] as a condition for patentability.
> (3) Invalidity of the patent or any claim in suit for failure to comply with—
>> (A) any requirement of section 112 ["Specification"], except that the failure to disclose the best mode shall not be a basis on which any claim of a patent may be canceled or held invalid or otherwise unenforceable; or
>> (B) any requirement of section 251 ["Reissue of Defective Patents"].
>
> (4) Any other fact or act made a defense by this title.[2]

[1]A study prepared in the late 1980s estimated that 80 percent of U.S. patent infringement lawsuits included an allegation of inequitable conduct. *See* Therasense, Inc. v. Becton, Dickinson and Co., 649 F.3d 1276, 1289 (Fed. Cir. 2011) (*en banc*) (citing Committee Position Paper, *The Doctrine of Inequitable Conduct and the Duty of Candor in Patent Prosecution: Its Current Adverse Impact on the Operation of the United States Patent System*, 16 AIPLA Q.J. 74, 75 (1988)).

[2]35 U.S.C. §282(b) (eff. Sept. 16, 2012) ("Defenses"). The America Invents Act of 2011 eliminated best mode as an invalidity defense as reflected in the quoted statutory text,

Several of the defenses enumerated in §282(b) are actually categories that encompass a variety of defensive theories. For example, the defense of unenforceability can be established on the basis of inequitable conduct or patent misuse. The defense of invalidity can be based on a failure of the patent to comply with the requirements of utility, novelty, nonobviousness, enablement, and the like.

Each defense encompassed within §282(b) is discussed below.[3]

B. Noninfringement

In accordance with 35 U.S.C. §282(b)(1), an accused infringer may assert that it does not infringe the patent in suit either literally or under the doctrine of equivalents. The alleged noninfringement may be based on the failure of the accused device to satisfy one or more limitations of the asserted claims, either literally or equivalently, or the accused infringer may raise a legal limitation to the patentee's reliance on the doctrine of equivalents, such as prosecution history estoppel. The substance of these theories of infringement was discussed in Chapter 9 ("Patent Infringement"), *supra,* and the reader is encouraged to review Chapter 9 before tackling this chapter.

Procedurally, the patent owner bears the burden of proof on infringement. The quantum of evidence required to carry that burden is a preponderance of the evidence (i.e., greater than half of the weight of the evidence of record). If a preponderance of the evidence does not establish infringement, then the patentee has failed to carry its burden and the accused infringer will prevail on the ground of noninfringement.

C. Absence of Liability for Infringement

Asserted in accordance with 35 U.S.C. §282(b)(1) (eff. Sept. 16, 2012), this category of defenses covers situations where there cannot be liability as a matter of law; for example, the patent in suit has been expired for more than six years before the filing of the infringement

effective September 16, 2011. Best mode compliance remains a requirement for obtaining a patent in the first instance, however, under 35 U.S.C. §112(a) (eff. Sept. 16, 2012).

[3]These defensive theories also may be raised as the affirmative allegations of an accused infringer who files a **declaratory judgment action** under 28 U.S.C. §2201. Such an action seeks to obtain a judgment that the putative infringer/declaratory plaintiff is not infringing and/or that the allegedly infringed patent is invalid and/or unenforceable. An important part of patent infringement litigation practice, declaratory judgment actions are considered in further detail in Section G, *infra.*

action.[4] It also can be viewed as encompassing the defenses of license, prior user right, experimental use, laches, equitable estoppel, state sovereign immunity, and temporary presence in U.S. territory. Each is discussed below.

1. License

Absence of liability for infringement under §282(b)(1) encompasses the defense of license. A **license** is simply an agreement or covenant between the patentee and the licensee that the patentee will not sue the licensee for acts that would otherwise constitute infringement; it is not a transfer of ownership of the patent (i.e., an **assignment**). In accordance with the language of 35 U.S.C. §271(a), if an accused infringer believes that it is a licensee, it will assert that it does not infringe because its acts were not "without authority" as required by the statute. In other words, the accused infringer will argue that it acted with the authority or permission of the patentee when it made, used, sold, offered to sell, and/or imported into the United States the patented invention or its substantial equivalent, and therefore cannot be liable for infringement.

Patent licenses may be express or implied. Each type of license is separately considered below.

a. Express License

An express license is formed when the parties agree, either in writing or orally, that the patent owner (licensor) will not sue the other party (licensee) for its acts of using, making, selling, offering to sell, or importing the claimed invention. A license is express if created by the actions of the parties themselves, rather than implied by operation of law.

Express licenses may be exclusive or nonexclusive. An *exclusive* license is one in which the patent owner agrees to grant a license to the licensee only, and to no other third parties. Moreover, an exclusive license usually presumes that the patentee will not compete with the exclusive licensee in making or selling the licensed product(s).[5] In contrast, a *nonexclusive* license does not give the licensee any right to control competition within the scope of the license; rather, it simply protects the licensee from being sued for infringement.[6]

[4] *See* 35 U.S.C. §286 (stating six-year limitation on period of time for which damages may be recovered for infringements that occurred prior to filing of lawsuit).

[5] *See* Jay Dratler, Jr., Licensing of Intellectual Property §8.01 (2008).

[6] *See id.*

b. Implied License

The existence of an implied license is a legal conclusion that the patent owner has impliedly waived its statutory right to exclude another from making, using, selling, offering to sell, or importing the claimed invention. The Supreme Court has stated the following with respect to implied licenses:

> No formal granting of a license is necessary in order to give it effect. Any language used by the owner of the patent, or any conduct on his part exhibited to another from which that other may properly infer that the owner consents to his use of the patent in making or using it, or selling it, upon which the other acts, constitutes a license and a defense to an action for a tort. Whether this constitutes a gratuitous [i.e., royalty-free] license, or one for a reasonable compensation, must of course depend upon the circumstances; but the relation between the parties thereafter, in respect of any suit brought, must be held to be contractual and not based on unlawful invasion of the rights of the owner.[7]

The Federal Circuit recognizes that an implied license may arise in at least four different circumstances: by acquiescence, by conduct, by equitable estoppel (i.e., estoppel in pais), or by legal estoppel.[8] *Wang Labs. v. Mitsubishi Elecs. Am.*[9] illustrates a successful assertion of the implied license defense under a theory of equitable estoppel, a recognized but rarely established defense in U.S. patent law.[10] Wang developed Single In-Line Memory Modules (SIMMs) in the 1980s and encouraged Mitsubishi to make 256K chips incorporating the SIMMs. Wang succeeded in its campaign to have an electronics industry standards organization, Joint Electronics Devices Engineering Council (JEDEC), adopt SIMMs as a standard, without informing JEDEC that it was seeking to patent the SIMMs technology.

When Wang subsequently sued Mitsubishi for infringement of Wang's SIMMs patent, the Federal Circuit affirmed a district court's holding that Mitsubishi was entitled to an irrevocable, royalty-free implied license based on six years of interaction between the parties that led Mitsubishi to reasonably infer Wang's consent to its use of the invention. Although Wang did not itself make SIMMs and had to buy them from other manufacturers such as Mitsubishi, Wang benefited from Mitsubishi's reliance in the form of lowered prices as the market for SIMMs grew. The Federal Circuit acknowledged its

[7] De Forest Radio Tel. Co. v. United States, 273 U.S. 236, 241 (1927).

[8] Wang Labs. v. Mitsubishi Elecs. Am., 103 F.3d 1571, 1580 (Fed. Cir. 1997).

[9] *Id.*

[10] *See id.* at 1582; A.C. Aukerman Co. v. R.L. Chaides Construction Co., 960 F.2d 1020, 1041-1044 (Fed. Cir. 1992) (*en banc*) (setting forth elements of equitable estoppel and reversing district court's grant of summary judgment that patentee was equitably estopped to assert patent infringement).

imposition of an implied license in *Wang* was "in the nature of" equitable estoppel, but determined "a formal finding of equitable estoppel [was not required] as a prerequisite to a legal conclusion of implied license."[11]

Another variety of implied license dispute arises when one who has purchased a patented device makes repairs so extensive that the patentee construes them as an infringing **reconstruction** of the claimed invention. As mentioned above, the "use" contemplated by §271(a) as an act of infringement is limited by the statute to use "without authority." By contrast, use of a patented device that has been legally purchased is not infringement. A purchaser is deemed to have obtained an implied license to use the purchased patented device, which includes a right to repair it.[12] When that **repair** expands to become reconstruction or a new making of the patented device, however, such acts are no longer considered within the scope of the purchaser's implied license.[13] Federal Circuit case law has not clearly distinguished between permitted repair and prohibited reconstruction; the cases are by necessity extremely fact-specific and must be carefully scrutinized.[14]

Another variation of an implied license is illustrated by *Anton / Bauer, Inc. v. PAG, Ltd.*[15] The patented invention in that case was a battery pack connection that joined a battery pack to a portable television video camera. The patent's claims recited a connection comprising both a male plate and a female plate that would be fitted together to form a mechanical and electrical connection. Neither the male plate nor the female plate was separately patented, however. In use, the female plate would be attached to a television camera or other electrically operated device and the male plate would be attached to the

[11]*Wang Labs.*, 103 F.3d at 1581. The implied license was not in the nature of legal estoppel, the Federal Circuit explained, which "refers to a narrower category of conduct encompassing scenarios where a patentee has licensed or assigned a right, received consideration, and then sought to derogate from the right granted." *Id.* (quoting Spindelfabrik v. Schubert, 829 F.2d 1075, 1080 (Fed. Cir. 1987)).

[12]*See* Aro Mfg. Co. v. Convertible Top Replacement Co., 377 U.S. 476, 484 (1964) (stating that "it is fundamental that sale of a patented article by the patentee or under his authority carries with it an 'implied license to use.'") (citing Adams v. Burke, 84 U.S. (17 Wall.) 453, 456 (1873)).

[13]*See* Hewlett-Packard Co. v. Repeat-O-Type Stencil Mfg. Corp., 123 F.3d 1445, 1451-1452 (Fed. Cir. 1997). The issue of permissible repair versus infringing reconstruction often arises in the context of disputes over contributory infringement under 35 U.S.C. §271(c), as further discussed in Chapter 9 ("Patent Infringement"), *supra*.

[14]*Compare* Bottom Line Mgmt., Inc. v. Pan Man, Inc., 228 F.3d 1352 (Fed. Cir. 2000) (affirming district court's conclusion that defendant's refurbishment of platens in hamburger grills was noninfringing repair) *with* Sandvik Aktiebolag v. E.J. Co., 121 F.3d 669 (Fed. Cir. 1997) (reversing district court's conclusion that defendant's retipping of drills was not infringing reconstruction).

[15]329 F.3d 1343 (Fed. Cir. 2003).

housing of a battery pack. Notably, the patentee did not sell the patented combination of male and female plates, but rather sold only the female plates to firms in the portable television video camera industry. These firms in turn sold the cameras with female plates attached to the public. The accused infringer sold battery packs incorporating the male plate (only) of the claimed invention. In its infringement suit the patentee theorized that direct infringement occurred when end-users connected their video cameras (incorporating the female plate) with the male plate of the accused battery pack, and that the battery pack manufacturer had induced or contributed to this infringement by selling the battery pack for use with the female plate and by urging end-users to employ it in that fashion.

The Federal Circuit in *Anton/Bauer* rejected the patentee's infringement theory and held that the end-users possessed an implied license that precluded liability. The court observed that a patentee grants an implied license to a purchaser when (1) the patentee sells an article that has no noninfringing uses and (2) the circumstances of the sale plainly indicate that the grant of a license should be inferred.[16] In the case at bar, the female plate had no noninfringing uses. The sale by the patentee of the unpatented female plate as a stand-alone item effectively extinguished the patentee's right to control the use of the plate, because the female plate could only be used in the patented combination and that combination had to be completed by the purchaser.[17] With regard to circumstances of the sale, the Federal Circuit stressed that the patentee had placed no restrictions on the use of the female plates it sold.[18] "By the unrestricted sale of the female plate, [the patentee] grants an implied license to its customers to employ the combination claimed in the [] patent." Thus there was no direct infringement to support the patentee's claim of inducing and/or contributory infringement by the battery pack manufacturer. The Federal Circuit rejected the patentee's argument that finding an implied license existed would "obviate the applicability of contributory infringement in every case." The key fact here was the involvement of the patentee, the court emphasized; its implied license holding in this case "merely limits a patentee's ability to assert contributory

[16]*Id.* at 1350 (citing Met-Coil Sys. Corp. v. Korners Unlimited, Inc., 803 F.2d 684, 686 (Fed. Cir. 1986)).

[17]*Id.* at 1351.

[18]*Compare* Mallinckrodt, Inc. v. Medipart, Inc., 976 F.2d 700 (Fed. Cir. 1992) (holding that sale to hospitals of patented nebulizer device for lung therapy with "single use only" restriction was not a per se antitrust violation nor patent misuse; defendant's violation of restriction would be remediable by action for patent infringement so long as sale of the device was "validly conditioned under the applicable law such as the law governing sales and licenses, and if the restriction on reuse was within the scope of the patent grant or otherwise justified . . .").

infringement where the patentee has chosen to sell part, but not all, of its patented combination."[19]

In *Zenith Elecs. Corp. v. PDI Commc'n Sys., Inc.*,[20] the Federal Circuit explained that an implied license defense "is typically presented 'when a patentee or its licensee sells an article and the question is whether the sale carries with it a license to engage in conduct that would infringe the patent owner's rights.' "[21] An implied license exists in such a case if two requirements are met: (1) the article involved must not have any noninfringing use, thus making it reasonable to infer that the patentee "relinquish[ed its] monopoly with respect to the article sold";[22] and (2) the circumstances of the sale should plainly indicate that a license should be inferred.[23]

Both prongs of this implied license test were satisfied in *Zenith Elecs.* The '301 patent in suit covered methods of remotely controlling televisions located in hospital rooms.[24] For safety and cost reasons, the remote control devices had to be hard-wired to the televisions. Because they also delivered audio signals to patients via internal speakers, the devices were known as "pillow speakers." The invention of the '301 patent advantageously enabled the transmission of digital (rather than analog) signals from the pillow speaker to the television while using existing wire interfaces already installed in hospital rooms.[25] Patentee Zenith entered into express licenses with three companies (Curbell, MedTek, and Crest) to make and sell pillow speakers specifically designed to operate Zenith televisions using Zenith control codes. When television manufacturer PDI began to sell a new hospital room television also designed for compatibility with the pillow speakers of the '301 patent (i.e., using Zenith's control codes), Zenith sued for infringement. According to Zenith, PDI directly infringed by operating its televisions with the pillow speakers and indirectly infringed

[19] *Anton/Bauer*, 329 F.3d at 1353.

[20] 522 F.3d 1348 (Fed. Cir. 2008).

[21] *Id.* at 1360 (quoting Jacobs v. Nintendo of Am., Inc., 370 F.3d 1097, 1100 (Fed. Cir. 2004)).

[22] *Id.*

[23] *Id.*

[24] *See* "Three-Wire Pillow Speaker with Full Television Remote Control Functions," U.S. Patent No. 5,495,301 (issued Feb. 27, 1996).

[25] Representative claim 1 of Zenith's '301 patent recited

> 1. A method of operating a television receiver wired to a remote housing including a speaker and a multi-function control signal encoder comprising:
>
> supplying operating power to said multi-function control signal encoder from the television receiver over first and second wires;
>
> supplying audio signals to said speaker from said television receiver over said first wire and a third wire; and
>
> supplying encoded control signals from said multi-function encoder to said television receiver over said first and second wires.

by supplying the televisions and encouraging its customers to operate them using the pillow speakers.

The Federal Circuit agreed with PDI and the district court that an implied license defense shielded PDI from liability for infringement of the '301 patent. First, the pillow speakers in question had no use other than in the method of the '301 patent. Second, there were no restrictions in the express licenses between Zenith and the three pillow speaker manufacturers; for example, nothing required them to affix a "use with Zenith televisions only" label to the pillow speakers they sold. Rather, the express licenses achieved a "clear, broad grant of patent rights" between Zenith and the three companies.[26] The Federal Circuit agreed that "customers who purchase pillow speakers from Curbell, MedTek, and Crest obtain an implied license to use those pillow speakers in combination with any compatible television," not just Zenith televisions, and that the implied license was "derived from the express licenses in place between Zenith and the [pillow speaker] manufacturers."[27] Thus, PDI did not infringe Zenith's patent by making or selling televisions that would work with the pillow speakers sold by the express licensees Curbell, MedTek, and Crest. Accordingly, the Federal Circuit affirmed the district court's summary judgment of no infringement of Zenith's '301 patent on the basis of an implied license.

2. Prior User Rights

The existence of a prior user right represents another, more recently recognized (at least in the United States) instance of an "absence of liability for infringement" under 35 U.S.C. §282(b)(1) (eff. Sept. 16, 2012). A prior user right is a personal defense to a charge of infringement, raised by a person who did not patent the invention herself but rather used it in her business prior to the patent owner's filing of his own application for patent on the same invention, typically maintaining the invention as a trade secret. Because they tend to ameliorate the sometimes harsh results of first-to-file patent systems,[28] prior user rights have long been recognized in Europe.[29] Because recognition of prior user rights reduces the economic value of a patent

[26] Zenith Elecs. Corp. v. PDI Commc'n Sys., Inc., 522 F.3d 1348, 1362 (Fed. Cir. 2008).

[27] *Id.*

[28] The first-to-file versus first-to-invent debate is discussed in further detail in Chapter 12 ("International Patenting Issues"), *infra.*

[29] *See, e.g.*, Germany Patent Law (as amended by the Law of July 31, 2009) §12(1), *available at* http://www.wipo.int/wipolex/en/text.jsp?file_id=238776 (providing without limitation as to scope of "invention" that "[a] patent shall have no effect against a person who, at the time of the filing of the application, had already begun to use the invention in Germany, or had made the necessary arrangements to do so").

by abrogating exclusivity, however, the United States historically opposed them.

The U.S. opposition to prior user rights weakened somewhat in 1998, when the Federal Circuit decided *State St. Bank v. Signature Fin. Group, Inc.*,[30] confirming the patentability of business methods. Firms that had long maintained their proprietary business procedures and processes as trade secrets suddenly faced the risk of infringing the exclusive rights of competitors who might legitimately obtain patent protection on the same methods. Responding to these concerns, Congress enacted as part of the American Inventors Protection Act of 1999 (AIPA) a limited form of prior user rights, codified at 35 U.S.C. §273.

The assertion of prior user rights under AIPA 35 U.S.C. §273, inaptly titled "Defense to Infringement Based on Earlier Inventor,"[31] was limited to those cases in which a defendant allegedly infringed a claim that recited a *method,* which the statute further defined as "a method of doing or conducting business."[32] The statute provided that

> [i]t shall be a defense to an action for infringement under section 271 of this title with respect to any subject matter that would otherwise infringe one or more claims for a method in the patent being asserted against a person, if such person had, acting in good faith, actually reduced the subject matter to practice at least 1 year before the effective filing date of such patent, and commercially used the subject matter before the effective filing date of such patent.[33]

Thus, an accused infringer asserting a defense under AIPA §273 had to establish that (1) it was acting in good faith when (2) more than one year before the effective filing date of the patent, it actually reduced to practice the subject matter of the asserted claim, and (3) before the effective filing date of the patent, it commercially used that subject matter. The statute defined "commercial use" of the method to mean a "use of a method in the United States, so long as such use is in connection with an internal commercial use or an actual arm's-length sale or other arm's-length commercial transfer of a useful end result, whether or not the subject matter at issue is accessible to

[30]149 F.3d 1368 (Fed. Cir. 1998). The *State Street Bank* decision is further discussed in Chapter 7 ("Potentially Patentable Subject Matter (35 U.S.C. §101)"), *supra.*

[31]Contrary to the title of §273, the party asserting a defense to infringement under that section of the Patent Act is *not* required to prove that it invented before the patent owner in accordance with the criteria of 35 U.S.C. §102(g) (2006). *See* 35 U.S.C. §273(b)(1) (2006) (requiring that defendant show actual reduction to practice more than one year prior to patent's effective filing date but not requiring a showing of prior invention sufficient to satisfy §102(g)).

[32]35 U.S.C. §273(a)(3) (2006).

[33]35 U.S.C. §273(b)(1) (2006).

or otherwise known to the public. . . ."[34] This definition permitted trade secret users of business methods to avail themselves of the §273 defense; their use of the allegedly infringed method need not have been known to the public, so long as it was used in connection with their business. For example, a mutual fund firm might develop a novel and nonobvious method for maximizing stock market returns and use this method to manage its clients' stock portfolios, but maintain the details of the method as a trade secret.

Because the §273 prior user defense was narrowly defined and largely untested in the federal district courts,[35] the Federal Circuit did not address the contours of the defense as implemented by the AIPA of 1999, particularly the question of its limitation to business methods.

The America Invents Act of 2011 significantly broadened the scope of the prior user rights defense to subject matter beyond business methods.[36] Now titled "Defense to infringement based on prior commercial use," the protection of post-AIA 35 U.S.C. §273 is potentially

[34]*Id.* §273(a)(1).

[35]The district court in *Sabasta v. Buckaroos, Inc.*, 507 F. Supp. 2d 986 (S.D. Iowa 2007), held the §273(b) defense inapplicable to the facts before it. At issue was whether Sabasta's patent in suit claimed a "method" within the meaning of §273(a)(3), which defines "method" as "a method of doing or conducting business." The patent's claims recited an article of manufacture, that is, a "roll bending die for being used with a roll bending machine for producing rib reinforced rolled material," and did not include any method or process claims. *See* "Roll Bending Die," U.S. Patent No. 6,751,995 (issued June 22, 2004). Nevertheless, accused infringer Buckaroos contended that the '995 patent's claims should be construed as method claims because they often referred to the intended use of the recited die. Buckaroos further argued that it should be considered within the protection of §273 because Buckaroos was "in business, and is using a roll-bending process as part of conducting its business." *Sabasta*, 507 F. Supp. 2d at 1002. The district court disagreed. The court noted the lack of any case law directly addressing the scope of §273, but concluded from the section's legislative history that Congress intended "the First Inventor Defense to have a limited scope, that is, the defense is designed to protect small businesses from patent infringement suits for methods of conducting business that use a novel process employing unpatentable subject matter, but that have 'useful, concrete and tangible result[s].'" *Id.* at 1005 (quoting *State St. Bank*, 149 F.3d at 1374). In light of this legislative history and the *State Street* decision, "[t]he fact that Buckaroos is in business and uses a process to manufacture ribbed pipe saddles does not . . . bring it within the intended purview of §273." *Id.*

The §273(b) defense to infringement was also asserted in *Seal-Flex, Inc. v. W.R. Dougherty & Assoc., Inc.*, 179 F. Supp. 2d 735 (E.D. Mich. 2002), a case involving a patented method for manufacturing an all-weather surface for an outdoor running track. Because the district court had previously granted summary judgment to the patentee on the issue of infringement, however, it refused to entertain the §273(b) defense as untimely raised. *Id.* at 742. The court did not discuss the merits of the defense or its potential applicability to the facts of the case.

[36]*See* Leahy-Smith America Invents Act, Pub. L. No. 112-29 (H.R. 1249), §5, 125 Stat. 284, 297 (Sept. 16, 2011) (titled "Defense to infringement based on prior commercial use") (amending 35 U.S.C. §273 (2006)). The amendment of 35 U.S.C. §273 became effective September 16, 2011, and applies to any patent issued on or after that date.

available to alleged infringers practicing "subject matter consisting of a process, or consisting of a machine, manufacture, or composition of matter used in a manufacturing or other commercial process."[37] Thus, post-AIA, the practice of *all* 35 U.S.C. §101 categories of subject matter is potentially shielded by prior user rights so long as the accused infringer was using the allegedly infringing subject matter in a "commercial process" by the requisite date. The defense is no longer limited to those who allegedly infringed patented business methods. The broadened version of the prior user rights defense became available for those accused of infringing patents that issued on or after September 16, 2011.

The post-AIA version of 35 U.S.C. §273 further requires that to assert the prior user rights defense, two primary criteria must be satisfied. First, concerning domestic "commercial use," the accused infringer asserting the §273 defense must have, "acting in good faith, commercially used the subject matter in the United States, either in connection with an internal commercial use or an actual arm's length sale or other arm's length commercial transfer of a useful end result of such commercial use. . . ."[38] Second, concerning timing, the accused infringer's commercial use must have "occurred at least 1 year before the earlier of either—(A) the effective filing date of the claimed invention; or (B) the date on which the claimed invention was disclosed to the public in a manner that qualified for the exception from prior art under [post-AIA 35 U.S.C.] section 102(b) [(eff. Mar. 16, 2013)]."[39]

Essentially carried over from the pre-AIA version of §273, the latter "time gap" requirement that an asserted prior use began at least one year before the patentee's effective filing date represents a significant difference (namely, one favoring patentees) between U.S. and European prior user rights defenses. European countries generally require that the prior use began any time before the patent owner's application filing date and do not mandate that the prior use began more than a year before it.[40]

[37]35 U.S.C. §273(a) (eff. Sept. 16, 2011).

[38]35 U.S.C. §273(a)(1) (eff. Sept. 16, 2011).

[39]35 U.S.C. §273(a)(2) (eff. Sept. 16, 2011).

[40]*See, e.g.*, Germany Patent Law (as amended by the Law of Oct. 8, 2017) §12(1), *available at* https://wipolex.wipo.int/en/text/461310 (providing that "[a] patent shall have no effect against a person who, *at the time of the filing of the application*, had already begun to use the invention in Germany, or had made the necessary arrangements to do so") (emphasis added); Great Britain Patents Act 1977 (as amended 2004) §64(1)-(2), *available at* https://wipolex.wipo.int/en/legislation/details/5417 (providing that "[w]here a patent is granted for an invention, a person who in the United Kingdom *before the priority date of the invention* does in good faith an act which would constitute an infringement of the patent if it were in force, or makes in good faith effective and serious preparations to do such an act, shall have the right[] . . . to continue to do or, as the case may be, to do that act himself . . .") (emphasis added).

Several aspects of the §273 prior user rights defense remain the same post-AIA as they stood pre-AIA. For example, an accused infringer still bears the burden of establishing the defense by clear and convincing evidence.[41] One major change benefits universities, however. Post-AIA 35 U.S.C. §273 includes a "University Exception" that prohibits an accused infringer from asserting the prior user rights defense if the allegedly infringed subject matter was, "at the time the invention was made, owned or subject to an obligation of assignment to either an institution of higher education . . . or a technology transfer organization whose primary purpose is to facilitate the commercialization of technologies developed by one or more such institutions of higher education."[42]

3. Experimental Use

Occasionally an accused infringer will assert that it is not liable for infringement because its activities constituted experimental use that should not be considered infringement. As explained below, this defense is construed very narrowly and has rarely succeeded.[43]

A U.S. patent grants its owner the right, *inter alia*, to prevent others from *using* the patented invention, without qualification as to the nature or purpose of the use.[44] Nonconsensual uses of patented inventions that lead to the development of other products may result in patent infringement liability, even though sales of the other products do not involve a making or selling of the patented invention itself. For example, a researcher may infringe if she uses without a

[41]35 U.S.C. §273(b) (eff. Sept. 16, 2011).

[42]35 U.S.C. §273(e)(5)(A) (eff. Sept. 16, 2011). The statute defines an "institution of higher education" in accordance with the text of "section 101(a) of the Higher Education Act of 1965 (20 U.S.C. 1001(a))." *Id.*

The AIA's legislative history explains that "Section 5 . . . clarifies that a person may not assert the [prior user] defense if the subject matter of the patent on which the defense is based was developed pursuant to a funding agreement under Chapter 18 of the Patent Act (patent rights in inventions made with Federal assistance) or by a university or a technology transfer organization affiliated with a university that did not receive private business funding in support of the patent's development." H.R. REP. 112-98 (June 1, 2011), at 75.

[43]The foundational article on the U.S. experimental use defense to patent infringement is Rebecca S. Eisenberg, *Patents and the Progress of Science: Exclusive Rights and Experimental Use*, 56 U. CHI. L. REV. 1017 (1989).

[44]*See* 35 U.S.C. §154(a)(1) ("Every patent shall contain . . . a grant to the patentee . . . of the right to exclude others from making, using, offering for sale, or selling the invention throughout the United States or importing the invention into the United States. . . ."); 35 U.S.C. §271(a) ("Except as otherwise provided in this title [35 U.S.C. §§1 *et seq.*], whoever without authority makes, uses, offers to sell, or sells any patented invention, within the United States or imports into the United States any patented invention during the term of the patent therefore, infringes the patent.").

license a patented "research tool," such as the biological receptor *Taq*[45] or a transgenic animal model[46] in the research and development of new drugs, therapies, or diagnostic products to be sold commercially.[47] Use liability arises under the U.S. patent laws even though the researcher has not physically incorporated the patented research tool into the new product that is ultimately marketed.[48]

Most of the world's patent systems recognize an exception to patent infringement liability for nonconsensual uses of patented inventions that are for experimental or research purposes, and many countries have statutorily implemented such an exception in their patent laws.[49] An experimental use exception to infringement has met with very little success in the United States, however. The only statutory

[45]*Taq* is a shorthand name for the thermostable enzyme *Thermus aquaticus* TY1 DNA polymerase, a widely used biotechnology tool. *See* PAUL RABINOW, MAKING PCR: A STORY OF BIOTECHNOLOGY 128-132 (1996) (describing identification, purification, and introduction of *Taq*). A receptor is a portion of a cell's surface that binds with specific molecules "like a lock accepting a key." *Human Pheromone Link May Have Been Found,* N.Y. TIMES, Sept. 28, 2000, at A22.

[46]For example, "Transgenic arthritic mice expressing a T-cell receptor transgene," U.S. Patent No. 5,675,060 (issued Oct. 7, 1997), discloses and claims transgenic arthritic mice that are useful as animal models for the evaluation of human arthritogenic and therapeutic anti-arthritic compositions. Genetically altered mice are preferred models for many human diseases because the mouse genome is similar to the human genome. David Malakoff, *The Rise of the Mouse, Biomedicine's Model Mammal,* SCIENCE, Apr. 14, 2000, at 248.

[47]*See* John H. Barton, *Patents and Antitrust: A Rethinking in Light of Patent Breadth and Sequential Innovation*, 65 ANTITRUST L.J. 449, 451 (1997) (suggesting scenario in which firm obtaining patent protection on biological receptor useful in schizophrenia research could preempt others from further research in schizophrenia, without itself having any truly "marketable product"); *see also* Eliot Marshall, *Patent on HIV Receptor Provokes an Outcry,* 287 SCIENCE 1375, 1375-1377 (2000) (describing academic researchers' criticism of patent issued to Human Genome Sciences, Inc. (HGS) on CCR5 cell-surface receptor that HIV uses as cell entry point, and reporting HGS's position that it will enforce patent against "anyone [who] wants to use the receptor to create a drug").

[48]Because the patented research tool is not incorporated into the commercial product, the researcher has not violated the "sells" prohibition of 35 U.S.C. §271(a).

[49]For example, French law provides that "[a]cts accomplished for personal or domestic purposes or for the purpose of testing the object of the patented invention shall not be considered as affecting the patentee's rights." French Patent Law Including Modifications of 1978, art. 29, reprinted in 2D JOHN P. SINNOTT ET AL., WORLD PATENT LAW AND PRACTICE (1999), at FRANCE-9. Germany provides that the "effects of the patent shall not extend to . . . acts done for experimental purposes relating to the subject matter of the patented invention." German Patent Act of 16 December 1980, §11.2, reprinted in 2D SINNOTT ET AL., *supra,* at WEST GERMANY-78.22. Great Britain exempts from infringement liability those acts "done privately and for purposes which are not commercial" as well as those acts "done for experimental purposes relating to the subject-matter of the invention." United Kingdom Patent Act 1977, §60(5), reprinted in 2D SINNOTT ET AL., *supra*, at GREAT BRITAIN-269. The Japanese patent laws provide that "[t]he effects of the patent right shall not extend to the working of the patent right for the purposes of experiment or research." Japanese Patent Law of 1959, as amended through May 6, 1998, effective June 1, 1998, §69(1), reprinted in 2F SINNOTT ET AL., *supra*, at JAPAN-194.

recognition of such a defense in the U.S. Patent Act is a very narrow exception from liability for nonconsensual uses of patented drugs in the preparation of test data to be submitted for regulatory approval by a government agency such as the Food and Drug Administration (FDA).[50] There is no general "fair use" provision in the U.S. Patent Act, in contrast with §107 of the U.S. Copyright Act.

The Federal Circuit has grudgingly recognized the existence of a common law–based experimental use defense, but characterizes it as "truly narrow" and applicable only to trifling, "dilettante affairs."[51] Excluded from the common law–based experimental use doctrine is any activity viewed as "commercialization" or otherwise grounded on profit motive.[52] The Federal Circuit's narrow interpretation of the doctrine virtually assures that it cannot be relied on by the rapidly growing number of university and industry collaborations whose research and development efforts are ultimately targeted at the commercialization of new biomedical products.[53]

Any prospects for a broader recognition of the common law–based experimental use defense were roundly refuted by the Federal Circuit's 2002 decision in *Madey v. Duke Univ.*[54] In that case, scientists at Duke University had used laboratory lasers to conduct basic research in nuclear physics without a license from Dr. John Madey, owner of patents on the laser equipment. The Federal Circuit concluded that the district court had erred in excusing the Duke scientists' activity as exempted from patent infringement liability under the experimental use doctrine.[55] The university's nonprofit status was not dispositive, for the university was engaged in its own "legitimate business" of attracting top scholars, students, and funding:

> Our precedent clearly does not immunize use that is in any way commercial in nature. Similarly, our precedent does not immunize any conduct that is in keeping with the alleged infringer's legitimate business,

[50]*See* 35 U.S.C. §271(e)(1), discussed *supra* Chapter 9, Section E.3.

[51]Roche Prods. v. Bolar Pharm. Co., 733 F.2d 858, 863 (Fed. Cir. 1984).

[52]*E.g., Roche Prods.,* 733 F.2d at 863 (refusing to adopt broader view of experimental use doctrine that would "allow a violation of the patent laws in the guise of 'scientific inquiry,' when that inquiry has definite, cognizable, and not insubstantial commercial purposes"); Pitcairn v. United States, 547 F.2d 1106, 1125-1126 (Ct. Cl. 1976) (rejecting government's experimental use defense because government's unauthorized use of infringing helicopters for testing, demonstrations, and experiments was "in keeping with the legitimate business of the using agency"); Deuterium Corp. v. United States, 19 Cl. Ct. 624, 633 (1990) (rejecting experimental use defense because government agency's participation in demonstration project with for-profit partner corporation "was not strictly intellectual experimentation, but development of technology and processes for commercial applications").

[53]For further development of this position, *see* Janice M. Mueller, *No "Dilettante Affair": Rethinking the Experimental Use Exception to Patent Infringement for Biomedical Research Tools*, 76 WASH. L. REV. 1 (2001).

[54]307 F.3d 1351 (Fed. Cir. 2002).

[55]*See id.* at 1352, 1361-1363, 1364.

> regardless of commercial implications. For example, major research universities, such as Duke, often sanction and fund research projects with arguably no commercial application whatsoever. However, these projects unmistakably further the institution's legitimate business objectives, including educating and enlightening students and faculty participating in these projects. These projects also serve, for example, to increase the status of the institution and lure lucrative research grants, students and faculty.
>
> In short, regardless of whether a particular institution or entity is engaged in an endeavor for commercial gain, so long as the act is in furtherance of the alleged infringer's legitimate business and is not solely for amusement, to satisfy idle curiosity, or for strictly philosophical inquiry, the act does not qualify for the very narrow and strictly limited experimental use defense. Moreover, the profit or non-profit status of the user is not determinative.[56]

In the aftermath of the *Madey* decision, the National Academies of Science (NAS) concluded in an important 2004 report that "most organized research using patented inventions is subject to demands for licenses and may in some cases be halted by an injunction or assessed money damages for infringement."[57] The NAS report recommended that at least some of these research uses be explicitly shielded from patent infringement liability,[58] but concluded that "[r]ealistically, the likelihood that Congress will pass research-exception legislation in the absence of compelling circumstances is small."[59] The National Academies' prediction has thus far proved correct; neither the 2005 nor the 2007 legislative proposals for U.S. patent law reform,[60] nor the America Invents Act of 2011, codified any experimental use defense.

4. Expiration of Damages Limitation Period of 35 U.S.C. §286

An accused infringer may assert absence of liability for infringement under §282(b)(1) (eff. Sept. 16, 2012) when the alleged infringing

[56]*Id.* at 1362. For an argument that the Federal Circuit's *Madey* decision fundamentally misapplied the "legitimate business" criterion of an earlier experimental use precedent, *Pitcairn v. United States*, 547 F.2d 1106, 1125 (Ct. Cl. 1977), *see* Janice M. Mueller, *The Evanescent Experimental Use Exemption from United States Patent Infringement Liability: Implications for University and Nonprofit Research and Development*, 56 Baylor L. Rev. 917 (2004).

[57]*See* National Research Council of the National Academies, A Patent System for the 21st Century 108 (Stephen A. Merrill et al. eds., 2004), *available at* https://www.nap.edu/read/10976/chapter/6#p2000af929970108001.

[58]*See id.* at 108-117.

[59]*Id.* at 115.

[60]*See* Patent Reform Act of 2007, H.R. 1908, 110th Cong. (2007), *available at* http://thomas.loc.gov/; S. 1145, 110th Cong. (2007), *available at* http://thomas.loc.gov; Patent Reform Act of 2005, H.R. 2795, 109th Cong. (2005), *available at* http://thomas.loc.gov.

activity ended more than six years before the filing of the infringement lawsuit. The defense raised here is not a statute of limitations, but rather is based upon the damages limitation provisions of 35 U.S.C. §286, which operate in a somewhat similar fashion.

Unlike its copyright counterpart,[61] U.S. patent law does not recognize a general statute of limitations in the sense of a statutory provision that bars the maintenance of an infringement suit following a delay in filing the suit for a certain number of years after the patentee had notice of the alleged infringing activity.[62] However, the Patent Act does provide a practical limitation on the time period in which infringement actions seeking the remedy of damages can be brought. Section 286, titled "Time Limitation on Damages," provides that except as otherwise provided by law, "no recovery shall be had for any infringement committed more than six years prior to the filing of the complaint or counterclaim for infringement in the action. . . ."[63] Thus, in an infringement action seeking damages (e.g., based on theories of lost profits and/or reasonable royalties),[64] the patent owner's damages recovery period extends retroactively to, at most, six years before the action was filed. This means that even if infringement was ongoing for ten years prior to the filing of suit, §286 provides that only the most recent six years of infringement damages accrued prior to the filing of the lawsuit are recoverable. If the patent expired more than six years prior to the filing of the infringement suit, §286 bars any monetary recovery.[65]

5. Laches and Equitable Estoppel in Initiating Patent Infringement Litigation

a. *Introduction*

The equitable doctrines of **laches** and **equitable estoppel** also may be asserted by accused infringers as the basis for "absence of

[61]*See* 17 U.S.C. §507 (three-year statute of limitations for copyright actions).

[62]The Patent Act includes a statute of limitations for actions seeking the provisional compensation remedy under 35 U.S.C. §154(d), based on infringements that occurred between the time of the publication of a patent application and its issuance as a patent. *See* 35 U.S.C. §154(d)(3) (providing that "[t]he right under paragraph (1) [of §154(d)] to obtain a reasonable royalty shall be available only in an action brought not later than 6 years after the patent is issued").

[63]35 U.S.C. §286, ¶1.

[64]*See* Chapter 11 ("Remedies for Patent Infringement"), *infra,* for discussion of theories of monetary recovery for patent infringement.

[65]An infringement suit that seeks only damages can be filed at any time in the six years after the patent expires. No injunctive remedy is available after a patent has expired, however, because the patentee no longer possesses the statutory right to exclude others from manufacture, use, sale, offering to sell, or importation of the invention.

liability for infringement" under §282(b)(1) (eff. Sept. 16, 2012). These judicially created doctrines permit the accused infringer to limit or negate its liability when a patentee has unfairly brought suit after an unreasonable delay or after misrepresenting that it would not do so. Laches and equitable estoppel are particularly important defenses in patent infringement litigation, which (unlike copyright law) does not have a statute of limitations *per se.*[66]

The defense of *laches* targets the plaintiff's unreasonable delay in filing suit. If successfully established, laches does not bar the plaintiff's action in its entirety but rather prevents the recovery of any damages accrued prior to the filing of the action. A successful laches defense may also impact the plaintiff's ability to obtain injunctive relief against an infringer; it will generally not prevent the award of an ongoing royalty when an injunction is inappropriate.[67]

Equitable estoppel is a separate defense that targets the plaintiff's misleading actions, which led the defendant to believe it would not be sued. If the defense of equitable estoppel is established, then the plaintiff's claim of infringement is entirely barred.

The foundational Federal Circuit case addressing the defenses of laches and equitable estoppel is the court's 1992 *en banc* decision in *A.C. Aukerman Co. v. Chaides Const. Co.*[68] In 2015, the Federal Circuit reaffirmed most (but not all) aspects of *Aukerman* in another important *en banc* decision, *SCA Hygiene Prods. Aktiebolag v. First Quality Baby Prods., LLC* ("*SCA Hygiene II*").[69]

In 2017, however, the U.S. Supreme Court vacated in a major part the Circuit's *SCA Hygiene II* decision and substantially repealed the laches defense. But equitable estoppel remains available. Given the importance of these defences, the *Aukerman* and *SCA Hygiene* cases are further examined in detail below.

(i) *Aukerman* (Fed. Cir. 1992) (*en banc*)

Aukerman, the owner of a U.S. patent on a device and method for forming concrete highway barriers, threatened to sue Chaides for infringement and offered it a license in 1979. Chaides responded that its alleged infringement was worth only $200 to $300 per year, and that it was not willing to take a license. The patentee Aukerman had no further contact with Chaides for over eight years. During that time, Chaides increased the volume of its business (which employed the allegedly

[66]*See supra* Section C.4 ("Expiration of Damages Limitation Period of 35 U.S.C. §286").

[67]*See* SCA Hygiene Prods. Aktiebolag v. First Quality Baby Prods., LLC, No. 2013-1564, 2015 WL 5474261, *15-*16 (Fed. Cir. Sept. 18, 2015) (*en banc*). The *SCA Hygiene* cases are examined further *infra.*

[68]960 F.2d 1020 (Fed. Cir. 1992) (*en banc*).

[69]No. 2013-1564, 2015 WL 5474261 (Fed. Cir. Sept. 18, 2015).

infringing process) twentyfold. When Aukerman finally sued Chaides in 1988, the district court granted summary judgment of nonliability to Chaides on both the defenses of laches and equitable estoppel.

On appeal, the Federal Circuit vacated the summary judgment grant as precluded by unresolved questions of material fact. The court also went *en banc* to clarify and restate the law of laches and equitable estoppel as described below. *Aukerman* set out the elements of each defense and applied them to the merits of the case as explained *infra*.

With respect to the laches defense, the *SCA Hygiene II* court conveniently summarized the five rules enumerated in *Aukerman* as follows:

1. Laches is cognizable under 35 U.S.C. §282 (1988) as an equitable defense to a claim for patent infringement.
2. Where the defense of laches is established, the patentee's claim for damages prior to suit may be barred.
3. Two elements underlie the defense of laches: (a) the patentee's delay in bringing suit was unreasonable and inexcusable, and (b) the alleged infringer suffered material prejudice attributable to the delay. The district court should consider these factors and all of the evidence and other circumstances to determine whether equity should intercede to bar pre-filing damages.
4. A presumption of laches arises where a patentee delays bringing suit for more than six years after the date the patentee knew or should have known of the alleged infringer's activity.
5. A presumption has the effect of shifting the burden of going forward with evidence, not the burden of persuasion.[70]

Moreover, in reliance on the Supreme Court's 1888 decision in the trademark case *Menendez v. Holt*,[71] the *Aukerman* court held that laches did *not* bar a patentee from obtaining post-filing damages or

[70]SCA Hygiene Products Aktiebolag v. First Quality Baby Products, LLC, No. 2013-1564, 2015 WL 5474261, at *3 (Fed. Cir. Sept. 18, 2015) (citing *Aukerman*, 960 F.2d at 1028).

[71]*See Aukerman*, 960 F.2d at 1040 (citing *Menendez*, 128 U.S. 514, 523-524 (1888)). The Court in *Menendez* held that

> [m]ere delay or acquiescence cannot defeat the remedy by injunction in support of the legal right, unless it has been continued so long and under such circumstances as to defeat the right itself.... Acquiescence to avail must be such as to create a new right in the defendant....
>
> So far as the act complained of is completed, acquiescence may defeat the remedy on the principle applicable when action is taken on the strength of encouragement to do it, but so far as the act is in progress and lies in the future, the right to the intervention of equity is not generally lost by previous delay, in respect to which the elements of an estoppel could rarely arise.

Menendez, 128 U.S. at 523-524.

injunctive relief, unless the elements of equitable estoppel were also established.[72]

The *Aukerman en banc* decision, authored by then–Chief Judge Helen Nies, was well regarded as a comprehensive synthesis and restatement of the law of laches and equitable estoppel in the patent context.[73] *Aukerman* was not questioned until 2014, when the Supreme Court considered the laches defense in a copyright case.

(ii) *Petrella* (U.S. 2014)

In 2014, the U.S. Supreme Court decided an important *copyright* infringement case involving a laches defense, *Petrella v. Metro-Goldwyn-Mayer, Inc.*[74] Because Petrella, owner of copyright in the screenplay for the film "Raging Bull," did not file her copyright infringement suit against MGM, the film's distributor, for some 18 years after attaining sole ownership of the copyright, a U.S. district court and the U.S. Court of Appeals for the Ninth Circuit agreed that the laches doctrine barred Petrella's complaint.

In a 6-3 decision, the Supreme Court in *Petrella* reversed the dismissal of the lawsuit. Petrella sought damages for the alleged infringements occurring for the three years prior to the filing of her suit, in accordance with the copyright statute of limitations codified at 17 U.S.C. §507(b). The Supreme Court held that "[t]o the extent that an infringement suit seeks relief solely for conduct occurring within the limitations period, . . . courts are not at liberty to jettison Congress' judgment on the timeliness of suit."[75] "Laches, we hold, cannot be invoked to preclude adjudication of a claim for damages brought within the three-year window."[76]

In short, under *Petrella* the defense of laches does not bar a copyright owner's claim for damages for infringements occurring during the Copyright Act's three-year statute of limitations. The Supreme Court resolved the case largely on "separation of powers" principles; that is, a defense such as laches, rooted in the common law, could not be allowed to trump Congress's enactment of a statute providing that

[72]*See* A.C. Aukerman Co. v. R.L. Chaides Const. Co., 960 F.2d 1020, 1040 (Fed. Cir. 1992).

[73]*Cf.* SCA Hygiene Prods. Aktiebolag v. First Quality Baby Prods., LLC, No. 2013-1564, 2015 WL 5474261, *5 (Fed. Cir. Sept. 18, 2015) (*en banc*) (observing that "[f]or over two decades, *Aukerman* governed the operation of laches in patent cases").

[74]134 S. Ct. 1962 (2014).

[75]*Petrella*, 134 S. Ct. at 1967.

[76]*Petrella*, 134 S. Ct. at 1967. The Court limited its holding to infringement damages by explaining that laches may still be a viable defense to requests for *equitable* relief in "extraordinary circumstances," *Petrella*, 134 S. Ct. at 1967, and that a plaintiff's delay "can always be brought to bear at the remedial stage, in determining appropriate injunctive relief, and in assessing the " 'profits of the infringer . . . attributable to the infringement.' " *Petrella*, 134 S. Ct. at 1967 (quoting 17 U.S.C. §504(b)).

copyright claimants have three years in which to bring their causes of action for copyright infringement.[77]

Although patent law does not have a direct counterpart to copyright's statute of limitations on actions, the Patent Act includes the six-year damages limitation period codified at 35 U.S.C. §286.[78] The *en banc* Federal Circuit acknowledged in *SCA Hygiene II* (further examined below) that "because patent infringement [like copyright infringement] is a continuous tort, there is no relevant functional difference between a damages limitation and a statute of limitations."[79]

Thus the patent law question raised by the Supreme Court's *Petrella* copyright decision was whether laches remains a viable defense in a patent infringement suit seeking damages for infringements occurring in the six years prior to filing of suit (i.e., within the six-year damages limitation period permitted by 35 U.S.C. §286). The Supreme Court in *Petrella* acknowledged the Federal Circuit's *Aukerman* rule that laches *can* bar damages incurred prior to the commencement of a patent infringement suit, but pointedly stated that the Court "ha[d] not had occasion to review the Federal Circuit's position."[80]

[77]*See SCA Hygiene II,* 2015 WL 5474261, at *5, explaining that in *Petrella,*

> [f]undamentally, the Supreme Court reasoned that "the copyright statute of limitations, §507(b), itself takes account of delay," crowding out the judiciary's power to decide whether a suit is timely. *Id.* [*Petrella,* 134 S. Ct.] at 1973. According to the Court, "[l]aches ... originally served as a guide when no statute of limitations controlled the claim." *Id.* at 1975. Historically, "laches is a defense developed by courts of equity; its principal application was, and remains, to claims of an equitable cast for which the Legislature has provided no fixed time limitation." *Id.* at 1973. Laches is thus "gap-filling, not legislation-overriding." *Id.* at 1974. In this respect, separation of powers concerns drove the result in *Petrella. Petrella* consequently held that "in face of a statute of limitations enacted by Congress, laches cannot be invoked to bar legal relief." *Id.*

[78]*See supra*, Section 4 ("Expiration of Damages Limitation Period of 35 U.S.C. §286").

[79]SCA Hygiene Prods. Aktiebolag v. First Quality Baby Prods., LLC., No. 2013-1564, 2015 WL 5474261, at *7. Copyright infringement is a continuous tort because

> [e]ach time an infringing work is reproduced or distributed, the infringer commits a new wrong. Each wrong gives rise to a discrete "claim" that "accrue[s]" at the time the wrong occurs. In short, each infringing act starts a new limitations period. *See Stone v. Williams*, 970 F.2d 1043, 1049 (C.A.2 1992) ("Each act of infringement is a distinct harm giving rise to an independent claim for relief.").

Petrella, 134 S. Ct. at 1969 (footnote omitted).

[80]*Petrella*, 134 S. Ct. at 1974 n.15. The entirety of the Supreme Court's commentary on laches in the patent law context was the following:

> The Patent Act states: "[N]o recovery shall be had for any infringement committed more than six years prior to the filing of the complaint." 35 U.S.C. §286. The Act also provides that "[n]oninfringement, absence of liability for infringement or unenforceability" may be raised "in any action involving the validity or infringement of a patent." §282(b) (2012 ed.). Based in part on §282 and

Unsurprisingly, the Federal Circuit soon accepted the Supreme Court's suggestion to review the impact of *Petrella.*

(iii) *SCA Hygiene II* (Fed. Cir. 2015) (*en banc*)

In the first Federal Circuit decision to consider the impact of the Supreme Court's *Petrella* copyright laches decision on patent cases, a three-judge panel held in 2014 in *SCA Hygiene Prods. Aktiebolag v. First Quality Baby Prods., LLC* (hereafter "*SCA Hygiene I*")[81] that "*Petrella* notably left *Aukerman* intact" and that "*Aukerman* remains controlling precedent."[82]

On the merits, the laches defense succeeded in *SCA Hygiene I.* Applying the *Aukerman* framework, as detailed below, the *SCA Hygiene I* panel affirmed a district court's grant of summary judgment of laches to accused infringer First Quality. The district court had erred, however, in granting First Quality's summary judgment motion as to the defense of equitable estoppel. The *SCA Hygiene I* panel determined that "competing inferences could be drawn as to the meaning of SCA's silence regarding the '646 patent,"[83] thus precluding summary judgment in First Quality's favor.

The *SCA Hygiene* dispute did not end there, however. Patentee SCA Hygiene asked the Federal Circuit to reconsider *en banc* the laches analysis of *Aukerman* in light of *Petrella.* On December 30, 2014, the

---

> commentary thereon, legislative history, and historical practice, the Federal Circuit has held that laches can bar damages incurred prior to the commencement of suit, but not injunctive relief. *A.C. Aukerman Co. v. R.L. Chaides Const. Co.*, 960 F.2d 1020, 1029-1031, 1039-1041 (1992) (*en banc*). We have not had occasion to review the Federal Circuit's position.

Petrella, 134 S. Ct. at 1974 n.15.

[81]767 F.3d 1339 (Fed. Cir. Sept. 17, 2014) (hereafter "*SCA Hygiene I*"), *reh'g en banc granted, opinion vacated*, No. 2013-1564, 2014 WL 7460970 (Fed. Cir. Dec. 30, 2014) (*en banc*) (order).

[82]*SCA Hygiene I*, 767 F.3d 1339, 1345 (Fed. Cir. Sept. 17, 2014) (rejecting patentee's argument that *Aukerman* was "no longer good law" based on Supreme Court's statement in *Petrella* that it had "never approved the application of laches to bar a claim for damages brought within the time allowed by a federal statute of limitations"). The Circuit observed that

> *Petrella* notably left *Aukerman* intact. *See id.* at 1974 n.15 ("We have not had occasion to review the Federal Circuit's position."). Because *Aukerman* may only be overruled by the Supreme Court or an *en banc* panel of this court, *Aukerman* remains controlling precedent.

SCA Hygiene I, 767 F.3d 1339, 1345 (Fed. Cir. Sept. 17, 2014) (citing, e.g., Tate Access Floors, Inc. v. Interface Architectural Res., Inc., 279 F.3d 1357, 1366 (Fed. Cir. 2002)).

[83]*SCA Hygiene II*, 2015 WL 5474261, at *2 n.1.

Federal Circuit vacated the panel's decision in *SCA Hygiene I* and ordered that the appeal be reheard *en banc.*[84]

In September 2015, the Circuit issued a 6-5 *en banc* decision in *SCA Hygiene Prods. Aktiebolag v. First Quality Baby Prods, LLC* (hereafter "*SCA Hygiene II*").[85] While admitting that *Petrella* "clearly casts doubt on several aspects of *Aukerman*,"[86] the *SCA Hygiene II* majority reaffirmed that the defense of laches remains available in patent infringement suits to bar *legal* relief (e.g., monetary damages) for infringements occurring in the six-year period before the filing of suit.[87] The *en banc* majority dealt exclusively with the threshold legal issue of whether the laches defense survived *Petrella*, concluding that it did; the court did not address *Aukerman*'s exposition of the law concerning the underlying elements of laches (i.e., the patentee's unreasonable delay and the accused infringer's material prejudice) nor review the *SCA Hygiene I* panel's application of those elements to the facts of the case.

On the law, the *SCA Hygiene II* majority departed from *Aukerman* in one important respect: it rejected *Aukerman's* holding that a successful laches defense cannot bar the imposition of *prospective* relief (e.g., injunctions and ongoing royalties imposed on the infringer).[88]

[84]*See* SCA Hygiene Prods. Aktiebolag v. First Quality Baby Prods., LLC, No. 2013-1564, 2014 WL 7460970 (Fed. Cir. Dec. 30, 2014) (*en banc*) (order granting SCA Hygiene's petition for rehearing *en banc*, vacating court's opinion of Sept. 17, 2014, reinstating appeal, and requesting briefing on two stated questions). The *en banc* order requested briefing from the parties on the following two questions:

> (a) In light of the Supreme Court's decision in *Petrella v. Metro-Goldwyn-Mayer*, 134 S. Ct. 1962 (2014) (and considering any relevant differences between copyright and patent law), should this court's *en banc* decision in *A.C. Aukerman Co. v. R.L. Chaides Const. Co.*, 960 F.2d 1020 (Fed. Cir. 1992), be overruled so that the defense of laches is not applicable to bar a claim for damages based on patent infringement occurring within the six-year damages limitations period established by 35 U.S.C. §286?
>
> (b) In light of the fact that there is no statute of limitations for claims of patent infringement and in view of Supreme Court precedent, should the defense of laches be available under some circumstances to bar an entire infringement suit for either damages or injunctive relief? *See, e.g., Lane & Bodley Co. v. Locke*, 150 U.S. 193 (1893).

Id. at *1.

[85]SCA Hygiene Prods. Aktiebolag v. First Quality Baby Prods., LLC, No. 2013-1564, 2015 WL 5474261 (Sept. 18, 2015) (*en banc*) (hereafter "*SCA Hygiene II*").

[86]*SCA Hygiene II,* 2015 WL 5474261, at *7.

[87]*SCA Hygiene II,* 2015 WL 5474261, at *17 (holding that "laches remains a defense to legal relief in a patent infringement suit after *Petrella.* Laches bars legal relief. . . .").

[88]In reliance on the Supreme Court's 1888 decision in the trademark case *Menendez v. Holt,* 128 U.S. 514, 523-524 (1888), the *Aukerman* court had held that a successful laches defense did *not* bar a patentee from obtaining post-filing damages or injunctive relief, unless the elements of equitable estoppel were also established. *See* Aukerman Co. v. R.L. Chaides Const. Co., 960 F.2d 1020, 1040 (Fed. Cir. 1992).

The Supreme Court's 2006 decision in *eBay* as well as *Petrella* required consideration of facts relevant to laches, such as the patentee's delay and the accused infringer's reliance thereon, as part of the "balance of the hardships" and "irreparable injury" factors that must be established for injunctive relief.[89] Thus, depending on the totality of findings made on the injunction factors, awarding the patentee an injunction might not be appropriate when the infringer has established laches in the initiation of the lawsuit. With respect to the remedy of an ongoing royalty, the *SCA Hygiene II* majority held that "absent egregious circumstances, when injunctive relief is inappropriate, the patentee remains entitled to an ongoing royalty."[90] In sum, under *SCA Hygiene II* a successful laches defense will bar money damages for pre-suit infringements, it may or may not impact the patentee's ability to obtain injunctive relief, and it will likely not bar any award of ongoing royalties in lieu of an injunction.

In the opinion authored by Chief Judge Prost for the six-judge majority in *SCA Hygiene II*, the Federal Circuit held firstly that *Aukerman* and the laches defense to pre-filing damages for patent infringement survived the Supreme Court's 2014 decision in *Petrella*. The *SCA Hygiene II* majority reasoned that Congress included Section 282, listing categories of defenses to patent infringement,[91] when it enacted the 1952 Patent Act. Although Section 282 did not expressly mention laches, the statute's use of broad, general language presumptively meant that Congress intended to continue the pre-1952 common law rule that laches could bar damages recovery in patent infringement lawsuits.[92] Thus, the 1952 Patent Act codified the laches defense

[89]*See SCA Hygiene II,* 2015 WL 5474261, at *15. These injunction factors are examined *infra* Chapter 11, Section B ("Injunctions").

[90]*SCA Hygiene II,* 2015 WL 5474261, at *18.

[91]The various defenses to infringement categorized in what is now 35 U.S.C. §282(b) (eff. Sept. 16, 2012) are the subject of this Chapter 10. *See* in particular *supra* Chapter 10, Section A ("Introduction") for further discussion of §282(b).

[92]*See SCA Hygiene II,* 2015 WL 5474261, at *11 (citing as examples the pre-1952 cases Banker v. Ford Motor Co., 69 F.2d 665 (3d Cir. 1934); Hartford-Empire Co. v. Swindell Bros., 96 F.2d 227 (4th Cir. 1938); Ford v. Huff, 296 F. 652 (5th Cir. 1924); France Mfg. Co. v. Jefferson Elec. Co., 106 F.2d 605 (6th Cir. 1939); Brennan v. Hawley Prods. Co., 182 F.2d 945 (7th Cir. 1950); Middleton v. Wiley, 195 F.2d 844 (8th Cir. 1952)). The *en banc* majority concluded:

> In sum, the case law strongly supports the availability of laches to bar legal relief. Section 282 codified whatever laches doctrine existed when Congress enacted the Patent Act in 1952. Although the development occurred over time, by 1952 nearly every circuit had approved of the proposition that laches could bar legal relief for patent infringement, and no court had held to the contrary. The Walker treatise — in 1937 [4 *Walker on Patents* (Deller's ed. 1937)] and then more authoritatively in 1951 [4 *Walker on Patents* (Supp. 1951)] — agreed that laches precludes recovery of legal damages. The laches doctrine codified in §282 must have meaning, and, absent any direction from Congress, it takes on its common

to patent infringement. Legislative history further supported the majority's reasoning.[93]

The *SCA Hygiene II* majority considered *Petrella* irrelevant to the question of applying laches to bar pre-suit damages, stating that "[w]hether Congress considered the quandary in *Petrella* is irrelevant—in the 1952 Patent Act, Congress settled that laches and a time limitation on the recovery of damages [i.e., 35 U.S.C. §286] can coexist in patent law. We must respect the statutory law."[94] Unlike *Petrella*, application of laches to patent infringement damages was authorized by statute and did not entail a "separation of powers" problem; that is, in recognizing laches in patent cases, courts do not override "'Congress' judgment on the timeliness of suit.'"[95]

In a dissenting opinion authored by Judge Hughes, five Circuit judges strongly disagreed with the majority's holding that laches remains a viable defense to pre-suit damages claims. The *SCA Hygiene II* minority contended that at the time of the 1952 Act, Supreme Court authority not involving patent infringement generally precluded applying laches to bar a claim for damages brought within a federal statutory limitations period. In the minority's view, a few "aberrational" regional circuit decisions holding laches applicable to bar damage claims brought within the statutory limitations period were not sufficient to have created a "well-established rule" that Congress could have intended to codify.[96]

> law meaning. Following a review of the relevant common law, that meaning is clear: in 1952, laches operated as a defense to legal relief. Therefore, in §282, Congress codified a laches defense that barred recovery of legal remedies.

SCA Hygiene II, 2015 WL 5474261, at *13.

[93]*See SCA Hygiene II,* 2015 WL 5474261, at *8 (citing the House and Senate Reports for the 1952 Act as confirming that "Congress intended §282 to have broad reach); *id.* (citing P.J. Federico, *Commentary on the New Patent Act*, 35 U.S.C.A. 1, 55 (West 1954)) (hereafter "*Federico Commentary*"). The *SCA Hygiene II* majority observed that Federico, a principal drafter of the 1952 Patent Act, stated in pertinent part:

> The defenses which may be raised in an action involving the validity or infringement of a patent are specified in general terms, by the second paragraph of section 282, in five numbered items. Item 1 specifies "Noninfringement, absence of liability for infringement, or unenforceability" (the last word was added by amendment in the Senate for greater clarity); *this would include* the defenses such as that the patented invention has not been made, used or sold by the defendant; license; and *equitable defenses such as laches*, estoppel and unclean hands."

SCA Hygiene II, 2015 WL 5474261, at *8 (quoting *Federico Commentary* (emphases added by Federal Circuit)).

[94]*SCA Hygiene II,* 2015 WL 5474261, at *1.

[95]*SCA Hygiene II,* 2015 WL 5474261, at *5 (quoting *Petrella,* 124 S. Ct. at 1967).

[96]*See SCA Hygiene II,* 2015 WL 5474261, at *17 (Hughes, J., concurring-in-part, dissenting-in-part), stating:

Despite their sharp disagreement on the viability of a laches defense to bar pre-suit legal (e.g., damages) relief, all members of the *en banc* Federal Circuit in *SCA Hygiene II* agreed about the impact of laches on equitable, prospective relief—e.g., injunctions and ongoing royalties. The court unanimously held that the 1992 *Aukerman en banc* holding that a successful laches defense could not bar injunctive relief or post-filing royalties for the patentee had to be revised in light of subsequent Supreme Court precedent. With respect to injunctions, a district court should consider laches as part of the four-factor *eBay* framework.[97] A patent owner's delay in suing and an accused infringer's reliance thereon could impact the "balance of hardships" factor as well as the irreparable harm factor. Thus, "laches in combination with the *eBay* factors may in some circumstances counsel against an injunction."[98] With respect to awards of ongoing royalties in lieu of injunctions, however, the Supreme Court's decisions in *Petrella* and *Menendez v. Holt*[99] dictated that "laches will only foreclose an ongoing royalty in extraordinary circumstances."[100] A patentee who has committed laches "typically does not surrender its right to an ongoing royalty."[101]

(iv) *SCA Hygiene III* (U.S. 2017): Substantial Repeal of Laches Defense

The Supreme Court thereafter granted a petition for *certiorari* in *SCA Hygiene*, hearing oral argument in November 2016. In March 2017, the Supreme Court issued a 7-1 decision in *SCA Hygiene Prods. Aktiebolag v. First Quality Baby Prods., LLC* ("*SCA Hygiene III*").[102] Rejecting 25 years of Federal Circuit patent laches case law stemming

---

the majority has no sound basis for finding that Congress intended to displace the uniform limitations period in §286 with the case-specific doctrine of laches. The majority's key logic—that Congress adopted the view of some lower courts that laches could bar legal relief in patent cases—requires us to presume that Congress ignored the Supreme Court. For in 1952, the Supreme Court had already recognized the common-law principle that laches cannot bar a claim for legal damages. I know of no precedent for inferring a congressional departure from a common-law principle recognized by the highest court based solely on aberrational lower-court decisions.

[97]The *eBay* factors are further examined *infra* Chapter 11, Section B.1 ("Permanent Injunctions").

[98]*SCA Hygiene II,* 2015 WL 5474261, at *17. *See also SCA Hygiene II,* 2015 WL 5474261, at *18 n.1 (Hughes, J., concurring-in-part, dissenting-in-part) (stating that "I agree with the majority that laches is available to bar equitable relief").

[99]128 U.S. 514 (1888).

[100]*SCA Hygiene II,* 2015 WL 5474261, at *1.

[101]*SCA Hygiene II,* 2015 WL 5474261, at *17 (citing *Menendez,* 128 U.S. at 523-525).

[102]137 S. Ct. 954 (Mar. 21, 2017) (Alito, J.) ("*SCA Hygiene III*"). The Supreme Court in March 2017 comprised only eight members following the death of Justice Scalia

from the 1992 *Aukerman en banc* decision (as well as pre–Federal Circuit patent case law dating from the late nineteenth century), the Supreme Court majority (in an opinion authored by Justice Alito) held that laches is *not* a defense to a patent infringement suit seeking damages for infringements that occurred during the §286 six-year period before filing suit.

To better understand the significant impact of *SCA Hygiene III,* consider a hypothetical in which Patentee P, manufacturer of a patented product, sends Competitor C, manufacturer of a competing product, a letter in the year 2020. Patentee P threatens in writing to sue C for patent infringement and offers C a license in lieu of the lawsuit. Because Competitor C believes in good faith that its product does not infringe P's patent and/or that the patent is invalid, Competitor C responds to P's letter by asserting these beliefs and rejecting the offer of a license. Thereafter the parties have no further communication for *eight years*. Meanwhile, C continues to manufacture and sell its successful product and to invest in new production facilities.

In 2028, Patentee P files a patent infringement lawsuit against Competitor C in federal district court. A jury finds that C's product *does* infringe and that C has *not* proven the patent invalid. The trial court refuses to disturb the jury's verdict and enters a permanent injunction against any further sales of C's infringing product. The jury also finds that Patentee P is entitled to lost profits damages in the amount of $25 million for infringements that occurred in the time period spanning the six years that elapsed before the filing of suit, i.e., during 2022-2028.[103]

Thus, Patentee P waited for eight years to bring its lawsuit after sending its original infringement letter to competitor C. Assume further that P's delay was unreasonable (for example, P was not involved in any other litigation or circumstances that would have excused its failure to sue earlier). Moreover, the delay materially economically prejudiced Competitor C (which had invested in new factories to make the accused product during the 2020-2028 time period).

The *SCA Hygiene III* decision means that Competitor C can*not* assert the defense of laches in an attempt to avoid paying the $25 million in lost profits damages. The Supreme Court ruled that the laches defense is no longer available to protect C from the damages incurred by its production and sale of what was later ruled an infringing product during the §286 six-year period before P filed its suit, despite P's unreasonable delay and the prejudice to C. Of course, Competitor C

(Justice Gorsuch was sworn in in April 2017). Justice Breyer was the sole dissenter in *SCA Hygiene III.*

[103]*See* 35 U.S.C. §286 (providing in part that "[e]xcept as otherwise provided by law, no recovery shall be had for any infringement committed more than six years prior to the filing of the complaint or counterclaim for infringement in the action").

can (and most likely did) continue to assert all the *other* defenses available to it, such as non-infringement, invalidity, and perhaps inequitable conduct. But those defenses did not persuade the jury in this hypothetical. Unless Competitor C can obtain relief on appeal, it must pay Patentee P the $25 million, despite P's eight-year delay and despite C's expenditures in building new factories to make a product now permanently enjoined.

In the above hypothetical, Patentee P and Competitor C both manufactured and sold the patented device. But the implications of the *SCA Hygiene III* decision sweep more broadly. The *SCA Hygiene III* decision is undoubtedly a boon for patent-assertion entities ("PAE"s, pejoratively termed "patent trolls"), which have become very active participants in the patent litigation landscape. Because they are not competing in the marketplace and are not losing customers to sales by manufacturers like C, a PAE has no incentive to sue earlier rather than later (and in fact, has every incentive to delay suit in order to maximize its potential damages recovery, which will be in the form of reasonable royalties rather than lost profits). Even though the validity of some patents asserted by PAEs may be questionable, in this hypothetical, the PAE's patent survived C's invalidity challenge. Consider also that the PAE's delay in bringing suit may mean that C suffered *evidentiary* prejudice (in addition to economic prejudice). The longer the PAE waits to sue, the more likely it is that C loses valuable documents and/or witnesses that might otherwise have helped it prove the invalidity of the PAE's patent.

Despite these negative results, it is important to understand that the *SCA Hygiene III* Court did *not* do away with the related but separate defense of equitable estoppel.[104] Henceforth accused infringers will likely attempt to rely on that equitable doctrine, discussed below.[105]

Realize also that the Supreme Court abrogated the laches defense in one particular (albeit substantial) part of patent litigation — as a means of seeking damages accrued during the six-year pre-filing time period set forth in 35 U.S.C. §286. The possibility of recouping such damages is an aspect of patent infringement actions brought under 35 U.S.C. §§281-299 (which sections comprise Chapter 29 of the Patent Act, titled "Remedies for Infringement of Patent, and Other Actions"). The *SCA Hygiene III* Court said nothing about revoking

[104]*See SCA Hygiene III,* 137 S. Ct. at 967 (noting that "the doctrine of equitable estoppel provides protection against some of the problems that [accused infringer] First Quality highlights, namely, unscrupulous patentees inducing potential targets of infringement suits to invest in the production of arguably infringing products. . . . Indeed, the Federal Circuit held that there are genuine disputes of material fact as to whether equitable estoppel bars First Quality's claims in this very case.") (citations omitted). Equitable estoppel is further examined *infra*, Section 5.c.

[105]The doctrine of equitable estoppel is addressed *infra*, Section 5.c.

the defense of laches as a means of recovering pre-suit damages for *other* types of patent-based actions, however, such as a lawsuit seeking correction of inventorship under 35 U.S.C. §256 ("Correction of named inventor"), subsection (b).[106] Presumably the laches defense remains available as a defense against pre-suit damages in such lawsuits.

Returning in more detail to the rationale of the *SCA Hygiene III* majority Supreme Court opinion, the majority vacated (in major part) the Circuit's 2015 *en banc* decision in *SCA Hygiene II,* which had reaffirmed the primary holding of *Aukerman*— that laches remained a viable defense against patent infringement actions seeking damages in the six years before suit was filed. Contrary to the Circuit's view, the *SCA Hygiene III* majority determined that the reasoning of its 2014 *Petrella* copyright decision, examined *supra,*[107] applied with equal force to preclude a defense of laches against the remedy of past damages in patent cases. Laches, the majority emphasized, is an *equitable* doctrine, while the remedy of damages is a *legal* remedy. The "well-established general rule," which the Court had repeatedly stated in a number of non-patent cases,[108] is that "laches cannot be invoked to bar a claim for damages incurred within a limitations period specified by Congress."[109]

To do otherwise would create a separation-of-powers problem, with judicial application of laches within the six-year pre-filing period effectively overriding congressional intent. The *SCA Hygiene III* majority determined that in 1952 when Congress enacted 35 U.S.C. §282 (enumerating defenses to infringement), if it "examined the relevant legal landscape . . . , it could not have missed our cases endorsing this general rule."[110] With this logic, the *SCA Hygiene III* majority refuted the writings of a co-drafter of the 1952 Patent Act. P.J. Federico wrote in his much-cited *Commentary* that 35 U.S.C. §282, by including the

[106] That subsection provides in part that "[t]he court before which such matter is called in question may order correction of the patent on notice and hearing of all parties concerned and the Director shall issue a certificate accordingly." 35 U.S.C. §256(b). Actions for correction of inventorship are examined *supra* Section M.3.

[107] *See supra* Section 5(a)(ii).

[108] *See SCA Hygiene III,* 137 S. Ct. at 963 (citing Holmberg v. Armbrecht, 327 U.S. 392, 395 (1946) ("If Congress explicitly puts a limit upon the time for enforcing a right which it created, there is an end of the matter[.]"); United States v. Mack, 295 U.S. 480, 489 (1935) ("Laches within the term of the statute of limitations is no defense at law[.]"); Wehrman v. Conklin, 155 U.S. 314, 326 (1894) ("Though a good defense in equity, laches is no defense at law. If the plaintiff at law has brought his action within the period fixed by the statute of limitations, no court can deprive him of his right to proceed[.]"); Cross v. Allen, 141 U.S. 528, 537 (1891) ("So long as the demands secured were not barred by the statute of limitations, there could be no laches in prosecuting a suit[.]")). Moreover, "*Petrella* confirmed and restated this long-standing rule. 572 U.S., at ___, 134 S. Ct., at 1973 ("[T]his Court has cautioned against invoking laches to bar legal relief[.]")." *SCA Hygiene III,* 137 S. Ct. at 963.

[109] *SCA Hygiene III,* 137 S. Ct. at 963.

[110] *SCA Hygiene III,* 137 S. Ct. at 963-964.

phrase "[n]oninfringement, absence of liability for infringement, or unenforceability," included a laches defense.[111]

The *SCA Hygiene III* majority was not concerned that the Patent Act does not provide a statute of limitations in the traditional sense of a time limit on bringing a lawsuit, but rather a limitations time period on recoverable past damages (i.e., 35 U.S.C. §286). In contrast, the Copyright Act includes a true statute of limitations (i.e., a forward-looking provision requiring that a copyright infringement cause of action be asserted within three years of the cause accruing) in 17 U.S.C. §507. The Patent Act includes merely a damages limitation statute (i.e., a backward-looking provision barring the remedy of damages for patent infringements that occurred more than six years before the complaint was filed, but not barring the filing of an action) in 35 U.S.C. §286. In the Supreme Court majority's view, the general rule that laches cannot bar damages incurred within a congressionally-specified "limitations period" (as broadly defined by the Court) still applied to patent cases, despite what the majority viewed as a "debatable taxonomy."[112]

In order to override the "general rule," the *SCA Hygiene III* majority required a showing that the case law demonstrated a "broad and unambiguous consensus" to the contrary. Specifically, the Court required that lower court decisions would have to clearly support the Federal Circuit's reasoning in *SCA Hygiene II*. Recall that the Circuit had determined that Congress's 1952 inclusion in the Patent Act of 35 U.S.C. §282(b), which enumerates the defenses of "[n]oninfringement, absence of liability for infringement or unenforceability," legislatively codified a well-established judicial understanding — that laches operated as a defense to *all* patent infringement claims, including claims for damages suffered during the six-year period specified in 35 U.S.C. §286. But after reviewing the cases, the Supreme Court majority in *SCA Hygiene III* concluded that they did not "constitute a settled, uniform practice" of applying laches to damages claims.[113]

[111]*See* P.J. Federico, Commentary on the New Patent Act, 35 U.S.C.A. 1 (West 1954), reprinted at 75 J. Pat. & Trademark Off. Soc'y 161 (1993), stating that:

> The defenses which may be raised in an action involving the validity or infringement of a patent are specified in general terms, by the second paragraph of section 282, in five numbered items. Item 1 specifies "Noninfringement, absence of liability for infringement, or unenforceability" (the last word was added by amendment in the Senate for greater clarity); this would include the defenses such as that the patented invention has not been made, used or sold by the defendant; license; *and equitable defenses such as laches*, estoppel and unclean hands.

Federico, 75 J. Pat. & Trademark Off. Soc'y at 215 (emphasis added).

[112]*SCA Hygiene III*, 137 S. Ct. at 962.

[113]*SCA Hygiene III*, 137 S. Ct. at 966.

Justice Breyer offered a solitary but forceful dissent in *SCA Hygiene III*. He asserted that "for more than a century courts with virtual unanimity have applied laches in patent damages cases."[114] When it wrote the 1952 statute, Congress was aware of and intended to codify that judicial practice in the "unenforceability" phrase of 35 U.S.C. §282, thus triggering the "[e]xcept as otherwise provided by law" preamble clause of §286. A trusted source of contemporaneous commentary by a co-author of the 1952 Patent Act, on which the Court had previously relied, supported Justice Breyer's position:

> At common law, the word "unenforceability" had a meaning that encompassed laches. *See, e.g.*, United States v. New Orleans Pacific R. Co., 248 U.S. 507, 511, 39 S. Ct. 175, 63 L. Ed. 388 (1919) (considering whether an agreement "had become unenforceable by reason of inexcusable laches"). We often read statutes as incorporating common-law meanings. *See* Neder v. United States, 527 U.S. 1, 21, 119 S. Ct. 1827, 144 L. Ed. 2d 35 (1999). And here there are good reasons for doing so. For one thing, the principal technical drafter of the Patent Act (in a commentary upon which this Court has previously relied, *e.g.*, Warner-Jenkinson Co. v. Hilton Davis Chemical Co., 520 U.S. 17, 28, 117 S. Ct. 1040, 137 L. Ed. 2d 146 (1997)) stated that §282 was meant to codify "equitable defenses such as laches." P. Federico, Commentary on the New Patent Act, 35 U.S.C.A. 1, 55 (West 1954).[115]

Justice Breyer also disagreed with the *SCA Hygiene III* majority's reading of the pre–1952 Act case law. In his view, "[t]he decisions that find or say or hold that laches can bar monetary relief in patent infringement actions stretch in a virtually unbroken chain from the late 19th century through the Patent Act's enactment in 1952."[116]

[114] *SCA Hygiene III*, 137 S. Ct. at 967 (Breyer, J., dissenting).

[115] *SCA Hygiene III*, 137 S. Ct. at 968 (Breyer, J., dissenting).

[116] *SCA Hygiene III*, 137 S. Ct. at 968 (Breyer, J., dissenting). He cited in support the following extensive list of cases "from the Federal Courts of Appeals alone":

> Lukens Steel Co. v. American Locomotive Co., 197 F.2d 939, 941 (2d Cir. 1952); Chicago Pneumatic Tool Co. v. Hughes Tool Co., 192 F.2d 620, 625 (10th Cir. 1951); Brennan v. Hawley Prods. Co., 182 F.2d 945, 948 (7th Cir. 1950); Shaffer v. Rector Well Equip. Co., 155 F.2d 344, 345-347 (5th Cir. 1946); Rome Grader & Mach. Corp. v. J.D. Adams Mfg. Co., 135 F.2d 617, 619-620 (7th Cir. 1943); France Mfg. Co. v. Jefferson Elec. Co., 106 F.2d 605, 609-610 (6th Cir. 1939); Universal Coin Lock Co. v. American Sanitary Lock Co., 104 F.2d 781, 781-783 (7th Cir. 1939); Union Shipbuilding Co. v. Boston Iron & Metal Co., 93 F.2d 781, 783 (4th Cir. 1938); Gillons v. Shell Co. of Cal., 86 F.2d 600, 608-610 (9th Cir. 1936); Holman v. Oil Well Supply Co., 83 F.2d 538 (3d Cir. 1936) (per curiam); Dock & Term. Eng. Co. v. Pennsylvania R. Co., 82 F.2d 19, 19-20 (3d Cir. 1936); Banker v. Ford Motor Co., 69 F.2d 665, 666 (3d Cir. 1934); Westco-Chippewa Pump Co. v. Delaware Elec. & Supply Co., 64 F.2d 185, 186-188 (3d Cir. 1933); Window Glass Mach. Co. v. Pittsburgh Plate Glass Co., 284 F. 645, 650-651 (3d Cir. 1922); Dwight & Lloyd Sintering Co. v. Greenawalt, 27 F.2d 823, 827 (2d Cir. 1928);

Justice Breyer criticized the majority for "tr[ying] to minimize the overall thrust of this case law by dividing the cases into subgroups and then concluding that the number of undistinguishable precedents in each subgroup is 'too few to establish a settled, national consensus.' "[117] But looking at the body of case law as a whole, rather than dissecting it into smaller groups, Justice Breyer found that "*all the cases say the same thing*: Laches applies."[118]

The majority and dissent in *SCA Hygiene III* disagreed sharply about the role and purpose of the laches defense as a "gap filler."

> George J. Meyer Mfg. Co. v. Miller Mfg. Co., 24 F.2d 505, 507-508 (7th Cir. 1928); Wolf Mineral Process Corp. v. Minerals Separation N. Am. Corp., 18 F.2d 483, 490 (4th Cir. 1927); Cummings v. Wilson & Willard Mfg. Co., 4 F.2d 453, 455 (9th Cir. 1925); Ford v. Huff, 296 F. 652, 654-655 (5th Cir. 1924); Wolf, Sayer & Heller, Inc. v. United States Slicing Mach. Co., 261 F. 195, 197-198 (7th Cir. 1919); A.R. Mosler & Co. v. Lurie, 209 F. 364, 371 (2d Cir. 1913); Safety Car Heating & Lighting Co. v. Consolidated Car Heating Co., 174 F. 658, 662 (2d Cir. 1909) (per curiam); Richardson v. D.M. Osborne & Co., 93 F. 828, 830-831 (2d Cir. 1899); and Woodmanse & Hewitt Mfg. Co. v. Williams, 68 F. 489, 493-494 (6th Cir. 1895).

SCA Hygiene III, 137 S. Ct. at 969 (Breyer, J., dissenting).

The *SCA Hygiene III* majority argued that this list of decisions proved little because nearly all of them came from the equity courts, which ordinarily applied laches to claims of an equitable nature for which Congress had not provided any fixed time limitation, Justice Breyer countered by reminding the majority that in 1870, Congress gave the equity courts power to award damages (a legal remedy) in patent cases. *See* Act of July 8, 1870, §55, 16 Stat. 206. From the late nineteenth century until 1938, when law and equity were merged, "nearly all patent litigation — including suits for damages — took place in courts of equity that were applying laches in conjunction with a statute of limitations [i.e., the precursor of 35 U.S.C. §286, limiting damages or profits recovery to the six years prior to filing suit]." *SCA Hygiene III,* 137 S. Ct. at 970 (Breyer, J., dissenting) (citing Mark A. Lemley, *Why Do Juries Decide if Patents Are Valid?,* 99 VA. L. REV. 1673, 1704 (2013) (discussing predominance of equity litigation)). Accordingly, Congress recognized that damages suits for patent infringement took place almost exclusively in the equity courts rather than the law courts. *SCA Hygiene III,* 137 S. Ct. at 970 (Breyer, J., dissenting). When enacting the 1952 Patent Act, "Congress, seeking to understand whether, or how, laches applied in patent damages cases, would almost certainly have looked to equity practice." *SCA Hygiene III,* 137 S. Ct. at 970 (Breyer, J., dissenting).

> Although Justice Breyer did not dispute the majority's contention that weaknesses existed in the reasoning of some individual cases, these were not sufficient to prevent a noted patent treatise author from concluding in 1951, "on the basis of the great weight of authority, that in patent cases, '[l]aches . . . may be interposed in an action at law.' " *SCA Hygiene III,* 137 S. Ct. at 970 (Breyer, J., dissenting) (quoting 3 A. Deller, WALKER ON PATENTS 106 (Cum. Supp. 1951)).

[117] *SCA Hygiene III,* 137 S. Ct. at 971 (Breyer, J., dissenting).

[118] *SCA Hygiene III,* 137 S. Ct. at 970 (Breyer, J., dissenting) (emphasis in original). He observed that "[t]he majority's insistence on subdivision makes it sound a little like a Phillies fan who announces that a 9-0 loss to the Red Sox was a 'close one.' Why close? Because, says the fan, the Phillies lost each inning by only one run." *SCA Hygiene III,* 137 S. Ct. at 971 (Breyer, J., dissenting).

According to the majority, the defense of laches developed in the equity courts in cases for which statutes provided no fixed time limitation. Because laches is a gap-filling doctrine, the majority reasoned, there is no gap to fill when there *is* a statute of limitations[119] (such as a traditional statute of limitations as in copyright law *or* a damages limitation statute as in patent law, which the majority considered a type of "statute of limitations").

Dissenting Justice Breyer countered that the nature of 35 U.S.C. §286, which limits the period of recovery for damages but not the time in which an infringement action must be brought, *does* create a gap. Thus, patent law continues to need a laches defense. Justice Breyer provided the following hypothetical highlighting the potential for prejudice to accused infringers in the absence of a laches defense:

> [Because there is no time-bar on filing the lawsuit,] a patentee, after learning of a possible infringement in year 1, might wait until year 10 or year 15 or year 20 to bring a lawsuit. And if he wins, he can collect damages for the preceding six years of infringement.
>
> This fact creates a gap. Why? Because a patentee might wait for a decade or more while the infringer (who perhaps does not know or believe he is an infringer) invests heavily in the development of the infringing product (of which the patentee's invention could be only a small component), while evidence that the infringer might use to, say, show the patent is invalid disappears with time. Then, if the product is a success, the patentee can bring his lawsuit, hoping to collect a significant recovery. And if business-related circumstances make it difficult or impossible for the infringer to abandon its use of the patented invention (i.e., if the infringer is "locked in"), then the patentee can keep bringing lawsuits, say, in year 10 (collecting damages from years 4 through 10), in year 16 (collecting damages from years 10 through 16), and in year 20 (collecting any remaining damages). The possibility of this type of outcome reveals a "gap." Laches works to fill the gap by barring recovery when the patentee unreasonably and prejudicially delays suit.[120]

b. Elements of Laches

This subsection details the underlying elements of the laches defense as laid out in the Federal Circuit's 1992 *Aukerman en banc* decision. As explained above, *Aukerman* (and its reaffirmance by the *en banc* Circuit in *SCA Hygiene II*) were rejected in large part by the Supreme Court's 2017 decision in *SCA Hygiene III*. Nevertheless, the material in this subsection is retained because of its historic importance and the possibility that Congress could legislatively

[119]*See SCA Hygiene III*, 137 S. Ct. at 961 (citing *Petrella*, 134 S. Ct. at 1974-1975).
[120]*SCA Hygiene III,* 137 S. Ct. at 968 (Breyer, J., dissenting).

overrule *SCA Hygiene III*. More importantly, the laches defense remains available in patent-related lawsuits for correction of inventorship under §256 (which do not involve the damages limitation period of 35 U.S.C. §286).

As held in *Aukerman,* the elements of a laches defense are:

1. unreasonable and inexcusable delay by the plaintiff in bringing suit; and
2. the defendant was materially prejudiced due to the plaintiff's delay.[121]

Each element is examined separately below.

Aukerman also clarified critical evidentiary aspects of the laches defense (that were not addressed in the 2015 decision *SCA Hygiene II*). Specifically, if the plaintiff brings suit *within* six years of learning about the alleged infringement, then the defendant must prove both of these factual elements based on the evidence of record. However, a *presumption* of laches arises in the defendant's favor when the plaintiff has delayed in filing suit for *more than* six years after the plaintiff knew or should have known of the alleged infringement.[122] If the presumption is triggered, both of the underlying laches elements of unreasonable delay and material prejudice are presumptively established in the defendant's favor without the need for submission of additional evidence.

Once the laches presumption is triggered, the burden of production (i.e., of going forward with the evidence) then shifts to the plaintiff, who must attempt to rebut the presumption.[123] If the plaintiff establishes facts that create a genuine issue of fact with respect to either one of the two underlying factors, then the laches presumption "bursts"[124] and the defendant is "put to its proof," meaning that the defendant must then attempt to establish the existence of both unreasonable delay and material prejudice based on the factual evidence of record.

[121]*See Aukerman,* 960 F.2d at 1028.

[122]*See* SCA Hygiene Prods. Aktiebolag v. First Quality Baby Prods., LLC, 767 F.3d 1339, 1343 (Fed. Cir. Sept. 17, 2014) (explaining that "[d]elays exceeding six years give rise to a presumption that the delay is unreasonable, inexcusable, and prejudicial") (citing Wanlass v. Gen. Elec. Co., 148 F.3d 1334, 1337 (Fed. Cir. 1998)), *reh'g en banc granted on other grounds, opinion vacated,* No. 2013-1564, 2014 WL 7460970 (Fed. Cir. Dec. 30, 2014) (*en banc*) (order).

[123]This procedural framework is in accord with Fed. R. Evid. 301. The burden of production, which shifts to the plaintiff when the laches presumption is triggered, should be contrasted with the burden of proof (i.e., persuasion). The defendant always bears the ultimate burden of proof on the defense of laches, and this burden never shifts to the plaintiff.

[124]This is referred to by law professors as the "double bursting bubble" approach to presumptions.

(i) Unreasonable Delay by Patentee

When attempting to rebut a presumption of laches, the plaintiff patentee may seek to establish a genuine issue of fact with respect to laches element (1), whether the delay in bringing suit was unreasonable, by offering evidence tending to show that its delay was in fact reasonable and justified under the circumstances. Such evidence might include proof of the plaintiff's participation in litigation against other infringers, ongoing negotiations with the defendant, poverty, illness, war, limited extent of infringement, dispute over ownership of the patent, or the like. In *Aukerman,* the plaintiff patentee offered evidence of its participation in other litigation, contending that this represented a legitimate excuse for its delay in suing Chaides. The Federal Circuit agreed that the evidence offered by Aukerman raised at least a genuine factual issue respecting the reasonableness of its conduct, and thus the laches defense needed to be tried rather than resolved prematurely on summary judgment.[125]

Although *Aukerman* instructed that involvement in "other litigation" may qualify as a valid excuse for a patentee's delay in filing suit so as to defeat an assertion of laches, the "other litigation" justification did not succeed in *SCA Hygiene Products Aktiebolag v. First Quality Baby Products, LLC* (*"SCA Hygiene I"*),[126] discussed in the previous section. The Federal Circuit held in that case that a patentee-initiated reexamination lasting three years, followed by an additional three-year delay in filing suit, amounted to an inexcusable delay. In the first instance, the appellate court agreed with the patentee that it was not required to give notice of the reexamination proceedings to accused infringer First Quality because the USPTO provides public notice of reexamination proceedings.[127] Nevertheless, although the three-year delay for reexamination might have been "excusable when viewed in isolation,"[128] the Circuit concluded that the patentee's delay *as a whole* was *not* excusable, for the following reasons.

Patentee SCA Hygiene, a global products company headquartered in Sweden, first sent a letter suggesting that its U.S. competitor First Quality's adult incontinence products might infringe SCA Hygiene's U.S. Patent No. 6,375,646 ('646 patent) in October 2003. In the following year, SCA Hygiene filed a request in the USPTO for *ex parte* reexamination of the '646 patent. The USPTO granted the request and in

[125]*Aukerman,* 960 F.2d at 1039.

[126]767 F.3d 1339 (Fed. Cir. Sept. 17, 2014), *reh'g en banc granted, opinion vacated,* No. 2013-1564, 2014 WL 7460970 (Fed. Cir. Dec. 30, 2014) (*en banc*) (order).

[127]*See SCA Hygiene I,* 767 F.3d at 1346, *reh'g en banc granted, opinion vacated,* No. 2013-1564, 2014 WL 7460970 (Fed. Cir. Dec. 30, 2014) (*en banc*) (order).

[128]*SCA Hygiene I,* 767 F.3d at 1346, *reh'g en banc granted, opinion vacated,* No. 2013-1564, 2014 WL 7460970 (Fed. Cir. Dec. 30, 2014) (*en banc*) (order).

2007, about three years later, confirmed all the patent's claims (SCA Hygiene never notified First Quality about the reexamination proceedings). Thereafter, SCA Hygiene did not file its infringement suit against First Quality until August 2010, almost seven years in total after SCA Hygiene had first contacted its competitor about the '646 patent. SCA Hygiene contended that its delay was justified because (1) the period of time during which its patent was in reexamination should not have counted as part of the delay period; and (2) following the reexamination, SCA Hygiene was occupied with evaluating new outside U.S. counsel, implementing new business management structures, and examining potentially infringing products on the market.

The Federal Circuit panel in *SCA Hygiene I* rejected these arguments. Viewing all facts in the light most favorable to patentee SCA Hygiene (First Quality having moved for summary judgment on its laches defense), the Circuit concluded that "no reasonable fact-finder could conclude that SCA's delay, viewed as a whole, was reasonable."[129] First, although SCA Hygiene not headquartered in the United States, it was represented by U.S. counsel when it sent its initial letters in First Quality in 2003-2004 and during the reexamination (2004-2007). In the Federal Circuit's view, there was no evidence to suggest that SCA Hygiene was unable to find counsel or reinitiate contact with First Quality shortly after the reexamination ended; rather, SCA Hygiene "should have been prepared to reassert its rights against First Quality shortly after the [patent in suit] emerged from reexamination."[130] The appellate court noted that "'personal lack of familiarity with the patent system... does not excuse... failure to file suit.'"[131] Instead, SCA Hygiene remained silent for more than three years after reexamination confirmed the viability of its patent. Even though the reexamination delay might have been excusable if viewed in isolation, the Circuit concluded that the totality of SCA Hygiene's delay was not excusable.[132]

After holding in September 2015 that laches remained a viable defense against legal relief in a patent infringement suit after *Petrella,*

[129]*SCA Hygiene I*, 767 F.3d at 1346, *reh'g en banc granted, opinion vacated*, No. 2013-1564, 2014 WL 7460970 (Fed. Cir. Dec. 30, 2014) (*en banc*) (order).

[130]*SCA Hygiene I*, 767 F.3d at 1346 (citing *Wanlass*, 148 F.3d at 1338 ("The availability of delay based on constructive knowledge of the alleged infringer's activities imposes on patentees the duty to police their rights."); 6A DONALD S. CHISUM, CHISUM ON PATENTS §19.05[2][a][iii] (2013) ("Many decisions in finding delay excused emphasize that the patent owner promptly filed suit after the excuse (such as other litigation) ceased.")), *reh'g en banc granted, opinion vacated*, No. 2013-1564, 2014 WL 7460970 (Fed. Cir. Dec. 30, 2014) (*en banc*) (order).

[131]*SCA Hygiene I*, 767 F.3d at 1346 (quoting Serdarevic v. Advanced Med. Optics, Inc., 532 F.3d 1352, 1360 (Fed. Cir. 2008)), *reh'g en banc granted, opinion vacated*, No. 2013-1564, 2014 WL 7460970 (Fed. Cir. Dec. 30, 2014) (*en banc*) (order).

[132]*SCA Hygiene I*, 767 F.3d at 1346, *reh'g en banc granted, opinion vacated*, No. 2013-1564, 2014 WL 7460970 (Fed. Cir. Dec. 30, 2014) (*en banc*) (order).

the *en banc* Federal Circuit in *SCA Hygiene II* remanded the case to the district court for further proceedings consistent with the *en banc* decision.[133]

(ii) Material Prejudice to Accused Infringer

With respect to laches element (2), whether the accused infringer was materially prejudiced by the delay, the prejudice may take the form of evidentiary prejudice, such as the loss of documents and the recollections of witnesses over time. The prejudice also may be economic, as where the accused infringer has encountered a change in its economic position during the period of the plaintiff's delay. For example, prior to the plaintiff's filing of the infringement suit, the accused infringer may have made substantial investments in manufacturing facilities and capital equipment needed to produce the accused product. However, there must be a "demonstrable nexus between the alleged economic prejudice [of the alleged infringer] and the patentee's delay."[134] The alleged infringer need not show *reliance* on the patentee's delay, but rather that economic prejudice *resulted from* the delay; that is, that the alleged infringer's economic losses " 'likely would have been prevented by an earlier suit.' "[135]

In attempting to rebut a presumption of laches, the patentee may attempt to create a genuine issue of fact with respect to element (2) by establishing that the evidence supporting the accused infringer's defenses (such as noninfringement and/or invalidity) remains available, or that the accused infringer has not suffered any substantial economic change during the period of the patentee's delay.

In the September 2014 *SCA Hygiene I* panel decision discussed above, the Federal Circuit agreed with the district court that accused infringer First Quality had suffered economic prejudice and that patentee SCA's attempt to rebut First Quality's contention of harm failed. During the period of SCA's delay before filing suit, First Quality made a number of capital expenditures and increased production capacity in its adult protective underwear business. This evidence "suggest[ed] that First Quality would have restructured its activities to minimize infringement liability if SCA had brought suit earlier."[136]

[133]*SCA Hygiene II,* 2015 WL 5474261, at *17.

[134]*SCA Hygiene I*, 767 F.3d at 1347, *reh'g en banc granted, opinion vacated*, No. 2013-1564, 2014 WL 7460970 (Fed. Cir. Dec. 30, 2014) (*en banc*) (order).

[135]*SCA Hygiene I*, 767 F.3d at 1347 (quoting *Aukerman*, 960 F.2d at 1033), *reh'g en banc granted, opinion vacated*, No. 2013-1564, 2014 WL 7460970 (Fed. Cir. Dec. 30, 2014) (*en banc*) (order).

[136]*SCA Hygiene I*, 767 F.3d at 1347, *reh'g en banc granted, opinion vacated*, No. 2013-1564, 2014 WL 7460970 (Fed. Cir. Dec. 30, 2014) (*en banc*) (order).

Moreover, First Quality should not be penalized for considering its business "important" and its initiatives in the market for adult underwear "highly successful." SCA Hygiene's argument that this evidence meant First Quality would have continued to expand its business regardless of infringement liability lacked evidentiary support. A statement by First Quality's president that the alleged infringement "was never thought of again" after First Quality sent its November 2003 response to SCA Hygiene's initial accusations did not suggest that First Quality planned to ignore the issue whether or not SCA Hygiene sued it. Rather, because First Quality never heard back from SCA Hygiene until the infringement lawsuit was filed almost seven years later, First Quality simply " 'did not consider it to be an issue because we did not know what, if any, issue existed for us to follow up on.' "[137] In the *SCA Hygiene I* Federal Circuit panel's view, SCA Hygiene's suggestions that First Quality would have continued its allegedly infringing activities regardless of when or whether SCA Hygiene filed suit was "pure speculation."[138]

As noted above, after holding in September 2015 that laches remains a defense to legal relief in a patent infringement suit after *Petrella,* the *en banc* Federal Circuit in *SCA Hygiene II* remanded the case to the district court for further proceedings consistent with the *en banc* decision.[139]

(iii) "Should Have Known"

The above discussion sets out the framework for analyzing a laches defense by assuming that the presumption of laches has been triggered, based on a delay in filing suit of more than six years after the patentee first knew or should have known of the alleged infringement. The "should have known" prong of the laches rule incorporates a degree of uncertainty, however. Whether the running of the six-year laches clock has been triggered is not always clear.

A good illustration is *Intirtool, Ltd. v. Texar Corp.*[140] There the Federal Circuit reversed a district court's conclusion that laches had presumptively arisen based on a patentee's delay in bringing suit that extended more than six years after a July 1993 conversation between

[137] *SCA Hygiene I,* 767 F.3d at 1348, *reh'g en banc granted, opinion vacated,* No. 2013-1564, 2014 WL 7460970 (Fed. Cir. Dec. 30, 2014) (*en banc*) (order).

[138] *SCA Hygiene I,* 767 F.3d at 1348, *reh'g en banc granted, opinion vacated,* No. 2013-1564, 2014 WL 7460970 (Fed. Cir. Dec. 30, 2014) (*en banc*) (order).

[139] *SCA Hygiene II,* 2015 WL 5474261, at *17.

[140] 369 F.3d 1289 (Fed. Cir. 2004).

employees of the patentee and the accused infringer. In that conversation, the chief executive officer of accused infringer Texar, a corporation that had previously purchased patented punch pliers from the patentee Intirtool, told an officer of Intirtool that he was "perfectly satisfied" with it as a supplier and "had no real desire to change vendors but [he] was under price pressure."[141] When Intirtool's officer refused to meet the competitive price, Texar stopped ordering from Intirtool and began placing orders with a competing manufacturer of punch pliers. The parties had no further contact after the July 1993 conversation until more than six years later, in April 2000, when the patentee filed its infringement lawsuit.

On these facts, the Federal Circuit held in *Intirtool* that the patentee could not be charged with actual or constructive knowledge of an act of infringement that would trigger the running of the laches clock.[142] At most, the July 1993 conversation may have indicated that accused infringer Texar was considering a change of suppliers; there was no indication that the patentee should have known at any point thereafter that the accused infringer had in fact acted on this plan. A contrary holding would place on the patentee the burden of policing the other party's subsequent conduct because of "speculative comments during a single phone conversation." The Federal Circuit was "unwilling to stretch the concept of due diligence so far."[143]

c. *Equitable Estoppel*

Importantly, the Supreme Court's 2017 decision in *SCA Hygiene III* abrogated laches but left intact the defense of equitable estoppel. Although the laches and equitable estoppel defenses were often asserted in tandem (at least prior to *SCA Hygiene III*), and while both are rooted in equity, they are separate and independent legal theories.

In addition to laches, the Federal Circuit in its foundational 1992 *en banc Aukerman* decision[144] also considered whether accused infringer Chaides had successfully established the defense of equitable estoppel. As with the laches defense, the appellate court vacated the district court's grant to Chaides of summary judgment of equitable estoppel as precluded by disputed fact issues.

The Federal Circuit in *Aukerman* explained that equitable estoppel focuses not on the plaintiff's unreasonable delay in suing (i.e., the basis of laches) but rather on the unfairness of the plaintiff's actions

[141] *Id.* at 1297.
[142] *See id.* at 1297-1298.
[143] *Id.* at 1298.
[144] A.C. Aukerman Co. v. R.L. Chaides Const. Co., 960 F.2d 1020, 1041 (Fed. Cir. 1992) (*en banc*). The laches analysis of *Aukerman* is examined *supra* Sections C.5.a.i and C.5.b.

in misleading the defendant into believing that it would not be sued and the defendant's detrimental reliance on those actions.[145] The following are required elements of equitable estoppel:

1. the plaintiff misleads the defendant into reasonably inferring that the plaintiff does not intend to enforce its patent against the defendant;
2. the defendant relies on the plaintiff's misleading conduct; and
3. due to its reliance, the defendant will be materially prejudiced if the plaintiff is allowed to proceed with its claim.[146]

In contrast with laches, there is no presumption applicable to the defense of equitable estoppel; a defendant must offer evidence sufficient to prove each of the three factual elements of the equitable estoppel defense. If the defense of equitable estoppel is sustained, the result is that the plaintiff's action is completely barred.[147] Thus, the penalty for equitable estoppel is considerably more severe than for laches, which limits damages but does not prohibit maintenance of the infringement suit, does not necessarily bar an injunction, and

[145]The *en banc* court noted, however, that the patent cases coming before it "involving the issue of a patentee's inequitable delay in suing have almost invariably raised the defense not only of laches but also of equitable estoppel." *Aukerman*, 960 F.2d at 1042 (Fed. Cir. 1992). Nevertheless, the elements of the two defenses should not be intertwined. "Delay in filing suit may be evidence which influences the assessment of whether the patentee's conduct is misleading but it is not a requirement of equitable estoppel. Even where such delay is present, the concepts of equitable estoppel and laches are distinct from one another." *Aukerman*, 960 F.2d at 1042.

[146]*Aukerman*, 960 F.2d at 1028. *See also* Radio Sys. Corp. v. Lalor, 709 F.3d 1124, 1131 (Fed. Cir. 2013) (holding that as to patentee Bumper Boy's U.S. Patent No. 6,830,014 directed to an electronic dog collar, district court did not abuse its discretion in concluding that "equitable estoppel barred Bumper Boy's infringement claims on the UltraSmart collar against [accused infringer] Innotek. With respect to Innotek, all three elements of equitable estoppel are present and Bumper Boy does not contest the district court's factual findings."). The Federal Circuit further held in *Radio Sys.* that the equitable estoppel defense may shield not only an originally accused infringer but also its acquiring company/successor-in-interest, so long as privity exists between the parties.

[147]*See* Scholle Corp. v. Blackhawk Molding Co., 133 F.3d 1469, 1473 (Fed. Cir. 1998) (holding plaintiff equitably estopped from asserting its patent where it had previously made an accusation of infringement followed by silence after inspection of defendant's redesigned product); ABB Robotics, Inc. v. GMFanuc Robotics Corp., 52 F.3d 1062, 1064-1065 (Fed. Cir. 1995) (sustaining equitable estoppel defense where four-and-a-half-year period of silence by plaintiffs misled defendants into believing plaintiffs would not enforce their patent rights, emphasizing that "[m]isleading action by the patentee may be silence, if such silence is accompanied by some other factor indicating that the silence was sufficiently misleading to amount to bad faith"); A.C. Aukerman Co. v. R.L. Chaides Const. Co., 960 F.2d 1020, 1028 (Fed. Cir. 1992) (*en banc*) ("Where an alleged infringer establishes the defense of equitable estoppel, the patentee's claim may be entirely barred.").

generally does not prohibit ongoing royalties when an injunction is inappropriate.

Additional distinctions exist between laches and equitable estoppel. In its 2014 panel decision *SCA Hygiene Products Aktiebolag v. First Quality Baby Products, LLC,*[148] discussed above, the Federal Circuit explained that

> unlike laches, equitable estoppel requires that a "plaintiff's inaction . . . be combined with other facts respecting the relationship or contacts between the parties to give rise to the necessary inference that the claim against the defendant is abandoned." [*Aukerman*, 960 F.2d] at 1042. Moreover, equitable estoppel requires that the defendant rely, to its detriment, on the patentee's abandonment. *See id.* at 1042-43. *See also Meyers v. Asics Corp.*, 974 F.2d 1304, 1308 & n.1 (Fed. Cir. 1992). And a court may not presume that the underlying elements of equitable estoppel are present, regardless of how much time has passed. *Aukerman*, 960 F.2d at 1043.[149]

Although it had affirmed a district court's grant of summary judgment of laches to the accused infringer in the 2014 decision discussed *supra*, *SCA Hygiene Products Aktiebolag v. First Quality Baby Products, LLC* ("*SCA Hygiene I*"),[150] the Federal Circuit panel in that case reversed the district court's grant of summary judgment of *equitable estoppel*. When the Federal Circuit reheard the case *en banc,* the dispute concerned the propriety of the laches defense in the aftermath of the Supreme Court's 2014 *Petrella* decision; equitable estoppel was not at issue. Accordingly, the *en banc* Federal Circuit in *SCA Hygiene Prods. Aktiebolag v. First Quality Baby Prods., LLC* ("*SCA Hygiene II*")[151] reinstated the *SCA Hygiene I* panel's reversal of the district court's grant of summary judgment to accused infringer First Quality on equitable estoppel, and "adopt[ed] [the] reasoning" of the *SCA Hygiene I* panel.[152] The Supreme Court did not displace equitable estoppel in its 2017 *SCA Hygiene III* decision; the defense remains good law.[153]

[148]767 F.3d 1339 (Fed. Cir. Sept. 17, 2014), *reh'g en banc granted, opinion vacated*, No. 2013-1564, 2014 WL 7460970 (Fed. Cir. Dec. 30, 2014) (*en banc*).

[149]*SCA Hygiene I*, 767 F.3d at 1343-1344, *reh'g en banc granted, opinion vacated*, No. 2013-1564, 2014 WL 7460970 (Fed. Cir. Dec. 30, 2014) (*en banc*).

[150]767 F.3d 1339 (Fed. Cir. Sept. 17, 2014), discussed *supra, reh'g en banc granted, opinion vacated*, No. 2013-1564, 2014 WL 7460970 (Fed. Cir. Dec. 30, 2014) (*en banc*).

[151]No. 2013-1564, 2015 WL 5474261 (Fed. Cir. Sept. 18, 2015).

[152]*SCA Hygiene II,* 2015 WL 5474261, at *17 ("[W]e reinstate the panel's reversal of the district court's grant of summary judgment on equitable estoppel and adopt its reasoning.").

[153]*See* SCA Hygiene Prod. Aktiebolag v. First Quality Baby Prod., LLC, 137 S. Ct. 954, 967 (2017) ("*SCA Hygiene III*").

With respect to the first equitable estoppel element of a misleading communication, the district court had found that patentee SCA Hygiene's failure to reply to First Quality's response letter addressing the validity of the '646 patent in suit and the fact that it wrote First Quality concerning a different patent and different products made it reasonable for First Quality to assume that SCA Hygiene was not pursuing its initial accusation of infringement of the '646 patent. The Federal Circuit panel in *SCA Hygiene I* disagreed. Admittedly, "the most common example of equitable estoppel is a patentee who objects to allegedly infringing activities and then remains silent for a number of years. . . ."[154] However, silence "must be 'coupled with *other* factors, [such that the] patentee's 'misleading conduct' is essentially misleading inaction.' "[155] In *SCA Hygiene I*, any interaction between the parties was "meager." After only two letters mentioning the '646 patent in suit or the accused products, First Quality "never solicited further comment from SCA [Hygiene]."[156] The record suggested that the parties had never been adversaries in prior related litigation, held no other close relationship, and never held "serious discussions" involving the accused products, the '646 patent in suit, or any related patent.[157] These facts did not amount to the required "misleading inaction." Moreover, SCA Hygiene's filing of its request for *ex parte* reexamination of the '646 patent in suit contravened First Quality's allegation that SCA Hygiene's silence was tantamount to an admission of the '646 patent's invalidity.

The Federal Circuit in *SCA Hygiene I* also disagreed with accused infringer First Quality's contention that its reliance on SCA Hygiene's misleading communication had caused it material prejudice. To show reliance for equitable estoppel, the Federal Circuit observed, the accused infringer's prejudice must be caused by *reliance* on the patentee's misrepresentation rather than merely *result from* the misrepresentation. In the case at bar, First Quality's asserted reliance was

[154]*SCA Hygiene I*, 767 F.3d at 1349, *reh'g en banc granted, opinion vacated*, No. 2013-1564, 2014 WL 7460970 (Fed. Cir. Dec. 30, 2014) (*en banc*).

[155]*SCA Hygiene I*, 767 F.3d at 1349 (quoting *Aukerman*, 960 F.2d at 1042) (emphasis added by Federal Circuit in *SCA Hygiene*), *reh'g en banc granted, opinion vacated*, No. 2013-1564, 2014 WL 7460970 (Fed. Cir. Dec. 30, 2014) (*en banc*). The Federal Circuit contrasted the facts of the case at bar with those of its earlier decisions finding equitable estoppel in *Scholle Corp. v. Blackhawk Molding Co.*, 133 F.3d 1469 (Fed. Cir. 1998) (parties' course of dealings was such that patentee's silence amounted to misleading inaction), and *Aspex Eyewear Inc. v. Clariti Eyewear, Inc.*, 605 F.3d 1305 (Fed. Cir. 2010) (patentee's three years of silence where parties had been embroiled in past related patent litigation made it reasonable for accused infringer to infer that patentee was not continuing its accusation of infringement).

[156]*SCA Hygiene I*, 767 F.3d at 1350, *reh'g en banc granted, opinion vacated*, No. 2013-1564, 2014 WL 7460970 (Fed. Cir. Dec. 30, 2014) (*en banc*).

[157]*SCA Hygiene I*, 767 F.3d at 1350, *reh'g en banc granted, opinion vacated*, No. 2013-1564, 2014 WL 7460970 (Fed. Cir. Dec. 30, 2014) (*en banc*).

not reasonable given SCA Hygiene's request for reexamination, which First Quality would have learned of by exercising "even the most rudimentary due diligence."[158] Unanswered fact questions as to whether First Quality relied on its own opinion that the '646 patent was invalid (or simply ignored the patent), rather than whether it relied on SCA Hygiene's silence, rendered erroneous the district court's grant of summary judgment of equitable estoppel.

6. State Sovereign Immunity

Under Supreme Court authority, state governments (i.e., states, instrumentalities thereof such as state universities, and state employees acting in their official capacity) enjoy constitutional immunity from infringement liability under the U.S. Patent Act.[159] As a general rule, state governments are immune from lawsuits under the Eleventh Amendment of the U.S. Constitution, which provides that the "Judicial Power of the United States shall not be construed to extend to any suit in law or equity, commenced or prosecuted against one of the United States by Citizens of another State, or by Citizens or subjects of any foreign state."[160] Congress in 1992 stripped (i.e., abrogated) the states of their immunity from patent infringement liability by enacting the Patent and Plant Variety Protection Remedy Clarification Act.[161] However, the Supreme Court in *Florida Prepaid Postsecondary Educ. Expense Bd. v. College Savings Bank*[162] subsequently struck down the Patent Remedy Act as unconstitutional based on the following reasoning.

Because Congress could not abrogate the states' Eleventh Amendment sovereign immunity under its Article I powers (which include

[158]*SCA Hygiene I*, 767 F.3d at 1351, *reh'g en banc granted, opinion vacated*, No. 2013-1564, 2014 WL 7460970 (Fed. Cir. Dec. 30, 2014) (*en banc*).

[159]Possible exceptions to states' immunity would include state and industry collaborations that are not sufficiently "instrumentalities of the state" to qualify for Eleventh Amendment immunity, and state officials acting in the scope of their official capacity who may still be subject to prospective injunctive relief under *Ex parte Young*, 209 U.S. 123, 167-168 (1908).

[160]U.S. Const. amend. XI.

[161]Pub. L. No. 102-560, 106 Stat. 4230 (1992) (codified at 35 U.S.C. §§271(h), 296(a) (1994)) (hereafter "Patent Remedy Act"). As codified by the Patent Remedy Act, §296(a) of the Patent Act provides in part that "[a]ny State, any instrumentality of a State, and any officer or employee of a State or instrumentality of a State acting in his official capacity, shall not be immune, under the eleventh amendment of the Constitution of the United States or under any other doctrine of sovereign immunity, from suit in Federal court by any person, including any governmental or nongovernmental entity, for infringement of a patent under section 271, or for any other violation under this title." 35 U.S.C. §296(a).

[162]527 U.S. 627 (1999).

the power enumerated in the Intellectual Property Clause),[163] the argument in *Florida Prepaid* for constitutionality of the Patent Remedy Act was premised on the Due Process Clause of the Fourteenth Amendment.[164] The petitioner contended that patents are private property and that to allow states to use them without authorization and without remedy was a deprivation of private property without due process. By a 5-4 vote, the Supreme Court rejected the Due Process theory on the grounds that there had not been a sufficient showing that state governments routinely infringe, that such infringement is willful rather than merely negligent or "innocent," or that such infringement results in a property deprivation without due process.[165] In support of its ruling, the Court pointed to the possibility of alternative remedies in state court such as unfair competition causes of action.[166]

Eleventh Amendment immunity not only protects states from liability for patent infringement but also shields them from other patent-related causes of action such a suit to correct a patent's inventorship. The Federal Circuit in *Xechem Int'l, Inc. v. Univ. of Texas M.D. Anderson Cancer Ctr.*[167] applied *Florida Prepaid* to hold that Eleventh Amendment immunity barred Xechem's claim for correction of inventorship under 35 U.S.C. §256 of two patents owned by the university, an entity of the state of Texas. The patents arose from a collaborative project between the university and Xechem; the sole named inventor on the patents was a university scientist. The Federal Circuit rejected Xechem's various arguments against Eleventh Amendment immunity as contrary to *Florida Prepaid* and its companion case, *College Savings Bank v. Florida Prepaid Postsecondary Educ. Expense Bd.*[168] In particular, the university's entry into commercial relationships and contracts with Xechem did not work a waiver of the university's Eleventh Amendment rights; this activity did not represent the necessary "clear declaration" by the state of its intent to submit to federal jurisdiction. Nor did the university constructively consent to federal jurisdiction by causing its employee (the named inventor) to apply for U.S. patents.

In contrast with *Xechem,* a state university lost its Eleventh Amendment immunity through waiver in *Vas-Cath, Inc. v. Curators*

[163]In *Seminole Tribe v. Florida*, 517 U.S. 44 (1996), the Supreme Court held that Congress cannot abrogate the states' Eleventh Amendment sovereign immunity under Congress's Article I powers. *Seminole Tribe* thus foreclosed reliance on congressional authority under the Intellectual Property Clause (or alternatively the Commerce Clause) to sustain the Patent Remedy Act.

[164]*See Florida Prepaid*, 527 U.S. at 636.

[165]*See id*. at 639-646.

[166]*See id*. at 643-644 & nn.8-9.

[167]382 F.3d 1324 (Fed. Cir. 2004).

[168]527 U.S. 666 (1999).

of the Univ. of Missouri.[169] The parties disputed priority of invention with respect to a type of dual lumen catheter. The University of Missouri initiated an interference proceeding in the USPTO between its pending patent application and a patent already issued to Vas-Cath. The university did not assert its Eleventh Amendment immunity at any stage of the proceedings before the USPTO. At the conclusion of the six-year interference, the USPTO awarded priority to the university and revoked Vas-Cath's patent. In accordance with 35 U.S.C. §146 (pre-AIA), Vas-Cath filed a civil action challenging the USPTO's decision in the U.S. District Court for the District of Columbia.[170] After the §146 action was transferred to the U.S. District Court for the Western District of Missouri, the latter court granted the university's motion to dismiss the action on the ground that the university had not waived its Eleventh Amendment immunity.

On appeal, the Federal Circuit reversed and remanded. The appellate court agreed with Vas-Cath that because the university had initiated and prevailed in the interference, it could not thereafter assert immunity from Vas-Cath's §146 action, which was effectively an appeal of the USPTO's decision:

> [T]he University cannot both retain the fruits of [the interference] and bar the losing party from its statutory right of review, even if that review is conducted in federal court. In the circumstances that here exist, the state's actions with respect to the interference include waiver with respect to the ensuing [§146] civil action. Having waived any potential immunity as to the interference contest in the PTO, we conclude that the University waived any Constitution-based objection to Vas-Cath's statutory right of judicial review.[171]

The Federal Circuit in *Vas-Cath* also distinguished *Xechem,* where no waiver was found. In *Xechem,* "the university . . . did not request the adjudication, did not initiate and participate in a PTO adversarial proceeding, did not engage in litigation like conduct, and there was no contested proceeding in which the university waived immunity and obtained the property of the losing party."[172]

[169]473 F.3d 1376 (Fed. Cir. 2007).

[170]Prior to the America Invents Act of 2011, section 146 of the Patent Act provided for a civil action in federal district court against the USPTO Director by a party who had lost an interference in the USPTO. *See* 35 U.S.C. §146 (2006). The AIA eliminated the filing of new interferences as of March 16, 2013. The post-AIA version of section 146 provides for civil actions against the USPTO Director when a party loses an AIA-implemented derivation proceeding. *See* 35 U.S.C. §146 (eff. Mar. 16, 2013) ("Civil action in case of derivation proceeding"); 35 U.S.C. §135 (eff. Mar. 16, 2013) ("Derivation proceedings").

[171]*Vas-Cath, Inc.*, 473 F.3d at 1385.

[172]*Id.* at 1383.

In contrast with state governments, the U.S. *federal* government has expressly waived its sovereign immunity from suit for patent infringement. Such lawsuits against the United States are brought exclusively in the U.S. Court of Federal Claims. The federal government retains the power to use any patented invention without injunction but must pay just compensation for the taking if infringement is proved.[173]

7. Temporary Presence Exemption

Section 272 of the Patent Act, titled "Temporary Presence in the United States," provides an exemption from patent infringement liability for certain uses of patented inventions in vehicles that temporarily enter United States territory. The statute provides that

> [t]he use of any invention in any vessel, aircraft or vehicle of any country which affords similar privileges to vessels, aircraft or vehicles of the United States, entering the United States temporarily or accidentally, shall not constitute infringement of any patent, if the invention is used exclusively for the needs of the vessel, aircraft or vehicle and is not offered for sale or sold in or used for the manufacture of anything to be sold in or exported from the United States.[174]

In a case of first impression, the Federal Circuit held in *National Steel Car, Ltd. v. Canadian Pac. Ry., Ltd.*[175] that the statutory exemption for "temporarily" entering the United States encompassed a non-permanent entry of a railroad car engaged in international commerce, even though the car was present in the United States for a majority of its useful life.[176]

National Steel Car's patent in suit was directed to a particular type of railway car used to haul lumber, known as a depressed-center-beam flat car. The Canadian defendant railroad's accused railroad cars, full of lumber, were brought into the United States from Canada on track owned by the defendant, and when that track ran out, the cars were sometimes shifted to locomotives owned by U.S. companies at locations such as Chicago, Illinois. After the lumber was unloaded at its U.S. destination, the accused railroad cars would return (empty) to Canada. A federal district court granted a preliminary injunction against the Canadian railroad, denying it the §272 exemption. In the

[173]28 U.S.C. §1498(a).

[174]35 U.S.C. §272.

[175]357 F.3d 1319 (Fed. Cir. 2004).

[176]For a comprehensive study of the *National Steel Car* decision and the growing importance of the §272 temporary presence exemption, *see* Ted. L. Field, *The "Planes, Trains, and Automobiles" Defense to Patent Infringement for Today's Global Economy: Section 272 of the Patent Act*, 12 B.U. J. Sci. & Tech. L. 26 (2006).

district court's view, the accused cars' presence could not be "temporary" because the cars were in the United States the majority of the time (i.e., about 57 percent of the useful lifespan of the cars). Moreover, the district court found, this U.S. presence significantly benefited the accused infringer.

On appeal the Federal Circuit vacated the preliminary injunction, concluding that a substantial question existed as to whether the accused rail cars were "temporarily" present. The Federal Circuit first held that as applied to the case at bar, the relevant "vessel" of §272 was an individual accused railroad car. Next, the Federal Circuit rejected both the metrics relied on by the district court — duration and benefit — in determining whether the accused cars were "temporarily" present in the United States. The Federal Circuit instead defined a vehicle entering temporarily as "a vehicle entering the United States for a limited period of time for the sole purpose of engaging in international commerce,"[177] based on the circuit's own interpretation of §272, an issue of first impression.

The Federal Circuit found the language of §272 ambiguous, so it turned to the statute's legislative history. That history reflected that §272 was drafted to codify the Supreme Court's 1857 decision in *Brown v. Duchesne,*[178] and to satisfy the obligations of the United States under the World Intellectual Property Organization (WIPO)–administered Paris Convention for the Protection of Industrial Property. Both of these sources suggested that the word "temporarily" in §272 should be interpreted "in light of a vehicle's purpose to participate in international commerce at the time of entry — namely, a purpose to enter the United States, engage in international commerce, and then depart."[179] The Federal Circuit explained that in *Brown,* the unauthorized use within U.S. jurisdiction of a patented invention related to the rigging of a French schooner was deemed beyond the scope of the patentee's right to exclude, where the challenged use was limited to the bare essentials of the contact with the United States required to engage in international commerce. Both *Brown* and Article 5*ter* of the Paris Convention[180] demonstrated a concern to leave the vessels and vehicles that pass through channels of international

[177]*National Steel Car,* 357 F.3d at 1329.

[178]60 U.S. (19 How.) 183 (1857).

[179]*National Steel Car,* 357 F.3d at 1330.

[180]Article 5*ter* of the Paris Convention for the Protection of Industrial Property, titled "Patents: Patented Devices Forming Part of Vessels, Aircraft, or Land Vehicles," provides that

> In any country of the Union the following shall not be considered as infringements of the rights of a patentee:
>
> (i) the use on board vessels of other countries of the Union of devices forming the subject of his patent in the body of the vessel, in the machinery, tackle, gear and other accessories, when such vessels temporarily or accidentally enter the

commerce free from the excessive burdens that would result if required to conform to the patent laws of all nations that the vessel or vehicle visited during its lifetime. The Federal Circuit concluded that "[i]f the cars are entering the United States for a limited time — that is, they are not entering permanently — and are entering only for the purpose of engaging in international commerce — that is, they are entering to unload foreign goods and/or to load domestic goods destined for foreign markets — they are entering 'temporarily' for the purposes of section 272 regardless of the length of their stay within the jurisdiction of the United States."[181]

8. Patent Exhaustion

The defense of patent exhaustion prevents a patent owner from getting a "second bite at the apple" once a particular patented device has been sold with the patentee's authority the first time.[182] For example, if a patent owner sells one of its patented widgets to retailer R, thereafter it is not an act of patent infringement for retailer R to resell *that* particular widget to customer C. The patent owner's right to control the disposition of the particular widget in question is said to have been "exhausted" at the time of its first sale, meaning that the patent owner does not have a right to a royalty payment or other monetary tribute for subsequent resales (nor a right to enjoin them).[183] Importantly, the sale of counterfeit or pirated items does not invoke patent exhaustion. Rather, patent exhaustion applies when the first sale of a patented item is authorized; that is, the item is sold by the patent owner or someone acting with the patent owner's permission such as a licensee. Assuming that the first sale was authorized, then the patent owner is viewed as having received its entire reward or "tribute" in the price it obtained for the first sale of the particular patented item.

The Federal Circuit's 2013 decision, *Keurig, Inc. v. Sturm Foods, Inc.*,[184] illustrates the principle that an unconditional sale of a

---

waters of the said country, provided that such devices are used there exclusively for the needs of the vessel;

(ii) the use of devices forming the subject of the patent in the construction or operation of aircraft or land vehicles of other countries of the Union, or of accessories of such aircraft or land vehicles, when those aircraft or land vehicles temporarily or accidentally enter the said country.

[181] *National Steel Car*, 357 F.3d 1331.

[182] The copyright law counterpart to patent exhaustion is the "first sale" defense, codified at 17 U.S.C. §109(a).

[183] The above discussion contemplates sales of patented items within a given country's market. Patent exhaustion in the international context is more complex, as discussed *infra* Chapter 12, Section F.

[184] 732 F.3d 1370 (Fed. Cir. 2013).

patented device exhausts the patentee's right to control the purchaser's use of that device. Patentee Keurig made and sold single-serve coffee brewers and beverage cartridges ("pods") for use in those brewers.[185] A consumer using Keurig's patented brewer inserted a cartridge, the brewer forced hot water through the cartridge, and the brewer dispensed a single serving of a beverage (such as coffee). Keurig obtained two patents reciting apparatus claims directed to the brewers themselves as well as method claims directed to methods of using the brewers to make beverages.[186]

Accused infringer Sturm made and sold its own cartridges (under the brand name Grove Square) that consumers could use with Keurig's brewers. Keurig thereafter sued Sturm for infringement of Keurig's *method* claims, not its apparatus claims to the brewers themselves.[187] (Nor did Keurig sue Sturm for infringing a separate Keurig patent directed to Keurig's cartridges.[188]) A representative method claim of one of the two asserted Keurig patents recited:

> 6. A method of brewing a beverage from a beverage medium contained in a disposable cartridge, comprising the following steps, in sequence:
> (a) piercing the cartridge with a tubular outlet probe to vent the cartridge interior;
> (b) piercing the cartridge with a tubular inlet probe;
> (c) admitting heated liquid into the cartridge interior via the inlet probe for combination with the beverage medium to produce a beverage; and
> (d) extracting the beverage from the cartridge interior via the outlet probe.

More specifically, Keurig's lawsuit contended that *consumers* directly infringed the method claims when they used the Keurig brewer with the Sturm cartridges to brew coffee. Keurig argued that Sturm's manufacture and sales of Sturm cartridges to consumers rendered Sturm liable for *inducing or contributory* infringement of the Keurig patents' method claims under 35 U.S.C. §271(b) or §271(c).[189]

[185]Notably, Keurig's sales of its brewers were unconditional; that is, Keurig did not purport to limit purchasers to using Keurig brewers only with Keurig cartridges. *See Keurig*, 732 F.3d at 1374 (stating that "Keurig sold its patented brewers without conditions").

[186]*See* U.S. Pat. No. 7,165,488; U.S. Pat. No. 6,606,938.

[187]*See Keurig*, 732 F.3d at 1374 (explaining that Keurig did "not dispute that its rights in its brewers were exhausted with respect to the apparatus claims of the asserted patents.... Instead, Keurig alleges that purchasers of its brewers infringe its brewer patents by using Sturm cartridges to practice the claimed methods and therefore that Sturm is liable for induced infringement").

[188]*See Keurig*, 732 F.3d at 1373-1374 ("Keurig did not assert its cartridge patent against Sturm . . .").

[189]These forms of indirect infringement are examined *supra* Chapter 9, Section E ("Aspects of Infringement Beyond 35 U.S.C. §271(a)").

C. Absence of Liability for Infringement

Affirming a district court's grant to defendant Sturm of summary judgment of noninfringement, the Federal Circuit agreed with Sturm that Keurig's method claims were exhausted by Keurig's authorized sales of its brewers. The brewers were covered by the asserted patents.[190] As the Supreme Court held in the nineteenth century, the purchase of a patented machine from the patentee or its assignee carries with it the right to use the machine.[191] "Keurig sold its patented brewer without conditions and its purchasers therefore obtained the unfettered right to use them in any way they chose, at least as against a challenge from Keurig."[192] Thus, Keurig's right to assert infringement of its method claims was exhausted by its initial authorized sale of its patented brewers.

The Federal Circuit majority in *Keurig* rejected Keurig's argument that the method and apparatus claims of the asserted patents should be treated differently for purposes of the exhaustion analysis. To do so, the majority reasoned, would allow patentees to make an "end run" around the exhaustion defense by "claiming methods as well as the apparatus that practices them and attempting to shield the patented apparatus from exhaustion by holding downstream purchasers of its device liable for infringement of its method claims — a tactic that the Supreme Court has explicitly admonished."[193] The appellate court refused to sanction Keurig's attempt to "impermissibly restrict purchasers of Keurig brewers from using non-Keurig cartridges by invoking patent law to enforce restrictions on the post-sale use of its patented product."[194]

[190]*Keurig*, 732 F.3d at 1372-1373. "Keurig acknowledges that its brewers are commercial embodiments of the apparatus claims of the [two asserted] patents." *Keurig*, 732 F.3d at 1373.

[191]*See Keurig*, 732 F.3d at 1374 (citing Quanta Computer, Inc. v. LG Elecs., Inc., 553 U.S. 617, 625 (2008) (citing Adams v. Burke, 84 U.S. 453, 455 (1873))).

[192]*Keurig*, 732 F.3d at 1374.

[193]*Keurig*, 732 F.3d at 1374 (citing *Quanta*, 553 U.S. at 630).

[194]*Keurig*, 732 F.3d at 1374 (citing *Quanta*, 553 U.S. at 638). *See also* Helferich Patent Licensing, LLC v. New York Times Co., 778 F.3d 1293, 1303 (Fed. Cir. 2015) (explaining that "[t]he allegation by the patentee in *Keurig* was that the defendant was inducing a brewer owner to infringe the asserted method claim. 732 F.3d at 1374. In that familiar context, the court held that exhaustion covered the method claim because it appeared in a patent that also contained an apparatus claim reading on the acquired brewer. *Id.* at 1374-75."); LifeScan Scotland, Ltd. v. Shasta Techs., LLC, 734 F.3d 1361, 1369 (Fed. Cir. 2013) (stating that "[w]e have recently rejected the contention that a potential non-infringing use prevents exhaustion where the use in question is the very use contemplated by the patented invention itself. *Keurig, Inc., v. Sturm Foods, Inc.*, No. 13-1072, 732 F.3d 1370, 1373, 2013 WL 5645192, *3 (Fed. Cir. Oct. 17, 2013)").

Circuit Judge O'Malley wrote separately in *Keurig* to concur in the result only. She agreed with the majority that Keurig's patent rights were exhausted by its authorized sales of its patented brewer because Keurig's asserted method claims involved the normal and intended use of the brewer. However, that conclusion "d[id] not . . . depend upon whether exhaustion should be assessed on a claim-by-claim or patent-by-patent basis." *Keurig*, 732 F.3d at 1375 (O'Malley, J., concurring). The majority's statement to the contrary was merely *dicta* because the longstanding rule that the first authorized sale of a patented item terminates all patent rights to that item disposed of the case at bar.

Keurig is one of a number of cases in which the exhaustion defense has been asserted when a patentee alleges infringement of its *method* claims. The exhaustion defense is less easily understood in this context because practice of a patented method (a series of steps) is not conceptually the same as the use of a patented, tangible article. The U.S. Supreme Court confronted a complex assertion of the patent exhaustion defense in response to alleged method infringement in *Quanta Computer, Inc. v. LG Elecs., Inc.*[195] The plaintiff LG owned a portfolio of patents on computer systems and methods. LG entered into a license agreement with Intel, the well-known computer chip manufacturer. Under the terms of the license, Intel had permission to make and sell microprocessors and chipsets that were components of the computer systems claimed in LG's patents. A dispute arose when Intel sold its microprocessor and chipset components to third-party computer manufacturers. Defendant Quanta (one of Intel's customers) made its computers by combining the Intel-supplied components with non-Intel components such as computer memory and buses. The claims of LG's patents read on these computers, that is, the overall combination of components assembled and sold by Quanta to consumers practiced LG's patents.

In the ensuing lawsuit between LG and Quanta, LG asserted that Quanta's computer sales infringed LG's patents, while Quanta contended that it was shielded from liability by the patent exhaustion defense. At the heart of the dispute were the terms of the LG-Intel license (even though Intel was not a party to the LG-Quanta lawsuit). The license authorized Intel to make and sell the licensed products (i.e., Intel's microprocessors and chipsets) to third parties, but also stipulated that LG was not granting any license (either express or implied) to any third party that combined the licensed products with non-Intel components. Intel gave written notice of these terms to Quanta, as required by a separate "Master Agreement" between LG and Intel. Nevertheless, Quanta proceeded to make and sell its computers on the theory that it was shielded by the patent exhaustion doctrine. Quanta's view proved correct.

First, the Supreme Court agreed with Quanta that the defense of patent exhaustion can apply to alleged infringements of *method* claims as well as to apparatus (in this case, system) claims, even though method claims are not linked to a tangible article but rather to a

---

Nevertheless, "[t]here could be instances where assessing exhaustion on a claim-by-claim basis — the same way we conduct almost every analysis related to patent law—would be necessary and appropriate." *Keurig*, 732 F.3d at 1375 (O'Malley, J., concurring).

[195] 128 S. Ct. 2109 (2008).

process. "It is true that a patented method may not be sold in the same way as an article or device, but methods nonetheless may be 'embodied' in a product, the sale of which exhausts patent rights."[196]

The more difficult issue in *Quanta Computer* was to what "extent a product must embody a patent in order to trigger exhaustion."[197] The Supreme Court's *Quanta Computer* opinion leaves ample uncertainty on this question. The Court concluded that even though the components sold by Intel to Quanta did not "completely" embody the claimed invention, they "essentially" did so in a manner sufficient to cause exhaustion of LG's patent rights when first sold by Intel to Quanta.[198] The Court reasoned that the Intel microprocessors and chipsets could not function unless connected to computer memory and buses. The only apparent object of Intel's sales was Quanta's combination of the Intel-supplied components with non-Intel computer memory and buses in order to make and sell computers. Moreover, the Intel-supplied components "constitute[d] a material part of the patented invention and all but completely practice[d] the patent." According to the Court, "making a product that substantially embodies a patent is, for exhaustion purposes, no different from making the patented article itself."[199] Neither did Quanta exercise any "creative or inventive" decision making in combining the Intel and non-Intel components; in fact Quanta had no choice but to follow Intel's specifications for incorporating the Intel components because their internal structures were Intel trade secrets.

The Supreme Court in *Quanta Computer* also confirmed that Intel's component sales to Quanta were "authorized" sales, which are required to invoke the patent exhaustion defense as explained above. Nothing in the LG-Intel license restricted Intel's right to sell its chipsets and microprocessors to purchasers, even to firms like Quanta that intended to combine them with non-Intel parts. In a much-noted footnote, the Court hinted that patentee LG might

[196]*Id.* at 2117.

[197]*Id.* at 2119.

[198]In this part of the *Quanta Computer* opinion the Supreme Court relied heavily on its decision in *United States v. Univis Lens Co.*, 316 U.S. 241 (1942). The Court in *Univis Lens* held that the sale of eyeglass lens "blanks" triggered patent exhaustion because the blanks' only reasonable and intended use was to practice the eyeglass lens patent in suit and because the blanks embodied essential features of the patented invention.

[199]It is interesting to contrast the Supreme Court's adoption of an uncertain "substantially embodies" standard in the exhaustion context with its rejection of the Federal Circuit's "substantially complete" standard for triggering the §102(b) on sale bar in *Pfaff v. Wells Elecs., Inc.*, 525 U.S. 59, 65-66 (1998) ("A rule that makes the timeliness of an application depend on the date when an invention is 'substantially complete' seriously undermines the interest in certainty.").

have had a claim to breach of contract damages but had no right to patent infringement damages against Quanta.[200] The point was moot, however, because LG's complaint did not include a breach of contract claim.[201]

[200]*Quanta Computer*, 128 S. Ct. at 2122 n.7. Footnote 7 stated in full:

> We note that the authorized nature of the sale to Quanta does not necessarily limit LGE's other contract rights. LGE's complaint does not include a breach-of-contract claim, and we express no opinion on whether contract damages might be available even though exhaustion operates to eliminate patent damages. *See Keeler v. Standard Folding Bed Co.*, 157 U.S. 659, 666, 15 S. Ct. 738, 39 L. Ed. 848 (1895) ("Whether a patentee may protect himself and his assignees by special contracts brought home to the purchasers is not a question before us, and upon which we express no opinion. It is, however, obvious that such a question would arise as a question of contract, and not as one under the inherent meaning and effect of the patent laws").

Quanta Computer, 128 S. Ct. at 2122 n.7.

The doctrinal difficulties spawned by the Supreme Court's *Quanta* decision continue to present complex, challenging cases for the Federal Circuit. *See, e.g.*, Helferich Patent Licensing, LLC v. New York Times Co., 778 F.3d 1293, 1311 (Fed. Cir. 2015) (in case involving asserted infringement only of "content claims," which recited a method of sending content to handsets (i.e., mobile wireless-communication devices) from remote servers, but where some of the asserted patents also contained "handset claims" that recited a "method of operating a wireless communication device in a communication system that includes a plurality of information storage systems, and a mobile radiotelephone network," rejecting "defendants' argument that the content and handset claims at issue are distinguished only by 'semantics,'... or 'artful drafting,'" and holding that "the two groups of claims here can [not] be collapsed into one"; seeing "no sound basis for expanding exhaustion doctrine to hold that authorized sales to persons practicing the handset claims exhaust the patentee's rights to enforce the asserted content claims against different persons"); LifeScan Scotland, Ltd. v. Shasta Techs., LLC, 734 F.3d 1361, 1377 (Fed. Cir. 2013) (in case involving asserted infringement of patent on a blood glucose monitoring system claimed as "[a] method of measuring the concentration of a substance in a sample liquid," holding that "patent exhaustion principles apply equally to all authorized transfers of title in property, regardless of whether the particular transfer at issue constituted a gift or a sale," and "further conclud[ing] that [patentee] LifeScan's OneTouch Ultra meters substantially embody the methods claimed in the '105 patent and that their distribution therefore exhausts LifeScan's patent rights").

[201]Based in part on the quoted footnote 7 of *Quanta,* some observers questioned whether the Federal Circuit's decision in *Mallinckrodt, Inc. v. Medipart, Inc.*, 976 F.2d 700 (Fed. Cir. 1992), permitting *conditioned* sales of patented products (as opposed to the *unconditional* sales of coffee pods in the *Keuring* case examined in the text), was still good law. More specifically, the Federal Circuit held in *Mallinckrodt* that a patentee's sale of a medical device bearing a "single use only" label was a permissible post-sale restriction on use of the patented invention, and that only *un*conditional sales trigger the patent exhaustion defense to infringement. The Supreme Court did not cite or discuss *Mallinckrodt* in its *Quanta* decision, but the Federal Circuit in April 2015 took the issue of permissible post-sale restrictions under *en banc* consideration in *Lexmark Int'l, Inc. v. Impression Prods., Inc.,* 785 F.3d 565 (Fed. Cir. 2015).

Lexmark International ("Lexmark"), a provider of printing and imaging products, software, and services headquartered in Lexington, Kentucky, sold toner cartridges for its inkjet printers. Several Lexmark-owned U.S. patents covered the cartridges and their use. Notably, Lexmark sold some of its patented toner cartridges under a "Returns Program." These cartridges were sold at a discount, but subject to an express single-use/no-resale restriction and a requirement that purchasers return the used cartridges to Lexmark for recycling. Accused infringer Impression Products (and others) purchased and then resold Lexmark cartridges that a third party had physically modified to allow re-use (in violation of Lexmark's single-use restriction).

A federal district court found in favor of Impression Products on the conditioned sale issue; i.e., concluding that Lexmark's sales had exhausted its patent right to prevent Impression Product's sales of the refurbished cartridges. The district court concluded "that *Quanta* overruled *Mallinckrodt* sub silentio." Lexmark Int'l, Inc. v. Ink Techs. Printer Supplies, LLC, 9 F. Supp. 3d 830, 2014 WL 1276133 (S.D. Ohio Mar. 27, 2014) ("Domestic Sale Opinion"), at *5, *6. Although the Return Program cartridges were sold under post-sale restrictions on reuse and resale, the district court held that "those post-sale use restrictions do not prevent patent rights from being exhausted given that the initial sales were authorized and unrestricted." *Id.* The district court thus dismissed Lexmark's claim of infringement based on Impression's acts involving Return Program cartridges that Lexmark had first sold in the United States. *See* Lexmark Int'l, Inc. v. Impression Prods., Inc., Nos. 2014-1617, 2014-1619, 2016 WL 559042 (Fed. Cir. Feb. 12, 2016), at *5 (*en banc*).

After a three-judge panel of the Federal Circuit initially heard Lexmark's appeal, the Federal Circuit in April 2015 *sua sponte* granted hearing *en banc* in *Lexmark Int'l.* The *en banc* court requested briefing on, *inter alia,* the following:

> (b) The case involves (i) sales of patented articles to end users under a restriction that they use the articles once and then return them and (ii) sales of the same patented articles to resellers under a restriction that resales take place under the single-use-and-return restriction. Do any of those sales give rise to patent exhaustion? In light of *Quanta Computer, Inc. v. LG Electronics, Inc.*, 553 U.S. 617, 128 S. Ct. 2109, 170 L. Ed. 2d 996 (2008), should this court overrule *Mallinckrodt, Inc. v. Medipart, Inc.*, 976 F.2d 700 (Fed. Cir. 1992), to the extent it ruled that a sale of a patented article, when the sale is made under a restriction that is otherwise lawful and within the scope of the patent grant, does not give rise to patent exhaustion?

Lexmark Int'l, 785 F.3d at 566 (order).

In February 2016, the Federal Circuit issued its much-anticipated *en banc* decision in *Lexmark Int'l, Inc. v. Impression Prods, Inc.*, 816 F.3d 721 (Fed. Cir. Feb. 12, 2016) (Taranto, J.). In a 99-page opinion, a ten-judge majority reversed the district court's determination that Impression's resales of the refurbished cartridges did not infringe, stating:

> [W]e adhere to the holding of *Mallinckrodt, Inc. v. Medipart, Inc.*, 976 F.2d 700 (Fed. Cir. 1992), that a patentee, when selling a patented article subject to a single-use/no-resale restriction that is lawful and clearly communicated to the purchaser, does not by that sale give the buyer, or downstream buyers, the resale/reuse authority that has been expressly denied. Such resale or reuse, when contrary to the known, lawful limits on the authority conferred at the time of the original sale, remains unauthorized and therefore remains infringing conduct under the terms of [35 U.S.C.] §271.

Lexmark Int'l, 816 F.3d at 726 (*en banc*). The Circuit further determined that the Supreme Court's 2008 decision in *Quanta Computer,* detailed *supra* this chapter, had not implicitly overruled *Mallinckrodt*:

> We find *Mallinckrodt*'s principle to remain sound after the Supreme Court's decision in *Quanta Computer, Inc. v. LG Electronics, Inc.*, 553 U.S. 617 (2008), in which the Court did not have before it or address a patentee sale at all, let alone

The Supreme Court in 2012 granted review of another patent exhaustion case involving very different facts from *Quanta and*

> one made subject to a restriction, but a sale made by a separate manufacturer under a patentee-granted license conferring unrestricted authority to sell.

Lexmark Int'l, 816 F.3d at 726 (*en banc*).

This portion of the *Lexmark Int'l en banc* decision rejected Impression's asserted defense of *domestic* exhaustion of patent rights. The *en banc* court also considered in *Lexmark Int'l* the separate question whether the Circuit's precedent, which has traditionally rejected the notion of *international* exhaustion, remained good law. The court answered affirmatively. *See Lexmark Int'l,* 816 F.3d at 727 (*en banc*) (holding that "a U.S. patentee, merely by selling or authorizing the sale of a U.S.-patented article abroad, does not authorize the buyer to import the article and sell and use it in the United States, which are infringing acts in the absence of patentee-conferred authority"). The difficult question of international exhaustion — whether the authorized sale of a patented item outside the United States should preclude the patent owner from thereafter enjoining its importation and sale into the United States and/or obtaining royalties for sales there — is examined separately *infra* Chapter 12, Section F.3.

The issue of primary concern here is domestic exhaustion, and more specifically whether *conditioned* sales of patented here products trigger domestic exhaustion. In other words, are patent rights exhausted if the patentee sells a product embodying the patented invention but the sale is subject to a post-sale restriction, e.g., "no resale" or "single use only"? Would a competitor who legitimately purchased the patented item with notice of the restriction, and thereafter used, sold, and/or reconditioned it for resale in violation of the restriction, still be shielded from patent infringement liability by the exhaustion defense?

As explained above, the Federal Circuit answered these questions in the negative in its 1992 panel decision *Mallinckrodt, Inc. v. Medipart, Inc.*, 976 F.2d 700 (Fed. Cir. 1992), and in 2016 reaffirmed *Mallinckrodt* in the *en banc* decision *Lexmark Int'l, Inc. v. Impression Prods.*, 816 F.3d 721 (Fed. Cir. 2016) (Taranto, J.). In these two decisions, the Federal Circuit adopted the view that the reconditioning and/or resale of patented items initially sold subject to a valid restriction (i.e., a "conditioned sale") was potentially actionable patent infringement.

Astonishing many in the patent law profession, the Supreme Court flatly rejected the Circuit's position on patent exhaustion in 2017. Reversing the *en banc* Circuit, the Court in *Impression Prods., Inc. v. Lexmark Int'l*, 137 S. Ct. 1523 (May 30, 2017) (Roberts, C.J.), held unanimously that patent rights were exhausted upon the domestic sale of Lexmark's Return Program toner cartridges. The Court concluded unequivocally that

> Lexmark exhausted its patent rights in the[] [Return Program] cartridges the moment it sold them. The single-use/no-resale restrictions in Lexmark's contracts with customers may have been clear and enforceable under contract law, but they do not entitle Lexmark to retain patent rights in an item that it has elected to sell.

Impression Prods., 137 S. Ct. at 1531.

Dramatically expanding the availability of the exhaustion defense, the Supreme Court's 2017 *Impression Prods.* decision essentially eviscerated a patentee's ability to enforce post-sale restrictions on the use of its patented products by suing violators for patent infringement. The Court announced in very broad terms that

> patent exhaustion is uniform and automatic. Once a patentee decides to sell — whether on its own or through a licensee — that sale exhausts its patent rights, regardless of any post-sale restrictions the patentee purports to impose, either directly or through a license.

Impression Prods., 137 S. Ct. at 1535. The Supreme Court's analysis of why Lexmark's conditioned sales of its Return Program cartridges triggered the domestic exhaustion defense proceeded in four primary points.

First, the Supreme Court viewed the well-established common law principle disfavoring restraints on alienation of chattels (items of personal property) as trumping patent rights. The Court cited its 1853 decision in *Bloomer v. McQuewan* as recognizing that the doctrine of patent exhaustion imposes limits on a patentee's right to exclude others. *Impression Prods.*, 137 S. Ct. at 1531 (citing *Bloomer*, 14 How. 539, 549-550, 14 L. Ed. 532 (1853) (when a patentee chooses to sell an item, that product "is no longer within the limits of the monopoly" and instead becomes the "private, individual property" of the purchaser, with the rights and benefits that come along with ownership)). The doctrine that patent rights are exhausted when the patentee sells its patented product had an " 'impeccable historic pedigree,' tracing its lineage back to the 'common law's refusal to permit restraints on the alienation of chattels.' " *Impression Prods.*, 137 S. Ct. at 1532 (quoting Kirtsaeng v. John Wiley & Sons, Inc., 568 U.S. 519, 538 (2013)). The Federal Circuit erred in viewing this common law principle "dismissively," improperly treating this "venerable" rule as "merely 'one common-law jurisdiction's general judicial policy at one time toward anti-alienation restrictions.' " *Impression Prods.*, 137 S. Ct. at 1532 (quoting *Impression Prods.*, 816 F.3d at 750.) Rather, Congress enacted and repeatedly revised the Patent Act "against the backdrop of the hostility toward restraints on alienation." *Impression Prods.*, 137 S. Ct. at 1532.

Second, more recent precedent supported the conclusion that Lexmark's patent rights were exhausted by its domestic conditioned sales of the Return Program cartridges. The Supreme Court had "long held that, even when a patentee sells an item under an express restriction, the patentee does not retain patent rights in that product." *Impression Prods.*, 137 S. Ct. at 1532-1533. Two antitrust resale price maintenance cases from the first half of the twentieth century served as illustrations. Even though *Boston Store of Chicago v. American Graphophone Co.*, 246 U.S. 8 (1918), and *United States v. Univis Lens Co.*, 316 U.S. 241 (1942), involved *illegal* resale price restrictions, which violated the antitrust laws at the time of decision, the Court applied the principle of patent exhaustion in both cases. Any doubts about the relevance of *Boston Store* and *Univis* were resolved by the Court's more recent decision in *Quanta Computer*, which had "settled the matter," *Impression Prods.*, 137 S. Ct. at 1533:

> In [*Quanta*], a technology company — with authorization from the patentee — sold microprocessors under contracts requiring purchasers to use those processors with other parts that the company manufactured. One buyer disregarded the restriction, and the patentee sued for infringement. *Without so much as mentioning the lawfulness of the contract*, we held that the patentee could not bring an infringement suit because the "authorized sale . . . took its products outside the scope of the patent monopoly." 553 U.S., at 638, 128 S. Ct. 2109.

Impression Prods., 137 S. Ct. at 1533 (emphasis added). Based on this "well-settled line of precedent," the *Impression Prods.* case admitted of only one answer: Lexmark could not bring a patent infringement suit against Impression Products to enforce the single-use-no-resale provision that accompanied its Return Program toner cartridges. Once Lexmark sold those cartridges, any rights it may have retained were a matter of contract law, not patent law. *Impression Prods.*, 137 S. Ct. at 1533.

Third, the Supreme Court charged the Federal Circuit with "g[etting] off on the wrong foot" by linking the common law exhaustion doctrine to the "without authority" phrase in the preamble of 35 U.S.C. §271(a). In its *en banc* decision, the Circuit had recognized a "presumption" of authority under §271(a). But according to the Circuit, the presence of an express, clear restriction on post-sale use would rebut that presumption. *Lexmark Int'l*, 816 F.3d at 742-743.

The *Impression Prods.* Court charged the Circuit with taking a "misstep" in logic by treating patent exhaustion as a mere presumption. Rather, "the exhaustion doctrine is not a presumption about the authority that comes along with a sale; it is instead a limit on 'the scope of the *patentee's rights.*'" *Impression Prods.*, 137 S. Ct. at 1534 (quoting United States v. General Elec. Co., 272 U.S. 476, 489 (1926) (emphasis added by Court)). Although the affirmative right to use, sell, or import a patented item derives from the common law and exists independently of the patent law, the Patent Act adds to the right by granting the patentee an exclusive but "limited" right to prevent others from engaging in those practices. Exhaustion extinguishes the patentee's exclusionary power. *Impression Prods.*, 137 S. Ct. at 1534 (citing Bloomer v. McQuewan, 14 How. 539, 549 (1853) (the purchaser "exercises no rights created by the act of Congress, nor does he derive title to [the item] by virtue of the . . . exclusive privilege granted to the patentee")). Hence, "the sale transfers the right to use, sell, or import because those are the rights that come along with ownership, and the buyer is free and clear of an infringement lawsuit because there is no exclusionary right left to enforce." *Impression Prods.*, 137 S. Ct. at 1534.

Fourth, the *Impression Prods.* Court asserted that the Federal Circuit erred in its concern about creating an artificial distinction between direct sales with restrictions by patentees and the same type of sales by patent licensees to downstream purchasers. The Circuit had read the Supreme Court's 1938 decision in *General Talking Pictures Corp. v. Western Elec. Co.*, 304 U.S. 175, *aff'd on reh'g*, 305 U.S. 124 (1938), to mean that when a patentee grants a license "under clearly stated restrictions on post-sale activities" by the downstream purchasers from the patentee's licensee, the patentee can sue for infringement the downstream purchasers who knowingly violate the restrictions. *See* Mallinckrodt, Inc. v. Medipart, Inc., 976 F.2d 700, 705 (Fed. Cir. 1992).

The Circuit's concern was "misplaced." *General Talking Pictures*, on which the Federal Circuit had relied, involved a "fundamentally different situation." *Impression Prods.*, 137 S. Ct. at 1535. The Supreme Court explained that patent licenses (a transfer of certain patentee rights) differ distinctly from sales of patented goods, in which title passes to the goods:

> A patentee can impose restrictions on licensees because *a license does not implicate the same concerns about restraints on alienation as a sale*. Patent exhaustion reflects the principle that, when an item passes into commerce, it should not be shaded by a legal cloud on title as it moves through the marketplace. But a license is not about passing title to a product, it is about changing the contours of the patentee's monopoly: The patentee agrees not to exclude a licensee from making or selling the patented invention, expanding the club of authorized producers and sellers. *See* General Elec. Co., 272 U.S., at 489-490, 47 S. Ct. 192. Because the patentee is exchanging rights, not goods, it is free to relinquish only a portion of its bundle of patent protections.

Impression Prods., 137 S. Ct. at 1534 (emphasis added).

Although the Supreme Court's 2017 decision in *Impression Products* stripped patentees who license their rights of the ability to use patent law to enforce post-sale restrictions, the decision clearly suggested that such restrictions are still enforceable under *contract law* (whether or not practical). *See Impression Prods.,* 137 S. Ct. at 1535 (proposing that a patent license might require the licensee to, for example, "hav[e] each customer sign a contract promising not to use" the purchased items in a particular field of use, acknowledging that "[t]he purchasers might not comply with the restriction," but concluding that "the only recourse for the licensee is through contract law, just as if the patentee itself sold the item with a restriction"). This outcome raises important questions and considerations. First, contract law is a matter of state, not federal law, thus seemingly removing the federal courts (including the Federal Circuit) from such

Impression Prods. and reaching the opposite result — that the exhaustion defense did *not* apply.[202] In *Monsanto Co. v. Bowman*,[203] the Federal Circuit had affirmed a district court's finding of infringement based on a farmer's act of planting the progeny of genetically altered soybean seeds covered by Monsanto's patents. More specifically, Monsanto marketed patented "Roundup Ready" soybean seed that had been genetically altered to confer resistance to glyphosate, the active ingredient in many herbicides (including Monsanto's Roundup herbicide product). Purchasing farmers signed a license agreement permitting them to plant the seed in only one season, but not to save the seed and replant it.

After purchasing the patented, genetically altered seed and signing a license agreement with Monsanto, Indiana farmer Bowman planted all his purchased seed and sold his entire crop to a grain elevator. However, Bowman also purchased (from grain elevators) and planted a second, "late season" crop of "commodity soybeans," many of which contained Monsanto's patented herbicide resistance trait. Not surprisingly, most of Bowman's second crop survived treatment with a glyphosate-based herbicide and produced in turn a new crop of soybeans with the same "Roundup Ready" trait. Bowman saved seed from his second crop, used it in his second planting the following year, and repeated the process until he had had harvested a total of eight crops.[204]

The Supreme Court in *Bowman v. Monsanto*[205] affirmed the holdings of the district court and the Federal Circuit that Bowman's conduct was not shielded from infringement liability by the patent exhaustion defense.[206] Bowman conceded that the exhaustion doctrine

---

lawsuits. Second, if a patentee attempts to sue in contract the downstream purchasers of its licensees, could the patentee establish privity with the purchasers? And what standards of notice and clarity for the post-sale restrictions would be required to enforce the restrictions (via contract law) against the downstream purchasers?

[202]Bowman v. Monsanto Co., 133 S. Ct. 420 (2012) (granting petition for writ of *certiorari* to the Federal Circuit).

[203]657 F.3d 1341 (Fed. Cir. 2011).

[204]*See Bowman*, 133 S. Ct. at 1765-1766.

[205]133 S. Ct. 1761 (2013) (Kagan, J., for a unanimous Court).

[206]The Supreme Court explained that the doctrine of patent exhaustion

> limits a patentee's right to control what others can do with an article embodying or containing an invention. Under the doctrine, "the initial authorized sale of a patented item terminates all patent rights to that item." *Quanta Computer, Inc. v. LG Electronics, Inc.*, 553 U.S. 617, 625, 128 S. Ct. 2109, 170 L. Ed. 2d 996 (2008). And by "exhaust[ing] the [patentee's] monopoly" in that item, the sale confers on the purchaser, or any subsequent owner, "the right to use [or] sell" the thing as he sees fit. *United States v. Univis Lens Co.*, 316 U.S. 241, 249-250, 62 S. Ct. 1088, 86 L. Ed. 1408 (1942). We have explained the basis for the doctrine as follows: "[T]he purpose of the patent law is fulfilled with respect to any particular article when the patentee has received his reward . . . by the sale of the

did not allow a purchaser of a particular patented item the right to "make" a new copy of that item. Nevertheless, Bowman argued that in planting the Roundup Ready seeds, he was merely "using" the seeds in the normal way that farmers do and have done for hundreds of years.[207]

The Supreme Court rejected Bowman's "use" argument. The Court observed that "[r]eproducing a patented article no doubt 'uses' it after a fashion," but explained that precedent had "always drawn the boundaries of the exhaustion doctrine to exclude that activity, so that the patentee retains an undiminished right to prohibit others from making the thing his patent protects."[208]

> article"; once that "purpose is realized the patent law affords no basis for restraining the use and enjoyment of the thing sold." *Id.*, at 251, 62 S. Ct. 1088.
>
> Consistent with that rationale, the doctrine restricts a patentee's rights only as to the "particular article" sold, *ibid.*; it leaves untouched the patentee's ability to prevent a buyer from making new copies of the patented item. "[T]he purchaser of the [patented] machine . . . does not acquire any right to construct another machine either for his own use or to be vended to another." *Mitchell v. Hawley*, 16 Wall. 544, 548, 21 L. Ed. 322 (1873); see *Wilbur-Ellis Co. v. Kuther*, 377 U.S. 422, 424, 84 S. Ct. 1561, 12 L. Ed. 2d 419 (1964) (holding that a purchaser's "reconstruction" of a patented machine "would impinge on the patentee's right '*to exclude others from making*' . . . the article" (quoting 35 U.S.C. §154 (1964 ed.))). Rather, "a second creation" of the patented item "call[s] the monopoly, conferred by the patent grant, into play for a second time." *Aro Mfg. Co. v. Convertible Top Replacement Co.*, 365 U.S. 336, 346, 81 S. Ct. 599, 5 L. Ed. 2d 592 (1961). That is because the patent holder has "received his reward" only for the actual article sold, and not for subsequent recreations of it. *Univis*, 316 U.S., at 251, 62 S. Ct. 1088. If the purchaser of that article could make and sell endless copies, the patent would effectively protect the invention for just a single sale.

Bowman, 133 S. Ct. at 1766 (footnotes omitted).

[207] *Bowman*, 133 S. Ct. at 1768.

[208] *Bowman*, 133 S. Ct. at 1768 (citing Cotton-Tie Co. v. Simmons, 106 U.S. 89, 93-94 (1882) (holding that a purchaser could not "use" the buckle from a patented cotton-bale tie to "make" a new tie)). The *Bowman* Court also relied on its more recent decision in *J.E.M. Ag Supply, Inc. v. Pioneer Hi-Bred Int'l, Inc.*, 534 U.S. 124 (2001) to support its holding. (The *J.E.M. Ag* case is further examined *supra* Chapter 7, Section H.1.) In *J.E.M. Ag*, the Court had observed that only a patent owner, not a Plant Variety Protection Act (PVPA) certificate holder, "could prohibit '[a] farmer who legally purchases and plants' a protected seed from saving harvested seed 'for replanting.'" *Bowman*, 133 S. Ct. at 1767 (quoting *J.E.M. Ag*, 534 U.S. at 140). Applying the patent exhaustion defense to Bowman's conduct would fly in the face of *J.E.M. Ag*:

> If a sale cut off the right to control a patented seed's progeny, then (contrary to *J.E.M.*) the patentee could *not* prevent the buyer from saving harvested seed. Indeed, the patentee could not stop the buyer from *selling* such seed, which even a PVP certificate owner (who, recall, is supposed to have fewer rights) can usually accomplish. See 7 U.S.C. §§2541, 2543. Those limitations would turn upside-down the statutory scheme *J.E.M.* described.

Bowman, 133 S. Ct. at 1767-1768.

The Supreme Court also rejected Bowman's "seeds-are-special" argument; i.e., that because soybeans will naturally sprout or self-replicate unless stored in a controlled manner, it was the planted soybeans themselves rather than Bowman that made replicas of Monsanto's patented invention.[209] Giving short shrift to Bowman's "blame-the-bean" defense, the Court emphasized that Bowman was not merely a "passive observer." Rather, he was the critical entity that facilitated and controlled the reproduction (into the eighth generation) of Monsanto's patented invention.[210] "[T]he seeds [Bowman] purchased . . . did not spontaneously create eight successive soybean crops."[211]

Lastly, the *Bowman* Court carefully constrained its rejection of the patent exhaustion defense to the unique facts of the case before it:

> Our holding today is limited — addressing the situation before us, rather than every one involving a self-replicating product. We recognize that such inventions are becoming ever more prevalent, complex, and diverse. In another case, the article's self-replication might occur outside the purchaser's control. Or it might be a necessary but incidental step in using the item for another purpose. *Cf.* 17 U.S.C. §117(a)(1) ("[I]t is not [a copyright] infringement for the owner of a copy of a computer program to make . . . another copy or adaptation of that computer program provide[d] that such a new copy or adaptation is created as an essential step in the utilization of the computer program"). We need not address here whether or how the doctrine of patent exhaustion would apply in such circumstances.[212]

In the case at bar, however, the patent exhaustion defense "provide[d] no haven" for Bowman's acts. He "planted Monsanto's patented soybeans solely to make and market replicas of them, thus depriving the company of the reward patent law provides for the sale of each article."[213] Accordingly, the Court affirmed the Federal Circuit's judgment that Bowman infringed and his patent exhaustion defense failed.

9. Plaintiff's Lack of Standing to Sue for Infringement

A lawsuit alleging patent infringement must be brought by the holder of the right to exclude that the patent conveys. The Patent Act provides that "[a] patentee shall have remedy by civil action for

[209] *Bowman*, 133 S. Ct. at 1768-1769.
[210] *Bowman*, 133 S. Ct. at 1769.
[211] *Bowman*, 133 S. Ct. at 1769.
[212] *Bowman*, 133 S. Ct. at 1769.
[213] *Bowman*, 133 S. Ct. at 1769.

infringement of his patent."[214] It further defines "patentee" as "not only the patentee to whom the patent was issued but also the successors in title to the patentee."[215] This statutory definition means that ordinarily, the party bringing an infringement suit must hold legal title in the patent.[216] When the plaintiff filing suit is the record title holder, standing is not a concern.

Questions about standing often arise, however, when a licensee under the patent attempts to file an infringement lawsuit in its own name without the participation of the patent owner/licensor.[217] If the plaintiff/licensee lacks standing, the accused infringer will assert this deficiency as a basis for dismissing the lawsuit. A *nonexclusive* licensee does *not* have standing to sue in its own name for patent infringement.[218] An exclusive licensee *may* have standing to sue in its own name, depending on the terms of the patent license.[219] In particular, the exclusive license must be a "virtual assignment" that confers standing to sue for infringements.[220] The license must transfer "all substantial rights under the patent" and it must be in writing.[221] If the exclusive licensee holds less than all substantial rights, the patentee/licensor must be joined as a party to the lawsuit.[222]

[214] 35 U.S.C. §281.

[215] *Id.* §100(d).

[216] *See* Enzo APA & Son, Inc. v. Geapag, A.G., 134 F.3d 1090, 1093 (Fed. Cir. 1998).

[217] As a practical matter, the patent owner/licensor may not want to be involved in litigation for any number of reasons, for example, not wanting to incur potential liability for counterclaims, an unwillingness to share the potentially high costs of patent litigation, or geographic inconvenience in the case of a patent owner based outside the United States.

[218] *See* Jay Dratler, Jr., Licensing of Intellectual Property §8.06 (2008). Indeed, "[a] nonexclusive license confers no constitutional standing on the licensee to bring suit or even to join a suit with the patentee because a nonexclusive licensee suffers no legal injury from infringement." Sicom Sys., Ltd. v. Agilent Techs., Inc., 427 F.3d 971, 976 (Fed. Cir. 2005).

[219] *See* Jay Dratler, Jr., Licensing of Intellectual Property §8.06 (2008).

[220] *See Enzo APA*, 134 F.3d at 1093.

[221] *See id.*

[222] *See Sicom Sys.*, 427 F.3d at 980 (stressing "the principle set forth in *Independent Wireless* [*Tel. Co. v. Radio Corp. of Am.*, 269 U.S. 459 (1926),] requiring that a patent owner be joined in any infringement suit brought by an exclusive licensee having fewer than all substantial rights.... Unlike an assignee who may sue in its own name, an exclusive licensee having fewer than all substantial patent rights and seeking to enforce its rights in a patent generally must sue jointly with the patent owner.") (citations omitted).

AsymmetRx, Inc. v. Biocare Med., LLC, 582 F.3d 1314 (Fed. Cir. 2009), provides a helpful illustration of these standing principles. After summarizing relevant precedent, the Federal Circuit in *AsymmetRx* concluded that "[a]lthough the AsymmetRx License effected a broad conveyance of rights to [plaintiff] AsymmetRx, [the patent owner, President and Fellows of] Harvard [College] retained substantial interests under the '256 and '227 patents [in suit], including the right to sue for infringement, and AsymmetRx therefore does not have the right to sue for infringement as a 'patentee' under the patent statute." *AsymmetRx,* 582 F.3d at 1320. Because AsymmetRx had not joined Harvard as a party to the lawsuit, AsymmetRx did not have standing to pursue its action against alleged infringer Biocare.

D. Unenforceability

The defense of unenforceability, asserted under 35 U.S.C. §282(b)(1) (eff. Sept. 16, 2012), has its roots in the equitable doctrine of "unclean hands."[223] In cases where ongoing infringement is alleged and the patent in suit is still in force, the patent owner will seek relief that includes an injunction against any further infringement. Because an injunction is an equitable remedy, however, courts will not grant the patentee an injunction if she has come to the court with unclean hands.

The Federal Circuit views the defense of unenforceability as encompassing several different equity-based theories: (1) **inequitable conduct**, (2) **patent misuse**, (3) **prosecution history laches**, or (4) **unclean hands independent of inequitable conduct in patent procurement**. Each is discussed separately below. If an equitable defense is successfully established, the result is that the federal district court will enter a judgment of unenforceability, which should be distinguished from a judgment of invalidity. If a patent is held unenforceable, *every* claim of the patent is considered unenforceable. Invalidity, by contrast, is determined on a claim-by-claim basis; some claims of a patent may be held invalid while others are sustained and may still be asserted as the basis for infringement.

Another distinction between unenforceability and invalidity is that the patent misuse form of unenforceability may be purged in some instances, such that the patent may again be enforced once the misuse has been alleviated.[224] In contrast, a judgment of patent invalidity (once affirmed on appeal) is final and cannot be lifted.[225]

1. Inequitable Conduct

The defense of inequitable conduct asserts that a court should refuse to enforce a patent if it was procured through improper conduct before the USPTO. The *ex parte* nature of patent prosecution before

[223]*See* Therasense, Inc. v. Becton, Dickinson and Co., 649 F.3d 1276 (Fed. Cir. 2011) (*en banc*). The *en banc* court observed that the judge-made doctrine of inequitable conduct, which if established results in the penalty of unenforceability, "evolved from a trio of Supreme Court cases that applied the doctrine of unclean hands to dismiss patent cases involving egregious misconduct: *Keystone Driller Co. v. General Excavator Co.*, 290 U.S. 240, 54 S. Ct. 146, 78 L. Ed. 293 (1933); *Hazel-Atlas Glass Co. v. Hartford-Empire Co.*, 322 U.S. 238, 64 S. Ct. 997, 88 L. Ed. 1250 (1944), *overruled on other grounds by Standard Oil Co. v. United States*, 429 U.S. 17, 97 S. Ct. 31, 50 L. Ed. 2d 21 (1976); and *Precision Instrument Manufacturing Co. v. Automotive Maintenance Machinery Co.*, 324 U.S. 806, 65 S. Ct. 993, 89 L. Ed. 1381 (1945)." *Therasense,* 649 F.3d at 1285.

[224]*See* Morton Salt Co. v. G.S. Suppiger Co., 314 U.S. 488, 493 (1942).

[225]*See* Blonder-Tongue Labs., Inc. v. Univ. of Ill. Found., 402 U.S. 313 (1971), discussed *infra.*

the USPTO drives the inequitable conduct defense. The USPTO rules require that all persons substantively involved in the patent application process owe a duty of candor to the agency, which includes a duty to disclose to the agency all known information that is material to patentability.[226] Rigorous compliance with the duty of disclosure may seem contrary to the self-interests of some patent applicants, and the USPTO has limited resources with which to police that compliance. Thus a severe penalty is set for violations of the duty that come to light in subsequent litigation of a patent: if the defense of inequitable conduct is proved, the entire patent (i.e., all claims, regardless of their validity) is rendered unenforceable (a result that courts have termed the "atomic bomb" of patent law).[227]

Because many foreign patent systems have robust opposition procedures allowing challenges to recently granted patents on any statutorily recognized ground of invalidity,[228] the U.S.-based notions of a strict duty of disclosure during prosecution and an inequitable conduct defense during litigation are not considered necessary there.[229] In the United States, however, the availability of the inequitable conduct defense is an essential method of ensuring that patent applicants "play by the rules." As a leading U.S. patent scholar observes, "[t]he most cogent practical argument for retaining the inequitable conduct defense is that unless a severe penalty exists for withholding information, practitioners and their clients will not be motivated to help the PTO in its job of examining applications thoroughly and allowing only valid claims."[230]

As with the invalidity defenses discussed below, the quantum of evidence required to satisfy a challenger's burden of establishing inequitable conduct is clear and convincing evidence. More particularly, the proponent of the inequitable conduct defense must prove by clear and convincing evidence each of two underlying factual elements:

[226] 37 C.F.R. §1.56 (2012).

[227] Therasense, Inc. v. Becton, Dickinson and Co., 649 F.3d 1288 (Fed. Cir. 2011) (*en banc*).

[228] *See, e.g.*, European Patent Convention arts. 99-105 (16th ed. 2016), *available at* https://www.epo.org/patents/law/legal-texts/html/epc/2016/e/ar99.html.

[229] *See* Paul M. Janicke, *Do We Really Need So Many Mental and Emotional States in United States Patent Law?*, 8 TEX. INTELL. PROP. L.J. 279, 292 (2000) (noting that "to date, no other country has adopted a private remedy for deceiving the patent-issuing authorities, with the exception of a German statutory provision whereby the Patent Office can request an applicant to disclose the state of the art truthfully as the applicant knows it"). Professor Janicke suggests that other countries have not adopted the inequitable conduct defense because they consider the possibility of invalidity a sufficient remedy, particularly in those foreign legal systems where the losing party pays the winning party's attorney fees. *Id.*

[230] Paul M. Janicke, *Do We Really Need So Many Mental and Emotional States in United States Patent Law?*, 8 TEX. INTELL. PROP. L.J. 279, 292 (2000).

(1) materiality and (2) intent to deceive the USPTO.[231] Each element is separately discussed below.

a. Materiality

To constitute inequitable conduct, a patent applicant's conduct before the USPTO must involve the nondisclosure or wrongful submission of information that is material to patentability. Such nondisclosure or wrongful submission typically occurs in one of the following three scenarios:

1. failure to disclose to the USPTO information known to the applicant[232] that is material to patentability;
2. submission to the USPTO of false information that is material to patentability; or
3. affirmative misrepresentations made to the USPTO that are material to patentability.

Thus, inequitable conduct can be based on either a patent applicant's omission (i.e., a failure to act) or commission (i.e., an affirmative act of submitting false information or making a misrepresentation).

The Federal Circuit has grown increasingly concerned about the "plague" of inequitable conduct assertions routinely encountered in patent litigation.[233] In its 2011 decision in *Therasense, Inc. v. Becton,*

[231]Dippin' Dots, Inc. v. Mosey, 476 F.3d 1337, 1345 (Fed. Cir. 2007) (stating that "[t]he party urging unenforceability must show by clear and convincing evidence that the [patent] applicant met 'thresholds of both materiality and intent'") (quoting Molins PLC v. Textron, 48 F.3d 1172, 1178 (Fed. Cir. 1995)).

[232]The information must be "known" to the applicant in order for the duty of disclosure to attach. There is no affirmative duty on a patent applicant to conduct a prior art search in order to seek out and find information material to patentability. However, "one should not be able to cultivate ignorance, or disregard numerous warnings that material information or prior art may exist, merely to avoid actual knowledge of that information or prior art. When one does that, the 'should have known' factor becomes operative." FMC Corp. v. Hennessy Indus., Inc., 836 F.2d 521, 526 n.6 (Fed. Cir. 1987).

[233]In *Therasense, Inc. v. Becton, Dickinson and Co.*, 649 F.3d 1276 (Fed. Cir. 2011) (*en banc*), the court observed that

> [l]eft unfettered, the inequitable conduct doctrine has plagued not only the courts but also the entire patent system. Because allegations of inequitable conduct are routinely brought on "the slenderest grounds," *Burlington Indus.*, 849 F.2d at 1422, patent prosecutors constantly confront the specter of inequitable conduct charges. With inequitable conduct casting the shadow of a hangman's noose, it is unsurprising that patent prosecutors regularly bury PTO examiners with a deluge of prior art references, most of which have marginal value.

Therasense, 649 F.3d at 1289; *see also* Burlington Indus., Inc. v. Dayco Corp., 849 F.2d 1418, 1422 (Fed. Cir. 1988) (remarking that "the habit of charging inequitable conduct in almost every major patent case has become an absolute plague").

Dickinson and Co.,[234] a majority of Federal Circuit judges determined *en banc* to "adjust" (that is, make more rigorous) the standard for establishing whether information is material to patentability.[235] The *Therasense en banc* majority read the Supreme Court's 1928 decision in *Corona Cord Tire Co. v. Dovan Chem. Corp.*[236] as supporting a heightened "but-for" materiality standard.[237] Applying this standard to the typical scenario of applicant failure to disclose prior art to the USPTO, the *en banc* Federal Circuit majority held that "prior art is but-for material if the PTO would not have allowed a claim had it been aware of the undisclosed prior art."[238] In other words, when assessing materiality of a withheld reference, "the court must determine whether the PTO would have allowed the claim if it had been aware

[234]649 F.3d 1276 (Fed. Cir. 2011) (*en banc*).

[235]The *en banc* court in *Therasense* was sharply divided. With 11 Federal Circuit judges participating in *en banc* review, 6 judges signed the opinion for the court (i.e., Rader (author), Newman, Lourie, Linn, Moore, and Reyna). Four judges dissented in full (i.e., Bryson (author), Gajarsa, Dyk, and Prost). Judge O'Malley authored an opinion concurring-in-part and dissenting-in-part. Notably, Judge O'Malley dissented from the materiality portion of the majority's opinion (and the majority's judgment to vacate and remand the district court's decision of inequitable conduct for further inquiry on the materiality determination). Thus, the "but for" materiality standard of *Therasense* became Federal Circuit *en banc* law by a 6-5 vote.

[236]276 U.S. 358, 373-374 (1928). The Supreme Court in *Corona Cord* considered two affidavits falsely stating that the claimed invention of the patent in suit had been used to produce rubber goods, when in fact the invention had been used only to make test slabs of rubber. Although perhaps "reckless," the false affidavits were not essentially material to the issuance of the patent in suit. Hence the *Corona* Court held that they did not destroy the patent's presumption of validity. *Corona Cord,* 276 U.S. at 374. The Federal Circuit majority in *Therasense* relied on the *Corona Cord* Court's "unwillingness to extinguish the statutory presumption of validity where the patentee made a misrepresentation to the PTO that did not affect the issuance of the patent," as well as the fact that the "severe remedy of unenforceability for inequitable conduct far exceeds the mere removal of a presumption of validity." *Therasense,* 649 F.3d at 1291.

[237]As a policy matter, the *Therasense* majority opined that "enforcement of an otherwise valid patent does not injure the public merely because of misconduct, lurking somewhere in patent prosecution, that was immaterial to the patent's issuance." *Therasense,* 649 F.3d at 1291. Four judges of the Federal Circuit sharply disputed this reasoning, writing in response to the majority's new "but for" materiality standard that

> [i]f a failure to disclose constitutes inequitable conduct only when a proper disclosure would result in rejection of a claim, there will be little incentive for applicants to be candid with the PTO, because in most instances the sanction of inequitable conduct will apply only if the claims that issue are invalid anyway.... Even if the nondisclosure or misleading disclosure is later discovered, under the majority's rule the applicant is no worse off, as the patent will be lost only if the claims would otherwise be held invalid.... Given the large stakes sometimes at issue in patent prosecutions, a regime that ensures that a dishonest but potentially profitable course of action can be pursued with essentially no marginal added risk is an unwise regime no matter how virtuous its subjects.

Therasense, 649 F.3d at 1305-1306 (Bryson, J., dissenting).

[238]*Therasense,* 649 F.3d at 1291.

of the undisclosed information."[239] In so determining, the court should follow the USPTO's "broadest reasonable construction" rule for patent claim interpretation,[240] and impose a "preponderance of the evidence" burden of proof on the question of materiality.

Application of these standards will usually require that in order to reach a conclusion of inequitable conduct, a court must also hold one or more claims of a patent invalid over the withheld reference(s). A judgment of invalidity will not *always* be required for inequitable conduct, however, because the withheld art (although not invalidating under federal court standards) might have prevented patent issuance by the USPTO under the agency's somewhat less rigorous evidentiary and constructional standards (i.e., "preponderance of the evidence" burden of proof and "broadest reasonable claim construction" rule).[241] In the view of this author, such cases will be few. In most cases, invalidity over the withheld prior art will be a prerequisite to a finding of materiality that supports inequitable conduct.

Though raising the standard for establishing materiality, the *Therasense* majority also recognized an exception to its general rule requiring "but for" proof. Based on the "unclean hands" doctrine of earlier Supreme Court cases, the *en banc* majority in *Therasense* held that the exception is triggered by "affirmative acts of egregious misconduct, such as the filing of an unmistakably false affidavit."[242] In such cases, the misconduct is material regardless of whether the "but for" rule is satisfied. Importantly, the egregious misconduct exception requires an *affirmative* act; neither "mere nondisclosure of prior art references to the USPTO nor failure to mention prior art references in an affidavit" qualifies for the exception (and hence still requires proof of "but for" materiality to establish inequitable conduct).[243]

[239]*Therasense,* 649 F.3d at 1291.

[240]*Therasense,* 649 F.3d at 1291-1292 (citing United States Patent and Trademark Office, Manual of Patent Examining Procedure §§706, 2111 (8th ed. rev. July 8, 2010)).

[241]Federal district courts need not apply the USPTO's more expansive "broadest reasonable construction" rule when interpreting patent claims, and the burden of proof to establish invalidity of patent claims before a district court (i.e., clear and convincing evidence) is considered higher than the USPTO's "preponderance of the evidence" burden of proof for rejecting application claims as unpatentable. For more on the "clear and convincing evidence" burden of proof in federal court validity litigation, *see infra* Section E.1 (discussing Microsoft Corp. v. i4i Ltd. P'ship, 131 S. Ct. 2238 (2011)).

[242]*Therasense,* 649 F.3d at 1292.

[243]In the post-*Therasense* decision *Powell v. Home Depot U.S.A., Inc.*, 663 F.3d 1221 (Fed. Cir. 2011), the court rejected an accused infringer's contention that a patentee's failure to update a Petition to Make Special amounted to inequitable conduct. The patentee Powell initially requested expedited prosecution based on a belief that he was obligated to manufacture and supply products embodying his invention to Home Depot. After Powell learned that Home Depot would be procuring the products from another company, he failed to update his Petition to Make Special. The Federal Circuit held that Powell's failure to update did not satisfy the *Therasense* affirmative egregious misconduct exception. "Where, as here, the patent applicant fails to update the record to inform

The facts of *Therasense* concerned Abbott Laboratories' (Abbott's) U.S. Patent No. 5,820,551 ('551 patent), directed to disposable blood glucose test strips used by diabetes patients. The claims recited strips for testing the concentration of a compound such as glucose in a "whole blood" sample (i.e., blood containing all its components, including red blood cells). Notably, the claims required that an "active electrode" on the strip be "configured to be *exposed to said whole blood sample without an intervening membrane* or other whole blood filtering member."[244]

A key focus of the '551 patent application's examination in the USPTO was whether the prior art taught that glucose sensors could be used to test whole blood without a protective membrane.[245] The asserted inequitable conduct by Abbott involved taking inconsistent positions before the USPTO and the European Patent Office (EPO) without disclosing the inconsistency to the USPTO. Specifically, Abbott failed to disclose to the USPTO examiner certain briefs that Abbott had previously submitted to the EPO during prosecution of the application leading to the European counterpart patent of the '551 patent. During a 13-year prosecution in the USPTO, Abbott submitted (in or after 1997) a sworn declaration from its technical expert (Abbott's then-Director of Research and Development) accompanied by statements from its patent counsel. These submissions "asserted unequivocally that one skilled in the art would *not* have read the prior art to say that use of a protective membrane with whole blood samples was optional."[246] However, "Abbott [had also] represented [to the EPO in briefs filed in 1994 and 1995] that it was 'unequivocally clear' that the same prior art language meant that the protective membrane *was*, in fact, optional."[247]

Because the district court found inequitable conduct on these facts but had applied the earlier, less rigorous materiality standard then codified in the USPTO's Rule 56,[248] the *en banc* Federal Circuit

---

the PTO that the circumstances which support a Petition to Make Special no longer exist — that conduct does not constitute inequitable conduct." *Powell,* 663 F.3d at 1235 (citing *Therasense*, 649 F.3d at 1290). "That is so because Mr. Powell's conduct obviously fails the but-for materiality standard and is not the type of unequivocal act, 'such as the filing of an unmistakably false affidavit,' that would rise to the level of 'affirmative egregious misconduct.'" *Powell*, 663 F.3d at 1235 (quoting *Therasense*, 649 F.3d at 1292-1293).

244 *Therasense,* 649 F. 3d at 1282 (quoting claim 1 of Abbott's '551 patent) (emphasis added).

245 *Therasense,* 649 F.3d at 1301 (O'Malley, J., concurring-in-part and dissenting-in-part).

246 *Id.* (emphasis added).

247 *Id.* (emphasis added).

248 The district court applied part of the USPTO materiality definition set forth in 37 C.F.R. §1.56 (1992). The rule provides in pertinent part that information is material when it is "inconsistent with [] a position that applicant takes in . . . [a]sserting an argument of patentability." 37 C.F.R. 1.56(b)(2)(ii) (1992). *See Therasense,* 659 F.2d at 1312, 1318 (Bryson, J., dissenting).

Therasense majority vacated and remanded the district court's decision for further consideration. On remand, applying the new "but for" materiality standard announced by the Federal Circuit, the district court reconfirmed its original determination that Abbott's '551 patent was unenforceable due to inequitable conduct.[249] The inconsistency of Abbott's position concerning what a critical prior art reference taught, or more precisely, Abbott's failure to disclose its inconsistent statements to the USPTO, was information material to patentability.[250]

Prior to its 2011 *Therasense* decision, the Federal Circuit's test for materiality was whether a hypothetical "reasonable examiner" would have considered the information "important" in deciding whether to allow the application to issue as a patent.[251] If that question was answered affirmatively, then the information satisfied the materiality element of the inequitable conduct defense, without regard to a "but for" inquiry. In other words, it was not necessary that the withheld information be invalidating, that is, that the information would have rendered the patent application's claims unallowable if the examiner had been aware of it.[252] A patent might be held unenforceable for inequitable conduct based on the applicant's act of withholding prior art with intent to deceive the USPTO, even though the patent's validity was sustained over that same prior art.[253] In such cases, the withheld prior art was not sufficiently relevant to invalidate the claims, but was

[249]*See* Therasense, Inc. v. Becton, Dickinson and Co., Nos. C 04–02123 WHA et seq., 2012 WL 1038715 (N.D. Cal. Mar. 27, 2012) (explaining that "[t]he court of appeals, sitting *en banc*, vacated a finding herein of inequitable conduct and remanded with instructions to redetermine specified questions under a new standard. Using the new standard, this order again comes to the same conclusion that the patent in suit was procured through inequitable conduct.").

[250]The district court also found that Abbott withheld the EPO briefs with specific intent to deceive the USPTO. *Therasense*, 2012 WL 1038715 at *11 (concluding that Abbott's explanation for not submitting the EPO briefs to the USPTO "simply lacked sufficient coherence and consistency compared to the rest of the record. There is not one shred of documentary evidence to corroborate their testimony that at the time in question they actually believed or documented or discussed the supposed reason for not submitting the EPO briefs. It surfaced for the first time in this litigation.").

[251]*See* Star Scientific, Inc. v. R.J. Reynolds Tobacco Co., 537 F.3d 1357, 1367 (Fed. Cir. 2008); Nilssen v. Osram Sylvania, Inc., 504 F.3d 1223, 1235 (Fed. Cir. 2007) (stating that "[i]nformation is material if there is a substantial likelihood that a reasonable examiner would have considered the information important in deciding whether to allow the application to issue as a patent"); Honeywell Int'l, Inc. v. Universal Avionics Sys. Corp., 488 F.3d 982, 1000 (Fed. Cir. 2007).

[252]*See* Molins PLC v. Textron, Inc., 48 F.3d 1172, 1179-1180 (Fed. Cir. 1995) (stating that "[n]or is a reference immaterial simply because the claims are eventually deemed by an examiner to be patentable thereover" and concluding as to case at bar that "the fact that the examiner did not rely on [the] Wagenseil [reference] to reject the claims . . . is not conclusive concerning whether the reference was material").

[253]*See, e.g.*, Critikon, Inc. v. Becton Dickinson Vascular Access, Inc., 120 F.3d 1253, 1255 (Fed. Cir. 1997) (finding that withheld McDonald prior art patent was material

nevertheless sufficiently material to patentability to form a basis for a judgment of inequitable conduct.

Post-*Therasense,* it remains the law that information is not considered material if it is merely *cumulative* of (i.e., adds nothing new or different to) other information already before the USPTO.[254] Similarly, if an applicant fails to disclose known information but that information is independently discovered by the USPTO examiner, such information is not considered material.[255]

USPTO rules mandate that patent applicants owe the agency a duty of candor and good faith, including a duty to disclose to the USPTO information known to applicants that is material to patentability.[256] The USPTO's definition of materiality has changed over time.[257]

The Federal Circuit's pre-*Therasense* "important to a reasonable examiner" standard for materiality in the inequitable conduct context was linguistically the same as the definition applied by the USPTO in the agency's rules from 1977 to 1992, referred to by patent practitioners as "old Rule 56."[258] Although the USPTO changed its materiality definition in 1992 in an attempt to provide patent practitioners with a standard that was more specific and less open-ended and vague,[259] the Federal Circuit retained the older "important to a reasonable examiner" standard of materiality in its inequitable conduct

---

to patentability, but affirming district court's judgment sustaining validity of the patents in suit).

[254]*See Star Scientific*, 537 F.3d at 1367.

[255]*See* Eli Lilly & Co. v. Zenith Goldline Pharms., Inc., 471 F.3d 1369, 1383 (Fed. Cir. 2006) (affirming district court's conclusion that patentee's nondisclosure to USPTO of "Chakrabarti 1980a" prior art reference "was neither a material omission nor done with an intent to deceive" in part because "the examiner found and relied on Chakrabarti 1980a during prosecution"); Molins PLC v. Textron, Inc., 48 F.3d 1172, 1185 (Fed. Cir. 1995) (stating that " '[w]hen a reference was before the examiner, whether through the examiner's search or the applicant's disclosure, it cannot be deemed to have been withheld from the examiner' ") (quoting Scripps Clinic & Res. Found. v. Genentech, Inc., 927 F.2d 1565, 1582 (Fed. Cir. 1991)); Orthopedic Equip. Co., Inc. v. All Orthopedic Appliances, Inc., 707 F.2d 1376, 1383-1384 (Fed. Cir. 1983) (affirming district court's finding that nondisclosed prior art was not material because "the examiner assigned to prosecution of the patent-in-suit independently ascertained the existence of the undisclosed prior art").

[256]*See* 37 C.F.R. §1.56(a) (2012).

[257]*See* Digital Control Inc. v. The Charles Mach. Works, 437 F.3d 1309, 1314-1316 (Fed. Cir. 2006) (describing history of USPTO changes to its definition of materiality).

[258]*See Digital Control*, 437 F.3d at 1315 (explaining that "in 1977, the PTO amended Rule 56 to clarify the duty of candor and good faith before the PTO. That version of Rule 56 required applicants to disclose 'information they are aware of which is material,' stating that information is material 'where there is a substantial likelihood that a reasonable examiner would consider it important in deciding whether to allow the application to issue as a patent.' ") (quoting 37 C.F.R. §1.56 (1977)).

[259]*Cf. Digital Control*, 437 F.3d at 1314 (noting that "in 1992, the PTO amended Rule 56, creating an arguably narrower standard of materiality").

jurisprudence. The court does not consider itself bound by the USPTO's current definition of materiality as set forth at 37 C.F.R. §1.56(b), referred to by patent practitioners as the "new Rule 56."[260]

Hence, the Federal Circuit pre-*Therasense* applied its "important to a reasonable examiner" standard of materiality even when USPTO rules would have provided a narrower definition of materiality during the time that the patent application in question was prosecuted.[261]

[260]Since 1992, USPTO regulations have defined information material to patentability as information that

> is not cumulative to information already of record or being made of record in the application, and
>
> (1) [i]t establishes, by itself or in combination with other information, a prima facie case of unpatentability of a claim; or
>
> (2) [i]t refutes, or is inconsistent with, a position the applicant takes in:
>
> (i) Opposing an argument of unpatentability relied on by the Office, or
>
> (ii) Asserting an argument of patentability.
>
> A prima facie case of unpatentability is established when the information compels a conclusion that a claim is unpatentable under the preponderance of evidence, burden-of-proof standard, giving each term in the claim its broadest reasonable construction consistent with the specification, and before any consideration is given to evidence which may be submitted in an attempt to establish a contrary conclusion of patentability.

37 C.F.R. §1.56(b) (2019).

In response to the Federal Circuit's *en banc* decision in *Therasense, Inc. v. Becton, Dickinson and Co.*, 649 F.3d 1276 (Fed. Cir. 2011) (*en banc*), the USPTO issued in July 2011 a notice of proposed rulemaking. The agency proposed to change its definition of materiality in 37 C.F.R. §1.56 ("Rule 56") to comport with the "but for" materiality standard announced in *Therasense*. *See* United States Patent and Trademark Office, *Notice of Proposed Rulemaking: Revision of the Materiality to Patentability Standard for the Duty to Disclose Information in Patent Applications*, 76 FED. REG. 43631 (July 21, 2011). The Notice stated in part:

> Specifically, the Office is proposing to revise the materiality standard for the duty to disclose to match the materiality standard, as defined in *Therasense*, for the inequitable conduct doctrine. While *Therasense* does not require the Office to harmonize the materiality standards underlying the duty of disclosure and the inequitable conduct doctrine, the Office believes that there are important reasons to do so. The materiality standard set forth in *Therasense* should reduce the frequency with which applicants and practitioners are being charged with inequitable conduct, consequently reducing the incentive to submit information disclosure statements containing marginally relevant information and enabling applicants to be more forthcoming and helpful to the Office. At the same time, it should also continue to prevent fraud on the Office and other egregious forms of misconduct. Additionally, harmonization of the materiality standards is simpler for the patent system as a whole.

76 FED. REG. at 43631. The USPTO did not implement the proposed rule.

[261]*See* Digital Control Inc. v. The Charles Mach. Works, 437 F.3d 1309, 1314-1316 (Fed. Cir. 2006) (applying "important to a reasonable examiner" standard of materiality while recognizing that USPTO in 1992 changed its definition of materiality as promulgated in 37 C.F.R. §1.56, and holding that the "reasonable examiner" standard and

To the extent that the Federal Circuit's standard was more searching and would have required a patent applicant to submit a greater amount of information than would otherwise satisfy the USPTO definition of materiality, risk-averse patent applicants acted in accordance with the broader Federal Circuit standard of "important to a reasonable examiner." In other words, when in doubt about a prior art reference's materiality, prudence recommends submitting the reference to the USPTO for its consideration.[262]

The facts of *Critikon, Inc. v. Becton Dickinson Vascular Access, Inc.*[263] illustrate another important principle of materiality: what must be disclosed to the USPTO is not merely limited to prior art, but rather includes all *information* known to the applicant that is material to patentability. Critikon sued Becton Dickinson for infringement of Critikon's patents on intravenous (IV) catheters (including the Lemieux patent). During the course of the litigation, the Lemieux patent was reissued; Critikon amended its complaint to assert infringement of certain claims of the reissue patent. Reversing the district court's conclusion of no inequitable conduct, the Federal Circuit found fault not only with Critikon's nondisclosure of a prior art reference (the McDonald patent) that was material to the original and reissue Lemieux patents,[264] but also with Critikon's failure to inform the USPTO reissue examiner that the original Lemieux patent was the subject of concurrent federal court litigation in which Becton Dickinson was challenging its validity and enforceability. The appellate court had "little doubt" that the concurrent litigation involving the Lemieux patent also would be relevant to its reissue proceeding.[265] Given the materiality of the information withheld, together with Critikon's "failure at any point to offer a good faith explanation of the

---

Federal Circuit's case law interpreting that standard "were not supplanted by the PTO's adoption of a new Rule 56").

The Federal Circuit's position found support in academic commentary. For example, Professor Carl Moy has argued that the USPTO's 1992 revision of Rule 56 was beyond the agency's rulemaking authority. Moy contends that the 1992 version of Rule 56 is merely a "hortatory statement" that the Federal Circuit is not bound to apply in the court's inequitable conduct jurisprudence. *See* R. Carl Moy, *The Effect of New Rule 56 on the Law of Inequitable Conduct,* 74 J. PAT. & TRADEMARK OFF. SOC'Y 257, 277-278 (1992).

[262]Patent applicants typically submit prior art references for USPTO consideration by attaching copies of the references to an "Information Disclosure Statement" submitted in accordance with 37 C.F.R. §§1.97-1.98.

[263]120 F.3d 1253 (Fed. Cir. 1997).

[264]It is interesting to note that although the withheld McDonald patent was deemed material to patentability, the Federal Circuit did not reverse that part of the district court's judgment sustaining the validity of the patents in suit. *See id.* at 1255. Thus, *Critikon* is a case in which the withheld prior art was not sufficiently relevant to invalidate the claims, but was nevertheless of sufficient materiality to form a basis for a judgment of inequitable conduct.

[265]*Id.* at 1258.

pattern of nondisclosure,"[266] the Federal Circuit was able to infer the patentee's requisite intent to deceive the USPTO. Accordingly, the court held Critikon's patents unenforceable.

A fine line sometimes separates "advantages advocacy" during patent prosecution from a failure to disclose material information to the USPTO, as demonstrated in *Purdue Pharma L.P. v. Endo Pharms. Inc.*[267] Purdue's three patents in suit were directed to controlled-release oxycodone medications for pain treatment, sold by Purdue as OxyContin®. In the written description of its patent applications and during prosecution thereof, Purdue repeatedly referred to its "surprising discovery" that its oxycodone formulations controlled pain over a fourfold range of dosages for 90 percent of patients, compared to an eightfold range for prior art opioids such as morphine. The patents also referred to the "clinical significance" of the fourfold dosage range as a more efficient titration process (by which a patient's dosage is adjusted to provide acceptable pain relief without unacceptable side effects). At no time prior to issuance of the patents did Purdue have clinical data to support these assertions, however. While Purdue never stated during prosecution that its discovery had been clinically tested, it discussed the fourfold dosage range under headings containing the phrases "Surprisingly Improved Results" and "Results Obtained." Based on this evidence a federal district court found that Purdue had failed to disclose material information to the USPTO because it did not inform the agency that its discovery was based merely on the inventor's "insight," without scientific proof. Moreover, the district court found, the record as a whole reflected a clear pattern of intentional misrepresentation.[268]

The Federal Circuit affirmed the district court's judgment that Purdue's patents were unenforceable due to inequitable conduct. Although Purdue admittedly had never stated that its discovery of the fourfold dosage range was based on the results of clinical studies, "that conclusion was clearly to be inferred from the language used by Purdue in both the patents and prosecution history,"[269] the court observed. "In the absence of any statements indicating the true origin of its 'surprising discovery,' Purdue's arguments to the PTO provide enough of a suggestion that clinical trials had been performed that failure to tell the PTO the discovery was based on [co-inventor] Dr. Kaiko's insight and not scientific proof was a failure to disclose material information."[270] The Federal Circuit rejected Purdue's argument that the fourfold dosage range was not material because it was simply a benefit of

[266] *Id.* at 1259.
[267] 410 F.3d 690 (Fed. Cir. 2005).
[268] *Id.* at 695.
[269] *Id.* at 698.
[270] *Id.* at 698.

the claimed invention to which the examiner would have given little weight. The court contrasted *CFMT, Inc. v. Yieldup Int'l Corp.*,[271] in which it had held that a patentee did not commit inequitable conduct by setting forth during prosecution a list of advantages of the claimed invention. In *CFMT,* such "'advantages advocacy recited only the natural, expected results of a closed system [for cleaning semiconductor wafers].'"[272] In the case at bar, however, Purdue's assertion concerning the fourfold dosage range was "much more" than advantages advocacy. Rather, it was "one of the key arguments Purdue made consistently and repeatedly during prosecution to overcome prior art cited by the examiner in an obviousness rejection."[273]

b. Intent to Deceive

A breach of a patent applicant's duty of disclosure to the USPTO, without more, does not establish the defense of inequitable conduct. The party asserting the defense also must establish that material information was withheld (or falsely submitted) with a specific intent to deceive the USPTO.[274] Materiality and intent are separate elements of inequitable conduct; materiality does not presume intent.[275] At least a threshold level of each element must be established by clear and convincing evidence.[276] When an inequitable conduct charge is based on an applicant's failure to disclose prior art to the USPTO, "clear and convincing evidence must show that the applicant *made a deliberate decision* to withhold a *known* material reference."[277]

In "tighten[ing] the standards" in order to "redirect" the inequitable conduct doctrine,[278] the *en banc* Federal Circuit majority in *Therasense, Inc. v. Becton, Dickinson and Co.*,[279] discussed *supra*, clarified the intent standard as well as the materiality standard. The "specific

[271]349 F.3d 1333 (Fed. Cir. 2003).

[272]*Purdue Pharma*, 410 F.3d at 699 (quoting *CFMT*, 349 F.3d at 1342).

[273]*Id.*

[274]*See* Therasense, Inc. v. Becton, Dickinson and Co., 649 F.3d 1290 (Fed. Cir. 2011) (*en banc*) (holding that "[t]o prevail on a claim of inequitable conduct, the accused infringer must prove that the patentee acted with the specific intent to deceive the PTO").

[275]Star Scientific, Inc. v. R.J. Reynolds Tobacco Co., 537 F.3d 1357, 1366 (Fed. Cir. 2008).

[276]*Id.* at 1365.

[277]*Id.* at 1366 (emphasis in original).

[278]*Therasense,* 649 F.3d at 1290. Professor Golden suggests that "[w]ithout a real option of repudiating the [inequitable conduct] defense, the Federal Circuit [in *Therasense*] has instead sought to guide and confine the defense's application in hopes of advancing legitimate aims at acceptable social cost." John M. Golden, *Patent Law's Falstaff: Inequitable Conduct, the Federal Circuit, and* Therasense, 7 Wash. J.L., Tech. & Arts 353 (2012).

[279]649 F.3d 1290 (Fed. Cir. 2011) (*en banc*).

intent" called for by the Federal Circuit mandates both knowledge and deliberate action by the patent applicant. When alleged inequitable conduct involves the withholding of prior art from the USPTO, an "accused infringer must prove by clear and convincing evidence that the applicant knew of the reference, knew that it was material, and made a deliberate decision to withhold it."[280] It is *not* enough that "the applicant knew of a reference, *should have known* of its materiality, and decided not to submit it to the PTO. . . ."[281]

The Federal Circuit *en banc* majority in *Therasense* also revoked any "sliding scale" analysis for inferring intent.[282] The inequitable conduct elements of materiality and intent must each be independently proved by clear and convincing evidence. Importantly, a district court may not infer intent solely from materiality, nor may a weak showing of intent be rendered sufficient when evidence of materiality is strong. The court "must weigh the evidence of intent to deceive independent of its analysis of materiality."[283]

Because "smoking gun" evidence of intent to deceive rarely exists, intent may be inferred from the circumstances,[284] as in *Critikon*.[285] But inferred evidence of intent nevertheless must satisfy the "clear and convincing" quantum of proof. Moreover, "the inference must not only be based on sufficient evidence and be reasonable in light of that evidence, but it must also be the single most reasonable inference able to be drawn from the evidence to meet the clear and convincing standard."[286] No inference of intent can be drawn if there is no evidence, either direct or indirect, that supports such an inference.[287]

Applying these standards, the Federal Circuit held that a district court had clearly erred in finding intent to deceive the USPTO in *Star Scientific, Inc. v. R.J. Reynolds Tobacco Co.*[288] In that case, accused infringer Reynolds asserted inequitable conduct in the procurement

[280]*Therasense,* 649 F.3d at 1290.

[281]*Therasense,* 649 F.3d at 1290 (emphasis added).

[282]*See Therasense,* 649 F.3d at 1290. Pre-*Therasense* Federal Circuit decisions permitted a sliding-scale approach. Under that approach, "[t]he more material the omission or the misrepresentation, the lower the level of intent required to establish inequitable conduct, and vice versa." Critikon, Inc. v. Becton Dickinson Vascular Access, Inc., 120 F.3d 1253, 1256 (Fed. Cir. 1997). *See also* Honeywell Int'l, Inc. v. Universal Avionics Sys. Corp., 488 F.3d 982, 999 (Fed. Cir. 2007) (stating that "[t]he more material the information misrepresented or withheld by the applicant, the less evidence of intent will be required in order to find inequitable conduct").

[283]*Therasense,* 649 F.3d at 1290.

[284]*See Therasense,* 649 F.3d at 1290 (holding that "[b]ecause direct evidence of deceptive intent is rare, a district court may infer intent from indirect and circumstantial evidence").

[285]For an example of inferred intent post-*Therasense, see* Aventis Pharma S.A. v. Hospira, Inc., 675 F.3d 1324 (Fed. Cir. 2012).

[286]*Star Scientific*, 537 F.3d at 1366.

[287]*Id.* at 1368.

[288]*Id.* at 1365.

of Star Scientific's '649 patent based on a "quarantine" theory.[289] Reynolds contended that Star Scientific switched law firms during prosecution of its '649 patent in order to prevent the first law firm from disclosing to the USPTO a potentially damaging letter describing certain prior art, and to purposely keep the second law firm ignorant of the letter.

The Federal Circuit in *Star Scientific* concluded that the accused infringer's quarantine theory of deceptive intent was not supported by clear and convincing evidence. Reynolds' evidence suffered from a "major gap" — no evidence indicated that Star Scientific knew what the letter said before switching law firms, or that the letter was a reason for changing firms.[290] Star Scientific gave two reasons for changing law firms: that a partner at the first firm had recently passed away, and that the inventor had observed unsatisfactory performance by an associate of the same firm in an unrelated patent prosecution. Although the district court found this testimony was not credible, the Federal Circuit emphasized that "even if Star's explanations are not to be believed, it remained [Reynolds'] burden to prove its allegation . . . [Reynolds] cannot carry its burden simply because Star failed to prove a credible alternative explanation."[291] In other words, a patentee "need not offer any good faith explanation unless the accused infringer first carried [its] burden to prove a threshold level of intent to deceive by clear and convincing evidence."[292] It is not incumbent upon a patentee to rebut evidence of deceptive intent by providing a good faith explanation for its alleged misconduct unless and until the accused infringer has met its burden.[293]

The foundational case for understanding the intent requirement for inequitable conduct is *Kingsdown Med. Consultants, Ltd. v. Hollister, Inc.*[294] There the Federal Circuit demonstrated its concern that inequitable conduct has been asserted routinely and virtually automatically in almost every patent infringement litigation. The court went *en banc* to clarify the type of conduct that rises to the level of an intent to deceive. After *Kingsdown,* conduct of the patent applicant characterized as "gross negligence" or "ministerial error" cannot constitute the level of deliberate intent needed to establish inequitable conduct.

Kingsdown filed a U.S. patent application directed to an ostomy appliance for use by patients with openings in their abdominal walls for release of waste. During a lengthy and complex prosecution that

[289]Star Scientific's U.S. Patent No. 6,202,649 ('649 patent) was directed to a method for preventing the formation of tobacco-specific nitrosamines (TSNAs), a hazardous chemical present in cured tobacco. *See Star Scientific*, 537 F.3d at 1360-1361.

[290]*Id.* at 1368.

[291]*Id.*

[292]*Id.*

[293]*Id.*

[294]863 F.2d 867 (Fed. Cir. 1988) (partially *en banc*).

lasted more than six years, Kingsdown filed a continuation application in which it carried forward certain claims from its original application. These claims had previously been indicated allowable by the USPTO examiner after Kingsdown amended them to overcome a §112, ¶2 indefiniteness rejection.[295] In renumbering and carrying forward the claims into the continuation application, Kingsdown's counsel inadvertently copied the earlier, unamended (i.e., broader) version of a certain claim, and the examiner did not notice the mistake before issuing the patent.

The Federal Circuit reversed the district court's decision that Kingsdown's "gross negligence" in not recognizing its mistake rose to the level of an intent to deceive the USPTO:

> [A] transfer of numerous claims *en masse* from a parent to a continuing application, as the district court stated, is a ministerial act. As such, it is more vulnerable to errors which by definition result from inattention, and is less likely to result from the scienter involved in the more egregious acts of omission and commission that have been seen as reflecting the deceitful intent element of inequitable conduct in our cases.[296]

The *Kingsdown* court went *en banc* for a portion of its opinion to conclude that

> "[g]ross negligence" has been used as a label for various patterns of conduct. It is definable, however, only in terms of a particular act or acts viewed in light of all the circumstances. We adopt the view that a finding that particular conduct amounts to "gross negligence" does not of itself justify an inference of intent to deceive; the involved conduct, viewed in light of all the evidence, including evidence indicative of good faith, must indicate sufficient culpability to require a finding of intent to deceive.[297]

Thus, the "intent to deceive" element of the inequitable conduct defense requires a clear and convincing showing of conduct that is culpable, not merely negligent.

c. *Balancing*

Once a patent challenger has established the underlying factual elements of materiality and intent, the district court must engage in an overall balancing of the evidence, including evidence of good faith,[298]

[295]The claim definiteness requirement of 35 U.S.C. §112, ¶2 was discussed *supra* Chapter 2 ("Patent Claims"). Effective September 16, 2012, the America Invents Act of 2011 renamed the second paragraph of §112 as "35 U.S.C. §112(b)."

[296]*Kingsdown*, 863 F.2d at 875.

[297]*Id.* at 876.

[298]*See id.*

to determine as a matter of law whether the scales tilt to a conclusion that inequitable conduct occurred. If they do, the court will hold the patent unenforceable for inequitable conduct.

Importantly, the balancing step comes only after both underlying elements of materiality and intent have been established by clear and convincing evidence. Once these underlying proofs have been made, "the district court must balance the *substance* of those now-proven facts and all the equities of the case to determine whether the severe penalty of unenforceability should be imposed."[299] This final balancing step is committed to the district court's discretion.[300] In exercising their discretion, courts should be mindful that the penalty for inequitable conduct is severe: "the loss of the entire patent even where every claim meets every requirement of patentability."[301] Given this severity, courts must ensure that the underlying factors of materiality and intent have been satisfactorily proven before they exercise their discretion to ultimately determine whether to render a patent unenforceable.[302] The Federal Circuit has cautioned district courts to be "vigilant in not permitting the [inequitable conduct] defense to be applied too lightly."[303] While it is unjust to allow a patentee "who obtained his patent through deliberate misrepresentations or omissions of material information to enforce the patent against others," it is also unfair "to strike down an entire patent where the patentee only committed minor missteps or acted with minimal culpability or in good faith."[304]

d. Burden of Proof and Standard of Review

The party asserting the defense of unenforceability based on inequitable conduct must establish each underlying factor of materiality and intent by clear and convincing evidence, in keeping with the burden of proof for invalidating an issued patent.

Because the overall conclusion of inequitable conduct is an equitable determination within the district court's discretion, the Federal Circuit's standard of review for the ultimate conclusion of inequitable conduct is quite deferential; that is, the Circuit will reverse only if the district court abused its discretion. Assuming that they were found

[299]Star Scientific, Inc. v. R.J. Reynolds Tobacco Co., 537 F.3d 1357, 1367 (Fed. Cir. 2008) (emphasis in original).

[300]*See id.*

[301]*Id.* at 1365. The penalty may be even more severe in some cases. Through the doctrine of "infectious unenforceability," inequitable conduct that involved one or more patents in a family (e.g., patents issuing from a chain of related continuing applications) can "infect" related applications and render the resulting patents unenforceable. *See* Nilssen v. Osram Sylvania, Inc., 504 F.3d 1223, 1230 (Fed. Cir. 2007).

[302]*See Star Scientific*, 537 F.3d at 1366.

[303]*Id.*

[304]*Id.*

by the district court (the usual case) rather than a jury, each of the underlying factors of materiality and intent is reviewed for clear error in accordance with Fed. R. Civ. P. 52.[305] If a jury made the findings of materiality and intent, the findings will be upheld so long as they are supported by substantial evidence.[306]

2. Patent Misuse[307]

a. Introduction

An accused infringer also may assert a defense of unenforceability under §282(b)(1) (eff. Sept. 16, 2012) on the ground that the patent owner has committed patent misuse. This basis for unenforceability is separate from inequitable conduct. Instead of the patent applicant's conduct before the USPTO, the patent misuse defense focuses on the manner in which the patentee has exploited her issued patent.

Patent misuse is a rather amorphous doctrine,[308] generally understood as a "method of limiting abuse of patent rights separate from the antitrust laws."[309] The misuse doctrine has its origin in judicial decisions that predate any significant development of U.S. antitrust law.[310] Procedurally, patent misuse is asserted as an affirmative defense to an allegation of patent infringement,[311] whereas antitrust violation is asserted by the accused infringer as a counterclaim.[312] Often the same conduct forms the basis for both a patent misuse defense and an antitrust allegation.[313] Substantively, however,

[305]*See* PerSeptive Biosys., Inc. v. Pharmacia Biotech, Inc., 225 F.3d 1315, 1318-1319 (Fed. Cir. 2000).

[306]*See* Juicy Whip, Inc. v. Orange Bang, Inc., 292 F.3d 728, 737 (Fed. Cir. 2002).

[307]Much of the material in this section is based on Janice M. Mueller, *Patent Misuse Through the Capture of Industry Standards,* 17 BERKELEY TECH. L.J. 623 (2002).

[308]Professor Chisum observes in the misuse area "the absence of a clear and general theory for resolving the problem of what practices should be viewed as appropriate exercises of the patent owner's statutory patent rights." 6-19 DONALD S. CHISUM, CHISUM ON PATENTS §19.04 (2008). But given that misuse is a doctrine based in equity, the lack of clarity is hardly surprising. *See* Robert Merges, *Reflections on Current Legislation Affecting Patent Misuse,* 70 J. PAT. & TRADEMARK OFF. SOC'Y 793, 796 (1988) (noting that "[t]he nature of equity is that it is somewhat 'messy' ").

[309]B. Braun Med. v. Abbott Labs., 124 F.3d 1419, 1426 (Fed. Cir. 1997).

[310]*See* USM Corp. v. SPS Techs., Inc., 694 F.2d 505, 511 (7th Cir. 1982).

[311]*See* Virginia Panel Corp. v. Mac Panel Co., 133 F.3d 860, 868 (Fed. Cir. 1997); Windsurfing Int'l, Inc. v. AMF, Inc., 782 F.2d 995, 1001 (Fed. Cir. 1986).

[312]Antitrust counterclaims are considered in Section F of this chapter.

[313]However, establishing that a patentee who has committed patent misuse also has violated the antitrust laws requires "much more": in addition to the fact of the misuse, there must be showings of power in the relevant market and anticompetitive effect. *See* Marina Lao, *Unilateral Refusals to Sell or License Intellectual Property and the Antitrust Duty to Deal,* 9 CORNELL J.L. & PUB. POL'Y 193, 207 (1999). *See also infra* Section F ("Antitrust Counterclaims").

different policies ground patent misuse and antitrust doctrine. Misuse focuses primarily on the patentee's behavior in expanding the scope of its rights beyond the statutory patent grant, whereas antitrust measures the impact of that behavior on the marketplace.[314]

Like inequitable conduct, the roots of patent misuse lie in the equitable doctrine of unclean hands, "whereby a court of equity will not lend its support to enforcement of a patent that has been misused."[315] Application of the misuse doctrine seeks to restrain practices that draw "anticompetitive strength" from the patent right.[316]

Although the patent misuse doctrine has been broadly defined as preventing a patent owner from using its patent in a manner contrary to the public interest, this characterization is too indefinite to provide any meaningful notice to a patentee of the boundaries of prohibited conduct.[317] In practice, determinations of patent misuse have been based on a fairly narrow range of specific practices or acts by the patent owner,[318] often (but not exclusively) in the context of patent licensing.[319] The key inquiry is whether, by imposing a challenged condition

[314]*See* Richard Calkins, *Patent Law: The Impact of the 1988 Patent Misuse Reform Act and* Noerr-Pennington *Doctrine on Misuse Defenses and Antitrust Counterclaims*, 38 DRAKE L. REV. 175, 187 (1988-1989) (explaining that the antitrust laws are "intended to foreclose unreasonable restraints of trade and illegal monopolies," and consequently bear severe punishments for violators, while patent misuse doctrine, which merely suspends patent owner's right to recover for infringement, "prevent[s] a patentee from projecting the economic effect of his admittedly valid grant beyond the limits of his legal monopoly," which effect can occur "regardless of whether the defendant in a patent infringement action is injured or a monopoly in trade and commerce results") (quoting Panther Pumps & Equip. Co. v. Hydrocraft, Inc., 468 F.2d 225, 231 (7th Cir. 1972)).

[315]B. Braun Med. v. Abbott Labs., 124 F.3d 1419, 1427 (Fed. Cir. 1997).

[316]*See* Mallinckrodt, Inc. v. Medipart, Inc., 976 F.2d 700, 704 (Fed. Cir. 1992).

[317]*See* USM Corp. v. SPS Techs., Inc., 694 F.2d, 505, 510 (7th Cir. 1982) (asserting that such a vague formulation, if "taken seriously . . . would put all patent rights at hazard").

[318]*Id.*

[319]*See generally* 6-19 DONALD S. CHISUM, CHISUM ON PATENTS §19.04[3] (2008) ("Acts of Misuse"). Important guidance on acceptable patent licensing practices is available at United States Department of Justice, *Antitrust Guidelines for the Licensing of Intellectual Property* (1995), *available at* https://www.justice.gov/atr/archived-1995-antitrust-guidelines-licensing-intellectual-property [hereinafter *Licensing Guidelines*]. The *Licensing Guidelines* provide helpful examples of the application of antitrust principles to particular licensing restraints (such as horizontal restraints, resale price maintenance, tying arrangements, and exclusive dealing) and to arrangements that involve the cross-licensing, pooling, or acquisition of intellectual property. *See id.* at §5. The *Licensing Guidelines* were updated in 2017. *See* United States Department of Justice and the Federal Trade Commision, *Antitrust Guidelines for the Licensing of Intellectual Property* (Jan 12, 2017), available at https://www.justice.gov/atr/IPguidelines/download. Although the majority of patent misuse cases have examined a patentee's licensing practices, the patent misuse defense also has been raised in a case involving restrictions placed by the patent owner on the conditions of post-sale use of its patented device. *See Mallinckrodt,* 976 F.2d at 709 (Fed. Cir. 1992) (reversing grant of summary judgment of unenforceability based on patent misuse and remanding for determination

(e.g., the imposition of an onerous term in a license granted under the patent), the patent owner has "impermissibly broadened the 'physical or temporal scope' of the patent grant with anticompetitive effect."[320]

In its 2010 *en banc* decision *Princo Corp. v. Int'l Trade Comm'n*,[321] the Federal Circuit reconfirmed that the patent misuse doctrine should be construed narrowly. The court observed that patent misuse "is a judge-made doctrine that is in derogation of statutory patent rights against infringement."[322] Even if a patentee has violated the antitrust laws, such conduct does not necessarily establish that it engaged in patent misuse.[323]

At issue in *Princo* was an allegedly anticompetitive agreement between U.S. Philips Corporation (Philips), intervenor in the ITC's case against Princo, and Sony Corporation. Philips and Sony worked together in the 1980s and 1990s to set standards for digital storage recordable and rewritable compact disc technology. The two companies faced a technical problem concerning how to encode position information in the discs. They ultimately chose an analog solution proposed by Philips and covered by Philips's "Raaymakers" patents over a digital solution proposed by Sony and covered by Sony's "Lagadec" patent. The Raaymakers approach was thus incorporated into the technology standard for making the compact discs, published in what was informally known as the "Orange Book." Philips and Sony commercialized their technology by offering "package" licenses for manufacturers of Orange Book–compliant compact discs. Philips, the licensing program administrator, included in the package of licensed patents not only its Raaymakers patents but also Sony's Lagadec patents (and other patents).[324]

---

of whether post-sale restriction was valid under applicable sales law and within scope of patent grant).

[320]Windsurfing Int'l, Inc. v. AMF, Inc., 782 F.2d 995, 1001 (Fed. Cir. 1986) (quoting Blonder-Tongue Labs., Inc. v. Univ. of Ill. Found., 402 U.S. 313, 343 (1971)). Commentators have identified *Windsurfing* as a merger by the Federal Circuit of patent misuse and antitrust theories. More specifically, they contend that *Windsurfing*'s requirement for an "anticompetitive effect" was a departure from the Supreme Court's decision in *Morton Salt Co. v. G.S. Suppiger Co.*, 314 U.S. 488 (1942), which did not require such a showing in order to establish patent misuse. *See* Robert J. Hoerner, *The Decline (and Fall?) of the Patent Misuse Doctrine in the Federal Circuit,* 69 ANTITRUST L.J. 669, 672-673 (2001) (suggesting that the *Windsurfing* court's citation of *Blonder-Tongue* after the words "with anticompetitive effect" could be regarded as "misleading," for only the phrase "physical or temporal scope" appeared in *Blonder-Tongue*).

[321]616 F.3d 1318 (Fed. Cir. 2010) (*en banc*).

[322]*Princo,* 616 F.3d at 1321.

[323]*Princo,* 616 F.3d at 1329 (stating that "[w]hile proof of an antitrust violation shows that the patentee has committed wrongful conduct having anticompetitive effects, that does not establish misuse of the patent in suit unless the conduct in question restricts the use of that patent and does so in one of the specific ways that have been held to be outside the otherwise broad scope of the patent grant").

[324]*See Princo,* 616 F.3d at 1322.

Princo was an initial licensee under the package license. When Princo thereafter ceased paying royalties, Philips filed a complaint with the ITC that Princo and other firms were violating the trade laws. Specifically, Philips alleged that Princo was infringing Philips's Raaymakers patents by importing certain compact discs into the United States without Philips' authorization.[325] Princo's answer raised an affirmative defense of patent misuse, contending that Philips had improperly forced Princo (and other licensees), as a condition of licensing patents (e.g., the Raaymakers patents) that were necessary to manufacture the Orange Book–compliant compact discs, to take licenses under other patents (e.g., Sony's Lagadec patent) that were not necessary for such manufacture. Princo further charged that Philips and Sony had agreed to suppress the technology embodied in Sony's Lagadec patent; that is, to anticompetitively eliminate the development of technology alternatives (such as Lagadec) to the Philips-patented Raaymakers approach.

The Federal Circuit rejected Princo's patent misuse argument. Even assuming that Philips and Sony had entered into a horizontal agreement to restrict the availability of Sony's Lagadec patent, Lagadec was an entirely different patent that was never asserted in the infringement action against Princo. These facts presented a "completely different scenario" from the Federal Circuit and Supreme Court precedent finding patent misuse. The *en banc* court in *Princo* held that "[e]ven if [the Philips-Sony] agreement [to suppress technology] were shown to exist, and even if it were shown to have anticompetitive effects, a horizontal agreement restricting the availability of Sony's Lagadec patent would not constitute misuse of Philips's Raaymakers patents or any of Philips's other patents in suit."[326]

The *Princo* court summarized the issue before it as follows: "When a patentee offers to license a patent, does the patentee misuse that patent by inducing a third party not to license its separate, competitive technology?"[327] The Federal Circuit found no authority or underlying policy concerns that would support a holding of patent misuse under the facts before it. "Such an agreement would not have the effect of increasing the physical or temporal scope of the patent in suit," the court concluded, and it "therefore would not fall within the rationale of the patent misuse doctrine as explicated by the Supreme Court and this court."[328]

[325]*See Princo,* 616 F.3d at 1323.
[326]*Princo*, 616 F.3d at 1331.
[327]*Princo*, 616 F.3d at 1331.
[328]*Princo*, 616 F.3d at 1331. Joined by Judge Gajarsa, Federal Circuit Judge Dyk authored an extensive dissenting opinion. Judge Dyk charged that "the relevant Supreme Court cases and congressional legislation . . . support[] a vigorous misuse defense, clearly applicable to agreements to suppress alternative technology.

b. *Historical Development*

(i) Tying

The foundational patent misuse case is *Morton Salt Co. v. G.S. Suppiger Co.*[329] The challenged conduct involved a patentee "tying" the grant of a patent license to the licensee's promise to purchase from the patent owner a nonpatented, staple commodity. The U.S. Supreme Court refused to enforce the patent in suit where the patent owner had conditioned the grant of licenses to use its patented machines, which deposited tablets of salt in a food canning process, on the licensees' purchase of the unpatented salt tablets from the patent owner rather than from any third-party salt supplier.

Although the Supreme Court concluded that this tying constituted patent misuse that justified nonenforcement of the patent,[330] the offense in *Morton Salt* did not necessarily rise to the level of an antitrust violation, because no evidence existed that the patent owner's licensing practice "substantially lessened competition or tended to create a monopoly in salt tablets."[331] Even though the patentee could not enjoin the infringement because of its own misuse, the patentee did not face antitrust remedies such as the imposition of treble damages.[332] Nor was the misused patent held permanently unenforceable, because misuse can be "purged" by alleviating a challenged condition.[333]

The majority cabins the doctrine in contravention of this Supreme Court authority." *Princo*, 616 F.3d at 1342 (Dyk, J., dissenting).

[329]314 U.S. 488 (1942).

[330]Older patent misuse precedent such as *Morton Salt* is historically important but should only be relied on today with caution. It is not clear that the patentee in *Morton Salt* would be guilty of patent misuse under current law. As revised by the 1988 Patent Misuse Reform Act, the patent laws now provide that conditioning the grant of a patent license on the licensee's promise to purchase even a staple article (such as salt) from the patentee will *not* be deemed patent misuse *unless* the patent owner has "market power in the relevant market for the patent..." 35 U.S.C. §271(d)(5). The §271(d) safe harbors from patent infringement are further discussed in Section D.2.c, *infra*.

[331]*Morton Salt*, 314 U.S. at 490. *See also* Richard Calkins, *Patent Law: The Impact of the 1988 Patent Misuse Reform Act and* Noerr-Pennington *Doctrine on Misuse Defenses and Antitrust Counterclaims*, 38 Drake L. Rev. 175, 183 (1988-1989) (concluding that "*Morton Salt* reinforced the Court's earlier rulings that the misuse defense was grounded on public policy underlying the patent laws and was not limited to a violation of the antitrust laws").

[332]*See* 15 U.S.C. §15 (§4 Clayton Act) (providing for treble damages recovery in private enforcement action brought by "any person who shall be injured in his business or property by reason of anything forbidden in the antitrust laws").

[333]*See Morton Salt,* 314 U.S. at 493, stating that

> [e]quity may rightly withhold its assistance from... [a misuse] of the patent by declining to entertain a suit for infringement, and should do so at least until it is made to appear that the improper practice has been abandoned and that the consequences of the misuse of the patent have been dissipated.

Notably, the defendant/accused infringer in *Morton Salt* was not itself a "victim" of the misuse, because it was not a licensee. In the Supreme Court's view, the true victim of the misuse was the public at large. Despite the defendant's seeming lack of standing to raise a misuse defense, the Court refused to enforce the patent on public policy grounds:

> [T]he public policy which includes inventions within the granted monopoly excludes from it all that is not embraced in the invention. It equally forbids the use of the patent to secure an exclusive right or limited monopoly not granted by the Patent Office and which it is contrary to public policy to grant.[334]

As *Morton Salt* made clear, the importance of preventing a patent owner from exploiting its patent in a way that improperly expands the scope of rights conveyed by the government justifies a liberal interpretation of the standing requirement to raise the misuse defense. Accordingly, an accused infringer need not have been personally impacted by the misuse in order to raise the patent misuse defense.[335]

(ii) Post-Patent Expiration Royalties

In a 1964 decision, the Supreme Court held in *Brulotte v. Thys Co.*[336] that "a patentee's use of a royalty agreement that projects beyond the expiration date of the patent is unlawful per se."[337] In 2015, the Supreme Court reaffirmed *Brulotte*'s prohibition on

[334]*Morton Salt,* 314 U.S. 492. *See generally* 6-19 DONALD S. CHISUM, CHISUM ON PATENTS §19.04[4] (2008) ("Purging and Dissipation of Misuse").

[335]Professor Lemley has criticized the lack of a standing requirement in the patent misuse area, asserting that it creates an economic windfall for infringers:

> The lack of an injury requirement often produces situations in which parties who are not injured by misuse are the ones who benefit from the doctrine. Besides annulling any compensatory effect the remedy might have, this undermines the goals of the patent system, since it unnecessarily rewards (and therefore encourages) infringement. Parties unrelated to the patentee's wrongful acts may infringe its patents with impunity, since they are protected from liability by the patent misuse doctrine. Indeed, because the bar on infringement suits continues until the wrongful consequences have been dissipated fully, a finding of misuse essentially gives a green light to infringers of that patent for the foreseeable future.

Mark A. Lemley, *The Economic Irrationality of the Patent Misuse Doctrine,* 78 CAL. L. REV. 1599, 1618-1619 (1990).

[336]379 U.S. 29 (1964).

[337]*Brulotte*, 379 U.S. at 32. Although the *Brulotte* Court did not explicitly state its holding in terms of a patent misuse violation, it did refer to a patent misuse defense having been raised in the state court contract litigation below. *See Brulotte*, 379 U.S. at 30 ("One defense was misuse of the patents through extension of the license agreements beyond the expiration date of the patents."). Moreover, the dissent in *Brulotte* characterized the Supreme Court's decision as one turning on the patent laws, not the antitrust laws. *See Brulotte*, 379 U.S. at 38 n.3 (Harlan, J., dissenting) (observing that the case at bar was

post-patent expiration royalty payments in *Kimble v. Marvel Entertainment, LLC.*[338] Both cases are examined below.

Thys Company (hereafter "Thys") owned a group of patents directed to machines for hop-picking (i.e., removing the flowers of a hop plant for use in making beer and other beverages). Brulotte and another farmer in Washington state purchased the machines from Thys for a lump sum[339] and also entered into license agreements with Thys for the farmers' use of the machines.[340] All the patents expired in 1957, but the license agreements required royalty payments for use of the machines beyond that date.[341] When the farmers refused to pay the license fees (both before and after patent expiration), Thys sued them in the Washington state courts for the unpaid royalties. The farmers raised, *inter alia*, the defense that the extension of the license agreements beyond the expiration dates of the patents constituted patent misuse.[342]

"a patent, not an antitrust, case, there being no basis in the record for concluding that Thys' arrangements with its licensees were such as to run afoul of the antitrust laws").

[338]135 S. Ct. 2401 (2015).

[339]One farmer paid $3,125 for "title" to a hop-picking machine and the other farmer paid $3,300. *Brulotte*, 379 U.S. at 29 n.1.

[340]"The royalties were to be paid at the rate of $3.33 1/3 per two hundred pounds of hops harvested with the machines, and in any event a minimum royalty of $500 per year was to be paid for the use of each machine." Thys Co. v. Brulotte, 62 Wash. 2d 284, 286, 382 P.2d 271, 272 (1963), *rev'd*, 379 U.S. 29 (1964).

[341]"The defendant Brulotte purchased his machine in 1948; his obligation to pay royalties extended through the 1958 harvest. The defendants Charvet purchased their machine in 1951 and agreed to pay royalties until the completion of the 1960 harvest." Thys Co. v. Brulotte, 62 Wash. 2d 284, 287, 382 P.2d 271, 273 (1963), *rev'd*, 379 U.S. 29 (1964).

[342]*See Brulotte*, 379 U.S. at 30 ("One defense was misuse of the patents through extension of the license agreements beyond the expiration date of the patents."). *See also* Thys Co. v. Brulotte, 62 Wash. 2d 284, 382 P.2d 271 (1963), elaborating:

> Mainly, the defenses urged by the defendants on appeal relate to the validity of the licensing contracts. It is contended that the contracts were illegal because (1) they placed restrictions on the subsequent free use of the patents after they were sold, (2) they conditioned the grant of a license on some patents on acceptance of a license on a larger group of patents, (3) they licensed the use of patents beyond the 17-year period of monopoly granted by the sovereign, and (4) they violated the antitrust laws of the United States. It is also contended that the contracts were terminated when the defendants first failed to pay royalties when they became due. For a last defense, the defendants allege that they were not obligated to pay royalties for the years when the machines were not in use.

Thys Co., 62 Wash. 2d at 285, 382 P.2d at 272.

Readers should note that *Brulotte* (and *Kimble*) are not cleanly "patent misuse" cases, although both cases challenged a purported attempt to extend a patent's power by charging royalties after its expiration. As discussed *infra,* the *Kimble* majority does *not* describe the case before it as sounding in misuse. Nevertheless, as in *Brulotte,* the *Kimble* majority emphasizes that the case before it arises under the patent laws rather than the antitrust laws. Accordingly, this text places its discussion of *Brulotte* (and

When the case ultimately reached the Supreme Court, the Justices (in an opinion authored by Justice Douglas, who was not a fervent fan of patents) concluded that the extension of royalties beyond patent expiration was "unlawful per se."[343] The *Brulotte* Court observed that the rights granted to a patentee "become public property once the [patent] period expires."[344] Licensor Thys was improperly "using the licenses to project its monopoly beyond the patent period."[345] To allow such licensing practices would mean that "the free market visualized for the post-expiration period would be subject to monopoly influences that have no proper place here."[346] In the *Brulotte* Court's view, the post-expiration royalty payments were "analogous to an effort to enlarge the monopoly of the patent by tieing the sale or use of the patented article to the purchase or use of unpatented ones."[347]

In so holding, the *Brulotte* Court reversed the Washington state Supreme Court decision in favor of the farmers on their defense of patent misuse through extension of the license agreements beyond the patents' expiration dates.[348] The Washington court had reasoned that spreading the royalty payments beyond the patent expiration date was "a reasonable amount of time over which to spread the payments for the use of the patent."[349] The Supreme Court disagreed strongly. In its view, the royalty payments due under the licenses were for use during the post-patent expiration period, rather than "deferred payments for use during the pre-expiration period."[350]

The *Brulotte* Court distinguished the case at bar, involving patents, from a situation involving the "sale or lease of unpatented machines on

---

Kimble) under the subtopic of "Patent Misuse," within the topic of "Unenforceability," as a defense to a charge of patent infringement.

[343] *Brulotte*, 379 U.S. at 32.

[344] *Brulotte*, 379 U.S. at 31. At the time of the *Brulotte* decision, patents expired 17 years after grant.

[345] *Brulotte*, 379 U.S. at 32.

[346] *Brulotte*, 379 U.S. at 32-33.

[347] *Brulotte*, 379 U.S. at 33 (citing Ethyl Gasoline Corp. v. United States, 309 U.S. 436 (1940); Mercoid Corp. v. Mid-Continent Inv. Co., 320 U.S. 661, 664-665 (1944) and cases cited)).

[348] *See Brulotte*, 379 U.S. at 30.

[349] *See* Thys Co. v. Brulotte, 62 Wash. 2d 284, 382 P.2d 271 (1963), stating:

> In this case, when the parties signed their agreements, the instruments showed on their faces that some of the patents would expire before the end of the period during which the payment of royalties was required. It was undoubtedly understood between them that a 17-year period was a reasonable amount of time over which to spread the payments for the use of the patent. They agreed that the value of the right to use the patents embodied in the machines was at least $500 per year, for the remaining years of the royalty period. There is no legal or equitable reason why they should not be required to perform their agreement.

Thys Co., 62 Wash. 2d at 291, 382 P.2d at 275 (1963).

[350] *See Brulotte*, 379 U.S. at 31.

long-term payments based on a deferred purchase price or on use. . . ."[351] The latter hypothetical would involve "wholly different considerations." Here, the machines were patented and thus the matter was in the "federal domain." Because the licenses in dispute drew no line between the term of the patent and its post-expiration period, the licenses were on their face a "bald attempt to exact the same terms and conditions for the period after the patents have expired as they do for the monopoly period."[352] In the *Brulotte* Court's view, this was unlawful *per se*.[353]

Despite frequent criticism,[354] the rule of *Brulotte* has not been overturned in over fifty years, nor has Congress acted to legislatively overrule it in that time. In 2014, however, the Supreme Court signaled its

[351] *Brulotte*, 379 U.S. at 32.

[352] *Brulotte*, 379 U.S. at 32.

[353] Justice Harlan dissented in *Brulotte*. He characterized the Court as holding that Thys "unlawfully misused its patent monopoly by contracting with purchasers of its patented machines for royalty payments based on use beyond the patent term." *Brulotte*, 379 U.S. at 34 (Harlan, J., dissenting). In Justice Harlan's view, a "more discriminating analysis" should have produced a different result. He saw the case as a "mixed" one "involving the sale of a tangible machine which incorporates an intangible, patented idea." *Brulotte*, 379 U.S. at 34 (Harlan, J., dissenting). Admitting that the patent laws "prohibit post-expiration restrictions on the use of patented ideas," he contended that there was "no substantial restriction on the use of the Thys idea." *Brulotte*, 379 U.S. at 34 (Harlan, J., dissenting). Justice Harlan also observed that the case was "a patent, not an antitrust, case, there being no basis in the record for concluding that Thys' arrangements with its licensees were such as to run afoul of the antitrust laws." *Brulotte*, 379 U.S. at 38 n.3 (Harlan, J., dissenting).

[354] *See* Kimble v. Marvel Enterprises Inc., 727 F.3d 856, 857 (9th Cir. 2013) (stating that "[t]his appeal calls on us to again construe the Supreme Court's frequently-criticized decision in *Brulotte v. Thys Co.*, 379 U.S. 29, 85 S. Ct. 176, 13 L. Ed. 2d 99 (1964)"), *cert. granted*, No. 13-720, 2014 WL 6993036 (U.S. Dec. 12, 2014). The Ninth Circuit in *Kimble* further observed that it had

> previously acknowledged these criticisms in *Zila*[, *Inc. v. Tinnell*, 502 F.3d 1014 (9th Cir. 2007)] at 1019 n.4 (collecting authorities). *Accord Brulotte*, 379 U.S. at 34-39, 85 S. Ct. 176 (Harlan, J., dissenting); U.S. Dep't of Justice & FTC, *Antitrust Enforcement and Intellectual Property Rights: Promoting Innovation and Competition* 12, 116-19, 122-23 (2007) (discussing criticisms of *Brulotte* and concluding that permitting patent holders to enter agreements requiring royalty payments beyond the expiration of the patent "can be efficient" in that it will "reduce[ ] deadweight loss associated with a patent monopoly and allow[ ] the patent holder to recover the full value of the patent, thereby preserving innovation incentives"), *available at* https://www.ftc.gov/sites/default/files/documents/reports/antitrust-enforcement-and-intellectual-property-rights-promoting-innovation-and-competition-report.s.department-justice-and-federal-trade-commission/p040101promotinginnovationandcompetitionrpt0704.pdf, Richard Gilbert & Carl Shapiro, *Antitrust Issues in the Licensing of Intellectual Property: The Nine No-No's Meet the Nineties*, in *Brookings Papers on Economic Activity: Microeconomics* 233, 322 (1997) (concluding that the "[l]egal reasoning here, based on the notion that extending the royalties in time is to 'enlarge the monopoly of the patent,' although rhetorically appealing, does not seem to reflect commercial reality or basic economics").

interest in revisiting the matter when it granted *certiorari* in a patent licensing case captioned *Kimble v. Marvel Enterprises, Inc.*[355] The sole

---

Kimble, 727 F.3d at 866 n.7. *See also* Scheiber v. Dolby Labs., Inc., 293 F.3d 1014 (7th Cir. 2002), stating that:

> *Brulotte* involved an agreement licensing patents that expired at different dates, just like this case; the two cases are indistinguishable. The decision has, it is true, been severely, and as it seems to us, with all due respect, justly, criticized, beginning with Justice Harlan's dissent, 379 U.S. at 34, 85 S. Ct. 176, and continuing with our opinion in *USM Corp. v. SPS Technologies, Inc.*, 694 F.2d 505, 510-11 (7th Cir. 1982). The Supreme Court's majority opinion reasoned that by extracting a promise to continue paying royalties after expiration of the patent, the patentee extends the patent beyond the term fixed in the patent statute and therefore in violation of the law. That is not true. After the patent expires, anyone can make the patented process or product without being guilty of patent infringement. The patent can no longer be used to exclude anybody from such production. Expiration thus accomplishes what it is supposed to accomplish. For a licensee in accordance with a provision in the license agreement to go on paying royalties after the patent expires does not extend the duration of the patent either technically or practically, because, as this case demonstrates, if the licensee agrees to continue paying royalties after the patent expires the royalty rate will be lower. The duration of the patent fixes the limit of the patentee's power to extract royalties; it is a detail whether he extracts them at a higher rate over a shorter period of time or a lower rate over a longer period of time.

Scheiber, 293 F.3d at 1017. *See also* Ayres & Klemperer, *Limiting Patentees' Market Power Without Reducing Innovation Incentives: The Perverse Benefits of Uncertainty and Non-Injunctive Remedies,* 97 MICH. L. REV. 985, 1027 (1999) ("Our analysis . . . suggests that *Brulotte* should be overruled"); Harold See & Frank M. Caprio, *The Trouble with* Brulotte*: The Patent Royalty Term and Patent Monopoly Extension*, 1990 UTAH L. REV. 813, 814, 851; Rochelle Cooper Dreyfuss, *Dethroning* Lear: *Licensee Estoppel and the Incentive to Innovate*, 72 VA. L. REV. 677, 709-712 (1986).

[355]No. 13-720, Kimble v. Marvel Enterprises, Inc., 2014 WL 6993036 (U.S. Dec. 12, 2014). In the decision under review, the Ninth Circuit observed:

> In *Brulotte*, the Court held that a patent licensing agreement requiring a licensee to make royalty payments beyond the expiration date of the underlying patent was unenforceable because it represented an improper attempt to extend the patent monopoly. *Id.* [379 U.S.] at 30-33, 85 S. Ct. 176. We have previously noted that *Brulotte* has been read to require that any contract requiring royalty payments for an invention either after a patent expires or when it fails to issue cannot be upheld unless the contract provides a discount from the alternative, patent-protected rate. *Zila, Inc. v. Tinnell*, 502 F.3d 1014, 1021 (9th Cir. 2007). We acknowledged that the *Brulotte* rule is counterintuitive and its rationale is arguably unconvincing. *Id.* at 1019-20 & n.4. Nonetheless, recognizing that we are bound by Supreme Court authority and the strong interest in maintaining national uniformity on patent law issues, we have reluctantly applied the rule. *Id.* at 1020, 1022. We are compelled to do so again. Accordingly, we join our sister circuits in holding that a so-called "hybrid" licensing agreement encompassing inseparable patent and non-patent rights is unenforceable beyond the expiration date of the underlying patent, unless the agreement provides a discounted rate for the non-patent rights or some other clear indication that the royalty at issue was in no way subject to patent leverage. *See Meehan v. PPG Indus., Inc.*, 802 F.2d 881, 884-86 (7th Cir. 1986); *Boggild v. Kenner Prods.*, 776 F.2d 1315,

question of the petition for *certiorari* in *Kimble* asked "[w]hether this Court should overrule *Brulotte v. Thys Co.*, 379 U.S. 29 (1964)."[356]

Kimble's U.S. Patent No. 5,072,856 ('856 patent) was directed to a toy glove that allowed "Spider-Man"[357] aficionados to role-play as a "spider person" by shooting a string of pressurized foam through an opening in the glove. An embodiment of the claimed invention is depicted in Figure 10.1.

Kimble in 1997 sued Marvel Entertainment LLC ("Marvel"), a wholly owned subsidiary of the Walt Disney Company, for infringing the '856 patent. The parties settled the case with Marvel agreeing to purchase the patent for a lump sum payment plus a 3 percent royalty on Marvel's future sales of its accused "Web Blaster" product. The parties' agreement did not set forth any sunset date for the royalty payments[358] (in other words, the royalty obligation would continue indefinitely).

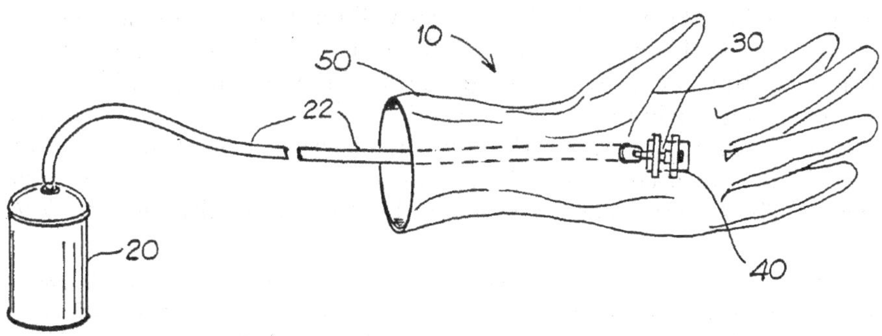

Figure 10.1

Toy Glove, U.S. Patent No. 5,072,856

1319-20 & n.5 (6th Cir. 1985); *Pitney Bowes, Inc. v. Mestre*, 701 F.2d 1365, 1371-72 (11th Cir. 1983).

Kimble v. Marvel Enterprises Inc., 727 F.3d 856, 857 (9th Cir. 2013), *cert. granted*, No. 13-720, 2014 WL 6993036 (U.S. Dec. 12, 2014).

[356]Petition for Writ of Certiorari, No. 13-720, Kimble v. Marvel Enterprises, Inc., 2014 WL 6993036 (U.S. Dec. 12, 2014), at i.

[357]*See* Marvel Entertainment LLC, *Spider-Man*, http://marvel.com/characters/54/spider-man (last visited Dec. 27, 2015) (explaining that "[when b]itten by a radioactive spider, high school student Peter Parker gained the speed, strength and powers of a spider. Adopting the name Spider-Man, Peter hoped to start a career using his new abilities. Taught that with great power comes great responsibility, Spidey has vowed to use his powers to help people.").

[358]*See Kimble,* 135 S. Ct. at 2406.

After executing the settlement agreement, Marvel discovered the 1964 *Brulotte* decision. Based thereon, Marvel initiated a declaratory judgment action against Kimble, asking a federal court to declare that Marvel would owe no further royalties once the '856 patent expired.[359] The district court agreed, holding that *Brulotte* rendered the royalty provision of the Kimble-Marvel settlement agreement unenforceable once the '856 patent had expired.[360] The U.S. Court of Appeals for the Ninth Circuit reluctantly affirmed.[361] *Certiorari* was granted.

In June 2015, the Supreme Court issued its decision in *Kimble v. Marvel Entertainment, LLC.*[362] Rather unexpectedly, a 6-3 majority of Justices declined to overturn *Brulotte,* instead reaffirming its bright-line rule that a patent owner cannot charge royalties for use of its patented invention after the patent has expired.[363]

The *Kimble* majority sustained *Brulotte* on the principle of *stare decisis*— "the idea that today's Court should stand by yesterday's decisions."[364] Although *stare decisis* in "not an inexorable command,"[365] it is the "preferred course."[366] The Court will not lightly overturn its earlier decisions absent "special justification."[367] Simply concluding in retrospect that a case was wrongly decided is not sufficient.[368]

Patentee/petitioner Kimble urged the Supreme Court to replace *Brulotte's* bright-line rule with an antitrust-style "rule of reason" standard that would consider all the facts and circumstances of each case.[369] The *Kimble* majority rejected the argument. Although *Brulotte*

[359]Application for the '856 patent was filed on May 25, 1990, and the patent issued on December 17, 1991. Under 35 U.S.C. §154(c), the '856 patent expired on May 25, 2010.

[360]*See Kimble*, 135 S. Ct. at 2406 (citing 692 F. Supp. 2d 1156, 1161 (D. Ariz. 2010)).

[361]*See Kimble*, 135 S. Ct. at 2406 (citing 727 F.3d 856, 857 (9th Cir. 2013) (observing that the rule of *Brulotte* "is counterintuitive and its rationale is arguably unconvincing")).

[362]135 S. Ct. 2401 (June 22, 2015).

[363]*Kimble*, 135 S. Ct. at 2405.

[364]*Kimble*, 135 S. Ct. at 2409.

[365]Payne v. Tennessee, 501 U.S. 808, 827 (1991).

[366]*Kimble*, 135 S. Ct. at 2409. *Stare decisis* is the "preferred course because it promotes the evenhanded, predictable, and consistent development of legal principles, fosters reliance on judicial decisions, and contributes to the actual and perceived integrity of the judicial process." *Payne,* 501 U.S. at 827.

[367]*Kimble*, 135 S. Ct. at 2409 ("To reverse course, we require as well what we have termed a 'special justification'—over and above the belief 'that the precedent was wrongly decided.'") (quoting Halliburton Co. v. Erica P. John Fund, Inc., 134 S. Ct. 2398, 2407 (2014)).

[368]*See Kimble*, 135 S. Ct. at 2409 ("an argument that we got something wrong—even a good argument to that effect—cannot by itself justify scrapping settled precedent").

[369]*See Kimble*, 135 S. Ct. at 2408-2409. "[M]ost antitrust claims are analyzed under a 'rule of reason,' according to which the finder of fact must decide whether the questioned practice imposes an unreasonable restraint on competition, taking into account a variety of factors, including specific information about the relevant business, its condition before and after the restraint was imposed, and the restraint's history, nature, and effect." State Oil Co. v. Khan, 522 U.S. 3, 10 (1997).

admittedly made some mention of economic consequences, the *Kimble* majority read it as a case decided under the patent laws rather than the antitrust laws.[370] Even though the Court has been willing to set aside *stare decisis* principles and overrule some of its earlier antitrust cases when economic consensus has changed over time, such was not the case with patent law.[371] Moreover, mandating an antitrust rule of reason analysis with full-fledged economic inquiry into market power, barriers to entry, and the like would make the law less workable. The elaborate antitrust inquiry proposed by Kimble would contravene the simplicity of *Brulotte*'s rule and introduce "notoriously high litigation costs and unpredictable results."[372]

The *Kimble* majority emphasized that *Brulotte* turned on the Supreme Court's application of a statutory provision — 35 U.S.C. §154, which governs a patent's term[373] — and accompanying patent policy that closely guards a patent's cut-off date. Section 154 provides

[370]The *Kimble* majority explained:

> *Brulotte* is a patent rather than an antitrust case.... [E]ven assuming that *Brulotte* relied on an economic misjudgment, Congress is the right entity to fix it. By contrast with the Sherman Act, the patent laws do not turn over exceptional law-shaping authority to the courts. Accordingly, statutory *stare decisis* — in which this Court interprets and Congress decides whether to amend — retains its usual strong force....
>
> [I]n any event, *Brulotte* did not hinge on the mistake Kimble identifies [i.e., assuming that post-expiration royalty payments are always anticompetitive]. Although some of its language invoked economic concepts, ... the Court did not rely on the notion that post-patent royalties harm competition. Nor is that surprising. The patent laws — unlike the Sherman Act — do not aim to maximize competition (to a large extent, the opposite). And the patent term — unlike the [Sherman Act] "restraint of trade" standard — provides an all-encompassing bright-line rule, rather than calling for practice-specific analysis. So in deciding whether post-expiration royalties comport with patent law, *Brulotte* did not undertake to assess that practice's likely competitive effects. Instead, it applied a categorical principle that all patents, and all benefits from them, must end when their terms expire.

Kimble, 135 S. Ct. at 2413 (citing *Brulotte*, 379 U.S. at 30-32).

As with *Brulotte,* the *Kimble* case is not cleanly a "patent misuse" case, although both cases challenged a purported attempt to extend a patent's power by charging royalties after its expiration. To be clear, the *Kimble* majority does *not* describe the case before it as sounding in misuse. Nevertheless, as in *Brulotte,* the *Kimble* majority emphasizes that the case before it arises under the patent laws rather than the antitrust laws. Accordingly, this text places its discussion of *Kimble* (and *Brulotte*) under the subtopic of "Patent Misuse," within the topic of "Unenforceability," as a defense to a charge of patent infringement.

[371]*See Kimble,* 135 S. Ct. at 2412 (noting that "[t]his Court has viewed *stare decisis* as having less-than-usual force in cases involving the Sherman Act").

[372]*Kimble,* 135 S. Ct. at 2411 (citing Arizona v. Maricopa County Med. Soc., 457 U.S. 332, 343 (1982)).

[373]*See supra* Chapter 1, Section C.7 ("The Patent Term").

a (relatively[374]) precise formula for determining a patent's date of expiration. The Court has "carefully guarded" that cut-off point, emphasizing in many decisions the policy that once a patent expires, the patented invention enters the public domain free of restrictions on its use.[375]

The *Kimble* Court explained that *stare decisis* holds special sway in cases interpreting statutes, because unlike provisions in the Constitution, Congress can amend statutes if it chooses.[376] Moreover, *stare decisis* concerns are "'at their acme'" in cases like *Brulotte* that involve the intersection of property law (e.g., patents) and contract law (e.g., license agreements).[377] Further, Congress has had many opportunities to change the rule of *Brulotte* but never amended the patent statutes to do so. Rather, "*Brulotte* has governed licensing agreements for more than half a century."[378] The fact that Congress has continually amended other parts of the Patent Act without amending §154 (or other provisions) to change the rule of *Brulotte* further supported leaving the rule in place.

Kimble advanced two additional arguments as the "special justifications" supporting a departure from *stare decisis* to overturn *Brulotte*. The *Kimble* majority rejected both. Firstly, Kimble contended that *Brulotte* wrongly assumed that post-expiration patent royalty payments were invariably anticompetitive. The *Kimble* Court did not disagree "with Kimble's economics — only what follows from it."[379] Even

[374]The *Kimble* court did not discuss patent term adjustment, which was not at issue with Kimble's '856 patent. When the current 20-year term was implemented, however, it was necessary to ensure that patent owners were not penalized for pendency delays caused by the USPTO rather than by the applicants themselves. Accordingly, the 1999 American Inventors Protection Act added to U.S. patent law the concept of patent term adjustment for such delays. *See* American Inventors Protection Act of 1999, Pub. L. No. 106-113, §4402 ("Patent Term Guarantee Authority"), 113 Stat. 1501 (1999). Patent term adjustment, governed by 35 U.S.C. §154(b), can be a notoriously complex computation. *See supra* Chapter 1, Section C.7 ("The Patent Term").

[375]*See Kimble,* 135 S. Ct. at 2407 (citing cases including *Scott Paper Co. v. Marcalus Mfg. Co.*, 326 U.S. 249 (1945) (determining that a manufacturer could not agree to refrain from challenging a patent's validity). "Allowing even a single company to restrict its use of an expired or invalid patent," the *Scott Paper* Court explained, "'would deprive... the consuming public of the advantage to be derived' from free exploitation of the discovery." *Kimble,* 135 S. Ct. at 2407 (quoting *Scott Paper,* 326 U.S. at 256). To permit such a result, whether or not authorized by express contract, would impermissibly undermine the patent laws. *Kimble,* 135 S. Ct. at 2407 (citing *Scott Paper,* 326 U.S. at 255-256).

[376]*See Kimble,* 135 S. Ct. at 2409.

[377]*Kimble,* 135 S. Ct. at 2410 (citing Payne v. Tennessee, 501 U.S. 808, 828 (1991); State Oil Co. v. Khan, 522 U.S. 3, 20 (1997)).

[378]*Kimble,* 135 S. Ct. at 2410 (citing Watson v. United States, 552 U.S. 74, 82-83 (2007) (stating that "long congressional acquiescence... enhance[s] even the usual precedential force we accord to our interpretations of statutes") (internal quotation marks omitted)).

[379]*Kimble*, 135 S. Ct. at 2412.

assuming *Brulotte* relied on economic misjudgment, it was up to Congress, not the courts, to change the patent laws.

More to the point, the *Brulotte* Court did not undertake to assess the likely anticompetitive effects of post-expiration patent royalties. "Instead, it applied a categorical principle that all patents, and all benefits from them, must end when their terms expire."[380] It was patent policy, not antitrust policy, which served as the basis of the *Brulotte* Court's conclusion that post-expiration royalty agreements are unenforceable — regardless of their economic impact.

Second, Kimble argued that the rule of *Brulotte* clashed with the patent policy of promoting innovation. He contended that some licenses may never be executed if the parties are not allowed to structure the timing of royalty payments over lengthened periods of time that extend beyond the patent's expiration date. The Court could not agree with Kimble's assertion that barring post-expiration royalties "imposes any meaningful drag on innovation,"[381] however. Although the *Kimble* Court recognized that "post-patent royalties are sometimes not anticompetitive,"[382] it maintained that *Brulotte* left open several alternative methods to accomplish payment deferral and risk-spreading.[383] Moreover, *amicus* United States "vigorously dispute[d] that *Brulotte* has caused any 'significant real-world economic harm.'"[384]

380 *Kimble*, 135 S. Ct. at 2413.
381 *Kimble*, 135 S. Ct. at 2414.
382 *Kimble*, 135 S. Ct. at 2414.
383 *See Kimble*, 135 S. Ct. at 2408, observing:

> [P]arties can often find ways around *Brulotte*, enabling them to achieve those same ends. To start, *Brulotte* allows a licensee to defer payments for pre-expiration use of a patent into the post-expiration period; all the decision bars are royalties for using an invention after it has moved into the public domain. See [*Brulotte*,] 379 U.S., at 31, 85 S. Ct. 176; *Zenith Radio Corp. v. Hazeltine Research, Inc.*, 395 U.S. 100, 136, 89 S. Ct. 1562, 23 L. Ed. 2d 129 (1969). A licensee could agree, for example, to pay the licensor a sum equal to 10% of sales during the 20-year patent term, but to amortize that amount over 40 years. That arrangement would at least bring down early outlays, even if it would not do everything the parties might want to allocate risk over a long timeframe. And parties have still more options when a licensing agreement covers either multiple patents or additional non-patent rights. Under *Brulotte*, royalties may run until the latest-running patent covered in the parties' agreement expires. See 379 U.S., at 30, 85 S. Ct. 176. Too, post-expiration royalties are allowable so long as tied to a non-patent right — even when closely related to a patent. See, *e.g.*, 3 Milgrim on Licensing §18.07, at 18-16 to 18-17. That means, for example, that a license involving both a patent and a trade secret can set a 5% royalty during the patent period (as compensation for the two combined) and a 4% royalty afterward (as payment for the trade secret alone). Finally and most broadly, *Brulotte* poses no bar to business arrangements other than royalties — all kinds of joint ventures, for example — that enable parties to share the risks and rewards of commercializing an invention.

384 *Kimble*, 135 S. Ct. at 2414 (quoting Brief for United States as *Amicus Curiae* 30).

Finding "many reasons for staying the *stare decisis* course and no 'special justification' for departing from it," the *Kimble* majority declined Kimble's invitation to overrule *Brulotte* and affirmed the judgment of the Ninth Circuit in Marvel's favor.

Justice Alito authored the dissenting opinion in *Kimble,* joined by Chief Justice Roberts and Justice Thomas. The dissent charged the majority with using *stare decisis* "to reaffirm a clear case of judicial overreach" rather than as a tool of restraint.[385] In the dissent's view, *Brulotte* was not based on "anything that can plausibly be regarded as an interpretation of the terms of the Patent Act." Rather, *Brulotte* turned on "an economic theory . . . that has been debunked."[386]

c. *Limitations on Patent Misuse: §271(d)*

Although the courts liberally construe the requirement of standing to assert patent misuse, other components of U.S. patent law provide exceptions or safe harbors that shield certain categories of patent owner activity from patent misuse liability. Section 271(d), added in the 1952 Patent Act and expanded by the 1988 Patent Misuse Reform Act, originated as a legislative attempt to resolve the tension between the defense of patent misuse and a patent owner's right to sue for contributory infringement in accordance with §271(c).[387] The history of

[385]*Kimble,* 135 S. Ct. at 2415 (Alito, J., dissenting).

[386]*Kimble,* 135 S. Ct. at 2415 (Alito, J., dissenting). The dissent interpreted the economics as follows:

> *Brulotte* misperceived the purpose and effect of post-expiration royalties. The decision rested on the view that post-expiration royalties extend the patent term by means of an anti-competitive tying arrangement. As the Court understood such an arrangement, the patent holder leverages its monopoly power during the patent term to require payments after the term ends, when the invention would otherwise be available for free public use. But agreements to pay licensing fees after a patent expires do not "enlarge the monopoly of the patent." 379 U.S., at 33, 85 S. Ct. 176. Instead, "[o]nce the patent term expires, the power to exclude is gone," and all that is left "is a problem about optimal contract design." Easterbrook, Contract and Copyright, 42 Hous. L. Rev. 953, 955 (2005).
>
> The economics are simple: Extending a royalty term allows the parties to spread the licensing fees over a longer period of time, which naturally has the effect of reducing the fees during the patent term. See *ante,* at 2407. Restricting royalty payments to the patent term, as *Brulotte* requires, compresses payment into a shorter period of higher fees. The Patent Act does not prefer one approach over the other.

Kimble, 135 S. Ct. at 2416 (Alito, J., dissenting).

[387]*See* Chapter 9 ("Patent Infringement"), *supra,* for a more detailed treatment of contributory infringement. Briefly, the doctrine of contributory patent infringement, statutorily codified at 35 U.S.C. §271(c) in the 1952 Patent Act, originated in judicial decisions such as *Wallace v. Holmes,* 29 F. Cas. 74 (No. 17,100) (C.C. Conn. 1871). Under a theory of joint tortfeasance, the *Wallace* court held liable for infringement the defendant supplier of a burner, which, when combined by consumers with a chimney,

§271(d) patent misuse limitations shows that they have primarily developed as a counterweight to contributory infringement. An assertion of contributory infringement challenges a defendant's supply of one or more components that make up less than the entirety of a claimed invention. The related patent misuse concern is that through such assertions, the patentee is attempting to expand the scope of its statutorily granted exclusionary right by restraining competition in these components, which are generally nonpatented items.[388]

After the Supreme Court's 1944 *Mercoid* decisions,[389] some courts viewed the very act of bringing a lawsuit that alleged contributory infringement as an act of patent misuse. In response to concerns that patent misuse was eradicating contributory infringement, Congress enacted §271(d) in the 1952 Patent Act.[390] Section 271(d) did not purport to affirmatively define patent misuse, but rather set forth three specific acts which, if the patentee were otherwise entitled to relief for direct or contributory infringement, would not be considered "misuse or illegal extension of the patent right."[391]

Attorney (later Judge) Giles S. Rich and others successfully lobbied for the inclusion of the §271(d) safe harbor provisions as a necessary counterbalance to the contributory infringement provision that had been contemporaneously enacted as 35 U.S.C. §271(c). In view of the Supreme Court's *Mercoid* decisions and the lower courts' reaction

---

resulted in direct infringement of the plaintiff's patent on the overall lamp device comprising burner and chimney. *See id.* at 79-80; *see also* Tom Arnold & Louis Riley, *Contributory Infringement and Patent Misuse: The Enactment of §271 and Its Subsequent Amendments,* 76 J. PAT. & TRADEMARK OFF. SOC'Y 357, 365 (1994) (discussing view of some courts that after *Mercoid* "the mere act of bringing a contributory infringement action was patent misuse").

[388]*See* Dawson Chem. Co. v. Rohm & Haas Co., 448 U.S. 176, 197 (1980) (noting that "an inevitable concomitant of the right to enjoin another from contributory infringement is the capacity to suppress competition in an unpatented article of commerce").

[389]*See generally* Mercoid Corp. v. Mid-Continent Inv. Co., 320 U.S. 661 (1944); Mercoid Corp. v. Minneapolis-Honeywell Regulator Co., 320 U.S. 680 (1944).

[390]The safe harbors provided in the 1952 Act are those that appear today at 35 U.S.C. §271(d)(1)-(3) (2008).

[391]*Id.* The three patent misuse safe harbors originally included in the 1952 Patent Act, for which "[n]o patent owner otherwise entitled to relief for infringement or contributory infringement of a patent shall be denied relief or deemed guilty of misuse or illegal extension of the patent right by reason of his having done one or more of the following," were that the patentee had

> (1) derived revenue from acts which if performed by another without his consent would constitute contributory infringement of the patent;
>
> (2) licensed or authorized another to perform acts which if performed without his consent would constitute contributory infringement of the patent; and
>
> (3) sought to enforce his patent rights against infringement or contributory infringement.

Act of July 19, 1952, ch. 950, §§1, 66 Stat. 811, codified at 35 U.S.C. §271(d)(1)-(3) (1952).

thereto, Rich and his colleagues believed that having a contributory infringement provision in the Patent Act was meaningless without a counterpart provision to make clear that the assertion of contributory infringement by a patent owner under limited conditions involving a defendant's supply of a nonstaple article should not be regarded as patent misuse. Congress ultimately agreed, enacting §§271(d)(1)-(3) as part of the 1952 Patent Act.

The U.S. Supreme Court did not have occasion to scrutinize the patent misuse safe harbors of 35 U.S.C. §271(d) until 1980. In *Dawson Chem. Co. v. Rohm & Haas Co.*,[392] the Court considered the propriety of a patent owner's refusal to license the defendant and other producers of the nonstaple but unpatented chemical propanil. The propanil was required to perform a patented process for inhibiting the growth of weeds in rice crops. The Court also scrutinized the patent owner's practice of tying the grant of implied licenses to rice farmers for use of the process based on the farmers' purchase of propanil from the patentee, rather than from the patentee's competitors that also manufactured the unpatented chemical. The defendant conceded that its sales of propanil with instructions for use amounted to contributory infringement of the process patent, but asserted the affirmative defense of patent misuse. The defendant argued that the patentee's acts of tying and refusal to license went well outside the three then-existing patent misuse safe harbors of 35 U.S.C. §271(d), and that by virtue of those acts the patentee was excluded from the category of patentees "otherwise entitled to relief" under the prefatory language of §271(d).

By a 5-4 vote, the Supreme Court majority in *Dawson Chem.* rejected the defendant's assertion of patent misuse, concluding that the patentee's acts, were "not dissimilar in either nature or effect from the [safe harbor] conduct that is clearly embraced within §271(d)."[393] With respect to the patentee's refusal to license the patented method, the majority provided little analysis except to note that the patentee "does *not* license others to sell propanil, but nothing on the face of the statute requires it to do so."[394] The Court focused much more

[392]448 U.S. 176 (1980).

[393]*Id.* at 202, 223.

[394]*Id.* at 202 (emphasis in original). The dissent in *Dawson Chem.* criticized this analysis as simplistic, pointing out that

> Section 271(d) does not define conduct that constitutes patent misuse; rather it simply outlines certain conduct that is not patent misuse. Because the terms of the statute are terms of exception, the absence of any express mention of a licensing requirement does not indicate that respondent's refusal to license others is protected by §271(d).

Id. at 234 (White, J., dissenting).

Contrary to the tenor of the *Dawson Chem.* dissent, and relying in part on the subsequent enactment of 35 U.S.C. §271(d)(4), the Federal Circuit maintains a strong stance

attention on the patentee's act of tying than its refusal to license its competitors. The majority held the tying acceptable because the tied product, propanil, was a nonstaple good, one that had "no use except through practice of the patented method."[395] In the majority's view, "the provisions of §271(d) effectively confer upon the patentee, as a lawful adjunct of his patent rights, a limited power to exclude others from competition in nonstaple goods."[396]

Congress in 1988 legislatively codified the holdings of *Dawson Chem.* by adding new subsections (4) and (5) to the three then-existing patent misuse safe harbors of 35 U.S.C. §271(d).[397] The new subsections address refusals to license and tying, respectively:

> No patent owner otherwise entitled to relief for infringement or contributory infringement of a patent shall be denied relief or deemed guilty of misuse or illegal extension of the patent right by reason of his having done one or more of the following:
>
> . . .
>
> (4) refused to license or use any rights to the patent; or
>
> (5) conditioned the license of any rights to the patent or the sale of the patented product on the acquisition of a license to rights in another patent or purchase of a separate product, unless, in view of the circumstances, the patent owner has market power in the relevant market for the patent or patented product on which the license or sale is conditioned.[398]

The language of the tying provision, §271(d)(5), reflects current economic and antitrust law thinking by providing that tying arrangements[399] will not constitute patent misuse or illegal extension of the

---

against placing on patent owners any affirmative obligations to license their patents. *See* In re Ind. Serv. Orgs. Antitrust Litig. (CSU, L.L.C. v. Xerox Corp.), 203 F.3d 1322, 1326 (Fed. Cir. 2000), discussed in further detail in Section F, *infra*.

[395] *Dawson Chem.*, 448 U.S. at 199.

[396] *Id.* at 201.

[397] Act of Nov. 19, 1988, Title II, Pub. No. 100-703, §201, 102 Stat. 4674; *see also* Robert P. Merges & Richard R. Nelson, *On the Complex Economics of Patent Scope,* 90 Colum. L. Rev. 839, 914 n.347 (1990) (describing legislation as "built on" *Dawson Chem.*). For a detailed description of the passage of the act, see Richard Calkins, *Patent Law: The Impact of the 1988 Patent Misuse Reform Act and* Noerr-Pennington *Doctrine on Misuse Defenses and Antitrust Counterclaims*, 38 Drake L. Rev. 175, 192-200 (1988-1989).

[398] 35 U.S.C. §271(d)(4)-(5).

[399] "A 'tying' or 'tie-in' or 'tied sale' arrangement has been defined as 'an agreement by a party to sell one product . . . on the condition that the buyer also purchases a different (or tied) product, or at least agrees that he will not purchase that [tied] product from any other supplier.'" United States Department of Justice, *Antitrust Guidelines for the Licensing of Intellectual Property* (1995) §5.3, *available at* https://www.justice.gov/atr/archived-1995-antitrust-guidelines-licensing-intellectual-property (quoting Eastman Kodak Co. v. Image Tech. Servs., Inc., 112 S. Ct. 2072, 2079 (1992)).The Antitrust Division of the U.S. Justice Department (DOJ) and the Federal Trade Commission (FTC) currently take the position that "[a]lthough tying arrangements may result in

patent right so long as the patentee does not have market power[400] in the relevant market[401] for the tying product.[402]

3. Prosecution History Laches

A third and more recently recognized basis for asserting the unenforceability of a patent rests on the notion that its owner improperly delayed the issuance of the patent by unreasonably extending the time

---

anticompetitive effects, such arrangements can also result in significant efficiencies and procompetitive benefits." *Id.* The agencies will, in the exercise of their prosecutorial discretion, "consider both the anticompetitive effects and the efficiencies attributable to a tie-in." *Id.*

[400]Market power is "the ability profitably to maintain prices above, or output below, competitive levels for a significant period of time." United States Department of Justice, *Antitrust Guidelines for the Licensing of Intellectual Property* §2.2 (1995), *available at* https://www.justice.gov/atr/archived-1995-antitrust-guidelines-licensing-intellectual-property. The DOJ and FTC "will not presume that a patent . . . necessarily confers market power upon its owner." *Id.* at §5.3.

[401]"Relevant market" is a term of art in antitrust law. The Federal Circuit has defined it as "the area of effective competition in which competitors generally are willing to compete for the consumer potential." Intergraph Corp. v. Intel Corp., 195 F.3d 1346, 1353 (Fed. Cir. 1999) (citing American Key Corp. v. Cole Nat'l Corp., 762 F.2d 1569, 1581 (11th Cir. 1985)). The *Intergraph* court summarized Supreme Court law on relevant market as follows:

> In *Brown Shoe Co. v. United States,* 370 U.S. 294, 324, 8 L. Ed. 2d 510, 82 S. Ct. 1502 (1962) the Court summarized that the relevant market has two dimensions: first, the relevant product market, which identifies the products or services that compete with each other; and second, the geographic market, which may be relevant when the competition is geographically confined. Thus "the 'market' which one must study to determine when a producer has monopoly power will vary with the part of commerce under consideration." United States v. E. I. du Pont de Nemours & Co., 351 U.S. 377, 404, 76 S. Ct. 994, 100 L. Ed. 1264 (1956).

Id.

[402]*See Indep. Ink, Inc. v. Ill. Tool Works, Inc.*, 396 F.3d 1342, 1349 n.7 (Fed. Cir. 2005) ("Proof of actual market power is required to establish a patent misuse defense based on patent tying."); Virginia Panel Corp. v. MAC Panel Co., 133 F.3d 860, 869 (Fed. Cir. 1997) (characterizing 35 U.S.C. §271(d)(5) as "provid[ing] that . . . in the absence of market power, even a tying arrangement does not constitute patent misuse"). *See also* Robert J. Hoerner, *The Decline (and Fall?) of the Patent Misuse Doctrine in the Federal Circuit,* 69 Antitrust L.J. 669, 672-683 (2001) (stating that "[t]ying is not patent 'misuse' or an 'illegal extension of the patent right' unless it meets the 35 U.S.C. §271(d)(5) standard"). The government's *Licensing Guidelines* provide that the DOJ and FTC "would be likely to challenge a tying arrangement if: (1) the seller has market power in the tying product, (2) the arrangement has an adverse effect on competition in the relevant market for the tied product, and (3) efficiency justifications for the arrangement do not outweigh the anticompetitive effects." United States Department of Justice, *Antitrust Guidelines for the Licensing of Intellectual Property* §5.3 (1995), *available at* https://www.justice.gov/atr/archived-1995-antitrust-guidelines-licensing-intellectual-property.

spent prosecuting it through the USPTO. A panel of the Federal Circuit in 2002 gave formal recognition to the defense of **prosecution history laches** in *Symbol Techs., Inc. v. Lemelson Med.*[403] There the patent owner first alleged infringement in 1998 of patents directed to bar code scanning technology, for which it claimed the benefit of the filing dates of two applications filed in 1954 and 1956. The *Symbol Techs.* majority held that as a matter of law, the equitable doctrine of laches may be applied to bar enforcement of a patent that issued after unreasonable and unexplained delay in prosecution, even though the patent applicant complied with all pertinent statutes and rules.[404] The majority found support for a prosecution history laches defense in Supreme Court precedent,[405] and further determined that the 1952 enactment of §§120 and 121 of the Patent Act (which entitle continuation and divisional applications to the filing dates of their parent applications[406]) did not foreclose the application of prosecution history laches to bar enforcement of a patent claim.[407]

Although the defense of prosecution history laches would seem to have fairly limited applicability to so-called "submarine patents" obtained under the pre-TRIPS 17-years-from-issuance patent term,[408] the federal district courts have thus far refused to constrain the defense to that context.[409] Moreover, prosecution history laches is not

[403]277 F.3d 1361 (Fed. Cir. 2002).

[404]The dissent charged that the majority's "judicial creation of a new ground on which to challenge patents that fully comply with the statutory requirements is in direct contravention to the rule that when statutory provisions exist they may be relied on without equitable penalty." *Symbol Techs.*, 277 F.3d at 1369 (Newman, J., dissenting).

[405]The *Symbol Techs.* majority read Supreme Court precedent as having recognized the doctrine of prosecution history laches in at least four decisions, including *General Talking Pictures Corp. v. Western Elec. Co.*, 304 U.S. 175 (1938); *Crown Cork & Seal v. Ferdinand Gutmann Co.*, 304 U.S. 159 (1938); *Webster Elec. Co. v. Splitdorf Elec. Co.*, 264 U.S. 463 (1924); and *Woodbridge v. United States*, 263 U.S. 50 (1923).

[406]*See supra* Chapter 1, Section H.5 ("Continuing Application Practice").

[407]A federal district court subsequently held Lemelson's patents unenforceable on the basis of prosecution history laches. *See* Symbol Techs., Inc. v. Lemelson Med., Educ. & Research Found., 301 F. Supp. 2d 1147, 1155 (D. Nev. 2004) (finding that "Lemelson's 18- to 39-year delay in filing and prosecuting the asserted claims under the fourteen patents-in-suit after they were first purportedly disclosed in the 1954 and 1956 applications was unreasonable and unjustified and that the doctrine of prosecution laches renders the asserted claims unenforceable against [accused infringers] Symbol and Cognex"). The Federal Circuit affirmed. *See* Symbol Techs., Inc. v. Lemelson Med., Educ. & Research Found., LP, 422 F.3d 1378 (Fed. Cir. 2005). Although the extreme facts of the case justified the district court's holding of unenforceability, the Federal Circuit cautioned that the doctrine of prosecution history laches should be "used sparingly lest statutory provisions be unjustifiably vitiated" and "applied only in egregious cases" of misuse of the statutory patent system. *Id.* at 1385.

[408]*See supra* Chapter 1, Section C.7 ("The Patent Term").

[409]*See* Cummins-Allison Corp. v. Glory Ltd., 2003 WL 355470, at *41 (N.D. Ill. 2003) (rejecting argument that doctrine of prosecution history laches, as a matter of law,

limited to patent infringement lawsuits in federal court; shortly after *Symbol Techs.* the Federal Circuit held in *In re Bogese* that the USPTO may rely on the doctrine as a basis for rejecting patent applications in appropriate circumstances.[410]

4. Unclean Hands Based on Misconduct Independent of Inequitable Conduct in Patent Procurement

All the unenforceability defenses examined above, including the most common unenforceability defenses of inequitable conduct in patent procurement[411] and patent misuse,[412] have their origins in the equitable doctrine of "unclean hands." That doctrine ' "closes the doors of a court of equity to one tainted with inequitableness or bad faith relative to the matter in which he seeks relief, however improper may have been the behavior of the defendant,' and requires that claimants 'have acted fairly and without fraud or deceit as to the controversy in issue.' "[413] The unclean hands doctrine " 'necessarily gives wide range to the equity court's use of discretion in refusing to aid the unclean litigant.' "[414]

In 2018, the Federal Circuit applied the "unclean hands" concept in a very concrete fashion by approving its use as the basis for a separate and independent unenforceability defense that did *not* involve inequitable conduct in the USPTO or patent misuse. In a panel opinion authored by Judge Taranto, the Federal Circuit in *Gilead Sciences, Inc. v. Merck & Co.*[415] affirmed the Northern District of California's judgment that declaratory judgment (DJ) defendant/patentee Merck could not enforce two of its drug patents against DJ plaintiff Gilead because Merck had acted with "unclean hands." The Circuit found no clear error in the district court's findings of "serious misconduct" by Merck both before and during its patent litigation with Gilead.

---

cannot apply to patents filed for after June 8, 1995, GATT TRIPS change to U.S. patent term, in agreement with *Digital Control*); Digital Control, Inc. v. McLaughlin Mfg. Co., 225 F. Supp. 2d 1224, 1226-1228 (W.D. Wash. 2002) (refusing to limit defense of prosecution history laches to patent applications filed before GATT TRIPS change in U.S. patent term).

[410]*See* In re Bogese, 303 F.3d 1362 (Fed. Cir. 2002) (affirming USPTO Board's decision that Bogese had forfeited his right to a patent by filing 12 continuation applications over an eight-year period while failing to substantively advance prosecution when required and given an opportunity to do so by the USPTO).

[411]Examined *infra* Section D.1.

[412]Examined *infra* Section D.2.

[413]Gilead Scis., Inc. v. Merck & Co., 888 F.3d 1231, 1239 (Fed. Cir. 2018) (quoting Precision Instrument Manufacturing Co. v. Automotive Maintenance Machinery Co., 324 U.S. 806, 814-815 (1945)).

[414]*Id.* (quoting *Precision Instrument,* 324 U.S. at 815).

[415]888 F.3d 1231 (Fed. Cir. Apr. 25, 2018) (Taranto, J.).

To summarize, "Merck's unclean hands bar[red] enforcement of the patents . . . because Merck improperly obtained the structure of PSI-6130 [a compound active against the Hepatitis C virus] from Pharmasset [another pharmaceutical firm later acquired by Gilead], drafted patent claims covering PSI-6130, and then lied about its conduct during this proceeding."[416]

Notably, patentee Merck's misconduct in *Gilead* did *not* involve a failure to disclose information material to patentability to the USPTO during the procurement of Merck's patents; thus the traditional unenforceability defense of inequitable conduct, examined *supra,*[417] was not asserted.

The *Gilead* Circuit deemed it "significant" that the case before it did *not* "involve[e] alleged deficiencies in communications with the PTO during patent prosecution." Rather, *Gilead* is a relatively rare and novel decision in which the Federal Circuit held patents unenforceable based on "unclean hands" independently of inequitable conduct in the USPTO. The appellate court observed that although its inequitable conduct decisions, "e.g., *Therasense, Inc. v. Becton, Dickinson & Co.*, 649 F.3d 1276 (Fed. Cir. 2011) (*en banc*), set important limits on conclusions of unenforceability through that doctrine," they were not relevant in *Gilead.*

In a footnote, the Circuit in *Gilead* emphasized that it had no reason in the case at bar to consider "issues that may arise in seeking to ensure that the unclean-hands doctrine operates in harmony with, and does not override, this court's inequitable-conduct standards governing unenforceability challenges based on prosecution communications with the PTO."[418] It thus appears that the Circuit currently sees the inequitable conduct defense (though locating its doctrinal roots in the unclean hands doctrine) as a different animal from the unclean hands defense imposed in *Gilead*, which was based on misconduct geared at the other litigation party rather than the USPTO. However, the tenor of the Circuit's observation suggests that questions remain to be more fully explored about overlap between the two doctrines.

The Supreme Court established the test for an unclean hands defense in its 1933 patent decision, *Keystone Driller Co. v. General Excavator Co.*[419] There the Court explained that a determination of unclean hands requires a relatively tight nexus between the purported misconduct and the subject of the litigation. A conclusion of unclean hands may be reached when "misconduct" of a party seeking relief "has *immediate and necessary relation* to the equity that he seeks in respect of *the matter in litigation*," i.e., "for such violations of

[416]Gilead Scis., Inc. v. Merck & Co, Inc., No. 13-CV-04057-BLF, 2016 WL 3143943, at *2 (N.D. Cal. June 6, 2016).

[417]*See supra* Section D.1 ("Inequitable Conduct").

[418]*Gilead,* 888 F.3d at 1240.

[419]*Gilead,* 888 F.3d at 1239 (citing *Keystone Driller*, 290 U.S. 240 (1933)).

conscience as in some measure affect the equitable relations between the parties in respect of something brought before the court."[420]

Based in equity, the unclean hands doctrine is certainly not limited to patent cases. But the Federal Circuit views it as "ha[ving] some distinctive features affecting the patent system."[421] For example, the Supreme Court's foundational *Keystone Driller* case involved the attempted enforcement of mechanical patents concerning parts of a ditching machine.[422] When the patentee in *Keystone Driller* became aware of a prior use that might have invalidated the patents, it paid the prior-using individual to prepare an affidavit that his use was merely an abandoned experiment, to keep secret the details of the prior use, and to suppress evidence about the prior use. When that individual was deposed, he did not disclose his arrangement with the patentee. When the defendants later reexamined him, they were able "to compel the plaintiff to furnish the details of the corrupt transaction."[423] The patentee's misconduct had allowed it to obtain a decree sustaining the validity of its patents in a prior case, which the patentee relied on in later enforcement efforts, including the case at bar. The *Keystone Driller* Court inferred that

> from the beginning it was plaintiff's intention through suppression of... evidence to obtain decree [of validity] in the [earlier] Byers Case for use in subsequent infringement suits against these defendants and others, it does clearly appear that the plaintiff made the Byers Case a part of his preparation in these suits. The use actually made of that decree is sufficient to show that plaintiff did not come with clean hands in respect of any cause of action in these cases.[424]

The following facts supported application of the unclean hands defense in *Gilead.* Because the Hepatitis C virus ("HCV") is a bloodborne virus that attacks and invades a patient's liver with the potential for serious harm, a number of pharmaceutical research firms investigated improved treatment options to fight HCV in the 1990s and 2000s.[425] DJ defendant/patentee Merck was one such company. Merck's U.S. Patents No. 7,105,499 ('499 patent) and No. 8,481,712 ('712 patent) claimed priority to 2001.[426] A Merck chemist and patent attorney, Dr. Phillipe Durette, handled the initial prosecution of the

[420]*Keystone Driller,* 290 U.S. at 245 (emphasis added).
[421]*Gilead,* 888 F.3d at 1239 n.2.
[422]*Keystone Driller,* 290 U.S. at 242.
[423]*Keystone Driller,* 290 U.S. at 244.
[424]*Keystone Driller,* 290 U.S. at 247.
[425]Gilead Scis., Inc. v. Merck & Co, Inc., No. 13-CV-04057-BLF, 2016 WL 3143943, at *4 (N.D. Cal. June 6, 2016).
[426]The '712 patent issued from a continuation of the application that became the '499 patent. The two patents shared a common specification.

patents. The patent claims as originally filed were broad in scope, included those in the *Markush* format,[427] and encompassed a "substantial number of possible constituents."[428]

Gilead (through Pharmasset, the pharmaceutical company it later purchased) developed its own Hepatitis C treatments. A Pharmasset chemist, Jeremy Clark, proposed a chemical compound called "PSI-6130," Pharmasset's first compound that was active against HCV. The PSI-6130 compound in turn led to the chemical compound sofosbuvir. Gilead ultimately obtained USFDA approval to sell the Sovaldi® and Harvoni® products based on sofosbuvir.

In the early 2000s, Merck and Pharmasset (later Gilead) discussed possible collaboration on discovery and development of antiviral agents against HCV. The two companies signed a nondisclosure agreement in 2001. Their interactions ultimately led to the misconduct forming the "unclean hands" determination against Merck.

The work of chemist Jeremy Clark allowed Pharmasset (later Gilead) to file in May 2003 its own patent application claiming PSI-6130 and numerous related compounds (referred to by the parties as the "Clark application"). The USPTO published the Clark application in January 2005. Notably, one month after the Clark application published, Merck (through its prosecution counsel Dr. Durette) filed a narrowing amendment to target PSI-6130 in the pending Merck application that later issued as Merck's '499 patent. As the Federal Circuit described it, "Merck seem[ed] to accept that the '499 patent claims include[d] PSI-6130" and Gilead "characterize[d] the claim as 'target[ing]' PSI-6130."[429] Merck's '499 and '712 patents issued in 2006 and 2013, respectively.

Gilead in 2013 brought an action in federal court seeking a declaratory judgment that (1) its sofosbuvir-based products, Sovaldi® and Harvoni®, did not infringe the Merck '499 and '712 patents; (2) the Merck patents were invalid based on non-compliance with the enablement and written description requirements of 35 U.S.C. §112, first paragraph, which assertions were tied to an allegation of derivation from Pharmasset's Jeremy Clark;[430] and (3) the Merck patents were unenforceable based on "unclean hands" grounded on Merck's misconduct both before and during the declaratory judgment lawsuit. Merck counter-claimed for infringement by Gilead of Merck's '499 and '712 patents.

[427]The *Markush* format for patent claim drafting is examined *supra* Chapter 2, Section E.4.

[428]*Gilead*, 888 F.3d at 1234.

[429]*Gilead*, 888 F.3d at 1237.

[430]In general terms, the concept of "derivation" in patent law refers to a person copying the invention of another and thereafter wrongly claiming the invention as her own. Derivation is examined *supra* Chapter 4, Section M.

A jury sustained the validity of Merck's patents and awarded damages to Merck, Gilead having stipulated to infringement based on the district court's claim constructions. Because validity under the enablement and written description requirements of 35 U.S.C. §112 was sustained, the issue of Merck's alleged derivation from Pharmasset's Jeremy Clark was not tried.

Nevertheless, the district court thereafter refused to enforce the Merck patents due to Merck's unclean hands. The district court held a bench trial on Gilead's equitable defenses and concluded that Merck could not enforce its '499 and '712 patents due to both pre-litigation business misconduct and litigation misconduct attributable to Merck. After balancing the equities, the district court applied its unenforceability remedy to both the '499 and '712 patents, although the latter '712 patent presented a "closer" question than the '499 patent.[431]

The misconduct identified by the district court focused on the actions of Merck's Dr. Durette, who prosecuted the '499 patent. Before publication of the Clark application in January 2005, Durette first learned about Pharmasset's PSI-6130 structure in a March 2004 "due diligence" conference call between Merck and Pharmasset representatives. The district court found that Dr. Durette's participation in the 2004 call violated a clear "firewall" understanding between the companies that the call participants would not be involved in Merck's HCV-related patent prosecutions.[432] The court further found that Dr. Durette knew before the call "that any information he learned about Pharmasset's PSI-6130 nucleoside analog compound would overlap with the subject matter of his patent prosecution docket for Merck, thereby creating a conflict."[433]

Even after the March 2004 conference call, Merck improperly continued to use Dr. Durette to prosecute the Merck patent applications. The district court found that "[i]nstead of withdrawing from prosecution, Dr. Durette continued to prosecute Merck's HCV patent applications and write new claims that targeted Pharmasset's work."[434] On appeal,

[431]*Gilead*, 888 F.3d at 1247. The '712 patent issued from a continuation of the application that became the '499 patent. The two patents shared a common specification. The district court determined that although another attorney took over the '712 patent's prosecution in 2011, Dr. Durette had filed the application. The misconduct in the '499 patent was severe enough to also prevent enforcement of the related '712 patent. "Merck and Dr. Durette's intentional litigation misconduct casts a darkness on this entire case that covers both patents-in-suit." *Gilead*, 2016 WL 3143943, at *36. The Federal Circuit agreed. *Gilead,* 888 F.3d at 1247 ("[W]e also see no abuse of discretion in the district court's ultimate conclusion that the unclean hands defense extends to that ['712] patent as well.").

[432]*Gilead*, 888 F.3d at 1240-1241. The firewall obligation "excluded anyone involved with Merck's internal HCV program." *Gilead*, 888 F.3d at 1242 (citing 2016 WL 3143943, at *9).

[433]*Gilead,* 888 F.3d at 1241 (citing *Gilead*, 2016 WL 3143943, at *9).

[434]*Gilead,* 888 F.3d at 1242 (citing *Gilead*, 2016 WL 3143943, at *10).

the Circuit found "adequate evidentiary support" for both these district court findings.

The Federal Circuit in *Gilead* also agreed with the district court's finding that the requisite direct connection or nexus existed between the challenged misconduct and the Gilead-Merck patent litigation at bar.[435] The appellate court concluded that Durette's "knowledge of PSI-6130, acquired improperly, influenced Merck's filing of narrowed claims, a filing that held the potential for expediting patent issuance and for lowering certain invalidity risks."[436] Durette would not have submitted new, narrower claims to target PSI-6130 in February 2005 "but for his improper participation on the March 17, 2004 patent due diligence call and learning the structure of PSI-6130 ahead of the structure being published."[437] Admittedly, Merck's broader pending claims before the February 2005 amendment *included* PSI-6130 and similar structures, but Merck obtained benefits from Dr. Durette narrowing its claims: prosecution was expedited; the scope of the Examiner's search was lessened; prior art would present less of an invalidity risk with narrower claims; and it became more likely that the "full scope" of narrower claims would be enabled.[438]

Merck argued that Gilead did not suffer any harm due to Dr. Durette's actions because "Merck did not obtain patent coverage that it would not have otherwise obtained."[439] Agreeing with the district court, the Federal Circuit rejected this argument. Merck's attempt to reframe or couch the *Keystone Driller* unclean hands standard in terms of "materiality," a concept central to the unenforceability defense of inequitable conduct in patent procurement, was not "helpful[].[440] Rather,

> for purposes of this case, which involves clear misconduct in breaching commitments to a third party and clear misconduct in litigation, the "immediate and necessary relation" standard, in its natural meaning, generally must be met if the conduct normally would enhance the claimant's position regarding legal rights that are important to the litigation

[435]*Gilead*, 888 F.3d at 1241.
[436]*Gilead*, 888 F.3d at 1241.
[437]*Gilead,* 888 F.3d at 1243 (citing *Gilead*, 2016 WL 3143943, at *11).
[438]*Gilead,* 888 F.3d at 1243-1244.
[439]*Gilead*, 2016 WL 3143943, at *36 (N.D. Cal. June 6, 2016).
[440]*See* Therasense, Inc. v. Becton, Dickson & Co., 649 F.3d 1276, 1287 (Fed. Cir. 2011) (*en banc*), explaining that

> [t]his court recognizes that the early unclean hands cases do not present any standard for materiality. Needless to say, this court's development of a materiality requirement for inequitable conduct does not (and cannot) supplant Supreme Court precedent. Though inequitable conduct developed from these cases, the unclean hands doctrine remains available to supply a remedy for egregious misconduct like that in the Supreme Court cases.

> if the impropriety is not discovered and corrected. Merck cites no authority holding such misconduct to be outside *Keystone*'s scope. Nor does Merck deny that the standard can cover at least some misconduct that ultimately fails to affect the litigation, as when it is discovered before it bears fruit, as long as its objective potential to have done so is sufficient.[441]

Applying this standard from *Keystone Driller*,[442] in order for Gilead to prevail on its unclean hands defense it would need to show that Merck's misconduct had "immediate and necessary relation" to the equity Merck sought in the case at hand — enforcement of its patents against Gilead. The Circuit determined that Gilead had successfully proved satisfaction of the *Keystone Driller* test. The district court's findings "establish[ed] serious misconduct, violating clear standards of probity in the circumstances, that led to the acquisition of the less risky '499 patent and, thus, was immediately and necessarily related to the equity" sought by Merck in the litigation — enforcement of its '499 and '712 patents against Gilead.[443]

It is important to realize that it is *not* improper to amend a pending patent application to cover a competitor's known product, assuming adequate §112 support for the amended claims in the application.[444] The Federal Circuit so held in its 1988 decision, *Kingsdown Med. Consultants, Ltd. v. Hollister Inc.*[445]

But the *Gilead* case went far beyond this. Merck amended its application one month after the publication of Gilead's application disclosing PSI-6130, adding narrower claims that included Gilead's PSI-6130. The issue in *Gilead* was not merely that Merck sought narrower claims to "target" Gilead's published sofosbuvir compound. Rather, the issue was that Merck acted improperly in gaining knowledge of the compound and its structure, thus allowing it to amend its claims in a way that gave it an improper advantage in the ensuing litigation.

[441]*Gilead,* 888 F.3d at 1240.

[442]*Gilead,* 888 F.3d at 1239 (citing *Keystone Driller*, 290 U.S. 240 (1933)).

[443]*Gilead*, 888 F.3d at 1240.

[444]*See* Kingsdown Med. Consultants, Ltd. v. Hollister Inc., 863 F.2d 867, 874 (Fed. Cir. 1988), explaining that

> there is nothing improper, illegal or inequitable in filing a patent application for the purpose of obtaining a right to exclude a known competitor's product from the market; nor is it in any manner improper to amend or insert claims intended to cover a competitor's product the applicant's attorney has learned about during the prosecution of a patent application. Any such amendment or insertion must comply with all statutes and regulations, of course, but, if it does, its genesis in the marketplace is simply irrelevant and cannot of itself evidence deceitful intent. *State Indus., Inc. v. A.O. Smith Corp.*, 751 F.2d 1226, 1235, 224 U.S.P.Q. 418, 424 (Fed. Cir. 1985).

[445]863 F.3d 867 (Fed. Cir. 1988).

According to the parties' "firewall" agreement, Dr. Durette should not have participated in the 2004 conference call, which first disclosed to Merck the structure of Pharmasset's PSI-6130 compound. Moreover, Durette continued after the conference call to act as the attorney prosecuting Merck's pending application that became the '499 patent. The district court in *Gilead* recognized the distinction between the proper amendment of pending claims à la *Kingsdown Med. Consultants, Ltd. v. Hollister, Inc.*[446] and Merck's improper conduct:

> Th[is court] finds *Kingsdown*'s holding is premised entirely on the assumption that a patentee learns of a competitors' product through legal and ethical means. Here, Merck learned of PSI-6130, Pharmasset's crown jewel, during its due diligence of Pharmasset. This information was provided to Merck in a confidential setting to Merck employees who were purportedly firewalled from the prosecution of Merck's HCV patents. The Federal Circuit's holding in *Kingsdown* does not permit individuals to disregard firewalls and confidentiality agreements; holding otherwise, would bring the marketplace to a halt as companies would be weary to engage in due diligence lest a competitor uses that information to obtain patents.[447]

The second form of "unclean hands" misconduct found in *Gilead* was Merck's litigation misconduct. This conduct involved Dr. Durette's participation as a witness in the Merck litigation with Gilead, which was held attributable to Merck.[448] Firstly, Dr. Durette in his deposition testimony "definitively" and "repeatedly" denied participating in the March 2004 conference call with Pharmasset. That denial was false; Durette later acknowledged at trial that he did participate and Merck did not dispute this.[449]

Secondly, the district court found un-credible Dr. Durette's testimony seeking to downplay the importance of the March 2004 conference call to the prosecution of Merck's '499 patent. In the Circuit view, the district court "reasonably found that [Durette] had in mind the information he learned in the March 2004 call, that he was waiting for publication of PSI-6130's structure to avoid violating the non-disclosure agreement, and that he filed the February 2005 amendment once publication of the Clark Application occurred [in January 2005]."[450] Based on those findings, the Circuit deemed reasonable

[446]863 F.2d 867 (Fed. Cir. 1988) (partially *en banc*).

[447]*Gilead*, 2016 WL 3143943, at *34.

[448]E.g., Merck designated Dr. Durette as its Fed. R. Civ. P. 30(b)(6) witness to represent the corporation during the litigation with regard to the prosecution of the application that issued as the '499 patent.

[449]*Gilead*, 888 F.3d at 1244-1245.

[450]*Gilead*, 888 F.3d at 1246.

the district court's characterization of Dr. Durette's trial testimony as "a misleading effort to downplay the role of Pharmasset's work in the February 2005 amendment."[451]

The *Keystone* standard for unclean hands was satisfied as to Durette's litigation testimony, which the district court found to be intentionally false. Moreover, the testimony had an "immediate and necessary relation" to the equity sought by Merck in the case at bar — patent enforcement against Gilead. The testimony was relevant to issues to be tried in the case; namely, Gilead's invalidity assertions under 35 U.S.C. §112. The *Gilead* Circuit explained that the jury verdict form made explicit that "lack of written description and lack of enablement were tied to the defense of 'derivation from Jeremy Clark' (the Pharmasset inventor of PSI-6130) — [derivation] to be addressed only if the jury found either lack of an adequate written description or lack of enablement."[452]

Additionally, Merck realized that the origin of the '455 patent claims could matter in eventual litigation over their validity, as confirmed by Merck's own policy of separating patent prosecutors from discussions like the ones held with Pharmasset. Dr. Durette's testimony downplaying the role of Pharmasset's Clark Application and the March 2004 conference call "naturally served to aid Merck's case that it did not derive the claimed inventions from Pharmasset's Jeremy Clark."[453] Thus it was reasonable for the district court to have determined that Dr. Durette's testimony "held a significant potential to give Merck an advantage in the litigation, satisfying the *Keystone* standard."

Because the district court had not abused its discretion in applying the unclean hands doctrine against Merck, the Federal Circuit affirmed the judgment that Merck's '499 and '712 patents were unenforceable.

In the view of this author, the *Gilead v. Merck* case tells a story of egregious falsehoods and acts of misconduct that were eventually brought to light when Merck tried to assert its patent. Notably, some of the misconduct involved acts that occurred during prosecution of Merck's patents in the USPTO. But because Merck did not mislead or otherwise convey false information to the USPTO, *Gilead* is not an "inequitable conduct" case. Rather, *Gilead* reinforces that the overarching doctrine of "unclean hands" has an active role to play as a tool to deter bad behavior in procuring and enforcing patents.

[451] *Gilead,* 888 F.3d at 1246.
[452] *Gilead,* 888 F.3d at 1246.
[453] *Gilead,* 888 F.3d at 1247.

E. Invalidity

Section 282(b)(2) and (b)(3) permit the defense of invalidity of an issued patent to be asserted on the same grounds that could have prohibited patentability in the USPTO, that is, a failure to satisfy one or more of the statutory criteria set forth at 35 U.S.C. §§101, 102, 103, and 112 (with the post-AIA exception of the best mode requirement of 35 U.S.C. §112(a)). Patents reissued in accordance with 35 U.S.C. §251 also are susceptible to invalidation under the same statutory grounds.

1. Burden of Proof

Section 282(a) of the Patent Act, 35 U.S.C., provides that

> **In general.**— A patent shall be presumed valid. Each claim of a patent (whether in independent, dependent, or multiple dependent form) shall be presumed valid independently of the validity of the other claims; dependent or multiple dependent claims shall be presumed valid even though dependent upon an invalid claim. The burden of establishing invalidity of a patent or any claim thereof shall rest on the party asserting such invalidity.[454]

An issued U.S. patent is thus entitled to a presumption of validity in accordance with 35 U.S.C. §282(a). This presumption is based, at least in part, on an assumption of "administrative correctness" — that the USPTO did a thorough, competent job when it examined the patent application and decided to issue the patent.[455] Because the patent owner benefits from the presumption of validity, it need not affirmatively establish that its patent is valid in order to bring an infringement lawsuit. Rather, the burden is on the accused infringer to rebut the presumption of validity created by 35 U.S.C. §282(a).

The statute does not specify what evidentiary quantum is needed to satisfy the burden of proof on invalidity. However, judicial decisions make clear that the burden in federal court litigation challenging patent validity is "clear and convincing" evidence, which means that the validity challenger (i.e., the accused infringer) can rebut the presumption only if it establishes invalidity by "clear and convincing"

[454] 35 U.S.C. §282(a) (eff. Sept. 16, 2012).

[455] *See* Applied Materials, Inc. v. Advanced Semiconductor Materials America, Inc., 98 F.3d 1563, 1569 (Fed. Cir. 1996) (explaining that "[t]he presumption of validity is based on the presumption of administrative correctness of actions of the agency charged with examination of patentability"); Interconnect Planning Corp. v. Feil, 774 F.2d 1132, 1139 (Fed. Cir. 1985) (stating that presumption of validity "derives in part from recognition of the technological expertise of the patent examiners").

evidence.[456] The quantum of evidence represented by the "clear and convincing" burden is understood to be somewhat more than a mere "preponderance" (or 51 percent) of the evidence, the typical burden of proof in civil litigation, and somewhat less than "beyond a reasonable doubt,"[457] the burden for criminal convictions. The Supreme Court has characterized clear and convincing evidence as "plac[ing] in the ultimate factfinder an abiding conviction that the truth of its factual contentions are 'highly probable.'"[458] It is a "heavy" burden.[459]

Twenty-first-century patent litigation reflects the growing impact of patent-enforcing "non-practicing entities" (NPEs), sometimes pejoratively referred to as "patent trolls."[460] NPEs own patents but do not manufacture or sell the products covered by the patents and do not compete in the marketplace through such manufacture or sale. The number of infringement lawsuits filed by NPEs rose sharply in the decade of 2000-2010.[461]

Several leading technology companies, including those frequently targeted by NPEs, took the position that the burden of proof to invalidate issued patents should be less than the "clear and convincing" quantum described above. The technology firms contended that accused infringers in infringement actions need only establish the defense of invalidity by a preponderance of the evidence. In particular, the firms asserted that the lesser preponderance standard should apply when an invalidity defense rested on "newly discovered" prior art, that is, evidence of invalidity that was never considered in the first instance by the USPTO during the patent examination process.

The Supreme Court in 2011 rejected this argument in *Microsoft Corp. v. i4i Ltd. P'ship*.[462] The Court in *Microsoft* affirmed the Federal Circuit's interpretation of 35 U.S.C. §282 that invalidity of a patent must be established by clear and convincing evidence. Relying on its

[456]*See* Microsoft Corp. v. i4i Ltd. P'ship, 131 S. Ct. 2238 (2011), discussed *infra*.

[457]*See* Buildex, Inc. v. Kason Indus., Inc., 849 F.2d 1461, 1463 (Fed. Cir. 1988).

[458]Colorado v. New Mexico, 467 U.S. 310, 316 (1984) (quoting C. McCormick, Law of Evidence §320, at 679 (1954)).

[459]Microsoft Corp. v. i4i Ltd. P'ship, 131 S. Ct. 2238, 2246 (2011).

[460]*See Intellectual Property: Patent Medicine*, The Economist, Aug. 20, 2011, at 50 (referring to "the growing problem of 'patent trolls,' or firms that treat patents as lottery tickets and file expensive, time-consuming lawsuits against companies that have supposedly infringed them"); Ted Sichelman, *Commercializing Patents*, 62 Stan. L. Rev. 341, 368 (2010) (stating that "nonpracticing entities (NPEs) — namely, firms that do not commercialize their patented inventions and perform little to no R&D — are often termed 'patent trolls,' because they tend to exploit litigation and licensing market defects to extract unwarranted rents from commercializers, usually on patents that the commercializer was completely unaware of before the NPE's demand for payment").

[461]*See Intellectual-Property Battles: Patent Lather*, The Economist, Sept. 4, 2010, at 90 (citing report by PatentFreedom, a body that tracks the activity of NPEs, stating that the number of court cases brought by NPEs rose from 109 in 2001 to 470 in 2009).

[462]131 S. Ct. 2238 (2011) (Sotomayor, J.).

earlier decision in *Radio Corp. of America v. Radio Eng'g Labs., Inc.*,[463] the Court reasoned that when Congress stated that a patent is "presumed valid" in §282 of the 1952 Patent Act, it implicitly incorporated the established common law meaning (i.e., as expressed in judicial decisions) of that phrase.[464] By the time of the 1952 Act, the presumption of patent validity had the "settled meaning" that "a defendant raising an invalidity defense bore 'a heavy burden of persuasion,' requiring proof of the defense by clear and convincing evidence."[465] With respect to the argument that the "clear and convincing" burden should not be required when an accused infringer's proffered evidence of invalidity was never considered by the USPTO, the Court responded that if Congress had intended the burden of proof to vary with the facts of every case, it would have said so expressly when enacting §282 (but it did not).[466]

The *Microsoft* Court recognized, however, that a number of appellate decisions predating the 1952 Act characterized the presumption of validity as "weakened" or "dissipated" in cases involving evidence never considered by the USPTO. The Court viewed these decisions as simply "reflect[ing] the same commonsense principle that the Federal Circuit has recognized throughout its existence — namely, that new evidence supporting an invalidity defense may 'carry more weight' in an infringement action than evidence previously considered by the PTO."[467] Accordingly, the *Microsoft* Court observed that "if the PTO did not have all material facts [e.g., prior art] before it, its considered judgment may lose significant force . . . [a]nd, concomitantly, the challenger's burden to persuade the jury of its invalidity defense by clear and convincing evidence may be easier to sustain."[468]

[463]293 U.S. 1 (1934).

[464]*Microsoft*, 131 S. Ct. at 2245 (explaining that "by stating that a patent is 'presumed valid,' [35 U.S.C.] §282, Congress used a term with a settled meaning in the common law").

[465]*Microsoft*, 131 S. Ct. at 2246.

[466]Scholars contend that the "clear and convincing" burden of proof to invalidate a patent in federal district court litigation makes a real difference, at least in close cases. *See* Christopher B. Seaman, *Empirical Studies Relating to Patents — Presumption of Validity,* Research Handbook on the Economics of Intellectual Property Law — Vol. II: Analytical Methods (P. Menell, D. Schwartz & B. Depoorter eds., Edward Elgar), (2015) (concluding that "the existing empirical scholarship suggests that the presumption of validity and the standard of proof to overcome it matters in patent litigation, at least in close cases").

[467]*Microsoft*, 131 S. Ct. at 2251 (quoting Am. Hoist & Derrick Co. v. Sowa & Sons, Inc., 725 F.2d 1350, 1360 (Fed. Cir. 1984) (Rich, J.)). The Court earlier observed that Judge Rich was "a principal drafter of the 1952 Act. . . ." *Microsoft*, 131 S. Ct. at 2243.

[468]*Microsoft*, 131 S. Ct. at 2251. The Court further observed that although it had

> no occasion to endorse any particular formulation, we note that a jury instruction on the effect of new evidence can, and when requested, most often should be given. When warranted, the jury may be instructed to consider that it has heard

2. Collateral Estoppel Effect of Invalidity Adjudication

In *Blonder-Tongue Labs., Inc. v. Univ. of Ill. Found.*,[469] the Supreme Court held that once a U.S. patent has been declared invalid by a federal court, the patent owner is collaterally estopped to assert validity of that patent against another accused infringer. In other words, once a U.S. patent has been declared invalid, it is dead and cannot be resuscitated. This rule assumes, of course, that the patentee had a full and fair opportunity to litigate the issue of invalidity in the earlier proceeding and did not obtain a reversal on appeal.

In announcing the rule of collateral estoppel for patent invalidity the Supreme Court in *Blonder-Tongue* specifically rejected the requirement of "mutuality of estoppel" that it had previously espoused in *Triplett v. Lowell*,[470] a decision roundly criticized by other courts and commentators. Continued reliance on the mutuality doctrine would work an economic harm on participants in the patent system, the Court reasoned. Among those who would bear the brunt of this harm were alleged infringers, who would be forced to choose between bearing the high cost of defending against a patent already declared invalid or accepting a license and making royalty payments as a cost of litigation avoidance. In the words of the President's Commission on the Patent System, the Court concluded that the patentee whose patent has been declared invalid has already "had his 'day in court' and should not be allowed to harass others on the basis of an invalid claim."[471]

3. Statutory Grounds for Invalidity

Section 282(b) (eff. Sept. 16, 2012) provides that invalidity of a patent can be based on "any ground specified in part II [35 U.S.C. §§100 *et seq.*] as a condition for patentability." These grounds include 35

> evidence that the PTO had no opportunity to evaluate before granting the patent. When it is disputed whether the evidence presented to the jury differs from that evaluated by the PTO, the jury may be instructed to consider that question. In either case, the jury may be instructed to evaluate whether the evidence before it is materially new, and if so, to consider that fact when determining whether an invalidity defense has been proved by clear and convincing evidence.

Microsoft, 131 S. Ct. at 2251.

[469] 402 U.S. 313 (1971).

[470] 297 U.S. 638 (1936). The Court in *Triplett* held that a determination of patent invalidity is not *res judicata* as against the patentee in subsequent litigation against a different defendant. The *Triplett* decision "exemplified the judge-made doctrine of mutuality of estoppel, ordaining that unless both parties (or their privies) in a second action are bound by a judgment in a previous case, neither party (or his privy) in the second action may use the prior judgment as determinative of an issue in the second action." *Blonder-Tongue*, 402 U.S. at 320-321.

[471] *Id.* at 340.

U.S.C. §101 (patent-eligible subject matter and utility); 35 U.S.C. §102 (novelty); and 35 U.S.C. §103 (nonobviousness). In accordance with §282(b), each of these statutory criteria for patentability (separately discussed in earlier chapters of this text) also can serve as a basis for alleging invalidity of an issued patent. Invalidity also may be based on a "failure to comply with . . . any requirement of section 112" other than failure to disclose the best mode, or "any requirement of section 251."[472] Thus, an issued patent may be held invalid under 35 U.S.C. §112(a) if the specification is non-enabling or fails to provide a written description of the invention, or under 35 U.S.C. §112(b) if the claims are indefinite. A patent reissued in accordance with 35 U.S.C. §251 is subject to the same constraints. A reissued patent is also subject to invalidation if the reissue broadened the claims by means of a reissue application filed more than two years after the original patent issued.[473]

4. Limits on Accused Infringer's Standing to Assert Invalidity: Licensee Repudiation and Assignor Estoppel

U.S. patent jurisprudence recognizes certain judicially created limitations on an accused infringer's ability to challenge patent validity in cases where the accused infringer is or was in a contractual relationship with the patent owner. These limitations have been raised when the accused infringer is or was a licensee under the patent, or was the assignor of the patent (typically an inventor who has transferred title in the patent to her corporate employer). Such cases present the courts with a conflict between enforcement of the defendant's contractual obligations to the patentee under the common law and the federal policy that supports the invalidation of U.S. patents not satisfying the statutory requirements of patentability. Although the courts originally treated licensees and assignors in the same manner, so as to preclude either category of defendant from challenging patent validity, the current state of the law permits licensees to challenge validity in instances where assignors may not. These

[472] 35 U.S.C. §282(b)(3) (eff. Sept. 16, 2012). The AIA abrogated best mode non-compliance as an invalidity defense as of September 16, 2011, while retaining it as a requirement to obtain a patent in the first instance. *See* Leahy-Smith America Invents Act, Pub. L. No. 112-29 (H.R. 1249), §15, 125 Stat. 284, 328 (2011); 35 U.S.C. §282(b)(3)(A) (eff. Sept. 16, 2011). This dramatic change means that even if a patent was very likely invalid on September 15, 2011, for failure to satisfy the best mode disclosure requirement, as of September 16, 2011, the patent could no longer be challenged on that basis (so long as litigation was not already underway). *See supra* Chapter 3, Section C.1 ("Best Mode Scale-Back by America Invents Act of 2011").

[473] *See supra* Chapter 8, Section C.4 ("Broadening Reissues").

doctrines, referred to as licensee repudiation and assignor estoppel, are addressed separately below.

a. Licensee Repudiation

Can the licensee of a patent stop paying royalties to the patent owner and challenge the patent's validity if the licensee has a good faith belief that the patent is invalid? The Supreme Court answered affirmatively in *Lear, Inc. v. Adkins.*[474] The Court in *Lear* abrogated the earlier doctrine of licensee estoppel, which had held that in a contract action for unpaid patent royalties the licensee of the patent was estopped from challenging its validity. After *Lear,* licensee repudiation of a license on the ground that the licensed patent is invalid is not only permissible, but perhaps even encouraged.

The facts of *Lear* are as follows. The plaintiff Adkins was a former employee of the Lear Corporation who patented an invention directed to aviation gyroscopes. While Adkins' patent application was pending in the USPTO, he entered into a license agreement with the Lear Corporation. Lear subsequently stopped paying royalties to Adkins, claiming that the invention was anticipated by the prior art. After a lengthy prosecution, the Adkins patent issued. Adkins then sued Lear in California state court for breaching the license agreement. The case eventually progressed to the California Supreme Court, which sided with Adkins and held Lear estopped from challenging validity.

The U.S. Supreme Court reversed, holding that the Lear Corporation could avoid payment of all royalties accruing after Adkins' patent issued in 1960, assuming that Lear could successfully prove invalidity of the patent.[475] The Court recognized the conflict between the obligations of contract performance, requiring that a licensee should continue to pay royalties in exchange for the use of a patented invention, and the public's interest in full and free competition in the use of ideas that are in reality part of the public domain. It concluded that the equities favoring the public far outweighed those favoring Adkins, the licensor/patentee. Often the licensee (frequently a marketplace competitor of the patentee) is the only party with sufficient resources and adequate incentives to challenge the patent under which it is licensed. For the sake of the public at large, the law should not prevent such challenges. Particularly in the absence of a robust, European-style opposition procedure,[476] licensee repudiation may be one of the

[474]395 U.S. 653 (1969).

[475]*Id.* at 674. The question whether the Lear Corporation was nevertheless contractually obligated to pay Adkins royalties for access to his ideas, prior to patent issuance, was a closer call that required remand to the state courts. *See id.* at 674-675.

[476]*See, e.g.*, European Patent Convention arts. 99-105 (13th ed. 2007), *available at* https://www.epo.org/patents/law/legal-texts/html/epc/2016/e/ar99.html.

most important vehicles for ensuring that the U.S. public is not burdened by invalid patents.[477]

The policies underlying *Lear* are consistent with the result in the Supreme Court's more recent decision in *MedImmune, Inc. v. Genentech, Inc.*[478] The *MedImmune* Court allowed a *nonrepudiating* licensee (i.e., one who continued to pay royalties to the patentee under protest) to challenge the validity of the licensed patent. In *MedImmune,* however, the licensee's vehicle for challenging validity was its own lawsuit filed under the Declaratory Judgment Act, rather than raising invalidity as a defense to the patentee/licensor's breach of contract action as in *Lear.*[479] The key issue in *MedImmune* was whether a licensee in good standing satisfied the constitutional "Case[]" or "Controvers[y]" requirement for bringing a lawsuit in federal court, an issue not raised by *Lear.* The *MedImmune* decision and declaratory judgment actions in patent disputes are examined in greater detail later in this chapter.[480]

b. Assignor Estoppel

The Supreme Court did not have occasion in *Lear* to address the companion doctrine of assignor estoppel, which operates to estop validity challenges not by a licensee, but rather by the inventor who has assigned her rights under the patent to another for valuable consideration. In light of different policy concerns that are implicated in the assignment context but absent from mere licensing, the Federal Circuit distinguished *Lear* and upheld the assignor estoppel doctrine in *Diamond Scientific Co. v. Ambico, Inc.*[481]

While an employee of plaintiff Diamond Scientific, Dr. Clarence Welter invented and applied for three patents directed to a vaccine for gastroenteritis in swine. Welter assigned his rights in the patents to Diamond Scientific. When Welter later formed his own company, Ambico, doing business in competition with his former employer, Diamond Scientific sued Welter and Ambico for infringement of the patents. In response to Welter/Ambico's defense that the patents in

[477]Not all agree. For cogent criticisms and proposed modifications of *Lear*, *see* Rochelle Cooper Dreyfuss, *Dethroning* Lear*: Licensee Estoppel and the Incentive to Innovate,* 72 VA. L. REV. 677 (1986).

[478]549 U.S. 118 (2007).

[479]*See id.* at 145 n.2 (Thomas, J., dissenting) (observing that *Lear* "has little to do with this case. [*Lear*] addressed the propriety and extent of the common-law doctrine of licensee estoppel, and the licensee in *Lear* had ceased making payments under the license agreement — a fact that makes the case singularly inapposite here. *Lear* did not involve the Declaratory Judgment Act because the case was brought as a breach-of-contract action for failure to pay royalties.") (citations omitted).

[480]*See* Section G, *infra.*

[481]848 F.2d 1220 (Fed. Cir. 1988).

suit were invalid, Diamond Scientific contended that the doctrine of assignor estoppel prevented Welter and his new company from challenging validity.

The Federal Circuit acknowledged the continuing debate over the vitality of the assignor estoppel doctrine in the aftermath of *Lear*'s renunciation of the "somewhat analogous" doctrine of licensee estoppel, but nevertheless upheld the application of assignor estoppel against Welter as well as Ambico, a party in privity with Welter.[482] In the Circuit's view, the *Lear* public policy favoring a licensee's freedom to contest the validity of a patent under which it had taken a license is not present in the assignment situation. "Unlike the licensee, who, without *Lear* might be forced to continue to pay for a potentially invalid patent, the assignor who would challenge the patent has already been fully paid for the patent rights."[483]

The monetary distinction drawn by the court in *Diamond Scientific* between assignor and licensee is not particularly compelling. Given the public policy of encouraging challenges to invalid patents as expressed in *Lear*, it is difficult to understand why the identity of the party challenging validity — whether licensee or assignor — should matter. The assignor is most likely in the best position to challenge validity, perhaps even to a greater degree than the licensee in *Lear*, because the assignor is the inventor.

The contrary result in *Diamond Scientific* no doubt reflects the Federal Circuit's discomfort with the inequity of allowing a named inventor, who actively participated in the prosecution of the patent, signed an oath (attesting to his belief that he was the first and sole inventor, that the invention was never known or used in the United States before his invention, and that it had not been previously patented or described in a printed publication anywhere),[484] and had been subject to the duty of disclosure while the application was pending, to thereafter attempt to prove that what he attested to and assigned for a valuable consideration was in fact a nullity:[485]

[482]*Id.* at 1224. The extent to which the assignor's company is in privity and bound by the estoppel depends on how close a relationship exists between the parties, and may vary depending on whether the inventor was a mere employee or the "alter ego" of the corporation.

[483]*Id.*

[484]*Id.* at 1225.

[485]One possible exception to the rule of assignor estoppel might be where the assignee controlled prosecution of the patent application and authorized the amendment of its claims so as to significantly broaden them, without the inventor/assignor's knowledge or participation. *See* Westinghouse Elec. & Mfg. Co. v. Formica Insulation Co., 266 U.S. 342 (1924), in which the Court suggested that

> [w]hen the assignment is made before patent [has been granted], the claims are subject to change by curtailment or enlargement by the Patent Office with the acquiescence or at the instance of the assignee, and the extent of the claims to

> In other words, it is the implicit representation by the assignor that the patent rights that he is assigning (presumably for value) are not worthless that sets the assignor apart from the rest of the world and can deprive him of the ability to challenge later the validity of the patent. To allow the assignor to make that representation at the time of the assignment (to his advantage) and later to repudiate it (again to his advantage) could work an injustice against the assignee.[486]

Because the equities weighed heavily in favor of Diamond Scientific, the Federal Circuit concluded that the doctrine of assignor estoppel should be applied against Welter and Ambico, even while admitting that "the doctrine of assignor estoppel may no longer be a broad equitable device susceptible of automatic application."[487]

Following *Diamond Scientific*, the Federal Circuit has confronted other assertions of the assignor estoppel doctrine and continues to apply it to preclude challenges to validity by patent assignors, while recognizing the doctrine's potential inapplicability in certain narrow circumstances such as an assignor's express reservation of the right to later challenge the assigned patent.[488] The assignor estoppel defense is commonly raised in the "departed inventor" scenario, where it may preclude the inventor's new employer from challenging a patent's validity:

> The doctrine [of assignor estoppel] often arises in factual scenarios similar to the facts of this case, where an employee invents something during his or her tenure with a company, assigns the rights to that invention to his or her employer, then leaves the company to join or found a competing

---

> be allowed may ultimately include more than the assignor [inventor] intended to claim. This difference might justify the view that the range of relevant and competent evidence in fixing the limits of the subsequent estoppel should be more liberal than in the case of an assignment of a granted patent. How this may be, we do not find it necessary to decide.

Id. at 353.

[486]*Diamond Scientific*, 848 F.2d at 1224.

[487]*Id.* at 1225.

[488]*See, e.g.*, MAG Aerospace Indus., Inc. v. B/E Aerospace, Inc., 2016 WL 1128100 (Fed. Cir. 2016) (affirming district court's determination that assignor estoppel barred accused infringer B/E from challenging validity of patents in suit because one of patents' inventors now worked for B/E and was in privity with B/E; inventor's former employer/assignee had assigned patents to MAG); Mentor Graphics Corp. v. Quickturn Design Sys., Inc., 150 F.3d 1374, 1378 (Fed. Cir. 1998) (affirming district court's application of assignor estoppel and concluding that exceptional circumstances justifying departure from doctrine, such as an express reservation by assignor of the right to challenge patent's validity or an express waiver by assignee of the right to assert patent's validity, were not present).

Professor Lemley criticizes the Federal Circuit for dramatically expanding the doctrine of assignor estoppel beyond its traditionally limited roots in Mark A. Lemley, *Rethinking Assignor Estoppel*, 54 Houston L. Rev. (2016).

company. *See, e.g., Westinghouse* [Westinghouse Elec. & Mfg. Co. v. Formica Insulation Co., 266 U.S. 342 (1924)], 266 U.S. at 345-46, 45 S. Ct. 117; Shamrock Techs., Inc. v. Med. Sterilization, Inc., 903 F.2d 789, 790 (Fed. Cir. 1990); Diamond Sci. Co. v. Ambico, Inc., 848 F.2d 1220, 1222 (Fed. Cir. 1988). In such situations, the employee's new company may be estopped because "[a]ssignor estoppel also prevents parties in privity with an estopped assignor from challenging the validity of the patent." *Mentor Graphics* [Mentor Graphics Corp. v. Quickturn Design Sys., Inc., 150 F.3d 1374 (Fed. Cir. 1998)], 150 F.3d at 1379; see also *Diamond Sci.*, 848 F.2d at 1224 ("The estoppel also operates to bar other parties in privity with the assignor, such as a corporation founded by the assignor.").[489]

In 2018, the Federal Circuit held that the assignor estoppel defense is not available to preclude *inter partes* review of a patent in the USPTO.[490]

F. Antitrust Counterclaims

Section 282(b) of 35 U.S.C. does not speak to the assertion of antitrust liability on the part of the patent owner as a defense to a charge of infringement. Therefore a patent owner's alleged violation of the antitrust laws is not asserted by an accused infringer as an affirmative defense, but rather as the subject of a counterclaim.[491] Nevertheless, antitrust counterclaims in patent infringement cases are included in

[489]Arista Networks, Inc. v. Cisco Sys., Inc., 908 F.3d 792, 801 (Fed. Cir. 2018) (Prost, C.J.).

[490]In *Arista Networks, Inc. v. Cisco Sys., Inc.*, 908 F.3d 792 (Fed. Cir. 2018) (Prost, C.J.), the Circuit held that the defense of assignor estoppel doctrine cannot be asserted to prevent one's patent from undergoing a post-grant patentability challenge in the USPTO such as *inter partes* review (IPR). These challenges are detailed *supra* Chapter 8, Section E ("AIA-Implemented Procedures for Challenging Issues Patents"). In *Arista,* the inventor of Cisco's challenged network device security patent, Dr. Cheriton, was employed by Cisco at the time of the invention and assigned all his rights therein to Cisco. Later in time, Cheriton and fellow Cisco employees left the company in order to found Arista, which became a competitor of Cisco. Arista thereafter filed a petition for IPR seeking to invalidate the Cisco patent on the grounds of anticipation or obviousness. The Federal Circuit affirmed the USPTO PTAB's holding that the defense of assignor estoppel is not validly raised to preclude IPR. The appellate court construed 35 U.S.C. §311(a), which allows "a person who is not the owner of a patent" to file a petition to institute IPR, and concluded that the statute "unambiguously dictates that assignor estoppel has no place in IPR proceedings," even when the person filing the petition to cancel the patent is the current employer of the patent's inventor. *See Arista,* 908 F.3d at 804. In the Circuit's view, the statutory language was not ambiguous and left "no room for assignor estoppel in the IPR context." *Arista,* 908 F.3d at 803.

[491]*See* Nobelpharma AB v. Implant Innovations, Inc., 141 F.3d 1059, 1067 (Fed. Cir. 1998) (stating that "an antitrust claim premised on stripping a patentee of its immunity from the antitrust laws is typically raised as a counterclaim by a defendant in a patent infringement suit").

this chapter because they are the subject of increasing interest among the antitrust bar and Federal Circuit watchers in general.[492]

Antitrust counterclaims in patent cases are most commonly brought under §2 of the Sherman Act, which prohibits acquisition or maintenance of monopoly power through anticompetitive conduct.[493] Patents have been viewed (in somewhat pejorative fashion) as "monopolies," such that accused infringers of patents have asserted (under certain limited circumstances) that patent owners' enforcement of their "monopoly" rights represented a violation of the antitrust laws. The mere assertion of patent rights is certainly not enough to give rise to antitrust liability, however; the party asserting a Sherman Act §2 monopolization must show (1) that the patentee has monopoly power in the relevant market, and (2) that it has acquired or is maintaining that power in an anticompetitive manner.[494] These elements are commonly abbreviated as "market power" and "anticompetitive conduct." Each element is addressed below.

1. Market Power

In practice, the requirement for a showing of market power[495] excludes much of typical patent owner behavior from antitrust prosecution.[496] The mere fact that a firm owns a patent on a particular

[492]A very useful resource on the topic of the patent-antitrust intersection and the Federal Circuit's growing role therein is the collection of articles published at *Symposium: The Federal Circuit and Antitrust,* 69 ANTITRUST L.J. 627-849 (2001).

[493]*See* 15 U.S.C. §2 (providing that "[e]very person who shall monopolize, or attempt to monopolize, or combine or conspire with any other person or persons, to monopolize any part of the trade or commerce among the several States, or with foreign nations, shall be deemed guilty of a felony . . .").

[494]*See* U.S. Philips Corp. v. Windmere Corp., 861 F.2d 695, 703 (Fed. Cir. 1988) (quoting United States v. Grinnell Corp., 384 U.S. 563, 570-571 (1966)). The Court in *Grinnell* held that

> [t]he offense of monopoly under §2 of the Sherman Act has two elements: (1) the possession of monopoly power in the relevant market and (2) the willful acquisition or maintenance of that power as distinguished from growth or development as a consequence of a superior product, business acumen, or historic accident.

Id.

[495]Market power is "the ability profitably to maintain prices above, or output below, competitive levels for a significant period of time." United States Department of Justice, *Antitrust Guidelines for the Licensing of Intellectual Property* §2.2 (1995), *available at* https://www.justice.gov/atr/archived-1995-antitrust-guidelines-licensing-intellectual-property. The DOJ and FTC "will not presume that a patent . . . necessarily confers market power upon its owner." *Id.* at §5.3.

[496]*See* Robert Merges, *Reflections on Current Legislation Affecting Patent Misuse,* 70 J. PAT. & TRADEMARK OFF. SOC'Y 793, 793 (1988) (noting that "the often very limited (or 'thin') markets for patented technology make it difficult to apply antitrust law's consumer-demand definition of the relevant market"). *See also* Richard Calkins, *Patent*

invention does not in and of itself demonstrate the requisite market power, because the antitrust law of market definition recognizes the possibility of noninfringing substitutes for the patented technology.[497] Moreover, the successful assertion of an antitrust counterclaim against a patent owner bringing an infringement suit is relatively rare because of certain antitrust protections given to intellectual property holders, discussed below.

The need for rigorous economic analysis of relevant market in patent/antitrust cases was emphasized in *Unitherm Food Sys., Inc. v. Swift-Eckrich, Inc.*[498] There the Federal Circuit vacated the judgment of a district court entered on a jury verdict that had found patent owner Swift-Eckrich (d/b/a ConAgra Refrigerated Foods) liable under the antitrust laws for attempted monopolization in the amount of $18 million in trebled damages. "The district court erred," the Federal Circuit concluded, "in allowing the jury to decide Unitherm's antitrust claims despite the total absence of economic evidence capable of sustaining those claims."[499]

Applying Tenth Circuit law to those antitrust issues not intertwined with patent law, the Federal Circuit in *Unitherm* explained that a relevant product market is composed of "products that have reasonable interchangeability for the purposes for which they are produced."[500] Market definition hinges on economic evidence, the

---

Law: The Impact of the 1988 Patent Misuse Reform Act and Noerr-Pennington *Doctrine on Misuse Defenses and Antitrust Counterclaims*, 38 DRAKE L. REV. 175, 187 (1988-1989) (noting that "[a]s a practical matter, requiring proof of an antitrust violation to check a patentee's economic extension of his patent monopoly may mean that such violations will go unchecked because excessive costs and uncertainty are inherent in proving a rule of reason violation or monopolization charge").

[497]*See* Ill. Tool Works Inc. v. Indep. Ink, Inc., 547 U.S. 28, 45-46 (2006) ("Congress, the antitrust enforcement agencies, and most economists have all reached the conclusion that a patent does not necessarily confer market power upon the patentee. Today, we reach the same conclusion. . . ."); Abbott Labs. v. Brennan, 952 F.2d 1346, 1354-1355 (Fed. Cir. 1991). As Justice O'Connor explained,

> A common misconception has been that a patent or copyright, a high market share, or a unique product that competitors are not able to offer suffices to demonstrate market power. While each of these three factors might help to give market power to a seller, it is also possible that a seller in these situations will have no market power: for example, a patent holder has no market power in any relevant sense if there are close substitutes for the patented product. Similarly, a high market share indicates market power only if the market is properly defined to include all reasonable substitutes for the product. *See generally* Landes & Posner, *Market Power in Antitrust Cases,* 94 HARV. L. REV. 937 (1981).

Jefferson Parish Hospital Dist. No. 2 v. Hyde, 466 U.S. 2, 33 (1984) (O'Connor, J., concurring).

[498]375 F.3d 1341 (Fed. Cir. 2004).

[499]*Id.* at 1344.

[500]*Id.* at 1363.

Federal Circuit observed. In this case, Unitherm's expert witness had defined the relevant product market as synonymous with the patented invention, a process for browning pre-cooked meats. The expert identified seven benefits of the patented process that no other similar process possessed and that, in his opinion, made the invention unique. The expert's testimony, "or at least the relevant excerpts in the appellate record, cannot sustain Unitherm's definition of a relevant market," the Federal Circuit concluded. The expert's testimony addressed *technological* substitutability but not *economic* substitutability. Nothing in the record addressed "whether potential customers of the patented process faced with a price increase would shift to other processes offering different combinations of benefits."[501] This determination "lies at the heart of market definition in antitrust analysis." "Not only is economic substitutability critical to market definition," the Federal Circuit explained, but also "it is improper to interpret 'the Sherman Act to require that products be fungible to be considered in the relevant market.' "[502] The minimal economic evidence in the record "suggested strongly" that Unitherm's expert's market definition was incorrect. In particular, the Federal Circuit found ConAgra's inability to attract any licensees indicative of a lack of pricing power — "the single most important element in defining a relevant antitrust market."[503]

Despite its economics-focused treatment of market power in the context of Sherman Act §2 cases such as *Unitherm,* the Federal Circuit in 2005 took a very different approach to market power in another patent/antitrust context, that of patent tying[504] under Sherman Act §1.[505] In *Indep. Ink, Inc. v. Ill. Tools Works, Inc.*,[506] the appellate court recognized a presumption of market power on the part of the patent owner

[501] *Id.* at 1364.

[502] *Id.* at 1364 (quoting United States v. E.I. Du Pont de Nemours & Co., 351 U.S. 377, 394 (1956), and citing generally U.S. Department of Justice, *Merger Guidelines* (1982), ch. 1.1 (describing the antitrust agencies' approach to product market definition in a merger analysis and the critical rule of economic substitutability)).

[503] *Id.* at 1364.

[504] A tying arrangement is "an agreement by a party to sell one product . . . on the condition that the buyer also purchases a different (or tied) product, or at least agrees that he will not purchase that [tied] product from any other supplier." Eastman Kodak Co. v. Image Tech. Servs., Inc., 504 U.S. 451, 461 (1992).

[505] Section 1 of the Sherman Act declares illegal "[e]very contract, combination in the form of trust or otherwise, or conspiracy, in restraint of trade or commerce among the several States, or with foreign nations." 15 U.S.C. §1. In the patent context, the types of contracts most typically encountered are agreements between patent owners and third-party licensees, or agreements between multiple patent owners to "cross-license" their respective patents or to form patent "pools." Generally such agreements are viewed as procompetitive, but antitrust concerns may arise. Section 1 principles may also be relevant with respect to mergers and acquisitions between patent-owning firms.

[506] 396 F.3d 1342 (Fed. Cir. 2005).

in a tying case, a presumption rejected shortly thereafter by the Supreme Court as discussed below. Defendant Trident (a wholly owned subsidiary of Illinois Tool Works) held a patent on printheads[507] and sold the printheads as well as ink (unpatented) used in the printheads. Trident's standard form licensing agreements with printer manufacturers (OEMs) granted the OEMs the right to "manufacture, use and sell... ink jet printing devices [printheads] supplied by Trident" only "when used in combination with ink and ink supply systems supplied by Trident." Thus, the licenses included an explicit tying provision conditioning the sale of the patented product (the printhead) on the sale of an unpatented product (the ink). Plaintiff Independent Ink, which competed with patent owner Trident in the manufacture and sale of ink, filed suit against Trident seeking a declaratory judgment that Trident's patent was invalid and not infringed. Independent Ink subsequently amended its complaint to allege that Trident had engaged in illegal tying under Sherman Act §1. A federal district court hearing the case rejected the notion of a presumption of market power on the part of a patent owner as contrary to modern economic thinking, and held that an antitrust claimant must affirmatively prove that a patentee has market power. Because antitrust claimant Independent Ink had not submitted any affirmative evidence defining the relevant market nor proving patentee Trident's power within it, the district court granted Trident's motion for summary judgment of no antitrust liability.

The Federal Circuit in *Indep. Ink* reversed the summary judgment for patentee Trident and remanded the case for further proceedings. After extensively reviewing the Supreme Court's tying jurisprudence, the Federal Circuit concluded that it was bound by the Court's holdings in *Int'l Salt Co. v. United States*[508] and *United States v. Loew's, Inc.*[509] to apply a presumption of market power in patent tying cases. Nor did any of the contrary authority relied on by the district court or Trident constitute an express overruling of the Supreme Court precedent.[510] "Even where a Supreme Court precedent contains many

[507]A printhead is the component of a printer that controls the flow of ink from the ink cartridge to the paper. The author thanks Neal McFarland of Lexmark for this insight.

[508]332 U.S. 392, 396 (1947) (without making inquiry of the defendant's market power, finding that "the admitted facts left no genuine issue.... [T]he tendency of the [patent tying] arrangement to accomplishment of monopoly seems obvious.").

[509]371 U.S. 38, 45 (1962) (stating that "[t]he requisite economic power is presumed when the tying product is patented or copyrighted").

[510]That contrary authority included contrary statements by the Supreme Court in *Walker Process Equip., Inc. v. Food Mach. & Chem. Corp.*, 382 U.S. 172 (1965), a §2 monopolization case discussed above; the statement of Justice O'Connor in her *Jefferson Parish* concurrence (joined by then–Chief Justice Burger, Justice Powell, and Justice Rehnquist) that it is a "common misconception... that a patent or copyright... suffices to demonstrate market power," 466 U.S. at 37 n.7 (O'Connor, J., concurring); statements by Justices White and Blackmun (both members of the *Jefferson Parish* majority)

'infirmities' and rests upon 'wobbly, moth-eaten foundations,'" the Federal Circuit noted, "it remains the 'Court's prerogative alone to overrule one of its precedents.'"[511] The Federal Circuit concluded that although "[t]he time may have come to abandon the doctrine," it is "up to the Congress or the Supreme Court to make this judgment."[512]

Not surprisingly, the Supreme Court accepted the Federal Circuit's invitation.[513] In *Ill. Tool Works Inc. v. Indep. Ink, Inc.*,[514] the Court vacated the Federal Circuit's decision and held that "in all cases involving a tying arrangement, the plaintiff must prove that the defendant has market power in the tying product."[515] In other words, market power cannot be presumed from the fact that a patent covers the tying product; the antitrust claimant charging illegal tying must make a satisfactory evidentiary showing of the patent owner's market power based on actual market conditions. The Court characterized the traditional presumption of market power by patent owners as a "vestige of [its] historical distrust of tying arrangements,"[516] which distrust has "substantially diminished" over time.[517] It explained that the presumption of a patentee's market power first arose in the context of the patent misuse doctrine, outside of antitrust law, but later migrated into antitrust jurisprudence. While the presumption's

---

in their dissent from denial of *certiorari* the following year in *Data General Corp. v. Digidyne Corp.*, 473 U.S. 908, 908 (1985) (White, J., joined by Blackmun, J., dissenting from denial of *certiorari*), noting that that case raised "several substantial questions of antitrust law and policy including . . . what effect should be given to the existence of a copyright or other legal monopoly in determining market power," *id.*; and the antitrust agencies' policy that they will not presume market power in the tying context from the mere fact of patent ownership, United States Department of Justice, *Antitrust Guidelines for the Licensing of Intellectual Property* §5.3 (1995), *available at* https://www.justice.gov/atr/archived-1995-antitrust-guidelines-licensing-intellectual-property.

[511] *Indep. Ink*, 396 F.3d at 1351 (quoting State Oil Co. v. Khan, 522 U.S. 3, 20 (1997)).

[512] *Id.* In further support of its decision recognizing a presumption of market power in patent tying cases based on the existence of the patent alone, the Federal Circuit in *Indep. Ink* also found it "noteworthy" that "Congress has declined to require a showing of market power for affirmative patent tying claims as opposed to patent misuse defenses based on patent tying," citing 35 U.S.C. §271(d)(5) (2000), which establishes a safe harbor for patentees from a charge of patent misuse "unless, in view of the circumstances, the patent owner has market power in the relevant market for the patent or patented product on which the license or sale is conditioned." The Federal Circuit noted that the version of this statute that originally emerged from the Senate contained language also abrogating the presumption of market power in antitrust patent tying cases, but that this language was removed in a House amendment and does not appear in §271(d)(5) as enacted, "making clear that Congress was not attempting to change existing law in this respect." *Indep. Ink*, 396 F.3d at 1349 n.7.

[513] Ill. Tool Works Inc. v. Indep. Ink, Inc., 545 U.S. 1127 (2005) (granting petition for writ of *certiorari*).

[514] 547 U.S. 28 (2006).

[515] *Id.* at 46.

[516] *Id.* at 38.

[517] *Id.* at 35.

applicability was expanding in the case law, however, Congress began "chipping away at the assumption in the patent misuse context from whence it came."[518] Most notably, Congress, in 1988, amended the Patent Act by adding §271(d)(5). This statutory provision eliminated the patent-equals-market-power presumption in the patent misuse context.[519] In view of Congress's judgment, the Supreme Court concluded that tying arrangements involving patented products should no longer be evaluated under the *per se* rule previously applied in cases such as *Loew's* and *Morton Salt Co. v. G.S. Suppiger Co.*[520] While some tying arrangements involving patented products remain unlawful, such as those stemming from a true monopoly or market-wide conspiracy, "that conclusion must be supported by proof of power in the relevant market rather than by a mere presumption thereof."[521]

The Court also observed that its rejection of the presumption of market power from the existence of a patent "accords with the vast majority of academic literature on the subject."[522] The lesson to be drawn from this literature, as already adopted by Congress and the antitrust enforcement agencies, is that "[m]any tying arrangements, even those involving patents and requirements ties, are fully consistent with a free, competitive market."[523] Hence, the Supreme Court reached the same conclusion: that a patent does not necessarily confer market power on its owner.

2. Anticompetitive Conduct

As applied by the Federal Circuit,[524] the antitrust *Noerr-Pennington* doctrine preserves the patentee's immunity from antitrust

[518]*Id.* at 41.

[519]Section 271(d)(5) of 35 U.S.C. (2012) provides (emphasis added):

> (d) No patent owner otherwise entitled to relief for infringement or contributory infringement of a patent shall be denied relief or deemed guilty of misuse or illegal extension of the patent right by reason of his having done one or more of the following:...(5) conditioned the license of any rights to the patent or the sale of the patented product on the acquisition of a license to rights in another patent or purchase of a separate product, *unless, in view of the circumstances, the patent owner has market power in the relevant market for the patent or patented product on which the license or sale is conditioned.*

[520]*See* Morton Salt Co. v. G.S. Suppiger Co., 314 U.S. 488, 490 (1942) (assuming without analyzing actual market conditions that by tying the purchase of unpatented goods to the sale of a patented good, the patentee was "restraining competition").

[521]Illinois Tool Works Inc. v. Indep. Ink, Inc., 547 U.S. 28, 42-43 (2006).

[522]*Id.* at 43 n.4.

[523]*Id.* at 45.

[524]*See* Nobelpharma AB v. Implant Innovations, Inc., 141 F.3d 1059, 1068 (Fed. Cir. 1998).

liability for asserting its exclusive rights unless the accused infringer establishes that (1) the patent was obtained from the USPTO through knowing and willful fraud within the meaning of *Walker Process Equip., Inc. v. Food Machinery & Chem. Corp.*,[525] (2) the infringement suit is a "mere sham" to cover what is in reality "an attempt to interfere directly with the business relationships of a competitor,"[526] or

[525]382 U.S. 172, 177 (1965). An antitrust counterclaim to patent infringement asserting "*Walker Process* fraud" is based on the concept of common law fraud as applied to the patentee's conduct before the USPTO. Traditionally *Walker Process* fraud was more difficult to establish than the affirmative defense of inequitable conduct. The antitrust claimant must show that the patentee acquired the patent by means of either a fraudulent misrepresentation or a fraudulent omission, evidencing a clear intent to deceive the examiner and thereby cause the USPTO to grant an invalid patent, and that the patentee was aware of the fraud when bringing suit to enforce its patent. Moreover, the necessary additional elements of a violation of the antitrust laws (e.g., monopoly power in a relevant market) must be established. *See Nobelpharma AB*, 141 F.3d at 1069-1070. *See generally* Peter M. Boyle et al., *Antitrust Law at the Federal Circuit: Red Light or Green Light at the IP-Antitrust Intersection?*, 69 ANTITRUST L.J. 739, 770-778 (2001) (discussing the proving of *Walker Process* claims under Federal Circuit precedent).

After 2011, it became less clear that establishing the *Walker Process* fraud component of a patent-antitrust counterclaim would be significantly more onerous than establishing the defense of inequitable conduct. The Federal Circuit's tightening of the standards to establish inequitable conduct in *Therasense, Inc. v. Becton, Dickinson & Co.*, 649 F.3d 1276, 1290 (Fed. Cir. 2011) (*en banc*), examined *supra* Section D.1, appears to have narrowed the gap. A case in point is *TransWeb, LLC v. 3M Innovative Properties Co.*, 812 F.3d 1295 (Fed. Cir. 2016). There the court candidly observed that "[a]fter *Therasense*, the showing required for proving inequitable conduct and the showing required for proving the fraud component of *Walker Process* liability may be nearly identical." *TransWeb*, 812 F.3d at 1307. A jury in *TransWeb* concluded that the asserted patents owned by declaratory judgment defendant 3M Co. were invalid under the public use bar of 35 U.S.C. §102(b) (pre-AIA), and the Federal Circuit agreed. In addition, the Circuit affirmed the district court's conclusion that the 3M patents were unenforceable for inequitable conduct under the *Therasense* standards of materiality and intent. Significantly, the Circuit also found properly supported the jury's finding that by enforcing its fraudulently obtained patents, 3M had violated the antitrust laws by committing *Walker Process* fraud. *See TransWeb*, 812 F.3d at 1306. Although the district court had concluded that 3M was liable as antitrust violator for only $34,000 in TransWeb's lost profits (trebled to $103,000), the Federal Circuit affirmed the district court's additional award of over $26 million in attorney fees to TransWeb as part of its antitrust damages under Section 4 of the Clayton Act, 15 U.S.C. §15(a) (2012). *See TransWeb*, 812 F.3d at 1308-1312.

Variations of *Walker Process* antitrust claims have been considered by the Federal Circuit. These include "*Handgards* claims," based on the assertion of a patent allegedly known to be invalid, *see* Bio-Technology Gen. Corp. v. Genentech, Inc., 267 F.3d 1325, 1333 (Fed. Cir. 2001) (concluding that district court's dismissal of *Handgards* claim based on *Noerr-Pennington* immunity was correct), and "*Loctite* claims," based on the assertion of a patent allegedly known not to be infringed. *See* Loctite Corp. v. Ultraseal, Ltd., 781 F.2d 861 (Fed. Cir. 1985), *overruled on other grounds, Nobelpharma AB*, 141 F.3d at 1068.

[526]*See* In re Independent Serv. Orgs. Antitrust Litigation (CSU, L.L.C. v. Xerox Corp.), 203 F.3d 1322, 1326 (Fed. Cir. 2000). The *Noerr-Pennington* doctrine of antitrust law provides that an attempt to influence the government (e.g., by the filing of a patent infringement lawsuit) is generally protected under the First Amendment and therefore immune from antitrust liability. Eastern R.R. Presidents Conf. v. Noerr Motor Freight,

(3) the patentee has engaged in illegal tying.[527] Thus, the owner of a patent who seeks to enforce its statutory right to exclude others by bringing suit against an accused infringer is presumptively immune from antitrust liability for bringing the lawsuit, even if maintenance thereof would have an anticompetitive effect. This immunity is only presumptive, however, not absolute; a patentee will be stripped thereof in certain situations. As affirmed by the Federal Circuit, "'[b]eyond the limited monopoly which is granted, the arrangements by which the patent is utilized are subject to general law.... The possession of a valid patent or patents does not give the patentee any exemption from the provisions of the Sherman Act beyond the limits of the patent monopoly.'"[528]

One type of anticompetitive conduct potentially resulting in a loss of antitrust immunity for patentees is the knowing enforcement of a patent obtained by common law fraud. In *Walker Process Equip., Inc. v. Food Machinery & Chem. Corp.*,[529] the Supreme Court held that the maintenance and enforcement of a patent obtained by fraud on the USPTO may be the basis of an antitrust action under Sherman Act §2, and therefore subject to a treble damages claim by an injured party under the Clayton Act §4.[530] Permitting such actions, the Court observed, would promote the policies it had earlier articulated in *Precision Instrument Mfg. Co. v. Automotive Maintenance Mach. Co.*:

> A patent by its very nature is affected with a public interest.... [It] is an exception to the general rule against monopolies and to the right to access to a free and open market. The far-reaching social and economic consequences of a patent, therefore, give the public a paramount interest in seeing that patent monopolies spring from backgrounds free from fraud or other inequitable conduct and that such monopolies are kept within their legitimate scope.[531]

Inc., 365 U.S. 127, 138-139 (1961); United Mine Workers v. Pennington, 381 U.S. 657, 670 (1965). An exception exists to *Noerr-Pennington* antitrust immunity for "sham litigation," where the defendant establishes that the litigation is objectively baseless. *See* Professional Real Estate Investors v. Columbia Pictures Indus., 508 U.S. 49, 60-61 (1993) (discussing the two-part definition of sham litigation). *See also* Filmtec Corp. v. Hydranautics, 67 F.3d 931, 937-938 (Fed. Cir. 1995) (detailing contours of sham litigation exception under *Professional Real Estate Investors* in patent cases); James B. Kobak, Jr., *Professional Real Estate Investors and the Future of Patent-Antitrust Litigation:* Walker Process *and Handgards Meet* Noerr-Pennington, 63 ANTITRUST L.J. 185 (1994).

[527] In re Independent Serv. Orgs. Antitrust Litigation (CSU, L.L.C. v. Xerox Corp.), 203 F.3d 1322, 1327-1328 (Fed. Cir. 2000).

[528] *Id.* at 1357 n.4 (quoting United States v. Singer Mfg. Co., 374 U.S. 174, 196-197 (1963)).

[529] 382 U.S. 172 (1965).

[530] *Id.* at 176-177.

[531] *Id.* at 177 (quoting Precision Instrument Mfg. Co. v. Automotive Maintenance Mach. Co., 324 U.S. 806, 816 (1945)).

The assertion of what has come to be known among patent lawyers as "*Walker Process* fraud" is based on the concept of common law fraud as applied to the patentee's conduct before the USPTO. The Federal Circuit has stressed that the fraud must be knowing and willful.[532] The antitrust claimant must show that the patent owner acquired the patent by means of either a fraudulent misrepresentation or a fraudulent omission, evidencing a clear intent to deceive the patent examiner and thereby cause the USPTO to grant an invalid patent, and that the patentee was aware of the fraud when bringing suit to enforce its patent.[533]

In 2004, the Federal Circuit in *Unitherm Food Sys., Inc. v. Swift-Eckrich, Inc.*,[534] held that *threatened,* if not actually consummated, enforcement of a patent procured by *Walker Process* fraud can also form the predicate for antitrust liability. The putative infringer Unitherm brought a declaratory judgment action[535] against patentee ConAgra, seeking a declaration that its patent was invalid and unenforceable; Unitherm's antitrust claim was an affirmative claim made with its declaratory judgment action (rather than presented as the more typical counterclaim to an allegation of patent infringement). "Strictly speaking," the Federal Circuit observed, "a *Walker Process* claim is premised upon 'the *enforcement* of a patent procured by fraud on the Patent Office.' "[536] However, a party such as Unitherm can bring a declaratory judgment action of patent invalidity even in the absence of overt enforcement actions. A parallel analysis should inform the antitrust claim. "As a matter of Federal Circuit antitrust law," the Federal Circuit concluded, "the standards that we have developed for determining jurisdiction in a Declaratory Judgment Action of patent invalidity also define the minimum level of 'enforcement' necessary to expose the patentee to a *Walker Process* claim for attempted monopolization." Whether sufficiently threatening actions have been taken by the patentee to create a reasonable apprehension

[532]*Walker Process* fraud was traditionally considered more difficult to establish than the affirmative defense to patent infringement of inequitable conduct, which requires a showing that the patent owner withheld from the USPTO information known to the patent owner that was material to patentability (or affirmatively submitted false material information), and that the withholding (or submission) was done with intent to deceive the USPTO. For further discussion of the defense of inequitable conduct, *see supra* Section D.1.

[533]*See* Nobelpharma AB v. Implant Innovations, 141 F.3d 1059, 1069-1070 (Fed. Cir. 1998). *See generally* Peter M. Boyle et al., *Antitrust Law at the Federal Circuit: Red Light or Green Light at the IP-Antitrust Intersection?*, 69 ANTITRUST L.J. 739, 770-778 (2001) (discussing the proving of *Walker Process* claims under Federal Circuit precedent).

[534]375 F.3d 1341 (Fed. Cir. 2004).

[535]*See infra* Section G for further discussion of declaratory judgment actions.

[536]*Unitherm,* 375 F.3d at 1357-1358 (quoting Walker Process Equip., Inc. v. Food Machinery & Chem. Corp, 382 U.S. 172, 174 (1965) (emphasis added)).

of suit in the putative infringer will control. "[I]f the patentee has done nothing but obtain a patent in a manner that the [declaratory judgment] plaintiff believes is fraudulent, the courts lack jurisdiction to entertain either a Declaratory Judgment Action or a *Walker Process* claim."

A second type of anticompetitive conduct potentially resulting in a loss of antitrust immunity for patentees is the enforcement of a patent for "sham" purposes, regardless of the facts of the patent's origin.[537] Sham patent litigation is thus consistent with the "sham litigation" exception to *Noerr-Pennington* antitrust immunity.[538] In order to establish this form of anticompetitive harm, the antitrust challenger must show that the patentee's "infringement suit was 'a mere sham to cover what is actually nothing more than an attempt to interfere directly with the business relationships of a competitor.'"[539] More specifically, the antitrust claimant must establish in accordance with *Prof'l Real Estate Investors, Inc. v. Columbia Pictures Indus., Inc.*,[540] that (1) the lawsuit was "'objectively baseless in the sense that no reasonable litigant could realistically expect success on the merits,'"[541] and (2) that the baseless lawsuit concealed "'an attempt to interfere directly with the business relationships of a competitor through the use of the governmental process — as opposed to the outcome of that process — as an anticompetitive weapon.'"[542]

A third type of anticompetitive conduct that has been the basis for antitrust claims against patentees involves what antitrust lawyers refer to as "refusals to deal." The essence of a patent as a government-granted property right is the right of its owner to exclude

[537]*See Nobelpharma AB*, 141 F.3d at 1071 (stating that "irrespective of the patent applicant's conduct before the PTO, an antitrust claim can also be based on a *PRE* [*Professional Real Estate Investors*] allegation that a suit is baseless . . .").

[538]The *Noerr-Pennington* doctrine of antitrust law provides that an attempt to influence the government (e.g., by the filing of a patent infringement lawsuit) is generally immune from antitrust liability. Eastern R.R. Presidents Conf. v. Noerr Motor Freight, Inc., 365 U.S. 127, 138-139 (1961); United Mine Workers v. Pennington, 381 U.S. 657, 670 (1965). An exception exists to *Noerr-Pennington* antitrust immunity for "sham litigation," where the defendant establishes that the litigation is objectively baseless. *See* Professional Real Estate Investors v. Columbia Pictures Indus., 508 U.S. 49, 60-61 (1993) (discussing the two-part definition of "sham" litigation). *See also* Filmtec Corp. v. Hydranautics, 67 F.3d 931, 937-938 (Fed. Cir. 1995) (detailing contours of "sham litigation" exception under *Professional Real Estate Investors* in patent cases); James B. Kobak, Jr., *Professional Real Estate Investors and the Future of Patent-Antitrust Litigation: Walker Process and Handgards Meet* Noerr-Pennington, 63 Antitrust L.J. 185 (1994).

[539]Nobelpharma AB v. Implant Innovations, 141 F.3d 1059, 1068 (Fed. Cir. 1998) (quoting Eastern R.R. Presidents Conference v. Noerr Motor Freight, Inc., 365 U.S. 172, 177 (1965)).

[540]508 U.S. 49 (1993).

[541]*Nobelpharma AB*, 141 F.3d at 1071 (quoting *Professional Real Estate Investors*, 508 U.S. at 60-61).

[542]*Id.*

others from practicing the patented innovation during the term of the patent. On the other hand, antitrust law recognizes that a monopolist's refusal to deal with other marketplace actors can be actionable in certain circumstances.[543] Accordingly, patent owners have been charged with anticompetitive conduct in the form of refusing to grant licenses under their patents and/or refusing to sell the patented items. A report by the Antitrust Modernization Commission on intellectual property issues recognized the existence of "substantial debate over whether and when licensing of intellectual property may appropriately be required under the antitrust laws."[544] The commission's report noted the contrasting approaches of the U.S. Courts of Appeal on this issue. Unlike the First[545] and Ninth[546] Circuits, the Federal Circuit has thus far rejected outright those antitrust claims based on refusal to license.

The Federal Circuit's negative view of such claims is best illustrated by *CSU, L.L.C. v. Xerox Corp.*,[547] in which the Federal Circuit summarily rejected an accused infringer's assertion that a patent owner's refusal to license or sell its patented products constituted a violation

[543] *See, e.g.*, Aspen Skiing Co. v. Aspen Highlands Skiing Corp., 472 U.S. 585 (1985).

[544] Intellectual Property Working Group, Antitrust Modernization Commission, *Memorandum re Intellectual Property Issues Recommended for Commission Study* (Dec. 21, 2004). The Commission's 2007 final report is *available at* https://govinfo.library/unt.edu/amc/report_recommendation/amc_final_report.pdf (April 2007).

[545] *See* Data General Corp. v. Grumman Sys. Support Corp., 36 F.3d 1147 (1st Cir. 1994) (adopting in a copyright case a rebuttable presumption that an intellectual property holder does not have any obligation to license its intellectual property).

[546] In *Image Tech. Servs. v. Eastman Kodak Co.*, 125 F.3d 1195 (9th Cir. 1997) (*Kodak II*) (appeal after remand in Eastman Kodak Co. v. Image Technical Serv., Inc., 504 U.S. 451 (1992)), the U.S. Court of Appeals for the Ninth Circuit borrowed the First Circuit's *Data General* presumption in a patent case but held that the presumption could be rebutted by evidence of pretext. "Neither the aims of intellectual property law, nor the antitrust laws justify allowing a monopolist to rely upon a pretextual business justification to mask anticompetitive conduct." *Id.* at 1219. The Ninth Circuit rejected Kodak's argument that its subjective motivation for refusing to sell its photocopier parts to the plaintiff independent service organizations was irrelevant. "Evidence regarding the state of mind of Kodak employees may show pretext, when such evidence suggests that the proffered business justification played no part in the decision to act." *Id.* at 1219. The court noted Kodak's "blanket" refusal, including both patent- and copyright-protected products and unprotected products. "Kodak photocopy and micrographics equipment requires thousands of parts, of which only 65 were patented," the Ninth Circuit observed. The trial court's failure to give any weight to Kodak's intellectual property rights in the instructions it had given to the jury was mere harmless error. *Id.* at 1218. Based on the evidence of record, the Ninth Circuit concluded, it was "more probable than not" that even had the instruction been given the jury would have found Kodak's presumptively valid business justification rebutted on the grounds of pretext. *Id.* at 1219.

[547] In re Independent Serv. Orgs. Antitrust Litigation (CSU, L.L.C. v. Xerox Corp.), 203 F.3d 1322 (Fed. Cir. 2000).

of the antitrust laws (as well as patent misuse). CSU, an independent service organization for photocopiers, sued Xerox for violation of the antitrust laws based on Xerox's refusal to sell it Xerox-patented replacement parts. The district court granted Xerox summary judgment and the Federal Circuit affirmed, concluding that

> [i]n the absence of any indication of illegal tying, fraud in the Patent and Trademark Office, or sham litigation, the patent holder may enforce the statutory right to exclude others from making, using, or selling the claimed invention free from liability under the antitrust laws. We therefore will not inquire into his subjective motivation for exerting his statutory rights, even though his refusal to sell or license his patented invention may have an anticompetitive effect, so long as that anticompetitive effect is not illegally extended beyond the statutory patent grant.[548]

The Federal Circuit's expanding jurisprudence at the intersection of patent law and antitrust, including the court's choice-of-law policy of applying Federal Circuit law to antitrust issues stemming from patent disputes,[549] was the subject of public hearings conducted in 2002 by the U.S. Department of Justice and the Federal Trade Commission.[550] This is an evolving area of Federal Circuit law that patent litigants should monitor closely.

G. Patent Declaratory Judgment Actions

Although typically asserted as defenses to a patentee's infringement lawsuit, the defensive theories discussed in Sections A through E of this chapter (i.e., noninfringement, absence of liability for infringement, invalidity, and unenforceability) alternatively may be raised as affirmative allegations of a party (such as an accused infringer) who

[548]*Id.* at 1327-1328. For criticism of the *CSU* decision by a former chairman of the Federal Trade Commission, *see* Robert Pitofsky, *Antitrust and Intellectual Property: Unresolved Issues at the Heart of the New Economy,* 16 Berkeley Tech. L.J. 535, 545-546 (2001) (characterizing Federal Circuit's decision in *CSU* as "[a] striking example of an approach that gives undue weight to intellectual property rights").

[549]*See* Nobelpharma AB v. Implant Innovations, 141 F.3d 1059, 1068 (Fed. Cir. 1998) (holding *en banc* that "whether conduct in procuring or enforcing a patent is sufficient to strip a patentee of its immunity from the antitrust laws is to be decided as a question of Federal Circuit law").

[550]*See* United States Dep't of Justice, Press Release: DOJ/FTC Hearings to Highlight U.S. Court of Appeals for the Federal Circuit Perspectives on the Intersection Between Antitrust and Intellectual Property Law and Policy (July 3, 2002), *available at* https://www.justice.gov/archive/atr/public/press_release/2002/11407.htm.

files an action (or counterclaim) under the Declaratory Judgment Act.[551] The plaintiff in a patent declaratory judgment (DJ) action affirmatively seeks a judicial declaration that it is not liable for infringement and/or that the patent in question is invalid and/or unenforceable. A patent DJ action can be thought of as the mirror image of a garden-variety patent infringement suit, because an accused infringer is the typical DJ plaintiff and a patentee is the DJ defendant. In certain circumstances discussed below, the party filing the DJ action may not be a formally "accused infringer" but rather a licensee that has not been explicitly threatened with an infringement action because it is currently paying royalties to the patentee. Nevertheless, the licensee believes that its product is not covered by the licensed patent and/or that the patent is invalid and/or unenforceable.

Because Article III of the U.S. Constitution mandates that federal courts adjudicate only "Cases" and "Controversies,"[552] the Declaratory Judgment Act requires that a "case of actual controversy" exist.[553] The Supreme Court has upheld the constitutionality of the Declaratory

[551]28 U.S.C. §2201(a). Congress enacted the Declaratory Judgment Act in 1934 "to prevent avoidable damages from being incurred by a person uncertain of his rights and threatened with damage by delayed adjudication." Minn. Mining & Mfg. Co. v. Norton Co., 929 F.2d 670, 673 (Fed. Cir. 1991) (citing EDWIN BORCHARD, DECLARATORY JUDGMENTS 803-804 (2d ed. 1941) [hereinafter Borchard]). Prior to the act's passage, "the patentee was the only one in a position to initiate a suit, usually an action for damages and an accounting, with or without an injunction, against the alleged infringer or his dealers." Borchard at 803. The patentee "could, without actually bringing suit, which might have placed in issue the validity of his patent, publicly and privately charge infringement and threaten to sue the manufacturer or any one who dealt with the product in issue. By continuous threat and coercion, [the patentee] could not only intimidate dealers and customers and gravely injure his competitor's business, but he could often force a settlement, without having risked an adjudication of his possibly unfounded claims of infringement." *Id.* (citations omitted).

[552]U.S. CONST., art. III, §2, cl. 1 (providing, "The judicial power shall extend to all Cases, in law and equity, arising under this Constitution, the laws of the United States, and treaties made, or which shall be made, under their authority; — to all Cases affecting ambassadors, other public ministers and consuls; — to all Cases of admiralty and maritime jurisdiction; — to Controversies to which the United States shall be a party; — to Controversies between two or more states; — between a state and citizens of another state; — between citizens of different states; — between citizens of the same state claiming lands under grants of different states, and between a state, or the citizens thereof, and foreign states, citizens or subjects").

[553]The Declaratory Judgment Act provides in pertinent part:

> In a *case of actual controversy* within its jurisdiction [except with respect to certain tax and trade actions], any court of the United States, upon the filing of an appropriate pleading, may declare the rights and other legal relations of any interested party seeking such declaration, whether or not further relief is or could be sought. Any such declaration shall have the force and effect of a final judgment or decree and shall be reviewable as such.

28 U.S.C. §2201(a) (emphasis added).

Judgment Act and explained that the act's use of the phrase "case of actual controversy" refers to the types of "Cases" and "Controversies" that are justiciable under Article III.[554] Satisfying the "actual controversy" requirement is thus a jurisdictional prerequisite for filing a declaratory judgment action.

The Federal Circuit's standard for determining the existence of a justiciable actual controversy changed in 2007 when the U.S. Supreme Court decided *MedImmune, Inc. v. Genentech, Inc.*, reversing the Circuit.[555] The *MedImmune* decision undoubtedly expanded the circumstances under which issued patents may be challenged.[556] "By liberalizing the availability of declaratory judgment relief concerning patent validity and scope, *MedImmune* tilts the patent landscape away from the interests of patent owners and toward those of licensees and other who may be threatened, rightly or wrongly, with the enforcement of patents."[557]

1. Federal Circuit's Pre-*MedImmune* "Reasonable Apprehension" Test

Prior to the Supreme Court's 2007 decision in *MedImmune,* the Federal Circuit considered a sufficient actual controversy to exist if the declaratory plaintiff had a "reasonable apprehension" of being sued for patent infringement. More particularly, the Federal Circuit applied a two-part inquiry for determining the existence of declaratory judgment jurisdiction:

(1) an explicit threat or other action by the patentee which creates a reasonable apprehension on the part of the declaratory judgment plaintiff that it will face an infringement suit; and
(2) present activity by the declaratory judgment plaintiff which could constitute infringement, or concrete steps taken with the intent to conduct such activity.[558]

[554]*See* MedImmune, Inc. v. Genentech, Inc., 549 U.S. 118, 126-127 (2007) (citing Aetna Life Ins. Co. v. Haworth, 300 U.S. 227, 240 (1937)).

[555]549 U.S. 118 (2007).

[556]*See* Micron Tech., Inc. v. Mosaid Techs., Inc., 518 F.3d 897, 902 (Fed. Cir. 2008) (observing that "[w]hether intended or not, the now more lenient legal standard [set forth by the Supreme Court in *MedImmune*] facilitates or enhances the availability of declaratory judgment jurisdiction in patent cases").

[557]Donald S. Chisum, *Licensee Challenges to Patent Validity After* MedImmune (Feb. 7, 2007). *See also* Eric Yeager, *BNA Conference Panelists Examine Pharma Legislation and Declaratory Judgment Trends,* 77 PAT. TRADEMARK & COPYRIGHT J. 92 (2008) (noting *MedImmune* decision's "sweeping impact" on declaratory judgment jurisdiction in pharmaceutical cases).

[558]Teva Pharms. USA, Inc. v. Pfizer, Inc., 395 F.3d 1324, 1332 (Fed. Cir. 2005).

Prong (1) of this inquiry focused on acts by the patentee; prong (2) examined acts by the DJ plaintiff.

The Federal Circuit clarified that prong (1) required the DJ plaintiff to demonstrate "that it has a reasonable apprehension of *imminent* suit."[559] The requirement of imminence meant that the injury had to be concrete, in other words, "actual or imminent, not conjectural or hypothetical."[560] In many cases, the prong (1) reasonable apprehension of imminent suit arose when the declaratory judgment plaintiff received a "cease and desist" letter or other express threat of suit for infringement from the patentee, although an express threat was not required to create declaratory judgment jurisdiction.[561] No such express threat was involved in *MedImmune.*

2. Supreme Court's Decision in *MedImmune*

The DJ plaintiff in *MedImmune*[562] was not the typical accused infringer that has received a cease-and-desist letter or otherwise been expressly threatened with an infringement suit. Instead, MedImmune manufactured the drug Synagis, for treatment of respiratory disease, under a license agreement with patent owner Genentech. Notably, Synagis accounted for 80 percent of MedImmune's sales revenues. When signed in 1997, the license agreement covered an existing Genentech patent and a then-pending application. When the application issued as the "Cabilly II" patent, Genentech sent MedImmune a letter asserting that Synagis was covered by Cabilly II and that MedImmune would owe Genentech royalties thereunder. MedImmune disagreed, believing the Cabilly II patent to be invalid and unenforceable, and in any event not infringed by Synagis.

MedImmune was unwilling to risk refusing to pay the royalties demanded, however. MedImmune anticipated that if it refused to pay royalties under the Cabilly II patent, Genentech would terminate the license and sue MedImmune for infringement. Knowing that an infringement lawsuit could potentially result in an injunction against further sales of its primary product, as well as the possibility of liability for enhanced damages and attorney fees, MedImmune paid Genentech the demanded royalties under protest. Thereafter MedImmune filed a DJ action against Genentech. A federal district court dismissed the action for lack of subject matter jurisdiction, and the Federal Circuit affirmed. Dismissal was based on the Circuit's precedent holding

[559]*Id.* at 1333 (emphasis in original).

[560]*Id.*

[561]*See* Vanguard Research, Inc. v. PEAT, Inc., 304 F.3d 1249, 1254-1255 (Fed. Cir. 2002).

[562]MedImmune, Inc. v. Genentech, Inc., 549 U.S. 118 (2007).

that a patent licensee in good standing cannot establish the requisite Article III case or controversy, because the license, "unless materially breached, obliterate[s] any reasonable apprehension" that the licensee will be sued for infringement.[563]

The Supreme Court granted review. By an 8-1 vote, it reversed the Federal Circuit in an opinion authored by Justice Scalia.[564] The Supreme Court agreed that as long as MedImmune continued to make the royalty payments, there was no risk that Genentech would seek to enjoin its sales of Synagis. Thus, the issue for decision was "whether this cause[d] the dispute no longer to be a case or controversy within the meaning of Article III."[565] The Court's earlier decisions required that a justiciable dispute be " 'definite and concrete, touching the legal relations of parties having adverse legal interests'; and that it be 'real and substantial' and 'admi[t] of specific relief through a decree of a conclusive character, as distinguished from an opinion advising what the law would be upon a hypothetical state of facts.' "[566] In summary, " 'the question in each case is whether the facts alleged, under all the circumstances, show that there is a substantial controversy, between parties having adverse legal interests, of sufficient immediacy and reality to warrant the issuance of a declaratory judgment.' "[567]

After reviewing this and other DJ precedent, which admittedly did "not draw the brightest of lines" between DJ actions that satisfied the case or controversy requirement and those that did not,[568] the Court concluded that the case at bar involved a sufficiently live dispute to establish the district court's jurisdiction over MedImmune's DJ action. MedImmune's continued payment of royalties was coerced by the threat of an infringement suit (and the potential negative consequences thereof) if it stopped payment. This coercion was sufficient to create DJ jurisdiction. "The rule that a plaintiff must . . . bet the farm, or (as here) risk treble damages and the loss of 80 percent of its business, before seeking a declaration of its actively contested legal rights finds no support in Article III."[569] The Court rejected

[563]Gen-Probe, Inc. v. Vysis, Inc., 359 F.3d 1376, 1381 (Fed. Cir. 2004).

[564]Justice Thomas dissented. *See MedImmune,* 549 U.S. at 137-146.

[565]*Id.* at 128.

[566]*Id.* at 127 (quoting Aetna Life Ins. Co. v. Haworth, 300 U.S. 227, 240-241 (1937)).

[567]*Id.* (quoting Maryland Casualty Co. v. Pacific Coal & Oil Co., 312 U.S. 270, 273 (1941)).

[568]*Id.* at 127.

[569]*Id.* at 134. Although it held that DJ jurisdiction existed, the Supreme Court did not reach the merits of the dispute or whether the district court should exercise its discretion to dismiss the action. "[I]t would be imprudent for us to decide whether the District Court should, or must, decline to issue the requested declaratory relief. We leave the equitable, prudential, and policy arguments in favor of such a discretionary dismissal for the lower courts' consideration on remand. Similarly available for consideration on remand are any merits-based arguments for denial of declaratory relief." *Id.* at 136-137.

Genentech's argument that the license agreement operated as an insurance policy or settlement that precluded MedImmune's challenge; "[p]romising to pay royalties on patents that have not been held invalid does not amount to a promise *not to seek* a holding of their invalidity."[570] The Court concluded that MedImmune "was not required, insofar as Article III is concerned, to break or terminate its . . . license agreement before seeking a declaratory judgment in federal court that the underlying patent is invalid, unenforceable, or not infringed."[571]

In the critical footnote 11 of its decision, the Supreme Court in *MedImmune* effectively overruled the "reasonable apprehension of suit" prong (1) of the Federal Circuit's test for DJ jurisdiction.[572] Several earlier Supreme Court decisions contradicted or conflicted with the Circuit's test,[573] and the test was at least "in tension" with other Supreme Court precedent.[574]

3. Post-*MedImmune* Federal Circuit Decisions

In *Teva Pharms. USA, Inc. v. Novartis Pharms. Corp.*,[575] the Federal Circuit acknowledged that its "reasonable apprehension of suit" test for DJ jurisdiction had been overruled in *MedImmune*'s footnote 11.[576] Henceforth, the Federal Circuit would apply the "all the circumstances" test of *MedImmune,* that is, "whether the facts alleged, under all the circumstances, show that there is a substantial controversy, between the parties having adverse legal interests, of sufficient immediacy and reality to warrant the issuance of a declaratory

[570] *Id.* at 135 (emphasis in original).

[571] *Id.* at 137.

[572] *Id.* at 132 n.11.

[573] *Id.* (citing Altvater v. Freeman, 319 U.S. 359 (1943) (holding that a licensee's failure to cease its payment of royalties did not render nonjusticiable a dispute over the validity of the patent); Maryland Casualty Co. v. Pacific Coal & Oil Co., 312 U.S. 270, 273 (1941); and Aetna Life Ins. Co. v. Haworth, 300 U.S. 227, 239 (1937)). In contrast with *MedImmune*, however, the licensees in *Altvater* were paying "under protests" royalties "required by an injunction the patentees had obtained in an earlier case." *Id.* at 130. In other words, *Altvater* involved the compulsion of an injunction. Based on this and other factual distinctions, Justice Thomas (as well as the Federal Circuit in *Gen-Probe, Inc. v. Vysis, Inc.*, 359 F.3d 1376 (Fed. Cir. 2004)) considered *Altvater* inapplicable to the *MedImmune* facts. *See MedImmune*, 549 U.S. 143-144 (2007) (Thomas, J., dissenting).

[574] *MedImmune*, 549 U.S. at 132 n.11 (citing Cardinal Chem. Co. v. Morton Int'l, Inc., 508 U.S. 83, 98 (1993) (holding that appellate affirmance of a judgment of noninfringement, eliminating any apprehension of suit, does not moot a declaratory judgment counterclaim of patent invalidity)).

[575] 482 F.3d 1330 (Fed. Cir. 2007).

[576] *See id.* at 1339.

judgment."[577] In *Caraco Pharm. Labs., Ltd. v. Forest Labs., Inc.*,[578] the Federal Circuit explained that proving a declaratory plaintiff's reasonable apprehension of suit (the Federal Circuit's pre-*MedImmune* test) "is only one of many ways a patentee can satisfy the Supreme Court's more general all-the-circumstances test to establish that an action presents a justiciable Article III controversy."[579] As with any "totality of the circumstances" type of legal standard, each case has to be evaluated on its particular facts, and no bright-line rule exists for determining whether a DJ action satisfies the case or controversy requirement.[580]

A series of post-*MedImmune* Federal Circuit decisions, including *Teva Pharms., Caraco Pharm. Labs.,* and others, have "reshaped the contours of the first prong of [the Federal Circuit's] declaratory judgment jurisprudence."[581] In particular, the Federal Circuit's post-*MedImmune* cases bring additional justiciability doctrines to bear in applying the *MedImmune* test for DJ jurisdiction. In *Caraco,* the Federal Circuit applied *MedImmune*'s all-the-circumstances test by utilizing a three-part framework developed in other Supreme Court cases. This precedent established that an action is justiciable under Article III

> only where (1) the plaintiff has standing, *Lujan v. Defenders of Wildlife,* 504 U.S. 555, 560, 112 S. Ct. 2130, 119 L. Ed. 2d 351 (1992), (2) the issues presented are ripe for judicial review, *Abbott Labs. v. Gardner,* 387 U.S. 136, 149, 87 S. Ct. 1507, 18 L. Ed. 2d 681 (1967), and (3) the case is not rendered moot at any stage of the litigation, *United States Parole Comm'n v. Geraghty,* 445 U.S. 388, 397, 100 S. Ct. 1202, 63 L. Ed. 2d 479 (1980).[582]

The Federal Circuit has explained that the standing, ripeness, and non-mootness doctrines are "more specific but overlapping doctrines rooted in the same Article III inquiry," and as such they represent "a helpful guide in applying the all-the-circumstances test" of *MedImmune.*[583]

[577]*Id.* at 1337.

[578]527 F.3d 1278 (Fed. Cir. 2008).

[579]*Id.* at 1291.

[580]*See* Prasco, LLC v. Medicis Pharm. Corp., 537 F.3d 1329, 1336 (Fed. Cir. 2008).

[581]Cat Tech LLC v. Tubemaster, Inc., 528 F.3d 871, 880 (Fed. Cir. 2008). The second prong of the Federal Circuit's pre-*MedImmune* test, that is, whether the DJ plaintiff has already engaged in potentially infringing activity or made meaningful preparation to conduct potentially infringing activity, "remains an important element in the totality of circumstances which must be considered in determining whether a declaratory judgment is appropriate." *Id.*

[582]Caraco Pharm. Labs., LTD v. Forest Labs., Inc., 527 F.3d 1278, 1291 (Fed. Cir. 2008).

[583]*Prasco*, 537 F.3d at 1336.

The Federal Circuit applied the standing requirement to affirm a district court's dismissal of a DJ action for want of actual controversy in *Prasco, LLC v. Medicis Pharm. Corp.*,[584] a post-*MedImmune* decision. *Prasco* demonstrates that *MedImmune* did not change the fundamental principle that parties in federal court must have a concrete dispute and not be seeking a mere advisory opinion based on hypothetical facts. The DJ defendant Medicis owned four patents covering a benzoyl peroxide cleansing product. The DJ plaintiff Prasco manufactured a generic benzoyl peroxide cleansing product marketed as Oscion in competition with the patentee's product. Prasco filed its DJ action in 2006, seeking a judicial declaration of noninfringement (it did not assert invalidity) after the following events had occurred: (1) Medicis marked the four patent numbers on its cleansing product in accordance with 35 U.S.C. §287(a); and (2) Medicis sued Prasco in 2005 for infringement of an unrelated patent based on Prasco's sales of a different cleanser product. After Medicis filed a motion to dismiss Prasco's DJ action for lack of a case or controversy, Prasco sent Medicis a sample of Oscion and requested that it sign a covenant not to sue Prasco for infringement under the Medicis patents. Medicis refused to sign the covenant. Based on Medicis' conduct, Prasco alleged that it had suffered an actual harm, namely, "paralyzing uncertainty" from fear that Medicis would sue it again, this time for patent infringement based on Prasco's sales of Oscion.

The Federal Circuit disagreed, affirming the district court's dismissal of Prasco's DJ action. Prasco had failed to allege a controversy of sufficient "immediacy and reality" to create DJ jurisdiction. The Federal Circuit explained that the "immediacy and reality" inquiry can be viewed through the lens of standing, which is satisfied when a DJ plaintiff alleges (1) an "injury-in-fact," meaning a harm that is concrete and actual or imminent, not conjectural or hypothetical; (2) the harm is fairly traceable to the DJ defendant's conduct; and (3) the harm is redressable by a favorable decision.[585] "Absent an injury-in-fact fairly traceable to the patentee, there can be no immediate and real controversy,"[586] the court explained. Although an injury-in-fact may exist even if the DJ plaintiff does not have a reasonable apprehension of suit (as in *MedImmune*), there must nevertheless exist a "case or controversy . . . based on a *real* and *immediate* injury or threat of future injury that is *caused by the defendants*— an objective standard that cannot be met by a purely subjective or speculative fear of future harm."[587] Generally, some affirmative act by the DJ defendant/patentee will be required to establish a justiciable controversy.

[584]537 F.3d 1329 (Fed. Cir. 2008).
[585]*See id.* at 1338 (citing *Caraco*, 527 F.3d at 1291).
[586]*Id.*
[587]*Id.* at 1339 (emphasis in original).

The Federal Circuit concluded in *Prasco* that the evidence was completely lacking as to a "defined, preexisting dispute between the parties concerning Oscion."[588] With respect to patent marking, the court noted that Medicis decided to mark its patent numbers on its cleansing product before it had any knowledge of Prasco's competing Oscion product. With respect to Medicis' 2005 infringement suit against Prasco, the Federal Circuit acknowledged that prior litigious conduct is one factor to be considered in assessing the totality of the circumstances for DJ jurisdiction. In this case, however, the prior lawsuit was entitled to only minimal weight. "[O]ne prior suit concerning different products covered by unrelated patents is not the type of pattern of prior conduct that makes reasonable an assumption that Medicis will also take action against Prasco regarding its new product."[589] With respect to Medicis's refusal to sign the covenant not to sue Prasco, although this too is one factor to be considered in the totality of the circumstances analysis, in this case it was "not sufficient to create an actual controversy — some affirmative actions by the defendant will also generally be necessary."[590] "A patentee has no obligation to spend the time and money to test a competitors' product nor to make a definitive determination, at the time and place of the competitors' choosing, that it will never bring an infringement suit."[591] The Federal Circuit concluded that

> where Prasco has suffered no actual present injury traceable to the defendants, and the defendants have not asserted any rights against Prasco related to the patents nor taken any affirmative actions concerning Prasco's current product, one prior suit concerning unrelated patents and products and the defendants' failure to sign a covenant not to sue are simply not sufficient to establish that Prasco is at risk of imminent harm from the defendants and that there is an actual controversy between the parties of sufficient immediacy and reality to warrant declaratory judgment jurisdiction. Although we understand Prasco's desire to have a definitive answer on whether its products infringe defendants' patents, were the district court to reach the merits of this case, it would merely be providing an advisory opinion. This is impermissible under Article III.[592]

Should a patent owner, by promising not to sue an accused infringer, be able to unilaterally divest a federal court's jurisdiction over the accused infringer's counterclaim for a declaratory judgment of patent invalidity? Before *MedImmune*, Federal Circuit precedent

[588]*Id.* at 1340.
[589]*Id.* at 1341.
[590]*Id.*
[591]*Id.*
[592]*Id.* at 1341-1342.

answered this question affirmatively.[593] In 2012, the Supreme Court granted *certiorari* in a trademark case that raised the same issue. The question presented in *Already, LLC v. Nike, Inc.*[594] was:

> Whether a federal district court is divested of Article III jurisdiction over a party's challenge to the validity of a federally registered trademark if the registrant promises not to assert its mark against the party's then-existing commercial activities.

The Supreme Court unanimously held that the broad, "unconditional and irrevocable" "Covenant Not to Sue" issued by Nike in the case at bar rendered the case moot.[595] Applying *Already*, the Federal Circuit in *Organic Seed Growers and Trade Ass'n v. Monsanto Co.* held that certain "binding representations" made by Monsanto, though not a covenant not to sue, had a "similar effect" and thus deprived the district court of DJ jurisdiction.[596]

[593]*See* Super Sack Mfg. Corp. v. Chase Packaging Corp., 57 F.3d 1054, 1055, 1059-1060 (Fed. Cir. 1995) (affirming district court's dismissal of case with prejudice for lack of a reasonable apprehension of a future infringement suit because "Super Sack's promise to assert neither U.S. Patent No. 4,143,796 ('796) nor U.S. Patent No. 4,194,652 ('652) against Chase as to any of its past or present products precludes the existence of an actual controversy").

[594]133 S. Ct. 24 (June 25, 2012) (order granting petition for writ of *certiorari*).

[595]*See* Already, LLC v. Nike, Inc., 133 S. Ct. 721, 729 (2013).

[596]*See* Organic Seed Growers and Trade Ass'n v. Monsanto Co., 718 F.3d 1350, 1352 (Fed. Cir. 2013).

Chapter 11

Remedies for Patent Infringement

A. Introduction

Patent infringement is a tort,[1] for which the patent owner may sue an accused infringer in a civil action.[2] Earlier chapters of this text addressed the substantive law of patent infringement[3] and the defenses that may be raised thereto.[4] This chapter concerns the types of relief that a successful patent owner may obtain if infringement is established and the patent's validity and enforceability are sustained.

To summarize, the available remedies for infringement of a valid, enforceable patent are

- an injunction (preliminary and/or permanent) against future infringement,
- ongoing royalties for future infringement that is not enjoined,
- damages (compensatory and/or enhanced) for past infringements,
- attorney fees,
- costs, and
- prejudgment interest.

In addition, the American Inventors Protection Act of 1999 created a new remedy for violation of a patentee's "provisional rights," which attach upon publication of its pending patent application.[5] Each type of remedy is addressed below.

[1]*See* Carbice Corp. v. American Patents Dev. Corp., 283 U.S. 27, 32 (1931) (stating that "infringement . . . , whether direct or contributory, is essentially a tort, and implies invasion of some right of the patentee").

[2]*See* 35 U.S.C. §281 (2020) (providing that "[a] patentee shall have remedy by civil action for infringement of his patent"). The Patent Act does not provide any criminal liability for acts of patent infringement.

[3]*See supra* Chapter 9 ("Patent Infringement").

[4]*See supra* Chapter 10 ("Defenses to Patent Infringement").

[5]*See* 35 U.S.C. §154(d).

B. Injunctions

An injunction is an order by the court commanding an infringer to cease any further infringement (direct, inducing, or contributory) in the United States during the term of the patent. The Patent Act provides for injunctive relief in §283, which states that

> [t]he several courts having jurisdiction of cases under this title [35 U.S.C.] may grant injunctions in accordance with the principles of equity to prevent the violation of any right secured by patent, on such terms as the court deems reasonable.[6]

In many patent infringement scenarios, the most important remedy for the patent owner is the award of an injunction against future infringement. The importance of injunctive relief reflects the fact that a patent's principal value lies in the right it conveys to exclude others.[7] Without the ability to enjoin infringement, the patentee's exclusivity is abrogated. A defendant's unchecked future infringement may impact the marketplace's perception of the patentee in ways that are never fully compensable by a monetary award;[8] continuing infringement may harm the patentee's reputation and result in loss of the patentee's goodwill if the public develops a mistaken belief that the inferior quality of an accused device is attributable to the patentee. Injunctions also are important for a very practical reason: some accused infringers may be judgment-proof and unable to pay damages. An injunction is the only meaningful remedy available in such cases.

Nevertheless, the patent property right should not be viewed as absolute. As further discussed *infra*, the Supreme Court clarified in *eBay Inc. v. MercExchange, LLC*[9] that injunctive relief is not automatic even though a patent is adjudged infringed and its validity sustained. As the Court explained, "the creation of a right is distinct from

[6] 35 U.S.C. §283 (2020).

[7] Emphasizing the importance of injunctive remedies in patent cases, the court in *Smith Int'l, Inc. v. Hughes Tool Co.*, 718 F.2d 1573 (Fed. Cir. 1983), observed that without them,

> [t]he patent owner would lack much of the "leverage," afforded by the right to exclude, to enjoy the full value of his invention in the market place. Without the right to obtain an injunction, the right to exclude granted to the patentee would have only a fraction of the value it was intended to have, and would no longer be as great an incentive to engage in the toils of scientific and technological research.

Id. at 1577.

[8] *See* Atlas Powder Co. v. Ireco Chems., 773 F.2d 1230, 1233 (Fed. Cir. 1985) (Rich, J.) (stating that "[t]he patent statute further provides injunctive relief to preserve the legal interests of the parties *against future infringement* which may have market effects never fully compensable in money") (emphasis in original).

[9] 547 U.S. 388 (2006).

the provision of remedies for violations of that right."[10] The use of the word "may" in 35 U.S.C. §283 makes clear that injunctions are optional, not mandatory, equitable remedies.

Section 283 also provides that the district courts have broad discretion in fashioning injunctions so as to do justice. That discretion is not unfettered, however. In awarding injunctive relief, the courts must comply with the requirements of Fed. R. Civ. P. 65. This rule requires that injunctive orders provide clear notice and specific detail concerning the conduct being enjoined. The rule provides in part:

> (d) Contents and Scope of Every Injunction and Restraining Order.
> (1) *Contents.* Every order granting an injunction and every restraining order must:
> (A) state the reasons why it issued;
> (B) state its terms specifically; and
> (C) describe in reasonable detail — and not by referring to the complaint or other document — the act or acts restrained or required.
> (2) *Persons Bound.* The order binds only the following who receive actual notice of it by personal service or otherwise:
> (A) the parties;
> (B) the parties' officers, agents, servants, employees, and attorneys; and
> (C) other persons who are in active concert or participation with anyone described in Rule 65(d)(2)(A) or (B).[11]

Two types of injunctions are encountered in patent cases: preliminary injunctions and permanent injunctions. Because permanent injunctions are more common, they are addressed first.

1. Permanent Injunctions

A permanent injunction is one that is issued after a final judgment of infringement and no invalidity or unenforceability. Prior to the Supreme Court's decision in *eBay Inc. v. MercExchange, LLC,*[12] federal courts virtually always granted permanent injunctive relief as a standard part of the final judgment when patent owners prevailed.[13]

[10]*eBay*, 547 U.S. at 392.

[11]Fed. R. Civ. P. 65(d) (eff. Dec. 1, 2009).

[12]547 U.S. 388 (2006).

[13]*See* Richardson v. Suzuki Motor Co., 868 F.2d 1226, 1247 (Fed. Cir. 1989) (observing that "[i]t is the general rule that an injunction will issue when infringement has been adjudged, absent a sound reason for denying it"); *see also* MercExchange, L.L.C. v. eBay Inc., 401 F.3d 1323, 1338-1339 (Fed. Cir. 2005) (reversing district court's denial of permanent injunction where court failed to "provide any persuasive reason to believe

Such relief permanently enjoined the infringing party from any further infringement during the remaining term of the patent. The Supreme Court's 2006 decision in *eBay* means that permanent injunctions are no longer granted to prevailing patentees on an essentially automatic basis.

Prior to *eBay*, courts refused to enter permanent injunctions against adjudged infringers only in rare cases, such as those clearly impacting the public's health and welfare. For example, the Seventh Circuit in *City of Milwaukee v. Activated Sludge, Inc.*[14] affirmed an award of damages for the city's infringement of a patent on a sewage purification process but refused to permanently enjoin the infringement. Making the injunction permanent "would close the sewage plant, leaving the entire community without any means for the disposal of raw sewage other than running it into Lake Michigan, thereby polluting its waters and endangering the health and lives of that and other adjoining communities."[15]

During patent reform discussions in 2005, a number of technology companies publicly urged that the availability of permanent injunctive relief for patent infringement be limited to those prevailing patent owners that had commercialized their patented inventions. Noncommercializing patentees would be limited to monetary damages.[16] The technology companies, such as Apple, Intel, Microsoft, and Hewlett-Packard, were the targets of patent infringement lawsuits by patent-holding companies or individuals (not infrequently referred to pejoratively as "patent trolls") that acquired patents (sometimes through bankruptcy proceedings) and sued or threatened to sue the technology companies for infringement, but that did not otherwise participate in the marketplace. These patent holders (also called "patent assertion entities" or PAEs) reportedly used the threat of then–virtually automatic injunctive relief to push their targets into settlements. The targeted technology companies contended that courts should consider whether such patent-holding firms would truly suffer irreparable harm in the absence of injunctive relief.[17] Because the 2005 patent reform proposals were never enacted into law,[18] concerns

---

th[e] case [wa]s sufficiently exceptional to justify the denial of a permanent injunction"), *overruled by* eBay Inc. v. MercExchange LLC, 547 U.S. 388 (2006).

14 69 F.2d 577 (7th Cir. 1934).

15 *Activated Sludge, Inc.*, 69 F.2d at 593.

16 *See infra* Section D ("Damages for Past Infringements").

17 *See* Brenda Sandburg, *A Modest Proposal,* THE RECORDER (May 9, 2005), *available at* http://www.dailyreportonline.com/id=900005543464/A-Modest-Proposal?slreturn=20160115101538.

18 The proposed legislation (titled the "Patent Reform Act of 2005") would have added the following language to the end of 35 U.S.C. §283:

> In determining equity, the court shall consider the fairness of the remedy in light of all the facts and the relevant interests of the parties associated with the

remained about the attempted enforcement of patents by holding companies, especially those with patents of questionable validity.[19]

a. The eBay v. MercExchange *Standard*

A landmark U.S. Supreme Court decision in 2006 effectively mooted the perceived need for congressional reform of injunctive relief in patent cases. In *eBay Inc. v. MercExchange, LLC,*[20] the Court announced that a permanent injunction is not to be automatically awarded in every case in which a patent is found infringed and its validity sustained. Rather, a district court's decision to impose or deny a permanent injunction in a patent case should be made after consideration of traditional equitable principles generally applicable to all types of cases. In other words, the equitable considerations for determining whether permanent injunctive relief is warranted should not be applied in a rigid fashion, nor should they be applied differently in patent cases than in non-patent cases.

Patentee MercExchange, a patent-holding company, licensed its patents but did not manufacture any products. It alleged that the "Buy It Now" feature of eBay's popular online auctions infringed MercExchange's '265 business method patent.[21] After eBay and its subsidiary Half.com (collectively "eBay") refused to take licenses, MercExchange sued for infringement. A jury sustained the '265 patent's validity, found that eBay infringed, and awarded damages to MercExchange. The district court thereafter denied MercExchange's motion for permanent injunctive relief against eBay, concluding that

---

> invention. Unless the injunction is entered pursuant to a nonappealable judgment of infringement, a court shall stay the injunction pending an appeal upon an affirmative showing that the stay would not result in irreparable harm to the owner of the patent and that the balance of hardships from the stay does not favor the owner of the patent.

H.R. 2795, 109th Cong., 1st Sess. §7 (2005).

[19]*See* ADAM B. JAFFE & JOSH LERNER, INNOVATION AND ITS DISCONTENTS: HOW OUR BROKEN PATENT SYSTEM IS ENDANGERING INNOVATION AND PROGRESS, AND WHAT TO DO ABOUT IT 15 (2004) (noting "worrisome development" of individual inventors, who in many cases have received a patent of "dubious validity," attempting to "hold up" established firms in their industries).

[20]547 U.S. 388 (2006).

[21]*See eBay*, 547 U.S. at 390; "Consignment Nodes," U.S. Patent No. 5,845,265 (issued Dec. 1, 1998). The '265 patent is directed to "[a] method and apparatus for creating a computerized market for used and collectible goods by use of a plurality of low cost posting terminals and a market maker computer in a legal framework that establishes a bailee relationship and consignment contract with a purchaser of a good at the market maker computer that allows the purchaser to change the price of the good once the purchaser has purchased the good thereby to allow the purchaser to speculate on the price of collectibles in an electronic market for used goods while assuring the safe and trusted physical possession of a good with a vetted bailee." *Id.* (abstract).

MercExchange's lack of commercial activity in practicing its patents coupled with its willingness to license them sufficiently established a lack of irreparable harm despite the denial of injunctive relief.[22] The Federal Circuit reversed, applying the appellate court's "general rule" that a permanent injunction should issue once infringement and validity have been adjudged.[23] In the Federal Circuit's view, the district court's citation of growing public concern over the issuance of business method patents was overly general and "not the type of important public need that justifies the *unusual* step of denying injunctive relief."[24]

The Supreme Court in *eBay* vacated the Federal Circuit's judgment, concluding that "[j]ust as the District Court erred in its categorical denial of injunctive relief, the Court of Appeals erred in its categorical grant of such relief."[25] The Court disagreed with the Federal Circuit's assumption that a patent owner's statutory right to exclude others under 35 U.S.C. §154(a)(1) is alone sufficient to justify a general rule favoring injunctive relief against adjudged infringers. The Court observed that "the creation of a right is distinct from the provision of remedies for violations of that right."[26] The Federal Circuit's approach was also contrary to copyright jurisprudence, in which the Supreme Court had "consistently rejected invitations to replace traditional equitable considerations with a rule that an injunction automatically follows a determination that a copyright has been infringed."[27]

Rather than following any general rule or presumption regarding injunctive relief in patent cases, the Supreme Court in *eBay* instructed that courts should instead apply "well established principles of equity."[28] These principles require that a patent owner seeking a permanent injunction must satisfy the following factors:

(1) that it has suffered an irreparable injury;
(2) that remedies available at law, such as monetary damages, are inadequate to compensate for that injury;

[22]*See eBay*, 547 U.S. at 393.
[23]MercExchange, LLC v. eBay Inc., 401 F.3d 1323, 1338 (Fed. Cir. 2005).
[24]*eBay*, 547 U.S. at 1339 (emphasis added). In contrast, some Supreme Court Justices harbored greater concerns about business method patents. *See eBay*, 547 U.S. at 397 (Kennedy, J., concurring) (stating that "injunctive relief may have different consequences for the burgeoning number of patents over business methods, which were not of much economic and legal significance in earlier times. The potential vagueness and suspect validity of some of these patents may affect the calculus under the four-factor test.").
[25]*eBay*, 547 U.S. at 394.
[26]*eBay*, 547 U.S. at 392.
[27]*eBay*, 547 U.S. at 392-393.
[28]*eBay*, 547 U.S. at 391.

(3) that, considering the balance of hardships between the plaintiff and defendant, a remedy in equity is warranted; and
(4) that the public interest would not be disserved by a permanent injunction.[29]

With respect to the irreparable harm factor, the Supreme Court cautioned courts not to assume that all nonpracticing patentees will be unable to satisfy the four-factor test. The Court observed that "some patent holders, such as university researchers or self-made inventors, might reasonably prefer to license their patents, rather than undertake efforts to secure the financing necessary to bring their works to market themselves. Such patent holders may be able to satisfy the traditional four-factor test, and we see no basis for categorically denying them the opportunity to do so."[30]

Because neither the district court nor the Federal Circuit had correctly applied the traditional four-factor framework governing the award of injunctive relief, the Supreme Court in eBay vacated the Circuit's judgment so that the district court could apply the framework in the first instance. The Court took no position on the merits of the case at bar, or on whether permanent injunctions should be awarded in "any number of disputes arising under the Patent Act."[31] It held "only that the decision whether to grant or deny injunctive relief rests within the equitable discretion of the district courts, and that such discretion must be exercised consistent with traditional principles of equity, in patent disputes no less than in other cases governed by such standards."[32]

b. "Causal Nexus" Requirement for Irreparable Harm

In a series of four decisions spawned by the much-publicized "smartphone wars" between consumer electronics giants Apple, Inc. and Samsung Elecs. Co., Ltd., the Federal Circuit in 2012-2015 placed new emphasis on the "irreparable harm" factor (for both permanent injunctions, examined here, and preliminary injunctions, detailed in the following subsection). The Samsung-manufactured smartphones and tablets accused of infringement in these cases involved a

[29] *eBay*, 547 U.S. at 391.

[30] *eBay*, 547 U.S. at 393. Other members of the Court were less willing to contemplate permanent injunctive relief for certain nonpracticing patentees. *See id.* at 396-397 (Kennedy, J., concurring) (stating that "[w]hen the patented invention is but a small component of the product the [accused] companies seek to produce and the threat of an injunction is employed simply for undue leverage in negotiations, legal damages may well be sufficient to compensate for the infringement and an injunction may not serve the public interest").

[31] *eBay*, 547 U.S. at 394.

[32] *eBay*, 547 U.S. at 394.

multitude of technical and design features, only a small number of which infringed utility and design patents owned by Apple. The *Apple v. Samsung* decisions establish that, at least when an accused device is a multi-component product with only a few infringing features, the patent owner's ability to show irreparable harm needed for an injunction against the product will not be automatic or easy.[33]

The Circuit's 2012 "*Apple I*" and "*Apple II*" decisions concerned Apple's requests for *preliminary* injunctions (i.e., injunctions until the date of a final judgment) against the Samsung smartphones and tablets. In these cases, further addressed below,[34] the Federal Circuit first recognized a "causal nexus" requirement as part of the irreparable harm factor. The causal nexus requirement means that a patentee seeking an injunction must show that the irreparable harm it has suffered (e.g., lost market share) was caused *by the infringement* rather than some other factor.[35] That is, the infringing feature(s) must in some way drive consumers' demand for the infringing product.

In *Apple Inc. v. Samsung Elecs. Co., Ltd.* ("*Apple III*"),[36] a unanimous panel of the Federal Circuit (in a 2013 opinion authored by Judge Prost) clarified that the causal nexus analysis applies equally to patentees seeking *permanent* injunctions. The *Apple III* court held that "[t]he reasoning in *Apple I* and *Apple II* reflects general tort principles of causation and applies equally to the preliminary *and permanent* injunction contexts."[37]

The *Apple III* decision offered a helpful synthesis of the Circuit's evolving law on the causal nexus component of the irreparable harm factor. The *Apple III* panel unanimously sustained the district court's denial of a permanent injunction against Samsung with respect to certain infringed Apple *design* patents, but vacated the trial court's denial of a permanent injunction with respect to three infringed Apple

[33]*See generally* Daniel Harris Brean, *Will the* "Nexus" *Requirement of* Apple v. Samsung *Preclude Injunctive Relief in the Majority of Patent Cases?: Echoes of the Entire Market Value Rule*, 51 San Diego L. Rev. 153 (2014).

[34]*See infra* Section B.2 ("Preliminary Injunctions").

[35]The Federal Circuit explained the reasoning behind the causal nexus requirement as follows:

> To show irreparable harm, it is necessary to show that the infringement caused harm in the first place. Sales lost to an infringing product cannot irreparably harm a patentee if consumers buy that product for reasons other than the patented feature. If the patented feature does not drive the demand for the product, sales would be lost even if the offending feature were absent from the accused product. Thus, a likelihood of irreparable harm cannot be shown if sales would be lost regardless of the infringing conduct.

Apple III, 735 F.3d at 1360 (quoting *Apple I*, 678 F.3d at 1324).

[36]735 F.3d 1352 (Fed. Cir. 2013).

[37]*Apple III*, 735 F.3d at 1361 (emphasis added).

utility patents.[38] The Circuit clarified that the causal nexus requirement "applies regardless of the complexity of the products . . . [but] [i]t just may be more easily satisfied (indeed, perhaps even conceded) for relatively 'simple' products."[39]

The Federal Circuit in *Apple III* confirmed that the district court had correctly required a showing "of *some* causal nexus between Samsung's infringing conduct and Apple's alleged harm."[40] Nevertheless, the Federal Circuit agreed with Apple that "certain of the standards arguably articulated by the district court [went] too far."[41] The appellate court modified the causal nexus requirement as the district court had applied it in two respects: by holding that (1) a patentee need not show that a patented (i.e., infringing) feature is the *sole reason* for consumers' purchases of the accused devices;[42] and that (2) there may be circumstances

[38]The utility patents were directed to user interface features of Apple's smartphones and tablets; namely, the "bounce-back" feature on Apple's iPhone and iPad (U.S. Patent No. 7,469,381); a "multi-touch display" functionality that distinguished between a user's single-touch commands for scrolling through a document and multi-touch commands for zooming in and out of the document's display (U.S. Patent No. 7,844,915); and a "double-tap-to-zoom" functionality that enlarged and centered the text of an electronic document (U.S. Patent No. 7,864,163).

[39]*Apple III*, 735 F.3d at 1362.

[40]*Apple III*, 735 F.3d at 1363-1364 (emphasis added). The "some" adjective would come back to haunt Chief Judge Prost in the Circuit's 2015 decision in *Apple Inc. v. Samsung Elecs. Co.*, 801 F.3d 1352, 1376 (Fed. Cir. 2015) ("*Apple IV*"). There, writing in dissent, Chief Judge Prost observed:

> In making these factual findings [that Apple's conjoint survey failed to demonstrate that features claimed in the patents in suit drove consumer demand for Samsung's infringing products], the district court followed our case law faithfully. Nothing in the district court's opinion suggests that it deviated from our precedent. *Rather, the majority deviates from our precedent by repeating as a mantra the phrase "some connection" in* Apple Inc. v. Samsung Electronics Co., 735 F.3d 1352 (Fed. Cir. 2013) ("*Apple III*") *detached from the causal nexus standard explained in our prior cases. See* Majority Op. at 1359, 1359, 1359-60 n.1, 1360, 1363. For example, we have held that
>
> > It is not enough for the patentee to establish some insubstantial connection between the alleged harm and the infringement and check the causal nexus requirement off the list. The patentee must rather show that the infringing feature drives consumer demand for the accused product.
>
> *Apple Inc. v. Samsung Elecs. Co.*, 695 F.3d 1370, 1375 (Fed. Cir. 2012) ("*Apple II*"). We quoted the precise language from the latter sentence above and explicitly acknowledged the continuing force of this requirement in *Apple III*. *Apple III*, [735 F.3d] at 1364 (quoting *id.*). The majority seems to ignore this consistent standard and concludes to the contrary that showing that a patented feature is a "significant driver of customer demand" is not necessary to prove causal nexus to the alleged lost sales. Majority Op. at 1363.

Apple IV, 801 F.3d at 1376 (Prost, C.J., dissenting) (emphasis added).

[41]*Apple III*, 735 F.3d at 1364.

[42]*See Apple III*, 735 F.3d at 1364.

in which it is logical and equitable to view the several patents in suit in the aggregate rather than on a patent-by-patent basis.[43]

In 2015, the Federal Circuit issued yet another injunction decision in the ongoing skirmish, *Apple Inc. v. Samsung Elecs. Co., Ltd.* ("*Apple IV*"),[44] a case concerning three different Apple utility patents.[45] In a panel opinion authored by Judge Moore, the Circuit majority vacated the district court's denial of a permanent injunction against Samsung. The *Apple IV* majority held that the district court had erred as a matter of law in "effectively requir[ing] Apple to prove," "in a case involving phones with hundreds of thousands of available features," that "[Samsung's] infringement was the sole cause of [Apple's] lost downstream sales."[46]

Chief Judge Prost, author of the *Apple III* opinion, responded with a vigorous dissent.[47] Judge Reyna offered a concurring opinion that

[43]*See Apple III*, 735 F.3d at 1365. With regard to its second modification of the causal nexus requirement, the Federal Circuit in *Apple III* explained that the district court had erred when it rejected Apple's arguments for irreparable harm stemming from infringement of each *group* of intellectual property rights; namely, its design patents, its utility patents, and its trade dress. Although the Federal Circuit had admittedly analyzed causal nexus on a patent-by-patent basis in *Apple I*, that analysis did not foreclose consideration of causal nexus for a group of patents in the aggregate. The *Apple III* court reasoned that "it may make sense to view patents in the aggregate where they all relate to the same technology or where they combine to make a product significantly more valuable." *Apple III*, 735 F.3d at 1365. Moreover, the inability of courts to consider patents in the aggregate could lead "to perverse situations such as a patentee being unable to obtain an injunction against the infringement of multiple patents covering different — but when combined, all — aspects of the same technology, even though the technology as a whole drives demand for the infringing product." *Apple III*, 735 F.3d at 1365. The Federal Circuit left it to the district court "to address this issue in the first instance on remand." *Apple III*, 735 F.3d at 1365.

[44]801 F.3d 1352 (Fed. Cir. Sept. 17, 2015).

[45]The patents at issue in the *Apple IV* appeal were U.S. Patent Nos. 5,946,647 ('647 patent); 8,046,721 ('721 patent); and 8,074,172 ('172 patent). Claim 8 of the '721 patent recited a touchscreen device that unlocks when the user makes contact with an "unlock image" and moves that image to a second, predefined location. Claim 9 of the '647 patent recited a system that detects "data structures" within text and generates links to specific actions that can be performed for each type of detected structure — for example, detecting a phone number in a text message and creating a link that would allow the user to dial the phone number or store it in an address book. Claim 18 of the '172 patent claims a method for automatically correcting spelling errors on touchscreen devices. *See Apple IV*, 801 F.3d at 1356. The Northern District of California held on summary judgment that Samsung infringed the '172 patent. Following trial, a jury found that nine Samsung products infringed one or both of Apple's '647 and '721 patents. The jury also awarded Apple a total of approximately $120 million for Samsung's infringement of the three patents. *See Apple IV*, 801 F.3d at 1356.

[46]*Apple IV*, 801 F.3d at 1360.

[47]*See Apple IV*, 801 F.3d at 1374-1381 (Prost, C.J., dissenting). Chief Judge Prost disagreed vehemently that the district court had erred as a matter of law in its application of the causal nexus component of the irreparable harm factor. Contrary to the majority's assertion, the district court never demanded that the infringing features be the "sole" or

focused primarily on Apple's asserted irreparable harm in the form of damage to the company's reputation as an innovator.[48]

In the view of this author, the *Apple III* and *Apple IV* decisions taken together reflect an unfortunate state of disarray in the Circuit's elucidation of the causal nexus component of the irreparable harm showing required for an injunction. The issue is particularly important in the context of multi-featured, multi-faceted technology. It appears that district courts are faithfully attempting to follow the Circuit's changing rules but are whipsawed on appeal when the Circuit "reinterprets" its earlier-stated pronouncements. Given the high profile and stakes of the *Apple v. Samsung* litigation, the Circuit's internal disagreements and lack of cohesive voice may warrant Supreme Court attention.[49]

2. Preliminary Injunctions

A preliminary injunction is "preliminary" because it is entered before trial, that is, before a complete adjudication on the merits of the infringement issue. Preliminary injunctions also are referred to as interlocutory or *pendente lite* (pending the lawsuit). The goal of a

---

"principal" cause of consumer demand for Samsung's products; Judge Prost observed that "the words 'sole' and 'predominant' [we]re not even present in the district court's opinion." *Apple IV,* 801 F.3d at 1375 (Prost, C.J., dissenting) (footnote omitted). Rather than improperly ignore the Apple-proffered "Hauser" survey due to a purported misunderstanding of the law, the district court had "simply weighed the evidence and found it lacking" in view of Samsung's challenges to the survey's "myriad deficiencies" and "nonsensical results." *Apple IV,* 801 F.3d at 1376 (Prost, C.J., dissenting) (noting the Hauser survey's conclusion that the patented word correction feature of Apple's '172 patent was "'worth about $102 on a phone that cost $149'") (quoting district court's *Injunction Order* at *13). In Chief Judge Prost's view, the majority had erred in reversing without deference the district court's rejection of the survey while "never mentioning that [it] was rejected . . . because Samsung's serious challenges to its techniques and conclusions were unrebutted by Apple." *Apple IV,* 801 F.3d at 1375 (Prost, C.J., dissenting).

[48]*See Apple IV,* 801 F.3d at 1366-1374 (Reyna, J., concurring).

[49]Two months after deciding *Apple IV,* the Federal Circuit denied rehearing *en banc* in *Apple III*, clearing the way for the filing of a petition for *certiorari* from *Apple III* in the Supreme Court. *See* Apple Inc. v. Samsung Elecs. Am., Inc., No. 2015-20188 (Fed. Cir. Nov. 19, 2015) (*en banc*) (denying Samsung's petition for rehearing *en banc*, on "[a]ppeal from the United States District Court for the Northern District of California in No. 5:11-cv-01846-LHK, Judge Lucy H. Koh."), *available at* http://patentlyo.com/media/2015/11/SamsungEnBancDenial.pdf (not published on Federal Circuit's website). The district court's decision in Case No. 11-CV-01846-LHK is reported at *Apple, Inc. v. Samsung Elecs. Co.*, 909 F. Supp. 2d 1147 (N.D. Cal. 2012), *aff'd in part, vacated in* part, 735 F.3d 1352 (Fed. Cir. 2013) ("*Apple III*").

The *App IV* opinion was slightly modified and replaced by *Apple Inc. v Samsung Elecs. Co., Ltd.*, 809 F.3d 633 (Fed. Cir. Dec. 16, 20150 (Moore, J.) ("*Apple V*"). The Supreme Court therefore denied *certiorari* in *Apple V*. *See Samsung Elecs. Co., Ltd., v. Apple Inc.*, 136 S. Ct. 2522 (June 27, 2016).

preliminary injunction is to protect the rights of the parties during pendency of the infringement lawsuit, which can take years, by preserving the *status quo* until final disposition of the case.

A preliminary injunction is an extraordinary remedy, not routinely awarded, and will only be granted on a strong showing of the necessary factors by the patentee (the preliminary injunction movant). Federal Circuit case law enumerates the following substantive factors that a district court must consider in evaluating whether to grant a preliminary injunction in a patent case:

i. whether the plaintiff patentee (i.e., the preliminary injunction movant) is " 'likely to succeed on the merits' " (i.e., that it will likely prevail at trial);
ii. that the patentee is " 'likely to suffer irreparable harm in the absence of preliminary relief' ";
iii. " 'that the balance of equities tips in [the patentee's] favor' "; and
iv. " 'that an injunction is in the public interest.' "[50]

The district court must consider the factors and balance all the elements; no one factor is necessarily dispositive.[51] The first two factors are deemed critical, however, such that if a district court finds that the preliminary injunction movant has failed to satisfy either of them, it may deny the injunction without making findings on the third and fourth factors.[52] Each factor is separately discussed below.

Procedurally, the patentee seeking a preliminary injunction against an accused infringer files a motion with the district court.[53] The court will usually hold a hearing with testimony, although the motion is sometimes decided based only on the affidavits and other documentary evidence. In either case, the party sought to be enjoined must be given advance notice. Federal Rule of Civil Procedure 65(a)(1) provides

[50]Apple Inc. v. Samsung Elecs. Co., 695 F.3d 1370, 1373-1374 (Fed. Cir. 2012) (quoting Winter v. Natural Res. Def. Council, Inc., 555 U.S. 7, 20 (2008) (citation omitted)).

[51]*See* Smith Int'l, Inc. v. Hughes Tool Co., 718 F.2d 1573, 1579 (Fed. Cir. 1983). *See also* Hybritech, Inc. v. Abbott Labs., 849 F.2d 1446, 1451 (Fed. Cir. 1988) (explaining that the preliminary injunction "factors, taken individually, are not dispositive; rather, the district court must weigh and measure each factor against the other factors and against the form and magnitude of the relief requested").

[52]*See* Reebok Int'l v. J. Baker, Inc., 32 F.3d 1552, 1556 (Fed. Cir. 1994) (stating that "[w]hile a district court must consider all four factors before granting a preliminary injunction to determine whether the moving party has carried its burden of establishing each of the four, we specifically decline today to require a district court to articulate findings on the third and fourth factors when the court denies a preliminary injunction because a party fails to establish either of the two critical factors").

[53]A motion for preliminary injunction in a patent case is sometimes preceded by an application for a temporary restraining order (TRO). *See* Fed. R. Civ. P. 65(b) (eff. Dec. 1, 2009).

that "[t]he court may issue a preliminary injunction only on notice to the adverse party." Rule 65(c) further requires that before an injunction is entered, the movant must give security; that is, the movant must post a bond, in an amount that the district court deems proper, for payment of costs and/or damages that could be suffered by the accused infringer if that party is later found to have been wrongfully enjoined.

a. Likelihood of Success on the Merits

Prior to the Supreme Court's landmark 2006 *eBay v. MercExchange* decision,[54] the Federal Circuit generally considered the likelihood of success factor the most important of the four preliminary injunction factors. If likelihood of success on the merits was "clearly established," the second preliminary injunction factor — irreparable harm — was presumed.[55] The irreparable harm factor would typically be presumed by the court if the patentee had made a "clear" or "strong" showing on the first factor.[56]

Post-*eBay*, however, the Federal Circuit gradually implemented the Supreme Court's guidance that categorical rules were not proper in the equitable realm of injunctive relief, and that each of the four injunction factors must be considered on its own merits. In 2008, the Federal Circuit admitted that "[i]t remains an open question whether there remains a rebuttable presumption of irreparable harm following *eBay*."[57] By 2011, the Federal Circuit had expressly jettisoned the presumption of irreparable harm (in the context of preliminary injunctions as well as permanent injunctions).[58] Thus, establishing likelihood of success remains essential in its own right, but satisfaction of this factor no longer guarantees that a court will also find irreparable harm.

[54]Discussed *supra* Section B.1 ("Permanent Injunctions").

[55]Smith Int'l, Inc. v. Hughes Tool Co., 718 F.2d 1573, 1581 (Fed. Cir. 1983) ("We hold that where validity and continuing infringement have been clearly established . . . immediate irreparable harm is presumed") (footnotes omitted).

[56]*See Smith Int'l*, 718 F.2d at 1581; *see also* Illinois Tool Works, Inc. v. Grip-Pak, Inc., 906 F.2d 679, 682 (Fed. Cir. 1990).

[57]Broadcom Corp. v. Qualcomm, Inc., 543 F.3d 683, 702 (Fed. Cir. 2008).

[58]*See* Robert Bosch LLC v. Pylon Mfg. Corp., 659 F.3d 1142, 1149 (Fed. Cir. 2011) ("We take this opportunity to put the question to rest and confirm that *eBay* jettisoned the presumption of irreparable harm as it applies to determining the appropriateness of injunctive relief."). Although *Bosch* involved a permanent injunction, the Federal Circuit clarified that it is reasonable not to presume irreparable harm in either context. The court observed that the standard for preliminary injunctions is "essentially the same" as the standard for permanent injunctions, except that the former requires a likelihood of success on the merits and the latter requires actual success. *See Robert Bosch LLC*, 659 F.3d at 1148 n.3.

Establishing likelihood of success at the preliminary injunction stage takes into consideration the presumptions and burdens of proof that will apply at trial.[59] More specifically, the patentee must show a reasonable probability of success that (1) it will establish infringement by a preponderance of the evidence, and (2) that the accused infringer will not be able to establish invalidity or unenforceability of the patent by clear and convincing evidence.[60] Although a patent owner does not ordinarily bear the burden of proof on validity or enforceability, "at the preliminary injunction stage, because of the extraordinary nature of the relief, the *patentee* carries the burden of showing likelihood of success on the merits with respect to the patent's validity, enforceability, and infringement."[61]

As to infringement, the patentee/preliminary injunction movant will often attempt to establish similarity between the accused product and other products that have previously been adjudicated as infringing the same patent. As to validity, the patentee's chances of success are strengthened if the validity of its patent was previously sustained against a challenge by a different defendant.[62] The patentee also may rely on evidence of public acquiescence in the patent's validity or conclusive direct technical evidence of validity.[63]

b. Irreparable Harm

To satisfy this factor the patentee must show that it will suffer irreparable harm if a preliminary injunction is not granted. The Federal Circuit has instructed that "the irreparable harm inquiry seeks

[59]*See* Titan Tire Corp. v. Case New Holland, Inc., 566 F.3d 1372, 1379 (Fed. Cir. 2009) ("when analyzing the likelihood of success factor, the trial court, after considering all the evidence available at this early stage of the litigation, must determine whether it is more likely than not that the challenger will be able to prove at trial, by clear and convincing evidence, that the patent is invalid"); Vehicular Techs. v. Titan Wheel Int'l, Inc., 141 F.3d 1084, 1088 (Fed. Cir. 1998) (stating that "[t]o establish a likelihood of success on the merits, [the patentee] must show that, in light of the presumptions and burdens that will inhere at trial on the merits, (1) it will likely prove that [the accused infringer] infringes the [] patent, and (2) its infringement claim will likely withstand [the accused infringer's] challenges to the validity and enforceability of the [] patent").

[60]*See Vehicular Techs.,* 141 F.3d at 1088 (stating that "[t]o establish a likelihood of success on the merits, [the patentee] must show that, in light of the presumptions and burdens that will inhere at trial on the merits, (1) it will likely prove that [the accused infringer] infringes the [] patent, and (2) its infringement claim will likely withstand [the accused infringer's] challenges to the validity and enforceability of the [] patent").

[61]Nutrition 21 v. United States, 930 F.2d 867, 869 (Fed. Cir. 1991) (emphasis in original).

[62]The prior adjudication on validity may be given considerable weight, although it does not necessarily bind the district court before whom the preliminary injunction motion is pending. *See* Hybritech, Inc. v. Abbott Labs., 849 F.2d 1446, 1452 (Fed. Cir. 1988).

[63]*See Smith Int'l*, 718 F.2d at 1578.

to measure harms that no damages payment, however great, could address."[64] Valid grounds for finding irreparable harm include price erosion, loss of goodwill, damage to reputation, and loss of business opportunities.[65]

The Federal Circuit holds that as the party seeking emergency relief, the preliminary injunction movant " 'must make a clear showing that it is at risk of irreparable harm, which entails showing a likelihood of substantial and immediate irreparable injury.' "[66]

The patentee succeeded in making this showing in *Celsis In Vitro, Inc. v. CellzDirect, Inc.*,[67] in which the patent in suit concerned methods for preparing multi-cryopreserved hepatocytes (a type of liver cell). The patentee marketed "pooled multi-cryopreserved hepatocyte products" with superior cell viability. The Federal Circuit highlighted evidence that these products, facing "irreversible" price erosion and lost sales to the accused infringer, were the patentee's "flagship products" and in their "growth phase," soon to be entering "the mature phase with the highest revenues and strongest market position."[68] The appellate court noted expert testimony concerning the difficulty of quantifying the harm to the patentee's reputation and business, for "[d]uring the growth stage of a product, it is particularly crucial

[64]Celsis In Vitro, Inc. v. CellzDirect, Inc., 664 F.3d 922, 930 (Fed. Cir. 2012) (citing Altana Pharma AG v. Teva Pharm. USA, Inc., 566 F.3d 999, 1010 (Fed. Cir. 2009); Sampson v. Murray, 415 U.S. 61, 90 (1974) ("The key word in this consideration is irreparable. Mere injuries, however substantial, in terms of money, time and energy necessarily expended in the absence of a stay, are not enough.") (quoting Va. Petroleum Jobbers Ass'n v. Fed. Power Comm'n, 259 F.2d 921, 925 (D.C. Cir. 1958))).

[65]*Celsis,* 664 F.3d at 930 (citing Abbott Labs. v. Sandoz, Inc., 544 F.3d 1341, 1362 (Fed. Cir. 2008); Sanofi-Synthelabo v. Apotex, Inc., 470 F.3d 1368, 1382-1383 (Fed. Cir. 2006)).

[66]Apple, Inc. v. Samsung Elecs. Co., Ltd., 695 F.3d 1370, 1374 (Fed. Cir. 2012) (*"Apple II"*) (quoting Apple, Inc. v. Samsung Elecs. Co., 678 F.3d 1314, 1325 (Fed. Cir. 2012) (*"Apple I"*) (citing Winter v. Natural Res. Def. Council, Inc., 555 U.S. 7, 22 (2008); Weinberger v. Romero-Barcelo, 456 U.S. 305, 311 (1982); O'Shea v. Littleton, 414 U.S. 488, 502 (1974))). *See also* Beacon Theatres, Inc. v. Westover, 359 U.S. 500, 506-507 (1959) ("The basis of injunctive relief in the federal courts has always been irreparable harm and inadequacy of legal remedies.").

In contrast, a "mere showing that [the patentee] might lose some insubstantial market share as a result of [the] infringement is not enough." *Apple I*, 678 F.3d at 1324-1325. The "clear showing" that a patentee must make "entails showing 'a likelihood of substantial and immediate irreparable injury.' " *Apple I*, 678 F.3d at 1325 (quoting O'Shea v. Littleton, 414 U.S. 488, 502 (1974)). The harm must be more than trivial. *See Apple I*, 678 F.3d at 1325 (citing Weinberger v. Romero-Barcelo, 456 U.S. 305, 311 (1982) (holding that an injunction should not issue as a matter of course for irreparable harm that is "merely trifling")).

[67]664 F.3d 922, 930 (Fed. Cir. 2012). Circuit Judge Gajarsa disagreed with the *Celsis* majority's decision to affirm the preliminary injunction grant. In Judge Gajarsa's view, the accused infringers had raised a substantial question concerning the nonobviousness of the patent in suit. *See Celsis*, 664 F.3d at 932 (Gajarsa, J., dissenting).

[68]*Celsis*, 644 F.3d at 930.

to be able to distinguish oneself from competitors. This includes building the brand, expanding the customer base, and establishing one's reputation and leadership in the market."[69] The Federal Circuit also highlighted the "particularly sensitive" nature of the market in which the parties competed, "because customers buy in bulk and at irregular times, such that the loss of a single sale in this market may be more harmful than for products purchased daily."[70]

An accused infringer may seek to rebut the irreparable harm factor by introducing evidence that it has stopped all infringing activity and has no plans to resume it in the future. A long period of delay by the patentee in moving for a preliminary injunction after learning of the infringement also may refute irreparable harm.[71] Likewise, evidence that the patentee has engaged in a pattern of licensing the patent to others, indicating that the receipt of royalties is sufficient remedy for the patentee's surrender of exclusivity, may be grounds for rebuttal of the irreparable harm presumption.[72]

In a series of four decisions spawned by the much-publicized "smartphone wars" between Apple, Inc. and Samsung Elecs. Co., Ltd., the Federal Circuit in 2012-2015 placed new emphasis on the "irreparable harm" factor (both for preliminary injunctions, examined here, and for permanent injunctions, analyzed in the previous section). The Samsung-manufactured smartphones and tablets accused of infringement in these cases involved a multitude of technical and design features, only some of which infringed utility and design patents owned by Apple. The *Apple v. Samsung* decisions establish that showing irreparable harm will not be automatic or easy, particularly when the accused device is a multi-component product with only a few infringing features.

In its two 2012 preliminary injunction decisions captioned *Apple, Inc. v. Samsung Elecs. Co., Ltd.*,[73] the Federal Circuit announced that

[69]*Celsis*, 644 F.3d at 931.

[70]*Celsis*, 644 F.3d at 930.

[71]On the other hand,

> [t]he period of delay exercised by a party prior to seeking a preliminary injunction in a case involving intellectual property is but one factor to be considered by a district court in its analysis of irreparable harm. Although a showing of delay may be so significant, in the district court's discretion, as to preclude a determination of irreparable harm, a showing of delay does not preclude, as a matter of law, a determination of irreparable harm. A period of delay is but one circumstance that the district court must consider in the context of the totality of the circumstances.

Hybritech, Inc. v. Abbott Labs., 849 F.2d 1446, 1457 (Fed. Cir. 1988) (footnotes omitted) (emphasis in original).

[72]*See* Polymer Techs. v. Bridwell, 103 F.3d 970, 974 (Fed. Cir. 1996).

[73]*See* Apple, Inc. v. Samsung Elecs. Co., Ltd., 678 F.3d 1314 (Fed. Cir. 2012) ("*Apple I*"); Apple, Inc. v. Samsung Elecs. Co., Ltd., 695 F.3d 1370 (Fed. Cir. Oct. 11, 2012) ("*Apple II*").

proving irreparable harm requires showing not only the extent of the harm (i.e., that it will be irreparable absent the grant of a preliminary injunction) but also a connection (i.e., a "causal nexus") between the asserted irreparable harm and the accused infringement:

> [W]here the accused product includes many features of which only one (or a small minority) infringe — a finding that the patentee will be at risk of irreparable harm does not alone justify injunctive relief. Rather, the patentee must also establish that the harm is sufficiently related to the infringement. *Apple I*, 678 F.3d at 1324. Thus, to satisfy the irreparable harm factor in a patent infringement suit, a patentee must establish both of the following requirements: 1) that absent an injunction, it will suffer irreparable harm, and 2) that a sufficiently strong causal nexus relates the alleged harm to the alleged infringement.[74]

Thus the 2012 *Apple v. Samsung* decisions of the Federal Circuit established that the irreparable harm prong of a preliminary injunction analysis has two parts: (1) the extent of harm itself — that it will be irreparable if not enjoined; and (2) a sufficiently strong causal connection between the alleged irreparable harm and the alleged infringing feature(s) of the accused device.[75]

c. *Balance of the Hardships Tipping in Movant's Favor*

The imposition of a preliminary injunction is a drastic measure. The accused infringer must stop making what may be its primary or only product, with the inevitable loss of assets and jobs that that entails. Some infringers have been forced to declare bankruptcy as a result of a court's injunction against patent infringement.

In the high-profile *Polaroid v. Kodak* instant photography litigation of the 1980s,[76] the accused infringer Kodak asked the district court to

---

In brief, the *Apple I* appeal involved three design patents directed to certain ornamental features of Apple's iPhone and iPad devices, as well as an Apple utility patent claiming a "bounce-back" software feature. Apple alleged infringement of these patents by Samsung's Galaxy S 4G and Infuse 4G smartphones and its Galaxy Tab 10.1 tablet computer.

The *Apple II* appeal involved a different Apple utility patent directed to an apparatus for a "unified search" feature. The feature allowed users to search the local memory of a smartphone device as well as the Internet by entering a single search query. Apple alleged that Samsung's Galaxy Nexus smartphone infringed this patent.

[74] *Apple II*, 695 F.3d at 1374.

[75] For additional discussion of the causal nexus requirement as further developed by the Federal Circuit in the 2013 *Apple III* and 2015 *Apple IV* decisions, *see supra* Section B.1.b.

[76] Kodak ultimately paid Polaroid $925 million to end a "decade-old court battle over Kodak's infringement of instant photography patents held by Polaroid. The $925 million consisted of a patent infringement verdict of $873 million plus $52 million in interest." Shawn K. Baldwin, *"To Promote the Progress of Science and Useful Arts": A Role for*

stay the entry of an injunction against it pending Kodak's appeal to the Federal Circuit.[77] Kodak contended that entry of the injunction would shut down Kodak's instant photography business, putting over 4,000 employees out of work and would result in lost investments in equipment and facilities of over $200 million.[78] Although admittedly "seductive," Kodak's claims of hardship did not persuade the district court to stay entry of the injunction pending appeal: "[t]o the extent Kodak has purchased [its] success at Polaroid's expense, it has taken a 'calculated risk' that it might infringe existing patents."[79] Thus, the district court found the potential harm to accused infringer Kodak outweighed by the harm that would result to patentee Polaroid had the injunction not been entered.

Because of the potentially significant consequences of its decision, a district court must weigh and balance the equities of the parties' respective positions before granting an injunction. The court must examine the hardships that may ensue if it grants the injunction versus those that will occur if it does not. If an injunction is to be entered, the district court should conclude that the balance of hardships tips in the patentee's favor.

d. Public Interest

Lastly, the district court should consider what, if any, impact the grant of an injunction would have on the public's interest. As with the previous factor, the court must weigh this factor from the perspective of both parties. The public always has an interest in ensuring that valid patents are enforced; this maintains the incentives for innovation that a strong patent system represents. On the other hand, the infringer may be supplying the public with an additional source of a critical product in short supply. For example, consider a breakthrough drug for a potentially fatal disease that a patentee is unable to manufacture in large quantities. Cutting off the infringer as a second source of supply would likely result in price increases and supply constrictions that could mean the difference between life and death to sick patients.

The Seventh Circuit's decision in *City of Milwaukee v. Activated Sludge, Inc.*,[80] discussed above, represents a rare example of a court

---

Federal Regulation of Intellectual Property as Collateral, 143 U. PA. L. REV. 1701, 1719 n.92 (1995) (citing *Kodak to Pay Polaroid $925 Million to Settle Suit*, WALL ST. J., July 16, 1991, at C13).

[77] *See* Polaroid Corp. v. Eastman Kodak Co., 641 F. Supp. 828, 1985 U.S. Dist. LEXIS 15003 (D. Mass. 1985).

[78] *See Polaroid Corp.*, 1985 U.S. Dist. LEXIS 15003, at *5.

[79] *Polaroid Corp.*, 1985 U.S. Dist. LEXIS 15003, at *6 (quoting Smith Int'l, Inc. v. Hughes Tool Co., 718 F.2d 1573, 1581 (Fed. Cir. 1983)) (footnote omitted).

[80] 69 F.2d 577 (7th Cir. 1934).

refusing to enjoin infringement (albeit permanently rather than preliminarily) because of public health concerns. In *Hybritech, Inc. v. Abbott Labs.*,[81] the Federal Circuit affirmed a district court's grant of a preliminary injunction that prevented the alleged infringer Abbott from continuing to sell certain accused products but permitted it to continue selling two others, namely Abbott's cancer test kits and hepatitis test kits. The district court had determined that the public interest was best served by the continued availability of those kits, and the Federal Circuit saw no basis for disturbing that finding.[82]

e. *Appellate Standard of Review*

The grant or refusal of a preliminary injunction is immediately appealable as an interlocutory order under 28 U.S.C. §1292(a).[83] Because the order to grant or refuse the injunction is an equitable decision, the appellate court may overturn it only if the district court abused its discretion. However, the Federal Circuit will not hesitate to vacate the grant of a preliminary injunction where the district court fails to sufficiently explicate its findings on infringement and validity.[84]

C. Ongoing Royalties for Future Infringements

After the Supreme Court's 2006 decision in *eBay Inc. v. MercExchange, LLC,*[85] district courts in certain cases have denied permanent injunctions (thus allowing ongoing infringement) while requiring that the infringer pay royalties for each infringing sale made during the remaining life of the patent.[86] As one commentator has observed,

[81] 849 F.2d 1446, 1458 (Fed. Cir. 1988).
[82] *See Hybritech*, 849 F.2d at 1458.
[83] The statute provides in part:

> (a) Except as provided in subsections (c) and (d) of this section, the courts of appeals shall have jurisdiction of appeals from:
>
> (1) Interlocutory orders of the district courts of the United States . . . granting, continuing, modifying, refusing or dissolving injunctions, or refusing to dissolve or modify injunctions, except where a direct review may be had in the Supreme Court. . . .

28 U.S.C. §1292.
[84] *See, e.g.*, Oakley, Inc. v. Int'l Tropic-Cal, Inc., 923 F.2d 167, 168 (Fed. Cir. 1991) (concluding that district court's findings were so limited and conclusory as to make meaningful appellate review impossible).
[85] 547 U.S. 388 (2006). *eBay* is examined further *supra* Section B.1.a.
[86] *See, e.g.*, Voda v. Cordis Corp., 536 F.3d 1311, 1329 (Fed. Cir. 2008) (affirming district court's denial of permanent injunction sought by prevailing individual patent owner; rejecting patent owner's argument that denial of permanent injunction would

"while understandably relieved that they may elect to continue their infringing conduct, [such adjudged infringers] are presented with an interesting conundrum if designing around the patent is not possible or practical: continue infringing the patent and risk paying onerous post-verdict ongoing royalties — and possibly enhanced damages — or stop infringing, thereby granting the patentee a de facto injunction."[87]

The Federal Circuit approved the imposition of ongoing royalties in *Paice LLC v. Toyota Motor Corp.*[88] Paice owned and licensed patents directed to drive train technology for hybrid cars but did not manufacture or sell any products.[89] After a jury found that Toyota's hybrid vehicles infringed certain claims of Paice's patents under the doctrine of equivalents, a district court denied Paice's motion for a permanent injunction against Toyota. Applying the four-factor test of *eBay*,[90] the district court found that Paice would not be irreparably harmed in its ability to license its patents absent a permanent injunction, that monetary damages were adequate given the relatively small dollar value of the infringing component as a subset of Toyota's entire accused vehicle, and that the balance of hardships favored Toyota.[91] In lieu of imposing a permanent injunction, the district court *sua sponte* imposed an "ongoing royalty" of $25 per infringing vehicle that Toyota would sell during the remaining life of the Paice patent. The court's $25/vehicle ongoing royalty rate was numerically the same as the jury's reasonable royalty award for past infringements.[92]

The Federal Circuit did not reject in principle the district court's imposition of an ongoing royalty, but nevertheless required remand because the district court's order did not explain how it had arrived at the $25/vehicle ongoing royalty. The Federal Circuit observed that

---

irreparably harm his exclusive licensee); Paice LLC v. Toyota Motor Corp., 504 F.3d 1293, 1313-1315 (Fed. Cir. 2007) (approving denial of permanent injunction but remanding for limited purpose of having district court reevaluate ongoing royalty rate).

[87]Chad S.C. Stover, *When Courts Deny Injunctive Relief Post-*eBay*: Winning the Injunction Battle but Losing the Ongoing Royalty War*, 79 BNA PAT., TRADEMARK & COPYRIGHT J. 18 (Nov. 6, 2009). Stover contends that the after the Supreme Court's *eBay* decision, the district courts have faced the "complicated, multifaceted" issue of ongoing royalties with "little guidance from the Federal Circuit." *Id.* Stover's article describes and critiques the "distinct" approaches taken by three different federal district courts.

[88]504 F.3d 1293 (Fed. Cir. 2007).

[89]*See Paice LLC.* 504 F.3d at 1302-1303 (discussing Paice's licensing business and noting that "Paice does not actually manufacture any goods").

[90]*See eBay*, 547 U.S. at 391 (listing factors that patentee seeking permanent injunction must satisfy as "(1) that it has suffered an irreparable injury; (2) that remedies available at law, such as monetary damages, are inadequate to compensate for that injury; (3) that, considering the balance of hardships between the plaintiff and defendant, a remedy in equity is warranted; and (4) that the public interest would not be disserved by a permanent injunction").

[91]*See Paice LLC*, 504 F.3d at 1302-1303.

[92]*See Paice LLC*, 504 F.3d at 1303 (noting that the reasonable royalty awarded by the jury "amounted to approximately $25 per accused vehicle").

awarding an ongoing royalty in lieu of an injunction may be appropriate under some circumstances, including patent infringement or antitrust violations. Such relief should not be awarded "as a matter of course," however.[93] Rather than acting *sua sponte* as in the case at bar, a court "[i]n most cases, whe[n] determin[ing] that a permanent injunction is not warranted, . . . may wish to allow the parties to negotiate a license amongst themselves regarding future use of a patented invention before imposing an ongoing royalty."[94] If the parties fail to negotiate a license, however, "the district court could step in to assess a reasonable royalty in light of the ongoing infringement."[95]

Some Federal Circuit judges take the view that an ongoing royalty award of the type imposed in *Paice LLC* should be deemed a "compulsory license," at least when the parties are not afforded a prior opportunity to negotiate the rate of the ongoing royalty. As a general matter, a **compulsory license** is a compelled (rather than voluntary) license, that is, one imposed by the government against the wishes of a patent owner. Historically, the U.S. patent system has strongly disfavored the general availability of compulsory licenses. According to Circuit Judge Rader, for example, "[t]o avoid many of the disruptive implications of a royalty imposed as an alternative to the preferred remedy of exclusion, the trial court's discretion should not reach so far as to deny the parties a formal opportunity to set the terms of a royalty on their own. With such an opportunity in place, an ongoing royalty would be an ongoing royalty, not a compulsory license."[96]

[93]*Paice LLC*, 504 F.3d at 1314-1315.

[94]*Paice LLC*, 504 F.3d at 1315. In *Telcordia Techs., Inc. v. Cisco Sys., Inc.*, 612 F.3d 1365 (Fed. Cir. 2010), the Federal Circuit again affirmed a remedy of ongoing royalties and approved a district court's direction to the parties to negotiate the ongoing royalty rate. *See Telcordia Techs.*, 612 F.3d at 1379 (stating that "after declining [patentee] Telcordia's motion for permanent injunction, the district court directed the parties to negotiate a reasonable royalty for ongoing infringement. An award of an ongoing royalty is appropriate because the record supports the district court's finding that Telcordia has not been compensated for Cisco's continuing infringement. Therefore, the district court did not abuse its discretion by directing the parties to negotiate the terms of the appropriate royalty.").

[95]*Paice LLC*, 504 F.3d at 1315. In *Amado v. Microsoft Corp.*, 517 F.3d 1353 (Fed. Cir. 2008), the Federal Circuit elaborated that "[t]here is a fundamental difference . . . between a reasonable royalty for pre-verdict infringement and damages for post-verdict infringement. . . . Prior to judgment, liability for infringement, as well as the validity of the patent, is uncertain, and damages are determined in the context of that uncertainty. Once a judgment of validity and infringement has been entered, however, the calculus is markedly different because different economic factors are involved." *Id.* at 1361-1362 (citations omitted).

[96]*Paice LLC*, 504 F.3d at 1316 (Rader, J., concurring). In *Atlas Powder Co. v. Ireco Chems.*, 773 F.2d 1230 (Fed. Cir. 1985) (Rich, J.), the Federal Circuit affirmed a district court's imposition of a preliminary injunction and stated that "[i]f monetary relief were the sole relief afforded by the patent statute then injunctions would be unnecessary and

Other Federal Circuit judges disagree, distinguishing an ongoing royalty like that awarded in *Paice LLC* from a compulsory license.[97] While a U.S. federal court may impose ongoing royalty payments on a particular adjudged infringer (e.g., Toyota in *Paice LLC*), a compulsory license as that phrase is understood internationally is potentially available to any applicant meeting applicable statutory or regulatory criteria as determined by a government's patent-granting authority. Unlike the United States, many foreign countries have implemented statutory frameworks under which domestic manufacturers may apply to their national patent offices for a compulsory patent license on grounds such as a public health crisis.[98] The TRIPS Agreement permits WTO member countries to grant compulsory licenses under specified conditions.[99]

D. Damages for Past Infringements

1. Introduction

In addition to an injunction, the other key form of relief for patent infringement is monetary, in the amount of the damages that the patentee suffered because of the infringement. Section 284 of the Patent Act, titled "Damages," provides:

> Upon finding for the claimant the court shall award the claimant *damages adequate to compensate for the infringement,* but in no event less than a reasonable royalty for the use made of the invention by the infringer, together with interest and costs as fixed by the court.

---

infringers could become compulsory licensees for as long as the litigation lasts." *Id.* at 1233.

[97]*Paice LLC*, 504 F.3d at 1313 n.13 (majority opinion authored by Prost, J.) (using phrase "ongoing royalty" to "distinguish this equitable remedy from a compulsory license"). The *Paice LLC* majority explained that "[t]he term 'compulsory license' implies that anyone who meets certain criteria has congressional authority to use that which is licensed," giving as an example the musical works "mechanical" license codified in U.S. copyright law at 17 U.S.C. §115. *See Paice LLC*, 504 F.3d at 1313 n.13. "By contrast, the ongoing-royalty order at issue here is limited to one particular set of defendants; there is no implied authority in the court's order for any other auto manufacturer to follow in Toyota's footsteps and use the patented invention with the court's imprimatur." *Id.*

Ongoing royalties have become an accepted remedy. *See, e.g., SRI Int'l, Inc. v. Cisco Sys., Inc.*, 930 F.3d 1295, 1312 (Fed. Cir. 2019) (Stoll, J.) (affirming district court's award of 3.5% ongoing royalties on all of infringers post-verdict sales of products found to infringe and those "not colorably different").

[98]*See, e.g.*, India Patents Act, 1970 (amended 2005) §§83-92A.

[99]*See* TRIPS art. 31. For additional discussion of compulsory licensing, *see infra* Chapter 12, Section D ("The World Trade Organization's Agreement on Trade-Related Aspects of Intellectual Property Rights (TRIPS)").

> When the damages are not found by a jury, the court shall assess them. In either event the court may increase the damages up to three times the amount found or assessed. Increased damages under this paragraph shall not apply to provisional rights under section 154(d) [35 U.S.C. §154(d)].
>
> The court may receive expert testimony as an aid to the determination of damages or of what royalty would be reasonable under the circumstances.[100]

The critical language of 35 U.S.C. §284, ¶1, "damages adequate to compensate for the infringement," is the subject of much case law interpretation. The statute does not explain how to determine an "adequate" amount beyond specifying that it must not go below the floor or minimum of a "reasonable royalty" (discussed separately below). Thus, the district courts "have been accorded wide latitude to choose a compensation mode that appears to them to fit the evidence presented."[101] The Federal Circuit has not hesitated to correct what it perceives as erroneous economic evaluation, however; since its creation in 1982, the appellate court has developed a detailed jurisprudence on the evaluation of patent infringement damages.

Damage awards may be of two basic types: compensatory and enhanced. Each is discussed below. To summarize, compensatory damages compensate the patentee by trying to approximate the actual monetary loss suffered.[102] Enhanced damages are in the nature of punitive damages and are intended to punish the accused infringer for willful conduct. Enhanced damages cannot be awarded for compensatory purposes; rather, they may be awarded "only as a penalty for an infringer's increased culpability, namely willful infringement or bad faith."[103]

In patent infringement actions, "[d]eciding how much to award as damages is not an exact science, and the methodology of assessing and computing damages is committed to the sound discretion of the

[100] 35 U.S.C. §284 (2020) (emphasis added).

[101] Paul M. Janicke, *Contemporary Issues in Patent Damages,* 42 Am. U. L. Rev. 691, 697 (1993). Professor Janicke's article is a valuable resource on all aspects of patent infringement damages. *See also* Robert S. Frank, Jr. & Denise W. DeFranco, *Patent Infringement Damages: A Brief Summary,* 10 Fed. Cir. B.J. 281 (2000).

[102] *See* Birdsall v. Coolidge, 93 U.S. 64, 68-69 (1876) (explaining that when patentee sued for infringement "at law" [before the merger of law and equity in the U.S. courts], "he would be entitled to recover, as damages, compensation for the pecuniary injury he suffered by the infringement, without regard to the question whether the defendant had gained or lost by his unlawful acts, — the measure of damages in such case being not what the defendants had gained, but what the plaintiff had lost") (citing Curtis, Law of Patents §461 (4th ed. 1873); 5 Stat. 123).

[103] *See* Beatrice Foods Co. v. New England Printing & Lithographing Co., 923 F.2d 1576, 1579 (Fed. Cir. 1991) (stating that "[d]amages cannot be enhanced to award the patentee additional compensation to rectify what the district court views as an inadequacy in the actual damages awarded").

district court."[104] The Federal Circuit has taken the position that any doubts as to the amount of a damages award are to be resolved against the infringer as the wrongdoer.[105]

2. Compensatory Damages

Federal Circuit authority expresses the basic goal of compensatory damages: putting the patentee in as good a position as it would have been in had there been no infringement. In the specialized terminology of patent damages, this condition or state is referred to as hypothetically returning the patentee to a "but for world."[106] In other words, U.S. patent law attempts to restore the patentee to its financial position but for the infringement.[107]

Unlike copyright infringement laws, the patent laws do not provide for an award of "statutory damages" within a specified range of dollars.[108] The amount of the patentee's compensatory damages must be determined based on the facts of each case. There are two primary analytical methods of computing the amount of compensatory damages for infringement of a U.S. utility patent: lost profits and reasonable royalty.[109] Each is discussed separately below.

[104]State Indus., Inc. v. Mor-Flo Indus., Inc., 883 F.2d 1573, 1576-1577 (Fed. Cir. 1989).

[105]*See* Kalman v. Berlyn Corp., 914 F.2d 1473, 1482 (Fed. Cir. 1990).

[106]*See* Grain Processing Corp. v. American Maize-Prods. Co., 185 F.3d 1341, 1350 (Fed. Cir. 1999) (observing that "trial courts, with this court's approval, consistently permit patentees to present market reconstruction theories showing all of the ways in which they would have been better off in the 'but for world,' and accordingly to recover lost profits in a wide variety of forms").

[107]*See* Aro Mfg. Co. v. Convertible Top Replacement Co., 377 U.S. 476, 507 (1964) (defining "damages" as the difference between the patentee's pecuniary condition after the infringement and what it would have been had the infringement not occurred).

[108]*Cf.* 17 U.S.C. §504(c) (2020) (providing that copyright owner may elect award of statutory damages of $750 to $30,000 for all infringements in the action (or up to $150,000 if willful infringement) rather than proving amount of its actual damages and profits).

[109]Historically, another method of compensation besides damages applied: an equitable accounting of the infringer's profits, sometimes referred to merely as "profits" but indicating the accused infringer's profits. (Such profits should be distinguished from the lost profits of the patentee, a form of damages. *See infra* Section D.2.a.) An accounting was based on a theory of disgorgement of the profits (i.e., ill-gotten gains) made by the defendant on its infringing sales. Use of this equitable accounting remedy for infringement of utility patents was eliminated by Congress in 1946. *See Aro Mfg.*, 377 U.S. at 505.

Although disgorgement of the defendant's profits is no longer available for infringement of a utility patent, 35 U.S.C. §289 (2020) still provides for recovery of such profits for infringement of a *design* patent:

> Whoever during the term of a patent for a design, without license of the owner, (1) applies the patented design, or any colorable imitation thereof, to any article of

a. *Lost Profits*

Damages computed on a theory of lost profits are intended to approximate the profits that the patentee lost because of sales diverted by the presence of the infringing product in the marketplace. The key element that a patentee must prove to attain a lost profits recovery is causation — that the infringement was the cause of the patentee's lost sales rather than some other cause such as the marketplace availability of noninfringing alternatives to the patented item. The patentee bears the burden of establishing causation; in other words, the patentee must show that but for the infringement, the patentee would have made the sales for which it seeks lost profits.[110]

To understand the computation of lost profits, consider the following simple example. Assume that it costs a patentee $5 to manufacture a patented widget and that the patentee sells each widget for $25, thus netting a profit of $20 per widget. Assume further that the defendant sold 100 infringing widgets. If the patentee can prove that but for the infringement, it could and would have made those 100 extra widget sales, then the lost profits to be awarded the patentee are computed as $20 × 100, or $2,000.[111]

(i) The *Panduit* Analysis

The foundational case of *Panduit Corp. v. Stahlin Bros. Fibre Works, Inc.*[112] set forth the following factors as the elements that a patentee must prove in order to obtain damages based on lost profits:

> To obtain as damages the profits on sales he would have made absent the infringement, i.e., the sales made by the infringer, a patent owner must prove: (1) demand for the patented product, (2) absence of acceptable

---

> manufacture for the purpose of sale, or (2) sells or exposes for sale any article of manufacture to which such design or colorable imitation has been applied shall be liable to the owner to the extent of his total profit, but not less than $250, recoverable in any United States district court having jurisdiction of the parties.
>
> Nothing in this section shall prevent, lessen, or impeach any other remedy which an owner of an infringed patent has under the provisions of this title [35 U.S.C.], but he shall not twice recover the profit made from the infringement.

See also supra Chapter 7, Section H.2.c ("Unique Remedy for Design Patent Infringement"), examining the dispute over design patent infringement damages in *Apple, Inc. v. Samsung Elecs. Co., Ltd.*, 786 F.3d 983 (Fed. Cir. 2015).

[110] *See* Water Techs. Corp. v. Calco, Ltd., 850 F.2d 660, 671 (Fed. Cir. 1988).

[111] A more robust analysis of the patentee's lost profits in this scenario should distinguish between the patentee's fixed and variable costs. As discussed below, lost profits must be computed using an incremental income approach that excludes the patentee's fixed costs, that is, those costs that do not vary with increases in production, such as management salaries, property taxes, and insurance. *See* Paper Converting Mach. Co. v. Magna-Graphics Corp., 745 F.2d 11, 22 (Fed. Cir. 1984).

[112] 575 F.2d 1152 (6th Cir. 1978) (Markey, C.J., sitting by designation).

> noninfringing substitutes, (3) his manufacturing and marketing capability to exploit the demand, and (4) the amount of the profit he would have made. . . .[113]

Each factor is separately examined below.

(a) Demand for the patented product. *Panduit* factor (1), demand for the patented product, is usually presumed from the fact of infringement. The Federal Circuit considers "a substantial number of sales" of infringing products containing the patented features to be, itself, "compelling evidence" of the demand for the patented product.[114] Under this analysis, the fact of the infringer's sales necessarily means that there were buyers who wanted the product and were willing to pay the infringer's price.[115]

(b) Absence of acceptable noninfringing substitutes. *Panduit* factor (2), absence of acceptable noninfringing substitutes, assures causation, that is, that the patentee lost its sales because of the defendant's infringement (i.e., the sales that the patentee would have made, but for the infringement, were diverted to the infringer), not because consumers were buying a third party's noninfringing substitute product. An award of lost profits must not be speculative; rather, the patentee's burden is to show a reasonable probability that, absent the infringement, it would have made the infringer's sales.[116] Establishing this under *Panduit* factor (2), and determining what products do or do not qualify as "acceptable substitutes" for the patented product, constitute the major battlegrounds in patent litigation over lost profits damages.

For example, in the long-running *Polaroid v. Kodak* battle over infringement of Polaroid's patents on instant photography,[117] Polaroid sought lost profits damages. The accused infringer Kodak argued that lost profits were not available because conventional (i.e., noninstant) photography represented an acceptable noninfringing substitute. The district court disagreed, finding that instant photography occupied a unique niche in the photography market and that consumers wanted the unique emotional "instant experience" of having the picture developed instantaneously.[118] Thus, *Panduit* factor (2) was satisfied, and lost profits were available.

[113]*Panduit Corp.*, 575 F.2d at 1156 (citations omitted).

[114]*See* Gyromat Corp. v. Champion Spark Plug Co., 735 F.2d 549, 552 (Fed. Cir. 1984).

[115]*See Gyromat Corp.*, 735 F.2d at 552.

[116]*See* Bic Leisure Prods., Inc. v. Windsurfing, Int'l, 1 F.3d 1214, 1218 (Fed. Cir. 1993).

[117]*See* Polaroid Corp. v. Eastman Kodak Co., 1990 U.S. Dist. LEXIS 17968, at *2 (D. Mass. 1990) (describing parties as "locked in a bitter, unyielding, exhausting and expensive litigation for over fourteen years").

[118]*See Polaroid Corp.*, 1990 U.S. Dist. LEXIS 17968, at *36-*42 (finding that conventional photography was not an acceptable substitute for instant photography during the period of infringement).

The Federal Circuit's conception of "acceptable noninfringing substitutes" has evolved over time. Earlier decisions appeared to require that an acceptable noninfringing substitute possess all the advantages or beneficial characteristics of the patented device.[119] It is rather difficult to see how a truly noninfringing device could ever satisfy this condition.

More recently, the Federal Circuit has focused on whether the proffered alternative "competes in the same market for the same customers" as the patented device. This analysis looks at prices as well as product features, and requires careful definition of the "relevant market." The court in *Bic Leisure Prods. v. Windsurfing, Int'l*[120] interpreted *Panduit* factor (2) as follows:

> [T]he second *Panduit* factor — absence of acceptable, noninfringing alternatives — presupposes that the patentee and the infringer sell substantially similar products in the same market. To be acceptable to the infringer's customers in an elastic market, the alleged alternative "must not have a disparately higher price than or possess characteristics significantly different from the patented product." Kaufman Co. v. Lantech, Inc., 926 F.2d 1136, 1142 (Fed. Cir. 1991).
>
> In *Kaufman,* for instance, the patent owner and the infringer sold substantially the same product. *Kaufman,* 926 F.2d at 1143. Thus *Panduit's* second factor, properly applied, ensures that any proffered alternative competes in the same market for the same customers as the infringer's product. *See* Yarway Corp. v. Eur-Control USA, Inc., 775 F.2d 268, 276 (Fed. Cir. 1985) (alternative products did not possess features of the patent owner's and the infringer's products, nor compete in the same " 'special niche' or mini-market").[121]

The Federal Circuit has explained that "[c]onsumer demand defines the relevant market and relative substitutability among products therein. . . . Important factors shaping demand may include consumers' intended use for the patentee's product, similarity of physical and functional attributes of the patentee's product to alleged competing products, and price."[122]

Must an acceptable noninfringing substitute be on sale in the marketplace at the time of the infringement? In *Grain Processing Corp. v. American Maize-Prods. Co.*,[123] the Federal Circuit held that it need not be. The court considered an acceptable noninfringing substitute to be "available," despite the fact that it was not actually being made nor

[119]*See* TWM Mfg. Co. v. Dura Corp., 789 F.2d 895, 901-902 (Fed. Cir. 1986).

[120]1 F.3d 1214 (Fed. Cir. 1993).

[121]*Bic Leisure Prods.*, 1 F.3d at 1219.

[122]Grain Processing Corp. v. American Maize-Prods. Co., 185 F.3d 1341, 1355 (Fed. Cir. 1999).

[123]*Grain Processing Corp.*, 185 F.3d at 1341.

offered for sale at the time, where the accused infringer possessed the capability to have made and sold the substitute but chose not to do so for economic reasons.[124] *Grain Processing* thus stands for the proposition that reconstruction of the "but for" world also must consider what the infringer might have offered as a noninfringing substitute, had the infringer known at that time that it was infringing.[125]

Although *Grain Processing* seemingly broadened an accused infringer's ability to escape payment of damages based on a theory of lost profits, the availability of acceptable noninfringing substitutes need not prohibit a patentee from *any* recovery of those profits. Although the traditional *Panduit* framework is best suited for two-supplier markets consisting only of the patentee and the infringer (in which it is reasonable to assume that the patentee would have made all the sales diverted by the infringer), subsequent decisions have recognized that the *Panduit* formulation can be modified to fit a multisupplier marketplace involving more sources of supply than just the patentee and the accused infringer. In *State Indus., Inc. v. Mor-Flo Indus., Inc.*,[126] the Federal Circuit approved a "market share" approach that permits a patentee to substitute evidence of its share of a multisupplier market in place of evidence that would satisfy *Panduit* factor (2), the absence of acceptable noninfringing alternatives.[127] Thus, strict application of

[124]*See Grain Processing Corp.*, 185 F.3d at 1353-1355 (upholding district court's finding that accused infringer "had the necessary chemical materials, the equipment, the know-how and experience, and the economic incentive to produce [the alternative product] throughout the entire accounting period"); *id.* at 1354 (approving trial court's explanation that "sole reason" accused infringer did not use alternative process during accounting period was economic; i.e., alternative was somewhat more expensive than accused product, and accused infringer "reasonably believed it had a noninfringing product").

[125]*See Grain Processing Corp.*, 185 F.3d at 1350-1351 (citations omitted):

> By the same token, a fair and accurate reconstruction of the "but for" market also must take into account, where relevant, alternative actions the infringer foreseeably would have undertaken had he not infringed. Without the infringing product, a rational would-be infringer is likely to offer an acceptable noninfringing alternative, if available, to compete with the patent owner rather than leave the market altogether. The competitor in the "but for" marketplace is hardly likely to surrender its complete market share when faced with a patent, if it can compete in some other lawful manner. Moreover, only by comparing the patented invention to its next-best available alternative(s) — regardless of whether the alternative(s) were actually produced and sold during the infringement — can the court discern the market value of the patent owner's exclusive right, and therefore his expected profit or reward, had the infringer's activities not prevented him from taking full economic advantage of this right. . . . Thus, an accurate reconstruction of the hypothetical "but for" market takes into account any alternatives available to the infringer.

[126]883 F.3d 1573 (Fed. Cir. 1989).

[127]*See* Bic Leisure Prods. v. Windsurfing, Int'l, 1 F.3d 1214, 1219 (Fed. Cir. 1993). Under the market share approach, a patentee should be awarded lost profits on its

the *Panduit* formula is not the only way of establishing the amount of lost profits damages.[128]

(c) Manufacturing and marketing capability. With respect to *Panduit* factor (3), capacity to meet the demand, the patentee seeking lost profits must show that it had or could have obtained the manufacturing capacity to make all the sales in question, that is, its own and the infringer's.[129] The patentee can satisfy this factor not only by reliance on its own manufacturing capability but also by evidence of the potential for licensing and contracting for the manufacture.[130]

(d) Amount of profit. With respect to the final *Panduit* factor, the amount of lost profits must be computed using an incremental income approach that excludes the patentee's fixed costs, that is, those costs that do not vary with increases in production, such as management salaries, property taxes, and insurance.[131] Thus, the precise formula for computing lost profits is

Amount of Lost Profits	=	Lost Revenues	–	Incremental Costs

where

Lost Revenues = the number of additional sales that the patentee would have made but for the infringement, multiplied by the plaintiff's historical prices (i.e., pre-infringement prices, so that the plaintiff is not penalized by any price erosion forced by the defendant's infringement); and

Incremental Costs = variable costs that have already been covered by the plaintiff's own sales (i.e., excluding fixed costs such as management salaries, research and development, and other amounts that would not vary with the extent of infringement).[132]

(ii) The *Rite-Hite* Expansion

Since the court's creation in 1982, the trend in Federal Circuit damages jurisprudence has been one of broadening acceptance for

market share percentage of the infringing sales and a reasonable royalty on the remaining infringing sales. *See* Atlantic Thermoplastics Co. v. Faytex Corp., 5 F.3d 1477, 1481 (Fed. Cir. 1993).

[128] *See* Rite-Hite Corp. v. Kelley Co., 56 F.3d 1538, 1545 (Fed. Cir. 1995) (*en banc*).

[129] *See* Datascope Corp. v. SMEC, Inc., 879 F.2d 820, 825 (Fed. Cir. 1989) (stating that "[t]he demand which a patentee must have the capacity to meet is measured by the total sales, by the patentee and the infringer, of the patented product").

[130] *See* Bio-Rad Lab. v. Nicolet Instrument Corp., 739 F.2d 604, 616 (Fed. Cir. 1984); Gyromat Corp. v. Champion Spark Plug Co., 735 F.2d 549, 554 (Fed. Cir. 1984).

[131] *See* Paper Converting Machine Co. v. Magna-Graphics Corp., 745 F.2d 11, 22 (Fed. Cir. 1984).

[132] *See* DONALD S. CHISUM ET AL., PRINCIPLES OF PATENTABILITY 1233 n.8 (2d ed. 2001).

new theories of "damages adequate to compensate for the infringement."[133] Emblematic of this expansion is the Federal Circuit's 1995 *en banc* decision in *Rite-Hite Corp. v. Kelley Co.*[134] Prior to *Rite-Hite,* Federal Circuit cases held that lost profits damages were to be based on diverted sales of the product covered by the infringed patent. In other words, the underlying analytical assumption was that each sale by the infringer meant a corresponding lost sale of the plaintiff's patented product. The Federal Circuit in *Rite-Hite* expanded damages law by holding that a patent owner also can potentially recover lost profits on lost sales of *unpatented* products (or products covered by patents other than the one in suit) that compete with the infringing device, so long as the patentee can establish causation.

The facts of *Rite-Hite* are these. Rite-Hite's patent in suit was directed to a manual safety device for securing a truck to a loading dock; it sold the patented device under the name MDL-55 for approximately $500 each. Rite-Hite also sold an automated version of the same device, known as ADL-100, for $1,000 to $1,500 each. Although the ADL was the subject of a U.S. patent, it was not covered by the patent in suit, and thus for purposes of the case was considered "unpatented."[135] The ADL device directly competed with Kelley's accused "Truk Stop" product, however.

Kelley's liability for infringement of Rite-Hite's patent on the manual MDL device had been affirmed on an earlier appeal to the Federal Circuit, and the issue remaining in the bifurcated case was damages. The district court determined that Kelley's sale of 3,825 infringing "Truk Stop" devices caused patentee Rite-Hite to lose the sales of (1) 80 patented, manual MDL-55 devices; (2) 3,243 unpatented APL-100 devices; and (3) 1,692 "dock levelers," unpatented devices frequently sold by Rite-Hite with both the MDL and the APL.[136] The district court awarded Rite-Hite lost profits based on the lost sales of all three products.

On appeal, Kelley argued that even assuming the *Panduit* factors had been met, as a matter of law, lost profits must be limited to lost sales of the *patented* device. In other words, Kelley contended, lost profits means that only lost sales of the patented product are compensable.

[133]35 U.S.C. §284.

[134]56 F.3d 1538 (Fed. Cir. 1995) (*en banc*).

[135]*See Rite-Hite Corp.*, 56 F.3d at 1543.

[136]While sustaining the award of lost profits damages for lost sales of the ADL device, the Federal Circuit also held that under the "entire market value rule," separately discussed below, Rite-Hite could not recover lost profits damages for lost sales of the dock levelers. *See Rite-Hite Corp.*, 56 F.3d at 1549-1551.

The Federal Circuit disagreed. A majority of judges affirmed the district court's award of lost profits damages for lost sales of the unpatented automatic APL-100 restraint, even though that device was not covered by the patent in suit.[137] In holding that damages based on lost sales of the APL were recoverable, the appellate court relied on tort-based theories of proximate cause (i.e., "legal" or primary or dominant cause) and reasonable foreseeability.[138] The court expansively held that in patent cases, "[i]f a particular injury was or should have been reasonably foreseeable by an infringing competitor in the relevant market, broadly defined, that injury is generally compensable absent a persuasive reason to the contrary."[139]

In the Federal Circuit's view, Kelley's accused device directly competed with the plaintiff's unpatented APL-100 device. In light of this competition in the marketplace, Kelley should have reasonably foreseen that its infringement would cause Rite-Hite not only a loss of the patented MDL device, but also lost sales of the directly competing but unpatented APL-100. The court distinguished those types of losses that are too "remote" to be compensable, such as "a heart attack of the inventor or loss in value of shares of common stock of a patentee corporation caused indirectly by infringement. . . .[140]

Judge Helen Nies (joined by then–Chief Judge Archer, Judge Mayer, and Senior Judge Smith) offered an extensive dissenting argument that "[t]o constitute legal injury for which lost profits may be awarded, the infringer must interfere with the patentee's property right to an exclusive market in goods embodying the invention of the patent in suit. The patentee's property rights do not extend to its market in other goods unprotected by the litigated patent."[141] She further pointed out that Kelley started selling its Truk Stop device two years before Rite-Hite's patent in suit issued.[142] Thus, there was no way that Kelley could have "foreseen" that it would infringe not-yet-issued claims and that its lawful competition with the ADL would be transformed into compensable injury for infringement of the patent in suit.

(iii) Territoriality Limitations

It is well settled that if patent infringement involves "making," "using" or "selling" an entire patented invention under *subsection (a)* of 35 U.S.C. §271, the direct infringement provision, damages are recoverable only for those uses or sales that occur within U.S. borders,

[137]*See Rite-Hite Corp.*, 56 F.3d at 1544-1549.
[138]*See Rite-Hite Corp.*, 56 F.3d at 1546.
[139]*Rite-Hite Corp.*, 56 F.3d at 1546.
[140]*Rite-Hite Corp.*, 56 F.3d at 1546.
[141]*Rite-Hite Corp.*, 56 F.3d at 1556 (Nies, J., dissenting-in-part).
[142]*Rite-Hite Corp.*, 56 F.3d at 1571.

not for any extraterritorial uses or sales.[143] That is, the reach of §271*(a)* is purely domestic.

A 2018 Supreme Court decision established a more expansive damages rule for infringement via the act of exporting component(s) of a patented invention from the United States with the intent that they be assembled abroad, which falls under 35 U.S.C. §271(f). The 7-2 majority in *WesternGeco LLC v. ION Geophysical Corp.* ("*WesternGeco IV*")[144] approved a jury's award of substantial lost profits damages[145] accrued for a patentee's loss of contract services performed by the accused infringer *outside* the United States.

More specifically, the infringer ION had exported key components of the patented underwater surveying system, so as to violate §271(f)(2). It manufactured the components of its competing system (including component(s) specially adapted for the claimed invention) in the United States, then shipped them abroad for offshore combination (hence, §271*(a)* liability was not triggered because a complete "making" did not occur in United States territory).

At trial, patentee WesternGeco proved that due to ION's infringement, it had lost ten contracts for surveying various ocean floor locations *outside* U.S. waters. Upon finding liability, the jury awarded WesternGeco damages of $12.5 million in reasonable royalties plus,

[143]*See* Power Integrations, Inc. v. Fairchild Semiconductor Int'l, Inc., 711 F.3d 1348, 1371 (Fed. Cir. 2013) (agreeing with district court that jury's award of "worldwide damages" for infringer's making or selling the patented invention in the United States under §271(a) was contrary to law; accordingly rejecting patentee's argument that "it was foreseeable that Fairchild's infringement in the United States would cause Power Integrations to lose sales in foreign markets"); *id.*, stating:

> Our patent laws allow specifically "damages adequate to compensate for the infringement." 35 U.S.C. §284 (emphasis added). They do not thereby provide compensation for a defendant's foreign exploitation of a patented invention, which is not infringement at all. *Brown* [Brown v. Duchesne, 60 U.S. (19 How.) 183 (1856)], 60 U.S. at 195 ("And the use of it outside of the jurisdiction of the United States is not an infringement of his rights, and he has no claim to any compensation for the profit or advantage the party may derive from it.")....
>
> Power Integrations' "foreseeability" theory of worldwide damages sets the presumption against extraterritoriality in interesting juxtaposition with the principle of full compensation. Nevertheless, Power Integrations' argument is not novel, and in the end, it is not persuasive. Regardless of how the argument is framed under the facts of this case, the underlying question here remains whether Power Integrations is entitled to compensatory damages for injury caused by infringing activity that occurred outside the territory of the United States. The answer is no.

[144]138 S. Ct. 2129 (June 22, 2018) (Thomas, J.) ("*WesternGeco IV*").

[145]The remedy of lost profits damages seeks to put a patentee back in the position it would have been in, but for the infringement. This includes profits the patentee would have made had the infringer not infringed. Lost profits damages are examined further *infra* Section D.2.a.

central to the parties' dispute, $93.4 million in lost profits for the value of the ten lost overseas contracts.

The *WesternGeco IV* Court held that the infringer's domestic act of exporting specially-adapted components of a patented undersea survey system in violation of §271(f)(2) was "the infringement" to be compensated for under the general patent damages statute, 35 U.S.C. §284.[146] In the Court's view, that *domestic* act of infringement was the focus or "solicitude" of §284, which requires awarding "damages adequate to compensate for *the infringement*."[147] Thus, a Texas jury's award of $93.4 million in profits lost on the ten foreign services contracts that the patentee would have made but for the infringement was a proper "domestic application of §284."

In contrast to the Supreme Court's 2007 *Microsoft v. AT&T* decision,[148] the Court in *WesternGeco IV* exercised its discretion *not* to decide the "difficult question[]" whether the presumption against extraterritorial application of U.S. statutes had been rebutted in the case at bar. Bypassing that threshold inquiry, the Court explained that " '[i]f the conduct relevant to the statute's focus occurred in the United States, then the case involves a permissible domestic application' of the statute, 'even if other conduct occurred abroad.' "[149] Given the nature of the defendant's violation of §271(f)(2), i.e., the domestic act of exporting the claimed invention's key components from the United States, the conduct relevant to "the focus" of the general damages statute §284 — "the infringement" — occurred in U.S. territory.[150] Hence,

[146]Section 284 authorizes in relevant part "damages adequate to compensate for *the infringement*..." (emphasis added).

[147]35 U.S.C. §284 (emphasis added).

[148]550 U.S. 437 (2007). *Microsoft* is examined *supra* Chapter 9, Section E.4.b.

[149]*WesternGeco IV*, 138 S. Ct. at 2137 (quoting *RJR Nabisco*, 579 U.S. at ___, 136 S. Ct. at 2101).

[150]The Court explained that its jurisprudence has established a two-step framework for deciding whether U.S. statutes should be applied extraterritorially (that is, for deciding when the general presumption against such application has been rebutted). The Court annunciated this framework in its 2016 RICO (Racketeer Influenced and Corrupt Organizations Act) decision, *RJR Nabisco, Inc. v. European Community*, 579 U.S. ___, ___, 136 S. Ct. 2090, 2101 (2016). Under *RJR Nabisco*, a court asks in step one "whether the presumption against extraterritoriality has been rebutted." Rebuttal occurs only if the statutory text provides a " 'clear indication of an extraterritorial application.' " *WesternGeco IV*, 138 S. Ct. at 2136 (quoting Morrison v. National Australia Bank Ltd., 561 U.S. 247, 255 (2010)). If the presumption against extraterritoriality has *not* been rebutted, the second step of the *RJR Nabisco* framework asks "whether the case involves a domestic application of the statute." Courts determine whether the statute is being applied domestically by identifying " 'the statute's "focus" and asking whether the conduct relevant to that focus occurred in United States territory.' " *WesternGeco IV*, 138 S. Ct. at 2136 (quoting *RJR Nabisco*, 136 S. Ct. at 2101). If it did, then the case involves a "permissible domestic application of the statute."

the Court found justified the jury's award to the patentee of its foreign lost profits.[151]

b. Entire Market Value Rule/Convoyed Sales

Patentees often will seek to recover damages for the lost profits they would have made, but for the infringement, on accessory items that typically would be purchased with the patented item. Such items also are referred to as "tag-along" or "convoyed" sales. For example, a manufacturer of a patented razor might contend that consumers who purchase this particular razor also frequently will buy the razor blades marketed by the patentee to operate with the razor.

In the *Rite-Hite* case discussed above,[152] the Federal Circuit considered whether the patentee could recover lost profits on diverted sales of its "dock levelers," unpatented items frequently sold as accessories with the patentee's MDL and ADL devices.[153] The court analyzed the allowability of such damages under a case law formulation known as the "entire market value rule."[154] Precedent held that damages for component parts used with a patented apparatus were recoverable if the patented apparatus "was of such paramount importance that it substantially created the value of the component parts."[155] Precedent also permitted recovery of damages based on the value of a patentee's entire apparatus containing several features when the patent-related feature was the "basis for customer demand."[156] The court characterized the entire market value rule as having "typically been applied to include in the compensation base unpatented components of a device when the unpatented and patented components are physically part of the same machine," acknowledging that the rule "has been extended to allow inclusion of physically separate unpatented components normally sold with the patented components."[157] In such cases, the *Rite-Hite* majority concluded, the "unpatented and patented components together were considered to be components of a single assembly or parts of a complete machine, or they together constituted a functional unit."[158]

In view of this authority, the Federal Circuit in *Rite-Hite* summarized the entire market value rule as follows:

151 *WesternGeco IV* is further detailed *supra* Chapter 9, Section E.4.c.

152 Rite-Hite Corp. v. Kelley Co., 56 F.3d 1538 (Fed. Cir. 1995) (*en banc*).

153 The dock levelers were described as "bridging platform[s] sold with the restraints and used to bridge the edges of a vehicle and dock." *Rite-Hite Corp.*, 56 F.3d at 1543.

154 *Rite-Hite Corp.*, 56 F.3d at 1549.

155 *Rite-Hite Corp.*, 56 F.3d at 1549.

156 *Rite-Hite Corp.*, 56 F.3d at 1549.

157 *Rite-Hite Corp.*, 56 F.3d at 1550.

158 *Rite-Hite Corp.*, 56 F.3d at 1550.

> [T]he facts of past cases clearly imply a limitation on damages, when recovery is sought on sales of unpatented components sold with patented components, to the effect that the unpatented components must function together with the patented component in some manner so as to produce a desired end product or result. All the components together must be analogous to components of a single assembly or be parts of a complete machine, or they must constitute a functional unit. Our precedent has not extended liability to include items that have essentially no functional relationship to the patented invention and that may have been sold with an infringing device only as a matter of convenience or business advantage. We are not persuaded that we should extend that liability. Damages on such items would constitute more than what is "adequate to compensate for the infringement."[159]

Under this formulation as applied to the facts of the case, patentee Rite-Hite could not recover damages for diverted sales of its dock levelers.[160] Although the dock levelers may have been used together with Rite-Hite's MDL and ADL restraints, "they did not function together to achieve one result and each could effectively have been used independently of each other."[161] The Federal Circuit concluded that Rite-Hite sold the dock levelers with the restraints "only for marketing reasons, not because they essentially functioned together."[162] Thus, lost profits–based damages were not available for lost sales of the dock levelers.

In contrast with *Rite-Hite*, lost profits were awarded on accessory sales in *Juicy Whip, Inc. v. Orange Bang, Inc.*[163] The claimed invention was a chilled drink dispenser of the type seen in convenience stores. The Federal Circuit reversed a district court's denial of lost profits on the patentee's asserted lost sales of flavored syrup used in the dispenser. The appellate court observed that the entire market value rule as articulated in *Rite-Hite* permits recovery for lost sales of components that are physically separate from, but which form a "functional unit" with, the patented item. Unlike the dock levelers in *Rite-Hite*, the syrup and dispenser in *Juicy Whip* were not sold together "only as a matter of convenience or business advantage"; rather, "the dispenser needs syrup and the syrup is mixed in a dispenser." The district court had erred in holding that the patented dispenser and the syrup did not share a functional relationship because the dispenser had been sold separately from the syrup on occasion and because other syrups could be used in Juicy Whip's dispenser.

[159] *Rite-Hite Corp.*, 56 F.3d at 1550.
[160] *See Rite-Hite Corp.*, 56 F.3d at 1551.
[161] *Rite-Hite Corp.*, 56 F.3d at 1551.
[162] *Rite-Hite Corp.*, 56 F.3d at 1551.
[163] 382 F.3d 1367 (Fed. Cir. 2004).

The Federal Circuit clarified that "a functional relationship between a patented device and an unpatented material used with it is not precluded by the fact that the device can be used with other materials or that the unpatented material can be used with other devices."[164]

Entire market value analysis can apply in damage computations based on a theory of reasonable royalty rather than lost profits, despite academic criticism of that application.[165] For example, a jury in *Lucent Technologies, Inc. v. Gateway, Inc.*[166] found that use of Microsoft's well-known Outlook software program infringed a Lucent patent. A method claim of Lucent's patent read on the "date picker" tool used in some components of Outlook.[167] The jury awarded Lucent a lump-sum royalty payment of $357,693,056.18 (excluding prejudgment interest). On appeal, the Federal Circuit sustained the jury's verdict that Microsoft had indirectly infringed the Lucent patent and that it had not been proved invalid, but vacated and remanded the damages award as not supported by substantial evidence. The Federal Circuit further held that, to the extent the jury relied on an entire market value calculation to arrive at the $358 million lump-sum damages amount, that award was likewise not supported by substantial evidence and was "against the clear weight of the evidence."[168]

In particular, the patentee Lucent had failed to carry its burden to establish that its patented invention was the basis for consumer demand of Microsoft's overall commercial product, Outlook. In the

[164]*Juicy Whip, Inc.*, 382 F.3d at 1372.

[165]*See* Lucent Technologies, Inc. v. Gateway, Inc., 580 F.3d 1301 (Fed. Cir. 2009), in which the court responded that such criticisms

> ignore the realities of patent licensing and the flexibility needed in transferring intellectual property rights. The evidence of record in the present dispute illustrates the importance the entire market value may have in reasonable royalty cases. The license agreements admitted into evidence (without objection from [accused infringer] Microsoft, we note) highlight how sophisticated parties routinely enter into license agreements that base the value of the patented inventions as a percentage of the commercial products' sales price. There is nothing inherently wrong with using the market value of the entire product, especially when there is no established market value for the infringing component or feature, so long as the multiplier accounts for the proportion of the base represented by the infringing component or feature.

Lucent, 580 F.3d at 1339.

[166]580 F.3d 1301 (Fed. Cir. 2009).

[167]*See Lucent*, 580 F.3d at 1317 (explaining that "[s]imilar to the number pad tool illustrated in [Lucent's] Day patent, Outlook's calendar date-picker tool enables the user to select a series of numbers, corresponding to the day, month, and year, using graphical controls. This date-picker calendar tool is incorporated in a few of Outlook's features. Microsoft Money and Windows Mobile [products also accused of infringement] have similar functionalities.").

[168]*Lucent*, 580 F.3d at 1324.

Federal Circuit's view, the only reasonable interpretation of the evidence was that

> the infringing use of the date-picker tool in Outlook is but a very small component of a much larger software program. The vast majority of the features, when used, do not infringe. The date-picker tool's minor role in the overall program is further confirmed when one considers the relative importance of certain other features, e.g., e-mail. . . . Lucent did not carry its evidentiary burden of proving that anyone purchased Outlook because of the patented method. Indeed, Lucent's damages expert conceded that there was no "evidence that anybody anywhere at any time ever bought Outlook, be it an equipment manufacturer or an individual consumer, . . . because it had a date picker." . . . And when we consider the importance of the many features not covered by the [Lucent] patent compared to the one infringing feature in Outlook, we can only arrive at the unmistakable conclusion that the invention described in claim 19 of the [Lucent] patent is not the reason consumers purchase Outlook.[169]

A second reason for rejecting the jury's apparent application of the entire market value rule in *Lucent* involved the royalty rate testimony of the patentee's licensing expert. The expert told the jury that an 8 percent royalty rate should be applied to a royalty base consisting of sales of the entire Outlook software program. Although "the base used in a running royalty calculation can always be the value of the entire commercial embodiment,"[170] this holds only "as long as the magnitude of the rate is within an acceptable range (as determined by the evidence)."[171] In the case at bar, Lucent's expert had improperly inflated his proposed royalty rate to 8 percent (from 1 percent) after the district court had granted Microsoft's *in limine* motion to exclude from the jury the expert's initial theory that the royalty base should be the value of an *entire computer* running Outlook software.[172] Yet the expert had admitted that "there was no evidence that Microsoft had ever agreed to pay an 8% royalty on an analogous patent."[173] Vacating the damages award, the Federal Circuit concluded that the Lucent expert's approach could "not be an acceptable way to conduct an analysis of what the parties would have agreed to in the hypothetical licensing context."[174]

[169] *Lucent*, 580 F.3d at 1337-1338.
[170] *Lucent*, 580 F.3d at 1338-1339.
[171] *Lucent*, 580 F.3d at 1339.
[172] *See Lucent*, 580 F.3d at 1338 (explaining that "Lucent's expert tried to reach the damages number he would have obtained had he used the price of the entire computer as a royalty base. Being precluded from using the computer as the royalty base, he used the price of the software, but inflated the royalty rate accordingly.").
[173] *Lucent*, 580 F.3d at 1338.
[174] *Lucent*, 580 F.3d at 1338.

c. *Reasonable Royalty*

Where lost profits cannot be proved,[175] the patentee is entitled to an award of damages based on a theory of reasonable royalty. A reasonable royalty has been defined as "an amount 'which a person, desiring to manufacture and sell a patented article, as a business proposition, would be willing to pay as a royalty and yet be able to make and sell the patented article, in the market, at a reasonable profit.' "[176] Recall that §284 of the Patent Act provides that the reasonable royalty is the minimum or floor below which the damages assessment cannot go.[177]

Consider a very simple example of a reasonable royalty-based award. Assume that the standard patent royalty in the widget industry is $5 per each widget sold. If an unlicensed defendant sold 100 infringing widgets, the patentee's reasonable royalty award on the infringing sales would be calculated as $5 × 100, or $500.

(i) Hypothetical Negotiation

In the majority of cases, there does not exist an "established royalty" based on an industry standard rate or extensive prior licensing by the patentee. In such cases, the district court must determine what royalty rate would have been "reasonable" in accordance with §284.

The key element in setting a reasonable royalty is to return to the date when the infringement began.[178] The district court must attempt to discern what royalty rate the patentee would have accepted at that time, knowing that the patent was valid and infringed. Courts attempt to do this by positing a "hypothetical negotiation" between a "willing licensor" of the patent and a "willing licensee," and on the basis of that hypothetical negotiation, approximating what royalty the parties would have agreed to.

[175]Sometimes the patentee will be able to establish the availability of lost profits for some, but not all, of the infringing sales. In such cases the patentee receives a reasonable royalty award for those infringing sales not included in the lost profits computation. *See* State Indus., Inc. v. Mor-Flo Indus., Inc., 883 F.2d 1573, 1577 (Fed. Cir. 1989) (stating that "the award may be split between lost profits as actual damages to the extent they are proven and a reasonable royalty for the remainder").

In other cases, the patentee may be a non-practicing entity that may license its patents but does not sell any products embodying the patented invention. Lost profits would not be available in such a situation.

[176]Panduit Corp. v. Stahlin Bros. Fibre Works, Inc., 575 F.2d 1152, 1157-1158 (6th Cir. 1978) (quoting Goodyear Tire and Rubber Co. v. Overman Cushion Tire Co., 95 F.2d 978, 984 (6th Cir. 1937) (citing Rockwood v. General Fire Extinguisher Co., 37 F.2d 62, 66 (2d Cir. 1930)), *appeal dismissed on motion of counsel for petitioners*, 306 U.S. 665 (1938)).

[177]"Upon finding for the claimant the court shall award the claimant damages adequate to compensate for the infringement, but in no event less than a reasonable royalty for the use made of the invention by the infringer, together with interest and costs as fixed by the court." 35 U.S.C. §284.

[178]*Panduit Corp.*, 575 F.2d at 1158.

The hypothetical negotiation is necessarily an exercise in fiction, because in light of the subsequent infringement, the parties, in reality, never entered into a license. As characterized by the court in *Panduit*,

> [t]he setting of a reasonable royalty after infringement cannot be treated . . . as the equivalent of ordinary royalty negotiations among truly "willing" patent owners and licensees. That view would constitute a pretense that the infringement never happened. It would also make an election to infringe a handy means for competitors to impose a "compulsory license" policy upon every patent owner.[179]
>
> . . .
>
> Determination of a "reasonable royalty" after infringement, like many devices in the law, rests on a legal fiction. Created in an effort to "compensate" when profits are not provable, the "reasonable royalty" device conjures a "willing" licensor and licensee, who like Ghosts of Christmas Past, are dimly seen as "negotiating" a "license." There is, of course, no actual willingness on either side, and no license to do anything, the infringer being normally enjoined . . . from further manufacture, use, or sale of the patented product.[180]

Thus, the Federal Circuit characterizes the hypothetical negotiation approach as an attempt to "do justice" to the patentee,[181] and in some cases has affirmed the award of royalty rates significantly above industry norms.[182]

In determining the contours of the hypothetical negotiation, district courts have traditionally considered evidence (typically in the form of testimony by patent licensing experts) on an extensive list of factors as set forth in the leading case of *Georgia Pacific Corp. v. United States Plywood Corp.*[183] A detailed examination of each of the 15 *Georgia Pacific* factors is beyond the scope of this text. Note, however, that

[179]*Panduit Corp.*, 575 F.2d at 1158.

[180]*Panduit Corp.*, 575 F.2d at 1159.

[181]*See* TWM Mfg. v. Dura Corp., 789 F.2d 895, 900 (Fed. Cir. 1986) (stating that "[t]he willing licensee/licensor approach must be flexibly applied as a 'device in the aid of justice'") (quoting Cincinnati Car Co. v. New York Rapid Transit Corp., 66 F.2d 592, 595 (2d Cir. 1933)).

[182]*See, e.g.*, Rite-Hite Corp. v. Kelley Co., 56 F.3d 1538, 1554 (Fed. Cir. 1995) (*en banc*) (affirming reasonable royalty rate determination based on approximately 50 percent of patentee's estimated lost profits per unit sold to retailers); Bio-Rad Lab. v. Nicolet Instrument Corp., 739 F.2d 604, 617 (Fed. Cir. 1984) (awarding royalty rate approximating one-third of infringer's sales price where industry rate was only 3 to 10 percent of sales).

[183]318 F. Supp. 1116 (S.D.N.Y. 1970), *modified by* 446 F.2d 295 (2d Cir. 1971). The *Georgia Pacific* factors are

> (1) The royalties received by the patentee for the licensing of the patent in suit, proving or tending to prove an established royalty;
>
> (2) The rates paid by the licensee for the use of other patents comparable to the patent in suit;

Georgia Pacific factor (15), the amount of the royalty, essentially subsumes all of the previous 14 factors. In other words, the evidence pertaining to factors (1) through (14) is what supports the ultimate determination of royalty rate in factor (15).

(ii) Analytical Approach

An alternative method of determining the amount of a reasonable royalty has been employed in some cases, referred to as the "analytical method." In this method, the court takes an infringer's anticipated net

---

(3) The nature and scope of the license, as exclusive or nonexclusive; or as restricted or nonrestricted in terms of territory or with respect to whom the manufactured product may be sold;
(4) The licensor's established policy and marketing program to maintain his patent monopoly by not licensing others to use the invention or by granting licenses under special conditions designed to preserve that monopoly;
(5) The commercial relationship between the licensor and licensee, such as, whether they are competitors in the same territory in the same line of business; or whether they are inventor and promot[e]r;
(6) The effect of selling the patented specialty in promoting sales of other products of the licensee; the existing value of the invention to the licensor as a generator of sales of his nonpatented items; and the extent of such derivative or convoyed sales;
(7) The duration of the patent and the term of the license;
(8) The established profitability of the product made under the patent; its commercial success; and its current popularity;
(9) The utility and advantages of the patent property over the old modes or devices, if any, that had been used for working out similar results;
(10) The nature of the patented invention; the character of the commercial embodiment of it as owned and produced by the licensor; and the benefits to those who have used the invention;
(11) The extent to which the infringer has made use of the invention; and any evidence probative of the value of that use;
(12) The portion of the profit or of the selling price that may be customary in the particular business or in comparable businesses to allow for the use of the invention or analogous inventions;
(13) The portion of the realizable profit that should be credited to the invention as distinguished from nonpatented elements, the manufacturing process, business risks, or significant features or improvements added by the infringer;
(14) The opinion testimony of qualified experts; and
(15) The amount that a licensor (such as the patentee) and a licensee (such as the infringer) would have agreed upon (at the time the infringement began) if both had been reasonably and voluntarily trying to reach an agreement; that is, the amount which a prudent licensee — who desired, as a business proposition, to obtain a license to manufacture and sell a particular article embodying the patented invention — would have been willing to pay as a royalty and yet be able to make a reasonable profit and which amount would have been acceptable by a prudent patentee who was willing to grant a license.

318 F. Supp. at 1120.

profit margin as the starting point and from this subtracts some "industry standard" or "acceptable" level of profit,[184] so as to leave that amount for the infringer; the remaining portion of the anticipated profit is awarded to the patentee as a reasonable royalty.[185] The analytical approach has been commended by commentators as one that "shifts from the fiction of hypothesizing what would have been negotiated in an imaginary licensing environment to the reality of determining what should be paid as fair compensation for patent infringement."[186]

In the Federal Circuit's 2012 decision, *Energy Transp. Group, Inc. v. William Demant Holding A/S*,[187] the appellate court upheld a $31 million jury award of reasonable royalty damages based in part on the patentee's expert's use of the analytical method.[188] The expert "compared the average expected profit margin on the infringing products, as set forth in [the accused infringers'] expert reports, to the industry average expected profit."[189] He determined that the infringing products garnered a 6.4 percent increase in expected profit margin based on the technology of the patents in suit. The expert's "suggested reasonable royalty rates were thus tied to the benefit accorded by the patents at issue."[190]

Notably, the Federal Circuit in *Energy Transp.* sustained the jury's award despite the fact that the patentee's expert had also testified about his "25 percent rule of thumb" analysis, an analysis that the Federal Circuit thereafter rejected as an inadmissible, "fundamentally flawed tool" in *Uniloc USA, Inc. v. Microsoft Corp.*,[191] further examined below. Unlike *Uniloc*, the patentee's damages expert in *Energy Transp.* provided additional analysis, independent of the 25 percent rule, which adequately supported his testimony (and the jury's award). The expert "offer[ed] acceptable alternative methods to support his damages calculation." The Federal Circuit concluded that the expert's

[184]*See TWM Mfg.*, 789 F.2d at 899 (affirming district court's adoption of analytical method in which special master "[s]ubtract[ed] the industry standard net profit of 6.56% to 12.5%" from infringer's anticipated net profit range).

[185]Paul M. Janicke, *Contemporary Issues in Patent Damages,* 42 Am. U. L. Rev. 691, 727 (1993).

[186]*Id.*

[187]697 F.3d 1342 (Fed. Cir. 2012).

[188]*See Energy Transp.*, 697 F.3d at 1356-1357 (explaining that in addition to his analysis under the 25 percent rule of thumb as well as consideration of certain factors from *Georgia-Pacific Corp. v. U.S. Plywood Corp.*, 318 F. Supp. 1116 (S.D.N.Y. 1970), patentee's expert "further performed an entirely separate analysis of a reasonable royalty using the method set forth in *TWM Mfg. Co. v. Dura Corp.*, 789 F.2d 895 (Fed. Cir. 1986)").

[189]*Energy Transp.*, 697 F.3d at 1357.

[190]*Energy Transp.*, 697 F.3d at 1357.

[191]632 F.3d 1292, 1315 (Fed. Cir. 2011).

"entirely separate damages analysis... supported the jury's verdict."[192]

In cases including *Energy Transp.* and many others, litigants and district courts adopted a "25 percent rule of thumb" to "approximate the reasonable royalty rate that the manufacturer of a patented product [i.e., the later-adjudged infringer] would be willing to offer to pay to the patentee during a hypothetical negotiation."[193] Based on empirical studies of actual licenses as well as general licensing practices, the 25 percent rule suggested "that the licensee [would be willing to] pay a royalty rate equivalent to 25 per cent of its expected profits for the product that incorporates the [intellectual property] at issue."[194] Although not without critics, the 25 percent rule was considered by certain organizations at least a valid starting point from which royalty rate could be adjusted up or down in accordance with the *Georgia Pacific* factors (described *supra*).

The Federal Circuit in 2011 strongly rejected the 25 percent rule of thumb in *Uniloc USA, Inc. v. Microsoft Corp.*[195] While admittedly "passively tolerating" the rule's use in earlier decisions, the Federal Circuit in *Uniloc* squarely considered the 25 percent rule of thumb in *Uniloc*. The appellate court concluded that evidence relying on the rule is inadmissible under the leading Supreme Court decision on expert witness testimony, *Daubert v. Merrell Dow Pharmaceuticals, Inc.*,[196] as well as the Federal Rules of Evidence.[197] In a nutshell, the 25 percent rule was not valid because it "fail[ed] to tie a reasonable royalty

[192]*Energy Transp.*, 697 F.3d at 1357.

[193]Robert Goldscheider, John Jarosz & Carla Mulhern, *Use of the 25 Per Cent Rule in Valuing IP*, 37 Les Nouvelles 123, 123 (Dec. 2002).

[194]*Id.*

[195]632 F.3d 1292, 1315 (Fed. Cir. 2011) (stating that "[t]his court now holds as a matter of Federal Circuit law that the 25 percent rule of thumb is a fundamentally flawed tool for determining a baseline royalty rate in a hypothetical negotiation").

[196]509 U.S. 579 (1993). In *Daubert*, the Supreme Court assigned to federal district courts the responsibility of ensuring that all expert testimony must pertain to "scientific, technical, or other specialized knowledge" under Federal Rule of Evidence 702. *Id.* at 589. This responsibility required district court judges to determine that the testimony was based on a firm scientific or technical grounding. *Id.* at 589-590.

[197]Titled "Testimony by Expert Witnesses," Rule 702 provides that

> [a] witness who is qualified as an expert by knowledge, skill, experience, training, or education may testify in the form of an opinion or otherwise if:
>
> (a) the expert's scientific, technical, or other specialized knowledge will help the trier of fact to understand the evidence or to determine a fact in issue;
>
> (b) the testimony is based on sufficient facts or data;
>
> (c) the testimony is the product of reliable principles and methods; and
>
> (d) the expert has reliably applied the principles and methods to the facts of the case.

Fed. R. Evid. 702 (eff. Dec. 1, 2011).

base to the facts of the case at issue."[198] *Daubert,* subsequent Supreme Court decisions concerning expert testimony, and the Federal Circuit's own prior case law demanded that

> there must be a basis in fact to associate the royalty rates used in prior licenses to the particular hypothetical negotiation at issue in the case. The 25 percent rule of thumb as an abstract and largely theoretical construct fails to satisfy this fundamental requirement. The rule does not say anything about a particular hypothetical negotiation or reasonable royalty involving any particular technology, industry, or party.[199]

Using the 25 percent rule as a starting point for adjustment was not valid, either. "Beginning from a fundamentally flawed premise and adjusting it based on legitimate considerations specific to the facts of the case nevertheless results in a fundamentally flawed conclusion."[200]

Concerns similar to those that led the Federal Circuit in its 2011 *Uniloc* decision to reject the 25 percent rule[201] also led the appellate court in its 2014 decision, *VirnetX, Inc. v. Cisco Sys., Inc.*,[202] to reject the use of a "Nash Bargaining Solution" as a tool for estimating reasonable royalty damages. Like the use of the 25 percent rule, the patentee's expert's reliance in *VirnetX* on the Nash Bargaining Solution,[203] a mathematical theorem based on a number of premises, "made too crude a generalization about a vastly more complicated world."[204] Because the expert's testimony was insufficiently tied to the particular facts of the case at bar, it could not be supported.

d. Price Erosion

In addition to lost profits and reasonable royalties, a third type of compensatory damages available to patent owners is an award of damages for depressed or "eroded" prices due to the infringement.[205] As with lost profits, the patentee seeking price erosion damages must prove causation, that is, that but for the infringement, it would have

[198]Uniloc USA, Inc. v. Microsoft Corp., 632 F.3d 1292, 1315 (Fed. Cir. 2011).

[199]*Uniloc USA, Inc.*, 632 F.3d at 1317.

[200]*Uniloc USA, Inc.*, 632 F.3d at 1317.

[201]*See* Uniloc USA, Inc., 632 F.3d at 1317.

[202]767 F.3d 1308 (Fed. Cir. 2014).

[203]For background on John Nash, the Nobel Prize-winning mathematician who developed the Nash Bargaining Solution, *see generally* Sylvia Nasar, A Beautiful Mind: A Biography of John Forbes Nash, Jr. (1998).

[204]*VirnetX*, 767 F.3d at 1332.

[205]*See* TWM Mfg. v. Dura Corp., 789 F.2d 895, 902 (Fed. Cir. 1986). *See also* Power Integrations, Inc. v. Fairchild Semiconductor Int'l, Inc., 711 F.3d 1348, 1378 (Fed. Cir. 2013) (stating that count "recognize[s] the economic principle of 'price erosion' in calculating compensatory damages for patent infringement").

sold its patented product at a higher price.[206] A patentee may fail to meet this burden if the accused infringer can establish that the patentee's price drop was influenced by factors other than the presence of the infringer in the marketplace, such as changing consumer preferences or an influx of foreign products.[207]

e. *Apportionment*

Federal Circuit decisions dealing with compensatory damages for patent infringement frequently emphasize the need for "apportionment." The concept of apportionment reflects a concern about computing damages recovery based on the entire price of an infringing product that has many features, when only one (or a few) of those features infringes.[208] This scenario is increasingly common as innovative products such as "smartphones" and semiconductors are introduced into the marketplace that include a multitude of features, only some of which are patent-protected. The Circuit has instructed that a patentee must "take care to seek only those damages attributable to the infringing features."[209] The statute confirms this; the Patent Act provides that a successful claimant is to be awarded "damages *adequate to compensate for the infringement*," with a floor set at "a reasonable royalty *for the use made of the invention* by the infringer. . . ."[210] In the case of multi-component infringing products, what the infringer is "us[ing]" may involve much more than the patented invention. The

[206]*See* SynQor, Inc. v. Artesyn Techs., Inc., 709 F.3d 1365, 1381 (Fed. Cir. 2013).

[207]*See* Bic Leisure Prods. v. Windsurfing Int'l, 1 F.3d 1214, 1220 (Fed. Cir. 1993).

[208]This same concern animates the entire market value rule (in its traditional role, allowing unpatented components of a device to be included in the compensation base when all the components are physically part of the same device and constitute a functional unit that produces a desired end result), as discussed *supra* Section D.2.b.

[209]VirnetX, Inc. v. Cisco Sys., Inc., 767 F.3d 1308, 1326 (Fed. Cir. 2014). As the Supreme Court observed in a nineteenth-century decision,

> [w]hen a patent is for an improvement, and not for an entirely new machine or contrivance, the patentee must show in what particulars his improvement has added to the usefulness of the machine or contrivance. He must separate its results distinctly from those of the other parts, so that the benefits derived from it may be distinctly seen and appreciated. The rule on this head is aptly stated by Mr. Justice Blatchford in the court below: "The patentee," he says, "must in every case give evidence tending to separate or apportion the defendant's profits and the patentee's damages between the patented feature and the unpatented features, and such evidence must be reliable and tangible, and not conjectural or speculative; *or* he must show, by equally reliable and satisfactory evidence, that the profits and damages are to be calculated on the whole machine, for the reason that the entire value of the whole machine, as a marketable article, is properly and legally attributable to the patented feature."

Garretson v. Clark, 111 U.S. 120, 121 (1884) (emphasis added).

[210]35 U.S.C. §284 (emphasis added).

goal of apportionment is to prevent a patentee in this situation from overreaching by seeking damages for features of an infringing product that do not in fact infringe.[211]

Thus, as a general rule, it is more accurate to compute damages based on the "smallest salable patent-practicing unit" rather than the value of the entire accused product.[212] Consider, for example, an infringer selling a laptop computer containing a battery, when only the battery infringed the patent in suit. The preferred approach would compute infringement damages based on the value of the battery rather than the entire laptop computer. However, in many multi-component products, the individual components are not sold separately or assigned a separate value.

When the smallest-salable unit concept is not applicable (and assuming the entire market rule examined *supra* does *not* apply[213]), then the default rule for multi-component products becomes *apportionment* of damages between infringing and noninfringing features.[214] Beyond its statutory underpinnings in §284, the

[211]*See* LaserDynamics, Inc. v. Quanta Computer, Inc., 694 F.3d 51, 70 (Fed. Cir. 2012) ("LaserDynamics' necessity argument also fails to address the fundamental concern of the entire market value rule, since permitting LaserDynamics to use a laptop computer royalty base does not ensure that the royalty rate applied thereto does not overreach and encompass components not covered by the patent.").

[212]As the court explained in *LaserDynamics, Inc. v. Quanta Computer, Inc.*, 694 F.3d 51 (Fed. Cir. 2012):

> By statute, reasonable royalty damages are deemed the minimum amount of infringement damages "adequate to compensate for the infringement." 35 U.S.C. §284. Such damages must be awarded "for the use made of the invention by the infringer." *Id.* Where small elements of multi-component products are accused of infringement, calculating a royalty on the entire product carries a considerable risk that the patentee will be improperly compensated for non-infringing components of that product. Thus, *it is generally required that royalties be based not on the entire product, but instead on the "smallest salable patent-practicing unit."*

LaserDynamics, 694 F.3d at 66-67 (emphasis added) (citing Cornell Univ. v. Hewlett-Packard Co., 609 F. Supp. 2d 279, 287-288 (N.D.N.Y. 2009) (explaining that "[w]ithout any real world transactions, or even any discernable market for CPU bricks, less intrepid counsel would have wisely abandoned a royalty base claim encompassing a product with significant non-infringing components. The logical and readily available alternative was the smallest salable infringing unit with close relation to the claimed invention — namely the processor itself.")).

[213]The entire market value rule was examined *supra* Section D.2.b. The rule allows damages to be computed based on the value of an entire product containing patented and unpatented components *if* the patented components are the reason for consumer demand. *See* Mentor Graphics Corp. v. EVE-USA, Inc., 870 F.3d 1298, 1300 (Fed. Cir. 2017) (Stoll, J., concurring in denial of rehearing *en banc*) (quoting Garretson v. Clark, 111 U.S. 120 (1884) (when "the entire value of the whole machine . . . is properly and legally attributable to the patented feature," the damages for infringement may be based on the value of the entire infringing product).

[214]VirnetX, Inc. v. Cisco Sys., Inc., 767 F.3d 1308, 1326 (Fed. Cir. 2014).

apportionment principle is grounded in the Supreme Court's 1884 decision in *Garretson v. Clark.*[215] There the Court held that "[t]he patentee . . . must in every case give evidence tending to separate or *apportion* the defendant's profits and the patentee's damages between the patented feature and the unpatented features."[216]

The Federal Circuit has ruled that the basic principle of apportionment applies in all of patent damages,[217] whether computed based on a patentee's lost profits[218] or a reasonable royalty.[219] Although reviewing a jury award of reasonably royalties, the Federal Circuit in its 2014 decision *Ericsson, Inc. v. D-Link Sys., Inc.*,[220] observed that

> [w]hen the accused infringing products have both patented and unpatented features, measuring this value requires a determination of the value added by such features. Indeed, *apportionment is required even for non-royalty forms of damages*: a jury must ultimately "apportion the defendant's profits and the patentee's damages between the patented feature and the unpatented features" using "reliable and tangible" evidence. *Garretson*, 111 U.S. at 121, 4 S. Ct. 291.[221]

Nevertheless, the Federal Circuit judges are not uniform in their view about the *application* of apportionment when lost profits damages are awarded. The appellate court's 2017 decision in *Mentor Graphics Corp. v. EVE-USA, Inc.*,[222] and the divided *en banc* court's refusal to rehear the case, illustrate the Circuit's disparate views on this economically complex topic.

The *Mentor* rehearing posture was unusual. The concurring and dissenting Circuit judges all agreed that apportionment is required whether patent infringement damages are based on a theory of reasonable royalty or a theory of lost profits. What could not be agreed on, however, was how to perform that apportionment. The *Mentor* panel, and the six judges concurring in the denial of rehearing *en banc*,

[215] 111 U.S. 120, 4 S. Ct. 291 (1884).

[216] *Garretson*, 111 U.S. at 121.

[217] Mentor Graphics Corp. v. EVE-USA, Inc., 851 F.3d 1275, 1283 n.3 (Fed. Cir. 2017) (Moore, J.).

[218] Lost profits damages are examined *supra* Section D.2.a.

[219] *Mentor Graphics*, 851 F.3d at 1287-1288 (agreeing that "apportionment is an important component of damages law generally, and we believe it is necessary in both reasonable royalty and lost profits analysis") (citing Ericsson, Inc. v. D-Link Sys., Inc., 773 F.3d 1201, 1226 (Fed. Cir. 2014) ("Apportionment is required even for non-royalty forms of damages.") (citing Garretson v. Clark, 111 U.S. 120, 121, 4 S. Ct. 291 (1884)); VirnetX, Inc. v. Cisco Sys., Inc., 767 F.3d 1308, 1326 (Fed. Cir. 2014) ("No matter what the form of the royalty, a patentee must take care to seek only those damages attributable to the infringing features." (citing *Garretson*, 111 U.S. at 120-121, 4 S. Ct. 291))). Reasonable royalty damages are examined *supra* Section D.2.c.

[220] 773 F.3d 1201 (Fed. Cir. 2014) (O'Malley, J.).

[221] *Ericsson,* 773 F.3d at 1226 (emphasis added).

[222] 851 F.3d 1275 (Fed. Cir. 2017) (Moore, J.).

determined that application of the well-established *Panduit* factors for determining entitlement to lost profits damages[223] implicitly incorporated the notion of apportionment, at least given the straightforward facts of the case at bar. Based on those specific facts, the Federal Circuit panel in *Mentor* answered the apportionment question affirmatively and affirmed a $36 million jury award of lost profits to the patentee.

When the Federal Circuit denied a subsequent petition for rehearing *en banc* in *Mentor,* six judges either disagreed or did not express an opinion. Two Circuit judges authored a dissenting opinion charging that the *Mentor* panel had improperly held that "when lost profits are awarded for patent infringement, there is no requirement for apportionment between patented and unpatented features, contrary to long-standing Supreme Court authority."[224] In the dissent's view, "the result here is that true apportionment will never be required for lost profits." Moreover, four Circuit judges did not join any opinion concerning the apportionment issue.[225] In light of the highly significant economic ramifications of the issue, the panel decision in *Mentor*, the Circuit's refusal to rehear the case *en banc*, and the dissent from that refusal are each examined in further detail below.

Filed in 1998, Mentor's U.S. Patent No. 6,240,376 ('376 patent) concerned generally the design of integrated circuits, and more specifically, methods for debugging synthesizable code at the register transfer level during gate-level simulation.[226] After Mentor obtained the '376 patent, the two named inventors left Mentor to form

[223]The four *Panduit* factors are detailed *supra* Section D.2.a(1).

[224]Mentor Graphics Corp. v. EVE-USA, Inc., 870 F.3d 1298, 1300 (Fed. Cir. Sept. 2017) (Dyk, J., dissenting from denial of rehearing *en banc*).

[225]Three opinions accompanied the order denying rehearing *en banc* in *Mentor*: (1) an opinion authored by Judge Stoll concurring in the denial of rehearing *en banc* on the apportionment issue; (2) an opinion authored by Judge Dyk dissenting from the denial of rehearing *en banc* on the apportionment issue; and (3) an opinion authored by Judge Moore concurring in the denial of rehearing *en banc* on the Circuit's refusal to abolish the doctrine of assignor estoppel. Chief Judge Prost and Judges Lourie (on the original panel) and Taranto did not join any of the three opinions that accompanied the order denying rehearing *en banc* in *Mentor*. Judge Chen joined the final opinion concurring in denial of rehearing *en banc*, but that opinion was limited strictly to the assignor estoppel issue. Thus Judge Chen, like Judges Prost, Lourie, and Taranto, did not express any opinion on the apportionment issue in *Mentor*.

[226]Representative claim 1 of Mentor's '376 patent recited:

> 1. A method comprising the steps of:
> a) identifying at least one statement within a register transfer level (RTL) synthesizable source code; and
> b) synthesizing the source code into a gate-level netlist including at least one instrumentation signal, wherein the instrumentation signal is indicative of an execution status of the at least one statement.

Mentor, 851 F.3d at 1281-1282.

EVE-USA, later acquired by accused infringer Synopsys. Mentor sued Synopsis for infringement of the '376 patent in the District of Oregon based on Synopsys's sales of "ZeBu" emulators. A jury found infringement and awarded Mentor approximately $36 million in lost profits damages. The jury computed the damage amount based on lost sales of Mentor's "Veloce" emulators due to Synopsys's infringing sales of its ZeBu emulators to electronics giant Intel.

On appeal, a panel of the Federal Circuit affirmed the jury's verdict on infringement and award of lost profits damages.[227] The *Mentor* court rejected accused infringer Synopsys's primary argument that the damage award should be vacated because the district court failed to apportion the lost profits.[228] Synopsis had asserted that Mentor did not deserve lost profits damages based on its lost sales of entire emulators because Mentor had invented only two out of thousands of features of the emulator.[229] The appellate court was not persuaded.

Although it agreed with Synopsys that "apportionment... is necessary in both reasonable royalty and lost profits analysis,"[230] the Federal Circuit disagreed that the jury below had not effectively apportioned the lost profits damages it awarded. Instead, and contrary to Synopsys's view, apportionment *was* properly incorporated into the *Mentor* jury's lost profits analysis because the *Panduit* factors for entitlement to lost profits were satisfied. On the first two *Panduit* factors, the jury had found that (1) there was a demand by customer Intel for the patented emulator because Intel would not have purchased the [infringing] Synopsis emulator system without the two patented features; and (2) there were no noninfringing alternative emulator systems acceptable to Intel.[231]

The *Mentor* Circuit reasoned that the first two *Panduit* factors, (1) demand for the patented product and (2) absence of acceptable noninfringing alternatives, "tie[d] lost profit damages to specific claim limitations and ensure[d] that damages [we]re commensurate with the value of the patented features."[232] It explained that

> [t]he first [*Panduit*] factor — demand for the patented product — considers demand for the product as a whole. *DePuy Spine, Inc. v. Medtronic Sofamor Danek, Inc.*, 567 F.3d 1314, 1330-31 (Fed. Cir. 2009). The second factor — the absence of non-infringing alternatives — considers demand for *particular limitations or features* of the claimed invention. *Id.* at 1331. Together, requiring patentees to prove demand for the product as a whole and the absence of non-infringing alternatives

[227] *Mentor*, 851 F.3d at 1280.
[228] *Mentor*, 851 F.3d at 1283.
[229] *See Mentor*, 851 F.3d at 1287.
[230] *Mentor*, 851 F.3d at 1287.
[231] *Mentor*, 851 F.3d at 1287.
[232] *Mentor*, 851 F.3d at 1288.

> *ties lost profit damages to specific claim limitations and ensures that damages are commensurate with the value of the patented features.*[233]

Importantly, the *Mentor* panel's conclusion that the jury's application of the *Panduit* factors necessarily incorporated apportionment turned on the particularly straightforward facts of the case. *Mentor* involved a "remarkably simple" two-supplier market in which only patentee Mentor and infringer Synopsys competed for sales of emulators to a single customer, Intel. Synopsys did not dispute that

> but for its infringement, Mentor would have made each of the infringing emulator sales to Intel. Nor does [Synopsys] dispute how much Mentor would have earned, the precise numbers of sales Mentor would have made, whether there were any alternatives that Intel may have preferred over the purchase of Mentor's product, or whether Intel would have chosen to purchase fewer emulators. In short, Synopsys does not dispute on appeal that for each infringing sale it made to Intel, Mentor lost that exact sale.[234]

Synopsys did not dispute on appeal the jury's findings that Mentor satisfied each of the four *Panduit* factors for lost profits. The Circuit found these facts critical because they made the case at bar "quite narrow and unlike the complicated fact patterns that impact so many damages models in patent cases."[235] The jury had answered in Mentor's favor the basic inquiry, "[h]ad the infringer not infringed, what would the [p]atent holder/licensee have made?"[236] Every sale that

[233]*Mentor*, 851 F.3d at 1285 (emphasis added) (citing Presidio Components, Inc. v. Am. Tech. Ceramics Corp., 702 F.3d 1351, 1361 (Fed. Cir. 2012) ("[P]roducts lacking the advantages of the patented invention can hardly be termed a substitute acceptable to the customer who wants those advantages." (quotations omitted)); Grain Processing Corp. v. Am. Maize-Prods. Co., 185 F.3d 1341, 1354 (Fed. Cir. 1999) (holding that customers would have found a particular claim limitation "irrelevant," so the patentee could not rely on that limitation for the second *Panduit* factor); Standard Havens Prods., Inc. v. Gencor Indus., Inc., 953 F.2d 1360, 1373 (Fed. Cir. 1991) ("If purchasers are motivated to purchase because of particular features available only from the patented product, products without such features — even if otherwise competing in the marketplace — would not be acceptable noninfringing substitutes."); SmithKline Diagnostics, Inc. v. Helena Labs. Corp., 926 F.2d 1161, 1166 (Fed. Cir. 1991) ("If purchasers are motivated to purchase because of particular features of a product available only from the patent owner and infringers, products without such features would obviously not be *acceptable* noninfringing substitutes.") (emphasis in original)).

[234]*Mentor*, 851 F.3d at 1286.

[235]*Mentor*, 851 F.3d at 1286.

[236]*Mentor*, 851 F.3d at 1290. The quoted language is found in the Supreme Court's 1964 *Aro II* decision:

> [T]he present statutory rule is that only "damages" may be recovered. These have been defined by this Court as "compensation for the pecuniary loss he (the patentee) has suffered from the infringement, without regard to the question whether

Synopsys made to Intel deprived patentee Mentor of a sale, because there were no other competitors in the market and because Intel did not consider any noninfringing alternatives to be acceptable.

Hence, the district court in *Mentor* did not err in refusing to further apportion lost profits after the jury returned its verdict in Mentor's favor. "We conclude that, when the *Panduit* factors are met, they incorporate into their very analysis the value properly attributed to the patented feature."[237] In other words, apportionment was subsumed into the jury's *Panduit* analysis for lost profits.

Synopsys thereafter sought rehearing *en banc,* contending that the *Mentor* panel had overstated (or misstated) the law of apportionment in lost profits cases. But the full Circuit denied rehearing *en banc.*[238] A total of six judges signed an accompanying opinion, authored by Judge Stoll, concurring in the denial. Judge Dyk, joined by Judge Hughes, issued an opinion dissenting from the denial. However, the remaining 4 judges (of 12 total) did not join either opinion. The tally in *Mentor* indicates that the issue of apportionment in lost profits cases may not yet be fully resolved. The issue is one to watch for further case law development.

In his opinion dissenting from denial of rehearing *en banc*, Judge Dyk charged the *Mentor* panel with improperly holding, contrary to longstanding Supreme Court authority, "that when lost profits are awarded for patent infringement, there is no requirement for apportionment between patented and unpatented features."[239] He rejected the panel's assertion that applying the first and second factors of the *Panduit* test "results in the required apportionment."[240] In Judge

---

> the defendant has gained or lost by his unlawful acts." Coupe v. Royer, 155 U.S. 565, 582, 15 S. Ct. 199, 206, 39 L. Ed. 263. They have been said to constitute "the difference between his pecuniary condition after the infringement, and what his condition would have been if the infringement had not occurred." Yale Lock Mfg. Co. v. Sargent, 117 U.S. 536, 552, 6 S. Ct. 934, 942, 29 L. Ed. 954. *The question to be asked in determining damages is "how much had the Patent Holder and Licensee suffered by the infringement. And that question [is] primarily: had the Infringer not infringed, what would Patent Holder-Licensee have made?"* Livesay Window Co. v. Livesay Industries, Inc., supra, 251 F.2d at 471.

Aro Mfg. Co. v. Convertible Top Replacement Co., 377 U.S. 476, 507, 84 S. Ct. 1526, 1543 (1964) ("*Aro II*") (emphasis added). *See also Mentor*, 851 F.3d at 1283-1284 (discussing *Aro II*).

[237] *Mentor*, 851 F.3d at 1290.

[238] Mentor Graphics Corp. v. EVE-USA, Inc., 870 F.3d 1298 (Fed. Cir. Sept. 1, 2017) (*en banc* order).

[239] *Mentor*, 870 F.3d at 1300 (Dyk, J., dissenting from denial of rehearing *en banc*).

[240] *Mentor,* 870 F.3d at 1301 (Dyk, J., dissenting from denial of rehearing *en banc*). Judge Dyk emphasized that simply complying with *Panduit* did not resolve the apportionment requirement. Firstly, *Panduit* was not apposite because the *Panduit* case itself did not concern apportionment; it was not a dispute about apportioning lost profits between patented and unpatented features. Rather, the patent in that suit was directed

Dyk's frank view, the panel's reasoning that apportionment was subsumed within the *Panduit* analysis " 'ignore[s] the ancient wisdom that calling a thing by a name does not make it so.' "[241] Rather, "the panel opinion simply does not apportion — even though it purportedly recognizes apportionment's importance."[242]

Judge Dyk acknowledged that the *Panduit* test's first two factors encapsulate "but-for causation"; that is, the concept that lost profits damages are not appropriate unless the patentee establishes that it would have sold the patented item but for the infringer's infringement. But Judge Dyk's reading of Supreme Court precedent made clear to him that "more than but-for causation is required for apportionment."[243] In addition to establishing that the infringing sale caused the patentee to lose a sale, the damages sought by the patentee must also be apportioned between patented and unpatented features:

> This principle was established by Supreme Court cases involving both the disgorgement of the defendant's profits (allowed before 1946) and the recovery of the patentee's own lost profits (the current rule). As the panel recognizes, both types of cases are pertinent because "the basic principle of apportionment which they espouse applies in all of patent damages." *Mentor*, 851 F.3d at 1283 n.3.[244]

Judge Dyk quoted language from the Supreme Court's decisions in *Seymour v. McCormick* (1853),[245] *Garretson v. Clark* (1884),[246] *Dobson v. Hartford Carpet Co.* (1885),[247] and *Blake v. Robertson* (1876)[248] to support his position that apportionment is mandatory and represents a step beyond simply establishing but-for causation.

Judge Stoll, writing for herself and five other colleagues who concurred in the Circuit's refusal to rehear the *Mentor* case *en banc*, asserted that "Mentor proved that the patented features were what imbued the combined features that made up the emulator with marketable value." Given these facts, she declared, further apportionment

---

to an electrical wiring duct that constituted the *entire* product in dispute. In other words, the accused product in *Panduit* was unlike the emulator at issue in *Mentor* because the patented features of the Panduit duct represented the entire claimed invention.

[241] *Mentor*, 870 F.3d at 1301 (Dyk, J., dissenting from denial of rehearing *en banc*) (quoting City of Madison v. Wis. Emp. Relations Comm., 429 U.S. 167, 174 (1976)).

[242] *Mentor*, 870 F.3d at 1301 (Dyk, J., dissenting from denial of rehearing *en banc*).

[243] *Mentor*, 870 F.3d at 1301 (Dyk, J., dissenting from denial of rehearing *en banc*).

[244] *Mentor*, 870 F.3d at 1301-1302 (Dyk, J., dissenting from denial of rehearing *en banc*).

[245] *See* Seymour v. McCormick, 57 U.S. (16 How.) 480, 489-490 (1853).

[246] *See* Garretson v. Clark, 111 U.S. 120, 121 (1884).

[247] *See* Dobson v. Hartford Carpet Co., 114 U.S. 439, 443-444 (1885).

[248] *See* Blake v. Robertson, 94 U.S. 728, 733-734 (1876).

was unnecessary.[249] Notably, Judge Stoll cited the *Ericsson* case's discussion of the entire market value rule in support of her position.[250]

Dissenting Judge Dyk countered that the entire market value rule was not in play in *Mentor*. Judge Dyk acknowledged that the Supreme Court's *Dobson* and *Garretson* cases both held (in addition to their discussion of apportionment) that recovery for *all* of the profits for a product is permitted *if* it can be shown that consumer demand is attributable to the patented features. This rule has become known as the "entire market value" rule, Judge Dyk explained.[251] When the entire market value rule applies, he agreed, no apportionment is required.

But in Judge Dyk's view, the panel opinion in *Mentor* did *not* invoke the entire market value rule; "[t]he panel never says or even suggests that the *Panduit* factors and the entire market value rule are the same."[252] Indeed, the district court had precluded Synopsys from introducing evidence that the entire market value rule was inapplicable.[253] Thus "the accused infringer here never had the opportunity to address the entire market value rule on the facts of this particular case."[254]

Accordingly, Judge Dyk rejected as "not tenable" Judge Stoll's attempt in her opinion concurring in denial of rehearing *en banc* to equate application of the *Panduit* factors with the entire market value rule. That an infringer's sale caused the patentee to lose a sale says nothing about whether the customer's demand for the product was driven solely by its patented feature(s), Judge Dyk explained:

> The combination of consumer demand and but-for causation (i.e., that customers would not have purchased the product without the two patented features) is not remotely the same as the entire market value rule.

[249] *Mentor*, 870 F.3d at 1300 (Fed. Cir. 2017) (Stoll, J., concurring in denial of rehearing *en banc*).

[250] *See Mentor*, 870 F.3d at 1300 (Fed. Cir. 2017) (Stoll, J., concurring in denial of rehearing *en banc*) (citing *Ericsson*, 773 F.3d at 1227 ("[W]here the entire value of a machine as a marketable article is 'properly and legally attributable to the patented feature,' the damages owed to the patentee may be calculated by reference to [the entire value of the machine.]") (quoting *LaserDynamics*, 694 F.3d at 67)); *VirnetX*, 767 F.3d at 1326). "Whether one views this in terms of what imbues value to the ultimate combination of features or what is a driver of demand for those combined features, the result is the same: the apportionment required by *Garretson* is satisfied." *Mentor*, 870 F.3d at 1300 (Fed. Cir. 2017) (Stoll, J., concurring in denial of rehearing *en banc*).

[251] *Mentor*, 870 F.3d at 1302 n.2 (Fed. Cir. 2017) (Dyk, J., dissenting from denial of rehearing *en banc*).

[252] *Mentor*, 870 F.3d at 1303 (Fed. Cir. 2017) (Dyk, J., dissenting from denial of rehearing *en banc*).

[253] *Mentor*, 870 F.3d at 1302 n.2 (Fed. Cir. 2017) (Dyk, J., dissenting from denial of rehearing *en banc*).

[254] *Mentor*, 870 F.3d at 1303 (Fed. Cir. 2017) (Dyk, J., dissenting from denial of rehearing *en banc*).

> Consumer demand for the patented feature and but-for causation may exist (and satisfy the *Panduit* factors), but this does not mean that *other* features do not contribute to consumer demand. The entire market value rule only applies if consumer demand is driven by the patented feature. Consumer demand for the patented feature and but-for causation do not establish that consumer demand is *only* attributable to the patented feature. Consumer demand may also be driven by other features in the product, which may be just as necessary to purchasing decisions, leading to the required apportionment.[255]

For dissenting Judge Dyk, the bottom line was that the *Mentor* panel decision meant apportionment would never apply in awards of lost profits damages. "Since the factual findings necessary to satisfy the *Panduit* factors are a necessary predicate for lost profits, the result here is that true apportionment will never be required for lost profits."[256]

3. Enhanced Damages and Willful Infringement

a. *Overview*

In accordance with 35 U.S.C. §284, a district court has the discretion to increase (or "enhance") damages up to three times the amount of the compensatory award.[257] "The paramount determination in deciding to grant enhancement and the amount thereof is the egregiousness of the defendant's conduct...."[258] Enhanced damages

[255]*Mentor*, 870 F.3d at 1303 (Fed. Cir. 2017) (Dyk, J., dissenting from denial of rehearing *en banc*) (emphasis added).

[256]*Mentor*, 870 F.3d at 1304 (Fed. Cir. 2017) (Dyk, J., dissenting from denial of rehearing *en banc*).

[257]35 U.S.C. §284, ¶2 (providing that "[w]hen the damages are not found by a jury, the court shall assess them. In either event the court may increase the damages up to three times the amount found or assessed."). The statutory phrase "up to" indicates that trebling damages is the maximum enhancement. In less egregious cases of willful infringement, a court may choose to enhance by doubling the compensatory damages (or by applying some other multiplier less than 3).

[258]Read Corp. v. Portec, Inc., 970 F.2d 816, 826 (Fed. Cir. 1992) (stating that such egregiousness is to be evaluated based on "all the facts and circumstances," i.e., a totality-of-the-circumstances analysis). The *Read* court enumerated the following factors "for consideration in determining when an infringer 'acted in [such] bad faith as to merit an increase in damages awarded against him,'... particularly in deciding on the extent of enhancement":

1. whether the infringer deliberately copied the ideas or design of another;
2. whether the infringer, when he knew of the other's patent protection, investigated the scope of the patent and formed a good-faith belief that it was invalid or that it was not infringed;
3. [the] [infringer's] behavior as a party to the litigation;
4. [the] infringer's size and financial condition;...

are frequently (but not always) awarded when a defendant's infringement is found to be "willful."[259]

As detailed below, the Federal Circuit's landmark 2007 decision in *In re Seagate Tech., LLC*[260] required that in order to prove willfulness a patentee must establish that the infringer acted in an objectively reckless manner.[261] The *Seagate* standard significantly raised the bar on willfulness, making it more difficult for a patentee to establish than under the Federal Circuit's previous standard.[262]

Seagate was not the last word on willfulness, however. The Supreme Court in 2015 granted writs of *certiorari* in two Federal Circuit decisions that had rejected assertions of willful infringement under the prevailing *Seagate* standard. In the June 2016 decisions, the Supreme Court rejected the complex, rigid test of *Seagate*, and replaced it with a far less formulistic and more discretionary inquiry favoring patent owners.[263] The Court's *Stryker* and *Halo* decisions are detailed below.

---

5. [the] closeness of the case;...
6. [the] duration of the defendant's misconduct;...
7. remedial action taken by the defendant;...
8. [the] defendant's motivation for harm; [and]
9. whether [the] defendant attempted to conceal its misconduct.

Id. at 826-827 (citations omitted). The court observed that using these factors is "in line with punitive damage considerations in other tort contexts." *Id.* at 827-828.

[259]*See Read Corp.*, at 826 (stating that "[a]n award of enhanced damages for infringement, as well as the extent of the enhancement, is committed to the discretion of the trial court.... [T]his court has approved such awards where the infringer acted in wanton disregard of the patentee's patent rights, that is, where the infringement is willful.... On the other hand, a finding of willful infringement does not mandate that damages be enhanced, much less mandate treble damages.") (citations omitted). *See also* In re Seagate Tech., LLC, 497 F.3d 1360, 1368 (Fed. Cir. 2007) (*en banc*) (noting that "a finding of willfulness does not require an award of enhanced damages; it merely permits it").

[260]497 F.3d 1360 (Fed. Cir. 2007) (*en banc*).

[261]*See Seagate,* 497 F.3d at 1371.

[262]*See* Carl G. Anderson et al., *Willful Patent Infringement: The First Year of the Post-*Seagate *Era*, 20 No. 9 INTELL. PROP. & TECH. L.J. 11, 13 (2008) (based on analysis of approximately 40 reported post-*Seagate* district court decisions analyzing willfulness issues, concluding that "*Seagate* has raised the bar with respect to succeeding on a claim of willful infringement"); *cf.* Eric Yeager, *Conferences/Patents: Judge Linn Discusses "Challenges Ahead" for Patentees, PTO at AIPLA Luncheon*, 77 BNA's PAT. TRADEMARK & COPYRIGHT J. 12 (2008) (stating that "there is no debate over the fact that patentees can 'no longer bank on a determination of willfulness and enhanced damages merely because infringement was found against an accused who had prior notice of the patent'") (quoting speech by Federal Circuit Judge Richard Linn).

[263]The heightened "objective recklessness" standard of *Seagate*, discussed *infra*, occasioned predictions that the decision would result in far fewer findings of willful infringement and awards of enhanced damages. *See* Christoper B. Seaman, *Willful Patent Infringement and Enhanced Damages After* In Re Seagate: *An Empirical Study*, 97 IOWA L. REV. 417 (2012). In an empirical study of district court cases involving willfulness and enhanced damages decided during the six-year time period encompassing

b. *Early Federal Circuit Decisions on Willfulness*

The Federal Circuit's 2007 *en banc* decision in *Seagate* is best understood in its historical context. After the Federal Circuit was created in 1982, its early decisions emphasized the importance of respecting patent property rights "at a time when widespread disregard of [such] rights was undermining the national innovation incentive."[264] In particular, Federal Circuit decisions during the 1980s established that once a potential infringer became aware of another's patent rights, it had an affirmative duty to proceed with due care to determine whether or not it was infringing.[265] That duty required seeking and obtaining competent legal advice *before* initiating any possibly infringing activity.[266]

In decisions such as *Underwater Devices, Inc. v. Morrison-Knudsen Co.*,[267] and *Kloster Speedsteel AB v. Crucible Inc.*,[268] the Federal Circuit went so far as to authorize district courts and juries to draw an "adverse inference" from an accused infringer's failure to produce an exculpatory opinion of counsel in response to a charge of willful infringement. In other words, if no opinion was produced, the fact finder could properly infer that the legal advice given had been negative (i.e., counsel had determined that the client was infringing) and that the accused infringer nevertheless continued to knowingly infringe.

Critics of the adverse inference rule charged that it was in tension with the principle of attorney-client privilege. An accused infringer was effectively forced to choose between producing its opinion of counsel and thereby waiving privilege, or maintaining privilege but being subject to the adverse inference (potentially leading to a finding of willfulness and an award of enhanced damages).

In its 2004 decision in *Knorr-Bremse Sys. v. Dana Corp.*,[269] the *en banc* Federal Circuit eliminated from U.S. patent law the adverse

---

three years before the Federal Circuit decided *Seagate* and three years after, Professor Seaman refutes these predictions. He finds that "willfulness was found only about 10% less often after *Seagate*, and this relatively small change was not statistically significant." *Id.* at 402 (footnotes omitted). Moreover, the data showed that judges and juries reached different decisions under the "objective recklessness" standard. "At trial, juries found willful infringement at similar rates both before and after *Seagate*. . . . In contrast, judges found willfulness only a small fraction of the time after *Seagate*, as compared to a majority of the time before *Seagate*." *Id.* (footnotes omitted).

[264] *Seagate*, 497 F.3d at 1369 (citing DEP'T OF COMMERCE, ADVISORY COMMITTEE ON INDUSTRIAL INNOVATION FINAL REPORT (Sept. 1979)).

[265] *See* Avia Group Int'l Inc. v. L.A. Gear Cal., Inc., 853 F.2d 1557, 1566 (Fed. Cir. 1988); Underwater Devices, Inc. v. Morrison-Knudsen Co., 717 F.2d 1380, 1389-1390 (Fed. Cir. 1983).

[266] *See Underwater Devices*, 717 F.2d at 1390.

[267] 717 F.2d 1380 (Fed. Cir. 1983).

[268] 793 F.2d 1565 (Fed. Cir. 1986).

[269] 383 F.3d 1337 (Fed. Cir. 2004) (*en banc*).

inference that had previously arisen from an accused infringer's failure to produce an exculpatory opinion of counsel. By the time of its decision, the *Knorr-Bremse* court had come to recognize that "the inference that withheld opinions are adverse to the client's actions can distort the attorney-client relationship," and that "a special rule affecting attorney-client relationships in patent cases is not warranted."[270] Thus entering the mainstream of judicial thought on attorney-client privilege, the Federal Circuit appeared to recognize that "patent law is not an island separated from the main body of American jurisprudence."[271]

In addition to rejecting the adverse inference based on the nonproduction of an opinion of counsel, the *Knorr-Bremse* court also eliminated the drawing of any adverse inference from the fact of an accused infringer's not seeking legal counsel or advice upon notice of potential patent infringement. The *en banc* court left open, however, the question whether the fact finder could be told of the nonrepresentation; this undecided issue has obvious resonance in the jury trial context.[272]

The *Knorr-Bremse* court did not go so far as to hold that the existence of a substantial defense to infringement would negate willfulness, as some *amici* had urged. Rather, the existence of a substantial defense was but one factor to be considered in the multifactor "totality of the circumstances" analysis for willfulness, the standard previously set forth in *Read Corp. v. Portec, Inc.*, discussed *supra.*[273]

[270]*Knorr-Bremse Sys.* 383 F.3d at 1344.

[271]*Knorr-Bremse Sys.*, 383 F.3d at 1351 (Dyk, J., concurring-in-part and dissenting-in-part). In his separate opinion Judge Dyk charged that the *en banc Knorr-Bremse* majority had not gone far enough. The majority should also have eliminated the duty of due care, Judge Dyk asserted, which effectively requires an accused infringer to prove a negative; that is, it shifts the burden of proof to the accused infringer to establish that its conduct was not willful. An infringer's failure to proceed with due care, without more, should not be enough to establish willfulness, Judge Dyk contended; rather, a court should require additional "bad acts" such as intentional copying before finding willfulness. In Judge Dyk's view, the *Knorr-Bremse* majority's retention of the duty of due care was inconsistent with Supreme Court decisions indicating that an award of punitive damages not based on truly reprehensible conduct may violate the Due Process Clause of the Constitution. Three years later, the Federal Circuit adopted Judge Dyk's view by abolishing the affirmative duty of due care in *In re Seagate Tech., LLC*, 497 F.3d 1360 (Fed. Cir. 2007) (*en banc*).

[272]A federal district court has held that even post-*Seagate*, a jury can be told that an accused infringer did not obtain an opinion letter from counsel. *See* Energy Transp. Group, Inc. v. William Demant Holding A/S, C.A. No. 05-422 GMS (D. Del. Jan. 7, 2008), (rejecting defendant's contention that *Seagate* effected a change in the law such that failure to obtain advice of counsel cannot be considered by the jury, and concluding that "nothing in *Seagate* forbids a jury to consider whether a defendant obtained advice of counsel as part of the totality of the circumstances in determining willfulness").

[273]*See* Read Corp. v. Portec, Inc., 970 F.2d 816, 826-827 (Fed. Cir. 1992).

c. Seagate *(Fed. Cir. 2007)* (en banc)

In 2007, the Federal Circuit again went *en banc* to consider willfulness. In *In re Seagate Technology, LLC* (*"Seagate"*),[274] the court revisited its willfulness framework in light of the "practical concerns facing litigants under the current regime" as well as guidance from Supreme Court decisions rendered since the Circuit's 1983 decision in *Underwater Devices*.[275] The *Seagate* court announced a substantially heightened burden for a patentee seeking to establish that an accused infringer acted willfully. The court abandoned its earlier imposition of an affirmative duty of due care on accused infringers, rejecting this "negligence"-type standard as "fail[ing] to comport with the general understanding of willfulness in the civil context" and as "allow[ing] for punitive damages in a manner inconsistent with Supreme Court precedent."[276] In its place, the court adopted an objective standard for willfulness that requires "reckless" conduct by an accused infringer, stating

> we overrule the standard set out in *Underwater Devices* and hold that proof of willful infringement permitting enhanced damages requires at least a showing of objective recklessness. Because we abandon the affirmative duty of due care, we also reemphasize that there is no affirmative obligation to obtain opinion of counsel.[277]

The *Seagate* court did not attempt to provide a comprehensive definition for objective recklessness, leaving this for further development in the case law. However, relying on the civil law's general definition of "reckless" conduct as acting "in the face of an unjustifiably high risk of harm that is either known or so obvious that it should be known,"[278] the Federal Circuit set forth the following two-part standard:

> [T]o establish willful infringement, a patentee must show by clear and convincing evidence that the infringer acted despite an objectively high likelihood that its actions constituted infringement of a valid patent. *See Safeco* [*Ins. Co. of Am. v. Burr*], 127 S. Ct. [2201,] 2215 ("It is [a] high risk of harm, objectively assessed, that is the essence of recklessness at common law."). The state of mind of the accused infringer is not relevant to this objective inquiry. If this threshold objective standard is satisfied, the patentee must also demonstrate that this objectively-defined risk (determined by the record developed in the infringement proceeding)

[274] 497 F.3d 1360 (Fed. Cir. 2007) (*en banc*).
[275] *Seagate*, 497 F.3d at 1370.
[276] *Seagate*, 497 F.3d at 1371 (citations omitted).
[277] *Seagate*, 497 F.3d at 1371.
[278] *Seagate*, 497 F.3d at 1371 (citing tort law treatises).

was either known or so obvious that it should have been known to the accused infringer.[279]

In addition to reframing the standard for willful infringement, the Federal Circuit in *Seagate* considered the appropriate scope of waiver of attorney-client privilege in willfulness cases. When an accused infringer asserts an advice of counsel defense in response to a patentee's charge of willful infringement, the scope of the resulting waiver of attorney-client privilege is typically put at issue. For example, after Convolve, Inc. and the Massachusetts Institute of Technology (collectively "Convolve") accused Seagate of willful infringement, Seagate notified Convolve that it intended to rely on three opinion letters Seagate had obtained concerning the patents in suit. Seagate made its opinion counsel available for deposition and disclosed all of that attorney's work product. In response to Convolve's motion, the district court ruled that the scope of Seagate's waiver extended beyond its communications with its opinion counsel to include all communications between Seagate and *any* counsel, including Seagate's trial counsel and its in-house counsel.[280]

The Federal Circuit rejected as a general matter the broad scope of waiver adopted by the district court in *Seagate*. Opinion counsel and trial counsel serve significantly different functions; the former provides an "objective assessment for making informed business

[279] *Seagate*, 497 F.3d at 1371. Although the *Seagate* court left it to future cases to "further develop the application of this standard," *id.*, it agreed with the suggestion of concurring Judge Newman that "the standards of commerce would be among the factors a court might consider." *Id.* at 1371 n.5.

In cases after *Seagate*, the Federal Circuit observed that *Seagate*'s threshold objective prong " 'tends not to be met where an accused infringer relies on a reasonable defense to a charge of infringement.' " Advanced Fiber Techs. (AFT) Trust v. J & L Fiber Servs., Inc., 674 F.3d 1365, 1377 (Fed. Cir. 2012) (quoting Spine Solutions, Inc. v. Medtronic Sofamor Danek USA, Inc., 620 F.3d 1305, 1319 (Fed. Cir. 2010)). An example is *Advanced Fiber*, in which the Federal Circuit affirmed a district court's dismissal of patentee AFT's motion for summary judgment that defendant J & L had willfully infringed. The district court's dismissal was properly based on "numerous factors" indicating that the accused infringer's acts were not objectively reckless. *Advanced Fiber*, 674 F.3d at 1377. These factors included "(1) the language of [AFT's] '072 patent [in suit], which 'leaves significant doubt as to the patent's validity'; (2) J & L's 'compelling non-infringement and invalidity arguments'; (3) the PTO's initial 'rejection of [AFT's] reissue application based on it being "structurally indistinguishable" from the Gillespie [prior art patent]'; and (4) the fact that the meaning of certain key claim terms in the '072 patent only became clear through AFT's arguments during reissue prosecution." *Advanced Fiber,* 674 F.3d at 1377 (quoting Advanced Fiber Techs. Trust v. J & L Fiber Servs., Inc., 751 F. Supp. 2d 348, 380-381 (N.D.N.Y. 2010)). "Taken together, these facts show that J & L's assertions of invalidity and noninfringement were, at minimum, objectively reasonable defenses to AFT's charge of infringement." *Advanced Fiber*, 674 F.3d at 1377-1378.

[280] *See Seagate*, 497 F.3d at 1366-1367.

decisions," while the latter develops litigation strategies as part of an adversarial process.[281] Moreover, communications of trial counsel have little relevance to pre-litigation conduct, upon which willfulness depends in ordinary circumstances.[282] Thus, the Federal Circuit held "as a general proposition [] that asserting the advice of counsel defense and disclosing opinions of opinion counsel do not constitute waiver of attorney-client privilege for communications with trial counsel."[283] Similarly, the appellate court held that waiver of opinion counsel's work product does not extend to waiver of trial counsel's work product, "absent exceptional circumstances."[284]

Willfulness was long considered a factual question amenable to jury determination. In 2012, the Federal Circuit concluded that the willfulness inquiry post-*Seagate* had become more complex than a single question of fact. The Federal Circuit held in *Bard Peripheral Vascular, Inc. v. W.L. Gore & Assoc., Inc.*[285] that the threshold objective prong of the willfulness standard enunciated in *Seagate* is a question of law based on underlying mixed questions of law and fact. A district court must determine the threshold objective prong, and its determination on that prong is subject to *de novo* review by the Federal Circuit.[286] Thus the *Bard Peripheral* court essentially reallocated the roles of the judge and jury in determining whether or not infringement of a patent is willful. The judge now determines whether a reasonable person would have found there to be a high likelihood of patent infringement.[287] If this threshold objective determination is met, only then does the jury determine the patent infringer's subjective intent.[288]

[281]*Seagate*, 497 F.3d at 1373.

[282]*See Seagate*, 497 F.3d at 1374.

[283]*See Seagate*, 497 F.3d at 1374. The Federal Circuit further explained that its announced rule on waiver was not absolute, and that "trial courts remain free to exercise their discretion in unique circumstances to extend waiver to trial counsel, such as if a party or counsel engages in chicanery." *Id.* at 1374-1375.

[284]*See Seagate*, 497 F.3d at 1375-1376.

[285]682 F.3d 1003 (Fed. Cir. 2012).

[286]*See Bard*, 682 at 1006-1007 (holding that "the objective determination of recklessness, even though predicated on underlying mixed questions of law and fact, is best decided by the judge as a question of law subject to *de novo* review").

[287]*See Bard*, 682 F.3d at 1008. The court explained that "[i]n considering the objective prong of *Seagate*, the judge may when the defense is a question of fact or a mixed question of law and fact allow the jury to determine the underlying facts relevant to the defense in the first instance, for example, the questions of anticipation or obviousness. But, consistent with this court's holding today, the ultimate legal question of whether a reasonable person would have considered there to be a high likelihood of infringement of a valid patent should always be decided as a matter of law by the judge." *Bard*, 682 F.3d at 1008.

[288]*See Bard*, 682 F.3d at 1008.

d. America Invents Act (2011) Codification

The America Invents Act of 2011 added a new section to the Patent Act in order to legislatively codify the holdings of *Seagate* and *Knorr-Bremse* regarding an accused infringer's failure to obtain advice of counsel.[289] Section 298 of the Patent Act provides:

> **§298. Advice of counsel**
>
> The failure of an infringer to obtain the advice of counsel with respect to any allegedly infringed patent, or the failure of the infringer to present such advice to the court or jury, may not be used to prove that the accused infringer willfully infringed the patent or that the infringer intended to induce infringement of the patent.[290]

The AIA's legislative history explains that the new §298 "is designed to protect attorney-client privilege and to reduce pressure on accused infringers to obtain opinions of counsel for litigation purposes. It reflects a policy choice that the probative value of this type of evidence is outweighed by the harm that coercing a waiver of attorney-client privilege inflicts on the attorney-client relationship."[291]

[289]*See* Leahy-Smith America Invents Act, Pub. L. No. 112-29 (H.R. 1249), §17, 125 Stat. 284, 329 (Sept. 16, 2011) ("Advice of Counsel") (amending Chapter 29 of 35 U.S.C. by adding at the chapter's end a new section designated §298).

[290]35 U.S.C. §298 (eff. Sept. 16, 2012). *See also* Leahy-Smith America Invents Act, Pub. L. No. 112-29 (H.R. 1249), §35, 125 Stat. 284, 341 (Sept. 16, 2011) ("Effective Date") (providing that "[except as otherwise provided in this Act, the provisions of this Act shall take effect upon the expiration of the 1-year period beginning on the date of the enactment of this Act and shall apply to any patent issued on or after that effective date").

[291]*See* H.R. REP. No. 112-98 [House Judiciary Comm. Rep. on the America Invents Act], at 63 (June 1, 2011). The legislative history further explains that "Section 298 applies to findings of both willfulness and intent to induce infringement — and thus legislatively abrogates the Federal Circuit's decision in *Broadcom Corp. v. Qualcomm Inc.*, 543 F.3d 683, 699 (Fed. Cir. 2008)." *Id.*

In the *Broadcom* litigation referenced by the AIA legislative history, a jury found Qualcomm liable for direct and inducing infringement of Broadcom's patents, and further found that Qualcomm's infringement was willful. *See* Broadcom Corp. v. Qualcomm Inc., 543 F.3d 683 (Fed. Cir. 2008). The jury had been instructed that

> considering whether Qualcomm acted in good faith, you should consider all the circumstances, including whether or not Qualcomm obtained and followed the advice of a competent lawyer with regard to infringement. The absence of a lawyer's opinion, by itself, is insufficient to support a finding of willfulness, and *you may not assume that merely because a party did not obtain an opinion of counsel, the opinion would have been unfavorable*. However, you may consider whether Qualcomm sought a legal opinion as one factor in assessing whether, under the totality of the circumstances, any infringement by Qualcomm was willful.

Broadcom, 543 F.3d at 698 (emphasis added by the Federal Circuit).

e. *Supreme Court Rewrites Law of Willful Infringement (2016)*

The Federal Circuit's 2007 *Seagate en banc* decision examined above adopted an objective standard for willfulness that required "reckless" conduct by an accused infringer. Patent litigators and academic commentators criticized the *Seagate* standard as overly rigid and raising the bar too high to find willful infringement (a prerequisite to obtaining enhancement of damages under 35 U.S.C. §284). The criticism accelerated in 2014 after the Supreme Court relaxed the standards for a prevailing party to obtain an attorney fee award in an "exceptional" case under 35 U.S.C. §285.[292] Such fees are sometimes awarded to patent owners based on willful infringement.

In October 2015, the Supreme Court granted writs of *certiorari* in two Federal Circuit decisions, *Stryker v. Zimmer* and *Halo v. Pulse.*[293] In both cases the Circuit had rejected assertions of willful infringement under the *Seagate* standard. They illustrated how difficult it was for patent owners to obtain an award of enhanced damages for willfulness under the very high bar set forth in *Seagate.*

On appeal, accused infringer Qualcomm argued that that the district court erred in allowing the inducing infringement verdicts to stand in light of the quoted jury instruction. Qualcomm asserted that the instruction improperly permitted the jury to consider failure to obtain an opinion of counsel as a factor in determining whether Qualcomm had the requisite level of intent for inducing infringement liability. The Federal Circuit disagreed, approving the jury instruction and sustaining the verdict of inducing infringement. The appellate court held that opinion of counsel evidence remains relevant to establishing the intent element of inducing infringement and that "the failure to procure such an opinion may be probative of intent in this context." *Broadcom,* 543 F.3d at 699. The Federal Circuit reasoned that "[i]t would be manifestly unfair to allow opinion-of-counsel evidence to serve an exculpatory function, as was the case in [the inducing infringement decision, *DSU Med. Corp. v. JMS Co.*, 471 F.3d 1293, 1307 (Fed. Cir. 2006) (*en banc* in relevant part)], and yet not permit patentees to identify failures to procure such advice as circumstantial evidence of intent to infringe." *Broadcom,* 543 F.3d at 699.

By legislatively overruling the *Broadcom* holding, the AIA-implemented §298 of the Patent Act clarifies that an accused infringer's failure to obtain advice of counsel may not be used to establish the intent required for inducing infringement liability. Inducing infringement and its intent requirement are further discussed *supra* Chapter 9, Section E.1 ("Inducing Infringement Under [35 U.S.C.] §271(b)").

[292]The Supreme Court's attorney fee shifting decisions in *Octane Fitness, LLC v. ICON Health & Fitness, Inc.*, 134 S. Ct. 1749 (2014) ("*Octane Fitness II*"), and *Highmark Inc. v. Allcare Health Mgmt. Sys., Inc.*, 134 S. Ct. 1744 (2014) ("*Highmark III*"), are examined *infra*, Section E ("Attorney Fees").

[293]*See* Halo Elecs., Inc. v. Pulse Elecs., Inc., No. 14-1513, 2015 WL 3883472 (U.S. Oct. 19, 2015) (mem.) (granting *certiorari* to review Halo Elecs., Inc. v. Pulse Elecs., Inc., 769 F.3d 1371 (Fed. Cir. 2014)); Stryker Corp. v. Zimmer, Inc., No. 14-1520, 2015 WL 3883499 (U.S. Oct. 19, 2015) (mem.) (granting *certiorari* to review Stryker Corp. v. Zimmer, Inc., 782 F.3d 649 (Fed. Cir. Mar. 23, 2015)). The Supreme Court consolidated *Halo* and *Stryker* for review.

In *Halo*, the Supreme Court granted *certiorari* on the following question presented:

> 1. Whether the Federal Circuit erred by applying a rigid, two-part test for enhancing patent infringement damages under 35 U.S.C. §284, that is the same as the rigid, two-part test this Court rejected last term in *Octane Fitness, LLC v. ICON Health & Fitness, Inc.*, 134 S. Ct. 1749 (2014) for imposing attorney fees under the similarly-worded 35 U.S.C. §285.[294]

In *Stryker*, the Supreme Court granted *certiorari* on the following two questions presented:

> 1. Has the Federal Circuit improperly abrogated the plain meaning of 35 U.S.C. §284 by forbidding any award of enhanced damages unless there is a finding of willfulness under a rigid, two-part test, when this Court recently rejected an analogous framework imposed on 35 U.S.C. §285, the statute providing for attorneys' fee awards in exceptional cases?
>
> 2. Does a district court have discretion under 35 U.S.C. §284 to award enhanced damages where an infringer intentionally copied a direct competitor's patented invention, knew the invention was covered by multiple patents, and made no attempt to avoid infringing the patents on that invention?[295]

In the Supreme Court's 2016 decision in *Halo Elecs., Inc. v. Pulse Elecs., Inc.*,[296] decided together with *Stryker Corp. v. Zimmer, Inc.*, the Court answered these questions in the affirmative. The result was a substantial rewrite of the law on willful infringement, making it easier for patentees to establish. The Supreme Court's decision and both of the underlying Federal Circuit decisions are analyzed below in chronological fashion.

(i) *Halo v. Pulse* (Fed. Cir. 2014)

In *Halo*,[297] a jury found that it was "highly probable that [accused infringer] Pulse's infringement was willful. . . ."[298] Nevertheless, a district court held Pulse's infringement was *not* willful because the

[294]Petition for Writ of Certiorari, Halo Elecs., Inc. v. Pulse Elecs., Inc., No. 14-1513 (June 22, 2015), at *i*, *available at* http://www.scotusblog.com/wp-content/uploads/2015/10/Halo-cert-petition-final6.pdf.

[295]Petition for Writ of Certiorari, Stryker Corp. v. Zimmer, Inc., No. 14-1520 (June 22, 2015), at *i*, *available at* http://www.scotusblog.com/wp-content/uploads/2015/10/Stryker-Petition-for-Certiorari.pdf.

[296]136 S. Ct. 1923 (June 13, 2016) (Roberts, C.J.).

[297]769 F.3d 1371 (Fed. Cir. 2014).

[298]*Halo*, 769 F.3d at 1376.

Seagate objective prong had not been satisfied. Specifically, the district court determined that Pulse had not acted in an objectively reckless manner when infringing because the obviousness defense that Pulse presented at trial was not objectively baseless.[299]

In an opinion authored by Judge Lourie, the Federal Circuit agreed, affirming the district court's judgement that Halo's infringement was not willful. Although Pulse's invalidity defense was ultimately unsuccessful, the Federal Circuit concluded that Pulse had raised a "substantial question" as to obviousness.[300] Specifically,

> Pulse presented evidence that the prior art disclosed each element of the asserted claims, that it would have been predictable to combine and modify the prior art to create the claimed electronic packages, and that there were differences between the prior art considered by the PTO and the prior art introduced at trial. . . . Pulse also challenged Halo's evidence of secondary considerations.[301]

[299]*See* Halo Elecs., Inc. v. Pulse Elecs., Inc., No. 2:07-CV-00331-PMP, 2013 WL 2319145, at *15 (D. Nev. May 28, 2013), stating:

> [E]ven though Pulse conceded infringement of some claims and some of Pulse's defenses failed at summary judgment, Pulse also asserted and consistently relied on defenses that ultimately were presented at trial, including its defense of invalidity for obviousness. (Jury Verdict at 9-10.) Although the jury ultimately rejected all of Pulse's defenses, Pulse reasonably relied on at least its obviousness defense. (Id.) Pulse's evidence on obviousness consisted of its infringement expert's testimony that the prior art disclosed each element of the asserted patent claims, that it would have been obvious and predictable to combine and modify the prior art references to create the asserted patent claims, and that there were differences between the prior art before the PTO and the prior art Pulse introduced at trial. Pulse also presented evidence of the secondary considerations of obviousness, such as that the commercial success of the patented design was tied to litigation-driven licenses, that there was only a single instance of skepticism by one of Halo's potential customers, and that Pulse already had solved the problem of cracking due to exposure to high heat years before the Halo invention.
>
> Pulse did not prove obviousness by clear and convincing evidence, but presented enough evidence of obviousness such that this defense was not objectively baseless, or a "sham." See Bard, 682 F.3d at 1007 (stating that a suit is a sham if it was "objectively baseless in the sense that no reasonable litigant could realistically expect success on the merits"). Pulse reasonably relied on its obviousness defense, and it did not act in the face of an objectively high likelihood that Pulse was infringing. See Spine Solutions, 620 F.3d at 1319 (finding, despite the jury's implicit finding that one of skill in the art would not have found the combination obvious based on the prior art, that the infringer raised a substantial question as to obviousness and therefore was not objectively reckless in relying on that ultimately unsuccessful defense).

[300]*Halo*, 769 F.3d at 1382.

[301]*Halo*, 769 F.3d at 1382-1383 (citing Halo Elecs., Inc. v. Pulse Elecs., Inc., No. 2:07-CV-00331, 2013 WL 2319145, at *15 (D. Nev. May 28, 2013) (summarizing evidence presented by Pulse on obviousness)).

In light of the record as a whole, the Federal Circuit "agree[d] with the district court that Pulse's obviousness defense was not objectively unreasonable."[302]

Patentee Halo focused on timing grounds to challenge the district court's conclusion that Pulse's obviousness defense was not objectively baseless — namely, by contending that Pulse should not be able to rely on its obviousness defense to defend against willfulness because Pulse did not develop that defense until after Halo sued it. Rather, when Halo first made its patents known to Pulse and offered it licenses, an engineer for Pulse spent merely two hours reviewing the patents before concluding that they were invalid in view of earlier Pulse products.[303] Pulse did not obtain an opinion of counsel on the Halo patents' validity at that time.[304]

The Federal Circuit was not swayed by the litigation-induced nature of Pulse's defensive strategy. The appellate court summarily reiterated that "'*Seagate*'s first prong is objective, and [t]he state of mind of the accused infringer is not relevant to this objective inquiry.'"[305] The district court had properly considered the "totality of the record evidence," which included the obviousness defense that Pulse developed during the litigation, to determine whether there existed an objectively defined risk of infringement of a valid patent.[306]

Circuit Judges O'Malley and Taranto each authored separate opinions in *Halo* identifying many questions that remained unanswered in the willfulness analysis.[307] The Supreme Court's subsequent 2016 decision in *Halo* did not address all the aspects of willfulness and

[302] *Halo*, 769 F.3d at 1383.

[303] *See Halo*, 769 F.3d at 1376.

[304] *See Halo*, 769 F.3d at 1376.

[305] *Halo*, 769 F.3d at 1382 (quoting DePuy Spine, Inc. v. Medtronic Sofamor Danek, Inc., 567 F.3d 1314, 1336 (Fed. Cir. 2009)).

[306] *Halo*, 769 F.3d at 1382. Joined by Judge Hughes, Federal Circuit Judge O'Malley authored a concurring opinion in *Halo* in which she agreed with the majority's "thoughtful" conclusion that all aspect of the district court's decision should be affirmed. Judge O'Malley wrote separately, however, to urge the full appellate court "to reevaluate our standard for the imposition of enhanced damages in light of the Supreme Court's recent [attorney fee] decisions in *Highmark* . . . and *Octane Fitness* . . . , and the terms of the governing statutory provision, 35 U.S.C. §284 (2012)." *Halo*, 769 F.3d at 1383 (O'Malley, J., concurring) (citations omitted) (citing Highmark Inc. v. Allcare Health Management System, Inc., 134 S. Ct. 1744 (2014) and Octane Fitness, LLC v. ICON Health & Fitness, Inc., 134 S. Ct. 1749 (2014)). *Highmark* and *Octane Fitness* are analyzed in the following section.

[307] On March 23, 2015, the full Federal Circuit denied rehearing *en banc* in *Halo*. Halo Elecs., Inc. v. Pulse Elecs., Inc., 780 F.3d 1357 (Fed. Cir. Mar. 23, 2015) (*en banc*) (order denying panel rehearing and rehearing *en banc*). Judge O'Malley, again joined by Judge Hughes, wrote an opinion dissenting from the denial in which she reiterated and expanded on the points raised in her concurrence in the *Halo* panel opinion. *See Halo*, 780 F.3d 1357, 1361-1364 (Fed. Cir. 2015) (O'Malley, J., dissenting from denial of reh'g *en banc*). Judge Taranto, joined by Judge Reyna, wrote an opinion concurring

compensatory damages enhancement raised in the O'Malley and Taranto opinions. But the grant of *certiorari* in *Halo* (and *Stryker*) in the year following the Court's overhaul of exceptional case/attorney fee award law in *Octane Fitness* and *Highmark,* suggested (correctly) that the Court clearly took notice of the many questions at stake.

(ii) *Stryker v. Zimmer* (Fed. Cir. 2015)

In *Stryker,* a jury found that Zimmer, Inc. had willfully infringed three Stryker Corp. patents directed to pulsed lavage devices used in medical therapies for delivering pressurized irrigation to wounds.[308] The jury awarded Stryker $70 million in lost profits damages. Based on the jury's willfulness finding, a district court trebled the damages. The district court also found the case exceptional and awarded Stryker attorney fees.[309]

---

in the denial of rehearing *en banc* in *Halo. See Halo*, 780 F.3d 1357, 1358-1361 (Fed. Cir. 2015) (Taranto, J., concurring in denial of reh'g *en banc*).

[308]*See* Stryker Corp. v. Zimmer, Inc., 782 F.3d 649 (Fed. Cir. Mar. 23, 2015). The Federal Circuit issued an initial panel opinion in *Stryker* on December 19, 2014, which was published at 774 F.3d 1349. That opinion was withdrawn and superseded by the March 23, 2015 opinion in response to Stryker's petition for rehearing *en banc*. The Federal Circuit panel granted Stryker's petition "for the limited purpose of clarifying the discussion of the standard of review of the objective reckless[ness] prong of willful infringement." *Stryker*, 782 F.3d at 652. The only new matter added to the March 23, 2015 opinion was the following footnote addressing the standard of review issue:

> This court has not yet addressed whether *Octane Fitness, LLC v. ICON Health & Fitness, Inc.*, ___ U.S. ___, 134 S. Ct. 1749, 188 L. Ed. 2d 816 (2014), or *Highmark Inc. v. Allcare Health Mgmt. Sys., Inc.*, ___U.S. ___, 134 S. Ct. 1744, 1746, 188 L. Ed. 2d 829 (2014), altered the standard of review under which this court analyzes the objective prong of willfulness. However, as the district court failed to undertake any objective assessment of Zimmer's specific defenses, the district court erred under any standard of review and thus this court need not now address what standard of review is proper regarding the objective prong of willfulness.

Stryker, 782 F.3d at 661 n.6.

[309]*Stryker*, 782 F.3d at 653. On appeal, the Federal Circuit vacated the grant of attorney fees, explaining:

> As the court reversed the district court's determination of willful infringement, and the district court's award of attorneys' fees was based on that determination, we vacate the district court's grant of attorneys' fees. However, because there exist further allegations of litigation misconduct in this case and because the standard for finding an exceptional case has changed since the district court issued its finding regarding attorneys' fees, we remand this issue for further consideration by the district court.

Stryker, 782 F.3d at 662. The change in the law of exceptional case referenced in the above quotation is the Supreme Court's 2014 decisions in *Highmark Inc. v. Allcare Health Mgmt. Sys., Inc.*, 134 S. Ct. 1744 (2014), and *Octane Fitness, LLC v. ICON Health*

Although the Federal Circuit affirmed the *Stryker* jury's verdict of infringement of all three patents, the appellate court reversed the determination of willful infringement and thus vacated the district court's award of trebled damages.[310] Stating firstly the threshold prong of the two-part *Seagate* test, the Federal Circuit explained that to establish willful infringement a patentee must show by clear and convincing evidence that the infringer acted " 'despite an objectively high likelihood that its actions constituted infringement of a valid patent.' "[311] Further, "[o]bjective recklessness will not be found where the accused infringer's 'position is susceptible to a reasonable conclusion of no infringement.' "[312]

In the case at bar, although Zimmer infringed, the Federal Circuit's "objective assessment . . . show[ed] that Zimmer presented reasonable defenses to all of the asserted claims of Stryker's patents."[313] Zimmer's defenses "were not objectively unreasonable, and, therefore, it did not act recklessly."[314] More particularly, Zimmer had raised reasonable defenses as to claim construction, infringement, and obviousness.[315]

& Fitness, Inc., 134 S. Ct. 1749 (2014). These decisions are analyzed *infra* Section E ("Attorney Fees").

[310]*See Stryker*, 782 F.3d at 662.

[311]*Stryker*, 782 F.3d at 660 (quoting In re Seagate Tech., LLC, 497 F.3d 1360, 1371 (Fed. Cir. 2007) (*en banc*)).

[312]*Stryker*, 782 F.3d at 661 (quoting Uniloc USA, Inc. v. Microsoft Corp., 632 F.3d 1292, 1310 (Fed. Cir. 2011)).

[313]*Stryker*, 782 F.3d at 661.

[314]*Stryker*, 782 F.3d at 662.

[315]*See Stryker*, 782 F.3d at 661-662:

> First, with respect to the '329 patent [Stryker's U.S. Patent No. 6,022,329], the motor in the Zimmer's Pulsavac Plus [accused device] is located in the nub at the rear of the barrel of its pistol-shaped device. Stryker's infringement case relied on first persuading the district court to broadly construe the claim term "handle" to include the barrel of a pistol-shaped device — even though the patent specification only describes the handle and barrel separately. Then, Stryker had to persuade the jury that the barrel nub was a part of the device "designed to be held by hand," even in light of prosecution history in which Stryker distinguished between the location of the motor in the handle as opposed to the barrel. Though Stryker ultimately prevailed, Zimmer's arguments were not unreasonably founded on the plain meaning of "handle" in the context of a pistol-shaped device, the specification's exclusive disclosure of pistol-shaped devices, and the prosecution history — all on which it could have relied to provide notice of what the patent claims covered.
>
> Second, with respect to the '807 patent [Stryker's U.S. Patent No. 6,179,807], the specification only disclosed female nozzles on the front end of the device and male nozzles on the removable tip, which would be consistent with the claim requiring that the front end "receive" the tip. Zimmer's devices had the exact opposite configuration: tapered male nozzles on the front end and female nozzles on the tip. Furthermore, the prior art Var-A-Pulse devices included all of the asserted claims' limitations except one. In light of the district court's claim construction, Stryker's defense to Zimmer's argument relied on persuading the jury

Hence, Zimmer's infringement was not willful and the district court had erred in affirming the jury's finding to the contrary. The Federal Circuit thus vacated the $210 million award of trebled damages.

The Supreme Court thereafter granted *certiorari* in *Stryker* (consolidating it with *Halo*) in October 2015.[316] The following subsection examines in detail the Court's important 2016 decision.

4. *Halo v. Pulse* (U.S. 2016)

The Supreme Court's June 2016 decision in *Halo Elecs., Inc. v. Pulse Elecs., Inc.*,[317] decided together with *Stryker Corp. v. Zimmer, Inc.*, delivered a unanimous result highly favoring patent owners. Emphasizing first principles gleaned from over 180 years of patent case law, the *Halo* Court stressed that enhanced damages are fundamentally a penalty for those "pirates" whose infringement amounts to "egregious" culpable behavior.[318] It refused to allow formalistic multi-part tests to constrain the federal district courts' discretion to enhance damages when faced with such behavior. Accordingly, the Court rejected the complicated framework of the Federal Circuit's 2007 *en banc* decision in *Seagate Techs.*, analyzed above.[319] In particular, the Supreme Court dismissed *Seagate*'s threshold requirement for wilfullness — that an infringer acted with "objective recklessness." Because it viewed the *Seagate* test as inconsistent with the governing statute for patent damages, 35 U.S.C. §284,[320] the

---

that even though the tip's nozzles could fit into the handpiece and be held in place through friction with internal housing grooves, that did not mean they were "secured or fastened." Again, though Stryker prevailed, Zimmer's defenses were not unreasonable.

Third, with respect to the '383 patent [Stryker's U.S. Patent No. 7,144,383], Zimmer's obviousness argument relied on a combination of references that was also raised by a PTO examiner during Stryker's prosecution of a related patent application — in an office action that occurred during discovery in this litigation. Zimmer's reliance on this combination was not without reason, in particular since the references related to pressured water irrigation systems used in hospitals and clinics. Therefore, even if Zimmer's defenses failed at trial, it still made a reasonable case that the '383 patent's asserted claims were obvious and thus invalid.

[316] Stryker Corp. v. Zimmer, Inc., No. 14-1520, 2015 WL 3883499 (U.S. Oct. 19, 2015) (mem.).

[317] 136 S. Ct. 1923 (June 13, 2016) (Roberts, C.J.).

[318] *Halo,* 136 S. Ct. at 1932.

[319] *Seagate Technologies* is examined *supra* Section D.3.c.

[320] 35 U.S.C. §284 (providing in part that "[w]hen the damages are not found by a jury, the court shall assess them. In either event the court may increase the damages up to three times the amount found or assessed."). Note the paucity of the statutory language, which does not even use the word "willful." Although the statute speaks of a court's power to "increase the damages," most patent case law refers to this concept as

Supreme Court vacated the Federal Circuit's decisions in *Halo* and *Stryker*.[321]

The Supreme Court in *Halo* first reviewed awards of enhanced damages under the Patent Act from "over the past 180 years," observing that "[e]nhanced damages are as old as U.S. patent law."[322] Precedent established that such awards

> are not to be meted out in a typical infringement case, but are instead designed as a "punitive" or "vindictive" sanction for egregious infringement behavior. The sort of conduct warranting enhanced damages has been variously described in our cases as willful, wanton, malicious, bad-faith, deliberate, consciously wrongful, flagrant, or — indeed — characteristic of a pirate.... District courts enjoy discretion in deciding whether to award enhanced damages, and in what amount. But through nearly two centuries of discretionary awards and review by appellate tribunals, "the channel of discretion ha[s] narrowed," Friendly, Indiscretion About Discretion, 31 Emory L.J. 747, 772 (1982), so that *such damages are generally reserved for egregious cases of culpable behavior*.[323]

While acknowledging that "the channel of discretion ha[s] narrowed" over the years, the *Halo* Court nevertheless determined that the Federal Circuit's two-part *Seagate* test for establishing willfulness[324] was "unduly rigid" and impermissibly encumbered the district courts' discretion, in a way that could "insulat[e] some of the worst patent infringers from any liability for enhanced damages."[325]

The *Halo* Court's primary problem with the *Seagate* test was that it required a threshold showing of "objective recklessness" in *every* case. This requirement allowed some of the most culpable offenders to

---

awarding "*enhanced* damages." Notably, the statute provides absolutely no restrictions or limitations on a court's optional determination to increase (i.e., enhance) damages, up to trebling the actual amount of damages found by the jury or assessed by the court.

[321]The Court explained that "[b]ecause both cases before us [*Halo* and *Stryker*] were decided under the *Seagate* framework, we vacate the judgments of the Federal Circuit and remand the cases for proceedings consistent with this opinion." *Halo,* 136 S. Ct. at 1935-1936. Although the Court summarized the facts of *Stryker v. Zimmer* separately from those of *Halo v. Pulse, see Halo,* 136 S. Ct. at 1930-1931, its analysis and reasoning did not distinguish between the two cases.

[322]*Halo*, 136 S. Ct. at 1928.

[323]*Halo,* 136 S. Ct. at 1932 (emphasis added).

[324]Under *Seagate,* a patentee had to show, by clear and convincing evidence, that (1) the infringer acted despite an objectively high likelihood that its actions constituted infringement of a valid patent, and (2) the risk of infringement was either known or so obvious that is should have been known to the accused infringer. *See Halo,* 136 S. Ct. at 1930.

[325]*Halo*, 136 S. Ct. at 1932.

escape enhancement, such as a malicious "pirate" who merely sought to steal a patentee's business with no consideration of the patent's validity or any potential defenses. The *Halo* Court noted that "[i]n the context of such deliberate wrongdoing,... it is not clear why an independent showing of objective recklessness — by clear and convincing evidence, no less — should be a prerequisite to enhanced damages."[326]

Thus, the *Halo* Court jettisoned "objective recklessness" as a requirement for finding willful infringement. Instead, as the Court's 2014 attorney fees decision in *Octane Fitness. LLC v. ICON Health & Fitness Inc.* had already suggested,[327] "[t]he *subjective* willfulness of a patent infringer, intentional or knowing, may warrant enhanced damages, without regard to whether his infringement was *objectively* reckless."[328] By "subjective," the Court indicated that a proper willfulness inquiry would focus on the extent of the infringer's culpability and maliciousness. Potential inquiries might ask whether the infringer deliberately act badly, and if so, what was its motivation? Did it *know* it was infringing? Was it aware of the patent in suit, or have a basis for thinking it invalid?[329]

The *Halo* Court also rejected the Federal Circuit's heightened "clear and convincing" burden of proof to establish willfulness under both the rejected objective prong and the retained subjective prong of *Seagate.* The text of the damages statute, 35 U.S.C. §284 (unlike other sections of the Patent Act, namely, §273(b)[330]), imposes no specific evidentiary burden. Henceforth, a mere "preponderance of the evidence" (i.e., more than half the weight of the evidence) would be required to establish willfulness, the same quantum of evidence as "regular," non-willful infringement (and the same burden of proof generally used in all types of civil litigation). Again, the Court cited its 2014 attorney fees decision in *Octane Fitness* as instructive:

> There too [in *Octane Fitness*] the Federal Circuit had adopted a clear and convincing standard of proof, for awards of attorney's fees under §285 of

[326]*Halo,* 136 S. Ct. at 1932.

[327]572 U.S. ___, ___, 134 S. Ct. 1749, 1755 (2014), examined *infra* Section E.5.a.

[328]*Halo,* 136 S. Ct. at 1933 (emphasis added).

[329]Note that, as further discussed *infra* this subsection, the *Halo* Court referred to "subjective willfulness of a patent infringer, intentional or *knowing*" (emphasis added), but did not say "knowing *of the patent*."

[330]Section 273(b) of 35 U.S.C. is part of the AIA-established prior user rights defense provision, titled "Defense to infringement based on prior commercial use." 35 U.S.C. 273 (eff. Sept. 16, 2011 for any patent issued on or after that date). Subsection (b) of Section 273, titled "Burden of proof," provides that "[a] person asserting a defense under this section shall have the burden of establishing the defense by clear and convincing evidence."

> the Patent Act. Because that provision supplied no basis for imposing such a heightened standard of proof, we rejected it. *See* Octane Fitness, 572 U.S., at ___, 134 S. Ct., at 1758. We do so here as well. Like §285, §284 "imposes no specific evidentiary burden, much less such a high one." *Ibid.* And the fact that Congress expressly erected a higher standard of proof elsewhere in the Patent Act, see 35 U.S.C. §273(b), but not in §284, is telling. Furthermore, nothing in historical practice supports a heightened standard. As we explained in *Octane Fitness*, "patent-infringement litigation has always been governed by a preponderance of the evidence standard." 572 U.S., at ___, 134 S. Ct., at 1758. Enhanced [or increased] damages [e.g., for willful infringement] are no exception.[331]

The *Halo* Court additionally rejected the Federal Circuit's cumbersome "tripartite framework for appellate review" of damages enhancement decisions under §284.[332] Because §284 gave the district courts discretion to determine whether enhanced damages are warranted, that discretionary determination should be reviewed by the Court of Appeals under a unitary "abuse of discretion" standard.[333]

Of course, a trial court's exercise of discretion has limits, as demonstrated by "[n]early two centuries of exercising discretion in awarding enhanced damages in patent cases." The *Halo* Court instructed the Federal Circuit to review district courts' exercises of discretion in light of the "longstanding considerations" identified by the Court that have guided the courts and Congress.[334]

The Supreme Court in *Halo* acknowledged but rejected the infringers'/respondents' arguments for retaining the *Seagate* standard. First, Congress's reenactment of 35 U.S.C. §284 in the America Invents Act of 2011 did *not* ratify the *Seagate* test. Rather, it "unambiguously confirmed discretion in the district courts."[335] "Isolated snippets" and "morsels" of the AIA's legislative history were contradictory and did not show a uniform intent by Congress to ratify the *Seagate* standard.

[331]*Halo*, 136 S. Ct. at 1934.

[332]The *Halo* Court explained that under Federal Circuit precedent, an award of enhanced damages had been subject to a three-part appellate standard of review:

> The first step of *Seagate*— objective recklessness — is reviewed *de novo*; the second — subjective knowledge — for substantial evidence; and the ultimate decision — whether to award enhanced damages — for abuse of discretion.

Halo, 136 S. Ct. at 1930 (citing Bard Peripheral Vascular, Inc. v. W.L. Gore & Assoc., Inc., 682 F.3d 1003, 1005, 1008 (Fed. Cir. 2012); Spectralytics, Inc. v. Cordis Corp., 649 F.3d 1336, 1347 (Fed. Cir. 2011)).

[333]*Halo,* 136 S. Ct. at 1934.

[334]*Halo*, 136 S. Ct. at 1934.

[335]*Halo*, 136 S. Ct. at 1935-1936.

Nor did Congress's enactment in the AIA of 35 U.S.C. §298, which refers to the concept of "willful[]" infringement,[336] signal that Congress had endorsed the *Seagate* test. Rather, "willfulness has always been a part of patent law, before and after *Seagate.* Section 298 does not show that Congress ratified *Seagate*'s particular conception of willfulness."[337] Instead, §298 merely clarifies that if an accused infringer does not obtain an opinion of counsel concerning infringement, that lack of an opinion letter can*not* be used to establish willful infringement. The statutory section says nothing about *how* one establishes willful infringement on the merits.

The infringers'/respondents' primary argument for retention of the *Seagate* test was one of policy. In their view, more readily available enhanced damages would embolden patent "trolls." The *Halo* Court explained that "in the patois [i.e., jargon] of the patent community, [trolls] are entities that hold patents for the primary purpose of enforcing them against alleged infringers, often exacting outsized licensing fees on threat of litigation."[338] The Court recognized the "seriousness" of these policy concerns, but did not find them sufficiently compelling to be case-dispositive. Rather, the *Halo* Court emphasized that enhancement should not be awarded in "garden-variety" or "typical" infringement cases:

> Respondents are correct that patent law reflects "a careful balance between the need to promote innovation" through patent protection, and the importance of facilitating the "imitation and refinement through imitation" that are "necessary to invention itself and the very lifeblood of a competitive economy." Bonito Boats, Inc. v. Thunder Craft Boats, Inc., 489 U.S. 141, 146, 109 S. Ct. 971, 103 L. Ed. 2d 118 (1989). That balance can indeed be disrupted if enhanced damages are awarded in garden-variety cases. As we have explained, however, they should not be. The seriousness of respondents' policy concerns cannot justify imposing an artificial construct such as the *Seagate* test on the discretion conferred under §284.[339]

[336]AIA-implemented Section 298 provides:

§298. Advice of counsel

> The failure of an infringer to obtain the advice of counsel with respect to any allegedly infringed patent, or the failure of the infringer to present such advice to the court or jury, may not be used to prove that the accused infringer willfully infringed the patent or that the infringer intended to induce infringement of the patent.

[337]*Halo,* 136 S. Ct. at 1935.
[338]*Halo,* 136 S. Ct. at 1935.
[339]*Halo*, 136 S. Ct. at 1935. In his concurring opinion, Justice Breyer was particularly concerned about the troll problem. He cited the risk that

> [t]he more that businesses, laboratories, hospitals, and individuals adopt this approach [i.e., to settle infringement disputes initiated by trolls rather than risk treble damages], the more often a patent will reach beyond its lawful scope to

The *Halo* Court concluded by reaffirming that the *Seagate* test "unduly confine[d] the ability of district courts to exercise the discretion conferred on them." Accordingly, post-*Halo*, the two-part test of *Seagate* is no longer good law; instead, the award of enhanced damages should be "limit[ed] . . . to egregious cases of misconduct beyond typical infringement."[340] Because the *Halo* and *Stryker* cases were decided at the district court and Federal Circuit levels under the rejected *Seagate* test, the Supreme Court vacated the judgments in both cases and remanded them to the Federal Circuit for further proceedings consistent with the Supreme Court's guidance.[341]

It now remains up to the district courts (and the Federal Circuit) to determine in future cases when infringement is sufficiently culpable or egregious under the more expansive *Halo* standard to warrant damages enhancement. Objective recklessness (encompassing the question whether the infringer's litigation-developed defenses were objectively reasonable) is no longer the proper inquiry; rather, subjective willfulness alone may be sufficient to justify enhancement. Willfulness need be established only by a preponderance of the evidence, not by clear and convincing evidence. The remands in the *Halo* and *Stryker* cases presented some of the first opportunities for district courts to consider and apply the new, more liberal standard.[342]

> discourage lawful activity, and the more often patent-related demands will frustrate, rather than "promote," the "Progress of Science and useful Arts." U.S. Const., Art. I, §8, cl. 8; see, e.g., Eon-Net LP v. Flagstar Bancorp, 653 F.3d 1314, 1327 (C.A. Fed. 2011) (patent holder "acted in bad faith by exploiting the high cost to defend [patent] litigation to extract a nuisance value settlement"); In re MPHJ Technology Invs., LLC, 159 F.T.C. 1004, 1007-1012 (2015) (patent owner sent more than 16,000 letters demanding settlement for using "common office equipment" under a patent it never intended to litigate); Brief for Internet Companies as Amici Curiae 15 (threat of enhanced damages hinders "collaborative efforts" to set "industry-wide" standards for matters such as internet protocols); Brief for Public Knowledge et al. as Amici Curiae 6 (predatory patent practices undermined "a new and highly praised virtual-reality glasses shopping system"). Thus, in the context of enhanced damages, there are patent-related risks on both sides of the equation. That fact argues, not for abandonment of enhanced damages, but for their careful application, to ensure that they only target cases of egregious misconduct.

Halo, 136 S. Ct. at 1937-1938 (Breyer, J., concurring). Justices Kennedy and Alito joined Justice Breyer's concurrence.

340 *Halo*, 136 S. Ct. at 1935.

341 *Halo*, 136 S. Ct. at 1935-1936. In August 2016, the Federal Circuit issued its remand decision in *Halo*, in turn remanding the willful infringement portion of the case to the district court with a strong suggestion that that court revisit its earlier refusal to enhance damages. *See* Halo Elecs., Inc. v. Pulse Elecs., Inc., 831 F.3d 1369, 1381 (Fed. Cir. Aug. 5, 2016).

342 *See, e.g.,* Halo Elecs., Inc. v. Pulse Elecs., Inc., 831 F.3d 1369, 1381 (Fed. Cir. Aug. 5, 2016) (remanding willful infringement aspect of case to district court with strong suggestion that it revisit its earlier refusal to enhance damages).

The Supreme Court's *Halo* decision left open a number of subsidiary questions to be grappled with by the lower courts. For example, the Court did not discuss the use of juries to decide willfulness, a practice that some Federal Circuit judges have questioned.[343]

Although the *Halo* Court noted that juries had found willfulness in both the *Halo* and *Stryker* cases,[344] it did not comment further on that fact. In reviewing the history of damages enhancement in patent law, the Court quoted its 1854 decision in *Seymour v. McCormick*.[345] There the Court stated "where the injury is wanton or malicious, a *jury* may

---

Not surprisingly, initial post-*Halo* decisions of the Federal Circuit looked with favor upon enhanced damages awards against willful infringers in light of the newly deferential "abuse of discretion" standard of review. However, more case law development is needed before empirical evidence can establish the true impact of *Halo*. An early post-*Halo* illustration is *WBIP, LLC v. Kohler Co.*, 829 F.3d 1317 (Fed. Cir. July 19, 2016) (Moore, J.) (affirming a Massachusetts district court's determination, based on a jury's verdict, that the defendant Kohler's infringement was willful). The Circuit observed that "[p]roof of an objectively reasonable litigation-inspired defense to infringement is no longer a defense to willful infringement. Thus, Kohler's arguments on appeal that the district court erred in concluding that its obviousness defense was objectively unreasonable [are] not a basis for concluding that the district court abused its discretion in enhancing damages." *WBIP*, 829 F.3d at 1341. In addition, the *WBIP* Circuit did *not* "interpret *Halo* as changing the established law that the factual components of the willfulness question should be resolved by the jury." *WBIP,* 829 F.3d at 1341 (citing Richardson v. Suzuki Motor Co., 868 F.2d 1226, 1250 (Fed. Cir. 1989) ("Absent sufficient basis for directing the verdict, Richardson has the right of jury determination of this factual question. Willfulness of behavior is a classical jury question of intent. When trial is had to a jury, the issue should be decided by the jury.") (citations omitted); Halo Elecs., Inc. v. Pulse Elecs., Inc., 769 F.3d 1371, 1386 (Fed. Cir. 2014) (O'Malley, J., concurring) ("[W]e have long held that a willfulness determination contains issues of fact that should be submitted to a jury.")).

The Supreme Court in *Halo* also did not address the manner in which district courts, having determined that infringement is willful, should decide whether to enhance a patentee's compensatory damages and in particular, how to determine the extent of that enhancement. In *WBIP*, the district court had applied the factors from *Read Corp. v. Portec, Inc.*, 970 F.2d 816 (Fed. Cir. 1992), to determine that WBIP's actual damages should be enhanced by 50 percent. On appeal, the Federal Circuit noted but did not analyze the district court's use of the *Read* factors (other than to affirm its award of enhanced damages). *WBIP,* 829 F.3d at 1325, 1342. Hence, the *Read* multi-factor approach for determining the amount of enhancement remains good law post-*Halo*.

[343]*See* Halo Elecs., Inc. v. Pulse Elecs., Inc., 769 F.3d 1371, 1368 (Fed. Cir. 2014) (O'Malley, J., concurring) (questioning "whether the Circuit's current practice of allowing juries to decide willfulness . . . is sound or should be reassigned to the court in view of the 'plain language' of §284 providing that '[*T*]*he court* may increase the damages' up to three times the amount found or assessed.' ") (quoting 35 U.S.C. §284) (bracket and emphasis added by Judge O'Malley)); *Halo,* 780 F.3d at 1360 (Taranto, J., concurring in denial of reh'g *en banc*) (questioning whether willfulness should be decided by a jury or a judge).

[344]*Halo*, 136 S. Ct. at 1931 (stating that in *Halo v. Pulse*, the jury found that "there was a high probability that [Pulse] had [infringed] willfully," and that in *Stryker v. Zimmer,* the "jury found that Zimmer had willfully infringed Stryker's patents . . .").

[345]16 How. 480, 488, 14 L. Ed. 1024 (1854).

inflict vindictive or exemplary damages, not to recompense the plaintiff, but to punish the defendant."[346] Again, the *Halo* Court did not comment further on the use of juries that it had appeared to approve in *Seymour*. Thus, it appears that district courts can continue to give juries the question whether infringement is willful. Jury participation also seems logical given the *Halo* Court's reference to "intentional or knowing" infringement,[347] issues of *scienter* that are typically the province of juries.

Another question not explicitly answered by the *Halo* Court is whether infringement can be willful if the infringer did not have knowledge of the patent at the time it infringed. The Court referred to "subjective willfulness of a patent infringer, intentional or *knowing*" (emphasis added), but did not say "knowing *of the patent*." For example, consider a hypothetical "pirate" who maliciously copied a competitor's product with intent to steal its market share, but did so without knowing that the product was patented. Why should such a culpable actor not be considered a willful infringer under *Halo*'s more lenient standard? In the view of this author, *Halo* should not prevent liability for willfulness under these facts. In other words, a lack of knowledge about a patent should not operate as a complete defense to a charge of willful infringement. (It would, however, be a fact to be considered and weighed in a district court's exercise of discretion under §284.) But, at least three Federal Circuit judges disagree with this author's position.[348]

[346]*Seymour,* 16 How. at 489 (emphasis added).

[347]*See Halo*, 136 S. Ct. at 1933 ("The subjective willfulness of a patent infringer, intentional or knowing, may warrant enhanced damages, without regard to whether his infringement was objectively reckless.").

[348]*See* WBIP, LLC v. Kohler Co., 829 F.3d 1317, 1341 (Fed. Cir. July 19, 2016) (Moore, J., joined by O'Malley, J., and Chen, J.) (stating that [post-*Halo*,] "[k]nowledge of the patent alleged to be willfully infringed continues to be a prerequisite to enhanced damages") (citing *Halo*, 136 S. Ct. at 1932-1933 (discussing knowledge requirement for intent)).

In this author's view, the cited discussion from *Halo*, which refers to "[t]he subjective willfulness of patent infringer, *intentional or knowing*, [which] may warrant enhanced damages..." (emphasis added), does not necessarily mandate *knowledge of the patent*. Moreover, the language quoted from *Halo* is stated in the disjunctive; the Court used the phrase "intentional *or* knowing." Setting aside any ambiguity in the meaning of "knowing," willfulness could turn on "intent" alone. In this author's view, the requisite intent could be to copy a competitor's product with intent to harm it in the marketplace, whether or not the infringer actually knew it was covered by a patent.

Moreover, the Federal Circuit's discussion of the point in *WBIP* could be viewed as *dicta*, because in that case "Kohler [did] not contest that it, in fact, had pre-suit knowledge of the patents in suit." *WBIP*, 829 F.3d at 1341. Rather, infringer Kohler argued that "no evidence of its knowledge was presented to the jury," an argument rejected by Circuit. *See WBIP,* 829 F.3d at 1341 (concluding "that there was substantial evidence for the jury's finding that Kohler had knowledge of the patents in suit at the time of infringement").

E. Attorney Fees

1. Overview

"The default rule in litigation in U.S. federal courts is the American Rule under which both sides, win or lose, must bear their own attorneys' fees."[349] The default rule applies in U.S. patent litigation. But in rare cases, courts order attorney fee shifting (that is, imposing the patentee's attorney fees on the infringer, or vice versa) in patent cases that are deemed to be "exceptional" under 35 U.S.C. §285.[350]

When willful infringement has been found (as examined in the previous section[351]), patent owners will frequently seek not only enhancement of their damages under 35 U.S.C. §284 but also payment of their attorney fees by the infringer under 35 U.S.C. §285. A number of Federal Circuit decisions have affirmed the imposition of patentee attorney fees on accused infringers when their infringement was found to be willful.[352]

Lastly, the language that the Federal Circuit in *WBIP* cites from *Halo* is stated in the disjunctive; the Court used the phrase "intentional *or* knowing." Setting aside the meaning of "knowing," willfulness could turn on "intent" alone. In this author's view, the requisite intent could be the intent to copy a competitor's product, whether or not the infringer knew it was patented.

349 Mark Liang & Brian Berliner, *Fee Shifting in Patent Litigation*, 18 VA. J.L. & TECH. 59, 84 (2013).

350 *See* Mark Liang & Brian Berliner, *Fee Shifting in Patent Litigation*, 18 VA. J.L. & TECH. 59, 64-65 (2013) (describing frequency of attorney fee shifting in U.S. patent cases as "very rare").

351 Willful infringement is addressed *supra* Section D.

352 *See, e.g.*, SSL Servs., LLC v. Citrix Sys., Inc., 769 F.3d 1073 (Fed. Cir. 2014) (after district court found that patentee SSL proved willful infringement of the three asserted claims of its U.S. Patent No. 6,158,011 involving multi-tier virtual private networks, for which jury awarded lump-sum damages of 10 million dollars and district court enhanced to a total of 15 million dollars, reversing district court's determination that SSL was not the prevailing party under 35 U.S.C. §285 (as well as under Fed. R. Civ. P. 54(d)) and remanding case to district court for assessment of the amount of attorney fees (and/or costs) to award to SSL in connection with the claims on which it had prevailed); Powell v. Home Depot U.S.A., Inc., 663 F.3d 1221 (Fed. Cir. 2011) (affirming district court's award of enhanced damages based on Home Depot's willful infringement and award of attorney fees based on Home Depot's "litigation misconduct and vexatious and bad faith litigation"); nCube Corp. v. Seachange Int'l, Inc., 436 F.3d 1317 (Fed. Cir. 2006) (affirming district court's finding of willful infringement and awards of patentee's actual damages and two-thirds of its attorney fees); Golden Blount, Inc. v. Robert H. Peterson Co., 438 F.3d 1354 (Fed. Cir. 2006) (affirming district court's finding that accused infringer Peterson willfully infringed and district court's award of attorney fees "based principally thereon"); Bott v. Four Star Corp., 807 F.2d 1567, 1574 (Fed. Cir. 1986) (stating that "[i]n view of the finding of willful infringement, the discretionary award of attorney fees was entirely proper") (citing Kori Corp. v. Wilco Marsh Buggies & Draglines, 761 F.2d 649, 657 (Fed. Cir. 1985)), *overruled on other grounds by* A.C. Aukerman Co. v. R.L. Chaides Const. Co., 960 F.2d 1020 (Fed. Cir. 1992) (*en banc*); Cent. Soya Co. v. Geo. A. Hormel & Co., 723 F.2d 1573 (Fed. Cir. 1983).

Importantly, Section 285 of the Patent Act requires that a case be found "exceptional" to merit attorney fee shifting, as detailed below. The two types of awards — enhanced damages under 35 U.S.C. §284 and attorney fees under 35 U.S.C. §285 — are not necessarily linked; nor does the grant of one preclude denial of the other.[353] Attorney fees incurred by patent owners also may be imposed on infringers for reasons other than willful infringement, such as the infringers' litigation misconduct.[354]

The remedy of attorney fee shifting is certainly not limited to patent owners; a prevailing defendant/accused infringer may also seek attorney fees based on a lack of merit in the patentee's lawsuit or various types of misconduct by the patentee as detailed below.[355] Targets of patent assertion entities (pejoratively referred to as "patent trolls") may seek this form of relief.

2. Statutory Basis

Section 285 of the Patent Act, titled "Attorney Fees," provides,

> The court in *exceptional* cases *may* award reasonable attorney fees to the prevailing party.[356]

[353]*See* Advanced Cardiovascular Sys. v. Medtronic, Inc., 265 F.3d 1294, 1303 (Fed. Cir. 2001) (affirming district court decision in which damages were enhanced based on jury finding of willful infringement but attorney fees were denied).

[354]Awards of attorney fees against infringers for litigation misconduct (as opposed to willfulness) are less frequent than those against patent owners, but an example is *Beckman Instruments, Inc. v. LKB Produkter AB*, 892 F.2d 1547, 1551-1552 (Fed. Cir. 1989) (affirming district court's finding that case was exceptional because infringer LKB's litigation strategy was "vexatious" and because LKB had "deliberately and repeatedly violated the permanent injunction"). *See also* Takeda Chem. Indus., Ltd. v. Mylan Labs., Inc., 549 F.3d 1381, 1388 (Fed. Cir. 2008) (affirming in Hatch-Waxman Act litigation district court's finding of exceptional case and award of attorney fees against defendant/ANDA filer/generic drug manufacturer Alphapharm; "[g]iven the district court's familiarity with the parties and the issues and its thorough discussion of Alphapharm's [Paragraph IV] certification letter and litigation strategy, we cannot say that the court committed clear error in finding that this was an exceptional case due in part to the misconduct of Alphapharm"); *Takeda Chem.*, 549 F.3d at 1389 (also affirming district court's finding of exceptional case and award of attorney fees against co-defendant/ANDA filer/generic drug manufacturer Mylan; concluding that "the [district] court did not commit clear error in finding that Mylan's misconduct contributed to this being an exceptional case. In fact, Mylan's invalidity argument in its [Paragraph IV] certification letter appears even more baseless than Alphapharm's. . . . Similarly, the finding that Mylan engaged in litigation misconduct was well-supported and explained by the district court.").

[355]*See infra* Section E.5 (discussing *Octane Fitness* and *Highmark* litigations reviewed by Supreme Court).

[356]35 U.S.C. §285 (emphasis added).

Parsing the quoted statutory language, an attorney fees award under 35 U.S.C. §285 (1) is discretionary with the district court, (2) is limited to "exceptional cases," (3) requires that the award be made to the "prevailing party," and (4) must be "reasonable" as to the amount of fees.

3. Discretionary

Because the wording of §285 is permissive rather than mandatory (i.e., a court "may" award attorney fees), the plain language of the statute indicates that even finding a case exceptional need *not* compel a district court to award attorney fees to the prevailing party.

However, the Federal Circuit has adopted a general rule that when willful infringement has been found, a district court that decides a case is nevertheless not exceptional under 35 U.S.C. §285 should explain why it is not.[357] Similarly, if the district court concludes that a case is exceptional under §285 but refuses to award attorney fees, it must normally explain that decision as well. The court recognizes an exception to these rules, however, where the record sets forth adequate grounds for affirming the district court's decision making.[358]

4. Prevailing Party

Attorney fees are awarded under 35 U.S.C. §285 only to the "prevailing party." In *Gentry Gallery v. Berkline Corp.*,[359] the Federal Circuit affirmed a district court's ruling that the patent in suit was not infringed, and the accused infringer Berkline Corp. had not proved the patent invalid. Under these circumstances, the patentee Gentry Gallery was not a "prevailing party," and thus did not qualify for an award of attorney fees under §285. Merely overcoming a defense does not elevate a party to prevailing status; the party must obtain some affirmative relief, for example, an injunction or damages for the patentee, in order to be considered prevailing for attorney fee purposes.[360]

Difficulties arise when district courts must determine which party was the prevailing party in "mixed judgment" cases; that is, when both

[357]*See* Transclean Corp. v. Bridgewood Servs., Inc., 290 F.3d 1364, 1379 (Fed. Cir. 2002).

[358]*See Transclean Corp.*, 290 F.3d at 1379.

[359]134 F.3d 1473 (Fed. Cir. 1998).

[360]*See Gentry Gallery*, 134 F.3d at 1480.

parties "prevail" or win on some aspects of the case and lose on others.[361] In *Shum v. Intel Corp.*,[362] the Federal Circuit explained that

> [t]o be a "prevailing party," our precedent requires that the party have received at least some relief on the merits. That relief must materially alter the legal relationship between the parties by modifying one party's behavior in a way that "directly benefits" the opposing party. *Farrar v. Hobby*, 506 U.S. 103, 111-13, 113 S. Ct. 566, 121 L. Ed. 2d 494 (1992); *Manildra Milling*, 76 F.3d at 1182; *see also Inland Steel*, 364 F.3d at 1320; *Former Emps. of Motorola Ceramic Prods. v. United States*, 336 F.3d 1360, 1364 (Fed. Cir. 2003). A party is not required, however, to prevail on all claims in order to qualify as a prevailing party under Rule 54. *See Kemin Foods, L.C. v. Pigmentos Vegetales Del Centro S.A. de C.V.*, 464 F.3d 1339, 1347-48 (Fed. Cir. 2006).[363]

Even in mixed judgment cases, a district court's designation of "prevailing party" allows for only one "winner." In other words, the Federal Circuit explained in *Shum*, "[a] court must choose one, and only one, 'prevailing party' to receive any costs award."[364] This follows from the "unambiguous" language of Fed. R. Civ. P. 54(d) that refers to "*the* prevailing party" in the singular. "Rule 54(d) has no special rule or exception for mixed judgment cases, where both parties have some claims decided in their favor. . . ."[365]

5. "Exceptional" Case

The law on attorney fee shifting in patent cases took a dramatic turn in 2014, seemingly making the remedy more frequently available. In two unanimous decisions further examined below, the Supreme Court jettisoned as "overly rigid" the Federal Circuit's demanding standard for district court determinations of "exceptionality" and reemphasized the district courts' discretion in assessing attorney fee awards.[366] The Supreme Court's 2014 decisions in *Octane Fitness,*

[361] *See, e.g.*, *Manildra Mill.*, 76 F.3d at 1182 (observing that "[i]n those cases in which one party wins completely on every claim at issue, determining which party has prevailed is a straightforward task. The inquiry becomes more difficult when each party has some claims adjudicated in its favor.").

[362] 629 F.3d 1360 (Fed. Cir. 2010).

[363] *Shum*, 629 F.3d at 1367-1368.

[364] *Shum*, 629 F.3d at 1367.

[365] *Shum*, 629 F.3d at 1367.

[366] *See* Octane Fitness, LLC v. ICON Health & Fitness, Inc., 134 S. Ct. 1749 (2014) ("*Octane Fitness II*") (Sotomayor, J.) (unanimous except for Justice Scalia's refusal to join footnotes 1-3, which concerned the legislative history of 35 U.S.C. §285 and its predecessor provisions); Highmark Inc. v. Allcare Health Mgmt. Sys., Inc., 134 S. Ct. 1744 (2014) (*Highmark III*") (Sotomayor, J.) (unanimous).

LLC v. ICON Health & Fitness, Inc. ("*Octane Fitness II*"),[367] and *Highmark Inc. v. Allcare Health Mgmt. Sys., Inc.* ("*Highmark III*"),[368] decidedly changed the law of attorney fee awards in patent cases, potentially making the awards easier to attain.[369]

Notwithstanding the 2014 change in judicial standard, the §285 requirement that a case be "exceptional" to merit the remedy of attorney fee shifting remains — it is the statutory mandate. Hence, fee shifting in patent cases is by no means automatic, even in cases of proven misconduct. Notably, Professor Chien's empirical research indicates that, at least prior to *Octane Fitness II* and *Highmark III,*

> [a]ttorney's fees are awarded infrequently: from 2005 to 2011, there were on average fifty-six awards per year; in comparison to around 3,000 patent case filings on average per year. The majority of the attorney fee awards are made in cases that go to trial. Slightly less than half of the awards are to prevailing defendants.[370]

Future litigation will determine whether these statistics will be altered to any significant extent by the Supreme Court's 2014 loosening of the law on what constitutes an exceptional case under 35 U.S.C. §285.

Tracking the evolution in the case law concerning attorney fee shifting highlights the impact of the Supreme Court's 2014 decisions in *Octane Fitness II* and *Highmark III.* Before 2005, courts approached exceptional case determinations in patent litigation with a flexible, discretionary, holistic view.[371] In 2005, however, the Federal Circuit

[367]134 S. Ct. 1749 (2014).

[368]134 S. Ct. 1744 (2014).

[369]*Cf.* Summit Data Sys., LLC v. EMC Corp., No. CV 10-749-GMS, 2014 WL 4955689, at *2 (D. Del. Sept. 25, 2014) (observing that "[t]he Supreme Court recently commented on §285 and loosened the preexisting standard for what makes a case 'exceptional'") (citing Octane Fitness, LLC v. ICON Health & Fitness, Inc., 134 S. Ct. 1749 (2014)), *aff'd sub nom.* Summit Data Sys. LLC v. NetApp Inc., No. 2015-1103, 2015 WL 5894214 (Fed. Cir. Oct. 9, 2015) (non-precedential Rule 36 affirmance).

[370]Colleen V. Chien, *Reforming Software Patents*, 50 HOUS. L. REV. 325, 377 (2012) (footnotes omitted).

[371]*See* Octane Fitness, LLC v. ICON Health & Fitness, Inc., 134 S. Ct. 1749, 1753-1754 (2014) (footnotes omitted), observing:

> For three decades after the [1952] enactment of [35 U.S.C.] §285, courts applied it — as they had applied [its 1946 Patent Act predecessor provision] §70 — in a discretionary manner, assessing various factors to determine whether a given case was sufficiently "exceptional" to warrant a fee award. See, *e.g.*, *True Temper Corp. v. CF & I Steel Corp.,* 601 F.2d 495, 508-509 (C.A.10 1979); *Kearney & Trecker Corp. v. Giddings & Lewis, Inc.,* 452 F.2d 579, 597 (C.A.7 1971); *Siebring v. Hansen,* 346 F.2d 474, 480-481 (C.A.8 1965).
>
> In 1982, Congress created the Federal Circuit and vested it with exclusive appellate jurisdiction in patent cases. 28 U.S.C. §1295. In the two decades that

adopted a significantly more stringent framework for establishing exceptionality. In *Brooks Furniture Mfg., Inc. v. Dutailier Int'l, Inc.*,[372] the Federal Circuit instructed that a case could be deemed exceptional only "when there has been some material inappropriate conduct related to the matter in litigation, such as willful infringement, fraud or inequitable conduct in procuring the patent, misconduct during litigation, vexatious or unjustified litigation, conduct that violates Fed. R. Civ. P. 11, or like infractions."[373]

With respect to imposing attorney fees on *patent owners* (in other words, awarding attorney fees to prevailing accused infringers), the Circuit in *Brooks Furniture* further (and more controversially) held that "[a]bsent misconduct in conduct of the litigation or in securing the patent, sanctions may be imposed against the patentee *only* if both (1) the litigation is brought in subjective bad faith, *and* (2) the litigation is objectively baseless."[374] Thus under *Brooks Furniture* an

---

followed, the Federal Circuit, like the regional circuits before it, instructed district courts to consider the totality of the circumstances when making fee determinations under §285. See, *e.g.*, *Rohm & Haas Co. v. Crystal Chemical Co.*, 736 F.2d 688, 691 (C.A. Fed. 1984) ("Cases decided under §285 have noted that 'the substitution of the phrase "in exceptional cases" has not done away with the discretionary feature'"); *Yamanouchi Pharmaceutical Co., Ltd. v. Danbury Pharmacal, Inc.*, 231 F.3d 1339, 1347 (C.A. Fed. 2000) ("In assessing whether a case qualifies as exceptional, the district court must look at the totality of the circumstances").

In 2005, however, the Federal Circuit abandoned that holistic, equitable approach in favor of a more rigid and mechanical formulation. In *Brooks Furniture Mfg., Inc. v. Dutailier Int'l, Inc.*, 393 F.3d 1378 (2005), the court held that a case is "exceptional" under §285 only "when there has been some material inappropriate conduct related to the matter in litigation, such as willful infringement, fraud or inequitable conduct in procuring the patent, misconduct during litigation, vexatious or unjustified litigation, conduct that violates Fed. R. Civ. P. 11, or like infractions." *Id.*, at 1381. "Absent misconduct in conduct of the litigation or in securing the patent," the Federal Circuit continued, fees "may be imposed against the patentee only if both (1) the litigation is brought in subjective bad faith, and (2) the litigation is objectively baseless." *Ibid.* The Federal Circuit subsequently clarified that litigation is objectively baseless only if it is "so unreasonable that no reasonable litigant could believe it would succeed," *iLOR, LLC v. Google, Inc.*, 631 F.3d 1372, 1378 (2011), and that litigation is brought in subjective bad faith only if the plaintiff "actually know[s]" that it is objectively baseless, *id.*, at 1377.

[372] 393 F.3d 1378 (Fed. Cir. 2005).

[373] Brooks Furniture Mfg., Inc. v. Dutailier Int'l, Inc., 393 F.3d 1378, 1381 (Fed. Cir. 2005) (citing, *e.g.*, Cambridge Prods. Ltd. v. Penn Nutrients, Inc., 962 F.2d 1048, 1050-1051 (Fed. Cir. 1992); Beckman Instruments, Inc. v. LKB Produkter AB, 892 F.2d 1547, 1551 (Fed. Cir. 1989)), *abrogated by* Octane Fitness, LLC v. ICON Health & Fitness, Inc., 134 S. Ct. 1749 (2014).

[374] Brooks Furniture Mfg., Inc. v. Dutailier Int'l, Inc., 393 F.3d 1378, 1381 (Fed. Cir. 2005) (emphasis added) (citing Professional Real Estate Investors v. Columbia Pictures Industries, 508 U.S. 49, 60-61 (1993); citing also Forest Labs., Inc. v. Abbott Labs., 339 F.3d 1324, 1329-1331 (Fed. Cir. 2003)), *abrogated by* Octane Fitness, LLC v. ICON Health & Fitness, Inc., 134 S. Ct. 1749 (2014).

exonerated accused infringer had to establish not only an objective prong but also a subjective prong in order to establish that the case brought against it was "exceptional."

As to the first, objective prong, the Federal Circuit clarified in cases decided after *Brooks Furniture* that litigation was objectively baseless only if it was "so unreasonable that no reasonable litigant could believe it would succeed."[375] As to the second, subjective prong of the *Brooks Furniture* test, the appellate court also established that litigation was brought in subjective bad faith only if the plaintiff "actually kn[ew]" that it was objectively baseless.[376]

This very restrictive *Brooks Furniture* standard for awarding attorney fees in exceptional cases, particularly with regard to the extremely narrow window for a prevailing defendant/accused infringer to obtain attorney fees from the patentee that sued it, was controversial. The criticism was closely linked to the rise of patent "troll" litigation.[377]

Eventually the Supreme Court took note and dramatically changed the law. The Court in *Octane Fitness, LLC v. ICON Health & Fitness, Inc.* ("*Octane Fitness II*")[378] rejected the Federal Circuit's *Brooks Furniture* standard as "unduly rigid" and impermissibly encumbering the district courts' grant of discretion as set forth in 35 U.S.C. §285.[379] Although the Supreme Court's decision in *Octane Fitness II* was not limited in its applicability to fee awards imposed against patent owners, the facts of *Octane Fitness* involved assertions of exceptionalness under §285 based on the patentee's conduct as analyzed below.

[375] iLOR, LLC v. Google, Inc., 631 F.3d 1372, 1378 (Fed. Cir. 2011).

[376] *iLOR, LLC,* 631 F.3d at 1377.

[377] *See, e.g.*, Darin Jones, *A Shifting Landscape for Shifting Fees: Attorney-Fee Awards in Patent Suits After* Octane *and* Highmark, 90 Wash. L. Rev. 505, 506 (2015) (observing that "[o]ver time, the rigid interpretation of §285 under *Brooks Furniture* garnered an increasing amount of criticism from prominent commentators, who argued that patent litigants — particularly defendants — needed a "flexible" rule that would "discourage aggressive suits and frivolous demands") (footnote omitted) (quoting Randall R. Rader, Colleen V. Chien & David Hricik, *Op-Ed, Make Patent Trolls Pay in Court*, N.Y. Times, June 5, 2013, at A25 (noting that "[f]rivolous suits are costing billions and hurting innovation," and urging federal judges to exercise their discretion under 35 U.S.C. §285 to award attorney fees against "patent trolls")); Emily H. Chen, *Making Abusers Pay: Deterring Patent Litigation by Shifting Attorneys' Fees*, 28 Berkeley Tech. L.J. 351, 362 (2013) (commenting that "[r]ecent litigation has highlighted defendants' growing desire to use fee-shifting to recoup costs and deter future abusive litigation; it has also highlighted the difficulty of meeting the current "exceptional case" standard for fee-shifting in patent cases").

[378] 134 S. Ct. 1749 (2014).

[379] *Octane Fitness II*, 134 S. Ct. at 1755.

a. Octane Fitness II *(U.S. 2014)*

The litigation in *Octane Fitness* concerned alleged infringement of ICON Health's U.S. Patent No. 6,019,710 ('710 patent), directed to an elliptical exercise machine. The machine's design required less floor space than prior art models and its settings could be adapted to the stride path of individual users.[380] A representative embodiment is depicted in Figure 11.1. ICON Health reportedly never commercialized the invention of the '710 patent.[381]

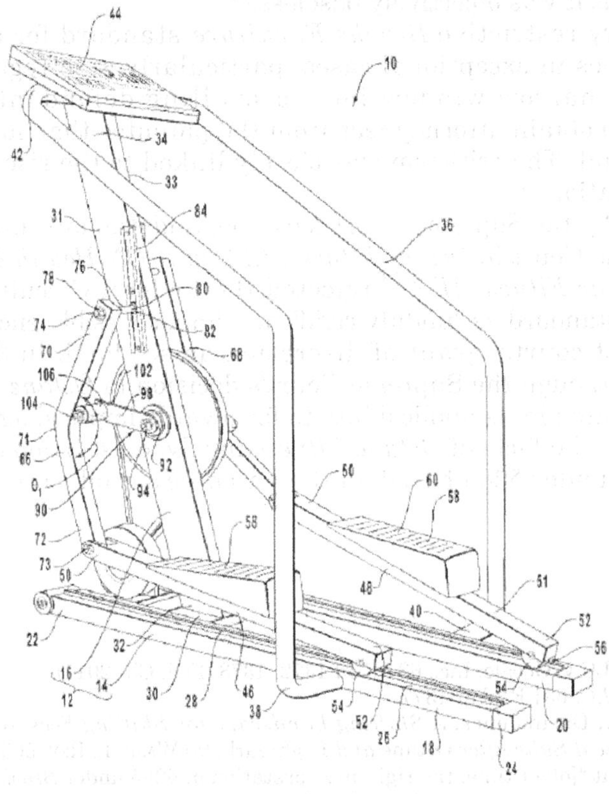

Figure 11.1

Embodiment of Claimed Invention in *Octane Fitness*

[380]*See* Icon Health & Fitness, Inc. v. Octane Fitness, LLC, No. CIV 09-319 ADM/SRN, 2010 WL 5376209, at *1 (D. Minn. Dec. 22, 2010).

[381]*See* Icon Health & Fitness, Inc. v. Octane Fitness, LLC, 576 F. App'x 1002, 1004 (Fed. Cir. 2014) (non-precedential) (on remand from Supreme Court's 2014 decision in *Octane Fitness II*) (stating Octane Fitness's argument that "ICON is a larger company that never commercialized its '710 patent").

A Minnesota district court in 2011 granted summary judgment that an accused elliptical machine sold by Octane Fitness, LLC did not infringe. Octane Fitness thereafter sought a determination of exceptional case and imposition of attorney fees against patentee ICON Health under 35 U.S.C. §285.[382] Nevertheless, the district court denied prevailing party Octane Fitness's motion for attorney fees.[383] The district court determined that Octane Fitness had not established either prong of the Federal Circuit's demanding *Brooks Furniture* standard for awarding attorney fees against a patentee;[384] that is, Octane Fitness had not shown that ICON Health's infringement claim was "objectively baseless" nor that it was brought in "subjective bad faith."[385]

[382]The Federal Circuit summarized Octane's position as follows:

> Octane . . . moved the district court to find the case exceptional under the "totality of the circumstances" and to award attorney fees under §285. Def.'s Mem. Supp. Mot. Att'y Fees & Costs, No. 09-0319, 2011 WL 11734262 (D. Minn. July 18, 2011), J.A. 2633-34 (citing *Yamanouchi Pharm. Co. v. Danbury Pharmacal, Inc.*, 231 F.3d 1339, 1346-47 (Fed. Cir. 2000)). Octane argued that ICON's infringement action was objectively baseless because the district court had rejected ICON's purportedly frivolous contentions relating to the construction of certain means-plus-function claim limitations and infringement of Octane's accused elliptical machines. Octane asserted that ICON's allegations were "unreasonable and unsupportable" because the court's noninfringement determination "should have been a foregone conclusion to anyone who visually inspected its machines." *ICON*, 2011 WL 3900975, at *2 (citations omitted). Octane also argued that ICON's case was brought in subjective bad faith as supposedly evidenced by: (i) an email exchange between two ICON sales executives suggesting that the litigation was undertaken as a matter of commercial strategy; and (ii) the fact that ICON is a larger company that never commercialized its '710 patent. *Id.* at *4.

Icon Health & Fitness, Inc. v. Octane Fitness, LLC, 576 F. App'x 1002, 1003-1004 (Fed. Cir. 2014) (non-precedential) (on remand from Supreme Court's 2014 decision in *Octane Fitness II*).

[383]*See* Icon Health & Fitness, Inc. v. Octane Fitness, LLC, No. CIV 09-319 ADM/SRN, 2010 WL 5376209 (D. Minn. Dec. 22, 2010).

[384]*See* Brooks Furniture Mfg., Inc. v. Dutailier Int'l, Inc., 393 F.3d 1378 (Fed. Cir. 2005).

[385]*Octane Fitness II*, 134 S. Ct. at 1755. As later summarized by the Federal Circuit,

> The [district] court specifically determined that, although ultimately unsuccessful, ICON's rejected claim construction arguments and infringement contentions were not objectively baseless, frivolous, or unreasonable. *Id.* at *2-3. The court concluded that the claim construction issues were not easily resolved and stated that it did not agree with Octane that the conclusions relating to noninfringement were so easily reached and that it had no reason to doubt ICON's pre-suit investigation because "[t]he visible differences" between Octane's machines and the patented invention "did not make it unreasonable to rely on testing and expert opinions as to infringement." *Id.* at *2-3.
>
> Although noting that "the inquiry could end [t]here," the district court further determined that ICON had not brought suit in bad faith and that attorney fees

In a 2012 non-precedential decision, the Federal Circuit affirmed the denial of attorney fees. The appellate court in *Octane Fitness, LLC v. ICON Health & Fitness, Inc.* ("*Octane Fitness I*"),[386] rejected Octane Fitness's cross-appeal argument "that the [district] court applied an overly restrictive standard in refusing to find the case exceptional under §285" and that the district court should have "lower[ed] the standard for exceptionality to 'objectively unreasonable.' "[387] The Circuit found "no reason to revisit the settled standard for exceptionality."[388]

Octane Fitness sought Supreme Court review of the Federal Circuit's refusal to impose attorney fees on patentee ICON Health. The question presented in Octane Fitness's petition targeted the merits of exceptionality, and in particular, the Circuit's two-pronged *Brooks Furniture* standard.[389] It asked:

> [w]hether a district court, in exercising its discretion to award attorney fees to prevailing accused patent infringers in "exceptional cases" under Title 35, United States Code, Section 285, should use traditional equitable factors guided by the purposes of patent law to protect legitimate patent interests in reasonable ways rather than the Federal Circuit's rigid test requiring both objective baselessness and subjective bad faith?[390]

On October 1, 2013, the Supreme Court granted *certiorari* in *Octane Fitness.*[391] On the same day the Court also agreed to review *Highmark, Inc. v. Allcare Health Mgmt. Sys., Inc.,* concerning the appellate court standard of review for exceptional case determinations by federal district courts.[392] This degree of Supreme Court attention

---

were not warranted. *Id.* at *3-4. The district court therefore denied Octane's §285 motion.

Icon Health & Fitness, Inc. v. Octane Fitness, LLC, 576 F. App'x 1002, 1004 (Fed. Cir. 2014) (non-precedential) (on remand from Supreme Court's 2014 decision in *Octane Fitness II*).

[386]496 F. App'x 57 (Fed. Cir. 2012) (non-precedential).

[387]Icon Health & Fitness, Inc. v. Octane Fitness, LLC, 496 F. App'x 57, 65 (Fed. Cir. 2012) (non-precedential), *rev'd and remanded sub nom.* Octane Fitness, LLC v. ICON Health & Fitness, Inc., 134 S. Ct. 1749 (2014).

[388]Icon Health & Fitness, Inc. v. Octane Fitness, LLC, 496 F. App'x 57, 65 (Fed. Cir. 2012) (non-precedential), *rev'd and remanded sub nom.* Octane Fitness, LLC v. ICON Health & Fitness, Inc., 134 S. Ct. 1749 (2014).

[389]*See* Brooks Furniture Mfg., Inc. v. Dutailier Int'l, Inc., 393 F.3d 1378 (Fed. Cir. 2005).

[390]Brief for Petitioner at *i*, Octane Fitness, LLC v. ICON Health & Fitness, Inc., No. 12-1184 (2013), *available at* http://sblog.s3.amazonaws.com/wp-content/uploads/2013/12/Merits-Brief-Final.pdf.

[391]*See* Octane Fitness, LLC v. Icon Health & Fitness, Inc., 134 S. Ct. 49 (2013) (mem.).

[392]134 S. Ct. 48 (Oct. 1, 2013) (mem.).

signaled that the law of exceptional case and attorney fee awards under 35 U.S.C. §285 was potentially subject to significant change.

The predicted transformation occurred in April 2014, when the Supreme Court in *Octane Fitness, LLC v. ICON Health & Fitness, Inc.* ("*Octane Fitness II*") reversed the Federal Circuit and remanded the case to the appellate court.[393] The Court jettisoned the Federal Circuit's *Brooks Furniture* test as "overly rigid" and inconsistent with the discretion granted to district court judges by 35 U.S.C. §285.

The Supreme Court in *Octane Fitness II* first noted that the Patent Act does not define "exceptional" in §285, so the adjective should be construed consistently with its ordinary meaning. Dictionaries (from 1952, when §285 was codified in 35 U.S.C., as well as current dictionaries) defined "exceptional" as "uncommon," "rare," or "not ordinary." Accordingly, the Supreme Court held that

> an "exceptional" case is simply *one that stands out from others with respect to the substantive strength of a party's litigating position (considering both the governing law and the facts of the case) or the unreasonable manner in which the case was litigated*. District courts may determine whether a case is "exceptional" in the case-by-case exercise of their discretion, considering the *totality of the circumstances*. . . . As in the comparable context of the Copyright Act, " '[t]here is no precise rule or formula for making these determinations,' but instead equitable discretion should be exercised 'in light of the considerations we have identified.' "[394]

Parsing the quoted holding, *Octane Fitness II* means that an exceptional case under 35 U.S.C. §285 is one that "stands out" based on *either* (1) the strength (or more precisely, the weakness) of a party's litigating position; *or* (2) the unreasonableness of the party's litigation conduct.

In terms of deciding when a case "stands out" for purposes of determining exceptionalness, the Court "drew from a copyright case to

[393] 134 S. Ct. 1749 (2014) ("*Octane Fitness II*").

[394] Octane Fitness, LLC v. ICON Health & Fitness, Inc., 134 S. Ct. 1749, 1756 (2014) ("*Octane Fitness II*") (emphasis added) (footnote omitted) (quoting Fogerty v. Fantasy, Inc., 510 U.S. 517, 534 (1994)). In the footnote omitted from the quoted text, the Court elaborated that

> [i]n *Fogerty v. Fantasy, Inc.*, 510 U.S. 517, 114 S. Ct. 1023, 127 L. Ed. 2d 455 (1994), for example, we explained that in determining whether to award fees under a similar provision in the Copyright Act, district courts could consider a "nonexclusive" list of "factors," including "frivolousness, motivation, objective unreasonableness (both in the factual and legal components of the case) and the need in particular circumstances to advance considerations of compensation and deterrence." *Id.*, at 534, n.19, 114 S. Ct. 1023 (internal quotation marks omitted).

Octane Fitness II, 134 S. Ct. at 1756 n.6.

present a non-exclusive list of factors for the district courts to consider, including 'frivolousness, motivation, objective unreasonableness (both in the factual and legal components of the case) and the need in particular circumstances to advance considerations of compensation and deterrence.' "[395]

Contrary to the correct, supple "totality of the circumstances" approach announced by the Supreme Court, the Federal Circuit's *Brooks Furniture* standard had impermissibly "superimpose[d] an inflexible framework onto statutory text that is inherently flexible."[396] With respect to those cases in which the Circuit allowed attorney fee awards against patentees, the Supreme Court explained that the proper test should be disjunctive rather than conjunctive: "a case presenting *either* subjective bad faith *or* exceptionally meritless claims may sufficiently set itself apart from mine-run [average or common] cases to warrant a fee award."[397] In the Court's view, "[s]omething less than 'bad faith'... suffices to mark a case as 'exceptional.' "[398] In short, two separate elements — objective unreasonableness *and* subjective bad faith — need no longer be established in order to justify an award of attorney fees under §285; something less may suffice.

In support of maintaining the *Brooks Furniture* test, patentee ICON Fitness argued that the Federal Circuit had appropriately imported into patent attorney fee cases the same two-pronged objective/subjective standard followed by the Supreme Court in certain aspects of antitrust law. More specifically, ICON Fitness contended that the *Brooks Furniture* test correctly adapted for patent litigation attorney fee cases the "sham exception" to an antitrust claimant's *Noerr-Pennington* immunity for engaging in conduct, such as litigation, aimed at influencing governmental decision-making.[399] As developed in the Supreme Court's 1993 antitrust decision *Professional Real Estate Investors, Inc. v. Columbia Pictures Industries, Inc.* ("*PRE*"),[400] the "sham exception" is a two-part framework mandating that an antitrust plaintiff loses its petitioning immunity only when it "brought

[395]Summit Data Sys., LLC v. EMC Corp., No. CV 10-749-GMS, 2014 WL 4955689, at *3 (D. Del. Sept. 25, 2014) (quoting *Octane Fitness II*, 134 S. Ct. at 1756 n.6 (citing Fogerty v. Fantasy, Inc., 510 U.S. 517, 534 (1994))), *aff'd sub nom.* Summit Data Sys. LLC v. NetApp Inc., No. 2015-1103, 2015 WL 5894214 (Fed. Cir. Oct. 9, 2015) (nonprecedential Rule 36 affirmance).

[396]*Octane Fitness II*, 134 S. Ct. at 1756.

[397]*Octane Fitness II*, 134 S. Ct. at 1757 (emphasis added).

[398]*Octane Fitness II*, 134 S. Ct. at 1757.

[399]The *Noerr-Pennington* immunity doctrine was established by *Eastern Railroad Presidents Conference v. Noerr Motor Freight, Inc.*, 365 U.S. 127 (1961), and *United Mine Workers v. Pennington*, 381 U.S. 657 (1965).

[400]508 U.S. 49 (1993) ("*PRE*"). *See also supra* Chapter 10, Section F.2 ("Anticompetitive Conduct"), analyzing the *PRE* standard for "sham litigation" antitrust liability.

[objectively] baseless claims in an attempt to thwart competition (i.e., in bad faith)."[401]

The Supreme Court summarily rejected ICON Fitness's argument. The Court observed that "the *PRE* standard finds no roots in the text of §285."[402] Moreover, any potential chilling of a patentee's right to petition the government in a case in which it might be subject to attorney fees does not rise to the same magnitude as the situation of a litigant potentially subject to antitrust liability and treble damages should it lose its *PRE* immunity. In the latter context, "defendants seek immunity from a judicial declaration that their filing of a lawsuit was actually unlawful"; in the former, patentees merely seek immunity "from a far less onerous declaration that they should bear the costs of [the litigation they initiated] in exceptional cases."[403] In other words, the stakes for a patentee in a §285 attorney fee determination are far lower than they were for the hotel operator antitrust counterclaimants in a potential "sham" litigation such as *PRE*.

Lastly, the *Octane Fitness II* Court cited an exception, "inherent" in the American default rule against attorney fee shifting, that applies in instances of "willful disobedience of a court order" or when a losing party has acted in "bad faith, vexatiously, wantonly, or for oppressive reasons. . . ."[404] Based on the existence of that inherent exception to the general rule in the United States that each side of a litigation pays its own attorney fees, the Supreme Court had twice previously declined to construe fee-shifting provisions on a narrow basis so as to render them "superfluous."[405] It again refused to do so in *Octane Fitness II*.

b. Highmark III *(U.S. 2014)*

In view of its rejection of the *Brooks Furniture* standard, the Court in the companion case of *Highmark Inc. v. Allcare Health Managements Sys., Inc.* ("*Highmark III*")[406] also rejected the Federal Circuit's

[401] *Octane Fitness*, 134 S. Ct. at 1757.

[402] *Octane Fitness*, 134 S. Ct. at 1757.

[403] *Octane Fitness*, 134 S. Ct. at 1757-1758.

[404] *Octane Fitness*, 134 S. Ct. at 1758 (citing Alyeska Pipeline Service Co. v. Wilderness Society, 421 U.S. 240, 258-259 (1975)).

[405] *Octane Fitness*, 134 S. Ct. at 1758 (citing Christiansburg Garment Co. v. EEOC, 434 U.S. 412, 419 (1978); Newman v. Piggie Park Enterprises, Inc., 390 U.S. 400, 402 n.4 (1968) (per curiam)).

[406] 134 S. Ct. 1744 (2014). In Highmark, Inc. v. Allcare Health Management Sys., Inc. ("*Highmark I*"), 687 F.3d 1300 (Fed. Cir. 2012), a divided panel of the Federal Circuit reversed-in-part a district court's judgment that a case was exceptional under 35 U.S.C. §285 based on a patentee's assertedly frivolous claims of infringement. In December 2012, the full Federal Circuit rejected a petition for rehearing *en banc* in *Highmark I*. *See* Highmark, Inc. v. Allcare Managed Healthcare Sys., Inc., 701 F.3d 1351 (Fed. Cir. 2012) (order denying panel reh'g and reh'g *en banc*) ("*Highmark II*").

de novo (i.e., no deference) standard of review for a district court's determination under *Brooks Furniture* whether a litigation was "exceptional" so as to warrant the award of attorney fees.[407] Rather, the far more deferential "abuse of discretion" standard should govern attorney fee determinations in patent cases.[408] *Highmark III* thus marks another Supreme Court adjustment of the balance of power away from the Federal Circuit and to the district courts.

The Supreme Court in *Highmark III* first observed that § 285 by its terms commits the determination of whether a case is "exceptional" to the discretion of a district court. Moreover, for reasons the Court had already explained in *Octane Fitness II*,[409] a district court's determination that a case is "exceptional" so as to justify fee-shifting is a matter of discretion, rather than a question of law or a question of fact.[410]

In addition, the Court had previously held that similar fee-shifting determinations in certain non-patent cases should be reviewed deferentially.[411] The Court observed further that as a matter of the sound administration of justice, district courts are better positioned to determine whether a case is "exceptional," because (unlike the Federal Circuit) they have "live[d] with the case over a prolonged period of time."[412]

The *Highmark III* Court accordingly held that "an appellate court should review *all* aspects of a district court's §285 determination for abuse of discretion."[413] The Court concluded by observing that

---

However, 5 of 12 Circuit judges dissented in *Highmark II*. The *en banc* court's order was accompanied by three opinions. The opinions and the divided vote indicated a great deal of disagreement within the Federal Circuit.

[407]*See Highmark III*, 134 S. Ct. at 1748 ("Our holding in *Octane* settles this case: Because §285 commits the determination whether a case is 'exceptional' to the discretion of the district court, that decision is to be reviewed on appeal for abuse of discretion[.]").

[408]Highmark Inc. v. Allcare Health Mgmt. Sys., Inc., 134 S. Ct. 1744, 1748 (2014) ("*Highmark III*").

[409]134 S. Ct. 1749 (2014) ("*Octane Fitness II*"), analyzed *supra*.

[410]Of course, the abuse of discretion standard of review does not prevent the Federal Circuit from correcting a district court's factual or legal error. *See Highmark III*, 134 S. Ct. at 1748 n.2.

[411]*See Highmark III*, 134 S. Ct. at 1748 (citing Pierce v. Underwood, 487 U.S. 552, 559 (1988) (determinations whether a litigating position is "substantially justified" for purposes of fee-shifting under the Equal Access to Justice Act are to be reviewed for abuse of discretion); Cooter & Gell v. Hartmarx Corp., 496 U.S. 384, 405 (1990) (sanctions under Federal Rule of Civil Procedure 11 are to be reviewed for abuse of discretion)).

[412]*Highmark III*, 134 S. Ct. at 1749.

[413]*Highmark III*, 134 S. Ct. at 1748 (emphasis added).

On remand from the Supreme Court to the Federal Circuit, the appellate court in September 2014 vacated the district court's award of $4.7 million in attorney fees to declaratory plaintiff/accused infringer Highmark and remanded the case to the district court for reconsideration of its §285 exceptional case determination under the new

"[a]lthough questions of law may in some cases be relevant to the §285 inquiry, that inquiry generally is, at heart, rooted in factual determinations."[414]

6. No Attorney Fee Shifting to Patent Office in §145 Actions

By a 7-4 *en banc* vote,[415] the Federal Circuit in 2018 decided an issue of first impression concerning attorney fee awards to the federal government. The majority held in *NantKwest v. Iancu*[416] that the USPTO is *not* entitled to have its attorney fees reimbursed in civil actions to obtain a patent brought by disappointed applicants under 35 U.S.C. §145, whether the government wins or loses.[417] Recall that in a §145 action, an applicant who has not been able to obtain a patent initiates a trial *de novo* in the Eastern District of Virginia, in which new evidence may be introduced, rather than appealing directly to the Federal Circuit based only on the USPTO record.[418] Section 145 actions are relatively rare but typically involve high-value cases. As of the October 2019 writing of this edition, the U.S. Supreme Court is reviewing the Circuit's decision in *NantKwest.*[419]

More specifically, the *en banc* Federal Circuit majority affirmed the Eastern District of Virginia's judgment that the §145 plaintiff NantKwest, Inc. was not compelled by the relevant statutory language to pay the USPTO's attorney fees, regardless of which party prevailed on the merits (in the case at bar, the USPTO). Recall that §145 provides (emphasis added):

---

standard articulated in *Octane Fitness. See* Highmark, Inc. v. Allcare Health Mgmt. Sys., Inc., 577 F. App'x 995, 997 (Fed. Cir. 2014) (non-precedential) (vacating Highmark, Inc. v. Allcare Health Mgmt. Sys., Inc., No. 4:03-CV-1384-Y, 2010 WL 6432945 (N.D. Tex. Nov. 5, 2010)).

[414] *Highmark III*, 134 S. Ct. at 1749 (quoting Cooter & Gell v. Hartmarx Corp., 496 U.S. 384, 401 (1990)). *Cooter* held that sanctions under Fed. R. Civ. P. 11 are to be reviewed for abuse of discretion. *See Cooter*, 496 U.S. at 405.

[415] Circuit Judge Chen (former USPTO Solicitor) did not participate in the case.

[416] 898 F.3d 1177 (Fed. Cir. July 27, 2018) (*en banc*) (Stoll, J.).

[417] Such actions are currently brought, in lieu of a direct appeal to the Federal Circuit, in the U.S. District Court for the Eastern District of Virginia. The general nature and procedures of §145 actions are detailed *supra* Chapter 1, Section G.1.b ("Civil Actions Against the USPTO Director in the Eastern District of Virginia").

[418] Actions under 35 U.S.C. §145 were detailed *supra* Chapter 1, Section G.1.b ("Civil Actions Against the USPTO Director in the Eastern District of Virginia").

[419] *See* Supreme Court of the United States, Granted and Noted List, October Term 2019 Cases for Argument, No. 18-801, Peter v. NantKwest, Inc. (Mar. 4, 2019), at 2, *available at* https://www.supremecourt.gov/orders/19grantednotedlist.pdf. The Court held oral argument in *NantKwest* on October 7, 2019. *See* Oral Argument Transcript, *available at* https://www.oyez.org/cases/2019/18-801.

> An applicant dissatisfied with the decision of the Patent Trial and Appeal Board in an appeal under section 134(a) may, unless appeal has been taken to the United States Court of Appeals for the Federal Circuit, have remedy by civil action against the Director in the United States District Court for the Eastern District of Virginia if commenced within such time after such decision, not less than sixty days, as the Director appoints. The court may adjudge that such applicant is entitled to receive a patent for his invention, as specified in any of his claims involved in the decision of the Patent Trial and Appeal Board, as the facts in the case may appear and such adjudication shall authorize the Director to issue such patent on compliance with the requirements of law. *All the expenses of the proceedings shall be paid by the applicant.*

Interpreting the italicized language in *NantKwest,* the *en banc* Circuit majority observed that

> [n]ow, 170 years after Congress introduced §145's predecessor [in the 1839 Patent Act], the agency argues that §145 also compels applicants to pay its attorneys' fees. We hold that it does not, for the American Rule prohibits courts from shifting attorneys' fees from one party to another absent a "specific and explicit" directive from Congress. The phrase "[a]ll the expenses of the proceedings" falls short of this stringent standard.[420]

As the quoted language illustrates, the *NantKwest en banc* majority relied chiefly on the presumption that the "American Rule" against attorney fee shifting applies in the absence of an explicit congressional directive to the contrary. In the majority's view, the "all the expenses" language of §145 did not rise to the level of a contrary directive clear enough to rebut the anti-fee-shifting presumption. It explained that congressional authorization to rebuff the American Rule must be "specific and explicit."[421]

In the *NantKwest* majority's view, no such "specific and explicit" evidence was present in §145's statutory award to the government of "all . . . expenses." To satisfy the Supreme Court's "strict standard," the USPTO had to show that the statutory phrase "all the expenses of the proceeding" specifically and explicitly included attorney fees.[422]

[420] *NantKwest,* 898 F.3d at 1180.

[421] *NantKwest,* 898 F.3d at 1187 (citing Summit Valley Indus., Inc. v. Local 112, United Bhd. of Carpenters, 456 U.S. 717, 722-723 (1982); citing also *Summit Valley,* 456 U.S. at 721, 726 (declining to deviate from American Rule after finding no "express statutory authorization" in statute's text to support contention that "damages" includes attorney fees); *Key Tronic,* 511 U.S. at 819 (requiring "explicit statutory authority" to depart from American Rule)).

[422] *NantKwest,* 898 F.3d at 1187.

The agency had failed to make this showing. At best, the *NantKwest en banc* majority acknowledged, the text of §145 was "ambiguous as to attorneys' fees."[423] The cases and word definitions relied on by the government showed "at most [that] this language is merely capable of *implicitly* covering attorneys' fees."[424] The "specific and explicit" requirement for displacing the American Rule against attorney fee shifting required "more than language that merely *can be* and *is sometimes used* broadly to implicitly cover attorneys' fees."[425]

Notably, the *NantKwest en banc* majority (like the district court below) distinguished the statutory term "expenses" from "fees," which it viewed as the traditional term triggering an award of attorney fees. The majority concluded that the generally understood, common meanings of "expenses" and "attorneys' fees" refer to two separate elements.

Joined by three colleagues, Circuit Chief Judge Prost authored the dissenting opinion in *NantKwest*.[426] In the dissent's view, "all the expenses" of §145 should include the USPTO's "personnel expenses," which in this case included the USPTO attorney time costs actually incurred (not billed at market rate).

As a policy matter, the *NantKwest* dissent urged, §145 litigation diverts USPTO time and resources. It is expensive and time-consuming. The dissent believed that the dissatisfied applicant choosing the §145 option should justly bear the cost of the agency's expended personnel/labor resources (i.e., including attorney fees, whether incurred in-house or by outside counsel). In its view,

> [a]n applicant's choice to proceed under §145 diverts the agency's resources from the PTO's principal mission of examining patent and trademark applications at the agency. The purpose of §145's expense-reimbursement provision is to ensure that these expenses fall on the applicants who elect the more expensive district court proceedings over the standard appeal route [i.e., a direct appeal from the USPTO to the Federal Circuit under 35 U.S.C. §141].[427]

The Supreme Court granted the USPTO's petition for *certiorari* in *NantKwest* in March 2019.[428] It agreed to consider the following Question Presented:

[423]*NantKwest,* 898 F.3d at 1187.

[424]*NantKwest,* 898 F.3d at 1187 (emphasis in original).

[425]*NantKwest,* 898 F.3d at 1187 (emphasis in original).

[426]*See NantKwest,* 898 F.3d at 1196 (Prost, C.J., dissenting). Judges Dyk, Reyna, and Hughes joined Chief Judge Prost's dissenting opinion.

[427]*NantKwest,* 898 F.3d at 1202 (Prost, C.J., dissenting).

[428]Supreme Court of the United States, Granted and Noted List, October Term 2019 Cases for Argument, No. 18-801, Peter v. NantKwest, Inc. (Mar. 4, 2019), at 2, *available at* https://www.supremecourt.gov/orders/19grantednotedlist.pdf.

Whether the phrase "[a]ll the expenses of the proceedings" in 35 U.S.C. 145 encompasses the personnel expenses the USPTO incurs when its employees, including attorneys, defend the agency in Section 145 litigation.[429]

The Supreme Court heard oral argument in the *NantKwest* case, recaptioned as *Peter v. NantKwest, Inc.*, in October 2019.[430] Commentators reporting on the oral argument described the Court as "skeptical" of the USTPO's position.[431]

The Supreme Court unanimously affirmed the Federal Circuit on December 11, 2019. *See* Peter v. NantKwest Inc., 140 S.Ct. 365 (2019) (Sotomayer, J.). The next edition of this text will analyze the Court's decision.

F. Prejudgment Interest

Prejudgment interest (sometimes referred to as "delay compensation") is awarded under 35 U.S.C. §284[432] in order to make the patentee whole, by compensating it for "the forgone use of the money [owed by the infringer to the patentee] between the time of infringement and the date of the judgment."[433] In other words, had the infringer paid the infringement damages (in the form of reasonable royalties or lost profits) to the patentee at the time they were actually incurred (i.e., the time of the infringement), the patentee presumably could have earned interest by investing this money. An award of prejudgment interest attempts to approximate the interest that the patentee would have earned during the period of time between the infringement and the judgment.[434] The U.S. Supreme

[429]Petition for a Writ of Certiorari, No. 18-801, Iancu v. NantKwest (Dec. 21, 2018), at (I), *available at* https://www.supremecourt.gov/DocketPDF/18/18-801/77342/20181221133549209_PETITION%20NantKwest%20Inc.pdf.

[430]A transcript of the October 7, 2019 Supreme Court oral argument in *Peter v. NantKwest, Inc.* is available at https://www.oyez.org/cases/2019/18-801.

[431]*See* Ronald Mann, *Argument analysis: Justices seem hesitant to award attorney's fees to government in litigation challenging denial of patent applications*, SCOTUSblog.com (Oct. 7, 2019), https://www.scotusblog.com/2019/10/argument-analysis-justices-seem-hesitant-to-award-attorneys-fees-to-government-in-litigation-challenging-denial-of-patent-applications (observing that "[i]n general, with a few discordant notes, the justices seemed skeptical of the government's position. For some of the justices, it seemed remarkable — a 'radical departure' in the words of Justice Brett Kavanaugh — for Congress to force a successful litigant to pay the attorney's fees of the other.").

[432]"Upon finding for the claimant the court shall award the claimant damages adequate to compensate for the infringement, . . . together with *interest* and costs as fixed by the court." 35 U.S.C. §284, ¶1 (emphasis added).

[433]General Motors Corp. v. Devex Corp., 461 U.S. 648, 656 (1983).

[434]*See* Whitserve v. Computer Packages, Inc., 694 F.3d 10, 36 (Fed. Cir. 2012) ("An award of prejudgment interest carries out Congress's 'overriding purpose of affording patent owners complete compensation' since a patentee's damages also include the

Court has provided that "pre-judgment interest should ordinarily be awarded."[435]

The Federal Circuit has held that prejudgment interest is available only for that portion of a damages award representing compensatory (actual) damages, not for any portion representing enhanced damages.[436]

In *Sanofi-Aventis v. Apotex Inc.*,[437] the Federal Circuit interpreted a settlement agreement between two parties involved in a long-running Hatch-Waxman dispute over patented clopidogrel bisulfate tablets. The agreement provided that if the U.S. Food and Drug Administration denied generic manufacturer Apotex's Abbreviated New Drug Application (ANDA), the previously stayed litigation between the parties would resume and "[i]f the litigation results in a judgment that [Sanofi's] '265 patent is not invalid or unenforceable, Sanofi agrees that its *actual damages* for any past infringement by Apotex, up to the date on which Apotex is enjoined, *will be 50% of Apotex's net sales* of clopidogrel products."[438] Under the facts of the case and applying New York state contract law, the Federal Circuit concluded that the patentee's agreement to limit itself to "actual damages" foreclosed any award of prejudgment interest. In the Federal Circuit's view, "the parties intended that the phrase 'actual damages' include all damages necessary to compensate Sanofi for Apotex's infringement."[439] Prejudgment interest is a form of compensatory damages under 35 U.S.C. §284. Hence the "50% of net sales" figure referred to in the agreement was Sanofi's full measure of damages. The Federal Circuit accordingly vacated the district court's award of approximately $108 million in prejudgment interest.[440]

'forgone use of the money between the time of infringement and the date of judgment.' ") (quoting *General Motors Corp.*, 461 U.S. at 655-656).

[435]*General Motors Corp*, 461 U.S. at 655. *See also Whitserve*, 694 F.3d at 36 (holding that when district court judge specifically instructed jury that it could "not award any interest on any damages," "[t]he jury's award could not, accordingly, constitute compensation for interest and the trial court abused its discretion in denying prejudgment interest without further analysis or justification"); Ecolab, Inc. v. FMC Corp., 569 F.3d 1335, 1353 (Fed. Cir. 2009) (holding that on remand, district court "must award [prejudgment] interest or provide a valid justification for withholding [it]").

[436]*See* Underwater Devices, Inc. v. Morrison-Knudsen Co., 717 F.2d 1380, 1389 (Fed. Cir. 1983).

[437]659 F.3d 1171 (Fed. Cir. 2011).

[438]*Sanofi-Aventis*, 659 F.3d at 1177 (emphasis added).

[439]*Sanofi-Aventis*, 659 F.3d at 1178.

[440]*Sanofi-Aventis*, 659 F.3d at 1176. The district court had reached that amount by starting with 50 percent of the patentee's net sales of the patented product over an approximately four-year period during 2006-2010, then computing prejudgment interest on that figure at the average annual prime rate, compounded quarterly. *See id.* at 1176 n.2.

Rather surprisingly, there is no statutorily mandated interest rate for the award of prejudgment interest in U.S. patent cases. The issue of the proper interest rate and method of compounding are separately litigated in each case where interest is awarded. District courts have substantial discretion in determining the interest rate to be applied, as well as whether simple or compounded interest should be awarded.[441]

G. Costs

The availability of "costs" under 35 U.S.C. §284[442] refers to Fed. R. Civ. P. 54(d)(1), which creates a presumption that a prevailing party shall be awarded costs.[443] The types of expenses that a federal court may award as costs under its Rule 54(d)(1) discretionary authority are listed in 28 U.S.C. §1920, and include fees for the court reporter, witnesses, court appointed experts, copying costs, and the like.

The Federal Circuit has adopted a choice-of-law rule in which the court applies its own law, rather than that of the regional circuit for the geographic territory from which a case arose, to define the meaning of prevailing party in the context of an award of costs in patent litigation.[444] In *Manildra Milling Corp. v. Ogilvie Mills, Inc.*,[445] the issue was whether a declaratory judgment plaintiff that "receive[d] no money damages at all but instead 'receive[d] a hard fought declaration that its competitor's patents are invalid,' and survive[d] the competitor's counterclaim for $17 million in patent infringement damages,"[446] was a prevailing party for purposes of awarding costs. Although the declaratory judgment plaintiff, Manildra Milling, failed to prevail on its claims under the Sherman (Antitrust) Act, the Lanham (Trademark) Act, and state common law claims, its victory on the patent issues was "complete." In the Federal Circuit's view, such

[441]*See* Gyromat Corp. v. Champion Spark Plug Co., 735 F.2d 549, 556-557 (Fed. Cir. 1984).

[442]"Upon finding for the claimant the court shall award the claimant damages adequate to compensate for the infringement, . . . together with interest and *costs* as fixed by the court." 35 U.S.C. §284, ¶1 (emphasis added).

[443]*See* Manildra Milling Corp. v. Ogilvie Mills, Inc., 76 F.3d 1178 (Fed. Cir. 1996) (holding that declaratory judgment plaintiff that successfully invalidated patent was a prevailing party for purposes of awarding costs in accordance with Fed. R. Civ. P. 54(d)(1), and affirming award of approximately $83,000 in costs).

[444]*See Manildra Milling Corp.*, 76 F.3d at 1181-1182.

[445]76 F.3d 1178 (Fed. Cir. 1996).

[446]*Manildra Milling Corp.*, 76 F.3d at 1182-1183.

a victory qualified Manildra Milling as a "prevailing party,"[447] entitling it to an award of costs of approximately $83,000.[448]

The Federal Circuit again explored what is required to qualify as a "prevailing party" entitled to an award of costs under Fed. R. Civ. P. 54(d) in its October 2019 decision, *B.E. Tech., L.L.C. v. Facebook, Inc.*[449] The case teaches that a party can be considered "prevailing" even when the lawsuit against it is dismissed for mootness rather than on the merits.

After B.E. sued Facebook and other technology companies for patent infringement in federal district court, the accused infringers sought and obtained *inter partes* review of B.E.'s asserted patent claims in the USPTO. While the district court stayed its proceedings, the PTAB determined that all the B.E. patent claims were unpatentable. Thereafter, the district court dismissed with prejudice B.E.'s lawsuit under Fed. R. Civ. P. 12(c)[450] on the ground of mootness. The district court reasoned that because the USPTO had cancelled its patent claims, B.E. no longer had a basis for its infringement lawsuit. The district court further determined that given this outcome, Facebook was the Rule 54(d) "prevailing party" and entitled to an award of its costs.

When B.E. appealed the award, the Federal Circuit agreed with the district court's analysis and affirmed the award of costs against B.E. Contrary to B.E.'s argument, the fact that the district court dismissed the case for mootness in light of the USPTO's determination of unpatentability, rather than on the basis of any merits determination by the district court, did not mean that Facebook had not "prevail[ed]." Rather, the Circuit explained, a defendant can be deemed a prevailing party even if the case against it is dismissed on procedural grounds rather than on the merits. Such a rule helps deter the bringing of frivolous or unreasonable lawsuits.

The district court had correctly relied on the Supreme Court's 2016 decision in *CRST Van Expedited, Inc. v. E.E.O.C.*[451] There the Court held that "a merits decision is not a prerequisite to a finding of prevailing party status."[452] In accordance with the requirements of *CRST,* Facebook was the prevailing party in the case at bar because it "obtained the outcome it sought via the mootness dismissal; it rebuffed

[447] *See Manildra Milling Corp.*, 76 F.3d at 1183 (holding that "as a matter of law, a party who has a competitor's patent declared invalid meets the definition of 'prevailing party'").

[448] *See Manildra Milling Corp.*, 76 F.3d at 1180.

[449] 940 F.3d 675, (Fed. Cir. Oct. 9, 2019) (Lourie, J.).

[450] Rule 12(c) permits a federal district court to dismiss a lawsuit in response to a party's motion for judgment on the pleadings, so long as the motion is made "[a]fter the pleadings are closed — but early enough not to delay trial."

[451] 136 S. Ct. 1642 (2016).

[452] *B.E. Tech.*, 940 F.3d at 678.

B.E.'s attempt to alter the parties' legal relationship in an infringement suit. This [wa]s true even though the mootness decision was made possible by a winning a battle on the merits before the PTO."[453]

H. Patent Marking

The U.S. Patent Act strongly encourages (but does not require) patentees and/or those who manufacture, sell, offer to sell, or import patented articles for them to mark the articles with the corresponding U.S. patent number(s).[454] This is why many patented items sold in the marketplace bear a patent number, either on the items themselves or on their packaging. The purpose of the marking provisions of the Patent Act is to provide the public with some degree of notice of patent rights (albeit an imperfect degree, because marking is optional). In order to accomplish this purpose, §287(a) of Title 35 provides that without adequate marking, "no damages shall be recovered by the patentee in any action for infringement, except on proof that the infringer was notified of the infringement and continued to infringe thereafter, in which event damages may be recovered only for infringement occurring after such notice."[455] The filing of the infringement lawsuit constitutes notice.[456] Thus, notice under §287 can be constructive notice, through marking the patent number on the patented product, or actual notice, through certain communications with the infringer or the actual filing of the lawsuit.[457] In cases where the patented articles were not marked and no other notice was given to the accused infringer, the operation of §287 means that the patentee will not be able to recover any damages for infringements that occurred prior to the filing of the lawsuit.

[453]*B.E. Tech.*, 940 F.3d at 679.

[454]The statute provides in part:

> Patentees, and persons making, offering for sale, or selling within the United States any patented article for or under them, or importing any patented article into the United States, may give notice to the public that the same is patented, either by fixing thereon the word "patent" or the abbreviation "pat.", together with the number of the patent, or by fixing thereon the word "patent" or the abbreviation "pat." together with an address of a posting on the Internet, accessible to the public without charge for accessing the address, that associates the patented article with the number of the patent, or when, from the character of the article, this cannot be done, by fixing to it, or to the package wherein one or more of them is contained, a label containing a like notice.

35 U.S.C. §287(a) (eff. Sept. 16, 2011).

[455]35 U.S.C. §287(a).

[456]35 U.S.C. §287(a).

[457]*See* Gart v. Logitech, Inc., 254 F.3d 1334, 1345 (Fed. Cir. 2001).

A number of Federal Circuit decisions address whether particular prefiling communications between patentees and accused infringers established that the "infringer was notified of the infringement" within the meaning of 35 U.S.C. §287(a) so as to start the damages recovery period. The fact that an accused infringer was merely aware of or even possessed a copy of the patent allegedly infringed is not sufficient, without more, to satisfy §287.[458] As the Federal Circuit explained in *Amsted Indus. v. Buckeye Steel Castings Co.*,[459] the determination of notice under 35 U.S.C. §287 "must focus on the action of the patentee, not the knowledge or understanding of the infringer."[460] In order to meet §287's actual notice requirement, an "affirmative communication [to the alleged infringer] of a specific charge of infringement by a specific accused product or device" is required.[461] This standard was not met in *Amsted Indus.* by a letter that notified the entire industry, including the accused infringer, only of the patentee's ownership of the patent and generally advised companies not to infringe.[462]

The §287(a) marking statute does not apply to patents that claim only processes or methods,[463] because in such cases there is usually no tangible article to mark; the marking provisions may be applicable to patents that include both method and apparatus claims, however.[464]

Section 292 of the Patent Act, titled "False Marking," provides that a fine of $500 per offense shall be assessed against those who, without the consent of the patent owner, intentionally mark the patentee's name or its patent number on their own products.[465] The false

[458]*See* Amsted Indus. v. Buckeye Steel Castings Co., 24 F.3d 178, 187 (Fed. Cir. 1994).

[459]24 F.3d 178 (Fed. Cir. 1994).

[460]*Amsted Indus.*, 24 F.3d at 187.

[461]*Amsted Indus.*, 24 F.3d at 187.

[462]*See Amsted Indus.*, 24 F.3d at 187.

[463]*See* American Med. Sys., Inc. v. Medical Eng'g Corp., 6 F.3d 1523, 1538 (Fed. Cir. 1993).

[464]*See American Med.*, 6 F.3d at 1538 (stating that "[w]here the patent contains both apparatus and method claims, however, to the extent that there is a tangible item to mark by which notice of the asserted method claims can be given, a party is obliged to do so if it intends to avail itself of the constructive notice provisions of section 287(a)").

[465]*See* 35 U.S.C. §292(a) ¶1 (2020) (providing that "[w]hoever, without the consent of the patentee, marks upon, or affixes to, or uses in advertising in connection with anything made, used, offered for sale, or sold by such person within the United States, or imported by the person into the United States, the name or any imitation of the name of the patentee, the patent number, or the words 'patent,' 'patentee,' or the like, with the intent of counterfeiting or imitating the mark of the patentee, or of deceiving the public and inducing them to believe that the thing was made, offered for sale, sold, or imported into the United States by or with the consent of the patentee . . . [s]hall be fined not more than $ 500 for every such offense").

marking penalty also applies to those who intentionally mark "patent" or "patent pending" on articles that are not patented or for which no patent application has been filed.[466]

Following a 2009 Federal Circuit decision holding that the $500 fine is assessed for *each article* falsely marked,[467] the federal district courts confronted a surge of false marking *qui tam* actions brought by third parties having no relation to the owners of the patents involved. In many instances, the *qui tam* plaintiffs sued when a patent covering a product expired but the patent owner continued to sell the product without removing the patent number.[468] In the America Invents Act of 2011, Congress amended the false marking statute to eliminate such *qui tam* lawsuits. Effective Sept. 16, 2011, only the United States government, not private individuals, can sue for the false marking penalty.[469]

[466]*See* 35 U.S.C. §292(a) ¶¶2-3 (2020) (providing that "[w]hoever marks upon, or affixes to, or uses in advertising in connection with any unpatented article, the word 'patent' or any word or number importing that the same is patented, for the purpose of deceiving the public; or [w]hoever marks upon, or affixes to, or uses in advertising in connection with any article, the words 'patent applied for,' 'patent pending,' or any word importing that an application for patent has been made, when no application for patent has been made, or if made, is not pending, for the purpose of deceiving the public — [s]hall be fined not more than $500 for every such offense").

[467]*See* Forest Group, Inc. v. Bon Tool Co., 590 F.3d 1295, 1301 (Fed. Cir. 2009) (concluding that "the statute clearly requires that each article that is falsely marked with intent to deceive constitutes an offense under 35 U.S.C. §292").

[468]*See* H.R. Rep. No. 112-98 [House Judiciary Comm. Rep. on the America Invents Act], at 62 (June 1, 2011) (observing that "a recent survey of such suits found that a large majority involved valid patents that covered the products in question but had simply expired. For many products, it is difficult and expensive to change a mold or other means by which a product is marked as patented, and marked products continue to circulate in commerce for some period after the patent expires. It is doubtful that the Congress that originally enacted this section anticipated that it would force manufacturers to immediately remove marked products from commerce once the patent expired, given that the expense to manufacturers of doing so will generally greatly outweigh any conceivable harm of allowing such products to continue to circulate in commerce.").

[469]*See* Leahy-Smith America Invents Act, Pub. L. No. 112-29 (H.R. 1249), §16(b)(1), 125 Stat. 284, 329 (Sept. 16, 2011) ("Civil Penalty") (amending 35 U.S.C. §292(a) to add at end of subsection (a) that "[o]nly the United States may sue for the penalty authorized by this subsection"). Also permitted are civil actions by persons (such as patent owners) who can prove a "competitive injury" resulting from false marking. *See* Leahy-Smith America Invents Act, Pub. L. No. 112-29 (H.R. 1249), §16(b)(2), 125 Stat. 284, 329 (Sept. 16, 2011) ("Civil Action for Damages") (adding to 35 U.S.C. §292 a new subsection (b) authorizing such suits in federal district courts "for recovery of damages adequate to compensate for the injury"). Lastly, Congress clarified that the false marking statute is not violated by the marking of a product with an expired patent number that once covered the product. *See* Leahy-Smith America Invents Act, Pub. L. No. 112-29 (H.R. 1249), §16(b)(3), 125 Stat. 284, 329 (Sept. 16, 2011) ("Expired Patents") (adding to 35 U.S.C. §292 a new subsection (c) providing that "[t]he marking of a product, in a manner described in subsection (a), with matter relating to a patent that covered that

I. Provisional Compensation Remedy

The American Inventors Protection Act of 1999 (AIPA)[470] created a new remedy for violation of patent-related rights. A U.S. patentee is now entitled to retroactively seek damages for infringement of the claims that appeared in its published patent application,[471] when that infringement occurred on or after the date of publication of the pending application by the USPTO but prior to patent issuance. Pursuant to 35 U.S.C. §154(d)(1), the provisional compensation remedy is limited to a reasonable royalty.[472] The Federal Circuit has described the §154(d) remedy as a "narrow exception" to the general rule that "patent owners may only collect damages for patent infringement that takes place during the term of the patent."[473]

Since passage of the AIPA, U.S. patent applicants have possessed the ability to "opt out" of automatic publication of their applications at 18 months after filing by attesting that they will not seek to patent the same invention in other countries.[474] Some U.S. applicants may want to exercise their option to avoid 18-month publication on the ground that there is no way to *enjoin* another who makes, uses, sells, offers to sell, or imports the subject matter of the published claims before the application has issued as a patent. The provisional compensation remedy creates an alternative remedy — a retroactive right to damages in the form of a reasonable royalty — that is intended to protect patent applicants from unchecked pre-issuance infringement and to encourage publication of their pending applications.

In order to qualify for the provisional compensation remedy of §154(d), the invention as claimed in the issued patent must be "substantially identical" to the invention as claimed in the published patent application.[475] The statute does not define "substantially identical,"[476] but the phrase is a term of art in reissue and

---

product but has expired is not a violation of this section"). These AIA amendments took effect for "all cases, without exception, that [we]re pending on, or commenced on or after, the date of the enactment of this Act [September 16, 2011]." Leahy-Smith America Invents Act, Pub. L. No. 112-29 (H.R. 1249), §16(b)(4), 125 Stat. 284, 329 (Sept. 16, 2011).

[470]Pub. L. No. 106-113 (Nov. 29, 1999).

[471]Pending U.S. patent applications are now published 18 months after their effective filing dates unless certain exceptions apply. *See* 35 U.S.C. §122(b) (2020).

[472]The computation of a "reasonable royalty" is examined *supra* Section D.2.c.

[473]Rosebud LMS Inc. v. Adobe Sys. Inc., No. 2015-1428, 2016 WL 494591, at *2 (Fed. Cir. Feb. 9, 2016).

[474]*See* 35 U.S.C. §122(b)(2)(B).

[475]35 U.S.C. §154(d)(2).

[476]Section 154(d)(2) provides that "[t]he right under paragraph (1) to obtain a reasonable royalty shall not be available under this subsection unless the invention as claimed in the patent is substantially identical to the invention as claimed in the published patent application."

reexamination practice,[477] so the courts may look to such cases for guidance in interpreting 35 U.S.C. §154(d). Professor Chisum has observed that

> [t]he "substantially identical" standard will undoubtedly create difficult issues. If prosecution of an application is not substantially complete by the time [of] the publication, the claims in the application may be amended by the addition of narrowing limitations. The claims may also be broadened. To take full advantage of the provisional right, an applicant must take care to include claims of adequate scope in the application as it is published.[478]

Moreover, in order for the patentee to seek a reasonable royalty under §154(d), the alleged infringer must have had "actual notice" of the patentee's published patent application;[479] again, the statute does not define "actual notice," leaving the courts to interpret the phrase based on case law experience.

In 2016, the Federal Circuit for the first time defined the meaning of "actual notice" as used in §154(d) in *Rosebud LMS Inc. v. Adobe Sys. Inc.*[480] In short, the "ordinary meaning" of "actual notice" in §154(d) includes "actual knowledge" but not constructive knowledge. For example, the fact that a patent application was published on the USPTO's website and thus available to the public at large would not, by itself, be enough to qualify as "actual notice" — the website publication would be only constructive notice. The accused infringer would have to have actually gained knowledge of the published application through its own actions, those of a third party, or by communication from the patent applicant. On the other hand, the Circuit in *Rosebud* rejected accused infringer Adobe's position that the patent applicant must necessarily take an affirmative act (such as sending a copy of the published application to the accused infringer's attention) in order to create "actual notice" under §154(d).[481]

[477]Reexamination and reissue are discussed *supra* Chapter 8 ("Correcting and Challenging Issued Patents in the USPTO").

[478]Donald S. Chisum, 4-11 Chisum on Patents §11.02[4][e] n.145 (2008).

[479]*See* 35 U.S.C. §154(d)(1)(B).

[480]No. 2015-1428, 2016 WL 494591 (Fed. Cir. Feb. 9, 2016).

[481]On this point, the Circuit rejected accused infringer's Adobe's reading of the legislative history of 35 U.S.C. §154(d). Although that legislative history stated that "[t]he published application must give actual notice of the published application to the accused infringer . . . ," the same sentence concluded that the published applicant must also "explain what acts are regarded as giving rise to provisional rights." H.R. Rep. No. 106-287, pt. 1, at 54 (1999). Because the second stated requirement was not included in the text of §154(d), the Circuit refused to be bound by the first stated requirement. *See Rosebud,* 2016 WL 494591, at *3 (concluding that the "language enacted by Congress is not consistent with Adobe's interpretation").

Applying its newly announced definition of "actual notice" to the facts before it, the Federal Circuit in *Rosebud* affirmed a district court's grant of summary judgment to accused infringer Adobe of no liability for pre-issuance damages under §154(d). Patentee Rosebud's three arguments that Adobe had "actual notice" of Rosebud's application were not persuasive. First, Rosebud contended that Adobe actually knew of the application that issued as the patent in suit (U.S. Patent No. 8,578,280 ('280 patent)), because Adobe knew of the "grandparent" patent to '280 patent. That grandparent patent (U.S. Patent No. 7,454,760 ('760 patent)) was the subject of "*Rosebud I*," the first of three infringement lawsuits that Rosebud had filed against Adobe starting in 2010.[482] The Circuit responded that mere knowledge of related patents (which, as in the case at bar, typically share a common written description) cannot satisfy the "actual notice" requirement, because such knowledge does not meet the additional requirement of §154(d)(2) that the accused infringer also have notice of the *claims* of the published application and the fact that the applicant is seeking an issued patent on those claims.[483] In other words, knowledge of the claims of the grandparent '760 patent application does not equate to knowledge of the claims of the '280 patent application for which Rosebud sought §154(d) reasonable royalties.

The *Rosebud* court also refused to apply its construction of the notice provision of the marking statute, 35 U.S.C. §287(a), to the "actual notice" requirement of for §154(d) provisional compensation. Although the Circuit has interpreted §287(a) as requiring an "affirmative communication of a specific charge of infringement," Amsted Indus. Inc. v. Buckeye Steel Castings Co., 24 F.3d 178, 187 (Fed. Cir. 1994), the text of §287(a) refers to "proof that the infringer was notified of the infringement." Thus, §287(a) "explicitly requires an act of notification, unlike §154(d), which merely requires 'actual notice.'" *Rosebud,* 2016 WL 494591, at *3.

[482]The Circuit explained the litigation history between the parties:

> Rosebud has filed three suits against Adobe for patent infringement. Rosebud first sued Adobe for infringing U.S. Patent No. 7,454,760 in 2010, in a suit that was dismissed more than three years before this case was filed. *Rosebud LMS Inc. v. Adobe Sys. Inc.*, No. 1:10-cv-00404-GMS (D. Del., filed May 14, 2010, dismissed Nov. 29, 2010) ("*Rosebud I*"). Rosebud next sued Adobe for infringing U.S. Patent No. 8,046,699 in 2012, in a suit that was dismissed with prejudice a few weeks after this case was filed. *Rosebud LMS Inc. v. Adobe Sys. Inc.*, No. 1:12-cv-01141-SLR (D. Del., filed Sept. 17, 2012, dismissed Feb. 28, 2014) ("*Rosebud II*"). And on February 13, 2014, Rosebud brought suit against Adobe for the third time, alleging that it infringed the '280 patent [U.S. Patent No. 8,578,280, the patent at issue in the appeal at the Federal Circuit]. The '280 patent is a continuation of the '699 patent, which is a continuation of the '760 patent. The patents teach techniques for enabling collaborative work over a network of computers.

[483]*Rosebud*, 2016 WL 494591, at *4. These requirements go to the statutory mandate that the right to receive a §154(d) reasonable royalty is only available if "the invention as [ultimately] claimed in the [issued] patent is substantially identical to the invention as claimed in the [earlier] published patent application." 35 U.S.C. §154(d)(2).

Second, Rosebud argued that accused infringer Adobe "followed Rosebud and its product and sought to emulate some of the Rosebud product's features." On this point, the appellate court found the evidence [i.e., seven e-mails from Adobe employees] simply inadequate to support Rosebud's assertion. The Circuit concluded that "[n]othing in the evidence suggests that Adobe or its employees were monitoring Rosebud and its products, let alone to such an extent that they would have actively sought out Rosebud's published patent applications more than two years after the emails were sent."[484]

Rosebud's third and final argument was probably its strongest, but this too failed. Rosebud contended that the district court erred in granting Adobe summary judgement because a reasonable jury could have concluded that Adobe's outside counsel would have undoubtedly discovered the published '280 patent application while preparing for the litigation in the second of the three lawsuits ("*Rosebud II*") that Rosebud brought against Adobe. Rosebud contended that it was "standard practice during litigation to review related patents, applications, and prosecution history to evaluate possible claim constructions."[485] Although the Federal Circuit did not attempt to refute that accurate statement about standard litigation practices, it nevertheless rejected Rosebud's argument. Notably, the *Rosebud II* litigation "never reached the claim construction stage because Rosebud missed all of its court-ordered deadlines."[486] Even taking all the evidence into account, and making all reasonable inferences in favor of Rosebud (the summary judgment non-movant), the Federal Circuit "agree[d] with the district court that no reasonable jury could find that Adobe had actual knowledge of the published '280 patent application."[487]

Compensation for violation of provisional rights cannot be sought unless and until the patent issues. Thus, 35 U.S.C. §154(d) creates a retroactive remedy. The statute also creates a six-year post-issuance limitation on actions to recover damages for violation of provisional rights.[488] This is a true statute of limitations, in contrast with the temporal limitation on recovery of damages under 35 U.S.C. §286.[489]

[484]*Rosebud,* 2016 WL 494591, at *4. Moreover, five of the seven e-mail chains originated from "unsolicited emails Rosebud sent to Adobe employees about its product." *Rosebud,* 2016 WL 494591, at *4.

[485]*Rosebud*, 2016 WL 494591, at *5.

[486]*Rosebud*, 2016 WL 494591, at *5.

[487]*Rosebud*, 2016 WL 494591, at *5.

[488]*See* 35 U.S.C. §154(d)(3).

[489]Section 286 of 35 U.S.C., titled "Time limitation on damages," provides in part that "[e]xcept as otherwise provided by law, no recovery shall be had for any infringement committed more than six years prior to the filing of the complaint or counterclaim for infringement in the action."

I. Provisional Compensation Remedy

One of the first court decisions to award reasonable royalties under §154(d) was *Parker-Hannifin Corp. v. Champion Labs., Inc.*[490] The patent in suit covered oil filter assemblies for vehicles, and it was undisputed that the defendant, a former customer of the patentee, sold over 100,000 infringing filters during the provisional compensation right period. At issue was the appropriate reasonable royalty to award the patentee for violation of its provisional compensation right. The district court applied the 15 *Georgia Pacific* factors discussed *supra* to hypothesize a license negotiation between the patentee and the accused infringer.[491] The district court concluded that the parties would have conducted this negotiation at the beginning of the provisional rights period, when the patentee's "rights vested under the Patent Act."[492] The district court did not consider whether any uncertainty at that date concerning whether a patent would ultimately issue (with claims the same or substantially identical to those that had been published) might have impacted the hypothetical license negotiation. The district court also determined that the reasonable royalty for the provisional compensation right period should *not* be capped by the accused infringer's cost of designing around the patent, that is, the cost of implementing its own noninfringing alternative.[493]

[490]No. 1:06-CV-2616, 2008 WL 3166318 (N.D. Ohio Aug. 4, 2008).

[491]*See supra* Section D.2.c.1 ("Hypothetical Negotiation"), discussing factors enumerated in *Georgia Pacific Corp. v. United States Plywood Corp.*, 318 F. Supp. 1116 (S.D.N.Y. 1970).

[492]*See Parker-Hannifin*, 2008 WL 3166318, at *9. The provisional rights period began on June 16, 2005; the USPTO's Notice of Allowance was received on September 12, 2005, and the patent in suit issued on January 10, 2006. The district court rejected the accused infringer's argument that the Notice of Allowance date would have been the proper date for the hypothetical negotiation. *See id.*

[493]On this point the district court relied on *Mars, Inc. v. Coin Acceptors, Inc.*, 527 F.3d 1359, 1373 (Fed. Cir. 2008) (characterizing as "wrong as a matter of law" accused infringer's claim that "reasonable royalty damages are capped at the cost of implementing the cheapest available, acceptable, noninfringing alternative"). *See Parker-Hannifin*, 2008 WL 3166318, at *7-*8.

Chapter 12

International Patenting Issues

A. Introduction

The rise of global commerce requires that U.S. patent attorneys possess not only a thorough understanding of domestic patent law, but also an overall familiarity with the substance and procedure for obtaining and enforcing patent rights worldwide. Many of the fundamental aspects of patentability and infringement previously described in this text are approached differently by foreign patent systems. This chapter introduces the key distinctions. It also summarizes the primary multinational treaties, conventions, and agreements that simplify the task of protecting an invention in multiple countries around the world. The primary provisions of U.S. patent law that implement these treaties will be described. Size constraints limit the scope of this final chapter; however, a number of useful reference works provide a more detailed treatment of international and comparative patent law.[1]

1. Territorial Scope of Patents

Fundamentally, it must be understood that patents are national, not international, in scope. Patents are generally not enforced

[1]*See* ARNOLD & SIEDSMA, MANUAL FOR THE HANDLING OF APPLICATIONS FOR PATENTS, DESIGNS AND TRADEMARKS THROUGHOUT THE WORLD (Wolters Kluwer 2016); J.W. BAXTER & JOHN P. SINNOTT, WORLD PATENT LAW AND PRACTICE (LexisNexis 2015); GRAEME B. DINWOODIE ET AL., INTERNATIONAL AND COMPARATIVE PATENT LAW (Matthew Bender 2002); PAUL GOLDSTEIN & MARKETA TRIMBLE, INTERNATIONAL INTELLECTUAL PROPERTY LAW, CASES AND MATERIALS, FOURTH ED. (Foundation Press 2015); MARSHALL A. LEAFFER, INTERNATIONAL TREATIES ON INTELLECTUAL PROPERTY (BNA 2d ed. 1997); MICHAEL N. MELLER ET AL., INTERNATIONAL PATENT LITIGATION: A COUNTRY-BY-COUNTRY ANALYSIS (Bloomberg BNA Supp. 2015); R. Carl Moy, *The History of the Patent Harmonization Treaty: Economic Self-Interest as an Influence*, 26 J. MARSHALL L. REV. 457 (1993); TOSHIKO TAKENAKA, ED., PATENT LAW AND THEORY: A HANDBOOK OF CONTEMPORARY RESEARCH (Edward Elgar 2009).

extraterritorially.[2] This means that the patentee's right to exclude others is extinguished at the geographic borders of the granting country. For example, the owner of a U.S. patent cannot rely on that U.S. patent to stop an unauthorized third party from copying and selling the invention in Japan.[3] Rather, she must obtain a Japanese patent on her invention and enforce the Japanese patent against the infringer, most likely in the courts of Japan.[4] Compared to copyright law, which provides virtually automatic worldwide protection via the Berne Convention, obtaining multinational patent protection is anything but automatic or inexpensive.

Consequently, the title of this chapter, which refers to "international patenting," is something of a misnomer. Currently there is no such thing as an international patent, at least in any form other than academic proposals. There are, however, a number of international treaties, conventions, and agreements that make it much easier today than in the past to obtain patent protection in multiple countries. Understanding the historical background and economic context in which these various agreements were enacted is necessary to understanding the present system of multinational patenting.

[2]The negative property right conveyed by a U.S. patent grant is statutorily limited to prohibiting acts of infringement that occur within the United States. *See* 35 U.S.C. §154(a) (2008) (providing that U.S. patent conveys "the right to exclude others from making, using, offering for sale, or selling the invention *throughout the United States* or importing the invention *into the United States*, and, if the invention is a process, of the right to exclude others from using, offering for sale or selling *throughout the United States*, or importing *into the United States*, products made by that process") (emphases added). For scholarly analysis of territoriality in intellectual property law, *see* Curtis A. Bradley, *Territorial Intellectual Property Rights in an Age of Globalism*, 37 VA. J. INT'L L. 505 (1997).

Given the rise of global commerce and the increasingly complicated and expensive nature of enforcing patent rights to a given invention on a worldwide basis, some scholars have called for a reevaluation of U.S. patent law's traditional territorial view. *See, e.g.*, Timothy R. Holbrook, *Extraterritoriality in U.S. Patent Law*, 49 WM. & MARY L. REV. 2119 (2008) (advocating that U.S. courts consider enforcing U.S. patents extraterritorially if an explicit analysis of a relevant foreign jurisdiction's patent laws indicates that infringement has occurred there and that extraterritorial enforcement of the U.S. patent would not conflict with the foreign jurisdiction's laws).

[3]*See* Microsoft Corp. v. AT&T Corp., 550 U.S. 437, 441 (2007) ("It is the general rule under United States patent law that no infringement occurs when a patented product is made and sold in another country."). Section 271(f) of Title 35, U.S.C., which prohibits the export for assembly abroad of components of an invention patented in the U.S., is an exception to the general rule. *See id.*; *supra* Chapter 9.E.4 ("Component Exports Under 35 U.S.C. §271(f)").

[4]Alternatively, if the patent holder is already litigating infringement of her U.S. patent in a U.S. court, she may request that the U.S. court exercise supplemental jurisdiction under 28 U.S.C. §1367 to adjudicate her claim of infringement of a counterpart Japanese patent. The Federal Circuit has thus far rejected such attempts, however. *See* Section G ("Enforcement of Foreign Patents in U.S. Courts"), *infra*.

2. Obtaining Foreign Patent Protection Prior to the Paris Convention

The Paris Convention for the Protection of Industrial Property (Paris Convention),[5] which entered into force in 1883, was the first truly international agreement concerning industrial property (i.e., patents, trademarks, and industrial designs). The Paris Convention created important rights for nationals[6] of member countries that made it much easier for those persons to obtain patents in multiple countries. The complexities of multinational patenting prior to the Paris Convention's enactment demonstrate why this treaty was such an important advance.

Before the Paris Convention, it was extremely difficult and expensive to obtain patent protection for the same invention in different countries. Some countries (e.g., Country A) considered an application filed on the same invention in another country (e.g., Country B) *even one day* before the filing of the application in Country A to be prior art that would destroy the novelty of the invention under the patent law of Country A. Thus, patent applicants had to arrange to file multiple applications on the same invention in multiple countries *on the same day*. The cost and complexity of accomplishing this, particularly before the invention of the telephone, fax machine, and Internet, are self-evident.

Prior to enactment of the Paris Convention, the various national patent systems differed in some very fundamental aspects of substantive patent law. For example, the United States did not substantively examine patent applications for novelty between 1793 and 1836. France did not do so until the 1960s. Italy, for a time, examined only those patent applications that were related to foods and beverages. Many of the world's developing and least-developed countries refused to grant patents altogether on pharmaceuticals or agricultural inventions.[7]

[5]Paris Convention for the Protection of Industrial Property, Mar. 20, 1883, as revised at Stockholm, July 14, 1967, 21 U.S.T. 1583, 828 U.N.T.S. 305, *available at* http://www.wipo.int/treaties/en/ip/paris (as amended Sept. 28, 1979).

[6]In international law terms, a "national" of a country is generally considered to be a natural or legal person who is domiciled or who has a commercial establishment in the country in question (generally referred to as a "state" in international law). Nationality is broader than and should be distinguished from citizenship. "A citizen under national law is generally a national for purposes of international law, but in some states not all nationals are citizens." RESTATEMENT (THIRD) OF THE FOREIGN RELATIONS LAW OF THE UNITED STATES §211, cmt. h (1987).

[7]*See, e.g.*, Janice M. Mueller, *The Tiger Awakens: The Tumultuous Transformation of India's Patent System and the Rise of Indian Pharmaceutical Innovation*, 68 U. PITT. L. REV. 491 (2007).

Procedures for prosecuting patents also varied widely between countries. Patent applications were published at varying times. Some countries published patent specifications immediately upon the filing of an application, others during the application's pendency, and some countries (such as the United States) did not publish the content of patent applications at all prior to the patent grant.[8]

By the late 1800s, national governments and economists determined that these differences between national patent systems could be used as tools to manipulate national wealth. More specifically, they realized that granting patents to foreign nationals generally results in a net outflow of national wealth.[9]

To understand why this is so, consider the example of a U.S. national who obtains a U.S. patent on her invention, a useful, novel, and nonobvious widget. The price of the widget that the U.S. national can obtain in the marketplace will reflect the fact that the widget is covered by patent, which price we would expect to be higher than if the widget were not patented and could be made and sold by multiple competing parties.[10] In this domestic patenting scenario, the link between the costs and benefits of the government's decision to grant patent rights to its own national is relatively tight. Presumably the sales revenues received by the U.S. national will be reinvested domestically, to fund the construction of additional widget factories in the United States or to further U.S.-based research and development in widgets. This business expansion will likely employ other U.S. nationals.

In contrast, when a country makes the decision to grant a patent to a foreign national, the link between cost and benefits is significantly weakened or decoupled. For example, consider a national of Germany who obtains a U.S. patent on her widget. The royalties obtained by the German national from the U.S. sales of her widget will generally be invested not in the U.S. economy but rather in the economy of Germany, the foreign national's home country. Thus, the domestic economy of the granting country generally does not benefit from awarding patent rights to foreign nationals to the same degree that it would have, had patent rights been granted to a national of the granting country.[11]

[8]Historically, the United States did not publish the contents of pending patent applications prior to the patent grant. With the enactment of the American Inventors Protection Act of 1999, however, the majority of patent applications are made public at 18 months after the application's earliest priority date. *See* 35 U.S.C. §122(b).

[9]Much of this section is based on the observations in R. Carl Moy, *The History of the Patent Harmonization Treaty: Economic Self-Interest as an Influence*, 26 J. MARSHALL L. REV. 457 (1993).

[10]*See supra* Chapter 1 ("Foundations of the U.S. Patent System") for a general discussion of the economics of patenting.

[11]Of course, the granting country gains some minor economic benefits in the form of the filing and maintenance fees paid to its national patent office and any taxes levied by the granting country on sales of the patented product made in that country.

As national governments realized the economic impact of granting patent protection to foreigners, they began to implement in their laws various protectionist measures that were intended to reduce these costs. Such measures made patenting by foreigners less attractive by decreasing the value of the patents obtained and thus reducing the outflow of national wealth. These measures discriminated against foreign nationals, either expressly or, in some cases, in application even though the provisions were facially neutral.

A pre-America Invents Act of 2011 (AIA) provision of the Patent Act, 35 U.S.C. §104 (2006), is an example of a law that, at least initially, discriminated widely against foreign inventors. Prior to its amendments in connection with U.S. participation in the World Trade Organization (WTO) and the North American Free Trade Agreement (NAFTA), §104 prohibited the admission of evidence into USPTO interference proceedings[12] (and *ex parte* prior art antedating procedures) of inventive activity (such as conception, diligence, reduction to practice) that took place in any foreign country. Under this earlier version of 35 U.S.C. §104, even if a foreign inventor made an invention in her home country before a U.S. inventor independently made the same invention in the United States, the foreign inventor would not be allowed to rely on her earlier home country activity in order to prevail in an interference with the U.S. inventor. As a result, the U.S. inventor would be awarded the patent on the invention, even though the U.S. inventor was not the first to invent on a worldwide basis.[13]

Examples of facially neutral measures that were discriminatory in application included "working requirements." A working requirement mandates that a patentee "work" (or practice) the patent in the granting country; that is, the patentee is obligated to manufacture and/or sell the patented invention in the granting country. While the United

[12]As explained in further detail *supra* Chapter 4 ("Novelty, Loss of Right, and Priority Pre- and Post-America Invents Act of 2011 (35 U.S.C. §102)"), interferences are pre-AIA *inter partes* administrative proceedings conducted in the USPTO to determine which of two or more rival claimants was the first to invent a particular claimed invention. The AIA eliminated interference proceedings effective March 16, 2013.

[13]Section 104 of the U.S. Patent Act was amended as a consequence of the U.S. signing of the North American Free Trade Agreement with Mexico and Canada, and the TRIPS Agreement of the World Trade Organization. In accordance with these amendments, inventive activity that occurred on or after December 8, 1993, in the NAFTA countries of Canada and Mexico, or inventive activity that occurred on or after January 1, 1996, in any WTO member country (other than the United States, Canada, and Mexico), was admissible in a U.S. interference proceeding, or in antedating prior art in *ex parte* prosecution, just as if the activity had occurred in the United States. *See* 35 U.S.C. §104 (2006); 37 C.F.R. §1.131 (2008); UNITED STATES PATENT AND TRADEMARK OFFICE, MANUAL OF PATENT EXAMINING PROCEDURE §715.07(c) (9th ed., Nov. 2015) ("Acts Relied upon Must Have Been Carried Out in This Country or a NAFTA or WTO Member Country"); *supra* Chapter 4, Section N ("Prior Invention Under 35 U.S.C. §102(g) (Pre-AIA)").

States has never implemented working requirements, many other countries have.[14] Although such a requirement would be facially neutral because of its applicability to both foreign applicants and nationals of the granting country, the practical reality was that it was much more difficult for a foreign entity to obtain the funding and regulatory permits necessary to set up factories for manufacture of an invention in the granting country than it would be for a domestic entity to do so.

B. The Paris Convention

1. Introduction

The Paris Convention is the oldest body of multinational industrial property[15] law with the widest membership. The Paris Convention first came into force in 1883, and the United States has been a signatory to the Paris Convention since 1903. The Convention has been modified through various revisions; the current version is that which was revised in Stockholm in 1967.[16] The World Intellectual Property Organization (WIPO) in Geneva, a specialized agency of the United Nations, administers the Paris Convention. As of 2019, 177 countries are signatories to the Paris Convention.[17]

[14]For example, the U.S. government in 2001 requested that WTO dispute resolution proceedings be initiated against the government of Brazil, on the ground that Brazil's patent laws violated the TRIPS Agreement by requiring local working of Brazilian patents. Specifically, the United States contended that "Article 68 of Brazil's 1996 industrial property law (Law No. 9,279 of 14 May 1996; effective May 1997), . . . imposes a 'local working' requirement which stipulates that a patent shall be subject to compulsory licensing if the subject matter of the patent is not 'worked' in the territory of Brazil. Specifically, a compulsory license shall be granted on a patent if the patented product is not manufactured in Brazil or if the patented process is not used in Brazil." *Request for the Establishment of a Panel by the United States, Brazil — Measures Affecting Patent Protection*, WT/DS199/3 (Jan. 9, 2001), *available at* http://docsonline.wto.org. The United States and Brazil later reached agreement on the dispute. *See Notification of Mutually Agreed Solution, Brazil — Measures Affecting Patent Protection*, WT/DS199/4 (July 19, 2001), *available at* http://docsonline.wto.org.

[15]Although the United States refers to "intellectual property" as encompassing the subject matter protected by patent law, trademark law, and copyright law, many foreign jurisdictions prefer the use of the phrase "industrial property" when speaking of the subject matter of patents, trademarks, and industrial designs, and "copyright" when referring to copyrightable subject matter.

[16]*See* Paris Convention for the Protection of Industrial Property, Mar. 20, 1883, as revised at Stockholm, July 14, 1967, 21 U.S.T. 1583, 828 U.N.T.S. 305, *available at* wipolex.wipo.int.

[17]*See* World Intellectual Property Organization, *Contracting Parties > Paris Convention*, https://www.wipo.int/treaties/en/ShowResults.jsp?lang=en&treaty_id=2.

The Paris Convention is the basic international agreement dealing with the treatment of foreigners under national patent laws. It addressed some, but not all, of the obstacles to international patenting discussed above. For example, the Paris Convention did not set up any "substantive minima" for industrial property protection, meaning that it was silent as to the technical criteria for patentability or the types of subject matter for which patents should be available. In fact, a country could be a signatory to the Paris Convention while not granting patents at all; Switzerland and the Netherlands did not have patent systems in the latter part of the nineteenth century, although both countries were signatories to the Paris Convention.[18]

The Paris Convention was fairly silent on the propriety of protectionist measures. For example, the original version of the Paris Convention specifically allowed the continued existence of national working requirements and said nothing at all about **compulsory licensing**. Later versions of the Paris Convention contain only very limited restrictions on the ability of a signatory country to grant compulsory licenses.[19]

Despite the absence of substantive minima and its few limitations on protectionist measures, the Paris Convention did establish two key rights that made it much easier to obtain patent protection in foreign countries than had previously been the case. These rights, which have become cornerstones of all subsequent international patent agreements, are the principles of **national treatment** and the **right of priority**.

2. National Treatment

The national treatment provision is found in Article 2 of the Paris Convention.[20] National treatment simply means that each signatory

[18]*See* ERIC SCHIFF, INDUSTRIALIZATION WITHOUT NATIONAL PATENTS (Princeton 1971). Switzerland and the Netherlands became parties to the Paris Convention in 1884. *See* World Intellectual Property Organization, *Contracting Parties > Paris Convention*, https://www.wipo.int/treaties/en/ShowResults.jsp?lang=en&treaty_id=2.

[19]*See* Paris Convention art. 5(A).

[20]Article 2, "National Treatment for Nationals of Countries of the Union," provides in part that

> (1) Nationals of any country of the [Paris] Union shall, as regards the protection of industrial property, enjoy in all other countries of the Union the advantages that their respective laws now grant, or may hereafter grant, to nationals; all without prejudice to the rights specially provided for by this Convention. Consequently, they shall have the same protection as the latter, and the same legal remedy against any infringement of their rights, provided that the conditions and formalities imposed upon nationals are complied with. . . .

Paris Convention art. 2(1).

country to the Paris Convention must treat foreigners seeking industrial property protection in that country as well as (or, optionally, better than) it treats its own nationals. For example, the national treatment principle prevents the United States from charging U.S. nationals a patent application filing fee of $500 while demanding a filing fee of $1,000 from nationals of other countries. The foreign nationals must be charged the same filing fee of $500 (or, optionally, a lower fee).

The drafters of the Paris Convention chose national treatment over the competing principle of "reciprocity." In a system governed by reciprocity principles, Country A treats foreign nationals of Country B in the same manner as Country B treats the nationals of Country A, regardless of how Country A treats its own nationals (or how it treats the nationals of Country C). For example, if Country B charges nationals of Country A a patent application filing fee of $1,000, then under a reciprocity system Country A will charge the nationals of Country B a patent application filing fee of $1,000 (regardless of whether Country A charges its own nationals only $500 or charges the nationals of Country C a filing fee of $2,000). Implementing a reciprocity-based system imposes significant administrative costs and burdens, because Country A must become intimately familiar with the patent laws and procedures of every other country and vice versa. These heightened burdens led the drafters of the Paris Convention to reject the principle of reciprocity in favor of national treatment.

3. Right of Priority

The other key right established by the Paris Convention is the right of priority, found in Article 4 of the convention.[21] This right greatly

[21]Article 4 of the Paris Convention provides in part:

> A. (1) Any person who has duly filed an application for a patent, or for the registration of a utility model, or of an industrial design, or of a trademark, in one of the countries of the Union, or his successor in title, shall enjoy, for the purpose of filing in the other countries, a right of priority during the periods hereinafter fixed.
>
> (2) Any filing that is equivalent to a regular national filing under the domestic legislation of any country of the Union or under bilateral or multilateral treaties concluded between countries of the Union shall be recognized as giving rise to the right of priority.
>
> (3) By a regular national filing is meant any filing that is adequate to establish the date on which the application was filed in the country concerned, whatever may be the subsequent fate of the application.
>
> B. Consequently, any subsequent filing in any of the other countries of the Union before the expiration of the periods referred to above shall not be

simplifies the process of obtaining industrial property protection in multiple signatory countries. By filing a patent application on an invention in a single Paris member country (typically in the inventor's home country, because it is the most convenient), an inventor can obtain the benefit of that same initial filing date (referred to as her *priority date*) in any other Paris Convention signatory countries in which she files additional patent applications on the same invention within the period of time called the *priority period.* For patents, the relevant priority period is 12 months, starting from the date of filing of the first application.[22]

For example, consider an inventor named Mayumi, a Japanese national, who filed a patent application on her invention X in Japan (a signatory to the Paris Convention) on January 1, 2002. On December 15, 2002, Mayumi filed an application for the same invention X in the USPTO. Assume that the Japanese application adequately supports the invention that Mayumi is claiming in her U.S. application in accordance with 35 U.S.C. §112, ¶1 (2000), and that Mayumi makes a formal claim for the benefit of her foreign priority date under 35 U.S.C. §119 (the U.S. implementation of the Paris Convention right of priority, discussed further below). If these criteria are satisfied, the USPTO examiner will treat the U.S. application as if it had been filed on January 1, 2002, for purposes of examining it against the prior art for novelty and nonobviousness. In practical terms this means that the U.S. application will "relate back" to the Japanese filing date; the USPTO will ignore any intervening, potentially patentability-destroying developments that occurred between January 1 and December 15 of 2002. Such developments could include, for example, the publication of a description of the same invention or the filing of another U.S. patent application on the same invention, whether these events were triggered by Mayumi or a third party.

The foreign priority right means that such intervening events are not considered prior art against Mayumi's U.S. application. More specifically, and under pre-AIA rules, Mayumi's January 1, 2002 Japanese filing date would be treated by the USPTO as Mayumi's presumptive invention date in the United States for purposes of applying the novelty provisions of 35 U.S.C. §102 (2000)

---

invalidated by reason of any acts accomplished in the interval, in particular, another filing, the publication or exploitation of the invention, the putting on sale of copies of the design, or the use of the mark, and such acts cannot give rise to any third-party right or any right of personal possession. Rights acquired by third parties before the date of the first application that serves as the basis for the right of priority are reserved in accordance with the domestic legislation of each country of the Union.

Paris Convention art. 4.

[22] *See* Paris Convention arts. 4.C(1), 4.C(2).

(i.e., §102(a), (e), and (g))[23] and 35 U.S.C. §103 (2000) (nonobviousness). Figure 12.1 illustrates this practice.

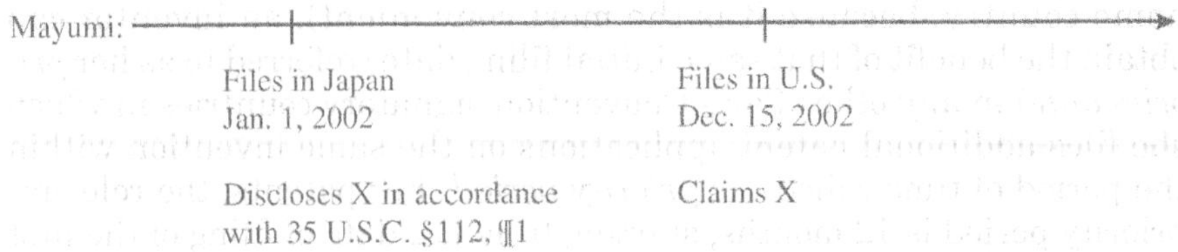

Figure 12.1
Paris Convention Priority Right

Following implementation of the AIA's first-inventor-to-file system on March 16, 2013,[24] the foreign priority date is treated as the U.S. application's "effective filing date," assuming all requirements for attaining the foreign priority right are satisfied.[25]

[23]Prior to the AIA, foreign priority under 35 U.S.C. §119 could not be relied on to overcome a loss of right under 35 U.S.C. §102(b) (2000). Thus, in the above example in the text, if Mayumi had placed her invention "on sale" in the United States within the meaning of §102(b) (2000) by making U.S. sales of the invention for commercial purposes beginning in July 2001, then claiming the benefit of her earlier Japanese filing date for her U.S. application filed more than one year after those sales would be of no use. The on sale bar of §102(b) (2000) was considered absolute in the sense that it could not be overcome by relying on foreign priority. *See* 35 U.S.C. §119(a) (2000) ("[B]ut no patent shall be granted on any application for patent for an invention which had been patented or described in a printed publication in any country more than one year before the date of the actual filing of the application in this country, or which had been in public use or on sale in this country more than one year prior to such filing.").

The AIA deleted any reference to pre-AIA statutory bars from §119(a). *See* Leahy-Smith America Invents Act, Pub. L. No. 112-29 (H.R. 1249), §3(g)(6),125 Stat. 284, 288 (Sept. 16, 2011); 35 U.S.C. §119(a) (eff. Mar. 16, 2013).

[24]The AIA-implemented first-inventor-to-file priority system is discussed *infra* Section E.1 ("First-to-File Versus First-to-Invent"); *see also supra* Chapter 4, Section R ("Presumptively Novelty-Destroying Events Under Post-AIA 35 U.S.C. §102(a)(2) (First-Inventor-to-File Rule)").

[25]Foreign priority operates in the same manner post-AIA. Assume, for example, that Mayumi files her Japanese priority application on January 1, 2014, and files her U.S. application for the same invention X on December 15, 2014. So long as the requisite formalities are complied with and the disclosure in Mayumi's Japanese application satisfies 35 U.S.C. §112(a) (eff. Sept. 16, 2012) with respect to the claims of her U.S. application, Mayumi's Japanese filing date will be treated as the effective filing date of the claims in her U.S. application under 35 U.S.C. §100(i)(B) (eff. Mar. 16, 2013) for purposes of examination for novelty under 35 U.S.C. §102 (eff. Mar. 16, 2013) and nonobviousness under 35 U.S.C. §103 (eff. Mar. 16, 2013). *See also* 35 U.S.C. §100(i)(B) (eff. Mar. 16, 2013) (defining "effective filing date" for a claimed invention in a patent or patent application to include "the filing date of the earliest application for which the patent or application is entitled, as to such invention, to a *right of priority under section 119*, 365(a), or 365(b) or to the benefit of an earlier filing date under section 120,

Thankfully, claiming the benefit of one's Paris Convention priority date does not reduce the term of protection by the length of the priority period.[26] In the above example, Mayumi's U.S. patent would expire 20 years from its earliest effective U.S. filing date, not any earlier foreign priority date. Thus, the U.S. patent would expire on December 15, 2022. Claiming entitlement to the benefit of a Paris Convention foreign priority date is an exclusively positive benefit. Mayumi benefits from being able to avoid any potentially patentability-destroying activity that occurred during the priority period (i.e., events that took place between January 1, 2002, and December 15, 2002), while not facing the start of the 20-year patent term clock until her actual U.S. filing date of December 15, 2002.

The ultimate fate of Mayumi's Japanese application is not relevant to the status of her U.S. application. The Japanese application need not issue as a Japanese patent in order for Mayumi to claim the benefit of its filing date for her U.S. application. All that the Paris Convention requires is that the priority application be "[a]ny filing that is equivalent to a regular national filing under the domestic legislation of any country of the Union or under bilateral or multilateral treaties concluded between countries of the Union. . . ."[27] The convention defines a "regular national filing" as "any filing that is adequate to establish the date on which the application was filed in the country concerned, whatever may be the subsequent fate of the application."[28]

4. U.S. Implementation of the Paris Right of Priority: 35 U.S.C. §119

Section 119(a)-(d) of the U.S. Patent Act is the domestic implementation of the Paris Convention right of priority in patent cases. These provisions of 35 U.S.C. §119 were added to our patent law by virtue

121, or 365(c)") (emphasis added). The "right of priority under section 119" includes foreign priority under §119(a).

[26]*See* Paris Convention art. 4*bis*(5) (providing that "[p]atents obtained with the benefit of priority shall, in the various countries of the Union, have a duration equal to that which they would have, had they been applied for or granted without the benefit of priority").

[27]Paris Convention art. 4.A(2).

[28]Paris Convention art. 4.A(3). The USPTO considers a U.S. provisional patent application filed under 35 U.S.C. §111(b) to be a regular national filing under the Paris Convention, such that "an applicant has 12 months from the filing date of a provisional application to file an application abroad or under the PCT to preserve the right to priority under the Paris Convention based on the filing date of the provisional application." Charles E. VanHorn, *Effects of GATT and NAFTA on PTO Practice*, 77 J. PAT. & TRADEMARK OFF. SOC'Y 231, 238 (1995).

of the 1952 Act, but similar provisions existed in predecessor statutes since 1903.[29]

Section 119 provides in pertinent part that

> (a) An application for patent for an invention filed in this country by any person who has, or whose legal representatives or assigns have, previously regularly filed an application for a patent for the same invention in a foreign country which affords similar privileges in the case of applications filed in the United States or to citizens of the United States, or in a WTO member country, shall have the same effect as the same application would have if filed in this country on the date on which the application for patent for the same invention was first filed in such foreign country, if the application in this country is filed within twelve months from the earliest date on which such foreign application was filed.[30]

This rather complex statutory language can be mastered by understanding a few basic points. Section 119(a) confers an important benefit to U.S. patent applicants who have previously filed a patent application on the same invention in another country. In sum, 35 U.S.C. §119(a) means that if an applicant first files a patent application in a foreign country that is a WTO member or conveys similar privileges to the United States (i.e., in any Paris Convention signatory country or in any of the other countries with which the United States has established bilateral treaties on this point), and then files a second patent application "for the same invention"[31] in the United States within 12 months of the foreign filing date, then the applicant can claim for that U.S. application the benefit of the earlier foreign filing date (foreign priority date).

[29]*See* In re Hilmer, 359 F.2d 859, 872-876 (C.C.P.A. 1966) (Rich, J.) (describing history and purpose of §119).

[30]35 U.S.C. §119(a) (eff. Mar. 16, 2013). The AIA deleted the last clause of 35 U.S.C. §119(a) (2006), which had prohibited reliance on foreign priority to overcome statutory bars by including the proviso "but no patent shall be granted on any application for patent for an invention which had been patented or described in a printed publication in any country more than one year before the date of the actual filing of the application in this country, or which had been in public use or on sale in this country more than one year prior to such filing." *See* Leahy-Smith America Invents Act, Pub. L. No. 112-29 (H.R. 1249), §3(g)(6),125 Stat. 284, 288 (Sept. 16, 2011).

[31]Federal Circuit case law has interpreted the meaning of "same invention" as used in §119. The claims set forth in a U.S. patent application are entitled to the benefit of a foreign priority date under §119 to the extent that the corresponding foreign application supports the claims in the manner required by the first paragraph of 35 U.S.C. §112. *See* In re Gosteli, 872 F.2d 1008, 1010 (Fed. Cir. 1989), discussed in the text. Post-AIA, this most likely means that the foreign application must provide an enabling disclosure of the invention as claimed in the U.S. application as well as a written description of that invention. Under pre-AIA rules, the foreign application arguably had to also reveal the best mode of the invention.

Obtaining this benefit means that, in the words of the statute, the U.S. application "shall have the same effect" as the same application would have if actually filed in the United States on the foreign filing date. In practice, this means that the USPTO will treat the application as if filed on the foreign priority date for purposes of examining it against the prior art. In other words, the foreign filing date will be taken as the "effective filing date" for purposes of examination for novelty and nonobviousness under post-AIA 35 U.S.C. §102 and 35 U.S.C. §103.[32] Events occurring in the time between the foreign priority date and the U.S. filing date that might otherwise anticipate the claimed invention or render it obvious will not "count" against the application, as explained above.

Although we assumed in the example of the previous section that Mayumi's U.S. application was for the "same invention" as that disclosed in her Japanese application, this is not always the case. Often, an inventor will make improvements over time and claim her invention more broadly in a later-filed application. The Federal Circuit case law has faced this scenario in interpreting the meaning of the phrase *same invention* as used in 35 U.S.C. §119(a). Claims set forth in a U.S. patent application are entitled to the benefit of a foreign priority date under §119(a) to the extent that the disclosure of the corresponding foreign application supports the claims in the manner required by §112, ¶1.[33] This means that the foreign application must provide an **enabling** disclosure of the invention as claimed in the U.S. application and include a **written description of the invention**. In pre-AIA situations, the foreign priority application arguably has to also reveal the **best mode** of carrying out the invention (assuming that a best mode existed).

These requirements were not satisfied in *In re Gosteli*,[34] where the applicant Gosteli first filed a patent application in Luxembourg that disclosed certain species of chemical compounds having antibiotic properties. Within one year, he filed an application in the United States with broader claims to a genus of compounds that encompassed the original species plus other species. In ruling on his priority claim, the USPTO had to determine whether Gosteli's U.S. application claimed the same invention as that disclosed in his earlier Luxembourg application.

On appeal, the Federal Circuit agreed with the agency that it did not. Gosteli was unable to obtain the benefit of his Luxembourg filing

[32]*See* 35 U.S.C. §100(i)(B) (eff. Mar. 16, 2013) (effective filing date may be based on "a right of priority under section 119"); 35 U.S.C. §102 (eff. Mar. 16, 2013) (novelty); 35 U.S.C. §103 (eff. Mar. 16, 2013) (nonobviousness).

[33]*See Gosteli*, 872 F.2d at 1010 (citing In re Wertheim, 541 F.2d 257, 261-262 (C.C.P.A. 1976)).

[34]872 F.2d 1008 (Fed. Cir. 1989).

date for the genus claims of his U.S. application because the Luxembourg application did not provide a sufficient written description of the invention as claimed generically in the U.S. application. The content of the Luxembourg application did not demonstrate that Gosteli was in possession of the generically claimed invention as of his Luxembourg filing date. Thus, the genus claims of Gosteli's U.S. application would be entitled only to their actual U.S. filing date. Because there was an anticipatory prior art reference (i.e., a 35 U.S.C. §102(e) (1988) reference having an effective date after Gosteli's Luxembourg filing date but before his U.S. filing date), Gosteli's U.S. claims were not allowable.

5. The *Hilmer* Rule (Pre-America Invents Act of 2011)

The rule of *In re Hilmer*[35] ("*Hilmer I*") is a controversial aspect of pre-AIA U.S. patent practice that concerns the effective date of U.S. patents relied on as prior art references. For reasons explained below, the rule was routinely criticized as discriminating against foreign inventors. The America Invents Act of 2011 prospectively repealed the *Hilmer* rule,[36] but it still holds for patents being applied as prior art against claimed inventions in applications and patents having effective dates prior to the AIA's March 16, 2013, first-to-file implementation. Hence, understanding the *Hilmer* rule will remain important for many years to come.

In a nutshell, the *Hilmer* rule states that when a U.S. patent (or published application) is being relied on as a prior art reference under 35 U.S.C. §102(e) (pre-AIA), its effective date is its U.S. filing date, *not* any earlier foreign priority date the benefit of which was claimed in the process of obtaining the reference patent. *Hilmer* requires that

[35] 359 F.2d 859 (C.C.P.A. 1966) (Rich, J.) [hereinafter *Hilmer I*].
[36] *See* 35 U.S.C. §102(d) (eff. March 16, 2013), which provides (emphasis added):

> (d) PATENTS AND PUBLISHED APPLICATIONS EFFECTIVE AS PRIOR ART. — For purposes of determining whether a patent or application for patent is prior art to a claimed invention under subsection (a)(2), such patent or application shall be considered to have been effectively filed, with respect to any subject matter described in the patent or application —
>
> (1) if paragraph (2) does not apply, as of the actual filing date of the patent or the application for patent; or
>
> (2) *if the patent or application for patent is entitled to claim a right of priority under section 119*, 365(a), or 365(b), or to claim the benefit of an earlier filing date under section 120, 121, or 365(c), based upon 1 or more prior filed applications for patent, *as of the filing date of the earliest such application that describes the subject matter.*

Subparagraph (d)(2) repeals the *Hilmer* rule implicitly by including foreign priority under 35 U.S.C. §119 in its scope.

we distinguish between patent-obtaining and patent-defeating uses of foreign priority under 35 U.S.C. §119(a), the United States' implementation of the Paris Convention right of priority. Only patent-*obtaining* uses of foreign priority are permitted under the *Hilmer* rule, not patent-*defeating* uses.

The facts of *Hilmer* are illustrative. Two foreign inventors, Hilmer (a German national) and Habicht (a Swiss national), sought a U.S. patent on the same invention. Habicht won an interference against Hilmer; thereafter, Hilmer reentered *ex parte* prosecution claiming a variant of the lost count of the interference. The disclosure of Habicht's patent was cited as a §102(e) reference against Hilmer's application claims, in combination with another prior art reference (Wagner), to form a §103 rejection for obviousness.[37] The timeline in Figure 12.2 depicts the pertinent dates.

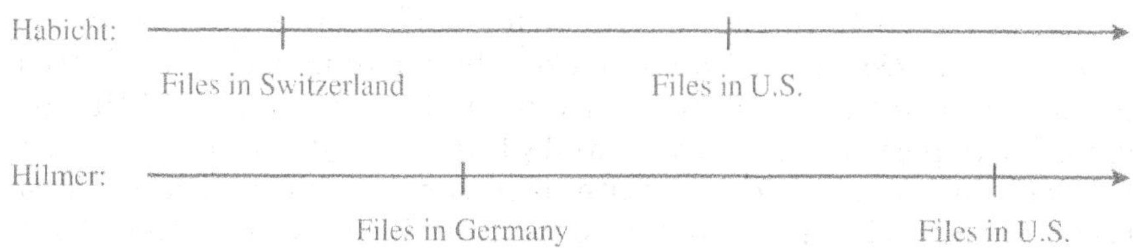

Figure 12.2

Timeline for *In re Hilmer*

Hilmer was able to overcome Habicht's earlier U.S. filing date by claiming the benefit of Hilmer's German priority date in accordance with 35 U.S.C. §119(a). This was a *patent-obtaining* use of foreign priority by Hilmer. The USPTO took the position that Habicht was nevertheless §102(e)/§103 prior art to Hilmer, by virtue of Habicht's earlier Swiss priority date. This was an attempted *patent-defeating* use of foreign priority by the USPTO. The agency argued that the "shall have the same effect" language of 35 U.S.C. §119(a) should be read broadly

[37]Recall that a 35 U.S.C. §102(e) (pre-AIA) rejection relies on subject matter that is *described but not claimed* by the reference patentee. If the reference patent *claims* the same invention as the applicant, an interference may be declared under §102(g) (pre-AIA). In this case, an interference had previously been declared between certain interfering *claims* of Habicht and Hilmer. Habicht prevailed because Hilmer conceded priority to Habicht of the subject matter of what became the interference "count." *See Hilmer*, 359 F.2d at 861. The invention for which Hilmer later sought a patent in *In re Hilmer* was not the same invention as the subject matter of the earlier interference, but rather a variant thereof. *See Hilmer*, 359 F.2d at 862 (quoting Board's statement distinguishing interfering subject matter from Hilmer's appealed application claims 10, 16, and 17, directed to a cyclohexyl substituted compound).

as having the "same effect" for all purposes, including that of modifying the "in this country" language of 35 U.S.C. §102(e).

The Court of Customs and Patent Appeals (CCPA), one of the Federal Circuit's two predecessor courts, reversed. The effective date of Habicht's disclosure when used as a §102(e) reference in this fashion was Habicht's U.S. filing date, *not* his earlier Swiss filing date. The court read the "filed in the United States" language of 35 U.S.C. §102(e) literally,[38] and refused to impute the patent-obtaining concept of §119(a) into the patent-defeating provision, §102(e). Thus, the *Hilmer* decision means that foreign priority can be used only to affirmatively obtain a patent (in *ex parte* prosecution or an interference), and not for patent-defeating purposes such as dedication of technology to the public through disclosing without claiming it.

The CCPA posited several rationales for the rule it announced in *Hilmer*, but the most compelling was the court's public policy–based refusal to exacerbate the "secret prior art" problem of *Alexander Milburn Co. v. Davis-Bournonville Co.*[39] by pushing back the effective date of a 35 U.S.C. §102(e) reference by up to another year of the foreign priority period. The court viewed §119(a) foreign priority as a benefit, not a burden. It is only a patent-preserving device, while the 35 U.S.C. §102 provisions are patent-defeating. In the view of the CCPA, these statutory provisions were enacted at different times, for very different purposes.

The practical result of the *Hilmer* decision was that Habicht's U.S. patent was rendered considerably less valuable than it might have otherwise been because Hilmer was allowed to obtain his own U.S. patent on an arguably obvious variant of that which Habicht had already patented. Habicht had attempted to dedicate the variant to the public, and thereby prevent others from patenting it, by means of disclosing it in his patent application; under the rule of *Hilmer*, however, Habicht (and the USPTO in its examination of Hilmer's application) were not permitted to rely on Habicht's disclosure in this fashion.[40]

[38]At that time, 35 U.S.C. §102(e) provided that a person would be entitled to a patent unless "the invention was described in a patent granted on an application for patent by another filed in the United States before the invention thereof by the applicant for patent. . . ." *Hilmer*, 359 F.2d at 864.

[39]270 U.S. 390 (1926). The *Milburn* rule, codified as 35 U.S.C. §102(e), is discussed in further detail *supra* Chapter 4 ("Novelty, Loss of Right, and Priority Pre- and Post-America Invents Act of 2011 (35 U.S.C. §102)"), Section L ("Description in Another's Earlier-Filed Patent or Published Patent Application Under 35 U.S.C. §102(e) (Pre-AIA)").

[40]In a subsequent decision involving the same application, *In re Hilmer*, 424 F.2d 1108 (C.C.P.A. 1970) ("*Hilmer II*"), the court reaffirmed the reasoning of *Hilmer I*, holding that the "shall have the same effect" language of §119 was not intended to modify the "in this country" language of §102(g). The court held that the USPTO cannot treat the foreign filing date of a U.S. patent, when used as a prior art reference, as evidence

The *Hilmer* rule was frequently criticized as protectionist and discriminatory against foreigners because the foreign patentee (e.g., Habicht) is prevented from using his disclosure (as of its foreign priority date) in a defensive manner.[41] Some experts questioned whether the United States' continued adherence to the *Hilmer* rule was consistent with its national treatment obligations under the Paris Convention and the TRIPS Agreement.[42] In the pre-AIA context, however, the *Hilmer* rule remains the law in the United States.

6. Limitations of the Paris Convention

The primary criticisms of the Paris Convention are (1) that it lacks any substantive minima for patentability, and (2) that it provides no meaningful enforcement mechanism by which to challenge the failure of signatory countries to comply with the standards that are contained in the Convention.[43] By the late 1980s, growing dissatisfaction of Western countries with the WIPO's inability to enforce patent and other intellectual property rights led a number of countries

of a constructive reduction to practice on that date, and thereby convert that foreign filing into a §102(g) event (i.e., the making of the invention in this country by another) to be relied on in a §103 rejection.

[41]To see more clearly the discriminatory effect of the *Hilmer* rule, imagine Hilmer as a U.S. national who first filed in Germany, then (within 12 months) filed in the USPTO. Hilmer (hypothetically the U.S. inventor) is entitled to rely on his German priority date under §119(a) in order to overcome Habicht's U.S. filing date and thereby remove Habicht as §102(e) prior art, but the disclosure in Habicht's Swiss priority application (filed before Hilmer's German priority date) is not recognized as prior art that the USPTO can cite in a §102(e)/§103 rejection against Hilmer's claims.

[42]*See, e.g.*, Heinz Bardehle, *A New Approach to Worldwide Harmonization of Patent Law*, 81 J. PAT. & TRADEMARK OFF. SOC'Y 303, 310 (1999) (suggesting that *Hilmer* rule should be challenged under TRIPS); Harold C. Wegner, *TRIPS Boomerang: Obligations for Domestic Reform*, 29 VAND. J. TRANSNAT'L L. 535, 556 (1996) (stating that "in international circles, the second target after first-to-file has been the elimination of the notorious *Hilmer I* decision, which unfairly denies foreign patentee's their patent-defeating right guaranteed by the Paris Convention"). *See also* TRIPS art. 27.1 (stating that "patents shall be available and *patent rights enjoyable* without discrimination as to the place of invention . . .") (emphasis added). The *Hilmer* rule may not explicitly violate national treatment obligations because the rule applies to U.S. and foreign patent applicants alike. *See Hilmer*, 359 F.2d 878 n.9 (stating that "[i]t is the first filing in a foreign convention country that creates the priority right, *not the nationality of the applicant*") (emphasis in original). *De facto* discrimination results, however, because many foreign inventors are likely to have first filed in their home country before filing in the United States. Some patent-sophisticated foreign corporations avoid the effects of the *Hilmer* rule by making their first filings in the USPTO.

[43]Theoretically, a Paris Convention signatory country could seek review of another member country's alleged failure to satisfy provisions of the Convention by petitioning the Court of International Justice. However, no country has ever done so. *See* Ralph Oman, *Intellectual Property After the Uruguay Round*, 42 J. COPYRIGHT SOC'Y U.S.A. 18, 26 n.11 (1994).

(spearheaded by the United States) to turn to multilateral trade talks, in the form of the Uruguay Round of the General Agreement on Tariffs and Trade (GATT).[44] This round produced the TRIPS Agreement, discussed below, which is administered by the WTO.[45]

Although the WTO, with its elaborate dispute resolution mechanisms and expertise in that area, has come to be viewed as the preferred forum for resolution of country-versus-country disagreements on intellectual property matters, the WTO has not in any way displaced the WIPO's specialized intellectual property expertise. The WIPO remains a central player in the international intellectual property framework, administering many important intellectual property treaties and conventions in addition to the Paris Convention. One of the WIPO's most active and important roles is its administration of the Patent Cooperation Treaty, discussed in the next section.

C. The Patent Cooperation Treaty

The Patent Cooperation Treaty (PCT), which entered into force on January 24, 1978, provides a procedural framework for efficiently exploiting the right of priority created by the Paris Convention. In short, the PCT greatly simplifies the procedures for obtaining patent protection for an invention in multiple countries. The PCT has proven popular; 253,000 international applications were filed in 2018 under the treaty.[46] The PCT, like the Paris Convention, is administered by the WIPO, headquartered in Geneva, Switzerland. The text of the PCT and a list of PCT contracting states (i.e., signatory countries) are available on the WIPO's website.[47]

[44]For a firsthand account of the unsuccessful efforts to modernize the Paris Convention in the WIPO during the 1980s and the subsequent shift of U.S. efforts toward including intellectual property in multilateral trade talks, ultimately leading to the TRIPS Agreement, *see* Ralph Oman, *Intellectual Property After the Uruguay Round*, 42 J. Copyright Soc'y U.S.A. 18, 26 n.11 (1994).

[45]*See* Agreement on Trade-Related Aspects of Intellectual Property Rights, Apr. 15, 1994, Marrakesh Agreement Establishing the World Trade Organization, Annex 1C, Legal Instruments-Results of the Uruguay Round, 1869 U.N.T.S. 299, 33 I.L.M. 81 (1994), *available at* http://www.wto.org/english/docs_e/legal_e/27-trips.pdf [hereinafter TRIPS Agreement]. The GATT organization, formed in the late 1940s following World War II, was superseded by the WTO, which entered into force on January 1, 1995. The WTO, located in Geneva, Switzerland, administers the TRIPS Agreement.

[46]World Intellectual Property Organization, *Patent Cooperation Treaty Yearly Review, The International Patent System* (2019), at 3, *available at* https:/www.wipo.int/edocs/pubdocs/en/wipo_pub_901_2019.pdf.

[47]*See* Patent Cooperation Treaty, June 19, 1970, 28 U.S.T. 7645, 1160 U.N.T.S. 231, *available at* http://www.wipo.int/pct/en/texts/articles/atoc.htm [hereinafter PCT]. The list of PCT contracting states is *available at* (16 Jan. 2020), *available at* https://www.wipo.int/pct/en/guide. Helpful resources on PCT practice include World Intellectual

The PCT created a system of "one-stop shopping" in which an applicant, so long as she is a national or resident of a PCT contracting state, can file a single "international application"[48] with the patent office of her home country (acting as a PCT "receiving office") or with the International Bureau of the WIPO in Geneva. Through designation of any or all of the PCT contracting states, the international application will have the effect of a national patent application in each designated contracting state.[49] The applicant also may claim for the international application the benefit of the filing date (priority date) of an earlier-filed application in a Paris Convention country, if applicable.[50] In such cases, the applicant will file her international application within 12 months of filing an application on the same invention in her home country patent office.

The international application will be searched against the prior art by a PCT international searching authority.[51] A copy of the application, together with the results of the search, will be published approximately 18 months after the priority date,[52] and these materials will be transmitted by the WIPO's International Bureau to the national patent offices of each designated contracting state.[53] An applicant additionally has the option of requesting an International Preliminary Examination of the application.[54]

The key cost-saving feature of PCT practice is that the treaty permits the applicant to delay entry into the "national phase," that is, entry into patent prosecution in the national patent office of each designated contracting state, for a considerable period of time: up to 30 months after the priority date in most cases.[55] This ability to delay

---

Property Organization, *The PCT Applicant's Guide* https://www.wipo.int.pct/en/guide/index.html (10 Feb. 2020). World Intellectual Property Organization, *Protecting Your Inventions Abroad: Frequently Asked Questions About the Patent Cooperation Treaty (PCT)* (April 2012), *available at* http://www.wipo.int/export/sites/www/pct/en/basic_facts/faqs_about_the_pct.pdf; World Intellectual Property Organization, *Basic Facts About the Patent Cooperation Treaty (PCT)* (2002).

48 *See* PCT art. 3.

49 *See* PCT arts. 4, 11.

50 *See* PCT art. 8.

51 *See* PCT arts. 15-18. For international applications filed on or after January 1, 2004, the international searching authority (ISA) also prepares a written opinion (WO) on patentability. *See* World Intellectual Property Organization, *Regulations Under the Patent Cooperation Treaty (as in force from July 1, 2019)*, Rule 43*bis*.1, *available at* https://www.wipo.int/pct/en/texts/rules/rtoc1.html. The WO will be sent to the PCT applicant but not otherwise published unless and until the applicant enters the national phase. *See id.*, Rules 44.1, 44*ter*.1.

52 *See* PCT art. 21.

53 *See* PCT art. 20.

54 *See* PCT art. 31.

55 *See* PCT art. 22. The 30-month time limit has been in effect since April 1, 2002. A few countries (specifically Luxembourg and United Republic of Tanzania continue to apply the 20-month time limit that was in effect before that date, however. *See* World

entry into the national phase gives the patent applicant more time to assess the marketplace for the invention and temporarily postpones incurring the considerable costs of the translations, filing fees, attorney fees, and the like that are required to prosecute patent applications to issuance in each national patent office.

The most important aspect of the PCT to keep in mind is that the PCT procedure results in only a single international application, *not* a single granted patent or even a bundle of national patents (as does the European Patent Convention). The PCT authorities of the WIPO do not issue patents. It is up to the domestic patent systems of the designated PCT contracting states to decide whether to ultimately grant or refuse a national patent based on the PCT international application, the PCT international search report, and (in some cases) the results of the PCT international preliminary examination. These reports are not binding on the national offices.[56]

D. The World Trade Organization's Agreement on Trade-Related Aspects of Intellectual Property Rights (TRIPS)

In the 1980s, the primary forum for legislating multinational intellectual property (IP) agreements shifted from the WIPO, an exclusively IP-focused organization, to the WTO, an independent body with its roots in post–World War II efforts to reduce trade barriers between nations.[57]

Intellectual Property Organization, *PCT Reservations, Declarations, Notifications and Incompatibilities* (Dec. 19, 2019) (table), *available at* https://www.wipo.int/pct/en/texts/reservations/res_incomp.html.

[56]*See* PCT art. 27(5) (providing that "[n]othing in this Treaty and the Regulations is intended to be construed as prescribing anything that would limit the freedom of each Contracting State to prescribe such substantive conditions of patentability as it desires. In particular, any provision in this Treaty and the Regulations concerning the definition of prior art is exclusively for the purposes of the international procedure and, consequently, any Contracting State is free to apply, when determining the patentability of an invention claimed in an international application, the criteria of its national law in respect of prior art and other conditions of patentability not constituting requirements as to the form and contents of applications.").

[57]The WTO's website provides the following overview of the organization's structure:

> The WTO is run by its member governments. All major decisions are made by the membership as a whole, either by ministers (who meet at least once every two years) or by their ambassadors or delegates (who meet regularly in Geneva). Decisions are normally taken by consensus.
>
> In this respect, the WTO is different from some other international organizations such as the World Bank and International Monetary Fund. In the WTO, power is not delegated to a board of directors or the organization's head.
>
> When WTO rules impose disciplines on countries' policies, that is the outcome of negotiations among WTO members. The rules are enforced by the members

D. The World Trade Organization's Agreement on TRIPS

The Uruguay Round[58] of GATT brought IP rights (including patents, copyrights, and trademarks) into the GATT WTO system for the first time. The Uruguay Round resulted, *inter alia*, in enactment of the Agreement on Trade-Related Aspects of Intellectual Property Rights (TRIPS Agreement).[59] The TRIPS Agreement entered into force on January 1, 1995.

TRIPS is a landmark agreement for a number of reasons. For example, TRIPS is the first international IP treaty to mandate minimum standards for enforcement of rights by individual IP holders. TRIPS mandates that procedures for enforcing IP rights shall be fair and equitable.[60] Decisions on the merits shall preferably be in writing.[61] Accused infringers shall have the right to timely and sufficiently detailed notice.[62] Injunctions[63] and damages[64] shall be available.

As part of the WTO Agreement, TRIPS also provides procedures for the settlement of disputes between member countries when one country believes that another's IP laws are not in compliance with the provisions of TRIPS. These procedures involve country-to-country consultations, the establishment of WTO panels to consider disputes and produce written reports, and the possibility of appellate review within the WTO. The considerable details of these dispute settlement procedures are set forth in the Dispute Settlement Understanding

---

> themselves under agreed procedures that they negotiated, including the possibility of trade sanctions. But those sanctions are imposed by member countries, and authorized by the membership as a whole. This is quite different from other agencies whose bureaucracies can, for example, influence a country's policy by threatening to withhold credit.

World Trade Organization, *The Organization: Whose WTO Is It Anyway? (2016)*, http://www.wto.org/english/thewto_e/whatis_e/tif_e/org1_e.htm.

[58]The international multilateral trading system in goods and services was developed through a series of trade negotiations, or "rounds," held under the auspices of the General Agreement on Tariffs and Trade. The first GATT rounds dealt mainly with tariff reductions, but later negotiations included other areas such as antidumping and nontariff measures. More recently, the 1986-1994 Uruguay Round led to the WTO's creation and included intellectual property as a trade issue, generating the TRIPS Agreement. *See* World Trade Organization, *The Multilateral Trading System: Past, Present, and Future (2016)*, https://www.wto.org/english/thewto_e/whatis_e/inbrief_e/inbr01_e.htm.

[59]The Uruguay Round resulted in an umbrella agreement that created the WTO, known as the "Agreement Establishing the World Trade Organization." This umbrella agreement, popularly known as the WTO Agreement, included several "annexed" side agreements. The text of the TRIPS Agreement is officially "Annex 1C" of the WTO Agreement. *See* TRIPS Agreement, *available at* http://www.wto.org/english/docs_e/legal_e/27-trips.pdf.

[60]*See* TRIPS art. 41.2.

[61]*See* TRIPS art. 41.3.

[62]*See* TRIPS art. 42.

[63]*See* TRIPS art. 44.

[64]*See* TRIPS art. 45.

(DSU) of the WTO.[65] The United States has invoked the WTO dispute settlement procedures in patent cases involving such topics as India's "mailbox" rule, "local working" and compulsory licensing in Brazil, and Canada's term of patent protection.[66]

The availability of the DSU procedures put real "teeth" into TRIPS. If a country is unsuccessful in a WTO dispute proceeding and does not timely bring its intellectual property laws into compliance with the WTO's ruling, trade sanctions (e.g., tariffs, import quotas, and taxes) can potentially be imposed on the offending country's exported products that have nothing to do with the intellectual property dispute at issue. This is known as "cross-sectoral retaliation."[67] For example, consider a hypothetical in which the United States, contending that France is not providing sufficient patent protection for computer software, prevails in a WTO dispute settlement proceeding against France, but France does not subsequently bring its laws into compliance with the decision. The WTO could decide to permit the United States to impose sanctions on France by increasing the tariffs imposed on exports of French wine to the United States. It is irrelevant that computer software and wine are unrelated products and that wine was not the subject of the WTO dispute.

TRIPS also is critically important because it is the first international IP treaty to establish "substantive minima" of protection for all types of intellectual property. With respect to patents, TRIPS provides that, subject to certain important exceptions,[68] "[p]atents shall be available for any inventions, whether products or processes, in all

[65]*See* Understanding on Rules and Procedures Governing the Settlement of Disputes, Apr. 15, 1994, Marrakesh Agreement Establishing the World Trade Organization, Annex 2, 1869 U.N.T.S. 401, 33 I.L.M. 1226, *available at* http://www.wto.org/english/docs_e/legal_e/28-dsu_e.htm [hereinafter DSU]. For a helpful flowchart of the WTO panel process for settling disputes, *see* World Trade Organization, *The Panel Process* (2016) http://www.wto.org/english/thewto_e/whatis_e/tif_e/disp2_e.htm. *See also* TRIPS art. 63 ("Transparency") and art. 64 ("Dispute Settlement").

[66]For the details of these disputes, *see* World Trade Organization, *Index of Disputes Issues (2016),* http://www.wto.org/english/tratop_e/dispu_e/dispu_subjects_index_e.htm (heading "Patents").

[67]*See* DSU art. 22.3, *available at* http://www.wto.org/english/docs_e/legal_e/28-dsu_e.htm.

[68]The categories of subject matter that member countries may exclude from patentability under the TRIPS Agreement are enumerated in TRIPS Article 27 ("Patentable Subject Matter"). More specifically, Articles 27.2 and 27.3 provide

> 2. Members may exclude from patentability inventions, the prevention within their territory of the commercial exploitation of which is necessary to protect *ordre public* or morality, including to protect human, animal or plant life or health or to avoid serious prejudice to the environment, provided that such exclusion is not made merely because the exploitation is prohibited by their law.
>
> 3. Members may also exclude from patentability:
>
> (a) diagnostic, therapeutic and surgical methods for the treatment of humans or animals;

fields of technology, provided that they are new, involve an inventive step and are capable of industrial application."[69] This language was targeted at developing and least-developed countries that had previously refused to grant patents on pharmaceuticals and agricultural inventions; if such countries want to become TRIPS signatories, they must bring their national patent laws into compliance with TRIPS within certain designated time periods by providing patent protection (or at least pipeline protection) on this subject matter.[70]

The quoted language of TRIPS Article 27 also establishes three substantive criteria of patentability (novelty, inventive step, and industrial application) that parallel the U.S. criteria of novelty, nonobviousness, and utility. TRIPS does not explicitly define these substantive criteria, however, leaving member countries certain flexibilities in interpretation.

TRIPS also reflects the United States' historic antipathy toward **compulsory licensing**, which involves a government-compelled grant of a patent license to a third party without the consent of the patent owner. TRIPS permits (but does not require) countries to grant compulsory licenses under patents, but only upon satisfaction of an extensive list of criteria set forth in Article 31. This article requires that unless a national emergency or other extreme circumstance exists, or unless the compulsory use is a public noncommercial use, compulsory licenses cannot be granted before the proposed licensee has attempted but failed to obtain a consensual license from the patent owner on reasonable commercial terms and conditions.[71]

Moreover, the compulsory licensee's use of the patent must be predominantly for the supply of the domestic market of the country granting the compulsory license.[72] This means that, for example, if the

---

> (b) plants and animals other than micro-organisms, and essentially biological processes for the production of plants or animals other than non-biological and microbiological processes. However, Members shall provide for the protection of plant varieties either by patents or by an effective sui generis system or by any combination thereof. The provisions of this subparagraph shall be reviewed four years after the date of entry into force of the WTO Agreement.

TRIPS art. 27. These optional exclusions from patentability are discussed in further detail in Chapter 6 ("The Utility Requirement (35 U.S.C. §101)"), *supra*, and in Chapter 7 ("Potentially Patentable Subject Matter (35 U.S.C. §101)"), *supra*.

[69]TRIPS art. 27.1.

[70]The "transitional arrangements" provisions of TRIPS give these countries an extended "phase-in" period of time in which to amend their patent laws. *See* TRIPS arts. 65, 66. For example, under TRIPS art. 65.4, India had until January 1, 2005, to begin granting patents on pharmaceutical products. For additional background on the evolution of India's patent system since the nation joined the WTO, *see* Janice M. Mueller, *The Tiger Awakens: The Tumultuous Transformation of India's Patent System and the Rise of Indian Pharmaceutical Innovation*, 68 U. PITT. L. REV. 491 (2007).

[71]*See* TRIPS art. 31(b).

[72]*See* TRIPS art. 31(f).

Brazilian government granted a compulsory license to a Brazilian domestic drug company to produce and sell an AIDS drug previously patented in Brazil by a U.S.-based pharmaceutical corporation, the Brazilian company must manufacture the drug primarily for the supply of the Brazilian market and not for export to another country (such as South Africa).[73] Responding to concerns of developing and least-developed countries that lack the domestic manufacturing capacity to take advantage of compulsory licensing, the WTO in 2003 implemented a procedure under which the TRIPS Article 31(f) "predominantly for the supply of the domestic market" requirement can be waived in appropriate circumstances. Under this procedure, a country such as Brazil or India could obtain a compulsory license to manufacture and export patented pharmaceuticals to a requesting country such as South Africa, but only in specified amounts and only with appropriate protections against diversion of the pharmaceuticals to non-intended countries.[74]

The patent owner who is subject to a compulsory license must be paid "adequate remuneration in the circumstances of each case, taking into account the economic value of the authorization."[75] Decisions to grant compulsory licenses, and those that determine the patentee's remuneration, are subject to judicial review.[76]

E. Patent Harmonization

Efforts to harmonize the world's disparate patent systems have a long history.[77] An important example is WIPO's Patent Law Treaty

[73]Interpretation of the "predominantly for the supply of the domestic market" provision of TRIPS art. 31 was the subject of controversy stemming from the WTO Ministerial Declaration issued at Doha, Qatar, in 2001. *See* Ministerial Conference, *Declaration on the TRIPS Agreement and Public Health,* WT/MIN(01)/DEC/2 (Nov. 20, 2001), *available at* http://www.wto.org/english/thewto_e/minist_e/min01_e/mindecl_trips_e.pdf. Paragraph 6 of the declaration recognizes that "WTO members with insufficient or no manufacturing capacities in the pharmaceutical sector could face difficulties in making effective use of compulsory licensing under the TRIPS Agreement" and "instruct[s] the Council for TRIPS to find an expeditious solution to this problem and to report to the General Council before the end of 2002." *Id.*

[74]*See* WTO General Council, *Implementation of Paragraph 6 of the Doha Declaration on the TRIPS Agreement and Public Health*, WT/L/540 and Corr.1 (Aug. 30, 2003), *available at* http://www.wto.org/english/tratop_e/trips_e/implem_para6_e.htm. The 2003 Implementation Decision will become a permanent part of the TRIPS Agreement (as a new TRIPS art. 31*bis*) if two-thirds of the WTO's members accept the change. The current deadline for acceptance is December 31, 2017. *See* Word Trade Organization, *Members Accepting Amendment of the TRIPS Agreement*, https://www.wto.org/english/tratop_e/trips_e/mapamendment_e.htm (2020).

[75]TRIPS art. 31(h).

[76]*See* TRIPS arts. 31(g), (i), (j), and (k).

[77]"Harmonization" should be distinguished from "unification." Harmonization as applied to patent law refers to efforts to bring the patent law systems of different

(PLT), which entered into force on April 28, 2005.[78] The PLT aims to harmonize and streamline formality requirements of national and regional patent procedures, rather than target substantive harmonization issues.[79]

With regard to substantive issues, the international harmonization debate has placed primary focus on two issues: (1) whether timewise priority in patent rights is to be determined under a first-to-file system or a first-to-invent system, and (2) whether the novelty requirement should be "absolute" or "qualified." The priority issue considers whether, in cases of competing claimants to patent the same invention, a patent system should award the patent to the entity who was first in time to invent, or to the entity who was first to file a patent application for the invention. The absolute-versus-qualified novelty issue invokes the question of whether a patent system provides a pre-filing grace period. Each of these harmonization topics is addressed below.[80]

1. First-to-File Versus First-to-Invent

In the early 1990s the United States announced, after prolonged debate, that it would maintain its unique first-to-invent system.[81] Until 2013, when Section 3 of the Leahy-Smith America Invents Act of 2011 (AIA) took effect, the United States was the only country in the world that continued to operate under a first-to-invent system. Although first-to-invent is generally thought to be more fair to independent/small entity inventors, it made U.S. patent law on this point significantly more complex and administratively burdensome than the first-to-file system employed by the rest of the world.

To simplify the U.S. patent system and move toward substantive international harmonization, Congress repeatedly debated switching to a first-to-file system during the first decade of the twenty-first

---

countries into alignment by reducing or eliminating the differences between them. For example, one of the most contentious issues in patent harmonization debates was whether the United States would change from its historic first-to-invent system to the first-to-file system employed by the rest of the world. Harmonization is not unification, which seeks to establish one unified "world patent" system.

[78]The current text of the Patent Law Treaty, June 1, 2000, 28 U.S.T. 7645, 1160 U.N.T.S. 221, is *available at* http://www.wipo.int/treaties/en/ip/plt/trtdocs_wo038.html.

[79]*See* World Intellectual Property Organization, *Patent Law Treaty (PLT)*, http://www.wipo.int/treaties/en/ip/plt (last visited Feb. 16, 2016).

[80]For a helpful summary of USPTO views on a variety of patent harmonization topics, *see* USPTO, *Request for Comments on the International Effort to Harmonize the Substantive Requirements of Patent Laws,* 66 Fed. Reg. 15409 (2001), *available at* http://www.uspto.gov/web/offices/com/sol/notices/intpatlaws.pdf.

[81]*U.S. Says "Not Now" on First-to-File, Agrees with Japan on Patent Term*, 47 Pat. Trademark & Copyright J. (BNA) 285 (Jan. 27, 1994).

century.[82] After additional years of negotiation aimed at reaching consensus between various industry groups, Congress enacted the Leahy-Smith America Invents Act of 2011 (AIA).[83] The AIA was signed into law by President Obama on September 16, 2011. This landmark legislation transitioned the U.S. from its historic first-to-invent priority principle to a unique "first inventor to file" system.[84]

The AIA represents a hybrid of (or compromise between) pre AIA U.S. law and absolute novelty "first to file" European law (described *infra*). The AIA retained a one-year pre–filing date grace period, but only for disclosures made by the inventor (or persons directly or indirectly obtaining the invention therefrom), not third parties. The AIA first-inventor-to-file system went into effect on March 16, 2013 for patent applications filed on or after that date.[85] The mechanics of the post-AIA first-inventor-to-file system are detailed in Chapter 4 of this text.[86]

Critically, the AIA changes concerning first inventor to file were purely *prospective*. This means that for patents or applications already in existence on March 16, 2013, the traditional pre-AIA framework continues to control throughout the life of the patents or applications. For example, if federal court litigants or USPTO *inter partes* review petitioners in 2020 challenge the validity of patents that were already issued (or filed for) as of March 16, 2013, they will continue to mount those challenges under pre-AIA rules. Given the 20-year term of a patent,[87] the duration and complexity of patent litigation, and the possibility of appeals to the Federal Circuit and Supreme Court, it is necessary to know and apply pre-AIA rules for 30 years or more following the AIA's enactment.

Because U.S. patent law will operate on a dual (pre- and post-AIA) system for many years to come, the traditional first-to-invent

[82]*See* Patent Reform Act of 2005, H.R. 2795, 109th Cong. (2005); Patent Reform Act of 2007, H.R. 1908, 110th Cong. (2007); S. 1145, 110th Cong. (2007).

[83]Leahy-Smith America Invents Act, Pub. L. No. 112-29 (H.R. 1249), 125 Stat. 284 (Sept. 16, 2011).

[84]The phrase "first inventor to file" simply denotes a first-to-file system named so as to emphasize the requirement of originality; that is, in order to obtain a patent, the invention must be original to the inventor and not copied or derived from another. This originality requirement is not unique to the United States and is part of the first-to-file systems of other countries.

[85]*See* Leahy-Smith America Invents Act, Pub. L. No. 112-29 (H.R. 1249), §3(n) ("Effective Date"), 125 Stat. 284, 293 (2011).

[86]*See supra* Chapter 4 ("Novelty, Loss of Right, and Priority Pre- and Post-America Invents Act of 2011 (35 U.S.C. §102)"), Part III ("Novelty and Priority Post-America Invents Act of 2011").

[87]This phrase is a shorthand reference to indicate that since June 8, 1995, U.S. patents have a term that expires 20 years after their earliest U.S. filing date. *See supra* Chapter 1, Section C.7 ("The Patent Term").

principles remain relevant and important in the United States.[88] Operating a patent system under a first-to-invent principle means that when two (or more) persons apply for a patent on the same invention, each having independently made the invention (i.e., *not* copied it), the patent will be awarded (at least theoretically) to the person who was first in time to invent, regardless of the order in which the two filed their respective patent applications.

The use of "theoretically" in the previous sentence indicates that the process did not occur automatically. In the USPTO, the competing claimants had to participate in an **interference** proceeding, an *inter partes* adjudicatory proceeding within the USPTO to determine which party invented first.[89] Interference proceedings were available only until March 16, 2013, although first-to-invent priority principles will continue to apply to validity determinations for issued patents for many years beyond that date. In a USPTO interference, the party who is the last to file (the junior party) bore the burden of overcoming a presumption that the first to file (the senior party) also was the first to invent. As discussed in Chapter 4 ("Novelty, Loss of Right, and Priority Pre- and Post-America Invents Act of 2011 (35 U.S.C. §102)"), *supra,* the basic statutory provisions that governed interferences were 35 U.S.C. §102(g)(1) (2006) and 35 U.S.C. §135 (2006). The rules and procedures for interferences are quite complex and beyond the scope of this text.[90]

In countries other than the United States, timewise priority has long been established via a first-to-file system. This is much less

[88]Moreover, the AIA does not render irrelevant all aspects of the traditional U.S. first-to-invent priority system. For example, the pre-AIA concept of invention dates (including dates of conception) will likely remain relevant to the post-AIA (i.e., AIA-implemented) derivation proceeding under 35 U.S.C. §135 (eff. Mar. 16, 2013). For more on derivation proceedings, *see supra* Chapter 4, Section S.3.a. In addition, many patent licenses and assignments refer to an invention's date of conception, a pre-AIA concept.

[89]The U.S. patent system developed the interference proceeding as a means of determining priority of invention. *See generally* Edward Walterscheid, *Priority of Invention: How the United States Came to Have a "First-to-Invent" Patent System,* 23 AIPLA Q.J. 263 (1995). Adoption of the first-to-invent principle does not necessarily require interferences, however. Historically, England appears to have used the relative order of filing dates as an irrebuttable presumption of the relative dates of invention, thus avoiding protracted factual disputes over first-to-invent priority. The author thanks Professor Carl Moy for this observation.

[90]For further guidance on interference law and practice, *see* Practice Before the Board of Patent Appeals and Interferences, 37 C.F.R. §§41.200-41.208 (2016) (titled "Subpart E. Patent Interferences"); United States Patent and Trademark Office, *Interference Proceedings*, Manual of Patent Examining Procedure §§2301-2309 (9th ed., rev. Nov. 2015); Charles W. Rivise & A.D. Caesar, Interference Law and Practice (W.S. Hein 2000); Charles L. Gholz, *Interference Practice*, in 6 Patent Practice 24-1 (Irving Kayton & Karyl S. Kayton eds., 4th ed. 1989). A Federal Circuit judge has described Gholz's work as a "definitive text" on interference practice. *See* Brown v. Barbacid, 276 F.3d 1327, 1340 (Fed. Cir. 2002) (Newman, J., dissenting).

cumbersome from an administrative standpoint than the United States' historic first-to-invent system. No determination of dates of conception, diligence, and reduction to practice is necessary, as in U.S. interference proceedings; in the event of a conflict, the patent will be awarded to the party that has the earlier filing date. The concept of **invention date** thus has very little meaning in foreign patent systems.

The first-to-file system has been characterized as unfair for prejudicing the independent inventor with fewer resources and limited capacity to win the race to the patent office. This unfairness is ameliorated to some extent, however, by the longstanding recognition in many patent systems of "prior user rights."[91]

A **prior user right** is essentially a defense to infringement. Prior user rights operate as follows: Assume that party A, a German national, obtains a German patent on a process for brewing beer, and sues party B, an unrelated German national, for infringement of A's patent. B determines that she independently developed the same process before A did and began using it in B's beer-brewing business prior to the filing date of A's patent application. Under these facts the German national patent laws will sustain the validity of A's patent but grant B a prior user right,[92] which is essentially a license that permits B to continue using the beer brewing process without liability to A.[93]

[91]*See* Gary L. Griswold et al., *Prior User Rights: Neither a Rose Nor a Thorn*, 2 U. Balt. Intell. Prop. L.J. 233, 236 (1994) (stating that foreign countries that provide defense to infringement based on prior user rights "include our most important trading partners and account for approximately 85% of the world's gross domestic product outside of the United States. (In Europe: France, Germany, Italy, The Netherlands, Spain, the United Kingdom, and 12 other countries. In Asia: China, Hong Kong, Indonesia, Japan, South Korea, Malaysia, the Philippines, Singapore, and Taiwan. In North America: Canada and Mexico. And elsewhere: Australia, Egypt, and Israel).") (footnotes omitted).

[92]The German patent statute provides:

> §12. (1) A patent shall have no effect against a person who, at the time of the filing of the application, had already begun to use the invention in Germany, or had made the necessary arrangements for so doing. Said person shall be entitled to use the invention for the needs of his own business in his own workshops or the workshops of others. This right can only be inherited or transferred together with the business. . . .
>
> (2) When the patentee is entitled to a right of priority, the date of the prior application shall be decisive and not the date of the application referred to in subsection (1). However, this provision shall not apply to nationals of a foreign country that does not guarantee reciprocity in this respect, where they claim the priority of a foreign application.

Patentgesetz [Patent Act], Dec. 16, 1980, BGBI.I 1981 at 1, last amended Oct. 8, 2017, BGBI.I at 2030, §12 (F.R.G.), *translated in* https://wipolex.wipo.int/en/legislation/details/17611.

[93]Thus, prior user rights can be viewed as a variety of compulsory licensing.

The license to B is a personal one, such that B cannot transfer the license to third party C, other than in connection with a full, bona fide transfer of B's beer-brewing business.

Prior to 1999, the United States did not recognize prior user rights at all, most likely because they are viewed as reducing the economic value of patents through derogating the patentee's exclusivity. In response to concerns over the rising tide of business method patents, Congress created a very limited prior user right as part of enacting the American Inventor Protection Act of 1999. The misnamed "earlier inventor" defense, codified at 35 U.S.C. §273 (2006), was limited to infringements of claims to methods, which the statute defined as "a method of doing or conducting business."[94] To claim the defense, the prior user must have (1) actually reduced the invention to practice more than one year before the patentee's effective filing date (i.e., U.S. or foreign priority date), and (2) commercially used the invention at any time prior to that same date.[95]

The defense of prior user rights as applicable in U.S. patent litigation was significantly broadened by the America Invents Act of 2011. As described in further detail in Chapter 10 of this text,[96] the protection of the post-AIA version of 35 U.S.C. §273 (eff. Sept. 16, 2011) ("Defense to infringement based on prior commercial use") is potentially available to alleged infringers practicing "subject matter consisting of a process, or consisting of a machine, manufacture, or composition of matter used in a manufacturing or other commercial process."[97] Thus, post-AIA, the practice of *all* 35 U.S.C. §101 categories of subject matter is potentially shielded by prior user rights so long as the accused infringer was using the allegedly infringing subject matter in a "commercial process" by the requisite date. The defense is no longer limited to those who allegedly infringed patented business methods. The broadened version of the prior user rights defense became available for those accused of infringing patents that issued on or after September 16, 2011.

2. Absolute Versus Qualified Novelty: Grace Period

The second major issue addressed in patent harmonization debates is the need for an internationally recognized prefiling **grace period**. As introduced in Chapter 4, *supra*, a grace period in patent law is a limited period of time prior to the applicant's filing date in which the invention may be commercially exploited or otherwise injected into

[94] 35 U.S.C. §273(a)(3) (2006).
[95] *See* 35 U.S.C. §273(b)(1).
[96] *See supra* Chapter 10, Section C.2.
[97] 35 U.S.C. §273(a) (eff. Sept. 16, 2011).

the public domain without any loss of right to obtain a patent. United States patent law has recognized a grace period since 1839.[98]

The pre-AIA grace period, as provided for in 35 U.S.C. §102(b) (2006), was one year. During this year-long time period, an invention could be patented, described in a printed publication, in public use, or placed on sale, by the inventor or a third party, all without triggering a §102(b) loss of right.

Post-AIA, the one-year grace period continues but in a narrower form. The post-AIA grace period protects inventors only against their own prefiling disclosures (or disclosures made by another who directly or indirectly obtained the invention from the inventor), and not against third-party disclosures.[99]

Many countries other than the United States are "absolute novelty" systems, which do not recognize any significant prefiling date grace period (or when they do, the grace period is only for very limited times and purposes, such as particular types of international exhibitions[100]). For example, under European Patent Convention (EPC) Article 54, any activity that makes the invention part of the "state of the art" at any time prior to the filing of the European patent application will defeat novelty.[101]

Absolute novelty systems are particularly difficult environments for professors and researchers in the academic community, with its "publish or perish" ethos, who also seek patent protection for their research results. Under an absolute novelty system, the patent application must be filed before any publication of the invention, including oral divulgation, is made.[102]

In previous patent harmonization discussions, the United States proposed that it would consider shifting to first-to-file in exchange for worldwide recognition of a suitable prefiling grace period. Congress passed the AIA in 2011 without the United States having obtained that concession. Independently of U.S. proposals, however, European

[98]From 1839 to 1939, U.S. patent law recognized a two-year grace period. In 1939, the grace period was reduced to one year.

[99]*See* 35 U.S.C. §102(b) (1) (eff. Mar. 16, 2013) ("Disclosures Made 1 Year or Less Before the Effective Filing Date of the Claimed Invention"). For further analysis of this provision, *see supra* Chapter 4, Section S ("Novelty-Preserving Exceptions Under Post-AIA 35 U.S.C. §102(b)").

[100]*See, e.g.*, Convention on the Grant of European Patents art. 55 ("Non-prejudicial Disclosures"), Oct. 5, 1973, 13 I.L.M. 268, 2007 O.J. Eur. Pat. Off. (Spec. Ed. 4) 1, 57 [hereinafter European Patent Convention].

[101]*See* European Patent Convention art. 54(1) ("An invention shall be considered to be new if it does not form part of the state of the art."); *id.* at art. 54(2) ("[S]tate of the art shall be held to comprise everything made available to the public by means of a written or oral description, by use, or in any other way, before the date of filing of the European patent application.").

[102]*See* European Patent Convention art. 54(2).

patent experts continue to debate the international adoption of a grace period.[103]

F. Gray Market Goods and the International Exhaustion Debate[104]

Transborder patent disputes frequently involve "gray market" goods. Such goods, also termed "parallel imports," are not counterfeit, illegal, pirated, or products of the "black market." Rather, gray market goods are legitimate products, manufactured by or under the authority of the patent owner. Whether manufactured domestically or offshore, gray market goods are first sold in a foreign market by the patent owner or its authorized agent, then purchased by third parties for unauthorized importation to the patent owner's home market, where they compete with authorized (and typically higher-priced) channels of distribution. Because these goods are typically sold by the patent owner at discounted prices in foreign markets, they are attractive targets for purchase by gray marketeers, who will import them into the patentee's domestic market to undercut higher prices there.

The divisive legal issue raised by parallel imports is whether the patent owner, having first sold its patented goods outside its domestic market, can prevent their subsequent importation into that market by an unauthorized third party as a violation of the underlying patent right. The patentee's ability to use its patent as a weapon to prevent competition from gray market goods turns on a legal doctrine rather inaptly named "exhaustion of rights."[105] Three forms of exhaustion should be distinguished: (1) domestic exhaustion, (2) regional

[103]A 2014 report evidenced widespread support for a grace period in the United States and Japan, but generally negative opinions about a grace period in Europe. *See* Consolidated Report on the Tegernsee User Consultation on Substantive Patent Law Harmonization (May 2014), *available at* documents.epo.org/projects/babylon/eponet.nsf/0/C3407F28C924DA5CC1257CD80036DB61/$File/Tegernsee_user_consultation_consilidated_report_en.pdf. *See also* European Patent Office, Press Release, *The Case For and Against the Introduction of a Grace Period in European Patent Law* (July 25, 2000) (summarizing comments of Mr. Jan Galama and Professor Dr. Joseph Straus). *See also* European Research News Centre, *The Controversial "Grace Period"* (Aug. 28, 2002).

[104]Much of this section is based on ideas in Janice Mueller & Jeffery Atik, *New International Dimensions in the Gray Market Goods Debate*, 1 J. Marshall Center for Intell. Prop. L. News Source 6 (Summer 1999).

[105]The phrase "exhaustion of rights" is something of a misnomer. The intellectual property right itself (e.g., the patent owner's right to exclude others from making, using, selling, offering to sell, or importing the claimed invention) is never exhausted, at least during the term of the patent. Rather, what is exhausted is the IP owner's *right to control the disposition of a particular item* that was originally produced under authority of her patent in a foreign country, but subsequently purchased by a third party and imported without the patent owner's permission into the patent owner's home country.

exhaustion (e.g., within the European Union), and (3) international exhaustion. Each is discussed below.

1. Domestic Exhaustion

The concept of domestic exhaustion in the patent context is well established in the national laws of all countries and is not directly implicated in parallel imports disputes. Domestic exhaustion simply means that after the first authorized sale of a product in a given domestic market, the owner of the patent right(s) under which that particular item was produced no longer has any enforceable right to control the disposition or profit from the subsequent resale *of that same physical item* within the domestic market.[106]

For example, a consumer who purchases a new Ford-brand automobile in Michigan, which automobile contains one or more internal components covered by Ford patents in the United States, owes no further patent royalty or other remuneration to the Ford Motor Company if and when she resells the same car in California. Ford received full value or "tribute" for the value of its patented automotive inventions at the time of the first authorized sale of the car, and the purchaser obtained the right to dispose of the car in any manner without having to seek Ford's permission.[107] The principle of domestic exhaustion

---

Judge Giles Rich, a co-author of the 1952 U.S. Patent Act, found the use of exhaustion terminology illogical:

> When the patentee himself makes and sells, he is not exercising his patent rights; in selling, he is, therefore, not exhausting them. It is not a question of control over the thing sold but of control, if any, over the purchaser and others. Having once enjoyed the potential benefit of having made a sale of property without competition, does the statute give the patentee any right whatever to control the purchaser with respect to the property he bought? My answer is "No" and the courts have generally so held, at least for the last half-century. They have rationalized the results, however, on the "exhaustion" theory, which is, in my view, logically unjustifiable.

Giles S. Rich, *My Favorite Things*, 35 IDEA 1, 3-4 (1994).

[106]U.S. copyright law implements an analogous domestic exhaustion rule through the "first sale doctrine" of 17 U.S.C. §109(a). The Supreme Court considered domestic patent exhaustion as a defense to patent infringement in *Quanta Computer, Inc. v. LG Elecs., Inc.*, 553 U.S. 617 (2008). For analysis of the *Quanta* decision, *see supra* Chapter 10, Section C.8 ("Patent Exhaustion").

[107]She did not, however, obtain the right to infringe Ford's patent rights by reconstructing the patented items, effectively "making" the patent items a second time. Infringing **reconstruction** should be distinguished from noninfringing **repair** of a patented item, which is within the purchaser's implied license to use the item she has purchased. *See* Jazz Photo Corp. v. Int'l Trade Comm'n, 264 F.3d 1094, 1105 (Fed. Cir. 2001).

recognizes that the fundamental legal policy against restraints on alienation of personal property outweighs any patent right of Ford.

2. Regional (European Community-Wide) Exhaustion

A second variety of exhaustion theory applies within the 27 member countries ("member states") of the European Union (as of the writing of this edition in late 2019).[108] The European Court of Justice (ECJ) has adopted a "community-wide exhaustion" approach, which is in essence domestic exhaustion for a marketplace that comprises the entire European Union (EU). In practice, community exhaustion means that once a patented item is put on the market anywhere in the EU with the patent owner's consent, the patent owner cannot thereafter prevent the importation of that patented item into another EU member state.[109] The ECJ's adoption of community exhaustion reflects the Treaty of Rome's bedrock principle of "free movement of goods," which grounds the EU's antipathy toward barriers to trade between EU member states.[110]

3. International Exhaustion

The third and final variety of exhaustion, international exhaustion, is a more complicated and unsettled legal concept than the two

[108]*See European Union: Countries* (Oct. 29, 2019), https://europa.eu/european-union/about-eu/countries_en. The United Kingdom (consisting of England, Wales, Scotland, and Northern Ireland) withdrew from the Union on January 31, 2020. *Id.*

[109]*See generally* Case 187/80, Merck & Co. v. Stephar BV, 1981 E.C.R. 2063, *available at* http://eur-lex.europa.eu/smartapi/cgi/sga_doc?smartapi!celexplus!prod!CELEXnumdoc&numdoc=61980J0187&lg=en.

[110]*See* Consolidated Version of the Treaty Establishing the European Economic Community, 2006 O.J. (C321)E/37, *available at* https://www.cvce.eu/en/obj/treety_establishing_the_european_economic_community_rome_25_march_1957-en-cca6ba28-0bf3-4cc6-8a76-6b0b3252696e.html [hereinafter Treaty of Rome]. The interface (or tension) between the free movement of goods principle and the territorial nature of intellectual property rights is illustrated by reading Article 28 of the Treaty of Rome in conjunction with Article 30. Article 28 (formerly Article 30) provides that "[q]uantitative restrictions on imports and all measures having equivalent effect shall be prohibited between Member States." However, Article 30 (formerly Article 36) creates a qualified exception for intellectual property rights, providing that (emphasis added)

> [t]he provisions of Article[] 28 . . . shall not preclude prohibitions or restrictions on imports, exports or goods in transit justified on grounds of . . . *the protection of industrial* and commercial *property*. Such prohibitions or restrictions shall not, however, constitute a means of arbitrary discrimination or a disguised restriction on trade between Member States.

previous forms; international exhaustion is directly implicated in parallel imports disputes that span national borders. In contrast with domestic exhaustion, countries do not uniformly agree over whether to adhere to the principle of international exhaustion. Proponents of international exhaustion contend that a patent owner's rights are extinguished at the first authorized sale of a patented item anywhere in the world, and that subsequent importation of that same item into the patentee's home country cannot be a legal wrong. This faction, which includes discount retailers, consumer action groups, and some economists, contends that consumers benefit from the price competition created by parallel imports. Advocates of international free trade and international harmonization of IP rights also favor parallel imports, because permitting entry of gray goods will lessen if not eliminate the patent owner's ability to price-discriminate on an international scale.

International exhaustion is a controversial idea because it flies in the face of traditional thinking that patent rights are merely national, not international, in scope, and that such rights begin and end at national borders. Indeed, the U.S. Patent Act expressly provides that unauthorized importation of goods embodying a patented invention is actionable infringement.[111] Patent owners, particularly in the pharmaceutical industry, contend that sales of their patented product in a foreign market, usually at discounted prices, cannot exhaust their domestic patent rights, which are created by domestic statutes of restricted territorial scope and for which the patentees have not received full value in the lower-priced foreign sales.

Of all forms of IP protection, the complexity of patent law may make it the most territorial, as reflected historically by extensive substantive differences between national patent laws. Indeed, Article 4*bis* of the Paris Convention expressly recognizes the principle of independence of patents obtained for the same invention in different countries. Thus, the Japanese Supreme Court's 1997 decision in *BBS Kraftfahrzeug Technik AG v. Kabushiki Kaisha Racimex Japan and Kabushiki Kaisha JapAuto Prods.*,[112] which adopted and applied the international exhaustion doctrine against a Japanese patent owner, surprised many in the international patent community.

[111]*See* 35 U.S.C. §271(a) (defining patent infringement as including "import[ation] into the United States" of any patented invention "without authority").

[112]51 Minshu 2299 (Sup. Ct. July 1, 1997), *translated in* http://www.courts.go.jp/english/judgments/text/1997.07.01-1995-O-No.1988.html (last visited Aug. 11, 2012). For additional analysis of *BBS, see* Janice Mueller & Jeffery Atik, *New International Dimensions in the Gray Market Goods Debate*, 1 J. MARSHALL CENTER FOR INTELL. PROP. L. NEWS SOURCE 6 (Summer 1999).

F. Gray Market Goods and the International Exhaustion Debate

Until 2017, the United States had never recognized the principle of international exhaustion with respect to patent-protected items (in contrast with the U.S. courts' treatment of certain categories of copyrighted or trademarked goods[113]). For those novel and nonobvious products that could qualify, protection under U.S. patent laws thus held the greatest promise for domestic corporations seeking to stop parallel imports. However, the U.S. Supreme Court in 2017 drastically changed the law by recognizing international exhaustion of patent rights in *Impression Prods., Inc. v. Lexmark Int'l, Inc.*[114]

Because patent rights are increasingly sought, enforced, and challenged throughout the world, understanding this seismic change in the law is essential. The remainder of this section analyzes the historical case law development on international exhaustion in the realm of patent as well as copyright law, the Federal Circuit's 2016 *en banc* decision in *Lexmark Int'l* rejecting international exhaustion of patent rights, and the Supreme Court's dramatic 2017 reversal thereof in *Impression Prods.*

In its first decision touching on parallel imports of patented goods, the U.S. Supreme Court in *Boesch v. Graff*[115] enjoined the importation of a product covered by U.S. patent and acquired abroad from an authorized German source with prior user rights, broadly asserting that "[t]he sale of articles in the United States under a United States patent cannot be controlled by foreign laws."[116] The Federal Circuit relied on *Boesch*'s reasoning in *Jazz Photo Corp. v. U.S. Int'l Trade Commission*,[117] confirming that "United States patent rights are not exhausted by products of foreign provenance" and that for an accused infringer "[t]o invoke the protection of the first sale doctrine, the authorized first sale must have occurred under the United States patent."[118]

[113] *See* Kirtsaeng v. John Wiley & Sons, Inc., 133 S. Ct. 1351, 1355-1356 (2013) (holding that "the 'first sale' doctrine applies to copies of a copyrighted work lawfully made abroad."); Quality King Distributors, Inc. v. L'Anza Res. Int'l, Inc., 523 U.S. 135 (1998) ("round trip" copyrighted goods); K-Mart Corp. v. Cartier, Inc., 486 U.S. 281 (1988) (trademarked goods).

[114] 137 S. Ct. 1523 (May 30, 2017) (Roberts, C.J.). The other issue in *Impression Prods.*, pertaining to *domestic* exhaustion of patent rights, is examined *supra* Chapter 10, Section C.8 ("Patent Exhaustion").

[115] 133 U.S. 697 (1890).

[116] Boesch v. Graff, 133 U.S. 697, 703 (1890).

[117] 264 F.3d 1094 (Fed. Cir. 2001).

[118] Jazz Photo Corp. v. U.S. Int'l Trade Commission, 264 F.3d 1094, 1105 (Fed. Cir. 2001) (citing *Boesch* for proposition that "a lawful foreign purchase does not obviate the need for license from the United States patentee before importation into and sale in the United States").

In its 2012 decision *Ninestar Tech. Co., Ltd. v. Int'l Trade Comm'n*,[119] the Federal Circuit reaffirmed the *Jazz Photo* holding in a case involving the infringement of U.S. patents owned by Epson America Inc. (and related corporations) by Ninestar's unauthorized importation of ink printer cartridges manufactured in China.[120] The Federal Circuit in *Ninestar* roundly rejected Ninestar's defenses that "national patent rights are exhausted by the manufacture and sale in a foreign country of a product covered by a national patent, and thus the importation of that product cannot violate the national patent,"[121] and that "the sale in a foreign country of a product manufactured in the foreign country extinguishes any right to enforce a United States patent against that product if it is imported into the United States."[122] Notably, the Supreme Court denied *certiorari* in *Ninestar* in March 2013,[123] even though it had recognized the international exhaustion defense for unauthorized importation of *copyrighted* works in a separate decision issued one week previously: namely, *Kirtsaeng v. John Wiley & Sons, Inc.*[124]

In 2015, the debate over international exhaustion of U.S. patent rights returned to the front burner, due largely to the Supreme Court's 2013 *Kirtsaeng* decision recognizing international exhaustion for copyright law.[125] The Federal Circuit took up the issue in April 2015, when it voted to hear *en banc* the case of *Lexmark Int'l, Inc. v. Impression*

[119]667 F.3d 1373 (Fed. Cir. 2012).

[120]*Ninestar*, 667 F.3d at 1376.

[121]*Ninestar*, 667 F.3d at 1378.

[122]*Ninestar*, 667 at 1378. The Federal Circuit also rejected Ninestar's argument that the Supreme Court's decision in *Quanta Computer, Inc. v. LG Elecs., Inc.*, 553 U.S. 617 (2008) had changed the law:

> Ninestar states that this case and the precedent on which it relied were incorrectly decided, and were overruled by the Supreme Court in *Quanta Computer, Inc. v. LG Elecs., Inc.*, 553 U.S. 617, 632 n.6, 128 S. Ct. 2109, 170 L. Ed. 2d 996 (2008). However, neither the facts nor the law in *Quanta Computer* concerned the issue of importation into the United States of a product not made or sold under a United States patent. In *Fujifilm Corp. v. Benun*, 605 F.3d 1366, 1371 (Fed. Cir. 2010), the court remarked that "*Quanta Computer, Inc. v. LG Electronics, Inc.* did not eliminate the first sale rule's territoriality requirement." The patents, products, and methods in *Quanta Computer* all concerned products manufactured and first sold in the United States, and the Court held that method patents as well as product patents are subject to exhaustion upon sale of product or components in the United States.

Ninestar, 667 F.3d at 1378.

[123]Ninestar Tech. Co., Ltd. v. Int'l Trade Comm'n, 133 S. Ct. 1656 (Mar. 25, 2013) (mem.).

[124]*See* Kirtsaeng v. John Wiley & Sons, Inc., 133 S. Ct. 1351 (Mar. 19, 2013).

[125]*See Kirtsaeng*, 133 S. Ct. at 1355-1356 (2013) (holding that "the 'first sale' doctrine applies to copies of a copyrighted work lawfully made abroad").

Prods., Inc.[126] The key facts are these: Lexmark International ("Lexmark"), a provider of printing and imaging products, software, and services headquartered in Lexington, Kentucky, made first sales outside the United States of toner cartridges for its inkjet printers. Several Lexmark-owned U.S. patents covered the cartridges and their use. Third parties outside the United States acquired and refurbished the cartridges so they could be re-used. Other parties, including defendant/accused infringer Impression Products, then sold the refurbished cartridges to customers in the United States without Lexmark's permission. When Lexmark sued Impression for patent infringement, a district court refused to dismiss the case, holding that "the Supreme Court [in deciding the copyright case *Kirtsaeng*] did not intend to implicitly overrule *Jazz Photo* and . . . *Jazz Photo* remains controlling precedent on patent exhaustion abroad."[127]

After a three-judge panel of the Federal Circuit heard oral argument in the appeal from the district court's decision in *Lexmark Int'l,* the Circuit *sua sponte* granted hearing *en banc.* The appellate court requested briefing on, *inter alia*, the following:

> (a) The case involves certain sales, made abroad, of articles patented in the United States. In light of *Kirtsaeng v. John Wiley & Sons, Inc.,* ___ U.S. ___, 133 S. Ct. 1351, 185 L. Ed. 2d 392 (2013), should this court overrule *Jazz Photo Corp. v. International Trade Commission*, 264 F.3d 1094 (Fed. Cir. 2001), to the extent it ruled that a sale of a patented item outside the United States never gives rise to United States patent exhaustion.[128]

[126]785 F.3d 565 (Fed. Cir. Apr. 14, 2015) (order *sua sponte* granting hearing *en banc* after three-judge panel heard argument on March 6, 2015).

[127]Lexmark Int'l, Inc. v. Ink Techs. Printer Supplies, LLC, 9 F. Supp. 3d 830, 838 (S.D. Ohio 2014).

[128]*Lexmark Int'l*, 785 F.3d 565, 566 (Fed. Cir. Apr. 14, 2015) (order *sua sponte* granting hearing *en banc*).

A second question for which the *en banc* court requested briefing concerned "(i) sales of patented articles to end users under a restriction that they use the articles once and then return them and (ii) sales of the same patented articles to resellers under a restriction that resales take place under the single-use-and-return restriction." *Lexmark Int'l,* 785 F.3d at 566. The question addressed the patent implications of Lexmark's practice of selling other of its patented toner cartridges in the United States, but at a discount and subject to an express single-use/no-resale restriction. In its February 2016 decision, the *en banc* court also found in favor of patentee Lexmark on this restricted sale question, holding:

> [W]e adhere to the holding of *Mallinckrodt, Inc. v. Medipart, Inc.*, 976 F.2d 700 (Fed. Cir. 1992), that a patentee, when selling a patented article subject to a single-use/no-resale restriction that is lawful and clearly communicated to the purchaser, does not by that sale give the buyer, or downstream buyers, the resale/reuse authority that has been expressly denied. Such resale or reuse, when contrary to the known, lawful limits on the authority conferred at the time of the

The *en banc* Circuit heard oral argument in *Lexmark* in October 2015.[129]

The Federal Circuit issued its *en banc* decision in *Lexmark Int'l, Inc. v. Impression Prods, Inc.* in February 2016.[130] In an exhaustive opinion, a ten-judge majority affirmed the district court's determination that *Jazz Photo* remained good law; that is, U.S. patent rights were *not* exhausted by a patentee's first sale of the patented product abroad. Thus, Impression's unauthorized imports and sales in the United

---

> original sale, remains unauthorized and therefore remains infringing conduct under the terms of [35 U.S.C.] §271.

Lexmark Int'l, Inc. v. Impression Prods., Inc., Nos. 2014-1617, 2014-1619, 2016 WL 559042 (Fed. Cir. Feb. 12, 2016) (*en banc*). The Circuit determined that the Supreme Court's 2008 decision in *Quanta Computer,* detailed *supra* Chapter 10, Section 8 ("Patent Exhaustion"), did not implicitly overrule *Mallinckrodt*:

> We find *Mallinckrodt*'s principle to remain sound after the Supreme Court's decision in *Quanta Computer, Inc. v. LG Electronics, Inc.*, 553 U.S. 617 (2008), in which the Court did not have before it or address a patentee sale at all, let alone one made subject to a restriction, but a sale made by a separate manufacturer under a patentee-granted license conferring unrestricted authority to sell.

Lexmark Int'l, 2016 WL 559042, at *1 (*en banc*).

The Supreme Court later granted *certiorari* and in 2017, overruled the Federal Circuit on this issue of *domestic* exhaustion. *See* Impression Prods. v. Lexmark Int'l, 137 S. Ct. 1523 (May 30, 2017) (Roberts, C.J.). The domestic exhaustion aspect of the Court's decision is examined *supra* Chapter 10, Section C.8 ("Patent Exhaustion").

[129]An oral transcript is available at http://oralarguments.cafc.uscourts.gov/default.aspx?fl=2014-1617_1022015.mp3. The American Intellectual Property Law Association reported that the attorney representing the patentee made the following arguments against adoption of international exhaustion for U.S. patents:

> On the *Jazz Photo* question, [Federal Circuit] Judge Moore asked why *Kirtsaeng* isn't dispositive, notwithstanding the Federal Circuit case law finding no international exhaustion. It is not dispositive, according to [counsel for Lexmark, Constantine L.] Trela, first because *Kirtsaeng* was a copyright case and not a patent case, and second because the decision was based on a statutory construction of the phrase "lawfully made under this title" at 17 U.S.C. 109(a). He rejected the argument that the [Supreme] Court's starting point was the common law, explaining that the Court simply wanted to determine if Congress meant to import into the copyright statute any territorial limitations from the common law.
>
> [The] Patent Act is territorial in a way that the Copyright Act is not, Trela stated, pointing out that copyrights don't depend on examination but rather come[] into existence when and wherever a work is created. By contrast, patent rights differ from country to country in patentability terms and scope, Trela explained, adding that the U.S. amicus brief conceded patents to be territorial. He maintained that logically a foreign sale should not exhaust U.S. rights because the foreign transaction has nothing to do with the U.S. patent.

American Intellectual Property Law Association, *International Patent Exhaustion Is Argued to* En Banc *Federal Circuit* (Oct. 12, 2015).

[130]Nos. 2014-1617, 2014-1619, 2016 WL 559042 (Fed. Cir. Feb. 12, 2016) (*en banc*).

States of the printer cartridges that Lexmark had first sold abroad constituted patent infringement. The Federal Circuit *en banc* majority stated:

> [W]e adhere to the holding of *Jazz Photo Corp. v. International Trade Comm'n*, 264 F.3d 1094 (Fed. Cir. 2001), that a U.S. patentee, merely by selling or authorizing the sale of a U.S.-patented article abroad, does not authorize the buyer to import the article and sell and use it in the United States, which are infringing acts in the absence of patentee-conferred authority. *Jazz Photo*'s no-exhaustion ruling recognizes that foreign markets under foreign sovereign control are not equivalent to the U.S. markets under U.S. control in which a U.S. patentee's sale presumptively exhausts its rights in the article sold. A buyer may still rely on a foreign sale as a defense to infringement, but only by establishing an express or implied license — a defense separate from exhaustion, as *Quanta* holds — based on patentee communications or other circumstances of the sale.[131]

The *en banc* Circuit in *Lexmark Int'l* also concluded that the Supreme Court's decision in *Kirtsaeng* did not implicitly overrule *Jazz Photo*. The no-exhaustion principle of *Jazz Photo* remained good law.[132] In contrast, *Kirtsaeng* was a copyright case that did not address patent law. Unlike copyright law, patent law does not have a statutory provision that allows imports of "gray market" articles without the intellectual property right holder's permission:

> We conclude that *Jazz Photo*'s no-exhaustion principle remains sound after the Supreme Court's decision in *Kirtsaeng v. John Wiley & Sons, Inc.*, 133 S. Ct. 1351 (2013), in which the Court did not address patent law or whether a foreign sale should be viewed as conferring authority to engage in otherwise infringing domestic acts. *Kirtsaeng* is a copyright case holding that 17 U.S.C. §109(a) entitles owners of copyrighted articles to take certain acts "without the authority" of the copyright holder. There is no counterpart to that provision in the Patent Act, under which a foreign sale is properly treated as neither conclusively nor even presumptively exhausting the U.S. patentee's rights in the United States.[133]

The Federal Circuit's *en banc* decision in *Lexmark Int'l* thus allowed patent owners to continue to use their patents to stop unauthorized third-party imports of products first sold outside the United States by or under authority of the patent owners. This result favored not only manufacturers of printer cartridges first sold abroad, but also the many pharmaceutical, biotech, agricultural, and high-tech

[131] *Lexmark Int'l*, 2016 WL 559042, at *2 (*en banc*).
[132] *Lexmark Int'l*, 2016 WL 559042, at *2 (*en banc*).
[133] *Lexmark Int'l*, 2016 WL 559042, at *2 (*en banc*).

companies that engaged in similar international sales and sought to preserve segmentation of international markets.[134]

Despite the appellate court's scholarly and thorough opinion in *Lexmark Int'l,* joined by ten judges, U.S. patent owners' ability to stop gray market imports by asserting their patent rights was short-lived. On December 2, 2016, the Supreme Court granted *certiorari* in the case, now captioned *Impression Prods., Inc. v. Lexmark Int'l, Inc.*[135] Two questions were presented,[136] the second presenting a referendum on international exhaustion of patent rights:

> Whether, in light of this Court's holding in *Kirtsaeng v. John Wiley & Sons, Inc.*, 133 S. Ct. 1351, 1363 (2013), that the common law doctrine barring restraints on alienation that is the basis of exhaustion doctrine "makes no geographical distinctions," a sale of a patented article — authorized by the U.S. patentee — that takes place outside of the United States exhausts the U.S. patent rights in that article.[137]

In May 2017, the Supreme Court issued its decision in *Impression Prods., Inc. v. Lexmark Int'l, Inc.*[138] To the surprise of many in the patent practitioner and academic community, the Court answered the quoted question affirmatively. By a 7-1 vote, the Court reversed the Federal Circuit on the international exhaustion issue.[139] The Court ruled summarily that "[a]n authorized sale outside the United States, just as one within the United States, exhausts all rights under the Patent Act."[140] Accordingly, Lexmark had exhausted its patent rights and could no longer sue for infringement to stop imports of the toner cartridges it had sold outside the United States.[141]

[134]For additional commentary on the impact of the *Lexmark Int'l* decision, *see* Susan Decker, *Lexmark Wins Closely-Watched Patent Case on Refurbished Products,* BloombergBusiness (Feb. 12, 2016), https://www.bloomberg.com/news/articles/ 2016-02-12/lexmark-wins-closely-watched-patent-case-on-refurbished-products.

[135]No. 15-1189, 2016 WL 1117396 (U.S. Dec. 2, 2016) (mem.).

[136]The first question presented addressed the other issue in *Lexmark Int'l*, i.e., whether exhaustion was avoided by domestic sales of patented products (i.e., Lexmark's Return Program toner cartridges) bearing post-sale restraints or limitations of use. This issue is further examined *supra* Chapter 10, Section C.8.

[137]Petition for a Writ of Certiorari, No. 15-1189, Impression Prods, Inc. v. Lexmark Int'l, Inc. (Mar. 21, 2016), at i, *available at* http://www.scotusblog.com/wp-content/uploads/2016/04/Impression-Products-v.-Lexmark-cert-petition-no-appendix.pdf.

[138]137 S. Ct. 1523 (May 30, 2017) (Roberts, C.J.).

[139]Justice Ginsburg was the sole dissenter to the majority's adoption of international exhaustion for U.S. patent rights, as detailed below. Justice Gorsuch did not participate in the decision.

[140]*Impression Prods.*, 137 S. Ct. at 1535.

[141]On the other issue in the *Impression Prods.* case, exhaustion of patent rights for *domestic* sales made subject to post-sale restrictions, the Court unanimously reversed the Circuit, as detailed separately in this treatise. *See supra* Chapter 10, Section C.8.

F. Gray Market Goods and the International Exhaustion Debate

In the view of this author, the Supreme Court's adoption of the international exhaustion doctrine for U.S. patent rights was the much more far-reaching and troubling result of the two questions decided in *Impression Prods.*; the majority's analysis erroneously treated patent rights as global, ignoring their fundamentally territorial nature. Nevertheless, international exhaustion for U.S.-patented products sold abroad by the patent owner is now the "law of the land" in the United States. As a result, U.S. law now conflicts with that of other important jurisdictions such as the European Union, which does not accept the international exhaustion doctrine for patents.[142]

The Supreme Court majority's analysis in *Impression Prods.* proceeded along four primary grounds. First, the majority relied heavily on its 2013 *Kirtsaeng* copyright decision, examined above, and the "historic kinship" between patent and copyright law. On these bases the Court concluded that that "the bond between the two leaves no room for a rift on the question of international exhaustion."[143]

Recall that in adopting international exhaustion for *copyrighted* goods in *Kirtsaeng v. John Wiley & Sons, Inc.*,[144] the Supreme Court majority in that case first considered the statutory first sale doctrine of copyright law, 17 U.S.C. §109(a). That textual provision was indecisive because it is silent on geographic limits.[145] Nevertheless, the *Impression Prods.* majority read *Kirtsaeng* to have found in the common law a geographic hook (that is, an absence of any geographic restrictions) for international exhaustion of copyrighted items sold abroad:

> What helped tip the scales for global exhaustion [in *Kirtsaeng*] was the fact that the first sale doctrine originated in "the common law's refusal to permit restraints on the alienation of chattels." [*Kirtsaeng*, 568 U.S.] at 538, 133 S. Ct. 1351. That "common-law doctrine makes no geographical

[142]*See* Vincenzo Franceschelli, International Report, International League of Competition Law 2014 Congress, *To what extent does the principle of exhaustion of IP rights apply to the on-line industry?* (Sept. 14, 2014) at para. 4.4 (stating that "the principle of exhaustion — at the moment — is not applied if the first sale is made by the legitimate holder outside the territory of the [European] Union. Indeed, no 'extracomunitary exhaustion,' or, if you prefer, no 'international exhaustion' currently exists."), *available at* http://www.ligue.org/uploads/documents/2014RapportinternationalB15septembre.pdf; 11 Intellectual Property Law and Policy 683 (Hugh C. Hansen, ed.) (Hart Pub. 2010) ("By placing the patented product on the market outside the European Union, no exhaustion takes place. According to the Federal Supreme Court [of Germany] and the European Court of Justice case law, there is at present no worldwide or international exhaustion of German/European industrial property rights[.]").

[143]*Impression Prods.*, 137 S. Ct. at 1356.

[144]568 U.S. 519 (2013).

[145]*Impression Prods.*, 137 S. Ct. at 1356 (citing *Kirtsaeng*, 568 U.S. at 528-533) (statute neither restricted scope of first sale doctrine geographically nor clearly embraced international exhaustion).

> distinctions." *Id.*, at 539, 133 S. Ct. 1351. The lack of any textual basis for distinguishing between domestic and international sales meant that "a straightforward application" of the first sale doctrine required the conclusion that it applies overseas. *Id.*, at 540, 133 S. Ct. 1351 (internal quotation marks omitted).[146]

Transposing the same rationale to patents, the *Impression Prods.* majority believed that applying exhaustion to foreign sales of U.S.-patented products was "just as straightforward." It observed that "nothing in the text or history of the Patent Act shows that Congress intended to confine that borderless common law principle to domestic sales." Viewing the common law principle as "well established," the majority took it "as a given that Congress ha[d] legislated with an expectation that the principle will apply except when a statutory purpose to the contrary is evident."[147]

Second, the *Impression Prods.* Supreme Court majority was not impressed by the "reward" argument. Because a U.S. patentee is not protected by U.S. exclusionary rights in foreign countries, it may often have to sell its products in those markets at lower prices than the prices it could command in the United States. The argument proceeds that the U.S. patentee who sells abroad has not received its just "reward" under the U.S. patent system. Accordingly, its U.S. patent rights should not be considered to have been exhausted by its foreign sales. Rejecting this argument, the *Impression Prods.* majority again assimilated patent rights to copyright protection. It observed that "[t]he territorial limit on patent rights is . . . no basis for distinguishing copyright protections; those protections " 'do not have any extraterritorial operation' either."[148]

More fundamentally, the *Impression Prods.* Supreme Court majority simply did not accept the idea that U.S. patent laws should offer patent owners a "premium" or guarantee a particular amount of return. The Court stated:

> Exhaustion is a separate limit on the patent grant, and does not depend on the patentee receiving some undefined premium for selling the right to access the American market. A purchaser buys an item, not patent rights. And exhaustion is triggered by the patentee's decision to give that

[146]*Impression Prods.*, 137 S. Ct. at 1356 (citing *Kirtsaeng*, 568 U.S. at 539).

[147]*Impression Prods.*, 137 S. Ct. at 1536 (citing Astoria Fed. Sav. & Loan Assn. v. Solimino, 501 U.S. 104, 108 (1991)).

[148]*Impression Prods.*, 137 S. Ct. at 1536-1537 (quoting 5 M. Nimmer & D. Nimmer, COPYRIGHT §17.02, p. 17-26 (2017)). While the quoted statement is literally true, this author observes that multinational copyright protection is essentially automatic for U.S. copyright-protected works under the Berne Convention. In contrast, multinational protection under patent law is an exceedingly more complex, laborious, and expensive process fraught with formalities; the ultimate decision on patentability is made by each national patent system where protection is sought.

> item up and receive whatever fee it decides is appropriate "for the article and the invention which it embodies." *Univis*, 316 U.S., at 251, 62 S. Ct. 1088. The patentee may not be able to command the same amount for its products abroad as it does in the United States. But the Patent Act does not guarantee a particular price, much less the price from selling to American consumers. Instead, the right to exclude just ensures that the patentee receives one reward — of whatever amount the patentee deems to be "satisfactory compensation," *Keeler* [Keeler v. Standard Folding Bed Co., 157 U.S. 659 (1895)], 157 U.S., at 661, 15 S. Ct. 738 — for every item that passes outside the scope of the patent monopoly.[149]

Third, the *Impression Prods.* majority rejected as inapposite the Supreme Court's only prior decision involving imports of U.S. patent–protected products by foreign purchasers, the 1890 decision examined above, *Boesch v Graff*.[150] The majority explained that U.S. patent rights were *not* exhausted in *Boesch* because the U.S. *patentee* never sold (or authorized the sale of) its product abroad. In *Boesch*, the product, an improved lamp burner, was legally made and sold in Germany by a Mr. Hecht, who held prior user rights superior to the German patent rights on the burners.[151] The burners legally made by Hecht in Germany were then imported into the United States, where they were also protected by U.S. patents. The *Boesch* Court held that the unauthorized importation of the U.S. patent-protected burners was actionable infringement. In other words, the patentee's rights had not been exhausted by the foreign sales of Hecht.

Importantly, the sale of the patented products abroad in *Boesch* was not by or with the authority of the patentee, thus distinguishing *Boesch* from the case at bar (in which Lexmark, the patentee, chose to sell its toner cartridges abroad).[152] As the *Boesch* Court summarized the case before it, "[t]he exact question presented is whether a

[149] *Impression Prods.*, 137 S. Ct. at 1537. Notably, both the cited *Univis* and *Keeler* cases involved the question of domestic, not international, sales of U.S.-patented products.

[150] 133 U.S. 697 (1890).

[151] Prior user rights, a defense to infringement recognized historically by many foreign patent systems, are explained *supra* Section E.1 ("First-to-File Versus First-to-Invent").

[152] *See Impression Prods.*, 137 S. Ct. at 1537; *see also Lexmark Int'l*, 816 F.3d 721, 784 (Dyk, J., dissenting), stating:

> [*Boesch*] did not even involve an authorized sale by the holder of U.S. patent rights but rather a sale by a third party under a foreign law's prior use exception. . . . Thus *Boesch* does not apply here because the foreign sales were made by Lexmark — the U.S. patent rights holder — itself. The accused infringer does not rely on foreign law as the source of its authority but the doctrine of exhaustion resulting from an authorized sale by a U.S. rights holder.

Lexmark Int'l, Inc. v. Impression Prods., Inc., 816 F.3d 721, 784 (Fed. Cir. 2016) (Dyk, J., dissenting).

dealer residing in the United States can purchase in another country articles patented there, from a person authorized to sell them, and import them to and sell them in the United States, *without the license or consent of the owners of the United States patent*."[153] Although the *Boesch* Court stated broadly that "[t]he sale of articles in the United States under a United States patent cannot be controlled by foreign laws,"[154] that statement did not help Lexmark because it was not addressing the same type of international transaction in dispute in *Impression Prods*.

Fourth, the *Impression Prods.* Supreme Court majority rejected the United States' *amicus* "middle-ground" position that foreign sales authorized by a U.S. patentee should exhaust the U.S. patent rights *unless* those rights are expressly reserved.[155] It disagreed with the government's assertion that the lower courts had "long ago coalesced" around this position. In the Supreme Court's view, two courts of appeals decisions in the 1890s,[156] certain district court decisions,[157] and the Federal Circuit's 2001 *Jazz Photo* decision[158] represented a mere "smattering" of "sparse and inconsistent decisions." These decisions provided "no basis for any expectation, let alone a settled one, that patentees can reserve patent rights when they sell abroad."[159]

The *Impression Prods.* Supreme Court majority concluded its opinion by reasserting the primacy of the common law real property policy against restraints on alienation. This was its primary basis for adopting an international exhaustion regime for U.S. patents. The majority explained:

> More is at stake when it comes to patents than simply the dealings between the parties, which can be addressed through contract law. Instead, exhaustion occurs because, in a sale, the patentee elects to give up title to an item in exchange for payment. Allowing patent rights to stick remora[160]-like to that item as it flows through the market would violate the principle against restraints on alienation. Exhaustion does not depend on whether the patentee receives a premium for selling in

[153] *Boesch*, 133 U.S. at 702 (emphasis added).

[154] *Boesch*, 133 U.S. at 703.

[155] *Impression Prods.*, 137 S. Ct. at 1537-1538.

[156] *See* Dickerson v. Tinling, 84 F. 192, 194-195 (8th Cir. 1897); Dickerson v. Matheson, 57 F. 524, 527 (2d Cir. 1893).

[157] *See* Sanofi, S.A. v. Med-Tech Veterinarian Prods., Inc., 565 F. Supp. 931, 938 (D.N.J. 1983).

[158] *See* Jazz Photo Corp. v. International Trade Commission, 264 F.3d 1094 (Fed. Cir. 2001).

[159] *Impression Prods.*, 137 S. Ct. at 1538.

[160] A "remora," also known as a "shark-sucker," is "[a] slender marine fish which attaches itself to large fish by means of a sucker on top of the head." English Oxford Living Dictionaries (2019), https://en.oxforddictionaries.com/definition/remora.

the United States, or the type of rights that buyers expect to receive. As a result, restrictions and location are irrelevant; what matters is the patentee's decision to make a sale.[161]

In this author's view, the Supreme Court majority in *Impression Prods.* over-emphasized the common law principle disfavoring restraints on alienation of chattels at the expense of ignoring the complex territorial nature of U.S. patent rights. The majority was certainly not forced to do so — it was not bound by any precedent on the question of international exhaustion. Not one of the cases it relied on dealt with foreign sales of U.S.-patented products by a U.S. patentee. Moreover, the U.S. Patent Act did not control because it is silent on exhaustion (at least according to the majority's rejection of the Federal Circuit's interpretation of "authority" in 35 U.S.C. §271(a)), discussed *supra*[162]). As the Court in its 2013 *Kirtsaeng* copyright decision had admitted, the common law policy was silent on cross-border transactions; no earlier case law had balanced the disfavor of restraints on alienation with the multinational, territorial nature of copyright (or patent) law.[163]

Writing on an essentially blank slate, then, the *Impression Prods.* Supreme Court majority simply chose to default to the common law policy against restraints on alienation. The best the majority could offer was that that policy made no geographic distinctions; Lord Coke's seventeenth-century pronouncements did not address global transfers of chattels.

In this author's view, Justice Ginsburg offered a far superior analysis in her dissenting opinion in *Impression Prods.*[164] She would have held that a foreign sale does *not* exhaust a U.S. inventor's U.S. patent rights.[165] She emphasized the fundamental fact that U.S. patents provide no protection in foreign countries; patent law is territorial. As

[161] *Impression Prods.*, 137 S. Ct. at 1538.
[162] *See supra* Chapter 10, Section C.8.
[163] Recall that the Supreme Court observed in *Kirtsaeng*:

> The common-law doctrine makes no geographical distinctions; nor can we find any in *Bobbs-Merrill* (where this Court first applied the "first sale" doctrine) or in §109(a)'s predecessor provision, which Congress enacted a year later. See supra, at 1360. Rather, as the Solicitor General acknowledges, "a straightforward application of *Bobbs-Merrill*" [Bobbs-Merrill Co. v. Straus, 210 U.S. 339 (1908)] would not preclude the "first sale" defense from applying to authorized copies made overseas. Brief for United States 27. And we can find no language, context, purpose, or history that would rebut a "straightforward application" of that doctrine here.

Kirtsaeng v. John Wiley & Sons, Inc., 568 U.S. 519, 539-540 (2013).
[164] *Impression Prods.*, 137 S. Ct. at 1538-1539 (Ginsburg, J., dissenting-in-part).
[165] *Impression Prods.*, 137 S. Ct. at 1538 (Ginsburg, J., dissenting-in-part).

Justice Ginsburg rightly asked the *Impression Prods.* majority, when a sale abroad operates independently of the U.S. patent system, how can one sensibly hold that such a sale exhausts an inventor's U.S. patent rights?[166] "U.S. patent protection accompanies none of a U.S. patentee's sales abroad — a competitor could sell the same patented product abroad with no U.S.-patent-law consequence. Accordingly, the foreign sale should not diminish the protections of U.S. law in the United States."[167]

Dissenting Justice Ginsburg also faulted the *Impression Prods.* majority for its reliance on the *Kirtsaeng* copyright decision (from which she also dissented). Although copyrights and patents may have a "historic kinship," she noted, they are "'not identical twins.'"[168] Unlike patent protection, copyright protections are "harmonized across countries."[169] Thus, she explained, "the copyright protections one receives abroad are . . . likely to be similar to those received at home, even if provided under each country's separate copyright regime."[170] That is *not* the case for patent protection. Rights must be formally applied for in each country for which patent protection is sought, and each country has flexibility in interpreting the prerequisites for patentability.[171]

[166]*Impression Prods.*, 137 S. Ct. at 1539 (Ginsburg, J., dissenting-in-part).

[167]*Impression Prods.*, 137 S. Ct. at 1539 (Ginsburg, J., dissenting-in-part).

[168]*Impression Prods.*, 137 S. Ct. at 1539 (Ginsburg, J., dissenting-in-part) (quoting Sony Corp. of America v. Universal City Studios, Inc., 464 U.S. 417, 439 n.19 (1984).

[169]*Impression Prods.*, 137 S. Ct. at 1539 (Ginsburg, J., dissenting-in-part). Here Justice Ginsburg referred to the Berne Convention's provision of national treatment, citing *Golan v. Holder*, 565 U.S. 302, 308 (2012) (Berne members "agree to treat authors from other member countries as well as they treat their own") (citing Berne Convention for the Protection of Literary and Artistic Works, Sept. 9, 1886, as revised at Stockholm on July 14, 1967, Arts. 1, 5(1), 828 U.N.T.S. 225, 231-233). But the Paris Convention for the Protection of Industrial Property (which governs patents) also provides for national treatment.

The more relevant distinction between multinational copyright and patent systems is that under Berne, an author in a Berne country receives automatically, without any formalities, national treatment protection in other Berne countries "as well as the rights specially granted by this Convention," including the exclusive right of reproduction (art. 9), certain moral rights (art. 6*bis*), and other rights. In contrast, the Paris Convention does not set forth any "substantive minima" of protection for inventions, and certainly does not provide for patent protection in other Paris member countries without formalities.

[170]*Impression Prods.*, 137 S. Ct. at 1539 (Ginsburg, J., dissenting-in-part).

[171]Although the TRIPS Agreement of the WTO for the first time set forth substantive minimum standards for patentability, *see* TRIPS art. 27(1) (setting forth "novelty," "inventive step," and "industrial application"), TRIPS does not define those criteria. *See* World Trade Organization, Trade-Related Aspects of Intellectual Property Rights (1994), WTO member countries have a great deal of freedom in interpreting those criteria to comport with their individual economic and social policies. Moreover, TRIPS expressly provides member countries with multiple options for excluding certain types of inventions from patentability. *See* TRIPS arts. 27(2)-27(3).

F. Gray Market Goods and the International Exhaustion Debate

The *Impression Prods.* majority did not concern itself with the practical result of its decision to adopt the international exhaustion doctrine for U.S. patents. In the view of this author, the impact is far-reaching and negative for U.S. patentees, whose exclusionary rights have been weakened. Commentators have suggested that "[w]hile the dispute . . . involved articles of manufacture, the decision has strong implications for the biotechnology and pharmaceutical Industry, and may make it easier for drugs sold legally overseas to make their way back to the U.S. market."[172] A former director of the USPTO suggested that "the impact of [*Impression Prods.*] on the ever-greater globalization of sales and manufacture could be profound."[173] And finally, a former USPTO Deputy Commissioner for Patent Examination Policy observed that

> [t]his weakening of patent owner rights may result in patent owners seeking to raise prices for goods sold abroad, but for price regulated products such as pharmaceuticals it may not be so easy to do. Thus, patent owners may need to further rely on regulatory authorities to impose restrictions on products regulated by the FDA or other regulatory bodies to prevent importation of patented goods purchased at lower prices in foreign markets. Otherwise, patent owners will have to be very wary of selling large volumes of patented products in foreign markets where the likelihood is that they are being purchased at low costs for resale in the U.S. to compete with the domestic supply chain.[174]

[172]*Patent Exhaustion and Pharmaceuticals* (Aug. 22, 2017), *available at* https://www.lexology.com/library/detail.aspx?g=46c92db5-a0a1-43ed-91f0-5f4a831eef50.

[173]Gene Quinn, *Patent Exhaustion at the Supreme Court: Industry Reaction to Impression Products v. Lexmark* (May 30, 2017) (quoting Q. Todd Dickinson), *available at* http://www.ipwatchdog.com/2017/05/30/patent-exhaustion-supreme-court-industry-reaction-impression-products-v-lexmark/id=83822.

[174]Gene Quinn, *Patent Exhaustion at the Supreme Court: Industry Reaction to Impression Products v. Lexmark* (May 30, 2017) (quoting Stephen Kunin), *available at* http://www.ipwatchdog.com/2017/05/30/patent-exhaustion-supreme-court-industry-reaction-impression-products-v-lexmark/id=83822.

For a more favorable view of the *Impression Prods.* decision, *see* Sarah R. Wasserman Rajec, *Impression Products, Inc. v. Lexmark Inc.: Will International Patent Exhaustion Bring Free Trade in Patented Goods?* (June 1, 2017), https://patentlyo.com/patent/2017/06/impression-international-exhaustion.html, stating that

> [t]he greater impact of an international patent exhaustion rule . . . is that it makes U.S. patent law more consistent with free trade principles and is likely to increase competition by lowering barriers to trade in patented goods. Companies will no longer be able to use patent rights . . . to engage in geographic price discrimination between U.S. and foreign markets, and supply-chain-participants, resellers, and consumers will not be subject to the information costs associated with determining the provenance and travels of all articles of commerce they purchase.

G. Enforcement of Foreign Patents in U.S. Courts

The U.S. Supreme Court's 2007 decision in *Microsoft Corp. v. AT&T Corp.*[175] reinforced a strong presumption against extraterritorial application of U.S. patents.[176] Because a U.S. court is unlikely to hold that acts occurring abroad infringe a U.S. patent, the conventional strategy for combating such acts requires that one has obtained patent protection in foreign countries and thereafter enforces the foreign patents in the courts of the foreign jurisdictions where the acts of infringement allegedly occurred. As commerce expands globally, the expense and complexity of conducting patent litigation in multiple foreign fora loom large.[177]

As a result, U.S. patent holders owning counterpart foreign patents on a particular invention have asked U.S. courts not only to decide the question of domestic infringement but also to exercise supplemental jurisdiction under 28 U.S.C. §1367 in order to decide whether the counterpart foreign patents have been infringed by foreign acts.[178] This strategy has not proved successful thus far, however, because the Federal Circuit continues to reject district court exercises of supplemental jurisdiction over foreign patent issues.[179]

For example, the Federal Circuit held that a district court abused its discretion in exercising supplemental jurisdiction over foreign patent claims in the closely watched *Voda v. Cordis Corp.*[180] The plaintiff

[175] 550 U.S. 437 (2007).

[176] *See* Microsoft Corp. v. AT&T Corp., 550 U.S. 437, 454-455 (stating that the presumption that United States law "governs domestically but does not rule the world" applied "with particular force in patent law") (citing 35 U.S.C. §154(a)(1), and *Deepsouth Packing Co. v. Laitram Corp.*, 406 U.S. 518, 531 (1972)). The Supreme Court's *Microsoft* decision is examined in further detail *supra* Chapter 9, Section E.4 ("Component Exports Under 35 U.S.C. §271(f)").

[177] *See* Fairchild Semiconductor Corp. v. Third Dimension (3D) Semiconductor, Inc., 589 F. Supp. 2d 84, 99 (D. Me. 2008) (observing that "[i]n a globalized marketplace, intellectual property disputes can involve many countries' patent laws. Uncertainty and complexity in resolving those disputes can increase the cost of doing business and, as a result, the cost to the consumer.") (footnotes omitted).

[178] Section 1367 ("Supplemental jurisdiction") of 28 U.S.C. provides in part that "[e]xcept as provided in subsections (b) and (c) or as expressly provided otherwise by Federal statute, in any civil action of which the district courts have original jurisdiction, the district courts shall have supplemental jurisdiction over all other claims that are so related to claims in the action within such original jurisdiction that they form part of the same case or controversy under Article III of the United States Constitution." *Id.* §1367(a).

[179] *See* Voda v. Cordis Corp., 476 F.3d 887 (Fed. Cir. 2007) (vacating district court's acceptance of supplemental jurisdiction); *cf.* Mars, Inc. v. Kabushiki-Kaisha Nippon Conlux, 24 F.3d 1368 (Fed. Cir. 1994) (affirming district court's decision to decline supplemental jurisdiction over claim of infringement of Japanese patent).

[180] 476 F.3d 887, 904 (Fed. Cir. 2007).

Dr. Voda owned U.S. and foreign patents (the latter issuing from the same PCT application) directed to guiding catheters for use in interventional cardiology. Although the parties disputed whether Voda's U.S. and foreign patents differed in any material aspects, the same accused Cordis catheter was sold in the United States as well as in France, Germany, the United Kingdom, and Canada. The Federal Circuit discussed but declined to decide under §1367(a) whether Voda's assertion of foreign patent infringement involved a "common nucleus of operative fact" with the question whether Voda's U.S. patent was infringed.[181]

Rather, the Federal Circuit held that the district court had abused its discretion under 28 U.S.C. §1367(c) by not declining to exercise supplemental jurisdiction.[182] According to the *Voda* majority, "considerations of comity, judicial economy, convenience, fairness, and other exceptional circumstances constitute compelling reasons to decline jurisdiction . . . in this case."[183] The majority first observed that nothing in the Paris Convention, PCT, or TRIPS Agreement "contemplates or allows one jurisdiction to adjudicate patents of another."[184] With respect to comity, the majority saw "no reason why American courts should supplant British, Canadian, French, or German courts in interpreting and enforcing British, Canadian, European, French, or German patents."[185] Judicial economy would not be realized by the exercise of supplemental jurisdiction because U.S. courts "lack . . . institutional competence in the foreign patent regimes" at issue, and separate trials would likely be required to deal with potential jury confusion in applying the different regimes.[186] The district court had not articulated any analysis regarding factors of convenience.[187] Lastly, the act of state doctrine potentially made

[181]*See Voda*, 476 F.3d at 896.

[182]Section 1367(c) provides that "[t]he district courts may decline to exercise supplemental jurisdiction over a claim under subsection (a) if—(1) the claim raises a novel or complex issue of State law, (2) the claim substantially predominates over the claim or claims over which the district court has original jurisdiction, (3) the district court has dismissed all claims over which it has original jurisdiction, or (4) in exceptional circumstances, there are other compelling reasons for declining jurisdiction." The Federal Circuit in *Voda* held that the district court erred by not declining supplemental jurisdiction under subpart (4) of §1367(c), because the case presented "exceptional circumstances" involving "compelling reasons" for declining. *See Voda*, 476 F.3d at 898.

[183]*Voda*, 476 F.3d at 898.

[184]*Voda*, 476 F.3d at 899. The dissent pointed out that none of the treaties affirmatively prohibits resolution by a national court of private disputes that include foreign patent rights. *See id.* at 915 (Newman, J., dissenting).

[185]*Voda*, 476 F.3d at 901.

[186]*See Voda*, 476 F.3d at 903.

[187]*See Voda*, 476 F.3d at 903.

the district court's exercise of supplemental jurisdiction over foreign patent claims fundamentally unfair. The doctrine might prevent U.S. courts from inquiring into the validity of foreign patents and might require the courts to adjudicate patent claims regardless of validity or enforceability.[188]

The Federal Circuit concluded by noting that the reasons it had stated as compelling the district court to decline supplemental jurisdiction in *Voda*, namely, limitations imposed by international treaties and considerations of comity, judicial economy, convenience, and fairness, comprised a "non-exhaustive list, not a test, for district courts to consider under §1367(c)."[189] The *Voda* court held out some slight possibility that other cases raising different facts might support the exercise of supplemental jurisdiction over foreign patent claims, "especially if circumstances change, such as if the United States were to enter into a new international patent treaty or if events during litigation alter a district court's conclusions regarding comity, judicial economy, convenience, or fairness."[190] In the case at bar, however, the factors considered by the majority compelled it to conclude that the district court had abused its discretion in exercising supplemental jurisdiction.[191]

[188]*See Voda*, 476 F.3d at 904. The dissent responded that "the grant of a patent is not an Act of State, whether done by the United States or a foreign country." *Id.* at 914 (Newman, J., dissenting). "Patent validity and infringement are legal and commercial issues, not acts of state." *Id.* at 915 (Newman, J., dissenting).

[189]*Voda*, 476 F.3d at 904-905.

[190]*Voda*, 476 F.3d at 905.

[191]The dissent in *Voda* observed that, *inter alia*, U.S. courts routinely decide issues of foreign law. The majority's "extreme barrier to exercise of the district court's discretion when foreign patents are involved stands alone among the vast variety of causes in which such determinations have been made." *Id.* at 906 (Newman, J., dissenting). The dissent charged that the majority's ruling "essentially eliminates [the] discretionary option in foreign patent cases." *Id.* at 910. Moreover, it contravened *eBay Inc. v. MercExchange L.L.C.*, 547 U.S. 388 (2006), in which the Supreme Court "discouraged the carving out of an exception uniquely for patent cases, and required that the equitable discretion of the district court be as available in patent cases as in other cases." *Voda*, 476 F.3d at 910 (Newman, J., dissenting).

Echoing the *Voda* dissent, a federal district court has read the *Voda* majority's decision as "seem[ing] vehement that a United States court should almost always decline to hear a dispute about foreign patents, at least if its jurisdiction is discretionary." Fairchild Semiconductor Corp. v. Third Dimension (3D) Semiconductor, Inc., 589 F. Supp. 2d 84, 85 (D. Me. 2008). The district court in *Fairchild* distinguished *Voda*, however, because *Fairchild* involved a licensing dispute in which the parties had agreed to a forum selection clause for resolution of disputes involving the licensed U.S. and Chinese patents. The district court held that its diversity of citizenship jurisdiction (rather than §1367 supplemental jurisdiction) applied to this contractual dispute, and that the court should exercise that jurisdiction even though doing so might require consideration of Chinese patent law. *See Fairchild*, 589 F. Supp. 2d at 98 (concluding that "the concerns expressed in *Voda* do not prevent enforcement of the forum selection clause for this royalty dispute").

H. Patent Protection in Europe

The European market is important to many U.S. patent holders; patent attorneys are frequently tasked with obtaining an international portfolio of patent protection for their clients. Europe has developed a sophisticated system of patent protection that is well worth study by U.S. practitioners. Accordingly, this section briefly overviews the options for obtaining and enforcing patent rights in Europe.

1. Routes to Obtain Protection

Presently there are at least four ways for a U.S. entity to obtain patent protection in Europe: (1) file an international application under the Patent Cooperation Treaty (PCT)[192] designating the European Patent Organization (this is referred to as the "Euro-PCT route[193]); (2) file a European patent application in the European Patent Office; (3) file an international application under the PCT designating individual European nations of interest; or (4) file a patent application directly in the domestic patent office of the European nation of interest (this is referred to as the "national route"[194]).

Options (1) and (2) involve the European Patent Office (EPO), which is headquartered in Munich, Germany, with a branch in The Hague, Netherlands. The EPO examines patent applications in accordance with the provisions of the European Patent Convention (EPC),[195] which was adopted in 1973 and entered into force in 1977.[196]

[192]The PCT is discussed *supra* Section C. The PCT international application is often filed in conjunction with (and within one year of) the applicant having filed its "priority" application in the applicant's home country patent office. *See* PCT art. 8(1) (providing that "[t]he international application may contain a declaration, as prescribed in the Regulations, claiming the priority of one or more earlier applications filed in or for any country party to the Paris Convention for the Protection of Industrial Property").

[193]*See* World Intellectual Property Organization, *PCT Applicant's Guide—International Phase* §§4.022-4.026 (Nov. 14, 2013), *available at* http://www.wipo.int/pct/en/appguide/text.jsp?page=ip04.html#_regional_patents (section titled "Regional Patents Via the PCT"). *See also* European Patent Office, *Euro-PCT Guide: PCT Procedure at the EPO* (12th ed., Jan, 2019), available at https://www.epo.org/applying/international/guide-for-applicants/html/e/index.html.

[194]Option (4), the "national route," may be preferable if an applicant "intend[s] to apply for a patent in just a few European countries. . . ." European Patent Office, *National Applications* (Mar. 14, 2011), http://www.epo.org/applying/national.html.

[195]*See* European Patent Convention, 15th ed. (Sept. 2013), *available at* http://documents.epo.org/projects/babylon/eponet.nsf/0/00E0CD7FD461C0D5C1257C060050C376/$File/EPC_15th_edition_2013.pdf.

[196]*See* European Patent Office, *The History of the EPO: 1973* (Nov. 27, 2014), http://www.epo.org/learning-events/40epc/timeline.html#year19731977, explaining that

The EPO operates as a centralized system for the filing and examination of a single application to procure a "European patent"[197] that may be thought of as comprising a bundle of national "parts."[198] More specifically, the EPC provides that each "European patent shall, in each of the Contracting States for which it is granted, have the effect of and be subject to the same conditions as a national patent granted by that State, unless this Convention provides otherwise."[199] Assuming the EPO grants a European patent, the patentee must then ensure that the patent is "validated" in each European country where patent protection is sought.[200]

Notably, the European Patent Organisation (which includes the EPO and an Administrative Council) is not an agency of the European Union but rather an autonomous international organization. The roster of EPO contracting states is not identical with that of the European Union, although there is substantial overlap.[201] Patent applications

---

> On 5 October [1973], after more than 20 years of negotiations and debate, 16 countries sign[ed] the European Patent Convention [in Munich, Germany]. This multilateral treaty create[d] the European Patent Organisation and the European Patent Office (EPO) and provide[d] for an autonomous legal system to review and grant European patents.
>
> When the EPC c[ame] into effect in 1977, applicants c[ould] file a single patent application with the EPO that, if granted, [wa]s applicable in all the member states that they choose. Member states retain[ed] the right to enforce and revoke individual patents.
>
> The EPC greatly reduce[d] fees and paperwork associated with filing in several European countries. Previously this required costly translations and time-consuming search and grant procedures in each country.

[197] *See* European Patent Convention art. 2(1) ("Patents granted under this Convention shall be called European patents.").

[198] *See* European Patent Convention art. 3 ("The grant of a European patent may be requested for one or more of the Contracting States.").

[199] European Patent Convention art. 2(2).

[200] *See* European Commission, *Patent Reform Package: Frequently Asked Questions* (Dec. 11, 2012), https://ec.europa.eu/commission/presscorner/detail/en/MEMO_12_970, stating in response to Question 4 that

> the grant of the European patent is not enough for it to take effect in most Contracting States to the EPC. The patent proprietor must choose the countries in which he/she wishes to have protection and validate the European patent in these states within a short time limit after grant. A number of different validation requirements may apply. For example, the patent proprietor may have to pay a fee to the national patent office, comply with various formal requirements and provide a translation of the patent to the official language of the State.

[201] *See* European Commission, *The EU Single Market: Patents: Frequently Asked Questions* (Dec. 11, 2012), https://ec.europa.eu/commission/presscorner/detail/en/MEMO_12_970 (stating in response to Question 4 that the EP Organisation includes 27 EU member states plus 11 other European countries); *see also* European Patent Office, *Member states of the European Patent Organisation* (Apr. 22, 2013),

must be processed in one of the EPO's three official languages—English, French, or German.[202]

2. Routes to Enforce Patents

Although the European Patent Convention revolutionized the process of obtaining patent protection in multiple European nations, the *enforcement* of patents in Europe has remained thus far a domestic process. In other words, infringement actions are brought in the courts of the European nation where the alleged infringement occurred.[203] This holds whether the patent being enforced was granted by a national patent office in Europe or is a "national part" of a European patent. The European Patent Convention provides a system of centralized procurement, but does not include a framework for centralized enforcement.[204]

a. Unitary Patent System

In 2012, after a number of prior attempts,[205] European legislators approved the creation of a European Union-administered Unitary

---

http://www.epo.org/about-us/organisation/member-states.html (providing roster of EPO members).

[202]European Patent Office, *European Patent Guide: How to get a European Patent* §4.1.006 (19th ed., April 2019), *available at* https://www.epo.org/applying/european/Guide-for-applicants/html/e/ga_c4_1_3.html.

[203]*See* Kevin P. Mahne, *A Unitary Patent and Unified Patent Court for the European Union: An Analysis of Europe's Long Standing Attempt to Create a Supranational Patent System*, 94 J. PAT. & TRADEMARK OFF. SOC'Y 162, 167 (2012) (stating that "a patent holder must sue an alleged infringer in the national courts of each country where the alleged infringement has occurred").

With respect to remedies, however, some attempts at enforcing injunctions across European borders have succeeded, particularly in the Dutch courts. *See* Gretchen Ann Bender, *Clash of the Titans: The Territoriality of Patent Law vs. the European Union*, 40 IDEA 49 (2000) (analyzing "the European cross-border injunction phenomenon and its potential future").

[204]*See* European Patent Convention art. 64(3) ("Any infringement of a European patent shall be dealt with by national law.").

[205]*See* Kevin P. Mahne, *A Unitary Patent and Unified Patent Court for the European Union: An Analysis of Europe's Long Standing Attempt to Create a Supranational Patent System*, 94 J. PAT. & TRADEMARK OFF. SOC'Y 162 (2012):

> For over forty[]years European countries have held numerous conferences and signed several international agreements aimed at either creating a unitary patent which would be valid in all European countries upon issuance or establishing a specialized European court with jurisdiction over patents. While the European Patent Organization "EP Organization," established by the European Patent Convention (EPC), was a significant milestone toward the creation of a supranational patent system for Europe, other attempts by European countries to reach an agreement which would resolve the problems that are inherent in the European fragmented patent system have failed. This is partly because of the

Patent System.[206] The system is intended to create a "European Union patent" or "unitary" patent having effect throughout all EU member states (as the EU has previously implemented for trademarks and designs[207]). "Once established, a granted unitary patent will be valid in all participating countries and, unlike the existing European patent, will no longer be a collection of nationally enforceable patents bundled together."[208] As of late 2019, however, the Unitary Patent System was not yet in effect.[209]

> reluctance of some countries to relinquish their sovereign power over patent matters to an international body.

Mahne, 94 J. PAT. & TRADEMARK OFF. SOC'Y at 164 (footnote omitted). *See also* European Commission, Staff Working Paper: Impact Assessment: Accompanying Document to the Proposal for a Regulation of the European Parliament and the Council Implementing Enhanced Cooperation in the Area of the Creation of Unitary Patent Protection and Proposal for a Council Regulation Implementing Enhanced Cooperation in the Area of the Creation of Unitary Patent Protection, at 4 (Apr. 13, 2011), *available at* http://eur-lex.europa.eu/LexUriServ/LexUriServ.do?uri=SEC:2011:0482:FIN:EN:PDF, stating that

> Today patent protection in Europe is fragmented. While the European Patent Office (EPO) ensures uniformity in granting patents under the European Patent Convention (EPC), the need for a coherent system of patent protection in the internal market has been apparent for decades. Efforts made since the 1970s, however, have not led to success.

[206]*See* Regulation (EU) No 1257/2012 of the European Parliament and of the Council of 17 December 2012 implementing enhanced cooperation in the area of the creation of unitary patent Protection (Dec. 17, 2012), *available at* http://eur-lex.europa.eu/LexUriServ/LexUriServ.do?uri=OJ:L:2012:361:0001:0008:en:PDF; Council Regulation (EU) No 1260/2012 of 17 December 2012 implementing enhanced cooperation in the area of the creation of unitary patent protection with regard to the applicable translation arrangements (Dec. 17, 2012), *available at* http://eur-lex.europa.eu/LexUriServ/LexUriServ.do?uri=OJ:L:2012:361:0089:0092:en:PDF.

[207]*See* Office for Harmonization in the Internal Market, *Trademarks and Designs* (2016), https://oami.europa.eu/ohimportal/en/home.

[208]European Patent Office, *The History of the EPO: 2012* (Nov. 27, 2014), http://www.epo.org/learning-events/40epc/timeline.html#year20082013.

[209]"The unitary patent is expected to enter into force at the end of the 2020. https://wwwepo.org/law-practice/unitary/unitary-patent/start.html. In October 2015, The European Patent Office reported that "[w]ith the exception of Croatia and Spain, 26 EU member states have embarked on enhanced co-operation with a view to creating unitary patent protection for their territories." European Patent Office, *Unitary Patent* (Oct. 26, 2015), http://www.epo.org/law-practice/unitary/unitary-patent.html. In December 2014, the select committee of the Administrative Council of the European Patent Organisation adopted Rules 1 to 24 relating to unitary patent protection. *See Rules relating to Unitary Patent Protection* (May 31, 2016), https://www.epo.org/law-practice/legal-texts/official-Journal/2016/05/a39.html.

b. Unified Patent Court

Importantly, the EU Unitary Patent System would also create a Unified Patent Court (UPC) for enforcement of patent rights throughout the EU. The UPC

> will be the future centralised patent jurisdiction of the participating [EU] Member States. It will be a court common to the participating Member States and thus subject to the same obligations under Union law as any national court of the participating Member States, in particular [to] refer, where necessary, questions on the interpretation of European Union law to the Court of Justice of the European Union.
>
> The UPC will have exclusive jurisdiction especially in respect of civil litigation related to infringement and validity for both the "classical" European patents and the European patents with unitary effect. . . .
>
> During a transitional period of 7 years, actions for infringement or for revocation concerning "classical" European patents without unitary effect can still be brought before national courts. A proprietor of or an applicant for a European patent granted or applied for prior to the end of the transitional period will also have the possibility to opt out from the exclusive competence of the Court (unless an action has already been brought before the Court). . . .
>
> The UPC will consist of a Court of First Instance, a Court of Appeal and a Registry. The Court of First Instance will comprise local and regional divisions as well as a central division. The Court of Appeal will be located in Luxembourg while the seat of the central division of the Court of First Instance will be in Paris. Specialised sections of the central division will be set up in London and in Munich. . . .[210]

In February 2013, 24 EU member states signed an international agreement for establishing the UPC.[211] At least 13 EU member states (including France, Germany, and the United Kingdom) must ratify the

[210]European Commission, *The EU Single Market: Patents: Frequently Asked Questions* (Oct. 3, 2014), http://ec.europa.eu/internal_market/indprop/patent/faqs/index_en.htm#maincontentSec14 (responding to Question 14: "What will be the role of the Unified Patent Court?"). *See also* European Patent Office, *Unified Patent Court* (Jan. 10, 2020), https://www.epo.org/law-practice/unitary/upc.html#tab1.

[211]*See* Council of the European Union, *Press Release: Signing of the Unified Patent Court agreement* (Feb. 19, 2013), http://www.consilium.europa.eu/uedocs/cms_Data/docs/pressdata/en/intm/135593.pdf. For the text of the UPC agreement, *see* Council for the European Union, Agreement on a Unified Patent Court (No. 16351/12) (Jan. 11, 2013), *available at* http://register.consilium.europa.eu/doc/srv?l=EN&f=ST%2016351%202012%20INIT. *See also* European Patent Office, *Unified Patent Court* (Jan. 10, 2020), https://www.epo.org/law-practice/unitary/upc.html#tab1 stating that the the Agreement on a Unified Patent Court was signed on 19 February 2013.

agreement before it can enter into force.[212] Although 16 member states (including the United Kingdom) had ratified the agreement by 2018, implementation of the UPC awaits resolution of litigation pending in the Constitutional Court of Germany.[213] As of December 2018, the Unified Patent Court was not yet in effect.[214]

[212]Council of the European Union, *Press Release: Signing of the Unified Patent Court agreement* (Feb. 19, 2013), http://www.consilium.europa.eu/uedocs/cms_Data/docs/pressdata/en/intm/135593.pdf. Ratification status is reported at European Commission, *Unitary Patent — Ratification Progress*, http://ec.europa.eu/internal_market/indprop/patent/ratification/index_en.htm. *See also* European Patent Office, *Unified Patent Court*, https://www.epo.org/law-practice/unitary/upc.html#tab1.

[213]European Patent Office, *The History of the EPO: 2013* (Oct. 30, 2013), http://www.epo.org/learning-events/40epc/timeline.html#year20082013 ("A committee charged with creating a roadmap for establishing the Unified Patent Court indicates that early 2015 is a realistic target date for the court and the unitary patent to take effect."). As of February 2016, nine European states have ratified the Agreement on a Unified Patent Court. *See* Council of the European Union, *Unitary Patent and Unified Patent Court — Information from the Presidency on the state of play*, at 9 (Feb. 18, 2016), data.consilium.europa.eu/doc/document/ST-6029-2016-INIT/en/pdf.

[214]Status of Unified Patent Court Project — 19 December 2018, https:/www.unified-patent-court.org/news/status-unified-patent-court-project-19-december-2018.

Glossary

Accused device, accused composition of matter, accused method: The allegedly infringing item (or composition or method) that was made, used, sold, offered for sale, or imported by one accused of infringing a patent (referred to as the **accused infringer**).

All-limitations rule: A doctrine requiring that in order to be found infringing, an accused device must satisfy (i.e., meet or match) each and every limitation of an allegedly infringed patent claim, either literally or under the doctrine of equivalents. The all-limitations rule, sometimes referred to as the all-elements rule, emphasizes that each and every limitation of a patent claim is material.

America Invents Act: Legislation (more formally known as the "Leahy-Smith America Invents Act of 2011") enacted September 16, 2011 that dramatically altered the U.S. patent laws (Title 35 U.S.C.) in several ways, including (1) changing the manner in which priority of invention is determined by prospectively switching the United States from its historic first-to-invent system to a unique first-inventor-to-file system (*see* 35 U.S.C. §102(a)(2) (post-AIA)); (2) as a consequence of (1), eliminating **interference** proceedings; (3) prospectively changing the definition of what counts as prior art to defeat patentability (*see* 35 U.S.C. §102(a) (post-AIA)) and recognizing certain limited exceptions thereto (*see* 35 U.S.C. §102(b) (post-AIA)); and (4) establishing new adjudicative proceedings for challenging the validity of issued patents in the USPTO — ***inter partes* review** (IPR) and **post-grant review** (PGR).

Analogous art: The prior art permissibly considered in an analysis of nonobviousness under 35 U.S.C. §103; that which, as a matter of law, the person having ordinary skill in the art reasonably would have consulted in attempting to solve the problem addressed by her invention. To be considered analogous to a claimed invention, the prior art in question must be either (1) prior art within the same field of endeavor as the invention, or (2) prior art from a different field of endeavor but reasonably pertinent to the same problem as that addressed by the invention. *See also* **Person having ordinary skill in the art (PHOSITA).**

Antedate: To "swear behind" a prior art **reference**. In accordance with the procedures set forth in 37 C.F.R. §1.131, a patent applicant may establish an **invention date** (pre–America Invents Act of 2011 (AIA)) predating the effective date of a prior art reference that has been cited against his claims in a rejection for lack of novelty under 35 U.S.C. §102(a) or (e) or for obviousness under 35 U.S.C. §103.

Anticipation: The negation (or opposite) of novelty, occurring through the triggering of one or more subsections of 35 U.S.C. §102. When one of the triggering events has occurred, it is said that the claimed invention has been anticipated. The necessary relationship between an anticipatory prior art reference and the claimed invention is one of **strict identity**; that is, in order to evidence anticipation under 35 U.S.C. §102, a single prior art reference must disclose every limitation of the claimed invention, arranged as in the claim. *See also* **Loss of right.**

Assignment: A transfer of ownership of a patent, patent application, or any interest therein. *See* 35 U.S.C. §261. *Compare with* **License.**

Best mode: A requirement of 35 U.S.C. §112(a) (eff. Sept. 16, 2012) that an inventor must disclose in a U.S. patent application the best way known to the inventor, as of the application's filing date, of carrying out the invention. The best mode is sometimes designated as the preferred embodiment of the invention. Post-AIA, patent applicants must continue to comply with the best mode disclosure requirement, but failure to satisfy the requirement is no longer a ground for challenging the validity of an issued patent in the federal courts or the USPTO.

Blocking patents: Two or more patents having claim coverage such that the practice of one patent infringes the other and vice versa. Patents are often said to be blocking when one patent issues covering a basic invention, a second patent issues covering an improvement of the basic invention, and the patents are owned by different entities. The blocking patents scenario is traditionally resolved by means of cross-licenses.

Central claiming: A patent claiming regime in which the patent claim recites the preferred embodiment of the invention but is deemed as a matter of law to include all equivalents to (i.e., substantially similar copies of) that preferred embodiment. *Compare with* **Peripheral claiming.**

Claims: Single-sentence definitions of the scope of a patent owner's right to exclude others from making, using, selling, offering to sell, or importing her invention, that appear at the end of the patent's specification. *See* 35 U.S.C. §112(b) (eff. Sept. 16, 2012). The individual elements or components of a patent claim are called **limitations.**

Commercial embodiment: The actual product or process, sold in the marketplace, that corresponds to (i.e., is made in accordance with) the invention as claimed in a patent. For purposes of determining infringement, however, it is improper to compare the commercial embodiment of the patented invention with the accused device. The *patent claims*, rather than the commercial embodiment of the invention, are what must be compared with the accused device in order to find infringement.

Composition of matter: A category of potentially patentable subject matter under 35 U.S.C. §101 that includes chemical compositions and mixtures of substances such as metallic alloys.

Compulsory license: A nonconsensual patent license that a government compels a patent owner to grant to a third party. Signatories to the GATT TRIPS Agreement may implement compulsory licensing systems under the conditions imposed by Article 31. The United States has historically opposed most forms of compulsory licensing.

Conception: The mental part of the act of inventing. Conception involves the formation in the mind of the inventor of the definite and permanent idea of the complete and operative invention, as it is thereafter to be applied in practice. *Compare with* **Reduction to practice.**

Continuation application: A patent application that encompasses all of the disclosure of an earlier (parent or original) application and that does not add any **new matter** to that disclosure. To the extent that it satisfies 35 U.S.C. §120, the continuation application "shall have the same effect" as if it were filed on the filing date of the parent application.

Continuation-in-part (CIP) application: A patent application that encompasses the disclosure of an earlier (parent or original) application and adds **new matter** to that disclosure. For purposes of patentability (i.e., examination for novelty and nonobviousness against the prior art), the claims of the CIP that are directed to common subject matter (i.e., subject matter disclosed in both the parent and the CIP) are entitled to the filing date of the parent, while those claims directed to new matter not disclosed in the parent are entitled only to the actual filing date of the CIP. For purposes of determining a patent's *expiration date*, however, if the patent application contains a specific reference to an earlier-filed application or applications under 35 U.S.C. §120 or §121, all claims of the patent will expire 20 years after the earliest such filing date.

Contributory infringement: A form of indirect infringement. *See* 35 U.S.C. §271(c). Contributory infringement is an intentional act of infringement committed by one who supplies (i.e., sells, offers to sell, or imports into the United States) a nonstaple *component* of a patented invention to another who directly infringes under 35 U.S.C. §271(a) by making, using, selling, offering to sell, or importing the *entire* patented invention. The supplied component must constitute a material part of the invention, and the contributory infringer must know that it is especially made or adapted for use in the infringement. Moreover, the supplied component must not be a staple article or commodity of commerce suitable for substantial noninfringing use. *See also* **Inducing infringement; Infringement.**

Covered Business Method review (CBM): The third and least common type of post-issuance patentability review implemented by the AIA. Its full name is "Transitional Program for Covered Business Method Patents" (TPCBM). The CBM proceeding operates similarly in many respects to post-grant review (PGR), but is much more limited in scope. It is available to challenge certain business method patents related to financial products or services. Only entities already sued or charged with infringement of a CBM patent may petition for review. CBM is scheduled to sunset on September 16, 2020. The provisions governing CBM review were not codified in the Patent Act; rather they are found in the enacting legislation (AIA §18) and USPTO implementing regulations in 37 C.F.R. §§42.300-42.304.

Critical date: Typically refers to the date that is one year prior to the date of filing a U.S. patent application. The date is considered critical for purposes of triggering the **"loss of right" provisions** (also called **"statutory bars"**) of 35 U.S.C. §102(b) (pre-AIA) or the "exceptions" set forth in 35 U.S.C. §102(b)(1) (post-AIA).

Declaratory judgment action: Under 28 U.S.C. §2201, an accused infringer may initiate a legal action against a patentee, seeking a declaration from a federal district court that he does not infringe the patent in suit and/or that the patent is invalid and/or unenforceable. Before a declaratory judgment action can be filed, an actual controversy must exist between the parties. The test is "whether the facts alleged, under all the circumstances, show that there is a substantial controversy, between the parties having adverse legal interests, of sufficient immediacy and reality to warrant the issuance of a declaratory judgment."

Definiteness: Shorthand name for the requirement of 35 U.S.C. §112(b) (eff. Sept. 16, 2012) that patent claims "particularly point[] out and distinctly claim[] the subject matter which the applicant regards as his invention." Claim definiteness is judged from the perspective of a **PHOSITA.** The Supreme Court interprets the statutory language to require that "a patent's claims, viewed in light of the specification and prosecution history, inform those skilled in the art about the scope of the invention with reasonable certainty."

Derivation: One who derives his invention from another is essentially a copyist, not an inventor, and is not entitled to a patent. Derivation involves the conception of an invention by party A and communication of that conception to party B. Under 35 U.S.C. §102(f) (pre-AIA), party B should not be granted a patent because "he did not himself invent the subject matter sought to be patented." AIA-implemented derivation proceedings are governed by 35 U.S.C. §135 (eff. Mar. 16, 2013).

Diligence: In order to establish a **conception** date as the invention date (an important pre-AIA concept) for a given invention, an inventor must have worked diligently following the conception to reduce the invention to practice (either actually or constructively). In determining priority of invention between two rival claimants for a patent under 35 U.S.C. §102(g) (pre-AIA), the party seeking to establish its conception date as its invention date must show reasonable diligence extending from "a time prior to conception by the other" to the party's own **reduction to practice** date. Reasonable diligence is established by evidence that the inventor was continuously active in working toward a reduction to practice of the invention she conceived, or that a legitimate excuse exists for any inactivity during the relevant time period.

Disclosure: The information included in a patent specification (in the form of text and, in many cases, drawings) in order to satisfy the requirements of 35 U.S.C. §112(a) (eff. Sept. 16, 2012): **enablement, best mode**, and **written description of the invention.**

Divisional application: A patent application that is divided or split from another (parent or original) application. When two or more "independent and distinct" inventions are claimed in a single original application, the USPTO may require that the original application be restricted to one of the inventions in accordance with 35 U.S.C. §121. The applicant may elect to prosecute the claims directed to one of the inventions (the elected claims) in the original application and file a "divisional" application directed to the other, nonelected invention. To the extent that it complies with 35 U.S.C. §120, the divisional application "shall be entitled to the benefit of the filing date of the original application." 35 U.S.C. §120. *See also* **Restriction requirement.**

Doctrine of equivalents: A judicially created theory of nonliteral patent infringement. The doctrine of equivalents extends the scope of the patentee's right to exclude others from making, using, selling, offering to sell, or importing the claimed invention beyond the scope of protection that is literally defined by the patent claims. The doctrine of equivalents evolved as a judicial response to the practical reality that if a party can avoid patent infringement liability by copying the claimed invention while making a minor, insubstantial change of just enough scope to take the copied matter outside of the literal boundaries of the claim, the economic value of the patent is significantly lessened. *See also* **Literal infringement.**

Double patenting: A prohibition against the issuance of more than one U.S. patent on a particular claimed invention. If an applicant attempts to obtain a second patent claiming the same invention or an obvious variant of the invention he has previously patented, he may confront a USPTO rejection of the second application's claims on the basis of double patenting. U.S. patent law recognizes at least two varieties of double patenting: (1) *same invention-type* (or *statutory*) double patenting, which is based on the wording of 35 U.S.C. §101 that "[w]hoever invents or discovers any new and useful process, machine, manufacture, or composition of matter... may obtain *a* patent therefor..."; and (2) *obviousness-type* double patenting, which is a judicially created doctrine intended to prevent a patentee from effectively extending his patent monopoly by obtaining a second patent on an obvious variant of the invention claimed in a first patent. Unlike same invention-type double patenting rejections, obviousness-type double patenting rejections may be overcome by the filing of a terminal disclaimer in accordance with 35 U.S.C. §253, ¶2. A rejection for double patenting can be conceptualized as the opposite of a **restriction requirement**, which is made by the USPTO in response to an applicant's attempted claiming of more than one invention in a single patent application.

Effective filing date (EFD): The effective filing date of a patent application is the filing date of an earlier-filed application, the benefit of which is accorded to the patent application in question under 35 U.S.C. §119 (Right of Priority [from foreign filing date or domestic provisional application filing date]), §120 (Benefit of Earlier U.S. Filing Date), or §121 (Divisional Applications) or, if no such benefit is accorded, the actual filing date of the patent application in question. The AIA added to the Patent Act an explicit definition of the "effective filing date for a claimed invention in a patent or application for patent." *See* 35 U.S.C. §100(i)(1) (eff. Mar. 16, 2013). *See also* **Foreign priority.**

Enablement: The requirement of 35 U.S.C. §112(a) (eff. Sept. 16, 2012) that a patent applicant describe in the **specification** how to make and use the invention claimed therein in such "full, clear, concise, and exact terms" as to permit any person skilled in the art of the invention to do so without undue experimentation.

Equitable estoppel: An equitable defense to a charge of patent infringement. Equitable estoppel is separate and independent from the defense of **laches** (although the two are frequently asserted together). Equitable estoppel targets the plaintiff's misleading actions that led the defendant to believe it would not be sued. If the defense of equitable estoppel is established, then the plaintiff's claim of infringement is entirely barred.

Experimental use: This judicially created doctrine negates (or excuses) certain activity occurring more than one year before a U.S. patent application's filing date that would *prima facie* appear to trigger the on sale or public use bars of 35 U.S.C. §102(b) (pre-AIA). In order to negate a statutory bar, the pre–critical date activity must involve use of the claimed invention "by way of experiment" and be "pursued with a bona fide intent of testing the qualities" of the invention. Presumably the common law-developed doctrine of experimental use remains viable post-AIA, but the Federal Circuit has not addressed this question as of early 2016. *See also* **Critical date; Statutory bar.**

Foreign priority: A benefit that may be claimed by patent applicants in countries signatory to the Paris Convention for the Protection of Industrial Property, wherein a later-filed application in Country B may be entitled to the benefit of the filing date of an earlier-filed application (i.e., the *priority date*) in Country A for the same invention, so long as the later filing is made during the priority period (i.e., 12 months under the Paris Convention) and all other formalities are complied with. In the U.S. patent system, this right of foreign priority is implemented under 35 U.S.C. §119(a).

Grace period: This term refers to the one-year period of time prior to the filing date of a U.S. patent application, during which the claimed invention may be put on sale or in public use in the United States or patented or described in a printed publication anywhere in the world without triggering a loss of right to a patent under 35 U.S.C. §102(b) (pre-AIA).

The AIA retains a more limited form of the one-year pre-filing grace period (now termed "exceptions") and narrows it to encompass only certain disclosures made by the inventor (or one who obtained the disclosed subject matter from the inventor) under 35 U.S.C. §102(b)(1) (post-AIA). Many (but not all) countries other than the United States do not provide such a grace period. *See also* **Critical date; Statutory bar.**

Inducing infringement: A form of indirect infringement. *See* 35 U.S.C. §271(b). Inducing infringement is an intentional act of infringement committed by one who induces (i.e., aids or abets) another to directly infringe under 35 U.S.C. §271(a). *See also* **Contributory infringement; Infringement.**

Inequitable conduct: A defensive theory of patent unenforceability. Under the equitable doctrine of "unclean hands," a court should not come to the aid of a patentee (e.g., by granting an injunction against ongoing infringement) if the patentee acted improperly in procuring his patent from the USPTO. Acts giving rise to inequitable conduct typically involve a violation of a patent applicant's duty of candor to the agency, which encompasses a duty to disclose known information that is material to patentability. Inequitable conduct may be proven by establishing that a patentee withheld known information material to patentability, and did so with a specific intent to deceive the USPTO.

Infringement: A violation of the patentee's right to exclude others. Acts that give rise to liability for infringement are enumerated in 35 U.S.C. §271. *Direct* infringement involves an unauthorized making, using, selling, offering to sell, or importing of the patented invention under 35 U.S.C. §271(a). No intent or knowledge of the infringement is required for liability; direct infringement is a strict liability offense. *Indirect* infringement involves inducing another to directly infringe under 35 U.S.C. §271(b), or contributing to the direct infringement of another under 35 U.S.C. §271(c) by supplying one or more nonstaple components of the invention. Intent is required for indirect infringement liability. *Divided* infringement refers to more than one entity performing the steps of a method claim; to find liability, a court must determine whether the acts of one entity are attributable to the other(s) such that a single entity is responsible for the infringement. *Technical* infringement may occur under 35 U.S.C. §271(e)(2) via the filing of certain applications seeking Food and Drug Administration approval for the manufacture of patented drugs. Certain acts of infringement that involve conduct outside U.S. borders are defined by 35 U.S.C. §271(f) and (g). *See also* **Contributory infringement; Inducing infringement; Literal infringement; Doctrine of equivalents.**

Intellectual property (IP): Intangible products of the human mind, such as inventions, ideas, information, artistic creations, music, brand names, product packaging, product design, celebrity persona, industrial secrets, and customer lists, which are the subject of patent, copyright, trademark, trade secret, or related form(s) of legal protection.

Intellectual property rights (IPRs): A variety of rights arising from patents, copyrights, trademarks, trade secrets, and the like.

***Inter Partes* Review (IPR):** An adjudicative proceeding implemented by the America Invents Act of 2011 for challenging the validity of issued patents in the USPTO. An IPR is intended as a less expensive and more streamlined alternative to federal district court litigation of patent validity. Petitions seeking IPR could be filed by any person (not just those threatened with infringement) beginning September 16, 2012 to challenge patents already issued on that date. An IPR petitioner can seek to cancel as unpatentable the claims of the targeted patent as anticipated or obvious based on prior art in the form of patents or printed publications. The decision to institute IPR as well as the ultimate decision on the merits of patentability is made by a three-judge panel of the USPTO's Patent Trial and Appeal Board (PTAB).

Interference: A pre–America Invents Act *inter partes* proceeding conducted in the USPTO to determine which of two (or more) rival claimants was the first to invent a particular claimed invention, and hence entitled to the patent on that invention. The interference proceeding was an essential element of the United States' pre-AIA historic first-to-invent priority system. Interferences were conducted in accordance with the priority rules of 35 U.S.C. §102(g)(1) (2006) and 35 U.S.C. §135 (2006). A losing party in an interference could appeal directly to the U.S. Court of Appeals for the Federal Circuit, or alternatively bring a civil action in case of interference under 35 U.S.C. §146 (2006) in U.S. District Court. The America Invents Act of 2011 prospectively eliminated interferences.

Invention date: The date on which an invention is reduced to practice, either actually or constructively, *unless* the patent applicant can "back date" the invention date to the date on which the invention was conceived through proof of conception coupled with reasonable diligence during the pertinent time period under 35 U.S.C. §102(g) (pre-AIA). For purposes of examining patent applications for novelty under 35 U.S.C. §102(a), (e), and (g), and for nonobviousness under 35 U.S.C. §103, the USPTO when operating under pre-AIA rules takes the application's filing date as the presumptive invention date of the invention claimed therein under a constructive reduction to practice theory. The burden is on the patent applicant to establish any earlier actual invention date, if such proof exists. In *ex parte* patent prosecution this may be accomplished by antedating §102(a) or (e) prior art references in accordance with the procedures set forth in 37 C.F.R. §1.131. In an interference proceeding, an earlier invention date is established under 35 U.S.C. §102(g)(1) and §135. *See also* **Conception; Diligence; Interference; Reduction to practice.**

Inventive Entity: When an invention is made jointly by two or more persons, patent law refers to those persons collectively as the "inventive entity." For an invention jointly made by Inventor A and Inventor B, the inventive entity of "A + B" is considered "another" (i.e., a different inventive entity) vis-à-vis A alone or B alone.

Inventor: One who substantively contributes to the **conception** of a claimed invention. The inventor is not necessarily the **patentee** or owner of the patent claiming the invention.

Laches: An equitable defense to a charge of patent infringement. Laches targets the plaintiff's unreasonable delay in filing suit after it became (or reasonably should have become) aware of the defendant's alleged infringement. If a patentee delays in filing suit for more than six years after this time, a presumption of laches arises and the burden shifts to the patentee to establish legitimate reasons for the delay (such as involvement in other litigation). If the defense is successfully established, laches does not bar the plaintiff's action in its entirety, but rather prevents the recovery of any damages that accrued prior to the filing of the action. *See also* **Equitable estoppel.**

License: An agreement or covenant between a patentee and a licensee that the patentee will not sue the licensee for acts that would otherwise constitute infringement. The license may be exclusive or nonexclusive, may include up-front lump-sum payments, and may be royalty-bearing or royalty-free. A license conveys lesser rights than an **assignment**, which is a transfer of ownership of the patent.

Limitation: An element or component of an invention as recited in a patent claim.

Literal infringement: One of two varieties of patent infringement (i.e., literal infringement and infringement under the doctrine of equivalents), in which an accused device falls precisely within the express boundaries of the asserted patent claim. *See also* **Doctrine of equivalents.**

Loss of right: The loss of a right to patent what may be an otherwise novel and nonobvious invention by delaying too long in filing a patent application after the invention has entered the public domain and/or been commercially exploited by the inventor. Such loss of right results from actions, either by the patent applicant or third parties, that trigger one or more statutory bar events enumerated in 35 U.S.C. §102(b) (pre-AIA) or §102(d) (pre-AIA). Abandonment of an invention under 35 U.S.C. §102(c) (pre-AIA) also is considered a loss of right. *See also* **Statutory bar.**

Machine: A category of potentially patentable subject matter under 35 U.S.C. §101. Synonymous with an apparatus, a machine generally has moving parts; an example is an internal combustion engine.

Manufacture: A category of potentially patentable subject matter under 35 U.S.C. §101. A manufacture in patent parlance is the "catch-all" category for human-made subject matter without moving parts, such as an insulating sleeve for a coffee cup or a foam football having spiral grooves to enhance flight performance.

National treatment: A principle of international law requiring that a country treat foreign nationals as well as (or better than) its own nationals.

New matter: A term of art representing a prohibition on changing the disclosure of an invention once a patent application has been filed. Under 35 U.S.C. §132, no amendment to a pending patent application shall introduce new matter into the disclosure of the invention. The new matter prohibition is the basis for the USPTO's objection to amendments to the abstract, specifications, or drawings that attempt to add new **disclosure** to that originally presented in the patent application as filed.

Nonobviousness: The ultimate condition or criterion of patentability in the United States. Even though novel, an invention nevertheless may not qualify for patent protection if it does not represent enough of a qualitative advance over the prior art. Pursuant to 35 U.S.C. §103, the nonobviousness of a given invention is evaluated from the perspective of a hypothetical person having ordinary skill in the art (i.e., technical field) to which the invention pertains, at the time the invention was made (pre-AIA) or at its effective filing date (post-AIA). In most foreign patent systems, the counterpart to nonobviousness is inventive step. *See also* **Person having ordinary skill in the art (PHOSITA); Novelty; Prior art.**

Nonprovisional application: A regularly filed (rather than provisionally filed) patent application that has been filed in accordance with the requirements of 35 U.S.C. §111(a).

Novelty: A patent law term of art for the requirement that a patented invention be new as defined by 35 U.S.C. §102.

Patent: A statutorily created, government-granted legal instrument that conveys to its owner a time-limited property right to exclude others from making, using, selling, offering to sell throughout the United States, or importing into the United States the invention recited in the claim(s) of the patent. *See* 35 U.S.C. §154(a)(1). *See also* **Claims.**

Patentee: The owner of a patent; the entity holding legal title in the patent. Patentees include not only the patentee to whom the patent was issued but also the successors in title to that patentee. 35 U.S.C. §100(d). The patentee is not necessarily the same entity as the **inventor** of the patented invention.

Patent-Eligible subject matter: Used synonymously with "**Statutory subject matter**."

Patent misuse: An affirmative defense to a charge of patent infringement that focuses on the patentee's behavior in improperly expanding the scope of its rights beyond the statutory patent grant. Determinations of patent misuse have been based on a fairly narrow range of specific acts or practices of the patent owner, often (but not exclusively) in the context of patent licensing.

Patent term: The enforceable life of a patent, that is, the period of time between a patent's issue date and its expiration date. For U.S. patent applications filed on or after June 8, 1995, the term of the patent ends on the date that is 20 years after the earliest U.S. effective filing date of the application. *See* 35 U.S.C. §154(a)(2). *See also* **Effective filing date.**

Peripheral claiming: A patent claiming regime in which the claim recites the precise literal boundaries of the patentee's right to exclude others. Accused subject matter falling outside the claim may infringe only the doctrine of equivalents, or not at all. The U.S. patent system presently employs a peripheral claiming regime. *Compare with* **Central claiming**.

Person having ordinary skill in the art (PHOSITA): A hypothetical person from whose perspective the nonobviousness criterion of 35 U.S.C. §103 must be judged. The PHOSITA is understood as the modern-day counterpart of the "ordinary mechanic" described by the Supreme Court in the famous doorknob case *Hotchkiss v. Greenwood*,

52 U.S. 248 (1850). The PHOSITA is presumed to have knowledge of all analogous prior art. *See also* **Analogous art; Nonobviousness; Prior art.**

Plurality: A term of art in patent law indicating a quantity of two or more.

Post-Grant Review (PGR): An adjudicative proceeding implemented by the America Invents Act for challenging the validity of issued patents in the USPTO. Like IPR, the PGR proceeding is intended as a less expensive and more streamlined alternative to federal district court litigation of patent validity. Petitions seeking PGR must challenge patents issued under the AIA regime ("AIA patents"); that is, those claiming inventions an effective filing date on or after March 16, 2013, and can only be filed within the nine-month window following such patent's issuance. A PGR petitioner can seek to cancel as unpatentable the claims of a targeted patent on a large number of invalidity grounds including patent-ineligible subject matter, lack of utility, anticipation, obviousness, non-enablement, failure to satisfy the written description of the invention requirement, and claim indefiniteness. *See* 35 U.S.C. 35 U.S.C. §321(b) (post-AIA). The decision to institute a PGR as well as the ultimate decision on the merits of patentability is made by a three-judge panel of the USPTO's Patent Trial and Appeal Board (PTAB).

Post-Issuance Proceeding: Umbrella term encompassing the three AIA-implemented adjudicatory proceeding conducted in the USPTO for reviewing the patentability of issued patents; namely, ***Inter partes*** **review (IPR)**, **Post-grant review (PGR)**, and **Covered Business Method review (CBM).**

Printed publication: General term for non-patent prior art references, such as treatises, periodicals, catalogs, technical documentation, mechanical drawings, photographs, and the like. To qualify as a printed publication, the content of the reference in question must be sufficiently accessible to that segment of the public interested in the art of which the reference is a part. To anticipate a claimed invention under 35 U.S.C. §102, the teaching of the printed publication also must be enabling in accordance with 35 U.S.C. §112(a) (eff. Sept. 16, 2012). *See also* **Anticipation; Prior art; Reference.**

Prior art: General term for the categories of prior technology or events against which the patentability of a claimed invention is evaluated. What qualifies as prior art in the U.S. system for purposes of novelty is cataloged by the various subcategories of 35 U.S.C. §102.

An analysis of nonobviousness under 35 U.S.C. §103 further narrows that universe of prior art to the subject matter that is considered analogous to the claimed invention. *See also* **Analogous art.**

Prior user right: A personal defense to a charge of patent infringement, raised by a person who did not patent the invention herself but rather used it in her business prior to the patent owner's filing of his own application for patent on the same invention. One asserting the prior user right has typically maintained the invention as a trade secret. Because they tend to ameliorate the sometimes harsh results of first-to-file patent systems, prior user rights have long been recognized outside the United States. The America Invents Act of 2011 significantly broadened the availability of prior user rights in the U.S. patent system. *See* 35 U.S.C. §273 (post-AIA).

Priority system: Although the term "priority" is used in several different senses in patent law, "priority system" is used in this text to refer to a system for determining time-wise priority of a patent between multiple applicants. Assuming each patent applicant has independently invented the same invention or an obvious variant thereof, only one applicant is entitled to a U.S. patent for the invention. Historically, the U.S. granted the patent to the first in time to *invent*, regardless of the order of filing of a patent application. For applications filed on or after the March 16, 2013, the effective date of §3 of the America Invents Act of 2011, U.S. patent law generally grants the patent to the first inventor to *file* her patent application. There are important exceptions to this general rule, however. *See supra* Chapter 4.

Process: A category of potentially patentable subject matter under 35 U.S.C. §101. Synonymous with a method, a process in patent parlance is a series of steps for carrying out a given task.

Prosecution: The process of obtaining a patent, which involves filing a patent application in the USPTO and responding to any rejections or objections made by the agency. Sometimes referred to as patent solicitation.

Prosecution history estoppel: A judicially created doctrine that operates as a legal limitation on the availability of the doctrine of equivalents. A patentee is estopped from seeking to obtain coverage under the doctrine of equivalents over accused subject matter that the patentee effectively surrendered during prosecution before the USPTO in order to obtain her patent. Sometimes referred to as file wrapper estoppel or file history estoppel. *See also* **Doctrine of equivalents.**

Prosecution history laches: A judicially created equitable doctrine under which a patent may be held unenforceable when it is issued after an unreasonable and unexplained delay in **prosecution**, even though the patent applicant complied with all pertinent statutes and rules. For example, refiling a patent application containing only previously allowed claims for the business purpose of delaying their issuance may trigger the defense of prosecution history laches. Courts should apply the doctrine sparingly, however, and only in egregious cases of misuse of the statutory patent system. Prosecution history laches should be distinguished from the equitable defense of **laches** (or "enforcement laches"), which is based on unreasonable delay in the *enforcement* of an issued patent.

Provisional application: A patent application filed under 35 U.S.C. §111(b), which must have a specification (and drawings, if necessary) but need not include any claims or an oath by the inventor(s). The filing fee for a provisional application is significantly less than that of a **nonprovisional** (i.e., regularly filed) **application** because the former is merely a "place holder" that is not substantively examined for patentability. The value of a provisional application is that it creates an early domestic priority date. If a nonprovisional application is filed under 35 U.S.C. §111(a) within one year of the provisional application's filing date for an invention disclosed in accordance with 35 U.S.C. §112(a) (eff. Sept. 16, 2012) (other than the requirement to disclose the best mode) in the provisional application, the nonprovisional application shall be entitled to the benefit of the provisional application's earlier filing date in accordance with 35 U.S.C. §119(e).

Reduction to practice: The final step in the act of inventing. A reduction to practice of an invention may be an actual reduction to practice or a constructive reduction to practice. An *actual reduction to practice* generally involves the construction of a physical embodiment of the invention that works for its intended purpose (testing is often required to verify whether that purpose is met). A *constructive reduction to practice* means that a patent application claiming the invention has been filed with the USPTO, which application satisfies the disclosure requirements of 35 U.S.C. §112(a) (eff. Sept. 16, 2012) for the claimed invention.

Reference: Term of art for a patent or printed publication that is being relied on as **prior art**.

Reissue: An administrative procedure conducted within the USPTO for correcting an issued patent that suffers from certain errors that render the patent wholly or partly inoperative or invalid. *See* 35

U.S.C. §251. Only the patentee (as opposed to a third party) can seek to reissue her patent.

Repair versus reconstruction: A purchaser of a patented device is deemed to have obtained an implied license to use that device, which includes the right to repair it. Thus, repair is not patent infringement. However, when that repair is so extensive as to be characterized as reconstruction or a new making of the patented device, such an act is no longer considered as being within the scope of the purchaser's implied license. Thus, reconstruction is patent infringement. The line between repair and reconstruction is a fine one and the pertinent cases are extremely fact-specific.

Restriction requirement: A requirement applied by the USPTO when a patent applicant claims two or more "independent and distinct" inventions in a single original application. In accordance with 35 U.S.C. §121, the agency may require that the original application be restricted to one of the inventions. If the applicant does not contest the restriction requirement, she will typically elect a claim (or claims) with which to proceed in the original application while canceling the remaining (nonelected) claims without prejudice to their later refiling in a **divisional application.**

Right of priority: A right provided to inventors in countries signatory to the Paris Convention for the Protection of Industrial Property, which permits them to file a patent application in one signatory country (typically an inventor's home country) and, within one year, file additional applications on the same invention in other countries that are also signatories to the Convention. The applicant exercises her right of priority by making a claim that her later-filed application(s) should be accorded the benefit of the filing date of her earlier-filed (typically home country) application. In the U.S. Patent Act, the Paris Convention right of priority is implemented by 35 U.S.C. §119(a).

Specification: The key documentary part of a patent application (which application under 35 U.S.C. §111(a) also includes an oath by the applicant and drawings if necessary for the understanding of the invention). Under 35 U.S.C. §112(a) (eff. Sept. 16, 2012), the specification must provide a disclosure of the invention that satisfies the requirements of (1) written description of the invention, (2) enablement, and (3) best mode. Under 35 U.S.C. §112(b) (eff. Sept. 16, 2012), the specification must conclude with one or more claims (unless the application is a provisional application, which need not include claims). Thus, the patent's claims are part of the specification. *See also*

Disclosure; Written description of the invention; Enablement; Best mode; Claims; Provisional application.

Statutory bar: The triggering of a statutory bar means that one (or more) of the four events listed in 35 U.S.C. §102(b) (pre-AIA) has occurred, and will result in a **loss of right** to patent what may be an otherwise novel and nonobvious invention. More specifically, a statutory bar is activated under 35 U.S.C. §102(b) (2006) if, more than one year before the patent application filing date, the claimed invention was (1) patented anywhere in the world, (2) described in a printed publication anywhere in the world, (3) in public use in the United States, or (4) on sale in the United States. Section 102(d) of 35 U.S.C. (pre-AIA), referred to as the foreign patenting bar, is another type of statutory bar.

Statutory subject matter: Subject matter that qualifies as potentially patentable in accordance with 35 U.S.C. §101 under one or more of the following categories: process, machine, manufacture, composition of matter, or improvement thereof. Inventions qualifying under §101 are only potentially patentable because, in addition to falling within a statutory category, they must be useful, novel, and nonobvious. Statutory subject matter is sometimes referred to as "patent-eligible" subject matter. The Supreme Court has ruled that "abstract ideas," "laws of nature," and "natural phenomena" are implicit exceptions to the patent-eligible subject matter categories enumerated in §101, but has not further defined these terms.

Strict identity standard: The necessary relationship between an anticipatory prior art reference and a claimed invention; that is, in order to evidence anticipation of a claimed invention under 35 U.S.C. §102, a single prior art reference must disclose each and every limitation of that invention, arranged as in the claim.

Utility: A requirement for patentability under 35 U.S.C. §101. Possessing utility means that an invention is useful in the patent law sense, that is, has some practical utility. Current USPTO guidelines require that a patentable invention have a "specific, substantial, and credible" utility.

Written description: That portion of a patent specification other than the claims, typically including a "background of the invention" section, a "summary of the invention" section, and a "detailed description of the invention" section explaining any drawings present in the patent application.

Written description of the invention: A legal requirement that a patent specification must satisfy under 35 U.S.C. §112(a) (eff. Sept. 16,

2012), recognized as independent from the enablement and best mode requirements. The genesis of this legal requirement is the concept of adequate "support"; that is, the language of patent claims newly presented or amended after the filing date of a patent application must be sufficiently supported in the written description of the patent document so as to be entitled to the application's filing date as the *prima facie* invention date for those claims. A test for compliance with this requirement is whether a PHOSITA reading the patent's specification as it existed on the filing date of the application would reasonably understand that the inventor was at that time in possession of the invention as later claimed. *See also* **Best mode; Enablement; Invention date.**

Table of Cases

Italicized page numbers indicate substantive discussions of cases in text. Alphabetization is letter-by-letter (e.g., "Newell Cos." precedes "New Marshall Engine Co.").

Index

B

E

N

U